CRIMINAL JUST

LONGMAN LAW SERIES

GENERAL EDITORS

PROFESSOR I. H. DENNIS, *University College London*
PROFESSOR R. W. RIDEOUT, *University College London*
PROFESSOR J. A. USHER, *University of Exeter*

PUBLISHED TITLES

PETER STONE,
The Conflict of Laws
CHRISTOPHER HARDING AND ANN SHERLOCK,
European Community Law: Text and Materials
ANDREW LE SUEUR AND MAURICE SUNKIN,
Public Law
ANDREW CHOO,
Evidence: Text and Materials
ROGER J. SMITH,
Property Law
WILLIAM WILSON,
Criminal Law
MARTIN WASIK, THOMAS GIBBONS AND MIKE REDMAYNE,
Criminal Justice: Text and Materials

MARTIN WASIK, THOMAS GIBBONS
and MIKE REDMAYNE

CRIMINAL JUSTICE
Text and Materials

LONGMAN

LONDON AND NEW YORK

Addison Wesley Longman Limited
Edinburgh Gate
Harlow
Essex   CM20 2JE
United Kingdom
and Associated Companies throughout the world

© Addison Wesley Longman Limited 1999

First published 1999

ISBN 0–582–28858–4

British Library Cataloguing-in-Publication Data

A catalogue record for this book is available from the British Library

Set by 35 in 10/12pt Plantin
Produced by Addison Wesley Longman Singapore (Pte) Ltd.,
Printed in Singapore

CONTENTS

PREFACE

This book examines the operation of criminal justice in England and Wales. It is a large and important area of study, reflected in the growth of courses which draw upon it. We have included a substantial amount of explanatory material, to guide those who are turning to this subject for the first time, but we have also tried to provide a critical analysis of the current state of criminal justice which we hope will prove useful to those who are embarking on more advanced study, and to criminal justice practitioners. We present our own analysis and discussion of contemporary issues, but we also make reference, through a wide selection of quotations and longer extracts, to the views of others.

This range of perspectives on criminal justice makes the subject well suited to the 'text and materials' style of treatment, allowing as it does for an intercutting of diverse and contrasting views. Everyone, it seems, has an opinion about criminal justice. Inevitably, we have had to be selective in the topics which we have covered and the viewpoints which we have examined. We have relied heavily upon government and other official reports, research studies, the writings of individual academics from different disciplines, and we have also included some statutory and case law material. In making these choices we have drawn upon a collective experience of teaching over a number of years on criminal justice courses for lawyers and for social workers, and on our involvement in training programmes for criminal justice professionals. A comprehensive bibliography has been provided at the end of the book, to assist those who wish to examine particular issues in greater depth.

The three authors have contributed in equal measure to compiling this work. Our grateful thanks are due to the publishers for their help and encouragement throughout, and to Professor Ian Dennis of University College London for initially supporting the idea of the book, and for his valuable advice and assistance thereafter.

Martin Wasik
Thomas Gibbons
Mike Redmayne

ACKNOWLEDGEMENTS

We are grateful to the following for permission to reproduce copyright material:

Academic Press Ltd, London, for an extract from D Dixon, K Bottomley, CA Coleman, M Gill and D Wall, 'Reality and Rules in the Construction and Regulation of Police Suspicion' (1989) 17 *International Journal of the Sociology of Law* 185, pp 185–92.

Addison Wesley Longman Ltd for extracts from S Savage and S Charman, 'Managing Change', pp 50–53; AJP Butler, 'Managing the Future: A Chief Constable's View', pp 220–23; and S Walklate, 'Equal Opportunities and the Future of Policing', pp 193–9, all in F Leishman, B Loveday and S Savage (eds), *Core Issues in Policing* (1996).

Andrew Ashworth for an extract from A Ashworth, 'Disentangling Disparity' in DC Pennington and S Lloyd-Bostock, *The Psychology of Sentencing* (1987) pp 24–7.

Arnold for extracts from P Manning, 'The Social Control of Police Work' in S Holdaway (ed), *The British Police* (1979) pp 53–9 and S Holdaway, *Inside the British Police* (1983) pp 89–101, pp 157–9.

The Audit Commission for extracts from *Streetwise – Effective Police Patrol* (1996) Exhibit 18; *Helping with Enquiries* (1993) Exhibit 20; and *Misspent Youth: Young People and Crime* (1996) Summary.

Blackstone Press Ltd for extracts from D West, 'Sexual Molesters' in N Walker (ed), *Dangerous People* (1996) pp 53–7 and D Miers, *State Compensation for Criminal Injuries* (1997) pp 156–61, 165–7, 170–76, 182–5.

Blackwell Publishers for extracts from N Lacey, 'Government as Manager, Citizen as Consumer' (1994) 57 MLR 534, pp 534–5, 543–5; D Miers, 'The Responsibilities and Rights of Victims of Crime' (1992) 55 MLR 482, pp 599–601; R Reiner, 'Policing a Postmodern Society' (1992) 55 MLR 761, pp 770–71, 777–9, 781; L Bridges and M McConville, 'Keeping Faith with their Own Convictions: The Royal Commission on Criminal Justice' (1994) 57 MLR 75, pp 80–83; A Sanders, 'Reforming the Prosecution System' (1992) 63 *Political Quarterly* 25, pp 30–32; D Dixon, CA Coleman and K Bottomley, 'Consent and the Legal Regulation of Policing' (1990) 17 *Journal of Law and Society* 345, pp 346–9, 352; A Sanders, 'Constructing the Case for the Prosecution' (1987) 14 *Journal of Law and Society* 229, pp 234–42; J Hodgson, 'Adding Injury to Injustice: The Suspect at the Police Station' (1994) 21 *Journal of Law and Society* 85, pp 92–5; R Evans and C Wilkinson, 'Variations in Police Cautioning Policy and Practice in England and Wales' (1990) *Howard Journal* 155, pp 163–75; S Holdaway, *Inside the British Police* (1983) pp 89–101, 157–9 and J Baldwin and M McConville, *Negotiated Justice* (1997) pp 32–3, 49–50.

Butterworths, London for extracts from A Sanders and R Young, *Criminal Justice* (1994) pp 234–6; G Maher, 'The Verdict of the Jury' in M Findlay and P Duff (eds), *The Jury under Attack* (1988) pp 45–6, 47–9, 50–52 and A Ashworth, *Sentencing and Criminal Justice* (2nd ed, 1995) pp 62–72.

Crown Prosecution Service for an extract from Code for Crown Prosecutors, paras 1.1, 3.1 and 3.2, 4.1 and 4.2, 5.1 and 5.2, 6.1–6.7. © Crown Copyright 1994.

Forensic Science Society for an extract from Blakey, 'Does Forensic Science Give Value for Money?' (1995) 35 *Science and Justice* 1, pp 2–4.

Franz Steiner Verlag Wiesbaden GmbH for extracts from J Jackson, 'The Value of Jury Trial' in E Attwool and D Goldberg (eds), *Criminal Justice* (1995) pp 81–3, 87–93 and M Ockelton, 'Rules of Evidence' in E Attwool and D Goldberg (eds), *Criminal Justice* (1995) pp 96–100. Published by Franz Steiner Verlag Stuttgart as *Beheft*, No 63, of Archiv für Rechts- und Sozialphilosphie.

Gordon and Breach Publishers for an extract from D Dixon, A Bottomley, C Coleman, M Gill and D Wall, 'Safeguarding the Rights of Suspects in Police Custody' (1990) 1 *Policing and Society* 115, pp 129–33.

Her Majesty's Stationery Office for extracts from *Criminal Statistics for England and Wales 1996* (Home Office, 1997) Cmnd 3764, table 1.1, figure 1.1, table 2A and paras 2.4–2.9, table 7.1, table 7E; *Prison Statistics for England and Wales 1996* (Home Office, 1997) figure – prison population policy, figures 1.1, 1.2, text relating to table 1.14, figure 2.4; Royal Commission on Criminal Justice, *Report* (HMSO, 1993) Cm 2263, paras 9–27, 50–52; H Pullinger, 'The Criminal Justice System Viewed as a System' in D Moxon (ed), *Managing Criminal Justice* (HMSO, 1985) pp 19–23; *The Victim's Charter: A Statement on the Rights of Victims* (Home Office, 1996) Introduction; Royal Commission on Criminal Procedure, *The Investigation and Prosecution of Criminal Offences in England and Wales; The Law and Procedure* (HMSO, 1981) Cmnd 8092-I, paras 3–4; W Skogan, *Contacts Between the Police and the Public: Findings from the 1992 British Crime Survey* (HMSO, 1994) Home Office Research Study No 134, table B.2; P Mayhew, C Mirlees-Black and N Aye Maung, *Trends in Crime: Findings from the 1994 British Crime Survey* (HMSO, 1994) HORSD Findings No 14, p 1; P Mayhew et al, *The British Crime Survey* (Home Office, 1993) Home Office Research Study No 132, p 25, including table 3.1; P Morris and K Heal, *Crime Control and the Police* (Home Office, 1981) Home Office Research Study No 67, pp 19–24, 25, 27–8, 30–32; *The Cautioning of Offenders* (HMSO, 1994) Circular 18/1994; M Maguire and C Norris, *The Conduct and Supervision of Criminal Investigations* RCCJ RS 5 (HMSO, 1992); J Baldwin and T Moloney, *Supervision of Police Investigations in Serious Criminal Cases* (HMSO, 1992) pp 74–7; T Newburn and S Merry, *Keeping in Touch: Police-Victim Communication in Areas* (HMSO, 1990) pp 37–9; D Brown, *Investigating Burglary: The Effects of PACE* (HMSO, 1191) p 40, table 4.1; D Brown, T Ellis and K Larcombe, *Changing the Code: Police Detention under the Revised PACE Codes of Practice* (HMSO, 1192) pp 96–7; J Baldwin, *The Role of Legal Representatives at the Police Station* (HMSO, 1992) table; J Baldwin, *Video-Taping Police Interviews with Suspects – An Evaluation* (Home Office Police Research Group, 1992) pp 15–17; *Police Complaints and Discipline England and Wales 95/96* (Home Office Research and Statistics Directorate, 1996) Home Office Statistical Bulletin 17/96, p 10; D Crisp and D Moxon, *Case Screening by the Crown Prosecution Service: How and Why Cases Are Terminated* (HMSO, 1994) p 20; Lord Chancellor's Department, *A New Framework for Local Justice* (HMSO, 1992) Cm 1829, figure; C Hedderman and D Moxon, *Magistrates' Court or Crown Court? Mode of Trial Decisions and Sentencing* (HMSO, 1992) Home Office Research Study No 125, table 3.1; *No More Excuses – A New Approach to Tackling Youth Crime in England and Wales* (Home Office, 1997) Cm 3089, paras 9.1–9.3; G Philpotts and L Lancucki, *Previous Convictions, Sentence and Reconviction* (Home Office, 1979) Home Office Research Study No 53, table 4.2; C Hedderman and L Gelsthorpe, *Understanding the Sentencing of Women* (Home Office, 1997) Home Office Research Study No 170, pp 21–2, 26–9, 41–3, 52–3, 58–9; Lord Chancellor's Department, *Judicial Statistics England and Wales for the Year 1996* (HMSO, 1997) Cm 1736, tables 1.7 and 1.8; Home Office Research and Statistics Directorate (1997) table and figure downloaded from RSD website; HM Prison Service, *Prison Service Annual Report and Accounts, April 1996 – March 1997* (HMSO, 1997) HC (1997–98) 274, table of performance statistics; *Three-Year Plan for the Probation Service 1197–2000* (Home Office, 1997) Annex D; E Mortimer and C May, *Electronic Monitoring in Practice: The Second Year of the Trials of Curfew Orders* (Home Office, 1997) Home Office Research Study No 177, pp 40–43, including figure 4.1, tables 4.1 and 4.2; Her Majesty's Chief Inspector of Constabulary, *Winning the Race: Policing Plural Communities* (1996–97) Thematic Inspection Report on Police Community and Race Relations, paras 2.62–2.94; Criminal Injuries Compensation Scheme, paras 1–16; Home Office, *Crime Statistics for the Metropolitan Police District by Ethnic Group, 1987: Victims, Suspects and Those Arrested*, Home Office Statistical Bulletin 5/89, table 4; and Home Office Circular, August 1993. Crown copyright is reproduced with the permission of the Controller of Her Majesty's Stationery Office.

Howard League for Penal Reform for an extract from D Faulkner, *Darkness and Light: Justice, Crime and Management for Today* (1996) pp 1–3.

Institute of Criminology and Mike Chatterton for M Chatterton, 'Police in Social Control' in J King (ed), *Control Without Custody* (1976).

Kluwer Academic Publishers for extracts from G Dworkin, 'The Serpent Beguiled Me and I Did Eat: Entrapment and the Creation of Crime' (1985) 4 *Law and Philosophy* 17, pp 30–34 and S Cohen, 'The Punitive City: Notes on the Dispersal of Social Control (1979) 3 *Contemporary Crises* 339, pp 346–50.

Law Society of Scotland for an extract from Lord Taylor CJ, Address to the Law Society of Scotland [1993] *Journal of the Law Society of Scotland* 129–31.

Macmillan Press Ltd and New York University Press for F Heidensohn, *Women and Crime* (1996, 2nd ed) pp 40–42.

Magistrates' Association for extracts from *Sentencing Guidelines* (1997) Guidelines – Taking a Vehicle Without Consent, Compensation.

Northeastern University Press for an extract from A von Hirsch and A Ashworth, *Principled Sentencing* (1992) pp 101, 103–5. © 1992 Andrew von Hirsch and Andrew Ashworth. Reprinted with permission of the editors and Northeastern University Press.

Open University Press for an extract from M Eaton, *Justice for Women?* (1986) pp 73–6.

Oxford University Press for extracts from M Maguire, 'Complaints Against the Police: The British Experience' in A Goldsmith (ed), *Complaints Against the Police – The Trend to External Review* (1991) pp 186–93; A Ashworth, *The Criminal Process* (1994) pp 43–5, 292–6; K Hawkins, (ed), *The Use of Discretion* (1992) pp 11–12, 27–32, 35–6; A Bottoms, 'The Philosophy of Politics of Sentencing Reform' in CMV Clarkson and R Morgan (eds), *The Politics of Sentencing Reform* (1995) pp 24–8, 34–7; DJ Smith, 'Ethnic Origins, Crime and Criminal Justice', pp 705–7, 732–9, 749–52, L Zedner, 'Victims', pp 599–600; R Reiner, 'Policing and the Police', pp 1030–34, all in M Maguire, R Morgan and R Reiner *The Oxford Handbook of Criminology* (2nd edn, 1997); M McConville, J Hodgson, L Bridges and A Pavlovic, *Standing Accused: The Organisation and Social Practices of Criminal Defence Lawyers in Britain* (1994) pp 225, 227–9, 237–8; I Dennis, 'Reconstructing the Law of Criminal Evidence' (1989) 54 *Current Legal Problems* 21, pp 35–8; P Rock, *The Social World of an English Crown Court* (1993) pp 33–7; R Hood, *Race and Sentencing: A Study in the Crown Court* (1992) pp 193–205; R Pattenden, *English Criminal Appeals 1844–1994* (1996) pp 3–4 and RD King and K McDermott, *The State of Our Prisons* (1995) pp 47–52. All reprinted by permission of Oxford University Press.

Policy Studies Institute for extracts from DJ Smith and J Gray, *Police and People in London: IV The Police in Action* (1983) pp 56–63, 232–3 and C Horton and DJ Smith, *Evaluating Police Work* (1988) pp 21–7.

Routledge for extracts from R Morgan, 'Policing by Consent: Legitimating the Doctrine' in R Morgan & DJ Smith (eds), *Coming to Terms with Policing* (1989) pp 217–20; A Cretney and G Davis, *Punishing Violence* (1995) pp 78–80, 137–40 and M McConville, A Sanders and R Leng, *The Case for the Prosecution* (1991) pp 70–71.

Sage Publications Inc. for an extract from T Bennett, 'Community Policing on the Ground: Developments in Britain' in Dennis P Rosenbaum (ed), *The Challenge of Community Policing: Testing the Promises* (1994) pp 229–30, 234–5, 239–41 (including table 13.1). Reprinted by Permission of Sage Publications Inc.

Sage Publications Ltd for extracts from M Feeley and J Simon, 'Actuarial Justice: The Emerging New Criminal Law' in D Nelken (ed), *The Futures of Criminology* (1994) pp 173–8; and M Fitzgerald, 'Racism: Establishing the Phenomenon' in D Cook and B Hudson (eds), *Racism and Criminology* (1993) pp 45–61.

Joanna Shapland for an extract from Joanna Shapland, 'The Criminal Justice System and the Victim' (1985) 10 *Victimology* 585, pp 586–9.

Sweet & Maxwell Ltd for extracts from C Pollard, 'Public Safety, Accountability and the Courts' [1996] Crim LR 152–61; A Ashworth, 'Crime, Community and Creeping Consequentialism' [1996] Crim LR 220–30; A Ashworth and Michael Hough, 'Sentencing and the Climate of Opinion' [1996] Crim LR 776, pp 780–86; R Evans, 'Cautioning: Counting the Cost of Retrenchment' [1994] Crim LR 566–75; A Sanders and L Bridges, 'Access to Legal Advice and Police Malpractice' [1990] Crim LR 498–501; C Hilson, 'Discretion to Prosecute and Judicial Review' [1993] Crim LR 739; M Zander, 'What the Annual Statistics Tell Us About Pleas and Acquittals' [1991] Crim LR 252, pp 253–4; A Morris and L Gelsthorpe, 'Not Paying for Crime: Issues in Fine Enforcement' [1990] Crim LR 839, pp 840–43, 846–7, 849–50; C Walker and D Wall, 'Imprisoning the Poor: Television Licence Evaders and the Criminal Justice System' [1997] Crim LR 173, pp 173–5, 177–9; A Morris, 'Sex and Sentencing' [1988] Crim LR 163–71; J Jackson, 'The Royal Commission on Criminal Justice: (2) The Evidence Recommendations' [1993] Crim LR 817, pp 818–20 and A Ashworth, 'The Criminal Justice Act 1991' in C Munro and M Wasik (eds), *Sentencing, Judicial Discretion and Training*, pp 77, 83–5.

West Group for an extract from *State v Ward* 869 P 2d 1062, 1966–1978 (Wash 1994). Reprinted from West's National Reporter System with the permission of the West Group.

TABLE OF CASES

Note. Cases are listed under the name of the accused whenever the usual method of citation would cause them to be preceded by 'R v' signifying prosecution by the Crown.

TABLE OF STATUTES

I

INTRODUCTION AND THEMES

The aim of this first chapter is to set the scene for the more detailed discussion of topics which follows in Chapters 2–5, and to identify a number of key themes which we see as running through the book. These themes are taken up again in Chapter 6.

1. CRIME STATISTICS AND THE 'CRIME PROBLEM'

Crime itself, and the fear of crime, are widely acknowledged to be massive social problems. Fear of crime, a term which is usually used to refer to perceived threats to personal safety rather than to fear of property crime, is known to blight the lives of many citizens, by causing (sometimes excessive) anxiety and by damaging trust and social relations. The fear of crime may deter people from going to public places, or being out after dark, and can affect drastically the quality of their lives. Elderly people, women, and some ethnic minority groups are particularly affected by fear of crime. Fifty-seven per cent of women report feeling 'very unsafe' when alone after dark (Mirrlees-Black et al, 1996). Media images tend to exaggerate the likelihood of crime occurring, especially violent or sexual crime. A survey commissioned by the BBC in 1995 found that people believed that there was about a 25 per cent chance of falling victim to a violent crime in the next 12 months, whereas the true level is around 1.5 per cent. (For discussion of the relationship between television viewing and fear of crime see Sparks (1992) and Reiner (1997).) The British Crime Survey, a regular biennial survey first conducted in 1982, which collects data by interviewing a large sample of citizens and asking them how often they have been a victim of a crime within a specified time period, has found that, on average, a person could expect to be the victim of a robbery once every 500 years, to be assaulted once every 100 years and to be the victim of a burglary once every 40 years. In the United States, where overall crime levels are significantly higher than in England and Wales, a person is four times as likely to be accidentally injured at home or at work as to be the victim of theft, twice as likely to be injured in a car accident as to be the victim of violent crime and 50 times more likely to die from heart disease than to be the victim of a homicide (Laub, 1997). Fear of crime cannot be dismissed as an irrational phenomenon, however, and there is a correlation between fears about crime and actual levels of crime, both generally and in the local area. As might be expected, fear of crime increases as crime itself increases. The British Crime Survey and comparable surveys in the United States do show, however, that those with the greatest fear of crime (such as the elderly) tend in fact to be at relatively low risk of crime while others (such as young, socially active men) may have little fear of crime but have lifestyles which carry a substantially greater risk of victimisation (see Hough, 1995, and for comparable findings in the United States, see Davis et al, 1997).

Important recent research has demonstrated the highly skewed nature of victimisation. For most citizens, victimisation is a quite rare event, whilst some 'repeat' victims may be affected by crime routinely, almost continuously (Farrell and Pease, 1993; Genn, 1988). Those living in inner city areas, for example, are much more at risk of burglary and theft than those living elsewhere. In his first speech as Prime Minister in June 1997, at a housing estate in Southwark, Mr Blair underlined this fact, observing that 'nearly a half of all crimes take place in only a tenth of the neighbourhoods'. Local crime surveys provide valuable data on these differential risks of crime (Zedner, 1997, p 583). A person's lifestyle is known to make a significant difference to magnitude of risk. Young, fit and socially active people who go out regularly in the evenings to visit pubs and clubs and meet new people are at increased risk of violent crime (for discussion, see Zedner, 1997). It should be remembered, however, that 'lifestyle' must be broadly construed here so as to include domestic living arrangements. Much violent crime takes place in the home rather than on the streets and in public places so for those, particularly women and children, who are subjected to domestic violence, there is no safety in staying at home (see Walklate, 1989, Ch 1).

According to the latest sweep of the British Crime Survey (BCS), there were an estimated 19.1 million offences committed against individuals and their property in 1995 (figures taken from Mirrlees-Black et al, 1996, see table 1.1 below). The survey focuses on issues such as the kinds of crime which have affected those questioned, whether incidents of crime were reported to the police or not, and matters relating to respondents' fear of crime.

It can be seen from this summary that, despite the media focus on violent and sexual crime, the incidence of property crime reported by victims, especially car crime, far outweighs the number of cases of violent crime in the survey. Figures issued by the insurance industry show that for every 1,000 cars on the road, 22 were stolen during 1995. Car owners in England and Wales are twice as likely to have their vehicle stolen as those in France, three times as likely as those in Spain and almost ten times as likely as those in Switzerland. The British Chamber of Commerce states that property crime costs small businesses a total of £5.8 billion a year (British Chamber of Commerce, 1997). Half the firms responding to the survey had been victims of

2

Table 1.1 Surveyed crime

Offences	(000s)
Vehicle vandalism	1,851
Vandalism to other property	1,564
Burglary	1,754
– Attempts with no loss	975
– Burglary with loss	779
All vehicle thefts	4,312
– Theft from motor vehicles	2,522
– Theft of motor vehicles	499
– Attempted thefts of and from motor vehicles	1,291
Bicycle theft	660
Wounding	860
Robbery and theft from the person	984
Other household theft	2,266
Common assault	2,820
Other personal theft	2,075
All BCS offences	**19,147**

Source: Mirrlees-Black et al (1996).

crime over the previous year. One quarter of those responding had their premises burgled during the year and one quarter had suffered from vandalism. These commercial offences do not show up in the British Crime Survey since that survey is concerned purely with private households.

The overall estimate of more than 19 million offences from the British Crime Survey can be compared with Home Office figures on the numbers of crimes which are *reported* to the police and *recorded* by them. The total of offences recorded and published in the latest volume of *Criminal Statistics England and Wales* for 1996 (Home Office, 1997a) is much smaller than the BCS assessment, running at not much more than a quarter of the offending level revealed by the British Crime Survey. That survey shows clearly that many crimes which occur are not reported to the police, and this goes a long way towards explaining the gap between the two figures. Indeed, the survey suggests that there are almost three times as many domestic burglaries, four times as many thefts from vehicles, four times as many woundings and eight times as many robberies and thefts from the person committed as are reported to and recorded by the police. The main reason for non-reporting (in over 40 per cent of cases) is that the victim thought the crime was too trivial to be worth reporting. Other significant reasons are the perception that the 'police would do nothing' or 'would not be interested'. A number of victims

3

in the survey said that they preferred to deal with the matter themselves, and a very few felt intimidated and feared reprisal if they notified the police. For the crime category of theft of vehicles the numbers in the British Crime Survey and in police recorded crime figures are much closer together, because victims more routinely report such offences to the police, in order to obtain help in recovering their vehicles and for insurance purposes. More detailed comparison of the BCS results with offences recorded by the police is provided by *Criminal Statistics* (Home Office, 1997a), set out and discussed further in Chapter 2 at p 167 below.

The highest ever level of officially recorded crime was 5.5 million in 1992, since when there has been a modest annual fall. The former Conservative Home Secretary, Michael Howard, when announcing successive yearly reductions from this peak level of recorded crime, claimed that the downturn in the figures clearly demonstrated the success of government strategies in the 'war on crime'. This included the increased use of crime prevention measures such as closed-circuit TV (CCTV) in town centres and the pursuit of strongly punitive sentencing policies. Mr Howard made political capital out of the figures, claiming them to be 'a real turning of the tide against crime'. A total of 5 million offences was recorded by the police in 1996, a sum which is again slightly down from the previous year. This overall fall, however, masked a rise in recorded violent crime which, although still making up only a small proportion (8 per cent) of overall offending, has been rising steadily in recent years and has increased by the order of 60 per cent between 1986 and 1996. Current levels of recorded crime are nearly 10 times greater than the level of recorded crime in the 1950s.

Figures generated by these official statistics are notoriously controversial. *The Times* columnist, Simon Jenkins, has commented that '[R]ecorded crime figures testify to one thing alone: the capacity of intelligent people in Whitehall to concoct any old rubbish when required by the black art of politics. A fourth category has been added to the notorious scale of mendacity: lies, damned lies, statistics and "police recorded crime figures"' (Jenkins, 1995). The statistics include all offences which must be tried in the Crown Court and most others which can be tried in either the Crown Court or in a magistrates' court, but many summary offences (triable only be magistrates) are excluded. Offences recorded but not prosecuted by non-police agencies, such as the Inland Revenue, Customs and Excise or the Department of Social Security are not included. Many offences which are not routinely reported or are not readily detectable are greatly under-represented in the figures. These include incidents of domestic violence, prostitution and drug offences. The recording practices of the police vary from one force to another (for a case study, see Farrington and Dowds, 1985), and may change over time.

So are the figures totally useless? Not entirely. Some criminologists have pointed out that although study of the recorded crime figures can tell us little about crime rates, it can tell us quite a lot about the officials who are doing the recording (see Kitsuse and Cicourel, 1963, for the famous observation

4

Home Office, *Criminal Statistics England and Wales* (1997) table 1.1

Summary of criminal justice statistics, 1951, 1961, 1971, 1981, 1991, and 1994–96

England and Wales	Thousands								
	1951	1961	1971	1981	1991[5]	1994[5]	1995[5]	1996[5]	1995–96 (% change)
Notifiable offences									
– offences recorded by the police[1]	525	807	1,666[2]	2,794	5,075	5,036	4,886	4,868	0
– offences cleared up	247	361	775[2]	1,056	1,479	1,320	1,277	1,288	+1
– clear-up rate (percentage)	47	45	45[2]	38	29	26	26	26	
Number of offenders cautioned[3]	*[6]	70	109	154	279	308	291	286	−2
of *which* Indictable offences[4]	*[6]	25	77	104	180	210	203	191	−6
Defendants proceeded against at magistrates' courts	736	1,161	1,796	2,294	1,985	1,970	1,928	1,919	0
of *which* Indictable offences[4]	122	159	374	523	510	497	464	465	0
Defendants found guilty at magistrates' courts	705	1,121	1,648	2,042	1,438	1,357	1,359	1,372	+1
of *which* Indictable offences[4]	115	151	282	402	269	249	234	234	0
Defendants sentenced at the Crown Court after summary conviction	3	4	14	14	7	3	4	5	+25
Defendants tried at the Crown Court	20	34	48	79	100	86	89	86	−3
Defendants found guilty at the Crown Court	18	31	40	63	81	68	70	69	−1
Total offenders found guilty at both courts	723	1,152	1,688	2,105	1,519	1,425	1,430	1,441	+1
of *which* Indictable offences[4]	133	182	342	465	347	314	302	301	0
Total offenders found guilty or cautioned[3]	723[6]	1,222	1,797	2,259	1,796	1,733	1,721	1,727	0
of *which* Indictable offences[4]	133[6]	207	419	568	527	524	505	491	−3

(1) Excluding other criminal damage of value £20 and under. Includes estimates for criminal damage over £20 for Merseyside and Metropolitan Police.
(2) Adjusted to take account of the Criminal Damage Act 1971.
(3) Excludes motoring offences. Cautions, written warnings and all fixed penalties for summary motoring offences are not covered in this volume but are published in the Home Office Statistical Bulletin 'Motoring offences'.
(4) Indictable offences include those triable either way.
(5) Includes allowances for missing data for those proceeded against, convicted, sentenced at magistrates' courts, see . . .
(6) Caution figures were not collected until 1954.

that crime rates are simply 'indices of organisational processes'). In contrast to the dismissive comments of Jenkins (above), Maguire takes the more balanced view that:

> . . . awareness of the shaky foundations of criminological knowledge does not mean that one should abandon the collection and use of statistical data about crime . . . [S]o long as their limitations are fully recognized, crime-related statistics undoubtedly offer a valuable aid to understanding and explanation, as well as to the very necessary task of description . . . [N]o conclusions should ever be drawn from any such data without a clear understanding of how they were compiled and what they represent. (Maguire, 1997, p 142)

Towards the end of 1997 the Home Secretary, Jack Straw, announced that a new accounting system for recorded crime would be introduced in future years 'to give the figures greater clarity and accuracy'. The changes would include crimes involving several victims as counting multiply rather than singly, and more summary offences being included. It was accepted that these changes would result in a substantial rise in the recorded figures. The revised statistics will be issued twice yearly in future, rather than annually. For further discussion of the considerable gap between patterns of offending disclosed by the British Crime Survey and the offences recorded by the police, see Chapter 2.

As can be seen from the table set out at Extract 1.1.1 above, the overall 'clear-up' rate for crime was 26 per cent in 1996. This term includes not only cases which have gone forward for prosecution, but also cases where suspects have agreed to be formally cautioned (see Chapter 2) and offences which were 'taken into consideration' (where an offender being sentenced for other matters accepted responsibility for these at the same time). The clear-up rate is much higher for offences against the person (around 95 per cent for homicides and 75 per cent for violent and sexual offences) than it is for property crime. The solving and clear up of many offences against the person requires little police effort, since very often the victim knows the assailant. Violence between people who know each other is much more common than violence between strangers. In cases of property crime, however, there will often be few clues as to the identity of the perpetrator. There is considerable variation in clear-up rates across different police forces, with Home Office league tables currently placing Lincolnshire at the top of the class for having the highest clear-up rate, at around 45 per cent of crimes reported to them. On the face of it, this suggests that Lincolnshire has the most efficient police force, but this kind of comparison is fraught with difficulty, since different police forces are known to vary in their recording practices. There is a substantial body of research evidence which shows that, even where crime is reported to the police, it may subsequently not be recorded or may be reinterpreted by the police as 'no-crime' (Bottomley and Coleman, 1981). The temptation to interpret an offence as a no-crime offence where seriousness is low and the chance of detection is very slim (such as in bicycle theft) is obvious. Forces may also differ in their policy on recording 'prison write-offs' – offences admitted by a prisoner serving a sentence for unrelated matters but with which he is never charged. According to a press report in 1992, a convicted 18 year-old robber in Gloucestershire confessed to more than 3,000 further offences and alone accounted for almost a quarter of the county's rise in recorded crime in 1990–91 (*The Times*, 1992). The creation of competition between police forces by the publication of efficiency 'league tables', while it may have other advantages, seems certain to exacerbate this problem, with individual forces anxious to present their results in the best possible light: 'Since [the police] are recording only a fraction of the crimes committed, they may as well record even fewer, boost the clear-up rate and do everyone a favour. It is great politics, but terrible statistics' (Jenkins, 1995).

The percentage of cases recorded by the police which subsequently results in formal action by caution or prosecution has been declining steadily in recent years, and since 1992 there has been a 10 per cent reduction in the number of cases reaching the courts. In 1995, 35 per cent of reported violent crime resulted in prosecution, compared with a figure of 59 per cent in 1979. Explanations for this highly significant change varies, with some commentators pointing to the substantial and increasing number of cases each year which are referred to the Crown Prosecution Service but not proceeded with. About 12 per cent of cases so referred are dropped, mostly because the evidence turns out to be too weak to justify prosecution or because defendants cannot be traced. Some trenchant criticism has been made of this level of discontinuance (see Rose, 1996) but commentators also point to the large number of cases where prosecutions are mounted but a weak case collapses quickly with the judge having to order the defendant's acquittal (see Baldwin, 1997). See further, Chapter 4. Looking again at the larger picture of the real level of offending (the so-called 'dark figure') derived from the British Crime Survey, and comparing that with official statistics on the processing of defendants through the criminal justice system, it becomes clear that, on average, only about 2 per cent of crimes committed actually result in conviction. Home Office figures suggest that about 10 per cent of wounding offences result in a conviction, as compared to about 3 per cent of burglary offences and 0.5 per cent of cases of vandalism (Home Office, 1993). (For discussion of these statistics, see p 13 below and, further, Ashworth, 1995, Ch 1).

2. CRIMINAL JUSTICE AND POLITICAL CHANGE

Discussion of criminal justice often takes places within a highly charged political arena. This is often fuelled by the media, which tend to focus on the facts of particularly upsetting cases involving violence or sex. Media focus on a particular kind of crime becomes a running story. Heightened awareness of the issue results in more such cases being reported to the press, creating the appearance of a crime wave. Once interest in the story wanes and the 'moral panic' (Cohen, 1972) subsides, it is often difficult to tell whether there really was a genuine problem or not. Political capital can be, and often is, made out of crime. Examples include the well-documented scare over 'mugging' in the early 1970s (Hall et al, 1978). More recent instances, where changes to the criminal law have taken place against the background of highly coloured press accounts, are computer hacking (Computer Misuse Act 1990), attacks on children by dangerous dogs (Dangerous Dogs Act 1991), actions involving trespass by squatters, new age travellers and ravers (Criminal Justice and Public Order Act 1994; Wasik and Taylor, 1995, Ch 4) and stalking (Protection from Harassment Act 1997; Wells, 1997). This is not to deny that particular incidents of these kinds can be serious and should properly excite public opinion. The problem, however, lies in the very skewed and selective nature in which crime stories are reported, which can lead to hasty and ill-thought-out legislation. To take one example, the provisions for mandatory destruction of dangerous dogs introduced by the Dangerous Dogs Act 1991 have since been softened, allowing judges and magistrates greater flexibility over whether to make a destruction order (see the powerful attack made on the original law by Rougier J in *Ealing Magistrates' Court, ex parte Fanneran* (1996) 160 JP 409, and changes made by the Dangerous Dogs (Amendment) Act 1997).

With criminal justice issues high on the political agenda, legislative activity in this area has been intense, with five major Criminal Justice Acts reaching the statute book in recent years (the Criminal Justice Acts 1991 and 1993, the Criminal Justice and Public Order Act 1994, the Criminal Procedure and Investigations Act 1996 and the Crime (Sentences) Act 1997), with further measures (in the Crime and Disorder Bill) currently before Parliament and expected to be implemented in 1998–9. The Criminal Justice Act 1991 was of particular importance. It introduced a legislative framework for sentencing, based on the philosophy of 'just deserts', an approach which stresses the need for sentencers to achieve a fair proportionality between the offence committed and the penalty imposed. A custody threshold was created by s 1(2)(a) of the Act, whereby sentencers could only pass a custodial sentence if the offence was so serious that nothing less (a community sentence or a fine, for example) would do (for discussion of the 1991 Act, see Ashworth, 1992 and the Extract 5.4.2. below). The Act required sentencers to pay more attention to the seriousness of the offence itself and, accordingly, to place less emphasis upon the record of the offender before the court. Part of the policy which lay behind the Act, as set out in the 1990 White Paper, *Crime, Justice and Protecting the Public* (Home Office, 1990) was to encourage the courts to favour non-custodial sentences for the general run of property offences, and thereby relieve pressure on the prisons (see Wasik and von Hirsch, 1990). On the other hand, s 1(2)(b) of the Act introduced a scheme of longer-than-normal sentences which could be imposed on a relatively small number of offenders convicted of violent or sexual offences, who were seen to represent a serious future risk to the public. The Act proved highly controversial, and a number of its key provisions (in particular, the unit fine scheme and s 29 on criminal record) were repealed by the Criminal Justice Act 1993 (for discussion see Chapter 5, and also Ashworth and Gibson, 1993). The sentenced custodial population was in a downward phase during the months before and after the implementation of the 1991 Act, but by 1993 it was increasing again, and has increased sharply year on year since then.

Criminal justice became an increasingly political issue during the mid-1990s. While traditionally there has been a recognisable difference between the criminal justice policies of the Conservative and Labour Parties, with the former proclaiming itself to be the Party of 'law and order', this period saw unprecedented competition between Left and Right in the generation of ever 'tougher' policies on crime. Of particular note was the then Home Secretary, Michael Howard's '27 point plan to crack down on crime' announced at the Conservative Party Conference in October 1993. A month later in a speech the Home Secretary called for the abandonment of '. . . trendy theories that try to explain away crime by blaming socio-economic factors. Criminals should be held to account for their actions and punished accordingly. Trying to pass the buck is wrong, counter-productive and dangerous.' The Criminal Justice and Public Order Act 1994 began the process of implementing that plan, focusing mainly on young offending. The maximum term for which juveniles could be sentenced to detention in a young offender institution rose from 12 months to two years, and Crown Courts were empowered to sentence offenders as young as 10 to long custodial sentences for serious crimes. Just before the General Election of 1997, the outgoing Conservative government secured passage of the Crime (Sentences) Act 1997. Key provisions in that Act are the introduction of presumptive life sentences for offenders convicted of a second 'serious offence' and presumptive sentences of seven years for commission of a third Class A drug trafficking offence. Provisions in the Act to impose presumptive minimum sentences on repeat domestic burglars are not to be brought into force at present. These provisions attracted much attention because of their similarity to some of the American 'three strikes and you're out' laws, which prescribe a mandatory sentence of life imprisonment after conviction for a third felony offence. They also attracted vehement criticism from senior members of the judiciary, who argued that such sentences would work serious injustice, preventing judges from taking account of the particular facts of the case. With the election of a Labour government in 1997 there seems likely to be no reduction in legislative activity. Labour has substantially implemented the sentencing provisions of the 1997 Act, but with an 'exceptional circumstances' provision which allows judges to avoid imposing the prescribed sentence. The Home Secretary, Jack Straw, has brought forward a range of further proposals, mainly in relation to the crimes of young offenders, in the Crime and Disorder Bill 1997. The Labour government's White Paper which heralds the Act, and which is ominously entitled *No More Excuses* (Home Office, 1997c), offers an analysis of young offending and a range of responses to it which are remarkably similar in tone (and in

9

some cases more punitive) to those adopted by the former Conservative administration.

All these developments have been taking place against the background of a burgeoning prison population, which has already reached record levels and which official sources predict will continue on an upward trend well into the next century. The Home Office estimates that the prison population will rise to 74,500 by the year 2005, even without taking account of any further increase occasioned by changes to sentencing arrangements, such as those in the Crime (Sentences) Act 1997 (Home Office, 1997c). The following graph, reproduced with some amendments from the Prison Statistics (Home Office, 1997d), traces the fluctuations in the prison population and places them alongside some of the key criminal justice developments described above.

Extract 1.2.1

Home Office, *Prison Statistics for England and Wales 1996* (1997)

Prison population policy interventions 1986–96

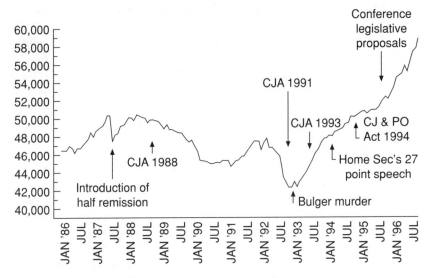

CJA = Criminal Justice Act
CJ & PO Act = Criminal Justice and Public Order Act

At the time of writing the prison population has reached record levels at over 60,000 convicted and remand prisoners. The government has said that nearly 10,000 more prison places will be made available by the year 2000, mainly by the construction of three privately run prisons. New blocks are being built in existing prisons and the refurbishment of existing prisons is being speeded up. According to then Home Office Minister, Ann Widdecombe, responding in a parliamentary answer in March 1997, an additional 8,500 places will be created by March 2000. A prison ship, originally called 'Resolution' but since renamed 'Weare', has been moored off Dorset, and is expected to be in use for at least three years to help cope with increasing numbers.

The two figures in Extract 1.2.2 are taken from the Prison Statistics (Home Office, 1997d), and relate to the prison population in 1996. The first gives information on the level of average population in custody over the last 10 years, the second sets out the main components of the current prison population by length of sentence. Finally, from the same source, Extract 1.2.3 provides a useful international comparison of prison population statistics.

Extract 1.2.2

Home Office, *Prison Statistics for England and Wales 1996* (1997)

Figure 1 Average population in custody

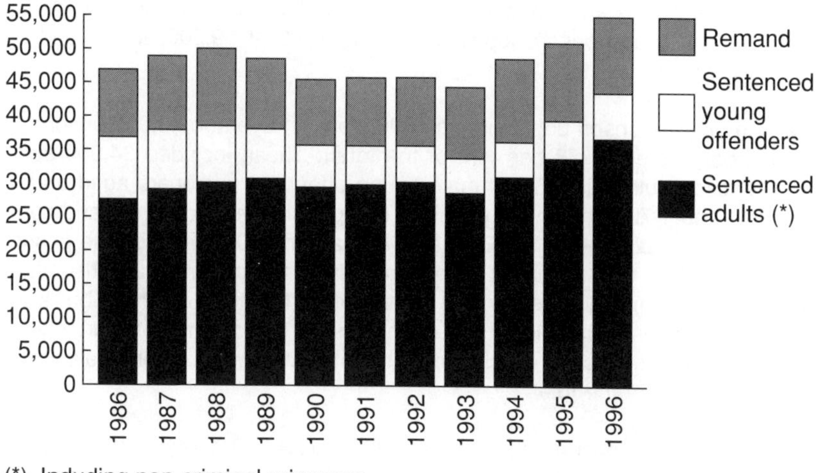

(*) Including non-criminal prisoners

The population in custody (. . .)

1.1 The average population in custody during 1996 was 55,300 which was greater than in any previous year. During the year the prison population rose steadily, from 52,000 at the end of January to 58,100 by the end of November. Between November and December the prison population reduced to 56,400, which is the usual seasonal pattern. Apart from that the only other month on month change which was not an increase was between July and August when the month end figures for the prison population reduced from 56,100 to 55,500. Seasonally adjusted

11

Figure 2 Main components of the prison population average during 1996

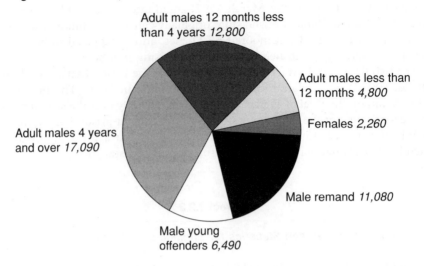

Adult males 12 months less
than 4 years *12,800*

Adult males less than
12 months *4,800*

Females *2,260*

Adult males 4 years
and over *17,090*

Male remand *11,080*

Male young
offenders *6,490*

figures, which are a better guide to the underlying trend, put the greatest month end prison population during 1996 at 59,000, at the end of December.

1.2 Among the prison population in 1996 were an average 43,000 prisoners under sentence (78 per cent of the total). These included 34,900 sentenced adult males, 6,500 male young offenders (prisoners aged under 21) and 1,700 sentenced females. The population held on remand consisted on average of 11,100 males and around 500 females. The prison population also included approximately 600 non-criminal prisoners, who were mainly persons held under the Immigration Act 1971 but also included prisoners held for civil offences such as contempt of court. Overall 2,300 females were included in the total prison population, making up 4 per cent of the total.

1.3 The average prison population in 1996 was 4,200 above that for 1995. This was an increase of 8 per cent and the largest year on year rise during the ten years since 1986. The recent growth in the prison population has mainly been among the population of sentenced prisoners. The average remand population during 1996 of 11,600 (males and females) was only a little more than the 11,400 average during 1995 and fewer than the average for 1994 when 12,400 prisoners were held on remand. Sentenced prisoners, by contrast, averaged 43,000 during 1996, compared with 39,100 during 1995, a rise of 10 per cent. Sentenced male young offenders increased by 15 per cent, from an average of 5,600 during 1995 to 6,500 during 1996. The sentenced female population increased by 16 per cent, from an average 1,460 in 1995 to 1,700 in 1996. Adult males under sentence increased by 9 per cent, from an average 32,000 in 1995 to 34,900 in 1996.

Extract 1.2.3

Home Office, *Prison Statistics for England and Wales 1996* (1997)

International comparisons (. . .)

1.18 International comparisons of prison population statistics are difficult to make because of differences in definitions and recording methods between countries. The main source of information is the annual survey by the Council of Europe of their member states (currently 40). This information has been supplemented by data obtained directly from individual countries. The results for September 1995 are shown in . . . In England and Wales there were 100 prisoners for every 100,000 members of the general population in 1995. This was more than some other western European countries such as Germany and France with 80 and 90 per 100,000 respectively. The greatest numbers of prisoners per 100,000 population were in Russia (695 per 100,000) and the USA (600 per 100,000). Many eastern European countries such as Belarus, Estonia, Latvia, Lithuania, Moldova, Romania and Ukraine had relatively high numbers of prisoners per 100,000 population – all of these had more than 200 per 100,000. Within western European countries the highest rate was in Portugal (125) followed by Scotland (110), Northern Ireland (105), Spain (105) and England and Wales (100). Since September 1995 there have been significant rises in several western European countries. The figure for England and Wales has risen to about 120 per 100,000 population and for Portugal to about 140. Figures for Belgium and the Netherlands have also risen sharply but, at about 85 and 70 per 100,000 respectively, they remain close to the western European average. Occupation of prisons was highest in Romania (145 for every 100 prison places), Greece (137) and Spain (135), and lowest in Slovenia (40). In England and Wales and Scotland the occupancy rate was 101, while in Northern Ireland it was 77.

In a speech given in July 1997 to the Police Foundation the Lord Chief Justice, Lord Bingham, commented that 'Given the temper of our society over the last five years, I do not find it surprising that the prison population has increased by 50 per cent, reflecting the more ready resort to custody by sentencers and an increase in the length of custodial sentences imposed. The tenor of political rhetoric has strongly favoured the imposition of severe sentences; this rhetoric has been faithfully reflected in certain elements of the media, and judges accused of passing lenient sentences have found themselves routinely castigated in some newspapers. So we have the extraordinary paradox that judges and magistrates have been roundly criticised for over-lenient sentencing during a period when they have been sentencing more defendants to prison for longer periods than at any time in the last 40 years.' (cited in NACRO, 1997)

We have seen that the number of offenders convicted and sentenced by criminal courts represents a very small and highly selective part of the total volume of criminal misconduct. Of course, conviction and sentence after a criminal trial is a public statement of the condemnation to be attached to the particular case, and its importance in symbolic terms is clear. But its instrumental significance is far from clear – can we really expect the sentences handed down by the judges to have any significant impact on the overall level of crime? In his first speech as Prime Minister, Mr Blair stated that 'we spend less than half of 1 per cent of the criminal justice budget on crime prevention, whilst we spend billions on courts and prisons to deal with people after they have committed crimes . . . Yet we know that many problems of later life stem from problems in the family, poor parenting and lack of support.' Rather than imposing ever 'tougher' sentences on those offenders who are caught, convicted and sentenced, should we rather think of the 'crime problem' as a matter requiring input from a range of agencies in which criminal justice can play a part but which primarily involves education, housing, planning, social services and so on? A recent report by the organisation Demos argues that rather than building more prisons we should be investing in a national crime prevention strategy, to address the factors which predispose to criminal behaviour – family conflict, alienation and lack of training and employment opportunities. The reduction of crime, and reduction of the fear of crime, might be achieved more effectively by measures such as improved security and design of housing and increasing community involvement in local policing initiatives (Bright, 1997).

Consider the following account of 'the problem of crime':

Extract 1.2.4

D Faulkner, *Darkness and Light: Justice, Crime and Management for Today* (London: Howard League, 1996) pp 1–3

The country is rightly concerned about the level and nature of crime, and about the state of the criminal justice system. Despite the welcome fall in the statistics for recorded crime, crime is seen to be a constant threat and the criminal justice system appears to be failing and in a state of perpetual crisis and organisational change. But a closer look shows that the problem is seen in different ways, in different places and by different people. The crisis is described in different terms, and the proposed solutions take different forms.

Confidence in criminal justice

Confidence in the criminal justice system has become an increasingly prominent theme of Government policy during the last fifteen years. Confidence may, however, mean different things to different people. For the general public, confidence is threatened if the police appear to be uninterested or unresponsive, if crime appears to be 'out of control', and if offenders seem to be 'getting away with it' by not being caught, prosecuted, convicted and sentenced – or if they are sentenced, because community sentences or prison conditions do not

14

seem to be sufficiently severe or demanding. To the government, the criminal justice system may seem expensive, inefficient and ineffective, either because of supposed structural or managerial weakness, or because the professionals who manage or work in it are thought to have had too great an influence or in some instances to be unduly 'liberal' in their outlook. Professionals themselves may feel undervalued, misunderstood, short of resources and constantly subjected to new legislation and demands for change. Police and ministers may perceive the system as balanced too much in favour of the offender, and therefore (it seems to follow) against the victim. Victims may feel that it gives them little or none of the recognition or respect they believe they deserve and have been led to expect, and sometimes even that they have been humiliated and betrayed. Offenders may see it as incomprehensible, unpredictable, arbitrary and capricious, but also easy to manipulate. Reformers are still concerned about actual or possible miscarriages of justice; discrimination against racial and cultural minorities, and sometimes against women; the criminalisation of children; the over-use of imprisonment and the degrading conditions which result from it; and the longer term social consequences.

Many of the views indicated in the previous paragraph are asserted vehemently and confidently by those who claim to represent public opinion, but more often on a basis of anecdote or impression than of systematic analysis or empirical evidence. Such evidence as is available from surveys or from practitioners' first-hand experience suggests that the situation may often be less straightforward than it is sometimes made to appear . . . But the demand for 'tough' action is undoubtedly a powerful political force, with strong public support.

Nature of the argument . . .

Arguments about crime and criminal justice tend to confuse two sets of issues. One is about crime and how to prevent or reduce it, and the other is about the process for dealing with crime once it has been committed. The latter has two aspects: measures for repairing, so far as possible, the harm that has been done, and the action to be taken with or against the offender. Much of the frustration in recent argument has arisen from the assumption that crime can be reduced, and its victims can be supported, simply by action against the offender. Not only that, but action against actual or supposed offenders is sometimes seen not only as the natural response to the problem of crime and the needs of its victims, but as the only response that is seriously required.

. . . of the proposed solutions . . .

The argument that the way to deal with crime is to prosecute more suspects and punish offenders more severely appeals to common sense and may sometimes be emotionally satisfying. It has a particular appeal to a managerial or consumerist approach to public services . . . All public services are quite properly required to demonstrate value for money in terms of measurable outputs, key performance indicators and satisfaction for the consumer. It is natural for a consumerist government and a cost conscious public to expect the criminal justice services to show improvements in efficiency and effectiveness, and that those improvements should be measured in terms of increased activity. It is equally natural for them to see a programme for reorganising those services or for changing the way in which they operate as a programme which will have that effect. Numbers of arrests and convictions, and even the length of prison sentences and the numbers serving them, are convenient measures of output. But crime is a complex phenomenon and criminal justice is an intricate process. Increased activity does not necessarily reduce crime and changes in structure or procedure can have unexpected and unintended results. Much depends on the way in which the process is managed, and on the outlook, attitudes and motivation of those who are engaged in it. These attitudes are themselves influenced by the extent to which staff feel valued, confident and secure, and by the relationships which they form among themselves and with those with whom they have to work.

An approach which relies on the criminal justice process as the principal means of preventing or reducing crime, or which expects changes in that process significantly to affect the general level of crime, reflects a misunderstanding of the nature of crime, and a misapprehension of the purpose of the criminal justice process and of what can properly be expected from it. As long ago as 1829, Sir Richard Mayne and Colonel Rowan, the first Commissioners of the Metropolitan Police, distinguished between the prevention of crime and the detection and punishing of offenders as complementary but separate functions when they wrote:

> 'The primary object of an efficient police is the prevention of crime; the next that of detection and punishment of offenders if crime is committed. To these ends, all the efforts of the police should be directed. The protection of life and property, the preservation of public tranquillity, and the absence of crime, will alone prove whether these efforts have been successful, and whether the objects for which the police were appointed have been attained.'

. . . and the consequences

Much of the pessimism, disillusion and cynicism which has characterised some of the recent debate . . . can be attributed to a failure to recognise the distinction between prevention and enforcement. The situation becomes even more serious if disillusion leads not to an attempt to construct more realistic and imaginative approaches to preventing or reducing crime . . . , but to simplistic demands for more repressive forms of enforcement and more severe punishment. These demands can lead in turn to a coarsening of standards not only of debate but also of justice itself.

3. THE ROYAL COMMISSION ON CRIMINAL JUSTICE

Even for those in substantial agreement with the sentiments expressed by David Faulkner, there remains the question of how to deal fairly and effectively with that percentage, however small it may be, of those suspected of having contravened the law and who are subsequently drawn through the criminal justice system. This is the issue with which the rest of this book is principally concerned. Faulkner speaks of the question of 'confidence' in the criminal justice system. How confident should we be that the system does deal fairly and effectively with suspects and defendants and, for that matter, with victims, witnesses and others who come in contact with it? A throughgoing inquiry into the state of criminal justice in England and Wales was carried out by the Royal Commission on Criminal Justice (1993). The Commission was established following a series of notorious cases in which serious errors in the criminal justice system had led to miscarriages of justice. These were the quashing by the Court of Appeal of the convictions of the Guildford Four (convicted in 1976; convictions quashed in 1979), the Maguire family (convicted in 1976; convictions quashed in 1992), the Birmingham Six (convicted in 1975; convictions quashed in 1991), Judith Ward (convicted in 1974; conviction quashed in 1992), the Tottenham Three (convicted in 1986; convictions quashed in 1991) and, under review at the time of the Commission, but not finally resolved until well after publication of its Report, the overturning of the convictions of those convicted of the murder of the newspaper boy, Carl Bridgewater (for further analysis of these cases see Rozenberg (1992) and Chapter 6 below). The subsequent Report of the Royal Commission was wide-ranging and included a total of 352 recommendations, many of which have subsequently been acted on.

The Commission's Report has been heavily criticised by academic commentators (see, for example, Ashworth (1996) and the essays in McConville and Bridges (1994) and Field and Thomas (1994)). A number of the Commission's proposals are considered more fully in later chapters. The following extract is taken from an early section of the Report, and it raises questions about a number of key issues of criminal justice:

(1) the relationship between wrongful convictions and wrongful acquittals;
(2) the question whether the English criminal justice system should move away from the 'adversarial' system of trial towards a continental 'inquisitorial' system (on this see further Sanders and Young (1994) and McEwan (1992));
(3) issues of resources and efficiency;
(4) training; and
(5) public confidence in the system as a whole.

Extract 1.3.1

Royal Commission on Criminal Justice, *Report* (1993) Ch 1, paras 9–27 (some footnotes omitted)

9. All law-abiding citizens have a common interest in a system of criminal justice in which the risks of the innocent being convicted and of the guilty

being acquitted are as low as human fallibility allows. For a person to be deprived of his or her liberty, perhaps for many years, on account of a crime which was in fact committed by someone else is both an individual tragedy and an affront to the standards of a civilised society. If innocent people are convicted, the real criminals, who may be very dangerous people, remain undetected. Conversely, justice is made a mockery in the particular case and the credibility of the system in general is undermined whenever a guilty person walks free because, for example, technical loopholes have been exploited, prosecution witnesses wrongly discredited, jurors improperly influenced, or victims intimidated. We recognise that there is no way of finding out, or even plausibly estimating, the frequency with which miscarriages of justice in either sense occur. It is widely assumed – and we are in no position to contradict it – that the guilty are more often acquitted than the innocent convicted. To some extent, an inevitable and appropriate consequence of the prosecution being required to prove its case beyond reasonable doubt must be that not every guilty person is convicted. But there is only a handful of cases in which it is possible to be certain, with hindsight, that the jury's verdict was mistaken. We have simply to acknowledge that mistaken verdicts can and do sometimes occur and that our task is to recommend changes to our system of criminal justice which will make them less likely in the future.

10.   Our terms of reference are not merely far-reaching, but closely interlinked. Any recommendation to change the rules and procedures governing one part of the criminal justice system will have a consequential effect on the others. It is not even possible to consider separately those which precede and those which follow the jury's verdict, since discussion of the rules and procedures of the Court of Appeal raises the question how far they could or should differ, · particularly in respect of the rules of evidence, from those of the court of first instance . . .

Adversarial or inquisitorial?

11.   The criminal justice system of England and Wales, in common with other jurisdictions which have evolved within the 'Anglo-Saxon' or 'common law' tradition, is often categorised as 'adversarial'. This is in contrast to the so-called 'inquisitorial' system based on the 'Continental' or 'civil law' tradition. In this context, the term 'adversarial' is usually taken to mean the system which has the judge as an umpire who leaves the presentation of the case to the parties (prosecution and defence) on each side. These separately prepare their case and call, examine and cross-examine their witnesses. The term 'inquisitorial' describes the systems where judges may supervise the pre-trial preparation of the evidence by the police and, more important, play a major part in the presentation of the evidence at trial. The judge in 'inquisitorial' systems typically calls and examines the defendant and the witnesses while the lawyers for the prosecution and the defence ask supplementary questions.

12.   It is important not to overstate the differences between the two systems: all adversarial systems contain inquisitorial elements, and vice versa. But it is implicit in our terms of reference that we should consider whether a change

18

in the direction of more inquisitorial procedures might not reduce the risks of mistaken verdicts and the need for subsequent re-examination of convictions which may be unsafe. For the reasons set out below we do not recommend the adoption of a thoroughgoing inquisitorial system. But we do recognise the force of the criticisms which can be directed at a thoroughgoing adversarial system which seems to turn a search for the truth into a contest played between opposing lawyers according to a set of rules which the jury does not necessarily accept or even understand. In some instances, such as our approach to forensic science evidence, our recommendations can fairly be interpreted as seeking to move the system in an inquisitorial direction, or at least as seeking to minimise the danger of adversarial practices being taken too far. But we have not arrived at our proposals through a theoretical assessment of the relative merits of the two legal traditions. On the contrary, we have been guided throughout by practical considerations in proposing changes which will, in our view, make our existing system more capable of serving the interests of both justice and efficiency.

13. We have sought information from a wide range of other countries' criminal jurisdictions (both adversarial and inquisitorial) in order to see whether there are lessons to be learned from them that might be applied with advantage to the criminal justice system in England and Wales. In particular, we have during two visits to Scotland looked in some depth at the Scottish system. We have not, however, found, either in Scotland or anywhere else, a set of practices which has so clearly succeeded in resolving the problems which arise in any system of criminal justice that it furnishes the obvious model which all the others should therefore adopt. Every system is the product of a distinctive history and culture, and the more different the history and culture from our own the greater must be the danger that an attempted transplant will fail. Hardly any of those who gave evidence to the Commission suggested that the system in another jurisdiction should be adopted in England and Wales; and of those who did, none argued for it in any depth or with any supporting detail. We have, accordingly, no evidence to suggest that there is somewhere a jurisdiction in which the rights and interests of the various parties involved are so uniquely well balanced as to give the system the best of all worlds. In the relevant chapters of this report, we make occasional reference to the features of other jurisdictions by which we have been influenced in arriving at our conclusions. But we make no attempt to give them either an 'adversarial' or an 'inquisitorial' label.

14. Our reason for not recommending a change to an inquisitorial system as such is not simply fear of the consequences of an unsuccessful cultural transplant. It is also that we ourselves doubt whether the fusion of the functions of investigation and prosecution, and the direct involvement of judges in both, are more likely to serve the interests of justice than a system in which the roles of police, prosecutors, and judges are as far as possible kept separate and the judge who is responsible for the conduct of the trial is the arbiter of law but not of fact. We believe that a system in which the critical roles are kept separate offers a better protection for the innocent defendant, including protection against the risk of unnecessarily prolonged detention prior to trial.

Moreover, there are 'inquisitorial' jurisdictions in which the system is moving, or being urged to move, in an 'adversarial' direction. For example, Italy has sought to introduce a more adversarial approach, and in France there has been widespread criticism of the role of the *judge d'instruction*.

15. We in no way suggest, as is sometimes done, that 'inquisitorial' systems presume suspects to be guilty until they are proved innocent. Nor do we suggest, as is also sometimes done, that 'adversarial' systems are not concerned to unearth the facts on which the guilt or innocence of the suspect depends. Both recognise the principle of the 'burden of proof' – that is, the obligation on the prosecution to establish the defendant's guilt on the basis of evidence which the defence is entitled to contest. We regard this principle as fundamental. This, as will become apparent in later chapters, is not incompatible with changes to our system which would require the defence to disclose the outline of whatever case it intends to put forward at an earlier stage than at present, or remove from the defendant charged with an 'either way' offence[1] the right to choose the mode of trial, or permit the judge to rule before the jury is empanelled on questions of admissibility of evidence or the production of statements of agreed facts. But defendants are always to be presumed to be innocent unless and until the prosecution has satisfied the magistrates or jury of their guilt beyond reasonable doubt.

Resources and efficiency

16. We are required by our terms of reference to have regard to the efficient use of resources – not, that is, to cost either the existing system or the changes we propose to it, but rather to satisfy ourselves that if our proposed changes were to be implemented the taxpayer could be reasonably assured of getting value for money. Although, as we have earlier remarked, every law-abiding citizen has an interest in a system in which the risk of mistaken verdicts is as low as it can be, there will always be argument about how much public money should be spent on arriving marginally closer to that ideal. But we have pointed out the scope for cost reductions where these can be made without, in our view, undermining the interests of justice; and we have kept in mind, even if no accurate calculations can be made, the prospect that the costs of our recommendations might be offset by consequential savings elsewhere within the system. We have been struck by the paucity of reliable information about the cost of the criminal justice system at present. While we recognise that the introduction of effective and reliable procedures of financial appraisal, monitoring and control would itself impose on the system a heavy additional burden of cost, we believe that more should be done to establish that value for money is being obtained.

17. Despite the absence of reliable information about costs, we have, during our examination of the system, become aware that in many areas there is a lack of adequate resources. We have been told, for example, that because of budgetary constraints the police may decide not to send samples collected at the scene of a crime for scientific analysis, or they may send such samples to their own laboratories or private sector laboratories rather than make use of

20

the Forensic Science Service, which is likely to have better facilities and more familiarity with the necessary requirements. There are also complaints about the quality of service provided by the Crown Prosecution Service (CPS). No one disputes that at its inception the CPS was seriously under-resourced and even now individual prosecutors may be required to undertake a heavier caseload than is consistent with the ability to prepare all cases thoroughly. There have also been well-aired complaints by the Law Society that the introduction of standard fees in the magistrates' courts is no more than an attempt to keep costs down. It is not within our remit to set levels of fees. But we think it worth noting that criminal work appears to be significantly less highly valued than civil work by those responsible for setting fees. We have also been told that legal aid does not always cover necessary correspondence with and visits to convicted defendants in order to complete applications for leave to appeal to the Court of Appeal. Furthermore, resource constraints are the major factor that prevents the training needs of the judiciary from being adequately met: there is too long a gap between refresher courses, and this in turn is because there are too few judges to allow the release of any greater number from their normal duties.

18.   The number of defendants proceeded against in the magistrates' courts in 1991 was 1,960,000, (the great majority of whom had been prosecuted for minor motoring offences). The number of defendants whose trial was completed in the Crown Court in the same year was about 100,000. The cost of the criminal justice system in that same year, excluding the prison and probation services, totalled £6.8bn, of which £5.4bn was attributable to the police and the Forensic Science Service. The Home Office Research and Planning Unit has estimated that the average cost of a contested trial in the Crown Court may be in the region of £13,500 while that of a guilty plea is about £2,500. The equivalent figures for magistrates' courts are £1,500 and £500. In the Crown Court, according to the Information Management Unit of the Lord Chancellor's Department, every day in 1991/92 cost nearly £7,000 even on a conservative assessment of the indirect overheads.

19.   It is immediately apparent from the published information that much the largest proportion of the total budget of the criminal justice system is spent on the police. In the Home Office Annual Report 1993 the expenditure on the police for 1991–92 is stated to have been £5,110m. In their evidence the Home Office told us that 80% of expenditure on the police is spent on police pay and allowances. Police pay is outside our remit, and has in any case been covered, along with structure, ranks, and conditions of employment, by the Inquiry into Police Roles and Responsibilities. But there are two points which we wish to make about the efficient use of police resources. The first is that if police officers are to be deployed as effectively as possible, every opportunity must be taken for replacing them with civilian employees in clerical, administrative or other tasks which do not require police powers or training. The second is that police officers need to be supported wherever possible by the most up-to-date technical aids. We have particularly in mind video cameras in custody suites, surveillance equipment at scenes of crime, computers in all areas of police work, and a fully automated national system of fingerprint recognition.

No doubt there are other means also by which investment in equipment of this kind can enable better use to be made of scarce investigative skills.

Training and sanctions

20.   During our examination of the criminal justice system, we have been struck by evidence of a disquieting lack of professional competence in many parts of it. There is, for example, a clear need for the police to improve their skills in interviewing suspects. The CPS, although greatly improved since its inception, could do more to prepare cases better and, in particular, ensure that weak cases do not get before the court. The services provided by solicitors at the police station are often inadequate. Not every member of the Bar knows how to present a criminal case fairly, clearly and without unnecessary repetition. Lawyers advising defendants on appeal do not always give their clients proper advice. Nor do all members of the magistracy and judiciary take sufficiently firm control of the cases in their courts. A number of our recommendations are addressed directly to these issues.

21.   Sanctions will only be effective if those empowered to apply them are willing to do so where necessary and the penalty is severe enough to function as a deterrent. Many of our recommendations will, if implemented, only succeed if these conditions are met. We accordingly look to chief constables to make full use of an amended discipline code covering police malpractice; to the Bar Council and Law Society to regulate the conduct of their members as well as to represent their collective interests; and to the judiciary to use their powers to implement wasted costs orders or refer cases to the taxing officer where lawyers have failed to perform to the minimum acceptable standard of conduct.

Public confidence

22.   The widely publicised miscarriages of justice which have occurred in recent years have created a need to restore public confidence in the criminal justice system. That need has not diminished since we were appointed. In addition to the terrorist cases where the convictions were quashed in 1990 and 1991, there has been since our appointment a fourth such case (Judith Ward) where the conviction was quashed in 1992. There has also been a number of cases not connected with terrorism, the most notable examples being those of the Broadwater Farm Three, Stefan Kiszko, and the Cardiff Three. We are particularly concerned that the last occurred after the implementation of the Police and Criminal Evidence Act 1984 (PACE) and its related codes of practice. There have also been a number of appeals allowed in cases which were originally based on evidence gathered by members of the West Midlands Police Serious Crime Squad as well as in cases where the convictions were said to arise out of alleged malpractice by officers based at Stoke Newington police station.

23.   The great majority of criminal trials are conducted in a manner which all the participants regard as fair, and we see no reason to believe that the great

majority of verdicts, whether guilty or not guilty, are not correct. The percentage of appeals against conviction both from the magistrates' courts and the Crown Court is very small. But the damage done by the minority of cases in which the system is seen to have failed is out of all proportion to their number. The maintenance of law and order is critically dependent on public goodwill, not only in the need for the law as such to command general assent but in the dependence of the police, whose duty it is to enforce the law, on the willingness of individual citizens to cooperate with them. The proportion of crimes solved by the police without help of any kind from members of the public is negligible, and the ability of the police to perform their function is impaired twice over if victims and witnesses are unwilling to give evidence in court because they no longer believe that trials are conducted fairly.

24. Those who have given evidence to us from the police service, the Home Office, the Lord Chancellor's Department, and the CPS are all as well aware of this as we are. The police, in particular, have pointed out to us that public concern about the integrity of police conduct in criminal investigations has increased at the very time when they themselves are doing more than ever before to improve and monitor standards. We fully recognise the burden which is placed on the police by the expectations which we, the public, have of them. We expect them to conduct themselves properly at all times, even while we know that they are frequently subjected to obstruction, abuse, and physical assault in the routine exercise of their duties. In the many contacts which we have had in the course of our enquiries with police officers of all ranks and in all parts of the country, we have been impressed both by their sense of commitment to their task and by their awareness of their dependence on public support. We recognise that police malpractice, where it occurs, may often be motivated by an over-zealous determination to secure the conviction of suspects believed to be guilty in the face of rules and procedures which seem to those charged with the investigation to be weighted in favour of the defence. Police officers must, however, recognise that, whatever the motive, malpractice must not and will not be tolerated. The remedy lies in a better-trained, better-equipped and better-supervised police force, not in the tacit acceptance of procedural rule-bending. And if the police are to claim, as they rightly do, that the burden of proof must apply to police officers charged with criminal offences no less than to anyone else, they must also accept that their disciplinary procedures should be such as to provide, and to be seen to provide, prompt and effective action against officers whose conduct has brought their force into serious disrepute.

25. Any member of the public who becomes involved in the system of criminal justice, whether as victim, defendant, witness, or juror should be treated fairly, reasonably and without discrimination. We are, however, acutely aware that confidence in the criminal justice system needs particularly to be restored among certain sections of the community. We have received evidence on behalf of both minorities and women that they do not feel that they are either fairly or reasonably treated. They allege that the system is discriminatory against them. It is a matter of statistical fact that members of the Afro-Caribbean community are represented in the prison population disproportionately to their

numbers in the population as a whole. Furthermore, there is evidence that in some Crown Court centres they may receive severer sentences if found guilty, and that discrimination may be a factor in this.[2] There is, however, no comprehensive information which would establish the extent to which members of the ethnic minority communities suffer discrimination within the criminal justice system.[3] This needs to be rectified by further research and we recommend that this should be carried out, even if, as we recognise, it may not be capable of providing a complete and conclusive explanation in so complex an area of behaviour.

26.   In any event, our recommendations are designed to improve the criminal justice system for all who become involved in it. We make some specific recommendations which we believe will help to restore the confidence of minorities in the criminal justice system. We are, however, strongly of the view that the most important need is to introduce a system of ethnic monitoring in order to establish how minorities are treated and thus to identify the measures which are needed to ensure as far as possible that the rules, procedures and practices of the criminal justice system are applied, and seen to be applied, in the same way to all. We so recommend. This should be seen as a means of enabling the Home Secretary to fulfil his statutory duty under section 95 of the Criminal Justice Act 1991 of publishing information annually to help those engaged in the administration of criminal justice to avoid discrimination against any person on the grounds of race, sex or any other improper ground.

27.   It may be argued that however practical our recommendations, and however cogent the reasoning behind them, there is a potential conflict between the interests of justice on the one hand and the requirement of fair and reasonable treatment for everyone involved, suspects and defendants included, on the other. We do not seek to maintain that the two are, or will ever be, reconcilable throughout the system in the eyes of all the parties involved in it. But we do believe that the fairer the treatment which all the parties receive at the hands of the system the more likely it is that the jury's verdict, or where appropriate the subsequent decision of the Court of Appeal, will be correct. As will become apparent from our recommendations, there are issues on which a balance has to be struck. But we are satisfied that when taken as a whole our recommendations serve the interests of justice without diminishing the individual's right to fair and reasonable treatment, and that if they are implemented they will do much to restore that public confidence in the system on which its successful operation so much depends.

---

[1] Offences in England and Wales are classified as summary, which means that they are triable only in a magistrates' court, or as indictable only, which means that they are triable only in the Crown Court, or as triable either way. An offence triable either way may be tried either in a magistrates' court or in the Crown Court. A defendant has a right in an either way case to elect trial on indictment. Subject to this the decision is for the magistrates . . .

[2] See R Hood, *Race and Sentencing: A study in the Crown Court*, Oxford, 1992.

[3] This is confirmed by M Fitzgerald, *Ethnic Minorities and the Criminal Justice System*, Royal Commission on Criminal Justice Research Study No 20, London, HMSO 1993. This Study reviews the key findings from existing research on ethnic minorities and the British criminal justice system.

The approach of the Commission has been criticised by Andrew Ashworth, who argues that the Commission has resorted too easily to the concept of 'balance' when trying to resolve competing arguments about criminal justice. Professor Ashworth is of the view that a better way forward would be for the criminal justice system to enunciate a set of 'principled priorities' among the various interests. These are, he says, to be derived from basic human rights (such as that of an innocent person not to be convicted) and that many of these basic rights are set out in the European Convention on Human Rights and Fundamental Freedoms. For the text of the Convention, and for information about the impending incorporation of the Convention into English law, see p 52 below.

Extract 1.3.2

A Ashworth, *The Criminal Process* (1994) pp 292–296 (some footnotes omitted)

The principled approach

The scourge of many debates about criminal justice policy is the concept of 'balance'. As it is often expressed, notably by the 1993 Royal Commission, the 'balancing' of conflicting interests is presented as if there is no particular weighting of or priority among the interests. They are all matters to be taken into consideration, and somehow a 'balance' emerges. Sometimes the process is given an apparent respectability by quoting probabilities that a certain consequence will ensue – for example, the low risk of innocent people being convicted. The existence of a low risk on one side of the equation may be thought to tip the scales in that direction, but herein lies the difficulty. It should not merely be a matter of utilitarian weighing, of calculating the balance of advantages, but rather a matter of social weighting, which involves deciding on principled priorities among the various interests. For this it is necessary to begin with a clear conception of the rights and duties that should be relevant.

It was argued in Chapter 2 that one of the most basic rights is the right of an innocent person not to be convicted. In Dworkin's theory the two rights associated with this are the right to procedures that place a proper valuation on moral harms (a right stated in broad and negotiable terms, yet which insists on the classification of certain harms as moral harms), and the right to consistent treatment within the declared policies. To this we added a third right, the right to be subjected to the minimum of restriction and inconvenience during the criminal process before conviction. All these rights remain at a rather general level, however, and do not cover in any specific form the many decisions to be taken in the criminal process. At this point it is possible to transfer the argument, as it were, from the philosophical level to a statement of positive law in the shape of the European Convention on Human Rights and Fundamental Freedoms. We saw in Chapter 3 that the European Convention, as interpreted by the judgments of the European Court of Human Rights, establishes a number of rights relevant to the criminal process: the right not to be subjected to torture or inhuman or degrading treatment, the presumption of innocence, the principles of legality, the presumption of liberty save for reasonable arrest or lawful detention, the right to a prompt court appearance, the right to prepare one's defence properly, the right to trial without unreasonable delay, the principle of equality of arms, the principle of non-discrimination, and the right to privacy.

In what way should this list of rights be used? First, it should be recognized that it cannot be regarded as exhaustive. It makes no reference to the rights of victims, although there are other declarations of the Council of Europe that do so. For many purposes it would be better if these rights of victims were incorporated into the European Convention on Human Rights, lest the separation should obscure their importance, but the process of declaring the rights of victims should be approached with circumspection. As argued in Chapters 2 and 7, the right to compensation, the right to respect, and the right to protection (at the remand stage) should be emphasized. Any procedural rights or powers that go further and incorporate the victim into decision-making should be rejected not merely as inappropriate but also on the ground that they may cast too great a burden on victims and increase the risk of intimidation. Second, it should be recognized that even within the European Convention some of the rights have greater force or priority than others. The most strongly weighted rights, then, are the right not to be subjected to torture or inhuman or degrading treatment (Article 3) and the right not to be held guilty of an offence that did not exist at the time of the act or omission charged (Article 7). These are absolute: there can be no justification for failing to observe them. On the other hand, we have seen that the right to privacy in Article 8 allows for derogation when 'necessary in a democratic society in the interests of national security, public safety . . . etc'. We have also seen that Article 15 allows member states to derogate from other obligations, notably Articles 5 and 6, 'in time of war or other public emergency threatening the life of the nation . . . to the extent strictly required by the exigencies of the situation'. The text of the European Convention demonstrates not only the importance of assigning weight or priority to the different rights and duties but also, in conjunction with the judgments of the Court, the practical possibility of doing so.

The contrast with the approach of the 1993 Royal Commission is marked. The Commission's terms of reference required it to have regard to 'securing the conviction of those guilty of criminal offences and the acquittal of those who are innocent, having regard to the efficient use of resources'.[1] At no stage in the Report is it stated how the Commission approached the question of priority among the three objectives in its terms of reference. In response to those who have criticized the Commission for giving undue weight to the reduction of public expenditure and insufficient weight to the protection of the innocent, one member of the Commission has stated that 'each [objective] had to be given its proper weighting in regard to every topic'.[2] This is a defective method, in that there is no suggestion of a clear standpoint from which the Commission began its deliberations on these issues of principle: no doubt the Commission might argue that this would have been a profitless exercise in abstraction, but that would miss the significance of the European Convention and its imperatives. Even if the Commission did follow some such method, its Report is defective in failing to articulate how its method was applied to each of the key decisions it reached. All too often the Report refers to the 'balance' favouring one solution rather than another, as if this were some ineffable mystery that requires no supporting explanation about how the conclusion was reached. Moreover, the assumption seems to be that in practice one can only decide on a policy by assessing the balance between different considerations. When there are so many conflicting interests how could one do otherwise?

The principled approach, evident from the structure of the European Convention and the judgments of the Court, does not adopt the utilitarian concept of balancing. Rather, it assumes that certain individual rights should be respected absolutely, and that several other individual rights should only be sacrificed in certain extreme circumstances. The process is different from balancing: it involves regarding certain principles as inviolable or as subject to derogation only where there is special justification, and then controlling the derogation so that it is kept to a minimum. Of course the European Convention says nothing about the interest of the community in ensuring that the guilty are convicted, and it would be wrong to conduct an argument, let alone to recommend policy, without recognizing this as a fundamental justification for having a formal criminal process. However, recognition of this fundamental justification does not return the discussion to the realms of balancing. It is clearly implicit in the European Convention that the individual rights it declares may operate to restrict the interest of the community in convicting the guilty, and that this of itself is not a sufficient reason to deny the rights. Once again the difference between a utilitarian form of balancing and a rights-based approach is evident. The 'balancing' approach tends to regard conviction of the guilty and acquittal of the innocent as matters to be weighed together, and empirical evidence of the effect of certain existing or changed procedures on convictions or acquittals would be important. The principled approach would assign priority to certain individual rights, and would then insist that any derogations be reasoned and minimal. Empirical evidence also plays a key role in this process, since it is important to verify claims about changes that are said to be 'necessary for public safety', or whatever community argument is advanced. For example, evidence such as that from research studies for the 1993 Royal Commission about the infrequency of 'ambush defences' or the infrequency of acquittals in cases where the defendant has relied on the right of silence should play an important part in assessing the strength of the arguments for derogation. Empirical evidence would continue to play a part in the monitoring of procedures, to ensure that they further rather than frustrate the values of the process: disclosure by the prosecution may be viewed as a prime example of the principle of 'equality of arms', but if it comes to be used as a defence tactic to delay proceedings or even to lead to the dropping of prosecutions, questions must be asked about the appropriateness of the rules.

There remains the point that the European Convention does not constitute an exhaustive statement of relevant rights. There are some central issues in the criminal process on which it contains little guidance at all, even apart from victim-related matters. There is little on the appropriate sanctions for breach by officials of rights declared either by the Convention or in domestic law. The Convention has little to say about dispositive decisions, and relatively little about the appropriate principles for remand decisions. There is nothing on such issues as confessions, controls on questioning by investigators, corroboration requirements, and mode of trial. On other issues, such as guilty pleas, there is no direct provision. However, this should not mean that in spheres not expressly covered by the European Convention there should be a return to 'balancing', even if it were conducted by a more explicit process than that evident from the Report of the 1993 Royal Commission. On some issues the spirit of the European Convention is clear, and is being developed already by the decisions of the European Court – for example, the presumption of innocence declared by Article 6(2) has been held to support the right of silence. At the very least the spirit of the Convention should be allowed to flow into the areas not covered, and to indicate directions in which the law and practice ought to move. It was argued in Chapter 9 that this would cast strong doubt on both existing practices of plea negotiation and the Royal Commission's proposals. A more difficult issue, as argued in Chapter 8, is whether the European Convention has any implications for the debate on mode of trial.

[1] RCCJ *Report*, Cm. 2263 (1993), p i, and paras 1.5–1.10.
[2] M Zander, 'Where the Critics got it wrong', [1993] *NLJ* 1338. Cf. N Lacey, 'Missing the Wood . . .', in M McConville (ed), *Criminal Justice in Crisis* (1994).

The next two extracts discuss a range of topical issues in criminal justice, providing contrasting analyses and hinting at very different solutions. The first is from an article by Charles Pollard, a senior police officer. He diagnoses a range of ills from which the criminal justice system is presently suffering. He stresses the high levels of fear about crime and public loss of confidence, and identifies this squarely with what he sees as the failings of the adversarial trial system to get to the 'truth' of criminal offending. The second extract is taken from a response to Pollard, by Professor Ashworth. He doubts whether it is possible to establish the 'truth' about offending, given the degree of selectivity and interpretation which occurs as cases are processed through the system. This issue is taken up again in Chapters 3 and 4 below. Even more importantly, Ashworth questions whether the pursuit of truth should be the central concern of criminal justice.

Extract 1.3.3

C Pollard, 'Public Safety, Accountability and the Courts' [1996] Crim LR 152–161 (footnotes amended and renumbered)

'Justice' must be one of the more loaded and ambiguous words in the English language. The Benthamite understanding of justice as the greatest happiness of the greatest number seems diametrically opposed to a view stressing the rights of the individual. Each definition has its limitations, but it is the 'civil liberties' one that underpins the adversarial system of trial, with the result that justice for the wider community is often relegated to the sidelines. Society's consent is essential for laws to be seen as 'just', but some social commentators claim the consensus underpinning the law and much of our social fabric is giving way. Others agree that society is fragmenting, albeit into communities

each characterised by their own moral code. This trend towards greater diversity between communities may have important implications for the adversarial
trial and its legitimacy in the eyes of communities whose moral claims to
justice it has so far failed to represent.

Entire communities are undermined by the fear of crime, despite evidence
that just 4 per cent of the population endure 44 per cent of offences.[1] As
victims, these people belong to a 'community' so far neglected by a trial system
dependent on their cooperation for its very existence. Far from equality before
the law, the defendant has become first among equals and it is his moral
claims to protection that are recognised by the law from the moment of arrest
onwards.

The courts are quick, rightly so, to express their abhorrence whenever they
learn of aggressive police questioning,[2] despite such occasions becoming
increasingly isolated. Paradoxically, they fail to apply these same standards of
protection to victims and witnesses in court. These are people, already vulnerable, who may find themselves harassed by lawyers[3] exercising an editorial
control reinforced by exclusionary rules that deny victims the right to give their
evidence in their own words. The point is that if the law refuses to tolerate any
abuse of power with regard to suspects under investigation in a police station,
should it not do the same for victims and witnesses co-operating under an
adversarial trial system?

A trial system that fails to search for the truth, where jurors are invited to
decide between one of two competing versions of events, is effectively organised around storytelling. All powerful stories are characterised by stereotyping
which, in the criminal trial, is used to label witnesses whose character is then
subjected to the routine attacks those stereotypes supposedly warrant.[4] This
tendency to stereotype victims and defendants thereby simplifying the issues,
inhibits a problem-solving approach to the underlying conflict. The key to finding the causes and treating the effects of crime therefore lies in reform of the
adversarial trial.

Many, both inside and outside the police service, seem agreed that the
adversarial system has 'more or less reached the limits of the present strategy of
checks and balances'.[5] The alternative scenario is one of greater co-operation
between defence and prosecution, but the greatest barrier to change remains
the principle that each of the two rival sides is the sole and rightful owner of
'its' evidence. Yet the extension of prosecution disclosure to the defence means
that this principle, so characteristic of an adversarial system, no longer holds
true. As McEwan has pointed out, 'if the trial were an entirely adversarial proceeding, it would be the responsibility of the parties to furnish their own evidence in support of their cases'.[6] Prosecution disclosure is certainly justifiable,
given that police investigations are like scientific research in that the pressure
to get results may sometimes tempt otherwise professional people to fit the
facts to the theory.[7] Despite that, there is now considerable evidence that the
current system of disclosure is in need of reform: existing practices may add
as much as 30 per cent to the costs of investigation,[8] an immense amount
of material is generated by the system, the time of witnesses, police and lawyers wasted, and victims suffer unnecessarily when trials are not focused on
the real issues. In addition, the absence until now of any requirement for the
defence to disclose an advance outline of their case, or to state the relevance

of prosecution material, has served to exacerbate or force the collapse of an unknown number of trials.[9] Mutual disclosure should be seen less in terms of its implications for lawyers and more as an opportunity to establish what victim and defendant agree on and where they disagree. This implies a new type of justice, shaped by the reciprocal rights and duties, not of lawyers, but of victims and accused: less confrontational and more of an attempt to solve issues that may reflect genuine problems within a community. Under the present rules, victims cannot be given legal rights without radically changing the structure of the trial. This is a consequence of an adversarial system which treats their rights as though in competition with those of defendants. While we need to acknowledge the betrayal felt by many victims when a defendant is acquitted on a technicality, it might be more practical in the short term to consider meeting their needs *outside* the formal structure of the courts. This could be done through mediation, reparation or diversionary schemes.

Public support is the oxygen of the criminal justice system, so a situation where only one in three people claim to be satisfied with the performance of the courts ought to give food for thought.[10] The probable reasons for this loss of confidence go beyond the well-publicised miscarriages of justice to include the failure of the adversarial trial to reconcile the differing needs of offenders and communities and the inadequacy of the criminal justice system in developing a coherent crime prevention strategy. All groups working within the criminal justice system must take their share of the blame for this loss of confidence: the police, who have become victims of their own insistence that the service could beat crime so long as it was given the resources; lawyers, who have tended to put legal accountability above social accountability; and the courts, for their remoteness and their poor treatment of victims and witnesses.

Change to the criminal trial must reflect four key characteristics. First and foremost, the trial must be designed to get at the truth in a way that is as transparent as possible. Many laymen are amazed that this is not already the case, having always assumed that finding out 'who did it', and perhaps 'why', is precisely what the trial is for. Secondly, the final decision must be based on all the facts (albeit some may need treating with caution as to their prejudicial value). Thirdly, the principle of value for money and accountability must be seen as relevant to the needs of justice: improper exploitation of the adversarial system can make this a very expensive way of dispensing justice. Fourthly, the process must become more people-centred: it must show itself willing to listen to the victims and witnesses once described by Jeremy Bentham as the eyes and ears of justice. In short, justice must become more 'user-friendly'.

For the courts to retain public support, each successive stage from investigation to trial must be opened up to public scrutiny; it is this 'transparency' that holds the key to public confidence. The law must play its part by recognising that justice is to be found in the reciprocal rights and responsibilities of all the participants, not simply in due process as it affects police and lawyers; in other words, justice must in future be grounded in *citizenship*. At present, too many aspects of the criminal law act as barriers to social accountability by emphasising procedural justice at the expense of substantive justice. Rather, justice should depend on both a fair process *and* a fair outcome.[11] A fair process means more than the objective and neutral application of rules; it also implies the moral obligation of the criminal justice system to work to prevent crime.

[1] G Farrell and K Pease, *Once Bitten, Twice Bitten: Repeat Victimisation and its Implications for Crime Prevention* (Home Office Police Research Group CPU Paper 46, 1993).

[2] On 21 November 1993, a jury at Leeds Crown Court acquitted George Heron of murder. During the trial, Justice Mitchell ruled some of the evidence inadmissible because of 'oppression and misrepresentation'. See also *Paris, Abdullahi and Miller* (1993) 97 Cr App R 99.

[3] P Rock, *The Social World of an English Crown Court*, 1993. See Chapter 2.

[4] See H Kennedy, *Eve Was Framed: Women and British Justice*, 1992, for a general discussion of stereotyping of women, both as victims and defendants.

[5] A Zuckerman, 'Bias and Suggestibility: Is There an Alternative to the Right to Silence?' in D Morgan and G Stephenson (eds), *Suspicion and Silence: The Right to Silence in Criminal Investigations*, 1994.

[6] J McEwan, *Evidence and the Adversarial Process*, 1992, p 19.

[7] M McConville, A Sanders and R Leng, *The Case for the Prosecution*, 1991.

[8] T Williamson, 'Police Investigation, The Changing Criminal Justice Context' in F Leishman, B Loveday and S Savage (eds), *Core Issues in Policing*, 1996.

[9] C Pollard, 'The Case for Disclosure' [1994] Crim LR 42 on the prosecution of three Animal Liberation Front activists which was dropped rather than disclose the names of informants.

[10] *The MORI State of the Nation Poll*, 1995. For police lack of confidence in the criminal justice system, see results of Police Federation Poll, 15 May 1995.

[11] See J Burnside and N Baker (eds), *Relational Justice: Repairing the Breach*, 1994.

Extract 1.3.4

A Ashworth, 'Crime, Community and Creeping Consequentialism' [1996] Crim LR 220–230 (footnotes amended and renumbered)

In his recent article Charles Pollard has presented a case in favour of several changes to the English criminal justice system. My aim here is to argue for a different emphasis. Whilst I agree that there remains a need for a fundamental reappraisal of our approach to criminal justice – a need recognised for many years, but not satisfied by the Report of the Royal Commission on Criminal Justice – I suggest that we should be fully conscious of the history of the matter, clear about the values to be upheld and clear about the dangers to be avoided. My task in this article is not to develop 'solutions', or alternative proposals[1] but to challenge common arguments, some used by Pollard, some used by others.

A particularly important point is that the police are nowadays expected – notably by politicians and by the media – to perform as the primary instrument of crime control. Thus the police are held 'responsible' for failing to prevent rises in crime, for failure to control certain kinds of offending, and for falling detection rates. Political concern about rising crime is met with the promise of more police officers. There is no shortage of research evidence to the effect that increasing the number of police officers by 5,000 is unlikely to have a discernible effect on the crime rate or on the clear-up rate.[2] This research is known to the Home Office and to the police. Yet politicians continue to suggest that increasing the number of police will alleviate the crime problem. The police therefore feel under (unreasonable) pressure. The police call for greater powers for the investigation of crime, partly as a response to the pressure for results which the expectations of their new paymasters place upon them . . . [I]t is wrong to hold the police responsible when any serious consideration of the problem would show that its causes go much wider and deeper. The police have not created the society in which we live, but they have to police it.

It is an important function of governments to take steps to ensure that citizens are adequately protected from criminal victimisation, but it is not simply a task for the criminal justice system – and it is certainly not, as already argued, a task that the police can be expected to perform single-handed. Crime prevention must be tackled on several fronts, and various public services (education, housing, environment, employment) have roles to play. The criminal process (police, prosecutors and courts) must then aim to deal properly with persons suspected or accused of crime. Where the disagreement occurs is in deciding what amounts to 'fair and just' treatment. A minimum notion of fairness is provided by the European Convention on Human Rights and Fundamental Freedoms, which the United Kingdom has ratified. It is worth recalling what some of the rights consist of:

(Professor Ashworth then refers to Articles 3, 5, 6, 7, 8 and 15 of the European Convention set out at pp 53–7 below.)

There is a police view, not expressed by Charles Pollard, that it might sometimes be in the interests of the public or the community at large to bend or ignore the rules so as to ensure the conviction of the real villains. Sir Paul Condon, the Metropolitan Police Commissioner, warned that this 'noble cause corruption' might occur if the law were perceived by police officers as unduly hampering their pursuit of criminals.[3] He did not condone it, but he clearly acknowledged this possibility. This accords with the consistent findings of policing research over the years, depicting a 'cop culture' in which certain values and goals are pursued which may or may not correspond with law and duty.[4] One of those values may be termed 'the police mission', a socially-motivated desire to secure the conviction of the guilty and to do so even in the teeth of laws designed to promote other values by restricting the methods which the police may use. The phrase 'rules are there to be bent' repeated by police officers to Maguire and Norris in their research,[5] shows how mere laws can be subordinated at the pursuit of this supposedly higher goal. The Royal Commission on Criminal Justice noted the phenomenon:[6]

> 'We recognise that police malpractice, where it occurs, may often be motivated by an over-zealous determination to secure the conviction of suspects believed to be guilty in the face of rules and procedures which seem to those charged with the investigation to be weighted in favour of the defence.'

In drawing attention to these practices I am not claiming that Charles Pollard supports them. Indeed he states that 'the courts are quick, rightly so, to express their abhorrence whenever they learn of aggressive police questioning, despite such occasions becoming increasingly isolated'. Rather, one of the aims of Pollard's article is to propose that the rules be changed so as to legitimate some investigative techniques that are now unlawful. The first two key characteristics in his conclusions are that 'the trial, must be designed to get at the truth in a way that is as transparent as possible' and that 'the final decision must be based on all the facts'. What are the implications?

32

First, there is the question of whose conception of 'the truth' and 'the facts' is to dominate. There seems little doubt that this will rest on the judgment of (often individual) police officers. That is worrying in view of research findings on the cultural opposition among many police officers to effective supervision, and the ingrained unwillingness to challenge fellow officers' judgments.[7] No doubt we will be assured that this research is out of date and that things have now changed; but, if the research tells us anything, it is that there is an enormous gap between what senior police officers say and what rank and file police officers do.[8] Moreover, reference to 'truth' and 'facts' carries an aura of objectivity and incontrovertibility that is often exaggerated. Two other terms need to be filtered into the discussion, 'selectivity' and 'interpretation'. In all cases that come to court, whether on a guilty plea or a not guilty plea, the prosecution's version of the facts is a selection. Both the Fisher Report[9] and the Royal Commission on Criminal Justice[10] commented on the tendency of police inquiries to neglect some lines of investigation and to view evidence in the light of one particular hypothesis. The notorious miscarriage of justice cases are graphic illustrations of these processes at work. It is unlikely that it has disappeared completely from everyday policing. Furthermore, the 'facts' that are selected and presented to the CPS and thence to the court may be open to different interpretations: events and statements can often be understood in divergent ways. One must therefore recognise that cases are 'constructed' in a particular way: the police do not make exhaustive inquiries on several hypotheses and then present all the evidence to some independent party to decide whether there is a sufficient case against any suspect.[11] No doubt it would be claimed that it is the rules of evidence that prevent the police and prosecution from putting forward more evidence, but that is a different point, examined in the next paragraph. Selectivity and interpretation are natural elements of investigative or 'fact-gathering' practices. Thus the defence case, too, is a construction dependent on selection and interpretation. What is important is to provide an adequate opportunity for each side to challenge the other's construction, and not to proceed as if the prosecution's version has an objectivity ('truth') which the defence version lacks.

Secondly, why does Charles Pollard assume that 'truth' is or should always be the overriding value in criminal justice? I have already questioned the practice of relying on the police or prosecution version of the truth. Even if the defendant's guilt were utterly clear, should a court convict if the evidence for it had been obtained by torture or by inhuman or degrading conduct on the part of the investigators? The principle of integrity insists that it is self-defeating if law enforcement agents themselves flout the law. This is often proffered as a justification for excluding evidence obtained in breach of PACE etc.[12] However, since the integrity principle insists on fidelity to rules, it is not inconsistent with the Pollard thesis, which is that the rules should be changed. However, while the United Kingdom remains a signatory to the European Convention on Human Rights, the scope for such change ought to be limited by the fundamental rights which the Convention guarantees. Unfortunately this did not prevent the curtailment of the right of silence in the Criminal Justice and Public Order Act 1994, for which the police lobbied strongly.[13] Moreover . . . the European Convention should be treated as a minimum: no less important is the right of an innocent person not to be convicted.[14] I fully accept that the existing laws of criminal evidence are far from perfect . . . However, any remodelling of them should insist on respect for this fundamental right, as well as for those rights in the Convention.

The same applies to references, not by Pollard but by some critics of the present system, to 'lawyers' games'.[15] Once again, the criticism must be assessed with care. Pointless technicalities and outmoded procedures should indeed be jettisoned, and codes of ethics for lawyers should be redrafted and then enforced. But procedures which give proper protection to rights must be preserved and, where necessary, strengthened. The 'games' caricature of the criminal trial often overlooks this. There is not the space here to develop these arguments in full;[16] my point is that sweeping references to the search for truth, and criticisms of lawyers' games, have far more glitter than substance.

Nor is this some remote academic view. There is anecdotal evidence that the experience of being arrested and questioned, or hearing of a friend or relative's experience may kindle an acute awareness of the significance of rights. More scientifically, there is ample evidence that people place great emphasis on the fairness of procedures, even where they disagree with the outcome.[17] I am not suggesting that Charles Pollard and ACPO adopt a truth-at-all-costs approach; but what is absent from their papers is any attempt to set out the principles and the rights of suspects and victims which a decent system of criminal justice ought to respect.

[1] For fuller discussion see A Ashworth, *The Criminal Process*, 1994.
[2] See e.g. M Hough, 'Thinking About Effectiveness' (1987) 27 *British Journal of Criminology* 70; R Reiner, *The Politics of the Police*, 2nd ed, 1992, pp 146–156.
[3] Evidence to the House of Commons Home Affairs Committee, 24 March 1993.
[4] For a summary of research see R Reiner, *The Politics of the Police*, 2nd ed, 1992, Ch 2; for more recent findings see M Maguire and C Norris, *The Conduct and Supervision of Police Investigations*, Royal Commission on Criminal Justice Research Study No 5, 1993.
[5] Ibid, and M Maguire and C Norris, 'Police Investigations: Practice and Malpractice' in S Field and P Thomas (eds), *Justice and Efficiency?*, 1994. For discussion see A Ashworth, *The Criminal Process*, pp 71–84 and P Scraton, 'Denial, Neutralisation and Disqualification' in M McConville and L Bridges (eds), *Criminal Justice in Crisis*, 1994, pp 102–106.
[6] *Report*, Cmnd. 2263 of 1993, Ch 1, para 24.
[7] See, e.g. Maguire and Norris (above) and J Baldwin and T Maloney, *Supervision of Police Investigations in Serious Criminal Cases*, Royal Commission on Criminal Justice Research Study No 4, 1992.
[8] For recent findings see P A J Waddington, *Liberty and Order*, 1994, Ch 6.
[9] The Confait Inquiry, 1977, discussed at [1978] Crim LR 117.
[10] *Report*, Ch 2.
[11] M McConville, A Sanders and R Leng, *The Case for the Prosecution*, 1991, Chs 4 and 5.
[12] Compare, for example, A Zuckerman, *The Principles of Criminal Evidence*, 1989, Ch 15 and the Note of Dissent by M Zander, Royal Commission on Criminal Justice, *Report*, 1993, p 234, with A Ashworth, *The Criminal Process*, 1994, pp 29–34 and 301–303.
[13] See also the arguments of I Dennis, 'Instrumental Protection, Human Right or Functional Necessity? Reassessing the Privilege Against Self-Incrimination' (1995) 54 *Cambridge Law Journal* 342.
[14] This proposition needs fuller argument than can be given here. See R M Dworkin, 'Principle, Policy and Procedure' in C Tapper (ed), *Crime, Proof and Punishment*, 1981, discussed in A Ashworth, *The Criminal Process*, 1994, Ch 2.
[15] Cf. Royal Commission on Criminal Justice, 1993, para 1.12.
[16] Cf. Ashworth, *The Criminal Process*, 1994, Ch 4.
[17] e.g. T Tyler, *Why People Obey the Law*, 1990.

4. SYSTEMS AND PROCESSES

The text and the extracts presented above clearly demonstrate a diversity of views about the criminal justice system, its failings, and the ways in which it should be reformed. Such diversity is mirrored among those who work within the different criminal justice agencies. Those who work within the system bring quite different perspectives to bear and have very different priorities and concerns. Little in the way of central planning went into the English criminal justice 'system', and different aspects of it have developed in very different ways. Yet there is a widespread and shared frustration at the lack of clarity over aims and objectives within criminal justice and at the constant switches of direction in criminal justice policy. Virtually every part of the criminal justice system has been subjected to institutional change over the last 10–15 years and more reforms are on the way.

The word 'system', when used above to refer to the criminal justice system, was placed in quotation marks. Given the range of different approaches which one can discern within criminal justice, an initial question that one might ask is whether the criminal justice system can properly be described as a 'system' at all, rather than a more loosely organised collection of state (and private) agencies. Of course there is some overall co-ordination in the day-to-day running of criminal justice, in that the Home Office oversees the police and the higher criminal courts. The Lord Chancellor's Department, on the other hand, is responsible for overseeing the magistracy. It has been suggested, from time to time, that a Department of Justice might be established to take over both, but progress in this direction seems unlikely at present. There is a Criminal Justice Consultative Council, established in 1991, which has a central committee which includes senior members of most of the criminal justice agencies, and 24 locally based committees, which brings together representatives from different agencies to provide a forum for discussion of strategic developments. But these are relatively cosmetic: underlying divergencies are deep-rooted.

Extract 1.4.1

H Pullinger, 'The Criminal Justice System Viewed as a System' in D Moxon (ed), *Managing Criminal Justice* (1985) pp 19–23

So what exactly is a *system*? The word 'system' may be used in many ways but the common core of the definitions includes the ideas of organisation, inter-connectedness and complexity. A system may be defined as 'an organised or connected group of objects' or 'a set or assemblage of things connected, associated or interdependent, so as to form a complex unity'. This concept is the focus for a wealth of theoretical and practical material which can be used as a framework for systems studies of the criminal justice system.

Figure 1 The criminal justice system and its environment

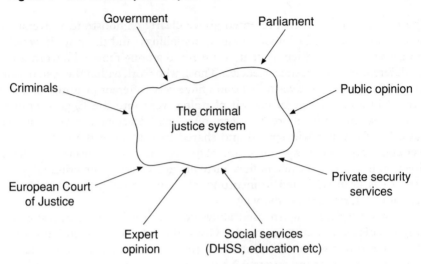

A system will possess channels of *communication and control*. In a human organisation, communication of the state of the system to the control centres will often trigger a response which will be communicated to the appropriate parts to attempt to change that state (*feedback*). The effectiveness of this process will depend on the system's monitoring capacity, the efficiency of its *information* channels and the degree of control which can be exercised.

When a system is observed as a whole it exhibits properties which its parts do not possess (e.g. a human being may have a sense of purpose, which cannot be said of the parts of the body). A system may be characterised as either *closed* (where interaction with its environment is minimal) or *open* (as is the case with social systems, where the environment has very important connections with the system).

Where does one draw the boundaries of the criminal justice *system*? For example, should Parliament, as the source of criminal law, be included? The choice of definition will depend on the purpose that it is intended to serve. However, the criminal justice system is commonly considered to be the combination of sub-systems concerning the police, the magistrates' courts, Crown Court and higher courts, the legal profession, the prison service and the probation and after-care service. The Home Office Research and Planning Unit computer model of the criminal justice system . . . explicitly specifies the parts of the system which the Home Office or the Lord Chancellor's Department can exert influence over and which significantly affect the passage of defendants through the system. All other elements of the criminal justice system are considered to be extraneous. It is clear that neat boundaries between sub-systems are impossible and also that there is no fixed delineation between the criminal justice system and its environment. We can see the 'open' nature of the criminal justice system in figure 1.

It is very strongly affected by outside influences – its input, in terms of offenders/defendants, is affected by social and environmental factors (so the requirement for criminal justice resources is largely determined from outside – it is largely demand-led); the laws which it has to uphold are imposed by Parliament; and there is a strong influence on the system's operational policies emanating from the Government and the public.

A further problem in attempting to describe the criminal justice system *as a system* is one of terminology. How does one refer to the people dealt with by the system? The names used at present include suspect, defendant, offender, inmate etc. These are all dependent on the stage of the criminal process at which the person finds himself – there is no general term for a 'person in the criminal process'. This has both advantages and disadvantages. It is right that the people are not tarred with the same brush. On the other hand, the use of the names 'defendant', 'suspect', etc will immediately put one's mind into 'court-think' or 'police-think' and will militate against considering that 'defendant' or 'suspect' as someone to be dealt with by the whole system. This is a small but important indicator that the advantages of systems thinking about the criminal justice system will not be easily won.

Some other questions may be asked. This extract is written from the perspective of a manager. Is this the best way to think about criminal justice? Also, do we really want a uniform view across the range? Would it be desirable for, say, the police agenda to dominate the entire criminal justice system, or is it better for there to be 'checks and balances', with different perspectives being brought to bear on the complex range of issues? Towards the end of Extract 1.4.1 Pullinger employs a different term when referring to criminal agencies – that of a 'criminal process'. The use of this term as a means of describing and explaining the complexities of criminal justice has been popular for some years. The approach is to examine the way in which a suspect is typically 'processed' by criminal justice agencies, initially by the police, then by the prosecution service, then by the courts through trial and sentencing, and then by the agencies assigned to deal with the offender after conviction. This has proved to be helpful in understanding criminal justice and, broadly, it is the one which is adopted in this book.

It is important, therefore, to grasp at the outset that criminal justice agencies operate in a *sequential* fashion, with each agency referring on to the next agency only a certain proportion of suspects/defendants/offenders whom it received at the previous stage of the process. Thus, the Crown Prosecution Service (CPS) receives files from the police with a view to deciding whether to institute a prosecution, or to drop the case. The police have, however, already made decisions not to pass large numbers of cases on to the CPS at all. Many suspects are dealt with informally by the police 'on the street', or they go through the formal cautioning procedure, without their case details ever reaching the prosecuting authorities. These cases are 'lost' in the sense that the CPS has no power to recapture and process them. Similarly, at the next stage of the process, the CPS will decide to proceed no further with prosecution in a substantial number of the cases which have been referred to them. This may involve a matter of judgment that the threshold of evidence needed to justify prosecution is not made out, or there may be other 'public interest' reasons for not proceeding. Cases which are proceeded with will ultimately reach the courts but those which the prosecution has dropped are 'lost', the court having no power to bring those persons before it. Again, when a defendant has pleaded guilty or has been convicted the judge, or the bench of magistrates, will impose sentence. The prison service, or the probation service, is simply required to receive those sentenced offenders from the courts and have no choice but to receive and accommodate them. One exception to this is where the sentencing court decides that the offender requires treatment in a hospital (Mental Health Act 1983, s 37). Since hospitals are part of the health service and not part of the criminal justice process, before making such an order, the sentencer has to make inquiries whether there is a hospital which is willing and able to take the sentenced person. If there is no space available, the order cannot be made.

In the extract from his essay, Pullinger refers to the need for 'feedback' from criminal justice agencies to the central authority. Information about the processing of cases is collected and published annually in *Criminal Statistics*, an important source of information about the criminal justice process in England and Wales. The flow chart on p 39 is taken from the 1997 publication, giving criminal statistics for 1996.

The description in the chart of the 'flow' through criminal justice agencies suggests an entirely 'one-way' process, with each criminal justice agency working largely in isolation from the others. While this kind of 'production line' analogy is useful, it can also be somewhat misleading. Inevitably, the routine operation of criminal justice does require a high degree of co-operation between different agencies. Communication and feedback takes place between the different criminal justice agencies in many important ways. The police and the CPS inevitably work closely together, whilst seeking nonetheless to maintain the important division of function between 'investigation' and 'prosecution' which was the rationale behind the setting up of the CPS by the Prosecution of Offences Act 1985. A Report on the problems of delay in the criminal justice system (Home Office, 1997f), noted that although fewer cases were now coming to court than before (see above) these cases were taking longer to process. The Report recommended, amongst other things, that CPS staff should have a permanent presence in police stations and should work alongside the police in preparing cases for court. The Lord Chief Justice, Lord Bingham, immediately criticised this suggestion, commenting that 'while relations between the police and the CPS should not be in any way adversarial nor should the CPS be . . . in the pocket of the police, and I have some fear that the permanent presence of a prosecutor in the police station would blur the important distinction between their roles . . .' (Lord Bingham, quoted in NACRO, 1997). The probation service,

Extract 1.4.2

Home Office, *Criminal Statistics England and Wales* (1997) figure 1.1

Flows through the criminal justice system, 1996

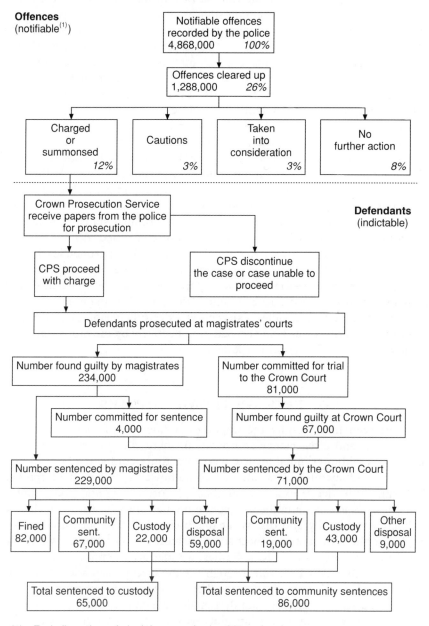

(1)   Excluding other criminal damage of value £20 and under

as well as receiving from the courts sentenced offenders placed on probation or given community service orders, provides the vital function of preparing pre-sentence reports on many of those who are to appear before the courts and who are intending to plead guilty. A probation officer, after interviewing the defendant and speaking to others who know him well, writes a report which, in addition to describing the circumstances of the offending will set out in some detail the offender's background, personal circumstances and diffi-culties, attitude to the offence, and so on. If the probation officer anticipates that the court will consider passing a community sentence, the report will also contain information about probation service facilities available locally for offenders. The links between the courts and the probation service are such that, in many local areas, relations are close and cordial. A recent Home Office survey found that 90 per cent of magistrates were 'fairly or very satisfied' with the work of the probation service in their area and felt that magistrates had a good or fairly good working relationship with the service (Home Office, 1997b). Sometimes, however, tensions can arise if the court thinks the probation service is too 'offender-biased' and is making unrealistic suggestions in its pre-sentence reports. Of course, anyone involved in crim-inal justice can make themselves aware of the criminal statistics relating to the part of the process with which they are most concerned. All this relates to communication and the dissemination of information at a general level. There is, however, little 'feedback' for decision-makers in the sense of their being routinely informed as to the outcome of particular cases they have dealt with. Thus in the survey cited above (Home Office, 1997b), many of the magis-trates questioned were unable to answer whether supervision or enforcement of community orders was being carried out effectively by the probation service in their local area. They did not know.

5. FIVE GENERAL THEMES

We have seen that, despite the important influences of management, sys-tematisation and inter-agency co-operation, there is a diversity of aims and approaches within criminal justice, with sometimes conflicting policies being pursued simultaneously. It would be wrong, however, to give the impression that criminal justice is in a state of chaos. In organising and presenting the material in this book a number of general themes press forward, which it will be helpful to identify and discuss at this point. It is not our purpose to re-emphasise these themes in a mechanical fashion at every point at which they subsequently appear in the text. Rather, we identify them here as a number of common threads which run through the detailed presentation of material in later chapters. To some extent, the themes are intended to provide a coun-terpoint to a sense of disunity and dysfunction which may otherwise have been the abiding impression of this introductory chapter. Particular aspects of the five general themes are taken up again in the final chapter of the book.

(a) The management of discretion

Management and control of discretion and decision-making by those working within criminal justice agencies is an important issue. At every stage of the criminal justice process the relevant criminal justice agency enjoys a degree of flexibility in decisions about the processing of individual cases. In the following short extract Professor Ashworth considers the extent to which the various criminal justice agencies are in fact subject to democratic control and accountability. He suggests that if the democratic ideal is to be taken seriously, 'there must be some overall plan or overall body with responsibility for general policies of law enforcement'.

Extract 1.5.1

A Ashworth, *The Criminal Process* (1994) pp 43–45

It will be evident in the course of the book that many stages of the criminal process are characterized by discretion. This is often justified by reference to the multifactorial nature of many decisions in the criminal process. However, this does not mean that values such as predictability, certainty, and principled decision-making have to be jettisoned: to a large extent they may be secured through systems of accountability.[1] Such values as the protection of declared rights (of victims and suspects or offenders) and the prevention of abuse of power by officials might be threatened if the policies or the practices of a law enforcement agency diverge from the purposes of the system. Methods of accountability include proper scrutiny of general policies, rules and/or guidelines for decision-making, active supervision of practice, avenues for challenging decisions, and openness rather than secrecy at key stages.

In a democratic form of society, issues of public policy should be decided by the legislature. However, in matters of law enforcement the tendency has been for Parliament to avoid such issues and to leave them to each agency itself, usually without any check other than the formal requirement to submit annual reports to the House of Commons. Thus agencies such as the Inland Revenue, Customs and Excise, and the Health and Safety Executive are relatively free to determine their own policies – 'semi-autonomous', as Dennis Galligan puts it[2] – although some of their procedures will be authorized by statute. The Crown Prosecution Service is similarly regulated: statute requires the Service to formulate a code and to report annually to Parliament, but there is no legislative guidance on substance. The police are also relatively free in this regard, although the Home Office sends guidance by circular to chief constables which is then used as a basis for appraisal by Her Majesty's Chief Inspector of Constabulary. It is, of course, possible for the Government to put pressure on agencies to modify their policies, but that hardly qualifies as a form of accountability. The Crown Prosecution Service has published its general guidelines, in the form of the *Code for Crown Prosecutors*, but this is only a significant step towards accountability if they are worded clearly and if they are followed in practice. The Crown Prosecution Service, in common with

41

other statutory bodies, is also open to scrutiny from various government and parliamentary sources. The Select Committee procedure applies, and thus the Home Affairs Committee has examined the performance of such organizations as the police, the Crown Prosecution Service, the Forensic Science Service, and the Prison Service. Within Government, there is also the role of the Audit Commission in assessing the performance of agencies. The existence of these bodies adds to accountability, even though their direct powers are limited.

Are these agencies accountable to the courts? There is a number of public law doctrines available, but the tendency has been to confine judicial review to the outer limits of unreasonableness (by applying the *Wednesbury* principle).[3] In recent years there have been some moves towards the scrutiny of certain policies for and against prosecution,[4] but the prevailing attitude remains one of reluctance. One could argue that the courts themselves, not being a democratic body, are unsuited to the task of reviewing operational policies. However, in a system with a declared set of rights (such as the US Constitution, or the European Convention on Human Rights if incorporated into English law), the courts could at least function to safeguard those rights against infringement.[5] Thus there is the potential for the courts to scrutinize decisions or policies on such matters as prosecution decisions, mode of trial, plea negotiation, and so forth, ensuring that they do not deprive individuals of procedural or substantive rights.

Claims for greater openness, as a step towards public accountability, are likely to be unwelcome in a sphere that has long known secrecy. Following the Scarman Report,[6] the Metropolitan Police developed local consultative committees, neighbourhood watch schemes, and other links with the community.[7] There are now schemes for lay visitors in police stations,[8] and 'appropriate adults' must be summoned to interviews of young people and of mentally handicapped people at police stations. Proposals for greater openness in plea bargaining might have similar benefits, in so far as they lead the participants in decision-making to take greater care to follow the rules.

However, it is in the nature of many pre-trial decisions that they involve wide discretion, offer the suspect or defendant a 'take-it-or-leave-it' choice, and may result in the case dropping out of the system altogether. Occasional *post hoc* review may well prove inferior to the articulation of policies, followed by thorough training, by internal supervision arrangements, and by opportunities for challenging decisions. It would certainly not be sufficient to assume that the formulation of guidelines for all the key decisions would ensure accountability and consistency, although that is a necessary step. But even then, there are further questions: who is to formulate the policies? If there is to be accountability at this stage, to whom should it be? There are varied histories of local accountability for the police and the Probation Service, but even a perfect system of local accountability might still lead to variations between one area and another. This suggests that, if the democratic ideal is to be taken seriously, there must be some overall plan or overall body with responsibility for general policies of law enforcement. This theme will be taken up again in the concluding chapter. For the present, it is sufficient to establish the strong arguments in favour of accountability, to point out the need for accountability at the different levels of general policy and individual decision-making,[9] and to advert to its limited and fragmentary nature in the existing system of pre-trial justice.

[1] D J Galligan, 'Regulating Pre-trial Decisions', in I Dennis (ed), *Criminal Law and Criminal Justice* (1987).

[2] Ibid.

[3] *Associated Provincial Picture Houses v Wednesbury Corporation* [1948] 1 KB 223.

[4] e.g. *R. v Chief Constable of Kent, ex p. L.* (1991) 93 Cr. App. R. 416, *R. v Inland Revenue Commissioners, ex p. Mead* [1993] 1 All ER 722, and *R. v Croydon Justices, ex p. Dean* [1993] Crim LR 759, discussed in Ch 5.

[5] For a recent judicial essay in favour of incorporating the European Convention into English law, see Sir Thomas Bingham, 'The European Convention on Human Rights: Time to Incorporate' (1993) 109 *LQR* 390.

[6] Lord Scarman, *The Brixton Disorders*, Cmnd. 8427 (1981).

[7] For general discussion, see R Reiner, *The Politics of the Police* (2nd ed, 1992), 253–261, and L Lustgarten, *The Governance of the Police* (1986).

[8] R Morgan, 'Policing by Consent', in R Morgan and D Smith (eds), *Coming to Terms with Policing* (1989).

[9] See G Richardson, *Law, Process and Custody: Prisoners and Patients* (1993), 43–45.

As is explained more fully in Chapter 2, a police officer on the street may, in a particular case, choose to 'turn a blind eye' to a minor incident of law-breaking or may decide to warn the person informally, rather than proceed officially with a view to prosecution. Clearly, principles of fairness and impartiality should inform these important choices. They should not be made so as to discriminate against minority groups, nor simply on the officer's whim, nor for his own convenience. A large degree of individual discretion does, however, seem inevitable in this situation – it is hard to see how such decisions could be monitored by Parliament or by the courts. However, the choice made by a police officer between a purely informal warning, a decision formally to caution a suspect, and a decision to press for prosecution is more amenable to guidelines and review. The current non-statutory system of cautioning has been under consideration for some time, and the Labour government proposes not only to tighten the criteria for cautioning, but also to place the whole practice on a statutory footing (see the Crime and Disorder Bill 1997). It remains to be seen to what extent statutory regulation of this area of discretion, rather than the present system of control by administrative arrangements (such as Home Office Circulars, which are authoritative advisory documents, not legislation), will affect the quality and consistency of decision-making in this area. Part of the impetus for change here derives from evidence of continuing diversity across different police forces in the exercise of cautioning powers (see Evans and Wilkinson, 1990), and partly from a government determination to 'tighten up' on certain aspects of the practice, especially repeat cautioning of young offenders (Home Office, 1994 and Evans 1994). See further, Chapter 2 below.

In those cases where the police do refer an incident for further official action, agents of the Crown Prosecution Service exercise an important discretion in deciding whether to prosecute or not and, if they choose to do so, over selection of the appropriate charge(s) to bring. (These matters are fully discussed in Chapters 3 and 4 below.) If a summary offence is charged, the matter must be heard in the magistrates' court. If the charge relates to an offence which is triable only on indictment, then ultimately it must be heard in the Crown Court. There is an important middle group of offences, however, offences 'triable either way', in respect of which magistrates exercise a discretion to determine in which court the matter will be heard. This procedure is known as 'mode of trial' selection. In this context, the discretion of the magistrates is limited by statutory authority and by mode of trial guidelines issued with the authority of the Lord Chief Justice and revised in 1995. These provide that '[in] general, except where otherwise stated, either-way offences should be tried summarily unless the court considers that the particular case has one or more of the features set out in the following pages *and* that its sentencing powers are insufficient'. This area of law is also currently under review and is considered in detail in Chapter 4 below.

There is also considerable opportunity for the exercise of discretion at the sentencing stage, which is the topic of Chapter 5 below. Magistrates and judges must select sentence from a menu which ranges from custodial sentences at the top, through community sentences (probation order, community service order, combination order, supervision order, curfew order and attendance centre order), down through the fine, to milder measures such as the conditional or absolute discharge and an order to bind the offender over in a stated sum for a specified period. In exercising their discretion over sentence, sentencers are constrained by statutory provisions. A few of these constraints take the form of clear legal rules, such as the availability of certain sentences only for offenders in specified age groups (a sentence of imprisonment is available only for offenders aged 21 or over; the minimum age for use of the probation order is 16, and so on), and the restriction on the power of magistrates' courts to impose custody (which, for most purposes, is limited to six months' imprisonment or detention in a young offender institution). Other legal rules require sentencers to abide by certain key sentencing principles such as the principle that, at least for non-sexual and non-violent offences, any custodial sentence imposed, and its duration, should be proportionate to the seriousness of the offence committed by the defendant (Criminal Justice Act 1991, ss 1 and 2). When passing a custodial sentence, judges and magistrates are required to state in open court that they have been faithful to that principle. They are also required by the Criminal Justice and Public Order Act 1994, s 48 to give a similar assurance in every case where the defendant has entered a guilty plea. The court must therefore make it clear that it has given some sentence reduction to reflect the guilty plea, with a prompt admission of guilt ordinarily attracting a higher 'discount'. Sentencers are also constrained by appellate guidance, primarily from the Court of Appeal, on sentencing principles and appropriate sentencing levels for particular offences. As we shall see in Chapter 5, lay magistrates have generated their own sentencing guidelines, through the offices of the Magistrates' Association. Section 28 of the 1991 Act gives sentencers a broad discretion to take into account mitigating factors personal to the offender, but, in that context, some Court of Appeal guidance may be found on the relevance of matters such as the offender's age, health, or previous good character.

It is often said that flexibility in criminal justice decision-making is inevitable, indeed desirable, since it is impossible to formulate rules in advance to cater for the wide variety of factors which can be relevant to individual cases. What the above brief description suggests is that decision-making becomes more 'visible' as we move through the criminal justice system, and hence becomes more amenable to control. Sentencing decisions are made in public, in open court so that decision-makers are much more accountable than, say, the police exercising 'on the street' discretion. But this point should not be taken too far. Even in apparently public settings, crucial aspects of the decision may be reached behind closed doors – an example is the persistence of the practice of informally canvassing sentence in the judge's chambers, in clear contravention of the Court of Appeal's strictures in *Turner* [1970] 2 QB 321. For discussion of this practice see Chapter 4, where there is also discussion of 'charge bargaining', another procedure where 'justice [is] done in corridors' (extract from Cretney and Davis (1997), set out at pp 376–8 below).

Consider the following discussion by Keith Hawkins of the uses of legal discretion. According to Hawkins, 'discretion is all pervasive in legal systems . . . [D]iscretionary power not only permits the realisation of the law's broad purposes, but also allows or even encourages officials sometimes to distort the word or spirit of the law, sometimes to ignore them'. Indeed, the working practices of decision-makers may often be at variance with the declared rules and principles, and it is these working practices which suspects, defendants, victims and witnesses actually encounter and which help to shape public attitudes towards the criminal justice system as a whole. While Hawkins' account has a wider relevance than criminal justice, his analysis is very helpful in that context.

Extract 1.5.2

K Hawkins, 'The Use of Legal Discretion: Perspectives from Law and Social Science' in K Hawkins (ed), *The Uses of Discretion* (1992) pp 11–12, 27–32, 35–36 (some footnotes and references omitted)

Discretion is a central and inevitable part of the legal order. It is central to law because contemporary legal systems have come increasingly to rely on express grants of authority to legal and administrative officials to attain broad legislative purposes. It is inevitable because the translation of rule into action, the process by which abstraction becomes actuality, involves people in interpretation and choice. Law is fundamentally an interpretative enterprise in which discretionary behaviour is compelled by what Denis Galligan has neatly summarized as the 'vagaries of language, the diversity of circumstances, and the

45

indeterminacy of official purposes' [D J Galligan, *Discretionary Powers: A Legal Study of Official Discretion* (Oxford: Clarendon Press, 1986)].

Discretion is the means by which law – the most consequential normative system in a society – is translated into action. One of the commonplaces of socio-legal studies is that the form such action takes may not necessarily be predictable from scrutiny of legal rules themselves. Discretion – which might be regarded as the space, as it were, between legal rules in which legal actors may exercise choice – may be formally granted, or it may be assumed. It is in the everyday discretionary behaviour of judges, public officials, lawyers, and others that the legal system distributes its burdens and benefits, provides answers to questions, and solutions to problems.

Discretion is all-pervasive in legal systems, though its extent in any particular instance may vary enormously. It is, however, difficult to contemplate the making of a legal decision that does not have at least a measure of discretion. As the role of the state has enlarged, dependence on bureaucracies of various kinds to advance the objectives of public order and welfare, matters of public or occupational health and safety, planning, the regulation of business, and so on, has increased. Legal systems rely heavily upon official grants of discretionary power for a variety of reasons: among them are the complexity of contemporary society, the sheer size and burden of the legislative task, and the growing dependence upon specialist, technical, or scientific knowledge and expertise. In the face of all of this, rules seem both inflexible and ill suited as a means of coping with uncertainty and change. Sometimes, of course, law-makers want to remain as silent as possible on controversial or complex matters of public policy; in these circumstances, awards of discretion to legal bureaucracies allow legislatures to duck or to fudge hard issues.

Considerable discretionary authority is vested in legal bureaucracies both to make and to implement policy. Indeed, discretionary power resides at all levels in such organizations, from the most senior officials at the centre who frame broad policy, to the most junior recruit at 'field' or 'street' level whose work as a 'screening' or 'gatekeeping' official means direct contact with the difficulties of the real world. This, the point at which the legal system touches the people or problems it is intended to address, is where the tensions, dilemmas, and sometimes contradictions embodied in the law are worked out in practice. It is here that discretionary power not only permits the realization of the law's broad purposes, but also allows or even encourages officials sometimes to distort the word or spirit of the law, sometimes to ignore them. And sometimes, of course, officials may assume a legal authority they do not in fact possess, or deny an authority which they do . . .

Elements of a holistic perspective

Case and policy decisions

If we wish to understand the nature of legal discretion empirically, it is important to take a systemic or holistic view of it. The individual case is usually taken as the unit of analysis in most social science studies of legal decision-making, though what is usually more appropriate, as the following section argues, is a broader focus which, *inter alia*, looks at the careers of cases within a decision-

46

making system, and at interactions between cases or groups of cases. The concern for the individual case is not surprising, since legal actors and legal bureaucracies typically assemble problems for decision into individual 'cases', each relating to a particular and concrete matter and consisting of physically segregated units by which they may be handled.

Even so, individual case determinations are themselves more complex than they might seem, even within an ostensible single decision point. As Lempert shows [R Lempert, 'Discretion in a Behavioural Perspective' in K Hawkins (ed), 1992, Ch 6], what may on the surface appear to be one simple discretionary decision quite often involves a rather more complex series of decisions. A legal decision may require a judgment first as to the nature of the problem for decision (questions concerned with 'what actually happened', or 'what the present position is', and so on), then whether the problem or event is addressed by, or constitutes a breach of, a rule. If a breach is found, or a rule applies, further decisions may be needed as to what action should be taken, and, if so, what precise action is required. Subsequent decisions are thus contingent upon earlier ones, suggesting that analytically it is possible to distinguish 'core' and subsequent 'contingent' discretion.

Discretion is also often regarded as a feature of decision-making by individuals. This, too, is not surprising, since individuals or panels of individuals are often allocated formal authority to make legal decisions. Decision-making in law is, however, to a greater extent than is apparent from much of the literature, a collective enterprise. Indeed, it is hard in reality to sustain the idea of the individual actor exercising discretion according to legal rules or standards alone, unencumbered by the decisions or influences of others. Some legal decisions are explicitly designed to involve groups, like boards, tribunals, and juries. Where a discretionary outcome is the product of a number of decision-makers acting together, discretion is exercised, as it were, in parallel. In the event that differences between individual decision-makers cannot be reflected in a majority vote, they have to be negotiated into an outcome that can be presented as the group's decision. In resolving individual differences, expertise, experience, status, and personal charisma are important matters shaping discretion, since they confer an interpersonal authority to have cases decided in particular ways . . .

A focus on the individual case and the activities of individual decision-makers often does not portray the reality of legal discretion in another way. A good deal of decision-making in legal bureaucracies is concerned with matters of policy – deciding in general how to decide in specific cases. Policy-making involves making decisions about the objectives and meaning of the law, and about how these ideas are to be shaped into strategies to permit their implementation. This is 'the very heart of the discretionary process' [Galligan, 1986, p 110]. Policy is the means by which discretion is at once shaped and transferred down through an organizational hierarchy. Policy decisions speak abstractly to the future in varying degrees of generality and exist in the form of series of statements often incorporating matters such as the objectives of a decisions, criteria to be taken into account, information to be used, and procedures to be followed. Policy, like legal rules, acts therefore as one of the constraints in the context or field within which individual decisions have to be made . . .

A serial view of discretion

An argument was made above for a view of discretion as part of a sequence of decisions and occurring as part of a network of relationships in the legal system . . . Substantial power is wielded by those making earlier determinations in the handling of cases, for discretion is exercised not only in parallel in legal systems, but also in series. A decision made at one point in the system may profoundly affect the way in which a subsequent decision is made, owing to the structural position of the individual at the point at which prior discretion is exercised (see Lempert, Chapter 6). It makes sense to see many legal decisions as comprised of a number of discretionary determinations following in sequence. Cases are processed over time by means of a referral system: the creation of any legal case and its subsequent career are shaped by decisions made in a dynamic, unfolding process. Once created, individual cases in the legal system are typically handed on from one decision-maker to another until they are resolved, discarded, or otherwise disposed of.

A serial perspective also draws attention to the fact that effective power to decide is frequently assumed by actors other than the person allocated formal authority to exercise discretion. What is described as a 'decision' reached is sometimes nothing more than a ratification of an earlier decision made in the handling of a case, even though that prior decision may appear in the guise of an opinion or a recommendation. The nature of a discretionary determination may change or be changed depending on where in the legal system authority to decide is located. In such circumstances, matters such as the flow of information from one point in the system to another become particularly important . . . Since discretion is diffused among those supplying information, evaluations, and recommendations to the proximate or ultimate decision-makers, it is important to distinguish the real exercise of discretion from mere ratification. Some people who supply information or assessment may have such an enormous influence on the subsequent handling of a case that it becomes difficult to conceive of the visible, official point of decision being the place at which real discretion was exercised.

The diffusion of discretion means that decision-making power is dispersed in legal systems. Power resides, *inter alia*, in the capacity of decision-makers to drop or divert cases. The primary concerns of decision-makers are often shaped by a concern to handle and manage a stream of cases seen in organizational context . . . Earlier decisions may serve to close off the scope of discretion afforded to subsequent decision-makers entirely or partially, either by excluding a subsequent decision-maker (by discarding the case) or by narrowing that decision-maker's range of choice. For instance, legal actors handling cases prior to trial take advantage of their structural position in various ways. The low visibility of many legal decisions (like arrest of disrespectful teenagers by the police), and the degree of credibility accorded the source of information used in formal decisions, are two illustrations . . . Officials have their own views on the merits of particular cases and are often able to dispose of them informally in ways that accord with their sense of justice, or that allow them to make or honour bargains over other cases. This is largely how plea-bargaining works in the United States (e.g. [M Heumann, *Plea Bargaining* (Chicago: University of Chicago Press, 1978; M M Feeley, *The Process is the Punishment* (New York: Russell Sage Foundation, 1979)]). Again, in trials or hearings, advocates

48

can exert considerable control over what is and (equally importantly) what is not put before the adjudicator. On the other hand, Lempert [1992] shows how decisions can be made contrary to a legal mandate because no opportunity is provided for review in the legal structure.

Another form of power resides in opportunities afforded by the legal system to those who create, assemble, or supply material relevant to a decision to formal decision-makers. These people are able, artfully or unwittingly, to frame the contents of reports or other information to give prominence to a particular point of view (see [K Hawkins, 'Assessing Evil: Decision Behaviour and Parole Board Justice' (1983) 23 *British Journal of Criminology* 101] for examples). The use of language in documentary reports may often reveal where the effective source of power or influence in the making of a decision actually resides. Officials may frame how discretion may subsequently be exercised, not only by describing or presenting the case in a particular fashion, but also by making related decisions in a certain way. Thus, for instance, the penalty imposed by the authorities for prison misconduct may well profoundly influence a subsequent determination about the prisoner's release by the parole board ... What has happened earlier in the processing of a case, or similar cases, has powerful indications for the present decision, as well as for future ones. Furthermore, from the point of view of the earlier decision-maker, one decision is not made independently, but in a way that takes account of the implications of other cases for the present one and vice versa ...

The matters attended to by decision-makers and the nature of the constraints to which they feel subject may change as time passes and cases move in the sequence of handling decisions. It follows that decision-makers at different points in the handling system might be expected to have different priorities; indeed, there may be not only different sets of resource constraints operating, but also quite different value systems. When discretion is viewed in serial perspective, the nature of the links between different parts of the decision-making system, and how they are bound together, become apparent. The history of a case is especially important because the legal method compels the selective social reconstruction of the past. In recreating history, the method of law is to pare down or remove the uncertainties of the real world 'in the course of successive transformations over time from the original event or act to final adjudication' [A Cicourel, *The Social Organisation of Juvenile Justice* (New York: John Wiley, 1968)]. What happens, to quote Cicourel's description of the juvenile justice system, is that

> 'Each encounter or written report affects the juvenile and events considered illegal in such a way that the contingencies in which the participants interpret what is going on, the thinking or 'theorizing' employed, are progressively altered or eliminated or reified as the case is reviewed at different levels of the legal process and reaches a hearing or trial stage.' (ibid.: p xiv)

One implication for policy here is that, because discretion in effect exists in legal systems in a certain equilibrium which may be disturbed if a rule is changed at one point in an effort to limit or extend discretion, discretionary play in one part of the system may be transposed elsewhere. This suggests that those who would change rules, policies, or procedures must adopt a holistic approach in appraising the legal system and seek to anticipate more effectively the precise impact of different structures and forms of rules on discretionary behaviour . . .

Discretion in using rules

In reality it is impossible to treat rules and discretion as discrete or opposing entities. Discretion suffuses the interpretation of rules, as well as their application. In thinking about the relationship between rules and discretion, it is important to distinguish between fact-finding and fact-defining decisions, on the one hand, and decisions about action, on the other. Rules themselves have to be defined as to their meaning and relevance. Even where the meaning of a rule seems clear, the facts upon which the application of a rule may depend have always to be interpreted. To claim that one is dispassionately following a rule is to take for granted the interpretative work – the choices – surrounding fact-finding, and to assume that the 'facts' assembled are relevant to the application of a particular rule.

Interpreting a rule involves, at the minimum, discovering its meaning, characterizing the present problem, and judging whether that problem is addressed by the rule. And, even where a rule is granted meaning, there will still be scope for the further exercise of discretion by officials, not only as to its applicability, but also as to the accuracy or genuineness of information relevant to the exercise of discretion. The facts, writes Galligan,

> 'can be ascertained only be imperfect means, relying on imperfect procedures – the evidence of others, one's own perceptions and understandings, and the classification of those perceptions; also, there are limits to the time that may be spent in the quest for factual accuracy . . . any decision requires assessment and judgment, both in fixing the methods for eliciting the facts and in deciding how much evidence is sufficient. Understood in this special sense, there is some justification for talking of discretion in settling the facts. Similarly, in applying a standard to the facts, the decision-maker has to settle both the meaning of the standard and the characterization of the facts in terms of that meaning.' (1986: 34–5)

The form and complexity of a rule have important implications for the degree of discretion created. Schneider [C E Schneider, 'Discretion and Rules: A Lawyer's View' in K Hawkins (ed), 1992, Ch 2] suggests that the simpler the rule the more likely it is that the principle embodied in it will be adhered to, while the more complex the rule the greater the discretion available to individual decision-makers in its interpretation and application. Similarly, complex systems of rules, though highly specific, may also have the effect of creating greater discretion in practice, as Long's study of US tax legislation suggests. This recalls Damaska's comment that 'there is a point beyond which increased complexity of law, especially in loosely-ordered normative systems, objectively increases rather than decreases the decision-maker's freedom' [M R Damaska, 'Structure of Authority and Comparative Criminal Procedure' (1975) *Yale Law Journal* 480]. On the other hand, a broad legal mandate, such as that typically granted to regulatory bureaucracies, will give rise to huge areas of administrative discretion.

What are the most appropriate strategies for the control of the discretion exercised by criminal justice agencies? One approach is to improve the training of the people concerned. If it is established that police decisions or prosecution decisions are influenced by the ethnic origin or social standing of the individual suspect, further training might re-educate the individual decision-maker, or make an impact upon a pervading discriminatory ethos. The provision for decision-makers of objective, accurate and up-to-date information can also assist towards the making of more consistent decisions (see the discussion on pre-sentence reports in Chapter 5 below), as can requirements for decision-makers always to give full reasons. A very different approach is for Parliament to legislate in such as way as to leave minimal discretion. One example is the highly complex legislative scheme established under the Drug Trafficking Act 1994 and the Criminal Justice Act 1988, for confiscation of profits from drug traffickers and other offenders. Every aspect of the procedure to be followed is detailed in the statutes, with the prosecution, the defence and the Crown Court judge required to follow precisely the procedural rules laid down by Parliament. One problem with this approach is that the operation of the scheme is very dependent on the design and drafting of the law, leaving little scope for judicial creativity to resolve anomalies or fill in gaps. For criticism of that scheme, together with a plea for reduction in the complexity and detail of sentencing statutes generally, see Thomas (1997).

A second approach to the management of discretion is by way of appeal to, or review by, the courts themselves. Judicial decisions are almost always made subject to the possibility of appeal to a higher court, but this 'right' may be hedged about with restrictions. Appeal may be available in law to one side but not the other, or it may be necessary to obtain leave before it can be exercised. These mechanisms are considered further in Chapter 6, p 557 below. When the procedures of appeal have been exhausted, or where a decision has been made by a criminal justice agency from which no appeal is available, someone personally affected by that decision may make application to the Divisional Court to challenge its fairness. The Divisional Court will strike down a decision where it finds that no reasonable agency could have made such a decision in the circumstances, the general legal principle being set out in *Associated Provincial Picture Houses v Wednesbury Corporation* [1948] 1 KB 223. So, the fact that the Divisional Court judges would themselves have taken a different line in the case in question is not sufficient to succeed – a remedy is forthcoming only where the decision is manifestly unreasonable, and this test can provide a difficult hurdle for the applicant to overcome.

The operation of criminal justice in England is also subject to the European Convention on Human Rights, the immediate significance of which will be increased by the impending incorporation of its provisions directly into English law (Home Office, 1997j). The European Convention for the Protection of Human Rights and Fundamental Freedoms, to give the Convention its full title, is a Treaty of the Council of Europe which was drawn up in 1950 and ratified by the United Kingdom in 1951. The Convention is one of a number of international human rights agreements to which the United Kingdom is a party, but in practice it has been the most important. This is because it provides for the judicial determination of disputes between a state which is party to the Convention and a citizen of that state. Where a citizen argues that the state has infringed one of the human rights declared by the Convention, and where that citizen has already gone through all the avenues of appeal available to him or her in the United Kingdom, he or she may submit a petition to the European Commission of Human Rights which will decide whether the petition is admissible. If the Commission decides in the applicant's favour and no settlement between the applicant and the state can be reached, it may refer the application to the European Court of Human Rights in Strasbourg for consideration. If the Court finds the complaint proved, it may make a formal finding to that effect, or award damages against the state, or make an award of costs and expenses. The repercussions of a decision of the European Court of Human Rights may well have the effect of causing the relevant state to amend the laws or procedures which were found to be in breach of the Convention. For a full account of the procedure and the case law, see Harris, O'Boyle and Warbrick (1995) and for the cases involving the United Kingdom, see Farran (1996).

Several of the human rights listed in the Articles of the Convention are of particular relevance to criminal justice. Important applications by individual UK citizens to the European Court of Human Rights have been successful, and these have required changes to be made to English criminal justice. For example, Article 3 states that 'No one shall be subjected to torture or to inhuman or degrading treatment or punishment'. The Court has held that Article 3 was breached by the use of corporal punishment in the Isle of Man (*Tyrer v Isle of Man* A.26, 1978) and by certain extreme methods of interrogation (*Ireland v UK* A.25, 1978, 67). Article 4(2) states that 'No one shall be required to perform forced or compulsory labour'. A question may arise under this Article in the United Kingdom, now that the government, in the Crime (Sentences) Act 1997, has abolished the requirement that a community service order can only be passed on an offender who consents to it. Imposing a community sentence on an unwilling offender is, on the face of it, in conflict with Article 4(2). Article 5 is concerned with a person's 'right to liberty and security'. Derogation from that right for criminal justice purposes, such as pre-trial detention and the use of imprisonment, must comply with the terms of the Article. The United Kingdom was found to be in breach of Article 5 by permitting detention for up to 44 hours of 'any person suspected of being a terrorist' under Northern Ireland legislation (*Fox, Campbell and Hartley v UK* (1990) 13 EHRR 157) and by permitting suspects to be detained by the police for up to seven days before bringing them before a court (*Brogan v UK* (1988) 11 EHRR 117). Article 6(1) requires for anyone charged with a criminal offence 'a fair and public hearing within a reasonable time by an independent and impartial tribunal established by law', and Article 6(2) states that 'Everyone charged with a criminal offence shall be

52

presumed innocent until proved guilty according to law'. It will be noted that this does not require the evidential standard of 'proof beyond reasonable doubt'. In *Funke, Crémieux, Miailhe and Dobbertin v France* (A.256, 1993) the Court referred to 'the right of anyone charged with a criminal offence to remain silent and not to incriminate himself' although, as we shall see in Chapter 4 below, legislative developments have undermined the practical significance of that particular 'right' in England and Wales. Article 7 states that 'No one shall be held guilty of any criminal offence on account of any act or omission which did not constitute a criminal offence under national or international law at the time it was committed, nor shall a heavier penalty be imposed than the one that was applicable at the time the criminal offence was committed'. Would a new legal requirement that all those convicted of a particular form of crime and currently serving sentence for such a crime be required on release to register their name and address with the police, constitute an infringement of Article 7? For discussion, see Chapter 6, p 618 below. Article 8(1) states that 'Everyone has the right to respect for his private and family life, his home and his correspondence' except where this is 'necessary in a democratic society . . . for the prevention of disorder or crime . . .'. At what stage would police surveillance of a crime suspect amount to a breach of Article 8(1)? See *Malone v UK* (1985) 7 EHRR 14 (on telephone tapping) and the decision in *Khan* [1996] 2 Cr App R 440, where the House of Lords held that evidence from a electronic listening device planted by the police on the outside wall of the suspect's home was admissible in English law, even though the means of obtaining it may well have been a breach of Article 8. Article 14 states that enjoyment of the rights and freedoms set out in the Convention 'shall be secured without discrimination on any ground such as sex, race, colour, language, religion, political or other opinion, national or social origin, association with a national minority, property, birth or other status'. Issues of discrimination in criminal justice are considered in Chapter 6, p 637 below. Articles 1–14 of the Convention follow:

Extract 1.5.3

European Convention on Human Rights 1950, Articles 1–14

Article 1

The High Contracting Parties shall secure to everyone within their jurisdiction the rights and freedoms defined in Section 1 of this Convention.

Article 2

1 Everyone's right to life shall be protected by law. No one shall be deprived of his life intentionally save in the execution of a sentence of a court following his conviction of a crime for which this penalty is provided by law.

2   Deprivation of life shall not be regarded as inflicted in contravention of this Article when it results from the use of force which is more than absolutely necessary:
  (a) in defence of any person from unlawful violence;
  (b) in order to effect a lawful arrest or to prevent the escape of a person lawfully detained;
  (c) in action lawfully taken for the purpose of quelling a riot or insurrection.

Article 3

No one shall be subjected to torture or to inhuman or degrading treatment or punishment.

Article 4

1   No one shall be held in slavery or servitude.
2   No one shall be required to perform forced or compulsory labour.
3   For the purpose of this article the term 'forced or compulsory labour' shall not include:
  (a) any work required to be done in the ordinary course of detention imposed according to the provisions of Article 5 of this Convention or during conditional release from such detention;
  (b) any service of a military character or, in case of conscientious objectors in countries where they are recognised, service exacted instead of compulsory military service;
  (c) any service exacted in case of an emergency or calamity threatening the life or well-being of the community;
  (d) any work or service which forms part of normal civic obligations.

Article 5

1   Everyone has the right to liberty and security of person.
No one shall be deprived of his liberty save in the following cases and in accordance with a procedure prescribed by law:
  (a) the lawful detention of a person after conviction by a competent court;
  (b) the lawful arrest or detention of a person for non-compliance with the lawful order of a court or in order to secure the fulfilment of any obligation prescribed by law;
  (c) the lawful arrest or detention of a person effected for the purpose of bringing him before the competent legal authority on reasonable suspicion of having committed an offence or when it is reasonably considered necessary to prevent his committing an offence or fleeing after having done so;
  (d) the detention of a minor by lawful order for the purpose of educational supervision or his lawful detention for the purpose of bringing him before the competent legal authority;
  (e) the lawful detention of persons for the prevention of the spreading of infectious diseases, of persons of unsound mind, alcoholics or drug addicts, or vagrants;

(f) the lawful arrest or detention of a person to prevent his effecting an unauthorised entry into the country or of a person against whom action is being taken with a view to deportation or extradition.

2 Everyone who is arrested shall be informed promptly, in a language which he understands, of the reasons for his arrest and of any charge against him.

3 Everyone arrested or detained in accordance with the provisions of paragraph 1(c) of this article shall be brought promptly before a judge or other officer authorized by law to exercise judicial power and shall be entitled to trial within a reasonable time or to release pending trial. Release may be conditioned by guarantees to appear for trial.

4 Everyone who is deprived of his liberty by arrest or detention shall be entitled to take proceedings by which the lawfulness of his detention shall be decided speedily by a court and his release ordered if the detention is not lawful.

5 Everyone who has been the victim of arrest or detention in contravention of the provisions of this article shall have an enforceable right to compensation.

Article 6

1 In the determination of his civil rights and obligations or of any criminal charge against him, everyone is entitled to a fair and public hearing within a reasonable time by an independent and impartial tribunal established by law. Judgment shall be pronounced publicly but the press and public may be excluded from all or part of the trial in the interest of morals, public order or national security in a democratic society, where the interests of juveniles or the protection of the private life of the parties so require, or to the extent strictly necessary in the opinion of the court in special circumstances where publicity would prejudice the interests of justice.

2 Everyone charged with a criminal offence shall be presumed innocent until proved guilty according to law.

3 Everyone charged with a criminal offence has the following minimum rights:
(a) to be informed promptly, in a language which he understands and in detail, of the nature and cause of the accusation against him;
(b) to have adequate time and facilities for the preparation of his defence;
(c) to defend himself in person or through legal assistance of his own choosing, or, if he has not sufficient means to pay for legal assistance, to be given it free when the interests of justice so require;
(d) to examine or have examined witnesses against him and to obtain the attendance and examination of witnesses on his behalf under the same conditions as witnesses against him;
(e) to have the free assistance of an interpreter if he cannot understand or speak the language used in court.

Article 7

1 No one shall be held guilty of any criminal offence on account of any act or omission which did not constitute a criminal offence under national or international law at the time when it was committed. Nor shall a heavier penalty be imposed than the one that was applicable at the time the criminal offence was committed.

55

2   This article shall not prejudice the trial and punishment of any person for any act or omission which, at the time when it was committed, was criminal according to the general principles of law recognized by civilized nations.

Article 8

1   Everyone has the right to respect for his private and family life, his home and his correspondence.
2   There shall be no interference by a public authority with the exercise of this right except such as is in accordance with the law and is necessary in a democratic society in the interests of national security, public safety or the economic well-being of the country, for the prevention of disorder or crime, for the protection of health or morals, or for the protection of the rights and freedoms of others.

Article 9

1   Everyone has the right to freedom of thought, conscience and religion; this right includes freedom to change his religion or belief, and freedom, either alone or in community with others and in public or private, to manifest his religion or belief, in worship, teaching, practice and observance.
2   Freedom to manifest one's religion or beliefs shall be subject only to such limitations as are prescribed by law and are necessary in a democratic society in the interests of public safety, for the protection of public order, health or morals, or for the protection of the rights and freedoms of others.

Article 10

1   Everyone has the right to freedom of expression. This right shall include freedom to hold opinions and to receive and impart information and ideas without interference by public authority and regardless of frontiers. This article shall not prevent States from requiring the licensing of broadcasting, television or cinema enterprises.
2   The exercise of these freedoms, since it carries with it duties and responsibilities, may be subject to such formalities, conditions, restrictions or penalties as are prescribed by law and are necessary in a democratic society, in the interests of national security, territorial integrity or public safety, for the prevention of disorder or crime, for the protection of health or morals, for the protection of the reputation or rights of others, for preventing the disclosure of information received in confidence, or for maintaining the authority and impartiality of the judiciary.

Article 11

1   Everyone has the right to freedom of peaceful assembly and to freedom of association with others, including the right to form and to join trade unions for the protection of his interests.
2   No restrictions shall be placed on the exercise of these rights other than such as are prescribed by law and are necessary in a democratic society in

the interests of national security or public safety, for the prevention of disorder or crime, for the protection of health or morals or for the protection of the rights and freedoms of others. This article shall not prevent the imposition of lawful restrictions on the exercise of these rights by members of the armed forces, of the police or of the administration of the State.

Article 12

Men and women of marriageable age have the right to marry and to found a family, according to the national laws governing the exercise of this right.

Article 13

Everyone whose rights and freedoms as set forth in this Convention are violated shall have an effective remedy before a national authority notwithstanding that the violation has been committed by persons acting in an official capacity.

Article 14

The enjoyment of the rights and freedoms set forth in this Convention shall be secured without discrimination on any ground such as sex, race, colour, language, religion, political or other opinion, national or social origin, association with a national minority, property, birth or other status.

The government has introduced a Human Rights Bill which will have the effect of incorporating the European Convention on Human Rights directly into English law. This will place a requirement through domestic law that public authorities exercising the powers of the state will have to exercise those powers in ways which are in accordance with the Convention. Public authorities include central and local government, the police, criminal justice agencies such as the Crown Prosecution Service and the prison service, and the courts themselves. The actions of Parliament, however, are excluded. A person who has been directly and adversely affected by a decision which he or she believes to be contrary to an Article of the Convention will, when the Bill becomes law in 1998, be able to challenge that decision in the courts of England and Wales, rather than having to apply to Strasbourg. If a public authority is found to have acted unlawfully by failing to comply with the Convention, the courts will be able to grant the injured party a remedy, such as by overturning a conviction, quashing a decision or by awarding damages. Criminal penalties will not be available. Where a court finds a statute to be in conflict with the Convention, it has been argued that the court should be able to strike down the statute, but the government has not accepted this suggestion. The Bill proposes, instead, that the statute should prevail, but that a higher court will be able to make a formal declaration that the law conflicts with the Convention, on the clear expectation that the government will then move swiftly to change the offending law. The Bill provides for a new 'fast-track' procedure in Parliament to enable this to be done. This may well be effective for future cases, but it seems strange that the court making a formal declaration will have no power to order a remedy for the individual applicant responsible for prompting change to the law.

In Extract 1.5.2 above, Hawkins stressed the importance of both the 'holistic' and 'serial' views of discretion. It is instructive to examine some examples from the field of criminal justice where official efforts have been made to eliminate, or significantly curtail, the level of discretion formerly enjoyed by a particular set of decision-makers. Of course, all decision-makers are reluctant to give up powers which they have formerly enjoyed, and the bridling of discretion can be a delicate exercise, particularly for a judiciary apt to regard such reductions in its power as a form of political interference and a threat to its independence (see Munro, 1992). The history of resistance by the English judiciary to key provisions of the Criminal Justice Act 1991 and, more recently, to the introduction of mandatory minimum sentencing laws, and its ultimate success in obtaining a broad 'exceptional circumstances' provision, has been described above. The Magistrates' Association's *Sentencing Guidelines* stress that they 'provide a method for considering individual cases . . . but they are not a tariff and should never be used as such' (Magistrates' Association, 1997, p 1). In part, of course, these are simply timely reminders to lay magistrates not to apply such guidance by rote (as it is sometimes suggested happens with the road traffic penalty guidelines). It is also significant, though, that until the 1992 version of the latter guidelines there was a steadfast refusal by the magistracy to accept the word 'guidelines' at all – the term 'penalty suggestions' being preferred. The mode of trial guidelines also emphasise that their object is to provide 'guidance, not direction'. Increasingly the model for criminal justice appears to be one of 'structured discretion', which recognises the inappropriateness of rigid rules, providing rather for a clearly-stated general policy together with a specified and limited number of reasoned exceptions.

To the extent that discretion may be successfully curtailed, however, there is a tendency for flexibility in a different part of the criminal justice process to increase, thereby preserving overall levels of discretionary power within the system. This is sometimes called the 'hydraulic' effect in criminal justice. In the United States during the late 1980s and early 1990s some states legislated to reduce greatly the amount of discretion traditionally accorded to sentencers. This was done by developing tight numerical sentencing guideline 'grids' which required sentencers to dispose of cases in particular ways. These grids did not go so far as to eliminate sentencing discretion – judges still retain power to depart from the 'presumptive' sentence – but they do seek substantially to curtail that discretion. At around the same period a number of these states also introduced tight guidelines for determining early release on parole or, indeed, abolished parole altogether. (For description, see Tonry, 1987 and 1992.) It has been noted by researchers that such dramatic reductions in discretionary powers, for judges and for parole authorities, tended to place greater power in the hands of prosecutors. Since, with the advent of guidelines, the prosecutor can predict accurately the sentence which the offender will receive for the offence, the prosecutor is in a strong position to 'plea-bargain' or 'charge-bargain' with the defence lawyer (Schulhofer, 1980; Nagel and Schulhofer, 1992). Perhaps to describe this effect as 'hydraulic' is to suggest too automatic a reaction. What is clear beyond doubt, however, is that alteration of the framework of rules within which one criminal justice agency works is bound to affect the practical operation of other agencies within the system. These interrelations can be complex and subtle. In the United States, Tonry has documented the ways in which mandatory 'three strikes' sentencing laws, seen by many criminal justice professionals as being inherently unjust, have been subverted by the police, by prosecutors and by judges (Tonry, 1996, Ch 5). He shows how the police have avoided application of a one-year mandatory sentence for carrying a gun by decreasing the number of arrests for that offence and increasing weapons seizures without arrest. Prosecutors may tend to file charges for different but roughly comparable offences which are not subject to the mandatory sentences, and substantive crimes can be bargained down to charges of attempt or conspiracy which do not carry the mandatory sentence.

Also, criminal justice agencies can sometimes react in unexpected ways to policy initiatives. This may be because the policy is poorly thought out in the first place, or there is inadequate consultation with those who are to carry it out. For instance, new community sentences have been introduced with little or no guidance for the courts as to the type of offence or offender for which the measure is suitable: introduction of the community service order in the early 1970s is a good example (Pease, 1981). Another is the ill-fated 'unit fine' system introduced by the Criminal Justice Act 1991 following very successful pilot schemes in magistrates' courts (Moxon, 1990), but fundamentally altered by the legislature prior to its being brought into force. The unit fine was a policy initiative with a great deal to recommend it (see Ashworth, 1995, pp 262–266) but the statutory scheme soon descended into chaos and was scrapped after eight months. A policy formulated by government to achieve a particular strategic goal may misfire when tried out in practice because the relevant agency, for one reason or another, disregards or subverts the policy. One of the main purposes of the introduction of the suspended prison sentence in the 1960s was to encourage sentencers to pass suspended rather than immediate sentences of imprisonment, thereby reducing the prison population. After implementation, however, research showed that many sentencers were using the suspended sentence as an alternative to probation, rather than as an alternative to custody. Since the suspended sentence places an offender at high risk of imprisonment on re-offending, the net effect of introducing the new measure was to increase the prison population, rather than to reduce it (Sparks, 1970). More recently, Parliament provided in the Criminal Justice Act 1991 that henceforth the courts were to make use of the suspended sentence only in 'exceptional' circumstances. While, no doubt, this effective reduction in their powers was disliked by many sentencers (see, for example,

Campbell, 1995) the rate of use of the suspended sentence fell dramatically after the 1991 Act came into force, from over 28,500 cases a year to around 3,500. Since then, however, there has been no effective guidance from the Court of Appeal as to the meaning of 'exceptional' circumstances, but a greater willingness to employ the suspended sentence on appeal. This lack of clarity may prompt something of a revival in its use.

(b) Issues of efficiency and economics

There is considerable pressure on all criminal justice agencies to operate in a cost-effective and efficient manner and to provide 'value for money'. It was a hallmark of the Conservative government's approach during the 1980s and early 1990s to squeeze public sector expenditure and to insist on rigorous financial planning and accountability (Jones, 1993; Faulkner, 1996). The Royal Commission (Royal Commission on Criminal Justice, 1993) argued that 'more should be done to establish that value for money is being obtained' (Extract 1.3.1, p 17 above). It is hard to argue against 'value for money' as a principle in itself. As Nicola Lacey points out in the following extract, however the pursuit of 'efficiency' is a misleadingly simple goal. The commercial style of management does not always fit well with the range of (sometimes conflicting) concerns of criminal justice.

Extract 1.5.4

N Lacey, 'Government as Manager, Citizen as Consumer' (1994) 57 MLR 534, at pp 534–535 (footnotes amended)

Over the last fifteen years, wider and wider areas of public administration in the United Kingdom have become infused with a discourse hitherto associated rather with the commercial world. The concern with efficiency, always an important one, has come increasingly to be approached on the assumption that the imposition of a market-type model can deliver improvement in the quality of public administration. Through full-scale privatisation, but also, more recently, via partial 'contracting-out' and 'market testing', government has adopted what might be characterised as a 'managerial approach': one in which an idealised image of the private sector is constantly held up as a model, to be compared favourably with the archaic and inefficient public sector. This has been true both in terms of the government's own strategies and in terms of the frameworks which it has imposed upon a wide range of bodies providing public goods and services.

One striking feature of this extended market approach is that, while the implicit goal is not straightforwardly profit or indeed necessarily exclusively financial, the instrumentalism which characterises the approach tends to assume that some relatively simple and measurable goal is being pursued. The figure of success becomes 'efficiency' or 'value for money', whilst the often complex and politically contested question of what constitutes 'value' in a particular area is moved away from the spotlight.[1] Hence, as I shall argue, all too often the actual specification of the relevant goals and values is avoided, being obscured within a discourse in which efficiency appears to become the end as well as the means. The ideological impoverishment which this entails is well illustrated by the way in which the managerial model of government as a direct or indirect provider of services finds its counterpart in a reconceptualisation of democracy itself. In this strand of policy and political discourse, measurable performance indicators become the ultimate test of democratic accountability, whilst citizenship is effectively reconstructed as a consumer status: a development which is perhaps best exemplified by the Citizen's Charter.[2]

---

[1] For a general appraisal and critique of these developments see Stewart and Walsh, 'Change in the Management of Public Services' (1992) 70 *Public Administration* 499; Jones, 'Auditing Criminal Justice' (1993) 33 *British Journal of Criminology* 187.

[2] See Barron and Scott, 'The Citizen's Charter Programme' (1992) 55 MLR 524; Cooper, 'The Citizen's Charter and Radical Democracy: Empowerment and Exclusion within Citizenship' (1993) 2 *Social and Legal Studies* 149.

It is the inevitable trade-off between economic stringency and the securing of justice which causes the greatest concern. The Royal Commission stated that while 'every law-abiding citizen has an interest in a system in which the risk of mistaken verdicts is as low as it can be, there will always be arguments about how much public money should be spent on arriving marginally closer to that ideal' (Extract 1.3.1, p 17). Financial pressure on the police to produce results, particularly in high-profile cases, has undoubtedly contributed on occasion to miscarriages of justice, and in Chapter 3 below we examine how imposing tighter constraints on police budgets has resulted in the police calling for fewer checks on forensic evidence. Questions of efficiency and economics, as measured against quality of justice, arise starkly when consideration is given to magistrates' courts, see Chapter 4. On the face of it, magistrates' courts offer a range of advantages over Crown Court trial, in terms of the speed of their proceedings and their relative cheapness. Yet magistrates' justice is regarded by many defendants and lawyers as a second-rate form of justice. In contrast to 'cheap and cheerful' summary jurisdiction, justice in its more elaborate Crown Court form can seem ponderous and highly inefficient. Consider, for example, the high percentage of Crown Court cases which 'crack' on or near the scheduled day of trial. 'Cracked' trials are those where the defendant, having previously indicated his or her intention to contest the case, at a late stage changes his or her plea to guilty. By that time, of course, much expenditure has already been undertaken in preparing for trial, ensuring the presence of witnesses, and so on. The reasons why at the last minute so many trials do not go ahead are complex, and are considered further in Chapter 4.

In Extract 1.5.5 below, Anthony Bottoms discusses further the growing importance of managerialism in criminal justice. His analysis draws us back to questions of 'system' within criminal justice, which were discussed at pp 35–40 above. To what extent do the various criminal justice agencies share the 'common purpose and common objectives' to which the author refers? The extract also develops a new and telling argument that, partly as a result of the infusion of management ideology, criminal justice is increasingly seen today as an instrument of risk management and social control, with a tendency to regard offenders in the aggregate (as a social problem to be managed) rather than dealing with them as individuals. The ideology of 'protection of the public' has come to predominate the criminal justice agenda, with an inevitable reduction in concern for the rights of suspects and defendants. Significantly, perhaps, while the influential 1990 White Paper on criminal justice was entitled *Crime, Justice and Protecting the Public* (Home Office, 1990), by 1996 an equivalent document describing the government's 'strategy on crime' could simply be called *Protecting the Public* (Home Office, 1996a).

Extract 1.5.5

A E Bottoms, 'The Philosophy and Politics of Punishment and Sentencing' in C M V Clarkson and R Morgan (eds), *The Politics of Sentencing Reform* (1995) p 17, at pp 24–28 (footnotes amended and renumbered)

Managerialism

... The growing importance of managerialism in criminal justice and penal systems has, perhaps, received less academic attention than it deserves, though in different continents Antonie Peters[1] and Feeley and Simon[2] have independently sought to highlight its significance[3] ...

One central feature of a managerialist approach is an emphasis on *the criminal-justice system*, conceived as a system rather than a collection of different parts. In most Western countries, conceptualization of this sort has become a great deal more prominent in the last thirty years in official discourse about criminal policy. To give only one example, in Britain a senior Home Office official, speaking at a conference on the probation service in the late 1980s, prefaced his main remarks with the following important introductory paragraph:

> 'The probation service is a *criminal justice service*. It is one of the five criminal justice services, the others being the police, the courts (perhaps more an institution than a service), the Prison Service and, a newcomer to the scene, the Crown Prosecution Service. All five services are about crime and what to do about it – preventing or reducing it, dealing with its consequences and with those who commit it, and mitigating its effect. The different tasks fall on different services in different ways, and at the operational level they are fairly clearly and rightly distinguished; but *at a more general level the services all share or ought to share a common purpose and common objectives*, even though their character is very different. Each can

62

frustrate any of the others, and action or lack of action by any of them can affect the workload and success of each of the others, *so they must understand one another and they must work together. The point is obvious*, but it does not easily happen (emphasis added).[4]

In most jurisdictions, this recent emphasis on the systemic character of the criminal justice tends to embrace some or all of the following features:

1. An emphasis on *inter-agency co-operation* in order to fulfil the overall goals of the system (see quotation above);

2. An emphasis on creating, if possible, *an overall strategic plan* for the whole of criminal policy in the given country (including the criminal-justice system), with each separate criminal-justice agency having its own *mission statement*, integrally related to the goals of the remainder of the system;[5]

3. The creation of *key performance indicators*, related to the overall 'mission statement' of each agency, in order to measure aspects of efficiency and effectiveness (such indicators might include, perhaps, 'clear-up rates' and 'response times' for the police; 'hours of constructive regime activity' and '% of population in overcrowded conditions' in the prison service; 'average length of time spent before trial' and 'average length of court hearing' in the courts, and so on);

4. Active *monitoring* of aggregate information about the system and its functioning, at various key decision points or service-delivery points, using modern information technology, and with special (though not exclusive) attention being given to information concerning the 'key performance indicators'.

This kind of systemic approach is often rather more pervasive in any given criminal-justice system than is apparent to the casual observer. So, for example, in England the Criminal Justice Act 1991, in its original form, has often been referred to as primarily a 'just deserts' statute (and indeed rightly so given some of the language in the White Paper that preceded it[6]), yet close analysis shows that in significant respects the Act also contained, or was backed up by, powerful elements of managerialist thinking. As an example of this, we may note the provisions of the Act relating to the setting up of the new Youth Court, which, *inter alia*, created what is often known as an 'overlapping jurisdiction' for community penalties for 16- and 17-year-olds, a concept which necessarily required an element of inter-agency co-operation or 'partnership'.[7] A government circular to local agencies was issued in March 1992, six months before the implementation of the Act, giving, *inter alia*, detailed guidance on the development of services relating to 16- and 17-year-old offenders[8] and emphasizing that in all local areas 'monitoring and evaluation are essential for the assessment of performance and to ensure the efficient and effective delivery of services and programmes'.[9] As an Annexe to the circular, a 'checklist of local action' was provided, in a much more detailed form than would have been contemplated twenty or thirty years beforehand; this checklist emphasized, among other things, the importance of partnership arrangements, target dates, and monitoring . . .

Given examples such as this, it is not hard to see that, as Feeley and Simon note, one result of what I have called the 'systemic' dimension of managerialism can be that, within criminal-justice systems, 'increasing primacy [is] given to the efficient control of internal system processes'.[10] Concentration on such matters can even, in some cases, result in the displacement of more traditional 'external' objectives such as the reduction of reoffending: hence in some contemporary criminal-justice systems, according to the same authors, 'the sense that any external social referent is intended at all is becoming attenuated'.[11]

. . .

Similarly, in the specific field of criminal policy Antonie Peters draws some analytically helpful schematic contrasts between the new systemic managerialism (what he calls the 'School of Social Control') and the earlier criminological 'schools' of classicism and positivism:

> 'The criminal law is no longer a moral code as it was in liberal market society, nor an instrument of social defence as in the period roughly from 1900 to 1950, but it has become one form, among other forms, of social control. The new approach is characterised by a withdrawal from the idea that the problem of crime can be eliminated, or even can be brought under complete control. Emphasis has shifted from maintenance of the criminal code . . . to more general control of volumes of delinquent activity. Criminal policy is no longer occupied primarily with concrete offenders, nor with problems of doing justice, but with the management of aggregate phenomena of social activity, with criteria for selective law enforcement, with quantitative regulation in the organisational processing of offenders . . . In the Classical School the main concern was with the definition of right and wrong. Punishment served the purpose of moral clarification. The [Positivist] School was intent on acting upon individual criminals, and punishment was conceived as treatment. In the School of Social Control the concern is with systems of action; punishment has become an instrument of policy . . . I believe that today legal rationality in criminal law has, in an important sense, dissolved in, and been replaced by the rationality of organisation.'[12]

As Feeley and Simon emphasize, all this can have very significant consequences for the implicit ways in which individual persons within the criminal-justice system are viewed. The tendency of the systemic approach is to 'target offenders *as an aggregate*' (emphasis added);[13] hence the individual within this kind of approach becomes, at least in some respects (see further below), simply a unit within a framework of policy.[14]

---

[1] A A G Peters, 'Main Currents in Criminal Law Theory', in J van Dijk, C Haffmans, F Ruter, J Schutte (eds), *Criminal Law in Action* (Arnhem, 1986).

[2] M M Feeley and J Simon, 'The New Penology: Notes on the Emerging Strategy of Corrections and its Implications', (1992) 30 *Criminology* 449–474.

[3] Managerialism in criminal justice has also been considered in some texts primarily aimed at a practitioner audience: see e.g. T Locke, *New Approaches to Crime in the 1990s: Planning Responses to Crime* (Harlow, 1990); R Statham and P Whitehead, *Managing the Probation Service: Issues for the 1990s* (Harlow, 1992).

[4] D E R Faulkner, 'The Future of the Probation Service: A View from Government', in R Shaw and K Haines (eds), *The Criminal Justice System: A Central Role for the Probation Service* (Cambridge, 1989), I. Since this speech was made, enhanced co-operation between the various services mentioned by David Faulkner has been sought by the British Government through the establishment of a national Criminal Justice Consultative Council and a series of 24 Area Criminal Justice Liaison Committees working under the umbrella of the national Council. This development follows a specific

recommendation made in Lord Justice Woolf's report on prison disturbances in England (*Prison Disturbances April 1990: Report of an Inquiry* (Cm. 1456; London, 1991)).

[5] On 'overall strategic plans', see esp. the Netherlands White Paper of 1985 and subsequent developments: see Netherlands Ministry of Justice, *Society and Crime: A Policy Plan for the Netherlands* (The Hague, 1985); A K Bottomley, 'Blue-prints for Criminal Justice: Reflections on a Policy Plan for the Netherlands', (1986) 25 *Howard Journal of Criminal Justice* 199–215.

[6] Home Office, *Crime, Justice and Protecting the Public* (Cm. 965; London, 1990).

[7] The concept of the 'overlapping jurisdiction' is that sentences previously available only for juveniles (i.e. persons aged 16 or less) were henceforth to be made available for 17-year-olds, who were to be brought within the ambit of the Youth Court; while conversely, sentences previously available for 17-year-olds, but not for juveniles, should be made available for 16-year-olds. Courts were then expected to select the most appropriate sentence for each individual 16- or 17-year-old defendant, from across this widened range of disposals. Since the probation service previously had sole responsibility for community penalties for 17-year-olds, and local-authority social-services departments had lead responsibility for some aspects of community penalty provision for 16-year-olds, a degree of inter-agency co-operation was required to make these provisions work effectively.

[8] Home Office, Department of Health, and Welsh Office, *Criminal Justice Act 1991: Young People and the Youth Court* (Circular 30/1992; London, 1992), paras. 6–28.

[9] Ibid, para 27.

[10] M M Feeley and J Simon, above, n. 2, 450.

[11] Ibid.

[12] A A G Peters, above, n. 1, 32, 34.

[13] M M Feeley and J Simon, above, n. 2, 450.

[14] W McWilliams, 'Probation, Pragmatism and Policy', (1987) 26 *Howard Journal of Criminal Justice* 97–121.

Professor Bottoms refers above to the important insights provided by Feeley and Simon in helping us to understand the functioning of the modern criminal justice system (Feeley and Simon, 1992). The following extract is taken from another essay by the same authors:

Extract 1.5.6

M Feeley and J Simon, 'Actuarial Justice: The Emerging New Criminal Law' in D Nelken (ed), *The Futures of Criminology* (1994) pp 173–178 (footnotes omitted)

Introduction

In a recent article we argued that there is a paradigm shift taking place in the criminal process. Focusing on selected issues of penology, we examined what we termed the Old Penology and the New Penology (M Feeley and J Simon, 'The New Penology: Notes on the Emerging Strategy of Corrections and its Implications' (1992) 30 *Criminology* 449). In this chapter we broaden this argument, and outline the features of this new development, which we term *actuarial justice*. In the earlier paper we argued that the Old Penology is rooted in a concern for individuals, and preoccupied with such concepts as guilt, responsibility and obligation, as well as diagnosis, intervention and treatment of the individual offender. It views committing a crime a deviant or antisocial act which is deserving of a response, and one of its central aims is to ascertain the nature of the responsibility of the accused and hold the guilty accountable.

In contrast the New Penology has a radically different orientation.[1] It is actuarial. It is concerned with techniques for identifying, classifying and managing groups assorted by levels of dangerousness. It takes crime for granted. It accepts deviance as normal. It is sceptical that liberal interventionist crime control strategies do or can make a difference. Thus its aim is not to intervene in individuals' lives for the purpose of ascertaining responsibility, making the guilty 'pay for their crime' or changing them. Rather it seeks to regulate groups as part of a strategy of managing danger.

In our article (Feeley and Simon, 1992) we addressed the general logic of the New Penology in terms of discourses, techniques and objectives. Here in our more general enquiry we explore how 'actuarial justice', is being institutionalised and survey the broader intellectual, political and social contexts which have facilitated its emergence. This shift, we believe, is shaping and will continue to shape the agenda of criminology. Indeed, as we show here, and in our earlier article, a new actuarial criminology has already emerged and made itself felt.

. . .

THE ELEMENTS OF ACTUARIAL JUSTICE

Actuarial justice is nebulous, but it is significant. Actuarial justice involves how we conceive of and talk about crime policy, but it is not an ideology in the narrow sense of a set of beliefs and ideas which constrain action. It involves practices, but is not reducible to a specific technology or set of behaviours. Indeed it is powerful and significant precisely because it lacks a well-articulated ideology and identification with a specific technology. Its very amorphousness contributes to its power. Below we outline an account of actual practices and discourses which are giving shape to this emerging formation in the criminal process. Following that we abstract some of the critical features of these developments. However, it is important to keep in mind that what we describe is not a mentality or a blueprint that can be cleanly separated from the material it analyses.

New practices

It is somewhat misleading to speak of new practices, since the practices we discuss are, in fact, partial practices which have had long and varied histories. Their newness lies in their particular combinations and the particular micropractices they are embedded in and the functions which they perform.

Incapacitation

Possibly the clearest indication of actuarial justice is found in the new theory of incapacitation, which has perhaps become the predominant model of punishment . . . Incapacitation promises to reduce the effects of crime in society not

66

by altering either offender or social context, but by rearranging the distribution of offenders in society. If the prison can do nothing else, incapacitation theory holds, it can detain offenders for a time and thus delay their resumption of criminal activity in society.

According to the theory, if such delays are sustained for enough time and for enough people, significant aggregate effects in crime can take place although individual destinies are only marginally altered. In this sense, incapacitation is to penology what arbitration is to investments, a method of capitalising on minute displacements in time; and like arbitration it has a diminished relationship to the normative goal of enhancing the value of its objects.

These aggregate effects can be further intensified by a strategy of *selective* incapacitation. This approach proposes a sentencing scheme in which lengths of sentence depend not upon the nature of the criminal offence or upon an assessment of the character of the offender, but upon risk profiles. Its objects are to identify high-risk offenders and to maintain long-term control over them while investing in shorter terms and less intrusive control and surveillance over lower risk offenders.

. . .

Preventive detention
Pre-trial decision making in the United States has always made evident a concern for preventive detention as well as for the task of assuring the presence of the accused at trial. Both concerns were pursued on an individual basis, albeit one which embodied plenty of collective stereotypes. The new logic of pre-trial detention operates in a manner similar to selective incapacitation. Preselected categories of information about an arrestee are collected and run through a collective algorithm.

The origins of this development are found in the bail reform efforts of the early 1960s, when liberal reformers and the courts rejected a constitutional 'rights strategy' for bail reform in preference to an 'administrative strategy' . . .

Once established 'pre-trial release agencies' developed a life of their own. What began as a reform calling attention to the problems of unnecessary pre-trial detention, quickly became 'part of that problem'. Seemingly without effort the pre-trial release agencies moved from developing actuarial-like models to predict appearance at trial to developing models to predict dangerousness and on to models to predict the consequences of testing dirty to various types of drugs . . . Once a rights strategy had given way to an administrative strategy, each of these moves was but a small step along the path of actuarial justice.

The conventional explanation for shifts in pre-trial release policy in the United States and Western Europe from the 1960s to the 1990s is that due process-oriented liberals were displaced by law-and-order conservatives. But this explanation is incomplete if not altogether wrong. Pre-trial release policies do not divide neatly along these lines. Indeed it was well-known liberal reformers who were responsible for first promoting actuarial justice in the form of administrative strategy of pre-trial release agencies. They set aside issues of rights, and once having claimed the ability to predict appearance at trial, it was a small step to applying their risk assessment models to the issue of dangerousness, the consequences of testing dirty, and the like. In hindsight one can trace the development of actuarial justice in this area and see how it cuts across traditional liberal-conservative lines.

. . .

Analysis of actuarial justice

What these forms have in common is not the repetition of a singular structure but a set of overlapping features.

The population itself, in its biological and demographic sense, is taken as the target of power The emergence of criminological positivism in the late nineteenth century divided between those who focused on crime as a set of prohibited acts (whether understood economically or morally) and those who focused on criminals as a set of dangerous individuals (embodied in both classicism and moral philosophies of punishment). As late as the 1970s it seemed as if the central tensions in criminal justice policy could be understood as a dialectic between these positions. We argue that the new practices radically reframe the issues, and target something very different, that is, the crime rate, understood as the *distribution* of behaviours in the population as a whole. In this sense actuarial justice should be seen as a part of the general movement noted by a number of scholars towards the exercise of state power as 'governmentality'.

This does not mean that individuals disappear in criminal justice. They remain, but increasingly they are grasped not as coherent subjects, whether understood as moral, psychological or economic agents, but as members of particular subpopulations and the intersection of various categorical indicators.

Power is aimed at prevention and risk minimisation Rather than seeking to respond to past offences, these techniques are mainly aimed at preventing future offences. Prevention has always been a concern of the criminal process and a justification of punishment. Some of the new techniques – selective incapacitation and pre-trial detention – present a possibly purer form of prevention. More important, however, prevention is aimed less at halting proscribed activities than reducing the likelihood and seriousness of offending.

Justice is increasingly understood not as a rational system but through the rationality of the system Criminal justice has always been concerned with how to distribute its own considerable powers. The classic theorists, such as Beccaria and Bentham, worried about the distribution between legislators, prosecutors and juries. Positivists defined the scientifically trained expert as the obvious repository of power. Until recently our debates on sentencing and other topics have operated as if this was still the fundamental set of choices. The new techniques discussed here suggest the rise of formal systems of internal rules, analogous in many respects to computer programs.

The new techniques we discussed above are a small subset of all criminal justice practices. They are attached to institutions that seem largely to operate in 'the old fashioned way', that is, responding reactively and often brutally to crime. Yet, while these measures are all in varying degrees defined as new and controversial, an examination of how the logic of actuarial justice has penetrated more venerable practices in criminal justice suggests that the future is already here.

(c) Community and community values

The third general theme identified for the purposes of this introductory discussion is that of 'community' and community values. The reassertion of local, community initiatives and values stands in some tension with the two previous themes. The first, the management of discretion, generally calls for greater uniformity in decision making across the country and the promulgation of national guidelines and standards, with only limited scope for variation in local application. The second, the quest for greater efficiency and economy, is also associated with enhanced uniformity and centralisation – see, for example, the discussion in Chapter 4 below on recent changes to the organisation of local magistrates' courts to make them more managerially accountable to central government. Christopher Compston, a circuit judge since 1986, puts a case for reversing the modern trend of centralisation in criminal justice:

> The justification for local justice surely lies in this – that only by breaking justice down into manageable units can it work effectively, for the defendant, the victim and the community. It implies closeness to the community and responsibility to the community . . . Only by dealing with matters locally will any sense of mutual responsibility be restored. (Compston, 1994, p 129)

The criminal justice system operates in the name of the public, and we have seen the importance which the Royal Commission on Criminal Justice attached to the need to preserve (or to recover) the confidence of the public in the institutions of criminal justice and, in particular, the decisions of the criminal courts (see Extract 1.3.1 above, at pp 22–25). Opinion survey research reveals significantly lower levels of public satisfaction with the performance of the police, and with other criminal justice agencies, than there was a number of years ago.

Part of government policy has been to promote local initiatives in response to the 'crime problem', particularly in the context of crime prevention efforts. At first sight, this trend sits uneasily with the increased politicisation of criminal justice, and the predominance of centralised 'law and order' policies. According to Downes and Morgan, the stress on 'citizenship' and 'the community' was '. . . evolved in the 1980s as a form of recognition by the government that reliance on the "rule of law" alone was no longer serving as a credible strategy' (Downes and Morgan, 1997). As the 1996 Home Office White Paper put it: 'Local crime problems essentially call for local solutions. In order to be effective, local crime prevention measures need the support and participation of the whole community, working in partnership. This vital work cannot be left to the police alone: communities themselves have a central role to play' (Home Office, 1996a, para 2.22). One of the best known initiatives was the 'Safer Cities' programme, begun in 1988 and designed to reduce crime and the fear of crime and to create safer cities in which community life could flourish, but wound up in 1995 (see Pease, 1997), in which year a new National Crime Prevention Agency was established. Another has been the widespread development of Neighbourhood Watch schemes, although research has shown there to be much variation in their impact on local crime levels and on the fear of crime (Bennett, 1990). A third has been the introduction of closed-circuit television (CCTV) in town centres and elsewhere (see Horne, 1996). This has been enthusiastically funded by government (see Home Office, 1996a, para 2.11: 'clearly, CCTV works'), to the extent that the bulk of Home Office expenditure on crime prevention is now devoted to it (Pease, 1997). Research on CCTV does suggest a clear reduction in crime committed within range of the cameras, but the use of technically deficient or inappropriate equipment can often undermine its usefulness for detection purposes. There are also unresolved questions over the extent to which CCTV, rather than really preventing crime, simply moves the crime elsewhere.

The importance of 'community' developments in contemporary criminal justice has been the subject of a comprehensive review by Adam Crawford, from whose work the following extract is taken.

Extract 1.5.7

A Crawford, *The Local Governance of Crime* (1997) pp 149–159

THE CONTESTABLE NATURE OF 'COMMUNITY'

. . .

'Community' . . . has become the policy buzzword of the 1990s . . . In this chapter, I will consider the nature of 'community' to which appeals are made in criminal justice discourse and policies, and the institutionalization of 'community' in actual practices. Or to rephrase this as a series of questions: why community? what is meant by community? and whose community? This will involve a consideration of the possible and actual contribution of 'community' to the practices of social order and crime prevention. In other words, what is it that 'community' has to offer crime control?

. . .

The nature of community in policy discourse

A close examination of Conservative government and opposition parties' publications and policy statements in the field of crime control and prevention, identifies a number of recurring assumptions upon which appeals to community are premised. These assumptions, it will be argued, derive from certain ideological understandings of the nature of crime, community, and their interconnections . . .

The following quotations from leading figures in the two major British political parties over recent years set the tone of dominant political appeals to 'community' and their connection with crime and its prevention . . .

'We need to look to individuals . . . to help us re-build those values and a sense of individual responsibility which prevents crime from taking a hold. It is only when these values fail that we come to rely upon the police and the courts. Rebuilding values will in many cases, also involve rebuilding communities. Crime flourishes in neighbourhoods with shallow roots, where there is little sense of pride or loyalty and where the disapproval of neighbours does not matter . . . In these places litter, for example, is not just a sign of local authority inefficiency but a potent symbol of the 'couldn't care less, let someone else clear it up' attitude to life. In many of these places the sense of community has been lost . . . The restoration of the values and standards of behaviour that should form the foundation for any 'community' is a moral imperative which we must pursue in the coming years . . . At the very centre of our ideas on how to control crime should be the energy and initiative of the active citizen. His or her contribution must be mobilised and should be the core of the radical rethinking we need on prevention and control of crime.' (Patten 1988)

'Aggressive begging, along with graffiti and, in some cities, "squeegee merchants" all heighten people's fear of crime on the streets . . . The result is a vicious circle in which people use the streets less, society becomes atomised, and community life breaks down.' (Straw 1995)

'We need to do what we can to recreate the sense of obligation through the generations. We also need to be aware of our duties as good neighbours . . . The strongest communities exist where voluntary collective action is most apparent. In rolling back the State we have rolled forward the scope for voluntary local collective action. We have given individuals far more scope for getting involved.' (Howard 1994)

'Britain must move back towards mutual responsibility if it is to re-establish vibrant community life . . . We need to break out of the language of dutiless rights and begin to insist upon mutual responsibility. Rights and duties go hand in hand . . . the community should expect responsible behaviour from all.' (Straw 1995)

The similarities and continuities in the above message both express the established mainstream political consensus on the appropriateness of a 'community' approach to crime, and the fact that 'community' signifies and references divergent attractions, meanings, and strategies. What the 'community' constitutes, its boundaries or the values and interests it prioritizes are rarely explicated. Nevertheless, a number of interconnected political and ideological assumptions can be identified.

A lack of community leads to a 'Spiral of Decline'
Underlying policy initiatives around crime in the community, as in the above extracts, is the prevailing idea that crime results from a failure or breakdown of community life. This degeneration is traditionally associated with a failure of processes of communal socialization and informal social control. Distant echoes from Chicago School sociologists can be heard in the notion that crime is associated with 'disorganised communities' . . . Community reorganization, from this viewpoint, acts to counter the degeneration associated with crime, on the presupposition that it is an inherent capacity of communities to mobilize their own resources of social control. Through informal community controls, it is anticipated that the primary of the normative, law-abiding consensus of the

community will be asserted. These ideas connect with, and reflect the influence of, Wilson and Kelling's [J Q Wilson and G Kelling 'Broken Windows: The Police and Neighbourhood Safety' (1982) *The Atlantic Monthly* 29–37, March] 'broken windows' thesis. According to this, communities are seen as occupying a pivotal role in halting moral decline, the regeneration of neighbourhood life, and the prevention of crime, by exerting their moral authority. Communities are identified, therefore, as a powerful site of social order and control.

Within the 'broken window' thesis, and British policy rhetoric which draws upon it, community degeneration is viewed as both the social cause and the effect of crime and the fear of crime. Crime is the product of disorganized communities and, at the same time, it is disorganized communities which create the conditions for crime to flourish. The regeneration of community is the proposed solution to halt and reverse the cycle. This process embodies a dual understanding of community. It assumes a definition of community as both a shared locality – in purely territorial terms – and a shared concern or 'sense of community' (both points to which I return). It starts from the premise that mere proximity generates – or at least should generate – shared concern. It goes on to propose that the combination of individual actions and behaviour, together with informal social processes of control to which those acts give rise, will help reconstitute and reassemble a 'sense of community'. Consequently, 'community' constitutes a means to an end, and an end in itself. It is both the vehicle to a better life and the better life. Means and ends have become badly confused. With such circularity, it is hard to recognize and separate off implementation problems associated with community programmes, as they constitute as much a failure of theory as of practice . . . It is not apparent, therefore, whether community regeneration or the reduction of crime is the primary aim, as they are seen to march hand in hand. In practice, however, they are not the same thing and, by contrast, they are often in tension, or at least ambiguously inter-related. This is especially problematic for practitioners – given the open-textured nature of both community and crime prevention – in that it exaggerates the multiple aims which often obscure strategies. The tension between means and ends, as a result, creates additional problems for monitoring and evaluation, as 'success' becomes so multi-layered as to be virtually meaningless . . .

Further, approaches that identify 'community' as a force of organization, tend to focus upon the *internal* attributes of 'community', its collective sense, social institutions, structure, demographic composition, and so on. Efforts at community organizing rarely, if at all, acknowledge, or seek to address, *external* forces and dynamics which often undermine – especially in high crime areas – those efforts. However, the power of private capital and property interests, resident mobility – particularly changing patterns of tenant allocation in public sector housing . . . – unemployment, social exclusion, and poverty, will all impact upon internal community relations, potentially increasing social and cultural disorganization . . .

More community equals less crime
The 'broken window' thesis assumes a direct causal relationship between a lack of informal social control – in other words a lack of 'community' – and the existence of high levels of crime. It is empirically questionable, however, whether

there is any direct link between incivilities, crime, fear of crime, and informal social control. 'Broken windows' do not necessarily have the same effects in different neighbourhoods. The way communities perceive crime and other social problems may be refracted through the political and social resources available to that community . . . Contrary to Wilson and Kelling's model, crime does not have a uniform impact upon community life. Foster's [J Foster, 'Informal Social Control and Community Crime Prevention' (1995) *British Journal of Criminology* 563] . . . ethnographic research on two crime-prone, public sector housing estates in England, exposes this fallacy of the 'broken windows' thesis. Foster found that informal control mechanisms were not absent in all high crime areas, challenging the assumption that they are lacking in poor communities torn by crime. Moreover, on one of the estates, the impact of crime was to a large degree contained, principally by local, mutual support networks. Crime, she concludes, is not always damaging *per se* so long as other mediating factors cushion its impact (Foster 1995: 580).

In addition, the logic behind this association between the lack of 'organized' community and crime is that, conversely, more community equals less crime. Community, in this context, is cleansed of any negative or crimogenic connotations and endowed with a simplistic and naïve purity and virtue. This benevolent understanding of community is highly misleading. In some instances 'community', i.e. its communal normative values, itself may be the source of crimogenic tendencies. Recent British research into criminal subcultures has reiterated the long established criminological truism that the collective values of a community may serve to stimulate and sustain criminality . . . This paradox has been particularly clearly noted in research on football hooliganism . . . For, in that context, it is the celebration of a particular (male) community and of cultural traditions, which is perceived as 'problematic' . . .

Community as a set of attitudes
As suggested earlier, the dominant discourse assumes 'community' to be a set of shared attitudes. Consequently, reference frequently is made to the importance of a 'sense of community'. 'Community', thus understood, is more than geographic location, it exists where members of a social grouping *feel* bound together by shared interests or identity. Therefore, communities take much of their character from the way in which their members think about and 'imagine' themselves . . . Community boundaries form around what its members share in common, or are 'imagined' to share, and how this differentiates them from others who are not members. Crime control policy (as identified in the extracts cited earlier) seeks to create and foster 'spatial communities', whereby a common sense of belonging to a geographical neighbourhood constitutes a defining criteria in the construction of communal identity and boundary formation. Consequently, a 'sense of pride or loyalty', 'mutual responsibility', and individuals showing that they 'care' about the place in which they live, are all prerequisites for a 'sense of community' and the local moral regeneration which it sustains. Here we see the 'activation of individual commitments, energies, and choices, through personal morality within a community setting' [N Rose, ' "The Death of the Social": Refiguring the Territory of Government' (1996) 25 *Economy and Society* 327]. The 'community' constitutes an acceptable collective imagery for energizing and catalysing individuals.

I will return to the issue of 'spatial communities' later. For the moment, however, I want to focus upon this generalized assumption that communities can, or should, be 'imagined', and therefore, that their construction and sustenance merely involve an attitude shift. Communities are, by and large, associations and groups of people which gather around certain interests, characteristics or identities, which may be based on lifestyle, culture, religion, ethnicity, occupation, place of residence, and so on . . . These social identities are accorded significance, both internally and externally. The process of ascribing significance involves the construction of 'boundaries' of inclusion and exclusion, but which need not be spatially constrained. An important element in this process is the establishment of a sense of 'belonging'. The way in which communities think about and imagine themselves and others is an evident part of community life . . . However, social identity, as a state of mind, whilst an important empirical aspect of 'community', fails sufficiently to explain the nature of a community's capacity for informal social control or its ability to address and organize around issues of crime and its prevention.

Currie (1988) has forcefully revealed the inadequacies of such a conception of 'community' in the field of crime prevention. He identifies two distinct 'visions' of community crime prevention in order to illustrate the very different understandings of 'community' upon which they are premised. The differences between the two visions impact upon, and contain, the capacity of communities to address issues of crime. In the Phase 1 vision, 'community' is understood, as in dominant policy discourse, in symbolic terms – a 'social-psychological view' – as a set of collective attitudes. Here, Currie suggests that

> 'Community, in brief, is in people's heads. Consequently, if you wish to improve community conditions you are in essence in the business of changing attitudes, or altering the symbols of community, in the hope that improved interpersonal relations will follow. In the ideal scenario you may thus start a benign cycle: improved attitudes lead to better behaviour, which in turn enhances people's conception of community, which in turn . . .' (1988: 280–1)

Phase 1 is most clearly typified by Wilson and Kelling's 'broken windows' model and by much situational crime prevention, particularly of the 'defensible space' type on large public sector housing estates. In my research, this notion – of community as attitudes which need to be implanted in a locality – was prevalent in all the case studies. For example, a council officer on the Illsworth Project articulated this approach:

> 'the function of community representation is to try, and by involving those opinion-formers in the local community, somehow spread the awareness that something is happening, to get the feeling out there that something is happening, that something is being done, that people do care about the area and to get the area *up* rather than *down*, and in order to encourage that feeling in the wider community you have to start with the rep[resentative]s.'

This 'trickle down' understanding of community representation suggests that an attitude shift is a, if not *the*, fundamental element in reversing the cycle of urban decline. Currie admits that this 'sense of identity' is a component of what a community is [E Currie, 'Two Visions of Community Crime Prevention' in T Hope and M Shaw (eds), *Communities and Crime Reduction* (London: HMSO, 1988)]. However, he suggests that this represents only a partial account. Further, it is arguably one that, by itself, does not constitute the most significant element for the purpose of crime control. This type of understanding of community, with its emphasis on the symbolic, lacks what Currie calls 'structural awareness'. This he illustrates by contrasting it with a Phase 2 vision. Here, 'community' is seen in:

> 'much more structural, or institutional terms not just as a set of attitudes we can "implant" or mobilise, but as an interlocking set of long-standing institutions which in turn are deeply affected by larger social and economic forces ... real communities thrive or fail to thrive, become healthy or pathological, mainly as a result of the strength or weakness of these basic institutions – work, family and kin, religious and communal associations, a vibrant local economy capable of generating stable livelihoods.' (Currie 1988: 282–3)

An understanding of 'community', particularly in the field of crime prevention, which fails to move beyond Phase 1 thinking and which lacks a structural or institutional awareness will only ever be partial. Unfortunately, much of the dominant policy analysis is locked into Phase 1 thinking alone ...

Community as place

The shift in criminological concern from *criminals* to *crimes*, people to places, has been dramatic over the last two decades ... Space, rightly, has come to be recognized as a critical variable in understanding and mapping the incidence of crime, together with its prevention. Urban geographers have been instrumental in asserting the importance of 'place' in criminological theory, both in terms of the spatial distribution of offences and offenders as well as their explanations ... As a result, the contemporary criminological talk is of the 'patterning of offence locations' ... the 'crime area distribution' ... 'hot spots' of crime ... and other spatial characteristics. However, theories of situational crime prevention in general, and 'defensible spaces' in particular, have come to revere the importance of the spatial. Often the result has been to focus exclusively upon spatial characteristics at the expense of social factors. In its excesses, crime and prevention have become overly 'spatialized'. Consequently, 'community' in crime prevention is defined, almost exclusively, in geographical terms and so spatial attributes are both the principal defining characteristics of scheme boundaries and the point of entry for most interventions.

At the level of practice this produces a number of tensions. These boundaries are often arbitrary – imposed by the constraints of funding or political niceties – and often mean little in human terms. They frequently create sources of local jealousy and conflict in relation to bordering areas. These largely revolve around whether vocal neighbouring residents wish to be included in, or excluded from, community crime prevention projects. For example, on the South Ornley Burglary Project a neighbourhood watch co-ordinator campaigned vigorously and successfully, for over a year, for the inclusion of his neighbouring area into the project. By contrast, other residents of his area were concerned about the association with crime that their locality might be given by the extension of the project. Consequently, there was little take up of the subject in his area.

75

Similarly, the Tenmouth project did not emerge around any 'natural' boundaries. The boundaries that were established arose as a consequence of local conflict and political expediency. Initially, the seconded probation officer had identified a small area of the city of Tenmouth as having a high rate of domestic burglary, based on an examination of police statistics. However, this created a local controversy when the chosen area became publicly known. Local residents expressed considerable concern at their area being the focus of a crime prevention initiative. Many of them thought that it would suggest that the locality was a 'high crime' neighbourhood and give it an adverse reputation. It was feared that the locality might subsequently become stigmatized and that house prices might be threatened. In response, the project leaders decided to broaden the scope of the initiative to include two additional police subdivisions of south and central Tenmouth, which included a further eight local authority wards, in an attempt to address the residents' concerns by watering down the focus of the project.

When placed in the context of competitive tendering for small amounts of government money, the emphasis on the spatial leaves local residents and workers in contradictory positions. In order to attract the funds, they are forced into cataloguing and highlighting the problems in the area. This often requires agency workers to over-emphasize the negative aspects of a given community. To use the language of the Illsworth council worker cited earlier, they need to put an area 'down' in order to get the resources to try and pull it 'up' again. The politics of attracting funds may involve media scrutiny and unwanted publicity. On the Churchway Project, for example, the publicity generated by the process of attracting funds was seen as involving an ambiguous logic, by the local residents. A tenants' association representative on the project explained:

> 'The media has been particularly useful at the beginning of the project when the residents had wanted to draw attention to the plight of [the area]. However, the media is a double-edged sword in that they also only ever want to hear bad news and always paint [the neighbourhood] as a terrible place.'

As the target of agency initiatives and public attention, the area developed what for many residents was an unwanted notoriety. The outcome of this process, other community representatives explained, was a desire on the part of some people to leave the area, particularly when insurance companies began refusing to renew contents insurance policies, a further product of the 'spatialization' of crime and risk assessment.

Other initiatives were plagued by similar problems and concerns about the fear of labelling a neighbourhood as a 'high crime' area, particularly through high profile interventions. Consequently, the connection between crime and 'spatial' communities is both inherently problematic and a 'double-edged sword'. It carries the imminent capacity to stigmatize whole areas. The very recognition that crime is a problem in a given area can be enough to set in motion a series of processes which may be eventually self-fulfilling, as an area gains a reputation for crime.

What is clear is that government policies and the actions of agencies can have an important influence upon the make-up and nature of communities. The provision of resources is particularly fundamental in this regard. Resources from governmental and other agencies may contribute to the construction of community boundaries and the promotion of either competition or collaboration between different groups ... On the one hand, the existence of scarce public resources can provide the basis for the establishment of an identifiable community and can encourage collaboration. This was the case in Churchway, which actually transcended two local authority boundaries but which was seen to be an ideal site to attract City Challenge funds. The two local authorities, as well as different subdivisions of the police and social services departments, consequently 'came together' and 'buried their differences' for the sake of mutual advantage. However, on the other hand, competition for resources, particularly of the type currently popular in government circles, can increase conflicts within and between groups and organizations. As we have seen, it can create intergroup jealousies and rivalries as well as further intensify social polarization ...

Reference should also be made at this point to the development and use of community sentences, although the topic is discussed in more detail in Chapter 5. Some community sentences, particularly the probation order, are of long standing but the range of community sentences has increased in recent years to include various forms of intensive supervision, curfew and electronic tagging of offenders. Community sentences are managed and enforced by the probation service, and have traditionally been associated with constructive and rehabilitative penal aims, and 'diversion' of the offender from the imposition of a custodial sentence. The passing of a community sentence required the offender's consent and his or her willingness to co-operate with the order's requirements. Formerly, community sentences were commonly referred to as 'alternatives' to custody, and were generally introduced by government in an attempt to steer judges and magistrates away from custodial sentences to more positive and constructive alternatives. The day-to-day task of persuading sentencers to use them fell to the probation service, by way of argument and recommendation in pre-sentence reports (formerly known as social inquiry reports) prepared by a probation officer and describing, amongst other things, the offender's circumstances and attitude to the offence. Persuasion was sometimes an uphill task, with community sentences derided in the press, and also by some politicians and judges, as 'soft options'. The rhetoric of 'alternatives' perhaps did not help, and the Criminal Justice Act 1991, in line with the predominance of desert theory at that time, changed the status of community sentences, so that they were henceforth to be regarded in law as punishments in their own right – measures admittedly less severe than imprisonment, but which offered a means of significantly restricting an offender's liberty without removal from the community from which he or she had come. The 1991 Act also recognised that community sentences can place considerable obligations of compliance on offenders and, by s 6(1), required sentencers to justify the use of such a sentence in every case by reference to the gravity of the crime – was the offence 'serious enough' to require a community penalty? If so, by s 6(2) of the 1991 Act, the form and duration of the order should take account of both the seriousness of the offence and the suitability of the offender. As already noted, the Crime (Sentences) Act 1997 has now dispensed with the requirement that offenders must 'consent' to the imposition of a community sentence.

These and other aspects of the 'community and community values' theme are identified in the following extract from Anthony Bottoms.

Extract 1.5.8

A E Bottoms, 'The Philosophy and Politics of Punishment and Sentencing' in C M V Clarkson and R Morgan (eds), *The Politics of Sentencing Reform* (1995) p 17, at pp 34–37 (footnotes renumbered and amended)

Community

. . . Without much doubt, the last thirty years have seen increased attention being given to what are now increasingly called 'community penalties' (sometimes 'intermediate penalties'). These are seen as ways of providing a credible sanction for the offender, but operated in the community rather than in prison. Some such penalties (most obviously the probation order) have a longer history, but in the period since 1970 we have seen the invention and very rapid spread of the community-service order,[1] and of the curfew order with electronic tagging,[2] as well as the development of a variety of different versions of intensive probation.[3] As often as not, the motivation in all this has been to avoid increased prison overcrowding, and/or new prison building, at a time of steadily increasing recorded crime rates; and hence to reduce the overall costs to the state at a time of fiscal crisis.[4] Critics[5] have argued that the new emphasis on 'community corrections' has become a way in which the state is exercising more, and more intrusive, control over the lives of its citizens, but in the wake of recent critique[6] this thesis now seems less attractive than it did.

A further, analogous, movement during the same period has been that of so-called 'diversion to the community', especially diversion from court.[7] This movement often shares some of the same philosophical features as the drive towards 'community penalties',[8] though at a 'shallower' point in the criminal-justice system. However, it is normally additionally associated with a labelling theory rationale, i.e. in the belief that diversion from court will provide a better opportunity than would formal entry into the criminal-justice system to help the offender avoid further criminality, because the stigma of conviction will tend to promote negative self-image and therefore enhanced risk of re-offending.[9]

It has to be said that this first element of the 'community' theme, though undoubtedly prominent in many jurisdictions in recent years, might have, in reality, little to do with real communities. That is most obviously the case when diversion from court simply entails non-prosecution, i.e. no action;[10] but it may also be so as regards some forms of community penalty, e.g. those forms of community-service order where the offenders are engaged, as a group, in a kind of 'public works' programme. In that connection, it is undoubtedly of great interest that McIvor's recent research in Scotland has shown that those forms of community-service order that are more oriented to a genuine 'community' theme tend to have higher compliance rates and (though the evidence here is more tentative) lower reconviction rates.[11]

In those instances where 'community penalties' or 'diversion' are only tenuously connected to any genuine sense of community, it is of some interest to ask why the 'community' concept is nevertheless applied to them. The answer to this appears to be that 'community', though an infuriatingly imprecise term, remains highly suggestive to most listeners, and with positive connotations of belonging, support, and identity. As such, it may be used in modern societies from a variety of political perspectives, including the left (in which the reference and appeal may be to the idealized working-class community, trade union, or friendly society, etc.) and the new right.[12] It may also be used, more or less consciously, as an attempt to evoke an image of a bygone and allegedly more tranquil/peaceful society, and in this respect there are some obvious potential linkages between the modern use of 'community' as an idealized concept, and the rise of the 'heritage' theme in modern societies.[13]

. . .

The second dimension of the 'community' theme derives directly from an intervention made by Michael Tonry at the Colston Symposium (see also Tonry's essay in this volume). Tonry pointed out that in the American context (where numerical sentencing guidelines have now been adopted in many states, and these constrain sentencers to a typically greater extent than the narrative guidance/directions embodied in statutes in, say, England or Scandinavia) it is a not infrequent occurrence to find statewide guidelines being resisted in particular local areas, because they are seen by local judges and others to be insufficiently sensitive to the particular local context. That sense of remoteness to local problems may be particularly marked in communities that are rather distant (physically or structurally) from the main locus of power in the given state – for example, remote rural communities or areas with a special concentration of residents from particular ethnic minorities. Relatively powerless groups of a non-geographical sort might also, and analogously, press their claims for a 'special' justice that has not been understood by the rational-legal state legislature, judiciary, or executive – and such groups might include interest groups such as women victimized by serious violent or sexual crimes, or environmental groups. The general point is that we live in an increasingly pluralist world – or at least, in a world where pre-existing pluralisms have become more overt and widely recognized – and that the demands generated by this pluralism do not always fit well with the rationalizing impulses created both by the 'fairness' critique of the rights approach, and by managerialism.

. . .

One possible response to the kinds of concerns highlighted in the preceding paragraph is to try to 'devolve' decision-making in the adjudication of criminal events into a more informal community-oriented forum, where, for example, the cultural norms of an ethnic minority group may be given greater weight than they can be in the formal context of a Western-style criminal court. Exactly this kind of thinking seems to underlie the interestingly widespread development, in different jurisdictions, of attempts to evolve victim–offender mediation schemes, in which the emphasis switches away from (to put the matter in stark terms to make the point) 'state punishment' and moves instead towards a 'negotiated settlement between parties to a dispute'. This kind of reform is sometimes presented as a necessary part of a broader social policy to recover the lost sense of community in modern life.[14]

Although experiments with mediation schemes have been widespread, it has to be said that reforms of this kind have usually been rather marginal to mainstream criminal-justice developments.[15]

[1] See e.g. W A Young, *Community Service Orders* (London, 1979); K Pease, 'Community Service Orders', in M Tonry and N Morris (eds), *Crime and Justice: An Annual Review of Research*, vi (Chicago, 1985); D C McDonald, *Punishment Without Walls* (New Brunswick, NJ, 1986); G McIvor, *Sentenced to Serve* (Aldershot, 1992).

[2] See J M Byrne, A J Lurigio, and J Petersilia (eds), *Smart Sentencing: The Emergence of Intermediate Sanctions* (Newbury Park, Calif., 1992), Part II; G Mair and C Nee, *Electronic Monitoring: The Trials and their Results* (Home Office Research Study No 120; London, 1990).

[3] See e.g. J M Byrne, A J Lurigio, and J Petersilia (eds), above, n. 2, Part I; N Morris and M Tonry, *Between Prison and Probation: Intermediate Punishments in a Rational Sentencing System* (New York: Oxford University Press, 1990) Ch 7; P Raynor, *Probation as an Alternative to Custody* (Aldershot, 1988).

[4] Whether costs are actually saved by an increase in community penalties is, however, not a wholly straightforward question: see N Morris and M Tonry, above, n. 3, 157–9 for a brief summary of the relevant issues.

[5] e.g. S Cohen, *Visions of Social Control* (Cambridge, 1985).

[6] M McMahon, *The Persistent Prison? Rethinking Decarceration and Penal Reform* (Toronto, 1992).

[7] See e.g. M Klein, 'Deinstitutionalization and Diversion of Juvenile Offenders: A Litany of Impediments', in N Morris and M Tonry (eds), *Crime and Justice: An Annual Review of Research*, i (Chicago, 1979).

[8] As it did in the 1980s in English juvenile justice, among a powerful practitioner-led alliance often referred to as developing a 'new orthodoxy': see generally A E Bottoms et al, *Intermediate Treatment and Juvenile Justice* (London: HMSO, 1990).

[9] The empirical evidence for this view is however less positive than is sometimes supposed: see e.g. D P Farrington, 'England and Wales', in M W Klein (ed), *Western Systems of Juvenile Justice* (Beverly Hills, Calif., 1984), 92.

[10] Some diversion schemes however entail an element of more community-oriented action, e.g. reparation or counselling.

[11] More specifically, in McIvor's (above, n. 1) research the work placements that were perceived most positively by the offenders were those which maximized the potential contact between the offender and the beneficiaries, those which offenders perceived as being of considerable benefit to the recipients, and those in which the offender him/herself was able to acquire new skills; and where there was positive rating of a placement by offenders, compliance and non-offending tended to be higher.

[12] The new right tends to operate with two rather distinct ideological strands: economic *neo-liberalism*, and social *neo-conservatism*, in which there is an appeal to a number of traditional values, including personal morality, the family, and the value of 'community'. See S Hall and M Jacques (eds), *The Politics of Thatcherism* (London, 1983).

[13] Often interestingly linked to consumer culture: see e.g. N Thrift, 'Images of Social Change', in C Hamnett, L McDowell, and P Sarre (eds), *The Changing Social Structure* (London, 1989); S Lash and J Urry, *Economics of Signs and Space* (London, 1994).

[14] N Christie, 'Conflicts as Property', (1977) 17 *Brit. J. Criminol.* 1–15.

[15] See e.g. T B Nergard, 'Solving Conflicts outside the Court System: Experiences with the Conflict Resolution Boards in Norway', (1993) 33 *Brit. J. Criminol.* 81–94; T F Marshall and S Merry, *Crime and Accountability: Victim/Offender Mediation in Practice* (London, 1990).

Extract 1.5.9

**S Cohen, 'The Punitive City: Notes on the Dispersal of Social Control'
(1979) 3 _Contemporary Crises_ 339, at pp 346–350 (footnotes omitted)**

Thinning the mesh and widening the net

On the surface, a major ideological thrust in the move against institutions derives from a desire to limit state intervention. Whether arising from the supposed failures of the treatment model, or the legal argument about the over-reach of the law and the necessity to limit the criminal sanction, or the implicit non-interventionism of labelling theory, or a general disenchantment with paternalism, or simply the pragmatic case for easing the burdens on the system – the eventual message looked the same: the state should do less rather than more. It is ironical then – though surely the irony is too obvious even to be called this – that the major results of the new movements towards 'community' and 'diversion' have been to increase rather than decrease the _amount_ of intervention directed at many groups of deviants in the system and, probably, to increase rather than decrease the total _number_ who get into the system in the first place. In other words: 'alternatives' become not alternatives at all but new progams which supplement the existing system or else expand it by attracting new populations.

I will refer to these two overlapping possibilities as 'thinning the mesh' and 'widening the net' respectively. No one who has studied the results of such historical innovations as probation and parole should be surprised by either of these effects.

Let us first examine community alternatives to incarceration. The key index of 'success' is not simply the proliferation of such programs, but the question of whether they are replacing or merely providing supplementary appendages to the conventional system of incarceration. The statistical evidence is by no means easy to decipher but it is clear, both from Britain and America, that rates of incarceration – particularly in regard to juveniles – are not at all declining as rapidly as one might expect and in some spheres are even increasing. Critically – as one evaluation suggests the 'alternatives' are not, on the whole, being used for juveniles at the 'deep end' of the system, i.e. those who really would have been sent to institutions before. When the strategy is used for 'shallow end' offenders – minor or first offenders whose chances of incarceration would have been slight – then the incarceration rates will not be affected.

The exact proportions of these types are difficult to estimate: one English study of community service orders shows that only half the offenders sent would otherwise have received custodial sentences. Leaving aside the question of the exact effects on the rest of the system, there is little doubt that a substantial number – perhaps the majority – of those subjected to the new programs, will be subjected to a degree of intervention higher than they would have received under previous non-custodial options like fines, conditional discharge or ordinary probation.

Turning now to the more explicit forms of diversion, it is once again clear that the term, like the term 'alternatives' is not quite what it implies. Diversion has

81

been hailed as the most radical application of the non-intervention principle short of complete decriminalization. The grand rationale is to restrict the full force of the criminal justice process to more serious offences and to either eliminate or substantially minimize penetration for all others.

Clearly, all justice systems – particularly juvenile – have always contained a substantial amount of diversion. Police discretion has been widely used to screen juveniles: either right out of the system by dropping charges, informally reprimanding or cautioning, or else informal referral to social services agencies. What has now happened, to a large degree, is that these discretionary and screening powers have been formalized and extended – and in the process, quite transformed. The net widens to include those who, if the program had not been available would either not have been processed at all or would have been placed on options such as traditional probation. Again, the more benevolent the new agencies appear, the more will be diverted there by encouragement or coercion. And – through the blurring provided by the welfare net – this will happen to many not officially adjudicated as delinquent as well. There will be great pressure to work with parts of the population not previously 'reached'.

All this can be most clearly observed in the area of police diversion of juveniles. Where the police used to have two options – screen right out (the route for by far the *majority* of encounters) or process formally – they now have the third option of diversion into a program. Diversion can then be used as an alternative to screening and not an alternative to processing. The proportion selected will vary. British research on police juvenile liaison schemes and similar measures shows a clear widening of the net and one survey of eleven Californian diversion projects suggests that only 51 per cent of clients were actually diverted from the system, with the rest receiving more processing than they would have received otherwise. Another evaluation of 35 police departments running diversion programs concludes:

'... the meaning of "diversion" has been shifted from "diversion from" to "referral to". Ironically, one of the ramifications of this is that in contrast to some earlier cited rationales for diversion as reducing costs, caseload and the purview of the criminal justice system, diversion may in fact be extending the costs, caseload and system purview even further than had previously been the case'.

The key to understanding this state of affairs lies in the distinction between *traditional* or *true* diversion – removing the juvenile from the system altogether by screening out (no further treatment, no service, no follow up) – and the *new* diversion which entails screening plus program: formal penetration is minimized by referral to programs in the system or related to it. Only traditional diversion is true diversion in the sense of diverting *from*. The new diversion diverts – for better or worse – *into* the system.

To conclude this section: whatever the eventual pattern of the emergent social control system, it should be clear that such policies as 'alternatives' in no way represent a victory for the anti-treatment lobby or an 'application' of labelling theory. Traditional deviant populations are being processed in a different way or else new populations are being caught up in the machine. For some observers all this is an index of how good theory produces bad practise:

82

each level diverts to the next and at each level vested interests (like job security) ensures that few are diverted right out. And so the justice machine enlarges itself.

If the criminal justice system operates in the name of the public, and needs to retain the confidence of the public in the decisions which are reached, to what extent should those who work within the system take account of public opinion when making their decisions? We need to reflect carefully on what is meant here by 'public opinion'. The Code for Crown Prosecutors (revised 1994) states that once the prosecutor is satisfied that there is enough evidence to provide a realistic prospect of conviction, in a case of any seriousness prosecution should take place 'unless there are public interest factors tending against prosecution which clearly outweigh those tending in favour'. However, public interest here does *not* mean canvassing and applying public opinion – it means taking account of wider social concerns than may be strictly relevant between the parties most immediately concerned in the alleged offence. Thus, for example, the attitude of the victim towards prosecution of the defendant, whether the victim is for or against that course of action, is influential but cannot be decisive in the decision to prosecute (see para 6.7 of the Code). Public interest criteria are capable of being specified with a fair degree of clarity, and set out in the Code (see Chapter 3 below).

What of public opinion on sentencing? The former Home Secretary, Michael Howard, when putting forward the proposals for tougher sentencing which subsequently became law in the Crime (Sentences) Act 1997 claimed that the changes he was proposing were 'vital if public confidence in the criminal justice system is to be maintained', so that people 'feel that the law is fair and just' (Howard, 1995). How can the Home Secretary know that the public, if asked, would support his policy? Are his comments anything more than political rhetoric? Individual sentencing judges, and the Court of Appeal, not infrequently also make reference to public opinion when passing sentence or reviewing sentencing policy. Judges, however, tend to call in aid the opinion of 'right-thinking' members of the public. In the leading case of *Cox* (1993) 14 Cr App R (S) 479 the former Lord Chief Justice, Lord Taylor, explained that a custodial sentence ought to be imposed for the kind of offence 'which would make right-thinking members of the public, knowing all the facts, feel that justice had not been done by the passing of any sentence other than a custodial one'. Does this test simply invoke 'popular punitiveness' (see Bottoms, 1995), is it a 'reasonable person' test, or is it simply meaningless and circular? (see further Ashworth and von Hirsch, 1997). In the following extract Ashworth and Hough subject the adoption of a 'public opinion' standard in sentencing decisions to detailed criticism.

Extract 1.5.10

A Ashworth and M Hough, 'Sentencing and the Climate of Opinion' [1996] Crim LR 776, at pp 780–786 (footnotes renumbered and amended)

Public opinion on sentencing

. . .

On the face of it, there is plenty of evidence to point to widespread public dissatisfaction with sentencing. In general, polls and surveys reveal a punitive public. Support for capital punishment has run at between 65 per cent and 75 per cent, depending on the precise wording of the question, for many years;[1] and a poll carried out for the *Daily Mail* found 92 per cent of a random sample supporting 'tougher sentences for criminals, especially persistent criminals'.[2] However, several research studies carried out mainly in the 1980s suggest that there is a need to qualify the picture of a public which is straightforwardly punitive.[3] Responses to questions pitched at a very general level, such as 'Are court sentences tough enough?' certainly *did* show a clear majority favouring tougher sentences; but when asked about suitable punishments for individual cases of specific types of crime, people's preferences tended to reflect the range of sentences actually imposed by sentencers. Although this research was limited, it was fairly consistent with work carried out in several other industrialised countries, notably Australia, Canada, the Netherlands and the United States.[4]

The most obvious explanation for the two sets of divergent findings lies in the lack of information which people have about crime and about sentencing practice. Walker et al found that people systematically underestimated how much the courts actually used imprisonment.[5] It is therefore arguable that the demand for tougher punishment stems, in part at least, from this misunderstanding. Another factor which might underlie the highly punitive responses to questions pitched at a general level could be ignorance about the characteristics of the average offender and of the circumstances under which he – or more rarely she – offends. Canadian research suggests that when people are asked to specify an appropriate punishment for a given crime, responses are highly dependent on the level of information about the offender. In general, people in these studies advocated tougher sentences the less information they were given about the offence and the offender's circumstances.[6] Arguably this was because, in the absence of adequate information, their responses were conditioned by stereotypes about 'criminals' gained from sources such as the popular press.

More recent qualitative research findings tend to confirm people's systematic ignorance of current practice as a factor fuelling dissatisfaction with the courts;[7] and the research also suggests that a majority of people advocate prison and community penalties for the same sorts of offence, respectively, as the courts. Moreover, when asked to consider a series of Court of Appeal judgments, participants generally expressed themselves as satisfied with the severity of sentences approved by the Court. However, in contrast to earlier survey-based research, this study also identifies some highly punitive views, with many participants calling for very long sentences for more serious crimes

84

such as rape, drug trafficking and serious wounding. Many advocated castration for rapists – not merely frivolously. There was also a consensus in favour of 'honesty in sentencing', whereby offenders serve prison sentences in full. It was not clear whether people saw this as a way of achieving a more transparent sentencing system, or a tougher one.

One survey of public reactions to court sentences is completely free of the criticism that people are asked to assess sentences in the absence of all the facts. This study, carried out for the Royal Commission on Criminal Justice, asked some 2,300 jurors what they thought about the sentence passed in the case on which they served. Almost a third (32 per cent) said the sentence was as they had expected, and exactly the same proportion said they had no expectation as regards sentence. The remaining one-third was divided between those who thought it was more severe (14 per cent) or less severe (23 per cent).[8] It is a reasonable assumption that these jurors constitute a representative sample of the population.

Debates about public opinion on sentencing have tended to focus on the overall congruence of opinion and practice on how tough sentencing should be. A possibility which tends to be overlooked is that people regard the courts not as overly lenient, but as erratic – imposing tough sentences when leniency is called for, and lenient sentences when toughness is called for. Walker and Marsh used the term 'cynicism' to refer to the belief that sentencers are creatively diverse in finding ways of reaching poor sentencing decisions.[9] Certainly, large proportions of the population think that judges and magistrates are 'out of touch with what ordinary people think' – three quarters, according to the 1992 British Crime Survey.[10] To the extent that this belief is rooted in a sense that sentencers are insufficiently *flexible* to respond appropriately to different sorts of cases, there is a great risk that current proposals for mandatory sentences will backfire.

A noteworthy feature of opinion about punishment is that it seems fairly fluid and malleable. Within limits, people will *tolerate* wide variations in sentencing severity. In an experimental survey design, Walker et al presented a random sample with facsimile newspaper cuttings of court cases in which sentences were systematically varied to be either severe or lenient. For most of the cuttings, large minorities of those presented with either tough or lenient sentences said that these were 'about right'; in some of the cases, majorities said that the sentence was about right, regardless of whether it was harsh or lenient. Tolerance for lenient sentences was less than for severe ones; but even when people did regard sentences as too tough or soft, substantial minorities did not feel strongly enough to want 'something done about it'. This finding carries the policy implication that *explaining* sentencing policy may be a more rational way of responding to public cynicism than *changing* current policy.

The views of victims of crime are arguably of particular importance. Some jurisdictions have gone so far as to allow or require sentencers to take account of 'victim impact statements', which may sometimes include the victim's view on what the sentence should be,[11] and there are soon to be experiments in England and Wales in providing prosecutors and courts with victim statements (excluding views on sentence).[12] Whether or not it is right for courts to attach particular weight to victims' views on punishment, the very fact that they are victims ensures that they have a detailed knowledge of the crime. Some victims will have actually considered the question of punishment at the time they suffered the crime. Most will not know the characteristics of the offender, of course, but they may be able to form a good idea of the sort of person he or she is likely to be. The few studies which have asked victims how they would like to see 'their' offender punished have failed to find evidence of widespread vindictiveness: on balance, views have tended to be consistent with those of the broader public, described above.[13]

The judiciary and public opinion

The statistics show that the courts rapidly increased their use of custody during 1993, following a fall in 1992. There was a sharp decrease from an average daily population of 47,000 for the first half of 1992 to a total of 40,606 people in prison at the end of the year. The fall was probably a response to the provisions about the use of imprisonment in the Criminal Justice Act 1991. Thereafter the trend was reversed. The prison population rose to 43,195 in March 1993, to 45,633 in August, and to 47,153 by the end of November. Readers will recall that this was the year of heightened media interest in crime and in 'law and order' issues. The killing of two-year-old James Bulger occurred in early 1993. In the months that followed, there was close media attention to several crimes that would hardly have been reported at other times, and a sustained attack on the provisions in the Criminal Justice Act 1991 discussed earlier in this article. Did the 'moral panic' evident during 1993 have any effect on judges and magistrates? Sentencers have rarely admitted this, but it would be hard to account for the increasing use of custody by reference to changes in the law (the Criminal Justice Act 1993 did not come into force until August 1993) or by reference to a sudden and exponential increase in the seriousness of the offences with which the courts were having to deal. The most straight-forward explanation is that judges and magistrates believed that the climate of opinion was changing, and attempted to reflect it to some degree. A more sophisticated version of the same argument is that they were in part responding to a shift in the climate of opinion, and in part anticipating the legislative changes which were announced in May 1993.

One example of the relationship between sentencing and notions of public opinion may be found in the interpretation of the statutory provision that is now section 1(2)(a) of the Criminal Justice Act 1991. The legislative purpose was to restrict the use of custodial sentences, and the sub-section states that a court may only impose custody if the offence is, or the offences are, 'so serious that only such a sentence can be justified'. The test that courts are expected to apply is, according to Lord Taylor C J, whether it is the kind of offence which 'would make right-thinking members of the public, knowing all the facts, feel that justice had not been done by the passing of any sentence other than a custodial one'.[14] Thus in *Cox* the Court held that the two offences (reckless driving and theft) were so serious that only custody could be justified, although the Court then found mitigating factors which took the case below the custody threshold. Among the subsequent cases in which the Court of Appeal has sought to apply this test is *Keogh*,[15] where the offender had been convicted of obtaining property worth £35 by deception from a do-ityourself store. In effect, this crime amounted to shoplifting, and the Court of Appeal, applying the *Cox* test, held that '. . . in our judgment in 1993, in the present climate of opinion, in relation to this sort of offence, that test is satisfied. We are, therefore, unable to interfere with the one month sentence for shoplifting.' One feature of this extraordinary judgment is that it implies that right-thinking members of the public may have become more punitive during 1993, even in relation to minor crimes of this kind.

It could be argued that the foundations of the *Cox* test have long been embedded in judicial culture. The Oxford pilot study found that, although the participating judges rejected the media as a true reflection of public opinion, they also took the view that it was not their proper function simply to reflect public opinion in their sentences. The proper approach was to be aware of public opinion but to pay attention only to 'informed public opinion'.[16] The research also suggested that judges were confident that they knew about informed public opinion, and a majority believed that it coincided with their own opinions. These are important issues, which are pursued more fully elsewhere.[17] For present purposes, it should be noted that the use of such adjectives as 'informed' and 'right-thinking' emphasises that the test has a normative element which straightforward opinion surveys cannot capture. Repeated findings that only a minority of the public would advocate imprisonment for offences of this kind[18] might be disregarded on the ground that the people surveyed were not 'right-thinking'. One result of this is that the judiciary can, in effect, keep the content of the test to themselves. There is no benchmark to determine whether or not it is being applied correctly.

Public opinion or populist punitiveness

Although the judges have increased the severity of their sentencing in the last few years, the statements of politicians and prevailing views in the mass media appear to favour even greater severity. At one level, this clearly chimes with popular sentiment. The majority of people think, in general terms, that sentences are far too soft. On the other hand, as we have shown . . . above, it is far from clear that public opinion and sentencing practice are out of step, when people are asked about their sentencing preference in particular cases.

The simplest explanation for this paradoxical set of findings lies in the tension between utilitarian sentencing aims such as deterrence and the requirements of proportionality or 'just deserts'. Crime rates have risen significantly over the last two decades, and it would hardly be surprising if some people responded to such changes by advocating tougher court penalties. In the absence of accessible information about current sentencing practice, some people may well infer that sentences are adequate in retributive terms but not likely to be effective in deterrent terms.[19] As discussed earlier, the news values of the mass media are likely to compound this process. Erratic sentencing decisions make better news than sensible ones, and reporting in the national press is likely to lead to systematic distortion of public perceptions of the courts. But this is not the whole story. Despite the claims often made by newspaper editors and proprietors that they simply reflect public opinion, some newspapers are transparent in their campaigning objectives. Sometimes the motivation for this may be the straightforward commercial one of boosting circulation; sometimes the agenda is more obviously political.

Politicians can certainly exercise leadership in shaping opinion. The surprising thing, perhaps, about the politics of criminal justice is how little attention – until recently – politicians have paid to the views of their electorate. The 1990s have seen a remarkable *volte-face*. At the beginning of the decade the Government was promoting a policy, embodied in the 1991 Act, that sought to increase the use of community sentences and to reserve custody for serious cases – in some ways a 'liberal' or at least a balanced approach.[20] Since 1993, however, appearing tougher and more decisive on 'law and order' than the other main parties has become a political priority. This makes it difficult for any politician to argue for a balanced approach to criminal justice: 'balanced' is regarded as a politician's synonym for 'mealy mouthed' or, worse still, 'soft'. It is at least conceivable that policy initiatives intended to demonstrate toughness and decisiveness may play a significant role in shaping public opinion on the substantive issues.

All these factors, however, may be insufficient to explain why so many people appear to be receptive to reporting that assumes the wisdom of severity and repressive measures against offenders. Tony Bottoms argues that deeper social insecurities may hold the key:

> 'The tendency of modern politicians occasionally to resort to populist punitiveness is relatively easy to understand. The disembedding processes of modernity . . . have not only probably increased the crime rate, they have also led to a fairly widespread sense of insecurity, especially among older people, as former social certainties are eroded . . . In such a context, a politician seeking popularity can reasonably easily tap into the electorate's insecurities by promising tough action on 'villains' – even if . . . the public are actually rather less punitive when confronted with real situations of criminality.'[21]

In this argument Bottoms takes care to separate the public's opinions 'when confronted with real situations' from the 'fairly widespread sense of insecurity'. It is the latter, which may be supported by findings on the fear of crime,[22] that Bottoms identifies as a major factor in ensuring a largely favourable public response to what he terms 'populist punitiveness' in the utterances of politicians and the media.

Conclusions

The views of sentencing held by people outside the criminal justice system – 'the general public' – will always be important even if they should not be determinative in court. Unfortunately, the concept of public opinion in relation to sentencing practices is often employed in a superficial or simplistic way. In this short article we have identified two major difficulties with the use of the concept. First, members of the public have insufficient knowledge of actual sentencing practices. Second, there is a significant but much-neglected distinction between people's sweeping impressions of sentencing and their views in relation to particular cases of which they know the facts. When it is proclaimed that the public think the courts are too lenient, both these difficulties are usually suppressed.

To construct sentencing policy on this flawed and partial notion of public opinion is irresponsible. Certainly, the argument is hard to resist that public confidence in the law must be maintained. It is also hard to resist the proposition that public confidence in sentencing is low and probably falling. However, since the causes of this lie not in sentencing practice but in misinformation and misunderstanding, and (arguably) in factors only distantly related to criminal justice, ratcheting up the sentencing tariff is hardly a rational way of regaining public confidence.

This is not to deny that there is political capital to be made, at least in the short term, by espousing sentencing policies which have the trappings of tough, decisive action. However, the underlying source of public cynicism will not have been addressed; and once politicians embark on this route, they may be committing themselves long-term to a treadmill of toughness, 'decisiveness', and high public expenditure. The political costs of withdrawing from tough policies, once embarked on, may be too high for politicians of any hue to contemplate. The United States serves as an example.[23]

---

[1] R Jowell, J Curtice, L Brook and D Ahrend, *British Social Attitudes: 11th Report* (1994).

[2] 1 April 1996.

[3] e.g. M Hough and D Moxon, 'Dealing with Offenders: Public Opinion and the Views of Victims', (1985) 24 *Howard J.C.J.* 160, and Chapters 3, 7, 10 and 11 of N Walker and M Hough (eds), *Public Attitudes to Sentencing: Surveys from Five Countries* (1988).

[4] See Chapters 2, 4, 5, 6 and 8 of Walker and Hough [N Walker and M Hough (eds), *Public Attitudes to Sentencing: Surveys from Five Countries* (Aldershot: Gower, 1988)]; also J V Roberts, 'Public Opinion, Crime and Criminal Justice', in M Tonry (ed), *Crime and Justice: a Review of Research*, Vol 16 (1992).

[5] N Walker, M Hough and H Lewis, 'Tolerance of Leniency and Severity in England and Wales' in Walker and Hough (1988), at p 185.

[6] A Doob and J Roberts, 'Public Punitiveness and Public Knowledge of the Facts', in Walker and Hough (1988).

[7] M Hough, 'People Talking About Punishment', (1996) 35 *Howard J.C.J.* 191. The research used 'focus group' methodology – essentially, structured group discussions with around 7–10 participants per group.

[8] M Zander and P Henderson, *Crown Court Study*, Royal Commission on Criminal Justice Research Study No 19 (1993), para 8.8.3. This question was only asked of jurors in cases which were sentenced immediately, which represented just over one-half of all cases.

[9] N Walker and C Marsh, 'Does the Severity of Sentence affect Public Disapproval?', in Walker and Hough (1988).

[10] Figure of 75 per cent supplied by the Home Office Research and Statistics Directorate.

[11] See A Ashworth, 'Victim Impact Statements and Sentencing', [1993] Crim.L.R. 498.

[12] *The Victim's Charter* (2nd ed) 1996, p 3.

[13] See, e.g. M Maguire, *Burglary in a Dwelling* (1982); J Shapland, C Willmore and P Duff, *Victims in the Criminal Justice System* (1985).

[14] *Cox* (1993) 14 Cr.App.R.(S) 479, at 481, adopting the words of Lawton L J in *Bradbourn* (1985) 7 Cr.App.R.(S) 180.

[15] (1994) 15 Cr.App.R.(S) 279.

[16] Oxford Pilot Study (1984) at p 31.

[17] A Ashworth and A von Hirsch, 'Recognising Elephants: The Problem of the Custody Threshold', [1997] Crim.L.R. (forthcoming).

[18] See Hough (1996), n. 7 above.

[19] The criminological research does not, however, support these rather simplistic assumptions about the operation of deterrence: see, e.g. N Walker and N Padfield, *Sentencing: Theory, Law and Practice* (2nd ed) 1996, Chs 7 and 8.

[20] For analysis, see Lord Windlesham, *Responses to Crime* (Vol 2), 1993, Chs 5 and 8; cf. also D Faulkner, *Darkness and Light* (Howard League) 1996, Ch 2 and *passim*. And see now Lord Windlesham, *Responses to Crime* (Vol 3) 1996, Pts I and II.

[21] A E Bottoms, 'The Philosophy and Politics of Punishment and Sentencing', in C Clarkson and R Morgan (eds), *The Politics of Sentencing* (1995), at p 47.

[22] See M Maxfield, *Fear of Crime in England and Wales* (1985) and M Hough, *Anxiety about Crime: Findings from the 1994 British Crime Survey* (1995).

[23] For analysis of recent U.S. sentencing policies and practices, see M Tonry, *Sentencing Matters* (1996).

There is an important degree of lay involvement in the criminal justice process itself, informally through assistance and information provided by the public to the police, and more formally through the lay magistracy and by citizens serving on juries in the Crown Court. Another example is 'special constables' – members of the public who volunteer to serve as police officers in their spare time. The practical importance of the lay magistracy in the English criminal justice system can hardly be over-stated, since magistrates deal with the vast majority of criminal matters coming before the courts (over 95 per cent, according to Darbyshire, 1997). Questions about the quality of magistrates' justice, and the process of their selection and training, are considered in Chapter 4. Juries are much less frequently called upon but, in the eyes of many, this element of lay involvement in the system has a profound, almost mystical, significance (see Darbyshire, 1991). The 'right' of a jury to return a verdict in defiance of law is considered in Chapter 4, and the function of the Court of Appeal in reviewing cases decided by jury is discussed in Chapter 6.

Finally in this section, it may be useful to consider briefly two recent instances in which the role of public opinion has been debated in relation to high-profile criminal justice decisions.

In 1997 the House of Lords ruled that the then Home Secretary, Michael Howard, was wrong to have taken into account a mass petition, in the form of cut-out coupons from the *Sun* newspaper, when making his decision to increase the tariff sentence which should be served by Venables and Thompson, the two juveniles convicted of the murder of Jamie Bulger (see *Secretary of State for the Home Department, ex parte Venables* [1997] 2 WLR 67). The two young defendants received the mandatory sentence of Detention during Her Majesty's Pleasure, a sentence imposed under s 53(1) of the Children and Young Persons Act 1933. It is solely applicable to offenders aged between 10 and 17 inclusive who have been convicted of murder. The sentencing judge has no choice but to impose that sentence. At the time of the case the law was that the sentencing judge had power to recommend a minimum period (the so-called 'tariff' period) to be served before the juveniles could first be considered for early release by the Parole Board, but that the period so recommended could be varied by the Home Secretary. The period of eight years set by the trial judge was varied to 15 years by Mr Howard. The House of Lords said that insofar as the Home Secretary had taken into account the mass petition organised by the newspaper his decision was an inappropriate exercise of his discretion and was unlawful. The English rules on release of juveniles sentenced under s 53(1) were the subject of criticism from the European Court of Human Rights in *Hussain v UK* (1996) 22 EHRR 1, and the relevant law has been amended by the Crime (Sentences) Act 1997, although not going so far as to remove the Home Secretary's power to set the tariff. In contrast, and also in 1997, the Divisional Court held in the case of *Secretary of State for the Home Department, ex parte Hindley, The Times*, Dec. 19, 1997, that the decision of the current Home Secretary, Jack Straw, to increase the tariff on Myra Hindley, the Moors murderer, to life from a period of 30 years set by one of his predecessors, was a proper exercise of his discretion. The court observed that the Home Secretary's powers were very broad in relation to adult prisoners convicted of murder and therefore serving the mandatory sentence for that crime of life imprisonment. The case is currently under appeal to the House of Lords.

(d) Fairness and discrimination

Questions of fair treatment and discrimination, particularly in relation to race and gender, arise and are discussed in a number of different contexts throughout this book and, therefore, only a brief introduction to these matters is provided here. The Royal Commission on Criminal Justice (Royal Commission on Criminal Justice, 1993, Ch 1, para 25) heard evidence 'on behalf of both minorities and women that they do not feel that they are either fairly or reasonably treated'. There has been a substantial amount of research in recent years into the extent to which criminal justice officials practise 'direct discrimination' by treating those coming into contact with the system (whether as suspects, defendants, victims or witnesses) less favourably on racial or other grounds. These findings have been 'contradictory and inconclusive' (Hudson, 1993, Fitzgerald, 1993 and Smith, 1997). A number of studies have demonstrated racist attitudes amongst rank-and-file police officers (Policy Studies Institute, 1983). The extent to which prejudice on the part of police officers and other agents of the criminal justice system may affect decisions over formal or informal cautioning, arrest and prosecution is considered in Chapter 2, and taken up again in Chapter 6. The racial, gender and class composition of those who staff criminal justice agencies, and their level of awareness and sensitivity to issues of discrimination, have been a matter of real concern (see further Chapter 6). The selection and representative composition of the lay magistracy is considered in Chapter 4, along with research which examines whether sentencing decisions in magistrates' courts are subject to racial and gender stereotypes. Discussion of discrimination at the sentencing stage is to be found in Chapter 5, and for further information on gender-related issues and criminal justice see Chapter 6 and Heidensohn, 1997.

It is well known that prisoners from some ethnic minorities make up a disproportionate part of the sentenced prison population. On 1 January 1997, 18 per cent of prisoners were from ethnic minorities, the great majority of them black, whilst the proportion of ethnic minorities in the population generally is around 5.5 per cent, with blacks constituting 1.6 per cent. The explanation for this disparity is, as yet, unclear. It might be claimed that blacks simply commit more crime, or a higher proportion of serious crimes, than whites. Taken together with the accounts of discriminatory treatment from those who have encountered it, however, this is unlikely to be an adequate explanation for differential treatment. The phenomenon of indirect discrimination is even harder to identify and evaluate than direct discrimination. Indirect racial discrimination, for example, arises where persons from racial minority groups are treated less favourably, not simply because they are part of that group, but because they belong to a particular sector of society, or to a particular group of suspects/defendants, where those from ethnic minorities are over-represented. For example, if defendants who are unemployed are over-represented amongst defendants as a whole, and a higher proportion of blacks are unemployed than whites, there will be over-representation of blacks within defendants as a group. Also, there is now substantial evidence that a higher proportion of black defendants than white defendants choose to plead not guilty to charges brought against them, and prefer to contest the case in the Crown Court rather than opt for summary trial (Hood, 1992; Walker, 1989). The reasons for these choices are as yet unclear, but the effect is that, if ultimately convicted, a higher proportion of black defendants will lose the sentence discount which is normally associated with a guilty plea, and will attract the higher sentence levels associated with the Crown Court. In addition, since pre-sentence reports are not normally prepared in respect of defendants who intend to contest their case, the court may choose to pass sentence on a convicted defendant immediately after the trial, without waiting to hear material in the offender's favour which such a report may provide. Some black defendants may opt for jury trial in the hope of securing a racially balanced jury, and this raises further questions of whether juries should be routinely vetted, in order to achieve such a balance. For further discussion, see Chapter 6, and Smith, 1997a.

The following extract explores further the issue of racism in criminal justice. The author is concerned to examine what distinguishes 'racial' from 'non-racial' criminal incidents, where much turns on the motivation with which decisions are made. The fact that a burglary victim is black clearly does not, in itself, make the burglary a racial crime. If, however, the victim has been targeted because of his or her race, then the offender's motivation does require the offence to be quantified as racial. Information about motivation, however, can rarely be derived from official crime statistics. If poorer housing estates are prone to substantially higher rates of burglary, and if a higher than average proportion of the residents on such estates are black, does that make such offending racist?

Extract 1.5.11

M FitzGerald, 'Racism: Establishing the Phenomenon' in D Cook and B Hudson (eds), *Racism and Criminology* (1993) Ch 3, pp 45–61 (footnotes omitted)

This chapter takes as given that 'racism' exists in British society. That is, certain groups suffer prejudice, discrimination and disadvantage on the basis of characteristics ascribed to them because of what others perceive as the racial group to which they belong (irrespective of whether they share that perception). The central concern of the chapter, however, is to explore some of the problems of establishing the phenomenon of racism in the field of criminology, both in terms of the concepts and the methods which tend currently to be used. It begins by looking critically at the convention of striving clearly to demarcate what is 'racial' from what is not; and it goes on to question the convention which strongly favours quantitative over qualitative research methods in this field.

Approaches which strive to distinguish the 'racial' from the non-racial have clear parallels in other social policy fields, both at the conceptual level and in terms of policy and practice. They have probably had their highest profile in policy areas associated with local authorities. They have created problems which are common to all fields but which manifest themselves differently in each.

. . . This chapter looks at three examples of issues where the question 'Is it racial or isn't it?' has been posed variously to practitioners, policy makers and researchers . . . The chapter explores the approaches which have been taken in each of the three examples and the confusion which has often resulted. From this, it goes on to draw some broad lessons about the reasons for this and to suggest ways in which prevailing approaches – both conceptual and methodological – may need to be adapted.

The first example, which links the local authority experience with more obviously criminological concerns, is the case of racial harassment in local authority housing. This draws largely on material from a research project for the Department of the Environment (DoE) which I worked on between 1986 and 1988. The second – the question of apparent ethnic differences in rates of general victimisation – draws on material from the 1988 British Crime Survey. And the third is the analysis of crime statistics by ethnic origin. The subsequent discussion aims to draw out the main issues raised by these three examples both at the conceptual level and in terms of methodology.

Racial harassment

At the time of the DoE research, key features of the prevailing orthodoxy on which local authorities based their racial harassment policies were: racial harassment was a discrete phenomenon which could clearly be identified as such; its perpetrators were assumed to be white; and its victims were non-white ethnic minorities. Any ambiguity about whether an incident was racial or not was conventionally resolved by adopting a 'victim-centred' approach. That is, it was to be treated as racial harassment if that was how the victim saw it.

93

A preliminary trawl of relevant local authority documents had begun to suggest that policy makers were not infrequently faced with requests from practitioners for further clarification of the definition of 'racial harassment'. And subsequent in-depth studies of individual authorities shed light on the reasons for this. The orthodox view was valid at the level of broad generalisation. Certainly the great majority of victims were non-white and those responsible (where they were identified) tended mainly to be white. However, it did not fully reflect the day-to-day experience of those responsible for carrying out the policy; nor did it provide them with sufficient guidance to deal with a significant number of cases which the orthodox view appeared not to encompass.

The general conceptual problems of this approach have been rehearsed elsewhere . . . Two are of particular relevance here. The first is that the study showed that racial harassment was *not* always discrete: on occasion it was an additional, exacerbating element to an issue which was not necessarily racial in its origins. At its most complex, it might arise in circumstances where the aggrieved party retaliated in a form which constituted racial harassment thereby (according to the policy) becoming the offender.

Secondly, despite the emphasis on the victim-centred approach, there was, at best, confusion when the ethnicity of the parties involved did not conform to the orthodox view. There were cases of white victims who were Jewish or who were being harassed because they had non-white partners or mixed race children. But such cases were recognised, if at all, only belatedly and with reluctance, lest they open up the possibility of whites more generally claiming racial victimisation. Certainly, there was enormous sensitivity where the perpetrators were themselves of minority ethnic origin. One housing officer I interviewed was in despair at her inability to help an Asian family. Although they were under siege in their flat, their tormentors were not white and she was told they were not, therefore, eligible for priority transfer on grounds of racial harassment.

The scope for refining policy to deal more effectively with the problem was further limited by the available data. There were several ways in which monitoring returns could be seriously misleading as a basis for reviewing policy. Already the picture they provided was distorted inasmuch as the categories they used and the variables they covered were limited by the prevailing orthodoxy. But they also posed difficulties in identifying the areas within the authority where the problem was most acute. In part this was because the areas where housing staff were least aware of and concerned about the problem were likely to produce low returns, reflecting both a lack of confidence among victims in reporting and a lack of official diligence in recording. In part also, it betrayed extreme crudeness in interpreting the figures: the areas with the highest numbers of incidents were often *de facto* assumed to be those where the problem was greatest, irrespective of whether the ethnic minority population of the area was 5 per cent or 50 per cent.

Victim surveys

In 1988 the British Crime Survey (BCS) for the first time included an over-sample of respondents of Afro-Caribbean and Indian subcontinent origin and found that these minorities were very significantly more likely than whites to

94

be victims of crime . . . It, therefore, appeared unsurprising that both groups perceived an element of racial motivation, particularly in the case of vandalism, assaults and threats.

However, by applying multivariate analyses to the figures for victimisation rates, the differences in victimisation between whites and Afro-Caribbeans became statistically insignificant; and, for Asians, only a small residue remained unexplained. That is, the greater victimisation of ethnic minorities appeared primarily – if not entirely – to be attributable to non-racial factors, such as area, age, tenure, employment and marital status.

This, of course, raised the further and somewhat sensitive question of why – if statistically it could be proved that race was not a factor – ethnic minority victims so often believed that it was. But the BCS also asked the *reasons* why some ethnic minority victims perceived racial motivation. Of these, the most common was that the incident had, in fact, been accompanied by racial abuse. The BCS authors concluded that Afro-Caribbeans in particular would not necessarily be 'less at risk of crime than similarly-placed whites if racially motivated offences were not counted' but acknowledged that 'it may be that in some incidents a racial element is an unfortunate, additional causal factor' . . .

However, police and local government officers whom I had found most resistant to the notion of racial harassment typically rejected the possibility that incidents which could have happened to 'similarly-placed whites' might also be racially motivated. The more unsympathetic (and less guarded) had told me squarely that ethnic minorities 'had a chip on their shoulders' and 'thought everything that happened to them was because they were black'. As already noted, they were reinforced in these attitudes by recording guidelines which were themselves based on assumptions that incidents could be divided into those which were racial and those which were not. The wider implications (including the relevance of alternative approaches) are drawn out in the discussion which follows. But it is also worth considering some further, methodological issues highlighted by the BCS data set and its analysis which are relevant to that discussion.

Mayhew et al (1989) presented the results for three main groups – whites, Afro-Caribbeans and Asians – because for most purposes the sample sizes of more disaggregated minority groups were too small to allow meaningful statistical analysis. Nevertheless, further analysis did succeed in identifying some statistically significant differences between sub-groups of Asians. This group is very heterogeneous. At one extreme, it comprises Indians who in socioeconomic terms, are not dissimilar to whites; and, at the other, it includes Pakistanis and Bangladeshis who occupy a still more disadvantaged position than Afro-Caribbeans. We found some evidence . . . that it was the Indians who suffered higher rates of crime; but the Pakistanis and Bangladeshis were more likely to say that crime against them was racially motivated. This suggests, although it does nothing to explain, a pattern which is distinctive from that for whites, but one in which the most important distinction is that between ethnic minorities themselves.

There was, however, no scope for testing two further hypotheses. The survey did not ask whites whether they thought their own victimisation was racially motivated. So the results did not cover harassment of whites who were victimised because of their own ethnicity or that of people they associated with.

Non-whites' perceptions of racial motivation, therefore, were presented in absolute rather than in relative terms. Further, a national sample survey of this type precludes refined comparisons between areas. Yet other studies suggest that local variations may have specific implications for ethnic minorities and, in particular, that those living in areas with sizeable populations of the same ethnic origin may have very different experiences – and, indeed, attitudes – from those who are more isolated.

Crime statistics

The only national crime statistics that have an ethnic breakdown are those that (in their present form) have been collected on the prison population since 1985. Tables based on these are published in the annual prison statistics; but the only official commentary appeared in 1986 in a Home Office Statistical Bulletin. Since 1977, however, the Metropolitan Police has been collecting information on the ethnic origin of those it arrests and prosecutes. These figures have been used in the work of Home Office and academic researchers ... and have also been the subject of several Home Office Statistical Bulletins ... But they were publicised most controversially in 1982 as the result of a press release from New Scotland Yard which highlighted the rise in reported offences of robbery and other violent theft between 1980 and 1981 and provided figures (based on victims' perception) apparently showing a dramatic over-involvement of Afro-Caribbeans in this type of crime.

The prison statistics and the Metropolitan Police data use slightly different forms of ethnic classification and neither is directly comparable with figures for the population at large, since the two main sources of this information up to the present ... also employ different ethnic categories ...

Notwithstanding these mismatches, the broad picture which emerges is very similar: Afro-Caribbeans are very significantly over-represented both in the Metropolitan Police figures and in the prison statistics relative to their presence in the population at large. Further, in the prison statistics, the over-representation is still greater for Afro-Caribbean women. The proportion of Asians in both data sets, however, appears to be broadly in line with their presence in the general population.

While some (including sections of the popular press) have readily taken the figures as proof of Afro-Caribbean 'criminality', others have taken them to indicate discrimination in the criminal justice system; and, indeed, have referred to 'double discrimination' against Afro-Caribbean women ... Most serious commentators have looked at possible 'structural' explanations for these differences; that is (like the British Crime Survey reports) they have focused on demographic and socioeconomic factors which, when adequately taken into account, might suggest that the differences are *not* racial after all; or that their racial component is much lower than it at first appears. And several have speculated about a combination of such 'explanations' and the likely balance within it ...

The data pose important and disturbing questions: most obviously why such a high proportion of Britain's Afro-Caribbean population is currently resident in its penal institutions; but they hardly begin to provide the answers. This is due to problems of interpreting the data which are partly conceptual and partly methodological ...

96

Discussion

Taken together, the problems highlighted by the three examples presented raise two broad sets of issues which are relevant to understanding questions of race and crime more widely. That is, their implications are both conceptual and methodological.

At the conceptual level, the examples appear to challenge a number of prevalent notions in political and academic discourse about what is racial. On the one hand, they show that the more other relevant factors are taken into account, the more one can whittle apparently racial differences into insignificance. On the other, they suggest that real world perceptions (and, indeed, experiences) of what is racial do not always fit comfortably into standardised boxes which are convenient for policy makers, practitioners and researchers.

This is not to suggest that attempts to establish the phenomenon should be abandoned. Rather, it is to argue strongly for a revision of the notion that there is a clear distinction between what is racial and what is not. The examples suggest that we need to expand our notion of what is racial, while recognising more explicitly that phenomena which are communal are not *de facto* exclusive. That is, what is racial, however generously defined, must be seen in a broader context.

. . . If we are serious about capturing the phenomenon, understanding how it occurs and developing and evaluating appropriate interventions, we must start by looking sceptically at the privileged status currently given to quantitative research. For once we try to reduce the issue to a set of discrete, measurable components we have already lost its essence. What is racial (in the broad sense used here) is not only multifaceted, it arises and manifests itself differently in different places at different times for different groups (and, indeed, subgroups of these groups). It is not a 'thing' of itself but is produced variously by a wide range of interactions between combinations of factors from within a very large set. The full range of factors will never come into play together; and what produces a racial result for one group in one situation at one time may comprise none of the elements which produce a racial result for another group in a different situation at another time or in a different place. In short, what is racial is much more than the sum of its component parts: it is the product of their various and complex interactions. This does not, of course, preclude trying to identify those component parts and to understand their interactions. Again, however, quantitative methods are of limited value. Neither task is initially suspectible to this type of approach, although at a second stage quantitative techniques can (in principle) play an essential verificatory role.

The pitfalls of starting from a quantitative approach are illustrated by the examples presented which show how, in various ways, we are missing the point by falling back on *a priori* assumptions to frame our analytical categories. Much of the information we have to draw on has, by default, been generated on the basis of received wisdom (not to mention political orthodoxy); for there has been little or no rigorous work to check whether these assumptions are relevant or sufficient for identifying, measuring and explaining inter-ethnic differences.

Apart from differential treatment of ethnic minorities and women there are many other, perhaps less obvious, issues of fairness and discrimination which afflict the criminal justice system. One is the question of variation of decision-making across different parts of the country, whether as a result of different police forces pursuing different policies on cautioning (see Chapter 2), lay magistrates having different local working practices on mode of trial decisions (Chapter 4) or local benches adopting different bench sentencing norms to cater for local conditions and local problems (Chapter 5). It is too easy simply to dismiss these differences as examples of unwarranted 'disparity' and to argue for clearer rules and tighter control over the discretion of decision-makers in these contexts. Is uniformity the ideal, or can arguments be made for variations according to local conditions and local traditions? Magistrates are selected, in part, to reflect community concerns and to deliver local justice, but is 'justice by geography' simply unjust? See further Turner (1992). Consider also the following examples of even-handedness which arise in the sentencing context. Sentencers have a broad discretion to take into account the individual circumstances of offenders when passing sentence (Criminal Justice Act 1991, s 28). Is it a sufficient argument against sending a person to prison for an offence which would otherwise clearly deserve that penalty that they are suffering from a serious illness (see *Bernard* [1997] 1 Cr App R (S) 135), pregnant (*Beaumont* (1987) 9 Cr App R (S) 342), that their family will suffer considerably as a result of incarceration (*Grant* (1990) 12 Cr App R (S) 441), that imprisonment will mean closing down the offender's business, with 23 people losing their livelihood (*Olliver* (1989) 11 Cr App R (S) 10), or that the offender on an earlier unrelated occasion tackled and arrested an armed robber (*Alexander* [1997] 2 Cr App R (S) 74)? For discussion of these and other cases, see Ashworth (1995), Ch 5.

(e) Victims

In recent years there has been a resurgence of interest in victims in the context of the criminal justice system and as a focus of criminal justice policy. In practical terms, it is widely acknowledged that crime victims have in the past been shabbily treated by the system, a form of additional insult sometimes referred to in the literature as 'secondary victimisation' by the system iself (see Shapland et al, 1985; Maguire and Corbett, 1987; Morgan and Zedner, 1992). While research has shown that many victims find their initial contact with the police to be helpful and reassuring, their level of satisfaction with the system tends to decline steadily as time (and the case) wears on (Shapland et al, 1985, pp 83–89; Newburn and Merry, 1990). Provision of information to victims is an obvious, but all too often overlooked, requirement. Victims may require advice on insurance, compensation or crime preventive measures. They may require emotional support or counselling, a task undertaken by Victim Support, an agency with small origins as a voluntary organisation but now a substantial enterprise which attracted Home Office funding in excess of £11 million in 1996–97 (see Rock, 1990). The

Royal Commission (Royal Commission on Criminal Justice, 1993) stressed the importance of treating *all* those involved in the criminal justice system, including victims of crime, 'fairly, reasonably and without discrimination'. One of the problems is that since the victim of a crime is not a party to the prosecution, criminal proceedings are brought by the state against the accused and the victim may not be strictly necessary to the proceedings unless required as a witness. While the victim will almost inevitably view the proceedings as 'their' case, the criminal justice system does not see it that way.

Extract 1.5.12

**J Shapland, 'The Criminal Justice System and the Victim' (1985)
10 *Victimology* 585, at pp 586–589 (footnotes omitted)**

The victim in the criminal justice system and criminal procedure

The victim's first contact with the criminal justice system is with the police. Very often the police remain the closest agency to the victim throughout the investigation and prosecution of the offense. Given the number of cases in which offenders are not caught, and the high rate of guilty pleas where they are caught, it is the police, rather than the courts, who will, in practice, structure most victims' experiences with the criminal justice system and delineate their role.

Victims are themselves vital to the police, as they play a major role in the reporting and investigation of cases and in the detection of offenders. In Britain, they have been shown to play a substantial role in the reporting of cases of violence, sexual assault and burglary . . . Very few cases are discovered by the police themselves . . . Information from the victim or civilian witnesses as to the identity of the offender is also the major factor in the detection of offenders in both property offenses and offenses of violence. For example, over 60 per cent of offenses of violence in one study were detected as a result of definite information supplied by the victim . . . The importance of the victim in these reports does not, of course, deny a role for the police. Without a quick response by the police where victims have themselves apprehended the offender, or fast action where a name and address have been supplied, offenders would not be caught. The police may not be the major detection agency, but they are still responsible for gathering evidence such that the offender, once caught, can be prosecuted.

The crucial role of victim co-operation in providing the input to the criminal justice system and in investigation and detection is not, however, always acknowledged by the police themselves. Although police officers recognize, at least in theory, the needs of victims for emotional support and help, they do not accord primacy to these needs nor give the victim status as an agent within the criminal justice system. Rather, police officers seem more concerned with fulfilling police organizational needs (including taking statements, filling out forms and the processing of offenders) than with victims . . . This is hardly surprising, given that individual officers are rewarded by the police service for meeting organizational needs, not victim needs. The result, in practice, is something of a paradox: the criminal justice system depends heavily upon victims for the reporting and detection of offenses and for the provision of evidence in court. Yet, it does not appear to value the victim. The victim is a non-person in the eyes of professional participants within the system. This can be seen in the problems faced by victims in reporting and investigation obtained from the results of studies of victims of physical violence, sexual assault and property offenses (particularly burglary and theft of motor vehicles) . . . These seem common to victims of different offenses and different countries and include:

1. A need for a positive and helpful attitude by police officers, particularly in their initial contacts with victims. The manner of the police, and whether they appear to take the case seriously are the most important determinants of victim satisfaction. Victims were very displeased if the police officer did not listen carefully or appear to take some action (such as looking for the suspect or dusting for fingerprints) or if he was dismissive or treated the case as routine. This emphasis upon process and attitudes recurred throughout the progress of the case through the criminal justice system.

2. In contrast, victims were not so concerned about the outcome of the case (whether the offender was caught or what the sentence was), provided that they felt that the proper procedures had been followed. They were, however, considerably upset by lack of information as to the progress of the case. Victims wanted to know whether the offender was caught, what the charges were, whether the offender was given pre-trial detention (a matter where, interestingly, the facts were less frightening than fear of the unknown), when court appearances would be, whether the victim would have to give evidence, whether the offender was convicted and what the sentence was. Even in jurisdictions with a public prosecutor, victims tended to expect the police to provide this information. There was a significant decrease in satisfaction if victims were not given sufficient information.

3. Victims did not necessarily want decision-making powers, but they did wish for consultation on particular decisions, such as whether to prosecute (as opposed to using some form of diversionary power, such as cautioning); whether charges should be changed or dropped; whether court appearances should be re-scheduled; and whether information about victims should be given to the press. There are few studies of the possible effects of such a process, but an experiment in Miami in which victims participated in plea negotiation seminars with judge, counsel and defendant indicated that victims who attended were not vengeful and had a beneficial rather than disruptive influence . . .

4. Victims wished for emotional support and reassurance from the police and for some consideration of their emotional reaction and practical difficulties when undergoing police procedures (for example, attending the police station, taking part in identification parades or undergoing medical examinations). This was not seen as a high priority by police officers. Officers tended to underestimate the degree of shock and other reactions suffered by victims of property offenses and to have incorrect beliefs about the reactions often suffered by sexual assault victims. Victims were also pleased to be referred to victim

support schemes (of most types). Police officers, though having an inadequate appreciation of the range of victims needing this type of help, also found these schemes valuable. The police are the only agency capable of informing victims about compensation, but this again was often not done.

Victims' reactions to the courts, in the common-law jurisdictions in which the research has been done, paralleled those to the police. Appearance in court for the small minority who gave evidence was regarded as a duty and a natural part of being a victim. The defence were, within limits, expected to give a different point of view on the facts of the offense to that of the victim. The actual experience in the witness box, contrary to some legal analyses, did not seem to cause great distress (though 'irrelevant' questioning in sexual assault cases was very upsetting). Any apparent lack of interest by the prosecutor (who may not even meet victims before the case) was much more seriously regarded. The major problem areas were peripheral to the court hearing itself: lack of facilities at court, cramped surroundings, sitting next to the defendant or his relations with consequent feelings of intimidation (actual intimidation in some instances), lack of notice of appearances, inadequate recompense for costs, and, above all, not being able to find out where or when the appearance was and what the victim would have to do. These are, equally, problems of status and of the attitudes of court personnel to victims.

. . . Addressing the problems of the victim in the criminal justice system and criminal procedures is not a matter of making fundamental structural changes to the system at the moment. It is a matter of changing attitudes, so that the victim is given a status by the system which matches his practical importance and which delineates him as a more equal partner. Changes in the written criminal procedure will then follow, as they have done in the case of the offender's rights. However, changing attitudes, particularly those in a complex bureaucratic system, is a hard task. It involves the implementation of some practical steps (discussed later), inputs to training of personnel, and a lead from governments and bodies such as the Council of Europe.

There is, however, a deeper question. Victim satisfaction and victim wishes are conditioned by their expectations and knowledge of the operation of the present system. It is difficult for victims to recommend major changes. We have moved, historically, far along the path towards public prosecution and a professionalized criminal justice system. Private prosecution is seen as vestigial, kept primarily to prevent abuse by prosecutors. There is now some feeling that the criminal justice system has become too isolated and too professional and there is exploration of alternative modes. Some of these, involving mediation or arbitration on a more civil law basis, have been a reaction against the problems of victims in the criminal law, inspired, however, perhaps more by social welfare considerations than by an exhaustive study of victim wants. Others, looking to customary law jurisdictions, have proposed a greater role for lay people (victim, offender and witnesses) within a criminal justice system. This might involve an inquisitional mode with some mediation. When considering questions of victim participation in prosecution, diversion and trials, it is necessary to examine what changes this would make to the existing model of the criminal justice system and the effects this would have.

Since 1985, when this extract was written, there have been a number of significant developments designed to improve the position of the victim in criminal justice which are sometimes collectively referred to as the 'victim movement'. The organisation, Victim Support, has been influential in placing the requirements of victims higher on the political agenda (see, for example Victim Support, 1995). The police are now generally identified as the main agency responsible for the provision of information to victims. A number of developments have flowed from this, including the provision of specialist training of police officers in the interviewing of crime victims, particularly victims of violent or sexual offences. The Home Office has issued a series of Circulars to police and to prosecution authorities indicating best practice for keeping victims in touch with developments. A key point perhaps was the publication of the first *Victim's Charter* in 1990 (which was revised and re-issued by the Home Office in 1996). The Charter sets out expected standards for the police and other criminal justice agencies to achieve in their response to, and interaction with, crime victims.

Extract 1.5.13

Home Office, *The Victim's Charter* (1996)

The Victim's Charter

A statement of service standards for victims of crime

INTRODUCTION

If you have been the victim of a crime, this Charter aims to explain, as clearly as possible, what happens after the offence has been reported to the police and the standards of service you should expect. There is also a section describing what other information is available and a list of addresses that you may find useful.

The way you are treated cannot make up for what you have suffered. But we aim to make sure that the unpleasant effects of the crime are not made worse by what happens later. We aim to treat you fairly and courteously and to provide a good service. However, things sometimes go wrong. If you feel that you have not received the standard of service you should have done, this Charter includes a section telling you how to complain. If you think there is more that could be done to improve the service, you should contact either the agency concerned or the Criminal Policy Directorate, Procedures and Victims Unit, Home Office, 50 Queen Anne's Gate, London SWIH 9AT.

The Victim's Steering Group will monitor the standards of service set out in this Charter. The Group is chaired by the Home Office and includes representatives from all the agencies involved in providing a service to victims. As part of their own monitoring the agencies may consult victims. Some of the results of this monitoring and consultation may be published locally. The Home Office will let you know each year how things are going by a summary in its Annual Report.

If you have received a very good service from any of the agencies you have dealt with you might like to nominate that agency for a Charter Mark award, which recognises excellent public service. Please send or fax your nomination to the Charter Mark Awards, Citizen's Charter Unit, Cabinet Office, Horse Guards Road, London SWIP 3AL. Fax: 0171–270 5968.

YOU CAN EXPECT

A crime you have reported to be investigated and to receive information about what happens

• The police will respond to your report as quickly as they can.

The police look into all crimes reported to them. If you phone them to tell them about a crime they will send an officer to see you if necessary.

• The police will give you the name and phone number of the officer or 'crime desk' responsible for your case.

The police are normally your first point of contact. If you have any questions at any time you can contact this person, who will either answer your question or put you in touch with someone who can.

• The police will give you a leaflet called 'Victims of Crime' as soon as you report the crime in person at a police station. In other cases they will send you one within five working days.

This leaflet explains what will happen during the investigation and if someone is caught.

• The police will do their best to catch the person responsible for your crime and to keep you informed of significant developments in your case.

The police will tell you if someone has been caught, cautioned or charged. You will be asked if you wish to receive further information about the progress of your case. If you do, you will be told about any decision to drop or alter the charges substantially. You will also be told the date of the trial and the final result, even if you are not required as a witness. The arrangements for doing this already exist in some areas. Where they do not, arrangements are being made and should be in place nationally by April 1997.

Victims of serious crime may also receive extra help.

• If a member of your family has been killed as the result of a crime, or you are the parent or carer of a child who has been the victim of a serious crime and who is a witness, the police will give you the relevant information pack to help you.

• In cases of rape, or where a child is the victim of a serious crime, a police officer who has received special training will be available if required.

103

YOU CAN EXPECT

The chance to explain how the crime has affected you, and your interests to be taken into account

- The police will ask you about your fears about further victimisation and details of your loss, damage or injury.
- The police, Crown Prosecutor, magistrates and judges will take this information into account when making their decisions.

We think you should be given the chance, if you wish, to explain more generally how the crime has affected you. Projects to test how this might be done are being put in place. Depending on the outcome of the evaluation the aim is to implement the system nationwide.

- The Crown Prosecution Service, on request, will meet the family of someone killed as a result of a crime, to explain their decision on prosecution.
- The probation service will tell you when someone sentenced to life imprisonment, or when someone who has committed a serious sexual or violent crime, is likely to be released.

Within two months of the sentence a probation officer will get in touch with you to find out whether you want to be told when the prisoner may be released from prison. They will ask you if you have any worries about them being released. Your worries can be taken into account when considering whether conditions need to be attached to the offender's release.

- You can use a phone helpline if you have received unwelcome contact from a prisoner, have any concerns about their temporary release or want to be informed when they are ultimately released.

The helpline number is 0345 585112 and all calls are charged at the local rate. The details of your concerns will be passed to the governor of the prison, who will take whatever action is needed.

YOU CAN EXPECT

If you have to go to court as a witness you will be treated with respect and sensitivity

- You will be offered the support of the Witness Service at the Crown Court.

Staff and trained volunteers from the Witness Service (run by Victim Support) can help you, your family and friends at the court before, during and after the trial.

- You can ask to see a courtroom before the case starts so that you know what to expect.
- You can reserve a seat in court for a relative or friend accompanying you.
- You can ask to wait separately from those involved in the case.

In some courts a lack of space may mean that you cannot reserve seats or wait in a separate area. Court staff will make suitable arrangements wherever possible. In the Crown Court these services are organised by the Witness Service and the Customer Service Officer. In a magistrates' court you should tell the police, who will put you in touch with the court.

- In the Crown Court we aim to make sure witnesses do not have to wait for more than two hours before being called to give evidence.
- However, if delays occur, court staff or a representative of the Crown Prosecution Service will explain why there is a delay and tell you how long the wait is likely to be.
- While you are waiting to give evidence a representative of the Crown Prosecution Service will introduce himself or herself to you (wherever possible) to tell you what to expect.

If you wish, the Crown Prosecution Service representative will normally give you the chance to read your statement again.

You will be paid travel and certain other expenses for the time you are at court to give evidence. The Crown Prosecution Service representative will give you a form so you can claim expenses. He or she will answer any questions you have about filling the form in.

- The Crown Prosecution Service aims to pay expenses where possible within five days but no later than ten working days from receipt of a correctly completed claim form.

Child witnesses

All Crown Court centres have a Child Witness Officer to make sure that everything runs as smoothly as possible. The Witness Service also offers help to child witnesses.

If you are the parent or carer of a child witness you can expect the following:

- the trial will be arranged for the earliest possible date;
- a Child Witness Officer will answer your questions about procedures in the Crown Court;
- a Child Witness Officer will meet you and the child when you arrive at court and take you to a private waiting area;
- the child will be able to give evidence over a live TV link or behind a screen in appropriate cases.

The Crown Prosecution Service can ask the judge for a TV link or screens to be used. If you want your child to use one of these facilities you should discuss this with the police as soon as possible and always well before the court hearing. If the judge agrees to the TV link, the child does not see the defendant or anyone in the courtroom except the judge and lawyers.

- If a TV link is to be used you and the child will see a demonstration of the TV link before the trial.

105

YOU CAN EXPECT

To be offered emotional and practical support

- Victim Support will normally send you a letter, phone you, or arrange a visit from a volunteer within four working days of you reporting the crime.

In most cases – such as burglary, assault, robbery, theft (except from and of cars), arson, harassment or damage to your home – the police will pass your details to Victim Support within two working days of the crime being reported, unless you ask them not to. In cases involving sexual offences, domestic violence and homicide, your details will only be given to Victim Support if you agree. In such cases individual arrangements will be made. You can also contact Victim Support directly.

- The Criminal Injuries Compensation Scheme will aim to give you a decision within 12 months of you making your application.

If you have been injured as a result of a violent crime you may apply for compensation under the Criminal Injuries Compensation Scheme. A leaflet called 'Victims of Crimes of Violence – a guide to the Criminal Injuries Compensation Scheme' explains how to claim compensation. You can get this leaflet from the police or the Criminal Injuries Compensation Authority.

- The court will consider making a compensation order in all cases if you have suffered loss, damage or injury. They will give reasons if they decide not to make an order.

This document is often described as a statement of victims' rights but, as can be seen, the Victim's Charter does not in fact furnish rights in any meaningful sense. It should rather be seen as a statement of good intentions and model practice (see Fenwick, 1995). Nonetheless, criminal justice agencies should now be more sensitive to the requirements of victims, and the Charter contains a number of fairly specific commitments that victims will be informed when a suspect is arrested, charged or cautioned, and when decisions are made about choice of charge. A key decision from the point of the view of the victim is whether the suspect is prosecuted or formally cautioned. Compensation orders can only be made by a court against a convicted defendant (see Chapter 6). So, if a suspect is formally cautioned, rather than prosecuted, the possibility of victim compensation is lost. As a result of inter-agency co-operation between the police, probation and social services and volunteer workers, a number of 'caution-plus' schemes have been developed in different parts of the country. These schemes employ the framework of formal cautioning but combine it with other elements, such as reparation, which can involve the perpetrator meeting with and apologising to the victim, repairing or replacing the victim's property, or compensating the victim financially. Such schemes (which all, of course, require the victim's agreement and willing co-operation) have a number of enthusiastic supporters but, so far, they remain rather marginal to the criminal justice system. The Crime and Disorder Bill 1997 will, when enacted, place such schemes, or at least those involving young offenders, on a statutory footing. Subsequent criminal justice decisions also impact significantly upon victims. Since magistrates' courts make compensation orders in a higher percentage of cases than the Crown Courts (see Chapter 6), it follows that choices over mode of trial decision can affect the victim's chances of obtaining compensation from the courts. Negotiations over charge also affect victims, in the sense that bargaining down the offence to which the defendant ultimately pleads guilty may save court time and costs, but may leave the victim with a feeling that their version of what happened has been disbelieved, and that their interests have been disregarded (see Chapter 4).

In other jurisdictions, especially the United States, there has been considerable lobbying on behalf of victims, which has prompted a range of initiatives going well beyond developments so far in England and Wales. US laws require state agencies to involve victims at virtually every stage of the criminal justice process and, in particular, they involve the routine presentation to the court of a 'victim impact statement' designed to ensure that the judge is fully aware of the effect which the crime has had upon the victim and his or her family. In some states victims are given the right to present such evidence in person, and to argue for what they regard as an appropriate sentence for the offender. The extent to which victims should be more intimately involved in criminal justice decisions about 'their' case is a matter of controversy. As we shall see next, Miers is generally sceptical of the value of these developments.

<hr>

Extract 1.5.14

D Miers, 'The Responsibilities and Rights of Victims of Crime' (1992) 55 MLR 482, at pp 499–501 (footnotes omitted)

Victim participation in criminal justice decisions

The *Victim's Charter*, despite the publicity surrounding its launch in 1990, was something of a disappointment. Much of it comprised a resumé of existing practices, some enshrined in Home Office circulars, together with brief descriptions of the scope of the CICB and of compensation orders, and of the work of *Victim Support*. In line with the recommendations of the Council of Europe, a number of propositions concerning good practice with regard to victims were included as a set of 'Standards for the Criminal Justice Services.' These address, among others, the police, the CPS and the courts, and concern such matters as giving information to victims, recording their losses and injuries for the purpose of compensation orders, providing facilities in court buildings for victims and their families, and being solicitous for victims who have to give evidence. Unlike New Zealand's Victims of Offences Act 1987, the *Victim's Charter* has no legal standing and, despite efforts in some courts to ease the experience of giving evidence, the criticisms of secondary victimisation are, it seems, still founded. Were the standards set by the *Victim's Charter* to be realised, they continue to cast the victim in a subservient role, as the recipient of services. Following the United States example, some favour a more active role for victims in pre- and post-trial decisions.

Pre-trial decisions

Choice of prosecution, plea-bargaining and bail decisions are the main areas in which it has been suggested that victims should be able to participate at the pre-trial stage. They all readily illustrate some of the main difficulties that attend such participation. Consider, firstly, plea-bargaining. The argument usually advanced here is that victims are often unpleasantly surprised to discover that what they perceived, or may have at an earlier stage of the case been informed was a serious offence, has been plea-bargained to a lesser offence. What is said to jar is that, without any consultation, their offence has, for reasons frequently dissociated from their interests, been downgraded and, in consequence, the public classification of their injuries devalued. What can be done to ameliorate this? A first response, that the offence charged and tried must be that for which the facts as known can *prima facie* bear (that is, as would satisfy examining magistrates), is surely so impracticable as not to merit further consideration. There is also an insurmountable legal objection, which is that there is no duty in law to enforce or prosecute any specific crime, even though the facts are known to the relevant authorities.

A second response, that the police or the prosecuting authorities should routinely consider the victim's preferences, is to some extent already met. Both the new cautioning guidelines and the DPP's *Code for Crown Prosecutors* include them within the list of public interest criteria, but guidance on what weight should be given to them is necessarily indeterminate. The cautioning guidelines say that the victim's views 'should not be overriding, but should be an important factor in the decision,' and Mott found that some prosecutions may be taken simply because the victim insisted, but what further prescription may be contemplated? The criteria could be amended to require consideration of the victim's preferences at every point at which the issue of what proceedings are to be taken is addressed, but that immediately raises a number of questions: how are victims' preferences routinely to be known and, since preferences can only be made on the basis of information, how much of the case investigation will be divulged to victims? Assuming their preferences are available, what weight is to be given to them and how, if at all, may victims be able to ascertain whether they were in fact considered? A further consideration is the role of the trial judge when faced with a guilty plea to a lesser charge. Currently, the judge must be satisfied that the arrangement is proper, which includes its being not offensive to the public interest; does routine consideration of the victim's preferences in the choice of indictment include asking the CPS whether it has consulted the victim (when, under present practices, it may not consult the police in all cases)? Though cumbersome, some control of this kind would need to be instituted if victims are to be sure that their interests have indeed been taken into account.

Coupled with the question of *what* information is to be given to the victim, is the question, *when* is it to be given? If new facts transpire following the initial charge which suggest alternative or additional charges, should the victim be informed, and kept informed, until the case actually comes to trial? And what of the offender's preferences? That the CPS refuse a guilty plea, thereby coinciding with the victim's preferences, is no ground on which the offender may argue that the charge is bad; but suppose the victim is quite happy with the plea to the lesser offence, because he or she doesn't wish to undergo the ordeal of giving evidence, or is afraid of having his or her own background challenged by the offender: what weight should the CPS give to the victim's desire for a quiet life where that happens to coincide with the offender's? Where, for example, a sexual offence is to be tried, the possibility of sparing the victim a distressing experience giving evidence is a good ground for the CPS agreeing a guilty plea to a lesser offence, but this cannot be in the public interest where the victim has something to hide that is relevant to the question of the offender's guilt. Ashworth concludes that there is a sound case for systematic and routine communication of information to victims about the progress of their case, and about the opportunities for compensation or the availability of other victim services; beyond this function, he sees the victim as having no active role in the decision to prosecute, or the determination of the charge finally to be tried. His conclusions are persuasive; it is no doubt in the public interest that the victim's preferences be acknowledged, and it may be that investigating officers can routinely ask for them, but these preferences are not to be equated with the public interest. Indeed, this point is emphasised by the *Victim's Charter*. The difficulty lies in obtaining preferences that are informed, while at the same time complying with the due process requirements for dealing with offenders. Besides these evaluative questions, there is also a substantial bureaucratic consideration, namely, communicating with and collecting a victim's preferences in time for decisions to be made within a processual framework. For an already overworked public sector service, the addition of this further layer of administrative activity will prove costly.

Probably the most controversial aspect of all this is the extent to which the views of the victim should be made known to, and taken into account by, the sentencer. In England, the courts have so far marked out a fairly clear distinction between receiving evidence at the sentencing stage which explains to the court the particular impact which the crime has had upon the victim, and hearing representations from the victim as to the proper sentence to pass. The Magistrates' Association's *Sentencing Guidelines* (Magistrates' Association, 1997) now require magistrates in every case to weigh the 'impact on the victim' when gauging offence seriousness. The leading Court of Appeal decision is *Nunn* [1996] 2 Cr App R (S) 136, where the court observed that it was '. . . an elementary principle that the damaging and distressing effects of a crime on the victim represent an important factor in the sentencing decision', but also said that it was inappropriate to listen directly to the subjective views of the individual who had suffered most as a result of the crime. Judge L J said that 'the opinions of the victim . . . about the appropriate level of sentence do not provide any sound basis for . . . sentence'. In a Scottish case it was held that it was invidious for a sentencer to seek the views of the victim as to the proper sentence, since that would 'expose the complainer to a risk of public pressure by passing comment on matters that lie outside her experience'. Perhaps the key problem in allowing victims to influence sentence, however, is that this would result in offenders who had committed otherwise identical crimes being sentenced quite differently depending upon whether the victim was willing and able to plead 'their' case and, if so, upon the force of their advocacy. While some victims may want the right to address the court many surely do not, and would not the expectation that they should do so create intolerable additional pressures upon them? The issue has arisen in acute form in several capital murder cases in the United States. For further discussion of the role of victims at the sentencing stage see Hall (1991), Ashworth (1993b) and Joutsen (1994)).

2

ENTRY TO THE CRIMINAL
JUSTICE SYSTEM

Entry to the criminal justice system is mainly controlled by the police. They are often described as 'gatekeepers' of the system because it is their decisions which determine whether individuals will be passed on to the other decision-makers in the process. But the role of the police is much wider than that of channelling suspects for prosecution, trial and sentencing. They also under-take responsibilities for maintaining order and for providing an emergency response service. All these aims are pursued by individual police officers as members of large, bureaucratic organisations and in working conditions which are often hostile, unsocial and tedious. The result is that policing decisions may be influenced by a host of considerations which are not directly related to criminal justice processing. Yet subsequent decision-makers in the process have to base their own choices on the people whom the police send to them. Whether the police manage to identify the suspects most suitable for process-ing is the question which we will explore in this chapter. After examining the aims and functions of policing, we will discuss the various criteria which are used for particular decisions. The outcome of those decisions is reflected in official statistics about crime and they provide an opportunity to reflect on how representative is the police sample of suspected offenders. Finally, work of the police will be assessed in terms of its effectiveness, its fairness and its legitimacy.

1. THE AIMS AND FUNCTIONS OF POLICING

A remarkable characteristic of the police is the variety of tasks that they perform. Yet there is no definitive statement of their duties. One of the more authoritative, constitutional pronouncements was that offered by the Royal Commission of 1962. It included the following objectives, all of which remain relevant today:

(1) The maintenance of law and order and the protection of persons and property.
(2) The prevention of crime.

111

(3) The detection of criminals.

(4) Controlling road traffic and advising local authorities about traffic questions.

(5) Carrying out certain duties on behalf of government departments.

(6) The befriending of anyone who needs help and being available at any time to cope with minor or major emergencies.

(Royal Commission on the Police (1962) para 59.)

Yet, in considering this range of police activities, it is difficult to discern a function that is exclusive to the police and differentiates them from other individuals or organisations. For example, in respect of apprehending offenders, members of the public play a significant role in identifying suspects if not actually catching them. In preventing crime, individuals usually take their own precautions to guard themselves and their possessions against offenders, and both central and local government play leading parts in crime prevention initiatives. More generally, most citizens and organisations contribute to maintaining the peace by attempting to diffuse disagreement and protest in order to avoid the outbreak of violence. This coincidence of functions, between the police and citizens, has often been emphasised but, while it has helped to provide a basis for the legitimacy of professional policing, its significance has been exaggerated. As the Philips Commission explained:

Extract 2.1.1

Royal Commission on Criminal Procedure, *The Investigation and Prosecution of Criminal Offences in England and Wales: The Law and Procedure* (1981) paras 3–4 (footnote omitted)

3. In England and Wales the individual police officer holds the office of constable under the Crown. He is thus independent in that his legal status is not, strictly speaking, that of an employee. But he is subject to a code of discipline laid down in Regulations approved by Parliament and is supervised by his superior officers. Above all, he is subject to the law for the way he carries out his duties. The traditional view of policing arrangements stresses this independence and the integration of the police with the community they serve. The essence of it is to be found in the report of the Royal Commission on Police Powers and Procedure of 1929 (and approved by the Royal Commission of 1962):

'The police of this country have never been recognised, either in law or by tradition, as a force distinct from the general body of citizens. Despite the imposition of many extraneous duties on the police by legislation or administrative action, the principle remains that a policeman, in the view of the common law, is only "a person paid to perform, as a matter of duty, acts which if he were so minded he might have done voluntarily".

Indeed a policeman possesses few powers not enjoyed by the ordinary citizen, and public opinion, expressed in Parliament and elsewhere, has shown great jealousy of any attempts to give increased authority to the police.'

4. This is too simple a view of the position now. The police officer is, as already noted, subject to a statutory scheme of control by his senior officers in addition to the general criminal and civil law. He does have greater legal powers than the ordinary citizen, as will become clear from the later parts of this volume, and he is a member of a large, disciplined and technologically advanced service, with all the resources and authority that brings.

(a) Maintaining social stability

Paragraph 4 of the above extract is a recognition of what those espousing the traditional position did not appreciate, that the police are public officials. Furthermore, it underscores what the common law has always recognised, that policing involves a public remit to maintain social stability in the broadest sense. Indeed, the current functions of the police are the accumulation of the tasks which they have accepted or grasped in the course of their history. Technically, policing powers are attached to the office of constable (see, for example, the drafting of the Police and Criminal Evidence Act 1984, continuing the tradition of all police powers legislation) and it was the development of that office which established, in a pragmatic way, what were the acceptable uses of official coercion. The Justice of the Peace Act 1361 had provided for the appointment of justices to maintain the King's Peace and constables were appointed as their agents (see Critchley, 1978, p 9). The constable's duty was to maintain order in the widest sense. Although the courts required that legal powers should be invoked to justify action which interfered with citizen's rights, the law did not set limits on the general role of policing. That continues to be reflected in contemporary law, where the rare statements about policing objectives are contained in rather vague dicta. For example, in *Rice v Connelly* [1966] 2 QB 414, at p 419, Lord Parker C J said that:

> It is also . . . clear that it is part of the obligations and duties of a police constable to take all steps which appear to him necessary for keeping the peace, for preventing crime or for protecting property from criminal injury. There is no exhaustive definition of the powers and obligations of the police, but they are at least those, and they would further include the duty to detect crime and to bring an offender to justice.

Historically and legally, then, the general function of the police is to maintain social stability and this provides the context for all their decisions. It is important to appreciate, therefore, that their work entails much more than processing suspects in the criminal justice system. Where criminal activity poses problems for individual victims or for public disorder, it will be normal to pursue and seek the prosecution of the most serious offenders if possible. But the main objective of policing will be to restore stability and calm. It may be that the use of informal methods, such as a warning or the negotiation of a truce in a dispute, will be equally effective solutions. Similarly, when accidents and misfortunes disrupt the normal functioning of society, the police

113

take responsibility for organising arrangements to deal with them, and it may be only fortuitous that criminal activity thereby comes to light. In fulfilling these functions, of controlling crime and providing general support for the public, the police have the advantage of possessing the authority to invoke force if the parties refuse to comply. Furthermore, in the immediate situation, the technical legality of that authority will often be less important than the symbolism of the police officer's uniform. Indeed, if there is one feature which does distinguish the police, it is their capacity to use coercion. As Egon Bittner observed, the police are specialists in the use of legitimate force. Such force is used to secure compliance with their solutions to the problems they encounter. Again, it is important to understand that this will not always involve popular notions of crime-fighting.

> [T]he police role is far better understood by saying that their ability to arrest offenders is incidental to their authority to use force. Many puzzling aspects of police work fall into place when one ceases to look at it as principally concerned with law enforcement and crime control, and only incidentally and often incongruously concerned with an infinite variety of other matters. It makes much more sense to say that the police are nothing else than a mechanism for the distribution of situationally justified force in society. (Bittner, 1970, p 123)

Most people will regard crime control as the central aim of policing. But, while the processing of individuals in the criminal justice system is one way of achieving that objective, in the context of maintaining social stability, it is not the only one for the police. Rather, as Bittner has observed, in US research which has widely influenced British work:

Extract 2.1.2

E Bittner, 'The Police on Skid Row: A Study in Peacekeeping' (1967) 32 *American Sociological Review* 699, at pp 700, 701, 714 (footnotes omitted)

... [T]here appear to exist two relatively independent domains of police activity. In one, their methods are constrained by the prospect of the future disposition of a case in the courts; in the other, they operate under some other consideration and largely with no structured and continuous outside constraint. Following the terminology suggested by Michael Banton, they may be said to function in the first instance as 'law officers' and in the second instance as 'peace officers.' It must be emphasized that the designation 'peace officer' is a residual term, with only some vaguely presumptive content. The role, as Banton speaks of it, is supposed to encompass all occupational routines not directly related to making arrests, without, however, specifying what determines the limits of competence and availability of the police in such actions.

... Policemen, when asked, insist that they merely use common sense when acting as peace officers, though they tend to emphasize the elements of experience and practice in discharging the role adequately. All this ambiguity is the more remarkable for the fact that peacekeeping tasks – that is, procedures not involving the formal legal remedy of arrest – were explicitly built into the program of the modern police from the outset. The early executives of the London police saw with great clarity that their organization had a dual function. While it was to be an arm of the administration of justice, in respect of which it developed certain techniques for bringing offenders to trial, it was also expected to function apart from, and at times in lieu of, the employment of full-dress legal procedure. Despite its early origin, despite a great deal of public knowledge about it, despite the fact that it is routinely done by policemen, no one can say with any clarity what it means to do a good job of keeping the peace. To be sure, there is vague consensus that when policemen direct, aid, inform, pacify, warn, discipline, roust, and do whatever else they do without making arrests, they do this with some reference to the circumstances of the occasion and, thus, somehow contribute to the maintenance of the peace and order. Peacekeeping appears to be a solution to an unknown problem arrived at by unknown means.

. . . Though our interest was focused initially on those police procedures that did not involve invoking the law, we found that the two cannot be separated. The reason for the connection is not given in the circumstance that the roles of the law officer and of the peace officer are enacted by the same person and thus are contiguous. According to our observations, patrolmen do not act alternatively as one or the other, with certain actions being determined by the intended objective of keeping the peace and others being determined by the duty to enforce the law. Instead, we have found that *peacekeeping occasionally acquires the external aspects of law enforcement*. This makes it specious to inquire whether or not police discretion in invoking the law conforms with the intention of some specific legal formula. The real reason behind an arrest is virtually always the actual state of particular social situations, or of the skid-row area in general.

Many practical policing decisions will depend on whether the officer considers a peace-keeping or law-enforcement response to be the best way of controlling crime. Informal warnings, for example, to the careless motorist or to the unruly adolescent, may be judged to be a better way of preventing a repetition of the offence than formal processing. As Chatterton explains, this requires the police officer to make a judgment about the 'trouble' that the offender is likely to cause in the future.

Extract 2.1.3

M Chatterton, 'Police in Social Control' in J King (ed), *Control Without Custody* (1976) pp 104–22

Broadly speaking there were two kinds of 'trouble' about which policemen on the Research Division were particularly concerned. The first kind I have called 'within-the-job trouble', which is bound up with the relationships between the patrol personnel and their superiors in the organisation. The second kind relates to their concern to control relationships between themselves and their various publics on the division, to maintain their capacity to intervene authoritatively in any incident and to preserve their own and others' beliefs that they are 'on top of the area', as they put it. For want of a better term this type of concern could be described as 'on-the-job trouble'. In some situations both types of trouble were relevant to how the policeman dealt with those situations.

The first kind of trouble is based upon policemen's appreciation of one of the basic facts about police-work, which is that one can never be absolutely certain that the action taken in a particular situation will later prove to be the most appropriate way of handling that situation. This important element of uncertainty stems partly from the fact that the police mandate is so widely defined that a certain course of action which may be deemed reasonable with reference to one of the aims of police work can be defined differently if it is viewed from another. For example a sergeant who directed his men to patrol their beats more 'aggressively' and engage in street stops and checks of persons, might be seen as contributing to the capacity of the police as a crime-prevention and thief-catching agency. But if complaints were made by persons living in and frequenting the area, and if the actions of his men destroyed the good relationships which his superiors were trying to build up between the police and local populace, then his actions and those of his men could be criticised as poor police-work.

Another source of uncertainty arises from the fact that policemen can rarely be certain that they have correctly assessed the circumstances of an incident and the parties to it. Through their inability to identify something which, it transpires, was of considerable relevance, the solution they may have proposed and worked to achieve may be rendered ineffective, and proved by the turn of events to have been inappropriate.

Although these sources of uncertainty are not unique to police-work, they take on a greater significance when subordinates appreciate how easily they can make mistakes and when they are also uncertain how such errors will affect their promotion and other job opportunities. It is this combination of factors which motivates policemen in the lower echelons to attempt to control the information about themselves which passes up the communications system to their superiors. Every attempt is made to ensure that only information which cannot damage their reputations is allowed to reach the higher echelons.

Hence, to the men on the Research Division, trouble in its mildest form meant allowing themselves to become involved in anything which could result in their superiors having to do more than routinely endorse a report which they had submitted on an incident. If the report 'bounced', i.e. was returned with comments requiring more details about the incident, that was seen as the fault of the report-writer. For controlling information also required the development of skills in report-writing, so that a report always provided a retrospective justification of the action which was reported to have been taken. Whenever possible the submission of a report was avoided. Instead one of several standard brief references was usually entered against the original entry in the station journal or in the radio-log, for example, 'parties advised', 'not a police matter', 'all quiet on arrival', 'unsatisfactory business transaction'. These observations on the concern to avoid 'within-the-job' trouble, by controlling information and handling of incidents and writing reports with the concern in view, will be particularly relevant to our subsequent discussion of incidents which result in no one being arrested or reported for an offence.

What I have called 'on-the-job trouble' requires an investigation of police-men's conceptions of the area where they work, their knowledge about types of premises and their conceptions of the types of persons who live upon or frequent the area. The use of this background knowledge is revealed in their responses to radio calls. Certain calls are guaranteed to produce a 'good turn-out': more than one officer will attend the incident even if one patrol-man only was directed to it by the communications officer. The response to these types of call is based upon an expectation that the officer dispatched to the scene might encounter difficulties and be exposed to a certain amount of danger in handling it alone. Those expectations are in turn inferred from the details provided in the radio message – details which are relevant to their *conceptions of significant locations and relationships*.

On the Research Division, '999' calls reporting trouble in a public house provided a good example of one type of significant location. When they heard the call, the patrolmen would interpret it in the light of their conceptions of the typical sequence of events leading up to the call (the trouble-maker will have been given more than one chance by the landlord), the types of persons likely to be present in the pub when they arrived (persons who will have a go at a policeman in difficulties and who will learn from how we deal with this one how much *they* can get away with in the future), and the likely outcome (if he is still there and he gives any trouble then he will be arrested).

In these kinds of location policemen are sensitive to the threat which the incident presents to their capacity to control the area, not only on the specific occasion but in the future. Taking an accused into custody who is defying their authority in such situations has to be interpreted in the context of those under-standings. Behaviour of which they might be more tolerant in different circum-stances consequently implies a high probability of arrest when it occurs in these significant locations.

The same observation applies in circumstances where the relationships between the complainant and the accused, and the situation of the complain-ant, were such that the police again considered that the incident in question threatened their control over the area. For example, there were certain occu-pations which exposed those who practised them in the area covered by the Research Division to a degree of personal risk from certain others who lived in the area. The policeman judged their success in keeping the area under control with reference to the confidence these people had that they could pursue their occupations without the fear of being victimised. In these incid-ents it was regarded as vital to prove, both to the complainant and the other party, that the police had the situation under control. If the trouble-maker was not prepared to co-operate with them, thus enabling them to resolve the issue in a way they thought appropriate, the power of arrest would be utilised, to teach him a lesson and to provide the complainant with the display or show of strength necessary to reassure him. In many circumstances their control was displayed without recourse to an arrest, by the compromise which they were able to negotiate once the person complained about accepted the legitim-acy of their intervention and complied with their demands. Thus a taxi client would be taken to his home to obtain the money to pay the fare knowing that the alternative, which had been spelled out to him in no uncertain terms, was a night in the cells and an appearance at court the next day charged with

'D and D'. An ambulance driver would receive an apology for the insults he had received because, in the view of the offending party, he had not arrived quickly enough. The dissatisfied customer would pay for the main course of the meal he had not enjoyed and contribute half of the cost of the meal his companion had eaten before running out of the restaurant without paying. The patient in the casualty department who had been blaspheming and threatening the medical staff would allow them to treat his wound without continuing the disturbance he had been creating.

The arrest powers given by the resource charges [that is, potential charges which could be brought in respect of the behaviour which the police wish to control] were therefore used as a threat and invoked when the other alternatives failed. This seems to answer the question posed at the beginning of the paper. Policemen appreciated the power which the resource charges provided, for they strengthened the probability of a settlement being achieved without resorting to an arrest and thereby made their interventions more effective. For these reasons, it has been suggested that policemen on the Research Division were particularly sensitive to the kinds of behaviour which threatened both their control over the specific incident in hand and their control over the area generally. Certain significant locations and relationships highlighted this concern and although an arrest in these situations was not inevitable, the probability of such a response was higher in these incidents than in others. Even in other incidents, however, failure to resolve the altercation by negotiating a satisfactory outcome might necessitate recourse to the arrest powers in order to retrieve the controlling position of the police . . .

Police judgments about the balance to be struck between peacekeeping and law enforcement may not always coincide with society's assessment of its best interests. A topical example is the way that the police regard domestic violence. At one time, policing practice subscribed to the view (possibly held by large sections of the population) that relationships between spouses or partners were so private that official intervention was to be discouraged. Responses to domestic violence tended to adopt the peacekeeping approach, therefore, by encouraging the aggressive party to keep his distance until he had cooled down or sobered up, and by not encouraging the victim to make a formal complaint. Now that social attitudes have started to progress beyond that stance, there has been a deliberate effort to alter the police approach (in Home Office Circular 60/1990) to encourage law enforcement as the usual response in such situations. Nevertheless, recent Home Office research showed that, although 'most officers were aware that arrest should be a priority in domestic violence cases, almost half of them put it below all other considerations (e.g. the safety of the victim and any children) when asked to prioritise their actions at a domestic violence scene'. (Grace, 1995, p 54) In deciding whether or not to arrest, the officers appeared to be strongly influenced by whether the complainant would support any police action, a consideration which also applies to the decision to prosecute (see the discussion in Chapter 3, pp 329–31). In addition, even where informal resolution of the problem had been rejected, there appeared to be a preference for proceeding on the basis that a breach of the peace had occurred, rather than treating the matter as an assault.

On the other hand, the need to maintain order will tend to favour a law-enforcement option against persons whom the police consider to be more likely to disrupt society. Historically, as Brogden has shown, the idea of what is an ordered society and who is likely to fracture it has led the police to concentrate on particular groups to the benefit of others. In particular, those who live on the margins of society and those who occupy public space will be vulnerable to enforcement activity. They encompass 'the inebriated, car-thieves, prostitutes, handbag-snatchers, street-pedlars, street gamblers, and brawlers outside the city-centre club' together with 'the unwaged, . . . drifting groups of teenagers, and . . . minority ethnic groups'. Measures against actual or anticipated street crime provide a demonstration, whether symbolic or real, that social disorder is being controlled. (See Brogden, 1982, pp 231–236.)

(b) Service to the community

The maintenance of social stability can be achieved in ways other than by the control of crime, whether or not that involves the use of force. One of the most important aspects of police work, at least from the citizen's viewpoint, is the 'service' role which they provide. Indeed, as the following table shows (and see also Waddington, 1993), a high proportion of policing activity is a response to requests from members of the public for assistance with problems which may have nothing to do with criminal behaviour.

Extract 2.1.4

W Skogan, *Contacts Between the Police and Public: Findings from the 1992 British Crime Survey* (1994) table B.2

Contacts initiated by the public

Type of contact (one or more times)	%
To report a crime of which you or someone in your household was a victim	13.1
To report a crime of which someone else was the victim	4.2
Because you were told or asked to do so (e.g. to show documents, give a statement)	3.6
To report a traffic accident or medical emergency	3.9
To report a burglar alarm ringing	2.8
To report a car alarm going off	0.4
To report any other suspicious circumstances or persons	5.6
To report any type of disturbance, noise or nuisance (apart from alarms going off)	3.7

Contacts initiated by the public (cont'd)

Type of contact (one or more times)	%
To report a missing person	0.4
To report that you had lost something (including animals)	3.2
To report that you had found something (including animals)	3.1
To tell them that your home was going to be empty	1.7
To report any other type of problem or difficulty	3.2
To ask for directions or the time	2.6
To ask for any other sort of advice or information	3.9
To give them any other sort of information	3.5
Just for a social chat	2.3
Total unweighted cases	5,184

Weighted data, half core sample. These are the categories listed on a show card presented to respondents.

The service role of the police is one contribution to their general function, to keep social stability, which does not have an immediate connection with the criminal justice process. But, insofar as it uses police resources when they could be deployed elsewhere, it will have an indirect effect on choices about whom to process. More importantly, from the police perspective, a good relationship with the community may be a practical requirement for success in law enforcement generally and, more abstractly, it is crucial in consolidating the legitimacy of police activity. These considerations can have a major influence on choosing the best course of action in particular situations.

2. FIRST ENCOUNTERS: CRITERIA FOR DECISION

(a) Legal powers and discretion

To legitimise the use of force in carrying out their functions, police officers, as constables, have extensive powers of stop and search, arrest, and detention. Police powers authorise police actions which would otherwise amount to assaults or false imprisonment in respect of citizens who are acknowledged to be free to conduct their affairs without official interference unless that is justified by law. Formally, it is possible to distinguish stop and search powers, which enable evidence of certain crimes to be sought without necessarily implying that the person searched may be an offender, and arrest powers, which do imply that the arrestee may have offended. In practice, there is considerable overlap between the two kinds of powers.

There are a variety of stop and search powers available to the police although, following the recommendations of the Philips Royal Commission

(Royal Commission on Criminal Procedure, 1981), the Police and Criminal Evidence Act 1984 (PACE) reduced the number considerably by replacing a panoply of local powers with a national power under s 1. A controversial national power, under ss 4 and 6 the Vagrancy Act 1824, had earlier been repealed by the Criminal Attempts Act 1981; this was the notorious 'sus' law which was the subject of some of the empirical studies to be discussed later. Under s 1 of PACE, a constable may search any person or vehicle, or anything which is in or on a vehicle, for stolen or prohibited articles, and may detain a person or vehicle for the purpose of such a search. However, by s 1(3), the search is not permitted unless the constable 'has reasonable grounds for suspecting that he will find stolen or prohibited articles . . .'. The category of prohibited articles includes offensive weapons, blades or sharply pointed objects whose possession in a public place is prohibited by s 139 of the Criminal Justice Act 1988, and implements made or adapted for use in committing the offences of burglary, theft, taking a vehicle without authority or obtaining property by deception. The stop and search may be conducted only in a public place or one to which the public have access. Other stop and search powers which are extensively invoked by the police are s 23 of the Misuse of Drugs Act 1971 and s 47 of the Firearms Act 1968, both dependent on reasonable suspicion of offending under the respective statutes. In respect of all these powers, ss 2 and 3 of PACE impose obligations on the constable to give reasons and make a record of the stop, and the Code of Practice on the exercise of statutory powers of stop and search applies.

In respect of arrest, PACE was also anticipated to rationalise what had been a complicated range of powers prior to 1984. However, although the majority of powers to arrest without warrant are contained in the Act, there are some significant ones in other legislation. Under s 24 of PACE, there is a comprehensive power to arrest without warrant for an 'arrestable offence'. Any person (not only but including a constable) may arrest somebody who is in the act of committing or whom he or she has reasonable grounds for suspecting to be committing an arrestable offence. Similarly, where an arrestable offence has been committed, any person may arrest without warrant somebody who is guilty or for whom he or she has reasonable grounds for suspecting to be guilty. Furthermore, a constable (but not any person) may arrest somebody who is about to commit an arrestable offence or somebody whom he or she has reasonable grounds for suspecting to be about to commit an arrestable offence. 'Arrestable offence' is defined generally as offences for which the sentence is fixed by law or ones for which a person of 21 years may be sentenced for a period of five years' imprisonment, together with a list of less serious offences, for example, relating to official secrecy, prostitution, taking a vehicle without authority, going equipped for stealing, and miscellaneous public order offences. Another category of arrest powers is contained in s 25 of PACE which provides a constable with a power to arrest where he or she has reasonable grounds to suspect that a non-arrestable offence has been committed or attempted, or is being committed or attempted, 'if it appears to him that the service of a summons is impracticable or inappropriate because any of the general arrest conditions is satisfied'. The general arrest conditions are, broadly, that the suspect's identity is unknown or cannot be readily confirmed or that the arrest is necessary to prevent physical injury or damage to property, to prevent an offence against public decency, to prevent an obstruction of the highway or to protect a child or vulnerable person. It will be noted that the s 25 power is *not* a general power of arrest. In addition to the powers contained in PACE, some of the more useful for everyday policing are those provided in public order legislation, for example, ss 4 and 5 of the Public Order Act 1986, enabling arrest for threatening, abusive or insulting words or behaviour likely to create fear or provocation of violence and for offensive conduct. There is also frequent resort to the common law power to arrest for an actual or apprehended breach of the peace (see *R v Howell* [1981] 3 All ER 383).

All such powers can be invoked only when certain conditions are satisfied; typically, there must be 'reasonable grounds for suspecting' that the suspect is connected with an actual or potential offence. However, the legal conditions for the exercise of these powers allows the police considerable choice as to which power they wish to invoke. From a civil liberties perspective, this may mean that safeguards which are built into particular powers can be avoided by the use of equally applicable alternatives. A good example is the relationship between stop and search powers and powers of arrest. The former have been constrained by fairly detailed duties to give reasons and make a record of stops, partly because the exercise of stop and search powers under previous legislation, including the 'sus' law, was widely regarded as unaccountable and discriminatory in its effect. But, in most cases where the police have reasonable grounds to suspect that an individual is carrying an object which would justify a stop and search, they will also have reasonable grounds to suspect that the individual has committed an arrestable offence. If they consequently arrest the individual, they may then search him or her following arrest (PACE, s 32(2)(ii)) and, if they consider no further action to be appropriate, they may release the individual before taking him or her to a police station (PACE, s 30(7)). The outcome will be similar to the use of the stop and search power but without the need to comply with the latter's safeguards. It may be questioned why stop and search powers are necessary therefore, or why they continue to be used. Indeed, the evidence is that their use has increased during the past decade. One explanation may be that there is some tendency to treat stop and search powers as being more appropriate for initial, on-the-street encounters, where suspicion of offending can be checked and resolved quickly, and to treat arrest powers as being more suitable where a suspect needs to be questioned further at a police station (see Sanders and Young, 1994, pp 73–75).

It is clear that these powers are given on the assumption that they will be used to enforce the criminal law. There is no requirement, however, that they must be used, simply because the conditions for invoking them do exist.

If the police wish to enforce the law and process a suspect, there is an expectation that it must be done by reference to their powers. But the powers will not prevent the police from choosing a peacekeeping option if they prefer. This discretion whether or not to invoke the criminal justice process is fundamental to an understanding of the police role. Its nature is explained by Davis in this classic passage.

Extract 2.2.1

K C Davis, *Discretionary Justice: A Preliminary Inquiry* (1969) p 4 (footnote omitted)

What is discretion? A public officer has discretion whenever the effective limits on his power leave him free to make a choice among possible courses of action or inaction.

Some elements of this definition need special emphasis. Especially important is the proposition that discretion is not limited to what is authorized or what is legal but includes all that is within 'the *effective* limits' on the officer's power. This phraseology is necessary because a good deal of discretion is illegal or of questionable legality. Another facet of the definition is that a choice to do nothing – or to do nothing now – is definitely included; perhaps inaction decisions are ten or twenty times as frequent as action decisions. Discretion is exercised not merely in final dispositions of cases or problems but in each interim step; and interim choices are far more numerous than the final ones. Discretion is not limited to substantive choices but extends to procedures, methods, forms, timing, degrees of emphasis, and many other subsidiary factors.

In fact, the exercise of discretion pervades policing because, as Quinney explains:

Extract 2.2.2

R Quinney, *The Social Reality of Crime* (1970) p 104 (footnote omitted)

Full enforcement of criminal law . . . is not a realistic expectation. Numerous limitations and circumstances preclude the possibility of enforcing the law to the fullest extent. First, *procedural* restrictions prohibit the enforcement of the law beyond the lawful rights of the individual citizen. Second, *interpretational* latitude, resulting primarily from ambiguity in the wording of many statutes, permits considerable discretion as to what constitutes a criminal offence. Third, *technical* difficulties confound law enforcement, such as limitation of police time, personnel, and equipment in the detection and investigation of crime. Fourth, *organisational* demands of local police departments provide guides for both the enforcement and non-enforcement of criminal law. Fifth, *ideological* orientations or values of policemen provide a basis for selective law enforcement. Sixth, numerous *societal* pressures prevent full enforcement of some criminal laws.

It is not always easy to discover how those extraneous factors have an influence on police choices, however. Many initial decisions are what have been described as 'low-visibility' (Goldstein, 1960) because they are taken by individual officers and, if they are decisions not to act – for example, to 'turn a blind eye' – they cannot be observed. The exercise of such a broad discretion, at the very point of entry to the criminal justice system, does not mean, however, that the system is not working properly – that police officers are somehow evading the controls that the law imposes on them. On the contrary, the law condones such wide discretion in two ways.

First, the common law recognises the office of constable as quasi-autonomous. This means that, although police officers are members of the disciplined hierarchy of a police force, as far as the law is concerned, their decisions whether or not to invoke process must be taken independently and personally. Constables are said to be accountable only to the law (see Lustgarten, 1986). Whilst it may be a rather foolhardy police officer who ignores the expectations of his or her superiors, the effect is to subvert the possibility of a comprehensive law enforcement policy imposed from above. In particular, it legitimises the area of greatest discretion for police officers, the decision not to invoke the criminal justice process.

Secondly, the law to which constables are accountable does not exert a tight control on individual decisions. The requirement for the police to act in accordance with their powers gives the impression that, provided that compliance by the police can be enforced, the law will act as a real constraint. The reality, however, is that the criteria for invoking powers are typically drafted in terms which are sufficiently broad to allow the subjective judgments of the police to pass unchallenged. The police do not need to evade their powers to enjoy wide discretion, therefore. For example, Southgate and Ekblom observed two vehicle stops, by different patrol-car crews, for the same offence of driving through a red traffic light. Both offenders were middle-aged with similar occupations and driving goods vehicles. 'Both reacted to the constables with deference, did not try to argue their way out of the situation and only spoke when questioned. Yet the outcomes were totally different. The first driver was "let off" with a verbal warning, but the second was reported.' (Southgate and Ekblom, 1986, p 103). As McBarnet emphasises, the design of the law itself allows plenty of scope for legally circumventing the principle of equality before the law. She points out that, where substantive offences are vague (what is a 'breach of the peace' or an 'offensive weapon'?) or where powers do not depend on a specific offence having been committed, the police are effectively being allowed to define the circumstances in which they will take action (McBarnet, 1981). While the courts have acknowledged that the police cannot act wholly irrationally, in the administrative law sense (see *Holgate-Mohammed v Duke* [1984] AC 437)

124

that is not of much assistance in police–public encounters on the street and there is a reluctance to impose retrospectively a standard of reasonableness derived from calm reflection in the courtroom rather than the urgency to act in the heat of the moment:

> The lawfulness of the conduct of the police must be judged at the time, and not by what happens afterwards.

(*Ghani v Jones* [1970] 1 QB 693, per Lord Denning MR. See also *Moss v McLachlan* [1985] IRLR 76).

Prior to the introduction of the Police and Criminal Evidence Act 1984 (PACE), research on policing in London showed that decisions to stop individuals on the street were often unrelated to a specific reason for suspecting the individual concerned:

Extract 2.2.3

D J Smith and J Gray, *Police and People in London: IV The Police in Action* (1983) pp 232–233

The following types of behaviour or circumstance have been counted as giving rise to a reasonable suspicion.

1. Odd driving, for example, quick acceleration away from traffic lights, or unusually slow driving (where no traffic offence is involved).
2. Running or moving quickly.
3. Behaving aimlessly ('hanging about'), moving very slowly, especially at night.
4. Specific odd circumstances, for example a man following a woman 20 yards behind at 3am.
5. Carrying valuable property by hand or in a vehicle (it is often possible to see, say, a television set in the back of a car).
6. Being out on foot in the small hours of the morning (this is, of course, a very weak reason for suspicion on its own, but we have counted it in some cases).
7. Having something in common with the description of suspects in a recently reported crime in the area.

On this basis, we find that there was a reason to make the stop in 44 per cent of cases (in addition to the 23 per cent where a traffic offence was committed). There was no specific reason to make the stop in 34 per cent of the cases, though among these are five per cent where the person stopped was 'known to police' – had, according to the officer, been recently arrested or convicted of an offence . . .

These findings show that the criterion of 'reasonable suspicion' does not act as an effective constraint on police officers in deciding whether to make a stop. It is true that in the case of people in vehicles there is a power to stop without 'reasonable suspicion', but there is no power to search; yet in many cases the person and vehicle was searched. Further, it is clear from the way that police officers talk about stops that the question of what their legal powers

125

may be does not enter into their decision-making except in the case of rare individuals. They do, of course, consider the chance of getting a 'result', but factors that they associate with the chance of getting a 'result' are often unconnected with the concept of 'reasonable suspicion' . . . Thus, they strongly tend to choose young males, especially young black males. Other groups that they tend to single out are people who look scruffy or poor ('slag'), people who have long hair or unconventional dress (who, they think, may use drugs) and homosexuals. We observed two cases where men were stopped purely because they appeared to be homosexual. In a few cases there appear to be no criteria at all, and the stop is completely random; this happens especially in the early hours of the morning when police officers tend to be bored.

Although the aim of PACE was to constrain the extent of discretion in initial encounters with the public, it has hardly affected policing practice outside the police station. Its approach was to provide more detailed advice for decision-making, accompanied by new procedures for recording any action taken. But the basic criterion for invoking a police power, that of 'reasonable suspicion', was retained and, significantly, it is interpreted differently by police officers and lawyers. On their face, the Act and its accompanying Code of Practice on Stop and Search demand objective reasons for intervention:

Extract 2.2.4

Code of Practice for the Exercise by Police Officers of Statutory Powers of Stop and Search 1995, paras 1.6, 1.7

1.6   Whether reasonable grounds for suspicion exist will depend on the circumstances in each case, but there must be some objective basis for it. An officer will need to consider the nature of the article suspected of being carried in the context of other factors such as the time and the place, and the behaviour of the person concerned or those with him. Reasonable suspicion may exist, for example, where information has been received such as a description of an article being carried or of a suspected offender; a person is seen acting covertly or warily or attempting to hide something; or a person is carrying a certain type of article at an unusual time or in a place where a number of burglaries or thefts are known to have taken place recently. But the decision to stop and search must be based on all the facts which bear on the likelihood that an article of a certain kind will be found.

1.7   Reasonable suspicion can never be supported on the basis of personal factors alone. For example, a person's colour, age, hairstyle or manner of dress, or the fact that he is known to have a previous conviction for possession of an unlawful article, cannot be used alone or in combination with each other as the sole basis on which to search that person. Nor may it be founded on the basis of stereotyped images of certain persons or groups as more likely to be committing offences.

126

But, as Dixon and his co-researchers show, this may not be sufficient to influence police practice (see also Dixon, 1997, pp 90–125).

Extract 2.2.5

D Dixon, K Bottomley, C A Coleman, M Gill and D Wall , 'Reality and Rules in the Construction and Regulation of Police Suspicion' (1989) *Int J Soc Law* 185, pp 185–192 (some references omitted)

A majority of the Royal Commission on Criminal Procedure accepted the need for a national stop and search power, if only to legalise existing police practices and to provide consistency between force areas . . . Consideration of the way in which such powers should be limited and controlled was decisively influenced by accounts of the abuse of stop and search (and, earlier, 'Sus' law powers) in the London Metropolitan Police area against young black people . . . A stereotype of the potential or actual criminal (above all, the 'mugger') had been constructed: this created the grounds for suspicion of black youth as a group, leading to the extensive use of stop and search powers against them. While this observation had become commonplace amongst many academics and black communities, it was given decisive weight by the Report on the Brixton Disorders . . . In consequence, the significant issue in the legislative control of stop and search became the attempt to exclude stereotyping as an adequate ground for suspicion justifying the use of coercive powers. Given the significance of the policing of Britain's black communities, this was understandable: however, its consequence was to lead to a misdirection of efforts to regulate police suspension.

Concentration on the problematic results of suspicion based on stereotyping induced a misunderstanding of the nature of suspicion in police patrol work: it failed to take account of, or provide for, a type of suspicion which is at least as significant as that based on stereotyping, and which is deeply rooted historically in the policing mandate and in the culture of police work. This suspicion is the product of what Sacks [H Sacks, 'Notes on the Assessment of moral character' in P Manning and J Van Maanen (eds), *Policing*, Santa Monica: Goodyear, 1978] called the 'incongruity procedure'. Here, individuals attract suspicion not because they accord to a stereotype, but because they fail to fit into variable contexts of activity, place and time considered by officers to be normal, according to criteria such as age, sex and class. Police officers are encouraged to learn, as a fundamental part of their professional skills, to see the world as divisible into the normal and the abnormal . . .

> 'The experienced patrolman . . . develops a set of background expectancies about his beat as a set of normal appearances, normal for particular times, days, seasons and so forth. He is sensitised in such a way that slight variations warrant an investigation of presented appearances.' [K Bottomley and C A Coleman, *Understanding Crime Rates* (Farnborough: Saxon House, 1981) p 105]

People who do not 'fit' will be checked – stopped and then searched if their account does not satisfy the officer. Only the experienced officer who really knows his/her area can use this procedure to its fullest extent, identifying, for example, the new 'window cleaner' and others who, despite appearances, do not in fact belong in the area. Newcomers to a beat or sub-division will rely on standardised indicators of incongruity, such as a scruffy person driving an expensive car or a black pedestrian in a white middle-class area ... As such examples suggest, there is an overlap with stereotyped suspicion: these people are suspicious both because they are out of place and because they fit a stereotype. However, the incongruity procedure is more subtle than simple stereotyping, and depends on a particular combination of variable factors of age, sex, race, behaviour, time and place. People in places at one time may be unremarkable: at another they appear incongruous, are suspicious, and may be checked. (The frequent use of the word 'checking' by officers as a synonym for stopping, questioning, and possibly searching is itself a good indication of the exercise's nature.)

As noted above, this kind of suspicion must be understood as an historical product ... Cohen has shown how, in London, relations between the police and working class communities developed in the first third of this century. A process of negotiation defined what was acceptable behaviour at various times and various places:

> 'The new norms in effect imposed a system of unofficial curfew, informal out-of-bounds, to define what were the wrong people, wrong age, wrong sex, in the wrong place and the wrong time.' [P Cohen, 'Policing the Working Class City', in B Fine et al. (eds) *Capitalism and the Rule of Law*, London: Hutchinson, 1979, p 131]

Suspicion, and then perhaps the criminal law, could be activated against those who transgressed these definitions. Police suspicion has to be seen as being created and reinforced in the historical process in which the control of socially marginal groups (and particularly their street activities) became a central feature of the police mandate ... The continuing significance of this is shown in the way in which police officers articulate social divisions ... In particular, there is the distinction between the 'respectable' and 'police property' ... People in this category include some of the unemployed, the socially marginal, and ethnic minorities:

> 'The prime function of the police has always been to control and segregate such groups, and they are armed with a battery of permissive and discretionary laws for this purpose. The concern with 'police property' is not so much to enforce the law as maintain order using the law as one resource among others.' [R Reiner, *The Politics of The Police* (Brighton: Wheatsheaf, 1985, pp 98–99]

This embedding of a working method in the culture of police work has implications for the possibility of effective reform which will be addressed below.

Some examples will illustrate the point. The first comes from the experience of a middle-class social explorer into the 1930s. Hugh Massingham lived as a participant observer in an East End street. Tramping around looking for work, he reports an occasion when he found himself in the City of London. This was where he worked in his 'real life': it was the 'world to which I imagined I belonged'. But he was without collar and tie, in the clothes of the East End unemployed: while he felt 'at home' in the City, a watching policeman saw him as out of place and 'was looking at me with suspicion and hostility'. By assuming his new identity and class, Massingham had changed his relations with the police officer:

'He was no longer my friend, but my enemy. I had unconsciously locked myself out of the world of busy preoccupied people, and for him I had become a disturber of the peace, a breaker of safes, a dangerous being.' [H Massingham, *I Took Off My Tie* (London: Heinemann, 1936) p 5]

The officer then moved him on, back to the East End 'where nobody would throw a stone at me because I had not a collar or tie and had not shaved for two days.' (ibid., 6). Similarly, Brogden & Brogden ['Postscript: The Toxteth Riots' in M Brogden, *The Police: Autonomy and Consent* (London: Academic Press, 1982)] cite an example in which a youth is considered suspicious because he has returned from the city centre to his normal area: theft is assumed to be the likely reason for a visit to the city centre and its shops. This deviation from perceived normality of place leads to a stop and search (1982, 246).

A second example comes from observation of a car-patrolling officer in the City Centre sub-division of our Research Force. At 9.35 on a Friday night, a researcher and the officer are discussing stop and search. On an industrial street, they pass a man walking with a canvas bag. The PC states that, if it were later at night, he would routinely stop and search a man walking with a bag in such an area. But at this time, a man carrying a bag is still not incongruous, and therefore not suspicious: he is probably someone going home from work. The PC comments that, if he stopped and attempted to search the man, strong objection would be likely. This makes a point suggested by the historical material noted above: that the construction of suspicion must be understood as taking place in the context of relations and negotiations of power. The man would not have regarded himself as 'fair game' to be stopped and searched: the officer would have been acting out of order if he had done so. The categories of suspicion are not created unilaterally by the police: they are a product of negotiation and interaction with their public.

A few minutes later, the officer's suspicion is aroused by three people. They are not carrying anything, or doing anything other than standing on a street corner. If the time had been 5.45 rather than 9.45, they would have been unremarkable. However, they are incongruous here at this time of night because of their age: they are all early teenagers. They are asked to account for themselves by the PC, who asks where they are from and what they are doing. They tell him that they are from a large council estate which is some distance away. They are now regarded as being out of place as well as out of time, and have to explain their presence. They are visiting a friend. This account satisfies the PC's suspicion: nothing that they have done or said, or that he has seen, has served to increase it. Similar examples are evident in the grounds provided on some PACE stop and search forms for the exercise of stop and search powers by officers in our Research Force: e.g., 'Time of day and location (being far from home address)' and 'Suspicion of reason to be in area because of age (15 years) and also because not direct route home for him.'

This use of suspicion, based on the recognition of incongruity, is highly valued in police culture (Reiner, 1985, Ch 3). Ability to work on instinct or 'commonsense' and to 'know the ground' are crucial characteristics of the 'good copper'. Attempts are made to teach suspicion to new officers . . . via 'streetcraft' courses and manuals such as Powis's *The Signs of Crime*. However, suspicion is a prime example of the kind of policing skill which, it is claimed, can only be learnt by experience, by doing the job on the street . . . This rooting of the practice of suspicion in the culture of policework makes it highly resistant to attempts at external influence and change. An attempt to change this working practice is likely to be resisted (actively or passively) as interference by a management which is seen by many junior officers as being out of touch with the realities of street policing . . .

A second reason why the PACE power of stop and search fits uneasily with the practice of policework is that PACE treats stop and search as an event, an artificially distinct activity, rather than as a social process. The Code of Practice specifically states that an officer has 'no power to stop or detain a person against his will in order to find grounds for a search' or to question a person in order to find reasonable ground for suspicion which will justify the stop retrospectively . . . The reasonable grounds for suspicion must exist *before* the stop is made with the intention of carrying out a search. However, the practice of policework is not so neatly segmented. Stops and searches have to be seen as potential parts of a social process stretching from informal contact between police and public, to arrest. Willis suggests that only a quarter of stops lead to searches being carried out (1983, 22). Suspicion is built up and dispersed, as in the example of the boys on the street corner noted above. Officers stop and talk to people in the street, and suspicion may be created or increased during this interaction. In an example from our Research Force, two PCs stopped a youth who was walking at night without shoes. When asked where he lived, he gave what one PC knew to be a false address. For the PC, this lie provided the reasonable grounds for suspicion which he had not had at the beginning of the encounter. He went on to search him under PACE. (The other PC considered that mere lack of shoes constituted reasonable grounds for suspicion: the problems of variable interpretation will be noted below.)

Suspicion is not just a preparatory stage of detection of a specific crime: it is also central to more general police duties of surveillance and crime prevention . . . Stops are used by the police to collect information: Willis notes that supervisory officers read patrol officers' records, inter alia, 'to identify potential witnesses or suspects stopped at or around the time and place of a subsequently reported crime' [C F Willis, *The Use, Effectiveness and Impact of Police Stop and Search Powers*, Home Office Research and Planning Unit Paper No 15 (London: Home Office, 1983) p 15] . . . In our Research Force, collators use a computer facility to collect and distribute information produced from informal stops and sightings of suspects. The role of stop and search in crime prevention is stressed in Powis's 'field manual' on suspicion: he argues that the potential benefit of crime prevention fully justifies intervention on the basis of suspicion, and indeed prefaces his book with a quotation from the 1829 instructions to the Metropolitan Police on the priority of crime prevention over other duties. From this perspective, a stop and search which does not lead to an arrest is not to be dismissed as unsuccessful:

'Never be disappointed because your 'stops' are not always recorded as arrests. Who is to say that an apparently unsuccessful stop is not a crime prevented? . . . Arrests and captures are important, of course, but activity by uniformed officers in speaking to loiterers and suspicious persons is what is required *to reduce the incidence of serious crime*.' [D Powis, *Signs of Crime* (London: McGraw Hill, 1977) p 104, original emphasis]

The issue of arrests raises a third problem with the attempt to restrict stop and search. Critics have complained that a low proportion of stops and searches produce arrests . . . In 1986, in both our Research Force and nationally, 17 per cent of recorded stops and searches were followed by arrests: in 1987, the respective figures were 14 per cent and 17 per cent. Whether these are regarded as low or as acceptable depends upon (1) one's views about the appropriate functions of stop and search in police work; and (2) the relationship between recorded and unrecorded stops and searches. (It is estimated that, before PACE, about 30 per cent of stops and searches in provincial forces were recorded . . .) However, at least as important are the statistics which show that a significant proportion of arrests in some areas (notably the Metropolitan Police district) result from stop and search . . . More information is needed about the *kind* of offences for which people are arrested: if many are traffic or 'knock-on' obstruction or public order offences, the utility of stop and search may be open to question . . . This general figure understates the importance of stop and search for uniformed patrol officers: it provides them with a rare opportunity to do proactive, self-motivated police work (rather than simply responding to the control room's directions to crimes reported by the public or, frequently, to non-crime duties). In any case, statistics may be less significant than the *belief* that stop and search provides an important source of arrests . . . In addition, the credit given for initiative and arrest record in probationers' assessment and in consideration for desirable postings to specialist departments (and, thereby, promotion) encourages patrol officers to stop and search, and undermines the attempt to regulate the activity.

This discussion should not lead to the conclusion that the PACE concept of reasonable grounds for suspicion must inevitably fail. This would be to succumb to seeing police culture as artificially constant, unchangeable and distinct from its legal environment . . . However, it does suggest some minimal conditions for success: for PACE to have had any realistic chance of success in this respect, at least some of the following would have been required:

(i) clear expression of the desired standards;
(ii) effective training in order to modify police culture;
(iii) favourable political circumstances;
(iv) the backing of effective sanctions for non-compliance; and
(v) public knowledge of rights and the limits of police powers.

In practice, the use of policing powers is not an issue in many initial encounters between the police and the public. We saw above that the police are inclined to engage in law enforcement as a last resort, once social support and peacekeeping options have been excluded in negotiations with suspects. It may be more convenient for officers, and may forestall the possibility of subsequent legal challenges, if suspects can be encouraged to consent to co-operate with the police instead of being coerced.

Extract 2.2.6

D Dixon, C A Coleman and K Bottomley, 'Consent and the Legal Regulation of Policing' (1990) *J Law & Soc* 345, p 346, 347–9, 352

Our concern here is with a major issue which the strategy of legal regulation has not yet adequately faced – the problem of consent. A police officer may be able to achieve her/his objectives (for example, to interrogate or search) not by using a legal power, but by securing the 'consent' of the suspect. If 'consent' is obtained, the legal relationship between the actors is not that between a state official and a private citizen, but rather that between two private citizens. This has long been used by police officers, in Britain and elsewhere, to supplement or replace what are regarded as inadequate or unclear powers.

As legal regulation comes to delimit police powers, 'consent' becomes increasingly significant. Some of the consequences of 'consensual' encounters are that statutory requirements for the exercise of powers do not apply (so that, for example, a suspect can be searched without reasonable grounds for suspicion); record-making is unnecessary (rendering supervision more diffi-cult); and the rights of the suspect do not have the protections which are the corollaries of the exercise of legal power. The discussion below will consider the ways in which 'consent' has created problems for legal regulation of stop/ search, search of premises, and arrest, detention, and questioning, and will also note some of the attempts to deal with these difficulties. The aim is not just to list various incidents of 'consent', but to illustrate a way of thinking about and doing police work which constitutes a social practice, policing 'by consent', which is distinct from 'policing by law'. It is hoped that the analysis is also of relevance to debates about 'consent' in a variety of other legal settings.

Up to this point, 'consent' has been put between quotation marks in order to acknowledge problems with bland uses of the term: it is clear that what is classified, in practice, as consent encompasses a range of states, which include approving agreement, unwilling acquiescence, submission, and a co-operation or compliance ignorant of the possibility of acting differently. There is a mass of philosophical and other literature on what constitutes consent (and correlative concepts such as coercion) which we do not intend to review here. It is enough for present purposes to suggest, not a definition, but an indication of two significant components of consent which must be considered in any discussion of the concept. These are (i) *knowledge*: that is, information and understanding about what is requested; and (ii) *power*: that is, an ability to make choices on the basis of knowledge and to use the available information . . .

Some of the most important provisions of PACE construct a legal frame-work for stop and search. These were both controversial and significant because of the clear evidence that abuse of stop and search was a major factor in worsening relations between police and public, notably young black people. PACE provides legal powers to stop and search for various articles: reasonable grounds for suspicion are required. Code of Practice A provides guidance on what can and cannot amount to reasonable grounds. The code requires officers to complete a record giving details of, among other things, themselves, the suspect, and the grounds for and purpose of the stop and search. These provisions were justified as providing the police with necessary but strictly regulated and supervised powers.

The conclusion of our research in this area is that PACE operates largely as what the Policy Studies Institute called 'presentational rules' which 'exist to give an acceptable appearance to the way that police work is carried out'. The apparently crucial changes in stop/search powers had little impact on the practice of many officers: in our interview study, seventy-one per cent of those with pre-1986 operational experience told us that PACE had not affected the way in which they carried out stop/searches. Our research force has almost 2,000 officers. In 1986, 1987, and 1988, they recorded 739, 722, and 590 stop/searches respectively. Similarly, in 1987, the total of 124,102 officers in England and Wales recorded 118,300 stop/searches. Of course, by no means all of these officers were operational: nonetheless, this amounts to fewer than one recorded stop/search each annually. This sits uneasily with reports from officers that they would expect to carry out four or five stop/searches when patrolling on a late shift. People walking late at night (particularly young people carrying bags) would be routinely stopped, asked who they were and where they were going, and often searched. This is not surprising, given the usefulness of stop/search as a source of arrests (despite the low 'success' rate) and especially its attractiveness to uniformed officers as one of the few methods by which they can engage in proactive crime work.

The major device which bridges the gap between the records and the reality is 'consent'. Suspects 'consent' to be stopped and searched: consequently, no power is employed and (subject to regulations to be noted below) no record need be made. In our research force, three-quarters of interviewed officers had done a consent stop/search since 1986, while only a quarter said that they had used statutory powers. Many distinguished between types of encounters. Some officers considered that a stop/search means a thorough search of the suspect's clothes: they classified simply looking in a bag as a (non-PACE) 'stop/check' for which legal authority was not provided and was, in any case, unnecessary, because 'consent' would be obtained. Several officers told us that they did not even bother to carry stop/search forms when they were on patrol. They, and many others, said that they would try to get consent from a suspect: if that was not forthcoming, they would arrest her or him. As elsewhere, the very process of trying to obtain consent allows officers to test their suspicion about a person. As the hoary truism insists, only the guilty have reason to refuse it. One officer explained: 'If they are decent law-abiding citizens they wouldn't mind being stopped because they'd appreciate the police being about.'

'Consent' here frequently consists of acquiescence based on ignorance. Many people assume that the officer who says 'What have you got in your pockets?' or 'Let's have a look in your bag' has a power to search. We asked

133

officers how often people whom they stopped and searched knew their rights: seventy-nine per cent said rarely or never. Such lack of knowledge must mean that their 'consent' has little substance. Familiar strategies are used to deal with those who do raise questions about the authority to search. As a sergeant put it: 'A lot of people are not quite certain that they have the right to say no. And then we, sort of, bamboozle them into allowing us to search.' Such 'bamboozling' is done by appealing to the willingness of the innocent to be searched, by threatening arrest, or by claiming the authority of fictional powers.

This is certainly the way in which some people are handled: however, it is too legalistic as an account of how many interact with police. The reality for them may not be acquiescence based on ignorance, but submission rooted in an appreciation of the contextual irrelevance of rights and legal provisions. 'Rights' are seen by officers as properly belonging to some people, but not to the young and unrespectable whom they usually encounter in the street. An officer made the point in explaining what he would do if someone refused to show what was in a bag: 'If it was someone of reasonable intelligence, I'd leave it at that. If it was a scruff, I'd probably have a look myself.' For a 'scruff' to assert her or his rights is 'buggering about' and itself suspicious: reference to rights may be regarded as a challenge to police authority and/or an indication of previous contact with police, and therefore as worth further investigation. Account must be taken of the substantive reality of the police mandate in order maintenance on the street and of material relations between police and policed (see below). A strategy of rights and legal regulation which overlooks them will be misleading and ineffective.

In the circumstances, it would be reasonable to ask why *any* stop/searches get recorded. First, some are recorded for operational purposes, notably drugs intelligence. Secondly, records are more likely to be completed if a probationary constable carries out the stop/search, if a supervisory officer is present, or if senior officers have commented on the lack of recorded stop/searches. Thirdly, if a prohibited article is found and an arrest is made, officers may cover their backs by completing a record. Fourthly, a record would be completed if other 'comeback' was a possibility: an officer explained that if, for example, a middle-class person who was aware of the law happened to be stopped, 'you would probably revert to the standard opening speech procedure' and complete a form. However, as suggested above, refusal of consent is a rare experience for officers. One commented: 'I have never had any problems with anyone refusing to be searched . . . so I have never had to fall back on proving my reasonable suspicion.'

As these points suggest, stop/searches usually come to be recorded because of contingent factors, rather than statutory criteria. It is important to note that many of these operate retrospectively: an officer begins operating by 'consent' and may only later reinterpret the encounter as being a PACE stop/search. Indeed, several officers *defined* a PACE stop/search as being one in which the suspect does not consent.

. . . The point must be emphasized that current practice in street policing is not to be understood simply as 'deviance': rather it is a normative product of the historical mandate of the police to control the streets and to reproduce social order. The central task of street police work is not law enforcement, but order maintenance: an essential part of the police's historical mandate has been the control of street economies, recreations, and people. This means employing wide discretionary powers against categories of the population which police culture distinguishes from 'respectable people' – the 'toe-rags', the 'rubbish', the 'shit', the 'scruffs'. Concepts such as rights and informed consent fit very uneasily with police images of such 'police property' as being stupid, low-status, marginal, and troublesome. Legislation like PACE (ironically, from a police perspective, a product of 'respectable' but socially naive people who are protected from the rubbish by the police) is widely regarded as being simply inappropriate as a means of carrying out this task. As one officer put it starkly, 'PACE was meant to protect decent people, but we don't deal with decent people'.

We may conclude that policing powers do not act as a significant constraint on early policing choices. This is not necessarily because the police are prepared to flout the law. Rather, the law gives the police a wide latitude to interfere with citizens' lives to maintain social order. It does impose some limits, of course, and they are illustrated in the arbitrary exercises of power which result in successful actions for wrongful arrest and false imprisonment, or the excessive use of force which results in actions for battery or prosecutions for criminal violence. Generally, however, legal considerations provide only the background against which particular individuals are selected for processing. It is at later stages in the criminal justice system that the law becomes more critical.

(b) The moral significance of the suspected behaviour

Most studies of policing confirm that suspicion of serious offending will normally result in decisions to enforce the law and pass the suspect on for further processing. In the occupational culture of policing, what counts as serious is reflected in the values that police officers apply to their work, values which are broadly traditional and conservative. As Reiner observes, police officers tend to see themselves as 'the thin blue line', safeguarding social order, preserving a valued way of life, and protecting the weak. Furthermore, police work is seen as a 'mission', more than a mere job but being a worthwhile occupation of protecting and serving the community (Reiner, 1992, pp 111–114). This means that the police value 'crime-fighting' as opposed to low status duties such as traffic duties, football-crowd control or 'social work' tasks such as dealing with domestic disputes, dealing with deaths, handling problem families or dealing with the old or the homeless (see Punch, 1979). This has an impact on the way the police prioritise their activities. There is a sense of personal satisfaction and public benefit in responding to 'real' crime:

135

Extract 2.2.7

**D J Smith and J Gray, *Police and People in London:
IV The Police in Action* (1983) pp 61–63**

Terms like 'good arrest' and 'good result' are used to describe what the lower ranks see as the objectives of police work; and such terms are also adopted by senior officers when making judgements about performance.

A 'good arrest' is one which demonstrated skill, determination or physical strength. It might be considered 'good', for example, because the officer noticed something apparently insignificant that led to the arrest, sensed that someone was uneasy, afraid or out of place and therefore suspected him, or had the physical speed or strength to catch and hold onto someone who might have got away. A 'good result' is similar, except that the emphasis is on building a good case against someone in connection with a reported crime rather than catching someone in the act. A 'good villain' is a successful criminal who, therefore, counts as a worthy antagonist; arresting a 'good villian' is counted a much greater success than arresting an incompetent or occasional law-breaker, even if the offence committed by the latter is fairly serious. 'Rubbish' is a matter that the police are required to deal with but which will either not result in any arrest or is an arrest of a kind that is not valued.

The following is an example of a 'good arrest' combined with a 'good result'. One night two PCs on a relief that DJS was working with stopped a youngish man of fairly conventional appearance. The PCs would claim that they sensed there was something suspicious about him, though in fact they were keen to make arrests and considered that any young person walking in that area late at night was likely to have cannabis on him. When they questioned him about where he had come from and where he was going to they did genuinely sense that he was uneasy. They therefore searched him very thoroughly. Most people would not have found anything, but these PCs were sure that the man was worried about something, were determined to find something if possible, and were good lookers. Eventually they found a single cannabis seed. Many PCs, even if they had noticed the seed, would not have known what it was, but these PCs did know. They then went with the suspect to his flat, which they searched (without a warrant). They found a large quantity of cannabis worth several thousand pounds and quantities of cocaine. It was evident that the man must be a drugs dealer. He was of course arrested, but in addition the relief inspector decided to mount a continuous observation on the flat. Early the next morning a respectable looking man came to call. When he was stopped and searched he was found to be carrying a large quantity of drugs. The case was then taken over by a central drugs squad, who may have been able to catch several more drugs dealers through the two already arrested. This was considered by everyone on the relief to be a very good arrest and result because many police officers would have missed the small initial clues, because the first stop was followed up intelligently and effectively, because it led to a further arrest, and (perhaps most of all) because a specialist central squad took an interest in the case and benefited from the spadework done by members of an ordinary uniform relief. (An interesting point to notice about

136

this case is that if the original suspect had refused to let the PCs into his flat they could not legally have gained entry without first getting a warrant. They could probably have legally detained the suspect for long enough to get a warrant, but as very often happens they 'fronted' their way in without one.)

Although this was undoubtedly a 'good arrest' and a 'good result', the suspects were not referred to as 'good villains' probably because drug dealers do not really fall into this category: they are not the kind of criminal that a police officer normally respects. The prototype of the 'good villain' would be a skilful safe-breaker or jewel burglar. However, most police officers have to settle for 'good villains' of a lower order: any young man who had done a large number of burglaries, or his 'fence', would qualify.

For serious matters, it will be unreasonable and irregular not to take a suspect into custody for further investigation. That will also be the case with specialised offending which is enforced through dedicated policing, such as drugs, vice, or robbery squads. For the less serious kinds of suspected offending, however, the emphasis in policing decisions shifts to the moral worth of the individual rather than his or her behaviour. The outcome of an encounter may depend on the officer's assessment of the extent to which the individual deserves to be processed. At a general level, this may be based on the tendency of the police to polarise the community into people like 'us' and 'them', the latter being described in such disparaging terms as 'rubbish', 'the filth' or 'slag' (for example, see Smith and Gray, 1983, p 232; Skolnick, 1975; Young, M, 1991). Where an individual is perceived to be a respectable member of the community, basically law-abiding and unlikely to repeat the offence or give further trouble, an informal warning may be sufficient to resolve the encounter. By contrast, somebody who is seen as having no strong commitment to the law and the community may not be thought to deserve the benefit of the officer's discretion not to invoke formal processing. If they seem likely to repeat the behaviour, or if they do not take the encounter seriously, the officer has no incentive to control crime through a lenient option. Inevitably, such judgments are impressionistic and they are crucially influenced by the nature of the interaction between the officer and the suspect. The conversation will reveal the latter's general demeanour, background and willingness to co-operate, together with any explanations or excuses. This process of negotiating the outcome of less serious kinds of encounter has been widely observed (for example, Piliavin and Briar, 1964; Chatterton, 1983) and it allows officers considerable latitude in deciding moral blameworthiness and implementing their personal notions of fairness. As we shall see, the importance of the moral significance of the suspected behaviour applies not only to interactions with members of the public. It also applies in decisions about recording the amount of crime which is reported to the police by the public, and it applies to decisions not to send the offender on for processing by the Crown Prosecution Service, but to administer a caution instead.

(c) Craftsmanship and professionalism

To succeed as a police officer 'on the street', certain practical skills are regarded as essential. In his seminal study of policing in the United States, Jerome Skolnick suggested that the police officer is therefore better described as a 'craftsman rather than a legal actor, as a skilled worker rather than as a civil servant obliged to subscribe to the rule of law' (Skolnick, 1975, p 231). Such craftsmanship is manifested in the 'working personality' of police officers, a personality characterised by concerns with 'danger' and with 'authority' and by a constant need to appear efficient (see Skolnick, 1975, pp 43–48).

The maintenance of authority and control is a central element of craftsmanship. All studies of policing show how police officers' main objective in dealing with the public is to control the situation. To achieve this, they require their authority not to be challenged and respect to be shown to them. There is a need to be seen to be competent, to be able to survive and handle a difficult situation satisfactorily. Often, they will be alone amongst a number of potential offenders, or of mere passers-by, and they cannot afford to have their instructions questioned. The mere demeanour of a group of juveniles (see Piliavin and Briar, 1964) or perhaps the law student's tactless inquiry about the officer's legal powers, could be sufficient to prompt a law-enforcement option, simply to maintain credibility with the audience. The response will be instinctive and legal justification may be found only later. As Holdaway (a former police sergeant who became a sociologist) describes, there are a variety of tactics for maintaining control and by no means all of them involve overt force. Taking up McBarnet's theme, mentioned earlier (see McBarnet (1981)), he notes that the law is drawn sufficiently vaguely to legitimate most decisions taken by the police:

Extract 2.2.8

S Holdaway, *Inside the British Police* (1983) pp 89–101

Very little is known about how police officers actually exercise their authority other than in formal, legalistic ways. It is often claimed that laws and rules are moulded within strategies and tactics which are meaningful to the lower ranks, but empirical evidence to back the assertion is rare . . . Strategies of control are the techniques employed regularly by Hilton's officers in encounters with people who may have committed an offence; tactics are the adjustment of strategies to meet particular contexts of police work . . . How does a police officer use this wide range of strategies to cajole, prompt, advise and force people – to him, disorderly people – into doing what he requires? In less academic terms, if chummy doesn't behave, what do you do?

Older officers tend to take the view that their younger colleagues have lost a lot of the finesse that they themselves possessed in their own day . . . Some of the home beat officers, whose specialist work could broadly be called 'community relations', feel that the aggressive approach of younger officers leaves much to be desired. Two of them discuss the issue and conclude that the ineffective juvenile court system and unit beat policing [whereby routine policing is conducted by an area constable assisted by other officers patrolling in Panda cars] are root causes:

'I can tell you, I hear more young men around this station talking about summary justice than I've ever done.'

'Yes, I agree with you, but more and more young men here are hitting people, because they don't think it's worth doing them at court.'

Later in the discussion:

'Yes, you're dead right, that's another old chestnut. The blokes here just don't know how to walk a beat. They never get out and meet anybody. They don't know how to talk to anybody. I think it's terrible. There is a proper way to walk a beat, you know. There's a proper way to do it, but do they know? No, they don't. They want to ride around in Panda cars, and they don't want to get out and walk around, meet people and talk to people. They just haven't got a clue.'

Following an incident during which a PC hit a coloured youth with his truncheon, a telephonist who had worked at Hilton for a considerable number of years made the following comments:

Since the old personal radio [PR] came in, I think that instead of talking their way out of trouble like the old coppers did and getting by that way, they just pull their truncheons out and shout for assistance on the PR. They don't talk their way out of it at all. They just ask for assistance and get their truncheons out.

Remember that the telephonist and the officers do not think that police use of physical force is always wrong; other data confirm this. Yet they are bothered by the dominance of unsubtle strategies of control which are used from day to day. We now consider five of these. (In the following discussion priority is accorded to crime work. My rank made it difficult for me to observe much peacekeeping work.)

Symbolic strategies
A uniformed constable standing on a street corner or driving a marked police car is representative of the pervasive character of state control . . . Doubtless you will have seen a police car and checked your speedometer immediately or watched an officer looking in your direction and wondered if you were the focus of interest. The police are a highly visible symbol of the political state.

In police work any separation of symbolism from instrumentalism is tenuous and analytical. A uniformed sergeant, temporarily employed in plain clothes, parks his car outside the station, leaving his truncheon on the rear seat, to him a symbol of control. An inspector notices the truncheon and is concerned about the sergeant abusing his authority: 'I don't know what he is trying to prove, but there's a Paddy going to nick his truncheon which is on the back seat round there.' A marked police car can also be used in a symbolic manner. Using the distinctive illuminated 'Police' sign on the roof of his Panda car,

139

an officer creates a setting in which his ability to control a motorist is first enhanced and then normalized.

> During a night-duty shift I patrolled as a passenger in a Panda, driven by a constable. We patrolled a well-lit street without the 'Police' sign illuminated. A car tried to overtake us at what the constable thought was an inappropriate moment. He switched the 'Police' sign on and said to me, 'I'll just let him know what's what.' Later he was patrolling with the sign fully illuminated. He noticed a vehicle being driven in an erratic manner and commented that the driver might have been drinking. As our car was positioned behind the suspect vehicle, the illuminated sign was switched off, making it virtually impossible for the suspect to realize the identity of the vehicle following him.

Control is here extended beyond, and then contracted to frame, the normal spatial boundaries of the car itself.

Symbols, then, extend an idea, a principle or some other notion beyond particular restrictive boundaries to a broader terrain. They penetrate physical and psychological barriers. In the following incident a uniform is used to extend police control beyond the physical frame of the officer, beyond a police vehicle, into a distant area.

> At 3.30 a.m. I was patrolling with a uniformed officer who was driving an unmarked police car. A coloured man was walking slowly along the pavement of a well-lit major route. The officer slowed his car to walking pace and on two occasions passed the man at this speed, gazing at him as he passed. The officer commented, 'These coloured people certainly ask for trouble from us. They seem to hang about and look suspicious.'

Other data suggest that the uniform, combined with a fixed gaze, enhances symbolic control . . .

> We noticed a vehicle that was double-parked. – [officer] chose to draw up behind it and continually flash his headlights. The vehicle did not move and so he rang the bell on our car. The offending vehicle moved off and we eventually went past it very slowly. As we did this the officer, wearing his cap and full uniform, glanced carefully at the driver.

In other settings officers use the uniform to imply that they are willing and able to deal with a situation when, in fact, their intentions are rather different. Someone telephones Hilton to complain that a car is obstructing the entrance to his garage. It is obvious that other than spending a long time waiting for the owner of the parked car to return, which is unacceptable, symbolizing a police presence is the only viable strategy. The constable assigned to attend the scene feels that there is little point in going to the car, but his colleague tells him, 'Well, that doesn't matter. Just go along there and show the flag. Tell them you can't do anything. Just show the flag.'

The symbolism of 'showing the flag', however, cannot always be easily separated from the aim of achieving a definite objective. When a robbery occurs in the subdivision a sergeant suggests that the officer in charge of the CID is in favour of 'getting all the villains in the station – just to let them know who's who'. Other incidents verify that arrests are sometimes made simply to symbolize police authority and power over criminals who commit serious offences. Indeed, 'professional criminals' are said to be quite in tune with such a strategy:

– [names officer] doesn't get civil claims against him because they [professional criminals] don't know what he knows about them. If they started complaining, then – would beat them at their own game and get them for other jobs which they were committing, and serious ones at that. Arrests like these hint at the possibility of wider-ranging police activity; they are certainly symbolic, but their symbolism finds expression in a highly instrumental context – the custody assured by arrest.

Strategies of containment

Strategies of containment are intended to limit situations which require some control but which the police cannot contain completely. A boundary of tolerance is drawn around particular behaviour, often with some symbolic flourish to signify a measure of police authority . . .

A number of 'dippings' (pickpocket offences) are reported, and in response the officer in charge of the CID allows uniformed constables to work overtime, patrolling the areas in question in plain clothes. During a chat about the CID chief, a sergeant explains the strategy of containment that he employs.

He's as good as gold. He's OK . . . We had a lot of dippings up at – [names location], and he wanted to stop it, and after a few days it did stop. The word got round that we were up there. Mind you, old – had a couple of sus [suspected] dippings, so that soon got around.

There is implicit acknowledgement that such patrols cannot stop the pickpocketing in the longer term; containment offers only a temporary and partial means of control. Something more than a symbolic 'showing of the flag' is offered because some arrests are made, but these are attempts to define a boundary of tolerance rather than to put an end to the offences.

In situations in which alternative strategies do not calm people who are causing trouble an arrest is sometimes made in the hope that it will contain the conflict and etch the boundary of police tolerance. On one occasion officers have been called to eject troublemakers from a party. One of them recalls:

– [names officer] went up there and was asked to evict a bloke from a party. When he got there the bloke took a swing at him and so – [officer] chucked him down the stairs and was going to nick him for drunk and disorderly outside on the street. Then a lot of them came down and had a go, and the urgent assistance call went up three times.

Later I had an opportunity to talk to a youth arrested at this incident. I asked him what had happened.

Youth: 'I was just standing on the pavement.'
SH: 'What do you mean, "just standing there"?'
Youth: 'I was just standing there. They were having a fight with one of the blokes, and I was just standing there, and a policeman came over to the crowd and said, "You're mine, you'll do," and I got nicked and was put in the van.'

141

Knowing the arresting officer, I repeated the account to one of his colleagues. He, in turn, repeated it to a sergeant and said, 'That sounds just about right doesn't it? Typical copper. That's just how it would have happened.'

Faced with what could have been an inflammatory incident, the PC certainly milked the event of all the drama he could but chose a strategy of control which, leaving a disorderly situation in progress, aimed at containment and a demonstration of police authority.

Containment is not restricted to highly dramatic settings:

Two traffic division officers stop a vehicle driven by a black youth outside a club frequented by blacks. They suspect the car is stolen and bring the driver and passengers to the station for questioning. One of them explains, 'I thought that for their good and for ours we had better bring them in, sarge. There were several others outside the club, and it was getting a bit difficult.'

Why do these officers act differently from those who dealt with the party? Perhaps it is because they are specialist traffic department officers who are less committed to the values and associated actions of the occupational culture than are their station patrol colleagues. They do not attribute as much value to action and hedonism. Their use of a containment strategy is designed to avoid conflict.

Crimes without readily identifiable victims are especially well suited to containment. A man is believed to be practising witchcraft and to be exhuming corpses from a local cemetery. An officer alleges that he also 'kills cats and drinks their blood'.

The press give him publicity and the Chief Superintendent gets into trouble. Our job is really to get rid of him, strip him naked and send him over the fence or send him over on to – [names bordering subdivision] ground and get rid of him that way.

Homosexuals are subject to broadly similar tactics:

While on patrol with a colleague I passed a public toilet where homosexuals were known to congregate throughout the day and night. My colleague looked at the toilet building and said, 'There's a couple having a right old wank in there. Two heads very close together.' He said no more, but when we soon passed another toilet, known to function in the same way, he mentioned a greengrocer who was known to visit the toilet frequently while on his way home from a wholesale market. 'I think I will have his van towed away sometime so that he will have to claim it. It will be a bit of a laugh anyway.'

Again, these are situations which would probably not be permanently resolved if an arrest were made; the crimes are difficult to detect but the police feel that they must do something about them and contain the situation, hoping that their action will provide sufficient warning.

Arrest and/or detention are not the only ploys used. When officers face situations in which their effort is likely to exceed the calculated benefits, they are often prompted to consider strategies of containment. This is particularly true if a considerable amount of documentation is required. Road traffic accidents are an example. As one officer puts it:

> I usually try to square them up unless there is some allegation. In that one [refers to accident he has just dealt with] the damage is more than the cost of the fine, so you pays your money and you takes your choice.

Further, containment can simply mean restraint. If someone who is mentally ill acts in a strange manner, it is clear that the police will not be able to change matters; they can only contain them. The moral culpability of the person is also in doubt. On occasions when patients have to be returned to mental hospitals it is noticeable that restraint rather than force is used: '– [names officer] has the patter. He'll go with him.' In a similar situation a supervisory officer tells his constables, 'Just restrain him, just restrain him.'

'Conning' and lying

The police always have a head start on us. We do not know how much information they have about us or how they might use what information they have. This access to private and potentially damaging information drives a wedge of uncertainty between police and public, which officers can manipulate to their advantage by 'conning' and lying . . . The difference between these is a fine one, save that lying involves more malice.

People are conned so that the police can settle a situation that could get out of hand. Pop music concerts which attract hundreds of young people are frequently held at a local theatre. They queue for ages waiting for a ticket, spilling on to the pavement outside the theatre. On one occasion I go to the theatre with an inspector, who asks his constables to disperse a sizeable crowd because all the available tickets have been sold. After the bulk of the crowd has dispersed he tells me:

> Oh well, they will probably only come back again, but that has done the job for the moment . . . They are very good in there. They still have fifty tickets to sell, and if any of the lads want one, they will sell them; just ring up.

Not all police work relies on illusion. It is possible to make an arrest by lying and conning. An officer holds two warrants for a suspect. One orders a fine to be paid on the spot; the other stipulates arrest with bail and appears the more serious. The officer explains: 'He can pay the money on the first one, and he can be granted bail on the second . . . but I'll show him the second one first.' Similarly, arrests can be made by telling people merely that they are required to come to the station, without any intimation that once there they will be questioned or charged with a specific offence.

> A woman is arrested for assault and she challenges the arresting officer: 'Well have I been arrested? Am I going to be charged? You only asked me to come down here to see about it. Am I being charged, then? Am I staying in all night? I want to get back home.'

The woman was later questioned and charged with a substantive offence; the arrest strategy ensured a minimum of trouble for the officer.

Finally, a con or lie can be used to protect an informant from the possible reprisals of an offender about whom he has given incriminating evidence.

After a youth was arrested for a burglary I asked the arresting officer for the evidence of offence and arrest in the presence of the suspect. I also asked, 'Have you got a statement?'

The officer mouthed silently, 'Yes, it was made by the other bloke.' After the suspect was put in a detention room he explained his unwillingness to provide all the evidence in the presence of the suspect: 'The other kid made a statement under caution implicating him. Would you like to read it?'

Verbal control and threat

Egon Bittner [E Bittner (ed), *Aspects of Police Work* (Boston: Northeastern University Press, 1970) p 46] argues that the central unifying feature of policing is the capacity of an officer to use 'non-negotiably coercive force employed in accordance with the dictates of an intuitive grasp of situational exigencies'. In the most mundane of encounters this access to force operates as a threat to strengthen the control that an officer is able to exert.

Shouting a threat is sometimes an adequate means of exercising control. Some youths are messing about outside the local theatre: 'Pack it up or you'll get nicked.' After dealing with a call to 'suspects in an empty house', the information log is marked up with the result: 'Two satisfactory stops'. I ask one of the officers for a more comprehensive explanation. 'Well, I'll quote – [other officer], shall I?' "Fuck off or you'll get nicked."'

The threat is not always one of possible arrest. Within the space of thirty minutes an officer stops two drivers who, he suspects, have been drinking. The first, a woman, is cautioned. The second, a man who has driven at high speed, is stopped. The officer mutters: 'I'll give him a blow, just to show him.' The threat of possible prosecution is used, although the officer knows that the man has not drunk enough alcohol to warrant his action. In other situations this non-negotiable threat can involve physical force.

> After a rather long observation during the early hours of the morning, two constables watch a man go into a school playground and steal some milk. At some stage of the arrest he hides in the school grounds and the officer uses a threat to finalize the apprehension. He shouts, 'We'll put the dogs in after you if you don't come out.'
> 'Do you know,' he later remarks, 'he jumped straight back out again.'

Prosecution and physical force are just two of the resources on which officers draw. A further expedient is to draw the suspect's attention to the implications of a court case. An inspector and a constable are discussing a difficult traffic case for which more evidence is required. They particularly need the name of the driver of a vehicle and consider using a threat: 'We'll go along and tell him that if he doesn't give us the name, he can get two years. Yes, that's good, we can do that.'

Of course, a threat need not relate to bona fide legal power. I am with an inspector who wants to stop some striking employees from blocking the road. They are cheeky, and he invites three of them to talk by his car. When he gets to the car he opens its back door asking, 'Do you want a seat?' They explain that the gathering is about to disperse – and it does.

Such threats permit officers some measure of control. They are sometimes symbolic, sometimes more instrumental; sometimes they are combined with conning people. Whatever the tactic, the threat of the non-negotiable power that is available to police underpins this strategy.

Education and punishment
All of the strategies which have been described contain an element of education and punishment. However, there are occasions when officers are more explicit about the sufficiency of these objectives.

A constable is called to deal with a woman who has been stabbed in the hand by her husband. She goes to the local magistrates' court and is advised to return to the police station for assistance with an application for a warrant of arrest. It is then discovered that the officer who dealt with the incident and recorded his action as 'Advice given' actually left the conflict because he thought that the couple should face the consequences of their dispute, not least because they seemed to take no notice of his attempts to quieten them. This strategy of education by default is more clearly illustrated by another incident:

> I was patrolling with a colleague and saw four young people – two girls and two boys – arguing and scrapping on the pavement. One of the males hit a girl in the face and her nose started to bleed. My colleague drove to them quickly and asked the girl what was happening. He then turned to the boy, and as his account was being given, the girl began to shout and argue. The officer said, 'Look, I'll talk with you if you speak one at a time, but if not, I'm wasting my time.'
>
> The boy started talking and the girl began shouting again. Officer: 'Look, you obviously aren't going to tell me. If you want to get on with it, get on with it yourselves. I'm not bothered.'
>
> He then went to his car and as he drove away said to me, 'What's the point of me standing there and listening? I can't get anywhere when they do that, can I?'

Much later, in the early hours of the morning, another officer reported over the personal radio system that he might require some assistance to arrest a youth who, so a female told him, had threatened her with a knife. The officer who dealt with the initial incident recognized the parties concerned as those whom he had tried to control and he replied, 'No, we were there when the first blow was struck. It's just an argument between themselves. I don't know about knives, but they'd been to a party and they're just having an argument. I'd leave it if I were you.'

By absenting themselves these officers leave people to educate and/or punish each other. The police officers are involved, but their strategy is to allow disorderly people to face the consequences of the tangles into which they get themselves.

On other occasions officers are somewhat more active in fulfilling their educational task. A schoolboy had been caught writing on the wall of a cinema. The officers who caught him made him wash the slogan off with hot water and a scrubbing brush, a reprisal that was both educational and demanding, as

145

was the following tactic when some demonstrators who sat in a road were removed:

> There was a bloody great puddle by the side of the road, and when they were nicked they were swept right through this puddle. At the nick they refused to speak English, so [the officers] just said, 'Unless you speak English you don't go home,' and they began speaking it straight away.

All of these strategies have to be related to the legal powers afforded the police; this much is basic and given [D McBarnet, *Conviction: Law, the State and the Construction of Justice* (London: Macmillan, 1981)]. Recent research by Doreen McBarnet suggests that all of the strategies that the police adopt in crimework and tasks related to it are not deviations from, but acceptable within, our very flexible framework of law. However, it is also important to take into account the rationale of the officers who appear in these cameos of police work. They are less certain that their actions are acceptable to the courts, senior officers or the local population. The apparent confidence of Hilton's officers veils hesitation about making their working rules and practices known. The PC who argues, 'It all depends on who is boss out there' indicates a touchstone of policy at Hilton – 'This is a place inhabited by people who are going to get out of hand if we don't do something.' By one strategy or another, by one tactic or another, the appearance of police control – or more precisely, as far as our officers are concerned, the reality of control – is maintained.

All strategies and tactics are supported by this fundamental view and by specific aspects of knowledge about 'prisoners' and figures. The strategies emphasize control, hedonism, action and challenge – constituents of the occupational culture. These cultural strands of policing are woven together as practical skills employed on the streets. They may provoke a critical response; however, as far as possible, in the first instance, we have to see things from a police perspective. Nevertheless, these strategies seem to distance Hilton's officers from the constraints of legal rules and force directives, from the criticisms of the public that is policed, from the influence of the least powerful groups living and working in Hilton. Hilton's rank-and-file officers are free to police in their own style, with their own assumptions and strategies intact.

Clearly, an important aspect of craftsmanship is the possession of good communications skills. It is by being able to engage with members of the public on a personal level that the police officer can make a diagnosis about potential 'trouble' in the future, or about the moral worth of the suspect, and can decide whether a peacekeeping option will be adequate to preserve social order. The outcome of such interactions will often be contingent on the way that the conversation develops, an uncertainty which is emphasised in the writings of the labelling theorists (see Hester and Eglin, 1992, pp 91–140). In some situations, the police may be provoked and their reaction may have the effect of exacerbating a tense situation and actually producing a challenge which necessitates law enforcement. In other situations, it is the police who may provoke the challenge, with the same outcome. Often, such confrontations develop when the police encounter groups of juveniles. The latter may tease or goad the officers; the police officers may wish to assert their authority. Whoever starts the process, the other side's response will aggravate the exchange and invite an ever more forceful rejoinder, probably resulting in a law-enforcement decision (see, for example, Welsh, 1981).

One reason why police behaviour may be interpreted as provocative is that another element of craftsmanship is a generally suspicious or hostile attitude to the world at large. Police officers are trained to view the unpredictable and the irregular as indicating disorder and, essential to their survival, the possibility of danger. Being aware of danger can intensify such hostility because the police are aware that, ultimately, they can rely only on other officers to protect them from harm. Such an operational approach to encounters with the public is only likely to increase officers' sensitivity to a lack of respect for authority.

The effect of all these elements of craftsmanship is to encourage the police service to retain an independence, often amounting to isolation, from the community it polices. Support and companionship within the force become a dominant goal. This is manifested in actions such as assistance in a physical fight, taking part in initiation rituals, and socialising at police functions. It is also revealed in the pressures on police officers to produce the paperwork to back each other up in the face of superiors' and external scrutiny (see Smith and Gray, 1983, pp 57–61).

Many of the dimensions of policing culture that we have examined so far – conceptions of seriousness, judging the moral worth of suspects, sensitivity to danger, isolation from the community – are brought together in another aspect of craftsmanship, the use of stereotypes to identify potential offenders. In fact, the word 'stereotype' is misleading to the extent that it suggests mechanical decision-making. The reality is that the police use certain cues to assist them in predicting possible trouble and they constitute working presumptions which may be rebutted in the course of the encounter. The use of such presumptions is justified as embodying the culmination of police experience and, while many of them would not create 'reasonable suspicion' in the legal sense, they indicate that the police would be unhappy to wait for the legal threshold to be cleared before they intervened. The problem with working presumptions, however, is that they may indeed become self-fulfilling stereotypes. The stereotype predicts likely trouble based on police experience and, every time the prediction is correct, it appears to validate the use of the stereotype. The police are not encouraged to look beyond the stereotyped situation to discover other sources of offending and, especially if police experience is based on discriminatory assumptions, the targeting of unrepresentative groups of the population becomes institutionalised. Although police managers are aware of these drawbacks, the practical police officer knows that the job is made easier by using such short-cuts and that is why factors, such as age, dress, demeanour and incongruity of situation, feature so strongly in police training manuals (for example, Powis, 1977) – but also research on the use of stop and search powers.

147

Finally, although we should not given it too much significance, craftsmanship also implies an ability to create amenable working conditions – knowing how to operate the system. This may result in acts of 'marginal' law enforcement. Some occur because the police wish to create some excitement for themselves or wish to get off the street to the warmth of the police station, for example, arresting vagrants or drunks (see Cain, 1973). Others may be inspired by financial considerations, for example, processing which creates overtime (see Holdaway, 1983).

Successful craftsmanship is obviously related to the broad police function to maintain social order, discussed earlier. This means that the exercise of legal powers is often incidental from the police perspective. As Chatterton observed, such powers are best seen as 'resources used in peace-keeping'; when a police officer recounted his or her use of a power, 'the grounds for the *decision to use it* were to be found elsewhere than in the reasons provided to *justify* its use to the courts': (Chatterton, 1976, p 115). This approach to policing can create tensions within the police service, however, because it does not coincide with the professional attitude that has been encouraged at the managerial level since the late 1960s. Such professionalism embraces a number of themes. It requires that peacekeeping and law enforcement should be carried out with an understanding of the role that the police play in a democratic society. It accepts that power must be exercised in accordance with legal and political limits, and it also recognises that policing will be improved by a knowledge of the wider social problems that are associated with crime.

Extract 2.2.9

S Holdaway, *Inside the British Police* (1983) pp 157–159

During the early 1960s an important basis of police status and authority was diminishing. Many senior officers who had joined the police force after serving as officers in the armed forces were retiring: the scheme by which they had entered the police at officer rank had been abandoned; all recruits now joined as constables. These new recruits lacked the educational qualifications of their superior officers and offered few other skills on which a new competency could be built. The Royal Commission on the Police, which finally reported in 1962, drew attention to the issue of the public accountability of the police, sensitizing chief officers and the Home Office to the questioning of public authority. A number of criminal trials which received national publicity – particularly the revelations of malpractice and violence during the interrogation of some suspects by the Sheffield CID . . . , and the case of Detective Sergeant Challenor . . . , charged with perjury and conspiracy to pervert the course of justice – cast doubt on the accountability and methods of policing. If the supposed rigidity of police discipline could not be assured by quasi-military styles of command, where might an alternative base of internal control be found?

At this very time, just as police status and authority were being called into question, the police found themselves increasingly required to liaise with, for example, social service agencies, traffic departments and community relations officers. On the whole, the representatives of these and other public agencies had professional status and were legitimately concerned with matters of direct relevance to police policy and decision-making. As the old basis of police status and authority was eroded, so new foundations for parity with the representatives of these agencies and a more secure public image had to be laid. This parity was deemed to be located in the notion of a 'professional police'.

No longer would police competence be based on ill-defined 'common sense'. With the aid of the resources of what was then called the National Police College at Bramshill, now the Police Staff College, the expertise of the few serving graduate officers and a revised basic training for recruits, a body of knowledge drawn from a range of academic disciplines was applied to operational policing. Although it was never formally collated in a single text, this body of knowledge embraced both law enforcement and peacekeeping aspects of policing, recognizing their equality . . .

The development of a diverse corpus of knowledge prompted greater specialization in the service. Police specialists in traffic management, computerization, communications, community relations – the list is extensive – could now use their particular knowledge to liaise with those doing similar work in central and local government. Technology is of importance here because as it was, and continues to be, employed in the traffic control, data collection and patrol spheres of police work; an appearance of competence and professional status was enhanced.

Specialist knowledge and technological innovation were further associated in the context of police discretion. Senior officers – Mark was probably the first – began to articulate the view that errors like those highlighted in the Sheffield and Challenor cases would, as far as possible, be controlled with rigour. Corrupt officers would be purged from the police service; the rule of law would receive due regard. Bad law, however, would be exposed, and the police would lobby for reform of the law.

'The police alone see the whole crime reported to them, most of which never reaches a court and they are no longer the semi-literate, unthinking mercenaries of long ago. No discussion of criminal justice can be complete without their participation, far too long delayed.' (Mark, 1977, p 261)

Particular attention was paid to the arrest and questioning of a suspect. The 'professional method' emphasized the slow accumulation of evidence, if necessary with the support of specialist and technical aids to provide evidence of guilt before rather than after arrest. Law was henceforth to be invoked within a framework of 'informed discretion'.

'We decided that it would be worthwhile to discover everything we could about [criminals'] movements, their associates, and their weaknesses simply as an insurance against the probability that they would commit further crimes. Thus the description "target criminals".' (ibid., p 312)

If the consequence of working in this way within the rule of law led to the acquittal of guilty persons, so be it; but no one should expect the police to retire from public debate and to cease pressing for reform . . .

149

While attention was paid to crime, the police also recognized that many of the problems with which they dealt were social problems. Officers of all ranks now make judgements about such matters and display a professional competence which matches that of social workers and probation officers. The police, it is argued,

'are what might be described as social diagnosticians. Their role is to recognize social crises or their incipient causes and to activate other social agencies where expertise is needed. As yet the formalization of the role of social diagnostician has not been fully developed but it is in this field that the police should be expected to continue to operate. In a society where social welfare services are rapidly developing the police should seek to help more in the field.' (Alderson, 1979, p 45)

The implication of these ideas about knowledge and 'informed discretion' is that when officers choose whether or not to enforce the law, they do so either on the basis of information which has been gathered prior to arrest, possibly with the aid of 'neutral' technology, or on the basis of an assessment founded less on common sense than on an understanding of the diagnostic practices of the social services. The likelihood that a suspect will be abused is reduced; the police retain parity with their fellow professionals.

Finally, the established militaristic style of command changed quite dramatically to one of 'management'. Discipline remained paramount but was to be maintained more by persuasion, consultation and encouragement than by enforcing blind obedience to authoritative commands. A profession manages itself, mobilizing all the skills of motivation, task determination, delegation and so on that it can muster. One of the Assistant Commissioners of the Metropolitan Police, writing about 'man management' during the 1960s, made this point:

'Studies have shown that a democratically led group may become highly disciplined and efficient. Under democracy, the will of the group dominates and social pressure will force individuals into line. In other words, the discipline is from within the group, that is to say, self-discipline. Such self-discipline is easier to maintain than a forced discipline under autocratic rule where the force must be wielded from outside.' (Mahir, 1966, p 823)

Importantly, these features of 'managerialism' were first fostered among the supervisory ranks. Policy was to be fed down the hierarchy to the officer on the street; a well-qualified body of police managers would gradually remould the attitudes and practices of the lower ranks. The process was to be one of gradual, disciplined education rather than militaristic prescription.

Holdaway points out that the expectation was that managerial professionalism would have an effect on the way that the rank-and-file work. There would be less emphasis on 'search, chase and capture', more stress on strengthening community relationships, and greater respect for legal constraints on law enforcement. For lower-ranking, operational police officers, however, such managerial professionalism is not always consistent with their sense of craftsmanship. For all that internal rules prescribe the way that procedures must be followed, there is little guidance about the way that individual officers actually deal with the public. So police officers have to translate their understanding of managerial objectives into action. They do this by applying the ground rules, the 'practical professionalism' that they learn from other more experienced officers. The occupational culture tends to dominate, therefore, with managerial policy being interpreted in accordance with the ideas of the lower ranks. It continues to be the case, as a police officer told Chatterton:

> In this job it's not always possible to work to the book. Common sense plays a large part in police work and that's the angle that the practical copper sees the rules from. That's one of the ways you can tell the good bobby from what we call the plastic policeman – the bookman who doesn't know what the job is all about. (Chatterton, 1979, p 83)

Although, in theory, policy is implemented – 'top-down' – through the hierarchical structure of police forces, in practice, many aspects of policing place effective power to make decisions in the hands of the junior ranks. As Wilson observed, the police service has the special property that:

> within it discretion increases as one moves *down* the hierarchy (Wilson, 1968b, p 7)

This does not mean that managerial objectives have no impact on practical policing. Rather, as Manning describes (and see also James, 1979), a compromise occurs between the craftsmanship of operational officers and the policing goals of senior management: this is 'organisational reality'.

Extract 2.2.10

P Manning, 'The Social Control of Police Work' in S Holdaway (ed), *The British Police* (1979) pp 53–59

1. Regardless of the present position and activities of an officer, certain types of events can serve as a warrant for the avoidance, setting-aside, ignoring, or otherwise finessing an on-going assignment or, conversely, taking on a job when one is presently occupied. That is, even with the fixed-points systems where an officer was to be in a certain place at an appointed time, it was considered proper to have taken a quick look around the back of a store to investigate a movement, to check a pub that was excessively noisy which had a reputation for fights, or in other words, to look into something which might call for action and about which only the police could properly act (cf. Bittner, 1974). In my observations, cars would speed to calls of burglary in progress, man on the premises or a private loading dock and the like, even though in so doing they would violate the boundaries of the subdivision, arrive late and after the fact (sometimes to find six or more pandas on the scene as well as an area car and a Q car from another subdivision), and fruitlessly search for the person (having taken 20–30 minutes to arrive when working as the area car for a subdivision).

2.   The police see and read events within the context of their understanding that they are expected to 'do something' and usually fairly quickly. As Bittner ['A Theory of the Police' in H Jacob (ed), *Potential for Reform of Criminal Justice* (Beverly Hills: Sage Publications, 1974) p 33] notes:

A policeman is always poised to move on any contingency whatever, not knowing what it might be, but knowing that far more often than not, he will be expected to do something. The expectation to do something is projected upon the scene, the patrolman's diagnostic instinct is heavily coloured by it, and he literally sees things in the light of the expectation that he somehow has to handle the situation. The quick-witted and decisive act of the police is connected with the fact that they are attuned to dealing with emergencies; and in many instances, the response-readiness of the policeman rounds out the emergency character of the need to which the response was directed.

Two bits of evidence can suffice at this point. When police are unable to act decisively because constraints interfere about which they can do nothing, mounting frustration and anger accompany the work.

One Sunday, a loud outside alarm within earshot of the subdivision was ringing. Calls were received at the station, and efforts were made to contact the keyholder. Since the store, a new supermarket, had just opened that week, there was no keyholder registered in the file. Calls were made to the regional manager of the store who was in church, to the present manager who did not have a key to the inner office where the bell had to be disconnected, to the alarm company (which had no key), and finally again to all concerned in a futile effort to obtain a lead to who might in fact have a key. The chief inspector in charge was more concerned about not having the keyholder in the register than the bell, and amid mounting confusion, called the fire department to break down the door to silence the bell. They did, having shattered two doors and the alarm box door. They entered and progressively axed their way into the inner office. As they stood in the middle of the room with debris around them the keyholder arrived, having been reached as he arrived home from church.

When something can be done, and it results in an arrest or the proper paper, then a good bit of police work has been accomplished. For the crime-oriented uniformed man, it is more satisfying if one can be in on the beginning of a crime and personally bring it to a conclusion with an arrest.

A fifteen year old girl was out after midnight drinking in a 'dram house' and came into the station alleging that she had been beaten and raped by two youths. The PC interviewed her and was able to extract the information that she would recognize the two if she saw them again. One was a 'half-caste' (that is, a person with one black, one white parent), the other a Scots lad. With this information, the PC went to the collator of information in the station and discussed the facts with him: they talked over the street where she lived, the families there, and the youths who might fit this description. The PC said at this time he was feeling the smell of the hunt! He went out to have a look around and spotted two lads she described playing pinball in a cafe. (He could see them in the back through the plate

152

glass windows of the cafe.) He went in and arrested them; they were subsequently charged with two crimes each. This investigation and arrest lead to a commendation for the PC.

3.   The officer in situations attempts to do at least two things – to succeed within the premises he understood to properly guide his work and to create, if necessary, the proper official paper which will present events within the officially sanctioned format for such events as they are administratively understood. If succeeding means avoiding paper, then that will be done. 'Necessary paper' is defined by external pressures as much as by features of the incident. In other words, paper that is written is written at such time that one needs to show paper work. Sometimes, this action of generating the proper paper is called 'covering your ass'. Thus, the remarkable discretion of the officer is constantly in working tandem with the complex web of internal rules and guidelines. Lacking paper when it is called for later, he must present an adequate account or rationalization for having taken an action . . .
4.   These actions, such as the original alteration of the *pro forma* expectations of patrol (going to investigate a suspicious noise or light in the back of a building) are understood in the context of the events at hand, not against an absolute set of priorities of work that must be accomplished on that turn of duty. Thus, the inability to raise an officer on the panda (as frequently occurred when I observed in the radio reserve room of the subdivision) in and of itself could never be understood as evidence that the officer was 'skiving' or 'easing' if other features of the work were present, and there was no evidence that they were not. That is, the radio could have been turned off for an investigation, or for observations, or the radio transmittal was not powerful enough to reach the officer's present location, or the radio (either at the subdivision or in the car, the officers PR) could have malfunctioned. The orientation of the officer and his priorities, understandably, were to crime-related work, even on the subdivision where there was very little crime.
5.   This phenomenology of police work means that a problematic is introduced. The work is known at the official level by what is said to have been done, largely by officer pairs. This means at least two inferences can be drawn. What was said to have been done may or may not have happened in that way, but must be seen in that way until facts to counter it are known. Administrative support for patrol officer's actions is often symbolic in the sense that they cannot do otherwise unless they admit to aspects of discretion which are not admitted publicly. What was done could always have been done otherwise (in another order, by another officer, resolved in another fashion), and since it could have been, the doing of the police work cannot be in and of itself grounds for criticism of a colleague. This feature of the work, something shared with medicine and law for example, complements the peer support system as well as constructing and maintaining the guildlike boundaries of the occupation.
6.   The situation is shared by those present and since their proximal definitions constitute the working reality of the episode, they must communicate this to each other. Those present become a team, a unit of social organization that exists situationally for as long as the relevant definition of the situation is maintained . . . From a role perspective, this may involve laying out, communicating

153

and carrying off scripts such as those suggested above. From the team perspective, the question is control of the definitions of the situation vis-à-vis each police officer, as well as the officer and the public.

An officer was walking a beat in a quiet residential neighbourhood when he encountered a middle-aged matron who had been locked out of her home. She had a load of groceries and obviously could not climb in the window she designated as open (it was above the porch, near the roof of the porch). He sat aside hat and truncheon, climbed in through the window, and came downstairs to let her in. As she was grateful and was going to write a letter informing his superiors of his meritorious service, he had to carefully explain to her that what he did was against police regulations and quite possible against the law (since he had no evidence that she actually lived in the house). Any mention of his actions would probably become a black mark in his personnel file.

A recent sympathetic biography of a young DC who served on the drugs squad of the Metropolitan Police describes in lovely detail the social construction of a team definition of work (he was among the constables charged with perjury in the Salah case but was acquitted). He writes of 'inaccuracies' which arose from co-operation on booking in and out (officers would book their fellows in and out by phone, and as a result, great freedom of concealed movement was possible), and calls the diary a 'general guide to our whereabouts' [G Honeycombe, *Adam's Tale* (London: Arrow Books, 1974) p 183]. He further details the collusive behaviour that governed the reporting of overtime, signing off duty, and reimbursement for expenses (Honeycombe, 1974, 183–4 ff.). Analogous behaviour occurs between partners on patrol, with the general rule being that if one cannot control the definition of events on the ground, then one attempts to construct the proper paper. This often involved, as Honeycombe writes, and I had observed, a vertical situational clique where officers tacitly accept officially unacceptable behaviour because it was considered the sanctioned practice on the station.

7. The points considered under (3) above – the relative demand for paper or its situationally justified status – and this latter point about the problematic nature of administrative support produce a special kind of *suspicion* of paper, and indeed of all kinds of official action, rhetoric and statements of organizational intent and policy.

For example, the evaluation of the performance of officers is problematic in that sergeants claim to 'know what their officers are doing' (yet rarely observe their behaviour). Most sergeants and most officers considered written evaluations to be ritual without meaning, while evaluations and other official paper is taken by senior officers who do not otherwise have contact with men, or do not have other negative or disconfirming evidence, to constitute evidence of 'activity' on the ground. Officers on this subdivision did not worry about activity, or showing evidence of it, because they viewed the chief superintendent as 'community-relations' oriented. Thus, what is counted, in the minds of the constables, does not count, and what counts for them (those who were crime-oriented) did not count for senior officers. Paper was something written to satisfy the situation-at-hand if senior officers might have an interest or if the event might 'come back on you'. To some degree paper stood independent of

the form of events, but was generated on the basis of situational understandings . . . The idealized myths and rituals symbolizing altruism and service and commitment to the welfare of the men, normally used to transcend the mere material basis of organizational attachment and commitment, are seen as serving the purposes of only legitimating existing authority. Gouldner, Ritti and Ference ['The Production of Cynical Knowledge in Organizations' (1977) *American Sociological Review* 539–551] argue that information that undercuts the idealized myths or knowledge used to explain unknown events (for example, rumours and gossip) and reduces altruistic explanation is cynical knowledge. Clearly, all members of police departments possess an abundance of cynical knowledge, and when internal conflict surfaces, it becomes the dominant mode of or content of interpersonal communication. Thus, the solid front presented to the public at large on public and ceremonial occasions, or in court for example, crumbles from the inside because of cynical knowledge. This reapparent cynicism increases individualism and decreases identification of collective purpose; thus loyalty tends to be restricted to one's partners or squad and rarely extends to the organization as a whole [J Van Maanen, 'Working in the Street: A Developmental View of Police Behaviour' in H Jacob (ed), *The Potential for Reform of Criminal Justice* (Beverly Hills, California: Sage, 1974)]. If one extends this inference, one could suggest that the defence, 'one can't police by the book', might be related to this cynicism insofar as 'the book' is not impossible, but that it is not truly seen as a respectable, relevant guide to action in the first place. It serves as another form of cynical self-protection, rather than a statement of fact concerning the inadequacy of formal, written rules as a basis for police decisions (Van Maanen, personal communication).
8.   Since the interests of the officer on the scene are principally to control that scene, and to produce outcomes consistent with his definition of what needs doing, deciding whether, what and how to write up (see 3 above) is based in part upon the officers' perceptions of their readings of the interests of the supervising officers. Sergeants are usually the most significant of these referent others. In the subdivision, there were two day sergeants and one inspector or chief inspector on every turn. On late turn, the duty sergeant (Sergeant A) was not needed in the station, and since the men were senior and needed very little supervision, he would drive the second or reserve area car. His interest was in being 'one of the lads'. Supervision was left to the chief inspector, who liked to take out an unmarked CID car and occasionally cross our path at a distance. Since the radio was unreliable (see above) and the area car covered the entire subdivision (some parts of which were not in fact penetrated by radio transmissions), it was not always possible for reserve or supervising officers at the station to know from time to time precisely *where* a given area car was located. Thus, a vertical situational clique operated whenever Sergeant A and the normally assigned driver and radio operator rode together in the reserve area car. What was in the sergeant's interest they did, whether it was to run an errand (as it turned out, several stops were required) to find the proper nails for some modifications of his house, clock a speeder, ignore a cab that ran a red light (it was said that a ticket goes on his record and that he might lose his licence), or stop for a drink at a hospital party after we had arrived to check on a man who had been taken to the hospital in an ambulance.

155

9. Insofar as a car (panda or area car) responds to radio calls, then the prospective definitions of meanings of call-events provide the actionable features of those events. Van Maanen (1974, 106) writing about the American police, provides a summary statement that is consistent with my London observations:

> One can divide . . . dispatched (radio) calls into a rush, non-rush dichotomy. Rush calls are those involving 'real' police work. Statistically, however, non-rush calls are much more common. The decision to rush is, of course, a learned one, developed as the patrolman learns his territory and gains knowledge of the patrol lexicon. There is not a universal code for rush calls. They are dependent upon the dispatcher's choice of words, the time, the place, and the particular unit receiving the call and perhaps even the mood of the officer.

Let us trace this out a bit further for the implications it contains. If the event is in fact truly a 'rush call' (that is, if one discovers upon arrival that it is 'a man with a weapon' – always a rush – as well as a 'domestic' – sometimes a rush, mostly a nuisance), and it is treated otherwise, no one is in a position to know how quickly the car arrived on the scene (technically it would be possible if the dispatch were from force radio, and it were recorded by the car, and the operator called in precisely on arrival, and that car was the only car on the scene, and closest, and not beaten there by another, and so on. The point is the force radio does not know where a car is when a call is sent or accepted, only where it ends, if at all!) Conversely, if it were *not* a rush call and were so treated, no one knows the difference:

> We were driving the Rover 2000 area car, a powerful machine. J. The driver mentioned that the car's shifting mechanism had not been working well previously, was sluggish when shifting from low to high speeds, and that the car recently had been in the shop for repairs. We received a call on the PR that a woman was locked *into* her house with small children and needed assistance to get out. We chuckled at the reversal of normal circumstances. The car flew into action suddenly, going from about 20 miles per hour to 60 in the course of a few blocks. The car's engine smoothly wound out, even as the tyres began to slip on the slick, damp pavement, recently wet from a late summer shower. As we dodged in and out of the traffic, playing guessing games with mums bringing home children from nurseries, pensioners on wheels, and three-wheeled disabled persons' cars, the speedometer hit seventy.
>
> We arrived at the house, and as the conversation on the way there had suggested a panda had 'beat' us and the panda officer was waiting at the curb. Since the area car had priority, we dashed up, forced a window and extracted the old lady. The children were happy and slightly embarrassed at the predicament. Later, when I asked the driver why he had sped there, suggesting that he might have thought she was 'crazy', or would harm the children, he replied that he had 'just wanted to see if they had fixed the shifter properly'.

However, the most important calls received by any officer are those that involve, by implication, if not directly, criminal activity in progress or a threat to the well-being of a fellow officer.

We received a call while on the Q car (a car with subdivisional priority assigned to 'crime work') of a crime in progress reported at the distant point (some ten miles away). We dashed there at speeds approaching 70 miles an hour. Upon arrival, we discovered two area cars from the subdivision there, five pandas, and two cars full of CID officers. The actual event had been put on the air by the force radio as being 'in progress', but the call had been garbled, and officers had said that they thought it was because the officers reporting thought they saw movement. Investigations showed that the place had been broken into earlier, and no signs of life had been discovered when the first 'back-up' arrived.

A similar chase resulted from information about a man on the docks in a lumber yard. After an hour's wandering on the docks in the dark (I did not have a torch, they did), we found nothing. (We had previously made another 15 minute run near the far end of the subdivision, marginally outside the metropolitan city limits.)

Chases of various kinds also typically draw a cluster of vehicles to the place.

We heard a call of 'mental escapee loose'. We jumped in the car, raced to the scene, and found no less than three pandas, another area car, and a CID car on the scene. A naked mental patient had hopped a fence when officers had come to retrieve him, and one off the officers put out a radio call almost as his partner captured the man.

These calls are important symbolically because the arrival of officers to the scene communicates peer solidarity, and are significant regardless of their specific official outcomes (no paper was written by the officers I rode with on any of the above items).

Finally, this patterning of activity ensures that the officer learns to 'cover his ass', to 'keep out of trouble', and to look for easing opportunities (sanctioned breaks from routine), 'easy numbers' (soft, undemanding, jobs such as inside work in the winter, riding as radio operator in the area car), and a little 'skiving' or avoidance of expected work. Since these activities stood in contrast to 'real police work', while one was not doing real police work (there was very little of it to be done on this subdivision), one eased with impunity. The contrast between easing and work was lightly marked because of the low work load, although the mesh of possible disciplinary violations was salient . . . Unlike active, crime-oriented officers, these officers, with very few exceptions, did not attempt to build up arrests by surveillance of pubs, and so occupied themselves observing traffic (and young women), running personal errands in the small shops, and endlessly talking and driving through the grey, ageing and tired streets of London.

Here, it is important to note that all police officers, no matter what rank, start from a common base; although there have been various schemes for accelerated promotion, there is no 'officer entry' to the service. This means that all officers have a sense of shared experience and solidarity. This helps police officers to maintain a careful balance between fulfilling the aims of practical policing and satisfying their superiors. The result of organisational

157

reality, however, is that the determinants of actual policing decisions are some-what fluid and unpredictable. Certainly, they may not always reflect the pol-icies or the criteria contained in the law that is being enforced. Furthermore, in recent years, the locus of organisational reality has extended as a result of developments in police powers. As many commentators have noted, arrest is no longer regarded as the culmination of an investigation. Instead, it is seen as a means of bringing a suspect into the sphere of police control in order to assemble evidence. Managerial professionalism insists that the inquiry is con-ducted in accordance with the procedures set out in PACE and its Codes of Practice. But, as we shall see in Chapter 3, practical professionalism constantly challenges those constraints.

(d) Organisational pressures

Organisational pressures operate at different levels within the police service. Overall policing policy is the responsibility of senior officers and, while there is a general tendency for objectives to be rationalised and centralised through Home Office Circulars, the advice of the Inspectorate of Constabulary and the guidance of ACPO (the Association of Chief Police Officers), there remains considerable potential for local priorities to be emphasised. Different police forces may have different styles of policing. Some senior officers may have particular enforcement objectives. Increasingly, the police are engaged in pro-active enforcement on a highly organised basis. We will examine these issues in turn.

(i) The ethos of the force

The most intangible organisational constraint on decision-making is the ethos which characterises every police force. But its influence may be significant, as Wilson's early research in the United States demonstrated (Wilson, 1968a). Wilson compared two cities, which he called Western and Eastern. The police force in Western City had a professional style, characterised by a bureaucratic organisation and political impartiality. In its day-to-day decision-making, it did not discriminate between different types of suspect. It was perceived to be more severe on them, however, because it tended to process more of them and did not 'let them off' or 'turn a blind eye'. Within the force, there was a well-developed system for checking decisions about processing. By contrast, in Eastern City, there was a non-professional, more 'fraternal', style of policing. It was decentralised and less bureaucratic, albeit more subject to political influences, and the neighbourhood was the focus of decision-making. While there was less formal processing, the officers, many of whom had grown up in the areas that they policed, maintained control by meting out a punitive form of rough justice.

158

In later work (Wilson, 1968b), Wilson refined his analysis and described three major styles of police administration. The first was what he called the 'watchman' style. It amounted to peacekeeping or order maintenance on an institutional scale. There was a greater tolerance of minor infractions of the law especially by juveniles who were 'expected' to misbehave and would be ignored or treated informally. There was less enforcement in support of black people (who were regarded as marginal members of the community). Traffic violations and private disputes would be dealt with informally also, provided they did not involve serious offences or a flouting of police authority. By contrast, the 'legalistic' style was characterised by law enforcement. There was an expectation that infractions, even minor ones, would result in arrests and a single standard of community conduct was applied to all groups. Not surprisingly, such police departments tended to produce high levels of arrest and formal processing. The third style was what Wilson described as the 'service' style. This referred to the police acting 'as if their task were to estimate the "market" for police services and to produce a "product" that meets the demand' (as opposed to the provision of community support services). Police departments characterised by this style were typically associated with stable, middle-class areas. They encouraged policing which was relaxed, courteous to residents but suspicious of outsiders, and tending to the frequent use of informal warnings and involvement of juveniles' parents.

Wilson's work showed that the general ethos of a force can influence the exercise of discretion. Although the context and organisation of policing is quite different, similar differences in style have been observed in British policing. One of the first studies, by Maureen Cain, compared a city and a country police force (Cain, 1973). She described how officers in the city force had little social contact with the community that they policed and were more inclined to process 'the rough', those members of the public who were not regarded as 'people like us'. By contrast, officers in the country force were much more involved in their local community. They relied on it for information and co-operation, as well as prestige for themselves and respect for their families. In terms of formal processing, therefore, they tended to be less severe on suspects and would resolve more problems informally.

These differences in ethos are the result, partly of policing traditions and partly of the circumstances of the police job. Occasionally, there are examples of attempts to instil a force ethos by managerial dictate. The leadership of Greater Manchester Police, by the charismatic James Anderton, was widely regarded as having an impact on the everyday policing of moral behaviour as well as other policies (see McLaughlin, 1994). One of the more concerted efforts to influence policing styles, however, has been the development of some kind of 'community policing' in all British police forces. Although there are different approaches to community policing, it typically involves local police becoming closely involved with their area, developing special knowledge of its inhabitants and their difficulties, and liaising with other agencies (such as social services, the local authority, the probation service, or schools) and seeking to deal with crime in the broader context of solving the community's problems.

The approach was developed most fully in Devon and Cornwall Constabulary when John Alderson was Chief Constable. He reorganised the force so that community policing permeated every aspect of decision-making to reflect his vision of a different approach to policing. Based on a liberal political philosophy, some aspects of that vision were especially relevant to police organisation. He saw the police as playing an important leadership role in their local communities, helping the community to dispel the social conditions which give rise to crime. He also saw the police as participating much more fully in community decision-making at all levels and encouraged police membership of relevant committees so that information could be fed into the force's policy making (see Alderson, 1979). Community policing is not attractive to traditional operational officers, however, because it does not entail the crime-fighting that the occupational culture values. But, as Alderson demonstrated, one way that management can make it significant is to show that it does actually have worth in terms of law enforcement (community liaison is a valuable source of criminal intelligence) or to provide career advancement through community policing (the post of liaison officer may be made into a necessary career rung). The effect of this policy was to encourage peacekeeping options, even in situations where the instinctive response of most police officers might be anticipated to be law enforcement (for an example, involving a public protest, see *R v Chief Constable of Devon and Cornwall, ex parte Central Electricity Generating Board* [1981] 3 All ER 826, at pp 831–2).

The appointment of 'community constables' has provided a different organisational role for such police officers and that has a direct effect on the way their discretion is exercised, as the research of Fielding and his colleagues showed (Fielding et al, 1989). Officers on the beat would respond to incidents in terms of a choice between peacekeeping or law enforcement. For example, when called to help evict a man from a woman's flat, they were concerned with helping the woman and removing the cause of her trouble as quickly as possible. They did not investigate the couple's relationship (they had both been patients at a local mental hospital) and were not interested in what would happen to the man once he had left, nor whether the incident might be repeated for another patrol to resolve some time later. The approach of the community constable was different. When called to assist a community worker who was being confronted by some angry youths who were about to be sacked from a training scheme, he acted more like an impartial referee between the two sides. He could have handled the problem through law enforcement because there was evidence of assault and threatening behaviour, but it would have cast him in a partisan role and would have aggravated the situation. Rather than seeking a quick solution, he spent some time in calming the confrontation. Such a response was possible because the organisation of the force allowed it. Community constables were former beat officers but they had the facilities and the time to develop investigative and negotiating skills, and success was not assessed in terms of process rates. However, organisational support was essential for the community policing role to be maintained. When managerial enthusiasm waned, and organisational resources were withdrawn, discretion was once more judged in terms of traditional policing norms.

(ii) Local objectives

Local objectives may develop as a response to public demand; there may be a spate of burglaries or muggings which require resources to be targeted. Other local, organisational objectives may be directed more at the management of police work than enforcement policy as such. Meeting those objectives will contribute to crime control, but only incidentally. For example, superiors will want to assess the work of their officers and, to the extent that they be efficient, but not so successfully that they remove the justification for their existence! Too many crime reports and arrests will also have implications for investigation and may increase the burden on the CID or require uniformed officers to be diverted away from work on the street. (As we shall see, later, there may be pressure for those reasons also to keep crime figures down). These considerations have implications for decision-making because they offer a set of quantitative measures with which police officers can demonstrate that they have achieved the tasks set by their superiors. But it does not follow that the outcome is qualitatively better for the criminal justice process in general, let alone the individual members of the public who are subject to such decisions. Practical police officers are well aware of the tension between quantitative and qualitative measures of their work (and for further discussion of this tension, see later in this chapter and in Chapter 6) and they resolve it through the organisational compromises discussed earlier. Sometimes, the result may be a paper exercise, whereby an arrest is attributed to an officer who did not make it. At other times, arrests may be generated in circumstances when they would not otherwise occur.

Extract 2.2.11

D J Smith, J Gray and S Small, *Police and People in London* (1983)
Vol 4, pp 56–61

'Figures' is the disparaging term used by police officers for the evaluation of their performance in terms of numbers: typically, the number of traffic process reports or the number of arrests made in a particular period. There are a number of reasons for the contempt associated with the term. One is resentment at what is seen as a crude attempt by senior officers to get constables to do something useful. Another is the conviction that certain kinds of arrest are far more valuable than others, and that assessment in terms of 'figures' confounds good and bad police work. Thirdly, police officers never fully accept without misgivings the idea that making arrests or doing traffic process reports should be taken as the objectives of police work: they argue that this will produce wrongful or unnecessary arrests and pointless traffic process reports.

. . . Looking at the matter from the viewpoint of the constables, 'figures' are not an objective that they recognise as springing from their own conception of police work; they are something you may have to get, on occasion, to satisfy more senior officers. It would, however, be a gross exaggeration to say that most constables are motivated from day to day by a need to get 'figures'. This only applies to probationers, to others who are at transitional stage (for example, trying to get into CID or a specialist group) and to officers working in units which they fear may be wound up unless they continue to show good results. Also, 'figures' have no relevance at all to promotion.

Probationers (officers in their first two years of service) have three-monthly meetings with their chief-superintendents when they are expected to produce returns of work and show that they have had experience of a range of policing activities. The sanction is that their appointment as police officers cannot be confirmed (even if they pass the final examination) without the support of their chief-superintendent. Few constables think that this system works to ensure that probationers undertake a reasonable balance of work. The usual view is that they tend to carry out certain simple operations in a mechanical fashion in order to produce 'figures'. In particular, most traffic process work that is done by officers outside the specialist traffic group is done by probationers, because it is easy to build up 'figures' that way, and because there is no pressure on confirmed constables to undertake this kind of work. A young PC who was two years out of probation put it this way.

> When you're a probationer you must get 'figures' so that you have something to show at your meeting with God's deputy (the chief-superintendent). You have to build up the figures with traffic process. But once you have passed your final exam, nobody cares whether you do one or a hundred traffic processes a month.
> DJS: Could you get away with doing nothing?
> PC: You probably could do, but luckily there is nobody on our relief like that, except for one who is not with us at the moment – he's in the Coroner's office.

That same night this PC took a probationer with him in his panda car, and at about 3 am they went down a long residential road while the probationer wrote out a process report for every car he found without an up-to-date tax disc. There were twelve of these cars in the single road, which was as many as the probationer needed to keep up his 'figures'. Of course, this was a purely clerical exercise that provided no experience of police work at all, since the probationer did not meet or talk to anyone. Not all chief-superintendents would give any credit for simply 'writing out tickets': in fact some told us plainly that they considered this kind of activity to be totally useless from every point of view. But this probationer would not have behaved like this if his own chief-superintendent had not encouraged him to.

On another District, the probationers said they were set a target of two process or arrests and five stops a day. A popular way of getting the process 'figures' was to stand by a bus lane and report the motorists driving in it. Once an officer was out of probation he would be very unlikely to do anything of this kind.

Probationers are responsible for keeping their own records of the work they have done so that they have something to show to the Chief-Superintendent. However, once they are out of probation, uniform officers are not expected to keep a record of this kind, and there is no ready way in which senior officers can pull out statistics, from all the forms filled in, showing the number of arrests, stops or traffic process reports done by an individual officer. (CID officers do, however, keep a record of their arrests at the back of their diaries.) Apart from probationers, the officers who have to show 'figures' are those working in crime squads and hoping to be selected for CID, and those trying to get into a uniform specialism. In both cases there is a selection procedure including a method of finding out what the officer's experience is and what kind of work he has been doing recently. Under the old system, whereby officers worked as Temporary Detective Constables for about two years before being selected for CID, this pressure was probably greater than it is now (though some of the stories told are exaggerated and romanticised).

At one Division the members of the crime squad thought that senior officers were less than fully committed to the continuance of the squad. All of them wanted to stay working in the squad either because they hoped to join CID or because they liked the nature of the work and the more flexible working environment (compared with a relief). They thought that their places on the squad were assured as long as they continued to make 5–10 arrests a week, but worried if they failed to achieve this 'quota'.

It is widely believed that 'figures' are a bad criterion of performances and that the use of such a criterion leads to unnecessary or unjustified arrests and stops. Police officers will prove that the criterion is crude and mechanical by finding ways of distorting the 'figures'. As the uniform sergeant in charge of a crime squad put it:

It's really quite simple. If anyone in the crime squad comes under attack for not getting figures, the rest of us make sure that anyone nicked for a two or three-day period is shown to the person criticised.

Unfortunately, the mildly mischievous practice of misleading a supervising officer can lead to the far more serious one of misleading a court: for 'showing the arrests to the person criticised' can mean fabricating evidence to make it appear that this person actually made the arrests when he did not ... It is significant that the motive has to do with the internal management of a police force rather than with any desire to increase the chance of conviction.

At the same Division, concern was suddenly expressed somewhere high up in the hierarchy about the numbers of burglaries, which had steeply increased in a large part of the ground. The message bumped all the way down to the sergeant in charge of the crime squad, which was expected to do something

about it. When members of the squad heard about this, one of them immediately volunteered a suspect who 'might be good for one or two jobs'. His
solution to the problem was 'Let's go round and nick Danny'. The only justification for doing so was that Danny 'had form' for burglary, that a particular
shop had been burgled three nights running and that Danny was the only local
criminal who was stupid enough to do a burglary three times in the same
place. The sergeant thought this was a good idea, and he went (with JG) to
arrest Danny at a building site, but could not find him there. To the annoyance
of the crime squad, someone on a uniform relief did arrest Danny later that
same day, and Danny did admit to the shop burglaries. We did not find out
how or why Danny came to be arrested.

We did not see police officers making unnecessary or wrongful arrests for
the sake of the 'figures', though we did hear stories about it, mostly going
back to the old Temporary Detective Constable system. A PC who had at one
time been in the CID said that when he was trying to get in, he and the other
TDCs had worked on a quota system, which meant that they had to achieve a
certain number of arrests a week.

> If you got to Friday and that space at the back of your diary wasn't filling
> up, you used to go out or were sent out in search of bodies (arrests).
> People got nicked for things like sus, just to make everything look right.
> I just couldn't do it and the DI (detective inspector) used to say to me
> 'Why have you got so few arrests and everybody else seems to be able
> to manage to get X per week?' I would say 'I just didn't see the crimes
> committed, Sir'. He would say 'Either you're calling your colleagues liars or
> you're just not looking hard enough'.

A uniform sergeant boasted about the success of his recent posting to the
Q car in terms of the number of arrests made: 'We had 64 bodies in eight
weeks'. At the same time he strongly criticised the use of arrests as a criterion of performance by management. He had at one time been an aide to CID
(a TDC) under the old system and told rather lurid stories about the methods
used to get 'figures'.

> There was a space in the back of your diary for arrests. The quota was
> two per week. If you didn't get the quota come Friday you had to grab
> just anyone or buy the DI a bottle of Scotch. It was wicked in those days –
> you could be back in a top hat on the Monday. What some of the aides at
> X Police Station used to do was suspend a jemmy from an archway by a
> piece of twine. The paddies would come out of the local pub, pissed, and
> one of them would grab the jemmy. Then he'd be nicked with his dabs all
> over it for the old offence of going equipped for house-breaking. I used to
> know an old DS (detective sergeant). When he worked in the Q car he
> used to carry a briefcase. In this briefcase he carried a Luger and ten
> rounds. They'd go out and pick up the first old drunk they saw and put him
> in the back of the car. The DS would say 'What you going to have? (What
> charge are you going to admit to?) You can have a bit of sus, a bit of
> burglary . . . or you can have this Luger and ten rounds.' So the bloke
> would put his hands up to something and the Q car had its body for the
> day. Mind you, I'm talking about some time ago.

J G: Does it still happen?
Sergeant: Of course it does. But it isn't as bad as the old days.

However exaggerated these stories are, they show that the junior ranks are extremely sceptical about 'management by figures' and hostile towards it. This is partly because they resent any attempt to set targets which may mean that they have to work harder; but it is partly because of genuine misgivings about the nature of the criterion and the abuse it could lead to.

(iii) Proactive planning

Thus far, we have emphasised the role of police officer as constable, exercising an independent discretion within the confines of practical policing. The general picture has been one of the police reacting to events, by responding to the public's requests for assistance or chancing upon suspicious activities. But a significant amount of law enforcement no longer follows that pattern. Increasingly, police actions are being planned as parts of strategies designed to tackle particular problems. The result is considerably less scope for individual officers to make decisions that are inconsistent with team objectives.

One manifestation of such proactive policing has been with us for some time. The work of the CID, especially when its resources are directed towards the investigation of one or two serious crimes, provides examples of officers' attention being focused on a single goal in preference to wider aims of crime control. Its natural development has been the creation of specialised squads to deal with, for example, murder, vice, drugs, robbery, organised crime, fraud, stolen vehicles or burglary, and the formation of a national crime squad was announced in mid-1996.

A second instance of proactive policing is a refinement of such specialisation. The use of criminal intelligence has become much more sophisticated. Sometimes, this involves high-profile criminals being targeted and evidence being carefully collected to maximise the chance of convictions. More mundanely, the use of intelligence allows the police to conduct investigations by elimination, whereby the matching of a crime to an offender profile (a development of the traditional use of the *modus operandi*) enables a pool of likely suspects to be identified and rounded up for interrogation. One side-effect of specialised, intelligence-gathering approaches to law enforcement is that fewer resources may be devoted to community-based beatwork. This may lead uniformed police to engage in more reactive 'fire-fighting', with a greater likelihood that problems may have to be solved by formal processing instead of peacekeeping methods. An important consequence of this approach to enforcement is that the focus of policing activity shifts from the street to the interrogation room; it is there that crime is 'discovered'. But the approach to policing on the beat may also be affected. Uniformed officers on patrol are playing a much more important role in collecting the intelligence which forms the basis of targeted enforcement. They are encouraged to secure the services of informants and to cultivate people who may be sources of information, such as shopkeepers, local officials, taxi-drivers, news vendors and other reliable members of the community. Much of this information may be hearsay or gossip but may be considered adequate to construct profiles of likely suspects who may, in terms of practical professionalism if not legal justification, merit further inquiries. (See Kinsey et al, 1986, especially at pp 137–143; see also Baldwin and Kinsey, 1982.)

The third expansion of proactive policing is the most controversial. To solve the problems of containing public disorder, the police have developed techniques of organised response which subsume the individual constable's discretion to the demands of a paramilitary force. All police forces now maintain riot squads and all police officers undergo riot training. This involves learning how to use anti-riot protection gear and weaponry and how to act in concert with other officers under the command of a superior. If peacekeeping occurs in situations of public disorder, it is of the crudest sort. If law enforcement ensues, it involves the most haphazard snatching of suspects from the crowd. In either case, individual officers have little or no opportunity to make personal judgments about the situation, of the kind that we noticed above in discussing ordinary patrol work.

Jefferson describes paramilitary policing of a public order event as having four stages. First, there is the 'preparation'. This requires the police to be ready for all eventualities and that includes not only physical readiness but also psychological preparation. Such preparation is often finalised while the officers wait, in vans, buses or police canteens, for the action to start, and the confined atmosphere may lead to the expectation that trouble will occur. To members of the public, however, such a well-prepared body of police may appear unduly provocative. The second stage of paramilitary policing is 'controlling space', separating the areas which the crowd may use and the ones which the police wish to defend. To do this, the crowd may have to be moved around and some may resent that. Their resentment may be interpreted as trouble by the police, confirming their expectations during preparation, and so will justify a firm response. The crowd may then react, in turn, against what they interpret as police excess. The third stage is 'controlling the crowd'. Here the techniques of paramilitary policing will be employed: the use of horses, dogs, riot shields and snatch squads. The latter, in particular, combine supportive team work with an apparently random and typically forceful enforcement. If this leads to further resentment from the crowd, the situation may escalate and serious violence may be perpetrated on both sides. Once control has been asserted, the fourth stage is 'clearance', as the crowd is dispersed. Again, there are many opportunities for confrontation. (See Jefferson, 1990, pp 84–86.)

Advocates of paramilitary policing maintain that negative attitudes to its adoption can be traced to its association with authoritarian state control. They argue that, on the contrary, the training in military-style responses actually introduces a discipline to law enforcement.

Instead of encouraging the use of excessive force, disciplined and concerted action is more likely to reduce the force required effectively to restore and maintain order. (Waddington, 1987, p 40)

But Jefferson's rejoinder is more convincing in the light of the research that we have examined so far.

How can we explain this apparent paradox – that the most supervised form of policing can produce the most apparently unconstrained type of police behaviour? The answer is that when police move on the offensive, the independence of the office of constable takes over. In such situations offences take precedence and the rank structure is effectively neutralized. In other words, supervisory powers become subordinated to constabulary ones. (Jefferson, 1990, p 55)

Given the operational independence of police officers, effective supervision becomes impossible once discretion is allowed to implement public order objectives.

3. IMPLICATIONS OF POLICE DECISIONS

(a) A select group: the relationship between suspects and the extent of crime

When the police decide to enforce the law, they are choosing the group of individuals which forms the basis of all subsequent decisions in the criminal justice process. It is difficult to quantify the relative size of the sample selected, but we can be confident that it is quite small. Statistics about the extent of crime show that a large proportion of criminality is not even known to the police. But, of the crimes which they do know about, a large number cannot be attributed to particular offenders. Official measures of the extent of crime rely on the annual *Criminal Statistics*. However, it has long been recognised that they provide a limited account of the total amount of crime committed. This is because the basis for measurement is 'notifiable crimes recorded by the police' and that is affected by three important variables. Most significant is the extent to which crimes are reported to the police. A second is the exercise of police discretion in compiling the record. A third factor, which will not be pursued here (but it is discussed in the appendices to the *Criminal Statistics*), is that inconsistencies in applying technical rules, dealing with the classification of offences and recording practice, can have an impact on the size and trends of the figures. The combined effect of these factors is to produce a discrepancy between the number of crimes actually committed and the number recorded; this is described as the 'dark figure of crime'. Since 1982, the British Crime Survey (BCS) has attempted to quantify the dark figure of crime in England and Wales on a systematic basis. The results of the sixth survey were reported in 1996.

Extract 2.3.1

C Mirrlees-Black, P Mayhew and A Percy,
The 1996 British Crime Survey 1996 **(1996) p 9**

. . . Earlier sweeps were carried out in 1982, 1984, 1988, 1992 and 1994. The survey asks a large, random sample of nearly 16,500 people aged 16 and more about offences they have experienced in the preceding year.

THE BCS AND POLICE COUNT OF CRIME

The BCS and offences recorded by the police both measure various aspects of crime at the national level. They are complementary series which together provide a better picture of the nature of crime than could be obtained from either series alone. The main features of the two measures are below.

The British Crime Survey

- Starting in 1982, it measures both reported and unreported crime.
- Provides an independent measure of trends in crime which is not affected by changes in reporting to the police.
- Does not measure crime at the small area level well.
- Does not generally include those under 16.
- Counts common assaults.
- Crime against commercial and public sector establishments are not counted in a household survey.
- Those in institutions are not covered. Their experiences of crime could differ.
- It cannot measure victimless crimes, nor those where a victim is no longer available for interview.
- Does not measure fraud. Nor does it measure sexual offences well (though information is collected).
- Collects information on what happens in crime: e.g., when crimes take place, and their effects in terms of injury and property loss.

Offences recorded by the police

- Have been collected since 1876. They comprise more serious offences for which suspects can be tried in court.
- They are a good measure of the workload of the police.
- Provide data at the level of 43 police force areas.
- Measure crime affecting those under 16.
- Common assaults are not recorded by the police for statistical purposes.
- Crimes against commercial and public sector establishments are counted by the police.
- Cover crimes reported by those in institutions.
- 'Victimless' crimes are counted (e.g., drug and alcohol misuse), and so is murder and manslaughter.
- Include fraud, as well as consensual and non-consensual sexual offences.
- Collect information about number of arrests, who is arrested, the number of crimes detected, and by what method.

168

The BCS does not provide a complete count of crime. Some crimes, such as fraud or drug offences, are unlikely to be covered in what is a household survey. Other sources of error are the difficulty of ensuring that samples are representative, respondents' inaccuracies in remembering information, respondents' reluctance to talk about their experiences as victims, and respondents' failure to realise that an incident could be considered a crime and is relevant to the survey. However, the BCS still provides a more complete picture than the figures recorded by the police and its results are now routinely incorporated into the commentary to the *Criminal Statistics*.

Extract 2.3.2

Home Office, *Criminal Statistics England and Wales 1996* (1997) p 35, table 2A, paras 2.4–2.9 (footnotes omitted)

Comparison of the results of the British Crime Survey with statistics of notifiable offences recorded by the police

England and Wales 1995

Offences	Notifiable offences recorded by the police		BCS best estimate of number committed (Thousands)	Best estimate of percentage recorded
	Total (Thousands)	Adjusted for comparison[1] (Thousands)		
Violence against the person:				
Wounding	203	174	860	20%
Other, not covered by BCS	9			
Burglary:				
Burglary in a dwelling	644	644	1,754	37%
Other, not covered by BCS	596			
Robbery and theft from person	128	123	984	13%
Theft and handling stolen goods:				
Theft from vehicle (with loss)	715	657	2,522	26%
Theft or unauthorised taking of a motor vehicle (with loss)	431	402	499	81%
Theft from vehicle and attempted thefts or unauthorised taking of a motor vehicle (no loss)	176	150	1,291	12%
Theft of a pedal cycle	169	183	660	28%
Other, not covered by BCS	961			
Criminal damage	914	461	3,415	13%
Other, not covered by BCS	154			
Total	5,100	2,794	11,986	23%

(1) Adjustments necessary because of the sample structure and coverage of the BCS. Details of the adjustments are given in '1996 British Crime Survey (England and Wales) Technical Report' (SCPR 1996).

The extent of recording

2.4   The statistics of offences recorded by the police provide only a partial picture of crime committed. This is because not all crimes are reported to the police and not all those that are, are recorded by them. Less serious offences are particularly under represented in recorded statistics. Moreover, the propensity of the public to report offences to the police is influenced by a number of factors and may change over time. Trends in the numbers of offences recorded may differ therefore from trends in the number of offences committed.

2.5   These factors are apparent when recorded crime statistics are compared with results from victim surveys such as the British Crime Survey and, for domestic burglary, the General Household Survey.

2.6   The 1996 British Crime Survey (BCS) provides estimates for offences committed in 1995 and shows that, for the sum of offences in categories which can be compared to those recorded by the police, the amount of crime actually committed is perhaps four times the number of crimes recorded by the police.

2.7   Comparison of BCS estimates of crimes committed with police recorded crimes reveals that there were:

- **almost three** times as many **domestic burglaries** committed as recorded;
- **almost four** times as many **bicycle thefts**;
- **four** times as many **thefts from vehicles**;
- **four** times as many **woundings**;
- **seven** times as many offences of **vandalism**; and
- **eight** times as many **robberies and thefts from the person**.

2.8   For **thefts of vehicles** BCS and police recorded figures are **similar**, because victims more readily report such thefts to the police in order to obtain help in recovering their vehicles and for insurance purposes.

2.9   Over the period 1981–1995, for those crimes which can be compared, recorded crime increased by 91 per cent. The BCS shows a lower rise of 83 per cent. This is equivalent to an annual average increase of 5 per cent in recorded crime and 4 per cent in the BCS. An increased proportion of crimes reported to the police and recorded by them is cited as the main reason for the overall discrepancy.

In accounting for the discrepancy between the police records and victims' accounts, the reporting of crime is critical. Much will depend on the attitudes of the parties involved and the way they define an incident: was it a joke? was it serious? For example, an apparent fight in the street could be characterised as a harmless piece of fooling around or as an assault. Then, the parties must decide whether the incident is worth doing something about. Generally, the victim will be the most influential person at this stage. Bottomley and Coleman reported that 80 per cent of recorded crime had been reported by the victim, compared with 3 per cent by the general public. Significantly, only 14 per cent of crimes were reported by the police themselves (Bottomley and Coleman, 1981). The reasons for the public not reporting crimes are revealed in the British Crime Survey (and compare also Jones et al, 1986).

Extract 2.3.3

C Mirrless-Black, P Mayhew and A Percy, *The 1996 British Crime Survey 1996* (1996) pp 23–25 (footnotes omitted)

Whether or not victims report offences they have experienced to the police is a critical factor for criminal justice. What is reported will largely determine the nature and size of the police workload, since the vast majority of offences remain outside the scope of action by the police unless notified by victims.

UNREPORTED CRIME

Different forms of crime have different reporting rates. Figure 1 shows the variation. Car thefts, burglaries and bicycle thefts are usually reported. Vandalism to cars and thefts of household and personal property are often not.

Figure 1 Percentage of incidents reported to the police (British Crime Survey, 1996)

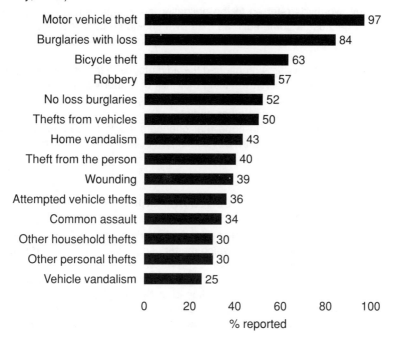

Why victims do not report

In the BCS, victims are asked this directly. They can give more than one reason. Mainly, they felt the incident was not serious enough (40 per cent said this), that the police would be unable to do much about it (29 per cent), or would not be interested (20 per cent). Some victims felt that what occurred was not a matter for the police, but better dealt with themselves (19 per cent). Overall, few people mentioned inconvenience of reporting (4 per cent), fear of reprisal (4 per cent), or fear and/or dislike of the police (<1 per cent).

The relative importance of these reasons varied between types of crime (. . .). Assaults, for instance, were particularly likely to be thought not a matter for the police, and more victims feared reprisals (11 per cent did so). These results do not differ in substance from previous sweeps of the BCS, and they are much in line with survey results from other countries.

Some reasons for not reporting are not without ambiguity. 'Nothing could be done' can mean that the harm, loss or damage cannot be rectified; that there is insufficient proof of what happened; or that it seems impossible that an offender could be apprehended. 'The police would not be interested' may signify that the victim feels uneasy about bothering the police; or that he/she feels the police would not want, or be able, to give the matter due attention.

Why victims report

Although most crime surveys ask victims why they did not report to the police, fewer ask why they *did* choose to. The 1996 BCS reinstated this question, used earlier in 1984 . . . In summary:

- Nearly two-thirds referred to the obligation on victims to notify the police, either because a crime such as their own should be reported, or that their incident had been a serious one, or that reporting might lessen the risk to others.
- Just over half of victims mentioned the advantages to themselves in reporting: recovery of property, reducing their risk of further victimisation, getting help from the police, and notifying the police to satisfy the requirements of insurance companies and other bodies.
- Retributive motives – the hope that offenders would be caught and punished – weighed with a third of victims, particularly victims of burglary with loss, theft of motor vehicles, and robbery.

REPORTING AND THE SERIOUSNESS OF CRIME

One facet of the relationship between recorded crime and the BCS is whether police figures represent crimes 'which matter': i.e., those crimes which people feel are sufficiently serious to report.

Seriousness can be gauged in one way through offence classification such as the group of serious crimes mentioned in Section 2 (wounding, robbery, burglaries with loss and thefts of vehicles). Such a classification is accessible, but not entirely reliable, since some crimes which would generally not be

172

considered serious may cause victims great upset (e.g., a common assault by a stranger), or substantial financial loss (e.g., some incidents of criminal damage). By the same token, some 'serious' crimes may carry low losses (e.g., some burglaries), or less distress than say a serious vandalism. Analysis shows, though, that of the serious crimes as defined, a third were *not* reported to the police. Most of the unreported incidents in this group were woundings (two-thirds were).

The BCS has another measure which may be better for assessing serious-ness in terms of the impact of crime. Victims were asked to rate what hap-pened to them using a 'seriousness scale' where zero represented a very minor offence, and twenty murder. Seriousness ratings are clearly influenced by objective factors such as financial loss, degree of injury etc and it is not surprising that ratings were higher for well-reported offences.

. . . Nearly two-thirds of the most serious incidents were reported, as against a quarter of the least serious.

. . . Seriousness is an overriding issue, but three other factors are at play.

- First, as seen, there are practical considerations of self-interest. Thus, for instance, at all levels of seriousness a much higher than average propor-tion of burglaries with loss, vehicle thefts and bicycle thefts were reported. A quarter of these victims said they reported because they wanted to make an insurance claim. And for those whose car or bike had gone missing, nearly two-thirds said they reported because they wanted police help in finding it.
- Secondly, victims' expectations of the police play a part. For crimes with higher seriousness scores, more victims felt that police would not be able to help, or would not be interested.
- Thirdly, when the victim knows the offender, he/she will often not bring in the police, even for offences considered serious. Thus, of the most serious assaults, many of which were related-party offences, more than half were not reported. Many were felt to be dealt with better privately, and more than one in five of the most serious assaults were not reported for fear of reprisal.

Whether incidents are actually recorded as crimes depends on the way that the police interpret the reports they receive. The statistics on the commission of crime include only 'notifiable' offences, which are the most serious ones (generally, indictable or triable either way). This means that the incidence of what the police regard as minor offending is not recorded by them. The first official indication of minor offending occurs, therefore, when statistics are compiled about convictions for summary offences, a figure which hides all earlier decisions about informal disposals or cautions. Of greater interest are police decisions to exclude notifiable offences from the official record. Where reports are notified by victims or other members of the public, there may be less discretion for the police to disagree with the initial definition of the incident as a crime. But decisions not to create a crime record, known as 'no-criming' or 'cuffing', have been found to account for up to 11 per cent of reports of crime and are explained by a variety of reasons (see Bottomley and

Coleman, 1981). In the main, reports are no-crimed where they are regarded as mistaken or false. But the lack of evidence or perceived unreliability of the victim or witnesses may also lead the police to discount the incident rather than generate an unsolvable crime. Similarly, another important reason for no-criming is the victim's withdrawal of his or her complaint. These decisions are important for the police because the crime report is a basic accounting unit of their work. It means not only that an offence has occurred but that resources have to be devoted to investigating it, and the police will be judged by their effectiveness and success in apprehending the offender. (See also Ackroyd, 1992, pp 124–134.)

Of the crimes which do enter the official records, only a small proportion are matched to offenders, or 'cleared up'. In 1994, for example, the figure was only 26 per cent. As we might expect, in the context of the dark figure of crime, the clear-up rate is even lower.

These various statistics about the relationship between the extent of crime and suspected offenders demonstrate what was implicit in the observational studies of police behaviour discussed earlier. Policing decisions result in a highly selective group of suspects being processed in the criminal justice system. The point has been succinctly put in the *Criminal Statistics*:

> Only 7 per cent of all offences committed (whether reported to the police or not) are cleared up with only 3 per cent resulting in a caution or conviction. (Home Office, 1995, para 1.5)

It is essential to the success and legitimacy of that system, therefore, that the police make the best possible choices at the point of entry.

(b) Effectiveness and efficiency

How effective are the police? The answer depends on the aims against which policing is assessed. In terms of law enforcement, that is, catching suspects with a view to further processing, the evidence shows that the police are not very effective in general, and only slightly more so for some kinds of offending. In terms of social stability, that is, preventing crime, maintaining public order and supporting the public in times of crisis, the evidence is equivocal because success on these criteria is difficult to measure and to attribute to the police alone. If we probe further, and ask whether the police are functioning efficiently, it becomes clear that there are trade-offs between law enforcement and social stability which make it difficult to quantify whether the police are using their resources in the most economic way.

We have already noted the considerable influence exerted by the public in drawing attention to crime. Although the police do engage in routine patrolling and also maintain specialist squads to detect the more serious kinds of crime, they generally *react* to information which they receive from other sources. As a consequence, policing activity in itself does not have a major impact on the crime problem generally.

Extract 2.3.4

P Morris and K Heal, *Crime Control and the Police* (1981)
pp 20–24, 27 (footnotes omitted)

It is a central tenet of policing that the probability of making an arrest is increased by swift responses to calls for assistance. Much effort and technological ingenuity has been devoted, both in this country and elsewhere, to reducing response time in the expectation that the number of arrests made would be increased, that the deterrent value of patrol enhanced, and that the public would be more satisfied with the service received . . . However, the results of a major study by Bieck [*Response Time Analysis* (Kansas City: Kansas City Police, 1977)] show that the outcome of a large proportion of more serious crimes is not influenced by the speed of response, and that on those occasions where a fast response is necessary, the time taken by members of the public to report the incident is crucial.

Bieck divided total response time into three components: the time taken to report an incident, to despatch police resources and to travel to the scene of the incident. He studied only 'Part I' crimes (those of a more serious nature) dividing these into two groups: those discovered after the crime had occurred and the suspect left the scene (62 per cent), and those in which a member of the public, either as a victim or witness saw, heard, or became involved at any point during the commission of the offence (38 per cent). For the first category, described as 'discovery' crimes, it was found – for obvious reasons – that the chances of making an arrest at the scene of the crime or locating a witness was not enhanced by rapid response. For the second category – 'involvement' crime – the importance of response time was found to vary with the nature of the incident. However, since for all crimes studied, reporting time amounted to nearly one half of total response time, the time taken by the public to report a crime was the primary determinant of the eventual outcome. Thus, where an involvement crime was reported within one minute, the chances of making an on-the-scene arrest were 10–15 per cent higher than in those cases where the public took five minutes to call the police. For burglaries the figure rose to 40 per cent. Where the public took longer than five minutes to call the police – and this was found to be so for half of the involvement crimes studied – reporting time was no longer associated with the chances of making an arrest. In summary, therefore, Bieck's study – which has the advantage of being based on more reliable data than earlier work discussed – leads to the conclusion that only a small proportion of even the more serious crimes warrant rapid police response.

On examining why delay occurred in calling the police, Bieck found that on many occasions the public, being unsure as to whether police intervention was necessary sought the advice of others (friends, relatives or superiors at work), or simply waited and observed the scene of the incident in the hope of gaining additional information. Public satisfaction with the service received was found to be unrelated to the actual time taken to respond – the important factor was whether response time was perceived to be faster or slower than that expected, 87 per cent of the public being satisfied with response time . . .

It has frequently been observed that the principal disadvantages of patrolling an area by car arises from the isolation of the police from the public and the area for which they are responsible. Under these circumstances contact with more than a handful of people is difficult, thus prejudicing police/community relations; it is also difficult for patrol officers to get to know their area or to establish more than a few sources of information. Many have noted that, freed from these disadvantages the officer patrolling on foot is likely to carry out the task of policing more effectively, particularly in busy congested city centres . . .

A study recently completed in New Jersey assessed the impact of foot patrol activity on both crime and the public's perception of crime and public behaviour [G Kelling and T Pate, *The New Jersey Foot Patrol Experiment: Executive Summary* (Washington DC: Police Foundation, 1980, unpublished)]. The study has shown that there appears to be little or no relationship between the level of crime occurring in a particular area and the number of officers patrolling there. It was found, however, that residents noticed changes in the number of officers patrolling the area in which they lived, and in those areas where the number of patrol officers was increased residents saw the severity of crime decreasing. This was not so for commercial respondents (shopkeepers, businessmen etc.). It was also found that residents in areas of increased foot patrol activity were more likely to forego protective measures against crime than residents in areas where the level of patrolling remained unchanged or had ceased. The authors conclude by noting that while foot patrol does not have a significant effect on crime levels, it does influence residents' fear of crime and the protective measures they take to avoid crime.

The most optimistic conclusion to be drawn regarding the effectiveness of patrolling on foot or by car, is that very substantial increases in patrol manpower, or alternatively the introduction of patrol to an area where none had previously existed may, on occasions, lead to a reduction in particular types of crime though for only short periods of time. It can of course be argued that until some of the more important studies have been replicated, it is difficult to judge how great the increase in manpower must be before an effect on crime patterns is likely to be observed . . . However, the more interesting and probably more useful line of enquiry would be to seek out the reasons accounting for the 'failure' of the traditional patrol.

. . . Some forces, both in this country and elsewhere, have devised complex duty rotas enabling increased patrol effort during those periods when calls for assistance are high, or by dividing total patrol strength into crime and non-crime divisions. However, while such tactics are likely to lead to some improvement in effectiveness, the major factor impeding police performance stems from the nature of crime itself. A number of authors have made the obvious, if often forgotten and useful point, that a patrol can only prevent or intercept those crimes occurring in places accessible to the patrol officer. While *some* crimes do most frequently take place in public places – for example robbery – it has been estimated that something in the order of 40 per cent to 45 per cent of all crimes are committed in public places, leaving some 55 per cent to 60 per cent of crime beyond the reach of even the most efficient patrol [J F Elliott, *Interception* (Springfield, Illinois: Charles Thomas, 1973)]. Moreover, the crime which occurs in public is often accomplished quickly, stealthily and without warning. Thus the chances of the police witnessing or being in a position to intervene even in these crimes are small. A second difficulty arises from the fact that while the aggregated crime statistics seem to represent an overwhelming problem, the number of incidents is *relatively* small if account is taken of the large number of opportunities for crime to be found in the activities of the population of even a moderately sized city during the course of a single day. Studies have shown that the likelihood of a uniformed patrol officer intercepting a crime in progress is very small; for example, a report of the president's Crime Commission estimates that a patrol officer in a large American city could expect to intercept a street robbery in progress once every fourteen years ... While in this country Mayhew et al [*Crime in Public View*, HORS No 49 (London: Home Office, 1979)] have noted that *on average* a household will be burgled once every 35 years – assuming that is, that around twice as many burglaries occur as are reported to the police.

... There is some evidence to suggest therefore that specialised police tactics may have an effect on crime. On the one hand tangible improvements in the status of a particular task, appears to lead to an improvement in police performance, though this may prove to be only a short term gain. On the other hand and of greater importance, are the gains which appear to be achieved as a result of differentiating between police tasks, and of developing specific police tactics. However, as the studies discussed have demonstrated, such a strategy may incur costs in the form of public alienation from the police, or rivalry between one group of officers and the next.

The ability of the police to detect crime is similarly lacking, not least when detection is associated with the work of the fictional detectives of crime novels and television programmes. In judging this, it should be noted that the clear-up rate, which is often taken to represent a detection rate, does not indicate police action to discover offenders.

Extract 2.3.5

**Home Office, *Criminal Statistics England and Wales 1996* (1997)
p 37, figure 2.4**

Notifiable offences by method of clear-up 1996

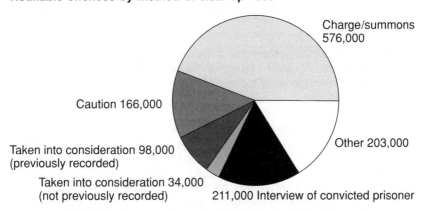

Charge/summons 576,000

Caution 166,000

Taken into consideration 98,000 (previously recorded)

Taken into consideration 34,000 (not previously recorded)

Other 203,000

211,000 Interview of convicted prisoner

1,288,000 offences cleared up (26% of recorded offences)

In 1996, 26 per cent of recorded crimes were cleared up. Of those crimes, 45 per cent were cleared up by issuing a charge or summons against a suspect; not all of these would have resulted in a conviction. Another 13 per cent were cleared up by issuing a caution; here, the required admission of guilt does not necessarily reflect police detection. Almost 30 per cent were categorised as cleared up when the police decided that no further action should be taken, usually where they were confident that they knew the identity of the offender but there was was insufficient evidence or an informal warning was considered adequate. Generally, for the majority of crimes, the most important factors leading to detection are whether the police or victims know the identity of the suspect or whether the suspect was caught. It is crucial for this evidence to be collected at the scene; as time passes, the identification of a suspect is increasingly less likely to occur. Unless there is strong public pressure for an investigation, the police tend to operate, therefore, by concentrating on the crimes for which such information is available and by then collecting evidence to present to a court to substantiate their suspicions (see also Bayley, 1994, pp 25–30).

Extract 2.3.6

P Morris and K Heal, *Crime Control and the Police* (1981) pp 30–32

It is therefore of interest to consider three . . . studies, the first by Steer [*Uncovering Crime: The Police Role*, Royal Commission on Criminal Procedure Research Study 7 (London: HMSO, 1980)], the second by Mawby [*Policing the City* (Farnborough: Gower, 1979)] and the third by Bottomley and Coleman ['Understanding Crime Rates' in R V G Clarke and J M Hough (eds), *The Effectiveness of Policing* (Farnborough: Gower, 1980)].

Steer reports findings similar to those of earlier American work. Thus with regard to the skills of detectives he reports that in the majority of cases the detection of crime involves little of what the public would perceive as real detective ability:

> 'The success of the police in the detection of crime depends for the most part on how much useful information the public is able to give the police about the circumstances of the events. It is difficult to see how the situation could be otherwise.'

In discussing the investigation of cases, Steer notes that it is the primary task for the investigating officer to look immediately for some indication of the suspect's identity. If an identification offering a reasonable chance of success is found, the case is pursued in the hope of clearing it. If, however, there is no immediate indication of identity the case is unlikely to be pursued much further. In qualifying this broad characterisation Steer notes that offences perceived as more serious attract more investigatory effort whatever the initial hope of success might be.

Around 57 per cent of offenders responsible for incidents studied by Steer were caught as a result of being at or near the scene of a crime, or actually committing a crime when the police arrived, or because the police were given their identity by the victim or witness. For this group, Steer suggests the detections could have been made by the average man in the street were he given the appropriate legal knowledge. Of the remaining 43 per cent of offenders, approximately 12 per cent were detected as a result of being stopped and checked by police, on the basis of information received from the public, as a result of local police knowledge, or from a fingerprint search. Between 12 per cent and 13 per cent of offenders were identified as a result of being implicated during the course of a police interrogation. The remaining 18 per cent were detected because they had the opportunity to commit the crime being investigated, were in possession of stolen property, caught while disposing of stolen property, or as a result of police observation or a police trap. On reviewing these and other findings Steer concludes that the business of detecting offenders was relatively straightforward in all but 25 per cent of the cases studied.

For Steer one of the principal investigatory skills of the police lies in knowing how to act upon information the public provide. He also points, however, to the skill of the police in interviewing suspects. In supporting this view Steer notes that a large proportion of offences studied were cleared as a result of interviewing the suspects at a police station following arrest for some *other* offence, or as a result of stolen property being found in the suspect's possession. Offences detected in this way comprise some 41 per cent of detections in a random sample of all indictable offences occurring during the study period, and 20 per cent of a sample of more serious offences.

The study by Mawby (1979) largely confirms the figures presented by Steer. On examining the way in which a sample of standard list offences committed in nine areas of Sheffield were detected, Mawby found that just under 40 per cent were detected 'indirectly', that is as a result of routine police interviews with offenders caught for *other* offences. Of offences detected 'directly', 62 per cent were solved as a result of information given by the public which led the police directly to the offender, leaving some 38 per cent of 'direct' detections – some 23 per cent of all detections – attributable to police investigatory effort.

Further evidence regarding the importance of the police interviews in detecting crime is to be found in a study of police interrogation by Softley et al (1980). On the basis of a study conducted in four police stations, Softley reports that nearly half of the suspects who were interviewed made a confession, and over two thirds gave information which would help secure a conviction. However, in considering the consequences of curtailing police powers to question suspects, Softley qualifies his findings regarding the importance of interviewing. He notes that in only 8 per cent of cases studied did the police officers interviewed admit that it would have been necessary to drop the case if the suspect had refused to answer questions.

Further insight into crime investigation work, and to some extent further qualification of some of the more interesting conclusions reported by Steer, is to be found in a paper by Bottomley and Coleman (1980). The authors, whose paper is principally concerned with the limitations of official crime rates as a measure of police effectiveness, note that in 26 per cent of detected cases studied the police were presented with a ready-made solution at the scene of the crime, and thus 'real' detective work was unnecessary. For a further 26 per cent of cases, detection occurred as a result of questioning by the police, while 24 per cent were detected by means of information from complainants, victims or witnesses. The number of cases detected as a result of activities more closely akin to public stereotypes of real detective work (e.g. on the basis of information received from informants, contacts – formal or informal – or intelligence systems), accounted for 5 per cent of detections. Special police enquiries, such as finger printing, forensic tests, house to house enquiries, accounted for 2 per cent, while 'set ups' or 'plants' accounted for a further 2 per cent. Three per cent were cleared up as a result of police vigilance (i.e. powers of observation and quick-wittedness of police officers). The remaining cases, where information was available, were accounted for either by the offender giving himself up or by admitting to the offence while in prison. The authors are, however, more sceptical than Steer of the investigatory skills of CID officers, and point to the fact that in those cases where suspects were identified by the police, much of the work was undertaken by officers from the uniform branch; an observation which clearly implies that in practice it is quite incorrect to see the 'expertise' for investigation residing solely in the hands of officers allocated to criminal investigation departments (cf. Chatterton, 1976). On a second point, when considering the importance of questioning procedures in terms of identifying suspects, Bottomley and Coleman note all but twelve of the 270 cases detected as a result of questioning were in practice cleared by use of the 'taking into consideration' (tic) procedure. The authors note that for all offence groups combined in their sample, one quarter of offences regarded by the police as being cleared up were dealt with in this way. Unfortunately, Steer gives little attention to this important aspect of investigation, a fact which undoubtedly contributes considerably to the rather more optimistic view of police investigatory skill to be drawn from his report.

If the police are not so effective when assessed by law enforcement criteria, this does not mean that they are ineffective in terms of the peacekeeping and support roles that contribute to social stability. While maintaining or increasing the existing police workforce may not lead to the processing of more offenders, it may be justified in the broader context of policing. Nevertheless, the police service consumes considerable public resources. How can we be sure that the police are performing adequately and using public monies efficiently? To answer this question, there has been a growth of various attempts to measure their achievement and to evaluate their performance as a contribution to the criminal justice system in general. None of the indicators have strong claims to objectivity, however. Bayley suggests that measures of police performance can be categorised as direct or indirect, and as hard or soft. Direct indicators show what the police have achieved: 'hard' examples would be crime rates, levels of victimisation, use of public space and commercial activity in the community, and numbers of substantiated complaints about police behaviour; 'soft' examples – more subjective perceptions – would be changes in the fear of crime, public confidence in the police, and willingness to help the police. Indirect indicators show what the police have done, albeit without showing that a discernible effect on community life has been achieved: 'hard' examples would be the number of police, response times, numbers of arrests and clear-ups, the value of property or drugs seized; 'soft' examples would be police morale and police knowledge of local communities. Bayley claims that the police managers in the United Kingdom tend to evaluate their own behaviour by reference to indirect, often 'soft', indicators which are readily available but do not tell them how effective they are being. (See generally, Bayley, 1994, pp 94–101). Obviously, the method of measuring police success will have an impact on police choices about the individuals that they send for further processing in the criminal justice system. Thus, Bayley would encourage the use of direct, 'hard' performance indicators of the police contribution to public safety. But other demands on the police may lead in different directions. For example, the public appear to value the mere presence of the police and, according to Skogan, what the public want is 'reassurance' that they are being protected and this can be provided by the sight of routine patrols on foot. But

> the popularity of foot patrol is an instance in which pressure for greater police effectiveness can run counter to public expectations. Foot patrol is expensive to mount, it is often in competition for the staffing needed to respond rapidly to 999 calls (which the public also wants), and it does not register well on performance indices such as making arrests and clearing up crimes. (Skogan, 1994)

Nevertheless, the last decade has witnessed a fundamental change in police organisation to take account of effectiveness and efficiency (see Weatheritt, 1993) and to focus on quality assurance from the consumers' perspective (see Waters, 1996). There are strong pressures to attempt to improve effectiveness by introducing principles taken from the practices of management and of accounting. Recent reports from the Audit Commission (beginning with Audit Commission, 1992), for example, have applied such thinking to such tasks as foot patrol and the investigation of crime, as the charts on pp 182 and 183 illustrate.

Extract 2.3.7

Audit Commission, *Streetwise – Effective Police Patrol* (1996) exhibit 18

Problems, causes and solutions

There are three major reasons why the police are unable to fulfil public expectations of patrol, especially foot patrol.

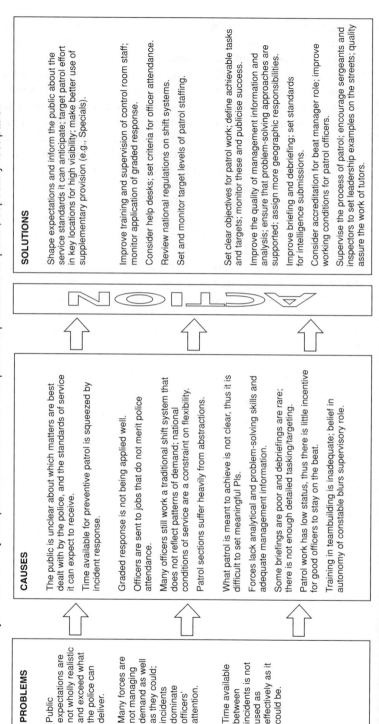

PROBLEMS

Public expectations are not wholly realistic and exceed what the police can deliver.

Many forces are not managing demand as well as they could; incidents dominate officers' attention.

Time available between incidents is not used as effectively as it could be.

CAUSES

The public is unclear about which matters are best dealt with by the police, and the standards of service it can expect to receive.

Time available for preventive patrol is squeezed by incident response.

Graded response is not being applied well.

Officers are sent to jobs that do not merit police attendance.

Many officers still work a traditional shift system that does not reflect patterns of demand; national conditions of service are a constraint on flexibility.

Patrol sections suffer heavily from abstractions.

What patrol is meant to achieve is not clear, thus it is difficult to set meaningful PIs.

Forces lack analytical and problem-solving skills and adequate management information.

Some briefings are poor and debriefings are rare; there is not enough detailed tasking/targeting.

Patrol work has low status, thus there is little incentive for good officers to stay on the beat.

Training in teambuilding is inadequate; belief in autonomy of constable blurs supervisory role.

ACTION

SOLUTIONS

Shape expectations and inform the public about the service standards it can anticipate; target patrol effort in key locations for high visibility; make better use of supplementary provision (e.g., Specials).

Improve training and supervision of control room staff; monitor application of graded response.

Consider help desks; set criteria for officer attendance.

Review national regulations on shift systems.

Set and monitor target levels of patrol staffing.

Set clear objectives for patrol work; define achievable tasks and targets; monitor these and publicise success.

Improve the quality of management information and analysis; ensure that problem-solving approaches are supported; assign more geographic responsibilities.

Improve briefing and debriefing; set standards for intelligence submissions.

Consider accreditation for beat manager role; improve working conditions for patrol officers.

Supervise the process of patrol; encourage sergeants and inspectors to set leadership examples on the streets; quality assure the work of tutors.

Audit Commission, *Helping with Enquiries: Tackling Crime Efficiently* (1993) exhibit 20

Problems, causes and solutions in crime management

Forces need to address a range of problems in order to secure improvements in performance . . .

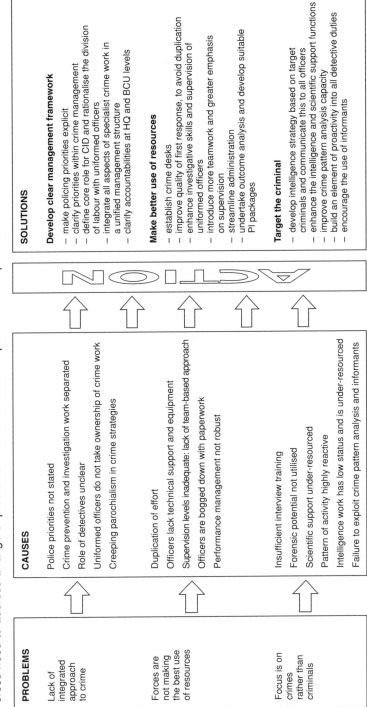

PROBLEMS

Lack of integrated approach to crime

Forces are not making the best use of resources

Focus is on crimes rather than criminals

CAUSES

Police priorities not stated
Crime prevention and investigation work separated
Role of detectives unclear
Uniformed officers do not take ownership of crime work
Creeping parochialism in crime strategies

Duplication of effort
Officers lack technical support and equipment
Supervision levels inadequate: lack of team-based approach
Officers are bogged down with paperwork
Performance management not robust

Insufficient interview training
Forensic potential not utilised
Scientific support under-resourced
Pattern of activity highly reactive
Intelligence work has low status and is under-resourced
Failure to exploit crime pattern analysis and informants

ACTION

SOLUTIONS

Develop clear management framework

– make policing priorities explicit
– clarify priorities within crime management
– define core role for CID and rationalise the division of labour with uniformed officers
– integrate all aspects of specialist crime work in a unified management structure
– clarify accountabilities at HQ and BCU levels

Make better use of resources

– establish crime desks
– improve quality of first response, to avoid duplication
– enhance investigative skills and supervision of uniformed officers
– introduce more teamwork and greater emphasis on supervision
– streamline administration
– undertake outcome analysis and develop suitable PI packages

Target the criminal

– develop intelligence strategy based on target criminals and communicate this to all officers
– enhance the intelligence and scientific support functions
– improve crime pattern analysis capacity
– build an element of proactivity into all detective duties
– encourage the use of informants

There are, however, grounds for being sceptical about advocating measures which do not take the context of policing and its various purposes into account. Indeed, the very complexity of policing makes the choice of appropriate performance indicators fraught with difficulties, as Horton and Smith demonstrated some years ago:

Extract 2.3.9

C Horton and D J Smith, *Evaluating Police Work* (1988) pp 21–27

Problems with measures

So far the discussion has considered the purposes of policing in broad and general terms, and those are the terms in which the discussion has generally been conducted in the past. There are considerable difficulties in moving from this general discussion to the definition of more specific objectives which would be linked with specific measures of performance.

1. If policing consists of a large number of diverse tasks, then clearly there can be no single or overall measure of police performance. The only possibility, therefore, is to find individual measures for the various tasks. For some aspects of police activity, such as the cost per mile of the police vehicle fleet, quite robust measures can be found. But for many services provided by the police it is by no means obvious what measures could be used. For example, it might seem reasonable to begin measuring the success of police crime prevention work by counting up the number of crime prevention surveys that had been done, or the number of talks given to groups in the community. But a crime prevented cannot be counted, and there is no obvious way of assessing the contribution to crime prevention of a uniform officer on foot patrol. Similar problems of assessment arise if we consider the success of the police in relation to:

    public reassurance, for example offering support to burglary victims;
    maintaining public tranquillity;
    schools liaison work;
    the impartial administration of the law;
    dealing with disputes between neighbours or family members.

2. Since choices must be made between possible uses of police resources, there needs to be some way of assessing the relative worth of different types of police work. But how can the moral or symbolic value of different police services be measured? Certainly, the task of chasing unpaid parking fines, which may consume hours of police time, cannot be justified on the grounds of economic rationality. Nor can the huge outlay of police resources in a murder hunt after the trail has 'gone cool' be justified, except by reference to the strength of public feeling. Yet a balance must somehow be struck, when allocating resources, between such diverse tasks as reassuring the elderly, investigating drugs suppliers, apprehending burglars, and catching speeding motorists.

184

3. It is generally assumed that policing should be evaluated in terms of ultimate policing goals, such as the prevention of crime, the apprehension of offenders or the maintenance of public tranquillity. However, such goals are too broad and general to be measured themselves. So rather than seeking 'final measures', it is more fruitful to look for 'intermediate measures' of specific kinds of activity. However, whether a high score on a particular 'intermediate measure' is an indication of success or not depends on the policy context. For example, a high arrest rate can be interpreted either as a good sign – that police officers are being diligent in enforcing the law – or else as a sign that the police are not succeeding in preventing crime or maintaining public order.

4. The link between the methods used by the police and the results of their efforts – or the link between police inputs and outputs – is not a straightforward one. Public order and crime rates are the product of a wide range of social influences. It is therefore extremely hard to isolate the contribution made by any one agency, such as the police, to particular changes in the level of public order and crime.

5. Much of policing has multiple aims. For example, the officer on point duty may at the same time be improving the traffic flow, giving directions to motorists, improving public relations, and helping to prevent crime. So if we were to assess this piece of work in terms of only one of the aims, then we would be underestimating what was actually being achieved. Conversely, if we wanted to measure what level of resources had been put into solving a particular crime, we might find that numerous individuals of different ranks and from different departments have contributed to the final outcome, and this multiplies the problems of assessment.

6. Another characteristic of the police officer's job is the amount of autonomy it involves. At the same time, police procedures require that only certain kinds of actions are recorded, so an officer may do a great deal of police work that no-one else at the police station gets to know about.

7. 'The problem with performance indicators', Ann James has written, 'is that they tend to become an end in themselves. They tend to measure a level of activity rather than a level of achievement' [A James, 'Performance and the Planning Process' (1987) *Social Services Insight*, 6 March, p 13]. Because the existence of performance indicators can cause a distortion in the pattern of policing, it is important that the chosen indicators measure activities which should be encouraged. In the words of the Deputy Director of the National Consumer Council, 'bad performance indicators will lead to badly directed resources' [M Healey, 'What Are Local Government Services For?' (1985) *Local Government Studies*, November/December, p 14].

8. If performance measures fail to win the confidence of the police officers who will be responsible for providing the data, then there will be costs to weigh against the expected gains in effectiveness from introducing performance measurement. Partly because of the traditional reliance on measures of dubious value, such as crime statistics, police officers tend to be instinctively suspicious of 'the numbers game'. They know, for instance,

how league tables of detection rates give an incentive to those low down in the table to 'massage' the figures in order to improve their rating. Police officers have a strong sense that many of the incidents they attend are 'unique', and that the quality of the service they give can be as important as any more tangible 'results'. But they know that these features of their work cannot be easily measured, and are wary of the introduction of measures that do not promise to give credit for them. Police officers tend to be particularly concerned about indicators which involve an increase in the amount of paperwork they have to complete; which involve a considerable amount of change and upheaval in their pattern of work; which might be used punitively against them; or which would reduce their discretion and autonomy.

9. There is a danger that measures will simply reflect passing fashions in policing, which subsequent experience and research show to be ineffective. For example, in the 1970s, there was considerable interest in reducing response times as a way of apprehending more offenders, but enthusiasm with this measure waned when it was discovered that the speed of response was critical in only a tiny proportion of cases.

These problems with performance measurement have a number of implications for the kinds of measures that might be appropriate for the police service.

a) The search for a single, overall measure of performance in the police service is futile and misleading, because policing consists of a wide range of diverse tasks. It follows that there will need to be a large number of specific measures for all the many different tasks involved in policing. For example, whilst an overall measure of success for crime detection may be of little practical use or meaning, the detection rate for burglaries can be used to gauge the success of fairly specific kinds of policing strategy directed at this objective.

b) It is probably equally misleading to seek measures of success in achieving the final objectives or outcomes of policing, such as the prevention of crime, the apprehension of offenders or the preservation of tranquillity, because these objectives are too general, and there are too many alternative policing strategies which might be pursued with these objectives in mind. Rather, it will be necessary to rely on 'intermediate measures' such as the number of man-hours spent on foot-patrol.

c) It will only be possible to interpret such intermediate measures, however, within some kind of policy context, and the process of interpreting the measures will require the exercise of judgement. The following conclusion of an earlier study of police effectiveness and efficiency by Ian Sinclair and Clive Miller, has won wide acceptance:

> 'In practice, measures have most usefulness within the context of a policy, a research design, a political debate or a management system'. [I Sinclair and C Miller, *Measures of Police Effectiveness and Efficiency*, Research and Planning Unit Paper 25 (London: Home Office) p 18]

Sinclair and Miller argue that context for individual measures can also be provided by 'creating "families of measures" in which one piece of statistical information provides a contextual background to another' (ibid, p 22). Either way, they argue,

> 'these two points mean that whoever interprets measures should have the relevant background information or judgement about the police to do so'. (ibid, p 22)

This leads them to endorse the 'Home Office policy of relying heavily on the professional judgement of HM Inspectorate in interpreting measures' (ibid, p 22).

These are strong arguments and we would substantially support them. However, if the relevant 'families of measures' were available to a wider audience than the Inspectorate, including police forces themselves, police authorities and the general public, then it would be possible for more people to acquire the 'background information' needed to make informed decisions about police effectiveness. It should be possible for a broader range of groups and individuals than just the Inspectorate to play a part in improving police effectiveness and efficiency.

d) There will need to be a large number of specific measures for all the many different tasks involved in policing. For example, whilst an overall measure of success for crime detection may be of little practical use or meaning, the detection rate for burglaries can be used to gauge the success of fairly specific kinds of policing strategy directed towards this objective.

e) Measures in policing are therefore best seen not as offering final judgement about police performance, but as providing information on the success or otherwise of a particular policing method or policy. This information can then be used to modify and improve on existing policies, as part of continuing management process. According to a major study of performance monitoring in the police by the U.S. Department of Justice, measurement can most usefully be thought of as 'a learning strategy'... [US Department of Justice, *Basic Issues in Police Performance* (Washington DC: National Institute of Justice) pp xi–xiii], ... 'that is more useful for asking better questions than for giving better answers' (ibid, p 22).

f) Sound research into the results of particular policing strategies, and evaluations of the way that particular objectives have worked in practice may help to avert the dangers of 'fashionable innovation'.

g) In view of the need to enlist the support of police officers for performance measures, it is a good idea if the measures are 'designed jointly by those responsible for collecting the data, those who will use the measures, and those who have technical expertise in designing measures and interpreting them' (U.S. Department of Justice, 1982, p 158).

h) In designing a recording system to assist with police performance measurement, it will be necessary to take account of the multiple aims of much of policing, and of the fact that individual officers have a good deal of autonomy in deciding what to do while on patrol.

Problems with objectives

The traditional view of policing saw it as being essentially determined by the law and by rules and regulations framed in the light of the duty to enforce the law impartially. The problem with this view is that the law does not specify any particular pattern of policing. Many contrasting styles and patterns of policing are possible within the limits set by the law.

The language of objectives is a reaction against the traditional way of thinking about policing. It aims to make policing more purposive and better directed to useful ends.

Yet the language of objectives is not always the most appropriate way of discussing policing. For example, members of the public may be interested in whether a particular practice, such as stop and search, is legitimate, as well as whether it is an effective way of achieving a particular objective. Uniform police patrol appears to be highly valued by the public and accounts for around 60 per cent of police manpower, and yet the objectives of patrol are extremely difficult to specify.

P A J Waddington has argued strongly against the police setting themselves objectives on practical grounds. In his view, the basic policing challenge is 'to respond flexibly to contingencies' [P A J Waddington, 'The "Objectives" Debate' (1986b) 2 *Policing* at p 230], and he warns that redirecting police efforts towards goals which cause them to neglect these basic duties could have 'disastrous practical consequences' [P A J Waddington, 'Defining Objectives: A Response to Tony Butler' (1986a) 2 *Policing* at p 20]. He points out that objectives may sometimes conflict with one another, and that choosing to pursue any one objective may have unintended and undesired side effects on other potential objectives (Waddington, 1986b, p 226). He argues that the real objectives of some worthwhile policing activities are 'undeclarable'. He says, for example, that the real reason for forces pursuing the policy of putting officers back 'on the beat' was 'to satisfy vocal public demands ... and to quell political criticism' – a reason that no force would be prepared to express in such terms to the general public (Waddington, 1986b, p 226).

Although the language of objectives has these limitations, policing is not a single, coherent set of activities that must always be discussed within the same conceptual framework. It may be that some police objectives are undeclarable, but most, such as trying to prevent crime, can be declared very clearly indeed. An important reason for thinking in terms of objectives ... is that police officers have a substantial amount of 'uncommitted time' when they could be tackling police problems in a planned, objective driven way. Moreover the language of objectives has the advantage of demystifying the subject of policing. We can all take part in a discussion about the results the police should be trying to achieve, and about the best means of achieving them; but only the initiated can take part in a discussion about the proper exercise of professional skills.

(c) Fairness

The selectivity of police decision-making places a premium on fairness. Three different aspects may be distinguished. The first is formal fairness, in terms of the legal criteria which justify police action. As we have seen, at least for initial encounters with members of the public, the responses of practical police officers are not determined by their powers but by craftsmanship. In respect of decisions to arrest, however, most evidence shows that the police are anxious to work within the general framework of the law, if only to cover themselves against criticism. But, in any event, the law does not impose a high threshold for formal fairness; it provides broad conditions for invoking powers and the courts tend to favour the way they are applied by the police on the spot.

The second aspect of fairness concerns the distribution of police processing. Given the general tendency of the police to choose not to invoke their powers in first encounters with the public, any decision to use those powers takes on added significance. The issue, and the courts' attitude to it, is illustrated in *Arrowsmith v Jenkins* [1963] 2 QB 561. The appellant was a nuclear disarmament campaigner who felt that her notoriety was one of the reasons for her being regularly arrested at the protests that she attended. But when she raised the question, why pick on me, the response was: 'That, of course, has nothing to do with this court. The sole question here is whether the defendant had contravened section 121(1) of the Highways Act 1959.' The decision shows that, where a police power can properly be invoked in respect of any one of a number of suspects, the courts will not question the way that discretion is actually exercised to select a particular one for processing. Since then, it has been held (see *Mohammed-Holgate v Duke* [1984] AC 437) that the police have a duty to comply with administrative law reasonableness (see pp 124–5 above) but, at present, there is no suggestion that it requires the exercise of powers to be distributed fairly between qualifying suspects. What all this means is that the law does not condemn the exercise of police powers against suspects from particular sections of the population; rather, it condones the use of working presumptions to produce self-fulfilling prophecies about likely suspects.

Nevertheless, it would be unfair, from a political and moral perspective, if the police used criteria which had a disproportionate effect on particular groups in the total pool of likely suspects. The PACE Code of Practice for Stop and Search recognises this (see p 126 above) but it is clear that the distribution of police action and processing is uneven. The implications of this have been considered most fully in relation to bias against racial and ethnic groups (in relation to social class, see Hester and Eglin, 1992, pp 141–165; in relation to gender, see Heidensohn, 1997). At issue is the question of whether the over-representation of such groups in the processing statistics is evidence of discrimination or whether it is evidence of a higher incidence of conditions which would legally justify stop and search, or arrest, or other action. There has been some official monitoring of police decisions for ethnic bias since 1993, by Her Majesty's Inspector of Constabulary and by some police forces. The results for 1996–97 show, for example, that ethnic minorities are more than four times as likely to be searched as white people and that, in 10 police forces considered, the proportion of black people arrested (out of the total black population) was consistently higher than the proportion of white people arrested (Home Office, 1997h). The official figures are derived from police records, however, and provide only limited information. But they are consistent with the current state of the research, which is analysed much more fully in the following survey by Smith:

<hr>

Extract 2.3.10

D J Smith, 'Ethnic Origins, Crime and Criminal Justice' in M Maguire et al, *The Oxford Handbook of Criminology* (1997) 2nd ed, pp 732–739

Police stops

Among those offenders who are processed by the criminal justice system, a considerable proportion are drawn into the net through the exercise of discretionary powers by the police, particularly stop and search. Thus, a survey of London police officers carried out in 1982 showed that 23 per cent of arrests arose from a stop [D J Smith, *Police and People in London: III A Survey of Police Officers* (London: Policy Studies Institute, 1983b) p 81, table V.3]. The proportion of arrests arising from a stop was particularly high for driving offences (64 per cent), taking and driving away a vehicle, or vehicle theft (47 per cent), and drugs offences (39 per cent) (Smith, 1983b: 87, table V.6). At that time, most of the stop and search powers were not consolidated within national legislation, although a variety of local powers existed. Consequently, police practice on stops may have varied widely between different parts of the country, and the use of stop and search was probably greater in London than in most other places. Since the Police and Criminal Evidence Act 1984 (PACE) came into force, police throughout England and Wales have had authority to stop persons or vehicles on the reasonable suspicion that they would find stolen goods or prohibited articles, and to carry out searches of vehicles and persons stopped. Other legislation also gives police authority to stop and search for other reasons, for example to look for controlled drugs. Hence, it seems likely that a substantial proportion of arrests now result from stops throughout the country. Clearly the over-representation of black people at later stages in the process could in principle arise partly because the police use their discretion to stop a larger proportion of black people than of other ethnic groups.

Pattern
A survey carried out in three parts of Manchester in 1980 found no significant difference between Afro-Caribbeans and whites in terms of the proportion who had been 'stopped, searched or arrested' within the last year, or in the number of times this had happened [M Tuck and P Southgate, *Ethnic Minorities Crime and Policing: A Survey of the Experiences of West Indians and Whites*, HORS No 70 (London: HMSO, 1981)]. These data do not distinguish between stops and arrests, and because of the rather small sample sizes, the 1.43:1

ratio between the 10 per cent of Afro-Caribbeans and the 7 per cent of white people who were 'stopped, searched, or arrested' does not reach statistical significance. This survey covered a single police division which extended over parts of five wards and had a population of 33,000. Other studies, which have all covered larger and more heterogeneous areas, have found differences in stop rates between black and white people. Willis (1983), who analysed stops recorded at four police stations, found that these were two to three times as high for black people as for the general population.[1] The PSI survey of Londoners carried out in 1981 found that the proportion stopped in the previous twelve months was 24 per cent for Afro-Caribbeans, 17 per cent for whites, and 7 per cent for South Asians. Also, among those who had been stopped at all, Afro-Caribbeans had on average been stopped twice as often as white people. The stop rate among young males aged 15–24 was found to be very high. Within this group, 66 per cent of the Afro-Caribbeans had been stopped an average number of 4.1 times in twelve months, while 44 per cent of the whites had been stopped an average number of 2.6 times [D J Smith, *Police and People in London: II A Survey of Londoners* (London: Policy Studies Institute, 1983a) pp 96–100]. In an observational study carried out in 1986–7 in three police divisions (two in London and one in Surrey), Norris et al (1992) ['Black and Blue: An Analysis of the Influence of Race on Being Stopped by the Police' (1992) 43 *British Journal of Sociology* 207–224] found that black people accounted for 28 per cent of persons stopped by the police, compared with 10 per cent of the local population. Among males aged up to 35, they calculated that the stop rate per 100 population was about thirty-three for blacks, compared with about ten for whites.[2] National data are available from the British Crime Survey 1988, which was carried out well after national stop powers were consolidated in PACE. Within the fourteen-month reference period, 15 per cent of white people, 20 per cent of Afro-Caribbeans, and 14 per cent of South Asians said they had been stopped by the police. The difference in stop rate between Afro-Caribbeans and white people or South Asians remained after taking account of a range of socio-demographic variables . . . An analysis of the 1992 BCS used a wider definition of 'stops', including, as well as traffic and pedestrian stops, orders to show documents or give a statement, and other police-initiated contacts in which respondents were under suspicion. On this basis, 36 per cent of Afro-Caribbean respondents had been 'stopped' during the reference period, compared with 22 per cent of whites and the same proportion of Asians . . .

Jefferson ['Race, Crime and Policing: Empirical, Theoretical and Methodological Issues' (1988) 16 *International Journal of the Sociology of Law* 521–539] and Walker ['Interpreting Race and Crime Statistics' (1987) *Journal of the Royal Statistical Society* A 150, Part I, pp 39–56] have suggested that the study of parts of Manchester (Tuck and Southgate, 1981) failed to find a difference between Afro-Caribbean and white people in stop rates because it was carried out in a relatively small and homogeneous area. They believe that what is being observed in the BCS and the PSI London survey is differences in policing practice between types of area: for example, higher stop rates in disadvantaged urban settings where concentrations of Afro-Caribbeans tend to be high. Jefferson (1993) has suggested in particular that the style of policing is more a response to the social and housing composition of the area than to the ethnic group of potential suspects. Whatever the merits of this argument in general terms, it is not needed to explain the Tuck and Southgate findings. These do not relate to stops alone, and . . . they do not necessarily indicate a different ratio between the rate of police-initiated encounters among Afro-Caribbean and white people from that shown by the BCS: the sample size in the Tuck and Southgate study was simply too small to demonstrate a contrast of the order shown by the BCS.

In a later article, Jefferson, Walker, and Seneviratne ['Ethnic Minorities, Crime and Criminal Justice: A Study in a Provincial City' in D Downes (ed), *Unravelling Criminal Justice* (London: Macmillan, 1992)] used police records of stops and searches to compare parts of Leeds where ethnic minorities accounted for more versus less than 10 per cent of the population.[3] They found that in areas of *low* ethnic concentration, the stop rate was *higher* for black than for white or South Asian people, whereas in areas of *high* ethnic concentration, the stop rate was *lower* for black than for white or South Asian people. However, the 1981 PSI survey of Londoners showed no difference in stop rates (all stops, regardless of whether there was a search) among either Afro-Caribbeans or South Asians according to the concentration of ethnic minorities in the local area, defined as a census enumeration district, which contains 150 households on average. Also, the survey showed no difference in stop rates among white people according to the concentration of ethnic minorities in the ward where they lived (unpublished data available from the author on request).

From a survey carried out as part of the Leeds study within census enumeration districts having a high concentration (10 per cent or more) of ethnic minorities, Jefferson and Walker (1992) found that the stop rate (in 1987) was *lower* among black and South Asian people than among white people living nearby. They interpreted this result as showing that the stop rate is determined by the social characteristics of the areas rather than the ethnic group of the individual. It is more likely, however, that the finding reflects the unusual characteristics of those white people who live in areas of high ethnic concentration. For example, Jefferson and Walker's own results show that a high proportion of this particular white population lives in rented accommodation and is transient, characteristics associated with police targeting.

On balance, there is a consistent body of evidence to show that Afro-Caribbeans are more likely to be stopped than white people or South Asians. There is some conflict of evidence about how marked these differences are, but they are much smaller than the differences in rates of imprisonment. They probably do make some contribution to explaining the high rate of imprisonment of Afro-Caribbeans, but they can only explain a small part of it. That is not only because the ethnic differences in stop rates are relatively small, but also because this kind of policing generates less than one-quarter of arrests.

Decision
Given that black people (but *not* South Asians) are more likely to be stopped by police than white people, the question that arises is how police officers take these decisions, and whether they amount to unequal treatment of black people . . . the most important factor here is that the vast majority of stops do not produce an arrest or prosecution. The BCS 1988 showed that of those

stopped on foot, only 4 per cent reported being arrested, and 3 per cent were prosecuted. The comparable figures for those involved in traffic stops were 1 per cent arrested and 10 per cent prosecuted – the prosecutions being mainly fixed penalty and vehicle defect notices . . . The low 'strike rate' is confirmed by local surveys in Merseyside [R Kinsey, *The Merseyside Crime and Police Surveys: Final Report* (Liverpool: Mersey County Council, 1985)] and London (Smith, 1983a), and by earlier national estimates from police records [C F Willis, *The Use, Effectiveness and Impact of Police Stop and Search Powers*, Home Office Research and Planning Unit Paper No 15 (London: Home Office, 1983)]. The implication of the low 'strike rate' is that the exercise of this kind of police power is highly discretionary. The law requires in principle that the police officer should have 'reasonable suspicion' to justify stopping or searching some-one, but in practice this criterion is extremely weak, and largely unenforceable.

The question whether the relatively high stop rate for black people amounts to unequal treatment is therefore very hard to answer. The PSI survey of Londoners found that the proportion of stops leading to an arrest or to an offence being reported was the same for Afro-Caribbeans and white people (Smith, 1983a: 116). In their observational study, Norris et al (1992) found that the police took 'formal action' in 40 per cent of cases following a stop of a black person, compared with 31 per cent of cases where the person was white, a difference that was not statistically significant. At one level these findings show that the higher stop rate of Afro-Caribbeans is 'justified by results', which may suggest that it does not amount to unequal treatment. As pointed out under the first heading in this chapter, however, decisions made within the criminal justice system tend to be self-validating. Decisions at later stages may be influenced by a need to justify a decision taken earlier. It remains possible that the police, having stopped a higher proportion of black than of white people, then work harder to find offences with which to charge the black suspects.

Observational research casts some further light on this. On the basis of extensive observations of policing in London, including 129 stops, Smith and Gray [*Police and People in London: IV The Police in Action* (London: Policy Studies Institute, 1983) p 233] concluded that 'from the way that police officers talk about stops . . . it is clear that the question of what their legal powers may be does not enter into their decision-making except in the case of rare indi-viduals'. Where there was no specific reason for making the stop (connected with the person's behaviour or appearance) police officers were nevertheless applying criteria which they associated with the chance of getting a 'result'. The researchers gained the impression that whether the person was black was one of these criteria, but that other criteria were more important.

The observational study by Norris et al (1992) is the only one to cast light on the question whether police decisions are influenced by the demeanour of black and white people. In all, Norris and colleagues, working in two police divisions in London and one in Surrey, observed 213 police stops which involved 319 people. A higher proportion of blacks than of whites (56 com-pared with 42 per cent) were stopped on general suspicion rather than tan-gible evidence.[4] There was no difference between white and black persons with regard to whether they were calm versus agitated, or civil versus antagon-istic. A significantly higher proportion of white than of black persons stopped appeared to be under the influence of alcohol (20 per cent compared with 8 per cent at the time of the stop). Police demeanour towards the person stopped was rated as 'negative' in a higher proportion of cases where the person was white than where he or she was black (27 per cent compared with 10 per cent at the time of the stop). These findings speak strongly against the theory that the high stop rate of black people is caused by their hostile behaviour towards the police. They suggest, instead, that stops of black people are rather more likely to be speculative than stops of white people.

The 1988 BCS found that once stopped, Afro-Caribbeans were substantially more likely to be searched than white people or South Asians ... In the case of traffic stops, this difference remained significant after controlling for the effects of a number of factors including past arrests within a multivariate model.

Police behaviour
The 1988 BCS found that Afro-Caribbeans who had been stopped were much more likely than white people or South Asians to think the police had been impolite ... People were more critical of police behaviour if the stop led to some sanction (such as arrest or a reported offence), but this did not explain the difference between Afro-Caribbeans and white people. Respondents were more likely to think the police had been polite where a reason was given for the stop, a finding which replicates the 1981 London survey (Smith, 1983a). Again, this did not explain the difference between Afro-Caribbean and white people.

The 1981 London survey found little or no difference between ethnic groups in the proportion who said the police explained the reason for the stop (Smith 1983a: 107–9). A smaller proportion of Afro-Caribbeans than of white people or South Asians thought the police were polite, and that they behaved in a fair and reasonable manner, but these differences were not striking (Smith, 1983a: 112).

Smith (1983a) conducted an intensive analysis of the relationship between critical views of the police (the belief that they fabricate evidence, use unnecessary violence, etc.) and patterns of contact with them. This showed a strong correlation between the amount of contact (of any kind) and critical views, although a later analysis (unpublished) showed that service contacts, primarily as a victim of crime, were associated with negative views only if those specific contacts were negatively evaluated. Within this general framework, stops tended to dominate the picture as (mildly) adversarial contacts that were very large in quantity and associated with critical views of the police. In a survey of parts of Leeds, Jefferson and Walker (1993) also found a relationship between the number of times stopped and critical views. From these findings it is likely that the large-scale practice of stop and search, and the disproportionate stopping of Afro-Caribbeans, has been among the causes of hostility between Afro-Caribbeans and the police. However, both the Leeds and London studies show that the relatively high level of criticism of the police among Afro-Caribbeans compared with white people cannot be wholly explained by their personal encounters with the police (see Smith ['Police and Racial Minorities' (1991) 2 *Policing and Society* 1–15], for further discussion of this point on the basis of the London findings).

194

Figure 1 Percentage of persons arrested who were black and South Asian: London, 1987

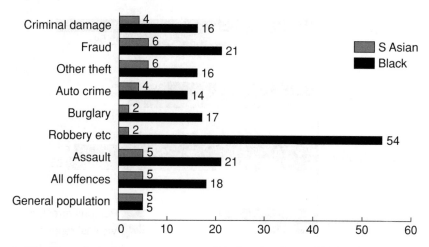

1. The figure includes persons arrested in London for notifiable offences that were followed by further action (caution, referral to juvenile bureau, charge).
2. The general population figures are estimates for 1984–86 of the black and South Asian population of London aged 10 and over as a percentage of the total population aged 10 and over.
3. 'Robbery etc' includes 'theft from the person' except for pickpocketing, which is included under 'other theft'.

Source [Home Office, *Crime Statistics for the Metropolitan Police District by Ethnic Group, 1987: Victims, Suspects and Those Arrested*, Home Office Statistical Bulletin 5/89 (London: Home Office, 1989a) table 4]

Arrests

No national statistics are available on the ethnic group of persons arrested, but data are available for London (the Metropolitan Police District) for certain years, starting in 1975.[5] Figure 1 summarizes the results for 1987. Black people formed a much higher proportion of those arrested than of the general population, whereas South Asians formed exactly the same proportion of the two groups, and this pattern had been broadly the same from 1975 onwards. The proportion of those arrested who were black varied little according to the offence, except that it was extraordinarily high for robbery (54 per cent in 1987).

For certain offences between 1975 and 1985, the Metropolitan Police also recorded the ethnic origin of the offender from the victim's description. For these offences, there is a fairly close correspondence between the proportion of offenders described as non-white by victims and the proportion of people arrested who were non-white (see figure 2). The statistics cover only a few specific offences, and they may well be influenced by police recording practices. None the less, they suggest that there was little or no tendency for police arrests, given a reported offence, to target black people.

Figure 2 Percentage who were non-white: victims' descriptions of offenders compared with police records of persons arrested, London, 1985

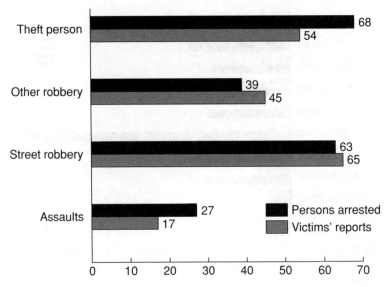

1. For victims' reports, the figure shows the percentage who were 'non-white', whereas for arrests it shows the percentage who were 'black or Asian'.
2. For victims' reports, the percentages are based on cases where the victim could describe the offender. They otherwise cover all recorded offences in the categories shown.

Source Home Office 1989a

Disregarding the victims' descriptions of offenders, the London statistics show such a large difference in arrest rates *per head of population* between black and white people that an explanation substantially in terms of biased policing is implausible. For example, using the 1983 London statistics, Walker (1987) calculated that if the actual rate of burglary by black and white offenders were the same, then the arrest statistics would imply that black burglars had four and a half times the chance of being arrested compared with white burglars; in the case of robbery the difference would be fourteen to one.

On any reasonable assessment, therefore, the London statistics reflect a much higher rate of offending among black than white people. They do not resolve the issue as to whether there is bias in policing practice. The comparison between victims' reports and arrest statistics (figure 2) tends to suggest that the overall effect of any such bias is fairly small, but this evidence is fragmentary.

Walker ['Arrest Rates and Ethnic Minorities: A Study in a Provincial City' (1992) *Journal of Royal Statistical Society*, 155, Part 2, pp 259–272] analysed the arrest rates of males aged 11–35 in six police sub-divisions within Leeds during a six-month period in 1987, when police recorded whether people arrested were white, black, or Asian. Like other elements within this research programme, this analysis compares white and black people living in the same very small areas (census enumeration districts (EDs), containing 150 house-holds on average). In the high ethnic concentration EDs (those with more than 10 per cent 'non-white households'), the arrest rate for black people was lower than for white people, while in the lower-concentration EDs the arrest rate was higher for black than for white people. This mirrors the pattern shown for stops (see earlier section). As before, the likely explanation is that white people in areas of high ethnic concentration are an unusual and high-crime group. In the city as a whole, the arrest rate was more than twice as high for black as for white people.

In the PSI London survey respondents who said they had been arrested were asked about their treatment under arrest by the police. A substantial minority had serious criticisms to make, including specific allegations of gross misconduct in many cases. However, Afro-Caribbeans were no more likely than white people to think they had been badly treated or to make serious allegations of this kind.

[1] She estimated that about half of the stops actually carried out were recorded.

[2] Because the same individuals are often stopped repeatedly, this does not equate with the proportion of the population who were stopped.

[3] The Police and Criminal Evidence Act 1984 requires the police to make a record where a member of the public is stopped *and* searched, and these are the records used by Jefferson et al. The earlier survey findings referred to stops as a whole, a far more inclusive category.

[4] This difference is significant at better than the 5 per cent level of confidence (calcu-lated by the present author from Norris et al's published results).

[5] These statistics cover arrests for notifiable offences (that excludes minor including most traffic offences) that were followed by further action (caution, referral to juvenile bureau, or charge).

Finally, a third aspect of fairness is the absence of deliberate discrimina-tion by the police. On this point, there is observational evidence to show that police attitudes do discriminate against non-white racial and ethnic groups. Smith and Gray, for example, found that black people were stopped more often than other ethnic groups but, while this was consistent with the finding that officers tended to assume that black people commit crime, it was also consistent with the proportion of offenders who were described as black by their victims. In addition, the number of suspects who were subsequently arrested and charged or reported for an offence did not vary between ethnic groups (Smith and Gray, 1983, p 128). Smith and Gray noted, however, that the effect of continued stopping was to increase feelings of hostility against the police by black communities in London, and it was a concerted policy of stopping and searching in Brixton which was cited by Lord Scarman as a major reason for the 1981 riots (Scarman, 1981). But, as Smith and Gray show, the attitudes did not appear to translate into discriminatory action.

For the lawyer, a typical approach to the problem of unfairness in police discretion has been to argue for the introduction of greater control over pol-ice decision-making (see, for example, Davis, 1969; Goldstein, 1960; Sanders and Young, 1994). The introduction of the Police and Criminal Evidence Act 1984 (PACE) was intended to put such a controlling mechanism in place. But, as Reiner points out, it is unrealistic to think that behaviour can be changed simply by superimposing legal controls on the cultural controls which influence the police (see Reiner, 1992a, pp 214–218). Ultimately, then, the way to change police behaviour will be to alter the terms of the organisational reality that comprises the police culture. That will require major changes in police attitudes and they can only be brought about by medium- to long-term changes in police education.

(d) Legitimacy

Early decisions by the police raise important questions about their legitimacy, that is, the extent to which their actions are worthy of respect, co-operation and compliance by the community. Indeed, the legitimacy of the whole criminal justice system rests on the ability and willingness of the police to choose the most deserving cases for processing, in the context of their broader remit to maintain social stability. To determine who should be selected, and yet to retain legitimacy, the police cannot rely on their own conceptions of deserving cases but must be sensitive to the community's views on the matter. At the level of practical policing, their relationship with the people that they police, and with the victims of crime, can give them some idea of acceptable priorities. At the level of policy-making, there is scope for more formal kinds of democratic accountability.

(i) Policing and the community

In respect of initial encounters with the public, considerable effort has been directed at different forms of community policing. The underlying philosophy is that the police should,

> consult with and take account of the wishes of the public in determining and evaluating operational policing and that they should collaborate with the public in identifying and solving local problems. (Bennett, 1994, p 229)

As Bennett's review shows, however, the various schemes have only an indirect effect on the kinds of suspects who are sent for further processing. They appear to have a generally favourable impact on public confidence in the police but it seems that it is independent police initiatives which have a greater impact on controlling crime.

Extract 2.3.11

T Bennett, 'Community Policing on the Ground: Developments in Britain' in D P Rosenbaum (ed), *The Challenge of Community Policing: Testing the Promises* (1994) pp 229–230, 234–235, 239–241

Table 1 Community policing philosophy and practice

Philosophy	Principles	Goals	Organizational strategies	General operational strategies	Specific operational strategies
		Consent			Consultative groups
	Consultation			Community meetings	
		Accountability			Foot patrols.
				Community contact	Contact patrols. Community
Community policing ideology			Decentralization		constables. Police shops.
		Problem identification			Police surgeries
	Collaboration			Community crime prevention	Neighborhood watch. Property marking. Security surveys. Partnerships
		Problem solving		Proactive policing	Problem-oriented policing. Targeted patrols

The principal elements of the philosophy of community policing as found in the literature are presented in table 1. The table aims to summarize some possible connections between the conceptual and practical elements of community policing. It is proposed in the table that the philosophy of community policing can be subdivided into two key principles: consultation and collaboration. These two principles can then be subcategorized into the primary goals of consultation (which include public consent and accountability) and collaboration (which include problem identification and problem solving).

Hence, on the basis of the descriptions of the relationship between the police and the public found in the literature, the main elements of a community policing philosophy might be summarized in a single sentence as a belief or intention held by the police that they should consult with and take account of the wishes of the public in determining and evaluating operational policing and that they should collaborate with the public in identifying and solving local problems.

The second component of community policing is the police organizational structure. It is widely reported in the literature that some organizational structures are more compatible with community policing than others . . . Compatible organizational structures include supportive career and management structures that reward community policing and police attitudes and occupational

199

cultures that accept community policing as a legitimate and desirable form of policing.

One of the most frequently reported organizational structures compatible with community policing is decentralization. It is believed that small command units that have small areas of operation will deliver community policing more effectively than large units with large areas of operation. Despite the fact that the concepts of 'small areas' and 'large areas' are relative terms (as is the concept of decentralization), it is presumed in this line of thinking that command units that are small enough to police individual communities are better placed than larger units to provide consultation and collaboration with local people.

The final components of community policing are the operational strategies used to implement community policing on the ground. The term *on the ground* is used here to refer both to the practice of the police in Britain to refer to their area of geographic responsibility as 'the ground' and also to highlight the fact that police reforms at some point hit 'ground level' (at least they should) and address the practical realities of policing.

. . .

Community meetings

Community meetings constitute community policing (when part of a community policing philosophy) to the extent that they offer an opportunity for the police to consult the public about their policing needs and to account for actions taken by the police.

The recommendations of the Scarman Report to establish statutory liaison committees in all police force areas were enacted in *The Police and Criminal Evidence Act, 1984* (HMSO, 1984). Section 106 of the Act specified that, 'Arrangements shall be made in each police area for obtaining the views of the people in that area about matters concerning the policing of the area and for obtaining their co-operation with the police in preventing crime in the area' (HMSO, 1984). In this sense community policing in general and community consultation in particular is a statutory requirement in Britain.

Although the Act did not specify the form of the consultation arrangements, guidelines were issued in the following year in a Home Office Circular that recommended that the police establish police consultative committees ... The major research on police consultative committees in England and Wales has been conducted by Morgan and Maggs [R Morgan and D J Smith, *Coming to Terms with Policing* (London: Routledge, 1989) and R Morgan and C Maggs, *Setting the PACE: Police Community Consultation Arrangements in England and Wales* (Bath: Centre for the Analysis of Social Policy, University of Bath, 1985)]. The authors concluded that all police authorities had followed Home Office advice and implemented some kind of consultative arrangement in their police force areas. Most police forces had a number of consultative committees with on average one for each division (or subdivision) or (in the case of the Metropolitan Police) one for each borough.

The research examined in detail consultative committees in nine police subdivisions and showed that in many respects the committees were not working as planned. Meetings were usually poorly attended and were usually held on police premises rather than community premises. The meetings were generally open-ended and unstructured and had no secretarial support or means of taking minutes or notes of the meetings. The community members were disproportionately male, middle-class, middle-aged, and existing community activists. Many of the members had little experience of the police or current policing issues and were fairly ignorant of day-to-day policing methods and procedures. As a result the meetings typically took the form of the police educating the community representatives about policing. The majority of the time of the meetings was devoted to police reports about the state of crime in the area and the paucity of police resources. The police accounts were generally accepted by the members (who according to Morgan had no basis to challenge them) and the meetings were generally supportive and sympathetic to the situation of the police.

The consultative committees set up under the Police and Criminal Evidence Act comprise the main form of formal community consultation arrangements in England and Wales. Nevertheless, there are other opportunities for consultation that are less well documented in the literature but should also be acknowledged. All police forces have community involvement officers or race relations officers who are tasked with making contact with the community or specific sections of the community . . . In addition, all forces operate some form of Neighborhood Watch scheme and many forces now have dedicated Neighborhood Watch liaison officers who coordinate Neighborhood Watch activities in their police force areas. Many forces also have generated multiagency partnerships involving the police, agencies, and sometimes community representatives in devising and implementing crime prevention methods.

There is little research on these informal arrangements for consultation with the community. The national survey found that more than three quarters of all forces had some kind of liaison arrangements involving patrol constables (arrangements involving other officers were not recorded) and the community's local businesses, and other professional agencies [T H Bennett and R Lupton, *National Review of Community-Oriented Patrols: Report* Report to the Home Office Research and Planning Unit (Cambridge: Institute of Criminology)]. The police also obtain the views of the public (particularly about their crime concerns) through public attitude and victimization surveys and through the use of community profiling techniques that involve the collection and analysis of information reported by the public or from local intelligence gathered by community constables or other officers. However, it is unknown to what extent these arrangements provide an effective forum for consultation between the police and the public . . .

Community crime prevention

Community crime prevention is often regarded as the heart of community policing as it comprises a working alliance between the police and the public in the prevention of crime. Although the term may be taken to cover almost any area-oriented (compared with individual-oriented or nation-oriented) initiative, community crime prevention has become associated with just a small number of programs. The most commonly cited programs (when operated at the area level) are: Neighborhood Watch, citizen patrols, home security surveys, property marking, and partnerships between the community and other groups in the prevention of crime. In this section I discuss just one of these programs that has now become the single most prolific community-oriented crime prevention program in Britain: Neighborhood Watch.

At the time of writing it is estimated that there are more than 90,000 Neighborhood Watch schemes in England and Wales [M McConville and D Shepherd, *Watching the Police Watching Communities* (London: Routledge, 1992)]. The results of the third British Crime Survey (BCS) showed that 90 per cent of the population of England and Wales had heard of Neighborhood Watch and it was estimated that at the beginning of 1988, 14 per cent of households were members of a Neighborhood Watch scheme covering approximately 2¹/₂ million households [P Mayhew, D Elliott and L Dowds, *The 1988 British Crime Survey*, HORS No 111 (London: Home Office, 1989)]. The BCS report also noted that two thirds of respondents not currently members of a Neighborhood Watch scheme reported that they would be willing to join one if one were set up in their area.

The BCS report also showed that there were marked regional differences in the coverage of Neighborhood Watch schemes throughout the country. Schemes were most common in 'affluent suburban areas' and 'high-status non-family areas.' Conversely, schemes were least common in 'less well-off council estates' and in 'poor quality older terraced housing' areas. The survey findings also suggest that Neighborhood Watch schemes tend to be most prolific in areas with little crime. High coverage areas tended to have lower burglary risks and low coverage areas tended to have higher burglary risks (with some anomalies in this trend). This latter finding gives some support to the argument that Neighborhood Watch is most frequently found in areas that need it least (although it is unclear what the phrase *need it least* means in this context).

Neighborhood Watch has been evaluated by both the police and by independent researchers. Police research in Britain has tended to produce favorable results in terms of both program implementation and outcome. Studies conducted in Bristol . . . and Stafford . . . each found some reduction in reported crime in the period following the implementation of Neighborhood Watch.

However, independent research in Britain has tended to produce less favorable results. The results of the detailed study of two Neighborhood Watch schemes in London showed that the programs had no impact on victimization rates, reporting rates, or police clear-up rates (although there was a reduction in worry about property crime in one of the Neighborhood Watch areas) (Bennett, 1990). The research concluded that the lack of program impact was a result (at least in part) of program failure and a weak program design that resulted in limited public involvement in it. Apart from attending the launch meeting and perhaps displaying a Neighborhood Watch sticker in their windows, local residents took little further active part in the scheme. The police found it difficult to service the increasing number of Neighborhood Watch schemes in their areas and little extra manpower or other resources were made available to conduct this task. Little encouragement was given to the public (beyond the initial launch meeting) to participate in policing their area, and few residents said that they looked out for anything suspicious or reported anything suspicious to the police.

Nevertheless, there was evidence that both the police and the public liked the schemes. The area coordinator of one of the schemes thought that it had improved the relationship between the police and the community and had brought the community closer together (which was confirmed by the survey analysis of the measures of social cohesion). Most of the street coordinators were convinced that crime had been reduced in their areas over the previous year (even though it had not) and believed that Neighborhood Watch had revitalized the community and had increased a sense of neighborliness. The local home beat officers who worked in the area and who helped administer the schemes enjoyed the fact they were now well known among the community and that the level of public contact had increased (although neither of them thought that the flow of useful information had increased) [T H Bennett, *Evaluating Neighbourhood Watch* (Aldershot: Gower, 1990)].

The findings of this research tend to reflect the findings of anecdotal and related evidence. There is no strong evidence that Neighborhood Watch has prevented a single crime in Britain since its inception in the early 1980s, yet it continues to grow in popularity and is now the most widespread community-oriented crime prevention strategy in this country.

However, Neighborhood Watch (and other community crime prevention programs) might be evaluated differently when discussed in the context of the debate about community policing. Neighborhood Watch facilitates the two central principles of community policing: namely an opportunity for consultation and opportunity for collaboration between the police and the public. In this sense Neighborhood Watch helps achieve the related goals of policing by consent and of police accountability. It also helps achieve collaborative problem identification and collaborative problem solving (albeit the problem-solving aspect of the alliance appears at this point not to be helped much by community involvement).

(ii) Victims

Another important source of legitimacy for police action is the attitude of victims of crime. In the past, their viewpoints have not been accorded high priority, despite their crucial role in reporting crime, identifying suspects and offering evidence in court. The growth of the victim movement has given them a higher profile (see Chapter 1 above; Rock, 1990) and, as Zedner explains, there have been strong pressures for the police to respond.

Extract 2.3.12

L Zedner, 'Victims' in M Maguire et al, *The Oxford Handbook of Criminology* (1997) 2nd ed, pp 599–600

As the first point of contact with the criminal justice system, the police play an important role in shaping the victim's experience. The first British Crime Survey found that satisfaction with the police response was generally good, but that the young, particularly young males, tended to be more critical . . . Shapland and her colleagues modified this view by showing that whilst initial levels of satisfaction with the police were generally high, this tended to decline steadily as the case progressed [J Shapland, J Willmore and P Duff, *Victims in the Criminal Justice System*, Cambridge Studies in Criminology LIII (Aldershot: Gower, 1985) pp 83–89] . . . Dissatisfaction arose from police failure to keep victims informed, perceived inefficiency, unhelpfulness, or unfairness. Disillusionment was a product, therefore, of a growing feeling that 'the police did not care and were not doing anything' (Shapland et al, 1985: 85). In a bid to respond to such criticisms, the Home Office now carries out regular surveys of public satisfaction with police services, each police force has issued a 'Statement of Policing Standards', and the Victim's Charter stipulates standards for police response to reports of crime by victims . . .

Particular efforts have been made to improve the police response to victims of sexual assault. Special interview suites in police stations, specially trained women officers, and joint interviewing with social workers in child abuse cases . . . are just a few of the innovations introduced in recent decades. Given these innovations, it is perhaps not surprising that victims of sexual assault appear to be more satisfied with the police than victims of physical assault or robbery (Shapland et al, 1985: 87). For the mass of property crimes where a suspect is never located, there is often little more the police can do than inform the victim of the reasons for ceasing their enquiries . . . However, in the case of more serious offences, victims look for sensitivity in the conduct of interviews, in the collecting of forensic evidence, in the handling of identification procedures, and for information about developments in the investigation.

In an attempt to ensure that victims are kept informed, both as a matter of routine and in response to personal enquiries, the Home Office has introduced a 'One Stop Shop' (OSS) initiative whereby the police become the single source of information to victims throughout the criminal process. Victims choosing to opt in to the OSS initiative are kept informed by the police about whether a suspect is cautioned or charged, whether the charge is altered, the date of any trial, the verdict, and sentence. Initially, the scheme applies only to crimes of domestic burglary, grievous bodily harm and attempted murder, robbery, sexual assault, criminal damage over £5,000, arson, and racially motivated offences. The scheme is a welcome move toward ensuring that the difficulties faced by victims in obtaining information from several different sources are overcome. This said, it is also open to criticism: many serious crimes (including domestic violence) have been excluded from the scheme and the police will be able only to inform victims of decisions made, not to offer any explanation of them.

But, in terms of legitimacy, the issue goes beyond keeping the victim happy. Many victims may feel aggrieved because the police do not share their views about the significance of the incident and the way to resolve it. For the most serious offences, the police are likely to adopt a law enforcement approach, regardless of the victim's wishes. For example, serious assaults which are reported to the police are usually followed up, even if the victim is reluctant to pursue the complaint or is unwilling to testify in court (Clarkson et al,

1994; see also Chapter 3 below). But where the police take a more lenient attitude to the complaint, they may require some assurance that the victim will co-operate with a formal processing, before they take action. If a victim is thought likely to be a poor or unreliable witness, the police may prefer to not even record a crime report. Even where the victim might be willing to assist, however, some victim's preferences are given low priority. As we noted earlier (see p 118), despite efforts to alter police attitudes, the police often choose to adopt an informal solution to domestic disputes. In doing so, they may be able to persuade the victim that it is the best course of action and then use her accedence to justify their decision (see generally, Edwards, 1989). On the other hand, some victims may be more influential than others and may present problems for the police if they are ignored. Thus, even when no criminality is involved, the police may invoke arrest powers to remove 'trouble-makers' at the request of publicans, security guards, shop or office managers, and security guards (see Kemp et al, 1992; Sanders and Young, 1994, p 93). The kinds of victim who are supported most by the police, therefore, are those who suffer from the types of crime which the police consider to be 'real crime'. This does not lay a firm basis for widespread support for the police in the community, but the impact of the victim movement has been to extend police interest to all kinds of victims, including those who may formerly have been regarded as undeserving, for example, the victims of sexual and violent crime or racial attacks (for a different view, see McLaughlin, 1994, pp 116–117). Nevertheless, it is still the case that, for those latter victims, it is the various victim support groups rather than the police who offer the most practical help.

(iii) Political accountability

While the victim's demands may not be the proper sole determinant of enforcement policy, they are an important element in identifying broader public wishes about the way the criminal justice system should operate. The traditional approach to policing has not recognised a role for direct democratic influence on operational policy, however. There have been suggestions for introducing some degree of local control over such policy (see Lustgarten, 1986; Jefferson and Grimshaw, 1984) but they have not succeeded in eroding the extensive discretion which the police enjoy in formulating and applying policing objectives. Since the prospect of political interference in prioritising enforcement choices is generally regarded as a threat to individuals' rights to fair treatment, the only formal control which is considered appropriate is accountability to 'the law' (see Lustgarten, 1986). Any further influence on policing policy is effected through a set of diffuse constitutional understandings which are known as 'policing by consent'. As Morgan shows, however, the existence and nature of that doctrine is by no means certain.

Extract 2.3.13

R Morgan, 'Policing by Consent: Legitimating the Doctrine' in R Morgan and D J Smith (eds), *Coming to Terms with Policing* (1989) pp 217–220

To clear the ground, and at the risk of stating the obvious, we need to be clear what policing by consent does not mean. It does not mean that suspects or offenders must assent to be acted against by the police. Were that the case there would be no need of police. Nor does it mean that the police should not act against offenders unless victims first assent. Victims' wishes are important considerations but they cannot be paramount. Policing is a public good. Offences are committed not just against individuals but against the Queen's, that is to say the state's, peace. There are good reasons for removing from individuals the capacity to determine prosecution and the allocation of punishment. Consent refers to policing policy rather than particular police decisions.

In relation to most public services we look to Parliament to find the core of consent to policy. Policing is no exception to this rule. We may call this the idea of contractual consent: it has two dimensions, the *legal* and the *political*. The police are established, governed, regulated, and empowered by statute. This body of law, approved by a democratically elected Parliament, ideally represents the will of the people. The law, however, changes but slowly, political parties seldom include detailed criminal justice proposals in manifestos, and governments need seek election only every five years. Further, traditionally we eschew the idea of elective dictatorship. In our system of democracy we subscribe to an ideal of continuing accountability (responsibility and answerability). Through ongoing processes of political accountability, mandates are allegedly refreshed. It is in this sphere that the arrangements in Britain for determining policing policy provoke argument. The law does not determine key aspects of policing policy and neither, directly, do elected politicians.

The law does not tell the police what priorities to pursue, what methods to use nor which of their many legal options to select. Within the tripartite structure for police governance – the chief constables, police authorities, and the Home Secretary – the police are stewards of delegated and independently exercised general policy responsibilities. Thus, in so far as there is *political* consent, it is realised through a delicately balanced mystery of influence brought to bear by politicians locally and nationally on what officers decide and on *ex post facto* accounting by the police.

It is possibly because of the unique political arrangements for the governance of the police that consent is used as much in a social as in a contractual sense. Social consent also has two dimensions. *Attitudinal* consent can be measured, in a more or less sophisticated fashion, through opinion surveys. It can also be gauged through public behaviour. Do people report offences to the police? Do they co-operate with the police by passing information, providing statements, appearing as prosecution witnesses, etc.? If they do, is this not an indication of trust and assent? Finally, what I shall call *operational* consent is often held to be the corollary of *attitudinal* consent. It is frequently suggested that we get the policing we deserve, the implication being that policing methods mirror public attitudes and behaviour. The extent to which

206

the police feel the need to patrol in pairs, arrest people, carry arms, deploy public order equipment, resort to physical force, etc., is indicative of public deference to their authority. According to this view, we can read consent, or its absence, into what the police do.

Declining consent?

Establishing the degree to which there is policing by consent and whether it has changed over time is as difficult an enterprise as one can imagine ... The public is not a homogeneous consensual whole. The law and policing, and thus consent to them, are not unitary entities. The authority of the police may be regarded as legitimate in spite of people's objections to particular police practices. People object differentially to *particular* laws, police priorities, powers, and methods. Moreover, the police and their methods are not a straightforward reflection of the society in which they operate. They may, for example, reflect the threat posed to order by a very small minority. Further, different sections of the community are more or less able to voice their views about policing and the degree to which they get a hearing is to some extent shaped by the structures of information exchange over which the police themselves exert a substantial degree of control ... Finally, it is doubtful whether too much should be read into public opinion surveys. We know from the British Crime Survey and other surveys that most people have little more than occasional fleeting contact with the police: only a small minority have prolonged and repeated, particularly adversarial, contacts ... It seems likely, therefore, that questions about what people think of the police will elicit, from most respondents, as much general attitudes about the state of the nation as informed judgements about what the police do.

There is not space to review these issues here. We can point only to the fact that during the last decade the claim that there is an acceptable level of consent, in all four senses of the term – *legal, political, operational* and *attitudinal* – has seriously been challenged.

The *legal* doctrine of 'officers as servants of no one save the law itself' is widely said to be built on sand and it is for this reason that left-wing critics have argued for repeal of the Police Act 1964 and the establishment of arrangements whereby democratically elected persons determine policy ... Moreover, the acrimonious passage of [PACE], the centrepiece of the Government's criminal justice record, indicated the divide (up to the 1987 general election) between the major political parties about what powers the police should have. There has also been a closely related breakdown of *political* consent. The tripartite arrangements, which used to give rise to no great concern, have in recent years seen an irruption of conflict. Indeed, in some parts of the country, police authorities have become almost ceremonial stages for the expression of dissent ...

Little need be said about *operational* consent. The police in mainland Britain are now provided with, trained in the use of, and routinely deploy, public order equipment the like of which would scarcely have been imaginable twenty years ago. The threshold for use of force against and by the police has been lowered. *Attitudinal* measures of consent are, for the reasons already cited, difficult to interpret. According to the general survey evidence, the police remain

among the most trusted of British institutions. However, the more sophisticated surveys show, first, that police powers, like stop and search, are used
disproportionately against particular groups and, second, that such adversarial
experience is associated with increased hostility to the police . . . The fact that
adversarial experience appears not to be associated with reduced willingness
to report offences is not necessarily reassuring: the possession of insurance
may be a more important factor. More significant is the evidence of reduced
willingness to assist the police, for without such willingness much police effort
is negated.

It is doubtful whether adequate mechanisms currently exist to enable the
concerns of those who are policed to have any direct effect on policing practice. A number of constitutional devices are available to allow political preferences to influence policy, but they operate at the level of senior management
and in rather abstract terms (the legislation is now consolidated in the Police
Act 1996). Thus, the tripartite arrangement, whereby police authorities, central government and the chief constables are responsible for the provision of
policing, acknowledges that the police have operational independence. This
applies, not only in respect of individualised exercises of discretion, but also
in respect of general enforcement objectives (see Savage, 1984; Lustgarten,
1986, pp 64–67); see also Reiner and Spencer, 1993). In securing the 'efficient and effective' maintenance of their forces, police authorities must take
into account the general policing objectives set by the Home Secretary as
well as the local policing objectives, performance targets and local policing
plans which they are obliged to determine. But the objectives are dominated
by managerial norms, for example, to maintain and, if possible, increase the
number of detections for violent crimes, and to increase the number of detections for burglaries of people's homes (see the Police (Secretary of State's
Objectives) Order 1994, SI 1994 No 2678; see also, Audit Commission, 1994a;
Audit Commission, 1994b). It was hoped that the introduction of Police Consultative Committees would provide more sensitive liaison between the police
and their communities but the evidence seems to suggest that their agendas
are typically defined by the police (see McLaughlin, 1994; Morgan, 1989). In
addition, the operation of the police complaints system has not been effective in deterring police misconduct, nor in sustaining public confidence (see
Maguire and Corbett, 1991; Clayton and Tomlinson, 1992).

Problems of political accountability are one instance of a broader set of
factors which, according to Robert Reiner, are contributing to a decline in
the legitimacy of the police and their social status. He suggests that the
traditional image of the British bobby, symbolised by PC Dixon in the television series, *Dixon of Dock Green*, has been inappropriate for many years. Such
an image of the police has been dented by the following: the uncovering of
police corruption during the early 1970s; the abuse of police powers – notwithstanding the introduction of PACE; the increased use of paramilitary
policing in public order situations and of firearms; a more partisan approach
by police of all ranks to issues of criminal justice policy; a failure successfully

to deliver the service and community aspects of policing to the public; the development of specialist policing at the expense of uniformed beat patrols; and, finally, a popular sense that policing is ineffective and unable to tackle the increasing fear of crime experienced by many members of the public (Reiner, 1992, pp 764–769). Reiner argues that these changes reflect deeper forces:

Extract 2.3.14

R Reiner, 'Policing a Postmodern Society' (1992) 55 MLR 761, pp 770–771, 777–779, 781 (footnotes omitted)

Police activity has always borne most heavily on the economically marginal elements in society, the unemployed (especially if vagrant), and young men, whose lives are lived largely in the street and other public places, 'police property.' Whereas the historical incorporation of the working class modified their resentment of policing, police conflict with the residuum at the base of the social hierarchy remained. Studies of policing in all industrial societies show this to be a constant. The police themselves recognise this and their argot contains a variety of derogatory epithets for their regular clientèle drawn from this stratum. In California they are 'assholes,' in Toronto 'pukes,' in London 'slag' or 'scum' and on Tyneside 'prigs.' Drawn mostly from the respectable working class, the police are responsive to their moral values and adopt a disdainful scorn for those whose lifestyles deviate from or challenge them. But however conflict-ridden, relations between the police and 'slag' have not usually been politicised. Membership in the marginal strata is temporary (youths mature, the unemployed find jobs) and their internal social relations are atomised, so a sense of group identity is hard to develop.

One important factor which politicised policing in the 1960s and 1970s was the development of social groups with a clear consciousness of antagonism towards (and from) the police. This owes something to the development of more self-conscious youth cultures, the return of long-term unemployment and the increasing militancy of industrial conflict.

The most crucial change, however, has been the catastrophic deterioration of relations with the black community. There is a long history of police prejudice against blacks and complaints of racial harassment. By the mid-1970s, clear evidence had mounted of blacks (especially black youths) being disproportionately involved in arrests for certain offences, largely but not only because of police discrimination. A vicious cycle of interaction developed between police stereotyping and black vulnerability to the situations that attract police attention, resulting from racial discrimination in society generally.

The burden of recent research on police-public relations suggests that while these still remain relatively harmonious with the majority of the population (including most of the working class), they are tense and conflict-ridden with the young, the unemployed, the economically marginal and blacks. What has happened to politicise policing since the 1970s is a growth in the size of these vulnerable groups, primarily due to economic failure and a heightening of their self-consciousness as targets of policing . . .

The police have lost the confidence of certain small but influential sections of the 'chattering classes,' what may be described roughly as *The Guardian* or *The Independent* reading circles. This process of a developing gulf with some educated middle-class opinion has a variety of roots, stretching back to the invention of the car. But the most significant are the growth of middle-class political protest since the early 1960s (CND, the anti-Vietnam War demonstrations, the 1960s' student movement and counter-culture) and the politicisation of forms of marginal deviance which involve some middle-class people, notably drug-taking and homosexuality. This conflict with highly articulate and educated sections of the population has been of enormous significance in converting policing into an overt political issue.

Underlying the change in educated middle-class opinion is a broader cultural trend: the decline of traditional patterns of deference and unquestioning acceptance of authority, a process which has been aptly termed 'desubordination.' This is reflected both in the attitudes of those at the receiving end of police powers and the general public audience of policing. Arrests are much less likely to be perceived as the legendary 'fair cop,' either by arrestees or by others. The police as symbols of social authority evidently suffer from a culture of desubordination.

The sources of declining public confidence in the police thus lie deeper than any changes in police tactics or policies. We can postulate an equation predicting public consent to policing in which public acceptance is largely a function of the extent of social and cultural consensus. Increasing social divisions and declining deference equal a decline in the public standing of the police. This is because police tactics will move up the menu of coerciveness to deal with the symptoms of division and to overcome the decline of consent. At the same time, controversial tactics, as well as outright abuse, are more likely to be perceived as malpractice by recipients, opinion-formers and policy makers, as well as the general public, due to declining deference.

... What are the implications for the prospects of success of current police initiative to restore their legitimacy? During the late 1970s and 1980s, as the creeping crisis of confidence in the police began to unfold, there emerged a succession of competing agendas for reform. In the late 1970s and early 1980s, debate became increasingly polarised between a conservative 'law and order' approach advanced by the police themselves and the Thatcher Government, and a radical rejectionist position, the organisational heart of which was in the Left-wing Labour Metropolitan local authorities elected in 1981. Whilst the Conservatives advocated greater powers for the police, Labour saw the problem as the unfettered autonomy the police enjoyed and sought to reinforce their accountability to elected local authorities. The Scarman Report in 1981 proposed a sophisticated synthesis of these two positions, but with strict law enforcement subordinate in the last analysis to the diplomatic requirements of keeping the peace. This was a policy of back to the future. The ideals of the British police tradition epitomised by Dixon [of Dock Green] remained intact in principle but had been undermined in practice. Scarman advocated a blend of community consultation and police professionalism, predicated upon an adequately maintained iron fist, to deal with disorder should the velvet glove tactics fail.

210

Scarmanism rapidly became the orthodox wisdom of government and police policy makers, to which at least lip-service had to be paid. In the hands of such influential police leaders as Sir Kenneth Newman and Sir Peter Imbert, it gave rise to a host of interrelated reforms throughout the 1980s. These were implemented in conjunction with innovations in management style which owed much to the new emphasis on professional management techniques and especially the concern for value for money, which increasingly pervaded the whole public sector. The style of the contemporary police chief correspondingly changed from bobby to bureaucrat.

Opposition to these approaches was rapidly won over, or bludgeoned over. Middle of the road opinion could not resist the *bien pensant* tones of the new philosophy of community policing. The radical end of the spectrum was subject to cruder tactics. The Local Government Act 1985 dealt with the radical critique of policing by abolishing its material base – the Metropolitan local authorities – and replacing them for police purposes with the more manipulable Joint Boards.

The problem with this accumulating avalanche of reforms was that while much changed in the leadership styles and presentational front of policing, the desired end products were not achieved. As discussed above, the end of the 1980s saw all-time record crime increases, renewed public disorder, spectacular scandals involving miscarriages of justice and plummeting public confidence in the police.

The leadership of the service has responded by seeking to model the mission of policing on the service style which their own research suggests is what the majority of the public wants. As described earlier, it has also sought to introduce a variety of managerial changes to monitor and improve the quality of service delivered. The key is seen as changing police culture to incorporate quality of service values. In short, the police elite has turned to the language and style of consumerism – market research, prominently displayed mission statements, codes of ethical service and the like. This chimes in with the general approach to the public sector promulgated by John Major, and is policing designed for the age of the Citizen's Charter.

Like its ideological first cousin, community policing, this consumerist ethos has the great virtue that it is almost impossible to be against it in principle. The issue is whether it fully confronts the realities of policing in the postmodern age. In so far as an emphasis of theorists of postmodern culture is on the centrality of style design and image rather than use-value, it is clear that the consumerist tack is itself a prime expression of postmodernism . . .

There are three strategies which must be adopted if the police are to achieve what legitimacy is available in the postmodern period. All are already in place as policy aspirations of the more progressive police leaders. The first is the recognition of the chimerical character of the Dixon ideal and its replacement by more pragmatic conceptions of acceptability. The police are providers of a mundane public service, not sacred totems of national pride.

Second, the personnel of the police must reflect the more diverse and plural demographics of postmodern societies. Specifically, the proportions of women and ethnic minorities must parallel at all levels in the police their numbers in the population policed. Third, local policing must be adjusted to the plural priorities and cultures of a much more diverse social world. Disaggregation downwards of policy making is already the main aspect of leading reforms such as the sector policing experiments in the Metropolitan Police. One vital ingredient which must be taken on board, however, is the integration of elected local authorities into the policy-setting process. For London, this means the creation of such a local authority. Opinion polls and market research techniques, on which the police increasingly rely, cannot substitute for the electoral process as a means of registering public opinion.

However, it remains a matter of debate as to whether improvements in political accountability alone can have a positive impact on practical decision-making. One of the lessons of the research reviewed in this chapter is that legislative and managerial efforts to control policing behaviour are constantly compromised by the operational culture. A combination of measures is needed – to increase the legitimacy of police action generally, in terms of the issues identified by Reiner, and to influence the policing culture to accept fairness and responsiveness to public wishes. The basis of police decision-making at the point of entry to the criminal justice system has obvious implications for the status and legitimacy of that system as a whole.

4. FURTHER ACTION: WARNINGS AND CAUTIONS

Once the police have apprehended a suspect and investigated his or her behaviour, they have a number of options for further decision. One is to take no further action and release the person concerned. Another is to administer a warning or a caution in circumstances where they are convinced that the individual has offended but where they have reasons for not taking the matter to court. The final option is to prepare a case for prosecution. In making these decisions, the police are able to take into account three sets of guidance: their own force policies, the current Home Office Circular on cautioning, and the Crown Prosecution Service's approach to prosecution. In addition, the working culture of the police reaches into this area of discretion as it does in respect of initial encounters with the public.

Following arrest and arrival at a police station, the custody officer is responsible for deciding whether the suspect should be detained or released (see, generally, Lidstone and Palmer, 1996, pp 316–387) and whether he or she should be charged with an offence. Here, the basis of any charge will be the information supplied to the custody officer by the arresting officer. Generally, the latter's view of the situation, including the seriousness of the alleged offence, will tend to be accepted by custody officers. As fellow 'practical professionals', they will also be sensitive to the concerns of beat officers that their authority is upheld. Consequently, public order offending may result in charges, whereas domestic violence may be followed by no further action (see Chapter 3, pp 254–9; McConville et al, 1991, pp 112–119). Similarly, decisions whether or not to charge will be influenced by the same considerations which apply to 'no-criming', discussed earlier at pp 173–4: perceived seriousness, likelihood of victim to co-operate, administrative workload. Another important factor is anticipation of future decisions by the Crown Prosecution Service; as will be discussed in the following chapter, the test for prosecution is that of a 'realistic prospect of conviction', which is a stricter standard than the 'reasonable suspicion' criterion for arrest and is a disincentive to proceed with suspects who have been subject to marginal and legally unjustifiable arrests.

In addition to these practical considerations of policing culture and administrative efficiency, an important policy objective in not processing suspects is that of 'diversion'. Diverting offenders from the formal process of prosecution, trial and sentence may be preferable where the human costs of the process are too great or where a different approach may better achieve a reduction in offending.

Extract 2.4.1

A Ashworth, 'Prosecution, Police and Public – A Guide to Good Gatekeeping' (1984) 23 *Howard Journal of Criminal Justice* 65, pp 66–67

It would be possible to have a system of criminal procedure whereby the prosecutor is obliged to bring a prosecution in all cases in which there is sufficient evidence against a person. This, indeed, is the Austrian system, and in West Germany the same obligation rests upon prosecutors when dealing with offences which carry a maximum of more than one year's imprisonment. There are strong arguments of principle in favour of mandatory prosecution. Criminal justice is seen to be administered in an even-handed way: the sense of unfairness sometimes generated by selective prosecution policies is avoided, as is the scope for prejudice, bias and even corruption among those who prosecute. All persons against whom there is sufficient evidence are dealt with in open court. Secondly, it would seem unconstitutional for members of the Executive, such as police and prosecutors, to dilute the laws laid down by Parliament by prosecuting for some and not for others. Thirdly, mandatory prosecution might be expected to have denunciatory and general deterrent effects, and thereby to promote greater observance of the law. Fourthly, since it is well known that most offences which the police record are brought to their attention by members of the public, mandatory prosecution might be supported as implementing the wishes of the public in relation to prosecution policy.

In view of these apparently weighty arguments of principle, why is it that not only has the English approach always favoured discretion in prosecution policy, but also that even those countries which proclaim mandatory prosecution appear nevertheless to find ways of avoiding the prosecution of certain offences and offenders? First and foremost, the argument based on justice may be turned on its head. Whilst inconsistent prosecution policies do strike citizens as unjust, it is not expected that every single person against whom there is sufficient evidence will be prosecuted. Indeed there might be a loss of public respect for the law if it were thought to be administered harshly and unsympathetically, as by prosecuting the old, the infirm or the afflicted. This may be linked to a second argument: prosecution in court may have a great human cost, even for a defendant who is ultimately acquitted. When the possible psychological consequences to the defendant, together with social and economic consequences, are placed in the scales, they should only be outweighed when there is demonstrable need to prosecute rather than to take some other action. This leads to the third argument, which is that there is no compelling evidence for the view that prosecution, conviction and sentence constitute the most effective means of preventing further crimes. Other approaches might be no less effective. Fourthly, the constitutional argument is less strong than it appears at first sight. In some instances Parliament has framed offences widely so as to allow room for sensitive and selective prosecution policies: the offence of unlawful sexual intercourse with a girl aged under 16 is the clearest example. On other occasions, as when enacting a single offence of theft with a maximum sentence of ten years, it might be said that Parliament did not expect every little dishonest taking to be prosecuted in court.

As a rationale for diversion, the avoidance of stigma has been especially important. It was given prominence by writers from the 'labelling' or 'interactionist perspective' (for an overview, see Downes and Rock, 1988, Ch 7; for an application, see Welsh, 1981) who argued that the official labelling of a suspect as an offender could have the effect of consolidating offending behaviour rather than deterring it. First offenders, especially juveniles, were considered particularly vulnerable to official stigma which could impede their ability or willingness to be re-integrated as law-abiding members of society. Diversion may also be regarded as being within the broad criminal justice process, however. For some offenders, it may be a suitable alternative to formal disposals, constituting a method in its own right for penalising offending by requiring, for example, apologies, reparation, compensation or community service. In the past, such an approach has not been encouraged in England and Wales although it does play an important part in some Continental legal systems, notably the Dutch (see Sanders, 1986; Brants and Field, 1995). However, as will be explained below, the Crime and Disorder Bill has introduced special provision for any child or young person who is diverted from prosecution: he or she will be expected to participate in a 'rehabilitation programme', the purpose of which is to rehabilitate and prevent re-offending.

Generally, however, diversionary policies have not been fully articulated in police decision-making prior to prosecution (for their application by the Crown Prosecution Service, see Chapter 3 below). Instead, police choices following arrest are based on a combination of factors – practical policing, administrative convenience, evidential considerations, as well as the reduction of stigma or the benefits of referring an offender to welfare agencies for support and guidance. Only in some police forces have the latter considerations been formalised in the shape of 'caution-plus' programmes. In this context, two concerns are frequently voiced. One is that an excessive use of decisions to divert offenders from prosecution will have the effect of bringing the whole criminal justice process into disrepute. This may occur where diversion is regarded as a 'soft' option which enables offenders to be 'let off'. The other concern is the lack of due process associated with police decisions prior to prosecution. Such decisions are 'low visibility', and enable the police effectively to act as prosecutor, jury and sentencer in disposing of the case. Moreover, in doing so, there is no guarantee that the police are deploying appropriate criteria. One worry, for example, is that there may be bargaining with a suspect to encourage the admission of an offence, so as to facilitate the issue of a caution; this would avoid the additional work and uncertainty of proceeding to prosecution, but it would secure another clear-up. Any diversionary decision necessarily involves the loss of some openness in criminal justice procedures, but this loss can be set against the expected benefits of individualised justice, institutional efficiency, or the more effective reduction of crime. Anxiety over this trade-off can be much reduced if the procedures for diversion are clear, and if they are carried out in a rational and transparent manner. As we shall see, however, current practice does not achieve those aims.

From the suspect's point of view, the most desirable option is that, after arrest, the police take no further action. It appears that about a quarter of arrests result in that outcome (McConville et al, 1991, p 104). Amongst those, however, there will be a proportion of arrestees who have been orally warned by the police that they will face more severe action should they come to police attention again. Such warnings are usually given informally (in the same way that they are given at street level) but they are becoming recognised explicitly, at the level of internal police procedure, as a stage in the process of dealing with offenders (in the Case Disposal Manual used by some forces: see Rose, 1996, pp 162–164; Evans and Ellis, 1997, p 3). Rather confusingly, such an informal warning is often described as an 'informal caution' (although such usage is disapproved by the Home Office: see Home Office, 1994, para 13) and is used where the suspect has admitted an offence but will not consent to being given a caution. Unlike a proper caution, however, an informal warning will not be mentioned in court, should there be further offending. But, where the suspect does not accept the warning, yet the case is not proceeded with further, the crime is counted as cleared up. The other option for the custody officer is to recommend that the suspect should be cautioned. The National Standards for Cautioning are contained in a Home Office Circular and extracts from the latest version, which was issued in 1994, are provided below. It should be noted that a caution may be administered by a senior police officer provided that (1) there is sufficient evidence of the suspect's guilt (on the reasonable prospect of conviction test), (2) the offence has been admitted, and (3) informed consent to the caution has been given. However, as mentioned above, cautioning provides a convenient way of processing offenders without the burdens and the risks of going to court and there is evidence that it is used despite the absence of the three preconditions of evidence, admission and consent (see Sanders, 1988; Dignan, 1992; McConville et al, 1991, pp 112–119).

Extract 2.4.2

Home Office, *The Cautioning of Offenders* (1994)

NATIONAL STANDARDS FOR CAUTIONING (REVISED)

Aims

1. The purposes of a formal caution are –

 – to deal quickly and simply with less serious offenders;
 – to divert them from unnecessary appearance in the criminal courts; and
 – to reduce the chances of their re-offending.

Note 1A A caution is not a form of sentence. It may not be made conditional upon the satisfactory completion of a specific task such as reparation or the payment of compensation to the victim. Only the courts may impose such requirements.

Decision to caution

2. A formal caution is a serious matter. It is recorded by the police; it should influence them in their decision whether or not to institute proceedings if the person should offend again, and it may be cited in any subsequent court proceedings. In order to safeguard the offender's interests, the following conditions must be met before a caution can be administered –

 – there must be *evidence of the offender's guilt* sufficient to give a realistic prospect of conviction;
 – the offender must *admit the offence*;
 – the offender (or, in the case of a juvenile, his parents or guardian) must understand the significance of a caution and give *informed consent* to being cautioned.

Note 2A Where the evidence does not meet the required standard, a caution cannot be administered.

Note 2B A caution will not be appropriate where a person does not make a clear and reliable admission of the offence (for example if intent is denied or there are doubts about his mental health or intellectual capacity).

Note 2C If an offence is committed by a juvenile under the age of 14, it is necessary to establish that he knew that what he did was seriously wrong.

216

Note 2D In practice consent to the caution should not be sought until it has been decided that cautioning is the correct course. The significance of the caution must be explained: that is, that a record will be kept of the caution, that the fact of a previous caution may influence the decision whether or not to prosecute if the person should offend again, and that it may be cited if the person should subsequently be found guilty of an offence by a court. In the case of a juvenile this explanation must be given to the offender in the presence of his parents or guardian, or other appropriate adult. The special needs of other vulnerable groups should also be catered for, in accordance with the Code of Practice for the Detention, Treatment and Questioning of Persons by Police Officers.

Public interest considerations

3. If the first two of the above requirements are met, consideration should be given to whether a caution is in the public interest. The police should take into account the public interest principles described in the Code for Crown Prosecutors.

Note 3A There should be a presumption in favour of not prosecuting certain categories of offender, such as elderly people or those who suffer from some sort of mental illness or impairment, or a severe physical illness. Membership of these groups does not, however, afford absolute protection against prosecution, which may be justified by the seriousness of the offence.

Note 3B Two factors should be considered in relation to the offender's attitude towards his offence: the wilfulness with which it was committed and his subsequent attitude. A practical demonstration of regret, such as apologising to the victim and/or offering to put matters right as far as he is able, may support the use of a caution.

Note 3C The experience and circumstances of offenders involved in group offences can vary greatly, as can their degree of involvement. Although consistency and equity are important considerations in the decision whether to charge or caution, each offender should be considered separately. Different disposals may be justified.

Views of the victim

4. Before a caution can be administered it is desirable that the victim should normally be contacted to establish –

- his or her view about the offence;
- the nature and extent of any harm or loss, and their significance relative to the victim's circumstances;
- whether the offender has made any form of reparation or paid compensation.

Note 4A If a caution is being, or likely to be, considered its significance should be explained to the victim.

217

Note 4B In some cases where cautioning might otherwise be appropriate, prosecution may be required in order to protect the victim from further attention from the offender.

Note 4C If the offender has made some form of reparation or paid compensation, and the victim is satisfied, it may no longer be necessary to prosecute in cases where the possibility of the court's awarding compensation would otherwise have been a major determining factor. *Under no circumstances should police officers become involved in negotiating or awarding reparation or compensation.*

Administration of a caution

5. A formal caution should be administered in person by a police officer, and wherever practicable at a police station. A juvenile must always be cautioned in the presence of a parent, guardian or other appropriate adult. Members of other vulnerable groups must be treated in accordance with Code of Practice C.

Note 5A The officer administering the caution should be in uniform and normally of the rank of inspector or above. In some cases, however, a Community Liaison Officer or Community Constable might be more appropriate, or in the inspector's absence the use of a sergeant might be justified. Chief Officers may therefore wish to consider nominating suitable 'cautioning officers'.

Note 5B Where the person is elderly, infirm or otherwise vulnerable, a caution may be administered less formally, perhaps at the offender's home and in the presence of a friend or relative or other appropriate adult.

Recording cautions

6. All formal cautions should be recorded and records kept as directed by the Secretary of State. The use of cautioning should also be monitored on a force-wide basis.

Note 6A Formal cautions should be cited in court if they are relevant to the offence under consideration. In presenting antecedents, care should be taken to distinguish between cautions and convictions, which should usually be listed on separate sheets of paper.

Note 6B Chief officers may also wish to keep records of cases in which action short of a formal caution has been taken, and the reasons for it. But care should be taken not to record anything about an individual which implies that he is guilty of an offence when the evidence is in any doubt. Offences dealt with by action short of a formal caution may not be cited in court.

The Home Office Circular stresses that the decision whether or not to caution is one solely for the police and it will be seen that the standards for cautioning allow the police considerable discretion. This has given rise to concern that the use of cautioning has not followed any consistent pattern.

Early research showed substantial differences in cautioning rates between different police forces and between adult and juvenile offending (see Laycock and Tarling, 1985) and this led to the Home Office issuing guidelines in the form of Circular 14/1985 (Home Office, 1985) with the intention of making cautioning policy and practice more consistent and effective and of encouraging the use of cautioning as a diversionary measure for juveniles. A few years later, in 1987–88, Evans and Wilkinson conducted a study to assess the impact of these guidelines and to review cautioning policy more generally. They found that there continued to be major discrepancies between forces in their cautioning policy and that those differences could not be explained solely in terms of variations in crime patterns. Rather, the Circular had encouraged 'tiered systems of pre-court decision-making', especially with juveniles (children and young persons). The first tier consisted of the pre-caution decisions to take no further action or to give an informal warning. The second tier consisted of decisions to caution, whether immediate, deferred (typically in order to consult with other agencies) or with a condition attached such as reparation or victim mediation (caution-plus). The third tier was the decision to recommend prosecution. However, there was no consistency of approach within forces or between forces in the way they applied particular tiers to types of offender or offence.

Extract 2.4.3

R Evans and C Wilkinson, 'Variations in Police Cautioning Policy and Practice in England and Wales' (1990) 29 *Howard Journal of Criminal Justice* 155, pp 172–175

Our examination of trends in average cautioning rates for all England and Wales forces shows that these were rising prior to Circular 14/1985 and have continued to rise since for all sex and age groups. The sharpest increase following the circular is for young adult males. Prior to the circular it was 'the policy of almost all forces to prosecute young adults and adults unless there were good and sufficient reasons not to do so' [G Laycock and R Tarling, 'Police Force Cautioning: Policy and Practice' (1985) 24 *Howard Journal* 81, at p 84]. This suggests that young adults and adults were treated as one group. In the period following the circular there has clearly been a change in policy with respect to young adult males which has affected average cautioning rates. We have already suggested that we are unable to assess whether this is due solely to the influence of the circular or due also to more general concerns about offence and custody rates in this group. It would appear that some forces are developing diversionary strategies for young adult offenders that are similar to those that they have developed for juveniles.

Our data on cautioning rate range trends suggests that if the circular has had any effect on consistency it has been neutral or negative for all age and sex groups. We need, however, to distinguish between consistency of outcomes in the form of cautioning rates and uniformity of approach in the form of policy and practice. We would argue that variations in caution rates between forces might be expected to continue as they are partly due to factors beyond the control of the police such as the proportion of offenders who are first offenders. We have documented, particularly with respect to juveniles, how cautioning policies and practices vary both between and within forces. Although we cannot measure precisely the effect of these differences on cautioning rates we would argue that it is reasonable to expect that some of the discrepancies in rates are due to these differences in policy and practice.

One of the most obvious sources or variations in juvenile policy and practice is that the circular encouraged forces to develop tiered systems of pre-court decision making. At the same time forces, or divisions or subdivisions within forces vary in the extent to which they make use of the available decision-making options. Given that the circular aims to increase effectiveness and consistency we suspect that the relationship between the two is that the effectiveness of cautioning for juveniles in some areas has been improved at the expense of overall consistency. There is some support for this argument from our trend data which shows that average rates have increased alongside a slight increase in the range in the period following the circular.

Whereas we do not have any answer to the vexed question of what would constitute acceptable variations in cautioning rates we think there are strong arguments for encouraging forces to have a uniform and therefore equitable approach to cautioning policy and practice. At the same time we would not wish to inhibit forces from experimenting and pushing back the boundaries of what is thought possible in the field of diversion. We agree with Sanders ['Rights, Remedies and the Police and Criminal Evidence Act' [1988] Crim LR 802] that there is still 'scope in England and Wales for increased diversion' so we would like to see a reduction in the number of 'rogue' forces with low but not high cautioning rates. Uniformity has to be balanced against encouraging the development of 'best practices'. With this in mind our research does suggest some further ways to achieve uniformity of approach.

Circular 14/1985 focusses on variations between forces whereas we think that the attention of chief constables should be drawn to our evidence concerning intra- as well as inter-force variations in policy and practice.

Their attention should also be drawn to the need for computerised recording of basic information about pre-court decisions. This is not only a question of monitoring the system but also of developing information for managing it. Forces ought to be able to tell how many pre-court decisions they are making, of what type, at what stage in an offender's career and with respect to what types of offences and offenders. Information ought to be recorded in a standardised way in order to facilitate intra- and inter-force comparisons and collected by division or sub-division.

It is hard to see how many forces can evaluate the effectiveness of their cautioning policies when they do not have the necessary basic information. Our interviews suggest that for the majority of forces evaluation consists of subjective judgments passed up and down the command structure and made during the process of internal review or inspection. Since the lack of hard data presented problems for us as researchers we can only assume that it presents similar problems to H. M. Inspectors of Constabulary when conducting external inspections.

There are a number of detailed ways in which recording pre-court decisions could be tidied up. For example our finding on no further action decisions suggest that they should be recorded in a way that distinguishes between those cases where there is an obstacle to prosecution and those where it is decided to take no further action even though the criteria for a caution or prosecution have been met. Consideration should be given to whether no further action decisions of the latter type and informal warnings should be recorded on personal records or solely as part of the monitoring process in order to avoid the dangers of net-widening.

Our research also suggests that there are a number of ways in which greater uniformity of policy and practice could be achieved. Circular 14/1985 treats no further action decisions as interchangeable with informal warnings and encourages diversion from the system by increased use of both. Our interviews suggest that in practice no further action is usually accompanied by informal words of advice so that greater uniformity might be achieved if all forces used either informal warnings or no further action in these circumstances. In either case they should meet the same criteria as those for a caution. Although the confusion between no further action and informal warnings makes it difficult to assess if the circular has achieved its aim of increasing their use and thus increasing diversion from the system our findings suggest that this aspect of the circular needs to be reinforced.

Our findings also suggest that the question of whether instant cautions are any more desirable than instant prosecutions should be reconsidered particularly if they are made in circumstances where an informal warning might be more appropriate, that is, when first offenders have committed trivial offences.

In setting out a wide range of pre-court decision options, at least with juveniles, and implying that forces could take up all or part of the range on offer, the circular arguably creates a situation where there is likely to be less rather than more uniformity of policy. Consistent policies, however, without mechanisms to enforce them are no guarantee of consistent practice. The circular is open to the criticism that it advises forces what to do but not how to do it. Even if it had suggested that forces adopt uniform cautioning policies, these would not be consistently implemented without placing limits on individual discretion and without mechanisms to regulate it in practice. The fact that forces are unable to define precise criteria for judging whether a caution or a prosecution is appropriate, even with respect to legal variables concerning the seriousness of the offence or the offender's record, is reflected in the belief among the majority of forces that 'each case should be judged on its merits'. How serious offences and serious records are defined in practice is central to the question of how to regulate discretion in order that it is exercised consistently. Sanders (1988) argues that:

'At present diversion decisions are generally made at the relatively low Inspector and Chief Inspector level. Low visibility in all contexts makes discretion almost impossible to regulate, producing the inconsistencies and abuses we all acknowledge.' (p 525)

There are, however, ways in which discretion could be better regulated for example by defining tight criteria for judging the seriousness of offences in terms of monetary values or degrees of violence scales, by subjecting individual decisions to consistent gatekeeping or by centralising decision making. Perhaps for guidance to be effective in producing uniform approaches to cautioning in practice greater attention needs to be given to this level of detail and to the question of enforcement.

Finally our research suggests that another potential source of a lack of a uniform approach to juvenile cautioning concerns consultation arrangements. These vary both between and within forces. For a major plank in cautioning policy surprisingly little is known about the effect of different systems on outcomes or about how discretion is exercised by the various professional interests involved although our findings, like other recent research, suggests that different professionals may have very different agendas . . .

We share Pratt's (1986) concern that the increased use of cautioning heralds a shift from 'judicial' to 'administrative' justice and so to some extent from the public to private domain where it is open to less scrutiny and more unfettered discretion. For this reason whatever the limits to achieving consistency of outcomes in the form of cautioning rates we ought at least to strive for consistency of approach in the form of uniform policies and practices. Circular 14/1985 has gone some way to achieving this and we have made some suggestions about how it might be further developed.

Following Evans' and Wilkinson's study, a revised version of the Home Office Circular on cautioning was issued in 1990, with the aim of further improving consistency between police forces and encouraging the greater use of cautioning for adults. In the meantime, the use of cautioning continued to increase at a marked rate. In 1985, the cautioning rate (offenders cautioned as a proportion of offenders found guilty or cautioned) was 26 per cent for all offenders. In 1990 it had risen to 33 per cent and, in 1992 it reached a peak of 41 per cent (Home Office, 1996e, p 104, table 5.3). However, in 1994, the current version of the Circular was published, ostensibly to refine the content of the earlier one, but actually to reflect a shift in the Conservative government's law and order policy. It was intended to alter the generally favourable attitude towards cautioning and to discourage its use in what were described as 'inappropriate cases'. The Circular states that 'cautions should *never* be used for the most serious indictable offences', such as attempted murder or rape, and should only be used for other indictable offences in 'exceptional circumstances', such as playground robbery. Other 'gravity factors' which suggest that an offence may be too serious to justify issuing a caution are 'the nature and extent of the harm or loss resulting from the offence, relative to the victim's age and means; whether the offence was racially motivated; whether it involved a breach of trust; and whether the offence was carried out in a systematic and organised way' (Home Office, 1994, paras 5 and 6). The Circular also deals with the issue of multiple cautions (the practice of giving a second or further caution to an offender who has already been cautioned once before) stating that more than one caution should only be considered where the subsequent offence is trivial or where there has been a sufficient lapse of time since the first caution to suggest that it had some effect.

222

Evans' response to the new Circular was critical of both the assumptions which underlie it and its anticipated effects. He argued that there were no grounds for believing that cautions were being administered when prosecutions would have been more appropriate and that the new policy against multiple cautioning, especially for juveniles, was contrary to both the research evidence and police experience.

Extract 2.4.4

R Evans, 'Cautioning: Counting the Cost of Retrenchment' [1994] Crim LR 566–575 (footnotes amended and renumbered)

Home Office Circular 18/1994 seeks to clarify key aspects of the existing guidance[1] pending Ministerial decisions on the Royal Commission's recommendations on diversion. The latter include the recommendation that cautioning should be governed by statute which, if accepted, is unlikely to be in place for some time. The purposes of the circular are:

- to discourage the use of cautions in inappropriate cases, for example offences which are triable on indictment only;
- to discourage the use of multiple cautioning because it brings this disposal into disrepute;
- to seek greater consistency between police force areas;
- to promote better recording of cautions;
- to encourage the police to monitor the use of 'caution plus' before a decision can be made on its future and to liaise with local statutory and voluntary agencies about the ways in which assistance might be offered to juveniles and their families to prevent re-offending.

Despite the claim that the circular seeks 'clarification' of existing guidance, the second of these points represents a significant departure from existing policy and practice.

Multiple cautions

Annex B to Home Office Circular 59/90 sets out national standards for cautioning applicable to adults and juveniles alike. With respect to multiple cautions Note 3D states that 'The offender's previous record (including any recent cautions) is an important factor although not in itself decisive. A previous conviction or caution should not rule out a subsequent one if other factors suggest it might be suitable'. These include an appreciable time lapse since the previous offence, whether the most recent offence and previous ones are different in character and seriousness, and the effect of a previous caution on the pattern of offending.

In addition Circular 59/90 lays considerable emphasis on the desirability of the police seeking the advice of multi-agency panels as an aid to improving the quality and consistency of decisions. It suggests that chief officers may find it helpful to consult other agencies both at a policy level, in order to agree broad objectives and strategy, and at the level of individual decisions, particularly in juvenile cases where the police are in doubt whether or not to caution. This raises the question of the extent to which 'straightforward' caution decisions are made at the police station by the police alone but decisions about second and subsequent cautions are made by multi-agency panels or bureaux. In some areas the police may in effect delegate to multi-agency groups the decision whether or not a further caution should be given.

The new circular states that research conducted into a sample of offenders cautioned in 1991 indicates that 8 per cent had already received two or more cautions.[2] A draft of the circular, which was sent out for consultation, contained the statement that 'it is only in *exceptional circumstances* that more than one caution should be given'. This does not appear in the final version as the Home Office was advised that the circumstances listed were by no means exceptional. They included where the subsequent offence is both minor and of a different nature from the first or where there has been an appreciable time lapse since the last offences. Nevertheless the circular is clearly designed to discourage the use of multiple cautioning. This is expressly stated and in addition a clear message was given by the Home Secretary at the press conference held to launch the Circular: 'From now on your first chance is your last chance. Criminals should know that they will be punished. Giving cautions to serious offenders, or to the same person time and again, sends the wrong message to criminals and the public.'[3]

The view that multiple cautioning has brought cautioning into disrepute has been voiced by sections of the police, the magistracy and the 'public' at least in the form of politicians. Plenty of anecdotal evidence has been offered in support of this view but the research evidence reveals a different picture. Questionnaire responses from the last national survey of cautioning policy and practice in the England and Wales police forces suggested that there is a wide variation in practice with respect to the number of cautions they were prepared to give the same offender.[4] In 19 forces there was no set number as 'each case is decided on its merits'; five forces prosecuted after one caution; 12 forces after two; two forces were prepared to consider more than two cautions and three forces declined to answer. More detailed interviews with policy and decision makers in 10 selected forces suggested that as a general rule of thumb juveniles were prosecuted after one or at the most two cautions. This was confirmed by data from the four forces that kept detailed statistical information on multiple cautioning. The proportion of third or subsequent cautions varied between 3 and 9 per cent. Seven forces, including these four, were able to supply data on second and subsequent cautions which indicated that the proportion of these varied from 16 to 37 per cent.

More detailed information is supplied by research conducted by Evans and Ferguson.[5] A sample of 367 juveniles was followed through the pre-court decision-making process. Arresting officers and custody officers were interviewed, crime files examined and inter-agency liaison panel and bureaux discussions observed. The latter suggested that there were often discrepancies between police and inter-agency records of previous offences. Indeed a considerable amount of time was spent clarifying criminal histories during inter-agency discussions since a key principle underlying decision-making was that the disposal should be in proportion to the seriousness of the current

Table 1 Number of previous cautions by disposal

Disposal	Number of previous cautions											
	0		1		2		3		4 or more		Totals	
	N	%	N	%	N	%	N	%	N	%	N	%
Prosecution	27	14	29	39	27	48	18	67	11	69	112	31
NFA	64	33	21	28	16	29	6	22	4	25	111	30
Caution	63	33	24	32	12	21	3	11	1	6	103	28
Informal warning	38	20	1	1	1	2	0	0	0	0	40	11
Totals	192	100	75	100	56	100	27	100	16	100	366	100

offence and the previous record. The time spent checking police records may be indicative of their inaccuracy. Reasons for this include the reliance on manual record-keeping and failure to collate information from different forces or subdivisions within the same force. Circular 18/1994 states that 'The accurate recording of cautions is essential both to avoid multiple cautioning and to achieve greater consistency.'

The Evans and Ferguson research is among the most detailed and comprehensive recent studies of pre-court decision-making. It is the only research that relates police and inter-agency decisions by looking at the prosecution process as a whole. In addition, although the research was carried out in a single force, this was chosen on the basis of the Evans and Wilkinson survey because it was typical of the types of multi-agency consultation arrangements that exist nationally. Estimates of multiple cautioning based on this research may therefore be more accurate than those based on police records alone.

Table 1 shows that the police force used for this study makes considerable use of informal warnings. These are equivalent to informal cautions as defined in Circular 59/90, i.e. where the evidence is sufficient and the offence is admitted but where a formal caution is considered inappropriate. Circular 18/1994 suggests that the use of the term 'informal caution' is confusing and not to be recommended but it does not wish to inhibit the use of oral warnings.

The Evans and Ferguson sample was constructed by taking all arrests over a period of time in three subdivisions served respectively by a juvenile liaison panel and two bureaux. Despite the fact that the force is supposed to have a uniform cautioning policy one of the bureaux had taken a policy decision that, since a caution is citable in court, and therefore a serious intervention, an informal warning could be given for first offenders committing minor offences. This particular subdivision accounts for 31 of the 40 informal warnings with another subdivision served by a bureau accounting for the remainder. This again illustrates that cautioning practice may be highly localised leading to differences within forces that are at least as great if not greater than those between them, a fact which is finally officially acknowledged in Circular 18/1994.[6]

The relationship between the number of previous cautions and the disposal for the current offence in the Evans and Ferguson sample is shown in table 1

Table 2 Number of previous cautions by age

No. previous cautions	Age 10–13		14		15		16		Totals	
	N	%	N	%	N	%	N	%	N	%
0	56	68	44	60	41	43	43	40	184	51
1	13	16	10	14	27	28	26	24	76	21
2 or more	13	16	19	26	28	29	39	36	99	28
Totals	82	100	73	100	96	100	108	100	359	100

and this is statistically significant ($p = <.0001$). The data provides further evidence that, as a general rule, juveniles are prosecuted after they have received two cautions. Of those cautioned the proportion receiving three or more cautions is less than 4 per cent and those receiving two or more is 16 per cent. The proportion of juveniles receiving two or more cautions in the Home Office research is 13 per cent, which is of the same order.[7] These estimates allow a 'worst case' scenario to be calculated based on the assumption that police forces implement the new guidance and that second cautions truly become exceptions and therefore insignificant in terms of their numbers. In 1992 the number of juveniles cautioned, for all offences excluding motoring offences, was 112,800.[8] On the basis of the Evans and Ferguson estimate, if all those currently receiving second or subsequent cautions were prosecuted, then the increase in numbers going to court would be approximately 18,000. The number of juveniles proceeded against in the same year was around 50,000 so the increase in the numbers of juveniles going into the youth courts would be 36 per cent.

It might be expected that the proportion of juveniles receiving two or more cautions will vary with age and that older juveniles are more likely to have received previous cautions. This relationship for the sample as a whole is shown in table 2 and as expected is statistically significant ($p = .018$). Of particular interest is the 16-year-old age group. This group is now dealt with in the youth courts along with 17-year-olds. The youth courts appear to have adopted an ethos and has a range of sentences for this age group which is more akin to adult courts than the juvenile courts which they have replaced. As a result 16-year-olds may be treated more harshly than they would have been had they remained in the juvenile courts. The increase in numbers going to court as a consequence of the implementation of the new cautioning guidance would be highest for this age group.

Subsequent 'trivial' offences

Under the new circular more than one caution may be considered where the subsequent offence is trivial, and the frequency of this occurrence will affect any estimates of increased numbers going to court. Having interviewed a considerable number of police officers in the course of various research projects over the years I would expect the use of this term in the circular to incense a significant proportion of them. I have lost count of the times I have been reprimanded by officers when I have referred to 'trivial' offences. 'It may be a trivial offence to you but the loss of £5 may be very serious for an old age pensioner. We prefer the term "minor"'.[9] Indeed this has been the preferred terminology in previous circulars including the draft of this one. Advice from the Home Office indicates that trivial is to be taken literally, with the proverbial theft of a Mars Bar given as an example. The change in terminology may therefore be of considerable significance. The former practice of forces with more liberal cautioning policies suggested that a commonly used threshold, distinguishing minor from serious offences, was burglary of a dwelling. The police tend to draw the line at cautioning offences of this seriousness.

The concept of seriousness has been relatively neglected in criminological analysis although Rossi et al suggest that the seriousness of criminal acts 'represents a conceptual dimension of criminality indispensable in everyday discourse, in legal theory and practice, and in sociological work'.[10] This begs the question of how seriousness should be judged. There has been considerable research on the question of whether there is any consensus about judgments of offence seriousness[11] from which Fitzmaurice and Pease have drawn two main conclusions.[12] First, individuals can make confident judgments of the seriousness of offences even though they are unable to describe how they have arrived at them. Secondly, there is a remarkable degree of consensus on these judgments across time, between cultures and among social groups. This is sufficient to encourage the recognition of 'seriousness' as a dimension of legal decision-making that is basic and comprehensible.

One problem with using the official labels attached to offences when measuring their seriousness is that these may 'fail to get behind these labels to where true seriousness is said to lie'.[13] For example the organised and systematic burglary of houses, in order to steal electrical equipment worth thousands of pounds, and the opportunistic theft of an empty tool box from an open garage may both be charged and recorded as burglary of a dwelling. In order to try to measure the 'true' seriousness of offences Evans and Ferguson used arresting officers' descriptions of the incident leading to the arrest including the money value of any loss or damage and the degree of any injuries sustained by victims. Randomly selected individuals were asked to rank these vignettes of the circumstances and nature of the offence for all cases in the sample. As expected from the results of previous research the level of statistical agreement between rankers was extremely high. The rank order was then used to assign a seriousness of offence score to each case in the sample using a score of one for the most serious offence and 367 the least. In order to simplify the analysis the scores for the sample as a whole were divided into eight groups containing an equal number of cases, i.e. approximately 45 in each. The group containing the most serious offences therefore consisted of scores one to 45 and so on. The most serious offence in each of the eight groups was then identified in order to construct an index of the seriousness of offences and this is shown in figure 1.

While a good proportion of the offences may be considered minor, arguably only those in the eighth group are trivial according to Home Office advice. Clearly on this basis the scope for giving second or subsequent cautions for trivial offences may be limited.

Figure 1 The incident with the highest seriousness rank score in each rank score group

1. Burglary of four dwelling-houses and the theft of two cars involving total value of £10,000.
2. Robbery by 'shoving' to obtain walkie talkie value £32.
3. Assault and criminal damage by punching in the face and kicking car door.
4. Juvenile caught by police climbing out of the window of an Educational Training Centre.
5. A 'scuffle' between a group of peers.
6. Criminal damage to school window value £45.
7. Theft from a shop of a digital alarm clock value £9.99.
8. Theft from a shop of a 75p packet of biscuits.

Another approach to this question is to explore whether second and subsequent offences in the sample are similar or different in character and seriousness to the first offence and to examine the current pattern of disposals in relation to them. As might be expected the majority of the offences in the sample were minor property offences including shoplifting, other types of theft, criminal damage, burglary other than from a dwelling and section 47 assaults usually arising from fights between peers. The fact that a significant number of 'trivial' offences are dealt with by the juvenile justice system has been commented on by various researchers.[14]

Assessments of whether the current offence was different in nature and minor compared to the previous offence for the sample as a whole relied on charges rather than detailed descriptions of the nature of the offence. This mirrors the real life situation as this is the information available to the police from criminal records. It is rare that either they, or members of inter-agency panels or bureaux, go back to full crime files to obtain more detail. There was no attempt to enter into complex judgments when making these assessments and simple rules were followed. Offences were categorised into those that were the same and those that were different and of greater, similar or lesser seriousness. For example robbery is treated as more serious than burglary which is treated as more serious than theft. In 34 per cent (N-67) of the 198 cases for which this judgment could be made the current and previous offence were the same and in a further 29 per cent (N = 57) the current offence was different but more serious than the previous one. Approximately 37 per cent of current offences were different or less serious than previous offences so that the increase in the number of cases that might be prosecuted under the new guidelines could be reduced by a factor of this order.[15]

Time lapse between cautions

The second circumstance in which a second or subsequent caution may now be given is where there is a sufficient lapse of time since the first caution to suggest that it has had some effect. Whilst this is vague enough to allow the police to exercise considerable discretion the research data indicate how it is

Table 3 Time lapse between offences by disposal

| Disposal | Time lapse in months | | | | | | | |
| | < or = 6 | | > 6 < or = 12 | | > 12 | | Totals | |
	N	%	N	%	N	%	N	%
Prosecution	58	60	10	37	9	37.5	77	52
NFA	20	21	5	19	6	25	31	21
Caution	18	19	12	44	9	37.5	39	27
Totals	96	100	27	100	24	100	147	100

currently defined in practice. Fifty-three per cent (N = 195) of the Evans and Ferguson sample had a previous conviction or caution and reliable information concerning the time lapse between the offences was obtainable for 76 per cent of these (N = 147). The relationship between the time lapse between offences and disposals is shown in table 3 and is statistically significant (p = .044). The mean time lapse for the sample as a whole is just over six months and the shorter the time lapse the more likely it is that prosecution will result. The chances of a prosecution or a caution become equal when there is a time lapse of over a year, so taking this factor into account, there is obviously some possibility of a further reduction of the original estimate of those with one or more cautions going to court under the new guidance.

Patterns of offending

Circular 59/90 suggested that a third criterion should be used when considering whether a second or subsequent caution is warranted, which is the effect of a previous caution on the pattern of offending. The new guidance omits this criterion and thus places a serious limitation on the exercise of discretion. The criminal careers of the juveniles in the Evans and Ferguson sample are typical. Forty-seven per cent of the sample are first offenders and a further 27 per cent have committed between one and three offences usually with a short time lapse between them. The remaining quarter are persistent offenders who account for the majority of the offences committed by the sample as a whole. Home Office research indicates that 85 per cent of those cautioned are not convicted of a standard list offence within two years so in that sense cautioning clearly works.[16] On this evidence police officers are right to take into account the pattern of offending. A 'normal' juvenile criminal career would appear to be one, two or at the most three offences committed in a relatively short space of time. After that the offender is likely to desist or at least not come to the notice of the police again. Only a minority continue into adulthood as career criminals.

Panels and bureaux

The Evans and Ferguson research suggest that there are significant differences between police referral rates to the juvenile liaison panel and the two bureaux. In the panel system decisions on first cautions were left to the police unless the offence was on the margins of being considered 'serious' or there were obvious 'welfare' aspects to the case. The main work of the panel was to advise the police on cases where a second or subsequent caution was a possibility. Both bureaux encouraged the police to adopt different referral policies. One argued that since a caution was citable in court, and therefore a serious intervention, the police should be discouraged from giving instant cautions at the station and encouraged to refer all cases for inter-agency consultation. The most notable model for this approach is the Northampton-shire Juvenile Bureau system. In systems of this type the police in effect delegate responsibility for decisions to the bureau. The other bureau adopted a slightly different approach. It was content to monitor police instant cautions by ensuring that they were notified to them and, like the panel, it focused on those cases where a second or subsequent caution was under consideration or the case was in some other way problematic. The Evans and Wilkinson national survey suggests that the Northamptonshire model is very much the exception and the referral policy adopted by the panel and second bureau is the more normal arrangement.[17]

One implication of the new cautioning guidance is that the work of juvenile panels and bureaux would be drastically reduced. Indeed this is indicated in the circular in so far as it states that 'The decision to caution is in *all* cases one for the police, and although it is open to them to seek the advice of multi-agency panels, this should not be done as a matter of course. It is important that cautions should be administered quickly, and where such advice is sought it must not lead to unnecessary delay.' Juvenile justice workers claim that their involvement in inter-agency consultation has been largely responsible for the increased use of cautioning.[18] This, allied to their commitment to minimalist intervention, makes it hard to imagine that they are easily going to relinquish the inter-agency power base which they have so carefully constructed. Neither is it easy to imagine that the police will unilaterally or instantly withdraw from these arrangements. All of this suggests practical difficulties in implementing the new cautioning guidance.

Conclusions

This question of implementation is a key one. Research into the effect of the previous Home Office guidance on cautioning (Home Office Circular 14/1985) found that forces responded in markedly different ways. There has been very little research into the effect of Home Office Circular 59/90 and it has focused on young adults.[19] Cautioning rates for young adults have risen since this circular was issued but whether this is a direct result of it, or the continuation of an already upward trend, is a more open question. Circular 59/90 aimed to ensure that forces comply with national standards for cautioning applicable to juveniles and adults alike but there is little evidence to suggest that this has been achieved. Significant differences between juvenile and adult cautioning rates remain and there are considerable inconsistencies in rates between and within police forces.

The Royal Commission on Criminal Justice recommended that cautioning should be placed on a statutory basis in the hope that this would lead to greater consistency. For those who advocate a liberal diversion policy, curtailing discretion in this way may be a dual-edged sword. At the moment the Home Office guidance is merely *guidance* which police forces, and their colleagues in inter-agency panels and bureaux, may choose to ignore. An assessment of the impact of previous guidance suggest that this is precisely what many forces did to a greater or lesser extent.[20] A more interesting question is whether forces ignore guidance when they disagree with it but comply when they agree. Since there is widespread dislike of the use of second and subsequent cautions amongst certain sections of the police they may choose to comply with Circular 18/1994 and avoid the use of multiple cautioning. A factor militating against this is that police discretion is exercised in conjunction with other agencies. Despite the fact that the circular reminds police that the decision to caution is theirs alone they are currently embedded in organisations which aspire to achieving liberal cautioning policies. This may be a positive barrier to full implementation of the new guidance for as long as they are unable or unwilling to untangle themselves from multi-agency structures. If the guidance had the force of statute, as desired by the Royal Commission, then it would almost certainly have the scale of effects which have been identified here.

This begs important questions concerning whether current cautioning practice is likely to bring cautioning into disrepute and whether there are alternatives to the measures proposed. The evidence that underpins the outcry against multiple cautioning is largely anecdotal. The research evidence suggests that juveniles receive more than two cautions in fewer than 4 per cent of cases. It is very rare indeed that more than one caution is given to adults, including young adults. Moreover when the police exercise their discretion in this way it appears to take into account the effect of a caution on the overall pattern of offending, mindful of the fact that cautioning appears to work. If the new guidance stated that third, rather than second cautions, would be given only in exceptional circumstances then this would both accord with the research evidence and the rule of thumb established on the basis of the practical day to day experience of police officers. This is not the first time that the current government has ignored research which it has commissioned or the informed advice of professionals working in the criminal justice system. Appealing to political and media pressure may have short term advantages but if a change in policy is likely to meet resistance, or to have unintended consequences, it may prove counter-productive. After all the already overloaded youth courts may be facing an increase of one-third in the number of cases they will have to deal with in future without any significant increase in financial resources given public expenditure plans.

[1] Home Office (1990) The Cautioning of Offenders, Home Office Circular 59/1990.
[2] Home Office Statistical Bulletin 8/94 (1994) *The Criminal Histories of those Cautioned in 1985, 1988 and 1991.*
[3] The Home Secretary, Michael Howard, reported in *The Guardian; The Independent; The Times*; and *The Telegraph*, March 16, 1994.
[4] R Evans and C Wilkinson, 'Variations in Police Cautioning Policy and Practice in England and Wales' (1990) 29 *Howard Journal of Criminal Justice* 155.
[5] R Evans and T Ferguson, *Comparing Different Juvenile Cautioning Systems in One Police Force Area* (Report to the Home Office Research and Planning Unit 1991).
[6] R Evans and C Wilkinson (1990) op cit. R Evans 'Comparing Young Adult and Juvenile Cautioning in the Metropolitan Police District' [1993] Crim.L.R. 572.
[7] See n. 2.

[8] *Criminal Statistics: England and Wales 1992.* London: HMSO.

[9] R Evans and C Wilkinson, *The Impact of Home Office Circular 14/85 On Police Cautioning In England and Wales* (Report to the Home Office Research and Planning Unit, 1988).

[10] P H Rossi, E Waite, C Bose and R E Berk, 'The seriousness of crimes: normative structure and individual differences' (1974) 39 *American Sociological Review* 224.

[11] T Sellin and M Wolfgang, *The Measurement of Delinquency* (1964). M Walker 'Measuring the seriousness of crime' (1978) 18 B. J. Crim. 384. K Pease, J Ireson, S Billingham and J Thorpe, 'The development of a scale of offence seriousness' (1976) 5 Int. J.Crim. and Penology 17. K Pease, *Judgments of Crime Seriousness: Evidence from the 1984 British Crime Survey* (Home Office Research and Planning Unit Paper No 44, 1988).

[12] C Fitzmaurice and K Pease, *The Psychology of Judicial Sentencing* (1986). Some would say this conclusion is rather optimistic including A Ashworth, *Sentencing and Penal Policy* (1983), p 85.

[13] H Parker, M Sumner and G Jarvis, *Unmasking the Magistrates* (1989).

[14] D Thorpe, D Smith, C Green and J Paley, *Out of Care: The Community Support of Juvenile Offenders* (1980). H Parker, M Casburn and D Turnbull, *Receiving Juvenile Justice* (1991).

[15] One word of warning is necessary. An analysis of differences in type and seriousness of current and previous offences in relation to disposals suggests that there is no statistically significant relationship. The implication is that the criterion of a sufficient time lapse is open to wide interpretation allowing police officers or members of juvenile liaison panels or bureaux to exercise considerable discretion.

[16] Home Office Statistical Bulletin 20/92 (1992) The Criminal Histories of those Cautioned in 1985 and 1988.

[17] R Evans and C Wilkinson (1990) op cit.

[18] H Blagg and D Smith, *Crime Penal Policy and Social Work* (1989).

[19] R Evans, *Evaluating and Comparing Young Adult Diversion Schemes in the Metropolitan Police Area* (Report to the Home Office Research and Planning Unit, 1992). R Evans, 'Evaluating Young Adult Division Schemes in the Metropolitan Police District' [1993] Crim.L.R. 490.

[20] R Evans and C Wilkinson (1990) op cit.

Evans' fear, that implementing the new Circular would lead to a reduction in diversion and an increase in prosecutions, is not wholly supported by recent statistics which show that, although the the overall cautioning rate has remained the same for the years 1992–94, at 41 per cent, there have been changes for the different age groups. There have been slight decreases in the cautioning of juveniles aged 10–17 but small increases in those aged 18–20 (Home Office, 1996e, para 5.17). In 1996, the overall cautioning rate fell to 40 per cent, the first fall since 1992 (Home Office, 1997a, para 5.15). This represented no change in the rate for all age groups except for males aged 14 to 17, for whom the rate fell from 58 per cent to 54 per cent, and females aged 14 to 17, for whom the rate fell by 3 per cent. However, it cannot be assumed that the reduction in cautioning indicates an increase in prosecution for all groups. The combined rate for juveniles who are found guilty or cautioned has been decreasing since 1986 and there is evidence that, for them at least, the police are resorting to greater use of informal warnings as a means of disposal (see Home Office, 1997a, para 5.8). The decrease in juvenile cautions could also be attributed to the effect of the current Circular on multiple cautioning which was most commonly used with juveniles. It appears that there has been some decrease in the number of repeat cautions (from 20 per cent in 1991 to 16 per cent in 1994) but the variation between police forces is significant and depends greatly on particular forces' arrangements for inter-agency co-operation (see Evans and Ellis, 1997).

Indeed, the research shows that the current Circular provides only a general guide for police decisions. The circumstances of each individual case and the localised practices of different police forces have a major impact on the detail of decision-making. This does not necessarily mean that cautioning decisions will be inconsistent; rather, disparities are difficult to detect because localised discretion mitigates the rationalising objective of centralised guidance. But such broad discretion may also conceal the role of practical policing in applying what may be inappropriate criteria in making decisions to caution. As Sanders and Young argue:

Extract 2.4.5

**A Sanders and R Young, *Criminal Justice* (1994) pp 234–236
(footnotes omitted)**

The cautioning 'rules' do not inhibit the police in any significant fashion. It follows that prosecution decisions must, if decision making is to be other than random and chaotic, be based on the informal working rules used by the police. The official public interest criteria are replaced in practice by the unofficial police interest criteria. These working criteria may, however, lead to three undesirable patterns of decision making: cautioning of those who should be NFAd [no further actioned], cautioning of those who should be prosecuted, and prosecution of those who should be cautioned or NFAd.

There are two types of suspect who are cautioned when they should be NFAd. There are those who, as we have already observed, do not meet the three pre-conditions, and there are those whose offences are so trivial that no action would have normally been taken against them. Caution is supposed to be an alternative to prosecution, not to no action. Yet there is evidence that at least some of the increase in cautioning represents more offenders being drawn into the system. This phenomenon – net widening – is warned against in the 1990 guidelines (para 3) and its existence is undeniable. Indeed, since it has happened with Scottish 'prosecutor fines' as well, it appears to be an endemic feature of all (so-called) alternatives to prosecution.

As far as the police are concerned, cautions are often as useful to them as are prosecutions and (especially in the case of instant cautions) they avoid a considerable amount of paperwork. It makes it worth arresting where it might otherwise not be worthwhile and, of course, where there is insufficient evidence it secures some kind of 'result'. Moreover, if the caution is presented as a favour to the suspect, it provides, or maintains, the basis of a relationship on which future 'deals' can be built. What is certain is that suspects are never given the choice between NFA and caution, even in cases where, if the suspect did not agree to a caution, the police would simply take no further action. Instead, in these cases, the choice is presented to the suspect as either caution or prosecution, and this usually produces the result the police

233

seek. If this is bargaining in the shadow of the law, it must be noted that the nature of the bargains struck will reflect the unequal status of the parties involved.

Cautioning those who should be prosecuted is advantageous for the suspects involved, but not for their victims. It is relatively easy for an officer to secure this result by constructing as trivial cases which are serious. Sometimes the offence is regarded as petty, or sometimes the offence is regarded as 'out of character'. Assessment of character, again as with stop-search and arrest, is fraught with difficulties. Middle class and white people particularly benefit from this. Informers are frequently cautioned rather than prosecuted as part of maintaining a mutually beneficial relationship. It is no accident that control of cautioning remains largely with the investigating officer, for cautioning can be an adjunct of other aspects of policing.

Where policing considerations such as order and authority point the other way, offenders are prosecuted and not cautioned. In one of McConville et al's cases [M McConville, J Hodgson, L Bridges and A Pavlovic, *Standing Accused: The Organisation and Practices of Criminal Defence Lawyers in Britain* (Oxford: Clarendon Press, 1994)], there was a fight outside a club which was notorious for minor disorder. The arresting officer said that the defendant would normally have been cautioned for his part in the fight but 'the reason he was charged was because we are objecting to the licence at [the club] . . . and the more charges we've got the better'. Kemp et al [C Kemp, C Norris and N Fielding, 'Legal Manoeuvres in Police Handling' in D Farrington and S Walklate (eds), *Offenders and Victims: Theory and Policy* (British Society of Criminology)] observe that it is not so much what the victim wants but who the victim is that counts. When business victims demand prosecution, they generally get their way, even where the police have reservations. And just as assessment of character and attitude to the offence can work to the benefit of some groups of people, it works in the opposite direction for those with a 'bad attitude' or 'suspect character'. In one case examined by McConville et al, a youth with previous convictions had picked up a Mars bar and broken a piece off. Asked why they had charged rather than cautioned, the police described the defendant as a 'toe-rag' who had been suspected of shoplifting on several occasions but never caught.

Research carried out in the 1980s found that very large numbers of cautionable cases were prosecuted. Now that, in the 1990s, caution rates are so much higher, it is likely that many fewer cautionable cases are being prosecuted (although net widening doubtless also accounts for an unquantifiable proportion of the higher numbers cautioned). However, there is no reason to believe that anything has changed in the cases where it is important for the police that a cautionable case be prosecuted. The same working rules that lead to the construction of 'suspiciousness' on the street, for example, still make prosecution more likely than caution for some types of suspect. Thus, the same patterns of race bias which can be observed in street policing seem to operate here. Evans ['Comparing Young Adult and Juvenile Cautioning in the Metropolitan Police District' [1993] Crim LR 572] found Afro-Caribbean juveniles to be prosecuted far more often than white juveniles in a study of the Metropolitan Police. He comments that 'this cannot be explained in terms of any differences in offence patterns for different ethnic groups or differences in the proportions of first offenders.' After reviewing several pieces of research carried out throughout the 1970s and 1980s (but not including the above study by Evans), Fitzgerald ['Ethnic Minorities in the Criminal Justice System', Royal Commission on Criminal Justice Research Study No 20 (London: HMSO)] concludes that: 'Once arrested, Afro-Caribbeans are less likely to be cautioned than whites and may be less likely than Asians to have no further action taken against them.' She does not conclude that direct discrimination is necessarily at work here. However, Afro-Caribbeans are less likely to admit the offence, are likely to be disadvantaged by the application of 'social' criteria (such as domestic circumstances) in an 'ethno-centric' way, and tend to have more previous convictions and cautions (possibly because of earlier biased decisions).

The custody officer is supposed to be a protection here. But as with evidential issues, the custody officer either acts as a rubber stamp or empathises with the arresting officer. Most custody officers, like police officers in general, are against extensive cautioning for adults in particular. One custody officer put it this way:

'When someone sits and looks at it in a file coldly the next morning it probably gives them a slightly different picture to what I see – the toe-rag coming in effing and blinding at all and sundry . . . Straight away you think "well yeah, okay, here we go", perhaps an independent would say no, no, NFA.'

However independent a custody officer might wish to be, however, as one told McConville et al, 'I'm dependent completely on what the officer says happened.' As with evidential matters, what the arresting officer does and does not say determines the construction of the case as serious or trivial, and the construction of the suspect either as a public enemy or as a temporarily lapsed paragon.

These insights about cautioning decisions are important to bear in mind when interpreting information about the effectiveness of cautioning. As the following extract shows, there is evidence that, in terms of reconviction rates, cautioning is effective. But it is not clear what effect the caution itself has on offenders' subsequent behaviour, as opposed to other options such as taking no further action or giving informal warnings, that is, the mere lack of prosecution. Another variable which needs to be considered is the influence of any support given by welfare agencies.

Extract 2.4.6

**Home Office, *Criminal Statistics England and Wales 1996* (1997)
paras 5.19–5.21**

Effectiveness of cautioning

5.19 Table 1 shows information drawn from studies of the past criminal histories of those cautioned for 'standard list' offences in 1985, 1988, 1991

Table 1 Sample of offenders cautioned in 1985, 1988, 1991 and 1994 percentage of the samples subsequently convicted[1] within 2 years of the sample caution

England and Wales	Percentages			
Age at sample caution	Percentage of sample subsequently convicted within 2 years			
	1985	1988	1991	1994
Males				
Under 18	20	22	25	22
18–20	20	25	25	24
21 and over	8	11	13	18
Total	19	20	21	21
Females				
Under 18	8	9	11	11
18–20	3	14	16	(9)
21 and over	5	5	7	(10)
Total	7	8	10	10
Persons				
Under 18	17	20	21	19
18–20	15	23	23	21
21 and over	7	9	11	18
Total	15	17	18	18

(1) Subsequently convicted of 'standard list' offences . . .
( ) Indicates percentage based on less than 50 offenders.

and 1994. The results suggest that cautioning is effective. Only 18 per cent of offenders cautioned in 1994 were convicted of a 'standard list' offence within 2 years of the caution. This was the same as 1991.

5.20 Table 2 shows that the effectiveness of cautioning appears to decline after the first caution. Only 11 per cent of offenders who were cautioned in 1994 who had no previous criminal history were subsequently convicted within two years, compared to 30 per cent of those with one previous caution and 42 per cent with two or more previous cautions.

5.21 Additional information from the Home Office Offenders Index, reveals that the percentage of those cautioned who had a previous caution was 15 per cent for those in the 1994 sample as opposed to 20 per cent for the 1991 sample . . . The 1994 sample was drawn in November after the Home Office circular 18/1994 had been issued. This circular specifically discouraged repeat cautioning and cautioning for the most serious offences . . .

Table 2 Offenders cautioned in 1991 and 1994, 2-year subsequent conviction rates following the caution

England and Wales	Percentages	
Criminal history before the sample caution	Percentage of offenders subsequently convicted within 2 years	
	1991	1994
No previous court appearances and		
– No previous cautions	11	11
– One previous caution	22	30
– Two or more previous cautions	45	42
Previous court appearances and		
– No previous cautions	24	32
– One previous caution	(33)	(40)
– Two or more previous cautions	46	(47)

( ) Indicates percentage based on fewer than 50 offenders.

Previous Home Office policy encouraged the development of inter-agency consultation (with the probation service and with local authority social work services) in juvenile cases. Although there is much variation between forces in the way that they consult (some referring to other agencies only if the case is complicated, others referring all cases routinely), the current Circular of 1994 has introduced uncertainty about the proper role of other agencies in deciding how to proceed with young offenders. The Circular emphasised that decisions whether or not to caution should be for the police alone, implying that other agencies' views should not be sought or taken into account. In addition, the discouragement of multiple cautioning had a direct impact on the cases where most inter-agency consultation occurred, and many police forces were concerned that the working relationships which they had fostered would be undermined (see Evans and Ellis, 1997: 2). Despite the official rhetoric, 24 of 42 forces are operating some form of caution-plus, and, in 17 of those forces, the willingness of an offender to participate in a caution-plus scheme is a factor which increases the likelihood of a decision to caution (Evans and Ellis, 1997, p 2; see also Brants and Field, 1995, p 132). But it is difficult to evaluate caution-plus because participation by the offender is voluntary, there is little information about its effectiveness, and its use is characterised by the inconsistencies in policy and practice which are common to cautioning generally.

Nevertheless, the new Labour administration's proposals in its consultation paper, *Tackling Youth Crime* (Home Office, 1997i, paras 46–63) and the

White Paper, *No More Excuses* (Home Office, 1997c, paras 5.9–5.15), are designed, in effect, to place caution-plus for juveniles on a statutory footing. The proposals are part of a broader package, which includes provision for parents to take responsibility for their children's offending, for the making of reparation to victims and for local authorities to make curfew orders in respect of children under 10 years. They are intended to reform youth justice by introducing measures which 'nip offending in the bud' before the young offender gets to court. It has been recognised that the majority of young offenders commit offences only once or twice, and that an informal warning or caution will often be the most effective way of preventing re-offending. In the government's view, however,

> [T]he trouble with the current cautioning system is that it is too haphazard and that too often a caution does not result in any follow up action, so the opportunity is lost for early intervention to turn youngsters away from crime. While some areas operate involuntary 'caution-plus' schemes, in others there is no backup to try to prevent further crime. Inconsistent, repeated and ineffective cautioning has allowed some children and young people to feel that they can offend with impunity. (Home Office, 1997c, para 5.10)

Detailed provisions to tackle this problem are set out in clauses 52 and 53 of the Crime and Disorder Bill 1997. The Bill will abolish cautioning for young offenders and replace it with a statutory scheme. The new process will apply when the following conditions are met:

(1) that the police have evidence that a child or young person has committed an offence,
(2) that, if the offender were to be prosecuted, there would be a reasonable prospect of conviction,
(3) that the offender admits the offence,
(4) that the offender has not previously been charged with an offence, and
(5) that the police are satisfied that it would not be in the public interest for the offender to be prosecuted.

Introducing further subtleties of terminology, the idea is to provide three choices in relation to a juvenile who admits an offence: he or she can be given a formal 'reprimand' by the police (where the offence is minor), given a 'final warning', or charged with a view to prosecution. When a final warning is given, the juvenile will be automatically referred to the local youth offender team and placed on a programme intended to help prevent re-offending. The new process is described in terms which do not include the caution, however, to distinguish it from the previous approach which is to be relevant only to adults, and clause 52(8) prohibits cautions from being issued to juveniles. By way of comparison, then, the reprimand for juveniles is analogous to that of issuing a (more formalised) informal warning to adults, and the final warning for juveniles is analogous to issuing a caution-plus for adults.

238

Consistent with the existing policy of discouraging multiple cautioning, a young offender will be able to receive only one reprimand, and only where he or she has not previously been given a final warning or where the offence is not so serious as to require a final warning. Once a reprimand has been issued to an offender, any subsequent offence must be met with a final warning or with a charge. Where a final warning has been given for a previous offence, including for a first offence, the expectation is that the offender should be charged and prosecuted for any later offence. However, where the later offence was committed more than two years after the date of a previous final warning, the police may issue one more final warning if the offence is considered to be not so serious as to require a charge to be brought. In due course, the Home Secretary will issue guidance as to the circumstances, including the level of seriousness, in which it is appropriate for reprimands and final warnings to be given.

Reprimands and final warnings are to be administered by a police officer, at a police station, in the presence of an 'appropriate adult' (a parent, guardian, local authority carer, a social worker, or other responsible adult not associated with the police). The police officer will also be required to explain the effect of a reprimand or final warning. In both cases, this will include the information that they may be cited in criminal proceedings in the same way as a conviction. Final warnings have more far-reaching implications, however. The offender must be referred to a youth offending team as soon as practicable after the final warning is given and, unless the team considers it inappropriate, they must arrange for the offender to participate in a rehabilitation programme, the purpose of which is to rehabilitate and prevent from re-offending. Again, in due course, the Home Secretary will issue guidance about the nature of such programmes and the consequences of failure to participate. A further effect of receiving a final warning will be that, if the young offender is convicted of an offence within two years of the warning, he or she will not be able to receive a conditional discharge in respect of the later offence, unless there are exceptional circumstances relating to the offender or the offence.

In seeking to introduce the reprimand and final warning scheme, the government is taking a more optimistic view of the success of caution-plus than the Home Office research would suggest (see Evans and Ellis, 1997), citing two schemes in the Thames Valley and Northamptonshire police forces where the effectiveness of diversionary initiatives appears to be promising (Home Office, 1997c, para 5.15). In fact, as Evans and Ellis suggest, there is still much research to be completed before the value of caution-plus can be assessed. In the meantime, it remains to be seen whether the police will continue to resort to informal means of dealing with juveniles after the new provisions come into force, or whether the statutory recognition of caution-plus will lead to yet further 'net-widening' (see p 81 above).

3

INVESTIGATING CRIME: PREPARING AND REVIEWING THE PROSECUTION CASE

1. INTRODUCTION

Between a crime's commission and its prosecution in a criminal court lies a process of investigation and case preparation, the conduct of which has a powerful impact on later phases of the criminal process. The majority of crime investigation is undertaken by the police and, like other aspects of police work, investigation is characterised by a large degree of discretion. However, the police do not have unlimited power in building the case which will be presented to the courts. Decisions made by victims, witnesses, suspects and defence lawyers will also affect the investigative process. Further, since its establishment in 1986 the Crown Prosecution Service has reviewed all cases before they are brought to trial.

In order to investigate crime, the police have powers which allow them to detain and question suspects. One of the key questions which we will consider in this chapter is whether suspects are adequately protected in the police station. Connected to this is the question of whether the rules governing police investigations are effective in guarding against miscarriages of justice, which are often caused by reliance on evidence of dubious quality at the investigative stage. It is sometimes suggested that the rules governing police investigations are too strict, that they hamper the police to the extent that the guilty are frequently able to evade conviction and that, as a consequence, the community is inadequately protected from crime (see Extract 1.3.3 above). Recent debates about the suspect's right to silence in the police station provide a good example of how the various concerns relevant to the investigative process – protecting suspects' rights, preventing miscarriages of justice and facilitating investigations – interact.

In order to understand this stage of the criminal process it is important to know something about the genesis of the rules and institutions that govern it. The structure of pre-trial decision-making in England and Wales has largely been shaped by two pieces of legislation which came into force during the 1980s: the Police and Criminal Evidence Act 1984 (PACE) and the Prosecution of Offences Act 1985. This legislation stems in turn from the report of the Royal Commission on Criminal Procedure (RCCP) which reported in

1981. Like the more recent Royal Commission on Criminal Justice (Royal Commission on Criminal Justice, 1993), the RCCP was established in response to a miscarriage of justice that had shaken people's faith in the criminal justice system: the *Confait* affair. In 1972 three boys were convicted of the killing of Maxwell Confait and of the arson of his house, their convictions being largely based on confessions they had made to the police. There was considerable disquiet about the case and in 1975 the Court of Appeal quashed the boys' convictions and an inquiry into the case was undertaken. The Fisher inquiry concluded that, although there had been a miscarriage of justice, two of the boys might have been involved in Confait's death (Fisher, 1977). However, in 1979 evidence emerged that completely exonerated all three. It seems that once the police had got confessions from the boys they simply made the other evidence in the case fit round the confessions, even persuading a pathologist to modify his estimation of Confait's time of death in order to negate the boys' alibi. The issues raised by the *Confait* case remain relevant today.

2. CHARACTERISTICS OF POLICE INVESTIGATIONS

(a) Case construction and investigative pressures

Pre-trial procedures need to be understood in the context of the way in which the police investigate crime in an adversarial system of criminal justice. Unlike their fictional counterparts, detectives rarely piece together clues to reveal the identity of an offender. Steer, who carried out research on police work for the RCCP, found that:

> the great majority of crime detections involve little of what the public would perceive as real detective ability. Information, forensic evidence even, contribute directly to very few detections. (Steer, 1980, p 71)

Steer found that suspects often came to police attention after having been identified by members of the public who reported the crime; many other suspects were already in police custody for a separate offence when they confessed to having committed other offences, allowing the police to clear up several crimes through questioning one suspect. The police played a direct role in identifying suspects in only about 10 per cent of cases in Steer's research.

A similar pattern was found by McConville and Baldwin:

How defendants were linked to offences	%
Police caught defendant in act	17.5
Victim or other civilian caught defendant in act	6.0
Police caught defendant in possession of stolen goods or in other suspicious circumstances	16.9
Victim or witness named or otherwise directly identified defendant	40.9
Defendant identified through interrogation of alleged accomplice	7.6
Defendant apprehended by other means	11.1

(Adapted from McConville and Baldwin, 1982, p 168)

The investigation of crime is often, then, a seemingly straightforward affair. The police will frequently have a suspect 'in the frame' as soon as a crime is brought to their attention. But this does not mean that police investigative work will end there, for if the police want to see their suspect successfully prosecuted they will have to collect convincing evidence against him or her. The *Confait* case is a good example of how the police tend to build a case around one or more suspects identified early in the inquiry. Sir Henry Fisher describes how, once three suspects had been found and confessions extracted from them, 'enquiries continued only to strengthen the evidence against them' (1977, p 203) at the expense of following leads which might have pointed to the boys' innocence. In an adversarial criminal justice system such practices are not unusual, and several commentators have argued that the archetypal police investigation involves the *construction* of a case against a suspect.

Extract 3.2.1

A Sanders, 'Constructing the Case for the Prosecution' (1987)
14 *Journal of Law and Society* 229, pp 234–242 (footnotes omitted)

[C]ases are not simply sets of objective facts which can be ascertained once and for all. Cases have to be *built* out of what people say or think about those facts. The content of cases is, therefore, fluid and uncertain. The police (and, of course, the defence) find that some cases change over time when crucial witnesses change their minds or disappear. Sometimes they make their cases change by *eliciting* thoughts and statements. Evidential strength is, therefore, determined by a complex and variable interaction between the events in question, witnesses to those events, and the police . . .

Creating the facts

. . . Crucial facts can often be far from concrete. Where, for instance, a suspect had been loitering it was not necessarily with any criminal intent; where someone refused to move along a pavement he did not necessarily obstruct it. These are matters of judgement, and judgements do not emerge from thin air. They are sought and provided in contexts that influence their very content. The judgement involved in eyewitness identification, for instance, is now known to be a partial product of promptings, expectations, and preconceptions.

Some facts are almost entirely lacking in substance. They are simply statements about facts – a confession, perhaps (which could be true or false), or an *opinion* about a fact. In *Confait* the police knew that their case against one of the defendants (Lattimore) would fail unless his alibi could be neutralized. Lattimore's alibi covered the whole period in which the pathologist originally estimated Confait had died. The police therefore persuaded the pathologist to alter his estimate. The time of death was a fact that was necessarily unprovable; the next best fact was an expert's opinion as to when that fact had most probably been. The police case against Lattimore rested on the successful re-negotiation of the pathologist's estimate of Confait's time of death. In other words, the strength of the police case rested on the police's ability to transform one set of facts (the pathologist's opinion) in order to nullify the effect of another set of facts (Lattimore's alibi).

Sir Henry Fisher was critical of the police in *Confait*. But to criticize individuals, rather than an institution balancing a dual role, was misconceived. We know that the police are entitled to try to build a case if it has a legally valid basis, and since most facts are vague and malleable one could argue that there is no distinction to be made between building and manipulating a case.

. . . facts sometimes, as in *Confait* have to be created as well as selected:

V and J had been friends. V had left his radio in the street by his car. From inside his house, he said, he saw J drive up and take his radio. J claimed that he had taken from the road by V's car some car components which he had lent to V earlier. The strength of the case rested in part on whether or not there really had been those components by V's car, for they provided J's reason for being in the vicinity of the alleged theft. After reporting J for the theft, the officer in charge was ordered to ask V about the components. In reply, V said that there had been none there.

As in other contexts where evidence is sought by the police, in the absence of knowledge about a fact (whether the components were there or not) an opinion had been sought. V's opinion, though, had to be *created* in the sense that he had to be asked specifically about the components; but in doing so, it would have been difficult for the officer to hide the significance of the question from V. The police cannot be criticized for asking V about the components, but it would be naive to assume that V's answers were unaffected by their context.

Since the essence of some cases is a set of facts which have to be created through police questioning, the police have also to be careful *not* to create certain facts:

243

H, a 64 year old man, was seen shoplifting. The arresting officer (X) asked him about psychological or medical problems in the interview. H replied that 'I had a lot of trouble with nerves'. He was cautioned. The sergeant said that he would 'talk to' X. When asked what this meant the Chief Inspector replied that X was wrong to ask H about his problems for it was 'giving him (H) a defence if it goes to court and he pleads not out.'

Constructing the file

Just as a case is not a simple summary of an incident, so prosecution files are not simply factual dossiers. They are argumentative documents, cast in a factual unidirectional mould. As Chatterton says, they present the action taken (for our purposes, the prosecution) 'as the only reasonable course of action available' [Chatterton, Organisational Relationships and Processes in Police Work (1975) unpublished Phd Thesis]. The 'Confait Affair' was, of course, an excellent example of this.

There are at least two reasons why files are generally constructed in this unidirectional way. First, supervisors prefer it when 'the thrust of the presentation is towards minimising uncertainty and maximising the strength of the case for the prosecution' [Moody and Tombs, *Prosecution in the Public Interest* (1982) p 45]. As one sergeant put it, it is no use having a file that 'left too much in the air' [Chatterton, op cit].

... the officer's adversarial task is to build his case clearly and unambiguously. So, in one case where several defendants could have been charged, the evidence against those not charged was simply 'discounted ... to prevent causing damage to the main charge' (officer in charge ...). This, of course, begs the question of what is the 'main charge'. The case which is selected to fulfill that role can only have its status questioned if something is known about *other* possible cases; but prosecution files are directed only at the case in question, and not any others:

D1 had an argument with D2, the father of D1's girlfriend (X). It was alleged that D1 hit D2 and that D2 damaged D1's car. Both the arresting officer and X stated that there was damage although they did not see it being done. Similarly neither saw the alleged assault. The Superintendent decided to summons D1 for assault and possession of an offensive weapon, and not prosecute D2. He then agreed with the Detective Inspector to 'strike from the statements all references to alleged criminal damage' by D2.

A second reason for files being unidirectional is that it minimizes the opportunities for criticism if the decision of the officer in charge turns out to be poor. The best thing to do about a poor choice is to pretend that there was no choice at all! The choice in question might be the prosecution decision, but it could also be a line of questioning leading to a defence ... or a denial. Hence, denials are sometimes omitted ... Nelken perhaps sums it all up in observing that material which could 'confuse' the issue is 'scrupulously rejected or amended in preparing court presentations' [Nelken, *The Limits of the Legal Process* (1983) p 127]. Officers who do not do this thoroughly pay the penalty:

P, a 38 year old woman with no record, stole items worth £10 from a store. It appeared a typical shoplifting, although P's confession stated that she took the goods to cheer up her daughter, her other daughter having recently died. She was arrested and charged with theft. When the Detective Chief Inspector saw the file he asked why the charge sergeant accepted the charge under these circumstances, whether P had medical problems, and what were the circumstances of the daughter's death. The officer in charge replied as follows: P was having medical treatment; the circumstances of the daughter's death were very distressing; P had told him all of this even though it was not recorded in her 'statement'; and the officer in charge had told the charge sergeant none of this. The case was dropped.

The arresting officer secured the charge by presenting a stereotyped oral report to the charge sergeant. This practice is not unusual. Had he constructed the file in the same way as his oral report no one seeing the file would have had any reason to question it. Consequently, we cannot ever learn how many cases of this kind there are, for it is precisely the absence of information in the files that makes their number unquantifiable. Constructions remain hidden forever in many guilty pleas where defendants simply wish to be rid of their cases as quickly as possible.

Paragraph 3.4 of the Code of Practice issued under Part II of the Criminal Procedure and Investigations Act 1996, states:

In conducting an investigation, the investigator should pursue all reasonable lines of inquiry, whether these point towards or away from the suspect. What is reasonable in each case will depend on the particular circumstances.

Another characteristic of police investigations which has been identified by a number of commentators is the importance of confession evidence. Questioning and the securing of a confession is often an easy and cheap way for the police to establish a case, as one police officer told Sanders et al (1989, p 134):

I make no bones about what my aims and objectives are; they're to get [the suspect] to talk to us . . . if he talks to us we can establish the truth much quicker.

The police secure confessions in about 60 per cent of cases. Confessions are usually determinative of case outcome: around 98 per cent of suspects who confess plead guilty or are found guilty after a contested trial (McConville, 1993, pp 32–33). However, confession evidence is not unproblematic: the suspects in the *Confait* case confessed to a crime that they did not commit, as did suspects in a number of other well-known miscarriage of justice cases. It seems that confession evidence is susceptible to being moulded by the constructive process of investigation (this aspect of confession evidence is discussed in more detail below).

Concerns about over-reliance on confession evidence have led to some attention being paid to increasing the use of other investigative strategies. Maguire and Norris (1992) suggest that, partly as a result of PACE, the CID may be moving towards the use of other types of evidence. For example, drug squads in particular often mount proactive investigations where a particular suspect is targeted. In this way an offender can be caught 'red handed' and perhaps filmed committing a crime, sidestepping some of the dangers of case construction and of the unreliability of confession evidence. The Audit Commission (1993) also proposed increasing the use of such proactive investigative strategies, especially the use of informers. However, an increase in the use of surveillance and 'sting' operations may raise fears about civil liberties and the propriety of entrapment (see the discussion of the entrapment cases in Chapter 4 below). Police dealings with informers also raise ethical questions. The Police Complaints Authority has noted that 'many informants are themselves involved in criminal activities' and that '[a] number of corruption allegations considered by the Authority have resulted from relationships between detective officers and informers' (Police Complaints Authority, 1996, p 33). See further Dunningham and Norris (1996).

In Chapter 2 we have seen how, in recent years, the police have come under pressure to provide 'value for money' and to carry out their work efficiently. Efficiency concerns have an impact on crime investigation (the Audit Commission's perception that the use of informers was cost-effective was the main reason why it recommended increasing their use). Although forensic science evidence provides an alternative to confession evidence (and is arguably more reliable), its use is affected by financial considerations. Since 1991 the police have had to pay a sum to the Forensic Science Service (FSS) every time they send an item of evidence to it for examination, a change which has forced police officers to ask themselves whether such evidence provides value for money.

Extract 3.2.2

Blakey, 'Does Forensic Science Give Value for Money' (1995) 35 *Science and Justice* 1, pp 2–4

I have to be sure that forensic science is a better use of the £2.4m of my £96m budget than spending it on informants, computers, more police officers, horses, dogs or helicopters. Is it?

Of the £2.4m of my budget spent on forensic science, £1.1m goes to fingerprints and photography and £1.3m to forensic science; of the £1.3m going to forensic science, half of that is my Forensic Science Service (FSS) budget and the other half is staff time on non-fingerprint work.

Now, £1.3m per annum would buy me a very big helicopter every year, or 70 extra police constables for the beat, and that is what the public demands. I have never yet had a politician or member of the public say to me. 'Chief, what we need is a bigger forensic science budget'. Let us assume that fingerprints and photography do give value for money – and I do assume that, not wishing to make any more enemies. That is not to say that there could not be efficiencies and savings. I remain ashamed that it took the Audit Commission, a set of accountants, to point out to Chief Constables some years ago that

246

it was time to sort themselves out in the management of fingerprints. There are new fingerprint technologies and equipment coming along to improve efficiency which we must adopt.

Does forensic science, excluding fingerprints, give value for money? We need to look at the recent history of the FSS, the biggest provider by far of forensic science to UK forces ... The Service rightly enjoys a high reputation for integrity, quality of work and for its research and development programme. As a government department it stood more exposed than any police force, and the same winds of political and management change which affected the police service have been at work on the FSS.

In 1991 the FSS, became an agency. It must now recover its costs by direct charging – it has to show value for money. In the words of Janet Thompson, Director of the FSS, 'The first three years as an Agency with a hard charging regime has resulted in changes in customer behaviour, which have required the adoption of new management procedures and disciplines in the Forensic Science Service'. [Forensic Science Service, *Annual Report and Accounts 1993/94*, HC 517 (London: HMSO, 1994)]. That is precisely why the change to agency status was advocated. The aim was to change customer behaviour and also to sharpen up, where needed, the practices of the FSS. Those aims have progressed and have produced the debate we are now engaged upon. Having focused the mind of customers on cost and continuing to improve internal practices, value for money considerations automatically appear. I have much respect for the FSS; it has come through a baptism of fire in the first three years as an agency and is the better for it. The quality is high and turn-round times are improved. There may be alternative providers of forensic science presently and in the future. The market forces concept expects that to happen and welcomes it, but however the market develops, Chief Constables are still left with the decisions to make on the allocation of resources, and they will make them on the basis of key objectives and policy plans.

In 1993, in my force, I spent £707,968 to help solve 90 burglaries through useful physical trace evidence. Every burglary/dwelling case cost nearly £10,000 and every burglary/other case something over £6,000 for forensic science. Those costs included Scenes of Crime Officers' time and FSS charges. By contrast, the total cost to identify 510 burglars by fingerprint was £541,706; every burglary/dwelling fingerprint identification cost £1,151 and burglary/other £983. So, fingerprints give much better value for money than physical trace evidence and they are a sole identifier, not just something 'useful', the definition of which varies from person to person and between groups of people.

With regard to violent crime, physical trace evidence resulted in conclusive or strong evidence to link suspect to offence in 30 assault cases and 14 sexual offences in West Mercia in 1993, again a very small proportion of the total number of such cases. Only 5 per cent of recorded crime is violent, although, of course, the more serious the violent crime, the greater the import of forensic science, partly because of the likely incidence of bodily fluids and also because of the amount of time which can be spent at the scene and in the laboratory. I do not dismiss the major contribution of forensic science to those high profile cases which concern the police and horrify the public.

Earlier I posed two tests for forensic science, namely that it should contribute to key objectives and likely policing plans, and that it should compare, in

247

terms of value for money, with other policing functions in the realization of the policing plan. My contention is that in burglary and in car crime – the volume crime which plagues the police and infuriates the public – forensic science plays no significant part. In this important, publicly-identified prominent area, forensic science is not presently giving value for money. It contributes little to the policing plans against volume crime now being produced.

The second question is more difficult. Of course, more police officers would help in visible policing, in response times and possibly in crime reduction and detection. I say possibly, but I think that 25 police constables in a burglary squad would solve me more than 90 burglaries a year. The £707,968 I spent on burglaries and forensic science last year would buy me 38 extra police constables, and the Head of my Criminal Investigation Department would drool at the thought of £700,000 more in his informants' fund and promise me more than 90 burglaries cleared up on the strength of it.

So, do I pull the plug on forensic science, at least for burglaries and car crime, as some forces apparently have done and others might be contemplating? I hope not.

I recognize that forensic science work is interdependent; we must think hard before cutting the budget so drastically and expecting our laboratories to continue to do the excellent work on serious crime and in research that the FSS does. Also, the whole thrust of investigations as expressed by the Royal Commission and by the Audit Commission in 'Tackling Crime Effectively' is to more, not less, reliance on intelligence work, surveillance and forensic science work, all suitably integrated. I readily admit that my somewhat simplistic presentations of figures and costs is not yet nearly as sophisticated as it should be. I am not setting out to prove conclusively that spending money on more 'coppers, cars or computers', and not on forensic science for burglary, would give better value for money. The evidence is still being gathered . . .

There are some fears about the effects that financial constraints have had on police use of forensic science evidence. In 1994 Her Majesty's Chief Inspector of Constabulary commented that: 'the provision of scientific services, whereby forces pay on an item by item basis, continues to be constrained by force budgets, with the result that forensic support is sometimes not obtained in cases where it could prove beneficial' (1994a, p 36). Research on police use of scientific evidence found that 'financial considerations' were the most common reason for officers choosing not to submit evidence to forensic science laboratories (given as a reason in 40 per cent of cases) (Saulsbury et al, 1994, p 32). See further Roberts (1996); Stockdale and Walker (1993, pp 86–87).

It is not only the police's use of certain evidence types or investigative strategies that is affected by efficiency concerns. The police must prove their overall efficiency in providing a service to the public and, when it comes to the investigation of crime, efficiency is measured in terms of clear-up rates. This inevitably puts pressure on police officers to secure convictions. In the following extract, Maguire and Norris describe how this pressure is part and parcel of the work of CID officers. (The CID (Criminal Investigation Department) of a police force is staffed by plain clothes officers who investigate the more serious types of crime, such as serious assaults, robbery and burglary, and do none of the community orientated work associated with uniformed officers.)

Extract 3.2.3

M Maguire and C Norris, *The Conduct and Supervision of Criminal Investigations* (1992) pp 33–35 (some footnotes omitted and amended)

A ... factor which looms large in the working environment of divisional CID offices is that of pressure to produce 'results'. This can take a number of forms. As noted earlier, the main currency by which success is measured in divisional crime work is the 'clear up'. The need to 'keep the Home Office happy', to quote the title of a recent article on the subject[1] (or, one could equally say, to keep police managers happy), by maintaining the clear up rate at an acceptable level, forms a background to the work which can never be ignored.

Although efforts are being made to devise alternative ways of measuring effectiveness and efficiency,[2] the clear up rate remains the key statistic in any assessment of how well a CID office is performing. In interviews with 26 detectives (of DC and DS rank) from six different forces, Maguire et al (1992) found that 22 were well aware of the latest rate in their own (sub)division. Moreover, while generally dismissive of its value as an indicator of performance (comments such as 'farcical', 'distorted' and 'open to abuse' being quite common), the majority saw it as a factor which could have a substantial negative impact on the work of the office: any significant fall in the rate was likely to produce not only a general 'bollocking' from managers and a fall in morale, but efforts to 'massage' the figures back to respectability in a number of fairly artificial (though not necessarily rule-violating) ways. Strategies mentioned – in both that and the current study – included ekeing as many separate charges as possible from minor criminal enterprises, detailing more officers to visit prisons to seek 'write offs', and concentrating more upon 'easy targets' (juvenile and other unsophisticated petty offenders) at the expense of more elusive offenders and more serious cases.

There are also other pressures to 'produce' which become particularly strong from time to time. One occurs when the subdivision is faced with a particular spate of offences which attract media attention: this in turn tends to bring pointed questions from CID managers at headquarters as to what the local DI is 'doing about it'. Other forms of pressure are partly self-generated by individual officers. One mentioned several times was the development of 'workaholic' tendencies, driven by an almost obsessive desire to detect crimes – although older officers claimed that this was now becoming a rarity among the 'new generation' of detectives, who tended to see investigative work 'more like a nine to five job'. A more common driving force, it was said, was ambition for promotion. The desire for promotion may lead officers to seek recognition as a 'good thief taker' (or as someone running a team of good thief takers), which is best achieved either through making noticeably large numbers of arrests or by making some unusually 'good arrests', i.e. of clever, serious or prolific offenders. As several interviewees remarked, to go before a promotion board with a poor arrest rate is not to improve one's chances – though it should be said that this is nowadays less likely to be a handicap than in the past.

Finally, and probably most important, there is the ever-present threat of being 'put back in uniform' (or, as it was wont to be put, 'made to wear a funny hat'). Despite all the rhetoric we heard from senior officers about uniform policing being as valuable as CID work and all being 'part of the same firm', we were left in no doubt that most detectives continue to regard working in the CID as a much more desirable job ('a form of promotion') and transfer back to uniform duties – except on promotion – as an indication of failure. According to several supervisors, as well as DCs, we spoke to, it is this fear above all which 'keeps them working'. At the same time, they recognised, there is a possibility that it will occasionally push some officers towards overzealousness or rule-bending in order to keep their individual results up. The point was nicely illustrated by an ex-DS who recalled a note pinned up in a CID office a few years ago:

'A sus a day keeps the helmet away.'

[1] R Reiner, 'Keeping the Home Office Happy: Can Police Effectiveness be Measured by Performance Indicators?' (1988) 4 *Policing* 28.
[2] See Audit Commission, *Effective Policing – Performance Review in Police Forces* (London: Audit Commission, 1990); S Love, *A Guide to Designing Performance Indicators* (Cambridge: HMIC, 1990); M Maguire, L Noaks, R Hobbs and N Brearley, *Assessing Detective Effectiveness* (Cardiff: Social Research Unit, SOCAS, University of Wales, 1992).

Maguire and Norris suggest that pressure to obtain convictions may encourage rule-breaking among officers. In his study of the West Midlands Serious Crime Squad, a specialist unit which was disbanded in 1989 following widespread allegations of police malpractice, Kaye (1991, pp 20–26) notes that there is evidence that officers in the squad first started to bend the rules when the number of convictions achieved by the squad began to fall. The pressure to obtain convictions means that tension exists between police objectives and the rules which govern, and constrain, investigative practices.

Maguire and Norris also note that the pressure to secure a conviction is likely to be especially strong in cases that have received a high public profile. In such cases it is not only the Home Office and other police officers who will be looking for a positive result: the community's faith in the police is also at issue. Along with other issues discussed here, this is well illustrated by the case of Colin Stagg. (The case was covered in the national newspapers on 15 September 1994 and during the following days.)

In 1992 Rachel Nickell was killed while walking on Wimbledon common in south London. The crime attracted enormous media attention. The Metropolitan Police responded with what was said to be the biggest murder inquiry ever carried out in the city. Most crimes that receive media attention when they are first discovered usually do not receive further press coverage until there is a trial, but there were periodic news reports about the investigation into Rachel Nickell's killing, some suggesting that the inquiry had stagnated. The only suspect the police did have was Colin Stagg, who lived near Wimbledon Common and who had first been located through the Crimewatch television programme by viewers who said that he resembled a photofit of a man seen on the common around the time of Nickell's death. Stagg had been questioned by the police, but this had not generated any evidence against him so he was released. Nevertheless, the police continued to try to build a case against him and they did so in a bizarre manner. A police officer wrote to Stagg pretending that she was the friend of someone whom Stagg had corresponded with through a dating agency. Over the next months the police used the letters exchanged between Stagg and the police officer – which revolved around a series of violent sexual fantasies – in an attempt to get Stagg to confess to Nickell's murder. Stagg never did confess, but he was eventually brought to trial. The main prosecution evidence was that his fantasies, as revealed in his letters, fitted the supposed 'psychological profile' of the killer. However, a judge at the Old Bailey ruled that the letters were inadmissible, criticising the police for showing 'not merely an excess of zeal, but a blatant attempt to incriminate a suspect by positive and deceptive conduct of the grossest kind'.

Accounts of the police investigation of the Nickell case suggest that the police were under immense pressure to bring someone to trial for the killing. In the absence of confession evidence they attempted to build a case around Stagg in an unusual undercover operation, which prosecution counsel claimed was justified due to 'the gravity of this case and the public interest'. Although Stagg's letters did contain some violent sexual fantasies, it appears that these had been drawn out of him through the encouragement of the undercover police officer in what the defence called a 'shaping process'. This clearly fits the case construction model discussed above; indeed, part of the prosecution case rested on evidence that inculpated Stagg (claiming that he knew facts about the position of the victim's body that only the killer would know) while ignoring exculpatory facts (some of the facts about the crime in Stagg's letters were plainly wrong). Although the Stagg case is exceptional, it is a good example of how pressure on the police can lead to the construction of a case out of dubious evidence.

(b) Supervision of criminal investigations

Given the pressure that the police face in investigating serious crimes, it might be expected that the CID would institute mechanisms for scrutinising the conduct of investigations. In fact, active supervision is very much the exception. In routine CID investigations, the potential for supervision exists in the rank structure of the CID: Detective Sergeants have responsibility for the investigative work undertaken by Detective Constables. Yet two research studies carried out for the Royal Commission on Criminal Justice (RCCJ) found the concept of supervision to be alien to most sergeants (Baldwin and Moloney, 1992; Maguire and Norris, 1992). It seems that the cohesive and supportive nature of police culture takes precedence over hierarchical supervision: Baldwin and Moloney found that most sergeants stressed that investigations were 'team work' and 'joint efforts', while supervisors stressed their co-ordinating rather than supervisory role. This means that sergeants will tend to be involved in the investigation of the cases which they are supervising and so may not find it easy to distance themselves from the pressures involved. At the end of the day, it seems that as long as a case produces a successful conviction, detectives will not be troubled by the quality of the investigation which secured it. Lack of supervision exists despite the fact that some aspects of detective work are amenable to later scrutiny: in particular, tape or video recordings of interviews could be reviewed by senior officers if they were so minded. What supervision there is tends to be managerial rather than qualitative: 'The actual practice of supervision is concerned more with ensuring that officers are working rather than "skiving", and with checking administrative matters (such as overtime and expense claims), than with ensuring legal or procedural propriety' (Maguire and Norris, 1992, p 114).

There are some exceptions to the 'hands-off' model of supervision which characterises routine detective work. The most serious cases (such as large-scale murder inquiries) do tend to be effectively supervised. In such cases the senior investigating officer, often a Detective Inspector, will assume responsibility for managing the inquiry and will not play an investigative role; at the same time the use of the computer based HOLMES (Home Office Large Major Enquiry System) enables effective scrutiny and cross-checking of evidence in the case.

Extract 3.2.4

J Baldwin and T Moloney, *Supervision of Police Investigations in Serious Criminal Cases* (1992) pp 74–75

Conclusion

Two distinct models of supervision emerge from this analysis of the investigative process. Major enquiries led by senior officers are supervised in the sense that the officer in charge of the investigation directs operations and assumes a full managerial role in the enquiry. By contrast, in investigations involving small numbers of officers, the ethos of teamwork prevails. The formal supervisor is usually no more than a name on the case papers. The dichotomy is such that it could almost be said that in the former case investigations are supervised, whilst in the latter they are not.

Our abiding impression is that too great a responsibility is being placed on the shoulders of junior officers. The cases included in this study were very serious in nature, and, as a detective constable in Birmingham observed of a section 18 assault case we had been discussing, 'If you try to equate the

252

weight or value of that particular job with something in industry, you wouldn't have someone on such a low echelon in a company dealing with that thing because it would be too big a responsibility.' The question that is raised in this research is therefore whether it is appropriate for officers of constable rank to be expected to investigate and supervise offences of this gravity.

We have noted that the detective constables we interviewed were confident about their own abilities to cope with running such investigations, but it is revealing that three quarters of them voiced reservations about the laxity of supervision in serious investigations within the police service as a whole. Almost all officers to whom we spoke could easily recount horror stories of working with others whose supervision was not highly regarded, and there are of course enough well-publicised instances of miscarriages of justice to indicate that there has been on occasions in the past a total breakdown in standards of supervision.

It is interesting that the criticisms of standards of supervision that were made by the officers we interviewed were not directed at immediate colleagues but instead at senior officers. The latter were often seen as being out of touch from the hurly-burly of investigations and so in a weak position to comment upon the way they were being conducted, still less to supervise them. However, it is likely that such attitudes reveal more about the prevailing police culture (a basic tenet of which is that officers have confidence in their immediate colleagues) than about how well these officers might have conducted enquiries.

The expression of such views is also indicative of the nature of supervision itself. Other than in the small number of military-style operations in the sample, supervision was superficial or non-existent, and it depended too heavily on small tight-knit groups of officers of detective constable rank operating as self-contained and largely autonomous entities with little direct supervision from above. While this may be an efficient and effective unit for most purposes, its performance is ultimately dependent on the competence and integrity of the individuals concerned. And if officers are incompetent, dishonest or even corrupt, the mechanisms of supervision currently in place provide little effective check on their activities. The 'cop culture' makes for strong and cohesive groupings, and, as long as things run smoothly to all outward appearances, the organisation itself is relatively powerless when it comes to controlling and supervising their activities.

The present problems of supervision, along with the pressures on the police to obtain convictions, have sometimes led to the suggestion that police investigations should be controlled and scrutinised by an independent agency. A popular model for reform is that of some continental jurisdictions in which the investigation of more serious crimes is controlled by a member of the judiciary such as the French *juge d'instruction* ('examining magistrate'). It is difficult to address the pros and cons of the institution of the examining magistrate without an in-depth examination of a legal system in which such a figure operates. Briefly, the two main criticisms of the concept are: (1) that the *juge d'instruction* plays a more limited role within the French legal system than is sometimes thought and (2) that the concept of judicial supervision is alien to our criminal justice system and thus risks being an unsuccessful 'transplant'. The RCCJ commissioned research from Leigh and Zedner (1992) on pre-trial criminal procedure in two Continental jurisdictions, but the authors were generally sceptical about the merits of examining magistrates, a view reflected in the RCCJ's own lukewarm attitude towards reform of criminal procedure along inquisitorial lines (Royal Commission on Criminal Justice, 1993, Ch 1, paras 11–16). However, Leigh and Zedner were more positive about the possibility of the Crown Prosecution Service (CPS) playing an increased role in decision-making prior to the charging of the suspect. Although the RCCJ recommended that the police should readily consult with the CPS about legal issues, such as the sufficiency of evidence, it rejected the idea that the CPS should play a supervisory role, recommending instead that internal supervisory procedures be strengthened:

> [W]e do not consider it appropriate for the CPS to supervise police officers in the investigation. It is the responsibility of the police to investigate crime. There is no reason to believe that another service, whose members are recruited and promoted for their legal skills and experience, would be more proficient at investigating crime or at supervising and monitoring investigations conducted by those specifically trained for the purpose. Moreover, serious confusion of roles would be likely to result to no good purpose if the CPS, whose task is to assess the results of investigations in terms of the prospects of prosecution to conviction for the offence involved, were to direct investigations themselves. Such a step would also remove accountability in this area from the police, with whom it most naturally belongs. Although, therefore, the CPS must be in a position to advise on the evidence that is required if the case is to go forward to trial, it should not be put in the position of supervising the gathering of evidence. (Royal Commission on Criminal Justice, 1993, Ch 2, para 67)

For a more positive view of external supervision, see Field (1994).

3. THE POLICE AND THE VICTIMS OF CRIME

Research on victims' experiences of the criminal justice system has alerted policy makers to the fact that, in the past, the needs of victims have tended to be ignored by the police. A common finding is that victims' satisfaction with the criminal justice system decreases as the case with which they are involved progresses through the system. This, and other problems, are discussed in the following extract:

Extract 3.3.1

T Newburn and S Merry, *Keeping in Touch: Police–Victim Communication in Two Areas* (1990) pp 37–39

Home Office circular 20/1988 states that: 'victims cannot realistically expect the police to apprehend every offender, nor that every prosecution will be successful. However, many victims welcome *information* about progress in the enquiries made into the offence against them, and in any resulting prosecution'. Accordingly the circular asks Chief Officers to review their arrangements for keeping victims informed of the progress and outcome of investigations and prosecutions resulting from offences against them, with a view to making these procedures as effective as possible within the constraints of existing resources.

Whilst it might be argued, ideally, that *all* victims should be kept updated about *all* developments in their case, or even regularly informed that there had not been any developments, this is unlikely to be a practical option. Consequently, any recommendations regarding changes in current practices in the provision of case-status information for victims must, as was suggested in the circular, take into account the considerable claims on finite police resources that already exist. This research, therefore, not only considered victims' experiences of their contacts with the police and their needs and priorities for information, but also police officers' experiences of dealing with victims of crime, and the constraints within which they have to do such work.

The major priority within the project was to identify those pieces or areas of information that victims most frequently or most strongly argue are important to their sense of wellbeing and satisfaction. This research suggests that the major problems experienced by victims in relation to information-provision occur in the later rather than the early stages of a case.

Satisfaction and dissatisfaction appeared to be related to the manner in which the police were perceived by the victim to be dealing with the case. Concern, sympathy and interest led to feelings of satisfaction: conversely, where these were missing dissatisfaction ensued. The general demeanour and behaviour of the investigating officer appeared to be crucial, and this reinforces the message of Shapland et al's (1985) research [J Shapland, J Willmore and P Duff, *Victims in the Criminal Justice System* (Aldershot: Gower, 1985)], that it is respect and concern that victims desire. Much of the research that has looked at the relationship between the police and victims of crime has suggested that in many ways the police look upon the victim as a resource, as a source of information and evidence which enables them to succeed in the primary task of policing – that of apprehending and prosecuting offenders. It is becoming increasingly apparent, however, that victims of crime find this relationship unsatisfactory. What they appear to desire is to be treated rather more like *customers* and rather less like an *informational resource*.

Whilst most victims found their initial meetings satisfactory the flow of information between police and victim tended to diminish substantially after an arrest had been made and as the case subsequently passed through the various stages of the criminal justice system. Although in most cases information about arrests was passed on to victims, details of the outcome of the case, particularly details from court, appeared to reach the victim, if at all, in a much more haphazard way. This was the greatest single source of dissatisfaction reported by the victims in the study. Two-thirds of victims said that they thought that the police *should* have let them know the outcome. The single most important piece of information victims wished to have was the knowledge that the case was 'closed'. This might simply mean that there had not been an arrest and that no further inquiries were to be made, that no charges were being made or, for example, that a conviction had been secured. 'Closure' was an extremely important component in the process by which victims came to terms with what had happened to them. Whatever the outcome, victims suggested, it was extremely important for them to be able to feel that the experience was over.

There was general agreement from the police officers in the study that it was important to pass on information about the outcome of the case to victims. Nevertheless, officers and victims had different perceptions of what constituted an 'outcome'. Officers rarely recognised that no arrest or no progress constituted an 'outcome' and they often assumed that victims would not expect or want to hear that nothing had happened. Given the importance of such information to the victim it would appear that the establishment of procedures by which victims are ensured of being informed of the closure of the case, whether that be marked by the discontinuation of enquiries, the decision not to bring charges or the sentence of the court, will be crucial to improved police–victim relations.

The lack of information and the consequent reduction in satisfaction were attributable not only to differing perceptions about 'outcomes' but also to organisational difficulties which made the passage of such information more complicated. As cases progressed, officers argued that they tended to have less information about them, a difficulty said to have been complicated by the introduction of the CPS, which had lessened the likelihood of officers attending court. The results of court proceedings could take up to two months to be fed back to the police. By this time, they felt it was too late to be of use, either because they assumed that the victim would have got the information from another source or simply because after such a period of time the officers were likely to be involved in other work and were consequently unable to keep track of all the cases they had previously been involved in. Potential solutions to this problem are likely to be complicated by the fact that several agencies are involved. Smoothing the flow of this information will necessitate liaison between the police, CPS and the courts. However, even if a method of passing the results back quickly to the police is negotiated, it would still seem to be impractical to expect the original investigating officers to feed this information to the victim. Therefore, making sure such information is regularly passed on is likely to require a central point where the information is collected, stored and then – by whichever means is decided upon but, possibly, case-status officers – passed on to the victim.

The standard of service that victims can expect from the police are now set out in *The Victim's Charter* (Home Office, 1996c). Apart from an expectation that the police will respond to a reported crime 'as quickly as they can' and 'do their best to catch the person responsible', the Charter primarily identifies the police as responding to victims' informational needs about the progress and outcome of a case. But, in reality, it seems that interaction between police and victims is more complex than the Charter makes out.

Cretney and Davis, who studied victims of assault, found that the police response to a victim's allegations was determined, in part, by their assessment of the 'worthiness' of the victim. In the following extract, the authors

256

describe how police perceptions of victim worthiness can be affected by the victim's social status:

Extract 3.3.2

A Cretney and G Davis, *Punishing Violence* (1995) pp 78–80 (footnotes omitted)

Victims least likely to receive an enthusiastic response are those members of the 'rubbish' class who make calls on the police which are 'messy, intractable, unworthy of attention, or the complainant's own fault' [R Reiner, *The Politics of the Police* (London: Harvester, 1985), p 95]. These victims will commonly have their private behaviour, their squabbles and disputes, exposed in public – including, very often, to the police. When they do so they are less likely than the rest of us to be accorded victim status. John Wheaton was treated as an in-patient after being knocked unconscious and having his arm broken in a street attack. Wheaton, who is alcoholic and frequents an area of the city populated by other addicts, asked to see a police officer while he was in hospital. Although he was interviewed, no crime was recorded. Wheaton, who claimed (not altogether convincingly) to be able to identify his assailant, spoke bitterly of this and other encounters with the police who took no account of him, he believed, because of his damaged status.

Along with 'rubbish' victims we must consider the impact of 'rubbish' areas. It has been found that in certain problem areas the proportion of reported offences not investigated by the police is much higher than in so-called 're-spectable' neighbourhoods [R Sparks, H Genn and D Dodd, *Surveying Victims* (London: Wiley, 1977) p 157]. An officer who worked in the St Paul's district of Bristol referred to this differential response as 'policing by consent'. It was defensible, he suggested, in terms of the differing expectations and under-standings of the respective populations:

> 'People's views, moral standards, and understanding of the law in Stoke Gifford, Little Stoke, Patchway and Hartcliffe are all different. That is why I think we police by consent. We are mindful of community needs.'

This puts a respectable gloss upon a policy which few officers would openly defend, as an offence which is decisively criminal in one area becomes only marginally so in another.

We ourselves did not find that the police response to assault was dramatic-ally different by area, but there were certainly instances where assault victims considered that their case had not been pursued because of unfavourable police judgements about *them*. For the most part they lived in the poorer areas of the city, but they also cited other reasons why, in their view, the police had been disinclined to pursue an investigation. Sally Chapman believed she had been discriminated against on several counts:

> 'I think because it happened in a club they weren't taking it seriously. And as I was drinking as well . . . I thought "I bet they think I'm a right trouble maker, typical sort of gay woman". You know, that sort of "hard woman" image.'

257

The police subsequently declined to charge Chapman's alleged assailant. The reasons given included the assailant's counter-allegations (which were strenuously denied by Chapman) and the fact that Chapman was only slightly injured.

It is not surprising that the operation of police discretion is most evident in relation to 'minor' violence [M Chatterton, 'Police Work and Assault Charges' in M Punch (ed), *Control in the Police Organisation* (London: MIT Press, 1983) p 220], or that it is in these instances that the perceived character of the victim appears to have most impact. Josephine Macdonald described with some amusement the problem of judgement which she felt she had posed to desk officers at the police station serving St Paul's:

> 'They were helpful to parts of me. They were helpful to the sort of articulate bit carrying a city council identity card. They were a bit . . . [pause for thought] perhaps the fact that I lived by myself and I didn't have my office suit on, I had sort of punkier clothes on and they were a bit . . . I felt that had I been, well, anything worse – homeless, unemployed – they could have been a lot less sympathetic. But as it was they *were* quite sympathetic in the end, although I did feel that I sort of insisted on it really.'

Macdonald, a city council clerk whose dress, hairstyle and perhaps manner hint at her former 'punk' lifestyle, was not easily pigeon-holed. Furthermore she had been assaulted by a former boyfriend, which meant that she was at risk of falling within the 'domestic' classification.

Walter Drobny on the other hand was one of Nils Christie's 'ideal' victims [N Christie, 'The Ideal Victim' in E Fattah (ed), *From Crime Policy to Victim Policy* (London: Macmillan, 1986)]. Drobny, in his late seventies, had been 'mugged' outside his house by a group of youths, the robbery taking place in broad daylight in a 'respectable' area of the city. He lost a substantial sum of money and he was also seriously, indeed tragically, affected in that his confidence was almost wholly destroyed. There was little hope of detection but the police nonetheless devoted much time and effort to the investigation, conducting house to house enquiries in the area. They also gave time to the personal care of Mr Drobny. The fact that the victim was so badly affected no doubt provides part of the explanation for the determined police response, but so too does the fact that Mr Drobny was archetypally innocent. An exemplary victim attracted an exemplary police response.

We can see from Cretney and Davis's examples that the police construct victims much as they construct other aspects of cases. The construction of good and bad victims is, in part, a product of the demands of the legal system. Police interaction with victims is carried out with the knowledge of the sorts of victim who are likely to prove to be impressive witnesses at court. The 'ideal victim' referred to by Cretney and Davis will not only have high social status, but will also have an unshakeable memory of events surrounding the crime (a victim who was drunk when the crime was committed may prove unreliable). Nor will the ideal victim be open to the criticism that he or she provoked the crime committed against them. We will see in Chapter 4 that victims who differ from these ideals will be open to attack in court.

Another factor which the police take into account when responding to victims of assault is whether the victim is committed to supporting a prosecution. If the police suspect that a complainant will later withdraw a complaint, or refuse to give evidence in court, they will be cautious about pursuing the case. Cretney et al (1994) suggest that the extent to which the police response is determined by the victim's decisions is rather ironic. Although in theory prosecution of crime conforms to an 'offence against the state' model, with offenders being prosecuted in the public interest, in practice victims are able to veto a prosecution by choosing not to support it. They found concerns about victim commitment to be reflected in police practice by a distinction which was drawn between a victim reporting an offence and a victim making an official complaint:

> The distinction between reporting and complaining is, not surprisingly, unclear to many victims. They suppose that in telling the police the circumstances of their victimization they are co-operating in the criminalization process. The police do not explain to them that reporting an assault is one thing, 'complaining' quite another. It is this second stage in the process which commits the victim (and the police) to an investigation of the offence and, where possible, to prosecution of the offender. 'Making a complaint' is a police term of art which means *you are prepared to take this all the way to court and, if necessary, to give evidence.* Only when they have this assurance will the police act. Quite often they will prefer to deflect the victim from this course, but it is characteristic of victim/police interaction that the fact that he or she has *been* deflected will not be made plain to the victim. (Cretney et al, 1994, p 19)

Cretney and Davis suggest that, to a certain extent, concerns about victim commitment explain the frequently criticised unenthusiastic police response to domestic violence cases. In police experience, many victims of domestic violence withdraw their complaints, and this colours their perception of all such victims: '[Victim unreliability] does not justify a cynical or grudging response, but it is difficult for the police not to be cynical because most measures of their effectiveness are geared to arrest, 'clear-up' and conviction. Given that the criminalisation of assault demands a victim who will remain committed to the prosecution effort, questions of victim *worth* and victim *effectiveness* are bound to be confused' (1995, p 85).

See further Shapland et al (1985).

4. THE TREATMENT OF SUSPECTS IN THE POLICE STATION

(a) Police and Criminal Evidence Act 1984

Interactions between police and suspects in the police station are a focal point of the criminal process. Because many suspects confess while in police custody, the conditions in which they are detained are closely related to the issues surrounding confession evidence. The police have considerable power over suspects in the police station and there is scope for abuse.

Before the Police and Criminal Evidence Act 1984 (PACE), the detention of suspects was subject to little strict regulation. In 1912 members of the judiciary had drawn up a set of guidelines called the Judges' Rules which governed detention and questioning, giving the police some guidance as to when evidence gained through such means was likely to be ruled inadmissible by the courts. In later years the rules were added to by the executive, becoming a Home Office Circular called *The Judges' Rules and Administrative Directions to the Police*. However, the status of the rules remained unclear.

The RCCP, whose report formed part of the basis of PACE, aimed to draw up clear and coherent rules to govern detention and questioning. As is the case throughout the RCCP's report, there is much emphasis on the concept of 'balance', in this context the balance between the rights of suspects and the interests of the police in investigating crime. More specifically, the Commission suggested that police investigations be subject to three principles: fairness, openness and workability (para 2.18). Insofar as these principles can be found in the framework of PACE, fairness means that suspects have certain rights, such as the right to legal advice, and that they should be made aware of those rights. Openness, or transparency, means that decisions should be recorded so that they can be effectively supervised and inspected at a later date. In PACE this is achieved primarily through the custody record which records the details relating to the detention of suspects. The police station will also be open to more scrutiny by the presence of more solicitors attending to advise suspects. Workability means that legal rules should not unduly inhibit the police in the investigation of crime and that (unlike the Judges' Rules) they should be clear. The balance sought by the RCCP can be seen in the following terms: PACE gave the police increased powers, particularly powers to arrest suspects and to detain them for questioning. To balance this, detention in the police station was regulated and suspects were given rights, such as the right to legal advice.

Since the introduction of PACE, an important question has been whether this balance has been achieved in practice. Just because PACE contains detailed rules governing the detention of suspects, we should not presume that these have been implemented as they were intended to be. Police officers still have discretion when implementing the rules which are meant to protect suspects. This discretion is sometimes overt: a number of the rules in PACE contain exceptions. Sometimes there is no overt discretion, but because the interaction between police and suspects takes place out of the public eye, it is possible that the police are able to negate the rules of PACE simply by not implementing them. Does this discretion mean that in practice suspects' rights are emptied of their content?

A considerable amount of research has been conducted to examine just how PACE has worked in practice (much of the research is summarised in

Brown, 1997). The findings of the research on the impact of PACE are not only of practical interest, they also have wider significance for debates about the ability of rules to influence the working practices of the police. The conclusions that have been drawn about the impact of PACE vary considerably. One police officer has talked of a 'sea change' in police practices: 'a new climate has been created and there is strict adherence to the rules' (Williamson, quoted in Dixon, 1992, p 518). However, the authors of one major study of post-PACE police work conclude that: 'the basic message of our research is of the *non-impact* of PACE on police practices' (McConville et al, 1991, p 189). They argue that this is because 'where legal rules cut across well-established cultural norms of actors to whom they are addressed, they are unlikely to have instrumental effect' (1991, p 200). McConville et al's conclusions are not supported by all of the PACE impact studies. Other researchers argue that PACE has had an effect on police work inside the police station, although the impact of the legislation varies. Some parts of PACE have had a more significant effect than others, and police practices may vary between different areas. There may also have been a 'learning curve' with PACE, as officers have come to accept the rules and as new officers, who have grown up with PACE, implement the rules more carefully. These factors should be borne in mind when considering the research findings related in this chapter (the debate over the research is explored in Dixon, 1992, in the papers discussing McConville et al's research in Noaks et al, 1995, pp 191–234, in Smith, 1997b and McConville et al, 1997).

Many of the rules in PACE are fleshed out in the Codes of Practice which are issued under s 66 of the Act; Code C governs the detention, treatment and questioning of suspects. The Codes do not have the force of law, but they can be referred to by the courts when considering the admissibility of evidence (PACE, s 67), so a breach of the Codes may lead to evidence being excluded from a trial. The Codes contain 'Notes for Guidance' which follow the main sections of the Code. These are not regarded as being part of the Codes, but it has been held that they may be relevant to decisions about the admissibility of evidence (see *Cox* [1993] Crim LR 382). The Codes of Practice have been revised twice (in 1991 and 1995) in the light of experience of their application and research on their effectiveness.

(b) Detention: authorisation and review

One of the key innovations of PACE is the creation of the post of custody officer. Every police station that detains suspects must appoint a custody officer who must be of at least the rank of sergeant (s 36). The custody officer has general responsibility for the welfare of suspects, and for making sure that their rights are implemented. The custody officer should keep a written record of the reasons for a suspect's detention and of any decision taken in relation to the suspect (the 'custody record').

39. Responsibilities in relation to persons detained

(1) ... it shall be the duty of the custody officer at a police station to ensure –

   (a) that all persons in police detention at that station are treated in accordance with this Act and any code of practice issued under it and relating to the treatment of persons in detention; and

   (b) that all matters relating to such persons which are required by this Act or by such codes of practice to be recorded are recorded in the custody records relating to such persons.

...

(6) Where –

   (a) an officer of higher rank than the custody officer gives directions relating to a person in police detention; and

   (b) the directions are at variance –

     (i) with any decision made or action taken by the custody officer in the performance of a duty imposed on him under this Part of this Act; or

     (ii) with any decision or action which would but for the directions have been made or taken by him in the performance of such a duty,

the custody officer shall refer the matter at once to an officer of the rank of superintendent or above who is responsible for the police station for which the custody officer is acting as custody officer.

On arrival at the police station, detention must be authorised by the custody officer. Under s 37(2) the custody officer should consider whether there is enough evidence to charge the suspect:

If the custody officer determines that he does not have such evidence before him, the person arrested shall be released either on bail or without bail, unless the custody officer has reasonable grounds for believing that his detention without being charged is necessary to secure or preserve evidence relating to an offence for which he is under arrest or to obtain evidence by questioning him.

This section appears to create a 'necessity principle' whereby the custody officer should refuse to permit the detention of a suspect unless he or she is satisfied that it is necessary for the purposes listed. The custody officer should keep the reasons for detaining the suspect under review and order his or her release if the reasons for detention no longer apply (s 34).

The custody officer should also order the release of a detainee where he or she:

(a) becomes aware, in relation to any person in police detention, that the grounds for the detention of that person have ceased to apply; and

(b) is not aware of any other grounds on which the continued detention of that person could be justified under the provisions of this Part of the Act, (s 34(2)).

A suspect should also be protected from unnecessary detention by the time limits which PACE imposes on detention. Under s 40, detention of suspects who have not been charged must be reviewed by an officer of at least the rank of inspector. The first review must be six hours after the suspect's detention was first authorised; further reviews are at nine-hour intervals:

Code C

15.1   The review officer is responsible under section 40 of the Police and Criminal Evidence Act 1984 . . . for determining whether or not a person's detention continues to be necessary. In reaching a decision he shall provide an opportunity to the detained person himself to make representations (unless he is unfit to do so because of his condition or behaviour) or to his solicitor or to the appropriate adult if available at the time. Other people having an interest in the person's welfare may make representations at the review officer's discretion.

Notes for Guidance

. . .

15C   If in the circumstances the only practicable way of conducting a review is over the telephone then this is permissible, provided that the requirements of section 40 of the Police and Criminal Evidence Act 1984 . . . are observed . . .

In addition to the reviews, PACE imposes time limits on detention. Section 41 creates what is sometimes called the 'PACE clock' – after the 'relevant time' the clock is ticking away, leaving investigating police officers with a limited time in which to question the suspect in custody.

41. Limits on period of detention without charge

(1)   Subject to the following provisions of this section and to sections 42 and 43 below, a person shall not be kept in police detention for more than 24 hours without being charged.

(2)   The time from which the period of detention is to be calculated (in this Act referred to as 'the relevant time') –

    (a)   in the case of a person to whom this paragraph applies, shall be –

        (i)   the time at which the person arrives at the relevant police station; or

        (ii)   the time 24 hours after the time of that person's arrest,

        whichever is the earlier;

The rest of s 41 further defines the way in which the basic 24-hour period is to be calculated, providing for a number of circumstances which may arise, for example if the suspect is taken to hospital while in police custody. This effectively creates exceptions to the 24-hour period; subs (2)(c) is significant:

    (c)   in the case of a person who –

        (i)   attends voluntarily at a police station; or

        (ii)   accompanies a constable to a police station without having been arrested,

        and is arrested at the police station, [the relevant time is] the time of his arrest.

The 24-hour period may be extended by the police:

42. Authorisation of continued detention

(1)   Where a police officer of the rank of superintendent or above who is responsible for the police station at which a person is detained has reasonable grounds for believing that –

    (a)   the detention of the person without charge is necessary to secure or preserve evidence relating to an offence for which he is under arrest or to obtain such evidence by questioning him;

   (b) an offence for which he is under arrest is a serious arrestable offence; and

   (c) the investigation is being conducted diligently and expeditiously,

he may authorise the keeping of that person in police detention for a period expiring at or before 36 hours after the relevant time.

Detention beyond 36 hours can only be authorised by a magistrates' court:

43. Warrants of further detention

(1) Where, on an application on oath made by a constable and supported by an information, a magistrates' court is satisfied that there are reasonable grounds for believing that the further detention of the person to whom the application relates is justified, it may issue a warrant of further detention authorising the keeping of that person in police detention.

. . .

(4) A person's further detention is only justified for the purposes of this section or section 44 below if –

   (a) his detention without charge is necessary to secure or preserve evidence relating to an offence for which he is under arrest or to obtain such evidence by questioning him;

   (b) an offence for which he is under arrest is a serious arrestable offence; and

   (c) the investigation is being conducted diligently and expeditiously

. . .

(11) Subject to subsection (12) below, the period stated in a warrant of further detention shall be such period as the magistrates' court thinks fit, having regard to the evidence before it.

(12) The period shall not be longer than 36 hours.

44. Extension of warrants of further detention

(1) On an application on oath made by a constable and supported by an information a magistrates' court may extend a warrant of further detention issued under section 43 above if it is satisfied that there are reasonable grounds for believing that the further detention of the person to whom the application relates is justified.

(2) Subject to subsection (3) below, the period for which a warrant of further detention may be extended shall be such a period as the court thinks fit, having regard to the evidence before it.

(3) The period shall not –

   (a) be longer than 36 hours; or

   (b) end later than 96 hours after the relevant time.

The provisions of PACE thus appear to provide strict controls on the circumstances in which suspects are deprived of their liberty. However, there are a number of factors which are likely to undermine the efficacy of PACE in controlling detention. Many of the provisions in PACE have a degree of flexibility built into them because they contain exceptions to the basic rules. This reflects McBarnet's (1981) argument that rules which apparently protect suspects are often undermined by the exceptions to them. The reviews of detention provided for in s 40 may be postponed under s 40(4) if 'it is not practicable to carry out the review at that time' or 'if at that time no review officer is readily available'; the review need then only be carried out 'as soon as is practicable' (s 40(5)). The ability of the police to authorise a further 12 hours' detention after the initial 24 hours hinges on the concept of a 'serious arrestable offence', defined in s 116. Section 116 leaves considerable room for interpretation: among other categories, an offence will be serious if it involves 'substantial financial gain to any person' or 'serious financial loss to any person', the seriousness of the latter depending on whether 'having regard to all the circumstances it is serious to the person who suffers it'. Brown found evidence that different police stations interpret s 116 differently: one station in his study classified all burglaries involving £1,500 or more as 'serious' and this probably led to it using the powers dependent on s 116 more frequently than other stations (1991, p 75).

The exception in s 41(2)(c) may encourage the police to persuade suspects to attend questioning in the police station voluntarily so as to avoid the pressure of the 24-hour detention limit coming in to play immediately. PACE and the Codes of Practice do include provisions that apply to volunteers. For example, under s 29 where a person is attending voluntarily at a police station:

(a) he shall be entitled to leave at will unless he is placed under arrest;
(b) he shall be informed at once that he is under arrest if a decision is taken by a constable to prevent him from leaving at will.

However, the police may still be tempted to make the most of the ambiguous status of volunteers. Just as the police are able to perform a stop and search on a person without resort to their powers under PACE by relying on that person's (implied) consent, suspects may be brought to a police station while being unaware of their volunteer status and right to leave at will. McKenzie et al (1990) found that the practice of using volunteers varied between police stations, but at one station that they studied a third of all suspects were dealt with as voluntary attenders. Although PACE does not require that the presence of volunteers be recorded, this force had instituted a recording system for volunteers.

The flexibility of PACE may be magnified by the way in which police officers approach the exercise of their discretion under it. All the studies on the impact of PACE agree that s 37, which requires the custody officer to scrutinise the reasons for detaining suspects as soon as they are brought to the police station, has had almost no effect in practice: it is exceptional for a custody officer to refuse to allow the detention of a suspect. This failing can be interpreted in a number of different ways. It might be argued that, being a police officer, the custody officer is unlikely to refuse to allow a suspect's detention owing to solidarity with the arresting officers. The 'solidarity' aspect of the custody officer's role is stressed by McConville et al (1991), but it has been contested by other researchers, such as Dixon (1992), who argue that in other areas of their work custody officers succeed in playing an independent role. Alternatively, it can be argued that, when scrutinising the reasons for detention, PACE leaves the custody officer in a weak position. The custody officer must rely on the arresting officers' version of events, and cannot question the suspect directly because such questioning might amount to an interview, and should only take place in the conditions laid down by PACE (see *Absolam* [1988] Crim LR 748).

In the following extract, Dixon et al emphasise the routinisation of decision-making in the police station and show how this affects the way in which suspects' rights are implemented:

Extract 3.4.1

D Dixon, A Bottomley, C Coleman, M Gill and D Wall, 'Safeguarding the Rights of Suspects in Police Custody' (1990) 1 *Policing and Society* 115, pp 129–133

[I]n almost all observed cases, custody officers did not inquire into the circumstances of arrest: they simply asked a question such as 'What has she been arrested for?', expecting and getting only the briefest of answers (for example, 'shop theft' or 'breach of the peace') needed to complete the custody record section for 'reasons for arrest'. At the beginning of the section of the custody record provided for a narrative account of the detention, the custody officer makes a standard entry based on s 37(2) – for example, 'detention necessary to secure or preserve evidence or to obtain such evidence by questioning'. The entry is not individualized to fit the particular case: indeed, in another force area, a rubber stamp is used to record the statutory formula. The duty to make such entries in the suspect's presence and to inform him/her of the grounds for detention (s 37(5)) are usually overlooked: typically, the entry is made as the suspect is being put in a cell by a warder.

We observed no instances of a custody officer refusing to accept a suspect into detention. This is consistent with the experience of researchers in other force areas. During one period of observation, an episode of ITV's *The Bill* showed a custody officer refusing to accept a suspect into custody because of lack of evidence against him. In discussion, this was cited by Research Force officers as a prime example of the programme's inaccuracy and unreality . . . Similarly, and not surprisingly given the above, we saw no suspects being charged at their reception: custody officers were concerned with booking the suspect in, not with assessing the weight of available evidence against him/her. Immediate charge would often be appropriate following, for example, arrests for minor public order offences, in which questioning is unnecessary and there is no evidence to secure or preserve: in such cases, pre-charge detention is used to allow a cooling-off period or to provide summary punishment.

Reception into custody has become an essentially routinized process: procedures are, generally, completed to the letter, but usually in a way which empties them of substance. The significance of this is that an important control over the entry of suspects into what may be lengthy periods of pre-charge detention has become of little real value. This situation can be partially accounted for by factors ranging from police attitudes towards procedural rules and paperwork, to standard features of bureaucracy. From these, it is worth picking two for comment.

First, the practical demands of charge room work encourage the tendency towards minimal compliance. At (often unpredictable) times, charge rooms are very busy and the staff have to deal with a number of suspects and other (for example, remand) prisoners. At other times, some custody officers have additional duties: in our rural subdivision for example, they were also responsible for the communications room. In consequence, the opportunity for the detailed, independent review of a case which PACE envisages is often simply impractical. At a more mundane level, the arrangement of the custody record encourages this approach. Reasons for detention are not considered until the induction sections of the form have been completed: in effect, the decision to detain has already been made. In some other forces, the custody officer's attention is drawn to consideration of immediate charge by the need to complete a section on the record which asks 'Sufficient evidence to charge: Yes/No'.

Reviews

The continuing necessity of pre-charge detention is supposed to be checked by a system of reviews at regular intervals (by an inspector after no more than 6 and 15 hours, by a superintendent after no more than 24 hours, and by a magistrates' court after no more than 36 and 72 hours). The suspect and his/her solicitor have the right to make representations to the review officer before continued detention is authorized (s 40(12)).

As with the checks on initial detention, the review procedure tends to be routinized and insubstantial, at least in its early stages; the opportunity to make representations can often consist merely of an inspector asking the suspect, 'All right mate?' through the hatch in the cell door. If the suspect does not appreciate the significance of what he/she is being asked, the question is valueless. Solicitors comment that their representations rarely influence review officers, who treat extension of detention as routine. The issue is particularly important in the case of reviews carried out by telephone. The Code of Practice allows this to be done if 'in the circumstances the only practicable way of conducting a review is over the telephone' (note 16B). This does not remove the duty to allow representations to be made, presumably requiring the inspector to speak by telephone with the suspect or his/her solicitor.

The observed usual practice in our Research Force when the shift inspector was not at the station was for the custody officer to seek authorization by telephone . . . The custody officer would then type a standard entry onto the custody record to the effect that continued detention was necessary to obtain evidence by questioning. Room would be left for the inspector's signature to be added when he/she next attended the station. The signature would not be timed, so on its face the record would suggest that the review had been carried out according to normal procedure. In one case, the custody officer instructed the warder to type an entry for subsequent signature onto a custody record giving standard reasons for continued detention. The shift was about to change, and the custody officer did not even know who the inspector required to sign the entry would be. In such circumstances, the inspector's role is purely presentational.

There was some difference of opinion as to whether or not a superintendent's review had to be done in person. PACE states that, when a superintendent authorizes detention beyond 24 hours: 'it shall be his duty – (a) to inform that person of the grounds for his continued detention: and (b) to record the grounds in that person's custody record' (s 42(5)). The issues in dispute were whether such a duty can be delegated, and whether a deliberate statutory contrast was made with inspectors' reviews, for which no such provision is made. One Research Force superintendent told us that he did all his reviews by telephone. In a case which we encountered, a review was authorized by telephone, with no opportunity being given to the suspect to make representations. The custody officer had told the investigating officer that such a review could not be carried out by telephone, but was overruled when they sought the superintendent's opinion. The draft revisions to Code C make clear that the custody officer had correctly interpreted the legislative intention: a superintendent's review 'must be carried out in person rather than over the telephone' (note 15C).

It must be acknowledged that, however they were carried out, such reviews were more rigorous than inspectors' reviews; investigating officers did not assume that such an extension would be granted (as they did with earlier reviews). Some superintendents record in some detail reasons for authorizing the continued detention: they reported being influenced by a court's criticism of unreasoned reviews in another Force area.

In general, our research suggests that the review system is conducted in a way which produces records apparently complying with the letter of PACE, but that its spirit is largely dissipated in the routinization of procedures. Particularly in the case of the earlier reviews, the quasi-judicial, independent role of the review officer which PACE seems to demand has been implemented as merely administrative routine. A vicious circle operates here; as lawyers see their representations having no effect, they too regard the procedure as a formality, and as they do not think it worth contesting the point, police practice is allowed to become entrenched.

Although the custody record has the potential to increase the transparency of decision-making in the police station by allowing challenges to and supervision of decisions, some commentators have suggested that this is not achieved in practice:

> Without exception, what is brought to notice by supervisors are *correctable* errors. Their pointing up is intended to ensure that inaccuracies and omissions in records which could serve as evidence in both trials, complaint investigations and discipline cases are kept to an absolute minimum. Mistakes of other kinds – errors of judgement, misinterpretation of the law or force policy – are commonly dealt with by 'words of advice'. To write them down would mean that they could potentially become documentary evidence in future trials, prejudicing the chance of a conviction. (McKenzie et al, 1990, p 26)

Similarly, McConville et al (1991, p 97) underline the 'self-validating' nature of police work, suggesting that the custody record plays a key part in the successful construction of a case: 'records create a self-serving reality whose connection with what happened is tenuous at best. . . . Once created the reality constructed is verified by the very existence of the record: the police narrative becomes for all practical purposes a source of indisputable accuracy.'

How long do suspects usually spend in police detention? The vast majority appear to be released before the end of 24 hours, the prima facie limit set by s 41. Research comparing the length of detention of suspects before and after the introduction of PACE suggests that the Act has had a mixed effect. In minor cases, length of detention may have increased slightly, owing to the fact that PACE requires time-consuming paperwork to be carried out by the police, and possibly because arrests are now better founded than prior to PACE. It is difficult to generalise because practice varies greatly between police stations and between different types of crime. Research by Bottomley et al (1991) found a slight increase in detention length after PACE. Research by Brown (1991) on those detained on suspicion of burglary, a crime of medium seriousness, found little overall change, though fewer suspects were held for longer than 24 hours after PACE than previously.

Extract 3.4.2

D Brown, *Investigating Burglary: The Effects of PACE* (1991)
p 40, table 4.9

Length of detention without charge for burglary suspects

Time detained	Chapeltown 1983	1987	Syston 1983	1987	Clapham 1984	1987	All areas 1983/84	1987
	Cumulative %							
up to 3 hrs	20	18	21	19	30	34	24	24
up to 6 hrs	48	39	51	45	63	69	55	53
up to 9 hrs	64	53	64	63	76	81	68	68
up to 12 hrs	70	60	76	75	84	85	77	76
up to 15 hrs	75	71	83	83	88	88	83	83
up to 18 hrs	78	74	86	85	93	92	86	85
up to 21 hrs	81	83	90	91	95	96	89	91
up to 24 hrs	88	91	91	95	96	98	92	95
up to 36 hrs	99	100	95	99	100	99	98	99
up to 72 hrs	100	100	100	100	100	100	100	100
Sample size	197	129	271	307	283	253	751	689
Mean length of detention	10h 3m	11h 34m	10h 5m	9h 23m	6h 46m	6h 19m	8h 50m	8h 40m
Median length of detention	6h 5m	8h 30m	5h 50m	6h 40m	4h 40m	4h 21m	5h 23m	5h 40m
Minimum	– 25m	– 47m	– 50m	– 10m	– 20m	– 13m	– 20m	– 10m
Maximum	43h 32m	34h 57m	66h 30m	48h 23m	27h 45m	44h 35m	66h 30m	48h 23m

The power to extend detention beyond 36 hours is used fairly infrequently. In 1995 the police applied for 220 warrants of further detention under s 43 of PACE. 209 were granted by magistrates. Regional variation is profound: several forces did not apply for any warrants, while just four of the 43 forces (Devon and Cornwall, Lancashire, Northumbria and West Midlands) accounted for 40 per cent of applications (Home Office, 1996b).

PACE is not the only piece of legislation under which suspects may be detained by the police. The Prevention of Terrorism (Temporary Provisions) Act 1989 (PTA) contains provisions under which people suspected of involvement with terrorism may be arrested and detained. Whereas those arrested on suspicion of having committed a serious arrestable offence may be held for 36 hours under PACE before being brought before a court, s 14 of the PTA provides an initial period of 48 hours. This period can be extended by the Home Secretary by a further five days. In 1988 this power was held to be in breach of the European Convention on Human Rights (*Brogan and Others v United Kingdom* (1989) 11 EHRR 117). The decision involved four suspects who had been detained for periods ranging from four days and six hours to six days and $16^{1}/_{2}$ hours. Article 5(3) of the Convention provides that anyone who has been arrested on suspicion of having committed an offence 'shall be brought promptly before a judge or other officer authorized by law to exercise judicial power'. The European Court of Human Rights held that the detention of all four suspects was in breach of this provision:

> In the Court's view, even the shortest of the four periods of detention namely the four days and six hours spent in police custody by Mr McFadden, falls outside the strict constraints as to time permitted by the first part of Article 5(3). To attach such importance to the special features of this case as to justify so lengthy a period of detention without appearance before a judge or other judicial officer would be an unacceptably wide interpretation of the plain meaning of the word 'promptly'. An interpretation to this effect would import into Article 5(3) a serious weakening of a procedural guarantee to the detriment of the individual and would entail consequences impairing the very essence of the right protected by this provision. The Court thus has to conclude that none of the applicants was either brought 'promptly' before a judicial authority or released 'promptly' following his arrest. The undoubted fact that the arrest and detention of the applicants were inspired by the legitimate aim of protecting the community as a whole from terrorism is not on its own sufficient to ensure compliance with the specific requirements of Article 5(3).
>
> There has thus been a breach of Article 5(3) in respect of all four applicants. ((1988) 11 EHRR 117, at pp 135–136)

The government responded to the Court's decision by announcing a derogation from its obligations under Article 5. Article 15 of the Convention permits derogations from the obligations imposed by some of the Articles in the Convention '[i]n time of war or other public emergency threatening the life of the nation'. Derogations should be limited 'to the extent strictly required by the exigencies of the situation'. The derogation was challenged in a later case (*Brannigan and McBride v United Kingdom* (1994) 17 EHRR 539) but the

Court held that the derogation was lawful. The incorporation of the Convention into English law will not affect the derogation, though the government has announced its intention to review the prevention of terrorism legislation which it hopes will allow it to end the derogation within the next five years.

The use of the PTA has been examined in a research study by Brown (1993). Brown examined all cases in which suspects had been held under the PTA between March 1989 and November 1990, 253 cases in all. Fifteen per cent of suspects were held for more than 48 hours, and 9 per cent for more than four days, the maximum that would have been allowed under PACE.

5. THE SUSPECT'S RIGHTS

(a) Giving effect to the right to legal advice

In the thinking of the RCCP, PACE was intended to balance the police's power over suspects in their custody against certain rights which are given to the suspect. The most important right provided by PACE is the right to legal advice, and we shall concentrate on this in the following discussion. PACE also contains a right to have someone informed when arrested (s 56) and Code C gives suspects the right to make a telephone call (C 5.6). All of these rights can legally be denied in certain circumstances. Section 58 of PACE provides as follows:

58. Access to legal advice

(1) A person arrested and held in custody in a police station or other premises shall be entitled, if he so requests, to consult a solicitor privately at any time.
. . .

(4) If a person makes such a request, he must be permitted to consult a solicitor as soon as is practicable except to the extent that delay is permitted by this section.

(5) In any case he must be permitted to consult a solicitor within 36 hours from the relevant time, as defined in section 41(2) above.

(6) Delay in compliance with a request is only permitted –
    (a) in the case of a person who is in police detention for a serious arrestable offence; and
    (b) if an officer of at least the rank of superintendent authorises it.

(7) An officer may give an authorisation under subsection (6) above orally or in writing but, if he gives it orally, he shall confirm it in writing as soon as is practicable.

(8) Subject to sub-section (8A) below an officer may only authorise delay where he has reasonable grounds for believing that the exercise of the right conferred by subsection (1) above at the time when the person detained desires to exercise it –
    (a) will lead to interference with or harm to evidence connected with a serious arrestable offence or interference with or physical injury to other persons; or
    (b) will lead to the alerting of other persons suspected of having committed such an offence but not yet arrested for it; or
    (c) will hinder the recovery of any property obtained as a result of such an offence.

271

It is difficult to underestimate the importance of the suspect's right of access to legal advice. The RCCP hoped that legal advice would go some way towards 'minimising the effects of arrest and custody upon the suspect' (1981, para 4.77). Legal advice can increase the openness of police practices by bringing an outsider into the station and is likely to provide considerable moral support to isolated suspects. Access to legal advice may also help suspects to understand the other rights that they have while in police custody, the precise nature of the offence they are accused of, and the effect of not answering police questions. The importance of access to legal advice at the police station has been recognised by the European Court of Human Rights which, in *Murray v UK* (1996) 22 EHRR 29 (the relevant parts of the judgment are reproduced in Extract 4.5.4 below), held that, in the light of changes to the law regarding a suspect's right to remain silent in the police station, access to a lawyer at this stage of the criminal process formed part of the right to a fair trial, guaranteed by Article 6 of the Convention.

The RCCP realised that giving suspects the right to legal advice might turn out to be empty rhetoric if solicitors were impossible to contact or too costly for (usually impecunious) suspects. Section 58 was backed up by a scheme providing free legal advice to suspects in the police station and accompanied by the implementation of a duty solicitor scheme whereby suspects without their own solicitors (or whose solicitors were unable to attend the police station) would be able to call an available duty solicitor at any time of day or night.

Prior to PACE, the rules governing access to legal advice were unclear: although the suspect could request a solicitor, the police were under no obligation to bring this possibility to the suspect's attention and could refuse the suspect's request. There was relatively little research on access to legal advice prior to PACE, but one study suggested that the right to legal advice was successfully secured by suspects in only about 7 per cent of cases and that requests to see a solicitor might be refused by the police about 75 per cent of the time (Baldwin and McConville, 1979).

How effective has PACE been in increasing the number of suspects receiving legal advice? Section 58 of PACE allows the police to *delay* access to legal advice for up to 36 hours in certain strictly defined circumstances. Despite the restrictions in s 58, there is evidence that after the introduction of PACE the police continued to delay access in a significant proportion of cases: Dixon et al (1990) found that in the force they studied delay was standard practice in all serious arrestable offence cases involving either more than one person or evidence which had still to be recovered. However, in *Samuel* [1988] 1 QB 615 (see Extract 4.5.1 below) the Court of Appeal drew attention to the strict provisions of PACE and held that the circumstances in which the exercise of 'this fundamental right' could be delayed were rare. The police would usually need evidence that the solicitor chosen by the suspect would commit a criminal offence by causing one of the circumstances in s 58(8)(a)–(c) to occur. Further, even if the police did have such information about the chosen solicitor, the suspect would still normally be allowed to contact a *duty* solicitor against whom the police would be even more unlikely to have evidence of misconduct. In *Samuel* the Court of Appeal excluded the confession obtained from the suspect after legal advice had been denied. However, the clear message sent to the police by *Samuel* has been somewhat diluted by the court's decision in *Alladice* (1988) 87 Cr App R 380 where it refused to exclude a confession made after a similarly ill-founded decision by the police (see Extract 4.5.2, and discussion of other cases, in Chapter 4 below). Despite the slightly contradictory nature of the messages being sent to the police by the Court of Appeal, Brown et al's research (1992) suggests that the police have taken the principle in *Samuel* seriously. Although earlier research on PACE found that advice was delayed under s 58(6) in about 1 per cent of cases (Brown (1989)), Brown et al's later study (1992) found only one case (in a sample of about 10,000) in which a suspect's access to legal advice was delayed. In another study:

> Detectives were interviewed after [*Samuel*] and they agreed that the case had made the power to delay legal advice a 'dead letter'. They did not envisage requesting delays in future, unless they had evidence that a specific lawyer was corrupt. (Brown, 1991, p 76)

However, the case law suggests that the police continue occasionally to delay access without good reason (see, for example, *Dunford* (1990) 91 Cr App R 150). There is also evidence in a report by JUSTICE (1994b) that legal advice is still sometimes unlawfully denied (see also Kaye, 1991, pp 48–50). Further, in cases where suspects are detained under the Prevention of Terrorism (Temporary Provisions) Act 1989, legal advice seems to be delayed more often (a quarter of cases in Brown's (1993) study). It should also be noted that in *Murray v UK* (1996) 22 EHRR 29 the European Court of Human Rights held that 'even a *lawfully* exercised power of restriction [of access to legal advice] is capable of depriving an accused, in certain circumstances, of a fair procedure' (at pp 66–7, emphasis supplied).

The exceptions in s 58 are not the only problem in the implementation of the right to legal advice. For s 58 to operate effectively, the police must inform suspects of their rights. Some suspects may be fully conversant with their statutory rights, but there must be a considerable number who are not. Even among those who know that they have a right to legal advice, some may not be fully aware of the duty solicitor scheme and some may not feel confident enough to ask the police to contact a legal adviser without being given a clear opportunity to do so.

Code C

3.1 When a person is brought to a police station under arrest or is arrested at the police station having attended there voluntarily, the custody officer must tell him clearly of the following rights and of the fact that they are continuing rights which may be exercised at any stage during the period in custody.

(i)   the right to have someone informed of his arrest . . . ;
(ii) the right to consult privately with a solicitor and the fact that independent legal advice is available free of charge; and
(iii) the right to consult these codes of practice.

3.2   In addition the custody officer must give the person a written notice setting out the above three rights, the right to a copy of the custody record . . . and the caution in terms prescribed in section 10 below. The notice must also explain the arrangements for obtaining legal advice. The custody officer must also give the person an additional written notice briefly setting out his entitlements while in custody. The custody officer shall ask the person to sign the custody record to acknowledge receipt of these notices and any refusal to sign must be recorded on the custody record.

. . .

6.4   No police officer shall at any time do or say anything with the intention of dissuading a person in detention from obtaining legal advice.

6.5   . . . If, on being informed or reminded of the right to legal advice, the person declines to speak to a solicitor in person, the officer shall point out that the right to legal advice includes the right to speak with a solicitor on the telephone and ask him if he wishes to do so. If the person continues to waive his right to legal advice the officer shall ask him the reasons for doing so, and any reasons shall be recorded on the custody record . . .

Paragraph 3.1 of Code C has been modified in the light of experience of its operation. This is because early research on PACE suggested that custody officers would attempt to dissuade suspects from requesting legal advice through the manner in which they informed suspects of their rights.

Extract 3.5.1

A Sanders and L Bridges, 'Access to Legal Advice and Police Malpractice' [1990] Crim LR 494, pp 498–501 (footnotes omitted)

Rule bending

Knowledge of rights – and what suspects make of that information – is influenced as much by:

> 'the way in which rights are explained to suspects . . . whether the choice is put as a "question expecting the answer yes or the answer no"' [M Maguire, 'Effect of the PACE Provisions on Detention and Questioning' (1988) 28 *British Journal of Criminology* 19]

as by whether the information is simply provided or not. Rule 'bending' (for want of a better term) can be as important as rule breaking. Our observation of suspect processing enabled us, uniquely, to assess systematically the nature and extent of rule bending through the use of various ploys . . .

Table 1   Types of ploy

Ploy	Amount used (principle ploy only)
1. Rights told too quickly/incomprehensibly/incompletely	142(42.9%)
2. Suspect query answered unhelpful/incorrectly	5(1.5%)
3. Inability of suspect to name own solicitor may affect his right to have one contacted	2(0.6%)
4. 'It's not a very serious charge'	1(0.3%)
5. 'You'll have to wait in the cells until the solicitor gets here'	13(3.9%)
6. 'You don't have to make up your mind now. You can have one later if you want to'	27(8.2%)
7. 'You're only going to be here a short time'	25(7.6%)
8. 'You're only here to be charged/interviewed'	14(4.2%)
9. (To juvenile) 'You'll have to (or do you want to) wait until/ an adult/gets here' (– before decision can be made)	18(5.4%)
10. (To adult) 'Juvenile/has said he doesn't want one'	8(2.4%)
11. Combination of 9 and 10	4(1.2%)
12. 'We won't be able to get a solicitor at this time/none of them will come out/he won't be in his office'	6(1.8%)
13. 'You don't need one for this type of offence'	2(0.6%)
14. 'Sign here, here and here' (no information given)	7(2.1%)
15. 'You don't have to have one'	4(1.2%)
16. 'You're being transferred to another station – wait until you get there'	6(1.8%)
17. CO interprets indecision/silence as refusal	9(2.7%)
18. 'You're not going to be interviewed/charged'	1(0.3%)
19. 'You can go and see a solicitor when you get out/at court'	9(2.7%)
20. 'You're (probably) going to get bail'	6(1.8%)
21. Gives suspect Solicitor's Directory or list of solicitors without explanation/assistance	3(0.9%)
22. Other	19(5.7%)
TOTAL	331(100.0%)

We observed one or more ploy being used in 41.4 per cent of cases, and two or more in 9.3 per cent. All of our 10 stations used these ploys, though some did so more than others. The most common ploy is the incomplete or incomprehensible reading of rights (ploy 1 and 14). According to one officer,

'Now under PACE you read them their rights as quickly as you can – hit them with it so quickly they can't take it in – say "sign here, here, and here" and there you are: nothing's changed, we all know that, though you wouldn't get any policeman to admit it to you.'

This sort of ploy is well documented. As one lay visitor has put it:

'Too often, a detained person was asked to sign "here and here" without being told what was printed on the lines directly above his/her signature. Very often, the detained person indicated that he/she had no idea what he/she signed, and did not realise the advice was free.'

The following typical example reproduces a complete exchange;

> (BA084) C.O.: 'While you're in police custody you have certain rights which are set out here. (He then indicated both leaflets, which he gave to the suspect, and read the three rights very quickly). Do you wish for any of these right now? If you don't you can exercise them later.'
> Silence from suspect.
> C.O.: 'O.K., sign there to say that I've read you your rights and there to say that you don't want a solicitor.'

This was one of many cases where silence, incoherence, or indecision were taken to mean that no solicitor was required (ploy 17). It is perfectly consistent with the letter of C.O.P. and PACE, where suspects are only entitled to advice if they so request. But this puts the onus on the suspect, even though the suspects who perhaps need advice most – young, simple, confused or in-experienced suspects – are those who are most susceptible to police ploys. The police realise this, and bend the rules to achieve their goals. Some suspects were clearly in need of advice – if only as to whether or not to see a solicitor:

> 'depends on how long it's going to take? Are you going to interview me?'
> 'What's going to happen to me? . . . If I'm going to be released . . . then I don't really need a solicitor.'
> 'If I get a solicitor what will happen to me? If I don't what will happen to me?'
> 'Do you know a local one?'
> 'Do I need one now?'
> 'What should I do?'
> 'Is it best to?'

But with only the police to seek this advice from, the answers were nearly always the same. The police very rarely advised, let alone attempted to per-suade, suspects to secure advice. No law prevents the police from giving advice, and many suspects would be distressed if the police refused to do so. But the scope for abuse is obvious.

> (MB020) D. was misled about costs (see later). The C.O. then said:
> '. . . if you could sign there (indicating custody record).'
> D.: 'What am I signing here?'
> C.O.: 'That's to say whether or not you want a solicitor.'
> D.: 'Well, I don't know that do I . . .'
> D. signed, without crossing out either '"I do" or "I do not" want a solicitor'. But, as always, ambiguity was taken by the police as negative, for no solicitor was contacted.

Of the other ploys, the most common cluster around juvenile difficulties (ploys 9, 10, and 11, discussed later), delay (mainly ploys 5 and 7), and failure to explain about the duty solicitor scheme (3, 12, 21). These ploys sometimes include lies, often about costs:

> (LC078) The suspect said that he was told: '. . . if you get a solicitor if you don't get legal aid you'll have to pay.'

276

(MB020) D.: 'Can I get it on the legal aid?'
C.O.: 'I don't know . . .'

But that is not all they lie about:

(MB110) 'When your daughter came to the station she was given her rights and indicated that she didn't want a solicitor.' In fact, after her rights were read this juvenile was told that her rights would be repeated in front of her mother and that she should 'sign there and there' without being given the chance to request a solicitor.
(LC082) D.: 'They said it would take nearly three hours to phone through to the solicitor but it didn't. It took just two minutes.'

A more inventive lie concerned one particular solicitor with a 'pro-suspect' reputation. For a while, suspects who requested him were wrongly told that he had retired. That solicitor was convinced that this was a deliberate ploy.

Ploys do not always dissuade suspects from requesting solicitors. This does not always bother the police. But when it does they make great efforts to persuade suspects to cancel their requests, which explains some of the gap between requests and actual advice received.

(LC041) D. appeared to be mentally retarded. He asked for a solicitor, despite various ploys. But he and his probation officer were then taken away somewhere private, after which the request was cancelled.
(EN022) D. hesitated about legal advice. Ploy 6 was used twice and the C.O. stressed that he could 'wait until his mother arrives.' D. signed away his right to advice without actually declining it. When his mother arrived she was informed by the D.C. that he 'didn't want a solicitor . . . we're just double-checking with you.' After the C.O. then read his rights properly she said she wanted a solicitor. The D.C. then took her somewhere private, after which the solicitor was cancelled.

Ploys sometimes take effect without formal cancellations. LC082 (above) was so disconcerted by the police stressing the probable delay that he did not wait for the solicitor to arrive. The complicity of the custody officers in all of these cases undermines their much-vaunted 'independence.'

When the Codes of Practice were revised in 1991, changes were made in an attempt to ensure that suspects would be adequately informed of their right to legal advice. The revised Code underlines the fact that suspects should be informed *clearly* of their right and that legal advice is free, that it can be given in private, that it is independent of the police and that it is a continuing right – after an initial waiver of the right suspects may change their minds at any time while in detention.

Research on the effects of the revised Codes of Practice suggests that they have had some effect. Brown et al (1992) were able to compare police practice before and after the revisions of Code C. After revision they found that 70 per cent of suspects were told that legal advice was free, as opposed to 4 per cent previously. Four per cent of suspects were still not informed of their right to legal advice at all (though in some cases this was because suspects were drunk or violent). As for the manner in which suspects were informed of their rights, Brown et al found that the proportion of suspects being informed unclearly increased after the revision of Code C, rising from 16 per cent to 26 per cent. However, Brown et al were reluctant to use the word 'ploy' to describe deficiencies in the manner in which rights were communicated to suspects, because the word suggests a degree of intent which they were cautious about ascribing to custody officers (1992, pp 29–30).

Overall, PACE has been successful in increasing the number of suspects requesting legal advice. It is unclear just what proportion of suspects asked for legal advice prior to PACE, but the figure was probably around 10 per cent (see Brown, 1997, p 95). Sanders et al (1989) found a request rate of around 25 per cent, and after the revision of Code C Brown et al (1992) found a rise in the request rate to 32 per cent. More recent research suggests that this has risen to around 38 per cent, though, as with most aspects of PACE, there is considerable regional variation (see Brown, 1997, p 97). This study also found that Afro-Caribbeans and Asians were more likely to request legal advice than whites.

There is still a considerable number of suspects who decide not to take advantage of free legal advice. Brown et al (1992) asked suspects about their reasons for this. The majority of those refusing advice (63 per cent) said that this was because advice would not assist them, but a significant number (12 per cent) were worried that requesting a legal adviser and waiting for one to turn up would delay their release. One suggestion for increasing the take up of legal advice is that duty solicitors should be present in police stations round the clock so as to be on hand to give immediate advice. Brown et al asked suspects refusing advice whether the existence of such a scheme would change their decision; many of them replied that it would. The authors calculated that this might lead to a request rate of around 50 per cent, but the RCCJ 'saw little prospect of introducing such a scheme in the foreseeable future' (Royal Commission on Criminal Justice, 1993, Ch 3, para 55).

The figures above are for suspects *requesting* legal advice. Not all of those who initially request advice will receive it. There are various reasons for this, though the research findings vary. Sanders et al (1989) found that the police simply made no attempt to contact a solicitor in about 10 per cent of cases, while in other cases they attempted to do so but had no success; overall they failed to contact a solicitor in about a quarter of cases where requests were made. Brown et al (1992) found that the police were more successful in contacting solicitors, achieving contact in 87 per cent of cases after Code C had been revised. Suspects inevitably face delays while waiting for the police to contact a solicitor and then for the solicitor to reach the police station, with waiting time likely to be longest where the request is for a duty solicitor (who will have to be contacted through a paging service and then ring back to the police station), or where the request is made during the night. A substantial number of suspects may find that the prospect of delay is worse than the prosect of being interrogated without legal advice and cancel their request, or consent to being questioned without advice: Sanders et al found that in about 20 per cent of cases suspects would cancel their requests for advice for reasons other than solicitor unavailability (1989, p 59). Code C is intended to act as a safeguard to prevent the police from manipulating this delay.

Code C

6.6 A person who wants legal advice may not be interviewed or continue to be interviewed until he has received it unless:

. . .

    (b) an officer of the rank of superintendent or above has reasonable grounds for believing that:
        (i) delay will involve an immediate risk of harm to persons or serious loss of, or damage to, property; or
        (ii) where a solicitor, including a duty solicitor, has been contacted and has agreed to attend, awaiting his arrival would cause unreasonable delay to the process of investigation; or
    (c) the solicitor nominated by the person, or selected by him from a list:
        (i) cannot be contacted; or
        (ii) has previously indicated that he does not wish to be contacted; or
        (iii) having been contacted, has declined to attend
        and the person has been advised of the Duty Solicitor Scheme but has declined to ask for the duty solicitor, or the duty solicitor is unavailable . . .
    (d) the person who wanted legal advice changes his mind.

In these circumstances the interview may be started or continued without further delay provided that the person has given his agreement in writing or on tape to being interviewed without receiving legal advice and that an officer of the rank of inspector or above, having inquired into the person's reasons for his change of mind, has given authority for the interview to proceed . . .

Notes for Guidance

6B A person who asks for legal advice should be given an opportunity to consult a specific solicitor or another solicitor from that solicitor's firm or the duty solicitor. If advice is not available by these means, or he does not wish to consult the duty solicitor, the person should be given the opportunity to choose a solicitor from a list of those willing to provide legal advice. If this solicitor is unavailable, he may choose up to two alternatives. If these attempts to secure legal advice are unsuccessful, the custody officer has discretion to allow further attempts until a solicitor has been contacted and agrees to provide legal advice.

Suspects who receive legal advice before they are questioned by the police do not always have an adviser present *during* questioning. Amidst much local variation, Brown et al (1992) found that the adviser only attended interviews in 57 per cent of cases where suspects secured legal advice. Before Code C was modified the rate had been 84 per cent suggesting that increased pressure on solicitors caused by the increased uptake of legal advice had led to this shortfall.

(b) Quality of legal advice

Up to this point in the book we have concentrated our discussion on the police as the key decision-makers in the criminal process. As we move through the criminal process the importance of decisions made by actors other than the police increases. One group of people who, until recently, have received relatively little academic attention are criminal defence lawyers. From the moment of their first engagement with a case, lawyers are likely to play a crucial role in influencing what happens to a suspect. Lawyers may advise suspects on what (not) to say to the police, on how to plead, and they may play a role in building a defence case to present at trial and in calling the police to account for the way in which they have treated a suspect. Like the police, lawyers exercise discretion and, though they are less bound by formal legal rules than the police, they are likely to be influenced by certain rules governing ethical behaviour and by the culture in which they operate. Criminal practice is also affected by economics: defence lawyers operate in a market where suspects are clients, potential sources of income. Since few suspects will be able to pay a lawyer out of their own funds, criminal practice will also be influenced by the way in which it is funded by the Legal Aid Board.

Although duty solicitor schemes were set up after PACE was introduced, provision of legal advice to suspects at the police station has remained problematic. There is evidence that duty solicitors in particular are reluctant actually to attend a police station to advise suspects (Sanders et al, 1989). Although the Legal Aid Board attempted to introduce stricter attendance requirements for duty solicitors, the board had to alter its proposals owing to pressure from solicitors, some of whom refused to implement the proposals (see Sanders and Bridges, 1993, pp 51–52; Cape, 1991). Many solicitors attempt to restrict their involvement to advice given to the suspect over the telephone. Telephone advice (often received by the suspect in the custody room in the hearing of police officers) is likely to be much less useful than advice given in private at the police station and presence at the interrogation. Brown et al (1992) found considerable variation between areas in the proportion of advice given over the telephone. Overall, 30 per cent of legal advice was given over the telephone rather than by personal attendance, and at one rural police station the proportion was as high as 78 per cent. As we have seen, the revision of Code C appears to have led to an increase in the number of suspects requesting legal advice; Brown et al point out that this is likely to have had some adverse effects because it has increased the pressure on firms of solicitors carrying out criminal work:

Extract 3.5.2

D Brown, T Ellis and K Larcombe, *Changing the Code: Police Detention under the Revised PACE Codes of Practice* (1992) pp 96–97

The response of the legal profession

The right to legal advice is only an effective right if the legal profession are able to deliver that advice adequately. The increase in demand for their services among suspects inevitably places additional strain on the profession. This comes at a time when there is already considerable debate among solicitors about the system of remunerating them for attendance at the police station. At one station in the present study, duty solicitors went on strike during phase two of the observational study (although this did not cause any obvious difficulties securing the attendance of solicitors).

There is clear evidence from the research that the coverage of advisory work at the police station by the legal profession is variable in the extreme and that this has suffered in some respects, almost certainly on account of rising demand. While more suspects are consulting legal advisers and they are attending the station more often, they are remaining for interviews between police and suspect far less frequently. Furthermore, a suspect's prospects of seeing a legal adviser at the police station and of having one present at interview vary considerably. Someone arrested at Peterborough or Wednesfield, for example, could virtually depend on seeing a legal adviser at the police station; however, someone taken to Weston Favell or Wellingborough would be fortunate to receive anything other than advice over the telephone. At the latter two stations, suspects would be even luckier to have a legal adviser present at a police interview: they attended only 11 per cent and 20 per cent of interviews at these stations in cases in which advice was requested. At Peterborough and Wednesfield, on the other hand, legal advisers were present at nearly two-thirds and 84 per cent of such interviews. There is some evidence to suggest, too, that suspects' decisions about legal advice may be affected by its availability. It is probably no coincidence that, at Peterborough, the proportion of suspects requesting solicitors was high and at Wellingborough low.

This variation in the provision of advice probably owes much to different local arrangements for providing advice: for example, the strength of the duty solicitor scheme, the proximity of firms to police stations, the number of firms prepared to carry out advisory work there and whether representatives are widely employed to provide such advice. Whatever the reason for the variation, it raises, . . . , issues about equitable treatment of criminal suspects and equality of access to legal advice. The revised Code has gone a considerable way towards ensuring that suspects (adults in particular) are treated equally in the provision of information about rights and providing the facility to request those rights. It is unable to ensure that the right to legal advice is implemented equitably. How this could be achieved is beyond the scope of the report. The answer may rest with some form of scheme under which legally qualified personnel are present at main police stations on a round-the-clock basis . . . [T]his might overcome the reservations of many about requesting a solicitor, as long as those who staffed the scheme did not become too closely identified with the police. It would also ensure that those who did want advice could depend on it being delivered without delay and in person, with the option of requesting attendance at police interviews if desired . . .

The giving of legal advice at the police station through the consistent presence of a solicitor would also eradicate a major difficulty with present arrangements, namely the provision of much advice by telephone and in conditions of considerable lack of privacy. Sanders et al [A Sanders, L Bridges, A Mulvaney and G Crozier, *Advice and Assistance at the Police Station and the 24 Hour Duty Solicitor Scheme* (London: Lord Chancellor's Department)], have pointed out that suspects tend to find telephone advice of lesser utility than advice at the station. Stations also do not generally possess dedicated facilities for private telephone consultations. *Ad hoc* arrangements were sometimes made, but conversations between solicitor and client were usually conducted in the custody area within the hearing of anyone in the vicinity, including investigating officers. The level of noise sometimes made such consultations extremely difficult, and police present often tended to make little effort to minimise the disruption. Bearing in mind that nearly one-third of all legal advice is given over the telephone, this is clearly an unsatisfactory state of affairs and detracts heavily from the value of this right.

Even if the suspect does meet a legal adviser in person, there is no guarantee that he or she will be a fully qualified solicitor with sufficient knowledge of the law to be able to give effective advice. Research examining the effects of PACE on the provision of legal advice to suspects in the police station has drawn attention to the use of non-qualified personnel to attend police stations. McConville et al (1994, p 84) found that 75 per cent of those attending the police station were not fully qualified solicitors. Although articled clerks were sometimes used, often those attending had no formal legal training at all, simply being clerks employed by the firm or sometimes ex-police officers. Qualified solicitors tended to see police station work as of relatively little importance: for them, the core of their job was advocacy in the magistrates' court rather than the less glamorous job of attending the police station to advise clients. When asked about the effects of PACE, one solicitor responded (McConville et al, 1994, p 85):

> It was a pain – all the calls used to come through to me initially. Once we got it organised and got the clerks on 24-hour call-out bleepers, it was okay. It works now. But solicitors shouldn't have to go out on it because it is too time consuming and it doesn't pay enough.

Given the central role of interrogations and confession evidence in police investigative practices, this attitude would seem to be inappropriate. In the following extract, Hodgson describes some of the factors which she sees as contributing to the use of non-legally qualified personnel to undertake such work.

Extract 3.5.3

J Hodgson, 'Adding Injury to Injustice: The Suspect at the Police Station' (1994) 21 *Journal of Law and Society* 85, pp 92–95 (footnotes omitted)

With statutory arrangements for the provision and financing of access to lawyers for those held at the police station, custodial legal advice became established firmly as part of the legal service offered by defence lawyers within the professional model. The broad expectation is that custodial legal advice under the duty solicitor scheme will be provided by solicitors. The rules allow the use of representatives in some instances, but they must first have passed a merits-test and each case requires personal consideration by a solicitor. These restrictions do not apply to firms of solicitors attending the police station on an 'own solicitor' basis, that is, having been named by the suspect as the particular solicitor who should be requested to attend. The Law Society states that such advice is best provided by a solicitor experienced in criminal work, but does not advocate the same individual consideration of each case, as in the duty solicitor scheme. Solicitors are advised that clerks may be given general authority to attend police stations. Although not specified, presumably only delegation to individuals sufficiently skilled to provide custodial legal advice is contemplated.

A minority of firms is able to ensure that most clients in custody are advised by qualified and experienced members of staff. Where solicitors are not able to attend personally, trained and skilled representatives are sent. In the majority of firms, however, it is never contemplated that a solicitor will attend. Instead, a range of non-legally qualified personnel are employed and without any formal training, relied upon to provide the bulk of custodial legal advice. Work is organized so that solicitors spend most of their time at court and, even when in the office, do not attend the police station. No filtering mechanism exists to enable delegation on the basis of the gravity of the offence or to monitor cases for any potential problems. Instead, police station work is automatically dealt with by whoever is on the firm's rota or is available. In some instances this is a solicitor but, more usually, it is a clerk.

Although wholly contradicting both the professional rhetoric and the expectations embedded in the legal provisions for custodial legal advice, there are clear benefits to solicitors in organizing their work in this way. As non-qualified staff are paid less than solicitors, it enables them to increase their profitability. This economic advantage to firms is most clearly demonstrated by the use of outside agencies (usually staffed by ex-police officers) who charge considerably less than legal-aid rates and are called upon when needed, removing the need for any continuing salary or overhead costs. Former police officers are considered ideal for custodial advice and are employed on the staff of many firms because of their familiarity with the routine of the police station and anti-social working hours together with their ability to maintain co-operative working arrangements with the police. The philosophies which many of these former police officers bring with them are not considered incompatible with defence practice and so, no attempt is made at reorientation.

For the client, there are clear drawbacks in being advised by non-qualified staff. Most representatives lack any real legal expertise and are often ignorant of the basic legal constituents of the offence and of legal concepts such as 'intent' or 'recklessness'. Neither are they capable of assessing the merits of adopting the various strategies available to the suspect such as whether or not to answer police questions. Combined with their relative inexperience, this means that many advisers lack confidence in their dealings with the client and more crucially, with the police. Many exhibit serious role conflict as, in the absence of any formal legal training, they develop their own working philosophies, frequently reflecting those of the police. For example, many clerks, without any consideration of the police evidence, thought that clients who claimed to be guilty should admit the offence in interview 'to get it over with' and were opposed to their exercising their right to silence . . .

The attendance of a solicitor may not place the suspect in any stronger position. Although some firms, or solicitors within firms, treat police station advice as the beginning of the construction of the defence case, meriting the use of legal skills and argument as well as strategic advice, most do not. Instead, they consider it routine and undemanding. Theirs is not an adversarial ideology of protecting the rights of the individual against the power of the state as manifested through the police. This is reflected in their limited aspirations in providing custodial legal advice: most see themselves as a referee between police and suspect rather than as a player in the game, and in the organizational context of legal defence practice, where the employment of non-qualified staff is not simply a phenomenon of police station work. This wholesale delegation and downgrading of work is part of a wider trend within criminal defence practice to employ non-solicitors to carry out the bulk of case preparation – client interviews in the office, advice on plea, preparation for trial, instructing counsel – while the solicitor increasingly acts exclusively as an advocate in the magistrates' court. The public aspect of criminal defence work shows solicitors in the lower courts and barristers in the Crown Court but magistrates' court advocacy has been criticized as routine and repetitive and much of it consists of remand hearings with some bail applications and pleas in mitigation. Where opportunities for skilled advocacy exist, they are missed by solicitors who, through discontinuous representation and deficient case preparation, resort to routinization. It is in the office or the police station that strategic legal decisions are made about the defence case and it is this work which is carried out for the most part by non-qualified staff.

The organization of criminal defence work is a key factor when reformers talk of suspects and defendants, as, in practice, this will be the representing defence lawyer. The traditional professional model described above is not appropriate when considering criminal defence services as it takes as its unit of analysis the adversarial solicitor, devoted to the representation of her client's interests, and employing her legal skills in a partisan way. The Commission itself takes note of this when rejecting as of limited value the requirement of the presence of a lawyer for any confession to be admissible in evidence [see Royal Commission on Criminal Justice, 1993, Ch 1, para 21]. Unfortunately, it is ignored in proposals to increase police and prosecution powers.

In an attempt to defend at least an aspiration to the professional model, spokespersons for the profession point to low levels of remuneration forcing solicitors to delegate work. Whilst poor rates of pay are an aggravating factor, they are not the sole cause, as evidenced by the fact that delegation of substantive legal work has been increasingly a feature of criminal defence practice since at least the 1970s when legal aid was expanding. Higher hourly rates, second only to those for magistrates' court advocacy, failed to alter substantially duty solicitor practices of offering telephone advice rather than personal attendance at the police station. It is the role definition of solicitors themselves which constitutes the key element in the organization of legal practice and for most criminal defence solicitors, the employment of non-qualified, untrained, and inexperienced staff is unproblematic. Professional training is inadequate in instilling the adversarial values which one would expect to govern the work of criminal defence solicitors. Instead, the criminal defence strand of the legal profession is highly atomistic with practices and values learned by trainee solicitors and non-qualified staff at the site of the firm itself and so producing wide variations. The dominant ideology is a belief in the guilt of the client and the desire for the effective management of clients towards a guilty plea.

The existence of firms exceptional to the standard legal practice provided further support for this thesis of a haphazard evolution of legal ideology. Existing within the same financial strictures, they provide a wholly different service to clients. They adopt an adversarial role, championing the rights and interests of their clients and complying far more closely with the traditional model set out by the profession. Where financial or recruitment pressures lead to the employment of non-qualified staff, the same adversarial ideology is fostered through training and supervision. It is firms such as these which are likely to be involved in appeal cases, some of which inevitably become high-profile, where original instructing solicitors consider the case to have run its course and have long since closed the file.

In response to some of the criticism levelled at the widespread use of unqualified legal advisers to do police station work, the Law Society has introduced a scheme of accreditation for non-solicitor advisers. Since 1995 legal aid payments for police station advice have not been available where a non-accredited adviser has been sent. The scheme does not apply to articled clerks, nor are solicitors required to undergo training in advising suspects at the police station (see Hodgson and Bridges, 1995).

Research on legal advice has also drawn attention to the attitudes that legal advisers take towards their role. The research suggests that most advisers take a passive, co-operative stance towards the police rather than an adversarial one. One illustration of this is Baldwin's figures on the role played by advisers during police questioning. He found that the majority of advisers remained silent throughout the interview; when they did intervene it was sometimes to help the police.

Extract 3.5.4

J Baldwin, *The Role of Legal Representatives at Police Stations* (1992)
p 28

	Bournville	Kings Heath	Belgrave Rd	Wednesfield	Edmonton	Redditch	Total	%
Says nothing in interview	17	19	27	19	29	10	121	66.5
Clarifies minor matters	1	4	6	1	1	2	15	8.2
Clarifies important matters	1	2	1	0	1	2	7	3.8
Pushes suspect's interests	0	0	4	3	4	3	14	7.7
Is obstructive	0	0	2	0	1	0	3	1.7
Plays role of third interviewer	5	3	8	0	0	0	16	8.8
Other type of role	2	0	2	2	0	0	6	3.3
No lawyer present	74	72	50	75	64	83	418	–

	100	100	100	100	100	100	600	100.0

The fact that many advisers say nothing during interviews does not necessarily mean that they are failing their clients. It may be that there is no need to intervene in most interviews. However, Baldwin argues that, given the impropriety of many police interview strategies, a more active role would be appropriate. A similar conclusion is drawn by McConville et al (1994). However, the authors' explanations of the passivity of legal advisers differ. Baldwin's explanation of the practices of defence lawyers is that they play a co-operative role in order to achieve good working relations with the police. At the end of the day, the police retain the upper hand in all dealings in the police station, and lawyers simply cannot afford to antagonise them. Lawyers do not have the right to see the custody record or to be told what evidence the police have against their client: their ability to extract such information depends on their good relations with the police. Sanders (1996, p 273) adopts a similar explanation of advisers' behaviour, arguing that they are in a 'catch-22' situation: '. . . if solicitors wish to do their best for suspects they have to compromise by becoming acceptable to the police; and if they wish to help their clients by retaining their adversarial purity, they forfeit cooperation and fail to do their best for their clients'. For McConville et al, however, the non-adversarial role of defence lawyers needs to be explained by something more than police dominance. They emphasise the attitudes and values of advisers, and the views they have of their clients:

> Looked at as a whole, advisers who attend police stations accept uncritically the propriety and legitimacy of police action, even when what they witness themselves, what they hear from clients, and what they suspect goes on, leaves them convinced that the police break the rules and in other ways are beyond the law. The reason

for this is that many advisers, like the police, instinctively believe, without requiring substantiation through evidence, that there is a case to answer, and that it is the client who must give the answer. This in turn springs from a working assumption that the client is probably factually guilty. In line with these ideologies, advisers permit the police free rein in interrogations and thereby legitimate dubious police methodologies. (McConville et al, 1994, pp 126–127)

McConville et al argue that the prevailing culture of criminal defence lawyers raises important questions about legal education and training. Lawyers, they suggest, are easily socialised into a culture where clients are believed to be guilty, prosecution evidence is accepted without question, and there is little attempt to construct a defence case. The authors call for 'a critical examination of the content of legal education and training . . . which [has] tended to be dominated by teaching about the technicalities of the criminal law and procedure, without sufficient attention to basic principles of adversarial justice and their links into more fundamental democratic values' (1994, p 296).

6. THE RELIABILITY OF EVIDENCE GATHERED DURING INVESTIGATIONS

One of the purposes of regulating the investigative process is to attempt to ensure that the evidence which is eventually presented to the courts is accurate and reliable. The use of unreliable evidence increases the probability that miscarriages of justice will occur. By regulating the way in which the police gather evidence and the way it is used in court, the legal system hopes to protect suspects from wrongful conviction. Most of our discussion in this section is of confession evidence, as this is the area where concern is currently greatest. However, we also consider two other common types of evidence: eyewitness identifications and witness statements. One of the common factors between all three is that psychological research suggests that they may be moulded by some subtle case construction processes.

(a) Identification evidence

In 1972 the Criminal Law Revision Committee stated that:

We regard mistaken identification as by far the greatest cause of actual or possible wrong convictions. Several cases have occurred in recent years when a person has been charged or convicted on what has later been shown beyond doubt to have been mistaken identification. (Criminal Law Revision Committee, 1972, para 196)

The problems of eyewitness evidence are well illustrated by the case of Laszlo Virag. Virag was convicted of shooting a police officer after having been surprised stealing coin boxes from parking meters. Eight witnesses picked Virag out at identity parades. When the real culprit was later caught, Virag was acknowledged to be innocent (see Devlin, 1976a). There is now a

287

considerable amount of psychological research on eyewitness identification which sheds light on why misidentifications occur (see, e.g. Gudjonsson, 1992, pp 83–91; Wells, 1993; Gross, 1987). People have a tendency to see what they expect to see: the visual process can be affected by preconceptions. Eyewitness identification depends on memory, but memory declines over time. Thus, the longer the gap between the crime and the time at which the eyewitness is called upon to make an identification, the more likely the witness is to make a mistake. Furthermore, human memory is malleable. The memory of an offender's appearance can be affected by 'post-event' factors: if the witness sees a picture of the supposed offender in the newspaper, this image may contaminate the original memory. Contamination could also occur if the witness is shown pictures of suspected offenders by the police, or if a police interviewer suggests information when talking to a suspect (for example, by asking a question such as 'did you see the gun', which suggests the information that the criminal had a gun). The psychological research also shows that there is no strong correlation between eyewitness confidence and accuracy: even the most confident witnesses may be mistaken.

The legal system has reacted to the problems posed by eyewitness evidence in two ways. First, following Lord Devlin's report on the *Virag* case (Devlin, 1976a), the Court of Appeal laid down guidelines, called the *Turnbull* guidelines, for cases which depend substantially on eyewitness evidence (*Turnbull* [1977] QB 224). In such cases, the judge is required to warn the jury about the dangers of mistaken identification and to draw to its attention the reasons for proceeding with caution. During the summing up, the judge should deal with the identification evidence in some detail, drawing attention to the particular circumstances in which the witness saw the offender and to any discrepancies between the witness's initial description of the offender and the accused's appearance. In cases where the identification evidence is especially weak, the case should be withdrawn from the jury unless there is supporting evidence. This does not go quite as far as Devlin's proposal, which was that in all identification cases the jury should be directed that only in exceptional circumstances would it be appropriate to convict on identification evidence alone.

The second way in which the legal system has responded to eyewitness evidence has been the regulation of the circumstances in which witnesses are asked to make identifications of suspects. This is dealt with in some detail by PACE Code of Practice D. Code D requires the procedures for witness identifications of a suspect to be undertaken by an 'identification officer' who must be of at least the rank of inspector and who must not be involved with the investigation. The Code sets out a rough hierarchy of identification procedures, starting with an identification parade. Less satisfactory procedures are group identification, where the witness views the suspect among an informal group of people, often outside the police station; video film identification; and confrontation, which should only take place where the other methods of identification are impracticable. The procedures laid down for the conduct of each identification method show an awareness of the dangers of memory contamination and suggestion. For example, witnesses called to an identification parade must be told that the person they saw may not be present; they should not be told whether a previous witness has made an identification; and they should be told not to make an identification until they have looked at every member of the parade twice (Code D, Annex A, para 14). There are also rules governing the showing of photographs to suspects. Asking witnesses to look at 'mug shots' is a procedure which carries the danger that the presence of a photograph in police records will suggest to the witness that the person pictured may have committed the crime they witnessed, thus permanently contaminating their memory. Witnesses should be shown photographs in private and should be shown at least 12 photographs which are, as far as possible, similar. Once one witness has made an identification from photographs, other witnesses should not be shown them; instead, an identification parade or some other identification method should be arranged. This procedure is intended to prevent all the witnesses having their memories contaminated before a superior method of identification can be used (Code D, Annex D, paras 2–5).

As with the other Codes of Practice, evidence gained in breach of Code D may be excluded by the courts. The Code D procedures, along with the *Turnbull* guidelines, have almost certainly reduced the danger of convictions being based on mistaken identifications. There are, however, still fears that poor quality identification evidence continues to reach the courts (see Davies, 1996).

(b) Confession evidence

As with eyewitness evidence, a series of miscarriage of justice cases have brought the problems of confession evidence to the attention of the legal system. The suspects in the *Confait* case confessed to a crime which they had not committed, and confessions formed part of the evidence against other well-known victims of miscarriages of justice, such as the Guildford four, the Birmingham six and the Bridgewater three. Again, we now have the benefit of psychological research on false confessions and the conditions which may produce them.

To understand false confessions we need to bear in mind the context in which police questioning takes place. Suspects are usually questioned while in detention, isolated from their everyday surroundings. This inevitably causes stress. The police have considerable power over suspects, being able to control most aspects of their surroundings and to reward co-operation by releasing a suspect from custody. The officers who question suspects will usually be looking for a confession and may be prepared to apply pressure to suspects to achieve this end. Questioning can be repetitive and forceful: it need not stop just because the suspect remains silent or denies the offence. But, even if no overt pressure is applied to suspects, it should be recognised that the context of police questioning makes it inherently coercive. Even so, one might question whether those who are not mentally ill are likely to confess to crimes they have not committed, as it is obviously against their long-term interests to do so. Psychologists, however, suggest that almost anyone will make a false confession if subjected to enough pressure: 'if the pressures are extreme then it is the characteristics of those who do not confess which are likely to be the most unusual' (Gudjonsson and Mackeith, 1988, p 193). In some of the notorious miscarriage of justice cases the pressures said to have been placed on suspects were extreme, including violence and threats of violence. But, even in the absence of severe pressure, some people will make false confessions. Gudjonsson (1992, Ch 11) presents a number of case studies where police questioning did not involve threats or violence, and draws the conclusion that: 'false confessions are not confined to the mentally handicapped or the mentally ill. The view that apparently normal individuals would never seriously incriminate themselves when interrogated by the police is totally wrong' (1992, p 259). Gudjonsson suggests that suspects will vary in their predisposition to confessing falsely: some otherwise normal people are particularly 'suggestible', that is, they will tend to adopt suggestions put to them by a questioner. Owing to suggestibility, a false confession may be detailed and convincing, containing facts about the crime thought to be known only by the criminal. The accuracy of details about the scene of crime in the confessions by the suspects in the *Confait* case led Sir Henry Fisher, who conducted the official inquiry into the convictions, to be convinced that two of the boys probably had been present at the death of Confait. Yet these details were almost certainly passed on to the boys inadvertently by the police.

Following Kassin and Wrightsman (1985), Gudjonsson (1992) suggests that false confessions can be divided into three main types (though he notes that there is some overlap between the categories). First, *voluntary confessions*: some people voluntarily confess to crimes that they have not committed, perhaps out of a desire for publicity or attention. One example of this is the Darvell brothers, who were convicted of murder but later released after a successful appeal. The brothers were well known to the local police for their propensity to walk into the police station and confess to crimes of which they were innocent (see *The Independent*, 14 and 15 July 1992). Some people may also confess voluntarily in order to protect others from suspicion. Secondly, *coerced-compliant confessions*: in these cases people confess to crimes which they know full well they have not committed. They confess because of the pressure they are under during the interrogation and hope to gain something through their confession, such as the end of the interrogation or release from custody. People who confess for such reasons may well believe that it will be easy to prove their innocence at a later stage. Thirdly, *coerced-internalised confessions*: like the person who makes a coerced compliant confession, a coerced-internalised confession is induced by the pressure of interrogation, but here the person actually comes to believe that the confession represents the truth.

In other words, such a person comes to distrust his or her own memory and instead internalises the version of events suggested by the police.

Extract 3.6.1

G Gudjonsson and J Mackeith, 'Retracted Confessions' (1988) 28 *Medicine, Science and Law* 187, p 191

It seems on the basis of the available evidence that most cases of false confession that come before the courts are of the compliant-coerced type. These confessions are best explained by the person's desire to escape from a highly stressful and aversive situation. The perceived immediate instrumental gains for confessing become a much more powerful influence on the individual's behaviour than the uncertain long-term effects of the confession, even when the alleged offence is serious.

Whether police pressure and coercion result in a coerced-compliant or a coerced-internalized confession depends on two sets of factors. The first are the idiosyncratic vulnerabilities of the individual. A tendency to become easily confused when placed under pressure, lack of confidence in one's memory and reconstruction of events, and marked susceptibility to suggestion, are probably the most prominent characteristics that make individuals prone to internalizing erroneous information communicated during police questioning. Secondly, there are the nature and circumstances of the police interviews. Coerced-compliant confessions are most easily elicited through aggressive interviewing techniques, whereas coerced-internalized confessions are produced by a more gentle, subtle and trusting form of interviewing. This is because the latter type of confession is dependent upon the individual actually coming to accept the police officers' account of events. Coerced-compliant confessions do not require any such private acceptance and the individual falsely confesses only in order to escape from an intolerable situation.

Another difference between the coerced-internalized and coerced-compliant types of confession has to do with the nature and duration of the confession. The coerced-compliant individual will stick to the false confession only while it has some instrumental value (e.g. until he or she is released from custody or when a solicitor arrives). The coerced-internalized individuals may not retract the confession for quite a while, because they continue to believe that they must have or might have committed the offence. In fact, the original memory of events may even become permanently distorted and the individual is unable for ever to recall what actually happened at the material time. More commonly, however, once the pressures of the police interview and detention are over and the person's confusional state is settled, the original memory comes back and the individual realizes with certainty that he or she is innocent.

Police interviewing techniques

The nature of the interviewing techniques used by the police are important in several respects. First, they may determine whether or not the accused

291

confesses to the crime in connection with which he or she is being questioned. Second, certain police interviewing techniques may increase the likelihood of a false confession occurring. Third, as discussed above, the type of false confession may be associated with the specific nature of the police interviewing (e.g. subtle v. aggressive). Fourth, it is evident from the Police and Criminal Evidence Act and the Codes of Practice that there is now more emphasis on police behaviour when considering the admissibility and reliability of self-incriminating statements.

Police officers in England and Wales receive little training in interviewing and commonly develop the necessary skills through experience. Various strategies for obtaining a confession from resistant suspects have been reported in the literature . . . These include confronting suspects with damaging evidence, employing 'information-bluff tricks', minimizing the seriousness of the offence, persuading suspects that it is in their best interest to confess, manipulating self-esteem, 'befriending' the suspect and showing a great deal of understanding and sympathy, and employing the 'Mr Nice and Mr Nasty routine'. The extent to which manipulative tactics are used by police officers can be seen from direct observational studies. For example, . . . Irving (1980) [B Irving, *Police Interrogation: A Study of Current Practice* (London: HMSO, 1980)] found that police officers in Brighton, England, were using interviewing techniques described in American textbooks on interrogation.

The danger of questioning producing false confessions is exacerbated by the fact that many suspects may be particularly at risk because of their mental state. Gudjonsson et al (1993) undertook a study of suspects at one police station and found that about a third of the suspects were 'intellectually disadvantaged', with 20 per cent suffering from an unusually high level of anxiety and distress and 35 per cent not in a 'normal mental state' owing to distress or drugs. The average IQ was 82, falling within the lowest 5 per cent of the population.

The regulation of confession evidence was a priority for the RCCP. Apart from the fact that it was aware of the possibility of suspects confessing falsely, there was a need to combat the problem of allegations of 'verballing', the police fabrication of statements attributed to suspects. The primary innovation of PACE in this area is the contemporaneous recording of police interviews with suspects (prior to PACE, interviews could be written up by police officers after the event). Code C, para 11.5 provides that an accurate record be made of all interviews. It should be made contemporaneously unless this is not practicable. Code E deals with the tape recording of interviews, now requiring that interviews with those suspected of indictable offences be tape recorded, unless 'it is not reasonably practicable to do so' (E 3.3), because, for example, no working tape recorder is available. Code C covers the circumstances of interviews, ensuring that suspects are given adequate rest if they are interviewed. They should be given at least eight hours of continuous rest in every 24 hours; 15-minute breaks in interviews should be made after two hours and there should be longer breaks at meal times.

While PACE regulates the *context* in which questioning takes place (tape recording, access to legal advice, number of hours rest), it is silent about the *manner* in which questioning should be carried out. Prior to PACE, research suggested that the police used a variety of strategies and tactics in order to induce suspects to confess (Irving, 1980). One study found many officers admitting that they were prepared to use violence or threats of violence during interrogation (Walkley, cited in Williamson, 1994, p 109). The RCCP felt that it could offer little guidance on the legitimacy of police questioning techniques, beyond condemning the use of violence or threats of violence. PACE gives the courts an indirect role in maintaining interviewing standards through s 76, by requiring them to exclude confessions gained in certain circumstances:

76. Confessions

(2) If, in any proceedings where the prosecution proposes to give in evidence a confession made by an accused person, it is presented to the court that the confession was or may have been obtained –

(a) by oppression of the person who made it; or

(b) in consequence of anything said or done which was likely, in the circumstances existing at the time, to render unreliable any confession which might be made by him in consequence thereof,

the court shall not allow the confession to be given in evidence against him except in so far as the prosecution proves to the court beyond reasonable doubt that the confession (notwithstanding that it may be true) was not obtained as aforesaid.

. . .

(8) In this section 'oppression' includes torture, inhuman or degrading treatment, and the use or threat of violence (whether or not amounting to torture).

Section 76 lays down a hypothetical reliability test: if anything said or done was likely to render a resulting confession unreliable, the confession must be excluded. In *Cox* [1991] Crim LR 276 it was held that it was irrelevant that the defendant admitted that his confession was true. 'Oppression' was defined in *Fulling* [1987] 2 All ER 65 in terms of a dictionary definition: 'exercise of authority or power in a burdensome, harsh or wrongful manner; unjust or cruel treatment of subjects'. The defendant had been arrested, and the police tried to undermine her will-power by telling her that her lover was having an affair with the person in the next cell; this was not held to be oppressive. In *Goldenberg* (1988) 88 Cr App R 285 it was held that 'anything said or done' did not include things done by the accused. The defendant claimed that as a result of his heroin addiction he was prepared to say anything to gain release from custody, but this was held to be irrelevant. It might have been different had the police deliberately taken advantage of his desperation because then *they* would have 'said or done' something. This decision is difficult to reconcile with *Everett* [1988] Crim LR 826, in which it was held that 'the circumstances existing at the time' included the defendant's very low mental age, even though this was not known to the police.

Unreliable confessions might also be excluded by the courts under s 78 of PACE, which gives a court the discretion to exclude evidence where its use would have an 'adverse effect on the fairness of the proceedings'. Aspects of the case law on s 78 are considered in Chapter 4 below. There is also a power at common law which could be used to exclude a confession where it is more prejudicial than probative: *Miller* [1986] 1 WLR 1191. Despite these various powers, there is evidence that unreliable confessions are still sometimes admitted by the courts (JUSTICE, 1994, pp 21–22).

Beyond the principles that can be gleaned from the cases, the law has given relatively little guidance to officers on how they should conduct interviews. Post-PACE, there are still fears that undue pressure may be brought to bear on suspects during police questioning. Interviewing sessions can still be extremely long: Baldwin (1993) reports one seven-hour interview, and JUSTICE (1994b, p 25) reports one case where a suspect was questioned for a total of 29 hours. A graphic example of post-PACE interviewing is the case of the Cardiff three. Three young men were convicted of the murder of a Cardiff prostitute in 1988. The main evidence against one of the men, Stephen Miller, was a confession made during police interrogation; the confession also implicated the other two defendants. Miller was interviewed by the police for 13 hours over a period of five days. During this time he denied his involvement well over 300 times until he eventually admitted being at the scene of crime. In the following extract, the Court of Appeal, which quashed the convictions of all three men, discusses the conduct of Miller's interrogation:

Extract 3.6.2

R v Paris, Abdullahi and Miller (1992) 97 Cr App R 99, pp 103–105

We are bound to say that on hearing tape 7, each member of this Court was horrified. Miller was bullied and hectored. The officers, particularly Detective Constable Greenwood, were not questioning him so much as shouting at him what they wanted him to say. Short of physical violence, it is hard to conceive of a more hostile and intimidating approach by officers to a suspect. It is impossible to convey on the printed page the pace, force and menace of the officer's delivery, but a short passage may give something of the flavour:

Stephen Wayne Miller:	'I wasn't there.'
D C Greenwood:	'How you can ever . . . ?'
Stephen Wayne Miller:	'I wasn't there.'
D C Greenwood:	'How you . . . I just don't know how you can sit there, I . . .'
Stephen Wayne Miller:	'I wasn't . . .'
D C Greenwood:	'Really don't.'
Stephen Wayne Miller:	'I was not there, I was not there.'
D C Greenwood:	'Seeing that girl, your girlfriend, in that room that night like she was. I just don't know how you can sit there and say it.'

Stephen Wayne Miller:	'I wasn't there.'
D C Greenwood:	'You were there that night.'
Stephen Wayne Miller:	'I was not there.'
D C Greenwood:	'Together with all the others, you were there that night.'
Stephen Wayne Miller:	'I was not there. I'll tell you already . . .'
D C Greenwood:	'And you sit there and say that.'
Stephen Wayne Miller:	'They can lock me up for 50 billion years, I said I was not there.'
D C Greenwood:	''Cause you don't wanna be there.'
Stephen Wayne Miller:	'I was not there.'
D C Greenwood:	'You don't wanna be there because if . . .'
Stephen Wayne Miller:	'I was not there.'
D C Greenwood:	'As soon as you say that you're there you know you're involved.'
Stephen Wayne Miller:	'I was not there.'
D C Greenwood:	'You know you were involved in it.'
Stephen Wayne Miller:	'I was not involved and I wasn't there.'
D C Greenwood:	'Yes you were there.'
Stephen Wayne Miller:	'I was not there.'
D C Greenwood:	'You were there, that's why Leanne is come up now . . .'
Stephen Wayne Miller:	'No.'
D C Greenwood:	''Cause her conscience is . . .'
Stephen Wayne Miller:	'I was not there.'
D C Greenwood:	'She can't sleep at night . . .'
Stephen Wayne Miller:	'No. I was not there.'
D C Greenwood:	'To say you were there that night . . .'
Stephen Wayne Miller:	'I was not there.'
D C Greenwood:	'Looking over her body seeing what she was like . . .'
Stephen Wayne Miller:	'I was not there.'
D C Greenwood:	'With her head like she had and you have got the audacity to sit there and say nothing at all about it.'
Stephen Wayne Miller:	'I was not there.'
D C Greenwood:	'You know damn well you were there.'
Stephen Wayne Miller:	'I was not there.'

and so on for many pages.

As to Miller standing his ground, it is significant that in the very next interview (tape 8) within an hour after the bullying, he was persuaded by insidious questioning to concede that under the effects of drugs, it was possible he was there and did not remember it clearly. Thus at tape 8, page 32, he said:

'I am just . . . I am just certain that I wasn't there that's all, I am, I am certain I wasn't there but it could . . . it could happen, it could have happened.'

Once he opened that chink, the officers kept up the questioning to open it further. Of course, it is perfectly legitimate for officers to pursue their interrogation of a suspect with a view to eliciting his account or gaining admissions. They are not required to give up after the first denial or even after a number of denials. But here, after the oppression in tape 7, Mr. Mansfield complains that the other officers were also guilty of a less blatant form of oppression. They made it clear to Miller on many occasions that they would go on questioning him until they 'got it right.' By that they clearly meant, until Miller agreed with the version they were putting.

Mr. Mansfield submits that additional pressure was applied by telling the appellant he was talking drivel and rubbish and telling him his alibi was blown away. The alibi had never been totally water-tight, but so far as it went, it was not, on the police information, blown away. The prosecution's version of events was said to be supported by a number of witnesses, which it was not. Vilday's account was put again and again as being wholly reliable. Miller was threatened with the prospect of a life sentence more than once. Much of the interviewing was taken up, not with questions put to the appellant but with the officers putting detailed descriptions of what they believed had happened and what role Miller may have played. Thus, they persistently suggested he was 'stoned' due to the effects of cocaine so as to persuade him that he might have been present even though he had no clear recollection of it. Having gained admissions by this approach, the officers then insisted that the appellant must know and tell them every detail of what occurred at the scene, e.g. which way Lynette fell, where the body was in the room, who came in, at what stage and so on. It is submitted that Miller was in effect brain-washed over these 13 hours into repeating back to the officers facts they had asserted many times to him.

It is clear on listening to the tapes that for extended periods, Miller was crying and sobbing, yet he was not given any respite. It is true that after some of the interviews concluded, he was asked if he wanted a break and he expressed willingness to continue. The context was that he was being led to believe the officers were seeking to eliminate him from participation in the attack and he wanted to get to the end of the questioning.

The treatment of Miller by the police raises problems beyond the reliability of any resulting confession. It was arguably inhuman and degrading treatment and thus a breach of Miller's rights under Article 3 of the European Convention on Human Rights.

The court's discussion of the tactics used by the police when questioning Miller are a reminder that investigation (including questioning) is a constructive process. The police had a clear idea of the role that they thought Miller had played, and worked to get Miller to assent to this. The interrogation of Miller is a fairly blatant example of the pursuit of case construction through questioning, but a similar strategy may be pursued through more subtle means. Several researchers have identified 'leading questions' as a key police interview strategy. These questions incorporate information which suggests the desired answer to the suspect, and they carry similar dangers to suggestive questions used in the questioning of eyewitnesses. A particularly subtle form of leading question plays on the police officer's superior knowledge of the legal elements of an offence to draw a suspect into supplying an incriminating answer without realising it. One detective told Maguire and Norris how he had been taught 'to use the law as a weapon' against suspects:

> He gave the example of the offence of possessing an offensive weapon, proof of which required more than simply demonstrating possession of, say, a knife: he had been taught to induce anyone found carrying a knife to state that it was for their own protection (which constituted sufficient evidence for the offence), by means of remarks such as 'I suppose this is a dangerous area to walk around in'. (1992, p 22)

Further examples are provided by McConville et al (1997):

Extract 3.6.3

M McConville, A Sanders and R Leng, *The Case for the Prosecution: Police Suspects and the Construction of Criminality* (1991) pp 70–71

CC-A002 – The defendant was alleged to have damaged a mini-cab windscreen in the course of an argument with his girlfriend. Both had been drinking heavily and the defendant had to sleep off the effects of the drink before being fit to be interviewed. He said that, in the course of the row, he had swung his arm out 'and hit the windscreen and it broke'. The police then turned their attention to the question of *mens rea*:

Police: 'Did you intend to smash the windscreen?'
Defendant: 'No.'
Police: 'So you just swung your hand out in a *reckless* manner?' (emphasis supplied)
Defendant: 'Yes, that's it, just arguing.'
Police: 'Why did you hit the window in the first place?'
Defendant: 'Just arguing, *reckless*, it wasn't intentional to break it . . .' (emphasis supplied)

Here, therefore, the suggestion of recklessness is first implanted by the police as a favourable, exculpatory alternative to the defendant, who accepts it as such and then adopts it. Although recklessness is a term of art and part of the definition of the offence with which A002 was charged (criminal damage) it is clear that A002 was not using the term in the technical sense, but rather was using the term colloquially to support a plea that the breakage was *accidental*. Thus, in providing A002 with the terminology in which to press his excuse, the police construct a key element of the case. Having made this key strategic gain, the officer does not explore the matter further; to do so would be to run the risk of showing that A002 had used the term reckless in a sense quite different from that contemplated in law.

CC-A069 – Here the defendant was arrested on suspicion of shoplifting.
Police: 'How did you take it?'
Defendant: 'I just put it in my shopping bag.'
Police: 'Then what did you do?'

Defendant: 'Walked out of the store.'
Police: 'So you stole the bag is that correct?'
Defendant: 'Yes.'

Case *CC-A069* is typical of a style of questioning that is common to much of police interrogation. Once the suspect has agreed to some act or acts, the police attribute the necessary state of mind and any other legal requirements of guilt by a 'question' which purports to *summarize* the legal effect of what the suspect has related: '*So* you stole . . .'. The suspect is being informed (incorrectly) of her *legal* position ('You are a thief') and the question form ('is that correct?') is effectively redundant.

> *CC-J45* – The defendant was arrested on suspicion of theft of chocolate. Under interrogation the crucial exchanges occurred as follows:
> *Police*: 'What did you do in Smith's?'
> *Suspect*: 'Took some chocolate.'
> *Police*: 'How did you take it?'
> *Suspect*: 'Put it in the shopping basket and then put it into the bag and then when we left put it into the trolley.'
> *Police*: 'Did you pay for anything in Smith's?'
> *Suspect*: 'No.'
> *Police*: 'So you stole the chocolate, is that correct?'
> *Suspect*: 'Yes.'

Here, the police introduce 'stole' without having established the legal elements which comprise stealing.

Baldwin's study of video-taped interviews provides a summary of the main deficiencies in interview practices post-PACE:

Extract 3.6.4

**J Baldwin, *Video-taping Interviews with Suspects – An Evaluation*
(1992) pp 15–17**

ineptitude: the image of police interviewers as professional, skilled and force-ful interrogators scarcely matched the reality. Officers sometimes emerged as nervous, ill at ease and lacking in confidence. Even in the simplest cases, they were unfamiliar with the available evidence, and the video cameras often showed them with their eyes glued to a written statement, clearly unacquainted with its contents. Some were slouched in chairs, scarcely looking the part of a professional interviewer. They may have assumed that such relaxed postures made for informality, but it suggested a general sloppiness pervading all aspects of the interview. Many interviews tended either to be short and breathless, with a quick-fire series of questions, or else they took the form of aimless and unfocused discussions, without structure and purpose.

assuming guilt: many officers evidently approach the interview anticipating a confession and much of the time they are not disappointed. It is often difficult for them to keep an open mind, and it is perhaps only natural that, at the

298

interview stage, they will have strong suspicions that the person before them is the offender concerned. But such assumptions can be dangerous, and many officers enter the interview room with their minds made up. They treat the suspect's explanation, if they bother to listen to it at all, with extreme scepticism from the outset. They are not predisposed, either from training or temperament, to think that they might be wrong. The questions asked (often leading questions starting, as they do, from an assumption of guilt) merely seek to persuade suspects to agree to a series of propositions. If this is unsuccessful, discussion tends to become unhelpfully polarised, with claims and counter-claims, allegations and denials following a familiar circular path, descending often into a highly repetitive series of questions. In several cases, one word admissions were obtained from suspects in response to leading questions, with the resulting admissions equivocal in character. Such admissions come close to officers putting words into suspects' mouths. Interviews can easily become self-confirmatory exchanges in which the interviewer's preconceptions are reinforced, no matter how the suspect responds.

poor interview technique: a hotch-potch of problems fell within this category and included instances of officers continually interrupting suspects and failing to give them a proper opportunity to put their version of events coherently; officers having only a fragile grasp of the legal elements that need to be proved in an offence, and officers losing control of an interview because they over-react to aggressiveness or provocation on the part of a suspect or else because they become unduly flustered at the intervention of a third party, particularly a legal representative.

unfair, questionable or unprofessional conduct: some interviews threw up more sensitive and controversial issues than those in the other categories. Some officers adopted an unduly harrying or aggressive approach in interviewing, and though this arose in a relatively small number of cases, these were the ones in which the present writer felt greatest unease about the outcome, particularly where they involved juveniles and young persons. There were another group of cases in which suspects were offered unfair inducements to confess to offences, particularly where offences taken into consideration were concerned. In a few cases at Wednesfield station, thoroughly misleading information was given to suspects about the likelihood of the sentence they might receive being affected if they agreed to have certain offences taken into consideration. Finally, there were three instances at the Belgrave Road station in Birmingham in which private exchanges between solicitors and suspects were recorded, despite the officer assuring both parties that the cameras were being turned off.[1] It goes without saying that, whether inadvertent or not, such practices are unacceptable.

Basic principles of good interview practice are as applicable in the police station as they are in the Job Centre or the TV studio. An unduly harrying style, persistent interruptions, continual use of leading questions, ineptitude or lack of planning are as much flaws in police interviews as in any other situation in which questioning skills are needed, and it is surely of greater importance to assess police interviews, since so much more is likely to be at stake – not least the liberty of individual suspects.

299

In talking to officers of all ranks in this study, it became apparent that there was a good deal of mythology surrounding the subject of police interviewing. Many of the assumptions that are made have found their way on to training programmes, and much training is blown off-course as a result. A main part of this mythology is that high level psychological skills are needed to 'turn' suspects who are as a rule reluctant to admit their involvement in an offence. It was remarkable to note, in examining interviews in a large number of cases, just how rare it was for suspects to be 'turned' in this way. This observation applied no matter how strong the evidence at the officer's disposal and regardless of the level of interviewing skill. Of the six hundred interviews observed, only twenty were cases in which suspects completely changed their story in the course of an interview and admitted the offence.[2]

It is clear, then, that in few interviews are suspects actually persuaded to admit participation in criminal offences. Yet much police training has focused on the methods that might be employed to produce that effect. The simple truth is that it is extremely difficult to induce reluctant suspects to confess by methods that are nowadays deemed to be acceptable. The paltry successes achieved by officers in these six hundred cases indicate that this focus is misguided. The upshot is surely that it is scarcely worth pursuing this course at all. Much of the public concern about police interview methods is the product of such 'persuasive interviewing' techniques. These results show that little will be lost by abandoning that preoccupation.

[1] Allegations that officers have 'eavesdropped' on solicitors in this way and that interview rooms have been 'bugged' were made in the local press, though the Chief Constable categorically denied that such practices were acceptable policy.

[2] In only nine of these cases was the change of heart attributable to the persuasive skills of the interviewer, and even here only three involved cases of any seriousness.

As other researchers have noted, there is a tendency for police officers to view the obtaining of a confession as the prime function of an interview with a suspect (e.g. Mortimer, 1994). In the light of the psychological research on false confessions this is problematic, because it will encourage officers to pressurise suspects. Baldwin concludes that: 'there is little an interviewer can legitimately do to induce a suspect to confess' (1992c, p 13).

As with identification evidence, attempts have been made to use some of the insights of psychological research to reform investigative strategies. Officers are now expected to adopt less incrimination-centred interview strategies, a style of questioning sometimes termed 'investigative' or 'cognitive' interviewing. Home Office Circular 22/92 defines the objectives of investigative interviewing as being 'to obtain accurate and reliable information from suspects, witnesses or victims in order to discover the truth about matters under police investigation'. Investigative interviewing 'should be approached with an open mind. Information obtained from the person who is being interviewed should always be tested against what the interviewing officer already knows or what can reasonably be established'. Officers should act fairly during questioning, but they do not have to 'accept the first answer given. Questioning is not unfair merely because it is persistent'. Some of the elements of investigative interviewing are fleshed out in a Home Office publication called *A Guide to Interviewing* (1992). The passages which follow give a flavour of how police officers should approach investigative interviews.

The 'Cognitive Approach'

The interviewee is asked to think back to the event and mentally re-live what happened; thus telling everything that is initially remembered with minimal inter-ference (Free Recall). This is followed with at least one more attempt at 'Free Recall' using a different order or perspective. Areas of specific interest can be pursued when the 'Free Recall' attempts are concluded. This approach is designed to make use of how memory works and the way in which information is stored and retrieved.

'Management of Conversation'

The interviewee is asked to provide an account of what happened. The interviewer subdivides this first account into a number of parts; each part being pursued in turn in a series of 'second accounts' to obtain more detail. Before each 'second account' is concluded, the interviewer can probe for more detail and then link that section to the next area of second account. (Home Office, 1992, p 19)

The management of conversation approach is said to be more appropriate for suspects than the cognitive approach.

Whether or not the introduction of PACE, and any related changes in pol-ice culture, have changed police interviewing strategies, PACE has increased the openness of police interviews through the introduction of tape recording and the increased presence of legal advice during interviews. However, there are weak spots in both these protections. We saw above that many suspects do not benefit from the presence of legal advice at interview. We also saw that doubts have been raised about the effectiveness of legal advice (it should be noted that one of the disturbing aspects of *Paris, Abdullahi and Miller* is that Miller's solicitor was present throughout the aggressive questioning re-produced in the extract above). As for tape recording, many tapes are never listened to by anyone other than the police. After an interview the police produce a written summary which will be used by the Crown Prosecution Service and the defence. There is considerable room for doubt about the status of the summary as an accurate representation of the factual content of the interview (see Baldwin, 1992a). The tape will only be heard in court if there is any dispute about the propriety of the interrogation.

A final weak spot in the regulation of interviewing is that some question-ing of suspects may take place off-tape. A graphic example is provided by a television film made about police work (see McConville, 1992). The film showed officers interviewing suspects politely and cautiously when they were aware that they were being recorded. However, sound recording also caught officers in less guarded moments as they visited suspects in the cells. Here suspects were aggressively offered inducements to confess, such as promises of bail and reduced charges. If such threats and promises were recorded, they would probably lead a court to exclude any resulting confession on the grounds of unreliability (PACE, s 76). Where crucial police–suspect interaction takes place off-tape, the recorded interview may be little more than a well-rehearsed routine, the dubious evidential value of which remains hidden. The custody officer should not allow officers access to suspects in the cells in order to question them, but some research suggests that visits do take place, and that these are not recorded on the custody record (McConville et al, 1991, pp 57–60). It should be noted that both police and suspects may have an interest in discussing such matters as bail and charge levels: suspects so that they can secure an advantage for themselves and police so that they can negotiate a confession in the later interview. This means that there is probably pressure on both sides to hold informal discussions off-tape.

Unrecorded conversations with suspects may also take place outside the police station. Code C, para 11.1 forbids the interviewing of suspects outside the police station, except in urgent cases. Suspects may, however, be legitimately *questioned* outside the police station: the distinction is that interviewing is the asking of questions of a suspect regarding his or her involvement in an offence. Research by Moston and Stephenson (1993), based on police responses, found that 8 per cent of suspects had been interviewed and 58 per cent questioned prior to arrival at the police station.

It will be apparent that the existing safeguards still leave room for convictions to be based on unreliable confession evidence. This may be because the suspect has confessed falsely or because the police have falsely claimed that the suspect confessed outside the police station. Continued concerns about confession evidence have led some commentators to suggest, as an additional safeguard, the adoption of a rule that a conviction should never be based solely on a confession. Instead, there would have to be corroborating evidence in all cases involving confession evidence. (There is no such requirement at present, though PACE, s 77 provides that where the case against a mentally handicapped person depends wholly or substantially on confession evidence, the jury should be told that there is a special need for caution.) A rule requiring the corroboration of confessions was considered by the Royal Commission on Criminal Justice (RCCJ), but rejected by the majority. The Commission summarised the most common argument against a corroboration requirement thus:

> The main argument against a requirement for supporting evidence is the likely effect on the numbers of people who are properly convicted on the basis of genuine confessions alone. A significant number of people plead guilty after a confession who might be strongly advised by their lawyers not to do so if the confession were the only evidence against them. There is no reason to believe that most of them are not in fact guilty. If they were to walk free, not only would justice not have been done in the individual case but there would be a cumulative adverse effect on the public's perception of the effectiveness of the criminal justice system. Furthermore, if there were a requirement of corroboration or supporting evidence,

some prosecutions that are properly brought now could not be brought at all for lack of such evidence. (Royal Commission on Criminal Justice, 1993, Ch 4, para 68)

However, attempts to quantify the number of cases which would fail were a corroboration requirement to be adopted suggest that the figure would be small: a Home Office study put the proportion of cases relying on confession evidence alone at 1.4 per cent (see Royal Commission on Criminal Justice, 1993, Ch 4, para 69), while a study by McConville (1993) suggested that around 3 per cent of convictions would be affected by the rule. Other reasons which the RCCJ thought told against a corroboration rule were the complexity of corroboration rules and the fact that the police might be able to fabricate corroborating evidence. The majority of the Commission recommended that, instead, there should be a mandatory warning in confession cases, along the lines of the *Turnbull* warning described above. No such rule has yet been adopted by the Court of Appeal.

See further Pattenden (1991), Dennis (1993), Leng (1994).

(c) Witness statements

Whereas eyewitness identification evidence and confession evidence have received considerable attention from researchers and academics, a third common type of evidence, the statements of witnesses, has been relatively neglected. Yet witness statements raise similar issues to eyewitness identifications and confessions, because similar psychological processes underpin their reliability. Witness accounts are malleable, and officers questioning witnesses may be looking for particular information. Trankell has described the problems which may result from the interaction of interviewer bias and interviewee suggestibility:

> On the one hand the interrogator . . . unintentionally directs the interrogation in accordance with his hypotheses concerning what has happened. On the other hand the witness . . . because of his feelings of inferiority and uncertainty, is extra keen to please the interrogator and filled with the desire to give an impression of reliability. In every question the interrogated listens for the interrogator's aims, and with each answer he favours these aims by slipping past the details in his observations which are not wanted. In building up his theory about what has occurred the examiner chooses those details which fit his preliminary hypotheses whilst he ignores those parts which contradict them. When he formulates his questions he bases them on the distorted results of his own listening. In this manner the witness's original perception gradually grows into a distorted picture which is more likely to gratify the interrogator's desire to prove his own theory than elucidate the interrogated's memory. (Trankell, 1972, p 27, quoted in Gudjonsson, 1992, p 15)

(Many of the points in this passage apply equally to confession evidence and eyewitness accounts.) That witnesses should be questioned cautiously is recognised by Home Office Circular 22/92 and the publication *A Guide to Interviewing*, which provide guidelines for questioning witnesses as well as suspects.

Witnesses statements are important pieces of evidence. In some circumstances, they may be used as evidence in court without the witness being called (see Criminal Justice Act 1967, s 9; Criminal Justice Act 1988, ss 23 and 26). Even if they are not so used, a witness will often be given the chance to re-read a statement before giving evidence in court or to refer to it while testifying. Although this practice is referred to as 'refreshing memory', this may be little more than a convenient fiction: many trials take place a long time after the events in issue occurred, and a witness's memory is probably more likely to be replaced than refreshed by reading the original statement.

Despite their evidential importance, there are very few safeguards governing the taking of witness statements. Officers will question witnesses, writing down what they say. The resulting statement is then given to the witness to sign. There is no requirement that the encounter be tape recorded or that the notes be made contemporaneously. A small study by McLean (1995), suggests that interviews with witnesses reproduce many of the worst aspects of interviews with suspects. McLean found that the majority of questions asked by officers were either leading questions or 'risky' questions (requiring only a yes or no answer). More worrying still was the fact that the written statements signed by witnesses often included distortions of what had actually been said. On average, each interview omitted 14 items of information, and on occasion officers actually wrote down the contrary of what the witness had said. Similarly, Cretney and Davis note that: '[S]everal of the victims whose cases we followed considered that the process of recording their statement had involved editing and transforming their account so that it might better meet the demands of the prosecution process' (1995, p 129). As with interviews with suspects, the questioning that produces a written statement may have been preceded by earlier questioning or by a statement given by the witness at the time the crime was reported. These interactions escape even the requirement of the production of written records. McLean recommends that witness interviews be tape recorded, as do Heaton-Armstrong and Wolchover (1992).

There are no legal rules requiring corroboration of witness statements or warnings to the jury about their reliability. Because the *Turnbull* rules only apply to the identification of people, a witness statement describing an action (e.g. 'I saw the defendant hit the victim') or an object (e.g. 'I saw a red Volvo drive away from the house') escapes the requirement of a warning.

7. THE RIGHT TO SILENCE

(a) The change in the law

In recent years one of the most controversial criminal justice issues has been the suspect's 'right to silence' during police questioning. What is meant by the right to silence in this context is the rule of evidence that an accused person's failure to answer questions when interviewed by the police cannot be used as evidence against him or her in court. The RCCP came down in favour of retaining the right to silence, but in the late 1980s the right was curtailed in Northern Ireland and the government announced plans to modify the right in England and Wales, establishing a working group to examine how this should be done. In the event, the air of crisis surrounding the criminal justice system following the release of the Guildford four and the Birmingham six meant that plans to curtail the right were shelved. An examination of the right to silence was included in the terms of reference of the RCCJ, but the Commission decided by a majority that the right should be retained. Despite the RCCJ's support for the status quo, in 1993 the Home Secretary, Michael Howard, announced that the government intended to abolish the right to silence. This led to ss 34–39 of the Criminal Justice and Public Order Act 1994 which allow a court to draw adverse inferences from an accused's silence in various circumstances. Section 34 permits inferences to be drawn from an accused's failure to mention facts when questioned or charged by the police:

34. Effect of accused's failure to mention facts when questioned or charged

(1) Where, in any proceedings against a person for an offence, evidence is given that the accused –

(a) at any time before he was charged with the offence, on being questioned under caution by a constable trying to discover whether or by whom the offence had been committed, failed to mention any fact relied on in his defence in those proceedings; or

(b) on being charged with the offence or officially informed that he might be prosecuted for it, failed to mention any such fact, being a fact which in the circumstances existing at the time the accused could reasonably have been expected to mention when so questioned, charged or informed, as the case may be, subsection (2) below applies.

(2) Where this subsection applies –

(a) a magistrates' court, in deciding whether to grant an application for dismissal made by the accused under section 6 of the Magistrates' Courts Act 1980 (application for dismissal of charge in course of proceedings with a view to transfer for trial);

(b) a judge, in deciding whether to grant an application made by the accused under –

(i) section 6 of the Criminal Justice Act 1987 (application for dismissal of charge of serious fraud in respect of which notice of transfer has been given under section 4 of that Act); or

(ii) paragraph 5 of Schedule 6 to the Criminal Justice Act 1991 (application for dismissal of charge of violent or sexual offence involving child in respect of which notice of transfer has been given under section 53 of that Act);

(c) the court, in determining whether there is a case to answer; and

(d) the court or jury, in determining whether the accused is guilty of the offence charged,

may draw such inferences from the failure as appear proper.

Inferences can also be drawn from a suspect's failure to account for suspicious objects, substances or marks (s 36) or presence at a particular place (s 37). None of these sections compels a suspect to answer police questions, so in one sense a 'right to remain silent' remains. However, the threat of adverse inferences puts some pressure on suspects to speak, as the new caution implies:

> You do not have to say anything. But it may harm your defence if you do not mention when questioned something which you later rely on in court. Anything you do say may be given in evidence.

Under s 38(3) a person may not be convicted solely on an inference from silence.

The impact of s 34 depends on its interpretation by the courts. The reference in s 34(1)(b) to facts which 'in the circumstances existing at the time the accused could *reasonably* have been expected to mention' (emphasis supplied) and in s 34(2)(d) to 'proper' inferences led some commentators to suggest that the courts might play an active role in policing the inferences to be drawn by a jury (see, for example, Pattenden, 1995). Thus, it was argued, if a suspect might have remained silent owing to legal advice or owing to some specific vulnerability (such as a mental disorder), then a court should hold that silence was not unreasonable and that no inference was proper. The Court of Appeal has not interpreted the section in this manner. So far its approach has been to leave the questions of reasonableness and the propriety of inferences to the jury. In *Condron* [1997] 1 Cr App R 185 the defendants had been arrested on suspicion of supplying heroin. Their solicitor, who was concerned that they were suffering the effects of opiate withdrawal, advised them not to answer police questions. At their trial the jury was invited to draw an inference from this refusal. The judge directed it along the lines of the following Judicial Studies Board specimen direction:

> If he failed to mention . . . when he was questioned, decide whether, in the circumstances which existed at the time, it was a fact which he could reasonably have been expected to mention.
>
> The law is that you may draw such inferences as appear proper from his failure to mention it at that time. You do not have to hold it against him. It is for you to decide whether it is proper to do so.
>
> Failure to mention such a fact at that time cannot, on its own, prove guilt, but depending on the circumstances, you may hold that failure against him when deciding whether he is guilty, that is, take it into account as some additional support for the prosecution's case. It is for you to decide whether it is fair to do so.

In *Condron* the Court of Appeal held that it had been proper to direct the jury that it might draw an inference from the defendants' silence during police questioning. However, the court held that in future cases, in addition to summarising the Judicial Studies Board direction, judges should direct juries along the following lines:

If, despite any evidence relied on to explain his silence or in the absence of any such evidence, you conclude the silence can only sensibly be attributed to the defendant's having no answer or none that would stand up to cross-examination, you may draw an adverse inference.

Another circumstance in which it has been suggested that a suspect might be justified in refusing to answer police questions, is where the police refuse to reveal the evidence against him or her prior to questioning. When they are questioned by the police, suspects may not know, and have no right to discover, the details of the evidence that the police have against them. Research suggests that the police are reluctant to give too much away to legal advisers prior to interview (McConville et al finding that they disclosed 'bare details' in 74 per cent of cases in which they were asked for information (1994, pp 91–92)). Both the RCCP and the RCCJ emphasised that, owing to this informational imbalance, it would be especially unfair to abolish the right to silence during police questioning (e.g. Royal Commission on Criminal Justice, 1993, Ch 4, para 24: 'it is when but only when the prosecution case has been fully disclosed that defendants should be required to offer an answer to the charges made against them'; and cf Zuckerman, 1994). Prior to the change in the law, some researchers drew attention to the fact that suspects and their advisers would sometimes use silence in a constructive manner, as a means of extracting information about the evidence against them from the police (Dixon, 1991; McConville and Hodgson, 1993). There is, of course, nothing to stop suspects and their advisers continuing to use this strategy now that the law has been changed. However, if the police refuse to disclose the evidence against a suspect, and the suspect responds by refusing to answer their questions, he or she runs the risk of adverse inferences at trial (see *Argent* [1997] 2 Cr App R 27).

(b) Was abolition justifiable?

Debate over changes to the right to silence reflect many of the arguments used more generally in debates about the criminal process. Advocates of the change to the law have stressed common sense and community faith in the criminal justice system. The following arguments appear in an article prepared on behalf of the crime committee of the Association of Chief Police Officers:

Under the present rule, a person suspected of committing an offence the previous night, arrested next morning and refusing to answer the question 'Where were you last night?' is able to conceal that silence from a jury. This does not provide the jury with all the facts, and it is not a sensible, rational basis upon which to proceed . . .

It is important to stress that the purpose of the right to comment on the right of silence is to create a more rational legal system. As the Royal Commission itself emphasised, we need to think more about victims and witnesses who presently lack faith in the process. One aspect of that lack of faith is an exclusionary rule which does not allow all the evidence in a case to be presented to a jury. (Neyroud, 1994, pp 17–18)

Another part of the argument for changing the law was that the right to silence allowed the guilty to escape conviction. This, in turn, prompted considerable debate about just how many suspects used the right to silence. Research prepared for the RCCJ by Leng (1993) suggested that the number was small, with 'significant' exercise of the right to silence in 4.5 per cent of cases. Further, when these cases were followed through the system, exercise of the right to silence did not appear to result in disproportionate numbers of discontinuances or acquittals. In cases where the police took no further action against a suspect, the right to silence had not been used in any greater proportion of cases than it was used overall. Other research for the RCCJ supported these findings, even suggesting that those suspects who refused to answer police questions are more likely to be convicted than their counterparts (Zander and Henderson, 1993, p 5). Later research, however, suggests that suspects' use of the right to silence increased in the 1990s (Leng's research used data collected in 1986–88). Brown (1997, p 174) suggests that by 1993 around 10 per cent of suspects were refusing to answer all police questions.

The debate about the number of suspects using the right to silence, and whether it rose after the introduction of PACE, is connected to another aspect of the argument for changing the law. This argument, called 'exchange abolition' by Greer (1990), was that the introduction of PACE gave suspects too many protections, so that a change in the law was needed to make the pre-trial process workable. For example, in *Alladice* (1988) 87 Cr App R 380, at p 385 the Lord Chief Justice commented on the suspect's right to legal advice in the following terms:

> The result [of the right to legal advice] is that in many cases a detainee, who would otherwise have answered proper questioning by the police, will be advised to remain silent. Weeks later, at his trial, such a person not infrequently produces an explanation of, or a defence to the charge, the truthfulness of which the police have had no chance to check . . . [I]t seems to us that the effect of section 58 is such that the balance of fairness between prosecution and defence cannot be maintained unless proper comment is permitted on the defendant's silence in such circumstances.

The exchange abolition argument hinges, in part, on the question of whether PACE has led to a significant change in the treatment of suspects in the police station. It was partly because of this that the majority of the RCCJ were sceptical about this that the majority rejected changing the law:

> It is the less experienced and more vulnerable suspects against whom the threat of adverse comments would be likely to be more damaging. There are too many cases of improper pressures being brought to bear on suspects in police custody, even

where the safeguards of PACE and the codes of practice have been supposedly in force, for the majority to regard this with equanimity. (Royal Commission on Criminal Justice, Ch 4, para 23)

The RCCJ's argument might be used to counter another part of the exchange abolition argument. That argument uses a metaphor of 'balance' to describe the criminal process: police powers should be balanced against suspects' rights so as to achieve a workable equilibrium. However, if we take the RCCJ's point, that the right to silence provides a protection for vulnerable suspects, we might ask whether this protection should be traded off in the search for balance. Those who see the criminal process in terms of rights argue that the balancing metaphor is inappropriate (see the discussion in Chapter 1). In this instance, if the right to silence is recognised as implementing the right of suspects not to be wrongfully convicted, it should not be removed in order to make it easier to convict the guilty.

However, identifying rights (in this strong sense of the word) that are protected by the right to silence is not easy. Take the right not to be wrongfully convicted: one might question whether the right to silence is an effective protection against wrongful conviction (the vulnerable suspects referred to by the RCCJ are probably those least likely to refuse to answer questions); or one might suggest other ways in which the right could be protected (for example, by introducing a rule requiring the corroboration of confessions).

There has recently been speculation as to whether the right to silence is recognised under the European Convention on Human Rights. Article 6(1) of the Convention establishes the right to a fair trial, and in *Funke v France* (1993) 16 EHRR 297 the European Court of Human Rights seemingly interpreted this provision so as to include a right to silence. Funke was investigated by French customs authorities on suspicion of breach of certain financial regulations, and the authorities brought a criminal action against him to force him to produce documents relating to bank accounts that he held abroad. In a rather elliptical judgment, the Court held that this was a violation of the Convention:

> 44. The Court notes that the customs secured Mr. Funke's conviction in order to obtain certain documents which they believed must exist, although they were not certain of the fact. Being unable or unwilling to procure them by some other means, they attempted to compel the applicant himself to provide the evidence of offences he had allegedly committed. The special features of customs law cannot justify such an infringement of the right of anyone 'charged with a criminal offence,' within the autonomous meaning of this expression in Article 6, to remain silent and not to contribute to incriminating itself.

In *Murray v United Kingdom* (1996) 2 EHRR 29 the Court ruled on whether provisions in Northern Ireland, allowing a court to draw inferences from refusals to answer police questions, constituted a breach of Article 6. The Northern Irish law in question is substantially similar to s 34 of the Criminal Justice and Public Order Act 1994. Murray had been arrested by police when he was found in a house in which a police informer was being held against his will. At his trial in a Diplock (non-jury) court he was convicted of aiding and abetting unlawful imprisonment. The judge drew adverse inferences (under art 6 of the Criminal Evidence (Northern Ireland) Order 1988, SI 1988 No 187) from the fact that Murray had not explained his presence in the house to the police (he had remained silent throughout police questioning).

Extract 3.7.1

Murray v United Kingdom (1996) 2 EHRR 29, paras 45–54
(footnotes omitted)

45. Although not specifically mentioned in Article 6 of the Convention, there can be no doubt that the right to remain silent under police questioning and the privilege against self-incrimination are generally recognised international standards which lie at the heart of the notion of a fair procedure under Article 6. By providing the accused with protection against improper compulsion by the authorities these immunities contribute to avoiding miscarriages of justice and to securing the aim of Article 6.

46. The Court does not consider that it is called upon to give an abstract analysis of the scope of these immunities and, in particular, of what constitutes in this context 'improper compulsion'. What is at stake in the present case is whether these immunities are absolute in the sense that the exercise by an accused of the right to silence cannot under any circumstances be used against him at trial or, alternatively, whether informing him in advance that, under certain conditions, his silence may be used, is always to be regarded as 'improper compulsion'.

47. On the one hand, it is self-evident that is incompatible with the immunities under consideration to base a conviction solely or mainly on the accused's silence or on a refusal to answer questions or to give evidence himself. On the other hand, the Court deems it equally obvious that these immunities cannot and should not prevent that the accused's silence, in situations which clearly call for an explanation from him, be taken into account in assessing the persuasiveness of the evidence adduced by the prosecution.

Wherever the line between these two extremes is to be drawn, it follows from this understanding of 'the right to silence' that the question whether the right is absolute must be answered in the negative.

It cannot be said therefore that an accused's decision to remain silent throughout criminal proceedings should necessarily have no implications when the trial court seeks to evaluate the evidence against him. In particular, as the Government has pointed out, established international standards in this area, while providing for the right to silence and the privilege against self-incrimination, are silent on this point.

Whether the drawing of adverse inferences from an accused's silence infringes Article 6 is a matter to be determined in the light of all the circumstances of the case, having particular regard to the situations where inferences may be drawn, the weight attached to them by the national courts in their assessment of the evidence and the degree of compulsion inherent in the situation.

48. As regards the degree of compulsion involved in the present case, it is recalled that the applicant was in fact able to remain silent. Notwithstanding the repeated warnings as to the possibility that inferences might be drawn from his silence, he did not make any statements to the police and did not give evidence during his trial. Moreover under Article 4(5) of the Order he remained a non-compellable witness . . . Thus his insistence in maintaining silence throughout the proceedings did not amount to a criminal offence or contempt of court. Furthermore, as has been stressed in national court decisions, silence, in itself, cannot be regarded as an indication of guilt.

49. The facts of the present case accordingly fall to be distinguished from those in FUNKE V. FRANCE where criminal proceedings were brought against the applicant by the customs authorities in an attempt to compel him to provide evidence of offences he had allegedly committed. Such a degree of compulsion in that case was found by the Court to be incompatible with Article 6 since, in effect, it destroyed the very essence of the privilege against self-incrimination.

50. Admittedly a system which warns the accused – who is possibly without legal assistance (as in the applicant's case) – that adverse inferences may be drawn from a refusal to provide an explanation to the police for his presence at the scene of a crime or to testify during his trial, when taken in conjunction with the weight of the case against him, involves a certain level of indirect compulsion. However, since the applicant could not be compelled to speak or to testify, as indicated above, this factor on its own cannot be decisive. The Court must rather concentrate its attention on the role played by the inferences in the proceedings against the applicant and especially in his conviction.

51. In this context, it is recalled that these were proceedings without a jury, the trier of fact being an experienced judge. Furthermore, the drawing of inferences under the Order is subject to an important series of safeguards designed to respect the rights of the defence and to limit the extent to which reliance can be placed on inferences.

In the first place, before inferences can be drawn under Articles 4 and 6 of the Order appropriate warnings must have been given to the accused as to the legal effects of maintaining silence. Moreover, as indicated by the judgment of the House of Lords in R. V. KEVIN SEAN MURRAY the prosecutor must first establish a prima facie case against the accused, i.e. a case consisting of direct evidence which, if believed and combined with legitimate inferences based upon it, could lead a properly directed jury to be satisfied beyond reasonable doubt that each of the essential elements of the offence is proved.

The question in each particular case is whether the evidence adduced by the prosecution is sufficiently strong to require an answer. The national court cannot conclude that the accused is guilty merely because he chooses to remain silent. It is only if the evidence against the accused 'calls' for an explanation which the accused ought to be in a position to give that a failure to give an explanation 'may as a matter of common sense allow the drawing of an inference that there is no explanation and that the accused is guilty'.

Conversely if the case presented by the prosecution had so little evidential value that it called for no answer, a failure to provide one could not justify an inference of guilt. In sum, it is only common sense inferences which the judge considers proper, in the light of the evidence against the accused, that can be drawn under the Order.

In addition, the trial judge has a discretion whether, on the facts of the particular case, an inference should be drawn. As indicated by the Court of Appeal in the present case, if a judge accepted that an accused did not understand the warning given or if he had doubts about it, 'we are confident that he would not activate Article 6 against him'. Furthermore in Northern Ireland, where trial judges sit without a jury, the judge must explain the reasons for the decision to draw inferences and the weight attached to them. The exercise of discretion in this regard is subject to review by the appellate courts.

52. In the present case, the evidence presented against the applicant by the prosecution was considered by the Court of Appeal to constitute a 'formidable' case against him. It is recalled that when the police entered the house some appreciable time after they knocked on the door, they found the applicant coming down the flight of stairs in the house where Mr L had been held captive by the IRA. Evidence had been given by Mr L – evidence which in the opinion of the trial judge had been corroborated – that he had been forced to make a taped confession and that after the arrival of the police at the house and the removal of his blindfold he saw the applicant at the top of the stairs. He had been told by him to go downstairs and watch television. The applicant was pulling a tape out of a cassette. The tangled tape and cassette recorder were later found on the premises. Evidence by the applicant's co-accused that he had recently arrived at the house was discounted as not being credible.

53. The trial judge drew strong inferences against the applicant under Article 6 of the Order by reason of his failure to give an account of his presence in the house when arrested and interrogated by the police. He also drew strong inferences under Article 4 of the Order by reason of the applicant's refusal to give evidence in his own defence when asked by the court to do so.

54. In the Court's view, having regard to the weight of the evidence against the applicant, as outlined above, the drawing of inferences from his refusal, at arrest, during police questioning and at trial, to provide an explanation for his presence in the house was a matter of common sense and cannot be regarded as unfair or unreasonable in the circumstances. As pointed out by the Delegate of the Commission, the courts in a considerable number of countries where evidence is freely assessed may have regard to all relevant circumstances, including the manner in which the accused has behaved or has conducted his defence, when evaluating the evidence in the case. It considers that, what distinguishes the drawing of inferences under the Order is that, in addition to the existence of the specific safeguards mentioned above, it constitutes, as described by the Commission, 'a formalised system which aims at allowing common sense implications to play an open role in the assessment of evidence'.

Nor can it be said, against this background, that the drawing of reasonable inferences from the applicant's behaviour had the effect of shifting the burden of proof from the prosecution to the defence so as to infringe the principle of the presumption of innocence.

312

The judgment of the European Court of Human Rights in *Murray* goes some way towards clarifying what it sees as the principle protected by the right to silence. This is the principle that people should not be compelled to produce evidence against themselves. Whereas the degree of compulsion in *Funke* was objectionable, that in *Murray* was not. This analysis, however, is problematic, because it would apply in cases where investigators obtained non-testimonial evidence (such as fingerprints or breath samples) from suspects through compulsion. In *Saunders v United Kingdom* (1996) 23 EHRR 313 the Court dealt with this point:

> 68. . . . The right not to incriminate oneself, in particular, presupposes that the prosecution in a criminal case seek to prove their case against the accused without resort to evidence obtained through methods of coercion or oppression in defiance of the will of the accused. In this sense the right is closely linked to the presumption of innocence contained in Article 6(2) of the Convention.
>
> 69. The right not to incriminate oneself is primarily concerned, however, with respecting the will of an accused person to remain silent. As commonly understood in the legal systems of the Contracting Parties to the Convention and elsewhere, it does not extend to the use in criminal proceedings of material which may be obtained from the accused through the use of compulsory powers but which has an existence independent of the will of the suspect such as, *inter alia*, documents acquired pursuant to a warrant, breath, blood and urine samples and bodily tissue for the purpose of DNA testing.

In *Saunders* the Court was considering the exercise of powers by inspectors from the Department of Trade and Industry in serious fraud cases. Under ss 434 and 436 of the Companies Act 1985 inspectors may question members of companies that are suspected of irregularities, and require the people who are being questioned to produce documents. A person's answers can be used as evidence against him or her, and a refusal to answer questions may be punished as contempt of court. The Court held that the use of these powers had amounted to a breach of Article 6. In a dissenting judgment, Judge Martens raises a number of important points about the Court's decision and its reasoning. Two of these relate to the distinction drawn, in para 69 of the judgment, between testimonial and non-testimonial evidence. Martens suggests, first, that this distinction appears to overrule *Funke* and, secondly, that the distinction, which seems to rest on respect for human dignity and autonomy, is not strong enough to endow the right to remain silent with the strength which the Court presumes it has. Martens also argues that there are pragmatic reasons for not regarding the right to remain silent as a strong right. This is because it may be in the public interest to give DTI inspectors wide powers to investigate serious fraud, especially as it may be difficult to establish that an offence has taken place without such powers. In addition, those questioned under the Companies Act 1985 have certain protections: they are not being questioned by police officers, they are encouraged to have legal representation and are usually told of the evidence against them. Finally, Martens makes the point that, if questioning under the Companies Act constitutes a breach of the right to remain silent, then facts discovered as a consequence of such questioning (such as the existence of a foreign bank account) would seem to have to be regarded as inadmissible.

One can identify problems with the Court's approach beyond those raised by Martens. The Court refers to 'evidence obtained . . . in defiance of the will of the accused'. But were the statements obtained from Saunders really in defiance of his will? There is a famous paradox here: any confession, even one obtained under threat of torture, is in some sense voluntary, because the suspect still chooses to confess. From this perspective, the right not to incriminate oneself that is protected by the Court is meaningless. One might attempt to salvage the right by arguing that suspects threatened with torture really do confess in defiance of their will, because they would rather not confess. But this threatens to make the right too broad, because any suspect might plausibly argue that he or she would rather not have confessed and, indeed, did not want to confess until questioned by the police. On this analysis, almost any police questioning violates the right. There are perhaps two ways of avoiding this paradox. The Court has taken the first: it has simply decided that certain forms of compulsion are wrong. So far, the use of criminal sanctions to compel testimony has been identified as a breach of the right, although other forms of compulsion might be held to be breaches in the future. This may leave the Court open to accusations of ad hoc line drawing; it also begs the question of just why it is wrong to compel testimony given that crime investigation is morally justified. The second way of avoiding the paradox is proposed by Thomas and Bilder (1991), who argue that one can make a distinction between first order desire and second order volition. A suspect threatened with torture may have a first order desire to confess (because of the threat), but a second order volition not to confess (because confessing means almost certain conviction). Thomas and Bilder argue that the right not to incriminate oneself protects suspects from being faced with a first order desire that conflicts with their second order volition. This analysis has considerable explanatory power, but it again begs a more fundamental question: why should we want to protect suspects from this conflict between desire and volition? As Thomas and Bilder note, on this analysis the right not to incriminate oneself may be morally unacceptable, 'because it sacrifices the good of the collective on the altar of [the individual's] autonomy' (1991, p 257).

It should be apparent that attempts to justify the right to silence, or the broader right not to incriminate oneself proclaimed by the European Court of Human Rights, are fraught with difficulty. For further discussion of self-incrimination, see Dennis (1995); Stuntz (1988); Greenawalt (1981) and Dolinko (1986). On the right to silence, see also Dixon (1990; 1991) and Morgan and Stephenson (1994).

314

8. CONTROLLING POLICE MALPRACTICE

We have seen that doubts have been raised about the ability of PACE to prevent police malpractice. When PACE was introduced, Sanders (1988) argued that its effectiveness would inevitably be compromised by the absence of sanctions for breach of the rules. What sanctions and controls are there to prevent police rule-breaking?

We have already seen that there is scant internal supervision of routine police investigations. Externally, the courts play some role in sanctioning the police for rule-breaking. Evidence obtained in breach of the rules in PACE may be excluded by the courts. An example of this, considered at p 273 above, is the Court of Appeal's decision in *Samuel* which had a significant effect on the application of s 58 of PACE. We also considered the use of s 76 to exclude unreliable confessions; this too may deter malpractice. The exclusion of evidence by the courts is further considered in Chapter 4 below. For the moment we will simply note that, although court decisions do have some deterrent effect, the case law does not approach the exclusion of evidence in disciplinary terms.

Another mechanism for controlling police malpractice, which operates both internally and externally, is the complaints and discipline system.

(a) The police complaints system and police discipline

In 1993 the Royal Commission on Criminal Justice (RCCJ) commented that:

> An effective system of police discipline is essential if police officers are to be deterred from malpractice or negligence, either of which may lead to miscarriages of justice, and if local communities are to have the necessary confidence in the integrity of the police. We doubt whether the existing arrangements for police discipline do now command general public confidence. (1993, Ch 3, para 96)

In addition to fostering community faith in the police, an effective complaints and discipline system has a role to play in ensuring that the rules of PACE and the Codes of Practice are adhered to.

The legal framework of the current system for investigating complaints against the police and for police disciplinary procedures is found in ss 83–106 of PACE. The complaints and discipline system are bound closely together: a complaint will be investigated and, if substantiated, may lead to disciplinary action being taken against an officer. The present system is complex, but in outline it operates as follows. Members of the public can lodge complaints against police officers (not against force policy) at any police station. When they do so PACE vests responsibility for investigating complaints with the Chief Constable, but this is usually delegated: most forces

315

now have a Complaints and Discipline Department under the control of the Deputy Chief Constable, and complaints will be investigated by an officer from this department. The investigating officer must be of at least the rank of chief inspector and no less senior than the officer against whom the complaint is made (PACE, s 85). The fact that complaints against the police are investigated by police officers (albeit officers from another force in the most serious cases) has often been criticised.

The Royal Commission on Criminal Procedure (RCCP) was well aware of the drawbacks of internal resolution of complaints, and following its report PACE provided for the establishment of the Police Complaints Authority (PCA) in the hopes of beefing up the external element in the system. Still, the 13 members of the PCA do not actually carry out the investigative legwork: their role is confined to the supervision of investigations, though this supervision may be more or less active. Even then, the PCA does not supervise the investigation of all complaints: under PACE, s 89 only complaints involving conduct which resulted in death or serious injury must be supervised. However, police forces can also refer other complaints to the PCA, which should supervise their investigation if it judges that this is in the public interest (s 89). In addition to this, police forces have a discretion to refer serious matters to the PCA even where they have not been the subject of a complaint. This might occur if there have been allegations of police corruption or if a person has been shot by the police. Again, the PCA can choose whether to supervise the investigations (s 89). Whether it has played a role in supervising the investigation or not, the files on all completed investigations into complaints are sent to the PCA for review.

During the process of investigation the complainant may decide to withdraw the complaint. In a number of other cases, the PCA grants the police force a 'dispensation', meaning that it does not have to investigate a complaint: this will occur where, for example, the complainant refuses to cooperate with the investigation. Otherwise the investigation continues much along the lines of any other police investigation. However, investigations of serious allegations may be hampered by several factors. An officer who is alleged to have committed a criminal offence can choose to exercise his or her right to silence when questioned (this remains the case, even though the right to silence in police investigations of crime has been abolished). More seriously, an investigating officer may find that a wall of silence surrounds the event being investigated. This is especially problematic where a complaint concerns the behaviour of a group of police officers, because if they all deny having committed an offence, and refuse to name any of their colleagues as wrongdoers, it will be very hard to prove a complaint.

At the end of the process of investigation complaints are classified as 'substantiated' or 'not substantiated'. The majority are unsubstantiated:

Extract 3.8.1

Home Office, *Police Complaints and Discipline England and Wales 1995/96* (1996) p 10, table 1

Outcomes of all completed complaints (1)

England and Wales				Number of complaints			
Year	Total complaints	Substantiated (%)	Unsubstantiated (%)	Withdrawn/ not proc (2) (%)		Informally resolved (3) (%)	
1973	12,886	1,144 (9)	7,579 (59)	4,163 (32)		–	
1974	13,373	1,141 (9)	7,645 (57)	4,587 (34)		–	
1975	14,258	1,254 (9)	8,057 (57)	4,947 (35)		–	
1976	15,653	1,334 (8)	8,572 (55)	5,747 (37)		–	
1977	16,935	1,107 (6)	7,911 (47)	7,917 (47)		–	
1978 (4)	28,234	1,559 (5)	13,720 (49)	12,955 (46)		–	
1979	29,383	1,338 (5)	13,326 (45)	14,719 (50)		–	
1980	31,009	1,288 (4)	13,476 (43)	16,245 (52)		–	
1981	32,443	1,542 (5)	14,660 (45)	16,241 (50)		–	
1982	32,086	1,787 (6)	14,702 (46)	15,597 (49)		–	
1983	30,681	1,448 (5)	13,570 (44)	15,663 (51)		–	
1984	31,174	1,561 (5)	15,549 (50)	14,064 (45)		–	
1985 (3)	28,253	1,155 (4)	11,650 (41)	13,286 (47)		2,162 (8)	
1986	29,178	1,129 (4)	12,676 (43)	11,335 (39)		4,038 (14)	
1987	27,932	924 (3)	10,432 (37)	11,491 (41)		5,085 (18)	
1988	28,758	853 (3)	9,848 (34)	12,144 (42)		5,913 (21)	
1989	29,312	765 (3)	8,464 (29)	12,958 (44)		7,125 (24)	
1990	34,894	847 (2)	11,864 (34)	14,225 (41)		7,958 (23)	
1991	35,346	813 (2)	11,329 (32)	14,224 (40)		8,980 (25)	
1992	34,922	760 (2)	10,038 (29)	14,984 (43)		9,140 (26)	
1993	34,894	750 (2)	9,734 (28)	14,284 (41)		10,126 (29)	
1994	36,521	793 (2)	8,797 (24)	14,658 (40)		12,273 (34)	
1995/96	35,840	749 (2)	7,904 (22)	15,535 (43)		11,652 (33)	

(1) [This table] . . . analyse[s] the disposal of individual complaints, since within any complaints case, some allegations may be substantiated and others not.

(2) Includes dispensations granted by the Police Complaints Authority under section 99(2)(c) of the Act. In 1995/96, 8,726 complaints were the subject of dispensations granted by the PCA.

(3) Part IX of the Police and Criminal Evidence Act 1984 introduced a procedure for dealing with less serious complaints informally (i.e. those where neither a criminal nor a disciplinary offence was involved). The effect can be seen in the statistics from 1985 onwards. Part IX was brought into force on 29 April 1985 so that the informal resolution figures for 1985 do not cover a full year.

(4) The basis on which complaints were recorded and arrangements for collecting statistics were changed in 1978. As a result, in any one case of complaint more individual complaints were likely to be identified and recorded, resulting in an otherwise unexplained increase in the figures between 1977 and 1978.

Police discipline regulations, which also came into force on 29 April 1985, stated formally for the first time that a discipline charge against a police officer was required to be proved beyond reasonable doubt. They also gave officers at risk of dismissal, requirement to resign or demotion, the right to be legally represented.

Substantiated complaints can be dealt with in a number of ways. If there is evidence that a criminal offence has been committed, the case can be referred to the CPS. Successful prosecutions of police officers are rare: not one of the police officers involved in the spate of renowned miscarriages of justice uncovered in the late 1980s and early 1990s was convicted of a criminal offence. In less serious cases, disciplinary proceedings may be set in motion. A distinctive feature of police disciplinary proceedings is that, at present, the standard of proof is beyond reasonable doubt (the civil standard of proof is applied in other disciplinary systems such as that of the fire brigade: see *Hampshire County Council, ex parte Ellerton* [1985] 1 All ER 599). Despite the fact that, until recently, a breach of PACE was a disciplinary offence, the RCCJ (1993, Ch 3, para 102) noted that the police appeared to be reluctant to meet breaches with disciplinary proceedings. For example, after *Canale* (1990) 91 Cr App R 1, in which the Court of Appeal reprimanded officers for 'deliberate breaches and cynical breaches' of PACE, officers involved were never formally disciplined (see Zander, 1994). If misconduct is proved at the disciplinary hearing, the most usual outcome is a fine, though dismissal is possible. Most commonly, officers will be subject to less formal disciplinary measures, such as being given 'advice'. The word 'advice' belies the serious nature of this outcome as far as the officer involved is concerned: advice may involve a formal admonishment of the officer, it will be recorded on his or her file and is likely to influence the officer's future chances of promotion. However, the purely internal nature of this outcome and the misleading nature of the word 'advice' mean that this process is less effective as far as instilling public confidence in the police is concerned.

The decision as to which outcome is appropriate for a substantiated complaint will be taken by the Deputy or Assistant Chief Constable. However, in all completed investigations the officer will send a memorandum to the PCA. If it has been decided that no formal disciplinary action will be taken, reasons must be given. The PCA can override the decision which has been taken by requiring the officer to refer the case to the CPS or to institute disciplinary proceedings.

An innovation stemming from the report of the RCCP means that not all complaints are now formally investigated. Formal investigation is bureaucratic and costly whereas many complaints about the police relate to relatively trivial matters, such as the allegation that an officer has been impolite. In such cases it may be better for both the officer and the complainant to resolve the matter informally: the complainant may be satisfied by an apology from the officer or an assurance that the misconduct will not reoccur. Informal resolution may only happen where no disciplinary offence is involved and the complainant consents (PACE, s 85(10)). If a complainant is dissatisfied with the outcome of the informal process, he or she may insist on the complaint being taken up formally. Informal resolution is used in a substantial proportion of cases (see the figures in Extract 3.8.1 above).

Information collected by the PCA (1997, p 19) shows that most complainants are male (81 per cent). Thirty-four per cent are aged under 25; 53 per cent are aged between 25 and 44. The majority are white, but ethnic minorities (18 per cent) are over-represented in comparison to their proportion in the population (around 5 per cent). There is an even more marked over-representation of blacks as complainants about the use of stop and search powers (26 per cent of stop and search complainants are black).

Extract 3.8.2

**M Maguire, 'Complaints Against the Police: The British Experience' in
A Goldsmith (ed), *Complaints Against the Police – The Trend to
External Review* (1991) pp 186–193 (footnotes omitted)**

THE EFFECTIVENESS OF THE CURRENT SYSTEM: SOME RESEARCH FINDINGS

As implied in earlier remarks, most complaints systems are intended to serve more than one purpose, although some of these may be in competition so that priority has to be given to one or more at the expense of others. Ideally, the police complaints system should meet all the following objectives:

1. The maintenance of 'discipline in the ranks'
2. The satisfaction of complainants
3. The maintenance of public confidence in the police
4. The provision of 'feedback from consumers' to police managers

In this section, we shall summarize research and other evidence on the effectiveness of the current system in achieving each of these goals. Particular attention will be paid to any impact made by the creation or activities of the PCA . . .

1. Discipline

The first objective above, the maintenance of discipline in the ranks, has always been regarded by the police themselves (or at least by senior officers) as one of the main priorities . . . A necessary condition for the system to work in this respect is that cases are dealt with fairly, consistently, and thoroughly, thus maximizing the chances that any officer who has breached police regulations will be 'brought to book' and others will consequently think twice before offending. One statistical indicator of whether this is occurring may be the substantiation rate for complaints, although it has to be recognized that an unknown proportion, made in error or in malice, should without question remain unsubstantiated, while many more are impossible to prove, however diligent the investigator. (This last point raises questions about the standard of evidence required, which will be referred to later.)

319

In fact, even taking the above provisos into account, the substantiation rate has always appeared to outsiders to be far too low to constitute a serious deterrent. Between 1979 and 1989, a total of 330,109 complaints were recorded, of which only 13,790 (4.2 per cent) were substantiated. The rate looks rather higher, though not impressively so, if one takes as a base only those complaints in which investigations were completed, that is, excluding those informally resolved, withdrawn or otherwise not proceeded with. Calculated this way, the annual substantiation rate ranged between 8 and 11 per cent over the same period.

It is also worthy of note that the advent of the PCA, like the PCB before it, has made no statistically significant difference to results overall. In 1989 there were only 765 substantiations among the 9,229 complaints fully investigated – a rate similar to earlier years. There are, however, two claims the PCA can make regarding their influence upon outcomes. First, in almost one in ten of those complaints in which some disciplinary action (in most cases, formal advice or admonishment) was taken, this followed a recommendation by the PCA, the Deputy Chief Constable having initially concluded that no action was warranted. And secondly – a possibility which will be discussed in the next section – there may be some effect where cases supervised by PCA members are concerned.

Probably a more reliable means of assessing the effectiveness of the system as a disciplinary tool is to examine the attitudes of junior officers towards it. In the course of the study, we interviewed fifty officers (mainly of constable rank) who had been the subject of a recent complaint. The majority told us that neither the existence of the complaints system, nor the fact of having received a complaint, had made any difference to how they behaved, largely because they did not consider that they engaged in misconduct anyway. About ten of these officers took a cavalier, even 'gung-ho' attitude to complaints, one asserting, for example, that they made 'good wallpaper'. Two in particular, who both admitted to us that they had handled people very roughly on arrest, seemed surprisingly sanguine. Both had received numerous (unsubstantiated) complaints over the years, mainly when serving in support units. Although they conceded that there was an outside chance that some of their actions could be interpreted as 'going over the top', they remained confident that investigating officers understood the 'pressures on the street' and that, so long as any roughness was in response to aggression from the arrested person, there was little danger of a charge of assault being brought against them. What they had always used, they claimed, was 'reasonable force' in the circumstances. As one of them put it, 'When you're in a scrum of fighting drunks, the last thing you worry about is complaints.'

However, at the other extreme, about one in five said that complaints had had quite a significant impact upon their style of policing. This was generally put to us in a negative light. For example: 'You start to back away from situations when you should be taking action . . . If there's an obvious risk of a complaint you tend to pass the buck. Why should I risk my mortgage by giving some little yobbo the chance to have a go at me?' Of course, the line between 'backing away' wrongly when firm action is required, and taking a more cool-headed approach to potentially violent situations, is extremely narrow. It could be argued that those who said that they no longer 'went in so hard' when trouble loomed – although themselves regarding this as a weakness and poor policing – had actually been deterred from using an unnecessarily tough response to violence or disorder in the streets.

It should also be noted that complaints investigations were regarded by many of the officers as unpleasant, and sometimes stressful, experiences. This was partly because of the fear of a 'blot on the record' (a handicap to promotion) and partly because of the uncomfortable experience of being 'put under the spotlight' by a Superintendent. Several said they were less concerned about the complaint itself being substantiated than about the possibility of some other misdemeanour – a pocket-book error, breach of PACE regulations, etc. – being turned up in the course of inquiries. Certainly, too, in preparing for situations in which complaints were thought likely, for example, raids on houses, officers spoke of efforts to 'cover their arses' by ensuring that in any subsequent investigation they could not be found to have made technical breaches in the 'paperwork'.

In sum, while only a minority admitted to altering their behaviour significantly as a result of complaints, and a few treated them very lightly indeed, most agreed that complaints were unpleasant enough to be worth avoiding if there was a simple way of doing so. The possibility of a complaint definitely impinged upon their consciousness when handling certain kinds of situation (for example, arrests, 'domestics', traffic stops, and raids), and hence could have a marginal influence on their conduct. Quite simply, as one officer put it, 'they are always there in the back of your mind ... they don't bother you, but obviously you avoid them if you can'.

2. Complainant satisfaction

Evidence about the performance of the system in meeting the second of the four objectives listed above – that of satisfying complainants – can be obtained from our interviews with 100 complainants in three police-force areas. Forty of these interviewees' cases had been fully investigated, thirty informally resolved, and thirty withdrawn by the complainant. When asked to rate their level of satisfaction with the outcome of their complaint, only 12 per cent declared themselves 'very satisfied' and 19 per cent 'fairly satisfied'. Almost half stated that they were 'very dissatisfied'.

As table 1 shows, the bulk of the dissatisfaction was to be found among complainants whose cases had been fully investigated: only four of the forty were even fairly satisfied. It might be thought that these responses merely reflect people's disappointment at 'losing their case'. This may account for some of the reactions, but it was interesting to discover that satisfaction was not closely correlated with outcomes: even those whose complaints had been substantiated were generally unimpressed. The main reasons given for dissatisfaction were the length of time taken to deal with the complaint, the absence of any apology, and the inadequacy or lack of explanation for the decision.

On the other hand, table 1 shows a more positive response from complainants who had experienced another part of the new system introduced by PACE, the informal resolution procedure. Over half of these declared themselves broadly satisfied with the outcome. A further indication of the relative attraction of this procedure was that almost half of the forty whose cases had

Table 1 Level of satisfaction by method used to handle case

Level of satisfaction	Type of case Investigated		Withdrawn		Informally resolved		All
	No.	%	No.	%	No.	%	%
Very satisfied	0	0	3	10	9	30	12
Fairly satisfied	4	10	7	23	8	27	19
A bit dissatisfied	9	22	7	23	5	17	21
Very dissatisfied	27	68	13	43	8	27	48
TOTAL	40	100	30	100	30	100	100

been fully investigated said that they would have preferred a less formal response to their complaint, most commonly a meeting with the officer and his or her superiors to discuss the incident in depth. This supports our conclusion from answers to other questions, as well as that of Brown (1987) [D Brown, *The Police Complaints Procedure: A Survey of Complainants' Views*, HORS 93 (London: HMSO, 1987)], that what complainants are seeking in most cases is not something akin to a trial and punishment of the officer concerned, but a full explanation, an apology, some pointed remarks to the officer from some-body in a senior position, and/or a clear assurance that steps will be taken to see that 'it does not happen again'. It also suggests that there is scope for wider use of informal resolution, which at present is employed in only about one in four of all cases, although, of course, judgements have to be made about the level of seriousness at which a 'justice'- or 'discipline'-oriented response becomes more appropriate than one geared primarily to the satis-faction of complainants.

3. Public confidence

. . . Some evidence about the current situation can be obtained from the answers to questions we inserted in the 1988 British Crime Survey.

Respondents from a random sample of households were asked, 'If you were to make a complaint against the police, how thoroughly do you think it would be investigated?' A total of 46 per cent answered either 'very' or 'fairly' thoroughly, but there was a substantial minority (25 per cent) who thought the opposite, the remainder being unsure. Similarly, when asked how happy they were with the present system, only 36 per cent declared themselves 'very' or 'reasonably' happy. And to the question of who they thought *should* investig-ate complaints, under one in six replied that he or she was content to leave it to the police: the most frequent response was 'an independent lay body'. It is also important to note that all the above questions drew negative answers from significantly higher proportions of black and ethnic minority respondents than of white respondents.

In the absence of comparable data from the period before the creation of the PCA, it is impossible to tell how much difference, if any, this development has made to the level of public confidence. However, some of the survey responses may be relevant. Under 10 per cent of the full sample of house-holders said that they knew of 'an independent organization which supervises the way police investigate complaints', only one in five of these could name it correctly, and, even when the name was put to them, only 38 per cent of the full sample claimed to have heard of the PCA. It will also be remembered that many complainants were fairly hazy about the Authority's role. All of this suggests that the PCA has some way to go before it can claim to have made a major impact upon public perceptions of the fairness of the system.

4. Feedback and change

Findings relevant to the last objective – the use of the complaints system as a provider of management information, leading to improvements in policy and practice – were again generally disappointing. It was rare for police forces to undertake any serious analysis of patterns of complaints or to make system-atic efforts to learn from them. Nevertheless, there were some signs of change here. 'Numbers of complaints' is now used regularly by Inspectors of Con-stabulary as one indicator of each force's overall performance, and senior officers at headquarters were watching complaints rates in local divisions more closely than in the past, asking questions whenever these rose signific-antly. One force had also started a monthly bulletin to all divisions, produced by the Complaints and Discipline department, in which points arising from recent complaints were disseminated to local commanders. Even so, the rich potential of case-files, in which can be found, for example, detailed accounts of how police–public encounters 'went wrong', has as yet hardly been tapped at all. These could provide excellent training material, as well as information on which to base management reviews of policy and practice (for further discussion, see [M Maguire and C Corbett, 'Patterns and Profiles of Com-plaints Against the Police' in R Morgan and D Smith (eds), *Coming to Terms with Policing* (London: Routledge, 1989)]).

However, perhaps the most important development in this area has come from the PCA. Members have made several public statements about lessons which can be learnt from high profile cases. For example, following one major investigation, they recommended that individual officers should be more easily identifiable when wearing riot gear. They have also recommended changes in regulations covering the use of firearms and access to the national police computer. This appeared to us to be one of the most valuable spin-offs from the role of the PCA, and one which might be developed further. In addition to commenting upon individual cases, members could more often use their experience of large numbers of cases to make general comments on themes which recur frequently in lesser cases. For example, more than one member expressed to us concern about the frequency with which complainants referred to excessive tightening of handcuffs: by drawing attention to this, they could perhaps stimulate changes either in the design of the equipment or in guide-lines for its use.

Many potential complainants are deflected from complaining officially or are persuaded to withdraw their complaints at some stage of the process. Maguire and Corbett (1991) used the 1988 British Crime Survey to try to probe the 'dark figure' of complaints never lodged. They found that about 20 per cent of respondents had been 'really annoyed' by the behaviour of a police officer in the past five years, but that only about a fifth of those who seriously considered complaining attempted to do so (this may reflect the lack of public confidence in the complaints procedure alluded to in the extract above). Even those who do attempt to complain often leave the police station without having had their complaint formally recorded. Police forces are under no obligation to record complaints, and if they refuse to do so, the PCA cannot overrule them. Maguire and Corbett found that 30 per cent of complainants said that at some stage the police had tried to persuade them not to follow through with their complaint.

Maguire and Corbett conclude that the present system for the investigation of complaints is failing on several levels. Above all it fails to instil public confidence in the police. Research conducted by the PCA confirms this picture of low public confidence. The most recent survey found that only 37 per cent of the public described the PCA as 'independent', and 32 per cent felt that it always comes down on the side of the police. Among ethnic minorities the figures show even less confidence in the PCA (PCA, 1995, p 48). This lack of confidence in the PCA and its investigatory powers led the Civil Liberties Trust to set up an independent investigation into allegations of widespread malpractice in the West Midlands Serious Crime Squad (Kaye, 1991, pp 11–16).

(b) Reform

There is considerable pressure for reform of various aspects of police complaints procedures. One of the most commonly proposed reforms is that the PCA be replaced by a totally independent system for investigating complaints, which would use civilians rather than police officers to carry out its investigations. The current system is often defended with the claim that only police officers have the investigative skills and knowledge of police procedures which are needed to undertake effective investigations. The Home Affairs Committee (HAC), which in 1997 published a report on police disciplinary and complaints procedures, has lent support to the calls for a completely independent investigatory process, though stopped short of recommending such a system, concluding instead that a study be undertaken to examine the feasibility of reforming the system in this manner. The Committee did, however, recommend that the PCA be given the power and funds to commission non-police investigations of complaints in cases where there is reason to believe that the present system is inadequate (HAC, 1997, p lvii). The latter proposal has also been endorsed by the PCA itself (PCA, 1996, p 45).

The other area where there is a general consensus that reform is needed is the police disciplinary process. In 1996, after a long consultation process, the Home Secretary announced his intention to replace the beyond reasonable doubt standard of proof in disciplinary hearings with a variable standard. The standard to be applied in each case would depend on the seriousness of the allegation and potential sanction, so that in the most serious cases the beyond reasonable standard would still apply, while the civil standard of proof (proof on the balance of probabilities) would be used in the least serious cases. The Home Affairs Committee recommended instead that the civil standard should be applied in all cases. It also called for the abolition of the double jeopardy principle and the modification of the right to silence in disciplinary proceedings, to allow inferences to be drawn against officers who refuse to answer questions (HAC, 1997, p lviii).

9. REVIEWING THE DECISION TO PROSECUTE

One of the most important reforms of the criminal process in recent times took place in 1986 with the creation of the Crown Prosecution Service (CPS), a national body charged with the prosecution of suspected offenders. Prior to 1986, prosecution decision-making lay almost entirely in the hands of the police. Thus, in addition to investigating crimes and charging suspects, the police were responsible for bringing cases to court. Prosecution policy was largely locally determined by each of the 43 police forces, though for a short period before the creation of the CPS force policy was co-ordinated by guidelines issued by the Attorney General. Most police forces had prosecuting solicitor departments to handle legal aspects of case preparation, but solicitors instructed by the police had no formal independent role in prosecutorial decision-making. The Royal Commission on Criminal Procedure (RCCP) was unhappy with these arrangements, criticising the conflation of investigative and prosecutorial roles and suggesting that the system might be unfair due to lack of uniformity. The Commission also pointed to high acquittal rates as evidence of the prosecution of weak cases.

Since the creation of the CPS, prosecutorial decision-making has been split between the police and the CPS. The police still take the initial decision as to whether or not to charge a suspect, but before the first court hearing the case file should be passed on to the CPS which takes all subsequent decisions. Under s 23 of the Prosecution of Offences Act 1985 the CPS can 'discontinue' cases (effectively dropping the prosecution). It can also decide what offence a defendant should be charged with, or refer a case back to the police suggesting that a caution would be more appropriate. Prosecutors can ask (but not require) the police to carry out further investigations.

(a) Criteria governing CPS decision-making

Central to the prosecutor's role is the exercise of discretion. The basis for the decisions made by prosecutors is the Code for Crown Prosecutors. These guidelines are issued by the Director of Public Prosecutions (DPP, the head of the CPS) and were updated in 1994. The Code sets out a 'two stage test' for prosecutors. Prosecutors must first consider whether there is sufficient evidence to justify a prosecution, and must then consider whether prosecution is in the public interest.

Extract 3.9.1

Code for Crown Prosecutors (1994) paras 1–6

THE CODE FOR CROWN PROSECUTORS

1 Introduction

1.1 The decision to prosecute an individual is a serious step. Fair and effective prosecution is essential to the maintenance of law and order. But even in a small case, a prosecution has serious implications for all involved – the victim, a witness and a defendant. The Crown Prosecution Service applies the Code for Crown Prosecutors so that it can make fair and consistent decisions about prosecutions.

3 Review

3.1 Proceedings are usually started by the police. Sometimes they may consult the Crown Prosecution Service before charging a defendant. Each case that the police send to the Crown Prosecution Service is reviewed by a Crown Prosecutor to make sure that it meets the tests set out in this Code. Crown Prosecutors may decide to continue with the original charges, to change the charges or sometimes to stop the proceedings.

3.2 Review, however, is a continuing process so that Crown Prosecutors can take into account any change in circumstances. Wherever possible, they talk to the police first if they are thinking about changing the charges or stopping the proceedings. This gives the police the chance to provide more information that may affect the decision. The Crown Prosecution Service and the police work closely together to reach the right decision, but the final responsibility for the decision rests with the Crown Prosecution Service.

4 The code tests

4.1 There are two stages in the decision to prosecute. The first stage is *the evidential test*. If the case does not pass the evidential test, it must not go ahead, no matter how important or serious it may be. If the case does pass the evidential test, Crown Prosecutors must decide if a prosecution is needed in the public interest.

4.2 This second stage is *the public interest test*. The Crown Prosecution Service will only start or continue a prosecution when the case has passed both tests. The evidential test is explained in section 5 and the public interest test is explained in section 6.

5 The evidential test

5.1 Crown Prosecutors must be satisfied that there is enough evidence to provide a 'realistic prospect of conviction' against each defendant on each charge. They must consider what the defence case may be and how that is likely to affect the prosecution case.

5.2 A realistic prospect of conviction is an objective test. It means that a jury or bench of magistrates, properly directed in accordance with the law, is more likely than not to convict the defendant of the charge alleged.

6 The public interest test

6.1 In 1951, Lord Shawcross, who was Attorney General, made the classic statement on public interest, which has been supported by Attorneys General ever since: 'It has never been the rule in this country – I hope it never will be – that suspected criminal offences must automatically be the subject of prosecution'. (House of Commons Debates, volume 483, column 681, 29 January 1951.)

6.2 The public interest must be considered in each case where there is enough evidence to provide a realistic prospect of conviction. In cases of any seriousness, a prosecution will usually take place unless there are public interest factors tending against prosecution which clearly outweigh those tending in favour. Although there may be public interest factors against prosecution in a particular case, often the prosecution should go ahead and those factors should be put to the court for consideration when sentence is being passed.

6.3 Crown Prosecutors must balance factors for and against prosecution carefully and fairly. Public interest factors that can affect the decision to prosecute usually depend on the seriousness of the offence or the circumstances of the offender. Some factors may increase the need to prosecute but others may suggest that another course of action would be better.

The following lists of some common public interest factors, both for and against prosecution, are not exhaustive. The factors that apply will depend on the facts in each case.

Some common public interest factors in favour of prosecution
6.4 The more serious the offence, the more likely it is that a prosecution will be needed in the public interest. A prosecution is likely to be needed if:

a a conviction is likely to result in a significant sentence;
b a weapon was used or violence was threatened during the commission of the offence;
c the offence was committed against a person serving the public (for example, a police or prison officer, or a nurse);
d the defendant was in a position of authority or trust;
e the evidence shows that the defendant was a ringleader or an organiser of the offence;
f there is evidence that the offence was premeditated;
g there is evidence that the offence was carried out by a group;

h the victim of the offence was vulnerable, has been put in considerable fear, or suffered personal attack, damage or disturbance;

i the offence was motivated by any form of discrimination against the victim's ethnic or national origin, sex, religious beliefs, political views or sexual preference;

j there is a marked difference between the actual or mental ages of the defendant and the victim, or if there is any element of corruption;

k the defendant's previous convictions or cautions are relevant to the present offence;

l the defendant is alleged to have committed the offence whilst under an order of the court;

m there are grounds for believing that the offence is likely to be continued or repeated, for example, by a history of recurring conduct; or

n the offence, although not serious in itself, is widespread in the area where it was committed.

Some common public interest factors against prosecution

6.5 A prosecution is less likely to be needed if:

a the court is likely to impose a very small or nominal penalty;

b the offence was committed as a result of a genuine mistake or misunderstanding (these factors must be balanced against the seriousness of the offence);

c the loss or harm can be described as minor and was the result of a single incident, particularly if it was caused by a misjudgment;

d there has been a long delay between the offence taking place and the date of the trial, unless:

- the offence is serious;
- the delay has been caused in part by the defendant;
- the offence has only recently come to light; or
- the complexity of the offence has meant that there has been a long investigation;

e a prosecution is likely to have a very bad effect on the victim's physical or mental health, always bearing in mind the seriousness of the offence;

f the defendant is elderly or is, or was at the time of the offence, suffering from significant mental or physical ill health, unless the offence is serious or there is a real possibility that it may be repeated. The Crown Prosecution Service, where necessary, applies Home Office guidelines about how to deal with mentally disordered offenders. Crown Prosecutors must balance the desirability of diverting a defendant who is suffering from significant mental or physical ill health with the need to safeguard the general public;

g the defendant has put right the loss or harm that was caused (but defendants must not avoid prosecution simply because they can pay compensation); or

h details may be made public that could harm sources of information, international relations or national security.

6.6 Deciding on the public interest is not simply a matter of adding up the number of factors on each side. Crown Prosecutors must decide how important each factor is in the circumstances of each case and go on to make an overall assessment.

The relationship between the victim and the public interest

6.7   The Crown Prosecution Service acts in the public interest, not just in the interests of any one individual. But Crown Prosecutors must always think very carefully about the interests of the victim, which are an important factor, when deciding where the public interest lies.

Previous versions of the Code contained more detailed guidelines relating to individual offences, but in the 1994 revision these were removed from the main code and are now to be found in confidential manuals issued to prosecutors. The CPS has issued charging standards for a number of offences (driving offences, public order offences and offences against the person). These are used by police and prosecutors when deciding the level of charge.

Research on discontinuance found that 58 per cent of prosecutions were discontinued on evidential grounds, and 34 per cent on public interest grounds. The remaining 8 per cent were discontinued owing to reasons such as the impossibility of tracing the defendant. The most common evidential reasons for discontinuance were the absence of corroborating evidence, the absence of evidence of a key element of the offence, unreliable identification evidence and problems with witnesses (including unreliability and reluctance to testify) (Crisp and Moxon, 1994).

The public interest grounds break down in the following manner:

Extract 3.9.2

D Crisp and D Moxon, *Case Screening by the Crown Prosecution Service* (1994) p 20

Reasons for terminating cases on public interest grounds

Reason	Non-motoring cases (n = 311) %	Motoring cases (n = 85) %
Nominal penalty likely	29	40
Accused being dealt with for other matters	42	46
Offence trivial	14	27
Complainant did not wish to proceed	16	1
Offence stale	7	25
Defendant mentally ill/stressed	11	8
Youth of defendant	12	1
Defendant of good character/suffered enough	7	4
Recompense made to victim	7	–
Case suitable for caution	4	1
Defendant old/infirm	2	5
Defendant on periphery of offence	2	–
Other	3	8
Reasons per 100 cases	163	167

329

The CPS should take the victim's interests into account when deciding whether or not prosecution is in the public interest: this includes considering the impact the crime had on the victim. However, victims have no right to be consulted about decisions to discontinue cases, and the CPS's policy of confidentiality means that it will not divulge the details of reasons for decisions in individual cases (Crown Prosecution Service, 1995b). In cases where a victim has died, however, prosecutors will meet relatives to discuss the basis on which a decision to drop a case was taken (Crown Prosecution Service, 1993). We will see below that victims are likely to find it difficult to gain a successful judicial review of a decision to discontinue a prosecution.

The victim's interest is not always in favour of prosecution: in some cases victims may want to prevent a prosecution from taking place. This is presumably a factor against prosecution, though victims have no right of veto. In such situations the question of the relationship between the public interest and the interests of the individual victim may be a delicate matter. This issue is well illustrated with reference to domestic violence cases. Since the early 1980s criminal justice institutions have made a concerted effort to treat domestic violence more seriously. We noted earlier in this chapter (see p 259) that police responses to domestic violence are shaped, in part, by their experience that many victims are reluctant to support a prosecution. There are several possible reasons why a woman may be reluctant to see her partner prosecuted. She may be pressurised into withdrawing the complaint through threats from her partner; she may become convinced that her partner has changed his ways and is no longer a threat to her; she may feel that, despite the possibility of continued violence, it is worth keeping the relationship going; she may recognise that the violence will continue but be worried that, if her partner is imprisoned, her family will lose its breadwinner.

In cases where a woman does withdraw her support for a prosecution, she can be compelled to attend court to give evidence (Magistrates' Courts Act 1980, s 97) and if she remains silent in the witness box or tells lies she is liable to be prosecuted for contempt of court or perjury. Spouses used to benefit from an exception to these rules, but s 80 of PACE made spouses compellable witnesses in cases involving the use of violence against them. In spite of these powers, Cretney and Davis found that prosecutors were reluctant to use them, so in practice victims were able to stop prosecutions. They conclude that: 'the most powerful determinant of prosecutorial decisions is *not* 'the public interest', as defined, but the possibly confused wishes and inclinations of the individual victim' (1997, p 83). If CPS submission to the victim's decision is indeed the general rule, then it would seem to be out of step with the CPS's own policy statement on domestic violence, which states that there are cases in which it will override the victim's wishes (Crown Prosecution Service, 1995a, p 5). Is the CPS neglecting the public interest if it drops a prosecution because of the victim's refusal to support it?

Society has an interest in prosecuting violence which, on the traditional analysis, is seen as a crime against the state rather than against an individual

330

victim (Ashworth, 1986). In some cases it will be in the woman's long-term interests to see her partner prosecuted: a single incident of domestic violence often forms part of a continued pattern of abuse which a successful prosecution may help to end. It might also be argued that, whether or not it is in the individual woman's interests to force her to co-operate in prosecuting her partner, it is in the interests of all women. This is because by taking forceful action against domestic violence, society expresses its condemnation of it and demonstrates that such violence is to be taken seriously. This will send a message to perpetrators; the police may also be encouraged to treat incidents of domestic violence less cynically if they know that they will definitely be prosecuted. These are all relevant issues, but should these long-term factors be considered to be part of the public interest which informs CPS decisions?

Against these arguments in favour of forcing women to co-operate in the prosecution of their violent partners, one can question whether it is right to do so. Victims' experiences of the criminal justice system are often described in terms of a process of secondary victimisation. To force them to co-operate in a prosecution against their will can only enforce the perception that, once the criminal justice system becomes involved, their interests are ignored. To place a woman in the witness box and face her with the choice of testifying against her will, committing perjury, or being in contempt of court seems cruel. The rare episodes where women are punished for contempt of court for refusing to testify are often accompanied by hostile media reaction. Further, in some cases women do face violent retaliation if they testify against their attackers. In others a prosecution risks splitting up a family. Perhaps it is not surprising that, in practice, these more immediate factors come to outweigh those discussed in the preceding paragraph.

There is no easy answer to the question of how the CPS should react to domestic violence cases where the victim is reluctant to testify, and it is doubtful that there can be any hard and fast rule that applies to all cases. There may be some scope for following a path between the two extremes of dropping cases and forcing co-operation: better investigatory procedures may mean that cases can be successfully brought without the victim's testimony; the exception to the rule against hearsay in s 23 of the Criminal Justice Act 1988 may allow an initial statement to the police to be used as evidence in cases where the victim does not testify through fear. If women are to be expected to testify against a violent partner, then the criminal justice system should support and protect them. However, our discussion of this topic demonstrates that the question of just what the public interest is is not straightforward; nor is the question of whether it should always prevail over the victim's interests. Crisp and Moxon's figures (Extract 3.9.2 above) suggest that victim withdrawal is one of the most common public interest reasons for discontinuance, so these issues have relevance beyond domestic violence cases.

See further Hanna (1996); Cretney and Davis (1996).

(b) Accountability for decision-making

What happens if a victim, suspect, or some other person is unhappy with a prosecution decision made by the CPS? There are two reasons why it is difficult to challenge CPS decisions: confidentiality and the width of CPS discretion. CPS policy is that:

> We cannot give details of the reasons for our decisions in individual cases. This is because it would break the confidentiality of those involved – the victim, witnesses and the suspect or accused. Public discussion about a case could lead to the suspect being tried without the protection which court proceedings provide . . . However, if we decide not to prosecute, we always tell the police which of the two tests in the Code for Crown Prosecutors, the case did not pass. (Crown Prosecution Service, 1995b)

This policy can be questioned. First, the CPS itself operates an exception in cases where a victim has been killed: prosecutors will meet with relatives to discuss a decision (Crown Prosecution Service, 1993, p 4). Secondly, few of the common public interest or evidential factors for discontinuance identified by Crisp and Moxon (see Extract 3.9.2 above) seem to involve any significant breach of confidentiality. This leaves the problem of trial by media. Failure to give reasons cannot *prevent* media discussion of a case, though giving reasons may allow *more detailed* media comment (and criticism of the CPS) in some cases. Finally, CPS policy is out of step both with many other administrative agencies (where giving reasons is accepted as good practice and is sometimes required by statute) and with practice in other jurisdictions: 'experience in Germany and the Netherlands has shown . . . it is possible to formulate a system of giving reasons for . . . prosecutorial decisions without prejudicing the course of justice' (Fionda, 1995, p 211).

The CPS's policy of confidentiality may make it difficult to challenge prosecution decisions. What makes it more difficult still is the width of discretion given to prosecutors, which has made the courts reluctant to intervene. A decision to prosecute (or not to prosecute) is an example of administrative decision-making, so in theory it is susceptible to judicial review. An action for judicial review would be successful if, for example, it could be shown that a prosecutor's decision was unreasonable or if it involved irrelevant considerations. Some of the case law predates the establishment of the CPS, but it remains important for its recognition of the wide discretion invested in prosecutors. In *Metropolitan Police Commissioner, ex parte Blackburn* [1968] 2 QB 118 the Court of Appeal considered the legality of the Metropolitan Police's policy of non-prosecution for certain gambling offences. Lord Denning explained the position:

> [The Commissioner of Police for the Metropolis] is not the servant of anyone, save the law itself. No minister of the Crown can tell him that he must, or must not, prosecute this man or that one. Nor can any police authority tell him to do so. He is answerable to the law and to the law alone. (at p 136)

However, this did not mean that the Commissioner's discretion was absolute:

> There are some policy decisions with which, I think, the courts in a case can, if necessary, interfere. Suppose a chief constable were to issue a directive to his men that no person should be prosecuted for stealing any goods worth less than £100 in value. I should have thought that the law would countermand it. He would be failing in his duty to enforce the law. (at p 136)

The High Court has since examined the reviewability of a decision by the CPS to prosecute young offenders. The Court heard two applications together, one from L, a 16-year-old boy charged with assault, who argued that, as his case fitted the criteria for a caution contained in Home Office guidelines, the CPS should have discontinued the prosecution. The other applicant, B, a 12-year-old girl charged with theft, argued that her case should be discontinued on public interest grounds:

Extract 3.9.3

R v Chief Constable of the Kent Constabulary [1993] 1 All ER 756, pp 770–771

I have come to the conclusion that, in respect of juveniles, the discretion of the CPS to continue or to discontinue criminal proceedings is reviewable by this court but only where it can be demonstrated that the decision was made regardless of or clearly contrary to a settled policy of the Director of Public Prosecutions evolved in the public interest, for example the policy of cautioning juveniles, a policy which the CPS are bound to apply, where appropriate, to the exercise of their discretion to continue or discontinue criminal proceedings. But I envisage that it will be only rarely that a defendant could succeed in showing that a decision was fatally flawed in such a manner as that.

The policy of cautioning, instead of prosecuting, has for some time now been well settled and plays a prominent part in the process of decision-making both by the police and by the CPS when consideration has properly to be given to whether, in any individual case, there should be (a) no action taken or (b) a caution delivered or (c) a prosecution and thereafter (d) a continuance or discontinuance of criminal proceedings.

That policy applied, obviously, to the case of L. It did not apply to the case of B because cautioning was not for her an option [B had not admitted the offence]. The policy, which can, I think, rightly be so called, which is applicable to her is another. It is that which is far more generally expressed, that is to say that a prosecution should not occur unless it is required in the public interest, regard being given to the stigma of a conviction which can cause irreparable harm to the future prospects of a young person and to his previous character, parental attitude and the likelihood of the offence being repeated: see the Attorney General's 1983 guidelines.

I find it very difficult to envisage, with regard to that policy, a circumstance, fraud or dishonesty apart possibly, which would allow of a challenge to a decision to prosecute or to continue proceedings unless it could be demonstrated, in the case of a juvenile, that there had been either a total disregard of the policy or, contrary to it, a lack of inquiry into the circumstances and background of that person, previous offences and general character and so on, by the prosecutor and later by the CPS. But here too I envisage the possibility of showing that such disregard had happened as unlikely. Therefore, although the CPS decision may in principle be reviewed, in practice it is rarely likely to be successfully reviewed.

I have confined my views as to the availability of judicial review of a CPS decision not to discontinue a prosecution to the position of juveniles because, of course, the present cases involve only juveniles. My view as to the position of adults, on the other hand, in this respect is that judicial review of a decision not to discontinue a prosecution is unlikely to be available. The danger of opening too wide the door of review of the discretion to continue a prosecution is manifest and such review, if it exists, must, therefore, be confined to very narrow limits. Juveniles and the policy with regard to them are, in my view, in a special position.

The arguments of both Mr Rhodes and Mr Cocks as to the merits, on the facts, of their applicants' cases were extensively deployed. Without, I hope, seeming to denigrate the force of them I believe the response to them can be brief.

I preface what follows with the observation that it is not suggested that the procedures for inquiring into the circumstances of juveniles are inadequate in any way.

I grant that L could be said to be the victim of what might be thought to be a stern decision. All the criteria, save for the seriousness of the offence, are on his side. However, the senior police officer who dealt with him felt that the circumstances of the offence warranted prosecution, the satisfactory criteria notwithstanding. That was a view which the CPS, as the affidavits show, felt able to share after a conversation with an even more senior police officer involved.

It may be that some other police officer would have taken the opposite view, but he who took the decision was very experienced in juvenile cases and advised cautions in about 98 per cent of them. I feel unable to say that, although there may be room for two views about the seriousness of the offence with which L is charged, the decision to continue the proceedings was in any way flawed. It was a proper exercise of discretion.

For those reasons I would dismiss L's application.

B's application is basically founded on, I suspect, sympathy as much as the alleged failure by the YACS [Youth and Community Service] to investigate circumstances adequately and likewise the CPS to ensure that that had been done. I do not think upon the affidavit evidence that it has come anywhere near being demonstrated that the CPS fell below the standard of care and inquiry to be expected in the circumstances, nor before the matter was referred to the CPS did the police. The prosecution evidence continues to be challenged and it reveals, if it were true, quite a determined and blatantly executed offence. I detect nothing to alert me to suppose that the CPS did not consider the public interest and all other matters which had to be borne in mind in deciding whether a 12-year-old girl should appear before the juvenile court. I would dismiss her application too.

The wide discretion enjoyed by prosecuting agencies, especially where adults are concerned, was again underlined in *Inland Revenue Commissioners, ex parte Mead* [1993] 1 All ER 772. The court acknowledged that the IRC's policy of 'selective prosecution' (prosecuting some offenders but not others in broadly similar cases) led to unfairness, but because the decision could not be termed 'irrational', the High Court refused to grant the application.

The *Kent Chief Constable* case and *Mead* both examined the reviewability of decisions to prosecute. In *DPP, ex parte C* [1995] 1 Cr App R 136 the High Court allowed an application for judicial review of a decision *not* to prosecute for an alleged offence of buggery. Heterosexual buggery is an offence under s 12 of the Sexual Offences Act 1956, but in practice prosecutions for consensual buggery are rare (even a successful prosecution is unlikely to result in anything other than a nominal penalty). In *C* the victim claimed that she had been buggered by her husband without her consent. The prosecutor's decision was held to be unreasonable because he had not followed the Code for Crown Prosecutors:

Extract 3.9.4

R v DPP, ex parte C [1995] 1 Cr App R 136, pp 141–145

Having identified what we have to look for I return to the evidence as to what caused Mr Naunton to decide as he did. It is to be found in paragraphs 5, 6, 7 and 8 of his affidavit, which read:

'5. I was satisfied that the evidential sufficiency criteria set out in the Code were satisfied in respect of the offence of buggery allegedly committed by C on his wife.

6. In considering the public interest criteria I had regard to:

(a) paragraph 7 of the Code, and in particular the words there attributed to Lord Shawcross.

(b) paragraph 8(vi) of the Code. In the light of the wording of that paragraph I considered the evidence on the issue of consent. In view of all the circumstances, and in particular the absence of any corroboration of the complainant's account on this issue and her failure to make a complaint over a long period, I reached the conclusion that the evidence of lack of consent would not have been strong enough to offer a realistic prospect of a conviction had the offence required proof of lack of consent. I therefore considered that paragraph 8(vi)(b) of the Code did not apply.

7. I also had regard to the fact that, by virtue of the Sexual Offences Act 1967, buggery in private between males aged over 21 is not an offence, unless proved to be non-consensual. Because of this provision, I also considered whether a prosecution was required for buggery of the alleged offender's wife in private, where both parties were over 21, and where the evidence of lack of consent would not have been sufficient to offer a realistic prospect of a conviction had the person buggered been male.

8. Approaching the case on the basis that the alleged buggery could not have been proved to have taken place without the complainant's consent,

I concluded that in all the circumstances the complainant's grievance could be more appropriately dealt with in the matrimonial court, and that the public interest did not require the institution of criminal proceedings. I was also aware that the police would consider whether disciplinary proceedings were appropriate.'

. . .

In my judgment this is one of those rare cases where the Director of Public Prosecution's decision is shown to be flawed because Mr Naunton on behalf of the Director of Public Prosecutions did not approach the question which he had to decide in accordance with the settled policy of the Director of Public Prosecutions as set out in the Code. Although buggery without consent and consensual buggery are both offences contrary to the 1956 Act they are in reality separate offences and here only the former was alleged, but the prosecutor's approach was, as it seems to me, to some extent clouded by the latter. Initially at least, as it seems to me, he should have disregarded it. He would then have had to bring his mind fully to bear on the question of whether the evidential sufficiency criteria were satisfied in relation to the more serious offence. In other words, he would have had to ask himself if there was a realistic prospect of a conviction. He would have had to look at the evidence available and consider those lines of defence plainly open to the accused. The accused had, up to that time, chosen to remain silent but there were, as it seems to me, looking at the matter from Mr Naunton's standpoint, two possible lines of defence. First, the accused might deny ever having had intercourse *per anum*. That was a possibility which, so far as I can see, was not considered at all by Mr Naunton, and of course if he had considered it the question of corroboration would have been easily satisfied. Instead he assumed that the second respondent's line of defence would be to admit buggery but to assert that it was consensual. In those circumstances it seems to me that Mr Naunton erred in that he failed in accordance with paragraph 4 of the Code to 'have regard to any lines of defence which are plainly open to . . . the accused.' What conclusion Mr Naunton would have reached if he had had regard to both of the lines of defence to which I have referred instead of to just one of them, as well as to the fact that the second respondent had not as yet indicated what his line of defence might be, is not a matter which in my judgment should be speculated upon in this court. The decision is one for the Director of Public Prosecutions not for this court. Accordingly, unless there are compelling reasons to do otherwise, I would set aside the decision and remit the matter to the Director of Public Prosecutions for consideration in the light of the judgment of this Court, and of course in the light of all that has happened since the original decision was made. It follows of course from what I have said that I need not deal with Mr Supperstone's submission that the decision under challenge was the result of the application of an unlawful policy, although I am far from satisfied about that, but he is entitled to say that the decision was unreasonable in that it failed to have regard to a material consideration. Primarily however I base my decision on what seems to have been a patent failure to act in accordance with the settled policy as set out in the Code.

In *C* the review was successful because the High Court thought that the prosecutor's affidavit revealed that he had been confused on the question of evidential sufficiency. Judicial review is much less likely to be successful where a prosecution is discontinued on public interest grounds. Two other successful reviews of non-prosecution decisions are worth noting: in July 1997 the DPP accepted that decisions not to prosecute police officers in two cases where suspects had died in custody were flawed (*Guardian*, 29 July 1997).

Is the current situation – in which the CPS operates using fairly vague guidelines and judicial review is difficult – satisfactory? Wide discretion leaves room for abuse and inconsistency in decision making. Defendants and victims may feel that they have been treated unfairly, defendants because they have been singled out for prosecution and victims because prosecutors have not done enough to pursue their cases. Davis (1969, Ch 7) has argued that, in the light of these factors, prosecutorial decision-making should be open, structured by clear guidelines, and that the courts should be prepared to review decisions. In the United Kingdom, it is generally recognised that the adoption of clear policies and the availability of judicial review are important means of holding decision-makers accountable. But is prosecution different?

Extract 3.9.5

C Hilson, 'Discretion to Prosecute and Judicial Review' [1993] Crim LR 739, pp 745–747

Should bodies adopt prosecution policies?

If all offences were prosecuted, a prosecution policy would be unnecessary. While it makes sense not to prosecute all offences for resource reasons, a prosecution policy is required if prosecution decisions are to be consistent. In other words, for the sake of fairness, a policy of selective prosecution must be accompanied by a policy for selecting prosecution. If cost and fairness are the respective advantages of these policies, what are the possible disadvantages? The principal one is a reduction in deterrence: if all crimes are prosecuted, deterrence is maximal; if there is a policy of selective prosecution, there may be a reduced deterrent to the extent that people can perceive a pattern in the offences which are not prosecuted. If, for reasons of fairness, an internal policy for selecting prosecution is introduced, deterrence may be further reduced because much more of a pattern will become discernible. In other words, with selective prosecution, there may be a trade-off between resources and deterrence; with a prosecution policy there may be a further trade-off between fairness and deterrence. However, as we shall see, not all bodies have to make this sacrifice.

The CPS *Code* and the cautioning guidelines are policies for selecting prosecution which state general principles for all crimes to provide some consistency. The price of this consistency may be a reduction in deterrence. More consistency would be provided by more detailed, crime-specific policies[1]

... ; but arguably at the cost of a further reduction in deterrence, because a detailed pattern would emerge. It is for policy makers to decide whether this increased trade-off between fairness and deterrence is worth making. As we will see later, other bodies such as the NRA [National Rivers Authority] and the Inland Revenue have not compromised deterrence by adopting their policies.

Should policies be open and should one be able to rely on them in review proceedings?

Even if crime-specific policies were not publicised they would eventually become visible through the public's experience of the system. With speeding for example, there are no open policies but many people know there are policies and hence drive above the speed limit. Nevertheless, making crime-specific policies open might increase such law-breaking, because more people would get to know about the 'licence' to commit offences within the policy threshold. The trade-off here is between allowing people to see that they have been treated fairly and extending the reduction in deterrence. Allowing crime-specific policies to be relied upon in review proceedings might make matters worse still, because if a policy is open but review is not allowed, there is always the chance that the police/CPS might ignore the policy. This uncertainty may serve as a deterrent. If, on the other hand, review is allowed, this deterrent is removed because one can take formal action if the police/CPS ignore the policy.[2]

The *Code for Crown Prosecutors* and the cautioning guidelines are already open policies – and there is evidence to suggest that many know that they can commit one or two minor offences and avoid prosecution. However, again, even if the policies were not open, they would eventually have become visible as an invitation to commit one or two minor offences with impunity.[3] Making the policies open may have created more petty crime because this invitation has become better known, but the trade-off between accountability and deterrence is probably small and would almost certainly be greater if crime-specific policies were made open. We saw earlier that the cautioning guidelines and the *Code for Crown Prosecutors* contain some specific provisions which could conceivably be used by an accused in review proceedings. In *theory*, as with crime-specific policies, allowing judicial review would reduce deterrence and thus increase crime levels still further. However, in *practice*, allowing review here is unlikely to have any effect on deterrence because, as we saw earlier, *successful* review by offenders is unlikely. This is because those accused will find it hard to prove that the *Code* or the cautioning guidelines have not been followed. The same is not true of crime-specific policies – if these were introduced, having a central plank at which to point ... would make successful review much more likely.

The above arguments about impunity and deterrence do not apply to all other prosecuting authorities. These bodies can create open prosecution policies and courts can scrutinise these in review proceedings without fear of inviting offending. Why is this? First, these other bodies may have recourse to enforcement techniques other than prosecution in order to maintain deterrence. With the Inland Revenue, for example, I may know that I will not be prosecuted for a tax offence but there is no invitation to offend because of the prospect of a civil penalty. Secondly, with our pollution example, many firms would not be able to tell what effect an increase in their emissions would have on the receiving water; even if they could calculate it, it is extremely unlikely that all discharges would rush to emit up to the threshold which attracts prosecution just once (in the policy, a continuous breach is a valid criterion for prosecution). It would hardly be worth it in financial terms. It is hard to think of an offence dealt with by the police and the CPS where the same might be said: it will usually be easy to establish the relevant thresholds and an excessive speed or a minor theft will look attractive to many even once. In other words, the practical consequences of drawing-up policies *and* publicising them or allowing them to be used in review actions are very different for the Inland Revenue and the NRA than they are for the CPS. With the first two bodies, their policies do not create invitations to commit offences; making these policies open and allowing judicial review does nothing to alter this.

Conclusion

To conclude, if prosecution is selective, like cases will not be treated alike without a policy to act as a yardstick in each case. However, if selective prosecution is adopted, then fairness ideally requires that this policy for selection is rational, visible and of practical use to third parties. Without a sufficiently detailed, open policy, one cannot be sure that fairness exists. If it is unenforceable by third parties, one might see unfairness, but be powerless to take formal action against it. For many prosecuting bodies, a requirement that they adopt detailed, open policies which can be relied upon by individuals in review actions would pose few problems. For the CPS, with the provisions of the *Code* and the cautioning guidelines, allowing review will probably do nothing to aggravate the impunity which already exists. However, while the development by the CPS of crime-specific policies may be warranted, for reasons of deterrence it would be inadvisable to publish these or to allow applicants to raise such policies in review actions.

[1] See, e.g. J Vennard, 'Decisions to Prosecute: Screening Policies and Practices in the United States' [1985] Crim.L.R. 20 at p 21.

[2] Detailed policies promote consistent decision-making; open, detailed policies would enable informal complaints to Crown Prosecutors . . . , drawing attention to inconsistencies with stated policy; open, detailed policies which could be mobilised in review proceedings would enable one to take formal action to alter prosecution decisions.

[3] This is not to say that the policy *of* cautioning should be abandoned – one must weigh the costs (reduced deterrence) with the benefits (e.g. resource savings from not prosecuting, and preventing 'labelling'); neither is it to say that the policy *on* cautioning should be abandoned – the benefits here (fairness) probably outweigh the costs (a possible further reduction in deterrence).

It should be noted that other European countries give victims specific rights to challenge prosecution decisions, for example the Netherlands and Germany (though in the latter, only in cases dismissed on evidential criteria) (Fionda, 1995, pp 127, 149). Fionda notes that although challenges are infrequent in these countries, they are an important means of ensuring accountability.

Victims who are disgruntled with a decision to terminate a prosecution can opt to bring a private prosecution. For most victims, the cost is likely to prove prohibitive. There have been some notable successes (see, for example

'Private Case Brings Rapist to Justice', *The Guardian*, 18 May 1995), but also failures, such as the Lawrence family's attempt to prosecute youths for the murder of their son (national newspapers, 26 April 1996). If a private prosecution is brought, the DPP has the right to take the case over and reduce charges or drop the case completely (Prosecution of Offences Act 1985, ss 6, 23). The Law Commission has recommended that the process of bringing a private prosecution be made easier (Law Commission, 1997).

(c) Problems with the prosecution process

How effective is the CPS? CPS performance is difficult to assess, in part because there are no agreed performance measures and in part because CPS effectiveness depends on other actors in the process, such as the police who investigate cases, barristers who prosecute them in the Crown Court, and witnesses who give evidence.

One way of measuring CPS performance is to look at the number of cases that it discontinues. Arguably, a large number of cases being dropped indicates that the CPS is actively reviewing the files passed on to it by the police. In 1987 the CPS discontinued 7.7 per cent of its cases (Crisp and Moxon, 1994, p 2), but this has now risen to 12 per cent (Crown Prosecution Service, 1996). In the same period, the proportion of offenders being cautioned by the police increased, suggesting that many trivial (thus discontinuable) cases were being weeded out before CPS review.

If the CPS is correctly targeting weak and trivial cases for discontinuance, we would expect to notice the effects of this later in the system. We might expect there to have been a decrease in the number of convicted defendants who are given minor punishments, but this does not appear to have happened (Crisp and Moxon, 1994, p 37). We might also expect fewer defendants to be acquitted by the courts. Crisp and Moxon note that this has not occurred, a result which they describe as 'disconcerting' (1994, p 40). More disconcerting yet is the fact that in the Crown Court many acquittals appear to be predictable. Around half of acquittals do not occur after a full trial, but are the result of the judge telling the jury to acquit the defendant because the prosecution case is not sufficiently strong. Sometimes the collapse of a case in court will be genuinely unpredictable: an important witness may not appear or may change his or her testimony. But moving beyond the bare figures, a study of ordered and directed acquittals by Block et al (1993) estimated that about a quarter of such acquittals could have been foreseen before committal (after committal, the CPS are not able to discontinue a case, but many cases will start to crumble between committal and trial: Block et al found that by the trial over half of the committals were foreseeable or possibly foreseeable). A later study by Baldwin (1997) concluded that around 80 per cent of non-jury acquittals (as well as the majority of jury acquittals) were foreseeable. These avoidable acquittals represent a substantial cost to the criminal justice system, and considerable stress and uncertainty for defendants. Where cases are dropped, this often occurs at the last minute: Crisp and Moxon (1994) found that 37 per cent of cases in the magistrates' court were dropped without prior notice to the defendant.

There is evidence, then, that despite the introduction of the CPS many weak cases are still prosecuted. This may, in part, be due to the powers that the CPS was given when it was set up. Although the CPS was intended to be independent of the police, some commentators have argued that it is not. This, it is argued, is because the police still take the initial charging decision so that prosecutors fall prey to 'prosecution momentum', continuing with the case because once the decision to prosecute has been taken it is easier to go along with it than to take the decision to stop it (Sanders, 1989). In the following extract Sanders, drawing on the research of McConville et al (1991), suggests other reasons why weak cases are prosecuted:

Extract 3.9.6

A Sanders, 'Reforming the Prosecution System' (1992) 63 *Political Quarterly* 25, pp 30–32 (some footnotes omitted)

The goals of the Crown Prosecution Service

It was because of the vested interest which the police have in their own cases that the Crown Prosecution Service was introduced. The CPS was to exercise a 'Ministry of Justice' role, dispassionately eliminating weak cases and counter-balancing the extra police powers in PACE by enforcing new guidelines on evidential strength and cautionability. It was to do this either by advising the police to take appropriate action on cases prior to the initiation of prosecution or by dropping those cases afterwards. Thus acquittals were to be reduced, as were trivial cases. An 'efficient' CPS has as few acquittals as possible. Hence the criterion in the CPS's own Code for Crown Prosecutors of 'a realistic prospect of conviction'.

The use of acquittal rates as performance indicators, however, distorts the primary goals of the CPS which are about the strength of the case or the likelihood of guilt or innocence. If it was really intended that the CPS drop as many weak and cautionable cases as possible this could be encouraged by using discontinuance rates – that is, cases dropped by the CPS – as performance indicators. Instead, in CPS Annual Reports, the performance indicators used are dismissal rates (by the courts) and 'judgement quality' tests (that is, cases dismissed with no case to answer).

Similarly, if it were really intended that the CPS counter-balance new police powers it should drop cases in which the police abused those powers. A year ago I talked to local prosecutors about the unpredictability of judicial decisions on the use of unlawfully obtained evidence. I asked the prosecutors whether the CPS would still rely on such evidence, bearing in mind the part played by unlawfully obtained evidence in *Confait* and many of the Serious Crime Squad cases (denial of access to legal advice, unlawful interrogation, and so forth).

341

They said that they would, if they thought they could get away with it. A concrete illustration of this is the case in our research where cannabis was found following an almost random stop-search. The prosecutor said that it was lucky that the defendant was pleading guilty as the stop 'might not have stood up in court'. As it was, a conviction was guaranteed, so he did not consider dropping the case. As another prosecutor told us, when asked why the CPS did not drop such cases: 'We are the Crown *Prosecution* Service!'

This attitude does not fit the due process 'Ministry of Justice' rhetoric of the CPS, but it does fit the operational criterion of treating conviction rates as 'success' rates. Nothing could be more rational for a prosecution service in an adversary system. So, instead of deciding whether or not a case is weak or unjust, the CPS simply looks for a 'realistic prospect of conviction'. There are several reasons why such a case may nonetheless be weak or unjust, which I shall now consider.

(i) *Case construction*... [T]he police construct strong evidence in order to convince courts to convict. This means that, at the same time, they try to convince the CPS of the probability of conviction. Police officers provide the evidence by which the CPS evaluates the work of those same police officers. Not surprisingly, disagreements are rare.

Whether or not the CPS is usually aware of different possible constructions is irrelevant. Its job is to prosecute as many strong cases – that is, likely convictions – as possible. So, in one case a woman was charged with criminal damage when she smashed a social services window. This was because she left her bed-sit after her landlord tried to rape her, and social services did not find her a new place to stay. The prosecutor neither pursued the rape allegation with the police nor dropped the damage prosecution on compassionate grounds. As part of the construction strategy in cases like this police officers often do not provide the CPS with the full background. But even if they did, the results would not necessarily be different. In terms of operational CPS goals, why should they be?

The problem is not just that the goal of eliminating 'weak' cases may not help the innocent. Through police case construction this goal can lead to the opposite result. In an adversary system the structural goal of the CPS is to assist the police achieve a maximum conviction rate. Hence in many cases they suggest extra interviews with witnesses or give advice about future conduct (suggesting that officers not ask questions of suspects which open up viable defences, for instance). The CPS aims to construct ever stronger cases, not to establish truth or innocence, guilt or lies, or to do 'justice' in the broadest sense.

(ii) *Justice is unpredictable*. In many cases it is difficult to predict what will happen in court. In our research we found that prosecutors who expected acquittals were sometimes surprised by convictions, and vice-versa. Thus, in one case, the prosecutor described the evidence in a public order case as a 'bit thin'. He speculated that the defendant was arrested just to get him off the street. The defendant, not surprisingly, was acquitted. In another case, the prosecutor complained bitterly to us about poor police investigation. He expected to lose the case, but in this case the defendant was convicted.

What is a prosecutor to do with a weak case? First, he may, as we have seen, advise the police how to construct it more strongly. Second, he may hope that at least some of these weak cases will succeed anyway. Why not press on? Every three dropped weak cases certainly constitute nil convictions, while every three weak cases prosecuted constitute one or two possible convictions. Why give up when you might succeed? The result is that many weak cases get prosecuted. There is, moreover, an ever-present third possibility.

(iii) *Guilty pleas.* The overwhelming majority of defendants plead guilty to all or some charges, which means that weakness is usually not put to the test. In one typical case of threatening behaviour the police agreed that 'the evidence is not particularly good'. When asked what precisely had been threatening about the defendants' behaviour the prosecutor just shrugged and replied 'they pleaded guilty'. Baldwin and McConville found that in 21 per cent of their sample of last-minute guilty pleaders acquittal would have been likely or possible because of weak prosecution evidence.[1]

Rather than dropping *weak* cases, then, the CPS only drops cases that are likely to *fail.* These are just those very weak cases, indeed, where it is clear that the defence lawyers will fight hard:

> (AT-A109) The CPS told the police that the charge was very weak and that the case should be dropped if the defendant pleaded not guilty.
> (BW-A002/J02) The CPS complained that the charges were too vague, and wanted them 'firmed up'. But the defendants pleaded guilty, making this unnecessary.
> (BW-A083) The CPS suggested that if the defendant pleaded not guilty they bargain over compensation instead of proceeding with prosecution.[2]

Only the defence lawyer acts in the interest of the defendant. This is not surprising in an adversary system, but clearly undermines the 'Ministry of Justice' role of the CPS.

With the CPS, as with the police, the 'due process' rhetoric is contradicted by the conviction-driven reality. As with the police, the reality is sometimes in breach of the rules and sometimes not, but it is consistently geared to operational goals grounded in 'crime control' norms.

---

[1] J Baldwin and M McConville, *Negotiated Justice*, Martin Robertson, Oxford, 1977.
[2] Cases drawn from M McConville [M McConville, A Sanders and R Leng, *The Case for the Prosecution* (London: Routledge, 1991)]. Similar instances are noted by D McBarnet [*Conviction* (London: Macmillan, 1983)], Ch 4.

More recent research on CPS decision-making by Baldwin (1997) tends to support Sanders' criticisms. Baldwin found that some prosecutors uncritically accepted police evidence and were aware that suspects were likely to plead guilty, even in cases with flawed evidence. Baldwin identifies a further reason why weak cases are prosecuted: in serious cases, prosecutors prefer not to take responsibility for dropping the case, preferring instead to leave the decision to the judge or jury.

Could the CPS be reformed so as to break it out of its reactive, police-dependent role? Sanders dismisses this possibility, arguing that in an adversarial system it is unrealistic to expect the CPS to play any sort of neutral role, or for it to act as a check on police case construction.

There are, however, possible reforms. One possibility is to enlarge the role of the CPS: if prosecutors fall prey to prosecution momentum then the initial decision to prosecute could be taken out of the hands of the police and given to the CPS. This reform was rejected by the Royal Commission on Criminal Justice:

> We saw certain advantages in such a change, not least because it would have the advantage of distinguishing unambiguously between the responsibility for the investigation of criminal cases and the responsibility for bringing a case against a defendant and presenting it in court. After closer examination, however, we concluded that the practical difficulties outweighed this theoretical advantage. It would not be practical to have CPS staff posted to police stations in order to frame the charge in every case, or even only in serious cases. There would still therefore have to be some procedure to mark the point at which the police concluded their investigation and the CPS took over. It seemed to us that this procedure would be bound to remain very similar in all but name to the present police charging process but that there might in addition have to be some procedure to mark the point at which the police concluded their investigation and the CPS took over. It seemed to us that this procedure would be bound to remain very similar in all but name to the present police charging process but that there might in addition have to be additional steps incorporated to accompany the proposed transfer of responsibility. This would bring with it the risk of extra bureaucracy and delay and on balance therefore we recommend no change to the present system. (1993, Ch 5, para 21)

A smaller scale reform which has been tried out attempts to give the CPS 'public interest' information about defendants so that they can make better informed prosecution decisions, without relying on the police for all of their information (which was the problem in Sanders' example in Extract 3.9.6 above, of the woman who broke the social services window). In some areas Public Interest Case Assessment (PICA) schemes have been piloted, using probation officers to interview defendants in an attempt to elicit information from them that may fit the public interest criteria considered by prosecutors. After initial schemes run by the Vera Institute of Justice (see generally Elliman, 1990), the Home Office ran a pilot study of PICA schemes in four areas (Crisp et al, 1995). In these areas, suitable cases were chosen and PICA forms prepared on the defendants. In terms of improving discontinuance rates, PICAs were successful: cases where a PICA report was prepared were twice as likely to be discontinued as other cases. Prosecutors appreciated the extra information provided by the schemes, and appeared to become sensitised to public interest criteria (in areas where PICA schemes operated there was an overall rise in discontinuance rates, i.e. even in non-PICA cases (Crisp et al, 1995, p 28)). Despite their qualitative success, the Home Office study judged the PICA schemes to be economically unfeasible: even the most efficient scheme was calculated to recover only 29 per cent of its costs.

344

We noted above that discontinuance rates have increased since the introduction of the CPS, and suggested that this may be evidence that the CPS is performing effectively. However, in some quarters there has been suspicion about the number of cases discontinued. The police have been critical of discontinuance rates (see, for example, police evidence to Home Affairs Committee, 1990). Rose (1996, Chs 3 and 4) has drawn attention to the fact that, at a time of rising crime rates, the proportion of people convicted for many offences has declined. This raises issues beyond the role of prosecutors, but Rose in part blames the CPS for discontinuing too many prosecutions, often on grounds of efficiency. Like other criminal justice agencies, the CPS is expected to operate efficiently and one way in which it can reduce its costs is by discontinuing more cases. This will also reduce costs for other parts of the system. Before the Code for Crown Prosecutors was amended in 1994, para 8(i) explicitly stated that, when considering public interest factors, the likely penalty should be weighed against the likely cost of proceedings, and this presumably remains a relevant consideration. Looking at the public interest factors which, in practice, result in discontinuance (see the figures in Extract 3.9.2 above), 'nominal penalty likely' is the second most common factor. Is justice being sacrificed for efficiency?

The arguments for not prosecuting trivial cases are similar to those for cautioning minor and first time offenders. Apart from the economic argument, it is possible that the stigmatising effects of prosecution and conviction will do more harm than good in a trivial case. But there is a difference between cautioning an offender (which has deterrent effects and signifies to the victim that something has been done) and simply abandoning a prosecution (though note that, unlike discontinuance, a caution is only possible where the offender admits the offence). Should prosecutors have the power to do something more than simply drop a case?

It may be that one of the problems with the prosecution system as it was created in 1986 is that prosecutors have too few powers in relation to trivial offences. At present a prosecutor faced with a trivial offence has few options: the case can be dropped or prosecuted. Prosecutors have no power to caution suspects, though they can request that the police do so. The Royal Commission on Criminal Justice (1993, Ch 5, para 82) recommended that the CPS be given the power to make the police caution a suspect, but this has not, so far, been taken up. Another option for dealing with minor offences, also recommended by the Commission (1993, Ch 5, paras 62–63), is to allow prosecutors the option of paying a fine as a means of avoiding prosecution.

'Prosecutor fines' are used in a number of other European jurisdictions. In the Netherlands prosecutors can offer offenders a fine in most cases, the prosecutors themselves choose the level of fine that will be offered. Fines are used in around 40 per cent of cases. The power to fine offenders was introduced in Scotland in 1988 after the Stewart Committee recommended it as 'an expedient and efficient method of removing a substantial number of cases from the courts' (1983, para 4.38). The level of fine was originally set at just £25, but since 1996 prosecutors have been able to choose between fines of £25, £50, £75 and £100. Prosecutors can offer a fine in cases that would otherwise be prosecuted; offenders need not accept the fine, but refusal is likely to result in prosecution. A fine does not count as a conviction and there is no requirement of an admission of guilt. Research on the use of the fine shows that it is used in 4.4 per cent of cases dealt with by prosecutors; the cases include such offences as theft, breach of the peace and assault (Duff, 1993). The introduction of the fine in England and Wales would raise a number of issues: it might be a suitable way of dealing with minor offences, and there would be efficiency gains for courts and prosecutors. However, some might see a small fine as an inappropriate way of dealing with crime. There are also questions about whether prosecutors in England and Wales are suited to having the power to fine. The CPS plays a much smaller role in the prosecution process than do prosecutors in other European countries (Scotland included) and their lack of public accountability might lead to fears that the power to fine was being abused. See further Duff (1994); Fionda (1995, pp 73–78 and Ch 7).

A rather different solution to the problem of trivial cases has been put forward in a recent Home Office report. As part of a proposed system to speed up CPS handling of cases, it has been suggested that the CPS should no longer be able to discontinue cases on the grounds that the offence is not serious or the likely penalty trivial. This, it is argued:

> would not only speed CPS review of the prosecution file, but, more importantly in my view, it would remove the potential for conflict between police and prosecutors. The decision on what type of offending behaviour is suitable for prosecution would once again be one for the police and would allow Chief Constables to make decisions about the targeting of particular crimes, often involving petty criminality of an anti-social nature.
>
> One Chief Constable suggested that this change to the public interest test had the potential to renew police officers' confidence in the criminal justice system by returning to them – so long as evidential requirements were met – the decision whether or not to prosecute. (Home Office, 1997f, pp 13–14)

4

COURTS AND TRIALS

Trial by judge and jury is a potent symbol of British criminal justice, but its symbolic status is at odds with reality. The vast majority of defendants are tried summarily in the magistrates' courts and most of those who are brought to trial at either court plead guilty, so their courtroom experience is of the court as sentencer rather than as tribunal of fact. The figures are instructive:

Table 4.1

	Proportion of cases	Proportion pleading guilty	Acquittal rate*	Cost of trial
Magistrates' court	98%	82%	25%	£1,500
Crown Court	2%	65%	40%	£13,500

* Acquittal rate is as proportion of contested trials.

Sources Lord Chancellor's Department (1997) pp 64, 90; Home Office (1995a) p 31; Crown Prosecution Service (1997) p 29. The figures for cost of trial are for contested trials and are taken from the Royal Commission on Criminal Justice report (1993) p 5: they include the costs of legal aid, prosecution, committal proceedings and the like.

The figures in this table provide the background to the first part of this chapter, in which we examine the two types of trial, the allocation of cases between the courts and the prevalence of guilty pleas. In the second part of the chapter we discuss some of the rules of evidence governing criminal trials and their relationship to the values underlying the criminal process.

1. SUMMARY JUSTICE: THE MAGISTRATES' COURTS

(a) Magistrates' courts and lay justice

In both magistrates' courts and Crown Courts there is an element of lay representation in the adjudicative process. In the Crown Court it is the jury, who sit in court to judge the factual issues in the case. In the magistrates' court it is the magistrates themselves – who act as judges of both fact and law and also sentence offenders – who are drawn from the local community. Magistrates usually sit in court in benches of three. They decide the case collectively, sometimes leaving the court to sit in the retiring room to deliberate. Although they are required to apply the criminal law and follow sentencing principles laid down in case law and statute, magistrates do not have to be legally qualified. On joining the magistracy, they must undergo a minimum of 34 hours' training within the first year. Lay magistrates are supported in court by clerks, who advise the bench on matters of law. Their role should simply be advisory, leaving all of the ultimate decisions to the magistrates (though there is evidence that clerks sometimes play a wider role than this: see McLaughlin, 1990). In the busier courts, some cases are tried by stipendiary magistrates, who are legally qualified. They sit alone, without a clerk, and try the more serious cases (in 1997 there were 90 full-time stipendiaries).

Should the vast majority of criminal cases be dealt with by lay people? It can be argued that the use of lay decision-makers involves the community in the application of the laws which govern it: it ensures that people are judged by their peers rather than by professionals whose day-to-day lives may be very different from their own. In this way, a space is opened up for 'local justice', an application of the criminal law that takes account of the attitudes of local communities. It is evident, then, that a defence of lay participation in the system of criminal justice in England and Wales presumes that magistrates are indeed representative of local communities. To what extent is this the case?

(b) The appointment of magistrates

Magistrates are officially appointed by the Lord Chancellor (or, in some areas, the Chancellor of the Duchy of Lancashire). However, with some 30,000 lay magistrates in England and Wales, it is obvious that the Lord Chancellor can play little more than a nominal role in deciding who to appoint. In practice, appointments are made in all but name by Local Advisory Committees. There are about 100 of these, one for every Commission of the Peace area. In the larger areas the LACs delegate much responsibility to advisory sub-committees. The Lord Chancellor's policy is that 'Advisory Committees must have due regard to obtaining a balance on benches in terms of age, gender, occupation, place of residence and political inclination in order that the bench may reflect the community it serves' (Home Affairs Committee, 1996b, p 149). However, in 1996 the Home Affairs Committee concluded that 'the aim of balancing the bench to take account of age, employment background and political leanings of magistrates has not, as yet, been achieved' (Home Affairs Committee, 1996a, para 205).

One criticism of the present appointments process focuses on the role of the advisory committees. Until recently, these committees were shrouded in secrecy, because it was felt that to publish details of the members would encourage lobbying. Since 1992 the Lord Chancellor has asked all committees to publish the names of their members. The majority of advisory committee members (80 per cent) are serving magistrates, and the Magistrates' Association has alleged that the system of recruitment to these important committees (which involves members being chosen by the chairperson) establishes a 'self-perpetuating oligarchy' (Home Affairs Committee, 1996b, p 241; see also Cooke, 1984). This may obviously have an effect on the profile of magistrates who end up being appointed: the Home Affairs Committee made much of the fact that, in 1983, no less than seven magistrates on the Sunderland bench lived in one middle class street containing only 43 houses (Home Affairs Committee, 1996b, p 269).

Although there are no statistics on all of the relevant characteristics of magistrates, the research (not all of it very recent) supports the contention that magistrates come from a fairly narrow range of backgrounds. As far as race is concerned, a 1987 survey by the Lord Chancellor's Department found that nationally just under 2 per cent of magistrates were black (compared to about 5 per cent of the population as a whole). This disparity may be particularly marked in some areas: a study by King and May in 1983 found that black magistrates in 23 out of 25 local areas studied were under-represented, when compared with their proportion in the community as a whole; in 18 of these areas even a doubling of the proportion of black magistrates would still have left them under-represented (1985, pp 101–102). However, in recent times the proportion of ethnic minority magistrates appointed has reflected that of the general population (Home Affairs Committee, 1996b, p 150). Forty-eight per cent of magistrates are women, an under-representation by some 5 per cent (Lord Chancellor's Department 1997, p 90), but this slight disparity is amplified when race and gender are combined: the 1987 figures showed that only 26 per cent of black magistrates were women. Class is another area that has received attention: it appears that the magistracy is dominated by the middle classes. The following table, summarising the results of four different studies, shows that this has changed remarkably little over the years despite efforts to recruit magistrates from a wider range of backgrounds:

Table 4.2

Registrar General's classification	Hood (1966) %	Baldwin (1971) %	Kapardis (1978) %	Henham (1982) %
Class 1	21.7	27.4	20.7	23.2
Class 2	55.2	56.5	60.0	56.6
Class 3	21.8	14.5	18.5	19.4
Class 4	0.0	0.8	0.8	0.8
Class 5	0.0	0.0	0.8	0.0
Not classifiable	1.3	0.8	0.0	0.0

(Class 1 = higher professional; Class 2 = managerial and other professional; Class 3 = clerical; Class 4 = skilled manual; Class 5 = semi-skilled. Dates are the dates of the authors' fieldwork. For the details of the studies, see Hood (1972), Baldwin (1976), Kapardis (1985), Henham (1990).)

Source Adapted from Henham, 1990.

Two more recent studies support this picture of an unrepresentative magistracy. Raine's figures for a number of benches suggest that magistrates' professions remain at odds with those of the communities they judge, with professionals and managers still significantly over-represented (1989, pp 46–47). Dignan and Wynne's (1997) study of one Midlands bench found that magistrates tended to be chosen from the more affluent sections of the community. How can the unrepresentative composition of the magistracy be explained? A factor which may go a long way to explaining the domination of the magistracy by the middle classes is that magistrates are not paid for the time they spend in court (apart from receiving expenses and sometimes a small loss of earnings allowance: for details see Home Affairs Committee, 1996a, para 213). All magistrates are expected to sit in court for half a day every fortnight (26 'sittings' a year), but in reality many will be expected to devote more time than this to their job: the average now seems to be 35 sittings a year, though this does not include time spent on training sessions (Lord Chancellor's Department, 1991, p 39). Thus magistrates will have to be prepared to take considerable unpaid time off from their jobs to sit on the bench, a requirement which means that those in less well paid and less secure employment will tend to be disinclined to join the magistracy (though employees are offered some protection by s 50 of the Employment Rights Act 1996). There was widespread agreement among those giving evidence to the Home Affairs Committee that many young people were discouraged from joining the magistracy because of fears that they would lose out on promotion at work, and that this leads to particular problems in recruiting those under 30 years of age.

The other significant factor determining the composition of the magistracy is the procedure and attitudes of advisory committees. It is for these committees to choose suitable candidates for the magistracy, and to attempt to create a representative and balanced bench. Throughout much of this century, concern about the balance of local benches has centred on the political composition of the magistracy, and with good reason. At the beginning of the century, Conservatives enjoyed a stranglehold on benches, particularly outside the cities where on average 83 per cent of magistrates were Conservatives (Vogler, 1990, p 66). When, in 1906, the requirement that magistrates be property owners was abolished, this marked the beginning of a long struggle to secure politically balanced benches. Has political balance been achieved? The evidence is mixed. Raine's study of three benches suggests that the Conservative domination has been ended (1989, pp 44–46), though Henham's slightly earlier study found that there was still a Conservative bias (an over-representation of 10 per cent in his 1982 study: see Henham, 1990, p 73). Dignan and Wynne, comparing magistrates' voting intentions with the number of local councillors from each party, found a marked over-representation of Conservatives. (For full details of the political affiliations of magistrates (at the time of joining their benches), see Home Affairs Committee, 1996b, pp 175–183). Whatever the current situation, it has been argued that a continued obsession with achieving political balance may act to the detriment of other conceptions of representativeness or balance. King and May, who studied the selection process as it affected black candidates, found that committees tended to rely on nominations from established groups, especially political parties, rather than attempting to foster links with community organisations which might have been able to suggest candidates. Thus the selection process tended to favour 'the professions and articulate, committee-minded people who are active in political, voluntary or charitable organisations' (1985, p 78). This not only counted against black candidates, but also meant that the black candidates who were selected tended to be those who had already gained the approval of established social groups. Advisory committees are now encouraged to advertise the possibility of joining the magistracy as widely as possible in order to attract a wider range of applicants.

King and May also expressed concern about two other aspects of the selection process. First was the fact that some committee members expressed racist views, referring to Asians as 'arrogant' and West Indians as 'volatile and excitable' (1985, p 60). Secondly, there was the fact that magistrates were expected to serve the whole community, and this requirement was consistently interpreted as excluding candidates who admitted to seeing themselves as representing a certain section of the community (although only black candidates were regularly asked if they saw themselves as representing their community). King and May saw as problematic, not only because the concept of representation is vague and open to misinterpretation, but also because it reflects some confusion on the part of the committees themselves. While committees were aware of the need to appoint black candidates in order to achieve a more balanced bench, they were not prepared to conceive that black candidates' community links or experience of life in a minority culture might be reasons for their appointment.

In an attempt to secure a more balanced bench, the current Lord Chancellor, Lord Irvine, has instructed LACs to disregard age balance, 'so as to give an overriding priority to achieving the right political and social balance'. To this end, he has increased the upper age limit for appointment from 55 to 65. He has also instructed LACs to carry out an experiment in widening the pool of possible magistrates by considering blind candidates (Irvine, 1997).

(c) The importance of lay justice

Having considered the extent to which magistrates are representative of their communities, we need to consider in more detail why it might be important for a criminal justice system to involve lay people in adjudicative decision-making. As we asked at the beginning of this section, the implementation of the criminal law is a serious business: why seek to involve lay people in it? And if we do use lay people in adjudicative decision-making, why is it important that all sections of the community are represented? If the bench is made up of white male professionals, are they not as well suited to the task of adjudication as any other social group?

Some of the arguments about lay involvement in criminal justice will be examined in more detail when we look at the role of the jury in the Crown Court. For the moment it is worth noting that the magistrates' role, which incorporates fact-finding, the application of the law and decision-making as to sentence, involves interpretation and evaluation rather than the simple application of rules to facts. King and May note that an understanding of the role that values and beliefs play in lay decision-making highlights the importance of the approach taken by committees in the selection process. They argue that: 'a system based upon [the] myth of objective, depersonalised justice is able to ignore the class, racial or cultural backgrounds of the decision-makers, while emphasising that they should be "well-balanced" people, endowed with "commonsense" and "the right motives"' (1985, p 145). It is for this reason that the requirement that magistrates not represent any particular section of the community is difficult to justify, for a black magistrate arguably should represent the black community's experience, and should bring their knowledge of that community to the bench. In the following extract Eaton describes how magistrates' decisions on appropriate sentences for defendants reflected the assumptions about gender and class that the magistrates drew from their daily lives:

Extract 4.1.1

M Eaton, *Justice for Women?* (1986) pp 73–76

Recognising a problem: women defendants

When talking about their work, Hillbury magistrates used a model of family life which employs many of the features noted in both the public rhetoric of pleas of mitigation, and the professional discourse of social inquiry reports. Women are expected to be home-centred with responsibility for domestic labour and child-care, while men are expected to be breadwinners:

> 'Sometimes if there are children involved one wonders why the woman is in full-time employment. Is it economic pressure or is it social pressure, because she desperately needs to be out at work and can't stand the family life and so on. One asks more questions about a woman being in a full-time job than one does about a man, because the assumption is that a man will be in a full-time job . . .' (Magistrate (woman))

This traditional division of labour also involves a hierarchy while the woman is held responsible for the running of the home, she is accountable to the man:

> 'I think something is said about the person in the home by their physical circumstances. If a place is left dirty, continually, at an unacceptable level, that tends to say . . . something . . . I think it is important to differentiate between what it says about the person and what it says about the person's problems . . . with a woman with a number of children and a husband in trouble . . . possibly the marriage itself in trouble, a dirty home and difficulties of that nature might present a picture of depression in her rather than the fact that she is a slut as such . . . most people on the bench look to the woman to maintain the standards of the home . . . (but) it says something about the man – the fact that he is indifferent to, or can tolerate, or *does nothing to encourage an alteration of these standards.*' (Magistrate (woman). Emphasis added.)

However, when talking about the family lives of defendants, magistrates were eager to distinguish between middle-class and working-class defendants. Gender-role was nearly always related to social class:

> '. . . you get a little more shock with some of the women when you know their background – when you see somebody who's really quite well dressed and obviously fairly cultured, it is a shock, even if you realise right from the start that it's a cry for help, because of some emotional disturbance. It's still a shock. But one can understand if it's a mother with several kids and she hasn't any money and she pinches a pair of shoes or the basic foods.' (Magistrate (woman))

Typically, that magistrate attributes gender-related motives to both women – the middle-class woman is recognised as emotionally disturbed, the working-class woman is caring for her children. However, the distinction between middle-class and working-class motivations is also a distinction between non-criminal and criminal behaviour. If a woman is middle class, it is much more difficult for the magistrate to believe that the actions are those of a criminal. For many magistrates any similarity between the defendant and themselves poses a problem:

'One woman, I remember, who'd never had any form of criminal background before, and had gone out on a major shoplifting spree, and in 24 hours had taken a mass of stuff, a really large amount of property – and one couldn't conceive what sort of brainstorm had brought this behaviour on to a woman of normal middle-class respectable background.' (Magistrate (woman))

Not only motivation, but also the judicial response has to be assessed in the context of the defendant's social position. One magistrate explained why, in her view, probation was not suitable for upper middle-class defendants:

'Very often a probation officer going into a home may be able to sort out an awful lot of problems, but there's a – I don't want to sound patronising because I don't feel it and I think the probation officers are marvellous. I think there's a very slight problem if you put them into an upper middle-class home – the way the upper middle-class home will regard the probation officer would work against the system, and if I, personally, could fine a woman in that position I would rather do that and get it out of the way, finished, clean cut, rather than risk putting a probation officer in her home. That might be a continuous shame on her.'

The magistrate then illustrated her point with the following example taken from her recent experience:

'. . . I had a shoplifter of that sort, a very upper middle-class lady, and we really wanted to give her probation, but she was already having psychiatric treatment, privately, and her husband had walked out on her anyway so she was alone at home, so there was no shame in bringing a probation officer in, but it was her first offence, it was shoplifting and in the end we said, "We'll slap a fine on her because if she's going to reappear, she's going to reappear again quite quickly and probation will still be suitable". But we agonised long over that because probation seemed very suitable, clearly the probation officers thought it was suitable too, and were only too keen to get in and help her. But in the end we decided the other way.'

The ready attribution of criminal motivation or the imposition of social work surveillance are, apparently, more appropriate for the working-class defendant. The origins of the probation service in nineteenth-century missionary work with the poor seem, here, a century later, to be an influence on the perception of magistrates dealing with middle-class offenders. Social work was, and apparently still is, something that the middle class do on behalf of the working class. When discussing their own role, most magistrates expressed a concern with helping those in need and the relative positions of middle-class magistrates and working-class defendants serve to perpetuate this nineteenth-century model. This was recognised by one magistrate, who had been appointed because of his work in a trade union. Speaking of his middle-class colleagues he said:

> 'They've got sympathy for the less well-off, the less fortunate. They've got sympathy but they tend to view them as, not the criminal class, but – "us and them".'

See further Hedderman and Gelsthorpe (1997) Chs 3 and 4.

Arguments for the use of lay magistrates also draw on the fact that magistrates' courts deliver local justice. It is argued that magistrates' decisions should reflect their knowledge of the local community and its particular needs and attitudes:

> [T]here remain some significant cultural differences between regions and localities of this country which are still reflected in community values and perceptions about crime and its treatment. In this respect, particularly in some of the more rural areas of the country, certain, if not all, forms of criminality are considered in more serious terms than elsewhere, and the communities concerned expect tougher sentences especially for offences which directly offend them, for example, vandalism. Similarly in some inner city neighbourhoods today, it appears that the community often perceives certain forms of criminality in a far less serious light than elsewhere, for instance, with regard to the possession of cannabis or other soft drugs. (Raine, 1989, p 174)

From this point of view, discrepancies in the practices of the courts between areas, and in particular discrepancies in sentencing levels, over which there has been considerable concern (for example, Tarling, 1979; Raine, 1989, pp 86–100), should, to a certain extent, be tolerated. But does the acceptance of local variation in the application of the law pose a threat to other important values in the criminal justice system, such as just deserts and the rule of law? At first sight it would seem that the notion of lay and local justice does just this, but it can be argued that the ideal of community justice is not completely incompatible with the rule of law because the legal system gains its legitimacy in a community through its ability to incorporate community values (Bankowski et al, 1987, Ch 1). Like many other aspects of the criminal justice system, the use of lay magistrates and the concept of local justice reflect conflicting values. Lay magistrates are valued for their local knowledge and lay status, but at the same time they are expected to operate within a framework of (increasingly complex) law. Bankowski et al (p 170) suggest that:

> Our society rests . . . on contradictory values and these are reproduced in its various institutions. In the legal system institutions like the jury and the lay magistracy enable the democratic pull of the system to be recognised while keeping its main and most important imperative, 'the government of laws and not men', intact.

If, then, the lay magistracy represents the benign community face of the criminal justice system, the selection procedures and the way the magistracy is composed can be seen as operating as a check on the 'democratic pull'. As we have seen, those who are selected as magistrates are not supposed to see themselves as representing the views of any particular section of the community, and in practice certain social groups end up dominating the magistracy. Given the checks on community justice produced by the present system, some commentators have argued that lay magistrates should be elected by their local communities (Pearson, 1980; Bankowski and Mungham, 1981). The proponents of an elected magistracy envisage that election would bolster the local nature of magistrates' justice. Elected magistrates would also be more likely to see themselves as having a mandate to represent a certain point of view and this would make magistrates' justice more visibly political. However, as shown below, at present the trend is towards increased central, not local, control of magistrates' courts.

(d) Efficiency in magistrates' courts

As the figures in table 4.1 above illustrate, magistrates' courts deal with the overwhelming majority of criminal cases and deal with cases much more economically than do Crown Courts. The efficiency of the service, which relies largely on unpaid adjudicators to process some two million defendants each year, is one of its attractions to those who manage the criminal justice system. At the same time, the efficiency gains of operating a system of unpaid justices should not be exaggerated: a stipendiary magistrate, sitting alone, could doubtless decide cases more quickly and without needing a clerk's advice on the law. Whatever the overall economics of relying on an unpaid magistracy, there have recently been moves to increase the efficiency of the system, in particular by reorganising the management of the courts. The administrative structure of the magistrates' courts is complex. The courts are funded by central government (80 per cent) and local authorities (20 per cent). In each Commission of the Peace area (of which there are around 100) there is a Magistrates' Courts Committee, which is responsible for the management of the service in that area, deciding on administrative issues such as the allocation of resources within it. There is also a smaller administrative level in the service, the Petty Sessional Division, which corresponds to the area over which each bench (essentially, court) has jurisdiction. Each bench is advised by a justices' clerk. Justices' clerks, usually aided by assistant clerks, have a dual role. Not only do they sit in court and advise lay magistrates on the law, they also have day-to-day administrative responsibility for the bench (deciding on the cases to be heard and the allocation of justices to each case).

Research carried out in the 1980s demonstrated that there was considerable variation in efficiency between different benches. The local nature of the service, seen as one of the strengths of the system, had meant that there was little accountability for the management of each bench and that different areas were run differently, depending on the practices of each Magistrates'

Courts Committee and justices' clerk (Raine, 1989, Ch 5). Magistrates' Courts Committees were staffed by magistrates, rather than by people with managerial expertise, and the clerks' dual role meant that they too might have had little administrative competence.

Unease about the efficiency of magistrates' courts culminated in a White Paper, *A New Framework For Local Justice* (Lord Chancellor's Department, 1992). The document followed a major scrutiny of the courts (Home Office, 1989), the findings of which are summarised in the following passage:

> The Scrutiny found that at the national level the Home Office had unclear respons-
> ibilities and limited powers, with the result that the 105 area services could go
> their own ways with widely varying results in terms of efficient performance and
> standards. The local structure was found to be just as confused, with over 250
> justices' clerks appointed by but not properly accountable to the 105 courts com-
> mittees, which in turn did not provide effective management supervision or direc-
> tion. The funding bodies – central government and local authorities – were judged
> not to provide effective budgetary controls. Justices' clerks themselves had little
> control over the resources with which they worked and insufficient management
> information; and there was no proper definition of the balance between their legal
> and management responsibilities. (Lord Chancellor's Department, 1992, para 8)

The Scrutiny report had suggested that the magistrates' courts be reorganised on a national basis as an executive agency. The government decided against this option, in part because it would have threatened the local nature of the courts which is traditionally portrayed as their strength. In the ensuing reform proposals and the debates about their worth, this tension between, on the one hand, efficiency and centralisation, and on the other, localisation and independence, was to play a major role. The proposals floated in the White Paper and later put before Parliament in the Police and Magistrates' Courts Bill would have greatly increased the Lord Chancellor's influence over the administration of magistrates' courts, and led some critics to suggest that the constitutional principle of the separation of executive and judicial powers was under threat. As a result, some of the more controversial proposals were dropped from the Bill. Nevertheless, the provisions enacted by the Police and Magistrates' Courts Act 1994 are a significant example of the extent to which the demands of efficiency and managerialism have had an impact on the criminal justice system. The provisions in that Act now form part of the Justices of the Peace Act 1997 (JPA), a piece of consolidating legislation: references here are to sections of that Act.

Section 32 of the JPA allows the Lord Chancellor, after local consultation, to amalgamate different Magistrates' Courts Committees (MCCs). At present, MCCs govern areas of widely differing size, and there is evidence that larger areas are run more efficiently (Raine, 1989, p 157). MCCs are also to be encouraged to appoint up to two members who are not magistrates (to allow people with managerial experience to be appointed) and the Lord Chancellor may appoint such members of his own accord (s 28). The Lord Chancellor has also been given a default power if he considers that an MCC is not running the courts in its area efficiently and effectively: 'the Lord Chancellor may give directions to magistrates' courts committees requiring each of them, in discharging their responsibilities . . . to meet specified standards of performance' (s 31(4)); in addition to this, he may sack the members of a MCC and replace them, for three months, with people nominated by him (s 38). One of the most controversial issues during parliamentary debates surrounded the dual role of justices' clerks. The Act increases the managerial responsibility of MCCs for the courts in their areas, but also puts day-to-day management of courts in the hands of a justices' chief executive. It was originally envisaged that the chief executive would still play the role of a clerk, giving legal advice to magistrates in court. However, there were fears that allowing the person responsible for the efficient business of the court to advise magistrates on legal points would be a dangerous erosion of the separation of powers. This led to provisions in s 40 to restrict the circumstances in which this might occur:

> (6) A person may not be appointed both as justices' chief executive and as justices' clerk for a petty sessions area unless the Lord Chancellor has agreed that he may hold both appointments.
>
> (7) Where, in accordance with subsection (6) above, a person holds an appointment as justices' chief executive with an appointment as justices' clerk for a petty sessions area, he shall not exercise any functions as justices' clerk for the petty sessions area unless authorised to do so (either generally or in a particular case) by the magistrates' courts committee for the area which includes that petty sessions area.

This section has already been used to make dual appointments, though the Magistrates' Association has announced its opposition to this (Magistrates' Association, 1996). Further, all clerks are under some pressure to ensure that their courts are run efficiently (and will doubtless be constantly reminded of the importance of this by MCCs and chief executives), so there is the ever-present danger that their dual role will lead to a conflict of interests. This was the reason for the inclusion of s 48:

48. Independence of justices' clerk and staff in relation to legal functions

> (1) When exercising the functions specified in subsection (2) below or giving advice to justices of the peace in an individual case –
>> (a) a justices' clerk shall not be subject to the direction of the magistrates' courts committee, the justices' chief executive or any other person, and
>> (b) any member of the staff of a magistrates' courts committee shall not be subject to the direction of that committee or of the justices' chief executive (when acting as such) . . .

Another significant change relates to the way in which magistrates' courts are funded. Before 1992 each MCC decided for itself how much money it needed to run the courts in its area. Funding is now performance related and is allocated in the following manner:

Extract 4.1.2

**Lord Chancellor's Department, *A New Framework for Local Justice*
(Cm 1829, 1992) p 11**

ARRANGEMENTS FOR DISTRIBUTING CASH LIMITED GRANT TO MAGISTRATES' COURTS COMMITTEES

Purpose   To ensure that the total amount of grant available to finance magistrates' courts in England and Wales is divided among magistrates' courts committees in a manner that reflects (on the basis of standard national assessments) the workload, efficiency and quality of service in each area.

The formula   Each area receives an allocation based on its performance (compared with other areas) measured in four key respects. The amount of the total national grant allocated to each measure is indicated below:

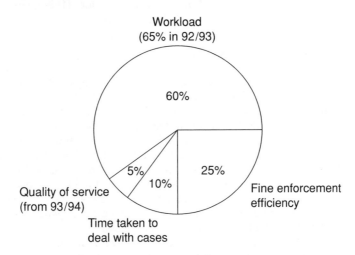

There is some evidence that this shift towards a managerial culture is affecting magistrates' decisions. Probation officers and court clerks have claimed that magistrates are disinclined to order psychiatric assessments of offenders. This is because an assessment would require an additional court hearing with its attendant costs (*Guardian*, 11 July 1996). Magistrates have also explained to researchers that:

> the Lord Chancellor's department has been putting pressure on the courts to have fines paid within a specified period of time, and that the Justice's Clerks in each court are enforcing this. As a result, magistrates are feeling forced to impose lower financial penalties than they thought appropriate in order to increase the chances of payment within a set period. (Hedderman and Gelsthorpe, 1997, p 41)

The tensions created by the push for efficiency are linked to those discussed in the previous section. Efficient practice has been encouraged through increasing central control over the magistrates' courts since the mid-1980s (Raine and Willson, 1993: Ch 6). There has been a move to iron out discrepancies in sentencing and administrative practices between magistrates' courts, but this might be seen as a threat to the ideal of community justice. Managerial interests coincide with increased professionalism, but this is at odds with the use of lay magistrates. Professionalisation could be achieved through the appointment of more stipendiary magistrates, but at present the solution has been, somewhat awkwardly, an increased emphasis on the administrative functions of justices' clerks. In the following extract, Faulkner considers some of the implications of these tensions for the future of the magistracy.

Extract 4.1.3

D Faulkner, 'The Functioning of Lay Justice' (1994) *The Magistrate*, 3 February, p 3

The quality of legal advice

The quality of magistrates' legal advice has always been crucial to the integrity and survival of lay justice. However unfairly, the argument is often heard that magistrates cannot be trusted with difficult points of law. An illustration is to be found in the Royal Commission's recommendation relating to the abolition of committal proceedings and their view that submissions of no case to answer should in the magistrates' courts be heard only by stipendiary magistrates. As the law becomes more complex and is changed more frequently, and as the environment of political, public and media interest becomes more demanding, the quality and accessibility of legal advice will become progressively more important. Quality, as distinct from independence, has however featured surprisingly little in the recent debate.

It should be no surprise if a future review of local justice recommends that for all 'serious' cases the chairman should be legally qualified, whether appointed as a stipendiary or on a part-time basis like recorders in the Crown Court. Lay members would still have an important part to play, as they do in some continental countries. A court composed in this way could be given greater powers than a present lay bench, and could dispose of many cases which are now committed expensively to the Crown Court. Court administration could be merged with the administration of the Crown Court as part of a national court service agency (the administration of the Crown Court is already to be based on an agency basis with effect from 1 April 1994), or contracted out to private operators. The attractions to a cost conscious, market oriented government would be obvious. It is not the purpose of this article to make a case for or against such a development, but it is to argue that much more attention should now be given to maintaining the long term quality of lay magistrates' legal advice and to the means by which it is delivered and structured. Few other organisations would make the same individuals responsible both for management and administration and for providing legal advice, and the culture and dynamics of today's managerialist environment will inevitably place more emphasis, and provide greater rewards, for the former than the latter. The present combination of functions, and the sometimes healthy symbiosis between magistrates and their clerks which results from it, has been an anomaly which was largely overlooked in the Le Vay Scrutiny, although the case was put to the Home Office in the early 1980s. In a few years time it will have become a dangerous anachronism.

(e) The quality of justice in magistrates' courts

Those who have studied the workings of the magistrates' courts are often critical of the standard of justice on offer. McBarnet's comments sum up the 'assembly line' image of summary justice:

> To enter the lower courts is to be taken aback by the casualness and rapidity of the proceedings. The mental image of law carried into the courts is shattered by observation. The solemnity, the skills of advocacy, the objections, the slow, careful precision of evidence, the adversarial joust, none of these taken-for-granted legal images are in evidence. It seems to be another world from the legal system we have learned about in books, films and television. Credibility in the ideology that the scales of justice are tipped to acquitting ten guilty men rather than convicting one innocent man is stretched to breaking point by the work of the lower courts. (McBarnet, 1981, p 123)

McBarnet labels the prevailing atmosphere in the magistrates' courts as an 'ideology of triviality', typified by the incredulity of practitioners that she was studying the lower courts at all: 'some were . . . genuinely concerned that I was wasting my time at the lower courts when I could be watching "juicy cases" and "real judges" elsewhere' (1981, p 144). However, the fact that magistrates' courts deal with large numbers of cases and have higher conviction and guilty plea rates than Crown Courts does not necessarily mean that they operate unjustly. The quality of justice is difficult to measure. We can never know the proportion of defendants before each court who are truly guilty. It may be that the higher acquittal rate in the Crown Court represents a large number of defendants who deserve to be found guilty but who are instead being acquitted. However, some support for concern about the quality of magistrates' justice is provided by the high proportion of appeals to the Crown Court which are successful: in 1996, 59 per cent of appellants had their appeals allowed or their sentences varied (Lord Chancellor's Department, 1997, p 66).

There are features of trials in magistrates' courts which mean that defendants are not as well protected by due process safeguards as they would be in the Crown Court. One possible disadvantage for defendants is the fact that magistrates sit as judges of both fact and law. If a defendant disputes the admissibility of a piece of evidence – for example, a confession – then the question of admissibility will be decided by the magistrates. This means that if the evidence is excluded, the magistrates will continue the trial still knowing of the existence of the incriminating evidence. In jury trials, questions of admissibility are decided by the judge in the absence of the jury, thus protecting the fact-finder from prejudicial knowledge. In a similar manner, a defendant with previous convictions poses problems in the magistrates courts' because it is harder to hide those convictions from the magistrates (see Wasik, 1996a; Darbyshire, 1997c).

Another frequent criticism of magistrates is that they are 'case hardened' and put too much faith in the police. A jury will generally come fresh to a case, and may be more likely to believe a defence put forward than a magistrate who may have heard similar defences advanced on countless occasions. The argument that magistrates are 'pro police' is common. The majority of magistrates come from sections of the community that are unlikely to have negative experiences of the police. Where a contested case involves a conflict of evidence between the defendant and a police officer, it is argued that magistrates will always believe the police (for example, King, 1982). As with many assertions about the quality of magistrates' justice, the 'pro police' and 'case hardened' arguments are difficult to test. Insofar as they involve a comparison with the Crown Court, they also rest on the similarly inscrutable assumptions that juries are less likely to believe the police, or that case hardened judges do not have considerable influence over jury verdicts. This said, there may be wider structural factors which help to explain why the routine outcome of magistrates' proceedings is a plea or finding of guilt. McConville et al (1994) point to both the advantages enjoyed by the prosecution, and the nature of defence work as explanations:

Extract 4.1.4

M McConville, J Hodgson, J Bridges and A Pavlovic, *Standing Accused: The Organisation and Practices of Criminal Defence Lawyers in Britain* (1994) pp 225, 227–229, 237–238

In general, . . . magistrates' court cases are not argued on legal issues, which are usually assumed to be inappropriate in such a forum. Instead, disputes are confined to competing versions of fact or competing interpretations of events in which the defence seek to undermine the prosecution through the evidence of defendants themselves and that of their immediate family or, exceptionally, with the assistance of independent witnesses. The outcome of most cases is, thus, dependent upon whether the prosecution is able to advance a convincing account to substantiate its allegations against the defendant.

. . . it is important to emphasise the *structural* advantages possessed by the prosecution in the overwhelming mass of summary cases.

Structural advantages of the prosecution

The first structural advantage of the prosecution is that police witnesses tend to be familiar with courtroom procedures and are skilled in the task of giving evidence. The 'flattening' effect of the uniform, creates an impression of police witnesses giving impersonal and 'objective' evidence, an impression heightened by the presentation of the evidence in a 'highly stylized manner ... frequently in a flat monotone' [La Trobe, *Guilty, Your Worship*, Occasional Monograph No 1 (Bundoora: Legal Studies Department, La Trobe University, 1980)]. This contrasts sharply with civilian witnesses:

> 'Their dress suggests a style of personality. Their demeanour in the box varies sharply. Their involvement is both unsurprising and unconcealed. The fact that they are playing what Carlen [P Carlen, *Magistrates' Justice* (London: Martin Robertson, 1976)] would recognize as "bit-roles" serves to suggest that they may, by chance or circumstances, be unreliable.'
> (La Trobe, 1980, p 53)

The possible psychological influence on magistrates of this contrast between police and civilian witnesses is not lost upon solicitors who are forever giving advice to their clients on how to dress ('be presentable', 'be smart', 'cover up those tattoos'), and on how to behave when giving evidence ('don't get riled', 'don't go piping off', 'don't lose your temper'). Thus, just before going into court, a solicitor suddenly caught sight of the defendant who had just arrived for trial and spoke to him in the following terms:

> SOLICITOR: Zip your jacket up. You should be doing better than a string vest for court. How much gold do you have on? Take some of that off – I don't want you looking flashy. [The client takes off neck chain and bracelet.] And when you're in court, I don't want you looking like you have an attitude problem; so keep your fucking mouth shut and let me do the talking.
> CLIENT: Yeah, yeah, I know.

The second structural advantage of the prosecution is that the evidence of police officers is almost invariably 'authenticated' by notes contained in the officers' notebooks. These notes purport to be a near-contemporaneous account of the alleged incident and, as such, appear to be more reliable than mere recollection and take on the flavour of 'facts' rather than 'opinions'. This impression may be reinforced in the witness-box where officers sometimes refer to their own evidence as an account of the 'facts' or 'what happened'. From a prosecution perspective, these notes have the added advantage that they need not be put to the defendant for comment at the time of the incident in question. The fact, therefore, that the notes are initially uncontroverted (for whatever reason) and can only be challenged by evidence of recollection (itself presumptively faulty), gives such police evidence enhanced status.

The third structural feature of prosecutions is that police evidence is usually supported by other police evidence. This 'mutual support' system renders much police evidence resistant to attack, even where the account might seem implausible. Thus, in *MCT-40* police evidence alleged that the defendant was behaving suspiciously and that he dropped something from his hand when the police arrived. Whatever the truth of this assertion, the officers stated that their

363

notes were prepared independently which, if true, would have reinforced the cogency of their evidence. Yet while both officers used identical language to describe the incident (e.g. both saying that, as they arrived, the defendant 'came out of the shadows') they flatly asserted that they had not collaborated in preparing their evidence, as in the following excerpt from the cross-examination of the second officer:

SOLICITOR: Have you discussed the case with [officer 1]?
OFFICER 2: No.
SOLICITOR: Not even to make up your notes?
OFFICER 2: No, I make the notes up independently.
SOLICITOR: Did you collaborate with him to make your statement?
OFFICER 2: No.
SOLICITOR: It's coincidence that you and [officer 1] both use the phrase 'came out of the shadows'?
OFFICER 2: Pure coincidence.

But the bullet-proof nature of police evidence goes far beyond this. Not only is it standard practice for police witnesses to have their evidence supported by that of other police officers, but the evidence itself can be constructed by the officers in a collaborative effort. Officers can *lawfully* write up their notes together to ensure that their accounts are synchronised and can even, as happened in several of our cases, sign the notebook containing the account compiled by one of their number thereby 'adopting' the note and allowing it to be relied upon by all the signatories in giving their testimony.

. . . Against this there is often no separate, competing case for the defence. The general lack of investigation and preparation by solicitors and their staff, throws the burden of the defence onto the defendant. The view that defendants hide behind their right to silence is revealed as a myth: defendants are commonly the front line of the defence, often the only witness called on the defence side. The nature of the defence case thus places solicitors under considerable restraint in the way they can confront prosecution witnesses, for fear that an attack upon the integrity of the police would let in their own client's character.

This general approach of the defence, tends to be rewarded only if the prosecution case is badly put together or if a significant element of chance intrudes. The failure of the defence to secure acquittals in cases in which the prosecution was badly damaged or in which there was, according to both defence and prosecution, more than a reasonable doubt, gives substance to the claim that, in magistrates' courts, there is a reverse onus of proof under which it is for the defendant to establish innocence rather than for the prosecution to prove guilt. It is, in a real sense, impossible to predict acquittals when all the evidence is in, and it is understandable that solicitors often speak of favourable outcomes as having been secured by 'luck'. Such expressions have nothing necessarily to do with their own evaluation of the client's guilt; rather they are expressions of surprise that the magistrates listened to the evidence and acted 'fairly'.

See further Darbyshire (1997b).

2. MODE OF TRIAL DECISIONS

It is a basic principle that the more serious criminal cases should not be tried summarily. Instead, they are tried by judge and jury in the Crown Court. How should it be decided which cases are the most serious and hence deserving of the more formal, and more costly, method of trial? There is no easy answer to this question, and it is one which has been a focus of attention in the criminal justice system for a considerable time. A brief survey of the issues involved will demonstrate the importance of mode of trial decisions.

Magistrates try the vast majority of criminal cases: some 98 per cent. This is an efficient way of dealing with the bulk of criminal litigation: trial by magistrates is much cheaper than trial by jury. But the efficiency gains of magistrates' trials are not confined to the cost of the trial itself. Magistrates have limited sentencing powers. They can impose no more than six months' imprisonment or a fine of £5,000 for any one offence. Research has shown that in practice, even in comparable cases, magistrates sentence less severely than Crown Court judges. One study found that, in comparable cases, magistrates imposed seven times less custody than Crown Court judges (Hedderman and Moxon, 1992). So, by steering more cases towards the magistrates, the prison population may be reduced. Further, there tends to be less pre-trial delay before a case is tried in the magistrates' court. This may also have an effect on the prison population by reducing the amount of time that some prisoners spend on remand. For those managing the criminal justice system, there seems to be much to be gained from keeping as many cases as possible in the magistrates' courts. However, efficiency is not the only consideration. If the criminal justice system is not to lose public confidence, then serious offences should be tried in the Crown Court where they can be punished appropriately. The problem of appropriate sentences is complicated by the fact that some defendants, after being found guilty in the magistrates' court, can be committed to the Crown Court for sentencing. In this way an efficient trial might be combined with an appropriate sentence in a serious case.

If we turn to examine mode of trial decisions from the defendant's perspective we will find a very different, and somewhat more complex, set of concerns. For the defendant the magistrates' limited sentencing powers are an attraction, but this must be weighed against the significantly greater chances of acquittal in the Crown Court: 40 per cent as opposed to 25 per cent. This might make it worth risking a harsher sentence to gain the greater chance of acquittal. But acquittal versus penalty is not the only difficult judgment that a defendant with a choice of trial venues would have to make. Pre-trial delays are a factor which are likely to be weighted differently by different defendants. In one sense the delay is a 'process cost' for defendants: it is a period of uncertainty and anxiety, to be avoided or diminished (see Feeley, 1979). Delay would appear to be an especially painful cost for defendants on remand, but this disguises another difficult judgment. Prisoners on remand benefit from more advantageous conditions than sentenced prisoners, and the amount of time spent on remand will be subtracted from any period of imprisonment imposed by the court when the defendant comes to be sentenced. So, remanded defendants who feel that they are likely to be found guilty *and* given a custodial penalty may wish to maximise pre-trial delay. But, if they do this by choosing Crown Court trial, they should weigh the advantages of a longer remand period against the harsher penalty which is likely to be imposed. Pre-trial delay may also have other advantages for defendants. It is thought that the longer the period between the commission of a crime and the trial of the criminal, the greater are the chances of acquittal. This is because the memory of witnesses is likely to fade over time, as may a victim's commitment to prosecution. Further, some defendants may wish to avoid facing the process cost of the trial for as long as possible, whether or not this is to their advantage in the long run.

Prosecutors and victims may also have an interest in the mode of trial decision. A victim's interests might be thought to be served by having a case tried in the Crown Court where the wrongdoing can be censured with a more severe punishment than in the magistrates' court. However, the speed and higher conviction rates of magistrates' courts may also be relevant factors. A study of decision-making in domestic violence cases found that prosecutors were aware of these concerns:

> [S]everal [prosecutors] said that they were very keen to use summary-only offences because it was better to prosecute cases in the magistrates' court where they would be dealt with more speedily and where, one prosecutor said, a conviction was more likely. The same prosecutor described this decision-making process as a balancing act between ensuring a serious enough charge was brought and making sure the case was dealt with swiftly and efficiently – 'for the victim's sake'. (Grace, 1995, p 46; see also Cretney and Davis, 1997)

Victims are also more likely to receive compensation from the defendant if a case is tried by magistrates: Hedderman and Moxon found that magistrates imposed a compensation order in 25 per cent of cases, compared with 10 per cent of Crown Court cases (1992, p 32).

In practice, magistrates, prosecutors and defendants all have some choice in some mode of trial decisions. The allocation of cases between the two courts is fixed primarily by the classification of offences into groups. *Offences triable only on indictment* can only be tried in the Crown Court. This category includes the more serious crimes such as murder, rape and some assaults. *Summary offences* can only be tried in the magistrates' court. These include many driving offences and some public order offences. However, between these simple classifications at the upper and lower end of the scale lies a large category of *either way offences* which can be tried in either the magistrates' or the Crown Court. These include many common offences such as theft, burglary and assaults under ss 20 and 47 of the Offences Against the Person Act 1861. Either way offences make up four fifths of the Crown Court's work load. The court which will try these offences is determined at a mode of trial

366

hearing. The decision-making process at a mode of trial hearing is governed by the Magistrates' Courts Act 1980:

> **19.** – (1) The court shall consider whether, having regard to the matters mentioned in subsection (3) below and any representations made by the prosecutor or the accused, the offence appears to the court to be more suitable for summary trial or for trial on indictment.
>
> (2) Before so considering the court
>
> (a) shall cause the charge to be written down, if this has not already been done, and read to the accused; and
>
> (b) shall afford the prosecutor and the accused an opportunity to make representations as to which mode of trial would be more suitable.
>
> (3) The matters to which the court is to have regard under subsection (1) above are the nature of the case; whether the circumstances make the offence one of serious character; whether the punishment which a magistrates' court would have power to inflict for it would be adequate; and any other circumstances which appear to the court to make it more suitable for the offence to be tried in one way rather than the other.

If the magistrates, after hearing representations from prosecution and defence, decide that the offence should be tried summarily, they should explain this to the accused (s 20(2)). However, the defendant has the right to refuse to be tried in the magistrates' court. This 'right to elect' trial by jury is an important and controversial feature of mode of trial decision-making.

(a) Guidance on mode of trial

We have seen that, in terms of efficiency, the state has an interest in channelling as many cases as possible into the magistrates' courts. For some time the number of either way cases tried in the Crown Court has been increasing, causing delays and contributing to a rising prison population (for example, in 1980 15 per cent of either way cases were committed to the Crown Court; this rose to 23 per cent in 1987, though it then fell to 17 per cent in 1992 (Home Office, 1995b, p 1)). Periodically, attempts have been made to reduce the number of either way offences being sent for trial in the Crown Court. This can be done most directly by reclassifying offences. For example, the Criminal Law Act 1988 reclassified criminal damage under £2,000 as a summary offence, and the limit was raised to £5,000 by the Criminal Justice and Public Order Act 1994. Attempts can also be made to influence the decision-making of magistrates, as it is they who are responsible for the initial decision on whether or not to send an either way offence to the Crown Court. Research carried out in 1986 found that a substantial proportion (40 per cent) of either way cases were sent to the Crown Court as a result of a decision by the magistrates under s 19 of the Magistrates' Courts Act 1980. The study also found that there was considerable regional variation in the number of cases so sent, suggesting that a reduction in the number of cases sent to the Crown

Court could be achieved by focusing on magistrates' decision-making (Riley and Vennard, 1988). To this end, national Mode of Trial Guidelines were issued in 1990 (the guidelines were revised in 1995). The guidelines flesh out the issues to be considered by magistrates under s 19.

Extract 4.2.1

**Mode of Trial Guidelines (revised edition, 1995) as set out in
Blackstone's Criminal Practice 1997 (1997) pp 1009–1011**

NATIONAL MODE OF TRIAL GUIDELINES

The purpose of these guidelines is to help magistrates decide whether or not to commit 'either way' offences for trial in the Crown Court. Their object is to provide guidance not direction. They are not intended to impinge upon a magistrate's duty to consider each case individually and on its own particular facts.

These guidelines apply to all defendants aged 18 and above.

General mode of trial considerations

Section 19 of the Magistrates' Courts Act 1980 requires magistrates to have regard to the following matters in deciding whether an offence is more suitable for summary trial or trial on indictment: (1) the nature of the case; (2) whether the circumstances make the offence one of a serious character; (3) whether the punishment which a magistrates' court would have power to inflict for it would be adequate; (4) any other circumstances which appear to the court to make it more suitable for the offence to be tried in one way rather than the other; (5) any representations made by the prosecution or the defence.

Certain general observations can be made: (a) the court should never make its decision on the grounds of convenience or expedition; (b) the court should assume for the purpose of deciding mode of trial that the prosecution version of the facts is correct; (c) the fact that the offences are alleged to be specimens is a relevant consideration; the fact that the defendant will be asking for other offences to be taken into consideration, if convicted, is not; (d) where cases involve complex questions of fact or difficult questions of law, the court should consider [transfer] for trial; (e) where two or more defendants are jointly charged with an offence each has an individual right to elect his mode of trial; (f) in general, except where otherwise stated, either-way offences should be tried summarily unless the court considers that the particular case has one or more of the features set out in the following pages *and* that its sentencing powers are insufficient; (g) the court should also consider its powers to commit an offender for sentence, under section 38 of the Magistrates' Courts Act 1980, as amended by section 25 of the Criminal Justice Act 1991, if information emerges during the course of the hearing which leads them to conclude that the offence is so serious, or the offender such a risk to the public, that their powers to sentence him are inadequate. This amendment means that committal for sentence is no longer determined by reference to the character or antecedents of the defendant.

368

Features relevant to the individual offences

Note: Where reference is made in these guidelines to property or damage of 'high value' it means a figure equal to at least twice the amount of the limit (currently £5,000) imposed by statute on a magistrates' court when making a compensation order.

[*Note*: Each of the guidelines in respect of the individual offences set out below (except those relating to drugs offences) are prefaced by a reminder in the following terms 'Cases should be tried summarily unless the court considers that one or more of the following features is present in the case *and* that its sentencing powers are insufficient. Magistrates should take account of their powers under s 25 of the Criminal Justice Act 1991 to commit for *sentence*'].

Burglary
1. Dwelling-house
   (1) Entry in the daytime when the occupier (or another) is present.
   (2) Entry at night of a house which is normally occupied, whether or not the occupier (or another) is present.
   (3) The offence is alleged to be one of a series of similar offences.
   (4) When soiling, ransacking, damage or vandalism occurs.
   (5) The offence has professional hallmarks.
   (6) The unrecovered property is of high value [see above for definition of 'high value'].

Note: Attention is drawn to para 28(c) of schedule 1 to the Magistrates' Courts Act 1980, by which offences of burglary in a dwelling *cannot* be tried summarily if any person in the dwelling was subjected to violence or the threat of violence.

2. Non-dwellings
   (1) Entry of a pharmacy or doctor's surgery.
   (2) Fear is caused or violence is done to anyone lawfully on the premises (e.g. nightwatchman; security guard).
   (3) The offence has professional hallmarks.
   (4) Vandalism on a substantial scale.
   (5) The unrecovered property is of high value [see above for definition of 'high value'].

Theft and fraud
   (1) Breach of trust by a person in a position of substantial authority, or in whom a high degree of trust is placed.
   (2) Theft or fraud which has been committed or disguised in a sophisticated manner.
   (3) Theft or fraud committed by an organised gang.
   (4) The victim is particularly vulnerable to theft or fraud (e.g. the elderly or infirm).
   (5) The unrecovered property is of high value [see above for definition of 'high value'].

Significantly, the guidelines suggest that there is a presumption in favour of trying either way offences summarily. Around the time the guidelines were published, the Home Office carried out more research on mode of trial decisions (Hedderman and Moxon, 1992). This confirmed the significant role played by magistrates in sending either way cases to the Crown Court: in 1990 nearly 60 per cent of such cases went to the Crown Court because magistrates declined jurisdiction. If the magistrates had not declined jurisdiction, most of the defendants said that they would have chosen summary trial. Hedderman and Moxon's study also uncovered some other facts about mode of trial decisions which increased concern about the process. It was found that in two thirds of either way cases sent to the Crown Court defendants ended up being given a sentence that was within the magistrates' range, implying that they need not have been sent to the Crown Court in the first place (estimates of the cost of the unnecessary Crown Court caseload to the criminal justice system as a whole range from £5 to £25 million a year (Home Office, 1995b, p 6)).

Another interesting finding related to the decisions made by defendants and solicitors about whether or not to elect Crown Court trial. The following table summarises the factors which were found to affect these decisions:

Extract 4.2.2

C Hedderman and D Moxon, *Magistrates' Court or Crown Court? Mode of Trial Decisions and Sentencing* (1992) p 20, table 3.1

Reasons defendants and solicitors gave for preferring Crown Court trial

Reason	Defendants %	Solicitors %
Better chance of acquittal	69	81
Magistrates on the side of the police	62	70
Lighter sentence	59	38
To get more information about prosecution case	48	45
Would be sent to the Crown Court for sentence	42	40
More likely to get bail	36	11
Crown Court would be quicker	34	6
Would delay start of trial	28	19
Co-defendant wanted case to go to Crown Court	26	19
To serve part of sentence on remand	24	(Not asked)
Easier to get legal aid	19	4

The figures invite several comments. First, a majority of defendants and solicitors listed the better chance of acquittal in the Crown Court as a reason for electing Crown Court trial. However, the majority of defendants who so elected ended up pleading guilty to all offences for which they were sentenced (Hedderman and Moxon's research did not allow a precise figure to be put on this, but it seems that the proportion is at least 70 per cent). Thus, most Crown Court electors never ended up benefiting from the higher acquittal rate, nor from any other advantages of trial by jury. Their formal experience of the Crown Court was purely as a sentencing venue. Secondly, many defendants and their solicitors thought that the eventual Crown Court sentence would be lighter than that in the magistrates' court. Hedderman and Moxon show that this is a mistaken impression: sentences are very much harsher in the Crown Court. In similar cases, Crown Court judges imposed more than seven times more custody than magistrates. A possible explanation for this connects to a third point: most defendants and solicitors have a dim view of the fairness of summary trial, believing magistrates to be on the side of the police. It may be that a general distrust of magistrates extends to the fairness of the magistrates' court as a sentencing venue. We noted above that there is a frequently expressed view that magistrates are 'pro police', but that it was practically impossible to prove such an assertion. At the end of the day, perhaps it matters little whether or not it can be shown that magistrates really are biased in favour of the prosecution. We know that many defendants *perceive* them to be so, and this in itself is cause for concern. People may judge the fairness of legal proceedings, not so much by their substantive outcome, as by the procedures employed to reach that outcome (see generally Stephenson, 1992, Ch 12). As long as defendants do not believe that they are getting a fair hearing in the magistrates' courts, summary trial will remain problematic. When convicted and sentenced by magistrates, defendants will not believe that justice has been done.

(b) Addressing the mode of trial problem

The research on mode of trial decisions is important because it provides a context within which to judge proposals to increase the number of cases tried summarily. We have seen that mode of trial guidelines were one way of attempting to influence the distribution of business between the two types of court, but the guidelines themselves have not been enough to forestall more radical proposals. There are three solutions to the mode of trial problem that deserve attention.

Either way offences can be reclassified so as to make them summary offences. This has been done with various offences in the past, but it now seems that any new reclassifications would be controversial. For example, the offence of possession of an offensive weapon is often dealt with by a sentence falling within the magistrates' range. In 1992, nearly 90 per cent of sentences passed at the Crown Court for the offence could have been imposed by magistrates (Home Office, 1995b, p 3). However, some instances of the offence might be thought serious enough to warrant a sentence of more than six months' imprisonment. Even more controversial is the partial reclassification of theft. Thefts of property worth less than a certain value could be reclassified as summary only (a similar scheme operates in criminal damage cases: up to damage valued at £5,000, the offence is summary). Many thefts are of minor value and a 1989 survey estimated that the reclassification of thefts of £100 or less as summary offences would divert about 9,000 cases a year from the Crown Court. A proposal along these lines was put forward by the James Committee in 1976, but proved so controversial that it appears not to have been seriously contemplated since. The reason is that a conviction for theft involves an imputation of dishonesty: this is true of the theft of £1 as much as of £1,000. The objection to reclassification is that a person accused of dishonesty should have the right to jury trial, in part because a group of fellow citizens is ideally suited to making judgments of honesty and dishonesty (in this context, note the definition of dishonesty in *Ghosh* [1982] QB 1053), and in part because a conviction for theft may have a severe impact on the defendant's future prospects of employment. A modified version of the theft proposal would involve reclassification up to a certain value, but retain the defendant's right of election if he or she had no previous convictions for offences involving dishonesty (see, for example, Block, Corbett and Peay, 1993, p 63). But this modification does not escape criticism: should the law presume that a defendant with a previous conviction has no reputation worth the protection of trial by jury?

The Royal Commission on Criminal Justice put forward what in many ways is an even more radical proposal. It suggested that defendants should no longer have the right to elect Crown Court trial: the decision should simply be for the magistrates, after having heard representations from the defence and the prosecution. The Commission made short shrift of objections based on the perceived fairness of summary trial:

> We do not think that defendants should be able to choose their court of trial solely on the basis that they think they will get a fairer hearing at one level than the other. Magistrates' courts conduct over 93 per cent of all criminal cases and should be trusted to try cases fairly . . . Nor in our view should defendants be entitled to choose the mode of trial which they think will offer them a better chance of acquittal any more than they should be able to choose the judge who they think will give them the most lenient sentence. (1993, p 88)

As far as the media were concerned, this proved to be the most controversial recommendation in the Commission's report; it was also criticised by academic commentators (see Bridges, 1994; Ashworth, 1993a). One objection is that the recommendation ignores the research evidence, in that it proposes attenuating the defendant's right to elect when the majority of either way cases are sent to Crown Court at the behest of the magistrates, even though they end up being punished within the magistrates' limits. Another criticism is that the Commission is drawing a false analogy between choice of court and choice of sentencer: the former involves choosing a different *form* of decision-making body while the latter does not. Despite the controversy which surrounded the Royal Commission's proposal, it has been revived in proposals put forward by the Home Office to reduce delay in the criminal justice system (Home Office, 1997f, Ch 6).

A third solution to the perceived mode of trial problem has now been put into practice. Since 1997, ss 17A–17C of the Magistrates' Courts Act 1980 have allowed defendants to indicate, at the mode of trial hearing, whether or not they intend to plead guilty when their case comes to trial (Hedderman and Moxon found that 65 per cent of defendants committed to the Crown Court by magistrates had been ready to plead guilty at the first opportunity). If a defendant indicates an intention to plead guilty, then this will be treated as a guilty plea and the magistrates can proceed straight to sentencing (though they retain the option of committing the case to Crown Court for sentence). This proposal presumes that most defendants will be happy to be dealt with by the magistrates and will not elect to be dealt with in the Crown Court even after magistrates indicate their readiness to accept the case, which seems to be in line with the research (Hedderman and Moxon's finding that three quarters of those committed by magistrates would have accepted summary trial). Why is it thought that an earlier plea will persuade magistrates to accept more either way cases? It might do so in two ways: first, magistrates concerned about a long and complex trial will know that there will be no trial, simply a consideration of the facts of the case for sentencing purposes. Secondly, defendants who plead guilty can receive a sentence discount of up to one third. That is, sentencers can give a lighter sentence in the event of a guilty plea than they would ordinarily do, because the guilty plea is regarded as a mitigating factor. So, if the magistrates considered that a defendant's crime merited nine months' custody and was thus only appropriate for Crown Court trial, a guilty plea might merit a discount of three months, bringing the sentence within the magistrates' sentencing range. It is difficult to judge whether this will have a substantial impact on the volume of Crown Court business. What is certain is that its impact will be minimal unless magistrates give more careful thought to their ability to try a large number of the cases which they are presently committing to Crown Court, something which previous research suggests they have not done. Further, magistrates will have to adapt to the practice of awarding a sentence discount. In the past, there has been no evidence that magistrates do award a discount for a plea of guilty (McConville et al, 1994, p 188). However, the discount has recently been recognised by s 48 of the Criminal Justice and Public Order Act 1994, and a timely guilty plea is listed as a mitigating factor in the most recent Magistrates'

Association *Sentencing Guidelines*. In summary, there is considerable doubt as to whether ss 17A–17C will alleviate the perceived overloading of the Crown Court (see further Redmayne, 1997, pp 89–92).

3. GUILTY PLEAS AND PLEA BARGAINING

The majority of defendants do not contest their cases. They plead guilty, foregoing their right to a trial (see table 4.1, p 347 above). At first sight this is puzzling, especially in the Crown Court where defendants have a good chance of being found not guilty. Another interesting fact is that the guilty plea rate varies. It varies over time: during the 1980s the guilty plea rate in the Crown Court rose by some 10 per cent (Zander, 1991). It varies between different offences: in the Crown Court in 1996 84 per cent of those charged with burglary pleaded guilty, but only 43 per cent of those charged with sexual offences and 54 per cent of those charged with offences against the person (Home Office, 1997b, table 12). The guilty plea rate also varies around the country. The regional variations are discussed by Zander:

Extract 4.3.1

M Zander, 'What the Annual Statistics Tell Us About Pleas and Acquittals' [1991] Crim LR 252, pp 253–254 (footnotes omitted)

The patterns of regional variation are remarkable not only in the extent of the differences but in their consistency over time.

In every year back to 1980 London had by far the lowest proportion of guilty pleas and the North East and the Midland and Oxford circuit had the highest. The figures for the proportion of defendants pleading guilty to all charges in the three years of 1989, 1985 and 1981 for instance were:

Percentage of defendants pleading guilty to all charges

	1989	1985	1981
London	50(1)	47(1)	40(1)
South East outside London	64(2)	65(2)	58(2)
Wales and Chester	72(3)	73(4)	69(5)
Western	72(3)	69(3)	62(3)
Northern	80(5)	73(4)	64(4)
Midland and Oxford	82(6)	78(6)	72(6)
North Eastern	86(7)	84(7)	80(7)
England and Wales	72	70	62

Note: the figures in brackets represent the ranking of the area that year.

Source Judicial Statistics, 1989 Table 6.8; 1985 Table 5.16; 1981 Table B.7(b).

374

These regional differences are extraordinary. The difference between the lowest guilty plea rate in London and the highest in the North East was 36 percentage points in 1989, 37 in 1985 and an astonishing 40 in 1981.

But the fact that the differences continue year by year is even more extraordinary. Each year London not only has the lowest guilty plea rate in the country, but the difference is dramatically lower than the next lowest (the South East outside London), which is again markedly lower than the next group, which in turn is distinctly lower than the Midland and Oxford and the North Eastern which year in year out have by far the highest rate. The position in the 1970s was just about the same.

These patterns defy any obvious explanation. Yet because they are so striking and so persistent they must have some rational explanation – though it may require sophisticated sociological research to dig it out.

Of course, some defendants will plead guilty because they accept their guilt, but this would not seem to explain the large numbers who do so, nor the extensive regional variation. To understand the role of guilty pleas in the criminal process we need to look more closely at the benefits derived from them. For defendants, there are often advantages to be gained from pleading guilty, and this may be the reason why so many do not pursue their chances of acquittal. In general terms, when a defendant offers to plead guilty in order to gain a perceived concession from the prosection or the judge, this can be called plea bargaining. Plea bargaining is comprised of a number of different practices.

(a) Charge bargaining

One form of plea bargaining is charge bargaining. Prosecutors have the power to drop or reduce charges; if they do so in return for a guilty plea from the defendant, this is a charge bargain. This may be in the prosecutor's interest, because rather than running the risk of losing the case at trial a definite conviction will be secured, albeit to a less serious charge than originally envisaged. The reduction or dropping of charges may also be in the defendant's interests, as the less serious offence will usually attract a more lenient sentence. Some recent studies suggest that charge bargaining is quite common. In their study of either way cases, Moxon and Hedderman asked defendants about their reasons for pleading guilty: 29 per cent said it was because the prosecution offered to drop or reduce some charges in return for a guilty plea (1992, p 24; of those who opted for Crown Court trial and then entered a late guilty plea, 51 per cent did so in the expectation that charges would be dropped or reduced: ibid). Some offences are particularly associated with charge reduction, because underneath one offence lies a similar, but less serious offence. For example, Moxon and Hedderman found that theft charges were often substituted for the less serious charge of handling stolen goods (Moxon and Hedderman, 1994, p 100). It is with offences against the person that we find the most fertile ground for charge bargaining: the Offences Against the Person Act 1861 (OAPA) creates a ladder of offences of varying seriousness. At the top is wounding with intent to cause grievous bodily harm (s 18, maximum sentence life imprisonment). Then comes inflicting grievous bodily harm without intent (s 20, maximum sentence five years), followed by assault occasioning actual bodily harm (s 47, maximum sentence five years) and then the common law offence of assault (a summary offence). The researchers found that:

> Only about one in five of the cases originally charged under section 18 were eventually dealt with in this way. This is reflected in the finding that 61 per cent of those convicted of wounding under section 20 of the 1861 Act had originally been charged under section 18. (The figure varied between areas, but was high at all courts, ranging from 48 per cent to 77 per cent.) Of the 447 section 47 (ABH) cases sampled, almost a quarter had originally been charged under section 20 (and a further 3 per cent under section 18). (Moxon and Hedderman, 1994, p 100; see also Shapland et al, 1985, pp 52–56).

The fact that charges are reduced does not necessarily mean that the defendant was offered a plea bargain, but these figures are certainly suggestive. The suspicion that some form of plea bargaining is a common feature of offences charged under the OAPA is confirmed by Cretney and Davis's study of the prosecution of violent offences. While so far we have suggested that plea bargaining may be beneficial to the system and to defendants, the authors draw attention to the effect that such deals have on victims and on the police:

Extract 4.3.2

A Cretney and G Davis, *Punishing Violence* (1995) pp 137–140 (footnotes omitted)

[O]ur sample included eleven initial s 18 charges (GBH with intent). CPS reduction of an initial s 18 charge appeared virtually standard. The eleven s 18 charges produced just one conviction on that count.

Police officers whom we interviewed claimed that the CPS commonly reduced charges to a level which no longer reflects the true gravity of the assault. Our own case monitoring bore this out. We should emphasise that this is not of itself reason to criticise the CPS: the circumstances surrounding assaults can be difficult to penetrate, while victims' commitment to the prosecution cause cannot be relied on. Many cases therefore present evidential problems. In these circumstances it is tempting to reduce the level of charge in order to induce a guilty plea. This may be done either at the stage of initial CPS case review or several weeks or months later, at court, as part of a plea bargain. Of the twenty-nine cases in our sample which were prosecuted, nine (31 per cent) were the subject of an immediate guilty plea; nine (31 per cent) were the subject of a not guilty plea but the defendant pleaded in due course to a lesser charge; six (21 per cent) were aborted when the prosecution offered no evidence (or, in mid-trial, offered no *further* evidence); four defendants (14 per cent) were tried and found guilty; and one defendant (3 per cent) was acquitted. These figures indicate a substantial use of the plea-bargain.

The question then arises: whose interests are served by the plea-bargain? The answer is not altogether clear. Take, for example, the case of Patrick Dashwood . . . Four suspects were charged with both assault and public order offences. The case was listed for trial at the Crown Court where, on the day of the trial, a bargain was struck: all charges were dropped against one defendant and the others pleaded to violent disorder. It is possible to analyse this and many other cases from a variety of perspectives. Taking first the defendants, the decision to allow one defendant to walk free (arguably, he was the prime mover in the whole affair) and to proceed against the other three smacked of expediency at best. The convicted men were indignant at this: they regarded their co-defendant as someone whom they had gone to help and who had then turned his back on them. From their point of view therefore justice was not served. The investigating officer, on the other hand, was more than content with the plea-bargain. He did not mind that the assault charges were dropped, because violent disorder is a serious charge in itself. He also did not mind that the charges against one defendant were dropped entirely. This was because he considered the case against him to have been weak. All in all he regarded three out of four as a good 'result'. The barristers, both prosecuting and defending, and the judge were likewise well satisfied. All were pleased at not having to conduct the trial.

If, however, we consider the *public* interest, there is reason to be less sanguine. Taking first the need to ensure efficient case management, the fact that the plea-bargain was secured only on the morning of the trial meant that considerable public expenditure had already been incurred, even if aborting the trial did assist the administration of the court: indeed, the fact that each of these defendants had his own barrister highlighted the waste of resources endemic in the court process. Second, in respect of the denunciatory or symbolic purpose of criminal justice, there was no public examination of this very violent event. As in so many other cases, justice was done in corridors. And what of the victims? As far as they were concerned the late plea-bargain brought only belated relief. They had experienced the burden of anticipating the trial over the preceding 12 months, their anxiety relieved only at the eleventh hour after they had endured a whole morning in the court waiting area, subject to verbal threats and menacing gestures from friends of their assailants. Nor had they been party to the negotiations leading to the plea-bargain. They were present, but not consulted. For the victims, therefore, the court experience constituted both a relief and a disappointment . . .

While victims may be affronted by their marginalisation in court, our research suggests that the technicalities of the law (represented, for instance, in the distinctions between s 18, s 20 and s 47 charges) have little or no meaning as far as most victims are concerned. Being only too well aware of the 'otherness' of the law as expressed in its rules, culture and language they are content to let the police and the courts decide these matters. But while victims may be happy to accept that the initial charge is the right one – they are unlikely to have any basis for deciding otherwise – they are much less likely to accept the legitimacy of the decision to *reduce* the charge [J Shapland,

J Willmore and P Duff, *Victims in the Criminal Justice System* (Aldershot: Gower, 1985) p 79]. A reduction in the charge gives the assault victim the message that prosecutor and court have downgraded the level of harm he or she has experienced. Considerations which carry weight with the CPS (as for instance that the new charge will permit a sentence similar to that which would have been imposed had the charge remained at its original level[1]) may not impress the victim. The Director of Victim Support has stated that:

> 'Victim Support receives frequent complaints that victims who have suffered a serious offence are distressed when the offender is convicted on a lesser charge to which he has pleaded. Many victims would prefer the seriousness of the offence against them to be recognised by a plea of guilty to the full charge.'[2]

This is consistent with the findings of our research. It reflects the fact that victims are seeking *vindication*. They will not feel vindicated if the defendant pleads to a lesser charge and is then 'let off' with what they consider a derisory sentence. Courts are all about symbolism, but the actual symbolic content is not necessarily that which is intended. Courts cannot avoid delivering vindication and humiliation, but they can determine *who* is vindicated and who is humiliated: it appears to some victims that they are treated as of no account while their assailant is accorded a minor triumph.

[1] Code for Crown Prosecutors, para 9.1.
[2] Letter to *The Times*, 12 January 1993.

Another type of offence where plea bargain related charge reduction may be common is rape, which may be downgraded to indecent assault. Grace et al's study of rape cases found some evidence of charge bargaining: 23 per cent of defendants whose cases came to court pleaded guilty to an alternative charge (1992, p 8; see also Gregory and Lees, 1996).

(b) The guilty plea discount

Another form of plea bargaining revolves around the offer of a lighter sentence to those who plead guilty. The Court of Appeal has long accepted that those who plead guilty will receive a sentence discount: they will be punished less harshly than they would have been had they pleaded not guilty. Originally, the mitigating effect of a guilty plea was justified in terms of remorse (for example, *Harper* [1968] 2 QB 108), but courts are now more likely to stress the benefits to the criminal justice system and to victims:

Hollington and Emmens (1985) 7 Cr App R (S) 281, 285, where the defendants changed their pleas to guilty at a late stage:

> The sooner it is appreciated that defendants are not going to get full discount for pleas of guilty in these sorts of circumstances, the better it will be for the administration of justice.

378

Billam (1986) Cr App R 347, 350, a guideline judgment on sentencing in rape cases:

> The extra distress which giving evidence can cause to a victim means that a plea of guilty, perhaps more so than in other cases, should normally result in some reduction from what would otherwise be the appropriate sentence. The amount of such reduction will of course depend on all the circumstances, including the likelihood of a finding of not guilty had the matter been contested.

If defendants know that they will definitely get reduced sentences on pleading guilty, this will encourage them to do so. The encouragement will be especially strong where the defendant knows exactly what the difference between the two sentences would be, in particular if a defendant is told that on a plea of not guilty a custodial sentence will result but that on a plea of guilty he or she will be given a non-custodial sentence. By confronting defendants with the details of their dilemma they will probably be encouraged to plead guilty: in this way the system benefits (by reducing the number of trials), as may defendants (by being better informed). The practice of sentence discounting thus gives rise to a form of plea bargaining called sentence canvassing. Here the defendant's counsel will go to talk to the judge before the trial to ask what the sentence is likely to be if the defendant pleads guilty, and how this would compare with a sentence after a contested trial. This information can then be conveyed to the defendant who may be persuaded to plead guilty. Of course, judges may exaggerate the not guilty sentence in order to induce a guilty plea; to the same end they may also be prepared to offer a lower not guilty sentence than they would normally do, because they know that the defendant is ready for trial but has not yet been persuaded to plead guilty. Sentence canvassing is frowned upon by the Court of Appeal:

Extract 4.3.3

R v Turner [1970] 2 All ER 281, pp 326–327

Before leaving this case, which has brought out into the open the vexed question of so-called 'plea-bargaining,' the court would like to make some observations which may be of help to judges and to counsel and, indeed, solicitors. They are these:

1. Counsel must be completely free to do what is his duty, namely to give the accused the best advice he can and if need be advice in strong terms. This will often include advice that a plea of guilty, showing an element of remorse, is a mitigating factor which may well enable the court to give a lesser sentence than would otherwise be the case. Counsel of course will emphasise that the accused must not plead guilty unless he has committed the acts constituting the offence charged.

2. The accused, having considered counsel's advice, must have a complete freedom of choice whether to plead guilty or not guilty.

3. There must be freedom of access between counsel and judge. Any discussion, however, which takes place must be between the judge and both counsel for the defence and counsel for the prosecution. If a solicitor representing the accused is in the court he should be allowed to attend the discussion if he so desires. This freedom of access is important because there may be matters calling for communication or discussion, which are of such a nature that counsel cannot in the interests of his client mention them in open court. Purely by way of example, counsel for the defence may by way of mitigation wish to tell the judge that the accused has not long to live, is suffering maybe from cancer, of which he is and should remain ignorant. Again, counsel on both sides may wish to discuss with the judge whether it would be proper, in a particular case, for the prosecution to accept a plea to a lesser offence. It is of course imperative that so far as possible justice must be administered in open court. Counsel should, therefore, only ask to see the judge when it is felt to be really necessary, and the judge must be careful only to treat such communications as private where, in fairness to the accused person, this is necessary.

4. The judge should, subject to the one exception referred to hereafter, never indicate the sentence which he is minded to impose. A statement that on a plea of guilty he would impose one sentence but that on a conviction following a plea of not guilty he would impose a severer sentence is one which should never be made. This could be taken to be undue pressure on the accused, thus depriving him of that complete freedom of choice which is essential. Such cases, however, are in the experience of the court happily rare. What on occasions does appear to happen however is that a judge will tell counsel that, having read the depositions and the antecedents, he can safely say that on a plea of guilty he will for instance, make a probation order, something which may be helpful to counsel in advising the accused. The judge in such a case is no doubt careful not to mention what he would do if the accused were convicted following a plea of not guilty. Even so, the accused may well get the impression that the judge is intimating that in that event a severer sentence, maybe a custodial sentence would result, so that again he may feel under pressure. This accordingly must also not be done.

The only exception to this rule is that it should be permissible for a judge to say, if it be the case, that whatever happens, whether the accused pleads guilty or not guilty, the sentence will or will not take a particular form, e.g., a probation order or a fine, or a custodial sentence.

Finally, where any such discussion on sentence has taken place between judge and counsel, counsel for the defence should disclose this to the accused and inform him of what took place.

Despite the Court of Appeal's admonition in *Turner*, sentence canvassing has continued: some judges are prepared to break the rules in order to induce guilty pleas. This judicial deviance is evidenced by a trickle of cases reaching the Court of Appeal, which often has to quash a defendant's conviction where plea bargaining has taken place and the defendant alleges that the deal has not been honoured (e.g. *Pitman* [1991] 1 All ER 468). Their Lordships have despaired that: 'despite frequent observations made in this court discouraging unnecessary visits to the judge's room, they appear to continue up and down the country' (*Smith* [1990] 1 WLR 1311, at p 1314; see also *Grice* (1977) 66 Cr App R 167). On occasion trial judges have allegedly gone so far as to tell counsel that the defendant has no chance of being acquitted (*Cain* [1976] Crim LR 464; *Inns* (1975) 60 Cr App R 231). Other evidence is more anecdotal, but suggests that strong local cultures of sentence canvass exist. Judge Pickles, giving evidence to the Royal Commission on Criminal Procedure in 1979, recounted that:

> Bargains between judges and defendants happen every day. It is in the interests of all concerned that they should ... The practice of Crown Court judges varies widely. Some see counsel in their rooms whenever they are asked. Some refuse to see counsel at all. One judge ... told me that he only sees counsel he can trust ... Some judges send for counsel before the case starts and virtually give directions for 'carving it up' ... Some judges negotiate more subtly, by sending or receiving messages through their clerks or their court clerks ... Judges miss life [at the Bar] and day after day see their former colleagues only across the formal courtroom. It is good to have a chat with the lads. How tempting to sit down and sort it all out sensibly, wigs off ... The tension of open court has gone. The short-hand writer is absent. No press or public. Even the accused – around whose fate it all revolves – is not there ... In this easy atmosphere [the formal rules] can be overlooked in a genuine effort to find a sensible short-cut, off the record. (Quoted in McConville and Baldwin, 1981, p 11; see also Pickles, 1988, pp 126–133 for a frank admission of his willingness to break the *Turner* rules)

Morison and Leith quote a similar remark (this time from a barrister) about varying judicial practices: '... plea bargaining is an art and it's all down to experience as well ... some judges you go into easy enough, some judges are delighted to give you an indication. You have to know by reputation, what you've heard' (1992, p 136). Judges and barristers are certainly unhappy with the strictures of the *Turner* rule. Of those questioned in the Crown Court study, 67 per cent of judges and nearly 90 per cent of barristers said they wanted to see the rule changed (Zander and Henderson, 1993, p 145).

While the Court of Appeal has not been prepared to overrule *Turner*, it has continued to insist that defendants who plead guilty should get the benefit of a substantial sentence discount. The court appears to favour a reduction of a quarter to a third, and research suggests that in practice guilty pleaders gain a reduction of some 22 per cent in the Crown Court (Moxon, 1988, p 32), though there is variation between courts (Robertshaw and Milne, 1992). There is evidence that the sentence discount operates across the custody threshold. Hood, in his research on race and sentencing, was able to calculate the effect of plea on risk of custody in his research area (the Midlands):

Holding all the variables constant, a not guilty plea was associated, over the whole range of cases, with an increased odds of receiving a custodial sentence, on average, of 1.7. . . . To put this in more graphical terms, an offender whose characteristics (other than plea) would predict a 50 per cent probability of a custodial sentence would, if he pleaded not guilty, have this predicted probability raised to 62 per cent. If the probability were 75 per cent it would be increased to 84 per cent. (Hood, 1994, p 87)

The sentence discount has now been recognised by statute in the Criminal Justice and Public Order Act 1994:

48. Reduction in sentences for guilty pleas

(1) In determining what sentence to pass on an offender who has pleaded guilty to an offence in proceedings before that or another court a court shall take into account –
> (a) the stage in the proceedings for the offence at which the offender indicated his intention to plead guilty, and
> (b) the circumstances in which this indication was given.

(2) If, as a result of taking into account any matter referred to in subsection (1) above, the court imposes a punishment on the offender which is less severe than the punishment it would otherwise have imposed, it shall state in open court that it has done so.

This may serve to make the practice of offering a discount to guilty pleaders more open and more uniform.

The report of a working party set up by the General Council of the Bar (Seabrook, 1992) recommended that the *Turner* rule be abolished, thus allowing official sentence canvassing. The Seabrook recommendations were broadly adopted by the Royal Commission on Criminal Justice (RCCJ). Both bodies linked the problem of pleas to another problem: that of 'cracked trials'. A trial is said to crack where a defendant changes his or her plea from not guilty to guilty at the last minute. Cracked trials cause problems for the administration of justice, because they will have been listed as contested cases, and court clerks will have allocated judges and court time on that basis. Where a case cracks on the day of the trial, witnesses may turn up at court, only to be told that they are no longer needed. The Crown Court Study, commissioned for the RCCJ, found that 26 per cent of all cases, and 43 per cent of cases not listed as guilty pleas, cracked. For this reason, the Seabrook working party and the RCCJ both recommended the institution of a system of graduated sentence discounts. The full discount would only be awarded to those who pleaded guilty at the first available opportunity; those who pleaded guilty at a later stage would receive a smaller discount, and those who waited until the last minute would only get a minimal sentence discount (see now the Criminal Justice and Public Order Act 1994, s 48, above). The graduated sentence discount would be combined with the opportunity to canvass the judge on the likely sentence. The RCCJ's sentence canvass recommendations follow:

Extract 4.3.4

Royal Commission on Criminal Justice, *Report* (1993) Ch 7, paras 50–52 (footnotes omitted)

50.   Many witnesses, particularly from the judiciary and the Bar, urged on us the desirability of reverting, in essence, to the system as it applied before the judgment in the case of *Turner*. The Crown Court Study also showed that, among the judges and barristers who responded, there was overwhelming support for change. We do not support a total reversal of the judgment in *Turner*, since we agree that to face defendants with a choice between what they might get on an immediate plea of guilty and what they might get if found guilty by the jury does amount to unacceptable pressure. But the effect of *Turner* and related judgments appears to have been to make judges reluctant to discuss sentence with counsel at all. We think that there is a case for a change of approach. We recommend that, at the request of defence counsel on instructions from the defendant, judges should be able to indicate the highest sentence that they would impose at that point on the basis of the facts as put to them. A request for such an indication might be made at a preparatory hearing, at a hearing called specially for this purpose, or at the trial itself.

51.   We envisage that the procedure which we recommend would be initiated solely by, and for the benefit of, defendants who wish to exercise a right to be told the consequence of a decision which is theirs alone. Where a defendant would need the protection of an appropriate adult during inquiries carried out at a police station, the system must be operated with particular care. The sentence 'canvass', as we have called it, should normally take place in the judge's chambers with both sides being represented by counsel. A shorthand writer should also be present. If none is available a member of the court staff should take a note to be agreed immediately by the judge and both counsel. The judge may give the answer to the question 'what would be the maximum sentence if my client were to plead guilty at this stage?' but to no other. The judge's indication should be based on brief statements from prosecution and defence of all the relevant circumstances, which should include details of the defendant's previous convictions if any and, if available, any pre-sentence report required by the Criminal Justice Act 1991.

52.   We emphasise that a judge should not be required to give an indication of the maximum sentence that would be imposed if he or she felt that to do so would be for any reason inappropriate. But we do not see the absence of a pre-sentence report as normally ruling out such an indication. The fact that the indication concerns maximum sentence leaves room for the pre-sentence report when available to be taken into account in mitigation. More likely reasons for the judge declining to give an indication of likely maximum sentence might be because there were co-defendants, or because the judge wished to defer the decision until more information had been obtained. In the case of co-defendants, if only one has instructed counsel to canvass sentence, the judge may take the view that that defendant's role is not identifiable until some or all of the evidence has been heard.

Insofar as concern about cracked trials was a motivating factor behind these proposals, there may be other solutions to the problem. The Crown Court Study highlighted a great degree of late case preparation, and this certainly contributes to the cracked trial problem (51 per cent of prosecution barristers, and 31 per cent of defence barristers only got their brief on the day of, or the day before, the hearing). The study found that late guilty pleas were rarely due to defendants simply changing their minds (only 6 per cent of cracked cases); in 78 per cent of cases it was due to advice from a solicitor or counsel, or due to a change in the prosecution's approach. It is barristers who are in the best position to give defendants realistic advice on their chances of conviction at trial; if this advice is not forthcoming until a very late stage, defendants cannot be blamed for delaying their final decision on plea. Yet in 60 per cent of cases, defendants met their barrister for the first time on the day of trial (Zander and Henderson, 1993, pp 30, 62, 150; see also JUSTICE, 1993). Therefore, earlier case preparation may be a more appropriate solution to the cracked trial problem than a system which would function by putting more pressure on defendants to plead guilty.

It should also be noted that ss 17A–17C of the Magistrates' Courts Act 1980, discussed above, will have an effect on cracked trials, because these sections allow defendants in either way cases to indicate their plea at the mode of trial hearing. Although defendants who indicate an intention to plead not guilty at the mode of trial hearing will be free to change their plea at a later stage, it is presumed that they will receive a reduced discount for doing so. However, our discussion of charge bargaining practices sheds new light on this and on the cracked trials problem. In Hedderman and Moxon's research, defendants who changed their intention as to plea after the mode of trial hearing were asked why they had done so: 51 per cent said that it was because they expected some charges to be dropped or reduced, resulting in a lighter sentence (1992, p 24). If, as would seem probable, this represents a large number of charge bargains offered to defendants at a late stage, then cracked trials would be the inevitable result. The suspicion that there is a connection between cracked trials and charge bargaining is supported by the Crown Court Study (Zander and Henderson, 1993). In 77 per cent of cases which cracked the Crown Prosecution Service said that charges had been reduced or dropped (Zander and Henderson, 1993, p 154). This suggests that defendants have a good reason for delaying their decision to plead guilty: they know that the prosecution may be tempted to do a deal and they will benefit from a conviction for a less serious charge. The effectiveness of ss 17A–17C in tackling the mode of trial problem will be diminished to the extent that defendants gamble on a late charge reduction, and this also raises questions about the system of graduated sentence discounts on which the effectiveness of the new scheme depends. Will defendants receive the full discount if, some time after the mode of trial hearing, they plead guilty in response to an offer to drop or reduce charges?

Other criticisms of the RCCJ and Seabrook recommendations need to be seen in the context of the more fundamental problems of plea bargaining practices in general. We have seen that plea bargaining and the sentence discount tend to benefit the criminal justice system by reducing the number of contested cases. The encouragement of guilty pleas may benefit victims by sparing them the ordeal of a court appearance; however, it may also be upsetting for a victim to see the label attached to an offender's wrongdoing downgraded in the interests of the smooth administration of justice. Plea bargaining and the sentence discount can obviously be to the advantage of some defendants: they will benefit from a reduced sentence. However, practices which encourage guilty pleas also operate to the detriment of defendants. The advantage conferred by the guilty plea is bought at the cost of not contesting some or all charges, charges which the defendant always has a chance of being found not guilty of (the Crown Court Study found that 26 per cent of defendants who pleaded guilty at a late stage had a good or fairly good chance of acquittal (Zander and Henderson, 1993, pp 156–157)). Is this too high a price for the criminal justice system to pay? Does the system inevitably result in improper pressure being placed on defendants?

The RCCJ admitted that 'it would be naive to suppose that innocent persons never plead guilty because of the prospect of the sentence discount' (1993, Ch 7, para 42). However, the Commission was prepared to trade off that risk in a stark calculation: 'Against the risk that defendants may be tempted to plead guilty to charges of which they are not guilty must be weighed the benefits to the system and to defendants of encouraging those who are in fact guilty to plead guilty' (1993, Ch 7, para 45). It is impossible to quantify the number of innocent people who may plead guilty in order to gain some benefit. The Crown Court Study questionnaire asked barristers whether they thought that their client had pleaded guilty when innocent: 53 answered 'yes'. Rounded up this would suggest 1,400 Crown Court cases a year where innocent people plead guilty in order to gain some perceived advantage (Zander and Henderson, 1993, p 139). However, it has been questioned whether the facts of these cases really do suggest that the defendants were innocent (see Zander, 1993 and the reply by McConville and Bridges, 1993).

While the dangers of plea bargaining can never be precisely quantified, there is evidence of the debilitating effects that incitements to plead guilty have on the relationship between defendants and their advisers. While carrying out a research project on Crown Court trials, Baldwin and McConville became interested in the large numbers of defendants who changed their plea to guilty at the last minute. They found that while 30 per cent of such defendants decided to change plea of their own accord, the majority had done so owing to pressure from their barrister or in order to take advantage of a plea bargain offered by the judge. The authors questioned whether the majority of defendants who changed their pleas could really be said to be doing so voluntarily. The authors' findings are best illustrated with quotations from the defendants they interviewed:

Extract 4.3.5

J Baldwin and M McConville, *Negotiated Justice* (1977) pp 32–33, 49–50

The judge sent for my barrister and the prosecution and said, 'As the case stands at the moment I'll be more inclined to give your defendant a suspended sentence but if he goes on pleading not guilty he will go to prison.' So when the barrister told me this I pleaded guilty. I believe it was because the judge didn't want the trial to go on and me to start saying anything against the police.

The barrister came back from seeing the judge and said, 'Well, the judge says we can argue as long as you like but you'll be found guilty anyway.' So I said, 'Where the hell do I stand here?' He said, 'We don't deal in the truth, we deal in facts.' I said, 'Well, British Justice is up the wall.' That really sickened me off completely did that. But what could I do? I think I was more forced into it than anything, personally. I was flogging a dead horse. I mean the judge had made up his mind before I even walked through the door.

I was really forced to plead guilty. I was feeling pleased because the witnesses didn't say much about me in their evidence; only one or two of them did and one of these said, 'It was just a few pounds.' But then my barrister and solicitor took me down below and they said, 'Look, you've got no chance, so you will plead guilty.' I said, 'I don't want to plead guilty, they are very bad charges against me and I didn't assault her and it was only a few quid.' The barrister then said, 'If you're found guilty you will get about 10 or 15 years but if you plead guilty you will get 4 or 5 years.' I was really shocked. I was so scared, sweating and nervous and he frightened me with this 10–15 years stuff and saying I had no chance. They then talked to my mother and frightened her as well. They brought her down to see me and they persuaded her and she said, 'if they think you are going to get 10–15 years if you plead not guilty you might as well plead guilty.' I agreed to plead guilty but it wasn't really my decision; I had no choice about it. I was very frightened by everything. It was a split second decision; I had to make a decision then and there, when I was very nervous and scared by 10–15 years.

My barrister compelled me to plead guilty. He threatened me saying, 'You will go to gaol for three years if you plead not guilty, the case will go on for a long time and you will have to pay the expenses which will come to £400. But if you plead guilty you will just get a fine.' He wouldn't listen to what I had to say; he compelled me to plead guilty.

It is obvious that in practice plea bargaining, whether it takes the form of reduced charges or the promise of a reduced sentence, does put pressure on defendants to plead guilty. This not only throws a critical light on the recommendations of Seabrook and the RCCJ; it may also lead us to ask whether the sentence discount itself can be justified. The discount, which can be up to 30 per cent for a timely guilty plea, can certainly not be ignored as a source of pressure on defendants. It is difficult to reconcile the discount with the Court of Appeal's warnings in *Turner* that to tell defendants explicitly of the differential between a guilty and not guilty sentence would be to place them under 'undue pressure' ([1970] 2 QB 321, at p 327). Can the sentence discount be justified? It is easy to regard the discount as an awkward fact of life: something that, while difficult to justify in principle, must be accepted, because if there was no discount everyone would plead not guilty and the system would collapse. But a system with no discount is not inconceivable. Although drawing comparisons with other jurisdictions can be problematic, Ashworth has pointed out that senior Scottish judges do not endorse a sentence discount, regarding it as irreconcilable with the presumption of innocence:

> It would be quite unacceptable that, in a legal system which presumes innocence and which permits every person to go to trial, a person who was found guilty after trial should be punished more severely simply because he had not pled guilty. (Sheriff-Principal Nicholson, quoted in Ashworth, 1993, p 837)

On the Scottish system, see further Moody and Tombs (1983), an article which suggests that charge bargaining plays a significant role in securing guilty pleas in Scotland.

Duff has suggested that inducements to plead guilty also devalue the plea of guilty:

> [A] guilty plea should properly express the defendant's recognition, and voluntary admission, of her guilt; it is *that* kind of admission which the court or police may properly seek from the defendant, or urge on her by citing the relevant reasons which justify the claim that she ought to plead guilty if she is guilty. But if we obtain a guilty plea by offering her irrelevant and improper inducements or threats, which are meant to provide her with a purely prudential motive for pleading guilty, that plea loses its meaning and its value; and we no longer address or respect her as a rational agent. Such induced guilty pleas . . . should have no place in a just and rational criminal process; for they are destructive of its proper ends and values. (Duff, 1986, p 141)

Another problematic aspect of the sentencing discount is that it may be discriminatory. It will discriminate against certain categories of offender: those found guilty of crimes with a mandatory sentence can receive no discount (at present the life sentence for murder is the only truly mandatory sentence, but s 2 of the Crime (Sentences) Act 1997 imposes a mandatory sentence of life imprisonment on defendants convicted of a second serious offence, as defined in the Act, unless there are exceptional circumstances). The Court of Appeal has also held that in certain situations no discount should be given, one example being where the defendant was caught red handed (*Morris* (1988) 10 Cr App R (S) 216). This exception is difficult to justify: a person arrested while committing an offence may have little to bargain with, but is this really a reason for sentencing him or her differently to the person against whom there is only equivocal evidence? There is also evidence that the sentence discount indirectly discriminates against black defendants. Hood's study found that 23 per cent of blacks pleaded not guilty at trial as opposed to 11 per cent of whites (Hood, 1994, p 51). A greater proportion of blacks than whites are penalised for contesting their cases.

4. CROWN COURT TRIALS

(a) The jury

In contested Crown Court trials, questions of fact are decided by a jury, a panel of 12 lay people drawn from the court's local area. Trial by jury has a long history, and during that history the functions and composition of the jury have changed. Before examining the modern jury in more detail, it is worth pausing to consider some of the significant changes that have occurred this century, as well as differences between jury trial in different jurisdictions.

At the beginning of this century the jury was not an especially representative body. Women were allowed to sit on juries in 1919, but the jury remained a 'male, middle-minded and middle-class affair' (Devlin, 1976, p 20), largely because there was a requirement that jurors be property owners and this effectively excluded women and the poorer members of society. The property qualification was only removed in 1972, when the minimum age for jury service was also lowered from 21 to 18. From 1972 potential jurors have been chosen from the electoral register, but this does not mean that the jury which comes to try a particular case will be a random selection of people. As we shall see, there are various reasons why a particular jury may not be very representative of the community. In the context of this brief historical sketch, it is worth noting that until 1988 the defence had the right of 'peremptory challenge', that is it could demand that up to three jurors be removed from the jury without giving any reasons for its choice. Probably the most important change in the operation of the jury since the war came in 1967 with the abolition of the requirement that verdicts be unanimous. Since then, a jury has been able to return a verdict when only 10 of its members are in agreement ('majority verdicts' occur in about 12 per cent of cases). If 10 jurors cannot agree on a verdict of either guilty or not guilty, then the jury is said to be 'hung' and the defendant may be retried by a different jury (the Crown Court Study suggests that 3–4 per cent of cases result in a hung jury (Zander and Henderson, 1993, p 159)).

Turning to look at jurisdictional variation, we find that the English model is not the only way in which lay participation in serious criminal cases can be achieved. For example, in the French *Cour d'Assises*, a jury of nine lay people sits with three judges; decisions are by a majority of eight. Several German courts use a mixture of lay and professional judges. In the United States the Federal jurisdiction and the majority of states require a unanimous verdict.

The High Court of Australia has also held jury unanimity to be a constitutional requirement (see the interesting discussion of the principle in *Cheadle v R* (1993) 177 CLR 541). Some American states have, at times, experimented with juries of only six people. A notable feature of the jury system in most Commonwealth countries is that defendants are able to waive their right to trial by jury and to opt for trial by judge alone. The Crown Court Study found that, given a choice, 30 per cent of English defendants would have chosen trial by judge alone (Zander and Henderson, 1993, p 172; see further Jackson and Doran, 1997).

Closer to home, in Northern Ireland since 1973 some offences have been tried by a judge sitting alone: these so called Diplock courts were a response to fears of 'jury nobbling' in terrorist trials. In Scotland, juries have 15 members; a majority of eight is required for a guilty verdict, but, as well as guilty and not guilty verdicts, the jury may also return a verdict of 'not proven'. However, if the jury cannot agree on one of these three verdicts, the defendant is acquitted and may not be retried. Maher has used the context of the Scottish jury and its voting patterns to question the procedures governing the English jury and the constitution of its verdicts:

<hr>

Extract 4.4.1

<hr>

G Maher, 'The Verdict of the Jury' in M Findlay and P Duff (eds), *The Jury Under Attack* (1988) pp 45–46, 47–49, 50–52

Majority verdicts and proof of guilt beyond reasonable doubt

It is generally accepted that the appropriate standard of proof in the criminal process, at least as far as proof of the guilt of an accused person is concerned, is proof beyond reasonable doubt (see Maher, 1983a) ['Reasonable Doubt and the Jury' (1983) *Scots Law Times* (*News*) 97]. This principle is one which has many defenders and few, if any, outright opponents. However, it has been argued (Freeman ['The Jury on Trial' (1981) *Current Legal Problems* 65]) that the change in the unanimity rule in English law has led to the weakening of the effect of the principle of proof of guilt beyond reasonable doubt. Where, it is suggested, the prosecution has failed to convince all members of a jury that the accused is guilty, then the jury as a collective body must be said to have a doubt about the guilt of the accused. Therefore a criminal process does not take sufficient account of proof of guilt beyond reasonable doubt where the unanimity rule for the constitution of a jury verdict does not apply.

Now, if this argument is correct as far as English law is concerned since 1967, then it is *a fortiori* true in respect of Scots law, for in Scotland unanimity has never been required for a jury verdict and for some considerable time the present rule has applied that a jury can return a verdict of guilty even when only eight out of a jury of 15 vote for conviction. But is the argument about the weight of the principle of proof of guilt beyond reasonable doubt as *requiring* jury unanimity correct? . . .

389

What is being argued here is that the ways in which we can understand the idea of practical certainty in relation to a group judgment depends on the size of the group in question. It is a general feature of group decision making that the larger the size of the group the more acceptable a majority outcome and the less the need for unanimity. There are several bases for this view but one of the more important is the idea that a large group is more representative of society in general, whereas a small group is less so.

Take first of all the question of the size of the jury. As we noted earlier this is a matter on which the rules of English and Scots law diverge and in Scots law a guilty verdict can be returned where eight members of a jury (of 15) vote for conviction, whereas in England a guilty verdict requires at least 10 votes (from a jury of 12). What is the important element here? Is it the total number of votes cast for the guilty verdict, in which case there is not that much difference between Scots and English law? Or is it the ratio of guilty votes to not guilty votes, in which case there are radical differences between the two legal systems? It is difficult to see why it should be the case that all that is required is unanimity no matter the size of the jury.

Consider the situation where one member of a jury of 12 in number is unable to continue to serve as a juror. The jury continues with 11 members who all vote for the conviction of the accused. Does it follow that because only 11 members of the jury believe in the guilt of the accused, then guilt beyond reasonable doubt has not been established? In these circumstances, English law says that a conviction can nonetheless be returned. The view can be defended on the basis that the missing member of the jury no longer counts as a juror and so does not have to be convinced of guilt, and that the verdict of the remaining jurors is still an unanimous verdict. But it is not clear why unanimity by itself should be vital in these circumstances. Are there any differences from the case instanced and that where a jury of 12 divided 11–1 on guilt? After all, a defendant can always argue that although 12 members of the jury were convinced of his guilt this does not indicate proof of guilt beyond reasonable doubt because if the jury had been 15 or 20 in size, there would not have been unanimity within the larger group, and thus proof beyond reasonable doubt would not have been reached. But such an argument about the *necessity* of unanimity to establish proof beyond reasonable doubt can be repeated for any size of jury. Thus even if we were to require unanimity for juries 120 members in size, a jury of 121 might still give rise to one dissentient and the fact of such disagreement would negate proof of guilt beyond reasonable doubt. Unanimity by itself does not appear to be a requirement of proof beyond reasonable doubt. Rather, the need for unanimity becomes greater the smaller the size of the jury but has less force the greater the size of the jury.

This position is reflected in a number of existing legal rules. It is implicit in the decision of the United States Supreme Court of *Johnson v Louisiana* 406 US 356 at 332 (1972) where the majority of the court upheld the validity of a conviction under State law according to which a jury verdict was competent on the basis of a 9 from 12 majority decision. The court held that this rule did not in itself contravene proof of guilt beyond reasonable doubt and added that although the prosecutor's case could be regarded as more certain if it had persuaded all 12 jurors, it would have been more certain still if it had been required to [convince] and had in fact convinced 24 or 36 jurors. The general position was explicitly adopted in Scotland during wartime provisions (*Administration of Justice (Emergency Provisions) (Scotland) Act* 1939, s 3) when juries were reduced in size from 15 (when eight votes for guilt suffices for a guilty verdict) to seven in number but a verdict of guilty required five votes (see *MacKay v H M Advocate* 1945 SLT 97).

However the argument that a unanimity rule can be relaxed where the size of the jury increases holds only on the assumption that the larger the jury the more representative it is of the community as a whole. It may be that in Scotland jury selection does operate in a way which ensures a better representation of different sections of the community than is said to occur in other countries but it is nonetheless difficult to avoid the conclusion that the rule of Scots law which allows guilty verdicts of eight votes from a jury of 15 does not give sufficient weight to the principle of proof of guilt beyond reasonable doubt. But it does not follow that Scots law must adopt a unanimity rule that all 15 members of a jury must vote for conviction before it can be asserted that guilt has been proved beyond reasonable doubt.

Once we accept that unanimity is not a prerequisite of proof of guilt beyond reasonable doubt, the question then becomes one of the weight to be accorded that principle in determining the voting pattern for juries to reach a verdict of guilty. One consideration has already been mentioned, namely that the greater the size of the jury the less need there is for unanimity in arriving at a verdict. Conversely the smaller the size of the jury the greater is the need for unanimity. But another factor concerning the weight of proof of guilt beyond reasonable doubt arises from the general context of the criminal process in which trial by jury operates. The principle of proof of guilt beyond reasonable doubt has the effect of giving the accused a right whereby he cannot be convicted unless guilt is established at a certain level of probability, namely that of practical certainty. But allowing jury verdicts to be constituted by majority decision weakens the force of this principle and a degree of weakening may arise which denies to the accused the right to which he is entitled by the principle of proof beyond reasonable doubt. However, a non-unanimous verdict will still cohere with the accused's right to proof of guilt at a level of practical certainty, where the criminal process provides other means of ensuring that particular level of proof. One example often cited in this context is from Scotland where the rule of Scots law that a guilty verdict from a jury can be based on a 8–7 majority is defended by the argument that the accused derives further benefits and safeguards, namely from the existence of the not proven verdict and the general requirement of corroboration of the Crown case (see e.g. Thomson Committee, 1975 [*Criminal Procedure in Scotland (2nd Report)* Cmnd 6218 (London: HMSO)] para 51–12 but also see Maher, 1983a) . . .

To sum up this part of the argument, it can be said that insisting on an unanimity rule is not always necessary in order to show that the principle of proof of the guilt of the accused beyond reasonable doubt is being taken seriously. For if a jury is large in size and is also representative of the community or society in general, then some relaxation of the rule may not frustrate the purpose of the principle which is to give the accused a right not to be convicted of a charge unless the case against him has been made out at a level

391

of practical certainty. The rule of unanimity may also be relaxed where this right receives adequate protection by other means, such as a rule of corroboration of prosecution evidence. But it can be said that if no such other safeguards exist for an accused then jury verdicts must be unanimous, or be near to unanimity, if the accused's right to proof of his guilt at the level of practical certainty is to be upheld ...

The symmetry rule and the presumption of innocence

... [A] feature of trial by jury which, somewhat surprisingly, has remained largely unexplored and is represented in the rule of English law that the constitution of a jury verdict for acquittal is identical to that of the constitution of a verdict for conviction, so that as a consequence, the jury can at times fail to reach a verdict at all. For example, in English law where a jury divides 9–3, even where the nine votes are for not guilty, the effect is that the accused is denied a not guilty verdict and may be tried again on exactly the same charge.

The trouble with this situation is that it does not cohere easily with the presumption of innocence or with the associated principle of double jeopardy (see Maher ['Jury Verdicts and the Presumption of Innocence' (1983) 3 *Legal Studies* 146]). The effect of the presumption of innocence, as expressed in the classic words of Viscount Sankey LC in *Woolmington v DPP* [1935] AC 462 at 481 is to give the accused the right to be acquitted, even if he has not proved his own innocence, where for any reason the prosecution does not prove his guilt. The presumption of innocence therefore closes the logical space between proof of guilt and proof of innocence, that is where neither guilt nor innocence has been established. The effect of the presumption of innocence is to treat as if on the same level both the situation where the accused has positively proved his innocence and that where the prosecution has failed to prove his guilt. In both situations, the accused is entitled to an acquittal.

Why this should be so can be found in the very nature of presumptions such as the presumption of innocence. According to Cross, the presumption of innocence is an example of that category of presumption whose effect is that a certain conclusion must be drawn until the contrary is proved [R Cross, *Evidence*, C Tapper (ed) (London: Butterworths, 6th ed, 1985) pp 131–132]. Thus it is crucial to the present argument to note that such presumptions are *determinative* of the issue to which they apply. If the contrary is proved, the presumption is rebutted and does not apply; if the contrary is not proved, the presumption remains applicable. The issue in a criminal trial which calls for proof is the guilt of the accused. Where the prosecution satisfactorily establishes guilt, the presumption of innocence is rebutted but it remains operative in all other circumstances. Accordingly it is impossible to apply the presumption of innocence to a criminal charge and at the end of the case leave the issue of guilt or innocence undetermined. But this is exactly the situation brought about by the failure of English law to acquit the accused whenever a jury cannot agree on his guilt.

It might be thought that the verdict of not proven in Scots law flies in the face of interpreting the presumption of innocence in this way, for the effect of the not proven verdict is not to provide the accused, against whom the prosecution has failed to make its case, with a clear-cut verdict of innocence. True, the not proven verdict results in an acquittal and also makes the charge to which it relates *res iudicata*. Nevertheless it is a form of second class acquittal which does not give full recognition of the accused's right to acquittal where his guilt has not been proved. But all that needs to be concluded from the existence of the not proven verdict in Scots law is that the presumption of innocence provides good grounds for recognising that the verdict is an historical anomaly which should be removed from the range of verdicts available in Scottish criminal trials.

As regards the English rule of symmetry in the constitution of jury verdicts of guilty and not guilty, a potential defence of the rule is to argue that where a jury fails to reach a decision, then the trial has not been completed and accordingly the full force of the presumption does not come into play. But this argument begs the question being asked. Once the stage is reached where all that remains is for the jury to decide upon its verdict, then the case by the Crown against the accused has ended, the evidence has been heard, and there is nothing to prevent the presumption from coming fully into play. If this evidence convinces the jury beyond reasonable doubt that the accused is guilty the jury should convict, but if the evidence does not so convince the jury it should acquit him. But in the situation where a jury cannot agree on its verdict, the prosecution has already had its time in court, and by definition if the prosecution case has not convinced the jury of the guilt of the accused, it follows that proof of his guilt has failed. Accordingly, the presumption of innocence dictates that the accused is entitled to his right to acquittal.

A better defence of the present rule on the constitution of jury verdicts in English law is that to allow failure by a jury to convict an accused to have the automatic result of his acquittal (even if say the jury divided 9–3 with the majority voting for guilt) would be to give the presumption of innocence too much weight (see Maher, 1983b: 156–7). It was noted earlier when discussing the principle of proof of guilt beyond reasonable doubt and the Scottish rules on constitution of jury verdicts that the issue of finding the appropriate weight of even fundamental principles of the criminal process does not necessarily lead to giving such principles total weight in all circumstances. It was argued in that earlier context that what must be done is to identify the right or rights which the principle seeks to protect and ask how that principle can withstand modification in a given context provided that the rights at its base still receive as equally strong protection by other means. But the objection to the present rule of English law is not that it gives too little weight to the presumption of innocence but rather that it gives no weight at all to that principle. It is perverse to argue that because a principle, such as the presumption of innocence, can be given too much weight therefore it should be given no weight at all. But English law could modify its rules about jury verdicts so as to recognise this fundamental principle without giving the presumption of innocence too much weight. For example it could adopt something like the position of Scots law and lower the majority needed to constitute a jury verdict of guilty (say to 8 from 12) but give the accused other forms of protection against unjust convictions (such as a general requirement of corroboration of prosecution evidence) and also recognise the right of the accused to be acquitted in all cases where the jury fail to reach the requisite majority for guilt. Perhaps what is surprising in recent debates about trial by jury in England is that this issue has not been discussed at all.

In his conclusion, Maher notes that his arguments draw on a conception of the trial that sees the accused as having certain fundamental rights, such as the right to be presumed innocent until proven guilty. He suggests that the failure of commentators to challenge features of trial by jury such as the symmetry rule may reflect a more general reluctance to think of the criminal process in terms of rights.

In general, juries are selected randomly from the area in which the trial takes place. There are, however, several reasons why the jury which finally comes to try a case may differ in composition from one that would be produced by a truly random selection. Most courts have a system for choosing names at random from the electoral register, but this does not ensure a completely random choice. There is some evidence that ethnic minorities are under-represented on the electoral register. Furthermore, a court may decide not to call jurors from a certain part of the jury catchment area on the grounds that jurors from that area have too far to travel, while other potential jurors may be excluded because their local council fails to send its electoral register to the court (Robertshaw, Cox and Van Hoen, 1992). The vagaries of the selection process apart, even those summoned by the court may not end up sitting on a jury. Some people are disqualified from jury service, notably those with recent or serious criminal convictions, lawyers and members of the clergy (Juries Act 1974, Sched 1). Others may request excusal from jury service if they show good reasons why it will be a particular burden on them (see Juries Act 1974, s 9(2) and *Practice Direction (Jury Service: Excusal)* [1988] 1 WLR 1162). Thus those who have demanding commitments – for example, caring for children or running their own businesses – will often be able to avoid jury service. It has been suggested that this has led to an over-representation of unemployed people and manual workers on juries (see *The Times*, 25 October 1988, reporting a survey by the Criminal Bar Association). More recent and thorough information about the make-up of juries is contained in the Crown Court Study. This suggests a slight under-representation of women (47 per cent of jurors as compared to 52 per cent of the population as a whole), but the occupational status of jurors was a fairly close match to that of the population as a whole.

Once a panel of jurors has been selected, prosecution or defence may seek to have certain jurors removed from the panel before the trial begins. Either side may challenge a juror for cause, that is, if it can show good reasons for having that juror excluded, such as that the juror knows the defendant. However, neither side is allowed to question jurors before challenging them in order to establish cause. Until 1989 the defence also had the right of peremptory challenge, which enabled it to ask up to three jurors to stand down without giving reasons. After much criticism, the peremptory challenge was abolished by the Criminal Justice Act 1988, s 118 (though there was little evidence that the peremptory challenge led to any advantages for defendants: research suggested that there were slightly higher conviction rates in cases where the challenge had been used: see Vennard and Riley (1988)). Although the prosecution has no right of peremptory challenge, it may 'stand-by' any number of jurors which amounts to the same thing. The use of this power caused controversy in the late 1970s when it was revealed that in a number of cases juries had secretly been vetted in order to allow the prosecution to stand by jurors who were deemed unsuitable (see Duff and Findlay, 1983). Jury vetting and the prosecution's stand-by should now only be used in circumstances laid down in guidelines issued by the Attorney General:

Extract 4.4.2

Attorney General's Guidelines on Jury Vetting and the Prosecution's Stand-by

Exercise by the Crown of its right of stand-by

5.   The circumstances in which it would be proper for the Crown to exercise its right to stand by a member of a jury panel are: (a) where a jury check authorised in accordance with the Attorney-General's guidelines on jury checks reveals information justifying exercise of the right to stand by in accordance with para 9 of the guidelines and the Attorney-General personally authorises the exercise of the right to stand by; or (b) where a person is about to be sworn as a juror who is manifestly unsuitable and the defence agree that, accordingly, the exercise by the prosecution of the right to stand by would be appropriate. An example of the sort of *exceptional* circumstances which might justify stand-by is where it becomes apparent that, despite the provisions mentioned in para 4 above, a juror selected for service to try a complex case is in fact illiterate.

Jury checks

3.   There are, however, certain exceptional types of case of public importance for which the provisions as to majority verdicts and the disqualification of jurors may not be sufficient to ensure the proper administration of justice. In such cases it is in the interests of both justice and the public that there should be further safeguards against the possibility of bias and in such cases checks which go beyond the investigation of criminal records may be necessary.

4.   These classes of case may be defined broadly as (a) cases in which national security is involved and part of the evidence is likely to be heard in camera, and (b) terrorist cases.

5.   The particular aspects of these cases which may make it desirable to seek extra precautions are (a) in security cases a danger that a juror, either voluntarily or under pressure, may make an improper use of evidence which,

because of its sensitivity, has been given in camera, (b) in both security and terrorist cases the danger that a juror's political beliefs are so biased as to go beyond normally reflecting the broad spectrum of views and interests in the community to reflect the extreme views of sectarian interest or pressure group to a degree which might interfere with his fair assessment of the facts of the case or lead him to exert improper pressure on his fellow jurors.

6. In order to ascertain whether in exceptional circumstances of the above nature either of these factors might seriously influence a potential juror's impartial performance of his duties or his respecting the secrecy of evidence given in camera, it may be necessary to conduct a limited investigation of the panel. In general, such further investigation beyond one of criminal records made for disqualifications may only be made with the records of police Special Branches. However, in cases falling under para 4(a) above (security cases), the investigation may, additionally, involve the security services. No checks other than on these sources and no general inquiries are to be made save to the limited extent that they may be needed to confirm the identity of a juror about whom the initial check has raised serious doubts.

7. No further investigation, as described in para 6 above, should be made save with the personal authority of the Attorney-General on the application of the Director of Public Prosecutions and such checks are hereafter referred to as 'authorised checks'. When a chief officer of police has reason to believe that it is likely that an authorised check may be desirable and proper in accordance with these guidelines he should refer the matter to the Director of Public Prosecutions with a view to his having the conduct of the prosecution from an early stage. The Director will make any appropriate application to the Attorney-General.

8. The result of any authorised check will be sent to the Director of Public Prosecutions. The Director will then decide, having regard to the matters set out in para 5 above, what information ought to be brought to the attention of prosecuting counsel.

9. No right of stand-by should be exercised by counsel for the Crown on the basis of information obtained as a result of an authorised check save with the personal authority of the Attorney-General and unless the information is such as, having regard to the facts of the case and the offences charged, to afford strong reason for believing that a particular juror might be a security risk, be susceptible to improper approaches or be influenced in arriving at a verdict for the reasons given above.

It is accepted that the police may need to run a check on jurors where it is suspected that a person who is disqualified under the Juries Act 1974 might sit on a jury panel (*Mason* [1980] 3 All ER 777). Jury vetting continues to be carried out in 'sensitive' cases: in *McCann, Cullen and Shanahan* (1990) 92 Cr App R 239, a case involving allegations of terrorist activity, the jury was vetted. The defence's argument that vetting was unconstitutional was rejected by the Court of Appeal.

Should there be more general exceptions to the principle of random selection? This question has recently received attention in the context of race. Even a perfectly randomly selected jury will not necessarily be statistically representative of the community in which a case is tried. The Crown Court Study found that, overall, the percentage of jurors from ethnic minorities roughly corresponded to the size of each minority in the population as a whole (Zander and Henderson, 1993, p 243). However, the majority of juries – 65 per cent – were all white, so many black defendants will be tried by all white juries, even in racially mixed areas (there will also occasionally be single sex juries: the Crown Court Study found that 0.1 per cent of juries were all male and 0.3 per cent all female). Are black defendants who are tried by all white juries really tried, as the rhetoric demands, by a jury of their peers? Before 1989 defendants in such situations could attempt to get a black person on their jury by using their right to peremptory challenge, but this is no longer possible. Some judges have been sympathetic to black defendants who have attempted to secure a racially mixed jury. Judges have used their own right to stand by jurors until a racial mix is achieved (*Binns* [1982] Crim LR 522), or have moved the trial to an area where a racially mixed jury is more likely to be chosen (*Broderick* [1970] Crim LR 155). The Court of Appeal has now expressed its disapproval of such practices:

Extract 4.4.3

R v Ford [1989] 3 All ER 445, pp 446–450

We deal first of all with the fact that the judge refused the application for a multiracial jury.

This is a problem which has arisen more than once in recent months, and it is likely to be a problem that will arise again. Consequently it seems to us that it is necessary to give careful thought to the way in which a judge should approach the problem.

At common law a judge has a residual discretion to discharge a particular juror who ought not to be serving on the jury. This is part of the judge's duty to ensure that there is a fair trial. It is based on a duty of the judge expressed by Lord Campbell CJ in *Mansell v R* (1857) 8 E & B 54 at 81, 120 ER 20 at 30, and he expressed it as a duty 'to prevent the scandal and the perversion of justice'. A judge must achieve that by, for example, preventing a juryman from serving who is completely deaf or blind or otherwise incompetent to give a verdict.

It is important to stress, however, that that is to be exercised to prevent individual jurors who are not competent from serving. It has never been held to include a discretion to discharge a competent juror or jurors in an attempt to secure a jury drawn from particular sections of the community, or otherwise to influence the overall composition of the jury. For this latter purpose the law provides that 'fairness' is achieved by the principle of random selection.

The way in which random selection should take place is a matter not for the judge but for the Lord Chancellor, as we endeavoured to point out in the course of argument to counsel for the appellant by citing the relevant portion of the Juries Act 1974, which is s 5(1). That reads as follows:

'The arrangements to be made by the Lord Chancellor under this Act shall include the preparation of lists (called panels) of persons summoned as jurors, and the information to be included in panels, the court sittings for which they are prepared, their division into parts or sets (whether according to the day of first attendance or otherwise), their enlargement or amendment, and all other matters relating to the contents and form of the panels shall be such as the Lord Chancellor may from time to time direct.'

There are several cases which give examples of this residual discretion. It may be exercised even in the absence of any objection by any of the parties. The basic position is that a juror may be discharged on grounds that would found a challenge for cause. In addition jurors who are not likely to be willing or able properly to perform their duties may also be discharged . . .

That discretion has now been confirmed by express statutory provision in the Juries Act 1974, s 10; and *Practice Note* [1988] 3 All ER 177, [1988] 1 WLR 1161 expressly provides for excusal of jurors at the court's discretion on grounds of 'personal hardship or conscientious objection to jury service'. It does not however envisage excusal on more general grounds such as race, religion or political beliefs.

On occasion however, as counsel for the appellant has pointed out to us by citing certain cases, in particular *R v Binns* [1982] Crim LR 522, trial judges have been invited to exercise their discretion not merely to remove an individual juror, but to go further and use the power of discretionary discharge to alter the composition of the panel or of a particular jury.

The most common cases in which this question has arisen have involved questions of ethnic groups where it has been suggested that the jury should consist partly or wholly of members of that same ethnic group. Those applications provide particular difficulty for the judge and the present case is a very good example. They arise without warning and are usually argued without any reference to authority, as indeed was very largely the case in the present instance.

There have been occasions on which it has been accepted that such a discretion exists, most notably *R v Thomas* (1989) 88 Cr App R 370, where the prosecution conceded, and the judge accepted, that such a discretion did exist, albeit, it was added, that it was only to be exercised sparingly and in very exceptional circumstances.

In the judgment of this court that concession made in *R v Thomas* was not correct. The trial judge had no discretion to interfere in that way with the composition of the panel or of an individual jury.

It is important to note the nature of the objection to the juries in question, and of the discretion that is supposed to meet that objection.

The racial composition of a particular panel or part panel would not be grounds for challenge to the array. A challenge to the array is a challenge to the whole panel on the ground of some irregularity in their summoning by the officer responsible.

In *R v Danvers* [1982] Crim LR 680 an application was made to challenge the array at the trial of a defendant of West Indian origin, when all members of the jury panel were found to be white. The application was made on the ground that the jury panel did not reflect the ethnic composition of the community, and on the further ground that an all-white jury could not understand the mental and emotional atmosphere in which black families live, so that a black defendant could not have unreserved confidence in an all-white jury. Not surprisingly, due to the fact that the challenge contained no allegation that the all-white jury panel was the result of bias or improper conduct on the part of the summoning officer, the challenge failed. It was held that there is no requirement in law that there should be a black member on a jury or jury panel.

It has never been suggested that the judge has a discretion to discharge a whole panel or part panel on grounds that would not found a valid challenge. Similarly, in the absence of evidence of specific bias, ethnic origins could not found a valid ground for challenge to an individual juror. The alleged discretion of the judge to intervene in the selection of the jury does not therefore fall within any acknowledged category of judicial power or discretion.

There are, moreover, strong reasons why such a discretion should not be recognised. The whole essence of the jury system is random selection, as the passage from Lord Denning MR's judgment in *R v Crown Court at Sheffield, ex p Brownlow* [1980] 2 All ER 444 at 452–453, [1980] QB 530 at 541, cited in the course of argument, shows. He said:

'Our philosophy is that the jury should be selected at random, from a panel of persons who are nominated at random. We believe that 12 persons selected at random are likely to be a cross-section of the people as a whole and thus represent the views of the common man ... The parties must take them as they come.'

The judgment was supported by Shaw LJ, who was sitting with Lord Denning MR in that case.

Secondly, it is worth noting that on occasions in the past when it has been thought desirable that the court should have a power of this kind it has been expressly granted by statute and equally subsequently abolished by statute.

Thirdly, such an application is in effect a request to the judge either to give directions as to the constitution of the panel or to order some individual jurors to be replaced without assigning a cause, that is peremptorily. It is true that in *R v Bansal* [1985] Crim LR 151, in response to an application of this type, Woolf J did give directions that the jury panel should be selected from a particular area known to contain members of the Asian community, but the judge does not appear to have had the benefit of full argument on the point.

Responsibility for the summoning of jurors to attend for service in the Crown Court and the High Court is by statute clearly laid on the Lord Chancellor. That is clear from s 2 of the Juries Act 1974 and from s 5, which I have already set out in this judgment. It is not the function of the judge to alter the composition of the panel or to give any directions about the district from which it is to be drawn. The summoning of panels is not a judicial function, but it is specifically conferred by statute on an administrative officer. That fact may not have been drawn to the attention of the court in the cases we have cited and others which have suggested that the judge has power to give directions as to the composition of the panel of juries.

It should also be remembered that the mere fact that a juryman is, for instance, of a particular race or holds a particular religious belief cannot be made the basis for a challenge for cause on the grounds of bias or on any other grounds. If therefore a judge were to exercise his discretion to remove a juror on either of these grounds, he would be assuming bias where none was proved. Such a course is not only unjustified in law, but also indeed might be thought to be seriously derogatory of the particular juryman himself. Further, any attempt to influence the composition of the jury on these grounds would conflict with the requirement that the jury to try an issue before a court shall be selected by ballot in open court from the panel as summoned (see the Juries Act 1974, s 11).

In *R v Chandler* [1964] 1 All ER 761 at 766, [1964] 2 QB 322 at 337 Lord Parker CJ held that earlier authorities that had been cited did not establish that the defendant in the particular case of a trial for misdemeanour had a right comparable to that of the Crown to ask a juror to stand by, but he did add:

> 'That . . . is not to say that, in an exceptional case, whether felony or mis-demeanour, a judge cannot in his discretion himself stand by a juror or allow a prisoner to do so.'

That was either a slip of the tongue or else it may be that Lord Parker CJ had in mind what was stated in *Mansell v R* in relation to individual incompetent jurors, because *Mansell v R* (and the judgment of Lord Campbell CJ) was cited to the court in that case.

We have been referred among other cases to *R v Binns* [1982] Crim LR 522. It is important to recollect and to note that in *R v Binns* the original report in the Criminal Law Review was supplemented by a corrigendum which puts the case in a very different light (see [1982] Crim LR 823). In so far as *R v Binns* conflicts with the principles which we have endeavoured already to state in this judgment, the opinion expressed in *R v Binns* must be said to have been wrong.

The conclusion is that, however well intentioned the judge's motive might be, the judge has no power to influence the composition of the jury, and that it is wrong for him to attempt to do so. If it should ever become desirable that the principle of random selection should be altered, that will have to be done by way of statute and cannot be done by any judicial decision.

We wish to make two final further points. It appears to have been suggested in some of the cases that there is a 'principle' that a jury should be racially balanced. One of those cases to which counsel for the appellant has referred us is *R v Frazer* [1987] Crim LR 418. There was a similar suggestion in *R v Bansal*. The existence of any such principle however was denied in a case which escaped the attention of counsel for the appellant, *R v McCalla* [1986] Crim LR 335. No authority is cited by those who have argued for the existence of the principle. In our judgment such a principle cannot be correct, for it would depend on an underlying premise that jurors of a particular racial origin or holding particular religious beliefs are incapable of giving an impartial verdict in accordance with the evidence.

Secondly, the principles we have already set out apply not only where it is argued that a jury of a particular composition ought to be empanelled because of the nature of the particular case or particular defendants, but also where complaint is made that the panel was not truly 'random', for instance that the population of a particular area contained 20 per cent of persons of West Indian origin but that only a much lower percentage of such persons was to be found on the panel. For the judge to entertain any such application would equally involve his seeking to investigate the composition of the panel in a manner which, for reasons already indicated, lies outside his jurisdiction, and lies within the jurisdiction of the Lord Chancellor.

So far as the mode of summoning the panel is concerned, the judge is limited, we repeat, to considering, in a challenge for cause, whether the summoning officer has displayed bias or other impropriety. If that cannot be established, the judge has no power to review or take action in respect of any procedures that are alleged to have led to the panel not being in fact 'random'. Any such complaint would be a complaint of administrative error and has to be tackled by means other than the judge's action. If the officer concerned is in fact not performing his duties properly, in circumstances that fall short of his displaying bias or impropriety, he must be corrected, in other words, by administrative means.

As emphasised above, action could certainly not take the form of directions by the judge as to how the task of selection should in fact be performed. That being the case, in the present instance, although the judge was not given the opportunity of argument on this point to any extent, he was right in the upshot to come to the conclusion that he should not order a multiracial jury to be empanelled, because he had no power so to do.

Extract 4.4.4

Royal Commission on Criminal Justice, *Report* (1993) Ch 8

63. We have ... found very relevant a proposal made to us by the Commission for Racial Equality (CRE) for a specific procedure to be available where the case is believed to have a racial dimension which results in a defendant from an ethnic minority community believing that he or she is unlikely to receive a fair trial from an all-white jury. The CRE would also like to see the prosecution on behalf of the victim be able to argue that a racial dimension to the case points to the need for a multi racial jury. In such cases the CRE propose that it should be possible for either the prosecution or the defence to apply to the judge before the trial for the selection of a jury containing up to three people from ethnic minority communities. If the judge grants the application, it would be for the jury bailiff to continue to draw names randomly selected from the available pool until three such people were drawn. We believe that, in the exceptional case where compelling reasons can be advanced, this option, in addition to the existing power to order that the case be transferred to another Crown Court centre, should be available and we so recommend. However, we do not envisage that the new procedure should apply (as proposed by the

CRE) simply because the defendant thinks that he or she cannot get a fair trial from an all-white jury. The defendant would have to persuade the judge that such a belief was reasonable because of the unusual and special features of the case. Thus, a black defendant charged with burglary would be unlikely to succeed in such an application. But black people accused of violence against a member of an extremist organisation who said they had been making racial taunts against them and their friends might well succeed.

A number of studies conducted in the United States (which means that they may not be applicable to the UK) have examined the effects of race on jury decision-making. These suggest that decisions are affected by race, with white jurors convicting black defendants more readily than white defendants (see Johnson, 1985, pp 1625–1634). See further Alschuler (1995).

(b) Secrecy and jury verdicts

The jury deliberates in secret and returns a verdict of guilty or not guilty without giving reasons for its decision. Under the Contempt of Court Act 1981, s 8 it is a contempt 'to obtain, disclose or solicit any particulars of statements made, opinions expressed, arguments advanced or votes cast by members of a jury in the course of their deliberations'. This section effect-ively prohibits research on jury decision-making in real cases, though the RCCJ has recommended that the Act be amended to allow such research (1993, Ch 1, para 8). The inscrutability of jury verdicts makes appeals on issues of fact difficult (see the discussion on appeals in Chapter 6 below); it also means that courts will not inquire into any improprieties that may have taken place in the jury room. This can be a harsh rule. In *Thompson* (1961) 46 Cr App R 72 evidence came to light that the jury had been in favour of acquittal until the foreman produced a list of the defendant's previous con-victions (such information is usually kept from the jury: the general rule is that a defendant's previous convictions should not be adduced as evidence in court). The Court of Appeal refused to see whether the allegation could be substantiated: 'It has for long been a rule of practice, based on public policy, that the court should not inquire by taking evidence from jurymen as to what did occur in either the jury box or the jury room.' In *Schofield* [1993] Crim LR 217, the defendant was convicted of affray, but there was evidence that the jury did not understand the definition of affray; again, the Court of Appeal refused to quash the conviction or to inquire into the matter. The rule is often justified in terms of finality: if the courts heard such evidence, every guilty verdict would be subject to appeal as soon as evidence came to light of some irregularity in the jury's reasoning. It is also suggested that the rule prevents pressure being placed on jurors to reveal their reasoning, but it should be noted that the rule could be modified and the Contempt of Court Act 1981 used to prosecute those who made ad hoc inquiries into the jury's decision. The *Thompson* rule does not apply to the actions of the jury outside the jury room. In *Young* [1995] QB 324 the jury in a murder trial retired to a hotel for the night during its deliberations. During the night, four jurors used an ouija board in an attempt to contact the deceased. The jurors believed that they were successful, and purportedly received an answer from the deceased, to the effect that the defendant had killed him. The Court of Appeal felt able to order an inquiry into the matter, because what happened in the hotel did not form part of the jury's deliberations. Had the ouija board session taken place in the jury room, the secrecy rule would presumably have prevented any inquiry at all. In an old case, *Vaise v Delaval* (1785) 1 TR 11, Lord Mansfield refused to hear evidence that the jury had reached its decision by tossing a coin.

(c) The value of jury trial

The cases on jury secrecy underline the fact that we know very little about how juries decide cases. Behind the doors of the jury room jurors may toss coins, or bully one another into accepting a verdict; on the other hand, jury deliberations may be the epitome of fair and reasoned argument. Without access to jury deliberations, however, we cannot tell which is the more accurate picture. Research has been carried out on jury decision-making using mock juries deliberating in mock trials. Though such studies give interesting insights into small group decision-making, the results are of less value when it comes to real juries in real trials (for an overview of such research, see Stephenson, 1992, Ch 10; Kapardis, 1997, Ch 5). Other jury studies have looked at real trials, focusing not on jury deliberation, but on its end product, the verdict, and have compared the jury verdict with the expectations of other actors in the trial. In England and Wales the most significant study of this type was carried out by Baldwin and McConville (1979). The authors studied 370 trials at Birmingham Crown Court, and questioned judges, police officers and prosecution and defence solicitors about the verdicts. The results of the research led the authors to conclude that 'trial by jury is a relatively crude instrument for establishing the truth' (p 67). Looking at acquittals, there were 41 cases where the judge and one other actor viewed the acquittal as questionable. The facts of most of these cases did not offer any obvious explanation as to why the defendant was acquitted: the acquittals did not seem to be attributable to jury equity (where, although the defendant has broken the criminal law, the jury considers his or her behaviour to be morally blameless – we discuss this in more detail below). As for convictions, in 15 cases guilty verdicts were questioned by respondents and in 13 of these cases even the police thought the conviction was questionable. Again, there appeared to the authors to be no obvious explanation for these doubtful convictions: it was not a case of the jury believing doubtful eyewitness or confession evidence. Baldwin and McConville comment (p 76):

We came to regard two other factors as being much more important [than the factors usually associated with miscarriages of justice]: *first*, that the jury appeared in many of these cases to be too easily satisfied of the defendants' guilt because they failed to appreciate the high standard of proof required in criminal cases; *second*, that the jury apparently convicted the defendant through lack of comprehension of the issues involved.

(More recently, the Crown Court Study has probed the views of judges and barristers about jury verdicts. Judges thought that 29 per cent of acquittals and 2 per cent of convictions were either against the weight of evidence or were inexplicable (Zander and Henderson, 1993, pp 164–167)). Although *Jury Trials* leaves the reader with a sense of the unpredictability of jury verdicts, Baldwin and McConville do not advance their findings as reasons for the abolition of the jury. This is in part because jury trial is not solely valued as a means of accurate fact-finding. The jury has a number of other functions. Several commentators point out that the jury helps to legitimate the criminal justice system. Some use the concept of legitimation here in a slightly cynical manner: the jury lets 'the judges and the whole judicial system to appear to be above the struggle, making judgments fairly in the event of conflicts between the state and its subjects' (Chambliss and Seidman, 1971, p 443). Similarly, Darbyshire suggests that the symbolic importance of trial by jury 'has fed public complacency with the English legal system and distracted attention from its evils' (1991, p 741). However, legitimation can also have a more positive meaning. Just as democracy legitimates government, so the use of lay fact-finders legitimates the application of the criminal law, by keeping it in touch with public opinion. This can happen in a number of ways. First, jurors will usually be faced with conflicting accounts presented by the parties at trial. Part of their function is to judge which accounts are plausible, and this will involve drawing on their general experience, which may differ from that of a professional trier of fact. For example, jurors with negative experience of the police may find a defendant's claim that the police have fabricated evidence more convincing than would a judge or magistrate. Secondly, many criminal cases involve evaluative fact-finding. For example, dishonesty – an element in theft cases – is defined in terms of the standards of 'reasonable and honest people', a person acting in self-defence must use 'reasonable force', and the common mens rea standard of recklessness involves an 'obvious' risk. None of these standards are defined precisely, so it is left to the jury to decide what is obvious and reasonable, and thus whether the defendant has broken the law.

There is a third, and more controversial, way in which the use of juries may keep the law attuned to public opinion. This is 'jury nullification' or 'jury equity' which occurs where a jury is convinced beyond reasonable doubt that the defendant has broken the law, but nevertheless returns a not guilty verdict. A jury might do this where it disagrees with the law, where it feels that a prosecution is unjust, or where it decides that the defendant's breach of the law should be excused. A frequently cited example of jury nullification is the trial of Clive Ponting (see Drewry, 1985). In 1985 Ponting, a civil servant in the Ministry of Defence, was prosecuted for breach of the Official Secrets Act 1911 after he had leaked information which revealed that Parliament had been misled about the sinking of an Argentine battleship during the Falklands war. The judge's direction to the jury on the law left it with little choice other than to convict, but it nevertheless returned a not guilty verdict. While the Ponting case is often used to demonstrate the value of jury trial, other possible examples of jury nullification are perhaps less laudable (though note that, owing to jury secrecy, it is usually impossible to be sure whether a particular case is an example of nullification). It has been remarked that during the 1960s and 1970s juries refused to convict defendants in drink/driving cases, perhaps because they thought that drink driving should not have been a crime or because the likely penalty was too harsh (see Enright and Morton, 1990, p 27). Given that the criminal law is made by a democratically elected Parliament, is nullification a desirable aspect of the jury system? Nullification appears to undermine the rule of law. It should also be noted that, while most of the examples of nullification which are cited involve juries being lenient, a jury might also exercise its power the other way and convict a defendant it believes to be innocent according to the law (though there are certain safeguards to prevent this, such as the judge's power to prevent a weak case going to the jury and the convicted defendant's possibility of appeal). In favour of the power to nullify is the argument that, when Parliament passes a law, it cannot foresee all the circumstances to which it might apply. What is more, even in a democratic system unjust laws may be passed and laws may remain on the statute books when they have lost public acceptability. Further, some law is judge-made or is interpreted in ways that will not have been foreseen by Parliament. Additionally, given that police and prosecutors have discretion not to apply the law, it might seem odd to deny that discretion to the jury. However, if it is accepted that jury nullification is a desirable feature of trial by jury, a further question arises: should juries be told (as they may be in two states in the United States) that they have the right not to convict a defendant who, on the evidence, is guilty? While some would fear that this would be an invitation to anarchy, the failure to apprise juries of their nullification power might seem to be duplicitous. As one American judge has remarked: 'Trust in the jury is, after all, one of the cornerstones of our entire criminal jurisprudence, and if that trust is without foundation we must re-examine a great deal more than just the nullification doctrine' (Bazelon J, dissenting, in *United States v Dougherty* 473 F2d 1113, at p 1142 (1972)). On jury nullification, see Freeman (1981); Devlin, (1991); Scheflin and Van Dyke (1980); Abramson (1994: Ch 2).

In the following extract, Jackson considers some of the other values of jury trial:

Extract 4.4.5

J Jackson, 'The Value of Jury Trial' in E Attwooll and D Goldberg (eds), *Criminal Justice* (1995) pp 87–93

[T]here are two important respects in which a lay tribunal may be able to guarantee defence participation [in the trial] more effectively than a professional tribunal . . . [Juries] are able to take a more wide-ranging view of the merits of the proceedings taken against the defendant. This has an important effect on the scope which the parties have to determine the ambit of the dispute. In a recent comparison of Diplock and jury trials in Northern Ireland, the substitution of the judge for the jury was found to effect a change in the nature of the arguments that were run, particularly by the defence against the prosecution case.[1] Counsel reported, and it was observed, that they were able to run 'sympathy points' much more easily in jury trials. Within more relaxed standards of relevance they were able to build up a more rounded picture of a defendant or a witness, which then enabled them to appeal to the merits of the case. In Diplock trials, by contrast, the scope of the context was much more restricted and there could be little consideration of the merits of conviction other than on the basis of the legal standards to be applied by the defendant. Judges, of course, may question the relevance of certain lines of inquiry in both modes of trial. Indeed the Royal Commission on Criminal Justice specifically urged judges to take a more interventionist approach in order to expedite the proceedings, to see that witnesses were treated properly and to control irrelevant questioning. But there seemed to be a certain reluctance on the part of judges to do this in Northern Irish jury trials. Certain judges admitted that they felt compelled to allow 'sympathy' points to be put before a jury because of the danger of being seen to be consistently interrupting counsel all the time in front of a jury. In professional trials where the jury is absent it is much easier for judges to curb counsel's questioning.

The second respect in which a lay tribunal such as the jury is able to maximise defence participation concerns the different position which lay triers occupy in court proceedings. Although the jury may take a more wide-ranging view of the merits of the proceedings at the end of the case, it is able to play a much less intrusive role than a professional trier of fact during the trial and pre-trial proceedings. By contrast the judge's professional role requires that the contest is confined within narrower boundaries than would be the case if a lay body were determining guilt, but the position of the professional judge permits him or her to exercise a more pervasive influence over the proceedings than lay triers can ever have. In a criminal context where evidentiary barriers are erected to enable the defendant to confront and challenge the prosecution case, this may put the accused at a disadvantage in a number of ways.

First of all, the evidentiary barriers rely heavily on keeping sources of prejudicial information away from triers of fact and it is much easier to keep information away from a lay tribunal than a professional tribunal. Juries usually come to the trial wholly ignorant about the details of the case. Damaska has said that jurors are the paradigmatic fact finders in a contest between parties because they enter the contest unprepared, with a 'virgin mind', to be 'tutored only through the bilateral process of evidentiary presentation and argument'.[2] This means that juries are likely to focus on the proofs and arguments adduced by the parties at trial rather than on other extraneous information. Professional triers in contrast as 'insiders' of the system have much greater access to knowledge about the case. They may become involved in sentencing discussions with counsel before the trial. They may have access to the prosecution papers on which the accused was committed for trial. Even if all sources of information have been kept away from the trial judge before trial, the professional judge's experience makes him or her better placed than a lay trier to pick up background about the case which may not be apparent to lay minds. Judges may very quickly work out, for example, whether a defendant has a good or bad character as a judge will be aware that a defendant who does not adduce evidence of his or her good character may have a bad character. Apart from this, of course, judges can much more easily become privy to inadmissible evidence during the trial. The process of exclusion works much less effectively when the trier of fact is privy to inadmissible evidence, which can happen when a professional tribunal acts as both the trier of fact and the trier of law. Whether the rules of evidence are properly described as the 'child of the jury', as has been claimed,[3] they have been tailored to suit the needs of jury trial.

Secondly, the jury system ensures that the non-exclusionary directions on the burden and standard of proof and on how certain kinds of evidence should be treated, are given a particular force when they are issued in the form of mandatory instructions to a group of lay persons who have not had cause to apply them before. When fundamental principles such as the burden and standard of proof are impressed upon the jury, one is incorporating in the decision-making process the commitment of the criminal justice system not only to the protection of the innocent from conviction but also to the principle that the prosecution must bear the burden of full proof at the defendant's trial. These principles cannot be conveyed so strikingly in a non-jury setting. A statement by the judge that the standard of proof has been met carries none of the solemnity of the message to the jury that it must eliminate all reasonable explanations consistent with innocence before finding in the prosecution's favour. The point is not that professional triers are unequipped to make a determination of guilt on the standard of proof beyond reasonable doubt. Indeed professional triers may be considered to have much more understanding of what the relevant principles mean. The difficulty, rather, is that when the standard has been expressed *ex post facto* as having been met at the defendant's trial, the defendant is given less assurance that it has truly been met than when triers of fact are directed to apply it before the deliberative process has begun.

Thirdly, the position of a lay tribunal during the trial process differs quite significantly from the position of a professional trier. In strict adversarial theory the parties present the proof and arguments and the trier of fact adopts a listening role rather than an active interrogative one. An active inquisitor is thought likely to skew the process of proof in favour of one side or another and to pursue lines of inquiry which the parties are unprepared for and unable to meet.[4] But a lay tribunal such as a jury is much more likely to perform a passive role during the contested trial than a professional judge because it is not so well placed to play an intrusive role. Professional triers of fact may be tempted to use the pre-eminent position they undoubtedly have in the trial to adopt a much more inquisitorial stance. There is evidence that while juries affect a relatively passive listening role during the trial,[5] judges who sit without a jury in common law trials can adopt an interventionist, even inquisitorial stance. Schulhofer's study of bench trials in Philadelphia concluded that judges typically played an active role in questioning witnesses and in closing submissions.[6] In the very different context of Diplock trials in Northern Ireland a comparison between judicial behaviour in these trials and judicial behaviour in jury trials revealed more interventionist tendencies in the former.[7]

Finally, there is a difference between the lay and professional deliberative process. A jury is unable formally to start deliberation until after it has been directed by the judge at the end of the case on the approach it should take. Individuals may, of course, form a view about the case before the jury retires and they may even speak amongst themselves about the case. But there will be no formal opportunity to form a collective judgment until they retire and at this stage views will be exchanged and the case for conviction will be talked out before a collective judgment is reached. Professional triers, on the other hand, have a much greater opportunity to form a judgment at an earlier stage. If there is a single judge, a decision may be reached before the case has begun on the basis of the papers in the case. Even if there is more than one professional hearing the case, there is much greater opportunity for them to discuss the case amongst themselves before it has finished. Once it has finished, moreover, steps are taken to ensure that no outside influences are brought to bear on the jury and if the jury raise matters about the case these must be aired in open court so that there can be no suspicion of any undue influence being brought to bear by the judge upon the jury.[8] No such restraints are placed upon judges who act as the trier of fact. After the case judges may reserve judgment and there is no requirement that they deliberate in private until judgment is reached.

All these factors are likely to have an effect on the level of party participation in the trial. Before a jury the parties' advocates must present their case in full as the jury will have no advance knowledge of it. The advocates have everything to play for in the dialectic of party debate. Before a judge things may be very different and indeed in our study of the Diplock trial process in Northern Ireland where the single judge acts both as trier of fact and law, they were observed to be very different. The advocates assumed that the judge had some knowledge of the case. There was more pressure to agree matters and to come to the nub of the case. The advocates as insiders of the system knew about the predilections of the particular judge and the judge's presence came to assume a dominance in the trial that a jury could never achieve. Even where judges maintained a conventionally passive role during the trial, as certain judges did, the dialectic inevitably shifted away from party to party towards party to judge. The difficulty for the parties in this situation, however, was that they received no feedback from the judge. Privy perhaps to information not brought out in the trial, judges could choose to remain silent and hold their fire until delivering judgment.

All this entails a considerable adversarial deficit for the accused. Defence participation is secured in the adversarial trial by the presentation of proofs and argument and by the assurance that these will be taken into account before the decision reached. But where professional triers decide the case, the defendant cannot be given the same guarantee that their proofs and arguments will be taken into account. The defendant is entirely at the mercy of professional insiders who may have access to information not before the trial, who may substantially influence the presentation of his or her case and who never have to justify their decision in the cut and thrust of reasoned debate. Judges usually have to give reasons for their decisions publicly and when reasons have to be given for findings of fact this may give more assurance that the findings have been based on the evidence presented at court.[9] At the same time all the written opinion has to do is convince an appellate tribunal which was not present at the instant proceedings and which therefore defers to the factual assessments of the judge who was there. Moreover, the reasons given have to relate to the evidence presented at court but they do not have to respond fully to the arguments presented by counsel and judges. Before a jury, by contrast, the case against the defendant has to be built up piece by piece, detail by detail in the open forum of the courtroom, with an opportunity for full challenge at every stage. Once the courtroom proceedings end the case will then be subjected to further deliberation by a body of people who have had no say in the presentation of the proofs and arguments in court but whose discussions may be presumed to be guided by the arguments they have heard on the basis of the directions they have been given.

All this suggests that the jury may be much more vital to the adversarial workings of the common law trial than is commonly thought. The two fundamental features of the common law trial – the adversary system and the jury – have tended to be considered in isolation from each other. The assumption appears to have been that the adversarial quality of trials need not be diluted in the absence of the jury. So when the system of trial by a single judge was recommended for Northern Ireland, the Diplock Commission assumed that the absence of the jury would not affect the adversarial quality of the trial, although it was against the introduction of a three-judge court on the ground that this would interfere with the adversary system of party presentation.[10] The argument here, however, is that the presence of the jury helps to make the adversary trial a genuinely participative proceeding between the parties in contest. A criminal trial which retains the trappings of the adversarial system without any recognition given to the absence of the jury is a much less participative proceeding.

This is not to argue that defence participation is as effectively secured as it might be in present jury trial procedure. The passive role that jurors play during the course of the trial has disadvantages for defendants because the defence remains ignorant about what the jury is really thinking and is unable to counter the assumptions it is making. After the trial juries deliberate in private and they never have to justify their decisions to the outside world. This means that the parties can never know for sure whether their participation in the decision has been real and whether the triers have understood and taken into account their proofs and arguments.[11] There is scope for opening a more formal channel of communication between triers of fact and the parties in both lay and professional trials. At a time, however, when jury trial is undergoing greater scrutiny than ever before, it is as well to appreciate what is lost when the jury is removed from the adversarial trial format as well as what is gained by jury trial. The arguments for the jury have tended to concentrate on the benefits that lay decision-making can bring to the criminal trial which include a more wide-ranging review of the merits of the case undertaken by 'fresh' minds. It has been argued here, however, that in addition to the qualities that juries can bring to the decision-making process, the institution of the jury cannot be abolished without profound procedural implications for the entire tradition of the adversary trial. We can at present only speculate about what goes on behind the closed doors of the jury deliberation room and how jurors reach the decisions that they do. But recent comparisons between professional and jury trials illustrate that a very different trial process emerges in a totally professional environment no matter how hard professionals try to simulate the conditions of jury trial in a professional setting.

[1] See J D Jackson and S Doran, *Judge without Jury: Diplock Trials in the Adversary System*, Oxford: Oxford University Press, 1995.
[2] M R Damaska, *The Faces of Justice and State Authority*, New Haven: Yale University Press, 1986, pp 137–8.
[3] W B Thayer, *A Preliminary Treatise on Evidence at Common Law*, Boston: Little Brown, 1898, pp 47, 266, 509.
[4] The dangers of active inquisition in adversary trials are well rehearsed by M Frankel, 'The Search for Truth: an Umpireal View', *University of Pennsylvania Law Review*, 123 (1975) 1031–1059 and S Saltzburg. 'The Unnecessarily Expanding Role of the American Trial Judge', *University of Virginia Law Review*, 63 (1978), 1–81.
[5] See M Zander and P Henderson, *Crown Court Study*, London: H.M.S.O., 1993; J Jackson, R Kilpatrick and C Harvey, *Called to Court: A Public View of Criminal Justice in Northern Ireland*, Belfast: S.L.S. Publications, 1991, pp 126–7.
[6] S J Schulhofer, 'Is Plea Bargaining Inevitable?', *Harvard Law Review*, 97 (1984), 1037, 1070–1073.
[7] J D Jackson and S Doran, 'Conventional Trials in Unconventional Times: The Diplock Experience', *Criminal Law Forum*, 4 (1993) 503–520.
[8] *R v Gorman* [1987] 1 W. L.R. 545.
[9] See M D Bayles, *Procedural Justice*, Dordrecht: Kluwer, 1990, 75.
[10] *Report of the Commission to consider legal procedures to deal with terrorist activities in Northern Ireland* (1972), Cmnd 5185, para 39.
[11] Fuller, [L Fuller, 'The Forms and Limits of Adjudication' (1978) 92 *Harvard Law Review* 353] p 388.

(d) The role of the judge in the criminal trial

There is a danger in paying too much attention to the role of the jury in Crown Court trials. This is partly because most defendants tried on indictment plead guilty, and about half of all contested cases end with a non-jury acquittal (see Block, Corbett and Peay, 1993 and discussion in Chapter 3 above). It is also because the jury plays its fact-finding role in an environment shaped by other actors. The evidence presented to it, as well as the charges which the defendant faces, will have been chosen by defence and prosecution lawyers. The crucial decision-making role of the prosecution and defence is part and parcel of the adversary system, but just as important is the role of the judge. The classic description of the role the judge should play in an adversary trial is to be found in a civil case, *Jones v National Coal Board* (1957) 2 QB 55, at pp 63–64:

> In the system of trial which we have evolved in this country, the judge sits to hear and determine the issues raised by the parties, not to conduct an investigation or

examination on behalf of society at large, as happens, we believe, in some foreign countries. . . . The judge's part . . . is to hearken to the evidence, only himself asking questions of witnesses when it is necessary to clear up any point that has been overlooked or left obscure; to see that the advocates behave themselves seemly and keep to the rules laid down by law; to exclude irrelevancies and discourage repetition; to make sure by wise intervention that he follows the points that the advocates are making and can assess their worth; and at the end to make up his mind where the truth lies.

In criminal trials judges do not have to decide where the truth lies because this is for the jury. They must, though, ensure that the jury is able to perform this task. To this end, judges may wish to question witnesses so as to clarify matters for the jury. At the end of the trial, judges nearly always sum up the facts of the case to remind the jury of the relevant issues. Some commentators have suggested that the judge's attitude, as expressed through such interventions in the trial, will have a considerable effect on the jury's view of the case (Mungham and Bankowski, 1976). Jackson and Doran have remarked that 'there is considerable uncertainty about the proper boundaries of the judicial role in criminal trials' (1995, p 290), and their research, which compared jury trials with Diplock (non-jury) trials supports this. They found considerable variation in the extent to which judges would intervene in the course of jury trials, but some judges consistently took an interventionist stance, on rare occasions even cross-examining witnesses. Judges who do go too far beyond the role described in *Jones* may pave the way for a successful challenge to a defendant's conviction in the Court of Appeal (see generally Doran, 1989). A recent example is *Whybrow and Saunders* (1994) 144 NLJ 124. The trial judge had cross-examined the defendants, and poured scorn on their story. Although he had stressed in his summing up that it was up to the jury to come to their own opinion on the case, the Court of Appeal decided that 'what had happened could not be cured in the summing up'. The defendants' convictions were quashed and a retrial ordered. Following the guidelines in *Matthews* (1983) 78 Cr App R 23, the Court of Appeal put particular stress on the tone (rather than merely the number) of the judge's interventions during the trial, because it is the overall tone that runs the risk of letting the jury see the trial judge's opinion of the evidence.

The summing up is a particularly delicate task for the judge. A judge may believe that the evidence presented during the trial clearly favours one side, but judges should be careful not to go too far in putting their views to the jury. A well-known example of a judge making his views plain is Mr Justice Bridge's summing up in the trial of the Birmingham six in 1975. At the start of the summing up, the judge told the jury that:

> Some judges tell juries that . . . they will express no views of their own on the weight of the evidence or on the conclusions which may or may not be drawn from the facts, [that] they will be utterly objective in their consideration of the facts. I never say that to any jury because I think that it is attributing to oneself a super-human capacity. I do not think that any of us can be detached. We all see things

411

differently but I have naturally formed an impression of the conclusions to which the evidence leads, as I dare say some of you have, and I think, however hard a judge tries to be impartial inevitably his presentation of the case, his summary of the evidence, is bound to be coloured by his own views. So I am of the opinion, not shared by all my brothers on the bench, that if a judge has formed a clear view it is much better to let the jury see that and say so and not pretend to be a kind of Olympian detached observer and try to hide the views that one has formed . . .

Bridge J was particularly scathing about some of the witnesses, including a doctor who had given evidence on injuries sustained by the defendants while in custody:

There are, inescapably many perjurers who have given evidence from that witness box. If Dr Harwood is one of them, is he not one of the worst?

He was also very critical of Dr Black, an expert witness called by the defence (whose fears about the scientific evidence in the case were vindicated years later):

I have read the transcript of Dr Black's evidence and I discover that there is a point when I ask him a question. I said to him 'Dr Black, is this conclusion of yours based on anything other than your own theorising?' and he said 'Oh, my Lord, to talk of theorising is rather unfair, is it not?' Is it? If Dr Black was not theorising, what was he doing? I am afraid that I have made my views on this issue . . . pretty plain.

At their first appeal, in 1976, the Court of Appeal did not object to the way in which Bridge J had let the jury know his views about the evidence, though it did acknowledge that his description of Dr Harwood's evidence 'unhappily went somewhat far' (see Dunne, 1989; Mullin, 1993; Mansfield and Wardle, 1993).

More recent cases show that the Court of Appeal will sometimes take a more robust line in cases where a judge's summing up has obviously not been neutral. *Wood* [1996] 1 Cr App R 207 is a good example of this. Wood was convicted of possessing explosives with intent to endanger life. He had asked an old friend to store a tea chest for him, but the friend discovered that the chest contained semtex. The police were alerted, and kept watch on Wood. Later Wood received a phone call at his place of work from a caller with an Irish accent who told him he was being watched. Wood's reaction was to leave work, go to his home and burn a map of the Huntingdon area; there was a mark on the map near the Prime Minister's residence.

Extract 4.4.6

R v Wood [1996] 1 Cr App R 207, pp 214–218

The judge's summing-up

We were told that the judge stamped his authority on the trial from the start. There is nothing inherently wrong in that, the judge is in charge of the trial. It

412

is said that he told the jury that they were not to take any notes, although they had been provided with materials for doing so. There are apparently two views held by judges on that point, and we have our own views. But they are not relevant to the determination of this appeal.

Miss Kennedy told us, in effect, that the tone of voice used by the judge and the physical expression of views by sighing, by the shrugging of his shoulders and raising his eyebrows were hostile to the defence. In our judgment we ought not to act on such information unless it is either agreed between counsel or supported by evidence. Indeed it may be that if the point is critical there should be sworn evidence. The rule should be enforced that a member of the Bar giving evidence can no longer act as counsel in the same case. (See Boulton's *Conduct and Etiquette of the Bar*, 6th ed (1975), p 39, and now, the *Code of Conduct of the Bar of England and Wales* (1990, 4th Amendment, 1994).)

We were referred to the case of *Mears v R* (1993) 97 Cr App R 239, and to this passage in the advice of the Judicial Committee delivered by Lord Lane at pp 243, 244:

'The Court of Appeal took the view that the trial judge was not putting forward an unfair or unbalanced picture of the facts as he saw them. In rejecting the appellant's submission that the comments of the judge were unfairly weighted against him, the court asked themselves whether the comments amounted to a usurpation of the jury's function. In the view of their Lordships it is difficult to see how a judge can usurp the jury's function short of withdrawing in terms an issue from the jury's consideration. In other words this was to use a test which by present day standards is too favourable to the prosecution. Comments which fall short of such a usurpation may nevertheless be so weighted against the defendant at trial as to leave the jury little real choice other than to comply with what are obviously the judge's views or wishes. As Lloyd LJ observed in *Gilbey* (unreported) January 26, 1990:

"A judge . . . is not entitled to comment in such a way as to make the summing-up as a whole unbalanced . . . It cannot be said too often or too strongly that a summing-up which is fundamentally unbalanced is not saved by the continued repetition of the phrase that it is a matter for the jury."

Their Lordships realise that the judge's task in this type of trial is never an easy one. He must of course remain impartial, but at the same time the evidence may point strongly to the guilt of the defendant; the judge may often feel that he has to supplement deficiencies in the performance of the prosecution or defence, in order to maintain a proper balance between the two sides in the adversarial proceedings. It is all too easy for a court thereafter to criticise a judge who may have fallen into error for this reason. However, if the system is trial by jury then the decision must be that of the jury and not of the judge using the jury as something akin to a vehicle for his own views. Whether that is what has happened in any particular case is not likely to be an easy decision. Moreover, the Board is reluctant to differ from the Court of Appeal in assessing the weight of any misdirections. Here their Lordships have to take the summing-up as a whole as Mr Andrade submitted, and then ask themselves in the words of Lord Sumner in *Ibrahim v R* [1914] AC 599, 615, whether there was:

"Something which . . . deprives the accused of the substance of a fair trial and the protection of the law, or which, in general, tends to divert the due and orderly administration of the law into a new course, which may be drawn into an evil precedent in the future."

Their Lordships consider that the judge's comments already cited went beyond the proper bounds of judicial comment and made it very difficult, if not practically impossible, for the jury to do other than that which he was plainly suggesting.'

It is interesting to note Lord Lane's reference to present day standards. We do not doubt that the degree of adverse comment allowed today is substantially less than it was 50 years ago. In recent times, elaborate measures have been taken to prevent miscarriages of justice, such as the Police and Criminal Evidence Act or rules as to the disclosure of unused material by the prosecution. But a fair trial is surely of far more importance than all those measures put together.

The passage in the summing-up which is critical for the purposes of this appeal relates to the events of October 28. The judge introduced them as follows:

'I turn, members of the jury, to what you the jury may regard, if you see fit, as an extremely important feature of the evidence you have heard in this case.'

He then referred to the telephone call and other matters and continued at p 29:

'According to him – we will look at his evidence later – when he got his call about being under surveillance, he was extremely agitated and upset and left the office and went home for no purpose other than, to use his words, "clear his head" and when he got into the house and only then did he suddenly notice the map which had been in his house for well over a month – indeed, nearer two months – which he had been minded originally to put in with the explosives when he repackaged them in the Reebok bag and the tea chest. He had forgotten about it, had not put it in the tea chest and it had completely escaped his memory until, as I understand his account and you saw him, going in his house that day to clear his head, he suddenly saw it, realised its presence within the house might heavily compromise him and for that reason and in those circumstances and only for that reason burned the map.

That is his account. You must give it such weight as you, the jury, see fit. You will also have to consider the opposing thesis that once he received the telephone call, in fact, he left in haste for his home for the specific purposes of destroying that map, for he knew – and he tells you he knew – it was an IRA map and a map the significance of which, I am confident, will not be lost to you. That is why – and I make no apology for repeating it – you, the jury, may think that his movements on that morning and his

414

destruction of the map are important features of this case. It is a matter, like all questions of fact, entirely for you.'

One should notice the degree of repetition in that passage. Not only is the point said twice to be important, there are two references to Wood clearing his head, two to his suddenly noticing the map, and two to the map having been forgotten, escaping his memory. That is the stuff of advocacy.

Later the judge, having rehearsed Wood's evidence, put a number of questions which the jury might ask themselves about his account, if they thought fit:

'That was his evidence. It will be a matter for you to make what you will of it. It is plainly of the greatest possible importance in making up your mind as to his alleged intentions. You may see fit, in your own judgment, to ask a number of questions which arise from that evidence. If you do not find these questions helpful, then you will not. It is a matter for you. What was the true purpose of all those trips to Ireland especially the two when he went by himself? What do you make of his account of the way in which he says that this lethal cargo arrived loose in a tea chest which was badly damaged perhaps by a fork lift truck? The telephone numbers of the Huntingdon public houses – why written in Gaelic language? To practise or to conceal? As I have already invited you to consider, as the Crown invite you to consider, why kept for so long after their purpose, on his own account, was no longer applicable. Why did Dock not contact him? Why did he wait all those weeks to front it out with Gerard as he said he did and what do you make of his explanation of the circumstances in which he came to burn the map?'

At the end of this, the judge's conclusion:

'There it is, Ladies and Gentlemen. Is it or may it sensibly be that this accused has told you the truth? Is it or may it sensibly be the case that he is a man who had been cruelly duped by and compromised by his brother-in-law in the republic and who, for some reason in circumstances he has explained, just could not rid himself of that deadly burden in the days and weeks that passed? If that is or may be your perception of the reality of the position you will acquit him of this charge. Or is his account a deliberate and detailed attempt to pull the wool over your eyes? Are you surely driven to the conclusion, Ladies and Gentlemen, that he was holding 2 of the 3 essential unlawful and lethal ingredients of an IRA bomb or bombs for the purpose of and until such time as they might be used in that way by themselves or by others? If your answer to that question is a sure yes, then he is guilty of this offence.'

That, again, we would describe as advocacy.

The Court of Appeal quashed Wood's conviction and ordered a retrial because he had not received a fair trial. This was partly because of the judge's summing up, and partly because of the effect that press reports might have had on the jury (see below).

Many jurisdictions in the US do not allow judges to express opinions about the facts of cases to the jury: the judge's summing up is restricted to a statement of the law. It is sometimes suggested that the same rule should be adopted in England and Wales (Wolchover, 1989). The RCCJ did not think that the law should be changed, though it did note that 'judges should be wholly neutral in any comment that they make on the credibility of the evidence' (1993, Ch 8, para 23). As to the more general issue of judicial intervention during the trial itself, the RCCJ was of the opinion that judges should play a more interventionist role, in part to increase the efficiency of trials (1993, Ch 8, para 2).

See further Jackson (1997).

5. CRIMINAL JUSTICE AND THE RULES OF EVIDENCE

Criminal courts must decide whether the defendants brought before them are guilty or innocent. What principles should inform the way in which they come to make these decisions? It is common ground that the verdicts of criminal courts may not always be accurate: some guilty defendants may be acquitted, and some innocent ones convicted. This risk of error is inherent in the trial process: courts make decisions about what happened in the past and complete accuracy cannot be guaranteed. The only way to avoid errors is to try no one. But what can be achieved through the rules of criminal evidence is a bias in favour of a certain type of error. Again, it seems to be common ground that it is worse to convict an innocent person than to let a guilty person go free. A well-known way of expressing this notion is that 'it is better that ten guilty men go free than that one innocent man be convicted'. But this can also be formulated in terms of rights: we can say that an innocent defendant has a moral right not to be wrongfully convicted, and that the state should acknowledge this right through the adoption of trial procedures which adequately protect the innocent (Dworkin, 1985). In practice, the legal system's preference for acquitting the guilty is embodied in the rule that the prosecution must prove the defendant's guilt beyond reasonable doubt. This rule helps to ensure that, when criminal courts make their inevitable errors, they are more likely to acquit the guilty than to convict the innocent. The rule is an expression of the presumption of innocence, which is included in Article 6 of the European Convention on Human Rights (see Extract 1.5.3 above).

So far we have seen that attaining accurate verdicts is not the only concern of the trial system. But if accuracy is to be sacrificed to protect the innocent, are there other concerns which are at play in the criminal trial and which may lead us to forego accuracy? The rules of criminal evidence often embody concerns other than verdict accuracy. The underlying principle of evidence law is that all relevant evidence will be admitted by the courts. But much of

416

the law of evidence consists of rules excluding certain types of relevant evidence. A useful way of thinking about these exclusionary rules is in terms of a distinction made by Galligan:

> [T]here are two distinct issues: (i) one concerns rules about the probative value of evidence; (ii) the other concerns rules about the exclusion of evidence for reasons other than reasons of evidentiary value. The question in (i) is how to deal with evidence the probative value of which is in doubt, or which, although of probative value, contains a degree of risk that it will be used improperly. . . . The guiding objective in these cases is rectitude of outcome. These are issues *internal* to proof. In (ii) the issue is whether certain kinds of evidence, which are likely to be of probative value and therefore relevant in achieving rectitude, should be excluded, in order to advance other values or policies . . . These are issues *external* to proof; they are based on values which compete with rectitude. The exclusion of evidence in order to uphold those values may mean the loss of probative evidence and thus a lower level of accuracy. The distinction between (i) and (ii) is fundamental, since (i) is concerned with the rationality of proof, while (ii) is concerned with the conflict of values. (Galligan, 1988, quoted in Choo, 1993: 14)

An example of a rule concerned primarily with probative value is the rule which excludes hearsay evidence (evidence by a witness of what a third party said, when that evidence is tendered as proof of the truth of what was said). Hearsay is thought to be unreliable, because if the third party is not called to give evidence in person, he or she will not give evidence on oath and cannot be cross-examined. Another example is the rule excluding evidence of a defendant's previous convictions. While previous convictions may be relevant evidence, their exclusion is said to be justified on the grounds that they are more prejudicial than probative, that is, that the tribunal of fact will give them too much weight. The rules of evidence also contain some rules designed to promote what Galligan terms external values. Sometimes courts refuse to admit relevant, reliable evidence because to admit it would undermine important values, such as fairness, privacy or respect for the law. As Galligan observes, these rules involve competing values: they therefore tend to be more controversial than rules of the first type because people disagree about the weight that should be given to the different values involved. It is partly because of this that rules of the second type leave more discretion to trial judges. An examination of some of these rules highlights the interplay of values which underlies the criminal process.

(a) The courts and the exclusion of evidence under PACE

Suppose that the police have broken the rules of the PACE Codes of Practice by interviewing a suspect outside the police station. The police claim that during the interview the suspect confessed to a crime. Should the court refuse to hear the confession evidence because it has been obtained as a result of police malpractice? When considering this question the Royal Commission on Criminal Procedure (whose report formed the basis of PACE) examined

417

three main principles for excluding evidence (Royal Commission on Criminal Procedure, 1981: 112–116). Each approaches the issue from a different perspective.

The first is the reliability principle: evidence should only be excluded if it is thought to be unreliable. In the example given, if the defendant disputes the confession, and the interview was not tape recorded by the police, the court would have good grounds for excluding it. However, if the confession could be independently corroborated (perhaps the defendant told the police that stolen goods were hidden in his or her attic and a police search found the goods in that place), then there would be no doubts about its reliability, and the confession would be admitted. It will be obvious that the reliability principle does not invoke any principles external to proof. Reliability appears to have been the main criterion considered by the courts prior to PACE.

Secondly, there is the disciplinary principle. Under this rationale evidence obtained as the result of police malpractice should automatically be excluded from the trial. The aim of the exclusion is to punish the police for their wrong-doing and to deter them from breaking the rules in future. In our example the defendant's confession would be excluded (although, under a variation of the principle, exclusion would only result from a *deliberate* breach of the rules by the police). There are many criticisms of the disciplinary principle, the first summed up in the phrase 'the criminal is to go free because the constable has blundered'. Imagine that in our problem the defendant confessed to a terrorist bombing. Should evidence bearing on such a serious crime be excluded because of a relatively minor breach of investigative rules? Another problem is that the excluded evidence may only punish the police for their wrongdoing in the most abstract sense. The suspect may be convicted without the confession evidence and, even if the case collapses, the loss of one conviction may not be felt as a particularly great blow to the police force concerned. Similarly, the individual officers who broke the rules by interviewing the suspect outside the station may feel no great loss in seeing the evidence excluded. In any case, why should the defendant benefit from the disciplinary exercise? Before the introduction of PACE the courts in England and Wales did not see their role as disciplining the police through the exclusion of evidence:

> It is no part of a judge's function to exercise disciplinary powers over the police or prosecution as respects the way in which evidence to be used at the trial is obtained by them. If it was obtained illegally there will be a remedy in civil law; if it was obtained legally but in breach of the rules of conduct for the police, this is a matter for the appropriate disciplinary body to deal with. (*Sang* [1980] AC 402, at p 436)

It is worth noting that, as the passage in *Sang* suggests, the fact that evidence has been obtained illegally was not seen as grounds for the exclusion of evidence prior to PACE. As the court in *Leathem* (1861) 8 Cox CC 498 said, 'if you steal it even, it would be admissible'.

418

A third rationale for excluding evidence has been put forward by Ashworth (1977), who calls it the protective principle. This differs from the first two rationales in that it draws on a rights-based conception of the criminal process. Under the protective principle, evidence is usually excluded when a suspect's rights have been infringed during the investigative process (Ashworth interprets rights in this context as protections stemming from procedures designed to safeguard individual liberty). The exclusion of evidence obtained in breach of those rights is regarded as the defendant's remedy for the disadvantage he or she has suffered. Pattenden (1990) has advocated a similar exclusionary rationale: the courts should exclude evidence to protect civil liberties. However, it is not immediately obvious why the remedy need take the form of the exclusion of evidence: there may be other ways of remedying the breach (such as the payment of damages) which do not involve a sacrifice of verdict accuracy. In our example the evidence would not be excluded unless (1) the rule against interviewing outside the police station was interpreted as protecting the suspect's rights and (2) the suspect suffered a disadvantage as a result of the breach.

The Royal Commission on Criminal Procedure recommended the adoption of a protective principle for the most serious cases of wrongdoing: confessions should automatically be excluded if obtained through violence or inhuman and degrading treatment. In other cases, the judge would merely warn the jury that a confession might by inaccurate. The rules which were eventually adopted in PACE are found in ss 76 and 78 of the Act. Section 76 was considered in Chapter 3 above. It only applies to confessions and embodies a protective principle (confessions are inadmissible if obtained by oppression) and a reliability principle (confessions obtained in conditions conducive to unreliability are inadmissible).

78. Exclusion of unfair evidence

(1) In any proceedings the court may refuse to allow evidence on which the prosecution proposes to rely to be given if it appears to the court that, having regard to all the circumstances in which the evidence was obtained, the admission of the evidence would have such an adverse effect on the fairness of the proceedings that the court ought not to admit it.

'Evidence' has been held to include confessions: *Mason* [1988] 1 WLR 139.

In practice, s 78 has been used more widely than s 76. To see how s 78 has been used in practice we will concentrate on a line of cases concerning the breach of s 58 of PACE (the suspect's right to legal advice in the police station). This both complements our discussion of the importance of legal advice in Chapter 3, and allows us to adopt a fairly narrow focus on the huge amount of case law generated by s 78. Our analysis cannot hope to capture all aspects of the case law. Our aim is to pick out some of the most salient themes, in particular those of judicial discretion and the role of rights-based reasoning in the case law.

Samuel (1988) 87 Cr App R 232 concerned a defendant who had been arrested on suspicion of armed robbery. He was interviewed at the police station, and during the second interview he asked to see a solicitor. The police denied the request under s 58(8) (this gives them the power to delay access for 36 hours in certain circumstances), and in the meantime interviewed Samuel a third time. The Court of Appeal decided that the police did not have the power to delay access, and doubted whether the police would ever genuinely believe that a suspect's contact with a solicitor would lead to one of the situations in s 58(8)(a)–(c) occurring (basically, contact would have to lead to the suspect's associates being tipped off). The Court of Appeal went on to consider the application of s 78:

Extract 4.5.1

R v Samuel (1988) 87 Cr App R 232, pp 243–244, 245–246

The more sinister side to the decision is, of course, this. The police had, over a period exceeding 24 hours, interviewed this young man four times without obtaining any confession from him in respect of the robbery. Time was running out for them. It was a Thursday evening. Thirty six hours from the relevant time would expire in the early hours of the morning; then access to a solicitor would have to be permitted. On the following day the appellant would have to be taken before the magistrates' court (section 46). As he had already been interviewed four times and been in police custody for over 24 hours, the expectation would be that a solicitor might well consider that, at least for that evening, enough was enough and that he ought to advise his client not to answer further questions. There were, therefore, very few hours left for the police to interview the appellant without his having legal advice. And, as events showed, that was something the police very much wanted to do; this one knows because, within 37 minutes, he was in fact interviewed. All previous interviews had been conducted by a Detective Sergeant with a Detective Constable as notetaker. The interview at 5.20 p.m. was conducted by a Detective Inspector, the Sergeant and Detective being present, so that the appellant now faced a different questioner and a total of three policemen. At that interview he made the confession to the robbery. Regrettably we have come to the conclusion that whoever made the decision to refuse Mr. Warner access at 4.45 p.m. was very probably motivated by a desire to have one last chance of interviewing the appellant in the absence of a solicitor . . .

Mr. Warner gave evidence. He said it was not his policy always to advise a client not to answer questions put to him by the police. In his view, in many cases, it was of advantage to someone in detention to answer proper questions put to him. However on this occasion, knowing that his client had already been interviewed on four occasions and at each had strenuously denied complicity in the robbery and had already been charged with two serious offences, he would probably, after consultation, have advised his client, for the time being at any rate, to refuse to answer further questioning. The probable result of allowing the appellant to exercise his right would therefore, in all probability,

420

have been that, had a further interview taken place (and we think it improbable that the police would, in those circumstances, have thought it worth their while to interview him further) no incriminating replies would have been given.

. . . It is undesirable to attempt any general guidance as to the way in which a judge's discretion under section 78 or his inherent powers should be exercised. Circumstances vary infinitely. Mr. Jones has made the extreme submission that, in the absence of impropriety, the discretion should never be exercised to exclude admissible evidence. We have no hesitation in rejecting that submission, although the propriety or otherwise of the way in which the evidence was obtained is something which a court is, in terms, enjoined by the section to take into account.

This Court is always reluctant to interfere with the exercise of a judge's discretion but the position is different where there was no discretion to exercise on the judge's ruling and all the court has is an indication of how the judge would have exercised it. This is particularly so in this case where, on the section 58(8) point, the judge failed properly to address his mind to the point in time which was most material and did not in terms give consideration to what his decision would have been had he ruled in favour of the defence on this more fundamental issue before him.

In this case this appellant was denied improperly one of the most important and fundamental rights of a citizen. The trial judge fell into error in not so holding. If he had arrived at correct decisions on the two points argued before him he might well have concluded that the refusal of access and consequent unlawful interview compelled him to find that the admission of evidence as to the final interview would have 'such an adverse effect on the fairness of the proceedings' that he ought not to admit it. Such a decision would, of course, have very significantly weakened the prosecution case (the failure to charge earlier ineluctably shows this). In those circumstances this Court feels that it has no alternative but to quash the appellant's conviction on count 1 in the indictment, the charge of robbery.

Shortly after *Samuel* the Court of Appeal again considered s 78 in the light of a breach of s 58. In *Alladice* (1988) 87 Cr App R 380 the suspect was again refused access to legal advice. The police evidence was that during his interview he confessed. The Court of Appeal held that the police were again in breach of s 58: they had no reasonable grounds for believing that accomplices would be tipped off, instead their concern was that the suspect would be advised to remain silent during the interview.

Extract 4.5.2

R v Alladice (1988) 87 Cr App R 380, pp 386–387

If the police have acted in bad faith, the court will have little difficulty in ruling any confession inadmissible under section 78, if not under section 76. If the police, albeit in good faith, have nevertheless fallen foul of section 58, it is still necessary for the Court to decide whether to admit the evidence would adversely affect the fairness of the proceedings, and would do so to such an extent that the confession ought to be excluded. No doubt in many cases it will, and it behoves the police to use their powers of delaying access to a solicitor only with great circumspection. It is not possible to say in advance what would or would not be fair.

In *Samuel*... for instance, the solicitor in question gave evidence. He said it was not his policy always to advise a client not to answer questions put to him by the police. He took the view that it was in many cases of advantage to a detainee to answer proper questions put to him. In that particular case, however, he knew that his client had already been interviewed on four occasions on all of which he had strenuously denied being involved in the crime and had already been charged with two serious offences. He took the view that in those circumstances he would probably have advised his client to refuse to answer any further questions. The Court came to the conclusion that the judge, had he arrived at a correct conclusion on the two points argued before him, might well have decided that the refusal of access to a solicitor compelled him to find that the admission of the evidence would have had 'such an adverse effect on the fairness of the proceedings' that he ought not to have admitted it.

The judge in the instant case decided that the authorisation of delay was properly given, and consequently did not have to consider the question whether section 78 was applicable in the light of a breach of section 58.

What the appellant himself said in evidence was that he was well able to cope with the interviews; that he had been given the appropriate caution before each of them; that he had understood the caution and was aware of his rights. Indeed he asserted that he had said nothing at all after the first four (innocuous) questions, and what had been written down by the interviewing officer was nothing that he said but had been invented by the writer. His reason for wanting a solicitor was to have some sort of check on the conduct of the police during the interview.

The judge rejected the allegations that the police had invented the admissions. He found as a fact that the interviews had been conducted properly. He concluded that the only difference the presence of a solicitor would have made would have been to provide additional advice as to the appellant's right to say nothing, a right which he knew and understood and indeed at times during the interview exercised.

It may seldom happen that a defendant is so forthcoming about his attitude towards the presence of a legal adviser. That candour does however simplify the task of deciding whether the admission of the evidence 'would have such an adverse effect on the fairness of the proceedings' that it should not have been admitted. Had the solicitor been present, his advice would have added nothing to the knowledge of his rights which the appellant already had. The police, as the judge found, had acted with propriety at the interviews and therefore the solicitor's presence would not have improved the appellant's case in that respect.

This is therefore a case where a clear breach of section 58 nevertheless does not require the Court to rule inadmissible subsequent statements made by the defendant.

This appeal is accordingly dismissed.

An important element in the decisions on s 78 is the role played by the trial judge's discretion. It has been held that the section gives the trial judge a discretion to exclude evidence, and the Court of Appeal will not lightly interfere with such an exercise of discretion. It will only fault the trial judge's ruling to admit the evidence if, as in *Samuel*, it decides that the judge did not consider the question in the light of all the relevant facts, or if it holds that the trial judge's decision was unreasonable. We will return to this issue later.

In *Walsh* (1990) 91 Cr App R 161, where the defendant had been convicted of robbery and possession of a firearm, the breaches went somewhat further than those in *Samuel* and *Alladice*:

Extract 4.5.3

R v Walsh (1990) 91 Cr App R 161, pp 162–164

It is common ground that there was a breach of section 58 of the Act. The appellant had therefore been arrested and was being held in custody at the police station. He requested a solicitor, but was denied access to one on grounds that the Crown do not seek to suggest fell within the exceptions set out in that section. It is also common ground that in breach of Code C the police conducted the interview with a person who had asked for but not received legal advice (para 6.3 of the Code), that they failed to make contemporaneous notes (para 11.3(*b*)(2) and 11.4 of the Code), that they failed to record in the officers' pocket books the reasons for not keeping a record in the course of the interview (para 11.6 of the Code), that they failed to give the appellant a chance to read and sign an interview record (para 12.12 of the Code). It was also suggested that since the interview was conducted in a cell there had therefore been a failure to conduct it in an interview room (para 12.4 of the Code), but this the Crown do not necessarily accept, on the grounds which the Code of course allows, that it was not practicable in the circumstances.

In his ruling after the *voire dire* in which he had heard evidence from the senior police officers involved, the trial judge concluded that none of the officers had acted in bad faith. The trial judge further expressed the view that he did not feel, as he put it, that the provision of a solicitor would have made any difference to what was said during the interview. Overall, the trial judge in effect concluded that it did not appear to him that (using the words of s 78) the admission of the evidence of the interviews would have such an adverse effect on the fairness of the proceedings that the court ought not to admit that evidence.

The main object of section 58 of the Act and indeed of the Codes of Practice is to achieve fairness – to an accused or suspected person so as, among other things, to preserve and protect his legal rights; but also fairness for the Crown and its officers so that again, among other things, there might be reduced the incidence or effectiveness of unfounded allegations of malpractice.

To our minds it follows that if there are significant and substantial breaches of section 58 or the provisions of the Code, then prima facie at least the standards of fairness set by Parliament have not been met. So far as a defendant is concerned, it seems to us also to follow that to admit evidence against him which has been obtained in circumstances where these standards have not been met, cannot but have an adverse effect on the fairness of the proceedings. This does not mean, of course, that in every case of a significant or substantial breach of section 58 or the Code of Practice the evidence concerned will automatically be excluded. Section 78 does not so provide. The task of the court is not merely to consider whether there would be an adverse effect on the fairness of the proceedings, but such an adverse effect that justice requires the evidence to be excluded.

In the present case, we have no material which would lead us to suppose that the judge erred in concluding that the police officers were acting in good faith. However, although bad faith may make substantial or significant that which might not otherwise be so, the contrary does not follow. Breaches which are in themselves significant and substantial are not rendered otherwise by the good faith of the officers concerned.

In our judgment, leaving aside the possible breach in respect of where the interview was conducted, it seems to us that the breaches in this case were both significant and substantial. For no good reason the officers concerned failed to follow the proper proceedings, denying the appellant legal advice and neither protecting or preserving his right in the way laid down in the Code.

The trial judge expressed the view that even if a solicitor had been present he did not feel that this would have made any difference. However, Mr. Kamlish pointed out that the trial judge had not heard the appellant and, what is more, it is the fact that after the appellant had eventually seen a solicitor he exercised his right to not answer questions. It may be that the judge was influenced by the fact that the appellant had been cautioned before the interview under attack, but this seems to ignore the fact that the appellant was not only entitled to be cautioned, but also entitled to the benefit of legal advice from a solicitor.

Having considered the matter, we can see nothing in this case which could properly lead the court to the conclusion that the breach of section 58 made no difference; or in other words that it was likely that the appellant would have made the admissions in any event. The very highest it could be put, to our minds, was that it was perhaps uncertain whether or not the presence of a solicitor would have made any difference. Added to this, of course, is the fact that it appeared through the cross-examination of the officers during the *voir dire* that the appellant was challenging root and branch that he had made any admissions at all. Accordingly, it seems to us that a major, if not the major, premise on which the learned judge exercised his discretion was a false premise. This distinguishes the present case from such decisions as *Smith and Campbell*, which was cited to us. We should observe at this point that a number of other authorities have been brought to our attention on the Act, but since we consider that the judge proceeded on a false basis, it seems to us that they are only of general assistance in the circumstances of this particular case.

424

In these circumstances, coupled with the failure of the police officers to comply with the Code in the respects that we have categorised as significant and substantial, we consider that to admit the evidence would have such an adverse effect on the proceedings that the judge should have excluded it.

This decision introduces the concept of a 'significant and substantial' breach of PACE and the Codes, a concept which has been important in later cases.

In *Dunford* (1990) 91 Cr App R 150 the Court of Appeal observed that s 58 had been breached, but decided not to interfere with the trial judge's discretion. It put particular emphasis on the reasoning in *Alladice*, under which a defendant's knowledge of his rights is important:

> If a man shows, as this man did, according to the words used, that he knew that he could answer 'no comment' and could refuse to sign an interview, and if a man has experience of arrest, we do not believe that a judge must or can simply pay no attention to those facts. (at p 154)

A good example of the effect of this accumulated case law is *Oliphant* [1992] Crim LR 40 (some of the quotations below are from a transcript of the case). The defendant was being interviewed about a bank robbery. During the interview he asked to talk to his solicitor. At this point the police officers should have stopped the interview (under Code C (6.6)). They did not: they continued to question the defendant, who then made extensive and damaging admissions. The trial judge had held that this was not a significant and substantial breach of the Codes, but the Court of Appeal disagreed: the defendant was denied 'one of his most important and fundamental protections as a citizen' and this was 'a serious inroad on his rights'. The Court cited *Walsh* as one of the most important decisions on the issue, but noted that not every significant and substantial breach would lead to the exclusion of evidence. This led the Court of Appeal to the heart of the problem: it would not usually interfere with the discretion of the trial judge, but here, as in *Samuel*, the judge had not exercised his discretion properly because he had not recognised the seriousness of the officers' misconduct. However, the Court of Appeal also considered the causal point referred to in *Alladice* and *Dunford*: although the defendant had not had prior experience of police interviews, he was a mature man and had been told what his rights were. The trial judge had concluded that: 'I am sure that the presence of a solicitor would have added nothing to [the appellant's] knowledge of his legal rights. The admissions made by him were made because he wanted to make such admissions.' In the light of this, the Court of Appeal would not interfere with the judge's exercise of his discretion:

> it is, in our judgment, not possible to say that the conclusion of the judge, that he was satisfied, so that he was sure, that the absence of a solicitor did not have an adverse effect on the fairness of the proceedings, was a conclusion to which the judge was not entitled to come. It was not a conclusion which this court would criticise in any way and certainly not interfere with.

What are the principles underlying the case law on s 78? The Court of Appeal decisions are certainly not motivated by an urge to discipline the police (see dicta to this effect in *Mason* [1988] 1 WLR 139), though of course, exclusionary decisions made on other grounds may still deter the police from misconduct (as we saw in Chapter 3 above, there is evidence that the decision in *Samuel* had a deterrent effect on the police). Nor are the courts particularly motivated by reliability: reliability concerns are dealt with under s 76, and the courts in *Samuel* and *Walsh* were not concerned about the reliability of the defendants' confessions. Are the courts trying to protect suspects' rights, or their civil liberties? This seems to come closer to being a description of the case law, but there is no protection of rights in the abstract. Alladice, Dunford and Oliphant all had a right to a solicitor, and insofar as their requests for legal advice were improperly denied, this right was infringed. What the courts want to know is whether this caused any identifiable detriment to the defendant: would a solicitor's advice have changed the way in which the defendant responded to the interviewer's questions? If so, this may render the trial unfair and justify exclusion, though in *Oliphant* the Court of Appeal expresses a final caveat:

> The task of the court is not merely to consider whether there would have been an adverse effect on the fairness of the proceedings but whether justice requires the evidence to be excluded. In other words, whether it would have 'such an adverse effect on the fairness of the proceedings that the court ought not to admit it'.

There is a lot of room for manoeuvre here. The trial judge has a large degree of discretion when deciding the fairness question. There is also much discretion in the trial judge's finding of fact on the causal issue: he or she must ask whether the solicitor's presence would have made a difference, a question of hypothetical causation which there is no obvious means of addressing. The appeal court also has discretion in deciding whether or not the judge's decision can be supported by the facts. In *Walsh*, the Court of Appeal, quashing the decision, remarks that: 'the very highest it could be put, to our minds, was that it was perhaps uncertain whether or not the presence of a solicitor would have made any difference'. Contrast the remarks in *Oliphant*, quoted above: 'it is not possible to say that the conclusion of the judge . . . that the absence of a solicitor did not have an adverse effect . . . was a conclusion to which the judge was not entitled to come'.

The suspect's right to legal advice has now been considered in a decision of the European Court of Human Rights. In *Murray v UK* (1996) 22 EHRR 29 (considered, in connection with the right to silence, in Chapter 3 above), the applicant had been denied legal advice for 48 hours while he was held in police custody. Murray's arrest and detention had taken place in Northern Ireland, and under the law in force in that jurisdiction the police had the power to do this. The Court held that this was a violation of Murray's right to a fair trial under Article 6 of the Convention. The Order to which the Court refers allows courts in Northern Ireland to draw inferences from a suspect's silence during police questioning: its effects are substantially similar to those of s 34 of the Criminal Justice and Public Order Act 1994 (see Chapter 3 above).

Extract 4.5.4

Murray v UK (1996) 22 EHRR 29, paras 63–68 (footnotes omitted)

63. National laws may attach consequences to the attitude of an accused at the initial stages of police interrogation which are decisive for the prospects of the defence in any subsequent criminal proceedings. In such circumstances Article 6 will normally require that the accused be allowed to benefit from the assistance of a lawyer already at the initial stages of police interrogation. However, this right, which is not explicitly set out in the Convention, may be subject to restrictions for good cause. The question in each case, is whether the restriction, in the light of the entirety of the proceedings, has deprived the accused of a fair hearing.

64. In the present case, the applicant's right of access to a lawyer during the first 48 hours of police detention was restricted under section 15 of the Northern Ireland (Emergency Provisions) Act 1987 on the basis that the police had reasonable grounds to believe that the exercise of the right of access would, *inter alia*, interfere with the gathering of information about the commission of acts of terrorism or make it more difficult to prevent such an act.

65. It is observed that the applicant did not seek to challenge the exercise of this power by instituting proceedings for judicial review although, before the Court, he now contests its lawfulness. The Court, however, has no reason to doubt that it amounted to a lawful exercise of the power to restrict access. Nevertheless, although it is an important element to be taken into account, even a lawfully exercised power of restriction is capable of depriving an accused, in certain circumstances, of a fair procedure.

66. The Court is of the opinion that the scheme contained in the Order is such that it is of paramount importance for the rights of the defence that an accused has access to a lawyer at the initial stages of police interrogation. It observes in this context that, under the Order, at the beginning of police interrogation, an accused is confronted with a fundamental dilemma relating to his defence. If he chooses to remain silent, adverse inferences may be drawn against him in accordance with the provisions of the Order. On the other hand, if the accused opts to break his silence during the course of interrogation, he runs the risk of prejudicing his defence without necessarily removing the possibility of inferences being drawn against him.

Under such conditions the concept of fairness enshrined in Article 6 requires that the accused has the benefit of the assistance of a lawyer already at the initial stages of police interrogation. To deny access to a lawyer for the first 48 hours of police questioning, in a situation where the rights of the defence may well be irretrievably prejudiced, is – whatever the justification for such denial – incompatible with the rights of the accused under Article 6.

67. The Government has argued, that in order to complain under Article 6 of denial of access to a lawyer it must be clear that had the applicant been able to consult with his solicitor earlier, he would have acted differently from the way he did. It is contended that the applicant has not shown this to be the case.

68. It is true, as pointed out by the Government, that when the applicant was able to consult with his solicitor he was advised to continue to remain silent and that during the trial the applicant chose not to give evidence or call witnesses on his behalf. However, it is not for the Court to speculate on what the applicant's reaction, or his lawyer's advice, would have been had access not been denied during this initial period. As matters stand, the applicant was undoubtedly directly affected by the denial of access and the ensuing interference with the rights of the defence. The Court's conclusion as to the drawing of inferences does not alter that.

It will be seen that the European Court of Human Rights approaches the question from a different perspective to the Court of Appeal. In paras 67–68 it explicitly rejects the causal reasoning which forms an important strand of the English case law. In part, this reflects the different functions of the two courts. The European court is concerned with the violation of the rights enshrined in the Convention. It has not, to date, ventured beyond this to consider questions about appropriate rules for the admissibility of evidence, seeing this as a matter for member states. This does not, though, mean that the Convention is irrelevant to a court considering the application of s 78. Both Article 6 and s 78 are concerned with fair trials. In *Khan* [1996] 3 WLR 162, at p 175 the House of Lords recognised that there was a large degree of overlap between them. Just how much overlap there is will become an important question when the European Convention on Human Rights is incorporated into English law. If the courts decide that the fairness concerns expressed in Article 6 and the jurisprudence of the European Court of Human Rights are identical to the fairness concerns protected by s 78, then, if the reasoning in *Murray* is accepted, the courts will have to exclude evidence in cases such as *Alladice* and *Oliphant*. The courts might avoid this outcome by opening up a gap between Article 6 and s 78, perhaps by stressing the words 'such an adverse effect on the fairness of the proceedings' in s 78, which imply that some degree of unfairness is condonable. If this approach is taken, the legal system will have to offer some other remedy to those defendants whose Article 6 rights are breached in circumstances that do not trigger the operation of s 78. If Article 6 and s 78 are held to cover identical ground, then the Court of Appeal may have to rethink the degree of discretion which has been granted to judges under s 78, because that discretion, with its concomitant freedom from review on appeal, hampers the protection of defendants' rights.

So far we have considered the exclusion of evidence in the light of the courts' interpretation of s 78 of PACE. Our analysis suggests that the English courts have developed a fairly narrow conception of fairness at trial, under which a trial will usually be fair unless there is some evidence that the defendant was materially affected by police misconduct. The exclusion of such evidence is one example of the impact of an issue external to proof on the trial process. It can be argued, however, that the criminal trial should reflect broader principles of fairness and equity.

Extract 4.5.5

I Dennis, 'Reconstructing the Law of Criminal Evidence' (1989)
Current Legal Problems **21, pp 35–38 (some footnotes omitted)**

The theory of the legitimacy of the verdict

Theorising about the law of criminal evidence needs to begin with the substantive law. Evidence, like procedure, is adjectival law; we cannot properly understand its purposes without reference to its context. Thus we should look first to the criminal law to which it forms an adjunct. Let me open therefore with some very basic propositions about the criminal law. First, its primary aim is to influence behaviour. In the words of Hart: 'The aim of making an act criminal is to announce to society that these acts are not to be done and to secure that fewer of them are done.'[1] Secondly, at the root of the principles of criminal liability is a moral concern to accord to all citizens equal respect and dignity.[2] As part of this concern the criminal law accords persons the status of autonomous moral agents with an entitlement to freedom of action and the ability to exercise self-determination in their choice of actions.[3] The fundamental doctrine that there is in general no criminal liability without *mens rea* is a clear expression of this moral principle. A person's freedom of action is not to be interfered with until it appears to have been knowingly abused. Thirdly, punishment involves the imposition of both a legal sanction, such as imprisonment or a fine, and a moral sanction in the form of the stigma of conviction. Fourthly, punishment should in general only be applied to a person who chose to break the law and who deserves to be punished.[4] . . .

Reminding ourselves of these basic propositions is helpful when we consider criminal trials. A criminal trial is a formal process of application of the criminal law to a citizen, and it is generally regarded as essential that that process should be public. The process should be open to all to see, hear and read about. This concern for publicity is an important clue to the purposes of trials and to the law of evidence which regulates them. It suggests amongst other things that the trial may be a medium of communication with the public at large. Within the trial the values attached to freedom and dignity require that the state should justify its claim that formal condemnation and punishment of the defendant should take place. Hence the principle that the burden of proof is on the prosecution to prove guilt beyond reasonable doubt. Now it seems to me that justifying the claim for condemnation and punishment contains both a factual and a moral dimension. The official imposition of a moral sanction calls for a moral justification. A verdict of guilty should reflect therefore the judgment of the tribunal not only that the defendant did in fact commit the alleged offence – a factual judgment – but also that he deserves to be convicted and punished for it – which is a moral judgment. Moreover it is essential that the verdict be publicly acceptable, in the sense that it is perceived as being factually accurate and as having moral authority.

The reasons for these claims have to do with the functions of the verdict and its relationship to the aims of the criminal law. A verdict of guilty or not guilty is more than just a factual statement. It is not like a pathologist's report any more than the criminal trial is like a diagnostic procedure.[5] The criminal trial in common law jurisdictions is a procedure which aims to be demonstrative *and* justificatory. When the defendant pleads not guilty he puts the prosecution to proof of their allegations. He requires them to demonstrate his *guilt* both to the satisfaction of himself and the public. At one level the verdict represents a conclusion that the factual demonstration has or has not been made out. But this is not the only message that the verdict carries. A verdict of guilty also conveys moral condemnation of the defendant. It is an expression of moral blame. At a deeper level the verdict is additionally an expression of the norms of the criminal law and of the consequences of breach of such norms. That is to say the verdict does not just communicate the result of one particular trial. Its further function is expressive. It emphasises the behavioural constraints imposed by the criminal law and points to the example of the defendant to increase the effectiveness of the message. This wider function of the verdict is perfectly well understood by the policy-oriented organs of the state. They frequently emphasise the importance of convictions in furthering the policy of crime control. Acquittals do little to reinforce behavioural constraints.

We may now explore further this notion of the several dimensions of the verdict. The factual judgment, that the defendant did or did not commit the offence, is a judgment on the probative value of the evidence. The moral judgment, that the defendant should or should not be convicted, is more complex. Clearly it is not independent of the factual judgment. A factual judgment that the defendant did not commit the offence should always result in an acquittal. A conclusion that the defendant deserved to be convicted despite not having committed the offence would be unacceptable. It would be inconsistent with the fundamental principles of responsibility and punishment I mentioned earlier. A judgment that the defendant did commit the offence should, presumptively, result in a conviction. It would tend to undermine the aims of the criminal law if those judged to have broken its terms in fact were not convicted. However, the moral authority of the verdict, and hence its justificatory and expressive value, is not necessarily to be equated with the factual judgment. We have only to return to the example of the confession obtained by torture to see this point. The confession may be perfectly reliable in proving that the defendant in fact committed the offence. But would a verdict of guilty be acceptable as a justification of punishment and as an expression of the values of the criminal law? I suggest that it would not. The use of torture amounts to a gross violation of the principle of according all citizens respect and dignity. Such a violation destroys the moral authority of the verdict. This is because a verdict which is derived from a disregard for the core principle of criminal law is self-contradictory. It cannot function as an expressive message that the criminal law incorporates values which it is necessary to uphold while appearing to be based itself on a deliberate flouting of those values. This must inevitably lead to a loss of respect both for the trial process and for the criminal law itself.

We are now in a position to appreciate more clearly the proper purposes of the law of criminal evidence. That law has as its goal not the discovery of some kind of historical truth about what the defendant did or did not do. The goal is rather the legitimacy of the verdict on whether the charge against him has been properly proved. Recognising that the verdict serves a number or important public functions, the law is constructed so as to ensure that the verdict will be able to discharge those functions. This means that it will be concerned both with factual accuracy, and hence with reliability of evidence, *and* with the moral integrity of the judgment. Translated into terms of admissibility these concerns mean that in principle all relevant evidence should be admitted because this will promote factually accurate judgments. Such judgments should be, and usually are, sufficient to satisfy the justificatory and expressive functions of the verdict. But equally, we may need principles of exclusion based on one or other of two grounds. Apparently *relevant* evidence may need to be excluded if it carries risks of unreliability outweighing its probative value.[6] Such evidence will tend to detract from the factual accuracy of the verdict. Apparently *reliable* evidence may need to be excluded if it carries significant risks of impairing the moral authority of the verdict. This is because it is not in the public interest that verdicts should be returned which lack moral authority. They are not satisfactory either for justifying individual punishment or for affirming the values of the criminal law. If relevant evidence is excluded on either ground it will be because we are giving effect to values which are internal, not external, to the process of proof.

A number of important conclusions follow from this approach. Truth-finding changes its character as an element in the trial process from that of the ultimate goal to that of an instrumental value. It becomes a means, in fact the major means, by which a legitimate verdict is secured, but it is the legitimacy of the verdict which is the ultimate goal. I want to emphasise at this point that I am not intending to enunciate some subversive or cynical doctrine. I do not want to associate myself with the judge who came to deliver judgment at the end of one particularly tricky case. After reviewing all the evidence the judge concluded:

'In summary I do not know whether you are guilty or not. There is an element of doubt in this case, but you are not getting the benefit of it. I am sending you to prison for six months. If you are guilty you have got off lightly. If you are innocent let it be a lesson to you.'

I repeat therefore that a factually inaccurate or doubtful conviction can never be legitimate. But I do want to stress that a factually accurate conviction may not be legitimate because it lacks moral authority.

---

[1] *Punishment and Responsibility* (1968) p 6.
[2] Gross, *A Theory of Criminal Justice* (1979) pp 32–33; Stein and Shand, *Legal Values in Western Society* (1974) pp 130 et seq.
[3] Walker, *Punishment, Danger and Stigma* (1980) Ch 7.
[4] Hart, op cit, Chs I and VII, esp at pp 8–13.
[5] See Duff, *Trials and Punishments* (1986) Ch 4.
[6] An obvious illustration is a voluntary confession by a person suffering from a mental disorder or mental handicap: *R v Stewart* (1972) 56 Cr App R 272; *R v Miller* [1986] 1 WLR 1191.

Dennis goes on to argue that the legitimacy principle provides a better explanation of how the courts are interpreting s 78 of PACE than any of the other theories so far outlined. A particularly telling point is that where the police have broken the rules contained in PACE, the fact that they have acted in bad faith has been held to weigh in favour of exclusion (there are dicta to this effect in *Walsh* and *Samuel*). If the concern is to remedy defendants for abrogation of their rights, then the issue of whether the police acted in good faith should be irrelevant. While the concept of legitimacy has considerable explanatory power, it should be noted that the courts do not refer to it specifically, and the principle is perhaps vague enough for it to serve as an explanation for almost any pattern of case law.

For similar arguments about the legitimacy of trial verdicts, see Zuckerman (1987), Duff (1986, Ch 4), Allan (1992; 1995) and Choo (1993, Ch 1).

One example of an application of the legitimacy principle is the doctrine of abuse of process. Under this doctrine a court may go further than excluding evidence: it may refuse to proceed with a case because it would be an abuse of the court's process to do so. An example is *Croydon JJ, ex parte Dean* [1993] QB 769. The defendant had been promised by the police that he would not be prosecuted for his part in destroying evidence which implicated friends of his in a murder. However, prosecution decisions do not rest ultimately with the police, and the Crown Prosecution Service prosecuted the defendant. The court ruled that the prosecution was an abuse of process because of the promise that had been made.

An example of the width of the abuse of process doctrine is the House of Lords' decision in *Bennett v Horseferry Road Magistrates' Court* [1993] 3 All ER 138. Bennett, who was a New Zealand citizen, was wanted by the police in England. He was arrested by police in South Africa, but in the absence of an extradition treaty he could not be extradited to the United Kingdom. Nevertheless, the South African police put him on a plane to London, handcuffed him to the seat, and on his arrival he was arrested. During committal proceedings Bennett argued that it would be an abuse of process for him to be tried in England because of the way he had been brought there. Faced with conflicting lines of authority on the issue, the Divisional Court had held that the behaviour of the authorities was irrelevant:

> The power which the court is exercising [in abuse of process cases] is one which is based on the inherent power of the court to protect itself against the abuse of its own process. If the matters which are being relied upon have nothing to do with that process but only explain how a person comes to be within the jurisdiction so that that process can commence, it seems to me difficult to see how the process of the *court* (and I emphasise the word 'court') can be abused by the fact that a person may or may not have been brought to this country improperly. ([1993] 2 All ER 474, at p 479)

The House of Lords took a different view:

Extract 4.5.6

Bennett v Horseferry Road Magistrates' Court [1993] 3 All ER 138, pp 150–151

LORD GRIFFITHS: Your Lordships are now invited to extend the concept of abuse of process a stage further. In the present case there is no suggestion that the appellant cannot have a fair trial, nor could it be suggested that it would have been unfair to try him if he had been returned to this country through extradition procedures. If the court is to have the power to interfere with the prosecution in the present circumstances it must be because the judiciary accept a responsibility for the maintenance of the rule of law that embraces a willingness to oversee executive action and to refuse to countenance behaviour that threatens either basic human rights or the rule of law.

My Lords, I have no doubt that the judiciary should accept this responsibility in the field of criminal law. The great growth of administrative law during the latter half of this century has occurred because of the recognition by the judiciary and Parliament alike that it is the function of the High Court to ensure that executive action is exercised responsibly and as Parliament intended. So also should it be in the field of criminal law and if it comes to the attention of the court that there has been a serious abuse of power it should, in my view, express its disapproval by refusing to act upon it.

Let us consider the position in the context of extradition. Extradition procedures are designed not only to ensure that criminals are returned from one country to another but also to protect the rights of those who are accused of crimes by the requesting country. Thus sufficient evidence has to be produced to show a prima facie case against the accused and the rule of speciality protects the accused from being tried for any crime other than that for which he was extradited. If a practice developed in which the police or prosecuting authorities of this country ignored extradition procedures and secured the return of an accused by a mere request to police colleagues in another country they would be flouting the extradition procedures and depriving the accused of the safeguards built into the extradition process for his benefit. It is to my mind unthinkable that in such circumstances the court should declare itself to be powerless and stand idly by; I echo the words of Lord Devlin in *Connelly v DPP* [1964] 2 All ER 401 at 442, [1964] AC 1254 at 1354:

'The courts cannot contemplate for a moment the transference to the executive of the responsibility for seeing that the process of law is not abused.'

The courts, of course, have no power to apply direct discipline to the police or the prosecuting authorities, but they can refuse to allow them to take advantage of abuse of power by regarding their behaviour as an abuse of process and thus preventing a prosecution.

In my view your Lordships should now declare that where process of law is available to return an accused to this country through extradition procedures our courts will refuse to try him if he has been forcibly brought within our jurisdiction in disregard of those procedures by a process to which our own police, prosecuting or other executive authorities have been a knowing party.

433

If extradition is not available very different considerations will arise on which I express no opinion.

Lord Oliver dissented, arguing that the courts had no authority to stay proceedings where wrongful treatment of the accused did not affect the fairness of the trial, and that to give them such authority would create hopeless uncertainty.

(b) Police tricks, entrapment and criminal trials

Now that we have examined some of the arguments surrounding the exclusion of evidence and the integrity of the courts, we turn again to examine one particular area of case law in more detail. In the cases concerning s 58 of PACE, which we considered above, the police had broken the rules of PACE. In some cases this leads the courts to exclude evidence. But what if the police have not broken the rules, but have simply played a trick on the defendant? In *Mason* [1987] 3 All ER 481 the defendant had been arrested on suspicion of arson. Fragments of glass had been found near the scene of the fire. These were from a bottle that had been used to carry the petrol that had started the fire. The police told Mason and his solicitor that Mason's fingerprint had been found on one of the fragments. This was a lie, but as a consequence the defendant admitted involvement in the crime. The Court of Appeal ruled that, under s 78, the confession should not have been admitted by the trial judge. The court did not explain why this would render a subsequent trial unfair, but it put particular emphasis on the fact that Mason's solicitor had also been tricked, which suggests that the effect on the solicitor's ability to advise his client was a particularly important factor. In *Bailey* [1993] 3 All ER 513 the police bugged the cell in which they placed the defendants, hoping that the defendants would make incriminating statements while alone together. In order to allay the defendants' suspicions, they pretended that putting the defendants in the same cell was the last thing they wanted, but that they were forced to do it by an unco-operative custody officer. The result of this was that the defendants did indeed make incriminating statements which were admitted at trial. The Court of Appeal refused to criticise the trial judge's decision: in contrast to *Mason*, there was no unfairness (see also *Jelen and Katz* (1989) 90 Cr App R 456, and note the case of Colin Stagg, discussed in Chapter 3 above, where the trial judge excluded evidence on account of 'a blatant attempt to incriminate a suspect by positive and deceptive conduct of the grossest kind').

Mason and *Bailey* involved tricks played upon suspects in order to obtain confessions, after the crime under investigation had been committed. What if the trick is played on a person in order to induce him or her to commit a crime? Here we enter the world of entrapment and *agents provocateurs*. We noted in Chapter 3 that, partly because of unease about confession evidence, the police are increasingly employing proactive methods for catching offenders.

434

Proactive enforcement may also be the only way to investigate some criminal activity, such as drugs offences, where there is no obvious victim to report the crime. A number of cases involving proactive tactics have come to the attention of the courts in recent years.

Entrapment occurs when a person is induced to commit a crime that he or she would otherwise not have committed. If this is to be seen as a defence, then the inducement would have to come from an *agent provocateur*, that is, someone acting on the authority of the police. The fact that X induces Y to commit a crime has no effect on Y's culpability in law (unless the inducement amounts to duress). Objections to such conduct generally only arise when the state is involved. In the leading case of *Sang* [1980] AC 402 the House of Lords held that in English law entrapment was not a defence to a criminal charge (though it might lead to mitigation of sentence). Nor would the courts exclude evidence that had been obtained through entrapment. In part this was because the exclusion of evidence would have the effect of creating the defence through the back door. But the House of Lords also held that judges only had a discretion to exclude relevant evidence in limited circumstances: (1) where the prejudicial effect of the evidence outweighed its probative value and (2) where the evidence (most often a confession) was obtained after the commission of the offence, in which circumstances it might be excluded if it had been obtained by unfair means (this reflects the privilege against self-incrimination). Beyond this, judges were held to have no power to exclude evidence simply because it was obtained unfairly, or even illegally.

Sang remains influential, but it will be obvious that the judgment should be read in the light of the power given to the courts under s 78 of PACE. Thus, in *Gill and Ranuana* [1989] Crim LR 358 (the quotation below is from a transcript of the case) the Court of Appeal held that s 78 might allow the courts to exclude evidence gained by entrapment; this was confirmed in *Smurthwaite and Gill* (1994) 98 Cr App R 437. In *Gill and Ranuana* the defendants had been convicted of conspiracy to murder. Gill claimed that his involvement in the conspiracy had been induced by a police informer who was described in the following terms by the Court of Appeal:

> There is no doubt that the informer John was a highly undesirable character, as indeed most informants of this type are. He had been a police informer for some considerable time and no doubt the matter which was uppermost in his mind was first of all to save his own skin so far as possible, and secondly to lay up such credit as he could with the police which might stand him in good stead when his own crimes came to light. Indeed he was at that very time subject to a proposed prosecution for various crimes of an unsavoury nature such as, we are told, the swindling of a charity and also suggestions of blackmail.

The trial judge had accepted that it may have been the informer who had put forward the idea of the murder conspiracy (though the Court of Appeal was more sceptical about this), but the crucial finding of fact was that the informer was not an *agent provocateur*. The trial judge had decided that, even if John had instigated the conspiracy, he did so on his own initiative, not on that of the police.

In *Christou and Wright* (1992) 95 Cr App R 264 the defendants fell victim to an elaborate police operation. Undercover officers set up a jewellery shop, 'Stardust Jewellers', in North London. Their aim was to attract people selling stolen jewellery, and in this they were successful. The defendants were convicted of handling stolen goods, but appealed, arguing that evidence of what they did while in the shop should have been excluded under s 78. Their appeals were dismissed, the Court of Appeal observing (at p 267) that this was not really a case of entrapment:

> The police were clearly engaged in a trick or deceit. However, they did not themselves participate in the commission of any offence; nor did they act as *agents provocateurs* or incite crime. The offences charged had already been committed before the appellants entered the shop and the police, so far from having any dishonest intent, were concerned to return the property to its rightful owners and bring offenders to justice. The police referred daily to the current price of gold announced by Johnson Matthey and pitched the prices they offered appropriately to the form of dealing in which they purported to be engaged. So, no market was provided which would not have been available elsewhere.

Or, as it was put more pithily, 'the trick was not applied to the appellants; they voluntarily applied themselves to the trick' (at p 269).

In *Williams* (1994) 98 Cr App R 209 the trick went a stage further. The police left a van parked on a street in an area with a high rate of vehicle crime. Visible through the partly open door of the van were what appeared to be a number of cigarette cartons. The police kept watch on the van, at one point having to intercept two eight year-old boys who had taken one of the cartons from it. Later the defendants noticed the van and, after observing it for 10 minutes, started to remove cartons from it.

Extract 4.5.7

R v Williams (1994) 98 Cr App R 209, pp 212–215

It is contended by Mr. Meikle for the appellants that the whole of the evidence of the activities of the two appellants on that day, as observed by the watching police officers, and therefore the entire sum of the prosecution evidence for practical purposes, should be declared inadmissible on the grounds that the appellants were unfairly incited, induced or provoked into committing an offence which they would not otherwise have committed by police officers acting, in effect, as *agents provocateurs* by leaving irresistible temptations in their path.

This contention is based either upon the general principles of the common law, at least so far as any admissions made by the appellants are concerned, or more particularly upon the specific provision of section 78(1) of the Police and Criminal Evidence Act 1984 with reference to the evidence of the appellants' behaviour generally. The justices came to the conclusion, as I have indicated, that the police officers were not acting as *agents provocateurs* within the meaning of that term whether as described in the Report of the Royal Commission on Police Powers, which was produced in 1928, nor in the sense described by Lord Salmon in *R v Sang* (1979) 69 Cr.App.R. 282, [1980] A.C. 402. The police did not incite, counsel or procure the commission of any offence, nor did they direct their operation at any particular individual and certainly not at the appellants.

In my judgment, these findings by the justices were plainly fully justified on the evidence. The justices accordingly came to the conclusion that in all the circumstances the admission of this evidence would not have such an adverse effect upon the fairness of the proceedings that they should exclude it, and it is this decision which is the subject of this appeal. The questions therefore that are posed for the opinion of this court are threefold: (1) whether the police officers on the admitted evidence of entrapment were acting as *agents provocateurs*; (2) whether the justices were right in law not to exclude the evidence of the police acting as *agents provocateurs*; (3) whether the justices failed properly to exercise their discretion under the common law and under section 78 of the Police and Criminal Evidence Act to exclude the evidence which any reasonable bench of magistrates properly directing themselves as to the facts would have done.

It is apparent from the justices' findings that counsel then appearing for the prosecution was prepared to concede that the circumstances in which the police were able to obtain this eye witness evidence against these appellants amounted to entrapment. For myself, I am far from satisfied that this was a concession properly made. But, given that the defence of entrapment is not one known to the law of England, in the event the concession may be of little consequence. The essential question for the justices, whether looked at from the common law standpoint or from that of section 78(1) of PACE, is whether the admission of the evidence would so prejudice a fair trial that it ought not to be admitted. The criterion of unfairness to be applied is the same in either case (see *Christou and Wright* (1992) 95 Cr.App.R. 264, [1992] 3 W.L.R. 228).

It is, in my judgment, clear from the justices' findings that the police officers were not acting as *agents provocateurs*. In no sense were they participating in or inciting, procuring or counselling the commission of any crime. That phraseology is taken from the Home Office circular number 97 of 1969 in which that phraseology is used, in my judgment rightly, to describe the essential characteristics of an *agent provocateur*. The police officers did nothing to force, persuade, encourage or coerce the appellants to do what they did. The appellants did the acts complained of voluntarily, of their own free will, in the absence of any pressure and with full understanding of their own dishonesty.

In one sense it may be said that the appellants were tricked into providing evidence against themselves by interfering with the van which they thought had been genuinely left unattended when in fact it was being kept under observation all the time by the police. But the true view of such a situation was neatly put by Lord Taylor of Gosforth C J in *Christou and Wright*. That was a case where an undercover police operation in London was set up in Hatton Garden in a shop which purported to buy and sell jewellery commercially and which was understood to be open for business to deal in stolen property. A situation very akin to the present arose at the trial of a number of people who had been detected as participating in either burglary or handling stolen goods as a result of the activities of undercover police officers in that shop. A very similar submission as to the admissibility of the evidence thus gleaned was mounted before the trial judge at the Crown Court at Wood Green and thereafter before this Court.

The learned trial judge, His Honour Judge McMullan, in his ruling said at p 269 and p 235:

'They were not tricked into doing what they would not otherwise have done, they were tricked into doing what they wanted to do in that place and before witnesses and devices who can now speak of what happened, I do not think that is unfair or leads to an unfairness in the trial.'

With reference to that part of the ruling by the learned trial judge, the Lord Chief Justice said this (at p 269 and p 235D):

'Putting it in different words, the trick was not applied to the appellants; they voluntarily applied themselves to the trick. It is not every trick producing evidence against an accused which results in unfairness. There are, in criminal investigations, a number of situations in which the police adopt ruses or tricks in the public interest to obtain evidence. For example, to trap a blackmailer, the victim may be used as an agent of the police to arrange an appointment and false or marked money may be laid as bait to catch the offender. A trick, certainly; in a sense too, a trick which results in a form of self-incrimination; but not one which could reasonably be thought to involve unfairness.'

The learned Lord Chief Justice went on to draw the obvious distinction between that situation and that which arose in such well-known cases as *Payne* (1963) 47 Cr.App.R. 122, [1963] 1 W.L.R. 637 and *Mason* (1988) 86 Cr.App.R. 349, [1988] 1 W.L.R. 139, which are plainly cases which are very different.

Mr. Meikle seeks to draw the distinction that in *Christou and Wright* what the police officers were doing was not seeking to induce or incite the commission of fresh offences but to obtain evidence of offences which had already and previously been committed by the customers of this bogus trading establishment.

That, as it seems to me, is to some extent a distinction without a difference and I am reinforced in that view by the similarity that, as it seems to me, arises between what happened in this case and what happens in other cases of a not dissimilar nature, as was mentioned in argument, where in an attempt to track down a molester of women, as from time to time occurs, a young policewoman who is usually not lacking in courage is dressed in plain clothes and set to walk about in the areas, usually at night, where the molester is thought to be operating in the hope that he will attack the young policewoman who is under the observation of her colleagues and will as a result be caught.

If Mr. Meikle's submissions are soundly based, any evidence gathered as a result of such an exercise would have to be excluded on the grounds of unfairness, notwithstanding the fact that the attack upon the young policewoman would itself constitute an offence which would no doubt give rise to

438

prosecution. Such a conclusion does not, I have to say, immediately appeal to common sense.

Further support in my judgment is provided by the views expressed by this court in *Director of Public Prosecutions v Marshall* [1988] 3 All ER 683, another case which in all significant respects, as it seems to me, bears a close similarity to the situation that obtained in this case. *Marshall* is a decision of this Court consisting of Woolf L J (as he then was) and Hutchinson J. I will read the headnote:

'Police officers in plain clothes purchased four cans of lager and a bottle of wine from the respondents' shop. The respondents were licensed to sell liquor by the case but not to sell individual cans or bottles of liquor. The respondents were charged with having sold the lager and the wine without having the requisite justices' licence, contrary to section 160 of the Licensing Act 1964. At the hearing before the magistrates the respondents contended that the police officers' evidence should be excluded under section 78(1) of the Police and Criminal Evidence Act 1984 as having "an adverse effect on the fairness of the proceedings" since it had been unfairly obtained because the officers had not at the time of the purchase revealed the fact that they were police officers. The magistrates accepted that contention and the prosecution was unable to proceed. The Director of Public Prosecutions appealed by way of case stated against the magistrates' decision . . .'

This Court held that the evidence of the police officers had been wrongly excluded by the magistrates since it had not been shown that the evidence of police officers who made test purchases in plain clothes would have an adverse effect upon the fairness of the proceedings.

In the course of his judgment Woolf L J pointed out that the police officers had made those purchases in plain clothes without revealing that they were police officers, presumably for the obvious reason that, if they had revealed the fact that they were police officers, they would not have been able to make the purchases that they did and thus establish the basis for the laying of the information. He went on to point out that, if the justices were entitled to exclude evidence on the basis on which the justices in this case decided to exclude the evidence, that could have wide-reaching implications on the methods adopted of obtaining evidence in a large range of criminal offences of this sort. He then went on to say, at p 685:

'Perhaps unfairly, I invited counsel for the respondents to indicate how it could be said that the admission of the evidence of the police officers in this case would have an adverse effect on the fairness of the proceedings. Counsel for the respondents was unable to give an indication as to why it would have any adverse effect on the fairness of the proceedings and was candid enough to accept that it is difficult to see, if those words of the section are focused on, how the evidence in question could have an adverse effect on the fairness of the proceedings.'

Equally unfairly, I fear, I asked Mr. Meikle the same question. He struggled manfully to answer the question, but, with all respect to him, I have to say that he was able to give me no more satisfactory answer than counsel in *Marshall's* case was able to give to Woolf L J. Also, the respondent in *Marshall's* case committed the offence in question under the eyes of and, in one sense, at the invitation of the police officers who tricked him into thinking that they were ordinary customers, but this Court took the view, unhesitatingly, that there was no sufficient adverse effect on the fairness of the proceedings as would lead the Court not to admit it. In my judgment entirely the same question can be asked and exactly the same answer can be given and should be given in the facts and circumstances of this case.

In the circumstances, in my view, the answers to questions (2) and (3) of those posed by the justices for the opinion of this Court were that the justices were right not to exclude the evidence of the police, whether under common law or by virtue of the provisions of section 78(1) of the Police and Criminal Evidence Act. In the circumstances, in my judgment, the appeal should be dismissed.

In *Smurthwaite and Gill* (1994) 98 Cr App R 437 the Court of Appeal again considered the application of s 78 to an entrapment situation. The defendants had both been convicted of soliciting murder, after asking undercover police officers to kill their spouses. The appeals were rejected, because in both cases the court held that the defendants had not played a passive role in the murder plans. However, the Court of Appeal did suggest some guidelines for consideration in entrapment cases:

> In exercising his discretion whether to admit the evidence of an undercover officer, some, but not an exhaustive list, of the factors that the judge may take into account are as follows: Was the officer acting as an *agent provocateur* in the sense that he was enticing the defendant to commit an offence he would not otherwise have committed? What was the nature of any entrapment? Does the evidence consist of the actual commission of an offence? How active or passive was the officer's role in obtaining the evidence? Is there an unassailable record of what occurred, or is it strongly corroborated? . . . [A] further consideration for the judge in deciding whether to admit an undercover officer's evidence, is whether he has abused his role to ask questions which ought properly to have been asked as a police officer and in accordance with the Codes. ((1994) 98 Cr App R 437, at pp 440–441)

The issue of entrapment came before the House of Lords in *Latif and Shahzad* [1996] 1 All ER 353. In Pakistan Shahzad was introduced to Honi, a police informer. On Shahzad's suggestion, Honi agreed to arrange to import 20 kilogrammes of heroin into the United Kingdom. Honi then came to England and the heroin was brought into the country by Customs and Excise officers. With some persuasion, Honi then managed to get Shahzad to come to England to receive the drugs. Shahzad was arrested during a meeting with Honi. He was later convicted of being knowingly concerned in the fraudulent evasion of the prohibition on importation of a controlled drug. He appealed to the House of Lords, arguing that the proceedings should have been stayed as an abuse of process and that the evidence should have been excluded under s 78 of PACE:

440

Extract 4.5.8

R v Latif and Shahzad [1996] 1 All ER 353, pp 360–362

It is now necessary to consider the legal framework in which the issue of abuse of process must be considered. The starting point is that entrapment is not a defence under English law. That is, however, not the end of the matter. Given that Shahzad would probably not have committed the particular offence of which he was convicted, but for the conduct of Honi and the customs officers, which included criminal conduct, how should the matter be approached? This poses the perennial dilemma (see W G Roser 'Entrapment: Have the Courts Found a Solution to this Fundamental Dilemma to the Criminal Justice System?' (1993) 67 ALJ 722 and Andrew L-T Choo 'Halting Criminal Prosecutions: The Abuse of Process Doctrine Revisited' [1995] Crim LR 864). If the court always refuses to stay such proceedings, the perception will be that the court condones criminal conduct and malpractice by law enforcement agencies. That would undermine public confidence in the criminal justice system and bring it into disrepute. On the other hand, if the court were always to stay proceedings in such cases, it would incur the reproach that it is failing to protect the public from serious crime. The weaknesses of both extreme positions leaves only one principled solution. The court has a discretion: it has to perform a balancing exercise. If the court concludes that a fair trial is not possible, it will stay the proceedings. That is not what the present case is concerned with. It is plain that a fair trial was possible and that such a trial took place. In this case the issue is whether, despite the fact that a fair trial was possible, the judge ought to have stayed the criminal proceedings on broader considerations of the integrity of the criminal justice system. The law is settled. Weighing countervailing considerations of policy and justice, it is for the judge in the exercise of his discretion to decide whether there has been an abuse of process, which amounts to an affront to the public conscience and requires the criminal proceedings to be stayed (see *Bennett v Horseferry Road Magistrates' Court* [1993] 3 All ER 138, sub nom *R v Horseferry Road Magistrates' Court, ex p Bennett* [1994] 1 AC 42). *Bennett* was a case where a stay was appropriate because a defendant had been forcibly abducted and brought to this country to face trial in disregard of extradition laws. The speeches in *Bennett* conclusively establish that proceedings may be stayed in the exercise of the judge's discretion not only where a fair trial is impossible, but also where it would be contrary to the public interest in the integrity of the criminal justice system that a trial should take place. An infinite variety of cases could arise. General guidance as to how the discretion should be exercised in particular circumstances will not be useful. But it is possible to say that in a case such as the present the judge must weigh in the balance the public interest in ensuring that those that are charged with grave crimes should be tried and the competing public interest in not conveying the impression that the court will adopt the approach that the end justifies any means.

In my view the judge took into consideration the relevant considerations placed before him. He performed the balancing exercise. He was entitled to take the view that Shahzad was an organiser in the heroin trade, who took the initiative in proposing the importation. It is true that he did not deal

441

with arguments about the criminal behaviour of the customs officer. That was understandable since that was not argued before him. If such arguments had been put before him, I am satisfied that he would still have come to the same conclusion. And I think he would have been right. The conduct of the customs officer was not so unworthy or shameful that it was an affront to the public conscience to allow the prosecution to proceed. Realistically, any criminal behaviour of the customs officer was venial compared to that of Shahzad.

In these circumstances I would reject the submission that the judge erred in refusing to stay the proceedings.

Section 78(1) of PACE

By way of alternative submission, counsel for Shahzad argued that the judge erred in not excluding the evidence of Honi and the customs officers under s 78(1) of PACE. Exclusion under s 76, which deals with confessions, does not arise. Section 78(1) reads:

> 'In any proceedings the court may refuse to allow evidence on which the prosecution proposes to rely to be given if it appears to the court that, having regard to all the circumstances, including the circumstances in which the evidence was obtained, the admission of the evidence would have such an adverse effect on the fairness of the proceedings that the court ought not to admit it.'

The judge found as a fact that Shahzad was not in any way prejudiced in the presentation of his defence. Counsel found it impossible to challenge that finding. Given that conclusion, counsel accepted that if his submissions on abuse of process failed, his separate argument based on s 78(1) of PACE must inevitably also fail. I need say no more about this aspect of the case.

The entrapment cases give plenty of food for thought. *Christou, Williams* and *Latif* are good examples of proactive police operations. They also show the courts grappling with the discretion given to them under s 78, and the development of guidelines by the Court of Appeal to help in this process. The cases also involve important issues of principle. In all of the cases the prosecution succeeds in convicting people who have committed crimes, in some cases, as the House of Lords points out in *Latif*, very serious crimes. But do the ends justify the means? Are we witnessing the criminalisation of those who are simply weak, led astray by the wiles of state agents?

In the Federal jurisdiction of the United States entrapment does exist as a defence to a criminal charge. However, on the approach consistently adopted by the Supreme Court, defendants must show that they did not have a propensity to commit the crime with which they have been charged. There is little rigorous discussion of propensity in the UK cases (e.g. *Williams* and the comment of the Court of Appeal in *Latif* that 'Shahzad should not be regarded as a total newcomer to the drug scene' ([1995] 1 Cr App R 270, at p 278)). Choo (1993, Ch 6) has argued that entrapment should operate as a defence in England and Wales, with a propensity test to be administered during a *voir dire*. An evidential burden would be placed on the defendant and if successful the proceedings would be stayed.

We noted above that the concept of entrapment involves activities incited by a state agent (an important issue in *Gill and Ranuana*). This troubled Lord Scarman in his judgment in *Sang*: 'It would confuse the law and create unjust distinctions if incitement by a policeman or an official exculpated him who they incited to crime whereas incitement by others – perhaps exercising much greater influence – did not' ([1980] AC 402, at p 451). The difference perhaps lies in the concept of legitimacy. It is the function of state officials to uphold the law, not to break it, and when a court admits the evidence of an official it signifies its approval of the official's action in a way it does not when admitting the evidence of a citizen. When we think of the courts upholding the legitimacy, not just of their own process, but of the criminal justice system as a whole, we find there are powerful criticisms of practices of entrapment:

Extract 4.5.9

G Dworkin, 'The Serpent Beguiled Me and I Did Eat: Entrapment and the Creation of Crime' (1985) 4 *Law and Philosophy* 17, pp 30–34 (some footnotes omitted)

Is it legitimate, and if so under what conditions, for the government to create criminal activity?

To answer this question one must have some general view about the underlying purpose and rules of fairness which are embedded in the particular system of criminal law-enforcement we have adopted. The legitimacy of particular law-enforcement techniques is necessarily relative to a particular conception or model of criminal justice. At most an argument for condemning particular modes of enforcement will be of the form 'If you accept a particular ideal of the purposes and fairness of attaching criminal sanctions to rules of conduct, then these methods will be inconsistent or not cohere with such an ideal.'

I shall sketch the outlines of what I believe to be an ideal of the principles of distribution applied to criminal sanctions embedded in our current practice and jurisprudence.

1. Criminal sanctions constitute an interference with the liberty of the members of a society.

2. They are justified, at least in part, by their contribution to the adherence of citizens to justifiable standards of conduct.

3. Individuals ought to have a broad area of autonomy, i.e. self-determination, in the choice of behavior and the formation of goals and purposes.

4. There is a conflict between maximizing autonomy and promoting fundamental human goods such as security of possessions, personal integrity and opportunity. One way of mitigating this conflict is to allow individuals to choose

whether or not to become subject to criminal sanctions by presenting them with reasons against certain conduct (sanctions) and letting them make the decision to comply or not. Individuals who are legitimately punished have self-selected themselves for such treatment.

5. The criminal law is not to be thought of as a price system, i.e. as it being indifferent whether a citizen obeys the law or violates it but pays the price of the sanction. The criminal law is meant to be obeyed. Certain behaviors are forbidden and others are required, and while the citizen is given a choice (in the sense that the behaviors are not made impossible) his will is constrained to make the correct choice.

These propositions have implications for very different aspects of the criminal justice system. They affect the substantive content of legal standards, e.g. standards which are very difficult or impossible to obey would be ruled out. They affect procedural issues, e.g. laws should be prospective in application. They affect the excusing conditions we ought to allow. And they affect the types of law-enforcement techniques we should regard as legitimate.

In light of the above propositions the normative issue may be phrased in the following manner: what methods of apprehending and detecting offenders are consistent with the view of a system of criminal sanctions as a choosing system and as the enforcement of law, i.e. authoritative rules backed by sanctions. I am claiming that it is not consistent with such a system that law enforcement officials attempt to see if they can cause a person to commit a crime by suggesting or encouraging in any way that a crime be committed.

It is not that such suggestions are improper only if they are such as to overwhelm the will. The use of coercion, excessive temptation, and fraud are obviously inconsistent with the view that we are only entitled to punish those offenders who willingly choose to commit crimes. I am arguing for the much stronger view that it is not proper to solicit, encourage, or suggest crime even if this is done by no stronger means than verbal suggestion. It is not that the offender can complain after the fact that his will was overborne. It is that we, any of us, can complain before the fact that it is not the purpose of officers of the law to encourage crime for the purpose of punishing it.

For the law is set up to forbid people to engage in certain kinds of behavior. In effect it is commanding 'Do not do this.' And it shows that it is commanding, as opposed to requesting or advising by saying that it will impose sanctions on those who refuse to conform. It will 'humble the will' to use Fingarette's language.[1]

But for a law enforcement official to encourage, suggest, or invite crime is to, in effect, be saying 'Do this.' It is certainly unfair to the citizen to be invited to do that which the law forbids him to do. But it is more than unfair; it is conceptually incoherent. Of course this incoherence does not appear to the person being entrapped since he is not aware of the official capacity of his entrapper. And the incapacity is concealed from the official since he thinks of himself as trying to detect a criminal – the thought being that an honest citizen will simply refuse the invitation. From the standpoint of one trying to understand and evaluate the system, however, the conflict is clear.

It is important to note that we are not literally involved in a contradiction as we would be, for example, if the Statutes both commanded and forbade that

444

a certain action be done. Nor is it a pragmatic contradiction, in the sense of being self-defeating. The person who says 'P but I do not believe P' takes back with the latter part of his assertion what he implies with the former part. Nor is it self-defeating in the sense that it cannot be useful to engage in such behavior in order to increase overall compliance with the legal system. It is not as if one part of the criminal justice system (the police) are trying to undo what another part (the legislature) is trying to accomplish.

It is not always incoherent to invite someone to do the very act which one is trying to get them to avoid doing. Consider a parent trying to teach a child not to touch the stove. In the case of a particularly recalcitrant child the most effective technique might be to encourage the child to touch the stove in one's presence. The slight pain now will teach the child to avoid a greater pain later. But this is surely not the model being used by the police. They are interested either in deterring others or in punishing guilty people. The end being served is not that of the person being invited to commit the crime.

I suppose we can (barely) make sense of a system of rules forbidding certain behavior which is enforced by inviting people to commit the forbidden acts and then punishing them for doing so. But such a system violates elementary standards of coherence and fairness.

To encourage the commission of a crime in the absence of any reason to believe the individual is already engaged in a course of criminal conduct is to be a tester of virtue, not a detector of crime.

As a way of insuring against such testing of virtue I suggest that whenever the action of creating an intent to commit a criminal act would render a private citizen liable to criminal charges as accessory or co-conspirator, public officials should be allowed to perform such acts as would create such an intent only if they have probable cause to suppose that the individuals approached are already engaged or are intending to engage in activity of a similar nature. If they offer to buy contraband from specific individuals they should have probable cause to believe those individuals are already engaged in such transactions. If they offer to sell stolen goods to individuals, they ought to have probable cause to believe such individuals are already buying stolen goods. If they offer bribes to public officials, then they should have probable cause to suppose that the officials are already corrupt; not just corruptible.

To use an analogy we do not think it proper for police to engage in random searches of homes in order to detect possible criminal activity. Why then should we allow random solicitation or encouragement of criminal activity? I have heard it argued that on grounds of equitable law enforcement it is wrong to allow those who may have corrupt dispositions, but have been fortunate enough not to have been given the opportunity to exercise them, to escape punishment when their less fortunate counterparts are caught. After all if we had offered them a bribe they would have taken it. This counter-factual seems to me an interesting piece of data for God, but not for the FBI. Suggesting the commission of a crime, even to wicked people, is not a legitimate function of a system of law enforcement.

[1] H Fingarette, *Punishment and Suffering*, Proceedings and Addresses of the American Philosophical Society, v. 50, 1977 p 510.

Dworkin's analysis raises some doubts about the propriety of the police operation in *Williams.*

Three more points about entrapment and the exclusion of evidence deserve
to be made briefly. First, the passage from *Gill and Ranuana* quoted above
raises fears about the actions and motives of some informers. One of the
Smurthwaite guidelines is that, if the conversations between the *agent provocateur* and the defendant are tape recorded, this should weigh in favour of
admitting the evidence. But, in cases like *Gill and Ranuana,* the initial contact is with a police informer who may not be acting on police instructions
and will be unlikely to record initial conversations. Defendants may face
problems in calling such informers to give evidence at trial, so they may not
even be able to cross-examine them about what took place: see *Mann* [1995]
Crim LR 647; *Smith* [1995] Crim LR 658. Secondly, in *Christou* the defendants argued that the questions asked by the police officers in the shop constituted a breach of the PACE Codes of Practice on the questioning of suspects.
This argument was rejected on the facts, but the court noted that it would be
wrong for the police to use an undercover situation as a means of interviewing suspects outside the PACE safeguards. Evidence was excluded on this
ground in *Bryce* [1992] 4 All ER 567. Thirdly, in *Latif* the Court of Appeal
remarked that: 'The Parliament that enacted section 78 of the Police and
Criminal Evidence Act 1984 for the purpose of protecting the innocent might
have been surprised to hear it invoked on behalf of an importer of heroin
worth £3.2 million into this country' ([1995] 1 Cr App R 270, at p 278).
Should the seriousness of the criminal conduct involved affect judgments
about the exclusion of unfairly obtained evidence? This is a difficult question. Suffice it to say that under the legitimacy principle crime seriousness is
relevant: a court which excludes evidence of serious crime owing to a minor
breach of the law fails to send an acceptable moral message to the public.
But, if we see the exclusion of evidence as having a deterrent effect, or as
serving to protect the rights of the whole community, the seriousness of the
crime is irrelevant: see Kamisar (1987). For a good example of a court quashing a conviction because of failure to exclude reliable evidence of a serious
crime, see *Nathaniel* (1995) 2 Cr App R 565.

On entrapment, see further Stitt and James (1984); Sharpe (1994); Robertson
(1994); Birch (1994); Choo and Mellors (1995) and Choo (1995).

(c) Judicial discretion

Our discussion of s 78 demonstrates the importance of judicial discretion
in the criminal trial. Section 78 has been interpreted as giving trial judges a
discretion to exclude evidence and, as long as the judge addresses the correct
questions, the Court of Appeal will not usually challenge his or her decision.
Many other rules of evidence give judges discretion. Some do so explicitly, as
in the case of s 78, while other rules bestow what has been called concealed

discretion (Pattenden, 1990). Section 76 of PACE (see Chapter 3 above) is an example of the latter: a judge must exclude a confession if it has been obtained by oppression or if it may be unreliable. Although the section is phrased in terms of an imperative, the trial judge has a concealed discretion in deciding whether the facts of the case do show oppression or the possibility of unreliability. In such cases the Court of Appeal will be less reluctant to overturn a trial judge's decision to admit evidence.

The arguments in favour of granting discretion to trial judges are summed up in a phrase in *Samuel*: 'Circumstances vary infinitely' ((1988) 87 Cr App R 232, at p 245). If the courts attempt to lay down strict rules on the exclusion of evidence this may lead to injustice when an unusual case falls outside the circumstances envisaged when the rule was made. The difficulty of formulating a precise rule is especially evident where the exclusion of unfairly obtained evidence is concerned, because the trial judge may have to balance different factors against each other, such as the gravity of the police misconduct and the seriousness of the crime being investigated. Nevertheless, the case law on s 78 gives judges little guidance even on the principles which underlie the exercise of the discretion. One criticism of this is that the resulting uncertainty may make it very difficult for the Crown Prosecution Service to judge whether or not a case will succeed in court, because prosecutors will find it difficult to predict whether or not important evidence will be excluded (see Mills, 1994).

The granting of wide discretions to trial judges has been criticised:

Extract 4.5.10

M Ockelton, 'Rules of Evidence' in E Attwooll and D Goldberg (eds), *Criminal Justice* (1995) pp 96–100 (some footnotes omitted)

Against discretions

It is clear that a balance does have to be struck between flexibility in the trial process on the one hand and the rule of law rather than unrestricted power of the judge on the other. It is not appropriate in the space available here to rehearse the large arguments for and against the general use of judicial discretions. Instead I shall consider the operation of two particular well-established evidential discretions in order to demonstrate a number of difficulties. The first is that given by section 78 of the Police and Criminal Evidence Act 1984, under which the trial judge may exclude prosecution evidence on the ground that:

'having regard to all the circumstances, including the circumstances in which it was obtained, the admission of the evidence would have such an adverse effect on the fairness of the proceedings that the court ought not to admit it.'

This is a modern discretion, contained in a statute: it therefore has perhaps the best possible pedigree for an evidential discretion. Yet everyone

447

knows that it poses a number of difficulties. The first is that it is apparent from the legislative history of the section that it was not intended to secure a fair *treatment* for the suspect, but only a fair *trial*. Judges have, however, used, or abused, their discretion under this section to exclude evidence obtained by police malpractice, where the only effect on the trial itself if the evidence were admitted would be that an undoubtedly guilty person would be convicted. In other words, the words 'including the circumstances in which it was obtained' have come to override the rather restrictive words 'effect on the fairness of the proceedings'. The discretion, which was not intended to, and read as plain English does not, allow or require the exclusion of evidence on the *ground* that it was unfairly obtained, is being used for exactly that purpose. And the introduction of this discretion certainly does not promote the efficient disposal of criminal trials, because the Court of Appeal spends a quite inordinate amount of its time reviewing its exercise.[1] Despite that, no clear positive direction has come from the Court of Appeal on when the discretion is, and is not, to be used. In a number of cases[2] the court has declared that mere breach of the Codes of Practice (which relate to such matters as the interviewing of suspects and holding identification parades), or even the use of a trick does not entitle the defendant to have the evidence excluded, and that therefore the judge's refusal to exclude was correct; but it has little opportunity to rule on the *wrong* exclusion of evidence, because of the imbalance of the appeals structure. Besides, if the matter is within the discretion of the trial judge, it is presumably not for an appellate court to make his decision for him. 'Guidelines' soon become rules, which no doubt the Court of Appeal is anxious to avoid creating. The result is that after countless hours of judicial time the position still is that the discretion 'is cast in terms of such vagueness and generality as to furnish little guidance to the court'.[3] Or, one might say, to those who have to advise persons who are to come before the court. One cannot help thinking that if the statute had contained a rule rather than a discretion the subsequent history might have been closer to the intention of the legislature, less of a waste of time, more predictable, and nevertheless relatively easy to correct if it was found to be unsuitable in some way. The Royal Commission takes the view that section 78 has worked satisfactorily in practice. In view of the foregoing, it is by no means clear what that comment means.

The second discretion I wish to examine is much older and has no statutory base, although it operates within the context of a statute. Under section 1, proviso f(ii) of the Criminal Evidence Act 1898, a defendant who gives evidence and either asserts that he is of good character or attacks the character of prosecution witnesses is liable to be asked questions about his own criminal record. It is well established that 'the defendant's character is indivisible'; that is to say that once this provision has come into play the defendant has no *right* to have any part of his record kept from the jury. But questions about his record are to be put only with the leave of the judge, who has a discretion in this respect.[4] He can disallow all questions, or he can allow those only relating to certain offences, to the exclusion of others.

The purpose of proviso f(ii) is clear, though admittedly not always easy to apply in practice. It is only when the defendant, as a witness, has made the credibility of the witnesses a particular issue for the jury that it is important that his own credibility be assessed by the same standards. The purpose of admitting his previous convictions is emphatically *not* in order to invite the jury to assume that, because he has previously committed crimes, he is more likely to have commited that for which he is now on trial. It is only:

> 'to show that when you have to rely on his word as contradicting something stated by somebody else, or as alleging something which is not corroborated, you have not the word of a person who has done nothing wrong, . . . ; you have only the word of a man whose career has been what you know it to have been.'[5]

It would appear to follow that, if the judge is minded to exclude some of the defendant's record, he should, other things being equal, allow the jury to hear about offences which might help them decide whether the defendant is honest, but prevent them from hearing about offences which have little relation to honesty but might well prejudice them in their consideration of the offence being tried. In *Selvey* the defendant was charged with buggery, and, as he had made serious allegations against some of the police witnesses, proviso f(ii) applied. The trial judge allowed his previous convictions for homosexual offences to be put to him, but not those for dishonesty: that is, exactly the reverse of what might have been expected. That course of action provoked no criticism in the House of Lords, and subsequent Court of Appeal decisions have taken a like view. The attitude seems to be that, since the defendant is liable to have his whole character put before the jury in these circumstances he obtains a benefit by any restriction on their knowledge and cannot complain. That is so even if the offences the jury do hear about are precisely those which might prejudice their deliberations without giving any assistance on the question of credit. No consideration is given to the fact that there is the danger that a person's record may be misrepresented by this sort of pruning. The judge is supposed to have applied his mind correctly to the exercise of his discretion; the appellate courts will not give directions, in general or in particular cases, on how the discretion should be exercised.

This state of affairs is bad enough by itself, but one should bear in mind also two other factors. The first is that the discretion may well be exercised not by an experienced criminal trial judge but by a recorder or assistant recorder. The second is that the rationale for making a division in the way set out above is by no means universally understood. Nevertheless whoever does the job, and however badly he does it, the matter is for him. There are no rules to govern him. A defendant may be lucky or he may not: there is no possibility of advising him in advance on the actual consequences of losing his shield.

[1] Of the cases reported under the heading 'Evidence' in the *Criminal Law Review* in 1992, exactly one-third (23 out of 69) were at least partly on this point.
[2] For example *Alladice* (1988) 87 Cr App R 380, *Christou and Wright* (1992) 95 Cr App R 264.
[3] *Cross on Evidence* (7th edn) 483.
[4] *Selvey v DPP* [1970] AC 304.
[5] Darling J's summing-up in *Morrison* (1911) *The Trial of Steinie Morrison* ed H Fletcher Moulton (1922) 278–279.

In the conclusion to his paper, Ockelton argues that trial judges should not be given unlimited discretions: powers such as that contained in s 78 should always be restricted, either by the statute which creates them or by appeal court judgments. He also argues that judges should be given specific training in exercising such discretions, and that the prosecution should be given the right to appeal the decision of Crown Court judges to exclude evidence (which at present they cannot do). For similar criticisms of s 78, see Robertson (1989); Carter (1997). For further discussion of judicial discretion, see Choo (1993, pp 119–130).

In response to Ockelton's criticisms, one might try to suggest ways in which the exclusionary discretion given to judges under s 78 could be more tightly structured. Judges might first look at two primary factors which reflect legitimacy considerations: (1) there should be a strong presumption of exclusion where evidence has been obtained because of deliberate breach of PACE or breach of the criminal law (whether deliberate or not); (2) there should be a strong presumption that credible evidence of guilt should be admitted. If these primary presumptions conflict, judges might then take the seriousness of the crime of which the defendant is accused into account. Judges might then consider a number of secondary factors which reflect the importance of protecting suspects. Thus, where a particularly important provision of PACE has been breached, there might be a presumption in favour of exclusion. The provisions of PACE designed to secure the integrity of the interviewing process or access to legal advice could be accorded particular importance. Under these guidelines, the 'causal' issue, which plays a prominent part in current case law, would be irrelevant as it tends to introduce discretion through the back door and leads to invidious distinctions between experienced and inexperienced suspects. If these guidelines seem too complex, or seem to leave out obvious factors, then that is an argument in favour of leaving judges the wide discretion they presently have.

(d) The media and the right to a fair trial

The public has an obvious interest in the criminal justice system, and this is reflected in the amount of media coverage devoted to criminal justice issues. There is an inherent fascination in crime stories, and public knowledge of the workings of the criminal justice system is important in a democratic state. Article 6 of the European Convention on Human Rights acknowledges the importance of the public nature of criminal proceedings, by requiring that trials be public. However, if a persons's guilt or innocence has been debated at length in the press, both before and during the trial, can he or she still be tried impartially? The problem is exacerbated by the use of juries as fact-finders in Crown Court trials. While we might believe that a professional judge, giving reasons for his or her decision, would be able to adjudicate fairly in spite of prejudicial media coverage, there are more doubts about the ability of a group of lay people to do so.

450

There has been some psychological research on the impact of media reports on jury verdicts. Though, like all research using mock juries, there are problems in generalising from such studies, this is the best evidence we have. It is not surprising that the research does suggest that media reports do influence jurors (for an overview, see Linz and Penrod (1992) and the special issue of *Law and Human Behaviour* (1990, Vol 14, No 5)). This is true both for case specific publicity (for example, where information about a defendant's criminal record appears in the press) and non-case specific publicity (for example, reports of a miscarriage of justice stemming from a mistaken eyewitness identification may make jurors more cautious about eyewitness evidence in other cases). The research suggests that measures commonly employed to counteract media influenced bias are of little help. It might be expected that during its deliberations the jury would come to concentrate on the evidence presented at trial rather than extraneous information, but in the experimental studies deliberation does not dissipate bias (indeed, some mock jurors referred to news reports during deliberations despite having been told not to do so). Warnings by the judge to the jury to ignore media reports also seem to be ineffective; one study concludes that: 'providing more specific and extensive instructions singling out pretrial publicity is probably pointless and might even be counterproductive' (Kramer, Kerr and Carroll, 1990, p 435). Time is the only factor which appears to have much impact on the effects of pre-trial publicity: a delay between news coverage and the trial will help to counteract jury bias (though the time lag effect is less pronounced for reports which affect juror's emotional reactions to a case rather than simply their degree of knowledge about the defendant).

Recent cases provide some good illustrations of the problem and the courts' reaction to it. In *McCann, Cullen and Shanahan* (1991) 92 Cr App R 239, the defendants were tried for conspiracy to murder the then Secretary of State for Northern Ireland, Tom King. The defendants exercised their right to silence at trial, and at the time the jury could not be invited to draw any inferences from this. However, during the trial the Home Secretary announced plans to change the law on the right to silence which inevitably attracted a lot of attention in the media. During news reports, King spoke in favour of the change in the law. One newscaster summarised his statements thus:

> Tom King says that the new rules were aimed at terrorists and racketeers. He said they were being taught how to refuse to answer police questions . . . Mr King said that under present rules justice was being thwarted. He said that it was a matter of concern and frustration to the majority of decent people in Northern Ireland that the absolute refusal by large numbers of people to answer questions cannot be taken into account by a court.

Lord Denning also spoke in favour of the change in the law. The Court of Appeal held that the publicity meant that there was a real danger that the jury would be prejudiced, and that the judge's instructions to the jury to disregard the news stories did not eliminate this danger. The defendants' convictions were quashed.

In *Taylor and Taylor* (1993) 98 Cr App R 361 the defendants, two sisters, had been convicted of murder. The victim was the wife of the former lover of the older sister, Michelle. The prosecution case was that the victim had been killed on account of Michelle's jealousy. The Court of Appeal accepted that media coverage of the case had been 'unremitting, extensive, sensational, inaccurate and misleading'. Particularly notable was the press treatment of a video of the victim's wedding, which showed Michelle kissing the bride and bridegroom. A still showing her kissing the latter was printed in the papers with headlines such as 'Cheat's Kiss' and 'Judas Kiss'. During the trial one headline read 'Love Crazy Mistress Butchered Rival Wife Court Told'. The Court of Appeal quashed the convictions (although this was partly because the prosecution had not disclosed important evidence to the defence, there is little doubt that the risk of prejudice would have been enough in itself). The court felt that the media treatment was such that a fair retrial was no longer possible.

The Court of Appeal had to consider the problem of press coverage again in *Wood* [1996] 1 Cr App R 207 (for the facts of the case, see p 412 above).

Extract 4.5.11

R v Wood [1996] 1 Cr App R 207, pp 211–214

1. Prejudicial material and the press

We were shown extracts from newspapers from Monday July 12, 1993 when the trial began, to Friday July 16 when it was nearing its end. Only a limited amount of this material was produced at the trial, and there is nothing to show that the remainder was known to the judge or the jury or the prosecution or the defence at the time. It might be thought wise if the Crown Prosecution Service or the police were to keep a careful watch on the national press when a trial of this importance is taking place. The defence might do the same. We do not know if that happened. But we bear in mind what was said by Mr Nutting, for the Crown, that in the aftermath of a trial it is easy to search and assemble extracts from the press which are arguably prejudicial. The Evening Standard of July 12 had a full page article (with pictures) by Sir Edward Heath MP about beating terrorists. It contained this passage:

> 'The authorities must be allowed to use the evidence that has been compiled against alleged members of the IRA more effectively. In the light of the appallingly low rate of conviction for terrorist offences over the past decade, this clearly has not been happening.'

The article then gave the example of an alleged terrorist who had been expelled from the country in the previous week because the evidence which was thought to establish his guilt would not be admissible in court.

Miss Kennedy, for the defence, complained to the judge about that article on the following day. She also had a complaint about an account of the trial in The Sun of July 13, but we need not go further into that. The judge's reaction was this:

'Unfortunately, commentary of a general kind on the activities of terrorists and the manner in which they are tried and indeed on the manner in which our society ought to cope with the ugly problem it continually presents are now the bread and butter of journalism and I have no difficulty in concluding that if it were not for this article then, in succeeding days and weeks, like comment will be made by people from all strata of society, including the great and the good, and will be the subject of publication . . . I see no purpose in discharging this jury and postponing the trial to allow the prejudice, which Miss Kennedy asserts, to die down for in the light of my assessment of the situation if it were not to be this article yesterday, it would undoubtedly be another article of a kindred kind tomorrow or the day after.'

The judge concluded:

'Such suggested mischief can be and will be effectively eradicated by telling this jury in the clearest terms that they will focus on the evidence they hear in this court and the submissions of learned counsel directed to it and on nothing else.'

The judge's first forecast proved only too true. The Sun of Thursday July 15 had a leading article and much other material on the acquittal of Joseph Elliot on a charge of killing Robert Osborne. The trial had taken place in the next door court to the trial of Vincent Wood, and uproar had been heard when the jury announced their verdict. The Sun article said:

'Did the jury who tried Joseph Elliot take leave of their senses? . . . That's not justice. It is madness.'

On the same day The Sun reported on its front page the dramatic capture of an alleged IRA bomber armed with a 10lb Semtex bomb.

On Friday July 16 The Sun had an article about a Detective Constable at the Old Bailey who had said:

'I felt as if I was entitled to a prize for getting a conviction. Every day in the police room, officers throw their case papers on the desk in disgust. They say, "It's not worth the effort any more. It has all become a big unfunny joke."'

On the same day a well-known columnist in the Daily Mail complained about many aspects of criminal justice in this country with reference to the Elliot case. The article contained this passage:

'Juries are thus representative of an increasingly undereducated and lawless population. But they are far less weighty and judicious. Most of them function surprisingly well in the circumstances; but a few display fellow-feeling with downtrodden criminals and behave rather more like zombies.'

In the same edition there was a full report of the Vincent Wood case. The Daily Express of that day had an article by the sports editor with the headline 'How I lost faith in British justice sitting on a jury'. He wrote of jurors:

'How many from poorly-educated, inner-city areas carry with them a mis-trust for the police and a near-determination not to convict? . . . No wonder criminals openly agree that the modern jury system gives them the best possible chance of beating the rest.'

Thus far it can be said that these extracts portray no more than discontent with the criminal justice system in general. There is some reference to terrorist cases but not to this case in particular. But also on July 16 there was an article in the Daily Star, which we must read in full. A letter to the Home Secretary:

'Dear Sir,
An IRA bomber was caught red-handed with a bag of Semtex. He was bang to rights. Yet there is a sinking feeling that he might get away with it. Unbelievable? Unfortunately not. The government, and what would be its legal Rottweiler, the Crown Prosecution Service, seem to be running scared in cases of terrorism. After the Birmingham Six and the Guildford Four they are terrified that the trial will end in defeat. In March 1991 Kevin O'Donnell was cleared at the Old Bailey of terrorist charges despite being arrested with two Kalashnikov rifles in the back of his car. After the case he was immediately served with an exclusion order signed by the then Home Secret-ary, and expelled from the mainland. Civil liberties groups led a chorus of protest saying that an innocent man had been pilloried. But a year later innocent O'Donnell was shot in County Tyrone in Northern Ireland leading a machine gun attack on a police station. He had been a lifelong supporter of the IRA.
Moral: Only days ago John Matthews was cleared of terrorist charges after being accused of hijacking a taxi to blow up 10 Downing Street. He was later thrown out of mainland Britain when the Home Secretary said that he was satisfied that Matthews had terrorist links. Here is the truth. The police believe there was a concrete case against him, and the Crown Prosecution Service at first told the court they had all the evidence needed to convict. But they suddenly decided to drop the charges with no real reason. In other words they did not have the courage of their convictions. We do not wish to prejudice the trial of the latest man to be arrested but the fact is that he was caught red-handed with a bag full of Semtex. If this man is not tried, convicted and sentenced to spend the rest of his life in jail justice will not have been done and the already shaky morale of the police will be even further eroded and the nation will have been betrayed.'

That is signed by the editor.
It is true that on a careful and fair reading one can detect that this piece referred to the man who had been caught with a Semtex bag earlier in the week. There was on the same page an article about that other case. But jurors reading the Daily Star that day could, in our judgment, have well concluded:

(i) that there was very likely to be evidence of guilt which could not be produced in court; and
(ii) that it was a duty which they owed to the nation to make sure that Vincent Wood was convicted.

454

> Whether it was the intention of the editor of the Daily Star to achieve that objective is not for us to say.
>
> If we are to have a free and independent press, we must allow and welcome general comment on the faults of our system of criminal justice and on the errors that are sometimes made in one direction or the other. But fairness demands that pressure should not be put on jurors in a particular case by the press or anyone else. Newspaper editors and their readers rightly require that those guilty of serious crime should be convicted and punished. That objective may be endangered by the very measures taken to achieve it, if they result in an unfair trial.

The Court quashed the defendant's conviction and ordered a retrial. However, the court held that the press coverage by itself was not enough to render the conviction unsafe and unsatisfactory: it was only in combination with the judge's summing up (see above) that this was the case.

It appears that trial judges themselves are now more aware of the dangers that media coverage poses to the cases they try. In recent years a number of trials have been stayed for this reason, including the trial of detectives involved in the Birmingham six case; the trial of Geoffrey Knights, the ex-boyfriend of a well known soap opera star, who had been charged with assault; and the trial of a number of prisoners who were charged with escaping from Whitemoor prison. This last episode led the Home Secretary to suggest that prosecutors might be given the right to appeal against a court's decision to abandon a trial (*Guardian*, 25 January 1997). In contrast, the trial judge and later the Court of Appeal held that it was not an abuse of process to try Rosemary West, despite press coverage that was described as 'extensive and hostile to the Wests'. The Court of Appeal said that 'providing the judge effectively warns the jury to act only on the evidence given in court, there is no reason to suppose that they would do otherwise', a statement which finds little support in the empirical research (see *West* [1996] 2 Cr App R 374, at pp 385–386).

The cases described above show different aspects of the problem of media coverage and its effect on trials. In *McCann* the defendants were prejudiced as much by accident as by anything else: plans to abolish the right to silence just happened to be announced during their trial, and this inevitably drew much media commentary. The Taylor sisters' case shows the press at its worst. As the Court of Appeal observed, the press coverage assumed the defendant's guilt: this was not reporting, it was comment. The comment was also lurid in the extreme, playing upon popular stereotypes of female deception and jealousy. *Wood* falls somewhere between the two situations. The press coverage complained of was not case specific, it was a response to the perceived failure of the criminal justice system to deal effectively with suspected terrorists. It cannot be denied that the press has an important role to play in such debates. Inevitably, the coverage would have some effect on anyone who was called to serve as a juror in a terrorist trial after having read it. Is this reason for criticism? The coverage will effect jurors, but the perceptions of all jurors in any trial are a product of their cultural background, of which the media are an important part. It is unrealistic, and undesirable, to argue that trials should take place in a cultural vacuum. This said, the letter by the editor of the *Daily Star* reproduced in the extract from *Wood* goes beyond general comment. By focusing on a specific case (albeit not *Wood*'s case) it prejudices a specific person's chances of a fair trial, and it is hard to believe that its author would not have realised this. A more difficult problem is posed by a case like *West*, of which the Court of Appeal said:

> [T]here can scarcely ever have been a case more calculated to shock the public who were entitled to know the facts. The question raised on behalf of the defence is whether a fair trial could be held after such intensive publicity adverse to the accused. In our view it could. To hold otherwise would mean that if allegations of murder are sufficiently horrendous so as inevitably to shock the nation, the accused cannot be tried. That would be absurd. ([1996] 2 Cr App R 374, at p 386)

In the Taylor sisters' case the Court of Appeal recommended that the Attorney General consider whether to take action against the newspapers concerned under the Contempt of Court Act 1981. No action was brought in that case, and the sisters were unsuccessful in an action for judicial review of the Attorney General's decision (*Solicitor General, ex parte Taylor* (1995) *The Times*, 14 August). The Attorney General has been accused of being unduly reluctant to bring actions against newspapers in these cases. The relevant law is found in s 2 of the Contempt of Court Act 1981. Although this section creates a strict liability offence (the publisher need not intend to cause prejudice to a defendant), it is difficult to bring a successful action because the Attorney General must prove that an individual publication created a *substantial* risk that the course of justice would be *seriously* impeded. Whereas in decisions whether or not to stay proceedings, or to allow an appeal as in *Wood*, it is the defendant's right to a fair trial which is in issue, proceedings under s 2 require the balancing of press freedom against the protection of the administration of justice. It is not, then, surprising that the cases sometimes reach inconsistent results.

Reported cases provide some good examples of actions under s 2, for example *Attorney General v Independent Television News Ltd* [1995] 2 All ER 370; *Attorney General v MGN Ltd and others* [1997] 1 All ER 456. The latter concerns the unsuccessful action brought against various newspapers for the publication of stories which led the trial judge to stay proceedings in the Geoffrey Knights case and contains a good discussion of the various issues involved.

On this issue see further Corker and Levi (1996), Naylor (1994).

(e) Victims and witnesses

Trials could not function without witnesses coming to the courts to give evidence. Some of these witnesses will also be the victims of the event around which the trial revolves. What are their experiences of the courts and what provisions are made for them?

The treatment of witnesses, especially victims, reflects many of the factors which we considered in previous chapters. Just as the police look for the ideal victim, so the adversarial trial functions in black and white terms: witnesses must be beyond all reproach if they are to be sure of being believed in court. Indeed, it is partly the demands made of victims during trials that lead the police to construct a model of the ideal victim and to favour only those who meet its demands. Trials are contests about truth and morality, and victims get accused of 'cheating, plotting, drunkenness, vindictiveness, quarrelling, muddle and mendacity' as a matter of course (Rock, 1993, p 83). It is defence counsel's job to win the case for his or her client, and the witness can become an unfortunate casualty in the adversarial joust. Rock spent a year observing a Crown Court in London; here are some of his observations about the treatment of witnesses in trials:

Extract 4.5.12

P Rock, *The Social World of an English Crown Court* (1993) pp 33–37 (some footnotes omitted)

It was the job of defence counsel to supply a rival way of explaining what had occurred, what might be called the antithesis, although that term was not used in the courts. The defence case did not have to be as solid or imposing as that of the prosecution. It was an attack that sought chiefly to so puncture the impression achieved by the prosecution and prosecution witnesses that it became difficult for the jury to be sure of what had been said and, indeed, of what may have happened (and, in the relatively sealed world of the courtroom, where stories and their tellers were all there was to judge, doubt did not seem very difficult to introduce). The defence would employ argument and questioning to reveal inconsistency, error, improper motives, forgetfulness, and falsehood in prosecution witnesses. The questions would often be searching. One counsel said: 'Anything that tends to mask the reality about the witnesses is hostile to the adversarial process. It should be stark. The choices that [the jury] have should be stark. The compulsion to tell the truth should be there.' The questions would probe minor contradiction after minor contradiction: 'You have to deal with things in detail, first of all to prevent anybody from saying that you didn't do that, but also ideally of giving a different account of even small details, raising a doubt as to the prosecution case . . . because [the jury] have been told they have to be sure.'

Almost as a matter of course, counsel would, as a judge put it, so 'blackguard' the witnesses that they were no longer believable. Under cross-examination, victims and prosecution witnesses could be asked about matters touching on their 'title to credit': their way of life, their associations, their past convictions, their disinterestedness, and their integrity. They could be vilified and shamed as they defended, in public and perhaps for the very first time, testimony about matters that were painful, embarrassing, and once personal. (Victim 20, for instance, had been questioned about events before she had had a miscarriage: 'He was going on about me and X . . . she was pregnant at the same time, going out together buying baby clothes. That upset me because I don't like talking about it.') At stake, wrote Ericson and Baranek, was the protection of valued aspects of identity.[1] Prosecution witnesses certainly experienced questioning by defence counsel as an assault on their identity. Those for whom public face was important (and it is important for most of us) found it harrowing (Victim 6 called it 'nerve wracking . . . I was shaking inside'). The techniques deployed were precisely those used by the prosecution in cross-examination of the defendant, and they seemed to put prosecution witnesses themselves on trial. Victim 20 told me after cross-examination, 'They made me feel like a criminal! It's the last time I'll come to court.' And Victim 17, a victim of assault by a cabdriver, said the worst thing about her routine cross-examination, in which she had been accused of lying, taking drugs, being drunk, and being provocative, was

'Being called a liar all the time, being accused of causing the affray. He asked me if I had been drinking . . . I knew what [defence counsel] was trying to do. I'm not stupid. When he said I was smoking cannabis, that's when I went, 'No way! This is getting out of hand!' I just felt that I was the one being proved wrong . . . How can he imply we were doing something with absolutely no proof!? How can he do that? Can he do that, suggest that we were taking drugs when we weren't? It's total rubbish! What was really upsetting was trying to convince them I was telling the truth. That's not fair.'

In promoting that antithesis, and to sow uncertainty in the jury's minds, the defence might produce their own witnesses, who could be 'blackguarded' by the prosecution in turn. Defence witnesses' motives, credibility, and credit-ability could be exposed to public examination, and that would be disagree-able for them too. A judge reflected: 'A close investigation of people's motives and actions may be very uncomfortable for those investigated.' So it was that advocates laid their tales and tale-bearers before jurors, inviting them to place a favoured construction on facts, arguments, and witnesses and deliver a verdict. The result, Pannick argued, was a choice between different con-structions. 'The reality is that the adversary process of a trial more than leaves the truth mysteriously hidden, covered over by the evasions and half-truths of competing contentions.'[2] . . .

Whatever lawyers and professionals might argue outside the courtroom, wit-nesses tended to take it that defeat signified that they had been disbelieved, that they had been taken for liars. And that was not a view discouraged inside the courtroom itself. Of one very routine trial, the prosecutor said to the jury, 'It's quite clearly a case of whom you believe. If you believe the defendant, then . . .', and a judge summed up in another such case: 'There it is, members of the jury, that's the evidence. That's the evidence on which you've got to decide this case . . . The prosecution say that unless you find all these police are telling lies, you'll have to find the defendant guilty.' Being publicly cast as tellers of untruths engendered distress. A barrister reflected that 'those who give their evidence orally are the most vulnerable. They don't expect their credibility to be challenged'. One witness, Victim 16, said: 'What really upset me was trying to convince them I was telling the truth. That's what upset me.' And another, Victim 1, said: 'I thought it would be straightforward. They kept asking me questions and trying to put them the other way around. It got confusing.' Even police officers who gave evidence regularly said, as one sergeant said, 'I don't think you ever get used to it . . .'

[1] See R Ericson and P Baranek, *The Ordering of Justice: A Study of Accused Persons as Dependants in the Criminal Process* (Toronto, Univ. of Toronto Press, 1982), 205.
[2] D Pannick, *Judges* (Oxford, Oxford Univ. Press, 1987), 53.

There are few limits to the lengths counsel may go to to discredit a witness. The only relevant part of the Code of Conduct of the Bar of England and Wales is para 610: a barrister 'must not make statements or ask questions which are merely scandalous or intended or calculated only to vilify insult or annoy either a witness of some other person'. Judges will seldom intervene in aggressive cross-examination. Preventing counsel from doing his or her job could be seen as the judge stepping into the arena (see the discussion of judicial neutrality, above, and for a case on this point, *Sharp* [1993] 3 All ER 225, at pp 234–240). The main limit to cross-examination is a purely pragmatic one. If counsel is too aggressive and bullying there is the danger that the jury will be alienated and sympathise with the witness, which would be the opposite of what is desired. Another consideration for defence counsel is that an attack on the credibility of a witness may mean that the judge will allow the defendant to be cross-examined on his or her previous convictions. This, though, is not a danger if the defendant has no previous convictions or if he or she has decided not to give evidence during the trial (the Royal Commission on Criminal Justice recommended that the defendant's previous convictions should be admissible in cases where the defendant chooses not to give evidence: (1993, Ch 8, para 34); see also Law Commission (1996) pp 223–234). In one area of the law an attempt has been made to prevent the assaults upon the character of witnesses described by Rock. The Sexual Offences (Amendment) Act 1976, s 2 prevents the defence from cross-examining a rape complainant about her previous sexual history, unless it would be unfair to the defendant not to allow such cross-examination. However, research shows that judges often do still allow cross-examination on sexual history, even when there is no obvious reason for it (Adler, 1982). This is not too surprising: judges have not traditionally seen their role as protecting witnesses, especially not at the expense of the defence's liberty to run its case in the manner it sees fit. Further, judges may feel that it is best to err on the side of favouring the defendant. If they restrict cross-examination, they run the risk of paving the way for a successful appeal. A decision to allow cross-examination could probably never be the subject of an appeal.

It is not only the experience of cross-examination about which witnesses complain. The whole process of being called to court can be frustrating and alienating. The date of a trial in which a witness is involved may change at short notice, and even after turning up at court the case may collapse owing to a last minute change of plea. At many courts there is no special provision for victims or witnesses. They may have little information about what is happening in the case they have been called to testify in and will simply have to wait until they are called. Rock found that the average waiting time was about four and a quarter hours, and that about two thirds of cases 'cracked' at court so that witnesses were sent home after having turned up (1993, pp 280–281). Victims, in particular, identify with the prosecuting barrister who is trying 'their' case, but any attempt to talk with the barrister is likely to be met with a rebuff. This is because any contact between the two might give the impression that the victim is rehearsing his or her evidence, so it has been forbidden by the Bar's Code of Conduct. Often victims and defence witnesses will end up waiting in close proximity to the defendant or his friends. A few victims in Shapland et al's study reported that they had actually been threatened while waiting to give evidence (Shapland et al, 1985). In the Crown Courts this situation has now been improved through a scheme run by Victim Support. Volunteers attend court in order to act as a point of contact with witnesses, to let them know what is going on and to prepare them for the experience of giving evidence (for a description of one such scheme, see Rock (1993) Chs 8 and 9). The Royal Commission on Criminal Justice recommended that prosecuting counsel be able to talk to victims and witnesses before they give evidence (1993, Ch 5, paras 50–52). It also recommended that the judge should play a more interventionist role to protect witnesses from aggressive cross-examination (1993, Ch 8, para 43).

5

SENTENCING

1. INTRODUCTION

Sentencing is the most highly visible decision-making stage in the criminal justice process. It is carried out in open court, and in public. It thus contrasts with earlier stages of decision-making discussed in previous chapters of this book, such as the decision made by a police officer on the street to deal with a case informally rather than formally, or the police decision to issue a formal caution rather than to press for prosecution, or a decision by the Crown Prosecution Service to discontinue proceedings rather than to prosecute. It must be appreciated from the outset that the operation of these various 'upstream' decisions means that only a small proportion of those who commit criminal offences actually find themselves before the courts. The Home Office estimates that sentencers probably deal with about 2 per cent of the total number of offences committed in any one year (see Chapter 1, at p 37). The great bulk of lawbreaking, as we have seen, goes unreported or undetected, or is otherwise dealt with by the police and prosecution authorities. When looking at statistics on sentencing it is important to remember that the figures are bound to reflect these other practices.

Despite this, it is obvious that sentencing is a very important part of the criminal justice process. In 1996, 1.44 million offenders were sentenced by the courts, the great majority by the lower courts. Sentencing matters take up much of the time and resources of magistrates' courts, the Crown Court and the Criminal Division of the Court of Appeal. Quite apart from the administration involved, it is clear that the sentencing of offenders serves an important 'symbolic' function in our society, providing the opportunity for a formal public denunciation of the offence (and the offender). It has long been established that criminal trials (including the sentencing stage) should normally take place in open court. The main exception is where a juvenile is being tried or sentenced in a youth court. Then the general public is excluded and the juvenile must not be named or otherwise identified by the press unless, exceptionally, the youth court magistrates order that reporting restrictions should be lifted (Children and Young Persons Act 1933, s 49). In recent years, as part of the government's view that young offenders should be seen to bear responsibility for their offences, youth courts have been encouraged to name young offenders more often than they have done in the past (Home Office 1997c, Ch 9). If the juvenile's case is heard in an adult magistrates' court or in the Crown Court (such as where an adult and a juvenile are jointly charged with an offence) then the court has power to make an order protecting the juvenile's anonymity (1933 Act, s 39). The sentencing decisions of magistrates' courts and the Crown Court do not appear in official law reports, but they are routinely reported (with varying degrees of accuracy) in the local press. Some high-profile Crown Court cases receive national attention in this way. Judges and magistrates sometimes receive fierce criticism for particular sentences which they pass especially where, in the views of the critics, they have been too lenient with the offender and have given insufficient weight to the sufferings of the victim. In the past judges were prevented from commenting on or responding to this kind of criticism, but this rule was eased during the mid-1990s when Lord Taylor was Lord Chief Justice. It is now not uncommon to find judges responding to criticism by making a clarificatory statement in court or by writing a letter to *The Times*. The response will often be along the lines that the press has reported only some of the facts of the case and thereby given a misleading impression. Occasionally judges will admit that the sentence which they have passed was lenient, but that their hands were effectively tied by an earlier 'guideline case' issued by the Court of Appeal (see further below). This kind of exchange demonstrates the deep disagreements which exist over what the aims of sentencing should be in a particular case, and what they should be in general.

2. SENTENCING IN THE MAGISTRATES' COURTS

Most sentencing is carried out in the lower courts, by lay magistrates (also known as 'justices of the peace' or 'justices'). There are about 30,000 lay magistrates in England and Wales. Lay magistrates are not paid a salary, but they are entitled to a travelling and/or subsistence allowance, and to compensation (up to a certain level) for loss of earnings. Although not legally qualified, these magistrates do receive training in matters relating to sentencing as part of their induction course when first appointed and in regular training updates. The clerk to the justices, who must be a barrister or solicitor of at least five years' standing, supervises the training programme of the local bench and also provides advice on the general sentencing powers of the magistrates when they are sitting in court. If invited to do so, after the defendant has pleaded guilty or has been convicted, the clerk may retire to the retiring room with the magistrates to provide them with further help on their sentencing powers, but the sentence decision must be that of the magistrates, not the clerk (see *Practice Direction (Justices: Clerk to Court)* [1981] 1 WLR 1163, para 2, and for research suggesting that clerks not infrequently transgress this boundary, see Darbyshire, 1980). It should be noted that each justices' clerk will have a staff of assistant court clerks to whom he or she can delegate functions, including that of sitting in court. Court clerks need not be qualified lawyers, but certain minimum qualifications are needed for the job (see further, Turner, 1992). In addition to the lay magistrates there are 90 full-time stipendiary (paid) magistrates, who are qualified lawyers (barrister or solicitor) of at least seven years' standing. The retirement age for magistrates (whether lay or stipendiary) is 70. For further information on the structure and organisation of magistrates' courts, see Chapter 4 above.

A defendant dealt with by magistrates who is dissatisfied with the sentence he has received has a right of appeal to the Crown Court. If this option is exercised the Crown Court judge, who will sit for these purposes with lay magistrates, will rehear the case. Having done so, the Crown Court then has power to decrease or increase the sentence which was originally passed. The power to increase sentence probably acts as a disincentive to appeals which have little hope of success. The prosecution has no equivalent right of appeal against what they might regard as an unduly lenient sentence. There is the possibility of challenging a sentence by making an application to the Divisional Court (see Wasik, 1984), but the sentence must be regarded as little short of a complete aberration before the court will intervene. At the end of the hearing of the appeal by the defendant, the Crown Court will issue a short explanation of the reasons for upholding or amending the decision of the magistrates, which is sent to the clerk of the relevant magistrates' court to be communicated to the justices concerned.

(a) The pattern of sentencing by magistrates

The pattern of sentences imposed by the magistrates' courts is clear from the table on pp 464–5 taken from *Criminal Statistics England and Wales 1996* (Home Office, 1997a).

This table compares the figures for 1995 and 1996, the latest years for which statistics are available. It will be seen that magistrates' courts select the fine as the appropriate sentence in a very high percentage of cases: 90 per cent of summary motoring offences, 83 per cent of summary (non-motoring) offences and 36 per cent of indictable offences dealt with summarily. In these terms, the percentage use of custodial sentences (detention in a young offender institution or immediate imprisonment) by magistrates' courts is low (9 per cent for indictable offences) whilst that of the Crown Court is much higher (61 per cent). On the other hand, far more offenders are sentenced by magistrates' courts than by the Crown Court. When comparison is made of the actual number of offenders sentenced to immediate custody, however, it will be seen that the numbers so sentenced by the two levels of courts are quite similar (41,200 for the magistrates' courts in 1996, as against 43,500 for the Crown Court in that year). After the fine, the conditional discharge is the next most frequently used sentencing option in the magistrates' courts, followed by the probation order and the community service order.

Extract 5.2.1

Home Office, *Criminal Statistics England and Wales 1996* (1997) table 7.1

Offenders sentenced by type of court, type of sentence or order and type of offence

England and Wales — Number of offences (thousands) and percentages

Type of sentence or order	1995 Total	1996 Number of offenders				Percentage of total offenders sentenced		
		Total	Indictable offences	Summary offences		Indictable offences	Summary offences	
				Offences (excluding motoring offences)	Motoring offences		Offences (excluding motoring offences)	Motoring offences
Magistrates' courts								
Absolute discharge	20.1	19.9	2.4	5.7	11.8	1	1	2
Conditional discharge	102.0	102.0	50.1	43.2	8.7	22	9	1
Fine	992.8	1,069.7	81.9	402.3	585.4	36	83	90
Community penalties								
Probation order	41.0	43.8	26.3	7.9	9.5	11	2	1
Supervision order	9.7	10.3	8.0	1.9	0.4	3	0	0
Community service order	37.8	36.8	19.7	8.1	9.0	9	2	1
Attendance centre order	7.4	7.4	5.3	1.9	0.1	2	0	0
Combination order	11.6	14.3	7.4	2.1	4.9	3	0	1
Curfew order	0.0	0.2	0.1	0.0	0.0	0	0	0
Young offender institution	10.6	11.2	7.4	1.9	1.9	3	0	0
Imprisonment								
Fully suspended	1.3	1.3	0.5	0.2	0.5	0	0	0
Unsuspended	28.2	30.0	14.6	4.4	11.0	6	1	2
Otherwise dealt with	17.6	17.3	5.6	6.6[(1)]	5.0[(1)]	2	1	1
Total	1,280.0[(2)]	1,364.1	229.4	486.3[(3)]	648.4[(3)]	100	100	100
The Crown Court								
Absolute discharge	0.1	0.1	0.1	0.0	0.0	0	0	0

Probation order	8.4	7.2	6.9	0.2	0.1	10	11	12
Supervision order	0.5	0.6	0.6	0.0	–	1	0	–
Community service order	10.5	9.0	8.6	0.4	0.0	12	19	6
Attendance centre order	0.1	0.1	0.1	0.0	–	0	0	–
Combination order	2.9	3.0	2.8	0.1	0.0	4	3	7
Curfew order	0.0	0.0	0.0	–	–	0	–	–
Young offender institution	8.2	9.5	9.3	0.1	0.0	13	7	3
Imprisonment								
Fully suspended	1.9	2.1	2.1	0.0	0.0	3	1	1
Unsuspended	32.2	33.4	33.5	0.3	0.2	47	16	24
S53 C&YP Act 1933	0.4	0.6	0.6	–	–	1	–	–
Otherwise dealt with	1.6	1.5	1.4	0.1[1]	0.0[1]	2	3	6
Total	74.3	73.7	70.9	2.0	0.7	100	100	100
All courts								
Absolute discharge	20.2	20.0	2.5	5.7	11.8	1	1	2
Conditional discharge	105.6	104.7	52.3	43.6	8.7	17	9	1
Fine	996.7	1,073.0	84.6	402.7	585.7	28	82	90
Community penalties								
Probation order	49.4	50.9	33.1	8.2	9.6	11	2	1
Supervision order	10.1	10.9	8.5	2.0	0.4	3	0	0
Community service order	48.3	45.9	28.3	8.5	9.1	9	2	1
Attendance centre order	7.5	7.5	5.4	1.9	0.1	2	0	0
Combination order	14.6	17.3	10.2	2.1	4.9	3	0	0
Curfew order	0.0	0.2	0.1	0.0	0.0	0	0	1
Young offender institution	18.8	20.6	16.7	2.0	1.9	6	0	0
Imprisonment								
Fully suspended	3.2	3.4	2.6	0.2	0.5	1	0	0
Unsuspended	60.3	64.0	48.1	4.7	11.2	16	1	2
S53 C&YP Act 1933	0.4	0.6	0.6	–	–	0	–	–
Otherwise dealt with	19.1	18.8	7.0	6.7[1]	5.1[1]	2	1	1
Total	1,354.3[2]	1,437.8	300.3	488.4[3]	649.1[3]	100	100	100

(1) Includes cases, where the result of the court proceedings was incorrectly recorded . . .

(2) It is estimated that there are shortfalls of 70,300 and 4,600 offenders sentenced for summary non-motoring and summary motoring offences in England and Wales . . .

(3) It is estimated that there are shortfalls of 800 and 2,000 offences for summary non-motoring and summary motoring offences in West Mercia in 1996 . . .

The table in Extract 5.2.1 above relates to all offenders sentenced in the magistrates' courts. One very important limitation on the powers of the magistrates' courts is that a custodial sentence of more than six months may not be imposed on an offender for any offence (Magistrates' Courts Act 1980, s 31(1)). There is an exception where the offender is being sentenced for two triable either way offences, where an aggregate sentence of 12 months may be imposed (s 32). A distinction needs to be drawn between the powers of magistrates' courts to impose custody on adults (aged 21 and over) and on young adults (under 21). For young adults the relevant custodial sentence is detention in a young offender institution, while for adults it is imprisonment. The normal six-months maximum applies to both. It should be noted that while a sentence of imprisonment can be suspended (Powers of Criminal Courts Act 1973, s 22), a sentence of detention in a young offender institution cannot. Some sentencing options (absolute discharge, conditional discharge, bind-over, and fine) are always available to the magistrates' court whatever the age of the offender. Availability of community sentences varies with the age of the person being sentenced. The attendance centre is applicable for offenders up to the age of 20, while the probation order, community service order and combination order have a lower age limit of 16 and no upper age limit. Powers to impose curfew orders (which can be enforced by electronic monitoring) were originally available where the offender was aged 16 or over, but have been extended by the Crime (Sentences) Act 1997 to include youngsters aged 10–15 inclusive. The powers of (adult) magistrates' courts to sentence juveniles (for this purpose defined to cover those aged 10–17 inclusive) are severely limited by statute (Children and Young Persons Act 1969, s 7(8)). These offenders are almost always dealt with in the youth court (see below).

Returning to the table in Extract 5.2.1, it is clear that the use of the fine dominates the sentencing practice of magistrates' courts, although its relative rate of use for indictable offences has been declining steadily in recent years (now 36 per cent as compared to 51 per cent in 1989). This decline seems to be associated with a relative increase in the use of community sentences rather than custody. The maximum fine which magistrates can impose is always limited by the category of the offence with which they are dealing. All summary offences are by statute allocated a place somewhere on the 'standard scale' of maximum fines, which is to be found in the Criminal Justice Act 1982, s 37(2). The maximum fine for a level 1 offence is £200, the maximum for level 2 is £500, for level 3 it is £1,000, for level 4 it is £2,500 and for level 5 offences it is £5,000. If the offence committed is one which is triable either way, the maximum fine available to the magistrates will normally be £5,000. These figures are, of course, maximum fine levels and the court has a duty in every case in which it imposes a fine to select a realistic level of fine which both reflects the seriousness of the facts of the case, and the ability of the offender to pay the fine (Criminal Justice Act 1991, s 18). They also have a duty to investigate the means of the offender. In many cases payment of a fine will involve some hardship for an offender (therein lies its penal 'bite'), but it should not be fixed at so high a level that the person simply cannot afford to pay. The Court of Appeal has often stated that to impose a fine which is unrealistically high is wrong in principle, since it may tempt the offender to commit further offences to pay off the fine. To send the offender to prison instead would be even worse, since this would mean that, for the same offence, a poor person would go to prison whilst a rich person would escape by paying the fine (a good example is *Reeves* (1972) 56 Cr App R (S) 366). The proper sentence is a fine scaled down to a level which the particular offender can manage to pay, bearing in mind that, for a person on low income, meeting even a small additional burden may involve hardship. While these principles are perfectly clear, this is one area in which there can be vehement criticism of magistrates by the press and public. If ability to pay is ignored, the imposition of a small fine, when compared to the facts of the offence, can look derisory.

Responsibility for following up outstanding fines and enforcing their payment is a further important function of magistrates' courts, and this applies whether the fine was imposed by a magistrates' court, or by the Crown Court. Although fines are meant to be paid as soon as they are imposed, magistrates' courts can (and often do) allow people time to pay. Payment by instalments can be arranged, usually over a period of up to a year, but longer periods of two, three or even four years can sometimes be appropriate (according to the Court of Appeal in *Olliver* (1989) 11 Cr App R (S) 10). Magistrates have a range of powers which they may use to enforce the fine. They may require the fine to be paid by sums deducted from the offender's wages (Attachment of Earnings Act 1971) or from their benefit payments (Fines (Deduction from Income Support) Regulations 1992). They can make a money payment supervision order, by which a probation officer is appointed to assist the offender to sort out his or her finances and ensure that priority is being given to paying off the fine. Magistrates may issue a warrant which authorises bailiffs to seize and sell off items of the offender's goods, using the proceeds to pay the outstanding sum. They may threaten imprisonment (by use of a suspended committal) and, ultimately, imprison if the court is satisfied that the default is due to the person's 'wilful refusal or culpable neglect'. It is generally agreed that the use of imprisonment is an inappropriate method of enforcing payment of a fine, and further alternatives to imprisonment have been introduced under the Crime (Sentences) Act 1997, which allow magistrates to impose a community service order, a curfew order, or even to disqualify the offender from driving, in lieu of sending him to prison. If none of these other methods work, the term which must be served in default is set according to the amount of the unpaid fine. Maximum terms which can be ordered are prescribed by statute (Powers of Criminal Courts Act 1973, s 31 (3A)). The serving of the term in default (or the successful completion of any of the alternatives listed above) wipes out the fine. The following two extracts describe the practical operation of arrears courts, and raise a number of important issues of sentencing fairness.

467

Extract 5.2.2

A Morris and L Gelsthorpe, 'Not Paying for Crime: Issues in Fine Enforcement' [1990] Crim LR 839, pp 840–851

There was a total of 178 listings in the period in which we were carrying out the research. This involved 166 different people, of whom 31 (19 per cent) were women. Almost half (45 per cent) of those cases listed did not result in an appearance in court (for example, because the defendant had paid the outstanding sum before the hearing or because he/she did not turn up for the hearing). Thus there were only 98 appearances (93 different people; 15 (16 per cent) were women and 19 (20 per cent) were young adults). We interviewed 66 (72 per cent) of those who appeared; 10 of these were women and 17 were young adults.

The majority of the offences which the defaulters had committed were not on the face of it particularly serious in comparison with the general work of the courts. More than half (52 per cent) of the women were in court for non-payment of TV licences (this applied to only eight per cent of the men) and two-thirds (66 per cent) of the men were in court for motoring offences or non-payment of vehicle excise licences (this applied to only about a third (35 per cent) of the women). Only just over a quarter (26 per cent) of the women and less than a quarter (22 per cent) of the men had been convicted of theft or deception offences. The majority (52 per cent) of the young adults were in court for motoring offences; the next most common offences committed by young adults were theft (26 per cent) and criminal damage (11 per cent).

Just over a quarter of the sample (27 per cent) had fines totalling more than £100. This figure, however, is substantially higher for young adults – 48 per cent – and substantially lower for women – 13 per cent. The lower level of fines for women reflects the nature of their offences (that is, the prevalence of convictions for not having a TV licence). Thus almost a quarter (23 per cent) of the women were fined less than £100 compared with 13 per cent of the total sample. Fines of over £1,000 were rare: seven per cent of the total sample. For almost a third of the sample (31 per cent), the total fines outstanding represented an accumulation of fines from previous court appearances. As we might expect it is in this group that we find the largest amount owed to the court. It is also in this group that we find fines which seem to be far in excess of the defendants' stated means.

For example, EN was convicted of various motoring offences and vehicle excise licence offences between 1986 and 1988. The total amount imposed was just over £12,000. At the time of this court hearing he had paid around £4,600. He had previously appeared on 14 occasions for default and at a hearing in 1987 the court set a rate of £100 per month out of his stated earnings of £400 a month. From the file it appears that his mortgage repayments then were £290 a month. In December 1988, he was given a sentence of nine months imprisonment suspended on payment of £600 by the end of the month and £200 per month thereafter. In May 1989, it appears from the file that the court intended to issue the committal warrant but that the defendant had broken his arm and so the committal warrant was held over until June for the defendant to appear. He did not attend that hearing and a warrant not backed for bail was issued. His appearance in September was the result of that warrant. The Arrears Court affirmed the sentence of nine months imprisonment suspended on payment of £200 per month. The defendant was a self-employed lorry driver. In his interview with us, he said that he had hoped for more time to pay or that the court would remit part of the fine. He continued 'I'm not a criminal. It's the business. They have no idea ... I can't deal with it really. I mean, where do you start to pay £7,000? I'll be paying for years.'

Almost a quarter (23 per cent) of those listed had not made any payment at all prior to the listing. This represents 35 people, almost three-quarters (26) of whom were adult men. Of the total sample, 13 per cent of the women had not paid anything compared with 22 per cent of the men and 17 per cent of the young adult men. We tried to determine whether or not complete non-payment was due to the level of fine(s) imposed. It seems not to be so. A high number of those who had not paid anything had received relatively low fines in the first instance. For example, more than a third (34 per cent) had been fined less than £100. Only 11 per cent had been fined more than £500.

Five (14 per cent) of those who had not made any payment prior to the court listing paid in full before the court date. This might suggest that they had had sufficient money to pay earlier, but had wilfully refused to do so. However, another interpretation is that the court listing – and fear of the consequences of court action – made them find the money from somewhere – for example, from relatives or money lenders. That is, we do not know from the fact that they paid that they could afford to do so ...

The issues of 'can't pay/won't pay' is at the heart of debates on fine enforcement. The dominant ideology in the Arrears Court seemed to us to be that defendants were unwilling to pay and had to be compelled to do so. Those we interviewed, on the other hand, presented their failure to pay in a quite different way. Two-thirds (66 per cent) felt that the initial fine was too high. As one defendant put it: 'It was adequate if you're a pop singer.' More particularly, they pointed to outgoings in excess of income and the continuing struggle to make ends meet:

'There are too many other things to pay for ... just living. I always have to juggle with money. You pay for one bill one month, another the next and sometimes they have to wait.'

'The problem is not enough money, not how to organise it.'

'We've nothing left in the second week and I end up borrowing from Mum and then I have to pay back at the beginning of the week.'

'You can't pay £25 a week out of £27.'

'I can't pay what I haven't got.'

'I can't pay the rent if I pay the fine.'

Indeed, more than a third (38 per cent) of the men and nearly half of the women we interviewed were on benefits at the time of the interview ...

What kind of case is this?

On average each case lasts about 10 minutes and so magistrates must reach their decision very quickly. They have to make choices: does a problem exist? what is the nature of the problem? what is the appropriate response to it? In order to do this, they look for cues or shorthand ways to assess the kind of case they are dealing with. Cases have to be made sense of – constructed – and crucial in this is the determination of 'moral character' – what type of *person* is this? Hence distinctions are drawn between 'deserving' and 'underserving' defendants, 'acceptable' and 'unacceptable' expenditures or explanations for non-payment and 'problems' and 'excuses.' For example, defendants were routinely asked if they drank, smoked or drove a car and, if so, whether the car was really necessary. Defendants were clearly expected not to own cars, not to drink and not to smoke.

Work and non-work was a major area in which this moral drama was played out. Magistrates held the view that it was not difficult to find work in the city and that defendants who were not in work were not trying hard enough to find it. One defendant, for example, was asked 'Why don't you do something about it? There are lots of jobs in the local paper.' Another defendant said: 'I didn't like the way they said I should get a job. They said it should be easy as a carpenter but it's not easy, especially with a criminal record. Lots of jobs are not available to me.' Yet another defendant (who told us that he had been advised by his GP not to leave his pregnant wife alone with their five children) was asked if there was any reason why he was not working and what he had done to get work. The chairman said that the court would like to hear that he was 'a bit more active' in getting a job. 'There are pages and pages of jobs in the paper. You must make more effort to support your wife and children.' Sometimes cases were adjourned for short periods specifically for defendants to return to court with evidence of job applications and searches for work. This was so even in cases where defendants had not worked for a long period of time and where they had no particular skills. The court, therefore, seems to have interpreted its task of ensuring that the fine was paid in a very broad way and saw it as appropriate to cajole defendants to find work and admonish those who did not 'perform' to the court's satisfaction . . .

Conclusion

It has been widely recognised for a long time that a major problem in the enforcement of fines is the fact that the sentencing courts did not fully take into account the means of the defendant. Current proposals to introduce a modification of the Scandinavian Day Fine system – the unit fine – are intended to ensure that fines more realistically reflect the defendants' means. The unit fine system involves two quite separate exercises: first the court considers the gravity of a particular offence and then it assesses individual offender's financial circumstances. This means that two shoplifters who have very different means could be fined very different amounts . . .

What our research also showed was that this Arrears Court made use of very few of its enforcement powers. Although the majority of the defaulters whom we interviewed were employed, an Attachment of Earnings Order was used only once; and, despite a range of financial and personal difficulties amongst many of the defaulters, the probation service was rarely involved and only one Money Payment Supervision Order was made.

The Arrears Court we attended relied more heavily on the use of suspended committals than many of its other enforcement powers. There are clear dangers in this, dangers which might continue to exist despite the introduction of unit fines. One of the objectives in the White Paper is to reduce the number of defaulters committed to prison for non-payment of fines. However, if suspended committals are relied on at the expense of the other powers available to the courts, committals to prison may not be reduced as much as it is hoped.

In their conclusion, Morris and Gelsthorpe refer to the 'day fine' system, a scheme for the computation of fines which developed in Scandinavia and which is now employed by courts in many other jurisdictions. These schemes require courts to go through an explicit exercise of:

(1) reflecting the seriousness of the offence by allocating a number of units and then

(2) multiplying that number by a sum which represents a proportion of the offender's disposable income.

Thus, although having committed the same offence, offenders with different disposable incomes will pay quite different levels of fine. A broadly equivalent system, known as 'unit fines' was introduced in England and Wales by the Criminal Justice Act 1991. The basic principles of the scheme attracted widespread support. Unit fines reflected the idea of 'equal impact' in financial penalties, and they should help to ensure that fine levels are set realistically, especially for the poor. There were, however, serious practical problems in the way in which the scheme was implemented in England. It attracted much unwelcome criticism for the government, and was abolished by the Criminal Justice Act 1993.

Extract 5.2.3

C Walker and D Wall, 'Imprisoning the Poor: Television Licence Evaders and the Criminal Justice System' [1997] Crim LR 173, pp 173–179

In December 1995, Yvette Griffiths, a 33 year-old mother of five who was unable to work because of severe kidney and liver illness, was sentenced to 14 days' imprisonment for failing to pay a £190 fine levied upon her for using 'apparatus for wireless telegraphy' (namely a television receiver) without a licence contrary to section 1 of the Wireless Telegraphy Act 1949 (W.T.A.). Once the sentence was passed, in a terrified state and unable to contact her family, she was taken directly to the Risley remand centre, from where she was released after five days. This case was exceptionally tragic, but the nature of the defendant and the ineluctable circumstances in which she found

Table 1

	1991	1992	1993	1994	1995
Male	258	405	553	487	508
	65%	71%	65%	67%	68%
Female	136	163	292	243	241
	35%	29%	35%	33%	32%
All (100%)	394	568	845	730	749

herself were by no means uncommon. Yvette Griffiths was one of several hundred people who face prison each year for fine default arising from failure to pay their television licence fee. Whilst it might appear that these people are intentional evaders who are abusing the system and therefore deserve their punishment, this article suggests that they are more likely to be helpless or hopeless victims of circumstances not of their making. Even worse, those individuals actually punished by the criminal justice system are *filtered unevenly* from a much wider non-paying public.

These allegations of injustice have not gone unnoticed. During the last few years the imprisonment of TV licence defaulters has featured widely in the media and pressure and professional groups, such as the Howard League for Penal Reform, the Magistrates' Association and the Penal Affairs Consortium have also pronounced on the issue . . . Yet the most recent statistics from the Home Office, shown below in table 1, illustrate that both the media interest and the public concern have had little impact upon overall rates of imprisonment. If anything, the number of imprisonments has increased during a period when there were supposed to be initiatives to reduce the imposition of imprisonment for minor offences.

One of the most significant observations to be derived from table 1 is that whilst there has been a gradual increase in the number of those imprisoned since 1991, the annual gender mix has changed very little. Just under one-third (32 per cent) of all those imprisoned in 1995 for TV licence fine default were women. However, as women comprise between 3 and 4 per cent of the total prison population, this proportion is eight to 10 times higher than what one would expect from nornal sentencing patterns . . . Almost two-thirds (63 per cent) of those prosecuted under the W.T.A. are women. More importantly, offences under the W.T.A. account for over two-thirds (69 per cent) of all summary prosecutions (excluding motoring offences) brought against women. These statistics contrast with the fact that W.T.A. offences account for only one-sixth (17 per cent) of all summary prosecutions brought against men . . .

What are the features in this system which seem to produce an over-representation of women defendants? At the initial investigation stage one simple reason for the large number of prosecutions against women is the timing of the initial contact between the suspect household and the Inquiry Officer. Though visting hours can be flexible, there is evidence that the officers tend to work during normal office hours which is when more women (especially women carers) tend to be at home . . . Thus, it is the occupier who

472

happens to be around to open the door and answer questions who will often be prosecuted.

... Just as the majority of prosecuted evaders are women, so it is more likely that they will be economically disadvantaged. Earlier research has revealed that patterns of evasion are in fact fairly uniform across socio-economic groups and that people tend to evade payment whenever thet feel that they can get away with it, regardless of income or social status. However, between detection and prosecution, evaders are given a number of opportunities to pay the licence fee, and so many defaulters (about one-half) do avoid prosecution or court appearance. The TVL Prosecution Policy document claims that it would not be in the public interest to prosecute certain groups, and one might readily concur with this categorisation as it applies to persons under 18 or over 65, and the infirm. However, other exemptions seem to disfavour the poor. Though there can be no 'negotiation' out of a prosecution, there are several circumstances in which a person with financial means can purchase a licence after detection and thereby escape from prosecution. The circumstances include: where in circumstances of non-renewal the licence is purchased and short-dated to cover the period of unlicensed use (unless there is a previous warning or conviction within three years); where a licence is purchased on the same day as the visit and the only provable use is for that day; and where there has been 'short-term' evasion, provided a licence is purchased immediately and (if evasion of six weeks or more is established) the period of unlicensed use is also covered. Those who fail to escape the system by these paths may be further condemned for this very failure: 'the court is frequently advised that [offenders] were told they would not be prosecuted if they obtained a licence', though official TVL policy is that Inquiry Officers should not make such comments. Not surprisingly, the people who do eventually make the transition from notice to prosecute to an appearance in the magistrates' court are disproportionately poor, unemployed, single parents – and females predominate in that social sub-group . . .

Therefore the chosen sanction of the imposition of fines for non-payment of licence fees, arising from a basic inability to pay the fee initially, only intensifies the fundamental problem and will continue to do so, so long as there is a substantial polarisation between the poor and the rich. This particular punitive path itself creates the circumstances for creating a secondary and more serious predicament, of fine default which then lies within the domain of the general sentencing powers of the criminal courts and not the W.T.A. The effects are to escalate the severity of the sanction to a custodial sentence and to impose the stigma of imprisonment for what in the beginning is a civil default.

(b) Rules, disparity and guidance

The rules which restrict the imposition of custody and of fines in magistrates' courts are, as we have seen, described in statutory form. The sentencing powers of the lower courts are further constrained in other ways. A range of sentencing principles has been developed over the years by the Court of Appeal. Since the Court of Appeal hears appeals against sentence from the

Crown Court, it is true that most of the guidance provided is of more direct relevance to that court than to the magistrates. For instance, many reported appellate decisions are concerned with the duration of long prison sentences for very serious offences which magistrates are not even empowered to try. There are some matters, however, such as the significance of particular aggravating and mitigating factors, which are of as much relevance to the magistrates court as to the Crown Court. Doubts have been expressed over the extent to which magistrates are aware of these principles. Ralph Henham, in research carried out in 1981, found that there was 'a significant level of misunderstanding' amongst lay magistrates as to what the Court of Appeal guidance actually was (Henham 1986; see also Henham 1990):

> This study demonstrates that out of a total of 13 sentencing principles considered, magistrates' views as to their application differed from the 'accepted view' in over 50 per cent of cases . . . The solution may be complex. It has already been pointed out many times that there is an uneasy relationship between the Court of Appeal's sentencing principles and the magistrates' courts, particularly because there are cases and difficulties encountered by the magistrates' courts which are not dealt with by the Court of Appeal. [One suggestion is] to establish a special Sentencing Division of the High Court, or a Magisterial Sentencing Division, to which specific problems relating to magistrates' sentencing practices could be referred. A related issue of equal, if not greater, significance to the sentencing system as a whole is the wider debate surrounding the reduction or control of discretion through some form of sentencing guidelines . . . The impression gained from this study is that magistrates are extremely wary of rules and guidelines, or anything which could be construed as an attempt to control their discretion in sentencing which they regard as essential in order to maintain an individualised approach to sentencing.

Sentencing in magistrates' courts has been the subject of much criticism over the years, much of it rooted in arguments about disparity (see, for example, Parker, Sumner and Jarvis, 1989). Numerous research studies carried out since the 1970s have shown what appear to be divergent sentencing practices for the sentencing of comparable cases. Most of these studies have focused on differential use of custody, or the fine, from one magistrates' court to another (so-called 'geographical justice'). It is argued that, unless these differences can be explained in terms of distinct patterns of crime being dealt with from one area to another, they are quite unacceptable. In principle, it is unjust for one offender to receive custody, but for another to escape, when the only difference between them is the location in which their offences were committed. An article published in 1988 (Cavadino, 1988) points out some striking differences: 20 per cent of adult male offenders in South Tameside received custodial sentences, compared with 9 per cent in Rotherham, 23 per cent in Manchester compared with 14 per cent in Liverpool, 26 per cent in Sunderland compared with 14 per cent in Newcastle, 27 per cent in Exeter compared with 16 per cent in Worcester, and 25 per cent in Oxford compared with 16 per cent in Cambridge. A Home Office Research Study published in 1985 but relating to sentencing patterns 10 years earlier found that the proportionate use of immediate custody for adult male offenders at that time varied from 5 per cent to 23 per cent. The study tried to take account of differences in the overall type of offending from one area to another, by comparing the rate of imprisonment for a particular type of crime. The differences were still striking. One court gave custodial sentences to 7 per cent of burglars while another gave custody to 47 per cent of such offenders (Tarling, Moxon and Jones, 1985). To some extent, the explanation for such differences lies in differing sentencing traditions held by differing benches. Each bench is, as we have seen, trained by a clerk to the justices, who may have a particular view on sentencing levels generally, or on sentencing for particular sentences. This view may well be communicated during the training programme. A senior magistrate (chairman) is likely to influence the sentencing practice of more junior colleagues (wingers), thereby confirming bench practice over time. The Home Office study found that neighbouring benches often knew little about one another's sentencing levels.

Figures taken from the *Criminal Statistics England and Wales* for 1996 may suggest somewhat less disparity in magistrates' sentencing than there was, though there are still significant differences. The *Criminal Statistics* (Home Office, 1997a) indicate that proportionate use of immediate custody for offenders over 21 varies from 14 per cent in London and 13 per cent in Manchester to 5 per cent in Wiltshire (average across England and Wales 10 per cent). Average sentence length varies from 3.6 months in Lincolnshire to 2.1 months in Essex (average across England and Wales 2.7 months). Such differences are easy to demonstrate. Do they really matter? In the following extract, Professor Ashworth takes a careful look at the arguments about disparity.

Extract 5.2.4

A Ashworth, 'Disentangling Disparity' in C Pennington and S Lloyd-Bostock (eds), *The Psychology of Sentencing* (1987) Ch 3, pp 24–27

Disparity in sentencing has for some time been both a matter of public concern and a subject which attracts considerable research. My purpose here is to offer some reflections on the concept of disparity and on what research can usefully achieve.

The concept of disparity

The enquiry must begin with perhaps the most difficult question – What is disparity? It is a word which calls attention to a form of injustice, to decisions which have resulted in an unfair distribution of burdens or benefits. The principle which seems to express the core of 'parity' against which various practices and decisions are measured is the widely accepted precept of formal justice: treat like cases alike. For completeness, the precept should be expanded so as to provide for 'unalike' cases thus: treat like cases alike and different cases differently. Even this formulation does not carry the argument very far, since 'disparity' cannot be used as a critical concept unless it is established which resemblances and which differences are to count as relevant and which as irrelevant. Otherwise the precept would remain an empty formula, which might be used as a basis for criticising our sentencing system for not treating all red-haired offenders in the same way or for dealing differently with mentally disordered offenders. Where might we find some 'given' categories of relevant resemblances and differences, so as to lend the concept some practical application as a critical tool?

One way of establishing such categories authoritatively is through legislation. Thus it could be said that Parliament has ordained that different criteria and measures should be used by courts when sentencing offenders under 17, those aged 17 to 20 and those aged 21 and over. Another authoritative source in England is the Court of Appeal, through its decisions in sentencing cases . . .

In sentencing generally, however, there are few spheres which are tightly regulated by legal rules or principles. Courts are generally left with a wide discretion. Some might say that the only constraints are that the sentence should not be unlawful or excessive. There are others who would protest at this: discretion does not confer such a wide freedom of choice, and courts are always bound by principles and conventions. The sentencer ascertains the 'going rate' for the offence, takes account of well-recognised mitigating factors, and the sentence emerges. But that view is probably true, if at all, only of the more serious Crown Court cases and the least serious cases in the magistrates' courts. It takes no account of the fact that about half of the sentences imposed by the Crown Court are non-custodial, and that many cases heard summarily require more than simply taking a fine from a well-established scale. Those who adopt this view may therefore be accused of distorting reality, even if the underlying proposition – that conferring a discretion on courts does not allow them a free choice according to their own whims and fancies – is a correct one.

Another view sometimes advanced is that the concept of disparity is inapplicable to sentencing. Any experienced sentencer knows, we are told, that no two cases are the same and that each has had to be dealt with on its own facts: the endeavours of academics and of appeal courts to propound general principles or to draw comparisons are therefore misguided because they are based on a misunderstanding of practical sentencing. This view was expressed by several judges in the Oxford 'pilot study' of sentencing in the Crown Court.[1] Yet the illogicality of the standpoint was exposed nearly a quarter of a century ago by Roger Hood:[2]

> 'Magistrates and judges . . . place particular value upon their experience in sentencing. Now, if this experience is to be of value, then all cases cannot be unique, they must be comparable at least in some respects; and even if it is agreed that all cases are unique in some sense, this cannot be decisive in the practice of sentencing, for frequently decisions are reached with the aid of 'experience'. There are, then, certain observable factors which magistrates will take into account in their consideration of the appropriate sentence.'

476

Thus the relevance of previous convictions, to give an obvious example, is a matter on which a sentencer is likely to adopt a general approach (though subject to defined and undefined exceptions, no doubt). Indeed, most decisions to take a factor into account or to leave it out of account are not simple responses to the 'facts of the case' but involve judgements based in part on the sentencer's approach to the task and preconceptions about what factors ought to be accorded significance. Perhaps what underlies the 'each case turns on its own facts' claim is that combinations of factors tend to differ from one case to another. As a matter of legal technique it is often regarded as more appropriate to confer a discretion than to attempt regulation by rules and exceptions when the decisions to be taken involve a range of relevant factors which may crop up in different combinations and different strengths. Sentencing decisions may be thus classified. The argument, then, is that there are general principles as to the effect on sentence of previous convictions, employment record, heroism in the Falklands war, etc. which courts should take into account, but that many cases have rare or unique combinations of factors which falsify the simple comparisons which researchers tend to make.

How strong is this claim about the rarity or uniqueness of the combinations of factors in sentencing cases? The tendency of the judge is to recount some wholly unusual facts from a recent case, whereas the academic asserts that the bulk of everyday cases involve only a few variables. How can we tell whether most cases involve little more than an application of general principles or whether most cases require a court to engage in some weighing and balancing in a context which is substantially 'one-off'? One escape route for the researcher who wishes to compare the practices of two or more courts is to argue that it is fair to assume that courts in broadly similar areas deal (over a period of time) with offenders who have broadly similar backgrounds. If this were accepted, then one could infer that any differences in sentencing patterns could be attributed to the different approaches of the courts. A more reliable escape route is to analyse the cases in terms of certain factors recognised as important in sentencing – such as type of offence, number of previous convictions – so as to discover whether the courts are imposing similar sentences on similar kinds of offender. This enables research to go behind an apparent similarity in the rate of using a particular measure (e.g. imprisonment) and to see whether it is used in a similar way. It also makes it possible to demonstrate to a certain degree whether the courts which are being compared are dealing with offenders of the same kinds. A further effect might be to cast doubt on the claims about rarity and uniqueness: if the research shows that in a majority of cases it is possible to predict the sentence by reference to type of offence and number of previous convictions (with or without certain other factors which the research might have coded for), might this suggest that sentencing is not so complex as some maintain, and that the many other factors which sentencers regard it as necessary to weigh in each case play only a minor role in fact?

Disparity identified – so what?

Let us suppose that research findings show a clear divergence of approach between two courts or groups of magistrates which cannot be accounted for by any major difference in the features of the cases sentenced; for example, it emerges that court A treats previous convictions as a stronger ground for increasing the sentence than court B, or that in a sentencing exercise groups V and X viewed previous convictions more severely than groups Y and Z. In order to draw any practical implications from this, it must be possible to state which is right and which is wrong. It is vacuous to conclude that disparity has been discovered and that a uniform policy must be adopted if there is no indication of what the right policy is. It is perhaps easier to articulate the principles which should be applied to the sentencing of persistent offenders than many other issues of sentencing principle, but the existing English principles could not give an unambiguous answer to the problems posed above . . . , and therein lies their condemnation.

Likewise, there is little guidance on the proper use of the various non-custodial measures and little indication of how sentencers should choose among the various aims of sentencing (individual or general deterrence, incapacitation, rehabilitation, retribution or just deserts) in their approach to the various types of case. To prove that disparity exists is not hugely helpful when it is not clear what the right course should be, although it may act as a spur to policy makers and reformers. In view of the dearth of guidance, it is hardly surprising that sentencers have improvised, and it is not really a cause for blame that these improvisations differ somewhat from court to court. It is a situation which might even be said to encourage the expression of sentencers' personalities and opinions, and those of bench chairmen and justices' clerks. Indeed, it would not be unreasonable to argue that the incompleteness and tentativeness of many English sentencing principles is a substantial *cause* of disparity.

---

[1] A Ashworth, E Genders, G Mansfield, J Peay and E Player, *Sentencing in the Crown Court: Report of an Exploratory Study*, Occasional Paper No 10 (Oxford: Centre for Criminological Research, 1984).
[2] R Hood, *Sentencing in Magistrates' Courts* (London: Tavistock, 1962).

As we have seen, lay magistrates are provided with advice and guidance on sentencing by their clerk and, of course, newer magistrates will be tutored informally in the sentencing conventions of their bench by their more experienced colleagues. In an attempt to provide more principled guidance to magistrates and to achieve greater uniformity of approach from one bench to another, the Magistrates' Association (to which over 90 per cent of lay magistrates belong) publishes a folder of *Sentencing Guidelines* for use in the lower courts. When first published these guidelines were confined to motoring offences, but in recent editions they have expanded to cover just about all offences which regularly come before the lower courts. The most recent revision was in 1997. The guidelines indicate various features of a case which might be regarded as making the particular offence before the court more or less serious than an 'average' case. The court is then reminded to look for matters of personal mitigation, and a 'starting point' for sentence is suggested.

Extract 5.2.5

Magistrates' Association, *Sentencing Guidelines* **(1997)**

Theft Act 1968 s 12 Triable only summarily Penalty: Level 5 and/or 6 months May disqualify	**Taking Vehicle** **without Consent**

CONSIDER THE SERIOUSNESS OF THE OFFENCE
(INCLUDING THE IMPACT ON THE VICTIM)

GUIDELINE: ➤   *IS COMPENSATION, DISCHARGE OR FINE APPROPRIATE?*
        IS IT SERIOUS ENOUGH FOR A COMMUNITY PENALTY?
        IS IT SO SERIOUS THAT ONLY CUSTODY IS APPROPRIATE?

⊕   CONSIDER AGGRAVATING AND MITIGATING FACTORS   ⊖

for example Group action Premeditated Related damage Professional hallmarks Vulnerable victim Offence committed on bail Previous convictions and failures to respond to previous sentences, if relevant *This list is not exhaustive*	**for example** Misunderstanding with owner Soon returned Vehicle belonged to family or friend *This list is not exhaustive*

CONSIDER OFFENDER MITIGATION

for example
Age, health (physical or mental)
Co-operation with the police
Voluntary compensation
Remorse

CONSIDER YOUR SENTENCE

Compare it with the suggested guideline level of sentence and reconsider your reasons carefully if you have chosen a sentence at a different level. Consider a discount for a timely guilty plea.

DECIDE YOUR SENTENCE

NB. COMPENSATION – Give reasons if not awarding compensation

Remember: These are GUIDELINES not a tariff

Extract 5.2.5 on p 479 sets out the current guideline for taking a vehicle without consent (known colloquially as TWOC: Taking Without Consent). This guideline is a typical one in scope and format, and it provides us with a chance to examine a number of sentencing issues in more detail, particularly as they affect the magistrates' courts.

The offence itself derives from s 12 of the Theft Act and is triable only summarily. Thus, as we have seen, the maximum penalty available to the magistrates is six months' imprisonment (or the equivalent term of detention in a young offender institution) or a fine not exceeding level 5 (see Theft Act 1968, s 12(2)). The offence is one for which the offender can, in an appropriate case, be disqualified from driving (Road Traffic Offenders Act 1988, Sched 2). The guideline does not say so, but these penalties and powers to disqualify are also applicable to a person who has been a willing passenger in a car which has been taken without authority. It may be noted that there is a more serious form of this offence (known as aggravated vehicle-taking). By s 12A of the 1968 Act, the offence is made out where, the basic offence having been committed, the vehicle is then driven dangerously, or an accident is caused resulting in injury or damage. This offence is triable either way and punishable with up to two years on indictment. If the accident causes a death, the maximum penalty rises to five years (see, further, the Aggravated Vehicle-Taking Act 1992).

The TWOC guideline offers magistrates guidance in the exercise of their sentencing discretion: a form of structured decision-making. It does not tell magistrates the 'answer': it provides them with a series of stages which must be gone through in a certain order. If faithfully followed by magistrates, the guideline on TWOC should achieve a uniformity of 'approach' but, of course, that is not same thing as uniformity of 'outcome'. There are bound to be differences between decision-makers in the assessments which they make of the facts of the case. This is true of all human decision-making. Starting from the top of the page and working down, the first thing which the magistrates are required to consider is the *seriousness* of the *offence*. In the plus and minus columns of the guideline are various factors which are regarded by the Magistrates' Association as making the individual offence of TWOC a more or less serious example of its kind. So, if in a case before the magistrates, one of the aggravating factors was present but there were no mitigating factors, the offence should be regarded as being somewhat more serious than average. Presumably, if two or more aggravating factors are present the case should be regarded as more serious still. Helpful though these lists undoubtedly are, it can be seen that they give no indication of relative weight. We should not assume that the most important aggravating factors appear at the head of the plus list (they are listed in alphabetical order), so we do not know whether some have more weight than others. If two or more of them are found together in a particular case, is their cumulative effect additive, or multiplicative? How should one or more of the aggravating factors be balanced against a mitigating factor? There are no clear-cut answers to these questions: in the end the bench of magistrates dealing with the case must come to an overall assessment of seriousness. Turning to the list of aggravating factors, one of the entries (offence committed on bail) can be found in all of the individual offence guidelines of the Magistrates' Association. It reflects a statutory provision, s 29(2) of the Criminal Justice Act 1991, which states that where an offence has been committed on bail, it must *always* be treated as aggravated by the breach of bail. Neither the statute nor the guidelines provide a justification for this rule. One reason for it might be that the offender, as well as committing the offence, has breached the trust which the court reposed in him when it granted bail. The final entry in the plus column relates to previous convictions of the offender and past failures of his to respond to earlier sentences. This is an important, and complex, matter of statutory authority and is discussed at p 507 below. The remaining factors in the plus list and the two factors in the minus list are not derived from statute, but from case law and the experience of magistrates in dealing regularly with such cases. Some of them are clearly offence-specific (misunderstanding with the owner of the car) while others might be important across a range of different offences (e.g. group action, premeditated, vulnerable victim). What does 'vulnerable victim' mean in this context? If the victim was more than usually dependent on their car (such as where it was essential for their livelihood), should this always make the offence more serious, or only where the offender *knew* at the time of taking it that this was the case?

After deciding upon the relative seriousness of the case the magistrates then have a discretion to adjust their sentence downwards in the light of 'offender mitigation'. Section 28 of the Criminal Justice Act 1991 states that 'nothing shall prevent a court from mitigating an offender's sentence by taking into account any such matters as, in the opinion of the court, are relevant in mitigation of sentence'. It will be seen that the examples in this box relate to the offender, while those in the minus-seriousness column relate to the offence. So, matters personal to the offender cannot be taken to increase the sentence: there is no 'offender aggravation' box. Thus, for example, the fact that the offender has annoyed the court by pleading not guilty in an utterly hopeless case is not a reason for increasing his sentence (*Spinks* (1980) 2 Cr App R (S) 335), nor is incurring the court's displeasure by falsely attacking the credibility of prosecution witnesses (*Scott* (1983) 5 Cr App R (S) 90). The guideline also refers to a 'discount' for a timely guilty plea, a matter frequently encountered in the courts. It was explained earlier that over 90 per cent of defendants who appear before the magistrates' courts plead guilty. The circumstances in which such a high rate of guilty pleas is received were discussed in Chapter 4 above. Are all of these offenders entitled to the 'about a third' discount on sentence which the guidelines indicate? This is one of the areas in which the case law generated by the Court of Appeal is of as much significance to the magistrates as to the Crown Court. The Court of Appeal has often indicated that there is a 'normal' discount of between one quarter and one third (see, for example, *Boyd* (1980) 2 Cr App R (S) 234 and other cases set out in Wasik, 1998). Although this is the norm, there is no absolute entitlement to a discount for pleading guilty. When might it be lost? A leading decision on this point is *Costen* (1989) 11 Cr App R (S) 182. The Court of Appeal said in that case that the 'normal' discount might be reduced or lost in any of the following circumstances:

(1) where the protection of the public requires the imposition of a long sentence and this imperative outweighs the normal effect of the plea;
(2) cases of 'tactical plea', where the defendant has delayed his guilty plea in a weak case in an attempt to squeeze advantage from the system; and
(3) where the offender has been caught red-handed and thus has no practical alternative but to plead guilty.

On the other hand, an offender might receive a greater-than-normal discount where he owns up in circumstances where he is not even under suspicion (*Hoult* (1990) 12 Cr App R (S) 180). The principles relating to the guilty plea discount have only quite recently been placed on a statutory footing, by the Criminal Justice and Public Order Act 1994, s 48. Parliament took the opportunity in that section to require sentencers, in every case in which a guilty plea has resulted in a less severe sentence than would otherwise have been imposed, to explain this in open court. The discount is normally referred to in terms of a percentage reduction. This language is appropriate when talking about custodial sentence length or the level of a fine, but it is less helpful when the court is thinking of imposing a community sentence (see p 486 below). Nor does it help very much when the question is whether one form of sentence (say, custody) should be reduced to another (say, a community sentence) by reason of the plea. See further Extract 5.4.3 below.

What about other forms of offender mitigation set out in the box in the guideline? The list is certainly something of a mixture, but it reflects a much wider and more diverse range of matters urged upon courts in mitigation of sentence. A comprehensive analysis of matters in mitigation was undertaken by Joanna Shapland in her book, *Between Conviction and Sentence* (Shapland, 1981), especially in Ch 3. Although based on empirical research carried out 20 years ago, this study remains the best of its kind. An analysis by Professor Shapland of pleas in mitigation given in 100 cases in magistrates' courts revealed a total of 123 different arguments relating to personal mitigation. Of these, 26 addressed the offender's attitude to the offence, 40 related to their personal circumstances at the time of court appearance, 19 related to their personal history and 37 made reference to their future prospects and plans. At the risk of over-simplifying, a three-fold distinction can be made. First, some of these considerations reflect a degree of *credit* upon the offender. Evidence of genuine remorse may do so, as may voluntary efforts to co-operate with the police or to rectify in some way the damage done to the victim. There is another factor reflecting credit which is, surprisingly, omitted from the list in the TWOC guideline. The Court of Appeal has on many occasions

482

said that a first offender, or a person with a light record, is normally entitled to some reduction in sentence (examples are *Walsh* (1980) 2 Cr App R (S) 224 and *Sykes* (1980) 2 Cr App R (S) 173). This form of personal mitigation was the one advanced most frequently of all in Shapland's study. A second batch of mitigating factors are designed to suggest that the offender is *less blameworthy* than might at first appear. The defendant may be very young or elderly, be suffering from serious physical or mental health problems. An example is *Green* (1992) 13 Cr App R (S) 613, where the offender's sentence was suspended on the ground that he was suffering from sickle cell anaemia in a severe form. Or, though this is not specifically mentioned in the TWOC guideline, the offence was committed at a time of exceptional personal stress. A remarkable example is *Jones* (1992) 13 Cr App R (S) 275 where a woman, severely depressed as a result of financial and domestic problems, carried out seven robberies at building society branches. A sentence of four years' imprisonment was varied to a probation order. The offender may have performed some meritorious conduct wholly unrelated to the offence which leads the court to take a different view of his character: in *Reid* (1982) 4 Cr App R (S) 280 the fact that the offender had earlier rescued three children from a fire was held to be relevant to sentence. The third group of consideration may reflect little credit upon the offender but be appropriate for other *criminal justice system reasons*, such as where the offender's co-operation in pleading guilty has saved witnesses the stress of appearing in court (especially in a rape case) in addition to the normal savings of time and money, or where the offender has been prepared to implicate others involved in the offence (for example, *Lowe* (1977) 66 Cr App R 122). The existence of a discount in this last group of cases helps to ensure that other offenders will follow suit in the future.

While it is common practice to take such matters of personal mitigation into account when passing sentence, there are no guarantees, and no *entitlement* to reduction. Sentencers are given a broad discretion to take account of personal mitigation, but they are in no case required to do so (see the terms of the Criminal Justice Act 1991, s 28(1), set out in Extract 5.4.3). The next stage in the process of structured decision-making, then, is for the magistrates to weigh their 'offence seriousness' assessment, on the one hand, with the matters in mitigation which they are taking into account, on the other. Depending on the facts of the case, this can be a very difficult exercise, especially in so-called 'borderline custody' cases. The Court of Appeal grappled with this issue in *Inwood* (1974) 60 Cr App R 70. The offender pleaded guilty to offences of obtaining money by deception, which had netted a total of £15,000, and numerous further unsuccessful attempts. An expert witness gave evidence that Inwood suffered from a personality disorder, often described as a 'Walter Mitty' personality. He indulged in unrealistic fantasies about himself and tried to attain a distinction and eminence in his life which was well beyond his abilities and means. The Court of Appeal upheld the original sentence of four years' imprisonment, Scarman L J commenting that:

We have listened, I hope with sympathy and understanding, to the mitigating factors urged upon us by Mr Buckley. But in the balance that the court has to make between the mitigating factors and society's interest in marking its disapproval for this type of conduct, we come to the irresistible though unpalatable conclusion, that we must not yield to the mitigating factors. The sentence was correct in principle when measured against the gravity of the offences.

The Magistrates' Association guideline offers little practical help here, beyond exhorting magistrates to: 'DECIDE YOUR SENTENCE', by comparing it with the suggested guideline (in the 'GUIDELINE' towards the top of the page). Because TWOC is a summary offence there is effectively no guidance from the Court of Appeal on how to address the issue. In fact, before 1988, TWOC was triable either way, so there is some guidance from before that date. Examples are *Bushell* (1987) 9 Cr App R (S) 537 and *Jeary* (1986) 8 Cr App R (S) 491. There is also some appellate guidance on the more serious version of the offence, aggravated vehicle-taking, when tried in the Crown Court.

3. SENTENCING IN THE YOUTH COURTS

When dealing with offenders under the age of 18 the magistrates' court is constituted as a youth court. Youth courts were known as juvenile courts prior to the Criminal Justice Act 1991. This change of name reflected the fact that from October 1992 (when the 1991 Act came into force) the jurisdiction of this court was extended to cover 17-year-olds, who were formerly dealt with in the adult magistrates' court. A youth court panel must be elected from each local bench of lay magistrates. Every time the youth court sits at least one of the magistrates must be female. All stipendiary magistrates are automatically eligible to deal with cases in the youth court, but when dealing with such cases they almost always sit with at least one other panel member. They are required to undertake additional training. Youth court proceedings must be kept separate from those of the adult magistrates' court wherever possible. A separate court room should be used for youth court business or, if a separate court is not available, there must be a time lag of at least an hour before and after the use of an adult court for the sitting of a youth court panel (Children and Young Persons Act 1933, s 47). The procedure in the youth court is less formal than in the adult magistrates' court, and there is some difference in terminology also. The youth court records a 'finding of guilt' rather than a 'conviction', and makes 'an order upon a finding of guilt' rather than passing 'sentence' (Children and Young Persons Act 1933, s 59).

All sentencing in the youth court is made subject to the general principle in s 44(1) of the Children and Young Persons Act 1933 that the court 'shall have regard to the best interests of the child or young person' and, more generally, the United Nations Convention on the Rights of the Child requires

484

that in legal proceedings against children the rights of the child shall be the primary consideration. The younger the offender the more significant this principle is, but there is an important and long-standing debate over the proper balance to be struck when sentencing juveniles between the 'justice' and 'welfare' approaches (Morris, Giller, Szwed and Geach (1980), Pratt (1989)). The former view stresses the need to use appropriate punishment for offences committed by juveniles (the so-called 'right to be punished', mitigated where appropriate to take account of a young person's reduced culpability), while the latter sees juvenile offending as a symptom of broader problems, sometimes requiring more lenient treatment (on the basis that young offenders often grow out of the offending phase) but sometimes requiring more active intervention in the family setting. The pendulum has swung back and forth between these different perspectives. The welfare approach predominated until the 1980s, since when the justice model has assumed more importance, but it has never had the same impact here as for adult offenders. Selection of the penalty proportionate to the offence remains an important objective for the youth court, but there is greater flexibility in the 'tariff' for juveniles than there is for adults (see Moxon, Jones and Tarling (1985); Stafford and Hill (1987)). The 1980s and early 1990s saw a marked decline in the number of juveniles who received custody. This was because of a policy of greatly increased use of community-based sentencing, partly because of a decrease of the number of juveniles in the population, and partly the result of statutory custody restrictions introduced in the Criminal Justice Acts of 1982 and 1988 (see further Ball (1992)). The sentencing pattern for juveniles must also be seen in the context of the very large number of young offenders who receive a formal caution, rather than being summoned to appear before the youth court, and the increasing proportion which have received conditional discharges in recent years. Recently there has been something of a downturn in the cautioning rate, associated with the issuing of revised cautioning guidelines. The whole area of cautioning is now subject to further change, with the impending introduction of 'final warning' schemes in place of formal cautioning for juveniles (Home Office, 1997c and see Chapter 2 above).

Specific sentencing powers available to deal with juveniles in the youth court are, at the lower end of the scale, the absolute and conditional discharge and the fine. The law states that the parent or guardian of a juvenile will be required by the court to pay the fine (or compensation order) where the juvenile is aged between 10–15. The court has a discretion to order the parent to pay where the juvenile is aged 16 or 17. The same can be required of a local authority if the juvenile was in the care of the authority when the offence was committed (Children and Young Persons Act 1933, s 55). Conservative and Labour administrations have strengthened these provisions in recent years, stressing the importance of 'parental responsibility' in keeping children out of trouble. The present government is convinced that 'the single most important factor in explaining criminality is the quality of a young person's home life, including parental supervision' (Home Office 1997c, p 5).

There is resistance to this approach from criminal justice pressure groups and from sentencers, many of whom take the view that it can be counter-productive to impose additional penalties on families which already have a range of economic and social problems. Perhaps reflecting this reluctance, parental orders to pay fines were made in only 9 per cent of eligible cases in 1996 (although the figure was 21 per cent for compensation orders). New powers for the courts to make a 'parenting order' are contained in the Crime and Disorder Bill. These orders, available where a young offender has been convicted of a crime, will require the parent to attend counselling or guidance sessions. Additional requirements can be written in to the order, designed to ensure that the child gets to school every day, or is at home by a certain time at night. The Bill, when enacted, will also contain powers to require young offenders to make reparation to their victims, such as by writing a letter of apology, apologising in person, or taking practical steps to repair the damage, such as by cleaning graffiti (Home Office 1997c, p 14).

Further up the sentencing scale, a juvenile may be dealt with by way of a community sentence. The Criminal Justice Act 1991 states that a community sentence should only be imposed where the offence itself was serious enough to justify it (rather than, say, passing a conditional discharge). The attendance centre order, the supervision order and the curfew order are available where the juvenile is aged between 10–17); the community service order, probation order and combination order are available for those aged 16 and upwards. Although *attendance centre orders* can also be made by the adult magistrates' court and by the Crown Court, by far the greatest number of such orders are made by the youth court, so that it is appropriate to say a little more about such orders here. The offender is required to attend a particular centre for a number of hours specified by the court normally between 12 hours and 24 hours (where the offender is under 16) and 36 hours (when aged between 16 and 21): Criminal Justice Act 1982, s 17. Attendance must be in a number of periods of time each of no more than three hours on any one day. A typical order would cover a series of Saturday afternoons. There are separate attendance centres for males and for females. The centres are usually run by police officers in their spare time. Juveniles should 'be given, under supervision, appropriate occupation or instruction' (Criminal Justice Act 1982, s 16(2)) and, according to the Home Office, the aim is to benefit the juvenile by 'bringing him under the influence of representatives of the authority of the state' and 'teaching him something of the constructive use of leisure' (Home Office Circular 69/1990). The *supervision order* may be imposed by the Crown Court as well as the youth court but, once again, the majority of such orders are made by the youth court. Powers to make supervision orders derive from the Children and Young Persons Act 1969. The order places the juvenile under the supervision of either a local authority social worker or a probation officer, the supervisor's duty being to 'advise, assist and befriend' the supervised person. A range of requirements may be written into the basic supervision order by the court. The relevant provisions are complex. They can be

486

found in ss 12–12C of the 1969 Act, and are just summarised here (for further details see Wasik, 1998). They include a requirement that the offender must reside with a person named in the order, must reside in local authority accommodation, must comply with specified arrangements for his education, or must observe a night restriction or curfew. Alternatively, the order may require the offender to take part in specified activities (known as 'intermediate treatment') for a period of up to 90 days. Activities might include individual counselling or group discussion, learning a new skill (such as horse-riding or canoeing or taking part in an adventure-type holiday). It will be seen that intermediate treatment is not really meant to be a punishment – its purpose is to encourage young offenders to use their time more constructively. Sending young offenders away on holiday has, however, been the subject of highly critical press campaigns.

Where a youth court decides that the offence is so serious that community measures are insufficient and that a custodial sentence must be passed, the only such sentence currently available to the court is detention in a young offender institution (not imprisonment, which can be used only for offenders aged 21 and over). The juvenile must be aged at least 15 to qualify for this sentence, and the maximum term available to the youth court is six months for a single offence (more on committal to Crown Court). In reponse to criticism from some quarters that youth courts lacked powers to deal with juveniles younger than 15 who were persistent lawbreakers, the Conservative government in 1994 created the secure training order, which represents a return to a more overtly punitive response to young offending. The sentence is directed at 12–14 year-olds who have three or more previous convictions and in respect of whom a supervision order has already been tried, but without stopping the offending (see Criminal Justice and Public Order Act 1994, ss 1–5). The sentence was made available only in 1998. Only one – privately run – secure training centre has so far been built. The Labour government has indicated that secure training orders will be scrapped in 1999, to be replaced in turn by a detention and training order.

· A Home Office document published in 1997 (Home Office, 1997c) presages further substantial changes to the administration of criminal justice in the youth courts of the future. The following proposals are currently open for consultation, but many of them seem likely to become law within the next couple of years:

Extract 5.3.1

Home Office, *No More Excuses – A New Approach to Tackling Youth Crime in England and Wales* (1997) paras 9.1–9.3

9.1. Underpinning the Government's reform programme is the belief that the right intervention at the right time can be highly effective at cutting short the criminal activities of young people. Previous chapters have highlighted plans for early intervention before a child or young person comes to court, for a range of new sentencing options to make young offenders take responsibility – and make amends – for their behaviour and for speeding up the youth justice system, including better case management. The Government has also been looking carefully at the way the youth court in England and Wales carries out its business, at the philosophy which underlies its proceedings and at the culture in which it operates.

9.2. A frank assessment of the current approach of the youth court must conclude that, all too often, inadequate attention is given to changing offending behaviour. This is not the fault of individuals working within the system. It is encouraged by the court's very structures and procedures. The Government is determined to tackle these failings head on. The purpose of youth justice must change from simply deciding guilt or innocence and then issuing a sentence. In most cases, an offence should trigger a wider enquiry into the circumstances and nature of the offending behaviour, leading to action to change that behaviour. This requires in turn a fundamental change of approach within the youth court system.

9.3. So, reform of the youth court is needed to provide:
- speedier decisions on guilt or innocence, much closer to the date of the offence and with less tolerance of adjournments;
- a system which is more open, and which commands the confidence of the victims and the public;
- processes which engage young offenders and their parents and focus on the nature of the offending behaviour and how to change it;
- a stronger emphasis on using sentencing to prevent future offending; and
- more efficient arrangements for the scheduling and management of cases.

Other, more specific, proposals in chapter 9 of the report include the following:

(1) Greater use of the youth court's powers to lift reporting restrictions on the case following conviction (that is, publicising the name of the offender, which could then be reported in the press).
(2) In the case where a juvenile pleads not guilty, but is convicted after conviction, a conditional discharge would not be available as a sentence if the juvenile had already received a final warning (see Chapter 2 above) and had re-offended within two years.
(3) If the juvenile pleaded guilty and it was his or her first offence, the case would be referred to a 'youth panel', comprising a magistrate, a member of a 'Youth Offending Team' and, perhaps, a police officer. Parents would be required to attend and victims would be encouraged (though not forced) to attend as well. The youth panel and the young offender would draw up a 'contract' setting out clear obligations on the juvenile,

488

and on his or her parents, for the future. These would always involve an element of reparation, to the victim directly or to the community more generally. Failure to comply would involve the juvenile being returned to the youth court for sentencing.

4. CROWN COURT SENTENCING

In the Crown Court, in contrast to the magistrates' court, sentencing is carried out by professional judges who are qualified lawyers of many years' standing. All Crown Court proceedings are heard before a single judge, with the exception of an appeal from a magistrates' court, where magistrates sit alongside the judge. There is a three-fold classification of Crown Court judge: High Court judges, circuit judges and recorders. Certain of the most serious offences, including murder, manslaughter and rape, are normally only listed before a High Court judge. Judges normally retire at the age of 72, but the Lord Chancellor has a discretion to allow High Court judges to continue to take cases until they are 75 (for further information see *Blackstone's Criminal Practice*, 1998, Part D2). The Judicial Studies Board is responsible for carrying out induction training seminars with newly appointed judges, and refresher courses for more experienced judges. The Board has always given prominence to training on matters relating to sentencing (see further Glidewell, 1992).

(a) The pattern of Crown Court sentencing

The table reproduced in Extract 5.2.1 above gives a good overall picture of sentencing by the Crown Court in 1996, the most recent year for which these figures are available. It will be seen that the Crown Court deals almost entirely with indictable offences. 'Indictable' means all offences which are triable only on indictment *and* offences which are triable either way but, following the decision on mode of trial (see Chapter 4 above) have been dealt with in Crown Court. A few summary offences do reach the Crown Court, where the offender is before the higher court for a different offence and there is a connected summary offence which it is appropriate to deal with at the same time (see Criminal Justice Act 1991, ss 40 and 41; there is an example in *Cox*, see Extract 5.4.3 below).

The sentencing pattern in the Crown Court is very different from that of the lower courts, as one would expect from the more serious offences being dealt with. In 1996 Crown Court judges imposed immediate custody (imprisonment for those over 21; detention in a young offender institution or long-term detention under s 53(2) of the Children and Young Persons Act 1933 for those under 21) in 61 per cent of the cases sentenced. A further 27 per cent were given community sentences (mainly community service orders and probation orders), and only 4 per cent of offenders received a fine. These figures should be seen against the background of some significant changes in Crown Court sentencing patterns in recent years. Changes in the proportionate use of immediate custody are complex. For adults the rate has been rising steadily, from around 45 per cent in 1990, while for younger age groups there was a reduction in the use of custody from 1984, which levelled out and is now increasing again. The proportionate use of community sentences by the Crown Court increased steadily from 20 per cent in 1989 to over 30 per cent in 1993, but has since fallen back below 30 per cent in 1996. The use of the suspended sentence of imprisonment has fallen dramatically, from around 16 per cent in 1992 to 3 per cent in 1996. This decrease results from a provision in the Criminal Justice Act 1991 which stated that the use of the suspended sentence was henceforth to be confined to 'exceptional' cases only. The proportionate use of the fine by the Crown Court has witnessed a steady decline in recent years, from around 9 per cent in 1989 to less than half that figure in 1996.

Sentencing decisions in the Crown Court are constrained, first, by statutory rules relating to the maximum penalty which can be imposed for each offence. While, as we have seen, magistrates' courts are generally restricted to six months' imprisonment, available custodial sentences in the Crown Court are very much higher. The availability of much higher sentences at Crown Court is an important consideration for both defendants and for magistrates in mode of trial decisions (see Chapter 4 above). Brief mention should be made here of the anomalous mandatory life sentence for murder. An offender aged 21 or over who is convicted of murder *must* be sentenced to imprisonment for life (Murder (Abolition of Death Penalty) Act 1965, s 1(1)). If the offender is aged under 21, the equivalent mandatory sentence is custody for life (Criminal Justice Act 1982, s 8). If the offender was aged under 18 at the time of the offence, the appropriate sentence is then detention during Her Majesty's pleasure (Children and Young Persons Act 1933, s 53(1)). All of these sentences are confined to the offence of murder, and do not apply to any other offences, not even attempted murder. When passing a life sentence for murder the judge may (and usually does) give an indication in open court of the period of time which he thinks should elapse before the offender's case is first referred to the Parole Board for consideration for early release. This recommendation goes to the Lord Chief Justice, and thence to the Home Secretary (Crime (Sentences) Act 1997, s 29). It is not binding on the Home Secretary, who can set a higher or lower tariff than the judges have indicated (see *Secretary of State for the Home Department, ex parte Doody* [1994] 1 AC 531). This is an arrangement which has long been subject to criticism, since it involves a politician interfering with a judicial decision. In *Secretary of State for the Home Department, ex parte Hindley* (1997) *The Times*, 19 December, the Divisional Court held that the current Home Secretary, Jack Straw, had been entitled to increase the tariff period which had to be served in the case of Myra Hindley, the Moors murderer, from 30 years to life.

The maximum penalty for a number of other very serious offences, including attempted murder, manslaughter, rape, robbery, and wounding with intent is life imprisonment. For these offences a life sentence *may* be imposed, but the judge has discretion to impose a lesser custodial sentence, or some other form of sentence, where appropriate (for the sentencing patterns for these offences, see Wasik, 1998). A life sentence imposed in such a case is known as a discretionary life sentence, to distinguish it from the sentence for murder. When imposing such a discretionary life sentence, the judge should normally make a statement in open court indicating what period of time he thinks the offender should serve in custody (the so-called 'tariff' period) before the case is first considered for early release by the Parole Board (Crime (Sentences) Act 1997, s 28). It can be seen that one effect of imposing a discretionary life sentence is to transfer a substantial amount of power to determine the offender's release date from the judiciary to the executive authorities, the Parole Board.

Other crimes attract lower maximum penalties. The maximum for burglary of a house is 14 years, while for burglary of a factory, office or shop it is 10 years. The maximum for theft is seven years. Burglary and theft are examples of offences which are triable either in the Crown Court or in the magistrates' courts. It can be seen that the maximum sentence available for the offence is very different depending upon which court deals with the case. A long-established sentencing principle of the Court of Appeal is that the available maximum sentence should be reserved for dealing with the worst cases. It follows that in any case where there is important mitigation, such as where the defendant has pleaded guilty, or has a clean record, to pass the maximum sentence available would be an incorrect sentence. Since there are relatively few examples of 'worst cases' with no mitigation, it is rare for maximum sentences to be imposed by the Crown Court. In *Carroll* (1995) 16 Cr App R (S) 488, the judge imposed the maximum sentence of two years' detention in a young offender institution for an offence of aggravated vehicle-taking, and justified this on the basis that the maximum provided by Parliament for the offence had been set too low. The Court of Appeal said that the courts must be faithful to the maximum sentences given, and reduced the sentence to 18 months.

While it remains true that, apart from the statutory maximum, Crown Court judges retain a fair degree of discretion as to the sentence to impose in a particular case, there have been important moves in recent years to curb that flexibility. Parliament has made many important changes to the law relating to sentencing. Sentencing issues figured prominently in the Criminal Justice Acts of 1991 and 1993, and in the Crime (Sentences) Act 1997. Further change is pending in the Crime and Disorder Bill. Two main developments can be seen. The first has been a burgeoning of the detail of sentencing provisions. Parliament has attempted to influence sentencers' discretion in numerous ways which may appear small in themselves but which cumulatively have increased the complexity of sentencing law and greatly increased the chances of sentencing mistakes being made. Of course, lawyers should know the law and such errors should not be made, but at times the techniques of statutory amendment have left matters less than clear, by the insertion of new sections into earlier statutes without the issuing of amending legislation, and the bringing into force of some changes and not others. There have been a number of recent sentencing cases in which the Court of Appeal has had to adopt 'saving' interpretations of statutory provisions. A remarkable example is *Moore* (1995) 16 Cr App R (S) 748, where the Court of Appeal held that when Parliament used the word 'following' in a particular section, it must have meant 'preceding'. There have been repeated calls for counsel to assist sentencers whenever they suspect that an error is about to be made. In *Kennedy* [1976] Crim LR 508 the Court of Appeal said that it was 'the duty of counsel to inform themselves what are the permissible sentences for the offences with which the defendant is charged, so as to be in a position to assist the judge if he makes a mistake', a comment repeated many times since. Dr David Thomas, a leading authority on sentencing law, has pointed to 'the grotesque deficiencies' of sentencing legislation. One example is provided by the Proceeds of Crime Act 1995 which, according to Dr Thomas (*Sentencing News* (1995), 4, p 6):

> Athough it is relatively short . . . manages to exhibit all the worst features of modern sentencing legislation . . . Section 71 of the 1988 Act, as amended, now has 12 subsections, numbered respectively 1, 1A, 1B, 1C, 1D, 1E, 4, 5, 6, 7A, 9 and 10. Section 72 begins at subsection 5 and is followed by section 72AA and then section 72A . . . There can be no possible justification for legislating in this way. Even before the reader begins to tackle the problem of what the Act means, the seeds of confusion have been sown.

A subsequent essay expands on the same theme (Thomas, 1997) and argues for consolidation of sentencing statutes to simplify matters, a call which has been heeded recently by the Law Commission. Apart from statutory material, the volume of reported guidance from the Court of Appeal in sentencing matters has also grown considerably. The relevant specialised law reports, the Criminal Appeal Reports (Sentencing), expanded to four issues per year in 1994 and then six in 1996, in which year 300 cases were fully reported. Further sentencing decisions (with commentaries by Dr Thomas) are reported in the *Criminal Law Review*, and yet others can be found in specialist reports.

The second main development has been the attempt by Parliament in the Criminal Justice Act 1991 to provide a set of guiding principles for the determination of sentences in both the Crown Court and in magistrates' courts. The Act failed to achieve all its objectives, and subsequent legislation has dismantled parts of it, but the basic scheme of sentencing is still to be found there. The provisions of the 1991 Act are considered further, below. It is appropriate first, however, to say something about the background to this important legislation. The seeds of the Act are to be found in a government

White Paper issued in 1990, *Crime, Justice and Protecting the Public* (Home Office, 1990). The White Paper advocated a new framework for sentencing based primarily upon the concept of 'desert' – proportionality between offence seriousness and penalty severity. Placing primacy upon the seriousness of the offence committed by the offender meant that relatively less emphasis would be given to the offender's previous record. A considerable training programme was implemented for judges and for lay magistrates to inform them of the principles of the Act. There was, from the first, significant opposition from practitioners and, subsequently, from the media. Mention was made, above, of the implementation and short-order abolition of the unit fine scheme. Other criticism focused on the relevance to sentence of the offender's previous record and, as a result of this pressure, the law was amended in the Criminal Justice Act 1993. This campaigning against the Act reflected a wider antipathy towards the whole exercise of legislative guidelines in the sphere of sentencing. The arguments are well illustrated by the following extract, from a speech made by the Lord Chief Justice to the Law Society of Scotland, six months after the Act's implementation in England and Wales:

Extract 5.4.1

Lord Taylor CJ [1993] *Journal of the Law Society of Scotland* **129–131**

The text of the address given at the Annual Conference of the Society at Gleneagles on 21st March 1993 by the Rt Hon the Lord Taylor, Lord Chief Justice of England.

If there is one topic in our time of equal concern north and south of the border, to lawyer and layman alike, it is the high level of crime and how to deal with it. So I propose to talk about sentencing policy.

What should be its aims? Surely they should include the following: to punish; to deter; to treat, reform or rehabilitate the offender; to compensate the victim; and to protect the public. It is at once evident that not all of these aims can be achieved by any given sentence. If it is necessary for the protection of the public to impose a long custodial sentence, reform and rehabilitation may be impracticable. If it is necessary to punish by imprisonment; compensation may not be available.

There are, I think, three propositions of fundamental importance. First, there is no such thing as an absolutely correct sentence. What the court has to do is to balance the aims I have mentioned against the factual background and achieve what it believes to be the best possible result in the public interest. Clearly, judges may differ in their perceptions as to how the balance should be resolved. There will, therefore, inevitably be a range of possible sentences in most cases.

That being so, my second proposition is that the sentence imposed must take account of public opinion and aim to leave all concerned with a feeling that justice has been done.

Thirdly, to achieve that, the court needs to have available the widest range of possible measures, and the broadest discretion to deploy them either individually or in combination. Courts, I suggest, should be concerned with deciding what sentence *ought* to be imposed rather than what sentence they are *allowed* to impose. In England and Wales I fear that the tendency has been to remove or unduly constrain judicial discretion. The complexity of the present legislation and the pitfalls created by petty prohibitions preoccupy the judge with avoiding technical errors rather than with doing justice.

You are fortunate in Scotland in having comparatively little legislation in your criminal law. The Lord Chancellor tells me that in Scotland most crimes are common law offences and you are spared most of the statutory limits and sentencing restrictions which we have south of the border. But your greatest advantage is to have been spared the Criminal Justice Act 1991 or any equivalent of it. Quite apart from the merits of its policies, its drafting has caused English criminal lawyers to tear their hair. At one seminar, a young assistant recorder rushed up eagerly to the senior judge presiding and said, 'I reread the Act last night and I now see that the sections we looked at yesterday *do* make sense.' The judge said, 'Go and read it again; you've obviously misunderstood it.'

I believe the fundamental error underlying the Act was a misconceived notion that sentencing should be programmed in detail so as to restrict the discretion of the sentencing judge. The laudable desire to reduce and confine custodial sentencing to cases where it is really necessary has led to restrictive provisions forcing the judge into an ill-fitting strait-jacket.

But, it may be said, unless the judges are forced by statute to apply certain sentencing policies, how will consistency be achieved and will they not resort to the use of imprisonment far too frequently? Ought we not at least to have a Sentencing Council?

In fact, there is already in place sufficient machinery to monitor and, where necessary, correct sentences passed by trial judges. First, there is the Court of Appeal which can review a sentence on the application of the offender if it is said to be too severe. Then, in England and Wales, the Attorney-General has power to refer a sentence to the Court of Appeal if he thinks it is unduly lenient and the court can then increase the sentence. You do not yet have this power in Scotland but I believe it is on the way. Again, the Court of Appeal lays down guidelines from time to time as to the appropriate levels of sentencing for specific crimes such as rape, drug importation and breaches of trust. These guideline cases merely set the general tariff, but judges are free to tailor the sentence to the facts of the particular case.

There is also the Judicial Studies Board in England which runs seminars for judges and publishes guidance on sentencing. Finally, there is an Encyclopaedia of Sentencing which is updated regularly and collates all the leading sentencing cases for easy comparison so that the bracket or tariff for particular types of offence is well established.

In my view, this range of moderating and guiding influences is sufficient to enable the system to work satisfactorily and consistently without interfering unduly with the judgment or discretion of the individual sentencing judge. A Sentencing Council would add nothing of value to the machinery I have described. It would, I fear, usurp the function of the independent judiciary and there would be a real danger of politicising the sentencing process. Who would be appointed to such a Council? Would not its function end up by imposing rigidity where there should be flexibility, and penal theory where there should be prognostism? I believe that a Sentencing Council would be a superfluous extra tier of control between Parliament and the judiciary.

But why, you may ask, if the judges can safely be left to exercise an unfettered judgment on sentencing do we have so many criticisms of individual sentences? I would be the first to concede that on occasions a judge does get the balancing exercise wrong – wrong to the extent that a sentence is passed which is wholly unacceptable. We are all human beings and we can all err on occasions. When *that* happens, the Court of Appeal can and usually does put it right whether the sentence was too high or too low.

However, apart from such cases, there are, I regret to say, many occasions when perfectly sensible and reasonable sentences are subjected to criticism unfairly. Often the press reports fail to state the facts completely or they slant their account of the case. I fully understand that good news is boring, while bad news is considered better copy. So we do not get a newsflash that a judge passed a sentence everyone agreed was correct. Instead, the tendency is to find someone who disagrees with it. If the sentence is on the light side, there is an interview with the victim or the victim's relatives who can usually be relied upon to say that the sentence was outrageously lenient. If, on the other hand, the sentence is on the heavy side, the defendant's wife or relatives will be interviewed to say how cruel and brutal the judge was. No wonder, in these circumstances, the impression the public gain from newspapers and television is that judges frequently impose unsatisfactory sentences. I do not for a moment doubt the right and duty of the media to comment on sentences and criticise judges. It is healthy that they should do so. But I wish that they would aim at scrupulous accuracy regarding the facts and moderation in their comments. There have been instances recently of wholly disproportionate condemnation of a judge over his sentencing. An examination of the transcript of what the judge actually said in full not infrequently shows the comment to have been excessive and unfair.

In my view, the best approach to sound sentencing is to leave it to the judiciary to exercise their experience and judgment subject to the monitoring and guidance I have mentioned. I deprecate the introduction of complex statutory curbs and braces to restrict judicial discretion. They inevitably lead to anomalous and often unjust embargoes preventing a judge from doing what the instant case clearly demands.

(b) The legislative framework for sentencing

The choice of sentence to be imposed in the Crown Court is, then, constrained by the general sentencing framework set out in the Criminal Justice Act 1991. The purpose of the Act, according to the White Paper which preceded it (Home Office, 1990, para 2.3), was to provide a 'new framework' for sentencing 'to achieve a more coherent and comprehensive consistency of approach in sentencing'. The Act creates what has been described as a pyramid of sentencing options, which is applicable both to the Crown Court and to magistrates' courts and is applicable to young offenders as well as adults:

Extract 5.4.2

A Ashworth, 'The Criminal Justice Act 1991' in C Munro and M Wasik (eds), *Sentencing, Judicial Discretion and Training* (1992) pp 77–85 (footnotes omitted)

There has been a plethora, some would say a surfeit, of Criminal Justice Acts in recent years. This one is different. It is not the usual rag-bag of minor reforms: it has general themes. In terms of changing the direction of sentencing, it is certainly the most important such statute since 1948, and perhaps the most important of the century. This is not to suggest, however, that it makes a clean break with the past on all issues. One of its features is to preserve a certain element of continuity in the English approach to sentencing policy and practice. For this reason, the outline of the Act's major provisions in this essay will seek to relate the new law to the system of which it will become part. It will focus less on the minutiae of the Act, which have received detailed consideration elsewhere and more on its major themes and their probable impact on English sentencing . . .

The new sentencing framework in outline

Although the Act is intended to install proportionality as the leading rationale for sentencing, it nowhere mentions the word. Nor does it mention 'just deserts,' desert or retribution. The style of the legislation is not to proclaim a leading aim, but to state at several points that 'the seriousness of the offence' should determine what type of sentence is justifiable, and how long or restrictive that sentence should be. Courts should infer from this that other sentencing aims, which do not regard the seriousness of the present offence as the key factor, are to be ignored. The most controversial of these is deterrence, particularly the aim of deterring others.

Over the years courts have sometimes passed, and the Court of Appeal has sometimes upheld, deterrent or exemplary sentences which are disproportionate in severity to the actual crime, but which are designed to deter others from following the offender's bad example. When the 1991 Act comes into force, such sentences will be unlawful. The sentence must be proportionate to the seriousness of the present offence, not based on offences which might possibly be committed by others in the future. Some might argue that a type of offence which is prevalent in a certain locality or at a particular time, like 'hotting' (stealing high-performance cars and racing them), should be treated as more serious because of its prevalence. However, this argument needs to be examined with care. Is it true that offences become more serious because many people commit them? Would this apply to speeding, or to shop thefts? Or is the argument really an attempt to smuggle deterrent reasoning into the

496

Act's framework, because the sentencer wants to pass an exemplary sentence? The White Paper wisely warned against over-stating the role of sentencing in preventing crime. Other agencies, not the courts, have this as a main function.

The leading aim of English sentencing under the 1991 Act is therefore proportionality. The hope is that this will produce consistency of approach. However, consistency is merely a formal value: the policy which the Act is designed to promote is the 'twin-track' approach, and particularly the wider use of financial penalties and community orders in appropriate cases. In broad terms, the framework of sentencing after the 1991 Act may be visualised as a kind of pyramid.

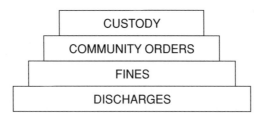

On the lowest level are orders such as absolute and conditional discharges, which are little altered by the Act. On the next level are fines, which may be regarded as the 'presumptive' sentence in most magistrates' court cases. On one further level upwards lie the various community orders – community service, probation, the new 'combination orders', curfew orders, attendance centres and supervision orders. If a court is to make an order on this level, it must first be satisfied that the offence was serious enough to warrant this; otherwise fines, discharges or compensation orders are the only possible measures. At the top level, and the narrowest part of the pyramid, come custodial sentences. In order to go up from a community sentence to a custodial sentence, a court must (in general) be satisfied that the offence is so serious that only custody can be justified . . .

What is important at this stage is to see just how central to the scheme the rationale of proportionality is. At every stage when a court moves up from one level to another, the move should be justified by reference to the seriousness of the offence. Indeed, the proportionality principle impinges even more strongly than that, because it is also central to decisions on how severe the fine should be, how stringent the restrictions on liberty imposed by a community sentence should be, and how long a custodial sentence should be. The pyramidal structure itself indicates that, starting from the lowest level, each higher level is not only more demanding for the offender but also more demanding for the sentencer – in the sense that there are more legislative restrictions and procedural requirements to be satisfied with each upward step.

Let us start at the top of the 'pyramid', with custodial sentences. Section 1 of the 1991 Act (as amended by subsequent legislation) provides the two reasons which may justify the imposition of a custodial sentence by the Crown Court, or by a magistrates' court:

(1) This section applies where a person is convicted of an offence punishable with a custodial sentence other than one fixed by law or falling to be imposed under section 2(2), 3(2) or 4(2) of the Crime (Sentences) Act 1997.

(2) Subject to subsection (3) below, the court shall not pass a custodial sentence on the offender unless it is of the opinion –

 (a) that the offence, or the combination of the offence and one or more offences associated with it, was so serious that only such a sentence can be justified for the offence; or

 (b) where the offence is a violent or sexual offence, that only such a sentence would be adequate to protect the public from serious harm from him.

A couple of points can be made quickly. Sub-section (1) excludes from the scope of this section the offence of murder which, as we have seen, carries a life sentence 'fixed by law'. It also excludes the recently introduced situations where the Crown Court is required under the Crime (Sentences) Act 1997 ('exceptional' cases apart) to pass a life sentence for a second serious offence, or to pass a minimum sentence of seven years for the third Class A drug trafficking offence committed by an offender. Section 1(3) covers the rare case where an offender will not accept a special condition which the court wants to write in to a community order, such as a condition that he undergo treatment for alcohol dependency. The main meat of s 1, then, lies in the alternatives in subs (2)(a) and (b). Paragraph (a) turns on 'seriousness': the question for the judge or the magistrates is whether the offence (or offences) for which the defendant is now being sentenced are '. . . so serious that only [custody] can be justified'. Many of the cases coming before the courts will be clearly above the custody threshold or clearly below it, but there will always be borderline cases. Here, the judge or the bench of magistrates has to exercise judgment, but there is some advice and guidance available to assist. As we saw from the Magistrates' Association *Sentencing Guidelines*, discussed above, a major problem is to achieve a balance between offence seriousness, which may point to a custodial sentence, and matters of personal mitigation, which may point the other way.

In one of the early cases decided after the 1991 Act came into force, the Court of Appeal offered the following general guidance:

Extract 5.4.3

R v Cox (1993) 14 Cr App R (S) 479, pp 480–482

LORD TAYLOR C J: On September 8, 1992, at Birmingham Crown Court this appellant pleaded guilty to theft and reckless driving. The case was put back for reports. On October 16 the appellant was sentenced to one month's detention in a young offender institution for theft, and four months' detention concurrently for reckless driving. His licence was endorsed and he was disqualified from driving for 12 months.

The appellant also pleaded guilty to an offence of using a vehicle while uninsured which was committed from the Magistrates' Court under section 41 of the Criminal Justice Act. No separate penalty was imposed in respect of that. He pleaded not guilty to a charge of driving without a licence, also committed to the Crown Court under section 41, and that was left on the file on the usual terms.

He now appeals against sentence by leave of the single judge.

The facts relating to the reckless driving were as follows. On April 7, 1992, at 11.35 at night police officers in a patrol car observed the appellant riding a trials motorcycle along the road with a pillion passenger. The motorcycle had no lights. The weather was wet. The visibility was poor.

The appellant saw the police car and rode off. The police car pursued him with flashing beacon. After 100 yards the appellant mounted the pavement and drove along it at about 25 to 30 miles an hour for some 50 metres. He then turned left into a walkway and across that on to another road. He overtook a car by going on to the pavement, turned left in front of the car, ignored a Give Way sign and went on to a narrow pathway towards some waste land. The appellant then lost control of the motorcycle and fell off. The police officers arrived and arrested him.

He was found to have in his possession a tan coloured haversack containing electrical hedge cutters, an electric drill, a portable vacuum cleaner, a spool of fishing line and a roll of white tape, all of which had been stolen from a domestic garage that evening along with other items not recovered. The theft charge was in respect of that property.

On interview the appellant claimed that he had panicked when he saw the police. He had found the stolen items in the field some 10 minutes before being seen by them. He said he knew it had probably been 'stolen, left abandoned or whatever.' He denied burglary.

The appellant was 18, single, and had been unemployed since February 1992. He had one previous conviction for taking away a vehicle without the owner's consent in 1990.

A pre-sentence report noted that he had an offer of part-time employment, and recommended a probation order.

In passing sentence the learned judge said:

'. . . this was a matter in which you were driving at speed on the pavement, trying to get away from the police, and you had no lights. It would be difficult to conceive a more dangerous form of driving.'

He indicated that because of the appellant's age and plea, the fact that he had not previously received a custodial sentence, and the short distance travelled during the chase, he would pass a shorter sentence than would otherwise be the case. He went on:

'But I am quite satisfied, having heard the facts of this case, that this is so serious that only a custodial sentence can be justified.
There is great public concern about driving of this sort.'

It is submitted that the judge erred in finding that the offence of reckless driving was so serious that only a custodial sentence could be justified. Mr. Welch,

499

who appeared for the appellant, relied on the provisions of section 1(2)(a) and section 3(3)(a) of the Criminal Justice Act 1991.

Section 1(2) provides that:

'. . . the Court shall not pass a custodial sentence on the offender unless it is of the opinion – (a) that the offence, or the combination of the offence and one other offence associated with it, was so serious that only such a sentence can be justified for the offence . . .'

Section 3(3) provides that:

'In forming any such opinion as is mentioned in subsection (2) of section 1 or 2 above a Court – (a) shall take into account all such information about the circumstances of the offence (including any aggravating or mitigating factors) as is available to it . . .'

Mr. Welch argues that when the circumstances of this offence of reckless driving are looked at in context, and all available information relating to the aggravating and mitigating factors is taken into account, a custodial sentence should not have been passed.

The Criminal Justice Act 1991 does not attempt a definition of the expression 'so serious that only such a sentence can be justified for the offence.' In *Bradbourn* (1985) 7 Cr.App.R.(S.) 180 another division of this Court had to consider the provisions of section 1(4) of the Criminal Justice Act 1982, and in particular the phrase, 'so serious that a non-custodial sentence cannot be justified.' Lawton L J said (pages 182–183):

'In our judgment the phrase, "so serious that a non-custodial sentence cannot be justified" comes to this: the kind of offence which when committed by a young person would make right-thinking members of the public, knowing all the facts, feel that justice had not been done by the passing of any sentence other than a custodial one. We think that is as good guidance as we can give to courts and that any attempt to be more specific would only add to the difficulties of courts and not help them.'

The form of words in section 1(4) of the 1982 Act differs from that of section 1(2)(a) of the 1991 Act, which applies not just to young offenders but generally. Nevertheless, we think that Lawton L J's formulation is appropriate to any consideration of the expression 'so serious that only such a sentence can be justified for the offence' and we adopt it.

Standing back and applying it to all the known facts of this case, we have reached the conclusion that only a custodial sentence could be justified for this offence.

Mr. Welch submitted in particular that the learned judge's observation, 'There is great public concern about driving of this sort,' was irrelevant. We do not agree. The prevalence of offences of a particular class and public concern about them are relevant to the seriousness of an instant offence, as we made clear in *Cunningham* (1992) 14 Cr.App.R.(S.) 444.

That, however, is not an end of the matter. Section 1(2) enjoins the court not to pass a custodial sentence unless it is of the opinion that the criteria of seriousness are met. The court is not *required* to pass such a sentence even when they are.

Although an offender may qualify for a custodial sentence by virtue of section 1(2), the court is still required to consider whether such a sentence is appropriate having regard to the mitigating factors available and relevant to the offender (as opposed to such factors as are relevant to the offence). Section 28(1) of the Act provides:

> 'Nothing in this Part shall prevent a court from mitigating an offender's sentence by taking into account any such matters as, in the opinion of the Court, are relevant in mitigation of sentence.'

It is submitted that even if the learned judge in the Court below was correct in holding as he did in regard to the seriousness of the offence of reckless driving, he nevertheless failed to give due weight to the mitigating factors personal to the offender. The appellant was 18 at the time of the offence charged and had one previous court appearance for taking a motor vehicle without the owner's consent, driving whilst disqualified and driving with no insurance. These offences were committed together in August 1990.

The pre-sentence report recommended probation. It said:

> 'Mr. Cox has not yet been the subject of a probation order and it is my belief that such a disposal would allow him the opportunity to examine his offending behaviour in more detail. It would also enable him to recognise the danger that he places both himself and the general public in, when he engages in this type of offence.
>
> He would be expected to attend supervision no less than 12 times in the first three months and then contact would be re-assessed according to the progress he had made in respect to the aims and objectives of the Order.'

We are of the view that, given the age and antecedent history of this appellant, this course would have been appropriate in the present case. Accordingly, if the appellant is willing to be placed on probation, we are prepared to quash the sentences of detention and substitute for them concurrent probation orders. In reaching this conclusion we are satisfied that the offence of reckless driving was serious enough to warrant the making of such orders pursuant to section 6(1) of the Act.

Accordingly, if the appellant is willing, and bearing in mind that he has served a month-and-a-half of custody, we are prepared to substitute a sentence of 12 months' probation for the sentences originally passed.

Many points for discussion emerge from this case. First, there is the expressed view of the trial judge, with whom the Court of Appeal agreed, that the offence *was* above the custody threshold. The Court of Appeal justifies this on two grounds. The first is public opinion. The Lord Chief Justice refers to 'public concern' about this kind of offence, and he adopts the *Bradbourn* test. This test appears to be circular. How is the Court of Appeal able to judge the public's perception of the seriousness of what Cox actually did? The Lord Chief Justice adduces no evidence of the public's attitude, so could the reference to 'right-thinking people' simply be replaced by 'right-thinking judges'? For a very interesting discussion of this test, see von Hirsch and Ashworth (1996). The second ground is the perceived prevalence of the offence. How does the court know the prevalence of such behaviour? Again, no evidence is cited. Even if it could be shown that riding trials motorcycles on pavements at night without lights is a regular occurrence up and down the country, was Cox's lawyer wrong when he argued that prevalence is unrelated to seriousness? If a particular form of lawbreaking is widespread, does this really make each instance of that form of lawbreaking more serious?

Another issue in the case is the balance which the Court of Appeal finds between seriousness and personal mitigation. The decision establishes the important point that personal mitigation may rescue an offender from the custodial sentence which the seriousness of the offence would otherwise deserve. What was the mitigation here? The Lord Chief Justice refers to Cox's age (18 at the time of the offence), his light record (one previous conviction) and his guilty plea. Some weight may also have been placed on the hint in the pre-sentence report, to the effect that moving straight to custody when Cox had not experienced the intermediate option of a probation order would be too great a step up in penalty for a young man on only his second court appearance.

This decision in *Cox* is concerned with para (a) of s 1(2): the 'seriousness' criterion. It says nothing about para (b), since Cox had committed neither a violent nor a sexual offence. We will return to para (b) in a moment.

Suppose that the sentencer has now made a determination, in accordance with s 1(2)(a) of the 1991 Act, that the offence is so serious that a custodial sentence must be imposed. The next step required of the sentencer is to fix the appropriate length of that sentence. Section 2 of the 1991 Act provides:

(1) This section applies where a court passes a custodial sentence other than one fixed by law or falling to be imposed under section 2(2) of the Crime (Sentences) Act 1997.

(2) Subject to section 3(2) . . . of that Act, the custodial sentence shall be –
   (a) for such term (not exceeding the permitted maximum) as in the opinion of the court is commensurate with the seriousness of the offence, or the combination of the offence and one or more offences associated with it; or
   (b) where the offence is a violent or sexual one, for such longer term (not exceeding that maximum) as in the opinion of the court is necessary to protect the public from serious harm from the offender.

Section 2(2)(a) was subject to an early assessment by the Court of Appeal in the following case:

Extract 5.4.4

R v Cunningham (1993) 14 Cr App R (S) 444, pp 445–448

LORD TAYLOR C J: On September 1, 1992, at Chichester Crown Court, this appellant pleaded guilty to two indictments and on October 2, 1992, was sentenced on the first indictment for robbery to four years' imprisonment and on the second indictment for theft to two years' imprisonment concurrently.

He now applies for leave to appeal against sentence, which we have granted.

The offence of theft was the first in time. It was committed jointly with co-accused Dunkerton, aged 29, and Cole, aged 26. Dunkerton was employed by a newsagent in Crawley as a deputy manager. On the morning of April 6, 1992, he staged a fake robbery. He pretended that he had been tied up against his will and was found secured to a chair. Cash, cigarettes and confectionery to the value of £1,500 had been stolen. The appellant, who was in possession of stolen cigarettes, was arrested initially for robbery. The police then discovered it had been a fake.

The appellant when first interviewed denied any involvement. Later he admitted being fetched to the shop by Dunkerton and Cole. They had all three stolen the property. He helped carry out the cigarettes and secured Dunkerton to a chair with his tie. He expected to get 'something' from Dunkerton for his part.

The offence of robbery took place on the evening of April 24, 1992. Whilst on bail for the offence of theft, the appellant, brandishing a knife and accompanied by Cole, went to a corner shop in Crawley. They demanded money from the shopkeeper who had a small child in his arms. There was a struggle during which the knife was bent against the counter. Cole grabbed the till containing some £2,700, and ran off. The till itself was worth £600. It was damaged when recovered. The shopkeeper managed to overpower the appellant and detained him, still holding the knife, until the police arrived. When interviewed, the appellant said he had been given the knife and some gloves by Cole. He admitted robbing the shopkeeper at knife point and claimed he had been threatened with death if he did not participate.

Cole pleaded guilty to the same offences as the appellant and was also sentenced to four years' and two years' imprisonment concurrently. Dunkerton pleaded guilty to the theft charge and two further thefts from his employers. He was sentenced to two years' imprisonment concurrently on each charge.

The appellant is 22. He had no previous convictions, whereas Cole and Dunkerton both had previous records for dishonesty. The appellant was unemployed and had been lodging with his co-defendant Cole whom he blamed for his involvement in these offences.

In passing sentence the learned judge indicated that in his view the offence of robbery was so serious that only a custodial sentence could be justified. No challenge is made to that finding and in our judgment it was right. Robbery committed in a small shop at knife point clearly falls within the scope of section 1(1)(a) of the Criminal Justice Act 1991.

The basis of this appeal is that the sentence passed upon the appellant was too long . . .

Mr. Meredith's . . . submission is that the learned judge was wrong in regarding deterrence as a legitimate consideration in passing sentence. The learned judge said in the course of his sentencing remarks:

'This was a robbery of a small shop at knife point. Such shops are very vulnerable and there are far too many such robberies. Others who might be tempted to follow your example must realise that a long deterrent sentence will follow such a robbery.'

Section 2(2) of the 1991 Act provides that where a court passes a custodial sentence other than one fixed by law or one involving a violent or sexual offence, that sentence shall be:

'(a) for such term (not exceeding the permitted maximum) as in the opinion of the court is commensurate with the seriousness of the offence, or the combination of the offence and other offences associated with it.'

Does that provision permit the sentencing judge to take the need for deterrence into account? In our judgment, it does. The purposes of a custodial sentence must primarily be to punish and to deter. Accordingly, the phrase 'commensurate with the seriousness of the offence' must mean commensurate with the punishment and deterrence which the seriousness of the offence requires.

In *Att.-Gen.'s Reference No. 9 of 1989* (*Lacey*) (1990) 12 Cr.App.R.(S.) 7, Lord Lane C J said:

'Businesses such as small post offices, coupled with sweetie shops – that is exactly what these premises were – are particularly susceptible to attack. They are easy targets for people who wish to enrich themselves at other people's expense. That means that in so far as is possible, the courts must provide such protection as they can for those who carry out the public service of operating those post offices and sweetie shops which fulfil a very important public function in the suburbs of our large cities. The only way in which the court can do that, is to make it clear that if people do commit this sort of offence then, if they are discovered and brought to justice, inevitably a severe sentence containing a deterrent element will be imposed upon them in order so far as possible to persuade other like-minded robbers, greedy persons, that it is not worth the candle.'

Although those remarks were made before the 1991 Act, we consider they still hold good. The sentence commensurate with the seriousness of an offence of this kind will be substantial to reflect the need both for punishment and deterrence. What section 2(2)(a) does prohibit is adding any extra length to the sentence which by those critieria is commensurate with the seriousness of the offence, simply to make a special example of the defendant.

Prevalence of this kind of offence was also mentioned by the learned judge. Is that a legitimate factor in determining the length of the custodial sentence to be passed? Again, our answer is yes. The seriousness of an offence is clearly affected by how many people it harms and to what extent. For example, a violent sexual attack on a woman in a public place gravely harms her. But if such attacks are prevalent in a neighbourhood, each offence affects not only the immediate victim but women generally in that area, putting them in fear and limiting their freedom of movement. Accordingly, in such circumstances, the sentence commensurate with the seriousness of the offence may need to be higher there than elsewhere. Again, and for similar reasons, a bomb hoax may at one time not have been so serious as it is when a campaign of actual bombings mixed with hoaxes is in progress.

In the present case we consider the learned judge was right to regard the robbery as very serious and to bear in mind both the need for deterrence and the prevalence generally of offences of this kind.

504

However, Mr. Meredith's final ground of appeal is that the learned judge did not sufficiently have regard to the mitigating circumstances in the appellant's case, especially when compared with that of his co-accused Cole, who received the same sentence. We think there is merit in this argument.

This appellant was younger than either of his co-accused. He was of previous good character, whereas both his co-accused had records for dishonesty. Furthermore, the appellant co-operated with the police from the start whereas Cole made no admissions and was putting forward an alibi until a very late stage. These were, in our judgment, matters relevant in mitigation of sentence within the meaning of section 28(1) of the 1991 Act.

Bearing them in mind, we consider that the sentence of four years passed by the learned judge was too long. We therefore quash that sentence and substitute for it a sentence of three years' imprisonment. The concurrent sentence of two years in respect of the offence of theft will stand. Accordingly the overall sentence is reduced to one of three years' imprisonment.

The maximum penalty for robbery is life imprisonment. In 1996 the Crown Court sentenced 5,500 offenders for robbery; 4,000 received immediate custody and a further 1,200 received community sentences. The offence varies in its seriousness from armed robbery with violence at the top of the scale to a bag snatch at the bottom of the scale. In *Cunningham* it was accepted on all sides without question that this offence of robbery, involving the use of a knife to demand money from a shopkeeper, was so serious that only a custodial sentence could be justified. Cunningham was aged 22, so the relevant custodial sentence was imprisonment. The sole issue before the Court of Appeal was whether the sentence of four years' imprisonment for this particular robbery was too long. The *Attorney-General's Reference (No 9 of 1989)*, to which the Lord Chief Justice refers, provided only very general advice on sentencing for this kind of offence. No other Court of Appeal decisions were referred to in the judgment, although there are numerous reported cases (see, for example, Thomas, 1982 B6–2.3B).

The main interest of the decision in *Cunningham* lies in the interpretation by Lord Chief Justice of s 2(2)(a) of the 1991 Act. In stating that the phrase 'commensurate with the seriousness of the offence' must mean 'commensurate with the punishment and deterrence which the seriousness of the offence requires', critics were quick to criticise Lord Taylor CJ for undermining the desert-based rationale of the Act, and for reintroducing deterrence into the assessment of sentence length (for example, Lacey, 1994). His Lordship also states, however, that s 2(2)(a) prohibits '. . . adding any extra length to the sentence . . . simply to make a special example of the defendant'. If we accept, as we must, that s 2(2)(a) effectively outlaws this kind of exemplary sentencing, there seems no purpose in referring to 'deterrence' here at all – a reference to it can only serve to confuse sentencers in the future. It will be recalled that in *Cox* his Lordship touched upon the question of offence prevalence. He has more to say about it here, explaining that the seriousness of an offence 'is clearly affected by how many people it harms and to what extent'. Is this

505

convincing? Harm is clearly an important dimension of crime seriousness and, if a particular offence is more than usually harmful, then it seems to follow that it is more than usually serious. But does the comparative frequency of corner shop robberies make each such robbery, per se, more serious?

Once again, we can see the court striving to effect an appropriate balance between offence seriousness and personal mitigation. One factor affecting offence seriousness is the commission of the offence in breach of bail (see Criminal Justice Act 1991, s 29(2), mentioned above). Other matters would be possession of the weapon, the use of violence, and perhaps the risk to the child as well as to the shopkeeper. Mitigation in this case included the offender's age, previous good character and co-operation with the police. There was also a guilty plea but, as we have seen, it would have had less than normal impact in this case, since Cunningham was detained by the shopkeeper. Presumably, the defendant's claim that he had committed the robbery under duress was, simply, not believed by the sentencer. This case stands in contrast to *Cox* in that here, although the mitigation was enough to effect a reduction in the term selected by the sentencer, it was insufficient to pull the offender back from the custody threshold.

The offenders in both *Cox* and *Cunningham* were being dealt with for more than one offence. In the former case sentences of one month's detention in a young offender institution (for theft) and four months (for reckless driving) were imposed by the trial judge, and ordered to run concurrently (i.e. at the same time). There were two other motoring offences, in respect of which no additional punishment was imposed. The Court of Appeal quashed the custodial sentences and imposed concurrent probation orders. In the latter case sentences of two years' imprisonment (for theft) and four years' imprisonment (for robbery) were passed by the trial judge, and ordered to run concurrently. The four-year sentence was reduced to three years on appeal. If these sentences had been made to run consecutively rather than concurrently, this would have made a considerable difference to the total custodial term required to be served. How is the sentencer to approach this matter?

There are two main sentencing principles which together determine whether custodial sentences are ordered to be served concurrently or consecutively. The first, which is derived entirely from case law, is that sentencers should impose distinct sentences for each count which is being dealt with. Then, generally, if the offences are related in the sense of arising out of the same set of events, the sentences should be concurrent (see, for example, *Matthews* (1987) 9 Cr App R (S) 1: TWOC and driving while disqualified). If the offences arise from separate matters, but are being dealt with together for convenience, then consecutive sentences may be appropriate. An example is *Attorney General's Reference (No 1 of 1990)* (1990) 12 Cr App R (S) 245, where the offender was sentenced for an indecent assault, and also for an attempt to pervert the course of justice, by writing a threatening note to the victim from prison, to discourage her from giving evidence. There are one or two situations in which the courts have said that consecutive sentences should be imposed even where the two matters are related. Examples are where violence is used by an offender against a police officer trying to arrest him for an offence (*Hill* (1983) 5 Cr App R (S) 214), or carrying a firearm on a robbery (*French* (1982) 4 Cr App R (S) 57). The reasoning in the exceptional cases is that if concurrent sentences were passed there would be no disincentive to committing the assault or to carrying the firearm. There is also authority to the effect that consecutive sentences should be imposed where the second offence was committed when the defendant was on bail for the first (*Young* (1973) Current Sentencing Practice A5–2F01). These authorities would suggest that while concurrent sentences were correct in *Cox*, they should have been consecutive in *Cunningham* (there were separate incidents, and the offender was on bail). There is, however, a second principle operating here, which is that sentencers must have regard to the total length of the sentence imposed, to ensure that the sentence properly reflects the nature and overall seriousness of the offending. This is a long-established principle of the Court of Appeal, but it has achieved statutory recognition in s 28(2)(b) of the Criminal Justice Act 1991. It applies to the totality of community orders and fines as well as custodial sentences. The so-called 'totality principle' is meant to ensure that an offender being sentenced for six like offences of, say, theft from a shop, does not simply receive the 'going rate' for that offence multiplied by six. If multiplication were the approach, then the sentence for the shoplifter would soon be on a par with that of the rapist, and this would compromise our sense of the relative seriousness of different offences. On the other hand, the totality principle contains a tension within it. A multiple offender convicted on six separate occasions can expect to fare much worse than if he had been dealt with for the same six offences together. Should the time frame for the offending make so much difference?

An issue which has presented considerable difficulty is the relevance of an offender's previous record to the sentencing decision. One thing is clear: that where an offender has no previous convictions, or is perhaps lightly convicted, some mitigation is normally available to him under s 28 of the 1991 Act. The continuing relevance of this was confirmed by the Lord Chief Justice in *Cox*. Suppose, however, that the offender has a string of previous convictions – such that any mitigation he might have had is now lost. In *Cunningham* the Court of Appeal drew a distinction between him and his co-defendants, at least partly on the ground of their different criminal records. Applying the test in s 1(2)(a) and s 2(2)(a), to what extent is the prior record relevant to the seriousness of the offence (or offences) committed this time? When the 1991 Act was implemented, s 29 declared that the fact that a person did have previous convictions, or the fact that they had 'failed to respond' to earlier sentences, would not normally be relevant to the seriousness of the new offence. Section 29 attracted a great deal of critical comment in the early days of the operation of the Act, much of it from practitioners, and the government took early opportunity to repeal and replace it. The new version, contained in s 29(1) simply says that

In considering the seriousness of any offence, the court may take into account any previous convictions of the offender or any failure of his to respond to previous sentences.

Some commentators take the view that this wording now gives sentencers a more-or-less free hand to take an offender's previous record into account when deciding whether to impose custody under s 1(2)(a) or in determining its length under s 2(2)(a). Others, however, have argued that since s 29 remains relevant only where the record impinges upon offence seriousness the new version is, in principle, little wider than before (see Wasik and von Hirsch (1994)). The Court of Appeal has, thus far, not issued any guidance on the operation of the new s 29. This may suggest that the courts are exercising a flexible approach over previous convictions and the Court of Appeal would prefer to leave things vague rather than fetter their discretion by the issuing of guidelines. The Magistrates' Association's *Sentencing Guidelines* (Magistrates' Association, 1997) advise magistrates to 'take care in using previous convictions or any failure to respond to previous sentences in assessing seriousness'. The guidelines recommend that 'courts should identify any convictions relevant for this purpose and then consider to what extent they affect the seriousness of the present offence'.

So far, in discussing the statutory framework for imposing and fixing the length of custodial sentences, we have been concentrating on the 'seriousness' question in s 1(2)(a) and s 2(2)(a). The second justification for imposing custody is contained in s 1(2)(b) – where the offender has committed a violent offence or sexual offence and the court makes an assessment that only a custodial sentence would be adequate to protect the public from serious harm from him. There is a corresponding provision in s 2(2)(b) relating to the length of a custodial sentence imposed for this reason. Its length shall be such as in the opinion of the court is necessary to protect the public from serious harm from the offender. The origins of these provisions can be found in the 1990 White Paper (Home Office, 1990), where the government advocated a 'sharper distinction' in sentencing, with non-violent and non-sexual offenders being accorded proportionate sentencing but with 'a small number of offenders who become progressively more dangerous and who are a real risk to public safety' receiving much longer sentences based upon public protection. Such sentence may be a determinate sentence which is longer than could be justified on the grounds of proportionality under s 2(2)(a) or it may be a discretionary life sentence. A life sentence is, of course, applicable only to those offences for which life is available as the maximum penalty. Also, the Court of Appeal has laid down preconditions for the imposition of a discretionary life sentence in any case:

(1) offence or offences must in themselves be grave enough to justify a very long sentence;
(2) defendant is a person of mental instability; and

(3) defendant will remain unstable and a potential danger for a long and/or indefinite period of time.

See *De Havilland* (1983) 5 Cr App R (S) 109 and *Attorney General's Reference (No 34 of 1992)* (1994) 15 Cr App R (S) 167.

Definitions of 'violent offence', 'sexual offence' and 'serious harm' are provided in s 31 of the 1991 Act. A 'violent offence' is one

> which leads, or is intended or likely to lead, to a person's death or to physical injury to a person, and includes an offence which is required to be charged as arson . . .

This definition was criticised by the Court of Appeal in *Richart* (1995) 16 Cr App R (S) 977 as being unduly narrow. In that case the court held that a case of threatening to kill (in which the defendant made abusive telephone calls and then sent the victim through the post a bullet with her name on it) was not a violent offence. See also *Khan* (1995) 16 Cr App R (S) 180 (carrying of unloaded firearm in the course of a robbery held not to be a violent offence).

'Sexual offence' is defined in the Act by listing a series of statutory offences in the Sexual Offences Act 1956 and various other provisions. The original list has been amended by subsequent legislation. The two categories of violent and sexual offences are not mutually exclusive, and so a single offence can qualify under both headings (*Robinson* [1993] 1 WLR 168: a case of attempted rape). 'Serious harm', as defined in s 31(3), means:

> death or serious personal injury, whether physical or psychological, occasioned by further such offences committed by him.

The wording establishes that the sentencer must believe the public to be at risk from this particular offender – it is not enough that the public needs protecting from offenders of his type. It is also clear that the perceived risk must relate to the commission of further 'such' offences (i.e. violent or sexual crimes). The sentencer is required to take into account any information about the circumstances of the offence, is entitled to have regard to any information about the characteristics of the offender (including his previous record) and, as usual, may consider matters of personal mitigation where appropriate, when making this complex decision.

The imposition of so-called 'longer-than-normal' sentences for violent and sexual offences has been the subject of a large number of appellate decisions, but the operative principles in this area of sentencing cannot yet be regarded as fully settled. Only a couple of examples can be given here. Much fuller treatment can be found in the sentencing texts such as Ashworth (1995) and Wasik (1998). Many of the decided cases are set out in Thomas (1982).

Consider first the decision of the Court of Appeal in *Bowler* (1994) 15 Cr App R (S) 78.

Extract 5.4.5

R v Bowler (1994) 15 Cr App R (S) 78, pp 80–83

SMITH J: On November 9 at the Crown Court at Southwark the appellant pleaded guilty to indecent assault on a female and was sentenced by His Honour Judge Butler, Q.C. to six years' imprisonment. An alternative count of indecency with a child was ordered to remain on the file on the usual terms. The appellant now appeals against his sentence by leave of the single judge.

On June 21, 1992, the appellant was at the Holy Cross Church in Cromer Street, London, where he had been helping to hand out books at the beginning of the service. He went downstairs to the lavatory at about 10.30 and, when he came out, came upon the Sunday school class which consisted of three children and the teacher. One of the children, whom he knew, a girl named 'Jenny' who was six years old, was leaning across a table. The appellant walked over to the children, patted each of them on the head, said 'Jenny', and put his hand up inside her dress. He touched her private parts over her knickers, whilst rubbing his penis on the outside of his trousers with the other hand. That was the evidence of the Sunday school teacher, although it was not accepted by the appellant that he had touched himself. He then sat down on the chair and pulled the girl on to his knee, at which point the Sunday school teacher tried to pull the girl off. Initially she failed, but she called for help. The appellant then let go of the little girl and ran out of the church. The complainant said that the appellant 'had tickled her near her bottom and her front bottom' and, while tickling her, he had said that he loved her.

The appellant was arrested shortly afterwards and interviewed. He admitted to having his hand up the girl's skirt and touching her over her knickers. He said he had been sexually excited and had had an orgasm, but he had not touched himself at the same time. He said he had done what he did because he had seen the girl's knickers.

The appellant was aged 27 at the time and had been before the court on eight occasions since the age of 16. All these convictions were for offences of indecent assault on women. From the information available it appears that none of the offences was of the most serious kind. They usually involved touching or grabbing at a woman's private parts, sometimes accompanied by masturbation. There was never any attempt at penetration; nor were any of the assaults prolonged. The offences had, until the instant offence, always involved adult women. This was the first offence involving a child.

For previous offences he had been dealt with by a variety of non-custodial measures in the earlier days, including probation in 1983, but he had also served custodial sentences; two of youth custody in 1984 and 1985 and two sentences of imprisonment, 18 months in 1988 and three years in 1990.

There was a wealth of material before the sentencing judge. A social inquiry report showed that the appellant was a single man living in a hostel. He had been in care from the age of 14. He was of limited intelligence. It was thought he had suffered from brain damage at some stage. He had no insight into his behaviour. He was a pathetic and inadequate young man. A medical disposal was suggested.

510

A psychological report described an attempt which had been made in 1983 to treat the appellant with a libido suppressant, which had been of very limited success, but a further attempt at treatment was suggested.

A psychiatric report showed that the appellant was unwilling to undergo any further drug treatment. This report recommended an assessment of the possibility of changing his conduct by psychological means.

Shortly before sentencing, two medical reports ruled out the possibility of a medical disposal by stating that there was no medical disorder within the meaning of that term in the Mental Health Act. One of those reports described the appellant as having paraphilia, a sexual preference for a specific behaviour or object. In his case it was the touching of knickers of women. He continued to offend, despite powerful deterrents, and it was said that he had a strong sex drive.

Counsel urged the sentencing judge to make a disposal which entailed medical treatment, but the judge rejected this because it had failed before. In any event, such a disposal was not practicable because the disposal required funding from a Health Authority, which was not forthcoming.

In the event, the judge decided upon a custodial sentence. No criticism is advanced of that decision.

The grounds of the appeal are that the sentence of six years was excessive in length and wrong in principle in that the judge used his powers under section 2(2)(b) of the Criminal Justice Act 1991 and passed a sentence which was longer than would be justified by the seriousness of the offence; the purpose of which sentence was to protect the public from serious harm. In passing sentence the judge said:

'I have concluded that it is now essential to pass a custodial sentence that will, so far as possible, protect the public from serious harm from you, that is to say, from serious physical or psychological injury that I believe will be occasioned by further offences committed by you. I have so concluded after giving the most careful consideration to the nature of your offending in the past, the particular facts of this case, and the numerous reports that I have relating to you and your offending. In all the circumstances, I sentence to you to a term of six years' imprisonment.'

The first ground of appeal is that the judge erred in principle in invoking his powers under section 2(2)(b) of the 1991 Act . . .

[Her Ladyship then set out the text of s 2(2), s 31(3) and s 3(3) of the 1991 Act.]

It has been submitted today that in this case there was no evidence that either on this occasion, or any previous occasion, the appellant had caused his victims any serious harm, either physical or pyschological. It is submitted, therefore, that there was no basis upon which the judge could reasonably have concluded that it was necessary to pass a longer sentence than was commensurate with the circumstances of the offence. It is further submitted that this provision, section 2(2)(b), should only be brought into operation in exceptional cases were the danger of serious harm is an obvious one.

We do not accept those submissions. We consider that it is not necessary for there to be evidence that serious harm has actually been caused in the

511

past for a judge reasonably to form the opinion that there is a danger that serious harm might occur in the future. It is the view of this Court that the risk of serious harm occurring in the future is sufficient to bring this provision properly into operation.

It appears to this Court that there was, in this case, material before the judge which entitled him reasonably to conclude that there was a danger that members of the public might suffer serious psychological harm. There was a wealth of evidence, indeed overwhelming evidence, that the appellant is likely to continue to commit offences similar to those he has committed in the past. Indeed in the prison report, which is available to this Court but was not available for the sentencing judge, there is evidence that he has continued with this type of conduct while in custody. There are worrying indications that the appellant has recently turned his attention towards young girls. In the view of this Court an indecent assault on a young girl might well lead to serious psychological harm.

In addition to that, as has been pointed out in the course of argument, there are some adult women who might be seriously disturbed by conduct such as this. Many women might shrug off this kind of unwelcome attention which this man gives to women indiscriminately, but some will not. It seems to us that the purpose of this section should include the protection of those women, less robust than average, who may be vulnerable to the kind of conduct that this man is likely to perpetrate and who might, in those circumstances, suffer serious psychological harm.

This Court considers that the judge was entitled to reach the conclusion that he did, on the evidence before him, that a longer sentence than was commensurate with the seriousness of the offence was necessary in this case. I add, for the sake of completeness, that the additional material available to this Court tends to confirm that the view that was taken by the judge was right.

The second ground of appeal is that the judge failed to give sufficient weight to the mitigating features of the case. These were principally the plea of guilty following frank admissions in interview. It was said that the offence was impulsive, not planned; that the circumstances were less serious than many offences of this kind. There were also factors in the appellant's personal circumstances, such as his limited intelligence and unsettled background, which the court would usually take into account.

In the judgment of this Court, where section 2(2)(b) is properly brought into operation, these mitigating factors will not carry the weight or have the same effect as they usually do in cases where the Court passes a sentence which is commensurate with the seriousness of the offence.

We draw attention to the fact that section 2(2)(b) is mandatory in a sexual or violent offence. The court shall pass such a sentence as is necessary for the protection of the public. That, of course, is not to say that mitigating factors are to be ignored, but the protection of the public from serious harm becomes, in the view of this Court, the overriding factor.

In the judgment of this Court, it cannot be said that this judge failed to take proper account of the mitigating factors. On the basis of all the material before him, he gave proper effect to section 2(2)(b) of the Act. In all the circumstances, we conclude that the sentence was neither wrong in principle, nor excessive in length. The appeal is dismissed.

Clearly, the sentencing exercise when imposing custody under s 2(2)(b) is quite different from the more usual case where a proportionate sentence is selected under s 2(2)(a). With para (a) the court is mainly concerned with seriousness of offence, but under para (b) the purpose is to remove the offender from society for a substantial period of time – to incapacitate him – and thereby to protect members of the public who would otherwise be at risk. Bowler received a sentence of six years' imprisonment. The indications are that if he had been sentenced under para (a) he would have received a sentence in the range of 18 months to two years (compare, for example, *Moghal* (1993) 14 Cr App R (S) 126 and *Aston* (1993) 14 Cr App R (S) 779). So, the defendant is being required to serve an extra period (of, say, four years) in prison in the belief that by so doing one or more women or young girls will avoid becoming a future victim of this defendant during that period. Was a longer-than-normal sentence justified in *Bowler*? Incapacitation as an aim of sentencing is considered further, below.

(c) Court of Appeal guideline judgments

It will be recalled that in the course of his speech to the Law Society of Scotland (Extract 5.4.1 above), Lord Taylor C J referred with approval to the now well-established practice of the Court of Appeal of 'lay[ing] down guidelines from time to time as to the appropriate levels of sentencing for specific crimes such as rape, drug importation and breaches of trust', and expressed a clear personal preference for that approach over the use of 'complex statutory curbs and braces to restrict judicial discretion'. Nearly all of the Court of Appeal's guideline cases are principally concerned with fixing custodial sentence length. This is, then, an appropriate point at which to consider in more detail two of those guideline judgments. The ones which we have selected are *Billam*, the guideline case for the offence of rape, and *Brewster*, the guideline case for burglary from a house.

Extract 5.4.6

***R v Billam* (1986) 8 Cr App R (S) 48, pp 49–51**

LORD LANE C J: We have had listed before us today a number of cases where there has been a conviction for rape or attempted rape, in order to give us an opportunity to restate principles which in our judgment should guide judges on sentencing in this difficult and sensitive area of the criminal law.

In the unhappy experience of this Court, whether or not the number of convictions for rape has increased over the years, the nastiness of the cases has certainly increased, and what would 10 years ago have been considered incredible perversions have now become commonplace. This is no occasion to explore the reasons for that phenomenon, however obvious they may be.

We would like, if we may, to cite a passage from the Criminal Law Revision Committee's 15th Report on Sexual Offences, Command Paper 9213 of 1984, which reflects accurately the views of this Court. It is as follows:

'Rape is generally regarded as the most grave of all the sexual offences. In a paper put before us for our consideration by the Policy Advisory Committee on Sexual Offences the reasons for this are set out as follows – "Rape involves a severe degree of emotional and psychological trauma; it may be described as a violation which in effect obliterates the personality of the victim. Its physical consequences equally are severe: the actual physical harm occasioned by the act of intercourse; associated violence or force and in some cases degradation; after the event, quite apart from the woman's continuing insecurity, the fear of veneral disease or pregnancy. We do not believe this latter fear should be underestimated because abortion would usually be available. This is not a choice open to all women and it is not a welcome consequence for any. Rape is also particularly unpleasant because it involves such intimate proximity between the offender and victim. We also attach importance to the point that the crime of rape involves abuse of an act which can be a fundamental means of expressing love for another; and to which as a society we attach considerable value."'

This Court emphasised in *Roberts* (1982) 4 Cr.App.R.(S.) 8, that rape is always a serious crime which calls for an immediate custodial sentence other than in wholly exceptional circumstances. The sort of exceptional circumstances in which a non-custodial sentence may be appropriate are illustrated by the decision in *Taylor* (1983) 5 Cr.App.R.(S.) 241. Although on the facts that offence amounted to rape in the legal sense, the Court observed that it did not do so in ordinary understanding.

Judges of the Crown Court need no reminder of the necessity for custodial sentences in cases of rape. The criminal statistics for 1984 show that 95 per cent of all defendants who were sentenced in the Crown Court for offences of rape received immediate custodial sentences in one form or another. But the same statistics also suggest that judges may need reminding about what length of sentence is appropriate.

Of the 95 per cent who received custodial sentences in 1984, 28 per cent received sentences of two years or less; 23 per cent over two and up to three years; 18 per cent over three and up to four years; 18 per cent over four and up to five years and 8 per cent over five years (including 2 per cent life). These included partly suspended sentences and sentences to detention centre or detention under section 53(2) of the Children and Young Persons Act 1933, as well as imprisonment or youth custody. Although it is important to preserve a sense of proportion in relation to other grave offences such as some forms of manslaughter, these statistics show an approach to sentences for rape which in the judgment of this Court are too low.

The variable factors in cases of rape are so numerous that it is difficult to lay down guidelines as to the proper length of sentence in terms of years. That aspect of the problem was not considered in *Roberts* (cited above). There are however many reported decisions of the Court which given an indication of what current practice ought to be and it may be useful to summarise their general effect.

514

For rape committed by an adult without any aggravating or mitigating features, a figure of five years should be taken as the starting point in a contested case. Where a rape is committed by two or more men acting together, or by a man who has broken into or otherwise gained access to a place where the victim is living, or by a person who is in a position of responsibility towards the victim, or by a person who abducts the victim and holds her captive, the starting point should be eight years.

At the top of the scale comes the defendant who has carried out what might be described as a campaign of rape, committing the crime upon a number of different women or girls. He represents a more than ordinary danger and a sentence of fifteen years or more may be appropriate.

Where the defendant's behaviour has manifested perverted or psychopathic tendencies or gross personality disorder, and where he is likely, if at large, to remain a danger to women for an indefinite time, a life sentence will not be inappropriate.

The crime should in any event be treated as aggravated by any of the following factors: (1) violence is used over and above the force necessary to commit the rape; (2) a weapon is used to frighten or wound the victim; (3) the rape is repeated; (4) the rape has been carefully planned; (5) the defendant has previous convictions for rape or other serious offences of a violent or sexual kind; (6) the victim is subjected to further sexual indignities or perversions; (7) the victim is either very old or very young; (8) the effect upon the victim, whether physical or mental, is of special seriousness. Where any one or more of these aggravating features are present, the sentence should be substantially higher than the figure suggested as the starting point.

The extra distress which giving evidence can cause to a victim means that a plea of guilty, perhaps more so than in other cases, should normally result in some reduction from what would otherwise be the appropriate sentence. The amount of such reduction will of course depend on all the circumstances, including the likelihood of a finding of not guilty had the matter been contested.

The fact that the victim may be considered to have exposed herself to danger by acting imprudently (as for instance by accepting a lift in a car from a stranger) is not a mitigating factor; and the victim's previous sexual experience is equally irrelevant. But if the victim has behaved in a manner which was calculated to lead the defendant to believe that she would consent to sexual intercourse, then there should be some mitigation of the sentence. Previous good character is of only minor relevance.

The starting point for attempted rape should normally be less than for the completed offence, especially if it is desisted at a comparatively early stage. But, as is illustrated by one of the cases now before the Court, attempted rape may be made by aggravating features into an offence even more serious than some examples of the full offence.

About one-third of those convicted of rape are under the age of 21 and thus fall within the scope of the Criminal Justice Act 1982, s 1. Although the criteria to which the Court is required to have regard by section 1(4) of that Act must be interpreted in relation to the facts of the individual case rather than simply by reference to the legal category of the offence, most offences of rape are 'so serious that a non-custodial sentence cannot be justified' for the purposes of that provision. In the ordinary case the appropriate sentence would be one

515

of youth custody, following the term suggested as terms of imprisonment for adults, but making some reduction to reflect the youth of the offender. A man of 20 will accordingly not receive much less than a man of 22, but a youth of 17 or 18 may well receive less.

In the case of a juvenile, the Court will in most cases exercise the power to order detention under the Children and Young Persons Act 1933, s 53(2). In view of the procedural limitations to which the power is subject, it is important that a Magistrates' Court dealing with a juvenile charged with rape should *never* accept jurisdiction to deal with the case itself, but should invariably commit the case to the Crown Court for trial to ensure that the power is available.

Extract 5.4.7

R v Brewster [1988] 1 Cr App R (S) 181, pp 183–186

LORD BINGHAM C J: There are before the court six appeals against sentence following pleas of guilty to offences of domestic burglary. By section 9(1) of the Theft Act 1968,

'A person is guilty of burglary if –
(a) he enters any building or part of a building as a trespasser and with intent to commit any such offence as is mentioned in subsection (2) below; or
(b) having entered any building or part of a building as a trespasser he steals or attempts to steal anything in the building or that part of it or inflicts or attempts to inflict on any person therein any grievous bodily harm.'

The offences referred to in subsection (1)(a) are offences of stealing anything in the building, or inflicting grievous bodily harm on or raping any person in the building, or doing unlawful damage to the building or its contents. Where the building is a dwelling, the maximum sentence is one of 14 years' imprisonment. The offence of domestic burglary is to be contrasted with aggravated burglary, where the burglar has with him a firearm or imitation firearm, or an offensive weapon or any explosive, and robbery, which involves the use or threat of force: in each of these cases the maximum sentence is imprisonment for life.

It is noteworthy that under the Larceny Act 1916 burglary (then defined as breaking and entering a dwelling-house of another, in the night, with intent to commit any felony) was punishable with life imprisonment. It is also noteworthy that when, in 1991, the maximum penalty for non-domestic burglary was reduced to 10 years' imprisonment, the maximum penalty for burglary of dwelling-houses was left unaltered.

All the present appellants entered as trespassers with intent to steal, or having so entered, stole.

The current pattern of offending and sentencing

Domestic burglary is a very common offence. Police figures for 1995 record 644,000 such offences. But many domestic burglaries are not reported to the police: victims may suffer no loss; or may be uninsured; or if insured may suffer a loss within the excess payable by themselves, or may wish to preserve their no-claim bonus. The British Crime Survey suggests that in 1995, 1,754,000 such offences were committed.

In 1996, 17,400 defendants were convicted of domestic burglary, of whom 12,800 were aged 18 or over. The Home Office estimate that of these 12,800 adult defendants, 5,700 were convicted for the first time and 2,800 for the second time; 4,300 had two or more previous convictions.

Provisional figures for 1996 (supplied to the court by the Home Office) suggest that rather more than half of all those sentenced, including those under 18, were sentenced in the Crown Court (7,871 in magistrates' courts, 9,517 in the Crown Court). Since the more serious offences would be committed to the Crown Court, one would expect some difference in the respective use of different penalties in magistrates' courts and the Crown Court, and in the length of custodial sentences imposed. The provisional figures show this to be so. Magistrates' courts discharged 12 per cent of defendants as compared with 1 per cent in the Crown Court; they fined 5 per cent of defendants as compared with none in the Crown Court; they imposed community sentences in 56 per cent of cases as compared with 20 per cent; and they imposed immediate custody in 26 per cent of cases as compared with 78 per cent. The average length of custodial sentences imposed in magistrates' courts was 3.8 months, as compared with 19.5 months in the Crown Court; but it must be recognised that any average figure in the Crown Court may conceal a considerable variation in the length of different sentences. Over the four years, 1993–1996 inclusive, the use of custody increased at both levels: in the magistrates' court, from 23 per cent to 26 per cent; in the Crown Court from 63 per cent to 78 per cent.

The Home Office has analysed the sentences imposed on a restricted group of domestic burglars aged 18 or over who were sentenced in March 1996. Of those convicted for the first time of this offence, 26 per cent were sentenced to immediate custody by magistrates' courts, and the average sentence length was 3.2 months; of those sentenced in the Crown Court, 68 per cent were sentenced to immediate custody and the average sentence length was 15.9 months. Of those convicted of the offence for the second time, 30 per cent were sentenced to immediate custody by magistrates' courts, and the average length of sentence was 3.6 months; 84 per cent were sentenced to immediate custody in the Crown Court and the average length of sentence was 14.8 months (a curious statistical anomaly). Of defendants with two or more previous convictions of this offence, 53 per cent were sentenced to immediate custody by magistrates' courts, and the average length of sentence was 3.8 months; 86 per cent were sentenced to immediate custody in the Crown Court, and the average length of sentence was 19.6 months.

The figures reveal some differences of practice between magistrates' courts and different Crown Courts. In 1995, two magistrates' courts sentenced between 12.5 per cent–14.9 per cent of domestic burglars to immediate custody, and at the other extreme one magistrates' court sentenced between 55 per cent–57.4 per cent of domestic burglars to immediate custody. In 1996, one Crown Court centre sentenced less than 60 per cent of domestic burglars to immediate custody; two Crown Court centres sentenced between 90 per cent–94.9

per cent of such defendants. These variations may, at least to some extent, be explained by different approaches to the committal of defendants to the Crown Court.

From 1987 to 1992, the use of custody generally declined, probably in response to legislation, ministerial speeches and the White Paper on 'Crime, Justice and Protecting the Public'. Since 1993 the use of custody has increased very sharply, in response (it would seem likely) to certain highly publicised crimes, legislation, ministerial speeches and intense media pressure. In 1996, the use of immediate custody in the Crown Court (for all offences, not only domestic burglary) reached 60 per cent, the highest level since the early 1950's.

The prison population is growing very rapidly. From a total of 48,000 in April 1994, it has now climbed to nearly 61,000. Of that total, some 10,000 are domestic burglars.

The framework of sentencing

The main statutory provisions relevant to these appeals are familiar but fundamental. By section 1(2)(a) of the Criminal Justice Act 1991 the court may not ordinarily pass a custodial sentence on an offender unless it is of the opinion that the offence, or the combination of the offence and one or more offences associated with it (as defined in section 31(2)), was so serious that only such a sentence could be justified for the offence. The test of seriousness has been expressed in terms of public, probably meaning judicial, perception: *Bradbourn* (1985) 7 Cr.App.R.(S.) 180; *Cox* (1993) 14 Cr.App.R.(S.) 479; [1993] 1 W.L.R. 188. This test has been criticised as imprecise, which it is; but it is not easy to devise a more satisfactory test. Section 28(1) of the 1991 Act provides that nothing in Part I of that Act shall prevent a court from mitigating an offender's sentence by taking into account such matters as, in the opinion of the court, are relevant in mitigation of sentence; and *Cox* (*supra*) confirms that the court is not required to pass a custodial sentence even when the criterion of seriousness is satisfied.

Section 29 of the 1991 Act permits the court, in considering the seriousness of an offence, to take into account any previous convictions of the offender and any failure to respond to previous sentences, and requires the court to treat commission of offences while on bail as an aggravating factor. The prevalence of an offence has been held to affect its seriousness and hence to be a legitimate matter to consider in determining the length of a custodial sentence: see *Cunningham* (1993) 14 Cr.App.R.(S.) 444; [1993] 1 W.L.R. 183.

Where a custodial sentence is imposed it must, for present purposes, be for such term, not exceeding the permitted maximum, as in the opinion of the court is commensurate with the seriousness of the offence, or the combination of the offence and one or more offences associated with it (1991 Act, sections 2(2)(a) and 31(2)). In forming its opinion under sections 1(2)(a) and 2(2)(a) the court is required by section 3(3)(a) to take account of all such information about the circumstances of the offence and offences associated with it (including any aggravating or mitigating factors) as is available to the court. It has been held that when a court is sentencing a young offender it would almost always be appropriate to impose a shorter sentence than would be imposed in the case of an adult, and that while a deterrent sentence might be appropriate in

518

the case of a young offender it is necessary to balance that aspect with the youth of the offender: *Marriott and Shepherd* (1995) 16 Cr.App.R.(S.) 428. A deterrent sentence may be imposed provided it is commensurate with the seriousness of the offence: *Cunningham* (*supra*).

Section 48 of the Criminal Justice and Public Order Act 1994 requires a court, in deciding what sentence to pass on an offender who has pleaded guilty, to take into account the stage in the proceedings for the offence at which the offender indicated his intention to plead guilty and the circumstances in which this indication was given.

The offence

Domestic burglary is, and always has been, regarded as a very serious offence. It may involve considerable loss to the victim. Even when it does not, the victim may lose possessions of particular value to him or her. To those who are insured, the receipt of financial compensation does not replace what is lost. But many victims are uninsured: because they may have fewer possessions, they are the more seriously injured by the loss of those they do have.

The loss of material possessions is, however, only part (and often a minor part) of the reason why domestic burglary is a serious offence. Most people, perfectly legitimately, attach importance to the privacy and security of their own homes. That an intruder should break in or enter, for his own dishonest purposes, leaves the victim with a sense of violation and insecurity. Even where the victim is unaware, at the time, that the burglar is in the house, it can be a frightening experience to learn that a burglary has taken place; and it is all the more frightening if the victim confronts or hears the burglar. Generally speaking, it is more frightening if the victim is in the house when the burglary takes place, and if the intrusion takes place at night; but that does not mean that the offence is not serious if the victim returns to an empty house during the daytime to find that it has been burgled.

The seriousness of the offence can vary almost infinitely from case to case. It may involve an impulsive act involving an object of little value (reaching through a window to take a bottle of milk, or stealing a can of petrol from an outhouse). At the other end of the spectrum it may involve a professional, planned organisation, directed at objects of high value. Or the offence may be deliberately directed at the elderly, the disabled or the sick; and it may involve burglaries of the same premises. It may sometimes be accompanied by acts of wanton vandalism.

The record of the offender is of more significance in the case of domestic burglary than in the case of some other crimes. There are some professional burglars whose records show that from an early age they have behaved as predators preying on their fellow citizens, returning to their trade almost as soon as each prison sentence has been served. Such defendants must continue to receive substantial terms of imprisonment. There are, however, other domestic burglars whose activities are of a different character, and whose careers may lack any element of persistence or deliberation. They are entitled to more lenient treatment.

It is common knowledge that many domestic burglars are drug addicts who burgle and steal in order to raise money to satisfy their craving for drugs. This

519

is often an expensive craving, and it is not uncommon to learn that addicts commit a burglary, or even several burglaries, each day, often preying on houses in less affluent areas of the country. But to the victim of burglary the motivation of the burglar may well be of secondary interest. Self-induced addiction cannot be relied on as mitigation. The courts will not be easily persuaded that an addicted offender is genuinely determined and able to conquer his addiction.

Generally speaking, domestic burglaries are the more serious if they are of occupied houses at night; if they are the result of professional planning, organisation or execution; if they are targeted at the elderly, the disabled and the sick; if there are repeated visits to the same premises; if they are committed by persistent offenders; if they are accompanied by vandalism or any wanton injury to the victim; if they are shown to have a seriously traumatic effect on the victim; if the offender operates as one of a group; if goods of high value (whether actual or sentimental) are targeted or taken; if force is used or threatened; if there is a pattern of repeat offending. It mitigates the seriousness of an offence if the offender pleads guilty, particularly if the plea is indicated at an early stage and there is hard evidence of genuine regret and remorse.

We are indebted to counsel for referring us to a very large number of sentencing decisions on domestic burglary over the past 20 years. But the decisions have to a very large extent turned on the facts of individual cases and the circumstances of individual offenders; they have often been influenced by the legislation in force at the time. While, therefore, the decisions have identified the aggravating and mitigating factors mentioned above, they do not fall into neat groups or lend themselves to the derivation of any precise arithmetical tariff. We do not think any detailed review of the cases will prove helpful.

The table in Extract 5.4.8 below is taken from the *Criminal Statistics England and Wales 1996* (Home Office, 1997). It compares a range of offences dealt with at Crown Court during that year, and compares the guilty plea rate, the percentage of use of custody, and the average sentence length in respect of those offences.

The table is useful in illustrating the generally high proportion of guilty pleas at Crown Court (see further Chapter 4 above), and the significance of the guilty plea 'discount' upon custodial sentence length. Bearing in mind the two guideline cases set out above, it can be seen that the offence of rape has the highest percentage use of custody, at 95 per cent of cases involving a guilty plea and 98 per cent where the case was contested. Sentences are also the longest for that offence, with an average term of nearly six and a quarter years after a guilty plea (nearly seven years where the case was contested). This represents a considerable increase upon the figures indicated by Lord Lane CJ in *Billam*. Perhaps the most striking statistic, however, is the (comparatively) very low percentage of defendants charged with rape who plead guilty. This suggests a high number of cases in which the defendant decides, or is advised by his lawyer, to put the prosecution to proof (which, of course, involves exposing the complainant to hostile cross-examination). The custody rate for house burglary is also high, at around 80 per cent. It can be seen that the sentencing pattern is somewhat different where the burglary was of non-residential premises. The table deals with Crown Court sentencing only. Some of the examples of triable either way offences, such as 'theft from shops' are normally deal with by the magistrates by non-custodial means. Shoplifting does attract custodial sentences at Crown Court, but this should only be the case where there are significant aggravating features, such as careful planning, working in groups and theft of high value goods. Such shoplifters are often 'professionals', with several previous convictions.

Extract 5.4.8

Home Office, *Criminal Statistics England and Wales 1996* (1997) table 7E

Males aged 21 and over sentenced for indictable offences at the Crown Court: plea rates and custodial sentencing for selected offences

England and Wales 1996

Offence[1]	Pleaded guilty (%)	Custody rate (%)		Average sentence length (months)	
		Guilty	Not guilty	Guilty	Not guilty
Violence against the person					
Causing death by reckless driving	57	73	81	35.9	29.1
Wounding or other act endangering life	57	84	94	42.9	54.4
Threat or conspiracy to murder	74	57	70	26.4	(33.4)
Other wounding, etc	78	52	60	14.3	15.1
All	73	58	73	21.9	32.5
Sexual offences					
Rape	39	95	98	74.7	83.8
Indecent assault on a female	67	64	83	25.3	23.7
Indecent assault on a male	72	68	84	30.5	29.1
All	64	69	88	33.7	46.2
Burglary					
In a building other than a dwelling	87	67	64	16.6	21.3
In a dwelling	91	80	83	21.1	26.8
All	91	77	78	20.4	25.6
Theft and handling stolen goods					
Other theft or unauthorised taking	80	56	55	11.4	17.4
Handling stolen goods	81	45	55	12.6	15.0
Theft from the person of another	82	51	54	11.9	15.0
Theft by an employee	85	58	54	11.5	(12.4)
Theft from shops	85	40	31	8.9	(7.4)
All	83	51	53	12.0	15.0
Fraud					
Other forgery	81	52	71	12.7	18.0
Other fraud	83	54	65	15.4	22.6
All	83	53	65	15.1	21.5

521

Males aged 21 and over sentenced for indictable offences at the Crown Court: (cont'd)

England and Wales 1996					
Offence[1]	Pleaded guilty (%)	Custody rate (%)		Average sentence length (months)	
		Guilty	Not guilty	Guilty	Not guilty
Criminal damage					
Arson	85	66	92	32.4	42.1
All	87	45	70	28.4	39.1
Drug offences					
Trafficking	83	71	90	27.2	54.7
Possession	93	23	35	11.3	(21.2)
All	84	63	86	27.0	52.3

(1) Only those offences where at least 100 pleaded guilty or not guilty are shown separately.

( ) Based on less than 50 cases.

5. SENTENCING AIMS AND RE-OFFENDING

In *Bowler* (1994) 15 Cr App R (S) 78, considered earlier, the sentencing judge and the Court of Appeal made their assessments of the risk posed by the offender to the community on 'common sense' grounds. They refer to Bowler's record, which shows a pattern of remarkably similar offending, and to the pre-sentence and psychological reports, which indicate that previous efforts to treat or to deter him from such offending have failed. On these grounds, the outcome certainly seems defensible. The defendant looks a sure bet to re-offend in the same way. Leslie Wilkins, a leading proponent of predictive methods in criminology, argues that (Wilkins, 1985):

> all persons predict the behaviour of others all the time. Indeed, if human behaviour were unpredictable all forms of social and economic life as we know them would cease. Almost always people do what they are expected to do . . .

But are social and economic decisions, such as whether a new brand of soap powder will find a niche in a mass market given a certain level of expenditure on aggressive advertising, of the same kind as a prediction of future offending? Even if we might be able to say that, for example, 20 per cent of a given cohort of convicted persons will re-offend within five years, would we be able to predict which 20 per cent?

What is known about patterns of re-offending? The leading research study in England was published by Philpotts and Lancucki in 1979. The researchers took a sample of 5,000 offenders who were originally sentenced for standard list offences in 1971. They collected information about other convictions received by those offenders between 1963 and 1976 inclusive.

Extract 5.5.1

G Philpotts and L Lancucki, *Previous Convictions, Sentence and Reconviction* (1979) table 1.2

Males convicted of standard list offences in January 1971 by offence in January 1971 and offence on first reconviction

Offence in January 1971	Total number of persons (= 100%)	Not reconvicted	Reconvicted: offence on first reconviction							
			Violence against the person	Sexual offences	Burglary and robbery	Theft and handling stolen goods	Fraud and forgery	Malicious damage	Motoring offences	Other offences
Violence against the person	435	51	16	1	7	13	2	3	5	2
Sexual offences	142	56	5	10	8	17	–	1	4	1
Burglary and robbery	812	32	6	1	26	26	2	4	2	1
Theft and handing stolen goods	2,072	51	4	1	10	25	2	2	3	2
Fraud and forgery	179	50	3	–(1)	7	23	11	1	3	2
Malicious damage	226	50	6	1	10	19	2	5	5	1
Motoring offences	442	74	2	1	2	8	1	2	8	–(1)
Other offences	117	53	4	–	5	19	1	2	4	12

Percentage of total number of persons

(1) Less than ½ per cent.

The table in Extract 5.5.1 gives the reconviction pattern for the male offenders (total sample 4,425), who were followed up for five years after 1971. The table shows the category of the original 1971 offence, and indicates that for most offence groups about half the offenders were not reconvicted at all within the follow-up period. Reconviction was more likely where the original offence was burglary or robbery, and significantly less likely where it was a motoring offence. For offenders convicted of a sexual offence in 1971, 56 per cent were not reconvicted at all. The table also shows the relative tendency for offenders convicted of a particular type of offence in 1971 to commit further offences of the same type. It will be seen that there is some tendency towards specialisation in offending. Those originally convicted of a violent offence were more likely than those originally convicted of other kinds of crime to commit a violent offence within the follow-up period (16 per cent as against 4 per cent where the original offence was theft, and 2 per cent where it was a motoring offence). Much the same pattern applies for fraud and forgery offending. The column showing the rate of reconviction for theft and handling stolen goods suggests that offenders of different persuasions are quite likely to 'turn to' theft or handling as their next offence. As far as sexual offences are concerned, we can see that very few offenders convicted of non-sexual offences were convicted of sexual offences within the five-year period. There is certainly some pattern of repetition in sexual offending, but it must be set in context. Remember that 56 per cent of those who originally committed a sexual offence did not re-offend at all, and of those who did, the further offence was more than three times as likely to be a non-sexual crime than a sexual crime.

Apart from the limited predictive power of a record of similar offending, statisticians have discovered that various other pieces of information about an offender will, when taken together with criminal history, help to generate a more sophisticated predictive model. These include information about their family circumstances and upbringing and whether they are drug-takers or not. There are two closely related problems inherent to techniques of prediction in re-offending. The first is the troubling rate of 'false positives' – individual offenders who fit the predictive criteria, but do not re-offend. The second is the ethical question of whether, or in what circumstances, it is justifiable to extend a convicted offender's punishment beyond the term which is deserved for the offence alone. These two issues are summarised in the following extract:

Extract 5.5.2

**A von Hirsch, 'Incapacitation' in A von Hirsch and A Ashworth (eds),
Principled Sentencing (1992) pp 101–105**

Incapacitation is the idea of simple restraint: rendering the convicted offender incapable, for a period of time, of offending again. Whereas rehabilitation involves changing a person's habits or attitudes so he or she becomes less criminally inclined, incapacitation presupposes no such change. Instead, obstacles are interposed to impede the person's carrying out whatever criminal inclinations he or she may have. Usually, the obstacle is the walls of a prison, but other incapacitative techniques are possible, such as exile or house arrest.

Incapacitation has, usually, been sought through predicting the offender's likelihood of re-offending. Those deemed likely to re-offend are to be restrained, for example by imposition of a term of imprisonment – or of a term of longer duration than they otherwise would receive . . . Who, then, is likely to re-offend? Prediction research in criminology has had more than a sixty-year history, beginning with S B Warner's statistical studies of recidivism among Massachusetts parolees in the 1920s and the Gluecks' prediction studies among juvenile delinquents in the 1930s. The basic research technique has been straightforward enough. Various facts about convicted criminals are recorded: previous arrests and convictions, school and employment history, prior drug use and so forth; and those factors that are, statistically, most strongly associated with recidivism are identified. The prediction instrument, based on these factors, is then constructed and tested. The studies suggest that a limited capacity to predict does exist. Certain facts about offenders – principally their previous criminal records, drug habits, and histories of unemployment – are (albeit only to a modest extent) indicative of increased likelihood of recidivism . . .

Although statistical forecasting methods can identify groups of offenders having higher than average probabilities of recidivism, these methods show a disturbing incidence of 'false positives.' Many of those classified as potential recidivists will, in fact, not be bound to offend again. The rate of false positives is particularly high when forecasting serious criminality – for example, violence. The majority of those designated as dangerous turn out – when the predictions are followed up – to be persons who are found not to commit the predicted acts of violence when allowed to remain at large. The tendency to over-predict . . . is not easily remediable because it results from the comparative rarity of the conduct to be forecasted. Serious crimes, such as acts of violence, are, statistically speaking, rather infrequent events. The rarer the event, the greater will be the incidence of false positives. When the conduct to be predicted occurs infrequently in the sample – and when the prediction method relies (as it must) on rough correlations between criminals' observed characteristics and their subsequent unlawful behaviour – the forecaster will be able to spot the actual violators only if he or she includes a large number of false positives. It is like trying to shoot at a small, distant target with a blunderbuss: one can hit the target only if much of the discharge hits outside it.

False positives put the justice of predictive sentencing into question. Ostensibly the offender classified as dangerous is confined to prevent him or her from infringing the rights of others. But to the extent the classification is mistaken, the offender would not have committed the infringement. The person's liberty is lost merely because people *like* him or her will offend again, and we cannot specify which of them will actually do so. It should be noted, however, that the false positives argument is only a conditional challenge to predictive sentence: it questions not the propriety *per se* of confining an offender to prevent injury to others in future, but only the propriety of doing so erroneously. Concern about false positives might thus conceivably diminish were it possible to make predictions more accurate.

The question of dangerousness became the focus of debate in Great Britain, after the publication of the so-called Floud Report (Floud, 1981). Floud concedes the recalcitrance of the false positive problem: in predictions of dangerousness, she admits, at least half of those classified as risks will mistakenly be so classified. With such a high incidence of error, how then can sentencing on the basis of dangerousness be justified? It can only be, she suggests, by the idea of shifting the burden of risk. An unconvicted dangerous person is entitled to remain at large, and any risk to potential victims must be borne by them. Once the person acts on their dangerous inclinations and is convicted for seriously harming others, however, we become entitled to shift the risk of victimization (in this case, of mistaken confinement) to the offender. Error is unavoidable, and the question is, who should bear the costs? However, Floud wishes to limit the scope of predictive sentencing. The protective sentence – which she defines as any duration of imprisonment exceeding the deserved term for the past crime – should be limited to cases where the predicted harm from the offender is quite severe . . .

False positives, however, may not be the central issue. What is fundamental, instead, is the extent to which predictive sentencing is consistent with notions of proportionality. Extending a person's *punishment* beyond his or her deserved term is problematic and it would remain so even if the predictions were quite accurate. If notions of desert are less precise, however – if they offer merely a range of permitted punishments – then relying on predictions within that permitted range could be morally permissible even if prediction errors inevitably do occur.

Let us return to the decision of the Court of Appeal in the case of *Bowler*. Here it was accepted that Bowler had not caused serious harm to his victims in the past: the sentence was based upon a prediction that he might do so in the future. It is important to appreciate the nature of the prediction which the sentencer is required to make under s 2(2)(b). The sub-section is geared not simply at the perceived likelihood of such offences recurring, but the anticipated seriousness of the future offending. Perhaps *Bowler* is a case where too much emphasis was given to the first of these considerations and not enough to the latter. The gap on seriousness was bridged by the Court of Appeal by postulating a more-than-normally susceptible victim. Is that approach correct? Note also the comment in the judgment that, where a custodial sentence is being imposed under s 2(2)(b), matters of personal mitigation will be accorded less weight than where the offender is being sentenced on the basis of proportionality. Would this include the guilty plea?

Bowler was one of the first decisions on longer-than-normal sentences after the 1991 Act came into force. Later decisions have established that a sentencer is not bound to pass a longer-than-normal sentence whenever a violent or sexual offence is being dealt with. The general rule in sentencing (violent and sexual cases included) is that the sentence should be proportionate to the seriousness of the offence but, exceptionally, the court may pass a longer-than-normal sentence where special risk to the public is made out and the imposition of a proportionate sentence would not provide adequate protection for the public (see also *Christie* (1995) 16 Cr App R (S) 469 and *Crow and Pennington* (1995) 16 Cr App R (S) 409). If, however, an offender was eligible for a longer-than-normal sentence on the relevant criteria, and the sentencer did not impose one, the sentence could be open to challenge as being an unduly lenient sentence (see *Attorney General's Reference (No 9 of 1994)* (1995) 16 Cr App R (S) 366, where the Court of Appeal said that a longer-than-normal sentence should have been passed in a case where the defendant had committed a series of sexual offences against young boys and, in the view of the court, represented a real and continuing danger). Appeals in sentencing cases are considered further in Chapter 6, p 557 below.

Extract 5.5.3

R v Bestwick and Huddleston (1995) 16 Cr App R (S) 168, pp 169–172

SMITH J: On August 20, 1992 at the Crown Court at Nottingham before his Honour Judge Hopkin, Stephen John Bestwick and Ian Jeffrey Huddleston pleaded guilty to offences of arson. Huddleston pleaded guilty to two offences of arson and an offence of handling stolen goods. Bestwick pleaded guilty to one count of arson. Bestwick was sentenced to 30 months' detention in a young offender institution, he being only 20 years of age at the time. Huddleston was sentenced subsequently to five years' imprisonment on each count of arson, and six months' imprisonment for the handling of stolen goods. Huddleston asked for two offences to be taken into account and Bestwick asked for nine offences to be taken into account, eight of which were for offences of arson and one of burglary. The total sentences were, therefore, five years' imprisonment in the case of Huddleston and Bestwick was sentenced to 30 months' detention.

The matters before the Court today are twofold. Bestwick appeals against his sentence by leave of the single judge. Huddleston renews his application for leave to appeal against sentence, his application having been refused by the single judge.

The facts of the matter in chronological order are as follows. On the evening of April 2, 1993 there was a fire at an open storage area at a British Rail depot at Toton near Nottingham. A number of plastic drainage pipes were destroyed. Among the crowd watching the fire was the applicant Huddleston and a girl named Temple. They both told a friend that Temple had lit the fire while Huddleston had stood nearby. Huddleston pleaded guilty to starting this fire.

Two days later a number of boys with whom Huddleston was friendly gathered at Huddleston's house. Bestwick was one of them. There was then some conversation between Huddleston and Bestwick about starting a fire and the two defendants, Huddleston and Bestwick, walked off from the group. It appears, and it is accepted by them, that they started a fire, again at the

British Rail depot at Toton. The nature of the material destroyed was electrical equipment and plastic equipment for use on the Intercity lines.

On April 4 the value of the materials damaged was probably only of the order of £5,000. The material before the sentencing court indicated that the damage in respect of both fires was of the order of £36,000. Bestwick was involved only in respect of the smaller of the two fires. Huddleston was involved in respect of both. Huddleston was also found, when arrested, to be in possession of a fire service pager and he pleaded guilty to the offence of handling in respect of that item. Nothing further need be said about that matter.

Bestwick initially denied his involvement in the fire of April 4 following his arrest. He then blamed Huddleston and another boy. However, in his second interview he admitted that he and Huddleston were both responsible. He said that it was Huddleston's idea.

Huddleston for himself denied any involvement in either fire but later implicated Bestwick in the fire of April 4. In the second interview when he was asked about the earlier fire, that of April 2, he initially denied involvement but then admitted that he had started it. Huddleston admitted that the pager had been stolen from the Fire Service during an open day.

So far as the other offences were concerned, Huddleston asked for two offences of arson to be taken into account, that of a straw barn and that of a Scania lorry. Those offences took place in November 1992 and March 1993 respectively, and the total estimated value of the property damaged was £6,000.

Bestwick, as we have indicated earlier, asked for nine offences to be taken into account but it is the eight offences of arson which appear to this Court to be a matter of some importance. The precise value of the property damaged in those eight offences is not clear to the Court from the records. However, the total damage from six of them was about £9,000 and they included arson of the straw barn, arson of the Scania lorry to which reference has already been made, and arson of wheelie bins and a garden shed.

In dealing with Bestwick, the learned judge had before him a psychiatric report from Dr MacKenzie which spoke of Bestwick's stable family background, his normal psychiatric condition and normal personality. He said that Bestwick found watching fires exciting but had no urge to light fires so as to experience the excitement it gave. He expressed regret to the doctor about the fire setting, and expressed a wish to put it behind him. The doctor was of the view that Bestwick had the personal and social resources to avoid further offences of arson. He proposed a probation order.

The judge accepted, and so does this Court, that Bestwick is not a man who is likely to commit further offences of this nature. He is mentally normal and not in any sense dangerous. He, therefore, fell to be sentenced in accordance with the seriousness of his offending.

It is said that the sentence imposed was too long and that insufficient account had been taken of his age, good character and plea of guilty. His age was 20. He was of virtually good character having only one wholly unrelated conviction of a minor nature and, of course, there was a plea of guilty. Those are significant personal mitigating features.

It has also been submitted that there were other mitigating factors which were not sufficiently taken into account. In particular it is submitted that the appellant was not the instigator of these offences and the judge accepted that that was so. Bestwick 'went along' with the suggestions of the applicant Huddleston, of whom we shall say more in a moment.

Also counsel has emphasised, quite properly, that the arson attack was not upon a building. That is true. However, it seems to this Court that this offence was still a very serious offence, and more particularly when viewed against the background of the eight other offences of arson which Bestwick asked the Court to take into consideration. In effect, between November 1992 and April 1993 Bestwick had 'gone along' with Huddleston's suggestion on nine occasions. This is a man who, although only young, is of normal intelligence and psychological profile. He does not suffer from any psychiatric illness or abnormality. We are urged to say that this is a mitigating factor. In our view it is not. A normal young man might be led astray once on an impulse but, in the view of this Court, not nine times. It follows that the view of this Court is that he must accept responsibility for his part in this serious course of conduct. The view of this Court is that the sentence is not so high as would permit us to interfere.

We turn now to deal with the case of Huddleston where, as we have already indicated, the single judge refused leave to appeal against the sentence of five years' imprisonment. In Huddleston's case the sentencing judge had before him a number of reports which indicated a seriously disturbed personality. There was a report from Dr Tombs who concluded that Huddleston's personality was abnormal and fulfilled the criteria for psychopathy in the Mental Health Act. He found that he had an obsession with lighting fires arising probably from an early interest in fires and a thwarted ambition to join the fire service.

The doctor was of the view that Huddleston was immature and had an impaired understanding of the impact of his behaviour on others. In short, he was dangerous. He was likely to continue to set fire to property because he gained an excitement from so doing. He disregarded the consequences to others.

Huddleston claimed that he did not plan his fire setting but the doctor was of the view that he did plan these activities, and that he would have a tendency to plan further and more serious fire setting incidents.

The judge came to the conclusion that Huddleston represented a danger to the public and must be sentenced under section 2(2)(b) of the Criminal Justice Ace 1991. In so doing he imposed a sentence which was longer than would have been warranted by the seriousness of the offences. In our view he was right to do so bearing in mind the material before him in the reports.

We have already referred to the report of Dr Tombs. There was, in fact, another report from Dr Earp who reached similar although less detailed conclusions.

One of the matters which this Court has been invited to consider is the question of whether Huddleston had learned his lesson from his convictions for these offences and would be unlikely to offend further. Huddleston had claimed that that was so during his final interview with the psychiatrist. However, information from Huddleston's father detailed in the report showed that that was not so. Whereas Huddleston had claimed that he had given up those interests, put his fantasies behind him and was facing the reality of life, (which

529

is that he will not be admitted to a job in the fire service,) and that he had given up the viewing of fire fighting videos and the wearing of a fireman's uniform which were all manifestations of the obsession to which we have referred, the information before the judge was that he had not, in fact, done so.

The further information before this Court demonstrates that this applicant is still failing to face the reality of his position. He has written a letter to this Court purporting to be written by his girlfriend, putting forward an explanation for his conduct based upon his distress at the termination by her of their relationship. Inquiries have revealed that that letter was not written by the girlfriend, but was written by Huddleston himself. We consider that that is a matter which demonstrates yet again that this applicant remains unrealistic about his condition and has no insight into the cause of his offending.

It follows that we have come to the conclusion that the judge was right when he concluded that the defendant was a danger and must be dealt with under section 2(2)(b). The mitigating effects of his previous good character, for such he had, his relatively young age, and his plea, must inevitably therefore be reduced.

The view of this Court is that there are no arguable grounds in support of an appeal, and the application for leave must be refused.

The main significance of this case is that it shows one co-defendant being sentenced on the basis of proportionality under s 2(2)(a) and the other receiving a longer-than-normal sentence under s 2(2)(b). The Court of Appeal rejected the claim that this amounted to an unfairness, or disparity, in the way in which the two men had been treated. It is clear, then, that the English sentencing system accepts that different sentencing objectives can be pursued, not only from case to case, but within the same case.

The four 'traditional' theories of punishment (and aims of sentencing) are deterrence (which is usually sub-divided into 'individual' and 'general' deterrence, rehabilitation, incapacitation and desert. Earlier reference has been made to all these concepts, but we can usefully conclude this section by considering Professor Ashworth's summary of these four approaches:

Extract 5.5.4

A Ashworth, *Sentencing and Criminal Justice* (1995) 2nd ed, pp 62–72 (footnotes omitted)

Deterrence

Deterrence is one of several rationales of punishment which may be described as 'consequentialist', in the sense that it looks to the preventive consequences of sentences. In fact, deterrence is merely one possible method of producing crime prevention through sentencing: it relies on threats and fear, whereas rehabilitation and incapacitation adopt different methods of achieving a similar end, as we shall see below. It is important to draw the distinction between

530

individual (or special) deterrence and general deterrence. The latter aims at deterring other people from committing this kind of offence, whereas individual deterrence is concerned with deterring this particular person from reoffending. A system which regarded individual deterrence as the main goal would presumably escalate sentences for persistent offenders, on the reasoning that if non-custodial penalties fail to deter then custody must be tried, and if one year's custody fails to deter two years must be tried etc. It would not be the gravity of the crime but the propensity to reoffend which would be the main determinant of the sentence. Although traces of this approach can often be discerned in the sentencing of repeat offenders, it is rarely adopted as the primary rationale of a sentencing system.

More significant is general deterrence. Jeremy Bentham was its chief proponent, and he started from the position that all punishment is pain and should therefore be avoided. However, punishment might be justified if the benefits (in terms of general deterrence) would outweigh the pain inflicted on the offender punished, and if the same benefits could not be achieved by non-punitive methods. Sentences should therefore be calculated to be sufficient to deter others from committing this kind of offence, no more and no less. The assumption is that citizens are rational beings, who will adjust their conduct according to the disincentives provided by sentencing law. Modern economic theorists such as Richard Posner adopt a similar approach, viewing punishments as a kind of pricing system. Less sweeping is the rational choice perspective, adopted by criminologists such as Derek Cornish and Ronald Clarke as an explanation of certain types of offending and used to generate specific preventive strategies. These authors argue that particular types of crime tend to result from a form of rational calculation, but they decline to extend this into a general theory.

Criticisms of deterrence theory may be divided into the empirical and the principled. The main empirical criticism is that the factual data on which a deterrent system must be founded does not exist. We lack reliable findings about the relative deterrent effects of various types and levels of penalty for various crimes. For example, sophisticated techniques have been applied in attempts to assess the deterrent efficacy of the death penalty, without yielding clear and reliable results. A necessary element in research is a proper definition of deterrence, to establish that fear of the legal penalty was the factor which determined conduct. The few studies which satisfy the criterion are no basis for broad policies. On the other hand, there is research which suggests that certain forms of offence which tend to be committed by people who plan and think ahead may be susceptible to deterrent sentencing strategies: Richard Harding, for example, found that robbers tended to desist from arming themselves with guns if there was a significant extra penalty for carrying a firearm. This may be taken to bear out the proposition that general deterrence is more likely to be effective for planned or 'professional' than for impulsive crimes, although Harding argues that deterrent sentences need to be combined with publicity and appropriate 'social learning' opportunities if they are to have significant preventive effects.

A counter-example is David Riley's study of drink drivers, in which he shows that the problems of a general deterrent strategy lie in drivers' optimism about the risk of not being caught, ignorance of the penalty, and ignorance of the amount of consumed alcohol to commit an offence. Further studies have examined the potential deterrent effect of increased enforcement by the police, but it seems that a general crime prevention strategy with publicity and attempts to change people's attitudes is likely to be more effective than either sentencing or enforcement changes alone. Another area in which the potential for legal deterrence appears not to be great is burglary: interviews with burglars suggest that most of them are not rational calculators but rather short-term hedonists or eternal optimists. The 1990 White Paper was concerned to point out that sentencers and others who talk about deterrence often overestimate the likely consequences of increases in penalty levels:

> 'much crime is committed on impulse, given the opportunity presented by an open window or unlocked door, and it is committed by offenders who live from moment to moment . . . It is unrealistic to construct sentencing arrangements on the assumption that most offenders will weigh up the possibilities in advance and base their conduct on rational calculation. Often they do not.'

One might wish to argue that armed robbery and, perhaps, drug smuggling are exceptions to this; but the reality is that reliable evidence of what types of offender can be deterred from what types of crime by what types of penalty is rare. The dearth of evidence leaves some authors undaunted, since they argue that 'commonsense reasoning about general prevention' can be used instead. But if the available research yields any conclusion, it is the danger of generalising from one's personal experience to the probable reactions of others – as the examples in the next paragraph suggest.

Principled criticisms of deterrence theory might be maintained whether or not there is satisfactory evidence of general deterrent effects. One such criticism is that the theory could justify the punishment of an innocent person if that were certain to deter several others: a simple utilitarian calculus would allow this to happen, without any respect for the rights of the innocent person. Another, more realistic criticism is that the theory can justify the imposition of a disproportionately harsh sentence on one offender in order to deter several others from committing a similar offence. This is the so-called 'exemplary sentence'. English judges have passed such sentences from time to time, and some would argue that such decisions have been the product of political or 'media' pressure to respond to public anxiety about a certain type of crime. One incident which has become part of judicial lore is the passing of exemplary sentences on certain offenders after the Notting Hill race riots in 1958. It is argued that such sentences may be justified by the consequences, which in this case were reductions in racial troubles in Notting Hill (although there were similar troubles in other cities in the following months). But who can assert that it was the exemplary sentences which caused the reduction in the number of offences which otherwise would have taken place? Might it not be the case that the police had arrested and charged the ringleaders, and without them there would be no continuation? Or that increased police patrols dramatically increased the perceived risk of being caught? The Notting Hill case serves only to emphasise the formidable difficulties of gathering evidence on the effectiveness of exemplary sentences as short-term deterrents. One can rarely be confident of interpreting a sequence of social events correctly, and that there are no other plausible explanations for changes in people's behaviour. These points emerge from the sequel to the Birmingham mugging case of *Storey* (1973) 57 Cr App Rep 840. A youth was ordered to be detained for 20 years for his part in the violent robbery of a drunken man. The sentence was widely publicised, both in Birmingham and in the national newspapers, as an exemplary sentence. Researchers were able to plot the rate of reported robberies in Birmingham and in two other cities during the months before and after the sentence was passed. The robbery rates seemed quite unaffected by the sentence in *Storey*: indeed, the rate of reported robberies in Birmingham had begun to rise before the trial and continued to increase before reaching a peak several weeks later. This calls into question the normal assumptions one would make about human behaviour, unless it is argued that the effect of *Storey* took several weeks to exert itself by reaching the ears of all potential robbers in Birmingham. The difficulty is that we do not understand the reasons, and this shows the problems of firm assertions about general deterrent effects.

The argument has returned to the empirical objection. The real test of the principled objection is this: even if one believes the Notting Hill anecdote, would this justify the extra long sentences on the first people to be sentenced for the crime? Should, for example, an extra two years of one person's liberty be sacrificed in the hope of deterring several others? The objection to this is often expressed in the Kantian maxim, 'a person should always be treated as an end in himself [or herself], and never only as a means'. Respect for the moral worth and autonomy of the individual means that citizens should not be regarded merely as numbers, to be aggregated in some calculation of overall social benefit. It may be true that the fundamental justification for the whole institution of punishment is in terms of overall social benefit, in the same way as this is the justification for taxes. There are also plenty of other examples of compulsion 'for the greater good', such as quarantine, compulsory purchase of property etc. These measures do not, however, have the censuring dimension which sentences have. If there is an argument for civil detention of individuals in the hope of deterring others from committing crimes, it has yet to be heard. Exemplary sentences, by heaping an undeserved portion of punishment on one offender in the hope of deterring others, are objectionable in that they condemn an individual in order to achieve a social goal – and do so without any real criterion of how much extra may be imposed. A deterrent theory which incorporates no restrictions to prevent this shows scant respect for individuals' choices and invests great power in the State and the judiciary.

A number of mixed theories of punishment have been advanced in an attempt to preserve elements of deterrence theory while avoiding the principled objections. The most notable is that of HLA Hart, who argued that the general justifying aim of punishment must be found in the prevention and control of crime, but that in deciding whom to punish and how much to punish the governing principle should be desert. That is, only the guilty should be punished, and then only in proportion to the seriousness of their offences. This does away with deterrence as a rationale for particular sentences, but on the other hand it finds no place for desert in the basic justification for punishment. There is a strong argument that punishment both incorporates and requires reference to individual desert as well as to overall social benefit.

Sentences are not the only form of general deterrent. In some cases it is the process which is the punishment – being prosecuted, appearing in court, receiving publicity in the local newspaper – rather than the sentence itself. In some cases the shame and embarrassment in relation to family and friends are said to have a more powerful effect than the sentence itself. On the other hand, the deterrent effects of sentencing and of the process may be diluted considerably by enforcement policy, or at least by beliefs about the risk of detection. Thus it is sometimes argued that it is beliefs about the probability of detection rather than about the quantum of punishment which are more likely to influence human behaviour. Once again, research suggests that a preventive strategy focused on detection probabilities has uncertain prospects at least for some types of offence. What matters, for deterrence theory, is potential offenders' beliefs about the risk of being caught, and we have little information about that. At a time when the clear-up rate for all crimes has fallen to 26 per cent and when burglary and robbery have clear-up rates of 19 and 22 per cent, respectively, there are grounds for believing that any deterrent effect which sentence levels have upon the reasoning of potential offenders may be diluted considerably by the fairly low risk of detection. These suggestions surely confirm that it is naive to assume a kind of hydraulic relationship between court sentences and criminal behaviour.

Rehabilitation

Like deterrence, rehabilitation as an aim of sentencing (sometimes termed reformation or resocialisation) is a method of achieving the prevention of crime. It proclaims that the principal rationale of sentencing is to achieve the rehabilitation of the offender. This usually requires a range of sentences and facilities designed to offer various programmes of treatment. Sometimes the focus is upon the modification of attitudes and of behavioural problems. Sometimes the aim is to provide education or skills, in the belief that these might enable offenders to find occupations other than crime. Thus the crucial questions for the sentencer concern the perceived needs of the offender, not the gravity of the offence committed. The rehabilitative approach is closely linked with those forms of positivist criminology which locate the causes of criminality in individual pathology or individual maladjustment, whether psychiatric, psychological, or social. Whereas deterrence theory regards offenders as rational and calculating, rehabilitative theory tends to regard them as in need of help and support. One key element in determining those needs is a report from an expert – for example, a pre-sentence report prepared by a probation officer or, occasionally, a psychiatric report. The sentencer should then decide on the form of treatment which matches the perceived needs of the offender, and make the appropriate order. Those jurisdictions which have operated a 'treatment model' of this kind have usually made their sentences indeterminate, on the basis that a person should only be released from obligations when, in the opinion of the experts, a cure has been effected.

This approach to sentencing reached its zenith in the 1960s, particularly in certain American jurisdictions, but the early 1970s are said to have brought the decline of the rehabilitative ideal. There seem to have been two major objections. One was the criticism that few of these treatment programmes seemed to be better at preventing reoffending than ordinary, non-treatment sentences. There had been many studies of the effectiveness of particular programmes, usually judging them on reconviction rates in subsequent years, and the conclusions of a widely-publicised survey of the research by Martinson and others were represented as 'nothing works'. In fact, Martinson disavowed such a totally negative conclusion, and an English survey by Stephen Brody was more circumspect in pointing out that only a limited number of programmes have been tried and evaluated. Research into intensive probation in England and in the United States has not been particularly encouraging, but there remains the possibility that research findings on rehabilitation conceal 'interaction effects'. In other words, there may be small groups of offenders for whom a certain kind of treatment has markedly better or markedly worse results, but such effects might not be apparent by looking simply at reconviction rates for all offenders. The early English survey of intensive probation was not encouraging in this respect either. Moreover, even if interaction effects are identified, there would have to be elaborate screening of offenders to discover which group or typology each of them falls into.

The second objection to rehabilitative policies is that they considerably increase the powers of so-called experts and recognise no right in individuals to be regarded as worthy of equal respect and concern. Indeterminate or even semi-determinate sentences place the release of offenders in the hands of prison or probation authorities, usually without firm criteria, clear accountability or avenues for challenge and reasoned decision-making. There is no question of recognising an individual's right not to be subjected to compulsory state intervention which is disproportionate to the seriousness of the crime committed. Even if the crime is relatively minor, an offender who is assessed as needing help might be subject to state control for a considerable period. The motivation may be benevolent and 'in the person's best interests'. In effect the individual offender may be regarded more as a manipulable object than as a person with rights.

Despite these two objections, it can be argued that rehabilitative approaches have not been properly tested, and a fuller commitment to its goals of treatment and resocialisation would result in a more humane and more effective sentencing system. There has never been adequate provision of the kinds of help and support which might be necessary. But this leaves several questions unanswered. Do we have rehabilitative programmes which could work for large numbers of offenders? Do we have programmes which could work for lesser, but still significant groups of offenders, whose suitability could be identified in advance? Should these programmes be available to courts, even in cases where the duration of the programme exceeds the proportionate sentence? Even if all these questions are answered in the negative, there are sound humanitarian reasons for continuing to experiment with rehabilitative programmes for offenders. However, respect for individual rights suggests that participation in programmes should be voluntary and that the duration of programmes should remain within the bounds set by proportionality.

Incapacitation

A third possible rationale for sentencing is to incapacitate offenders, that is to deal with them in such a way as to make them incapable of offending for

535

substantial periods of time. In its popular form of 'public protection', this is sometimes advanced as a general aim. However, it is usually confined to particular groups, such as 'dangerous' offenders, career criminals or other persistent offenders. Capital punishment and the severing of limbs could be included as incapacitative punishments, but there are formidable humanitarian arguments against such irreversible measures. The debate has usually concerned lengthy periods of imprisonment and disqualification for driving. Other measures such as curfews and additional requirements in probation orders may now raise similar problems.

What has been claimed for incapacitative sentencing strategies? The matter is discussed in greater detail elsewhere, but two such strategies can be mentioned here. One is the imposition of long, incapacitative custodial sentences on offenders deemed to be 'dangerous'. It is claimed that one can identify certain offenders as 'dangerous', i.e. as likely to commit serious offences if released into the community in the near future, and the risks to victims are so great that it is justifiable to detain such offenders for longer periods. The chief objection to this is overprediction: studies suggest that incapacitative sentencing draws into its net more 'non-dangerous' than 'dangerous' offenders, with a 'false positive' rate that has often reached two out of every three. Indeed, the main British study found that only 9 out of 48 offenders predicted as dangerous committed 'dangerous' offences within five years of release from prison, and, what is equally significant from the point of view of public protection, that an equal number of 'dangerous' offences was committed by offenders not classified as dangerous. This gives some cause for concern: there are hundreds of offenders serving discretionary sentences of life imprisonment in England and Wales, imposed on grounds of predicted dangerousness, and there is no way of telling whether the predictions on which these sentences rest are or are not over-cautious in a ratio of two-to-one.

The empirical basis of the second incapacitative strategy is likewise open to question. It was claimed by Greenwood in the United States that one can identify certain high-risk robbers and incarcerate them for substantial periods, achieving a reduction in the number of robberies and reducing sentence levels for other robbers. The crime preventive benefits of this are obvious, but the strategy has been shown to have major flaws. A subsequent report in America for the National Academy of Sciences demonstrates that Greenwood exaggerated the incapacitative effects and based his calculations on imprisoned robbers rather than robbers generally, and that a reworked version of his prediction method had disappointing results.

Apart from the empirical objections, there is also a principled objection to incapacitative sentencing, which parallels the objection to general deterrent sentencing: individuals are being punished, over and above what they deserve, in the hope of protecting future victims from harm. The force of such an objection is particularly strong where the successful prediction rate is low. The more difficult question is whether the objection should be given absolute force if a fairly high prediction rate could be achieved. There are some cases where the prison authorities, doctors and others feel sure that a certain prisoner presents a serious danger to others, in terms of violent or sexual assault. Should the Kantian objection be upheld even if there was an agreed high risk of serious offences? The Floud Committee thought that a just

536

redistribution of risk should result in the prolonged detention of the high-risk offender rather than an increased danger to victims. Some critics of their approach who would wish to uphold an individual's right not to be punished more than is proportionate to the offence(s) committed, also seem willing to concede that in cases of 'vivid danger' it would be justifiable to lengthen detention for incapacitative purposes. This means overriding the individual's right because of the danger to the rights of victims. The point is an important one because the emphasis of liberal theories on individual rights does not necessarily lead to absolute rights which ignore the social context and the possibility of conflicting rights. Thus, even the staunchest advocate of individual rights might concede that, where there is a conflict between the rights of two people (albeit that one of them is merely a potential or predicted victim), it is the right of the convicted offender which should yield. All this depends on an acceptably high rate of successful prediction. Even then, it is questionable whether it justifies the prolongation of incarceration in a prison: David Wood puts the case for transfer to a form of civil detention, if disproportionately long isolation of certain offenders is thought proper.

Desert

If the 1960s were the heyday of the rehabilitative approach, then the 1970s and 1980s were characterised by the re-emergence of desert as a primary rationale of sentencing. Desert theory is a modern form of retributive philosophy and, like retributivism, it has various shades and hues. Its leading proponent is undoubtedly Andrew von Hirsch, the author of the American report *Doing Justice* in 1976 and the writer of several subsequent articles and books. In his view, punishment has a twin justification. One element is that there is an intuitive connection between desert and punishment: thus, desert is 'an integral part of everyday judgments of praise and blame', and state punishment institutionalises this censuring function. Thus sentences communicate official censure or blame, the communication being chiefly to the offender but also to the victim and society at large. However, censure alone is not enough: the fallibility of human nature makes it necessary to attach a prudential reason to the normative one. Thus the second justifying element lies in the underlying need for general deterrence: without police, courts and a penal system, 'it seems likely that victimising conduct would become so prevalent as to make life nasty and brutish, indeed'. This preventive element of the rationale is regarded as subsidiary, operating only within a censuring framework.

The main thrust and chief contribution of desert theory is to the quantum of punishment, where proportionality is the touchstone. There is not one but two senses of proportionality, which must be distinguished with care. Ordinal proportionality concerns the relative seriousness of offences among themselves. Cardinal proportionality relates the ordinal ranking to a scale of punishments, and requires that the penalty should not be out of proportion to the gravity of the crime involved. Different countries have different anchoring points for their penalty scales, often evolved over the years without much conscious reflection and regarded as naturally appropriate. Yet it is possible to alter established penalty levels, as the experience of the Netherlands shows. Some have alleged that the rhetoric of desert is likely to lead to greater severity of penalties, but that is by no means the general outcome. In Finland, Sweden and Minnesota, for example, the change to desert did not lead to higher penalties, whereas in California and certain other jurisdictions it did. So much depends on general political trends and judicial disposition in the jurisdiction concerned: there is no natural connection between desert theory and severity, and in some states desert has been an integral part of policies of stabilising or reducing the use of custody.

Nevertheless, it must be conceded that to draw the theoretical distinction between cardinal and ordinal proportionality is not to provide much concrete guidance on the severity level which enables one to describe particular sentences as deserved. It does suffice to rule out extreme punishments such as ten-years' imprisonment for shoplifting; but the argument as to whether a person committing a particular house burglary deserves 18-months' imprisonment, three months or a community service order has to be conducted on penological and social grounds. In his writings, the leading exponent of desert theory has emphasised its role in reducing the use of imprisonment.

The parameters of ordinal proportionality are also difficult to establish. Most countries have a fairly traditional ordering of offences, but this has usually not come to terms with modern offences concerned with safety risks, environmental crimes etc. Changes in the relative positions of certain offences have taken place – for example, in England during the 1980s a more serious view was taken of rape and of causing death by reckless driving – but without any overall theory of what makes offences more or less serious. In justifying a reduction in sentence levels for social security fraud, Lord Lane CJ stated that such offences are 'non-violent, non-sexual and non-frightening' [*Stewart* (1987) 9 Cr App Rep (S) 135, at p 138]. Criteria of this kind need to be refined considerably if there is to be a framework which can cope not only with 'new' forms of criminality like breaches of safety regulations and incitement to racial hatred, but also with the longstanding contrast between property crimes and offences against the person. The subject calls for further philosophical and social enquiry, and important steps have been taken in a recent article by von Hirsch and Jareborg, where they advance a 'living standard' analysis of relative seriousness. They elucidate several steps in the process of assessing offence-seriousness, although their analysis is confined to crimes with individual victims . . .

Critics of desert theory have attacked it at various points. It is said to be unsatisfactory to rest such a coercive institution, even partly, on the mere intuition that punishment is an appropriate or natural response to offending. Furthermore, exactly what is deserving of blame and punishment – culpable acts or dispositions? It is also said to be unfair to rest desert partly on individual culpability when strong social disadvantages may be at the root of much offending. One answer to this is to recognise grounds for mitigation of sentence for any offender who has suffered significant social deprivation while maintaining that the unequal distribution of wealth and opportunity in society ought to be tackled by means other than sentencing. Where social injustices are widespread, this 'does not diminish . . . the harmfulness of common victimising crimes', although it strengthens the case for reducing overall punishment levels. Critics have also argued that the key concepts of ordinal and cardinal proportionality are too vague and open to divergent interpretations, but these criticisms are likely to apply to any approach to sentencing which invokes a notion of proportionality. Virtually all rationales rely on the notion in some shape or form, and it is significant that the Council of Europe's recommendation on 'Consistency in Sentencing' . . . states: 'A4. Whatever rationales for sentencing are declared disproportionality between the seriousness of the offence and the sentence should be avoided. The work done within desert theory to refine the key concept of proportionality surely outstrips the efforts of critics. For example desert theorists have tried to grapple with the awkward question of the relevance of previous convictions to sentence, rationalising the concessions to first offenders in terms of human frailty and evaluating the relevance of various types of previous record . . . Desert theorists have also tackled the problems of introducing proportionality into non-custodial sentencing . . . Many of the proposals require further refinement, but the strengths of desert theory are to be found in its apparent concordance with some widely held moral views, in its respect for the rights of the individual offender, and in its placing of limits on the powers of the state. Thomas Mathieson has attacked desert theory for the implicit claims of precision and objectivity embodied in terms such as 'commensurate', 'ordinal and cardinal proportionality', 'culpability' and 'offence seriousness'. An alternative evaluation would be that this analysis has enabled considerable advances in framing questions which should be asked about the justifications for punishing people and about the justifications for imposing different punishments on different offenders, with its proponents still seeking to refine the answers.

6. DISCRIMINATION IN SENTENCING

(a) Discrimination on grounds of race

There is now considerable evidence that people from racial minorities are dealt with differently from white people at many different stages of the criminal justice system. It has been claimed that blacks '. . . are more likely than whites to be arrested, charged, convicted and imprisoned and there are widespread concerns about remand conditions, bail conditions, stop and search, the police response to racial harassment complaints, deaths in custody, and police tactics particularly in relation to drug raids' (Dhakolia and Sumner, 1994), p 28. Questions of discrimination on the basis of ethnic origin through other stages of the criminal justice system are considered in Chapter 6 below. In this chapter, therefore, we confine the discussion to discriminatory practices in sentencing.

Some sentencing statutes are prefaced by a general policy statement that the operation of the sentencing principles contained therein must not operate in a discriminatory manner. A typical provision is that of the sentencing guidelines of the State of Minnesota, which provide that '. . . sentencing shall be neutral with respect to the race, gender, social or economic status of convicted felons'. There is no such statutory provision in England, and the government resisted pressure for writing such a general statement into the Criminal

Justice Act 1991. Instead, by s 95 of the Act, a duty was placed on the Home Secretary '. . . each year to publish such information as he considers expedient' for the purpose of enabling criminal justice agencies to avoid discrimination. One may regret the absence of a general statement in the English sentencing law, but Article 14 of the European Convention on Human Rights states that all the rights secured by the Convention (including the right to a fair trial) shall be accorded without discrimination (see p 57 above). In any event, deeds speak louder than words, and in recent years efforts have been made to provide training for magistrates, judges, the police, the probation service, and others, on race relations issues and to improving the quality of service which the criminal justice system as a whole offers to people from ethnic minorities (see further, Chapter 6).

Complete agreement is likely to the proposition that sentence decision-making should not be discriminatory. Non-discrimination is the clearest applica-tion of the principle of equality before the law and, put simply, sentencing should not turn upon irrelevant considerations. There is, however, much collected evidence to the effect that black people believe the criminal justice system to be biased against them (see, for example, Crow and Smellie, 1991). There is also one undoubted fact: that Afro-Caribbeans (but not Asians) are heavily over-represented within the prison system. Five per cent of the population in England and Wales is non-white, yet ethnic minority prisoners account for 18 per cent of the sentenced custodial population. The percentage within the remand population is higher still. Until recently little systematic research had been carried out into the question to what extent this over-representation can be explained by discriminatory sentencing practices. Research studies published in the late 1980s and early 1990s yielded rather contradictory results. Studies carried out by Walker (1988) and by Hudson (1989) did find some evidence of discriminatory practices in sentencing. Other studies, such as those by McConville and Baldwin (1982), Crow and Cove (1984), and Moxon (1988) found little or no such evidence. The latter studies suggested that while racism at earlier stages in the system (such as police decision-making) might explain why black defendants appeared in court in disproportionate numbers, once in court they were dealt with fairly. To the extent that there was some difference between the numbers of blacks and whites receiving custodial sentences, this seemed explicable for other reasons. First, in these samples blacks were being sentenced on the basis of somewhat more serious charges; secondly, that blacks were more likely to elect jury trial rather than be dealt with by magistrates; thirdly (and associ-ated with the last point), blacks were less likely than whites to plead guilty, and hence more often lost the sentencing discount associated with a guilty plea. It is very difficult to gain a clear picture from these studies. As Barbara Hudson puts it (1993, p 8):

> These attempts to establish or refute discrimination in criminal justice processes – especially in the courts – have been fraught with methodological difficulties.

The large samples needed to control the numerous legal and non-legal variables and to ensure an adequate number of black defendants; the fact that courts do not routinely record the race of defendants, the difficulty of generalising from studies of one court, or one judicial division, have made the studies vulnerable to criticism . . .

The most comprehensive research study so far carried out on the question of discrimination in sentencing was conducted by Roger Hood, on behalf of the Commission for Racial Equality. His report contains a very detailed analysis of over 3,000 defendants sentenced in five Crown Courts in the West Midlands during 1989. The methodology used, and the analysis of results is sophisticated and detailed. The following extract is taken from Dr Hood's summary of conclusions.

Extract 5.6.1

R Hood, *Race and Sentencing: A Study in the Crown Court* (1992) pp 193–205

Race differences to be explained

Ethnic minority defendants accounted for 28 per cent of the males sentenced at the West Midlands Crown Courts in 1989. This was two and a half times greater than their proportion in the population at large, which was about 11 per cent. This was because Afro-Caribbeans were generally over-represented, making up 21 per cent of the those found guilty at Birmingham and 15 per cent at the Dudley Courts (which sat in court rooms at Dudley, Wolverhampton and Birmingham) although they accounted for less than 4 per cent of the general male population in the age range of 16 to 64. Asian males, on the other hand, were convicted in the Crown Court only slightly more often than would be expected from their number in the population at large.

Differences in the proportions of each ethnic category – white, black or Asian – given a custodial sentence were marked. Taking the sample as a whole, the proportion of blacks sentenced to custody was just over 8 percentage points higher than for whites (56.6 per cent v 48.4 per cent). Asians, on the other hand, were sentenced to custody less often than either whites or blacks (39.6 per cent).

Variations between the proportions of ethnic minorities sentenced to custody at the different Crown Court Centres were even larger. The black: white 'custody ratio' was particularly high for those sentenced by the Dudley courts, amounting to a difference of 17 percentage points (65 per cent v 48 per cent). There was a similar high black: white ratio at Warwick and Stafford, although the numbers dealt with there were much smaller. Only at Coventry were more whites and Asians sentenced to custody than blacks.

It was possible to examine the pattern of sentences of 18 judges, (17 Circuit Judges and one Recorder) each of whom had dealt with at least 45 cases in the sample, and who, between them, had sentenced over half of all the cases.

541

They varied a great deal in their overall use of custody (i.e. for all cases irrespective of race) ranging from one judge who had sentenced 29 per cent of the cases he dealt with to custody to another who sentenced 69 per cent. As regards race, three judges had sentenced considerably fewer blacks to custody than whites, eight appeared to be relatively even-handed, and five sentenced a much higher proportion of blacks than whites to custody: the difference ranging from 11 to 42 percentage points, equivalent to a greater proportion of black offenders getting a custodial sentence of between 41 and 111 per cent. When judges were ranked in order of their severity (measured by proportion to custody) for each ethnic group, there was a very low level of concordance between them. In other words, they appeared to vary a great deal in their relative severity on defendants of different ethnic backgrounds.

Differences in patterns

To what extent could these disparities be accounted for by variability in the nature of the cases dealt with by these judges at the various courts covered by the study? A comparison was first made of the nature and circumstances of the offences and the legally relevant characteristics of the defendants in each ethnic group. This showed that, although more black offenders had appeared at the Crown Court charged with offences which could only be tried on indictment at such a court, there were no significant differences in the proportions of blacks and whites convicted of the most serious crimes of personal violence. More blacks were, however, charged with and convicted of robbery and of supplying drugs (mostly cannabis), although there were pro-portionately fewer sentenced for housebreaking, theft or fraud. Their *modus operandi* for illegally obtaining money was clearly often different. As far as social characteristics were concerned, more blacks were unemployed and in receipt of welfare benefits, but it appeared that fewer had an unsettled or disrupted social life or were impaired by alcohol at the time of the offence. Although fewer blacks had no prior convictions a higher proportion of whites had eight or more. The pattern of these convictions differed somewhat, the black offenders being more likely to have a record for robbery or a drugs offence. Nevertheless, a smaller proportion of them had been convicted in the past of the same broad type of offence as that of which they had cur-rently been convicted. It was particularly noticeable that more of the blacks pleaded not guilty and contested the case against them before a jury. As a consequence of this a considerably smaller proportion had a Social Inquiry Report (SIR) prepared about them by the probation service.

When the cases involving Asians were examined there was much to sug-gest that the lower proportion of them sentenced to custody was largely due to the fact that they were less involved in criminal acts than either whites or blacks. Although more had been charged with indictable only offences, fewer had more than one indictment laid against them and fewer had multiple charges or other offences taken into consideration. A much lower proportion had been previously convicted or had already served a custodial sentence. Further-more, considerably fewer were unemployed or came from obviously unsettled

542

backgrounds. They, too, had more often pleaded not guilty than had whites, and they too less often had an SIR.

Variations in the use of custody

In order to test whether the observed differences could be explained by the combination of factors in each case and the weighting given to them, a statistical method was used to 'match' cases as closely as possible in terms of those variables which were shown to have had the most significant impact on whether an offender was committed to custody or not. This was done by using standard multi-variate statistical techniques to calculate a 'probability of custody' score for each case, a score which summarised the probability of an offender with that particular combination of attributes getting a custodial sentence. In deriving this score more than 80 variables were analysed and 15 chosen which described 50 legally relevant attributes of the offence and the offender's criminal record. These variables correctly predicted whether an offender would receive custody or not in 75 per cent of cases. To what extent did the observed race differences in the proportion of blacks, whites and Asians sentenced to custody disappear when their probability of custody, as determined by these other factors, was taken into account?

A higher proportion of blacks than whites did fall into the category with the highest risk of custody, and fewer in the category with the lowest probability of receiving such a sentence. Asian offenders, on the other hand, were much less likely to be in the highest risk of custody group and were much more frequently in the lowest.

When this was taken into account the black-white difference in the sample as a whole of 8.2 percentage points in the proportion sentenced to custody was reduced to a difference of about 2.5 percentage points. Given the fact that the white custody rate was just under 50 per cent this amounts to a 5 per cent greater probability of a male black defendant being sentenced to custody than a white male. When a comparison was made on the basis of a probability of custody score derived only from the black defendants the difference was rather larger: whites being 7.6 per cent less likely to get a custodial sentence. Five per cent is not as large a 'residual race difference' as many commentators have suggested, but in a sample of this size it can be estimated that the number of blacks who received a custodial sentence would, if race had had no effect at all, have been 479 rather than 503 in the year 1989. It is important to bear in mind that this does not refer to any **particular cases**, only to the **aggregate difference** between the observed and expected **probability** of receiving a custodial sentence.

After taking into account the seriousness of cases, two other variables were related to racial differences in the use of custody. These were age and employment. There were no differences between the use of custody for blacks and whites aged under 21: all of the difference occurring amongst the adult offenders. The same pattern was found in relation to employment: the comparatively higher custody rate for blacks being found not amongst those who were employed but only amongst the unemployed. Indeed, if the defendant was black, being unemployed was a factor significantly associated with receiving

543

a custodial sentence, when all the other variables were controlled for, but not if he was white or Asian.

Variations between courts and judges

When the seriousness of the cases dealt with at the different court centres was controlled for, it was found that the observed differences between the proportions sentenced to custody by judges at these centres remained substantial and significant. In other words, the overall average relatively small 'race of defendant effect' concealed considerable variations between cases dealt with by judges sitting at different court centres.

At Birmingham Crown Court the proportion sentenced to custody was below what would have been expected, with no significant differences between the observed and expected rates for any of the ethnic groups. In other words, no overall 'race of defendant effect' existed amongst cases dealt with at that court. As half of the cases in the sample had been dealt with at Birmingham, this obviously had an impact on the overall findings.

The proportion of blacks committed to custody amongst those dealt with at the Dudley courts remained, however, considerably higher than expected from the characteristics of the cases: more than 12 percentage points higher than for whites, which is equivalent to an increased probability of receiving a custodial sentence of 23 per cent. Although the numbers were much smaller, and therefore the conclusions less reliable, the black defendants were similarly more likely to get a custodial sentence at Warwick and Stafford. Comparing blacks dealt with at the Dudley courts with those dealt with at Birmingham, the probability of receiving a custodial sentence was 29 per cent higher amongst cases at the former venue. Several other analyses and comparisons confirmed these findings.

Estimating the size of the race factor

A calculation was made to estimate the cumulative effect of race differences – in the proportion of cases sentenced to custody, in the proportion pleading not guilty, and in the average length of sentence imposed in such cases – on the substantial over-representation of black males in the prison population. Bearing in mind the difficulties of such an exercise and the degree of error therefore involved, it appears that, in this West Midlands sample, about 80 per cent of the difference between the proportion of black males in the general population and their proportion among those serving prison sentences, can be accounted for by the greater number of black offenders who appeared for sentence in the Crown Court and by the nature and circumstances of the crimes they were convicted of. The remaining 20 per cent could be attributed to their subsequent different treatment by the courts: one third of this (7 per cent) to more being sentenced to custody than expected and two-thirds (13 per cent) to more pleading not guilty and to the consequent longer sentences imposed.

Variations in the use of alternatives to custody

There were significant race differences in the way that sentences were distributed along the scale from imprisonment to discharge and in the alternatives to custody which were considered appropriate. Controlling for those variables which best explained severity of sentence, blacks were placed higher up the scale than were whites, especially amongst those sentenced at the Dudley courts.

Black offenders were more often given a fully suspended sentence of imprisonment and less often a probation order or a community service order than were whites. These differences were found to be concentrated amongst those blacks who had a medium risk of receiving a custodial sentence.

Asians were also less likely to be placed on probation but more likely to have been fined or conditionally discharged. They generally suffered less intrusive penalties than either blacks or whites.

For further discussion of the Hood study, see the criticisms by Halevy (1995) and the reply by Hood (1995), together with the further reflections by von Hirsch and Roberts (1997).

(b) Discrimination on grounds of gender

It is often claimed that female offenders are more leniently dealt with by the courts in sentencing, and that such lenience reflects a similarly favourable treatment at other stages of the criminal justice system: what has been called the 'chivalry hypothesis'. This kind of claim requires careful assessment. It is important to ensure when making any such comparison that similar offending is being compared. The number of women who are sentenced by the courts each year is very much smaller than the number of men. According to the *Criminal Statistics England and Wales 1996* (Home Office, 1997a), in 1996 there were 175,600 males over the age of 21 sentenced for indictable offences, compared to 27,200 women in the same category.

For males over the age of 21 sentenced for indictable offences in 1996:

(1) 26 per cent received custodial sentences (12 per cent for women);
(2) 24 per cent received community sentences (31 per cent for women);
(3) 33 per cent were fined (25 per cent for women); and
(4) 14 per cent were discharged (28 per cent for women).

On the face of it, then, women are far more frequently dealt with by way of discharges and community sentences, while men more frequently receive custodial sentences and fines. Clearly, however, any meaningful comparison of sentencing patterns for male and female offenders must match males and females with similar records being sentenced for similar offences in similar circumstances. The following figures are derived from table 7.6 in the *Criminal Statistics*, which compares the overall numbers of men and women sentenced during 1996 for a range of different kinds of offences, and relates that to the sentences received. Taking the category of 'theft and handling stolen goods', for example, 93,000 men were so dealt with as compared to 20,900

545

women. For men, this represented 35.6 per cent of total male offending, while it represented 55 per cent of total female offending.

Of the men sentenced for theft and handling stolen goods:

(1) 22.6 per cent received discharges (37 per cent for women);
(2) 28.6 per cent received a fine (21 per cent for women);
(3) 30.5 per cent received a community sentence (31.5 per cent for women); and
(4) 16 per cent received a custodial sentence (7.6 per cent for women).

Looking at the figures in this way suggests that the sentencing differential may not be quite so wide as it at first appears to be. To the extent that there remains a significant difference between the two sentencing patterns, one might argue that, within the category of theft and handling stolen goods, female offending may typically lie towards the lower end of the seriousness scale and hence attract more discharges and community sentences than the typically more serious male offending. Accepting for the moment, however, that women are sentenced differently from men and, in general, more leniently, the next question is whether this is an unacceptable disparity, or a recognition of relevant differences in personal mitigation between men and women. The sentencing system, as we have seen, does recognise that a wide range of mitigating factors may influence a judge in the circumstances of the case to a more lenient disposal. So if a judge takes account of the fact, say, that a female offender has been bringing up young children on her own, and that to send her to prison would mean that the children would have to be taken into local authority care, is the decision to impose a community sentence for an offence for which a man would have gone to prison a discriminatory sentence, or is it an appropriate use of the available flexibility to take account of mitigating factors – in this case the special hardship which would be occasioned to the family by the mother's imprisonment?

A quite different claim is also made about differential sentencing of men and women. This is the suggestion that women are, at least in some cases, dealt with more harshly than men, since a predominantly male judiciary tends to regard women who commit crimes as doubly deviant – breaching not only the criminal law but also sex-role expectations. As Allison Morris (1988) puts it:

> A woman who enters the criminal justice system is 'incongruous', 'out of place', 'invisible'. Hence explanations for her presence are sought and found within the discourse of the 'pathological' and the 'irrational': menstruation, mental illness, poor socialisation, broken home and so on. What is important here is that men are not 'out of place' and consequently their criminal behaviour is described in different ways, within the discourse of 'normality' and 'rationality'. Thus their behaviour is more likely to be viewed as due to such factors as boredom, greed and peer group pressure.

This is a complex issue, on which there is valuable observational research evidence. In the final two extracts in this chapter, a balanced summary of the issue is first provided by Allison Morris, and then evidence is presented from recent Home Office research on the attitudes of magistrates to the sentencing of women:

Extract 5.6.2

A Morris, 'Sex and Sentencing' [1988] Crim LR 163–171

The treatment of women and girls in the criminal justice system has been described as lenient. There is little evidence of this. Apparent differences in sentencing practices can be explained by differences in the extent and nature of men's and women's crimes. Their treatment has also been described as sexist, but it is more complex than this. First, such factors as race, family circumstances and commitments, type of offence and previous record all clearly mediate the treatment of both female *and* male defendants and it may be that some of these factors are as important as gender, if not more so. Heidensohn argues that it is, indeed, sex which is the key factor.[1] She acknowledges that women are not the only social group to be disadvantaged, but argues that women have a further disadvantage: the criminal justice system for them is 'a peculiarly alien and unfamiliar world.' It must surely be this too for young black and working-class men. It is wrong to present women's experiences in the criminal justice system as a unitary experience. We know that black women are over-represented in our prisons. We need to be able to account for this. Similarly the focus in both Eaton's[2] and Worrall's[3] work is women. But they seem to me to be saying much more about class than gender differences.

Secondly, sexism requires a context; sexism in every-day practice is mediated by organisational and administrative constraints. Research has not yet examined this in courts, but Gelsthorpe's research on the police shows that apparently sexist responses were shaped by such pressures as the need to be seen to be busy and to be doing 'real' police work.[4]

Thirdly, allegations of sexism assume that men are dealt with in non-sexist ways and sentenced equally and fairly. Patently this is false. Men and male defendants are also 'constructed' but in different terms from women and female defendants. References there are to 'breadwinners' and 'typical' men. For example, in Allen's description of the portrayal of male defendants in psychiatric reports, family pressures and personal frailties were ignored in contrast with the portrayal of female defendants. And clearly certain men are punished more harshly than others – black men are also over-represented in our prisons.[5]

Fourthly, allegations of sexism ignore the fact that a considerable body of research indicates that women are dealt with in much the same way as men: routine cases are routinely processed. On the other hand, there is some evidence that certain women and girls – for example, those who are divorced, sexual or black – are dealt with in a discriminatory way. In essence, those who fit stereotypical conceptions of 'ladies' or 'nice girls' seem to receive different sentences from those who breach these expectations.

The criminal justice system overtly controls both male and female defendants, but it seems more subtly to control female defendants by distinguishing among that population. To the extent that this is so, processing in the criminal justice system can be viewed as a way of patrolling and controlling the boundaries of the female gender role. The juvenile justice system, for example, seems more concerned with ensuring the appropriate behaviour of girls than with responding to their delinquency. Morris and Wilkinson suggested that the growth in secure facilities (the increase in the number of places for girls is greater than that for boys) reflected an easy answer to social workers' concerns about girls rather than a solution to the girls' problems.[6] Indeed, they suggested that secure placement had exacerbated the difficulties that many of the girls in the sample had.

This raises the question of whether or not we should aim for a sex-fair criminal justice system – a system which would mean the same dispositions for male and female defendants. There are now a number of Court of Appeal cases which indicate that this is the direction we should move in.[7] And some feminists argue this too, though there are many tensions in feminist writings on this point.[8]

Equal treatment, however, is not necessarily the right objective. There may well be differences between men and women which justify differential dispositions. Walker, in the discussion at the Cropwood Conference on Women and Crime, distinguished between paper and real justice. 'Paper justice,' he suggests, involves giving like penalties to women and men for like offences, but 'real justice' involves taking into account the consequences of a penalty: for example, the fact that, at least in this culture and at this time, child-rearing *is* primarily the responsibility of women and that their children suffer as a result of their incarceration. Thus it can be argued that a mother's responsibility to her children should take priority over her responsibility to the law and that, therefore, the imprisonment of mothers should be avoided at all costs. However, clearly the children of imprisoned men suffer too. There is no easy answer. What we can say with confidence is that simple allegations of 'chivalry' or 'sexism' obscure our understanding of the complex nature of sentencing both male and female defendants.

[1] F Heidensohn, 'Models of justice: Portia or Persephone? Some thoughts on equality, fairness and gender in the field of justice' (1986) 14 *International Journal of the Sociology of Law* 287.

[2] M Eaton, *Justice for Women* (1986).

[3] A Worrall, 'Out of place: female offenders in the court' (1986) 28 *Probation Journal* 90.

[4] L Gelsthorpe, 'Towards a sceptical look at sexism' (1986) 14 *International Journal of the Sociology of Law* 125.

[5] H Allen, 'Rendering them harmless: the professional portrayal of women charged with serious violent crimes' in P Carlen and A Worrall (eds), *Gender, Crime and Justice* (1987).

[6] A Morris and C Wilkinson, 'Secure care: just an easy answer?' (1983) *Community Care*, 8 December, 22.

[7] See, e.g., *Okuya and Nwaobi* (1984) 6 Cr App R (S) 253; *Hancock* [1986] Crim LR 697; *Ouless and Ouless* [1986] Crim LR 702.

[8] See A Morris and L Gelsthorpe (eds), *Women and Crime* (1981).

Extract 5.6.3

C Hedderman and L Gelsthorpe, *Understanding the Sentencing of Women* (1997) pp 21–22, 26–29, 43–44, 52–53, 58–59

The results reported in this [study] raise as many questions as they answer. There is certainly a *tendency* towards less use of custody for women offenders – but it is equally true that sometimes there is no difference in the treatment of men and women offenders. And why should women who are first-time violent offenders or recidivist drug offenders be treated no differently from their male counterparts while sentencers appear to avoid custodial sentences for the other groups of women?

Certainly it is not possible to explain this by positing a simple, direct relationship between the type of offence for which a woman is convicted and how she is perceived. Data on the seriousness of the offence and the remand status of the defendants may help to explain this further, but the safest conclusion (from this data) concerning the use of custody is that it is often but not always the case that women are less likely than men to be given a prison sentence.

However although the whole sentencing debate (perhaps inevitably) tends to focus around use of custody, this analysis shows that major discrepancies between the sentencing of men and women lie in the choice between non-custodial options. Women were consistently more likely than men to be discharged even when their circumstances appeared (on the basis of the available data) entirely comparable. This may stem from the fact that sentencers were (for whatever reason) reluctant to fine women. Equally though, it appears that this reluctance to fine women may sometimes result in a woman being given a more severe noncustodial penalty. Thus, this phase of the study shows different women being treated more leniently *and* more harshly. This leaves us with a number of questions: why are sentencers reluctant to fine women? Is it because they are reluctant to penalise the whole family for her misdemeanour if she is not working and her husband/partner provides the money for the household? Does this not also apply to men in similar circumstances – or is it that the results show up for women offenders simply because more of them are in this situation, as Farrington and Morris (1983) ['Sex, Sentencing and Reconviction' (1983) *British Journal of Criminology* 229–248] suggest.

In order to begin to resolve some of these questions, we extracted a subsample of magistrates' court cases involving men and women (N=363) matched on age, criminal history, offence and plea. We then asked the sentencing courts to provide information on whether the offender had been remanded in custody prior to sentence and details of their marital and economic status. Because the cases were sentenced in 1991, it was only possible to obtain full information in a small number of cases.

The questionnaire was returned for 137 pairs of offenders (an overall response of 37%) but even in these cases there was often missing information. So while it is noteworthy that married and single women were equally likely to be fined but married men were twice as likely to be fined than unmarried ones, one cannot draw any firm conclusions from this. Similarly, the fact that fines were given to 70 per cent of employed men versus 57 per cent of employed women and equal proportions of the unemployed were fined (40%) is interest-ing but inconclusive because of the numbers involved. However, even if this difference was found to be inspired by a desire not to financially penalise a woman's family, it carries the risk that, skipping a step on the sentencing ladder this time round, will lead to an even more severe sentence being imposed in the event of a subsequent conviction. To use probation where a fine would have been appropriate is also an ineffective use of resources . . .

As 96 per cent of men and women were bailed, we can say little about the impact custodial remands have on sentencing from this exercise, except that as half the matched pairs who were bailed and half of those remanded in custody were given the same disposal, and the others were given different ones, it seems unlikely that remand status had much impact on the senten-cing decision.

In the next section of this report Loraine Gelsthorpe and Nancy Loucks explore whether magistrates believe these factors should and do influence their decision-making and what other considerations affect their sentencing choices for men and women offenders . . .

Images of offenders: troubled or troublesome?

Think of them as greedy, needy or dotty. Group 3, Shelley court (F)

One explanation which magistrates gave for differences in the sentences given to men and women was that their motives were rarely similar. In their opinion, a 'typical' shop theft committed by a female defendant differed considerably from the 'typical' thefts which men committed:

> . . . *the women feed the family whereas the men, although they have to support their family, don't.* Mag. 13, Byron court (F)

'Troubled' offenders include those who steal items from shops which they, or particularly their children, need (mainly food, or sometimes clothing or shoes, but nothing very extravagant). This definition stretches to women (specifically) who steal tins of salmon, for example, as a treat for the family which they other-wise could not afford. Indeed, magistrates described this as the most typical scenario they dealt with when sentencing women convicted of shop theft. In contrast, those interviewed portrayed men as stealing out of greed rather than need:

> . . . *a shoplifting woman would probably be a single mother without enough money. A shoplifting man would very rarely be a single father without enough money and kids yapping around – they would be lads out on the town wanting to get a snappy pair of jeans . . .* Mag. 12, Shelley court (F)

Rather than food or shoes, men were characterised as stealing alcohol or CDs and videos to sell. Magistrates commonly referred to women as stealing to feed their children where men stole to support drug habits. Even offences relating to prostitution could often fall into this 'survival' category. Some magis-trates viewed it as something which was legally an offence, but which did little harm.

To some extent, fraud against the Department of Social Security was also seen as being for 'survival'. Magistrates generally sympathised with women

550

who 'did a couple of cleaning jobs on the side every once in a while' and 'didn't realise' that they were doing something wrong, or had become dependent on the extra income. Men were invariably seen as much more deliberate and profit-driven.

Although this was exceptional, women could be 'troublesome' rather than 'troubled'. Magistrates expressed least tolerance for women shoplifters whose offences were planned and/or done for profit − in other words, those whose offences were closer to the stereotype of the male shoplifter. They said that such women tended to work in groups and 'stole to order'. Some women were even believed to use their children either as a distraction or trained them to take the goods themselves (though magistrates thought that this was relatively infrequent).

Surprisingly perhaps, some violent offences were viewed by magistrates with a degree of understanding. To draw out the reasons for this, interviewees were asked to consider a real, but anonymised, case involving an assault by a female . . . In this case, 'Jane' attacked her husband's lover. Magistrates usually believed that Jane had been provoked and that the victim probably deserved what she got (to the extent that some magistrates did not think it was appropriate to award compensation).

Interestingly, a third (N=12) of the individual magistrates and a quarter of the groups (N=3) who were asked about this case vignette found her behaviour 'understandable' and several commented that they might well have done the same thing in her situation. On the other hand, magistrates who were asked to look at details of a case involving a man, 'Jason', who assaulted a man who made an obscene gesture at Jason's friend in a motoring dispute . . . , had little sympathy with him. Only four individual magistrates out of 28 and one group out of the 12 who looked at this case study could see any element of provocation.

One magistrate explained that where women commit violent offences, they tend to commit offences against people they know (an abusive partner, perhaps, or a neighbour or friend), with some identifiable cause. Men, on the other hand, are apt to be involved in offences against strangers, such as in pub brawls. These too may have an identifiable cause, but such causes tend to be unrelated to the victims of the offence. Examples those interviewed gave included expressions of frustration because of offenders' redundancy or continued unemployment, or their consumption of alcohol or drugs . . .

Factors relating to family background, such as a history of abuse during childhood, met with a mixed reception. Forty-six individual magistrates and 10 groups who mentioned such factors said they would take them into consideration. Fifteen individuals and three groups specifically said they would not; and nine individual and 10 groups of magistrates had no clear view on this matter.

While a small number of magistrates (four out of the eight who mentioned it) believed that male and female co-defendants would be regarded as equally culpable, others (three individuals and one group) commented that they were inclined to believe that a woman invariably played a lesser role or was perhaps coerced into committing an offence rather than sharing equal responsibility:

If a man and a woman come up together, there will be a tendency, unless you were told otherwise, [to assume] that the man was influencing the woman, that the man was the ringleader. This happens with juveniles, that a younger juvenile is influenced by the older juvenile . . . I think that is ingrained, a man and a woman together that you are expecting the man to be dominant. Mag. 10, Byron (M)

. . . there is a tendency to feel that women are more victims than men in that they are more vulnerable, the pressures of their various partners, and that they are following rather than instigating. Mag. 14, Byron (F)

Ten individual magistrates and two groups also mentioned that they believed male offenders used women in crimes – to steal pension books or pass stolen cheques for example – in the belief that, if caught, they would be dealt with more leniently. Interestingly, one magistrate commented that male offenders would never admit to being led by a woman, with the result that, at most, female co-defendants would share equal blame and probably much less. This in turn may produce disparity in the sentencing of men and women facing the same charge.

Magistrates expressed a general lack of tolerance of addiction to drugs or alcohol, which they viewed as self-inflicted problems. In addition only one group distinguished between binge drinking (which few would dispute is a matter of choice) and addiction (which is treated by the medical profession as an illness). Although magistrates said that they quite frequently recommended drug or alcohol programmes (16 individual magistrates and four groups mentioned this specifically), to some extent they viewed such programmes as an 'easy option'. Two magistrates also said that they would refer defendants to such programmes only once, after which they considered a more punitive response appropriate.

Magistrates very rarely viewed intoxication as a mitigating factor. Only one magistrate mentioned this possibility, whereas eight individuals and four groups were clear that it would *not* mitigate. In fact, eight individual magistrates and six groups thought that intoxication could well have an aggravating effect on sentence.

Drugs-related crime was generally viewed very seriously by the magistrates. Only possession of drugs for one's own consumption (with no other connected offences) was thought to warrant anything other than a very severe response. Few magistrates reported having any direct experience of sentencing women for dealing in drugs or even for possession. The main exception seemed to be women who resorted to prostitution to feed a drugs habit. This tended to be viewed as 'hurting no-one but themselves'. In contrast, men were characterised as likely to resort to burglary to feed a drug habit. If women were involved in selling drugs at all, then the magistrates believed that men were usually behind it (e.g., as pimps or suppliers).

Proof of some form of mental illness, on the other hand, was an acceptable form of mitigation. A further factor mentioned was 'hormonal problems' for older women. Male magistrates in particular tended to mention 'the Change' as an explanation of offending, especially shop theft. Only one female magistrate introduced this idea among the six individuals and four groups who mentioned it. Again, this perceived 'illness' generated sympathy rather than censure.

Magistrates' impression that most of those charged with not having a TV licence are women is confirmed by the sentencing statistics. All those interviewed described this offence as deserving of compassion. Magistrates believed that these women were doing their best in a bad situation: they could not afford their licence, or their husbands would not give them the money for it. Single mothers were particularly vulnerable as they relied heavily on the television to occupy their children. Magistrates also recognised that where women lived with partners, they were the ones who were most likely to answer the door while their children were watching the television (and thus they were the ones charged with having no TV licence).

In contrast there were a few particular offences which individual magistrates and groups said they could not understand and offenders with whom they could never empathise. The most commonly mentioned of these was having no motor insurance (mentioned by four individuals and three groups) – an almost entirely male offence in the view of those whom we interviewed. Despite earlier references to other magistrates finding some violent offences 'understandable', one group of magistrates and one stipendiary magistrate mentioned that they found violence of any sort anathema. Finally, three magistrates who had been burgled themselves mentioned burglary (one magistrate in particular blamed the death of his mother on the burglary of her house). All such offences were those usually committed by men . . .

Magistrates perceived their use of custody for women as a sentence of last resort, employed either because the crime was so serious that prison was the only option, or because they felt forced into it by the legislation, such as for non-payment of fines. In contrast, men were open to any sort of penalty, though tended to be given probation orders if their offence involved the use of drugs or alcohol, or involved motor vehicles. Male offenders reached the custody threshold much faster than women, either because of the motivation for the offence (e.g. it was inspired by 'greed' rather than 'need'), or because they had relatively limited mitigation compared to women (e.g. no direct responsibility for child care, at least in the view of the magistrates). We should acknowledge, however, that magistrates declared that custody was a rare option for both men and women.

Only a few magistrates (4 individuals and one group) believed that prison could help either male or female offenders in addition to punishing them, either through training or education, or by restricting access to drugs, alcohol, or people who were bad influences on their behaviour. Similarly, 'protection' was one of the grounds for remanding someone in custody. This could be protection from others who would try to avenge a crime or, in some cases, to help *prevent* someone from committing suicide. Prevention of suicide is included on Bail Forms as an exception to the Bail Act 1976 – in other words, as a justification for denying bail . . .

What emerges from the interviews with magistrates is a complexity that goes well beyond a simple male/female offender distinction, but appears to be closely tied to it. Magistrates generally seemed to make distinctions between offenders depending on whether they could understand the offence as a matter of survival, see it as a result of provocation or coercion, or attribute it to illness rather than irresponsibility.

How magistrates perceived defendants in the courtroom is influenced by considerations other than the simple 'facts of the case'. Appearance and demeanour, the novice status of first-timers or 'know it all' status of experienced offenders, the 'believability' of defendants, expressions and perceptions of remorse, and the reading or misreading of cues about ethnicity and culture all seemed to play a part in shaping magistrates' perceptions of the offenders before them. Such factors cut across simple sex differences, but we can surmise that the relative inexperience of female defendants and their concomitant 'nervousness' might lead magistrates to view them as more 'believable' than others – a point which reiterates the findings of Hedderman . . . in earlier research. Additionally, women's relative inexperience in offending might be reflected in their behaviour in court – showing deference and remorse – thus leading the magistrates to view them more sympathetically than some of the male defendants who were experienced offenders, well-rehearsed in courtroom procedures and thus seemingly less remorseful.

A distinction between 'troubled' and 'troublesome' offenders was, thus based on the perceived motivation for the offence and the demeanour of defendants in court. In turn, magistrates may make different decisions for bail and certainly choose different options for sentencing. They appeared to favour the use of probation orders or discharges for women – the 'troubled' offenders – as a means of assisting rather than just punishing them. Only occasionally did magistrates believe that male offenders merited assistance, and sometimes 'assistance' for men came in the form of CSOs or custody. Even allowing for the fact that women were more likely to be first offenders or less frequent offenders than men, and were more likely to behave respectfully in court, on the basis of these interviews it would seem that magistrates are less inclined to sympathise with men and to impose a sentence intended to address their underlying problems and needs . . .

The results of our discussions with magistrates about what sorts of factors might mitigate sentencing decisions for men and women suggest that female defendants were likely to find mitigation in dependants, primarily children, whereas men rarely benefitted from the fact of having dependent children.

Most magistrates had fairly firm views regarding the type of social structure which provided enough stability and discipline to influence a bail or sentencing decision in a positive way. The support of family or long-term partners, preferably in the same house, materially improved both male and female defendants' chances of avoiding custody and possibly mitigated against the eventual sentence as well. Family history too may have a bearing, but would depend more on its interaction with other features of the case.

Paid employment often mitigated in remand and sentencing decisions for those defendants fortunate enough to have it, but the lack of full-time employment seemed to be viewed less negatively for women than men because magistrates believed that most of the women they dealt with were mothers who were (and should be) occupied with childcare. On the other hand, paid employment often resulted in larger financial penalties for men . . . [H]owever, this does not always result in women being dealt with more leniently.

The locality and permanence of a defendant's address was acknowledged to play some part in bail decisions, but not on sentencing. Magistrates did not generally distinguish between male and female defendants in their comments about these factors.

While all of these factors – family circumstances and background, employment, and locality – may have a bearing on the decisions magistrates make, they will not necessarily in themselves have a material impact on a decision. For this reason, we asked magistrates whether each particular factor would push a potential penalty up or down if the case were on the borderline. Interestingly, and consistent with the results from Part I, the borderlines seemed to differ greatly for men and women. The custody threshold showed the clearest difference here, with magistrates doing everything possible to keep a woman out of custody, but sentencing men primarily in response to the seriousness of their offending. They also avoided using fines for women, but used them frequently for men. Much of this seemed to be based on the fact that magistrates considered family circumstances and responsibilities to be much more relevant when dealing with female than with male offenders. Therefore, although personal circumstances carried weight for both groups, they were given more weight with regard to female offenders.

The patterns of mitigation, particularly as they relate to men and women, clearly reflect the same divisions between 'troubled' offenders (those who deserve sympathy and assistance) and 'troublesome' offenders (those who deserve punishment). The issues are exceedingly complex, however, and reflect considerations of family responsibilities, family structure and the potential for social control through the family, the influence of family history as mitigation, employment and income and the links between these factors and the ability to pay fines and compensation. Some of these factors, but by no means all, appeared to carry differential degrees of influence depending on whether the magistrates were discussing men or women. Overall, magistrates appeared to consider family circumstances and responsibilities to be much more relevant in mitigation when dealing with female than with male defendants. This finding confirms the earlier research findings of Farrington and Morris ['Sex, Sentencing and Reconviction' (1983) 23 *British Journal of Criminology* 229–248] and Eaton . . . [*Justice for Women?* (Milton Keynes: Open University Press, 1986)] who describe family circumstances as a key factor in decision-making relating to women, but much less important in decision-making in relation to men . . .

Taken as a whole, these findings suggest that there remains a risk that some magistrates will resort to their 'common sense' (and a gendered 'commonsense' at that) as the best arbiter of what is right, despite the fact that new magistrates receive training designed to inform them of the inherent dangers of making decisions on the basis of stereotypes and on the dangers of relying on non-verbal cues.

The difficulty to be addressed is one of finding ways to challenge stereotypical pictures of men and women, without ignoring the fact that they often (but *not* always) do have different needs and responsibilities (and these are often precisely the needs and responsibilities which fuel the stereotypes). It may also be that the time to recognise such differences is in the shape and content of particular sentences rather than in the choice between different levels of sentence, but discussion of this is beyond our remit. A number of changes may be helpful here:

• Increased emphasis on gender issues in training to counteract the fact that so many magistrates have comparatively little experience of dealing with women in the courtroom. This is probably best accomplished through the 'human awareness' element of magistrates' training which encourages them to reflect on how cultural and gender specific stereotypes inform their practices and perceptions in the courtroom in ways which could lead to unfair sentencing. Currently, such training tends to focus on race issues and it would be unfortunate if combining race and gender in this way masked the importance of either issue. It is also important to note that while 'human awareness' training is popular, it does not appear to have been subject to any large scale or systematic evaluation.

- Training on gender (and race) should be made available to *all* magistrates rather than to new magistrates alone so as to ensure that resistant or reluctant magistrates are exposed to the issues as a matter of routine.

- Where magistrates may feel that their sentencing options are constrained by a (male or female) offender's childcare responsibilities, the Probation Service should use PSRs [pre-sentence reports] to draw attention to the fact that suitable childcare arrangements can be made.

- Increased feedback on sentencing patterns in each court – particularly patterns relating to men and women – may also assist magistrates in the general task of achieving consistency in approach.

Finally, we would suggest that there are at least three questions which require further exploration and discussion:

- to what extent does training help to address the tendency to use gender-stereotyping in sentencing?

- to what extent do gender, race and other factors have an interactive effect on sentencing?

- are the decisions of professional sentencers subject to the same influences as those of lay magistrates?

6

FIVE THEMES REVISITED

The final chapter of the book is divided into five sections, each of which revisits one of the key themes which we have identified.

1. POST-TRIAL REVIEW OF DECISION-MAKING: THE APPEALS PROCESS

(a) Appeals: overview of purposes and procedures

Appeals procedures provide a mechanism for reviewing the decisions of trial courts. We saw in Chapters 4 and 5 above that the lower courts have a degree of discretion when interpreting and applying the law governing trials and sentencing. For example, when considering an argument that evidence should be excluded under s 78 of the Police and Criminal Evidence Act 1984 (PACE), a court must decide whether admitting the evidence will have 'such an adverse effect on the fairness of the proceedings' that it ought not to be admitted; when considering whether to impose a custodial sentence for an offence, a court must consider whether the offence 'is so serious that only such a sentence can be justified' (Criminal Justice Act 1991, s 1(2)). By itself, the wording of these provisions gives little guidance as to their application, and this leaves considerable scope for different courts to interpret them differently. The appeals process therefore provides a means of increasing the consistency of decision-making in the lower courts through giving guidance on the meaning of provisions such as s 78 of PACE and s 1 of the Criminal Justice Act 1991. We saw examples of how these provisions have been interpreted (and thus how the discretion of judges in trial courts has been reduced) in earlier chapters. The promotion of consistency through the reduction of discretion, however, is not the only function of the criminal appeals process. Appeals also exist as a means of doing justice: sometimes judges make mistakes, such as when they misinterpret the law; appeals are an important means of correcting their decisions. Sometimes the decision of a trial court will lead to public outcry; an appeal offers a means of responding to public unease about the administration of criminal justice. Sometimes, although a court applies the law correctly, the magistrates or the jury make a mistake of fact and convict an innocent person; appeals offer a means of protecting the innocent by overturning such mistaken convictions.

An appeals system which took as its primary concern the oversight of judicial interpretation of the law would allow both the prosecution and defence to appeal at the end of any trial. By allowing as many appeals as possible, the rules applied by trial courts would be subjected to thorough review and judicial discretion would be controlled effectively. The criminal appeals system in England and Wales, however, does not work like this, because the control of trial court decision-making is not its sole concern. Other factors, such as efficiency, finality and justice, play a role in shaping the appeals system. The hypothetical appeal-maximising system outlined at the beginning of this paragraph would run the risk of swamping the appeal courts with unmeritorious appeals. The number of appeals must be limited, and to this end many appeals require leave from the appellate court before they will be heard: this acts as a sort of 'quality control' for the appeals heard. An appeal-maximising system would also undermine the finality of trial verdicts. If any and every verdict was subject to appellate revision, verdicts might come to be regarded as rather unauthoritative, as no more than first attempts to get the right answer. The resulting uncertainty would create concerns about justice. Defendants who were acquitted by trial courts could never be certain that an appeal would not result in their conviction, and prosecutors could attempt to ensure that the exercise of jury equity (discussed in Chapter 4) never prevailed. Because of such concerns, some verdicts are not subject to appeal.

The structure of the appeals system is depicted in Extract 6.1.1 below. The figures depict the appeal route from the Crown Court and the appeal route from the magistrates' court; they also show who can appeal and whether or not leave is needed. For more detailed accounts of appeals procedures, see Wasik (1998) on sentencing appeals, and Sprack (1995, pp 312–372) on both sentencing and verdict appeals.

Extract 6.1.1

R Pattenden, *English Criminal Appeals 1844–1994* (1996) pp 3–4

Figure 1

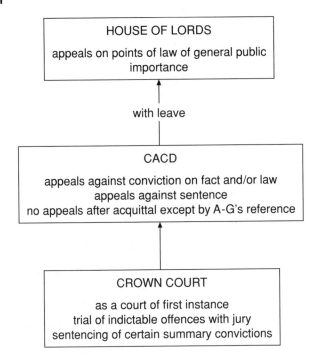

Figure 2

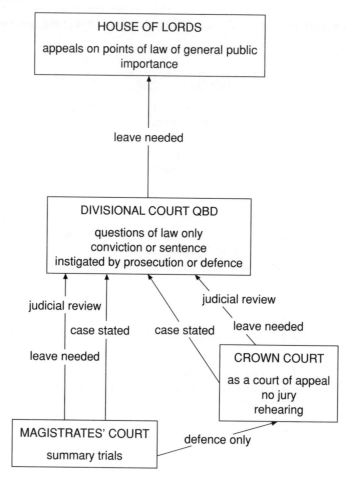

Some aspects of the structure of the appeals system merit further discussion. The first point to note is the asymmetry in appeal rights: generally, the defence are given more avenues of appeal than the prosecution. Consider appeals against sentence. After being sentenced in the Crown Court, and subject to leave being granted, a defendant can appeal to the Court of Appeal in the hopes that it will reduce his or her sentence. Defence appeals against sentence have provided the Court of Appeal with the means of developing a body of sentencing law and so have helped to give guidance to Crown Court judges on sentencing issues. The best illustration of this process is where the Lord Chief Justice has taken the opportunity offered by defence appeals to deliver guideline judgments, setting out the range of sentences appropriate for specific offences (for example, *Billam* (1986) 8 Cr App R (S) 48 (see Extract 5.4.6 above), a guideline judgment on sentencing in rape cases). Until 1989, however, the prosecution was unable to appeal in cases where it thought that a sentence was too lenient. So although defence appeals offered guidance on the maximum sentence appropriate for an offence, trial courts had less guidance on minimum sentences. Following disquiet about some cases where judges gave what seemed to be especially lenient sentences, s 36 of the Criminal Justice Act 1988 allowed sentences thought to be too lenient to be referred to the Court of Appeal by the Attorney General. Because of concerns about finality and unfairness to defendants, however, this procedure is perhaps less useful as a means of providing guidance to trial courts than it might otherwise be. On a reference, the court will only increase a sentence where it is judged to be 'outside the range of sentences which the judge, applying his mind to all the relevant factors, could reasonably consider appropriate' (*Attorney General's Reference No 4 of 1989* (1989) 11 Cr App R (S) 517, 521), and it will discount any increase to reflect the uncertainty experienced by the defendant during the referral process. The court is none too explicit about what the sentence should have been had these factors not been taken into account, and this blunts the effectiveness of these judgments as guidance for trial courts (see generally Shute, 1994).

The asymmetry in appeal rights is again marked when we consider appeals against verdicts. When a defendant has been acquitted following trial in the Crown Court, the prosecution has, in general, no right of appeal. There are two minor exceptions to this. The first is where the Attorney General refers a point of law that has been at issue in a case to the Court of Appeal for determination. This allows significant points of law to be addressed by the appellate courts, but, because of the importance of the finality of acquittals, the defendant's acquittal is unaffected by any decision made on a referral. The second exception is that where an acquittal is 'tainted' (for example, where jurors or witnesses involved with the case have been subjected to threats), a defendant may face a second trial on the original charge, but only after a complex process (Criminal Procedure and Investigations Act 1996, ss 54–57). We should note that the restriction on acquittal appeals exacts a

561

price. There is no remedy available when a defendant charged with a serious crime has been acquitted because of a misinterpretation of the law by a judge or because of a jury verdict which is against the weight of evidence. Additionally, the restriction on acquittal appeals means that the Court of Appeal has less opportunity to rule on the way in which trial courts interpret the law. For example, if courts are routinely interpreting the law of evidence so as to be overly lenient towards defendants, the Court of Appeal is deprived of the opportunity to lay down a different interpretation. Robertson (1989) argues that this has led to particular problems in the development of the law on s 78 of PACE (see the discussion in Chapter 4, pp 447–50). A similar criticism may be levelled at the interpretation of the Sexual Offences (Amendment) Act 1976, s 2. This provision restricts the circumstances in which defendants can explore the previous sexual history of rape complainants in court, but trial courts have often been accused of ignoring it (Adler, 1982).

Bearing these problems in mind, we should ask whether there are good reasons for restricting appeals against acquittal in Crown Court cases. Pattenden (1996, pp 283–289) has examined the arguments for the restriction, and suggests that they are not especially convincing. One justification is the double jeopardy principle, from which it is argued that it is unfair that a person should twice run the risk of conviction for the same offence. But it is not clear just why this is unfair, nor whether any unfairness outweighs the harm done (to society, to the victim and to the reputation of the legal system) by an unjustified acquittal. Further, the Crown does have the right to appeal on points of law after an acquittal in the magistrates' court, but this is not usually regarded as raising double jeopardy concerns. Other justifications for the restriction draw on the importance of trial by jury. It might be argued that Crown appeals from jury verdicts would undermine faith in the jury system. However, a similar argument applies to defence appeals as well, yet defence appeals are allowed. Alternatively, an argument against allowing Crown appeals might be that this would undermine jury equity (discussed in Chapter 4), which many take to be one of the key merits of the jury system. Pattenden considers the argument for jury equity to be the 'most sophisticated argument for the prohibition on Crown appeals' (1996, p 287). There are two responses to the argument. The first is to point to the controversial nature of jury equity itself. The second is to note that jury equity cuts both ways: it may result in the conviction of a person who is technically innocent. In this situation, the defendant could appeal. Therefore, unless 'acquittal' jury equity is regarded as more worthy of protection than 'conviction' jury equity, this argument against Crown appeals is flawed. But even if the arguments which appeal to a defence of jury trials are thought to be convincing, they do not apply to cases where the Crown wishes to appeal on the grounds that the judge made an error of law. Other common law countries do allow Crown appeals in such cases and some commentators have argued that they should be allowed in this country too (Robertson, 1989; Ockelton, 1995).

(b) Miscarriages of justice

The right of an innocent person not to be convicted of a crime must surely be regarded as fundamental. We noted in Chapter 4 that the high value accorded to this right means that the rules of criminal evidence and procedure are weighted towards acquitting the guilty rather than convicting the innocent. Yet in spite of this, we cannot guarantee that innocent people are never convicted. It is therefore important that there exist effective procedures for reviewing verdicts when it is alleged that a miscarriage of justice has occurred. It is apparent, however, that in the past the appeals system in England and Wales has not fulfilled this role as effectively as it might have done. The case that became known as the Birmingham six case serves as an example. In 1975 six men were convicted for their involvement in two serious terrorist bombings in Birmingham. The primary evidence against them was their confessions (which they alleged had been beaten out of them by the police) and forensic science evidence which purportedly showed that they had handled explosives. They immediately appealed to the Court of Appeal, but their appeal was dismissed in spite of the fact that the court agreed that the trial judge had 'unhappily [gone] somewhat far' in letting the jury know his views about the case during his summing up (see the related discussion in Chapter 4, pp 410–16). There continued to be unease about the men's convictions. In the mid-1980s a television documentary cast doubt on the reliability of the forensic science evidence in the case, an MP published a book in which he claimed to have tracked down and interviewed the real bombers, and a former police officer supported the claims of police violence. In 1987 the Home Secretary referred the case back to the Court of Appeal. The court dismissed the appeal, with the Lord Chief Justice remarking that 'the longer this hearing has gone on, the more convinced this court has become that the verdict of the jury was correct'. In 1990, however, the case was again referred to the Court of Appeal. On this occasion the appeal was allowed and the defendant's convictions were quashed on the grounds that both the confessions and the scientific evidence were suspect.

The Birmingham six case raises a number of important issues about miscarriages of justice. We can broadly divide the issues into two groups: (i) Why do miscarriages of justice occur? (ii) Are the procedures for correcting miscarriages of justice satisfactory?

(i) Why do miscarriages of justice occur?

The case of the Birmingham six is not the only high profile miscarriage of justice to have come to light in recent years. There have been a number of such cases, and many of them have features in common. Below is a table summarising the principal flaws in the evidence presented to the courts in some of these cases (a number of which have been mentioned briefly in

Table 6.1

Case	Date of conviction/ Date appeal allowed	Principal evidential problems	See further
Guildford four	1975/1989	Confessions Pressure on witness to change story Disclosure	Kee (1989) May (1994)
Birmingham six	1975/1990	Confessions Forensic science evidence	Mullin (1993) (1991) 93 Cr App R 287
Maguire family	1976/1991	Forensic science evidence Disclosure (forensic scientists)	Kee (1989) May (1990, 1992) (1992) 94 Cr App R 133
Judith Ward	1974/1992	Confession Forensic science evidence Disclosure (forensic scientists)	(1993) 96 Cr App R 1
Cardiff three	1990/1992	Confession	(1992) 97 Cr App R 99
Taylor sisters	1992/1993	Disclosure Media prejudice	(1993) 98 Cr App R 361
Bridgewater three	1979/1997	Disclosure Confessions	Foot (1993)

earlier chapters). The list of evidential flaws is not intended to be exhaustive, and one could easily point to other features shared by the cases. For example, several of the cases involved defendants charged with acts connected to IRA terrorist attacks, and in these cases the police were likely to be under considerable pressure to gain convictions.

Given that the same problems have occurred a number of times in these cases, it is worth reviewing those steps which have been taken, or which might be taken, to prevent their reoccurrence.

(1) *Confessions.* It is obvious that unreliable confession evidence has played a substantial role in several of these cases. We considered the problem of confession evidence in Chapter 3, pp 289–303. Owing to psychological research, there is now more awareness of the potential for false confessions. If the provisions of PACE and the Codes of Practice are strictly applied, the chances of false confession will be reduced, but not eliminated. The courts have not yet adopted a rule requiring the corroboration of confessions.

(2) *Forensic science.* Flawed forensic science evidence has played a role in a number of miscarriage of justice cases. In several of the cases in the table above the defence criticised the forensic science evidence that was presented

at trial, but, although many of the criticisms have now been shown to have been well founded, they were presumably not considered to be convincing by the jurors during the original trials. Where there are conflicts over scientific evidence in court, juries face obvious problems because they are not in a good position to choose between the conflicting claims of expert witnesses. To that extent, forensic science evidence will always cause problems for the criminal justice system. It is also important that defendants have access to experts who are able to challenge forensic science evidence used by the prosecution, and here the situation has probably improved since cases such as that of the Birmingham six occurred, because there is now a number of institutions, staffed by experienced forensic scientists, which exist primarily to undertake forensic science work for defendants.

(3) *Disclosure.* For some time, the prosecution has been under a duty to disclose relevant material to the defence. However, the prosecution may sometimes be tempted to gain a tactical advantage over the defence by choosing not to disclose evidence which undermines its case. In the cases in the table above, the failure to disclose was sometimes due to the police (failing to disclose an adverse witness statement in the Taylor sisters' case) and sometimes due to forensic scientists (failing to disclose test results which undermined their evidence). Because of adversarial pressures, non-disclosure will probably always be a problem in the criminal justice system. Recent reforms in this area are unlikely to have a significant effect. The Criminal Procedure and Investigations Act 1996 actually reduces the amount of information which must be disclosed to the defence by the prosecution, and campaigning groups such as JUSTICE have argued that this may lead to miscarriages of justice in the future (JUSTICE, 1995). A new Code of Practice issued under the 1996 Act may, however, clarify the obligations on police officers as regards the recording and disclosure of material relevant to their investigations (for discussion of the provisions and how they will affect defendants, see Leng, 1997).

(ii) Correcting miscarriages of justice

As already noted, the appeals system in England and Wales is not an 'appeal-maximising' system. Owing to concerns about efficiency and finality, there are various hurdles that appellants must surmount before their appeals will be heard. Similar concerns influence the way the Court of Appeal approaches those cases that it does hear. In addition to efficiency and finality, the court has to be aware of the relationship between its decisions and the original jury verdict. If it is too ready to overturn jury verdicts it may, by implication, cast doubt on the general ability of juries to make good decisions. Because of the impact of these concerns on the procedure and decision-making of the Court of Appeal, the court is often criticised for being too reluctant to acknowledge that a miscarriage of justice has taken place. An example of this is the 1987 appeal of the Birmingham six where, despite the fact that substantial doubt had been cast on the scientific evidence, the court did not overturn the convictions. In this section, we consider these criticisms in more detail.

(1) *The requirement of leave to appeal.* Defendants need leave from the Court of Appeal before it will hear the substance of their appeals. (There is an exception where the trial judge grants a certificate stating that the case is fit for appeal, but certificates are rarely granted (none were granted in 1994), and the Court of Appeal has discouraged their use.) The process of granting leave is usually delegated to a single High Court judge who considers the papers submitted by the defendant. It is not clear what test the judge should apply at this stage, though it has been suggested that it is whether the court feels the need to hear argument from the prosecution (Pattenden, 1996, p 98, citing *Mealey* [1975] Crim LR 154). Most applications (somewhat over half) are refused (see table 1 in Extract 6.1.2 below). Appellants who are refused leave at this first stage have the right to renew their applications, in which case the application is heard by a full court of two or three appeal judges sitting in public. At this second stage, the success rate is around 20 per cent.

Extract 6.1.2

Lord Chancellor's Department, *Judicial Statistics England and Wales for the Year 1996* **(1997) p 12**

Table 1 Court of Appeal (Criminal Division): Results of applications for leave to appeal, 1988–96[1]

	1988	1989	1990	1991	1992	1993	1994	1995	1996
Received:									
Conviction	1,644	1,821	1,705	1,957	2,118	2,134	2,342	2,393	2,288
Sentence	5,571	5,255	4,602	4,714	4,959	4,848	5,050	5,794	6,436
TOTAL	7,235	7,076	6,307	6,671	7,077	6,982	7,392	8,187	8,724
Considered by single judge:									
Conviction:									
Granted	346	366	443	569	517	601	514	472	419
Refused	997	1,052	1,009	1,038	1,035	1,088	1,376	1,444	1,429
Sentence:									
Granted	1,566	1,523	1,579	1,623	1,541	1,597	1,213	1,263	1,544
Refused	4,260	3,912	3,308	3,378	3,187	2,863	3,675	3,846	4,629
TOTAL	7,169	6,853	6,339	6,608	6,280	6,149	6,778	7,025	8,021

Table 1   (cont'd)

	1988	1989	1990	1991	1992	1993	1994	1995	1996
Applications renewed:									
Conviction	349	340	429	344	406	372	527	579	474
Sentence	833	770	679	672	505	347	573	635	823
TOTAL	1,182	1,110	1,108	1,016	911	719	1,100	1,214	1,297
Applications to renew granted by Full Court:									
Conviction	69	72	101	93	50	73	27	123	155
Sentence	135	166	209	196	95	49	56	151	146
TOTAL	204	238	310	289	145	122	83	274	301

(1) These figures relate to applications rather than cases.

Table 2   Court of Appeal (Criminal Division): Results of appeals heard by the Full Court, 1988–96[1]

	1988	1989	1990	1991	1992	1993	1994	1995	1996
Conviction:									
Allowed	223	211	256	269	299	402	351	253	250
Dismissed	255	240	337	308	370	524	577	521	469
Sentence:									
Allowed	1,149	1,314	1,526	1,219	1,049	1,309	1,384	1,222	1,379
Dismissed	554	508	492	514	439	600	643	538	603
Number of retrials ordered	n/a	1	3	15	12	20	51	52	53

(1) These figures relate to appellants rather than cases.

Of the appeals heard by the Full Court during 1996, 35 per cent (250) against conviction were allowed and 70 per cent (1,379) against sentence were allowed (33 per cent and 69 per cent in 1995). 53 retrials were ordered by the Full Court compared to 52 in 1995.

There exist two other mechanisms acting as a check on the number of appeals which will be considered by the court. The first is the time limit on appeals: an appeal must be lodged within 28 days of conviction. Although the Court of Appeal has the power to grant extensions, it does so rarely. Secondly, there is the 'loss of time' rule. By the time a defendant who is serving a custodial sentence has an application for appeal heard, he or she will have served part of the sentence. However, the Court of Appeal has the power to sanction appellants whose appeals are judged to be unmeritorious by ordering that part of the time that the defendant has already served (up

567

to a maximum of 90 days) does not count towards the sentence. This power is used infrequently, and in practice the Court of Appeal appears to have accepted a maximum of 28 days loss of time (JUSTICE, 1994a, p 7). In spite of this, the rule does seem to act as a deterrent, because the fact that it is rarely used does not appear to have filtered through to defendants or their legal advisers. JUSTICE (1994a, p 7) remarks that: '[t]he effect is to transform a minor check on wholly groundless applications into a major barrier in some meritorious cases'. The European Court of Human Rights has accepted that the rule is justifiable (*Monnell and Morris v UK* (1988) 10 EHRR 205).

The present system of granting leave to appeal is open to criticism because it leaves a large degree of unstructured discretion to the judges who decide the applications. Not all of these judges are specialist criminal judges. One indication of the width of discretion granted is the fact that there is 'considerable variation in the frequency with which leave is given by individual judges' (Pattenden, 1996, p 99). Another indication is that a considerable proportion of applications refused by the single judge go on to be granted by the full court, and some of these become successful appeals. A further example of the vagaries of the process is given by JUSTICE, commenting on a case in which a defendant appealed against sentence:

> [the] solicitor had in error sent in two sets of appeal papers in the same case. Two single judge decisions followed, one granting and one refusing leave. Both decisions had been made, at different times, by the same judge. The first decision was favourable and a custodial sentence was reduced to probation on appeal. (1994, p 8)

JUSTICE argues that there should be statutory criteria governing the decision to grant or refuse leave, which should also place a duty on the single judge to give detailed reasons for a refusal. It also calls for the abolition of the loss of time rule (1994a, pp 7–8).

(2) *Presenting fresh evidence in the Court of Appeal.* It is often noted that, rather than retrying or rehearing cases, the Court of Appeal *reviews* them. The appeal judges will consider the transcript of proceedings from the trial court, and hear argument from the Crown and the defence. Their decision will be based on these sources rather than on a thoroughgoing examination of all the evidence against the appellant. The court will not generally hear 'fresh evidence' (evidence that was not presented at the original trial), although under the Criminal Appeal Act 1968, s 23 it has a discretion to do so if this is 'necessary or expedient in the interests of justice'. This discretion is structured by the factors listed in s 23(2) which require the court to have regard in particular to:

(1) whether the evidence appears to the court to be capable of belief;
(2) whether it appears to the court that the evidence may afford any ground for allowing the appeal;
(3) whether the evidence would have been admissible in the proceedings from which the appeal lies on an issue which is the subject of the appeal; and

(4) whether there is a reasonable explanation for the failure to adduce the evidence in those proceedings.

Parts of the Criminal Appeal Act 1968, including s 23, were amended by the Criminal Appeal Act 1995. This Act modified the powers of the Court of Appeal in response to criticisms of the way it operated following the miscarriage of justice cases of the early 1990s and the report of the Royal Commission on Criminal Justice (which cautiously suggested that the court was interpreting its power to hear fresh evidence too restrictively (1993, Ch 10, paras 55–60)). Because these changes are fairly recent, it is difficult to assess what effect they will have on the working practices of the court. However, the amendments to s 23 are only minor, and to date the court has not interpreted them as introducing any substantive change to its powers (see *Jones* [1997] 1 Cr App R 86). However, this should be seen against the fact that Pattenden, in her review of the case law, detects a softening of the court's attitude towards fresh evidence in the years preceding the amendments (1996, pp 136–138; for an example, see *Ahluwalia* [1992] 4 All ER 889).

Is the Court of Appeal right to be reluctant to admit fresh evidence in criminal appeals? In *Stafford* [1973] 3 All ER 762, at p 753 the court remarked that:

> public mischief would ensue and the legal process would be indefinitely prolonged were it the case that evidence produced at any time will generally be admitted by this court when verdicts are being reviewed. There must be some curbs.

The Royal Commission on Criminal Justice (RCCJ) accepted that scepticism about fresh evidence was justifiable, because such evidence 'can, and often will be, manufactured' and because defendants should not be encouraged to see Crown Court trials 'as nothing more than a practice run' (1993, Ch 10, para 55), though it cited no evidence to support the former claim. On the other hand, Pattenden remarks that:

> An appellate court genuinely concerned to avoid miscarriages of justice should admit all evidence which could be believed by a reasonable jury, which could have affected the outcome of the case [and] that has not been deliberately saved up for appeal, should the accused be convicted. (1996, p 138)

These different points of view may perhaps be explained with reference to the fact that the Court of Appeal has to perform more than one role. On the one hand, the court should root out miscarriages of justice (the role emphasised by Pattenden), but, on the other hand, as a court of law it is aware that its decisions have an impact beyond the instant case (as recognised by the RCCJ and the *Stafford* court). The more the court receives fresh evidence, the more defendants may view trials as practice runs and may save up or manufacture evidence for the appeal. It is difficult to see how the court can reconcile these two roles.

(3) *The test for deciding the appeal.* Once a defendant has got leave to appeal and has presented the grounds of appeal and any fresh evidence, the court

must decide whether the appeal should be allowed. The court applies the test in s 2 (as amended) of the Criminal Appeal Act 1968:

(1) subject to the provisions of this Act, the Court of Appeal –
   (a) shall allow an appeal against conviction if they think that the conviction is unsafe; and
   (b) shall dismiss such an appeal in any other case.

This section was amended in 1995. The amendment constituted a significant simplification of the criteria for a successful appeal, but it seems that, in practice, there has been little substantive change (see the court's comments in *Hickmet* [1996] Crim LR 588). This means that the pre-1995 case law is still relevant to the interpretation of s 2.

Before s 2 was amended, conviction appeals would be allowed where there had been an error of law or material irregularity during the trial, or if the verdict was 'unsafe and unsatisfactory'. The leading case on the interpretation of 'unsafe and unsatisfactory' was *Cooper* [1969] 1 QB 267, which established what became known as the 'lurking doubt' test:

> In cases of this kind the court must in the end ask itself a subjective question, whether we are content to let the matter stand as it is, or whether there is not some lurking doubt in our minds which makes us wonder whether an injustice has been done. This is a reaction which may not be based strictly on the evidence as such; it is a reaction which can be produced by the general feel of the case as the court experiences it. (at p 271)

The subjectivity of the lurking doubt test is one reason why the Court of Appeal's practice in applying s 2 has been criticised. Even where there are good reasons for being suspicious of parts of the evidence against an appellant, this may not succeed in triggering a lurking doubt in the judges' minds. The subjectivity of the test means that, in practice, the general attitude which the court takes towards lurking doubt appeals is as important as any arguments about flaws in the evidence which the appellant may present. Commentators who have reviewed the court's handling of appeals against conviction agree that this attitude is one of reluctance to admit a lurking doubt. For example, in a sample of 204 successful appeals Malleson could identify only 11 which were allowed on the grounds of a lurking doubt (1993, p 22). In a survey of reported cases between 1973 and 1988, JUSTICE found only six lurking doubt cases. It concluded that 'the restrictive manner in which the Court of Appeal interprets its powers appears at times to be ineffective in curing miscarriages of justice' (1989, pp 49–50). The Royal Commission on Criminal Justice agreed that the court was too reluctant to quash convictions in the absence of any error of law, and suggested that this was due to its being too deferential towards jury verdicts (1993, Ch 10, para 3).

A closer look at the way the Court of Appeal has approached some cases will help to ground these criticisms. In the 1987 appeal of the Birmingham six there was much argument about the credibility of the scientific evidence which had been presented at the trial. Commenting on the 1987 appeal,

Nobles, Schiff and Shaldon suggest that the court was extremely reluctant to reject scientific evidence which had been accepted by the trial jury, unless the appellants could give a plausible explanation for the original test results:

> much of the evidence [at the appeal] concerned the unwillingness of scientific witnesses to reach the conclusion, on the basis of test results, that the appellants had been in contact with [explosives]. But this is not the question which concerned the Court. They asked: what other, more likely explanation can you give? (1993, p 14)

A court more willing to overturn jury verdicts would have accepted that the substantial doubt thrown on the scientific evidence rendered the verdicts unsafe. Similar criticisms have been levelled at the Court of Appeal in another case involving scientific evidence. The Maguire family was convicted in 1976 of offences involving the handling of explosives. The Crown case had been that the scientific evidence showed that the family had deliberately handled explosives. Later research cast considerable doubt on this evidence and the Maguire family's convictions were reviewed by the Court of Appeal in 1991. Although it quashed the convictions, the court did so on particularly narrow grounds, viz that it was possible that the appellants may have been innocently contaminated with explosives. Again, this suggests that the court was looking for alternative explanations of the evidence, rather than accepting that the flaws in the scientific evidence automatically rendered the verdicts unsafe and unsatisfactory. This reasoning has been criticised by, among others, Sir John May (1992, pp 2–3).

(4) *The test in fresh evidence cases.* The question of how the Court of Appeal should approach the original jury verdict is particularly pertinent in cases where the court admits fresh evidence. In such cases, there would appear to be three possible approaches. First, the court could conclude that the existence of fresh evidence automatically makes the conviction unsafe, because, had the jury heard the evidence, it might have come to a different conclusion. Secondly, the court could try to imagine how the original jury, or a reasonable jury, might have reacted to the fresh evidence. Thirdly, the court might simply rely on its own judgment of whether the new evidence, combined with the other evidence, makes the verdict unsafe. The question was considered by the House of Lords in *Stafford v DPP*:

Extract 6.1.3

Stafford v DPP [1973] 3 All ER 763, pp 765–766

Where such evidence is called, the task of the Court of Appeal may be extremely difficult. They have not heard the evidence the jury have heard. They can only judge of that from the shorthand note. They know, however, that the jury by their verdict have accepted some part, it may not be all, of the evidence for the prosecution and at least sufficient of it to satisfy them of the accused's guilt. They know too that the jury must have rejected the defence put forward.

Counsel for the appellant Stafford argued that all the Court of Appeal was entitled to do was to consider whether the fresh evidence was relevant and capable of belief. He based this argument primarily on some observations of Lord Parker CJ in *R v Parks* [[1961] 3 All ER 633, [1961] 1 WLR 1484] where Lord Parker CJ said that it was not for the Court of Criminal Appeal to decide whether the fresh evidence was to be believed or not. Lord Parker CJ was then stating the principles which the court would apply in relation to the exercise of its discretion to admit fresh evidence under s 9 of the Criminal Appeal Act 1907 (now replaced by s 23 of the Criminal Appeal Act 1968). He said the evidence must be relevant and credible. Then he said that it was not for the court to decide whether it was to be believed. I agree that in deciding whether to admit fresh evidence, the court, which at that stage has not heard the evidence, has not to decide whether it is to be believed but I do not agree that, when the court has heard the evidence, it has not to consider what weight, if any, should be given to it. Lord Parker CJ's fourth principle, as he called it, was that the court, after considering the evidence, would go on to consider whether there might have been a reasonable doubt in the minds of the jury as to the guilt of the appellant if that evidence had been given together with the other evidence at the trial. I cannot see how the court can consider this question without considering what weight should be given to the fresh evidence they have heard; and I do not see that this principle is applicable to the question whether the evidence is to be admitted. It is only after it has been admitted and, it may be, subjected to cross-examination, that its weight can be assessed and the court decide whether it might have affected the jury's verdict.

I do not suggest that in determining whether a verdict is unsafe or unsatisfactory, it is a wrong approach for the court to pose the question: 'Might this new evidence have led to the jury returning a verdict of not guilty?' If the court thinks that it would or might, the court will no doubt conclude that the verdict was unsafe or unsatisfactory. Counsel for the appellant Stafford in the course of his argument drew attention to the many cases in which, since 1908, and since the amendment made in 1966, the court has quashed a conviction saying that in the light of the fresh evidence the jury might have come to a different conclusion, but I do not think that it is established as a rule of law that, in every fresh evidence case, the court must decide what they think the jury might or would have done if they had heard that evidence. That it is a convenient approach and a reasonable one to make, I do not deny. When a court has said that, it means and can only mean that they think that the fresh evidence might have led to a different result to the case, and that in consequence the verdict was unsafe or unsatisfactory.

Counsel strongly urged that the court should recognise that reasonable men can come to different conclusions on contested issues of fact and that, although the court came to the conclusion that the fresh evidence raised no reasonable doubt as to the guilt of the accused, they should nonetheless quash the conviction if they thought that a jury might reasonably take a different view.

572

I do not agree. It would, in my opinion, be wrong for the court to say 'in our view this evidence does not give rise to any reasonable doubt about the guilt of the accused. We do not ourselves consider that an unsafe or unsatisfactory verdict was returned but as the jury who heard the case might conceivably have taken a different view from ours, we quash the conviction' for Parliament has, in terms, said that the court should only quash a conviction if, there being no error of law or material irregularity at the trial, 'they think' the verdict was unsafe or unsatisfactory. They have to decide and Parliament has not required them or given them power to quash a verdict if they think that a jury might conceivably reach a different conclusion from that to which they have come. If the court has no reasonable doubt about the verdict, it follows that the court does not think that the jury could have one; and, conversely, if the court says that a jury might in the light of the new evidence have a reasonable doubt, that means that the court has a reasonable doubt.

The approach endorsed in *Stafford* has been the subject of considerable criticism (Devlin, 1979, pp 148–176; Royal Commission on Criminal Justice, 1993, Ch 10, para 62) because it presumes that the opinions of judges are equal to those of juries. Yet one reason for having trial by jury, rather than trial by judge alone, is that it is widely believed that the collective experience of 12 lay people produces decisions different to those that would be obtained from professional judges. In addition to this, juries have the advantage of hearing the original evidence live, whereas appeal judges rely largely on transcripts.

If the Court of Appeal was to take the first approach outlined above (always quashing convictions in fresh evidence cases), it would not mean that defendants in fresh evidence cases would automatically escape liability. Since 1966, the court has had the power to order a retrial in fresh evidence cases (this was extended to all cases in 1988), where 'the interests of justice so require' (Criminal Appeal Act 1968, s 7). However, retrials have been rare in fresh evidence cases, and this itself may be due to the approach adopted in *Stafford*, because where the court has, under the test in that case, decided that a conviction is unsafe, it would be odd to order a retrial with the risk that the defendant will then be convicted (see O'Connor, 1990, p 621). On the other hand, the use of retrials in such situations would be congruent with a high degree of respect for the institution of trial by jury. In recent years, the court appears to have responded to its critics, because it is ordering an increased number of retrials (see Extract 6.1.2, table 2 above).

Whatever the approach that is taken towards retrials, there will always be some cases where a retrial is not a realistic option, such as where a long period of time has passed since the offence was committed, or where media coverage has made a fair trial impossible. While the RCCJ was unanimous in recommending that the court use the option of a retrial more often, it split (6:5) on how the court should approach cases where a retrial was unfeasible. The majority thought that the appeal should then be automatically allowed, while the minority thought that the court should attempt to resolve the matter by itself (1993, Ch 10, para 66). Neither retrials nor the test to be applied in fresh evidence cases are addressed in the amendments introduced by the Criminal Appeal Act 1995, so the resolution of these points is left to the Court of Appeal itself. In *Jones* [1997] 1 Cr App R 86 the court re-endorsed the *Stafford* approach to fresh evidence cases.

(5) *Post-appeal remedies.* If the court rejects an appeal, that is not necessarily an end to the matter. Where a point of law of general public importance is in issue, the defendant may, with leave, appeal to the House of Lords. In cases where the primary issue is that the original court made a mistake about the facts, this will not be an option. However, in such cases there is a possibility that the case will be referred back to the Court of Appeal. Before 1997, the power to make a referral was in the hands of the Home Secretary, who was also responsible for commissioning investigations of alleged miscarriages of justice. This system was frequently criticised. It was thought that the Home Secretary was often unduly reluctant to refer cases to the Court of Appeal. If the Home Secretary did refer a case to the Court of Appeal, there was an implication that the court had been wrong to refuse the first appeal. This raised issues about the separation of powers (should the executive be put in the position of suggesting that the judiciary has made a mistake?), and this probably led the Court of Appeal to take an extremely critical attitude towards referral cases. As we saw above, in the referral appeals of the Birmingham six and the Maguire family, the court appeared to be looking for any explanations that would justify the original verdict, rather than accepting that the appeal should be allowed once the evidence had been shown to be flawed. (For further discussion of the court's attitude in referral cases, see Pattenden, 1996, pp 367–377.)

In 1997 the Home Secretary's role in referring cases to the Court of Appeal was ended. A new body, the Criminal Cases Review Commission (CCRC) was set up. Broadly speaking, the CCRC's role is to investigate miscarriages of justice and refer possible miscarriages to the Court of Appeal for determination. The new arrangements raise several issues:

The role and powers of the CCRC. The CCRC has a wide jurisdiction. It will consider the claims of defendants that they have been wrongly convicted or sentenced in either the Crown Court or the magistrates' court. When it considers that a miscarriage of justice has occurred, it will refer the case to the Court of Appeal or, if the application involves a case heard in the magistrates' court, to the Crown Court. The CCRC will normally only consider cases where the defendant has already appealed unsuccessfully, but it may exceptionally consider cases where there has been no appeal. It has 14 members, though not all of these will work full-time. There are also 25 case workers to assist the commissioners. The CCRC will receive a large number of applications from defendants who allege that they have been the victim of a miscarriage of justice. Before 1997, the Home Office was receiving around 700–800

574

petitions a year, and it is expected that the CCRC will receive substantially more than this. At the end of its first year, the CCRC had received more than 1,300 applications (*The Guardian*, 21 March 1998). It will not be easy to review all of these cases in detail, and in practice, much will depend on the quality of application received. To have much chance of having their cases thoroughly reviewed, defendants will probably need a lawyer to help draft the application. Legal aid is available to pay for this under the Green Form (means tested) scheme. This allows a basic two hours of the solicitor's time; after this the solicitor will have to apply to the Legal Aid office to get an extension.

The CCRC will have two important decisions to make in each case it reviews. First, it will have to decide whether a decision will be made on the basis of the application form, along with any other information obtained from the defendant and his or her solicitor, or whether some further investigation is needed. The CCRC has the power to commission the police, or other agencies or individuals, to carry out investigations for it. Like the Police Complaints Authority (discussed in Chapter 3 above) the CCRC can supervise investigations and this may consist of more or less active involvement. However, although the ability to commission its own investigations is an important mark of the CCRC's independence, in practice the number of investigations commissioned will depend on the CCRC's budget, and so it will be indirectly affected by government funding.

Secondly, after investigating a case the Commission will have to decide whether or not to refer it to the Court of Appeal. The criteria governing this decision are set out in the Criminal Appeal Act 1995:

13. – (1) A reference of conviction, verdict, finding or sentence shall not be made under any of sections 9 to 12 unless –
  (a) the Commission considers that there is a real possibility that the conviction, verdict, finding or sentence would not be upheld were the reference to be made,
  (b) the Commission so consider –
    (i) in the case of a conviction, verdict or finding, because of an argument, or evidence, not raised in the proceedings which led to it or on any appeal or application for leave to appeal against it, or
    (ii) in the case of a sentence, because of an argument on a point of law, or information, not so raised, and
  (c) an appeal against conviction, verdict, finding or sentence has been determined or leave to appeal against it has been refused.

(2) Nothing in subsection (1)(b)(i) or (c) shall prevent the making of a reference if it appears to the Commission that there are exceptional circumstances which justify making it.

Under s 14(3):

In considering whether to make a reference under section 9 or 10 [cases tried on indictment] the Commission may at any time refer any point on which they desire the assistance of the Court of Appeal to that Court for the Court's opinion on it;

and on a reference under this subsection the Court of Appeal shall consider the point referred and furnish the Commission with the Court's opinion on the point.

The referral decision will be made by a quorum of three members. Where a referral is made, the CCRC must give the court and the parties a statement of the reasons for making a referral (s 14(4)). If it decides not to make a referral, the CCRC must give the applicant reasons for its refusal (s 14(5)). The criteria in s 13 invite consideration of a second important issue about the arrangements in miscarriage of justice cases:

The relationship between the CCRC and the Court of Appeal. The CCRC's decisions on referring cases to the Court of Appeal will be affected by the court's decisions in those cases it does refer. Under s 13, the Commission should not refer cases unless there is a 'real possibility' that the verdict will not be upheld. The court, therefore, remains the key player in the system. If it continues to display the same extremely sceptical attitude towards referrals that it has in the past, the CCRC will be discouraged from referring cases.

It is impossible to predict what the Court of Appeal's attitude towards referral cases, or conviction appeals in general, will be in the future. The reforms which were set in motion by the RCCJ's report were intended to make the court readier to allow conviction appeals in those cases where there had been no error of law. But the new test in s 2 of the Criminal Appeal Act 1968 (is the conviction unsafe?) will not achieve this by itself. When faced with reforms of criminal procedure, the judiciary can prove remarkably stubborn. In Chapter 5 we saw that the new sentencing regime instituted by the Criminal Justice Act 1991 was derailed, in part, by the sceptical attitude of judges towards some of the provisions in the Act. Similarly, the history of criminal appeals shows that numerous attempts to cajole the Court of Appeal into taking a less conservative attitude towards conviction appeals have failed (Malleson, 1994). Nobles and Schiff (1995) argue that this attitude towards appeals is inevitable, because allegations by outsiders that there has been a miscarriage of justice in a particular case threaten the court's power to decide for itself just what a miscarriage of justice is, as well as undermining the finality of convictions and the supremacy of jury verdicts. This sort of attitude is illustrated by the comments of Lord Denning, in a letter to *The Times* (31 March 1988):

> My opinion is that it is more important to uphold public confidence in our system of justice than to allow convicted people – whom the media on their own investigations allege to be innocent – go free.

In short, the court may see referrals by the CCRC as a threat to its independence and therefore prove reluctant to allow referral appeals.

Less pessimistically, it is possible that the Court of Appeal's attitude towards referrals will change. Some commentators have detected a change in the court's attitude towards conviction appeals after the widespread criticism of its role in the miscarriage of justice cases of the early 1990s. This may prove to be a permanent change. In addition, the Criminal Appeal Act 1968, s 23A gives the court the power to refer issues to the CCRC for investigation and this may help to provide the court with a rather more active role in the resolution of suspected miscarriage of justice cases.

Who should decide miscarriage of justice cases? The discussion of the attitude of the Court of Appeal towards referral cases leads into a final issue: is the Court of Appeal, as presently constituted, an appropriate body for deciding such cases? Some commentators would argue that the 1995 reforms did not go far enough, because they left the Court of Appeal – with its tarnished reputation in miscarriage of justice cases – as a central part of the process. The cases that have caused the appeals system the most problems over the years have been those, like the ones in table 6.1 above, where there are disputed questions of fact. Because these cases do not involve questions of law, some commentators have argued that lay people are as well placed to decide them as judges. This claim has inspired a number of proposals. One is to replace the Court of Appeal with a 'court of last resort' to hear miscarriage of justice cases, this court to include, or be entirely comprised of, lay people. Another proposal is to include lay assessors in the Court of Appeal to decide such cases. A slightly different proposal would require the Court of Appeal to order retrials in all cases referred to it by the CCRC, unless a retrial was unfeasible in which case the court would simply quash the conviction (see Legal Action Group, 1993, p 16; Thornton, 1993; Thornton et al, 1993, pp 24–35; Pattenden, 1996, pp 402–405).

The establishment of the CCRC is to be welcomed. As we have seen, though, there are a number of unanswered questions about the effect it will have on procedures for resolving miscarriage of justice cases. To date, criticism of the CCRC has centred on the fact that none of its 14 members have extensive experience of the criminal process from a defence perspective (Bindman, 1997). The Commission will have to be judged by its practice in the cases it considers; it will publish an annual report that will allow some evaluation of its effectiveness.

2. ALLOCATING RESOURCES IN CRIMINAL JUSTICE

A major constraint on formulating and implementing criminal justice policy is the amount of resources which can be devoted to the task. Yet the relationship between resources and policy has not been examined systematically. One reason is that the rhetoric of criminal 'justice' stresses a set of moral ideals which are usually regarded as too important to be compromised by expedience: on the one hand, crime is not to be tolerated and the criminal law must be enforced; on the other hand, the preconditions for imposing punishment are fairness and accuracy in identifying criminals. In practice, a lack of resources has often prevented those ideals from being achieved – for example, the police cannot afford to investigate all reports of crime, and the courts cannot afford to offer trial by jury to all defendants – but such failures have generally been regarded as unfortunate deviations from the ideal, and the need for pragmatism has rarely been conceded.

More recently, however, there has been a shift in the rhetoric of criminal justice itself. Partly, this has been prompted by the continual and ever-increasing demands being imposed on the criminal justice budget. But the main reason has been the willingness of the three Conservative administrations which held office from 1979 to 1997 to implement the recommendations of economics and of management studies in the public sector. Generally, economics is concerned with securing that wealth is used efficiently so that, when choices are made, the benefits are obtained for the least cost. Management studies includes the analysis of ways that human resources of time and skill can be used most effectively to realise the objects of an enterprise. These approaches to policy have been applied, not only to business and commercial activities, but also to public spending. In appraising policy, the reference point has become the three 'Es' – economy, efficiency and effectiveness – and the criminal justice process has not been immune to its application. The effect has been to transform thinking in all areas of policy, from policing, prosecution and trial to the delivery of different sentencing options. Whether the resource implications of policy choices have taken priority over the ideals of criminal justice is an issue which remains a matter of controversy. But, at the least, what the discussion of resource allocation serves to show is that those ideals can only be achieved at a price. By articulating the elements of that price, we can begin to appreciate the real value that we attach (or do not attach) to the aims of criminal justice.

(a) Economic approaches

The options are presented most radically in economic analyses of crime. These have not been applied directly in the British criminal justice process but they underpin the general approach known as cost-benefit analysis. Economic analyses stress the total social loss which results from crime: not only do criminal acts in themselves impose burdens on society, but so does the very enforcement of the criminal law. In the seminal work from this perspective, Gary Becker asked: 'How many resources and how much punishment *should* be used to enforce different kinds of legislation. Put equivalently, although more strangely, how many offenses *should* be permitted and how many offenders *should* go unpunished?' (Becker, 1968, p 170, original emphasis). Becker offered a formula which included all the elements that contribute to the total social loss from offending and then explored ways of minimising that loss by concentrating on the variables that he considered most easy to influence

578

through criminal justice policy, namely, the expenditure on resources used for law enforcement and penalties.

The aim of the economic analysis is to discover an efficient or optimal level of crime and the argument proceeds as follows. It is taken that society will benefit when money is spent on the reduction of crime. But where that expenditure is greater than the 'worth' of the crime which it prevents, society will be spending more than is necessary. It 'pays' society, therefore, to reduce expenditure on law enforcement and punishment to the point, at the margin, where an additional unit of spending is the same as the additional unit of social cost which would have been incurred if a crime had not thereby been prevented. This implies, however, that crime may be allowed to increase to that same point, at the margin, where the additional unit of social cost that it would impose is the same as the additional unit of expenditure which would be needed to prevent it.

Two broad policy recommendations flow from this analysis. One is that society should be prepared to tolerate a certain level of crime because it cannot afford to enforce the whole of the criminal law. The implication is that resources should only be allocated to those areas which society regards as priorities. This appears to be a rather alarming proposition because it runs counter to the deep assumption which underpins the criminal law, that to define behaviour as crime is to indicate that it is wrong and cannot be condoned. In reality, such an assumption is compromised in many ways in choices about the design of the criminal justice process. For example, police powers and codes of conduct place constraints on the ability of the police to apprehend all offenders. The rules of evidence and of criminal procedure place similar constraints on prosecution, and trial and conviction. But those compromises are based on the recognition of individuals' rights (to respect as humans and to fairness). The economic approach differs in allowing resource problems a similar weight, rather than treating them as pragmatic reasons for departing from the objective to reduce crime. Where cost-benefit analysis becomes a natural and pervasive way of planning and reviewing policy, the effect can be to allow economic considerations to function as an independent basis for policy decisions, possibly allowing them to dominate at the expense of more central values, such as the moral and political worth of symbolically emphasising the legal norms, the protection of victims' interests, or the maintenance of public order and security more generally.

The other policy recommendation which flows from economic analysis is its approach to reducing crime. Most economic studies of crime have concentrated on modelling individuals' rational responses to deterrence (see, for example, Erhlich, 1975; Pyle, 1983). Potential offenders are assumed to weigh their satisfaction from offending against the probability of being caught and punished combined with the severity of the sanction meted out. Law enforcement and sanctions are regarded as inversely related, so that offenders will be equally deterred by a high probability of apprehension followed by a mild punishment or a low probability of apprehension followed by a severe punishment. Leaving aside empirical doubts about the validity of this model (see Chapter 5 above; see also Beyleveld, 1980), the implications for resource allocation are that society can choose to spend either on law enforcement or on punishment, or on some combination of the two, yet achieve the same result in terms of crime reduction. At the extreme, if a cheap but very severe sanction could be devised, the economic approach suggests that that would enable spending on law enforcement to be reduced almost entirely. Less dramatically, when fiscal policy constrains the total amount that can be spent on law enforcement, the economic approach implies that the reduction in spending can be compensated by increasing the levels of penalties available and used by sentencers. Such possibilities clearly depend on an uncritical acceptance of the economists' preferred theory of criminal behaviour, that of the rational utility-maximiser. But some aspects of the economic analysis are implicit in many penal reform agendas: other things being equal, it makes sense to use a less costly penalty, for example a fine instead of imprisonment, where it achieves the same effect in terms of crime reduction as a more expensive one (see Walker, 1972; Becker, 1968).

(b) Managerialism

The application of economic theory to crime and the criminal justice process has paralleled the growth of a new approach to public administration during the 1980s. This has been variously described as 'managerialism,' or the 'new public management' or 'NPM,' and it involves the application of what is considered good commercial practice to the organisation of the public sector. The approach is characterised by a number of themes, all of which presuppose that market mechanisms are better than traditional styles of government. The aim is to reorganise the public sector so as to identify or to establish producer–purchaser relationships. The work of the public sector is divided into the roles of purchasers and providers, who are expected to compete with each other and with businesses in the private sector, and whose relationships are determined by contract. The exposure of the public sector to the wider market, for example, through compulsory competitive tendering and through the creation of internal markets, allows the provision of services to be driven by consumer demand. It is taken that this makes government more responsive and therefore more efficient. The new public management is often associated with the separation of political decision-making from management, with functions being allocated to quasi-independent agencies. Generally, accountability is sought to be measured, by adherence to procedures and by performance criteria, and success is typically audited by some form of external inspection. (See generally, Stewart and Walsh (1992), pp 504–508; Dunleavy and Hood (1994); Hood (1991).)

As Lacey argues, the Criminal Justice Act 1991 (discussed in Chapter 5 above) represented a significant application of the new public management to the criminal justice process.

Extract 6.2.1

N Lacey, 'Government as Manager, Citizen as Consumer: The Case of the Criminal Justice Act 1991' (1994) 54 MLR 534, pp 543–546 (footnotes omitted)

First, in important respects the sentencing and early release provisions themselves cohere with managerialist concerns. To take sentencing as our example, we have the imposition, not of a sentencing philosophy articulated in terms of a number of substantive sentencing principles, but rather of a framework, a process of reasoning which has to be gone through in every sentencing case. The values and goals which might inform this process are implied or alluded to ('commensurate,' 'seriousness,' 'public protection') rather than defined or fully articulated. In stark contrast, the process itself is spelled out in great detail. Whilst the principle of desert implicitly invoked by the ideas of seriousness and commensurability clearly predominates, references to public protection and even rehabilitation muddy the substantive waters to a significant degree. The implicit conception of good management here therefore consists mainly in an ideal of regularity and systematisation: of coherence, but coherence in a formal sense. This was an attempt to subject the courts themselves to the kinds of standards to which they hold other public bodies through the mechanism of judicial review. The Act sought to enhance the quality of decision-making by ensuring that a regular set of information is included and excluded, and that reasons are articulated. But the relevant criteria were implicitly rather than explicitly related to any dominant general conception of the nature of the enterprise itself: an approach which was reinforced by the national tradition of particularistic, detailed legal drafting. The approach was curiously technocratic: it assumed a practice in which everyone more or less knows what they are meant to be doing, and in which efficiency can simply be promoted by an outside and non-expert body designing a regularising system which is itself substantively indeterminate.

The second feature of the legislation which coheres with a managerial account does so in a somewhat different way. This is the miscellany of provisions in Parts IV and V concerning finance and the provision of services within the criminal process. Part IV provided, among other things, for the setting up of an Inspectorate of Probation (s 73); it gave the Secretary of State default powers to intervene where the minister considers that a probation committee is failing to discharge its statutory duty (s 74); it provided for the appointment of court security officers (s 76) and prisoners' escorts (s 80); and it provided for the contracting out and administration of new remand prisons (ss 84–91). Each of these last three sets of provisions constituted a significant reconstruction of areas of public administration as commercially structured enterprises operating within a statutory framework. At many points the language used by the Act is instructive in revealing just the kind of managerialist thinking to which I have referred. The heading of Part IV referred to the 'provision of services': admittedly not an entirely novel expression in public administration, but one which, in the context I have described, takes on a distinctive meaning in implicitly constructing the users of those services as consumers. These consumers, in a remarkable *reductio ad absurdum*, presumably include prisoners and offenders on probation – a figure vividly confirmed by Stephen Twinn, the former director of the first contracted out prison, the Wolds remand centre. In an interview with BBC radio in March 1993, Mr Twinn referred to prisoners as 'customers' who, in that ultimate test of market success, would prefer to return to the Wolds than to a state prison. Contracted out prisons have 'instead of a governor' a 'director' (s 85). The director acts alongside a 'controller' (truly Orwellian language) who is a crown servant.

When we move to Part V, the managerial preoccupations of the Act become yet more vivid, with provisions which impose cash limits on magistrates' courts (s 93) and probation services (s 94), and provision for the Secretary of State to publish regularly information 'enabling persons engaged in the administration of criminal justice to become aware of the financial implications of their decisions' (s 95(1)(a)). Perhaps most remarkably of all, in the very same subsection we find that the information to be published must also facilitate 'the performance by such persons of their duty to avoid discriminating against any persons on the ground of race or sex or any other improper ground' (s 95(1)(b)). This provision (itself added at a late stage) directly expresses equal opportunities as a managerial issue, and constructs what might generally be regarded as a civil right as merely another feature of good administration, on a footing with economic efficiency.

Clearly, the two parts of the Act which I have considered do not express the key themes of the new managerialism in the same way or to the same degree. The reform of the sentencing (and early release) systems is managerialist in the sense that it seeks to impose a regular, to some extent measurable and hence supervisable process on certain areas of public administration: it resonates with the ideas of accountability and regulation. It also, as I shall argue below, evokes the idea of the public as customer. The 'Principles of Public Services' enunciated in the White Paper on the Citizen's Charter are standards, openness, information, choice, non-discrimination, accessibility and redress: with the (highly significant) exception of choice, each of these is directly facilitated by the sort of sentencing reform which the Act attempts. There are clear resonances here with the thinking behind the Courts' Charter, which constructs both civil and criminal courts as providers of services. The provisions of Parts IV and V, on the other hand, evince not only these but also many of the other managerialist themes identified by Stewart and Walsh: separation of purchaser from provider roles, the growth of contractual arrangements, flexibility of pay and conditions, the separation of the political from the management process and the creation of quasi-markets.

As well as noting some of the managerial features of the CJA, we should observe that a managerialist account also generates some limited but nonetheless useful criteria for an assessment of the Act's success. Whilst these are not necessarily the criteria one would want to use in making any general assessment of the legislation, they do have a certain interest. For they generate a devastating critique of the impact of the legislation from the Government's own perspective, and in turn help, paradoxically, to show some of the limits of a managerial approach to the imposition of statutory frameworks for public administration.

Concentrating for the moment on the sentencing provisions, Part I was characterised by important deficiencies in terms of its antecedent likelihood of success in imposing a consistent sentencing practice. The failure to enunciate clearly the central rationale or goals underlying the statutory scheme has already been discussed. Moreover, poor, unduly cumbersome drafting of some of its central provisions exacerbated a general lack of clarity as to how some of the key provisions related to each other. For example, the Act, as we have seen, directed sentencers to give a custodial sentence only where the offence was so serious that only such a sentence was appropriate (s 1). But sentencers were then required to consider whether mitigating circumstances dictated that a less severe penalty could be given (s 28). The implication – one which became a crucial weapon in the assault on the Act's credibility – was that non-custodial penalties might be handed down in the case of offences already judged to be so serious that only a custodial penalty was suitable. Similarly, the nature of the circumstances in which previous convictions would and would not be relevant in fixing the length of a sentence was unspecified (s 29), which left the section open to ridicule as an obvious Parliamentary concession to those opposed to the ideas of commensurability and parsimony which had informed the Green and White Papers.

Also open to criticism was the complexity of the Act's provisions and of the reasoning process which, particularly when combined with other legislative provisions, they imposed on the courts. Conversely, there was a lack of mandatoriness in the instantiation of key aspects of the schema, notably the duty to give reasons for a particular sentence [see *R v Baverstock* [1993] 2 All ER 32]. Moreover, the Act failed to make the key notion of seriousness directly constraining by tying it to specific offence definitions. The impact of the provisions was therefore bound to depend on discretionary judicial decisions about both the absolute and the relative seriousness of offences within the wide boundaries of statutory maximum sentences.

Clearly, several of these weaknesses are closely related to the tensions between efficiency and political concerns mentioned above. Leaving aside more general questions about the real power of central Government directly to effect material changes in dispersed fields of administrative activity, it seems clear that a Government which avoids nailing its substantive colours to the policy mast is unlikely to be able to achieve its goals through a reform of processes. Yet a more explicit strategy – for example a more precise enunciation of the concept of seriousness sufficiently stringent to meet its fiscal concerns – would immediately have brought the Government into direct conflict with the judiciary, whose reaction (particularly as represented in a crime-conscious media) would have risked undermining the image of the Government's pro-law and order stance. To this delicate balancing act, we have to add the variety of views within both the Home Office and the Government as to the relative importance of the fiscal/managerial and desert principle bases for the sentencing and early release reforms.

As Lacey goes on to explain, the 1991 Act did not succeed in introducing a managerialist approach to sentencing reform, principally because of the judiciary's resistance to controls on their decision-making, but also because the parsimonious approach to custodial sentencing entailed by the Act's cost-cutting aspirations was inconsistent with the government's wider law and order policy. However, the Act's provisions which dealt with the financing and provision of services did pave the way for the consolidation of managerialist and economic rationales for change in the criminal justice process. The following discussion examines that trend in further detail. But first, some information is provided about the overall costs of the criminal justice process.

(c) The cost of criminal justice

One problem, as the Royal Commission on Criminal Justice noted in 1993, is that there is a 'paucity of reliable information' about the overall cost of the criminal justice process, (1993, para 16; see Extract 1.3.1 above). As the Commission itself recognised, 'the introduction of effective and reliable procedures of financial appraisal, monitoring and control would itself impose on the system a heavy additional burden of cost' (ibid). We have, therefore, only partial information about the costs involved and the extent to which spending on personnel, facilities and equipment is allocated effectively and efficiently to different parts of the process. This is understandable, because the major institutions in the process – the police, the prosecutors, the legal profession, the courts, the prison service and the probation service – are relatively autonomous. It is not easy to measure their comparative efficiency. Even if, as one economist claims, the cost of a period of imprisonment which has the same deterrent effect as policing work is considerably less than that of the police salaries involved (Pyle, 1995), it is difficult, politically, for governments to impose significant transfers of resources between criminal justice sectors.

Prior to the Commission's establishment, the Home Office had published a broad calculation of the overall costs of the system in 1988 (Home Office, 1988). That exercise has not been repeated regularly, but the information has been collated in occasional surveys (for example, Home Office, 1995a). Currently available figures show the following expenditure on the criminal justice process for 1995–96 with some preliminary amounts for 1996–97.

Extract 6.2.2

Home Office Research and Statistics Directorate, Expenditure on the Criminal Justice System (http://www.homeoffice.gov.uk/rsd/xexpend)

Expenditure on the Criminal Justice System (at current prices (£ million))

Service	1988/89	1990/91	1992/93	1993/94	1995/96	1996/97 (3)
Police	3,820	3,806	5,860	6,181	6,749	7,060
Magistrates' courts	275	300	356	410	416	321
Probation	250	329	424	480	491	(4)
Prisons	1,029	1,453	1,610	1,507	1,667	1,522
Lord Chancellor's Department (2)	(4)	528	707	716	744	1,003
Crown Prosecution Service	154	211	276	283	296	288
TOTAL (1)	(4)	7,627	9,233	9,577	10,363	(4)

(1) Total expenditure by central and local government, capital and current.
(2) Criminal work only.
(3) Estimated.
(4) Figures not available.

Expenditure on the Criminal Justice System 1995–96 (at current prices)

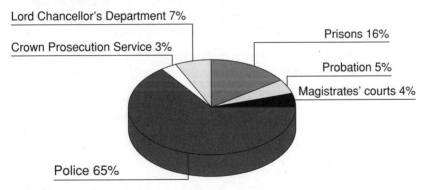

Lord Chancellor's Department 7%

Crown Prosecution Service 3%

Prisons 16%

Probation 5%

Magistrates' courts 4%

Police 65%

Total expenditure £10,363

Source Home Office, UK.

(d) Policing

During the 1990s, a series of initiatives were directed at reforming the organisation and management of the police. The police service had previously been protected from the more radical implications of the new public management, but at least three aspects of its work provided pretexts for attempting fundamental reform: it had absorbed an increasing share of public expenditure, its management was perceived to be top-heavy, and it had apparently failed to prevent a rise in recorded crime. The outcome of this process has been two seemingly contradictory trends in police organisation. One has been a move towards decentralisation. This is manifested in the devolution of policy planning to police authorities, within national objectives, and the delegation of operational responsibility to local commanders who are supposed to be responsive to community needs. Decentralisation is also the result of measures intended to privatise elements of police work, for example, vehicle fleet maintenance, prisoner escort duties or the running of the police national computer. One recurrent candidate for privatisation has been traffic patrolling, but an internal Home Office review, at the time of the Rosen inquiry (described below), concluded that such work could not be regarded as ancillary to mainstream policing objectives (see Butler, 1996, p 222). However, there has also been greater centralisation of management and finance, as Reiner describes in the following survey of recent reforms in the structure of police governance (see also Jones, 1993).

Extract 6.2.3

R Reiner, 'Policing and the Police' in M Maguire, R Morgan and R Reiner, *The Oxford Handbook of Criminology* (1997) 2nd ed, pp 1030–1034 (footnotes omitted)

The centralizing trend has become more apparent still as a result of the recent reforms of the structure of police governance. Originally announced by Kenneth Clarke in March 1993, and published by Michael Howard in June 1993 in the White Paper, *Police Reform*, these culminated in the Police and Magistrates' Courts Act 1994 (which received its Royal Assent in July after a conflict-ridden passage). The Police Act 1996 (which received Royal Assent on 22 May) consolidates the Police Act 1964, the Police and Criminal Evidence Act 1984, Part IX, and the Police and Magistrates' Courts Act 1994 into the currently definitive statutory statement of the structure of police governance.

The most controversial changes are to the structure of police authorities. Section 4 of the 1996 Act limits the normal size of police authorities to seventeen (although the Home Secretary has discretion to increase this under section 2). This uniform size, regardless of the area or population covered, itself signifies a departure from the conception of police authorities as primarily *representative* local bodies. The specified functions of police authorities are subtly altered from the 1964 Act's section 4 formulation, 'maintenance of an adequate and efficient' force. Section 6 of the 1996 Act changes this to 'efficient and effective'. The precise scope of this responsibility remains as gnomic as in the 1964 version, but the symbolism is obvious. The prime motif of the new-fangled police authorities is that they are to be 'businesslike' bodies, the local watchdogs of the managerialist, value-for-money, private enterprise ethos which the government has tried to inject into the whole public sector [F Leishman, S Cope and P Starie, 'Reinventing and Restructuring: Towards a "New Policing Order"' in F Leishman, S Cope and S Savage (eds), *Core Issues in Policing* (London: Longman, 1996)].

The democratically elected councillor component of police authorities has been reduced from two-thirds to just over a half (nine out of the normal total of seventeen members: Police Act 1996, Schedule 2, paragraph 1(1)(a)). Three members are magistrates (i.e. just under one-sixth instead of one-third: paragraph 1(1)(b)).

The remaining five members are appointed under the complex and arcane procedures detailed in Schedule 3 to the 1996 Act. The rationale running through the fourteen sections and umpteen sub-sections of the mind-numbingly labyrynthine selection game seems to be to allow the Home Secretary as many bites at the cherry as possible, without simply letting him or her choose. The original version of the Bill did indeed do precisely this, but so overtly centralizing a measure drew the wrath of a number of former Conservative Home Secretaries in the House of Lords, who staged a revolt against this aspect of the legislation. Hence the smokescreen of the tortuous process in the final version of the Act. The Home Secretary appoints one of the three-member selection panel, the police authority itself appoints another, and the two members thus selected appoint the third member. They then nominate four times as many people as the number of vacancies on the authority to the Home Secretary, applying criteria specified by the Home Secretary, and the Home Secretary short-lists half of them. If the selection panel nominate fewer people than twice the number of vacancies to be filled, the Home Secretary makes up the shortfall. This brief summary of the arrangements cannot do justice to their cumbersome complexity – but it does show how the Home Secretary remains the linchpin of the process.

The Chair of the authority is chosen by the members themselves. This was another concession resulting from the House of Lords revolt agains the clear centralizing thrust of the Bill. It was originally planned that the Chair would be chosen by the Home Secretary. Overall the final version of the Act leaves police authorities with a slight preponderance of elected members, but this is a fig-leaf to hide the centralization which was nakedly apparent in the Bill as originally presented to Parliament.

The intention is to make police authorities more 'businesslike', but the business they will be doing is that of central government rather than the local electorate. Police authorities have new duties to issue an annual policing plan for their area (Police Act 1996, section 8) and local policing objectives (section 7). The chief constable has the same general function of 'direction and control' of the force as in the 1964 Act, but this must be exercised with regard to the local policing plan and objectives which the authority draws up in liaison with him (section 10). This is an empowerment of the authority compared to the 1964 Act, but it largely has to act as a conduit for the Home Secretary's priorities. The Home Secretary decides the codes of practice for police authorities (section 39), sets national objectives and performance targets which local plans must incorporate (sections 37 and 38), determines the central government grant to police forces which covers most of their expenditure according to formulae which are at his discretion (section 46), and can direct police authorities about the minimum amount of their budgetary contribution (section 41) and any other matters (section 40).

Although it seems clear that overall the Police and Magistrates' Courts Act 'substantially shifts the balance of power away from local government towards central government' (Leishman, Cope, and Starie, 1996: 21), it has been officially represented by the government itself as doing precisely the opposite. This claim is based on the relaxation of the detailed controls which used to exist on precisely how chief officers spent their budgets. In future chief constables will be free to allocate their budgets in whatever way they feel is best suited to carry out the policing plan. The White Paper on *Police Reform* [Home Office, *Police Reform: A Police Service for the Twenty-First Century*, Cm 2281 (London: Home Office, 1993)] anticipates explicitly that chief officers will pay attention to the advice of the Audit Commission and the Inspectorate of Constabulary. These bodies have been encouraging devolution of decision-making to Basic Command Units in forces on the model of schemes like Sector Policing in the Met [B Dixon and E A Stanko, *Serving the People: Sector Policing and Police Accountability* (London: Islington Council)]. It is widely assumed that the pursuit of nationally determined performance targets will paradoxically drive chief officers to devolve a considerable measure of responsibility to local commanders [M Hough, 'The Police Patrol Function: What Research Can Tell Us' in W Saulsbury, J Mott and T Newburn (eds), *Themes in Contemporary Policing* (London: Police Foundation/Policy Studies Institute)].

This new independence may prove somewhat illusory, when the changes in police governance are considered in the context of the other elements of the government's police reform package. The Sheehy Inquiry into Police Responsibilities and Rewards, which reported in the same week of June 1993 as the *Police Reform* White Paper (Sheehy Report [Home Office, Northern Ireland Office and Scottish Office, *Inquiry into Police Responsibilities and Rewards*, Cm 2280 (London: HMSO, 1993)], recommended that all police officers should be appointed on short-term contracts and subject to performance-related pay (PRP). The criteria for successful performance and the assessment of whether these have been satisfied would be governed by the Home Secretary via the new police authorities (which on the White Paper's plan would be controlled by central government appointees).

This would have constituted a formidably centralized system of control over policing. Without abandoning the constabulary independence doctrine in any formal way, the Home Secretary would colour the use of discretion by constables by setting and assessing the criteria for performance which will determine pay and job security. The police would no longer be accountable in the gentlemanly 'explanatory and co-operative' style which (in Geoffrey Marshall's words) characterized the impact of the 1964 Police Act [G Marshall, 'Police Accountability Revisited' in D Downes (ed) *Unravelling Criminal Justice* (London: Macmillan, 1978)]. Nor would they be subject to the 'subordinate and obedient' style of accountability to democratically elected local authorities which was demanded by the Act's radical critics. Instead they would be subject to a new market-style discipline which can be called 'calculative and contractual' ... Whilst not concerned directly with the details of policing as the other modes of accountability purported to be it could penetrate the parts of policing which they could not reach, the day-to-day operation of discretion. This would be by attaching offers which could not be refused to the attainment of the targets specified in policing plans.

The clear centralization apparent in the original version of the reforms has not materialized . . . The Police and Magistrates' Courts Act reached the statute book in considerably modified form because of peer pressure exercised mainly by Conservative former Home Secretaries. The toughest aspects of Sheehy's recommendations were defeated by a storm of opposition from police representative associations. The watered-down versions of these measures which has resulted leaves a lot open to detailed argument and development . . .

There are likely to be all sorts of unintended consequences of the changes, rebounding on the reforms' framers . . . The new independent members of police authorities, for example, may well confound the expectations of both advocates and opponents of the legislation. Given their local concerns about the quality of service delivery they could well align themselves with elected police authority members and chief police officers against the central government on such matters as the effect of tight centrally set budgets.

Whatever the impact of the measures in practice, there has certainly been a profound transformation in the formal organization of police governance in the years since 1994. There has been as much criticism of the style in which these changes have been carried out as their substance. Unlike previous major changes in police accountability there was no Royal Commission (as many commentators advocated). The reforms emanated from internal Home Office enquiries with minimal outside consultation. Although the measures were predicated on a clear, contentious conceptualization of the police role as being primarily 'catching criminals' (as paragraph 2.2 of the White Paper, Police Reform, specifies) there was no public debate about this narrowing of the traditional police mandate. In theory and practice this had hitherto been seen as encompassing a much broader spectrum of concerns, including crime prevention and management, order maintenance and peace-keeping, emergency and other services . . . The narrow emphasis on crime detection, now pushed to the forefront by the government's White Paper, had hitherto been seen by most official enquiries, notably the Scarman Report of 1981, as a deformation of rank-and-file police culture to be rebutted by management as much as possible not actively promoted by policy and performance targets.

One very welcome response to the absence of public debate was the establishment in 1994 by the Policy Studies Institute and the Police Foundation of an Independent Inquiry into The Role and Responsibilities of the Police, chaired by Sir John Cassels . . . This reported in 1996 . . .

The Report endorsed the statement of the policing mission enshrined in 1991 in the police service's Statement of Common Purposes and Values (Police Foundation/Policy Studies Institute, 1996: paragraph 1.4). This encompassed upholding the law, crime prevention and detection, keeping the peace, and assisting the community: the broad conception of the police role advocated by the community policing philosophy of Lord Scarman, John Alderson, and others, which has become the dominant view of police leaders . . .

The Independent Inquiry, like the majority of the 'policing policy network' (Leishman, Cope, and Starie, 1996: 17–20) apart from the Home Secretary, recognizes the inherent limitations on the police capacity to control crime which has been revealed by research (including that of the Home Office itself). It also emphasizes the undoubted need for the police to be managed and targeted as efficiently and effectively as possible. This involves both enhancing accountability of the police to public concerns and priorities *and* public debate about policing to sensitize the public to the limitations of police capacity to re-solve the problems of crime, disorder and insecurity. This limitation arises only in small part from mismanagement or misdirection of the police. It is primarily due to the deep roots of policing problems in wider social, political-economic, and cultural processes . . .

It is not only government which has encouraged the adoption of the new public management style, however. The influence of three agencies in formulating acceptable practice in police management should not be under-estimated. These are Her Majesty's Inspector of Constabulary (HMIC), the Audit Commission (whose work has been noted in Chapter 2 above), and the Association of Chief Police Officers (ACPO).

Extract 6.2.4

S Savage and S Charman, 'Managing Change' in F Leishman, B Loveday and S Savage (eds), *Core Issues in Policing* (1996) pp 50–53

HMIC has undoubtedly become a more influential and interventionist body over the past decade . . . For example, the expansion of the process of civilian-isation throughout the police service since the mid-1980s owes much to the work of the Inspectorate, constituting as it does one element in the 'template' of best practice which HMIC disseminates through its inspections and recom-mendations for future action. Allied to the increasingly 'directive' nature of Home Office circulars . . . the Inspectorate has adopted a more forceful approach to its inspections, which now take three forms – 'Primary' (triennial), 'Performance Review' (annual), and 'Thematic' (ad hoc). Thematic inspections cover issues such as equal opportunities, complaints, and so on. HMIC reports are now published and widely circulated, a factor unlikely to be ignored by individual forces in determining a response to Inspectorate recommendations. HMIC has in recent years tended to recruit younger chief constables to its ranks, staff who have in a number of cases returned to the service after their period with the Inspectorate; it is no longer monopolised by former chief constables in the twilight of their careers. Indeed, HMIC has recently added two senior civilians to its inspection team. The work and influence of HMIC has been identified as a key factor in the 'centralisation' of policing policy and police activity . . . , although some commentators consider this to be an over-simplification on the grounds that its influence, while apparent at the stage of the *implementation* of policy, appears less significant at the *policy-making* phase . . . Nevertheless, what is still contentious is the extent to which HMIC may have become an extended arm of government policy for the police service at the expense of local determination of policing. Furthermore, a still under-research area lies in the perception and reception of HMIC activities at individual force level: how

Inspectorate views and recommendations on best practice are regarded by those responsible for local policing policy and actions.

An interesting line of inquiry in this regard would be to compare the relative influence of HMIC on the one hand and the *Audit Commission* on the other. It is almost impossible to over-estimate the influence of the Commission on the modern police service . . . [It] . . . began at the 'periphery' of policing activities – focusing on areas such as fingerprinting and vehicle fleet management – but it has since spread its tentacles into core policing functions and processes, such as crime detection, financial management, training, and communications. Such has been the expansion of the Commission's brief and its impact on police management that reference has been made to the 'Auditshire Constabulary' . . . What has emerged is something of a template of best management practice which stresses a number of core principles: that decision-making and budgeting be devolved to the lowest practical levels in the organisation; that managers maximise usage of performance measurement; that wherever possible police services be localised and draw upon local determination of priorities and preferences; that where possible and practical policing activities be organised around a client/contractor relationship. Increasingly, the work of the Commission has drawn closer to the philosophy of the 'social market' . . . , and herein lies a potential irony. It is quite clear that the work of the Audit Commission is highly regarded by many (if not most) senior police officers – early indications of a research project currently underway on the role of ACPO by the authors of this chapter are very much in this direction. Yet if indeed the philosophy of the Audit Commission points the way to many of the elements of the social market approach to the police and policing, then managers sympathetic to the approach taken by the Commission may be in danger of facilitating the very sorts of developments many senior officers have opposed when advocated by central government – in particular, the restriction of policing activities to core 'crime fighting' tasks and the stripping down and hiving-off of so-called 'service' or 'caring' functions . . .

Less clear than the role of the Audit Commission as an agency of and for change within the police service is the third major body: *ACPO*. One reflection of this is the frequent reference around the policing literature to ACPO as a 'staff association', alongside the other associations – the Police Federation and the Superintendents' Association. While ACPO does have as part of its function the protection of the pay and conditions of its members, it is also quite definitely a *policy-making* body, responsible not only for making policy for its members, but also for the service as a whole. In recognition of the importance of this qualification, ACPO as a body is, at the time of writing, considering formally separating the two wings of its organisation, i.e. to distinguish between the 'staff association' and 'policy/professional' aspects of its role, and at the same time to increase the explicit profile of the latter (see Johnson 1991). While at the time of writing the precise shape of this new constitution is yet to emerge, even symbolically this marks the growing significance of ACPO as a source of influence over policing policy nationally. To claim that an organisation which reflects the views of the most senior ranks of the service is influential may appear to state the obvious. What is more difficult to determine at this stage is the exact extent of that influence, the extent to which any such influence has grown in recent years and if so why and how, and the nature of the relationships between ACPO and other agencies such as HMIC and the Audit Commission – these are core concerns of the authors' ongoing research referred to above.

A number of organisational developments within ACPO in recent years do, however, shed light on the situation and certainly do point to the growing significance of the Association as a source of influence of police policy-making at individual force level. This relates not only to operational matters such as policy on traffic policing, but increasingly to 'quality of service' issues such as performance measurement. One key development was the establishment in 1990 of an expanded secretariat to service the Association. This would seem to have had a 'professionalising effect' on the workings of ACPO in terms of its decision-making processes and the dissemination of those decisions down to force level. The permanent staff of the secretariat now service the main 'coordinating committees' of the Association as well as the Chief Constable's Council. A second development has been the stance adopted by ACPO on 'dissenting members', i.e. those who choose not to follow individual policies agreed and approved by Council. Although individual chiefs are as 'free' as they have ever been to depart from collective policy on any particular matter, in order to do so they are now requested to state the grounds on which they have chosen this option to the President; this was not the case up until the mid-1980s, when ACPO's views on a policy issue could more easily be ignored by individual chiefs. Both of these developments point towards a more 'corporate' shape to ACPO, and a consequent enhancement of ACPO's role as a source of guidance on policing policy at force level. Furthermore, there is evidence that this corporacy is taking the shape of a more *proactive* approach to policy matters – of setting its own agendas rather than responding to those of others. In a small way, the establishment in 1994 of ACPO's journal *Policing Today* as a forum for debate on a wide range of policing issues bears witness to this. If it is the case that ACPO is establishing itself firmly as a corporate, proactive and highly influential body in terms of its effect on police policy-making as a whole, then inevitably questions of accountability will arise. The Association has no statutory basis and is not bound by any requirement to disclose its proceedings, although much of its work becomes public through press releases, evidence to bodies such as the Home Affairs Select Committee, advice to the police authority associations, presentations to the ACPO Annual Conference, annual reports, and so on. While clearly there would be practical problems if policing policy as 'advised' by ACPO were to be available for public scrutiny – motorists, for example, would be very interested in knowing if any guideline existed on which point above the speed limit charges rather than cautions were to be made – calls for some form of external scrutiny may well grow. Furthermore, public clarification of the role of ACPO vis-à-vis other bodies such as HMIC and the Home Office may be required.

The role of ACPO is particularly significant because its professional, expert support is necessary, in effect, for any political initiatives for reform to succeed. The following comments by a chief constable, albeit not speaking on behalf of ACPO, illustrate the kinds of reservations that senior officers retain about the benefits of the new public management.

Extract 6.2.5

A J P Butler, 'Managing the Future: A Chief Constable's View' in F Leishman, B Loveday and S Savage (eds), *Core Issues in Policing* (1996) pp 220–223

Personnel issues

A major source of criticism of the Sheehy Report was the very clear failure by the inquiry team to recognise the personnel needs and characteristics of police work. There was a degree of arrogance in the findings which seemed to see a direct translation of the personnel practices of industry to the police service. One of the members had been involved in the Fresh Start initiative in the prison service and had also been an architect of changes in the NHS. To put it bluntly, it was a confrontational style of management which sought to achieve by imposition what could not be achieved by negotiation. That is not to deny the responsibility of management to manage an organisation, but all the evidence shows the need, particularly in service organisations, to recognise that the motivation and attitude of staff are critical success factors.

Although many of the most damaging and impractical recommendations of Sheehy were rejected, there remain a number of themes which have the potential to cause problems for chief constables in the future. The concept of local pay bargaining has been introduced for the first time. Chief constables are required to set criteria for determining salary points for probationary constables; there are four grades on a scale for superintendents; and chief officers have to negotiate their own pay and conditions with their police authorities. In addition to local pay bargaining, performance-related pay is to be introduced for all ranks. PRP has been combined with FTAs [fixed term appointments] for chief officers as a new and potentially damaging change to their conditions of service. PRP is being implemented in the police at a time when research is questioning its value in other organisations. Furthermore, the nature of the police role and the paramount importance of maintaining public confidence in the impartial execution of their duties creates added difficulties with paying police officers on performance . . .

Only time will tell if these changes will bring benefits which out-weigh their disadvantages, but already it is difficult to see what benefits have been gained by 'buying out' the overtime payments to inspectors and chief inspectors, though the disadvantages are already apparent. It has substantially increased demands on force budgets because the total amount being paid was often considerably less than the increased salary costs caused as a direct result of the 'buy-out'. These additional costs will feed through into increased pension costs. Furthermore, it is already becoming difficult to find volunteers for some posts at these ranks where overtime working has long been the norm.

Funding

There were anomalies with the basis on which police forces were funded which have been exacerbated by the passage of time. One of the major weaknesses related to the funding of civilian support staff, with the Standard

Spending Assessment (SSA) being based entirely on police officer establishment, irrespective of the numbers of civilian staff employed. PMCA required a new formula to be developed to provide a basis for police funding. A working group attempted to produce a needs-based method seeking to identify those factors which would reliably predict the policing needs of a community and thus form the basis of the funds allocated as a proportion of the total police resources available. However, there are a number of major problems with this approach: there were very limited reliable and valid data on which to base calculations; the relationship between social and demographic factors was made on the basis of questionable regression analysis; and weighting techniques throughout the formula were based on questionable data and assumptions . . . Overall, the outcome of the first year failed to gain the full support of any member of the working group with the exception of the Home Office sponsors.

The formula approach did raise some issues of principle. The first was one of 'need'. This was not defined, but was said to be the result of establishing through regression analysis those factors which predicted the number of crimes which *should be* recorded in a police force area. It was accepted that this might be different to the actual number recorded, but this must be because the chief constable was less effective and allowed such an unreasonable crime rate to occur. The second principle was that need was not based on an objective assessment of what a police service costs to deliver in an area, rather, it was need based on the allocation of a set national figure for policing, which in turn expected new demands to be met from within those resources. The exception to this rule was to take funds from police forces when a service was privatised, for example the escort of prisoners to court. The final principle was cash-limiting. In the future, chief constables will have a set figure each year which, irrespective of emergencies, must not be exceeded. The chief constable will have to achieve performance measures which will be compared with other police forces which may receive more generous per capita funding, but nevertheless he/she will be told, 'if you have more demands on your resources, that is your fault: the formula predicts your crime should be much lower.'

Privatisation

The pursuit of better value for money (VFM) is a worthy goal, but if it takes on the mantle of a dogmatic mission, it has the potential to disrupt and damage other areas of police service. Privatisation of policing services has two principal themes: the first is the 'outsourcing' of internal services, compulsory competitive tendering (CCT); the second is the selling off of police services, such as the privatisation of prison escorts . . .

The problem with CCT lies in the 'compulsory' nature of the approach. At a time when chief constables are being said by the government to have greater freedom to manage, it is something of a paradox that they have to expend substantial resources going through an exercise of preparing tenders inviting bids for external companies to supply personnel and computer services. The folly of this compulsory approach has recently been acknowledged by the government with a relaxation of the CCT requirements for police vehicle maintenance. With a cash-limited budget and national performance indicators, chief constables are likely to look at outsourcing as a potential way of achieving greater VFM, but the extent of the financial advantages will depend to a great degree on local factors. CCT is unlikely to bring consistent benefits if it is imposed as a dogmatic solution looking for a problem.

The second theme is the privatisation of police work. This has a number of threads. The first was the privatisation of prisoner escorts which is now moving towards full implementation. The second approach was the hidden agenda behind much of the Home Office Core and Ancillary Tasks project. It was interesting that, during the course of this project, the government announced a change in the policy to privatise the registration and licensing of firearms and shotguns because their research had shown that the cost of privatising would have been substantially more than the current costs to the police service. The final report of the Core and Ancillary Tasks project did not achieve the anticipated opportunities to improve efficiency by removing tasks from the police, and it also demonstrated to the Home Office the complexity of police work, a complexity which had previously not been appreciated. In parallel with the Core and Ancillary Tasks project . . . has been a review of traffic policing work. There was a suspicion that this was searching for opportunities to privatise traffic policing, but once again the research challenged the simplistic views which had earlier been expressed about the nature of this work.

The final area for potential privatisation is police patrol. The massive and unregulated growth of the private security industry has created opportunities for communities, if they can afford it, to hire security patrols. The extent to which the government see this as an opportunity to cut spending on the public police has yet to be realised, but it does represent a significant trend which again could change fundamentally the nature of policing in Britain.

(e) The trial process

The recommendations of the Royal Commission on Criminal Justice have been discussed above. The Commission was set up in response to a number of well-publicised miscarriages of justice (which have been considered at p 563 above) but one of the more controversial aspects of its terms of reference was the requirement to consider the resource implications of the trial process. In particular, the Commission was asked:

> to examine the effectiveness of the criminal justice system in England and Wales in securing the conviction of those guilty of criminal offences and the acquittal of those who are innocent, having regard to the efficient use of resources. (Royal Commission on Criminal Justice, 1993, p iii)

Rather than giving priority to the values of fairness and accuracy in identifying offenders, however, the Commission adopted what amounted to an *economic* approach to its task.

Extract 6.2.6

L Bridges and M McConville, 'Keeping Faith With Their Own Convictions: The Royal Commission on Criminal Justice' (1994) 57 MLR 75, pp 80–83

The Commission's prospects of providing a coherent analysis of the criminal justice system in fact foundered at the very outset of its inquiry when it misread its own terms of reference. These, it will be recalled, enjoined the Commission 'to examine the effectiveness of the criminal justice system in England and Wales in securing the conviction of those guilty of criminal offences and the acquittal of those who are innocent, having regard to the efficient use of resources.'[1]

Whilst these terms are inartfully drafted in several respects,[2] they acknowledge the system's twin objectives of convicting those legally guilty of offences and acquitting any who might be innocent. Nonetheless, the Commission made the fundamental error of elevating the background resource context to co-equal status with these traditional concerns. The instruction to conduct their investigation 'having regard to the efficient use of resources' became, for them, not only an organising principle but a systemic *objective* of criminal justice which could, willy-nilly, take precedence over and frustrate the other conventionally-accepted objectives. As Michael Zander subsequently put it:

> 'Our conception . . . was to look at each part of the criminal justice process and to consider how it contributed to the three overall objectives we were asked to consider: securing the conviction of the guilty, the avoidance of convicting the innocent and efficiency in the use of resources.'[3]

The direct consequence of the Commission's framework of analysis was an idiosyncratic approach in applying what it took as the three main elements of its terms of reference. Despite claiming in the report that it saw these as 'closely interlinked,' so that changes to 'rules and procedures governing one part of the criminal justice system will have a consequential effect on the others,'[4] Professor Zander has since explained that 'when considering each separate topic we had to give due – which does not mean equal – weight to such of the three parts of our remit as were relevant to that topic.'[5] It now emerges, for example, that whilst most weight was given to protecting the innocent when recommending retaining the right to silence (i.e. preserving the status quo) and to conviction of the guilty when recommending the re-classification of saliva as a non-intimate sample (i.e. a change favouring the prosecution), efficiency of resources became the dominant concern in considering guilty pleas and in proposing direct judicial involvement in those pleas though the 'sentence canvass' (i.e. an innovation where resource considerations were explicitly placed above the need to protect the innocent). Through this approach, the Commission disregarded the burden of proof inherent in the adversarial system and the reason why it is placed on the State, and thus lost sight of the underlying purpose of the criminal justice process. It is rather like learning from your dentist that, in future, the completion of appointments in the fastest and cheapest way possible will from time to time and on an apparently arbitrary basis, take precedence even where it contradicts the normal concerns to preserve healthy teeth and treat or discard those which are decayed.

Unfortunately, the disclosures of Michael Zander, whilst troubling, do not provide an explanation of how the Commission decided which of the three elements of its remit were relevant – or irrelevant – to any given topic. The Commission itself says that it was 'guided throughout by practical considerations,'[6] but this does not get us much closer to the underlying rationale of its work.

A key to such understanding may be provided by a statement in the report, immediately following the disclaimer of interest in magistrates' courts quoted above, to the effect that 'convictions of the innocent and acquittals of the guilty in serious cases are always jury decisions.'[7] This is a remarkable statement since it implies that the Commission, insofar as it was concerned with miscarriages of justice, directed its attention exclusively to that small minority of criminal cases that result in jury trial. Otherwise the Commission, as a matter of definition rather than inquiry, assumed that the outcomes reached in the vast majority of cases dealt with through other court processes are correct or, at the very least, unproblematic in that, if mistakes do occur, they are not to be regarded as 'serious.' The statistics on criminal cases show just how narrow an application of the Commission's terms of reference this was. Even if we consider only the half million cases annually involving defendants charged with 'indictable/either way' offences, who currently would be eligible for jury trial, only 7 per cent of these cases ever reach the stage of Crown Court trial and less than 5 per cent are subject to an actual jury decision (as distinct from an ordered or directed acquittal). Of the remaining 93 per cent of defendants on these 'serious' charges, around a quarter have the cases against them dropped or dismissed at an early stage before trial or committal in the magistrates' court and two-thirds are convicted as a result of a guilty plea.

The Commission did, of course, give consideration to certain aspects of the criminal court process between the police station and the pinnacle of Crown Court trial. Two of its most controversial recommendations were that the right of defendants in 'either way' cases to elect jury trial should be abolished[8] and that the system of sentence discounts for early guilty pleas at Crown Court should be regularised and reinforced through direct judicial involvement under the 'sentence canvass.'[9] The Commission also proposed that committal proceedings in magistrates' courts should be ended.[10] But the minimalist basis of the Commission's concern with miscarriages of justice, as applicable only to jury trials, meant that it was able to address most of these intermediate issues primarily in terms of efficiency criteria and cost savings, with little or no evident regard for the 'consequential effects' its proposals might have in increasing the risks of innocent persons being convicted (or of the guilty being acquitted). And, given that the majority of non-jury cases actually result in convictions, for the most part on guilty pleas, this emphasis on efficiency would be bound to reinforce the bias of the criminal justice system in that direction, for example, by restricting more 'either way' cases to magistrates' courts where conviction rates are higher, or by inducing more defendants into guilty pleas through the sentence discount and canvass.

Underlying the Commission's pragmatic approach, therefore, is an unstated policy to minimise even further the number of criminal cases reaching the uncertain, fully adversarial stage of jury trial, where serious miscarriages of justice are deemed – and are seen – to occur. There is also an implicit

597

assumption on the part of the Commission that the vast majority of non-jury outcomes in criminal cases, especially convictions, are correct. The Commission does, of course, reaffirm the principle of an accused *individual's* presumed innocence in the face of criminal charges, even if its formulation of the related 'burden of proof,' as 'the obligation on the prosecution to establish the defendant's guilt on the basis of evidence which the defence is entitled to contest,'[11] may be regarded as so anodyne as to lose all moral force. But, overlaying this is a more general, system-based presumption of guilt, which is reflected in a number of otherwise unsubstantiated statements that the Commission uncritically adopts as 'facts':

> 'Nor do we recommend an absolute rule that a confession should be inadmissible unless tape-recorded. To do so would mean that some reliable confessions might be lost. Many witnesses suggested to us that spontaneous remarks uttered on arrest are often the most truthful. We agree.'[12]

> 'A significant number of people plead guilty after a confession who might [under a corroboration rule] be strongly advised by their lawyers not to do so if the confession were the only evidence against them. There is no reason to believe that most of them are not guilty.'[13]

> 'As the Seabrook Committee [the Working Party of the Bar Council] argued, the most common reason for defendants delaying a plea of guilty until the last minute is a reluctance to face the facts until they are at the doorway of the court.'[14]

[1] Royal Commission on Criminal Justice, *Report*, Cm 2263 (London: HMSO, 1993).
[2] For example, by failing to recognise that the objective of the system is to acquit those who *may be* innocent rather than simply those who *are* innocent, and by ignoring the burden of proof and the distinction between legal and factual guilt.
[3] Zander, 'Where the Critics Got it Wrong.' 143 *New Law Journal* 1364–1366, at p 1364.
[4] Ibid p 3.
[5] Zander, 'Where the Critics Got it Wrong,' *New Law Journal*, 24 September 1993, p 1338.
[6] RCCJ, p 3.
[7] RCCJ, p 2.
[8] Ibid pp 85–89.
[9] Ibid pp 110–114.
[10] Ibid pp 89–91.
[11] Ibid p 4.
[12] Ibid pp 60–61.
[13] Ibid p 65.
[14] Ibid p 112. Nor did the Seabrook Committee make any such statement.

Extract 6.2.7

J Jackson, 'The Royal Commission on Criminal Justice: (2) The Evidence Recommendations' [1993] Crim LR 817, pp 818–820

But apart from this concern, the Commission concentrates its chapter on trial procedures on how to improve the efficiency and cost-effectiveness of present procedures so that criminal trials reach an accurate outcome as speedily as possible. There is considerable emphasis, for example, on how to reduce the length of trials and make issues as comprehensible as possible for juries.

This concern for efficiency, as well as accuracy, is a constant theme throughout the report and provides the main motivation for removing the defendant's right to elect for jury trial in either-way offences. But it reflects a particularly limited view of what the purpose of a criminal trial is. Criminal trials play a key role in promoting public confidence in the entire criminal process not just by demonstrating the system's ability to convict the guilty and acquit the innocent, but also in setting standards of fair practice throughout the criminal process.[1] Whatever the level of public confidence in the ability of present trial procedures to reach accurate results, the Commission recognises that there is a need to restore public confidence in the investigation of criminal offences. But it does not appear to recognise that the criminal courts can help to restore confidence by demonstrating that they will not tolerate police malpractices, and there is little discussion of how the courts are to maintain the difficult balance between commanding public confidence in the system's ability to convict the guilty and at the same time commanding the public's confidence that persons are fairly treated by the system.

The adversarial system

The Commission devotes a mere five paragraphs in the introductory first chapter of its report to a general discussion of the appropriateness of adversarial or inquisitorial procedures. Instead of making a theoretical assessment of the relative merits of the two systems, the Commission preferred instead to be guided by, as it put it, 'practical considerations in proposing changes which will, in our view, make our existing system more capable of serving the interests of both justice and efficiency.'[2] But some of the Commission's recommendations sit uncomfortably beside the basic adversarial trial structure which the Commission sees as remaining intact. The Commission's concern to improve the efficiency of trial management prompts it to urge judges to take a more interventionst approach towards trial proceedings and it even recommends that judges should have the power to reduce counsel's fees where a trial has unreasonably exceeded its length because of time wasting tactics by counsel. The Commission also recommends that judges should be particularly vigilant to check unfair cross-examination by counsel of witnesses who are likely to be distressed or vulnerable and it would like to see judges taking a greater interest in the presentation of evidence, even where necessary exercising their little used power to call witnesses.

The problem with these recommendations, which would appear to move the trial in a more inquisitorial direction, is that they are made without any consideration as to how the adversarial trial might be restructured to accommodate this change in direction. The dangers of greater judicial intervention in adversary trials have been well rehearsed by a number of commentators,[3] and have recently been reiterated by the Court of Appeal.[4] One of the dangers is that judicial intervention runs the risk of unduly interfering with the party presentation of evidence. The adversarial system requires that counsel cross-examine opposing witnesses in a vigorous manner, and there may be a thin dividing

599

line between what a judge may view as a perfectly legitimate intrusion to prevent unfair or unnecessary cross-examination and what counsel may view as a completely unwarranted intrusion into the presentation of the case. Intervention is considered to be particularly problematic in jury trials where there is a danger that jurors will become over-influenced by the judge's view of the facts. Where interventions are aimed at restraining counsel's cross-examination, there is the danger that the jury will misread the judge's intention and believe that the judge is expressing a view about the credibility of the witness being cross-examined. The Commission proposes to prevent this by the judge telling juries in general terms before the trial that he may feel it necessary to prevent unnecessary delay and procrastination and that he will not hesitate to intervene to prevent harassment or intimidation by counsel for either side, but this may not prevent the jury in a particular instance inferring from the intervention that the judge holds a particular view about the case or about the particular witness being questioned. The Commission is rightly anxious that, when the judges sum up to juries at the end of the trial, they must be fair to both sides, but judicial intrusion during the trial also risks giving an impression of one-sidedness.[5]

Had the Commission been less concerned about questions of cost and efficiency and more concerned about the effect of adversarial procedures on witnesses, it might have conducted a more searching review of how adversarial structures could be modified to make them less intimidatory for witnesses. One issue that the Commission does not explore, for example, is whether there is greater role for judicial questioning during the trial and at what stage this may be best conducted.[6] There is also little discussion of the Pigot report's recommendation that child witnesses be cross-examined at a preliminary hearing before trial in the absence of the defendant in a less formal setting than at trial.[7] Such discussion would call for some evaluation of the importance of a defendant's right to cross-examination and whether a more inquisitorial role could be taken by judges in less formal settings. Pre-trial hearings also have the advantage of testing witnesses' testimony at a much earlier stage than at trial. One of the assumptions underlying the belief that the adversarial trial is the best method of discovering facts, for example, has been the view that witnesses' perceptions are crystallised at the time of events and that their versions of these events do not change much as they are reported and repeated.[8] But since it is now recognised that versions of reality change according to the interaction that takes place when they are described, it becomes increasingly important to provide conditions for the fair treatment of all witnesses during this interaction.[9]

---

[1] For discussion of the purpose of criminal trials, see Duff, *Trials and Punishments* (1986), Chap 4; Dennis, 'Reconstructing the Law of Criminal Evidence' (1989) C.L.P. 21; Zuckerman, 'Miscarriage of Justice and Judicial Responsibility' [1991] Crim.L.R. 492.

[2] *Report*, 1993, Chap 1, para 12.

[3] See, for instance, Frankel, 'The Search for Truth: An Umpireal View' (1975) 123 U. Pa. L.R. 1031; Saltzburg, 'The Unnecessarily Expanding Role of the American Trial Judge' (1978) 63 Va. L.R. 1.

[4] *Sharp* [1993] 3 ALL E.R. 225.

[5] For further discussion of the problems of judicial intervention in both jury and non-jury trials, see Jackson and Doran, 'Judicial Fact-Finding in the Diplock Court in Northern Ireland' (1990) University of Manchester Faculty of Law Working Paper, No 2, pp 12–20.

[6] For interesting comments on this, see *Sharp* [1993] 3 All E.R. 225, 235.
[7] Home Office, *Report of the Advisory Group on Video Evidence* (1989). See McEwan, [*Evidence and the Adversarial Process* (Oxford: Blackwell, 1992)] at pp 128–129.
[8] MacCrimmon, 'Developments in the Law of Evidence: The 1988–89 Term: The Process of Proof: Schematic Constraints' (1990) 12 Supreme Court L.R. 345, 381.
[9] Jackson, 'Two Methods of Proof in Criminal Procedure' (1988) 51 M.L.R. 549.

(f) The sentencing process: imprisonment

Although the sentencing process itself is not amenable to the influence of economic awareness or the new public management (see Lacey, Extract 6.2.1 above), their impact is apparent in the delivery of many types of sentence. Most notably, the prison service has been transformed from a government department to a quasi-autonomous government agency, and there have been a series of initiatives to privatise or 'contract out' aspects of its work.

Extract 6.2.8

R D King and K McDermott, *The State of Our Prisons* (1995) pp 47–52 (footnotes omitted)

Contracting out and agency status

Contracting out of court escort services and the running of remand prisons had been part of the agenda for criminal justice which Douglas Hurd had discussed with officials on his return to the Home Office in 1987. Woolf gave it scant attention, referring to it only once in his report (Lord Woolf, *Prison Disturbances April 1990*, 1991, paras 12.164–66) in the context of escort duties and then only to say it was not necessary for the Inquiry 'to be drawn into the argument'. Although the Home Office had contracted out the administration of its immigration detention centres and escort services associated with them to Securicor since 1970, serious attention to the involvement of private contractors in prisons was not given until the ideas of the Adam Smith Institute . . . received the enthusiastic (and not entirely disinterested) support of Gardiner, the Chair of the Home Affairs Committee . . . Since then there have been few arguments more divisive. The penal reform groups have been universally condemnatory of what they choose to call privatization and what the Government insists on calling contracting out. In this they have been supported by many academic voices, partly on moral grounds that it would be wrong for private profit to be made out of publicly inflicted misery, partly on historical grounds that private prisons had been abandoned (and with good reason) so long ago that imprisonment had come to be seen as an intrinsic function of the state, and partly on grounds that there would be dangers of a penal–industrial complex, with a vested interest in filling up prisons, becoming unduly influential in criminal justice policy . . .

Others had taken a more encouraging [M McConville and J E H Williams, *Crime and Punishment: A Radical Rethink* (London: Tawney Society, 1985)], or at least a more pragmatic [M Taylor and K Pease, 'Private Prisons and

Penal Purpose' in R Matthews (ed), *Privatizing Criminal Justice* (London: Sage Publications, 1989)] stand on the issue, not least because it would be hard to see how any kind of private contract could be drawn up which did not include a higher specification of service than was already provided in the public sector. Morgan and King ['Profiting from Prison' *New Society*, 23 October 1987] argued that the contracting out of services rather than whole prisons would offer opportunities entirely congruent with their prospectus for the normalization of the prison. In an attempt to bridge the gap between evolving Government policy and the rejection of the profit motive by penal reform groups, they also floated the possibility that non-profit bodies such as NACRO, already heavily involved in devising standards, might actually engage in the process of implementing them by bidding for a contract – but this was an idea not well received.

Although private prisons figured little in Woolf's deliberations, hardly had the report appeared before the Government issued invitations to tender for running The Wolds as a remand prison. The White Paper also made it plain that the Government proposed a rolling programme to contract out court escort services . . . As the tender documents for The Wolds made clear, the Woolf agenda had greatly heightened the validity of the argument that the Home Office would insist that private contractors provide standards considerably higher than those in the public sector and unlike anything previously experienced by remand prisoners . . . The award of the contract for The Wolds to Group 4 in November 1991 was followed by a competition for Blakenhurst, a 650-bed local prison, which was won by UK Detention Services, a consortium of Corrections Corporation of America, John Mowlem, and Sir Robert McAlpine, in 1992. In September 1993 Michael Howard announced that: '[the] private sector must be large enough to provide sustained competition and involve several private sector companies – a genuinely mixed economy' . . . The strategy was clear – to proceed quite quickly to contract with private sector firms for about 10 per cent of the prison estate, both new prisons and existing prisons, especially those which had most room for improvement, which would be 'market tested'. In this way, without becoming unduly dependent upon any one private sector company, considerable pressure could be exerted on the public sector prisons to become more economical and efficient, if not also more effective. It should be said that pressure has also been maintained on the private sector by the Government's determination to ensure that there will be several players in the field – as evidenced by the award of the third contract for Doncaster to Premier Prisons, a subsidiary of the American security company, Wakenhut.

It was probably always the case that one of the main planks in the Government's platform on contracting out prison services was the pressure that this would bring to bear on the Prison Officers' Association. Fresh Start had eliminated some opportunities for restrictive practices by prison officers, but opened up others. And one of the great failures of Fresh Start, as noted above, had been not first establishing appropriate staff complements for each prison. It was always evident that any savings which were to be made by private contractors would be in the area of staffing. If The Wolds could be seen to staff residential units with a ratio of one officer on duty to fifty prisoners, for how long could comparable public sector prisons continue to operate such units with a minimum of one senior and three basic grade officers? The contracting out of escort services, initially for East Midlands and Humberside in 1993–4, the Metropolitan Police District in 1994, and three further areas now identified as East Anglia, Transpennine, and North East, would remove what once had been a most lucrative perk for prison officers.

The mechanism for making sure that all public sector employees took these lessons to heart was 'market testing' which was pioneered at the rebuilt and refurbished Strangeways. In contrast to the competitions for The Wolds and Blakenhurst, the Prison Service was permitted to bid for the Strangeways contract. As Kenneth Clarke, who had succeeded Kenneth Baker as Home Secretary, put it:

> 'Market testing will, I believe, cause the Prison Service to examine its own performance in the light of the competitive pressure and encourage the spread of those reforms across public sector prisons much more quickly than would otherwise have been the case'. (quoted in McDonald ['Public Imprisonment by Private Means: The Re-emergence of Private Prisons and Jails in the United States, the United Kingdom and Australia' in R D King and M Maguire (eds), *Prisons in Context* (Oxford: Oxford University Press, 1994)])

The Prison Service [*Briefing No 54*, 10 November 1992 (London: Home Office, 1992)] got the message:

> 'A bid sticking to every detail of a central agreement dating back from 1987 [i.e. Fresh Start] is unlikely to beat the competition . . . Any agreements that hinder the chances of constructing an effective bid will have to be reconsidered in consultation with the unions.'

It also got the contract. It is unlikely that it was the lowest bid. But, as Derek Lewis, who by then had become the Director General, made clear, it represented 'levels of performance and value for money that we have not previously seen in the public sector [H M Prison Service, 'In-House Team to Run Manchester', *News Release* 15, July 1993 (London: Home Office, 1993)]. From the Government's point of view, the real measure of the success of The Wolds, therefore, may lie as much in the effect it may have had on Strangeways and other prisons subject to market testing, as it will in the normal application of what now have to be called performance indicators. Nevertheless, targets for cost savings in the public sector set for 1994–5 apparently take account of performance so far in the contracted-out sector.

In September 1994 the Prisons Board informed governors that twenty-one prisons with the poorest performance during 1993–4 were under consideration for market testing. None of our prisons was on the list, which excluded dispersal and local prisons. However, it seems unlikely that the lessons would have been lost on Birmingham but short of specific market testing quick improvements there will have been difficult to establish. Of somewhat greater import from the point of view of the research reported here may have been the effect of moving towards a purchaser rather than a provider of health care services, and the contracting out of education. It is by no means clear how far the first of these has proceeded, although on 1 May 1992 the Prison Medical Service was relaunched as the Health Care Service for Prisoners and the annual report for 1992–3 refers to the replacement of three medical officer posts at Belmarsh by psychiatric registrars on secondment from the NHS . . . Initial findings from inquiries by the Prison Reform Trust suggest that the most immediate consequence of changes in the education service has been the loss of many of the positive features that had previously prevailed . . .

On 1 April 1993, three years to the day after the prisoners took over the chapel at Strangeways, HM Prison Service became the third largest executive agency to have been formed since the 'Next Steps' programme was launched in 1988. Woolf had criticized the Prison Service's statement of purpose, adopted in 1988 and displayed in all establishments and virtually all official documents ever since, because it failed to take specific account of remand prisoners, it failed to make explicit that prisoners should be treated with justice whilst in custody, and it failed to relate the role of the Prison Service to the criminal justice system generally (Woolf 1991, paras 10.14–16). In spite of that the mission statement of the new agency remains unchanged: 'Her Majesty's Prison Service serves the public by keeping in custody those committed by the courts.

Our duty is to care for them with humanity and to help them lead law abiding and useful lives in custody and after release'.

Three key documents have set out the basis on which the newly formed agency works. The *Framework Document* . . . has a foreword by the then Home Secretary, Kenneth Clarke, and describes the procedures for accountability and the 'stand-off' relationship whereby the Home Secretary allocates resources and approves the corporate and business plans, and the Director General is responsible for day-to-day management of the service. It also declared six goals of the Prison Service and the key performance indicators against which success is to be evaluated. The *Corporate Plan* . . . has a preface from the Director General, Derek Lewis, and sets out strategic proposals for achieving the goals over a three year period, whilst the *Business Plan* . . . sets targets and action plans for the immediate financial year. Between them these documents replace the Statement of Tasks and Functions introduced under Circular Instruction 55/1984 . . .

In April 1994 HM Prison Service Agency celebrated its first birthday and ushered in yet more change. With the retirement of Ian Dunbar, his post and the Directorate of Inmate Administration was abolished as part of a review intended to produce a smaller strategic headquarters with a group of Central Services units supporting establishments in which governors will have greater devolved powers for budgets, contracts, staff recruitment, and regimes. Under this latest revision line management above establishment level now reports to just two directorates – Custody and Programmes – via a regrouped force of area managers.

These changes have had a major effect on the way that the work of prisons is officially assessed. It is illustrated by the following performance statistics.

Extract 6.2.9

HM Prison Service, *Prison Service Annual Report and Accounts, April 1996–March 1997* (1997) p 274

SECTION B: PERFORMANCE STATISTICS

Prison service performance against key targets 1996–97

Goal	Key performance target	Target	Performance
Keep prisoners in custody	KPI 1: The number of escapes from prisons and escorts	To ensure that no Category A prisoners escape and to ensure that the rate of escapes from establishments and from escorts, expressed as a percentage of the average prison population, is at least 10% lower than in 1995–96	No Category A escapes Escape rate reduced by 2% on 1995/6: 0.23%
Maintain order, control, discipline and a safe environment	KPI 2: The number of assaults on staff, prisoners and others which result in a disciplinary adjudication	To ensure that the rate of assaults on prisoners, staff and others, expressed as a percentage of the average prison population, is lower than 1995–96	Achieved. Assault rate reduced by 12% on 1995–96
	KPI 3: The rate of positive random drug testing	To ensure that the rate of positive random testing for drugs is lower in the fourth quarter of 1996–97 than in the first quarter of that year	Positive random testing rate in the first quarter was 24.0% and in the fourth quarter 24.2%
Provide decent conditions for prisoners and meet their needs, including health care	KPI 4: The number of prisoners held in units of accommodation intended for fewer numbers	To ensure that no prisoners are held three to a cell designed for one	Achieved. No prisoners were held three to a cell designed for one
Provide positive regimes which help prisoners address their offending behaviour and allow them as full and responsible a life a possible	KPI 5: The number of hours which, on average, prisoners spend in purposeful activity	To ensure that prisoners spend on average at least 26.5 hours per week in purposeful activity	23.8 hours per week

Prison service performance against key targets 1996–97 (cont'd)

Goal	Key performance target	Target	Performance
	KPI 6: The proportion of prisoners held in prisons where all prisoners on standard and enhanced regimes are unlocked for at least 10 hours on a weekday	To ensure that by 31 March 1997, at least 60% of prisoners are held in establishments which unlock all prisoners on the standard or enhanced regime for at least ten hours per weekday	Achieved: 65%
Help prisoners to prepare for their return to the community	KPI 7: The number of prisoners completing programmes accredited as effective in reducing re-offending	To ensure that at least 1,300 prisoners complete programmes accredited as being effective in reducing re-offending, of whom 650 should complete the Sex Offender Treatment Programme	Achieved: 1,373 completions of which 663 were sex offender treatment programmes
Deliver prison services using the resources provided by Parliament with maximum efficiency	KPI 8: The average cost of a prison place	To ensure that the average cost of a prison place does not exceed £24,388	Achieved: £24,271
	KPI 9: The amount of staff training	To ensure that on average, staff spend at least six days in training.	5.4 days of training per staff member

The principal advantage claimed for the private management of prisons is a gain in efficiency. Costs may be reduced through more flexible employment practices (for example, using fixed-term contracts with lower salaries than the comparable public sector), less bureaucracy, and more flexible use of capital (for example, using the market to attract cheaper and faster construction firms to build or adapt new prison accommodation). The major objection to such developments is that, as a matter of principle, it is the state which is responsible for the administration of justice and that it is wrong to allow profit from the infliction of punishment on others. There are also concerns that the commitment and training of privatised staff will be motivated by financial and career success, to the detriment of prisoners' welfare. Financially, it may prove difficult to compare privatised and public service because the contracts are considered commercially sensitive and are not published (and neither are staff costs included in the prison service's annual accounts). There are also hidden costs associated with the tendering process and supervising the arrangements in the public interest. In fact, contracted out prisons are not the cheapest in terms of operating costs per prisoner per annum (see Her Majesty's Prison Service, 1997a, table D) but they may achieve other objectives. Arguably, they are more accountable than state operated prisons because the terms of the contract, which include compliance with the Prison Rules and the implementing of national standards, can be enforced by the 'controller' which the prison service attaches to each contracted out prison. In addition, the government has been able to use privatisation as a means of moderating the power of the Prison Officers' Association and of galvanising the previous civil service management (see generally, Morgan, 1997).

Contracting out has been accompanied by other public management initiatives. Specific services, such as education, laundry, medical services and catering, have been contracted out. In addition, the acquisition of agency status enabled the introduction of goals and performance indicators for the prison service generally, as reproduced in Extract 6.2.9 above. These form the basis for individual governors' contracts to provide prison services, as recommended by the Woolf Inquiry (Woolf, 1991; see also Jones, 1993, p 198). It will be noted that performance is measured in ways which do not necessarily reflect the quality of regimes as expressed in the goals. However, in terms of quality, contracted out prisons have performed as well as state prisons and sometimes better (see James et al, 1997). Indeed, Taylor and Pease have suggested that they have the potential to provide 'an incentive to rehabilitate . . . and a commercial incentive to develop programmes which really change people' (Taylor and Pease, 1989). It remains doubtful whether that potential will be realised, however. Arguments about the future development of prison policy have been overshadowed by political interference and the dominance of law and order issues. Increasingly, security has resurfaced as a major priority, following some embarrassing lapses in the early 1990s, and that is diverting money in the cash-limited (indeed, reducing) prison budget away from spending which is designed to improve prisoners' regimes or to prevent them from offending in the future. Since the provision of security is expensive, it might be anticipated that private contractors will prefer to manage the less risky sectors of the prison population, leaving the state sector to deal with the more troublesome – albeit offering a lower quality of prison life (see Morgan, 1993).

(g) Community sentences

In the provision of community sentences also, the general concern with efficiency has prompted changes in organisation and management. In 1984, a *Statement of National Objectives and Priorities* for the probation service was published by the Home Office (Home Office, 1984), prioritising its objectives and emphasising accountability for expenditure on it and, since 1993, the Home Office has published a series of rolling three-year plans for the Service. This central government pressure, together with that of the Audit Commission (see Audit Commission, 1989), has forced local probation services to analyse their performance in the context of cash limits on their budgets (Field and Hough, 1993). More significantly, the importance of obtaining value for money has concentrated attention on the purposes of community sentences and their effectiveness (see Chapter 5 above; Lloyd et al, 1994) and the ethos of the service appears to have suffered as a result (see Humphrey, 1991; Humphrey and Pease, 1992). In particular, there has been concern that the underlying philosophy of the service is not reflected in the key performance indicators and targets but that they necessarily dominate officers' working lives. In the table reproduced in Extract 6.2.10 below, note the reservations about possible 'lax enforcement' in the column headed 'Progress': are probation officers really ignoring the requirements of the National Standards (see Home Office, 1995a) for initiating breach proceedings, or are they experiencing too much pressure to demonstrate success, or do they regard the willingness to institute breach proceedings as an inappropriate measure of success?

Extract 6.2.10

Home Office, *The Three Year Plan for the Probation Service 1997–2000* (1997) Annex D

Key performance indicators and targets

Indicator	1996–97 target	Progress	1997–98 target
KPI 1: Predicted and actual reconviction rates for persons subject to community orders by type of orders.	To maintain actual reconviction at a rate lower than predicted	No data available. Latest data are for those commencing community sentences in 1993.	To lower the actual reconviction rates for all types of order, and achieve rates lower than those predicted.
KPI 2: Number of community orders completed without early termination for breach or a further offence / total number of orders completed: • probation order • CSO • supervision order • combination order	To achieve the following completion rates: • probation order – 82% or more; • CSO – 71% or more; • supervision order – 80% or more; • combination order – 73% or more.	Targets are being exceeded in respect of all four types of orders. However, it remains of concern that these high levels of completion may be the result of lax enforcement which does not meet the requirements of revised National Standards.	To achieve the following completion rates within the framework of the enforcement requirements of National Standards: probation order – 82% CSO – 80% supervision order – 80% combination order – 80%
KPI 3: Number of licences completed without breach of licence including both breach leading to recall to prison and other breach / number of licences: • automatic conditional licence (ACR) • discretionary conditional licence (DCR)	To achieve a completion rate for ACRs of 85% or more. No target was set for DCRs	The target is being exceeded, but this again may reflect lax enforcement	To achieve the following completion rates within the framework of the enforcement requirements of National Standards: ACR – 85% DCR – 85%

KPI 4: a) cost per pre-sentence report; b) cost per welfare report; c) annual unit cost per community order; • probation order • community service order • supervision order • combination order d) annual unit cost/licence	To maintain or reduce estimated unit costs, at national level and in real terms, relative to the average estimates for 1994–95. The target figures are: • Cost per PSR – £250 • Cost per welfare report – £880 • Annual cost per probation order – £2,510 • Annual unit cost per CSO – £1,840 • Annual unit cost per supervision order – £2,420	The service nationally is currently maintaining unit costs in all five categories at levels below those targetted. However, there are wide variations in the performance of individual services.	To reduce unit costs in real terms in all four categories at national level. The target figures are: • cost per PSR [pre-sentence report] – £220 • cost per welfare report – £900 • annual cost per probation order – £2,360 • annual cost per CSO – £1,770 • annual unit cost per supervision order – £2,240 • annual unit cost per combination order – £3,500 • annual unit cost of licence – £1,120
KPI 5: a) Average number of working days to provide a pre-sentence report to the magistrates' courts b) Number of pre-sentence reports provided to the Crown Court within 7 working days of request by the Court / number of pre-sentence reports completed	a) Average number of working days to provide a PSR to the magistrates' court to be less than 16 No target set for KPI 5(b)	The service nationally is improving its performance but is still failing to achieve the target set in line with National Standards.	a) The average number of working days to provide a PSR to the magistrates' court to be less than 16 in 100% of cases. b) 11% or more of pre-sentence reports provided to the Crown Court to be provided within 7 working days.
KPI 6: Number of welfare reports completed within ten weeks of receipt of papers by the service / total number of welfare reports completed	95% or more of welfare reports to be completed within 10 weeks	Performance against the target continues to be poor. Very considerable improvement will be required for the service to achieve the target set in line with National Standards	95% or more of welfare reports to be completed within 10 weeks.
KPI 7: Number of occupied bedspaces in approved hostels	83% of approved hostel places should be occupied	Although service performance nationally is improving, further improvement will be required if the service is to achieve its target for 1996–97.	83% or more of approved hostel places to be occupied.
KPI 8: Number of hostel residents completing orders / number of departures	To raise the completion rate to 65%	The service is on target to achieve and better the target set.	To raise the completion rate to 80% within the framework of the enforcement requirements of National Standards.
KPI 9: Measure of court satisfaction (national sampling)	To maintain the overall satisfaction rate of 88% To improve the percentage of magistrates finding pre-sentence reports consistently useful	The level of overall satisfaction is being maintained nationally. (92% in latest 12 months). Owing to a change in the way in which magistrates views are surveyed, it has not proved possible to obtain information relating to the percentage that find PSRs consistently useful. However in the latest 12 months an estimated 34% of magistrates in areas inspected by HMIP were very satisfied with the overall usefulness of PSRs, compared with 31% in the previous 12 months.	100% of magistrates to express satisfaction with the work of the service overall. 80% of magistrates to be very satisfied with the overall usefulness of pre-sentence reports.

In developing the use of particular community sentences, considerations of efficiency may often prove more persuasive than the underlying penal objectives of the measure. The introduction of curfew orders with electronic tagging, under ss 12 and 13 of the Criminal Justice Act 1991, illustrates this well. Initially, electronic tagging was seen as a potentially useful condition of bail which might enable the order to be enforced more easily and therefore used more readily. Early trials demonstrated a number of technical problems with tagging (Mair and Nee, 1990) but they were not regarded as an insurmountable obstacle to introducing the curfew order and tagging as a sentence for offenders aged 16 and over, whereby they can be required to remain at specified places, typically their homes, for a minimum of two and a maximum of 12 hours each day, for up to six months. However, it was decided to conduct local trials of the new sentence before introducing it nationally and these began in 1995 (having been empowered by the Criminal Justice and Public Order Act 1994, Sched 9, para 42). The trials were conducted in Manchester, Reading and Norfolk, and later extended into Greater Manchester and Berkshire. A preliminary report on the trial dealt with the process of tendering for the tagging contract, the initial take-up of the order by magistrates, their attitude to the order and the experiences of offenders who had been tagged (see Mair and Mortimer, 1996). A report (Mortimer and May, 1997) on the second year of using the sentence in the trial areas brought that information up to date but also concentrated on two questions (interestingly, phrased in the language of the new public management): 'which sorts of sentences curfew orders were competing with (the "market share")?' and 'how much a national roll-out of electronic monitoring would cost?' Generally, during the second year in the areas concerned, curfew orders were rarely used: there were around 375 imposed, compared with 2,900 probation orders, 2,400 community service orders, 900 combination orders and 2,800 custodial sentences. Of those 375 orders, 28 per cent were imposed for theft and handling offences, 19 per cent for burglary and 13 per cent for driving whilst disqualified. The completion rate was 82 per cent. In terms of 'market share,' 'curfew orders with electronic monitoring were seen by magistrates as alternatives to custody and the higher end community penalties (community service orders and combination orders)'. The government has considered the trial to be a success and the Home Secretary, Jack Straw, highlighted the gradual willingness of magistrates to consider the sentence and its potential as a form of community punishment when he announced his intention, in November 1997, to extend the tagging scheme and to pilot its use with fine defaulters, young and petty persistent offenders. This has since been achieved in the Crime (Sentences) Act 1997. The Home Secretary did not mention the estimated costs and savings which would be involved but they actually formed an important element of the trial results:

Extract 6.2.11

E Mortimer and C May, *Electronic Monitoring in Practice: The Second Year of the Trials of Curfew Orders* **(1997) pp 40–43**

Comparison of the components of the cost estimates

Figure 1, based on costs in the first year, shows a comparison of the components of costs. The greatest cost is the field office running cost, which is necessarily high even with a low volume of offenders tagged. The next greatest cost, at least at higher volumes, is the total running cost for all offenders, which depends directly on the number of offenders dealt with. At the top end of the range of numbers tagged the cost of any extra equipment required becomes more significant. The chart shows that the costs of breaches and changes of term are a small percentage of total costs.

Figure 1   Components of first-year cost

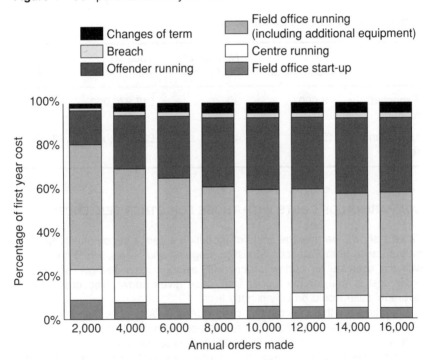

Each of the component costs shown in figure 1 recurs annually except the start-up costs of field offices.

Total costs versus costs per order

The model shows the way in which costs would vary for different values of the three main factors. Not surprisingly the total cost would increase with increasing numbers of offenders, with more field offices and with a long average length on curfew. However the cost per order shows a different pattern. For small numbers of offenders costs per order would be very high because the fixed costs are incurred for any number of offenders. Above an annual figure of about 6,000 offenders the cost per order varies little for a given average length of order.

Cost estimates

The model has been developed in order to be able to give cost estimates for a variety of possible uses of electronic monitoring. This section gives two estimates of the costs that would apply to the national extension of the current system. The first is based on an average or expected scenario, whilst the second is for an 'upper limits' scenario. Results are given in table 1. Should our expected number of annual orders prove to be an over-estimate then the total cost would be less, while the cost per order would be slightly higher.

Table 1 Cost estimates for two scenarios

	Annual orders made	Number of field offices	Total first year cost	Cost per order
'Expected' scenario	8,000	30	£13,970,000	£1,750
'Upper limit' scenario	12,000	40	£22,500,000	£1,900

COMPARISON OF COSTS WITH THOSE FOR OTHER SENTENCES

Table 2 shows the average costs of probation orders and community service orders (taken from *Probation Statistics, England and Wales, 1996*) compared with the estimate for curfew orders with electronic monitoring. The curfew order cost is that for the 'upper limit' case given above. The cost for the 'average' case would be only slightly less.

It can be seen that the cost of a curfew order is likely to be higher than that of a community service order, but rather less per order than probation. However, it must not be forgotten that additional costs will arise when probation and community service orders are imposed alongside a curfew order. The evidence from the second year of the trials in the Norfolk area (for which this information is most readily available) is that 24 per cent were given a probation order, 13 per cent community service and seven per cent a combination order, with the Crown Court much more likely to impose an additional order. (The numbers are too small to allow us to distinguish probation orders with added conditions.) Adding an element to allow for additional orders, the average cost of a curfew order would be about £2,700, rather more than a probation order.

Table 2 Average cost of different types of order, 1996/97 prices

Probation order	£2,200
Community service order	£1,700
Curfew order with electronic monitoring	£1,900

It is difficult to compare the *overall* costs of curfew orders directly with custody. However, in the report of the first year of the trials the *monthly* costs of curfew orders and custody were compared. The same approach is adopted here.

Where curfew orders replace custody, that custody would ideally have been spent in a category C prison. However, any time spent on remand or waiting for a move to a category C establishment means that some or even all of a custodial sentence would be spent in a local prison or remand centre. The monthly cost (at 1996/97 prices) of custody is about £1,420 in a category C prison and £2,040 in a local prison or remand centre. Comparing this with about £760 for a curfew order (including an element for additional community penalties), the cost of a curfew order is between a third and a half that of custody. Another way of expressing this is that the average cost of a curfew order would buy about eight weeks in a category C prison or six weeks in a local prison or remand centre.

OVERALL COSTS AND SAVINGS

The survey of sentencing choices described [above], though based on small numbers, gives an indication of the sentences that might have been imposed had curfew orders not been available.

Diversion from custody

Custody was 'seriously considered' for nearly two-thirds of those on whom a curfew was imposed. Taking the estimate of 8,000 curfew orders and assuming that two-thirds of these replace sentences of three month's custody we estimate that more than 1,300 prison places would be saved on national roll-out. These places would be spread over prison establishments in England and Wales so it is not possible to say that the costs of one or more prisons would be saved in the short term. In the longer term, however, the potential savings, based crudely on the current costs of custody (realised as reductions in the prison building programme and in running costs), could be in the order of £20,000,000 to £30,000,000 a year. Balanced against the costs of electronic monitoring, this implies an overall saving of several million pounds a year. It should be remembered that we are extrapolating from a small sample, with the likely take-up of curfew orders by the Crown Court being in particular doubt. However, the savings would be increased substantially if, firstly, the use of curfew orders were to prove greater than that indicated by the trials, and if, secondly, electronic monitoring were to be made available for types of offenders not eligible at present. With good management and continued successful operation the first of these possibilities should be achievable, whilst the second is already being actively pursued.

Diversion from other sentences

The sentencing survey showed that community sentences, in particular community service orders, were also often considered in cases when a curfew order was chosen. As the costs of community sentences are similar to those estimated for curfew orders, a reduction in their market share would yield neither significant savings nor extra costs.

There is no firm evidence from the sentencing survey that other sentences would be significantly diverted to curfew orders. It is unlikely, therefore, that there would be a large loss of revenue from fines.

(h) The context of resource allocation

The current prominence of questions about resources in criminal justice policy is not necessarily undesirable. It is right that expenditure should be targeted effectively and rendered accountable. But the starting point should not be an abstract notion of efficiency and value for money. The best use of resources can be assessed only by reference to the purposes which they are intended to serve. In other words, efficiency and value have to be understood in a context, in this case, the aims of criminal justice (see Lacey, 1994). When economics and the new public management are allowed to dominate policy planning, they distract attention from human priorities, such as reducing crime and victimisation, and securing fairness for suspects. Nevertheless, questions about resources can force us to think more deeply about the role of the criminal justice process in achieving those priorities. Policy choices may extend beyond the criminal justice process and, in terms of the broader allocation of society's wealth, it may be asked whether it is more cost-effective to tackle crime in other ways. One example of this approach is the work of Clarke in promoting crime prevention as the key to crime reduction. He has argued that the application of various measures to make crime more difficult or less profitable will have a much more dramatic impact on the rate of crime than processing offenders. Thus, personal and home security can defend victims from criminal acts. Controlling weapons (guns, knives, spray cans), enabling surveillance (by cameras or by designing spaces so that potential offenders cannot hide or take victims by surprise), identifying property and removing temptation (for example, reducing the amount of cash held on persons or premises and using electronic payment) all provide practical examples of creating disincentives for crime to take place (see Clarke, 1992; Mayhew et al, 1976). As Rock has noted (Rock, 1997), this approach is itself based on the rational choice theory which underlies economics, and it still does not deal with the experiences of victims and offenders. By contrast, the Audit Commission's recent report on young offending argues that prevention is a less costly way of tackling crime but extends the idea of prevention to include education, leisure opportunities, inter-agency co-operation, and consultation with local residents.

Extract 6.2.12

Audit Commission, *Misspent Youth: Young People and Crime* (1996)
pp 2, 4–6

PROCESSING AND DEALING WITH YOUNG OFFENDERS

'Public services spend around £1 billion a year on processing and dealing
with young offenders . . .'

1. Crime is high on the public agenda. Crimes against individuals – such as theft, burglary and assault – increased by 73 per cent between 1981 and 1995 in England and Wales, according to the British Crime Survey of households. A disproportionate number are committed by young people of 10–17 years, especially by a small number of persistent offenders. Public services spend around £1 billion a year on processing and dealing with young offenders; around £660 million of this is spent by the police, largely on identifying them . . .

2. Three out of five young offenders who are apprehended are given a warning or caution by a police officer, but very little else is done to challenge their behaviour. The police start proceedings against the remainder, a process which entails the completion of around 40 forms, and which can take half a shift. Four out of five court cases analysed by the Audit Commission were adjourned, leading to an average of four appearances in the youth court before a sentencing decision is reached. On average, the whole process takes from 70 days in some areas to 170 days in others . . .

3. Little or nothing happens to half of the young people proceeded against by the police: one-quarter have their cases withdrawn, discontinued or dismissed, and another quarter receive a conditional or absolute discharge. The rest are given a community sentence, fine or custody – but the effectiveness of different kinds of sentence on re-offending by young people is not monitored in most areas.

4. The court process costs, on average, around £2,500 for each young person sentenced. In many cases, resources could be used more effectively to address offending behaviour directly, through 'caution plus' action programmes, such as those developed by the Northamptonshire Diversion Unit. This scheme both arranges compensation for victims and addresses the behaviour of the young offender, at one-quarter of the cost of the youth court process. If one in five young offenders accepted a caution plus programme instead of being processed through the courts, about £40 million a year could be released to fund services that challenge offending behaviour and prevent crime . . .

PREVENTING CRIME BY YOUNG PEOPLE

'Local agencies need to pilot such interventions in the areas where they are most needed, and evaluate them to learn what works.'

5. While public services clearly need to deal effectively with offending behaviour by young people, it would be better to prevent the offending behaviour in the first place. Factors associated with offending include gender, with boys more likely to offend than girls; inadequate parenting; aggressive and hyperactive behaviour in early childhood; truancy and exclusion from school; peer group pressure to offend; unstable living conditions; lack of training and employment; and drug and alcohol abuse. These factors can be used to help target measures to prevent crime. Steps can be taken by a wide range of agencies to address such problems by intervening before those at risk start to offend. Local agencies need to pilot such interventions in the areas where they are most needed, and evaluate them to learn what works (Figure 1).

- **Parents**: Children brought up in families with lax parental supervision and which live in poor neighbourhoods are more likely to become offenders. A growing percentage of children are experiencing these factors. Parents who are bringing up their children in difficult circumstances can be helped by professionals (or by volunteer, experienced parents) to improve their parenting skills and produce better behaved, more trustworthy children who need less expensive supervision and intervention later on.
- **Schools**: Where parents fail to socialise their children adequately, schools end up coping with bad behaviour among their pupils. Young people who are excluded from school or who truant are more likely to offend – so it is worrying that the number of pupils permanently excluded from school has risen from around 3,000 to 11,000 over four years; and that one in ten pupils in years 10 and 11 truant at least once a week. Schools can be helped to deal with difficult pupils by support workers, and by advice from child and adolescent mental health services.
- **Leisure**: Young people at risk can be encouraged to mix with others who behave responsibly and engage in constructive activities, such as sport. Those activities that are most successful at reducing offending promote a positive and responsible self-image; improve reasoning skills; help young people to get on with others; and involve non-offenders. Summer activity schemes can help discourage juvenile nuisance and offending.
- **Housing**: Young people living in unstable conditions are more likely to offend. 'Foyers' – hostels which provide an integrated approach to housing, training and employment – have had some success in reaching young people who are homeless and unemployed.

616

Figure 1 Breaking into the cycle of antisocial behaviour

Local agencies need to pilot schemes which use these interventions in the areas where they are most needed, and evaluate them to learn what works.

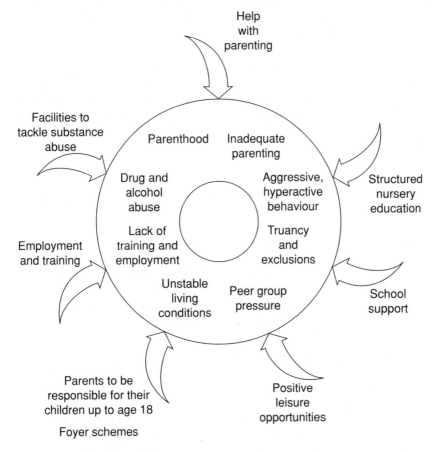

- **Training and employment**: Sixty per cent of young offenders on supervision orders have little to do, as they are not engaged in work, training or education. Many of them are absent from school for much of their last two years and so miss out on advice from the careers service offered there. Few young people who are not living with a parent attend school or college, while 72 per cent who are living with their parents do so. Those living in institutions are particularly likely to be unemployed.
- **Services for tackling drug and alcohol abuse**: Use of drugs and alcohol is high among young offenders – 70 per cent of those on supervision orders admit to taking drugs and over half get drunk at least once a week. Multi-agency Drug Action Teams need to ensure that some of the services developed locally cater for the needs of those under the age of 18.

617

DEVELOPING A STRATEGY

6. Resources need to be shifted from processing young offenders to dealing with their behaviour, while efforts to prevent offending and other antisocial behaviour by young people need to be piloted, evaluated, co-ordinated and targeted on the deprived areas with high crime rates . . .

7. Local authority chief executives should consider initiating forums in which all relevant local agencies participate. These groups should give priority to identifying areas where crime, juvenile nuisance and the risks of offending are high, and to co-ordinating a local response. They need to consider how a strategy for processing, dealing with and preventing offending by young people could be co-ordinated.

3. COMMUNITY, COMMUNITY VALUES AND SEX OFFENDERS

(a) Stigma and reintegration of offenders

The desirability of reintegrating ex-offenders into the community from which they have come has long been recognised. Conviction, particularly for a serious crime, carries with it in addition to the direct formal punishment imposed by the court a range of other forms of indirect deprivation and disqualification. Some of these are officially imposed, such as the many legal restrictions on the employment of ex-offenders (see von Hirsch and Wasik, 1997), but others are the result of informal stigma and prejudice which attend conviction and hamper a person's reintegration into the community (see Apex Trust (1994), McEvoy (1995) and Maxwell and Mallon (1997)). The Council of Europe has recognised as a general principle that 'if one is to prevent a convicted person from committing further offences, their social reintegration must be made as easy as possible' (Council of Europe, 1984). This principle is given legal force in England and Wales in the Rehabilitation of Offenders Act 1974, a statute designed to allow ex-offenders to 'live down' convictions after the expiry of a period of time free of further convictions. Many other countries have similar 'expungement' statutes, which either take their effect automatically on expiry of time, or which require the ex-offender to make application to a court to 'wipe the slate clean'. In general, the legal effect of expungement is to allow ex-offenders, when applying for employment, to declare that they have not been 'convicted' at all (see Walker and Padfield, 1996).

In recent years, however, the kind of liberal penal philosophy which lay behind the Rehabilitation of Offenders Act 1974 has come increasingly under attack, and the Act now has no more than a marginal impact on criminal justice. In Chapter 1 we discussed the increased influence of right-wing 'law and order' policies in criminal justice, and the rise of what Bottoms has called 'populist punitiveness' (Bottoms, 1995). On this approach, offenders are seen almost as a 'species apart' with whom ordinary persons need feel no sympathy at all (see Garland, 1996). We also noted the influence of the managerial model in criminal justice, where the attention moves away from the complexities of responsibility for individual crimes to the 'efficient' and 'cost-effective' management of offenders as a class. As Feeley and Simon have commented in an influential essay:

> Old Penology is rooted in a concern for individuals, and preoccupied with such concepts as guilt, responsibility and obligation, as well as diagnosis, intervention and treatment of the individual offender . . . In contrast the New Penology has a radically different orientation. It is actuarial. It is concerned with techniques for identifying, classifying and managing groups assorted by levels of dangerousness. It is sceptical that liberal interventionist crime control strategies do or can make a difference. Thus its aim is not to intervene in individuals' lives for the purpose of ascertaining responsibility, making the guilty 'pay for their crime', or changing them. Rather, it seeks to regulate groups as part of a strategy of managing danger. (Feeley and Simon, 1994)

The abandonment of traditional liberal concerns to reduce the stigmatic effects of conviction and to reintegrate offenders after their sentence has been completed, carries the danger that offenders become relegated to a form of general, and permanent, second-class citizenship (von Hirsch and Wasik, 1997). The predominance in political rhetoric of concerns about 'risk' to the community has meant that more and more exceptions to the operation of the Rehabilitation of Offenders Act have been created, in an ever-increasing range of employments. There has also been a substantial increase in the provision of information by the police about the criminal records of prospective employees (see Maxwell and Mallon, 1997). These trends, and the competing concerns of community safety, the rehabilitation of ex-offenders and 'populist punitiveness' all come together most starkly in the context of sex offenders in the community.

(b) Sex offenders: a special case?

As Donald West has pointed out in a recent essay, 'sex offenders have become modern folk devils . . . Those who perpetrate such crimes are hated and despised more than almost any other offender . . . The danger to children from sexual offenders has become a matter of obsessive public concern' (West, 1996). Given the enormity of such crimes when they do occur, it is very difficult to retain objectivity in any discussion about sex offenders, particularly sexual offending against children. Public anger and disgust at such offending is fuelled by the media and by politicians.

Extract 6.3.1

**D West, 'Sexual Molesters' in N Walker (ed), *Dangerous People* (1996)
Ch 4, pp 53–57**

Although sex offenders still comprise less than one per cent of all recorded crimes known to the police in England and Wales, there has been a significant increase (from 20,000 in 1983 to 31,000 in 1993), although this is less than the increase in the totality of violent crimes, which have nearly doubled over the same time-span. The number of offenders brought to court and found guilty of indictable sex offences in England and Wales has actually decreased over the same period (6,400 in 1983 to 4,300 in 1993). This suggests that at least part of the change is due to increased reporting and recording of less serious incidents that do not lead to conviction, rather than to an escalation of bad behaviour. The sharpest increase has been in recorded rapes, which have more than tripled, from 1,300 to 4,600, although the number of persons found guilty of rape (always a small fraction of the number of complaints recorded) has increased only moderately, from 330 to 482. Among reported rapes, the greatest proportionate increase has been in offences committed by friends and sexual intimates. Again, greater readiness of victims to complain and of police to record, even when the prospect of securing a conviction is slight, must be responsible in part.

Sex offenders are more widely distributed throughout the social classes than most other offenders, and many of those apprehended have no previous convictions for either sexual or non-sexual crime. This is consistent with the contention of some feminists that there is nothing unusual about men who rape. Given cultural support for macho ideals of sexual conquest, any man might become an offender. Against this, and notwithstanding the generally low reconviction rate of first offenders, there is a common belief, supported by some professionals, that all sex offenders have an enduring propensity for deviant behaviour. In a recent book on treatment for child sex abusers it is said: 'the goal of treatment is not cure, but the development and maintenance of self-control by the offender on a lifelong basis' [T Morrison, M Erroga and R C Beckett (eds), *Sexual Offending Against Children* (London: Routledge, 1994) p xix]. Long-term follow up lends some plausibility to the notion of ineradicable propensity, for although risk of reconviction for rape or aggressive molestation of children is relatively low it continues largely unabated for many years. Persistent reconviction for serious sex crime is characteristic of a small minority. In an large sample studied by Home Office researchers, the conviction rate of the totality of sex offenders was low, but men with two previous convictions were 15 times more likely to be reconvicted of a further sex offence than men with only one conviction [G Philpotts and L Lancucki, *Previous Convictions, Sentence and Reconviction*, HORS No 53 (London: Home Office, 1979)].

Because all but the most serious sexual incidents so often go unreported, especially where secretive behaviour involving children is concerned, convictions records underestimate the extent of offending. In a frequently cited research, Abel et al [G Abel, J Becker, J Cunningham-Rathner, J Rouleau and W D Murphy, 'Self-Reported Sex Crimes' (1987) 2 *Journal of Interpersonal*

Violence 3] assessed a large sample of sex offenders. Given elaborate assurances of confidentiality, many offenders admitted numerous and mostly undetected offences . . .

The nature of the misconduct is crucial. Peeping Toms, clothes-line thieves, obscene telephone callers and men who expose themselves to women without ever attempting closer contact, may all have multiple convictions, but remain more of a nuisance than a menace; but there are exceptions. The majority of nuisance offenders do not escalate to serious crime, but the minority of very violent offenders frequently have convictions for lesser sexual transgressions in their earlier years.

Professionals are often called upon to advise on the risk of future crime by offenders awaiting trial or being considered for parole. Since so much depends on the unforeseeable circumstances to which the offender may be exposed, predictions are necessarily uncertain. Nothing predicts future behaviour as well as past patterns of behaviour. Actuarial predictions, based on objective criteria derived from criminal histories (such as age, marital status, number and type of previous convictions (including convictions for non-sexual offences and violent offences) are generally more efficient than clinical judgments of attitude, personality or mental state. Such features are hard to assess when the offender is desperately trying to create a favourable impression, and clinicians tend to give them too much weight and, consequently, to over-estimate risk. It is relatively easy to group offenders into broad categories of relatively high or low risk, but for unusual individuals who have committed particularly nasty sex crimes the demand for certainty that they will never re-offend in a similar way is almost impossible to meet. Clinical assessments may not provide blanket predictions, but they are helpful in identifying particular vulnerabilities which serve both as indicators of situations linked with risk and as pointers to the type of supervision, welfare assistance or medico-psychological intervention that might help . . .

In spite of the emphasis by some researchers on the exceptions, the majority of sex offenders limit themselves, for the most part, to only one kind of deviant behaviour. The type of offence is important because it relates both to the nature of the danger to victims and to the likelihood of repetition. The highest recidivism rates are found among untreated exhibitionists. Men found guilty of violent heterosexual assaults have quite low reconviction rates, although in their case even a low statistical risk may be thought socially intolerable. Among child molesters, those who have offended against children in their own household are at lesser risk of reconviction than those who have targeted children outside.

A range of criminal justice measures specific to sex offenders has been put in place during the 1990s. Longer than normal sentences can be imposed on offenders who have committed sexual offences, and who appear to the judge to represent a risk to the public (see Chapter 5), and both the frequency and duration of custodial sentences for sex offenders has increased significantly in recent years. Sentencers can also order longer term supervision of sex offenders after release from their sentence (Criminal Justice Act 1991, s 44). Two consultation documents were published by the Conservative government in 1996, the first concerned with a range of general criminal justice measures to 'protect the public' (see Home Office, 1996a) and the second, *Sentencing and Supervision of Sex Offenders*, concerned specifically with sex offenders (Home Office, 1996d). In the latter document, the government argued that while 'the risk presented by sex offenders varies considerably . . . the physical and psychological effect upon victims, in both the short and long term, can be very significant' and indicated clearly its view that sex offenders are different, and do require special measures. The extract from West (1996) above, may be compared with the following summary from the report (Home Office, 1996d, pp 1–2):

> Sex offenders are not a homogeneous group, but it is possible to make some generalisations. Men convicted of sexual offences as adults will often describe a history of (mainly undetected) sexual offending which began in childhood or adolescence and which involved an escalataion to more and more serious offences. Once a pattern of repeated sex offending is established, the risk of re-offending persists over many years, perhaps for life. Whilst a small number of sex offences may genuinely be committed in an impulsive way, in the overwhelming majority of cases the offender has manipulated people and circumstances so as to set up the opportunity to offend. Convicted sex offenders typically seek to deny or minimise the seriousness of their offending and use their skills at manipulation to draw other people into accepting these minimalisations.

As a result of the latter report, a range of measures specific to this offending group were enacted during 1997. The Criminal Evidence (Amendment) Act 1997 introduces powers to obtain DNA samples from all convicted sexual offenders currently serving a prison sentence or detained under the Mental Health Act 1983. The Police Act 1997 places further obstacles in the path of ex-offenders seeking employment and, despite the Rehabilitation of Offenders Act 1974, requires many ex-offenders (not just sex offenders) to obtain and present full information about their past when applying for a job (see further Home Office, 1996c). The Crime (Sentences) Act 1997 contained provision for further extending the period of supervision for sex offenders, as part of wider changes to arrangements for early release of offenders. The Labour government decided not to implement the Part of the Act which contained that provision, but it has been revived in the Crime and Disorder Bill. Further changes are pending, such as the introduction of indeterminate sentences for sex offenders, where release will be entirely dependent on an assessment of risk, rather than the seriousness of the crime committed. Perhaps the most significant change, however, has been the establishment of the sex offenders register by the Sex Offenders Act 1997.

(c) Registration requirements

Part I of the Sex Offenders Act 1997 came into force in October 1997. It requires all those who have been convicted and are currently under sentence for one of a range of sexual offences to register their name and address and any subsequent changes, with the police. Those who have broken the criminal law do not normally have to register with the police, and so this Act continues the current policy of placing sex offenders in a distinct category. There was virtually no opposition to the Bill during its passage through Parliament. Understandably, much emphasis was placed on the need to protect vulnerable children from the attention of paedophiles, but in fact the definition of 'sexual offence' in the Act goes far beyond offences against children. Offences which have involved adult victims are likely to predominate, so that the register cannot be regarded as a paedophile register. There were also calls for the Act to be fully retrospective in its effect, so that everyone in the past who had been convicted of a sexual offence, no matter how long ago, should be required to register. Home Office estimates were that about 260,000 ex-offenders currently living in England and Wales had been convicted of a sexual offence and that about 110,000 of those had committed a crime involving a child. This proposal was therefore rejected, not on the basis that such retrospective law might infringe Article 7 of the European Convention on Human Rights (see Extract 1.5.3 above), but on the grounds of impracticality. The Act is, therefore, retrospective only in the sense that all those currently serving sentences (including early release supervision) for sexual offences have been required to register, whether their offence was committed before or after the Act was implemented. As a result, around 6,000 names have been placed on the register immediately, and it is estimated that about 3,500 further names will be added to it each year.

Extract 6.3.2

Sex Offenders Act 1997, ss 1, 2 and Sched 1

1. Sex offenders subject to notification requirements

(1) A person becomes subject to the notification requirements of this Part if, after the commencement of this Part –
  (a) he is convicted of a sexual offence to which this Part applies;
  (b) he is found not guilty of such an offence by reason of insanity, or to be under a disability and to have done the act charged against him in respect of such an offence; or
  (c) in England and Wales or Northern Ireland, he is cautioned by a constable in respect of such an offence which, at the time when the caution is given, he has admitted.

(2) A person becomes subject to those requirements if, at that commencement –
  (a) he has been convicted of a sexual offence to which this Part applies but has not been dealt with in respect of the offence; or
  (b) he has been found not guilty of such an offence by reason of insanity, or to be under a disability and to have done the act charged

against him in respect of such an offence, but has not been dealt with in respect of the finding.

(3) A person becomes subject to those requirements if, at that commencement –

- (a) he is serving a sentence of imprisonment or a term of service detention, or is subject to a community order, in respect of a sexual offence to which this Part applies;
- (b) he is subject to supervision, having been released from prison after serving the whole or part of a sentence of imprisonment in respect of such an offence;
- (c) he is detained in a hospital, or is subject to a guardianship order, having been convicted of such an offence; or
- (d) he is detained in a hospital, having been found not guilty of such an offence by reason of insanity, or to be under a disability and to have done the act charged against him in respect of such an offence;

and a person who would fall within paragraph (a), (c) or (d) above but for the fact that, at that commencement, he is unlawfully at large or absent without leave, on temporary release or leave of absence, or on bail pending an appeal, shall be treated as falling within that paragraph.

(4) A person falling within subsections (1) to (3) above shall continue to be subject to those requirements for the period set out opposite a person of his description in the second column of the following table.

TABLE

Description of person	Applicable period
A person who, in respect of the offence, is or has been sentenced to imprisonment for life or for a term of 30 months or more	An indefinite period
A person who, in respect of the offence or finding, is or has been admitted to a hospital subject to a restriction order	An indefinite period
A person who, in respect of the offence, is or has been sentenced to imprisonment for a term of more than 6 months but less than 30 months	A period of 10 years beginning with the relevant date
A person who, in respect of the offence, is or has been sentenced to imprisonment for a term of 6 months or less	A period of 7 years beginning with that date
A person who, in respect of the offence or finding, is or has been admitted to a hospital without being subject to a restriction order	A period of 7 years beginning with that date
A person of any other description	A period of 5 years beginning with that date

(5) Subsection (6) below applies where a person falling within subsection (1)(a), (2)(a) or (3)(a), (b) or (c) above is or has been sentenced, in respect of two or more sexual offences to which this Part applies –

(a) to consecutive terms of imprisonment; or

(b) to terms of imprisonment which are partly concurrent.

(6) Subsection (4) above shall have effect as if the person were or had been sentenced, in respect of each of the offences, to a term of imprisonment which –

(a) in the case of consecutive terms, is equal to the aggregate of those terms;

(b) in the case of concurrent terms, is equal to the aggregate of those terms after making such deduction as may be necessary to secure that no period of time is counted more than once.

(7) Where a person found to be under a disability, and to have done the act charged against him in respect of a sexual offence to which this Part applies, is subsequently tried for the offence, the finding, and any order made in respect of the finding, shall be disregarded for the purposes of this section.

(8) In this Part 'the relevant date' means –

(a) in a case of a person falling within subsection (1)(a), (2)(a) or (3)(a) to (c) above, the date of the conviction;

(b) in a case of a person falling within subsection (1)(b), (2)(b) or (3)(d) above, the date of the finding;

(c) in a case of a person falling within subsection (1)(c) above, the date of the caution.

(9) Schedule 1 to this Act (which lists the sexual offences to which this Part applies) shall have effect.

2. Effect of notification requirements

(1) A person who is subject to the notification requirements of this Part shall, before the end of the period of 14 days beginning with the relevant date or, if later, the commencement of this Part, notify to the police the following information, namely –

(a) his name and, where he also uses one or more other names, each of those names; and

(b) his home address.

(2) A person who is subject to those requirements shall also, before the end of the period of 14 days beginning with –

(a) his using a name which has not been notified to the police under this section;

(b) any change of his home address; or

(c) his having resided or stayed, for a qualifying period, at any premises in the United Kingdom the address of which has not been notified to the police under this section,

notify that name, the effect of that change or, as the case may be, the address of those premises to the police.

(3) A notification given to the police by any person shall not be regarded as complying with subsection (1) or (2) above unless it also states –

(a) his date of birth;

(b) his name on the relevant date and, where he used one or more other names on that date, each of those names; and

(c) his home address on that date.

SCHEDULE 1

SEXUAL OFFENCES TO WHICH PART I APPLIES

Offences in England and Wales

1. – (1) This Part of this Act applies to the following sexual offences under the law of England and Wales, namely –

    (a) offences under the following provisions of the Sexual Offences Act 1956 –

        (i)   section 1 (rape);

        (ii)   section 5 (intercourse with a girl under 13);

        (iii) section 6 (intercourse with a girl between 13 and 16);

        (iv) section 10 (incest by a man);

        (v)   section 12 (buggery);

        (vi) section 13 (indecency between men);

        (vii) section 14 (indecent assault on a woman);

        (viii) section 15 (indecent assault on a man);

        (ix) section 16 (assault with intent to commit buggery);

        (x)   section 28 (causing or encouraging prostitution of, intercourse with, or indecent assault on, girl under 16);

    (b) an offence under section 1(1) of the Indecency with Children Act 1960 (indecent conduct towards young child);

    (c) an offence under section 54 of the Criminal Law Act 1977 (inciting girl under 16 to have incestuous sexual intercourse);

    (d) an offence under section 1 of the Protection of Children Act 1978 (indecent photographs of children);

    (e) an offence under section 170 of the Customs and Excise Management Act 1979 (penalty for fraudulent evasion of duty etc) in relation to goods prohibited to be imported under section 42 of the Customs Consolidation Act 1876 (prohibitions and restrictions); and

    (f) an offence under section 160 of the Criminal Justice Act 1988 (possession of indecent photographs of children).

The development of sex offender registers in their modern form began in the United States in the 1980s and 1990s. Nearly every state now has a sex offender registration scheme (see Bedarf, 1995). At the Federal level, following President Clinton's famous remark that it was time to 'circle the wagons around our children', passage of the Violent Crime Control and Law Enforcement Act 1994 required all states to have registers in place by the end of 1997. According to Hebenton and Thomas (1996), in spite of the rapid development of registration schemes in the United States their effectiveness in checking future offending behaviour is largely untested, and in those states which have attempted to evaluate their schemes the results have suggested low offender compliance rates and inaccurate registers. One of the problems has been that, after initial official enthusiasm for setting up the register, the systems have been poorly financed and administered.

The introduction of a sex offender register in England and Wales has attracted only muted criticism. Some dissenting voices have expressed reservation at the inclusion of the offence of 'gross indecency' – a consensual offence involving homosexuals over the age of consent which is generally dealt with by way of formal caution rather than prosecution – within the list of scheduled offences in the Act, or have pointed out the practical problems involved in ensuring that sex offenders currently under supervision will actually register, despite the threat of a £5,000 fine for failing to do so. One more trenchant critic is the journalist, Matthew Parris, who, at the time the measure was introduced by the Conservative government towards the end of 1996, complained that:

> Few voices – and certainly not the Opposition's – have been raised to confront the central principle: that a great swathe of offenders who have served their sentences and returned – disgraced at the workplace, disgraced with landlords, disgraced among their families and their friends, and almost certainly unemployed – to try to begin their lives again, should now be bound to the 20th century equivalent of the leper's bell. This is primitive nonsense. Will nobody say so? It is shameful. (Parris, 1997)

Parris also pointed out the common misconception that sex offenders are uniquely persistent in their offending, stating that 'no category of offender has a lower percentage of re-offenders than that covering sexual offences'. For the relevant statistical evidence see Philpotts and Lancucki, 1979, referred to in the extract from West (1996) above, and also discussed in Chapter 5. A more recent Australian study found little evidence of 'specialisation' among offenders with a sexual offence on their record, but still concluded that 'there is sufficient evidence of repetition to warrant that special attention be given to offender tracking' (Broadhurst and Maller, 1992). In the United States, the various sex offender registration and community notification laws have been attacked on constitutional grounds by ex-offenders who have been required to register. So far these challenges have been largely unsuccessful. Consider, for example, the following extract from the decision of the Supreme Court of the State of Washington in *State v Ward* 123 Wn 2d 488 (March 1994). The sex offender registration statute in that state, one of the first to be established, was challenged on three grounds:

(1) that it imposed a retrospective penalty on the applicants, who had been convicted and sentenced for their crimes prior to the registration statute becoming law,
(2) that it breached due process rights which require that convicted persons be informed of the penal consequences of their conviction, and
(3) that it violated constitutional 'equal protection' guarantees which require even-handed treatment amongst persons similarly situated.

These arguments all failed.

Extract 6.3.3

State v Ward 123 Wn 2d 488 (March 1994), pp 488–96
(footnotes omitted)

GUY J. Appellants Jeffrey Ward and John Doe seek review of superior court decisions holding the sex offender registration statute, RCW 9A.44.130–.140, which requires appellants to register as sex offenders with the local county sheriff, does not violate ex post facto, equal protection, or due process provisions under the United States and Washington Constitutions. We granted review and affirm both decisions.

Background

In 1989, then Governor Booth Gardner formed a task force to study community protection. *See* Governor's Task Force on Community Protection, *Final Report*, at I-1 (1989). As a result of the Task Force's recommendations, the Legislature passed the Community Protection Act of 1990. Laws of 1990, Ch 3. Part 4 of the act provides for the registration of adult and juvenile sex offenders. Laws of 1990, Ch 3, §§ 401–409. The Legislature stated that its purpose in requiring registration was to assist local law enforcement, declaring:

> 'The legislature finds that sex offenders often pose a high risk of reoffense, and that law enforcement's efforts to protect their communities, conduct investigations, and quickly apprehend offenders who commit sex offenses, are impaired by the lack of information available to law enforcement agencies about convicted sex offenders who live within the law enforcement agency's jurisdiction. Therefore, this state's policy is to assist local law enforcement agencies' efforts to protect their communities by regulating sex offenders by requiring sex offenders to register with local law enforcement agencies as provided in [RCW 9A.44.130].'

Laws of 1990, Ch 3, § 401. The requirement for sex offender registration, codified at RCW 9A.44.130–.140, became effective February 28, 1990. RCW 18.155.902(1). In 1991, the Legislature amended the statute to clarify and amend the deadlines for sex offenders to register. Laws of 1991, Ch 274, § 2.

The statute requires all persons residing in Washington who have been convicted of any sex offense, as defined by RCW 9.94A.030(29), to register with the county sheriff in the county where the person resides. RCW 9A.44.130(1). When registering, the person must provide name, address, date and place of birth, place of employment, crime for which convicted, date and place of conviction, aliases used, and Social Security number. RCW 9A.44.130(2). Any person required to register under the statute who changes residence must either send written notice of the change of address to the county sheriff, if the person relocates within the same county, or reregister with the county sheriff in the new county, within 10 days of establishing the new residence. RCW 9A.44.130(4). The county sheriff must also obtain a photograph of the individual and a copy of the individual's fingerprints. RCW 9A.44.130(5). The county sheriff must forward the information and fingerprints obtained to the Washington State Patrol for inclusion in a central registry

628

of sex offenders. RCW 43.43.540. A person who knowingly fails to register is guilty of either a class C felony or gross misdemeanor, depending on the severity of the prior conviction. RCW 9A.44.130(7).

Each of the appellants was convicted of a sexual offense as defined in RCW 9.94A.030(29) . . .

Issue

The central issue before us is whether the sex offender registration statute, RCW 9A.44.130–.140, retroactively applied to Ward and Doe, violates the prohibitions against ex post facto laws under the federal and state constitutions. We hold that the statute's requirement to register as a sex offender does not constitute punishment and therefore does not violate ex post facto prohibitions. We also conclude that the statute does not violate appellant Doe's equal protection or due process rights under the federal and state constitutions.

Analysis

Ward and Doe claim that the requirement to register as sex offenders under a statute that had not yet been enacted at the time they committed their offenses violates the prohibition against ex post facto laws of both the federal and state constitutions. In addition, Doe claims that the statute as applied to him violates the equal protection and due process clauses of the federal and state constitutions.

While appellants claim the sex offender registration statute violates provisions of both the state and federal constitutions, there is no suggestion that analysis under both constitutions should not be the same.

A statute is presumed constitutional and the party challenging it has the burden to prove it is unconstitutional beyond a reasonable doubt . . .

Ex post facto clause

The ex post facto clauses of the federal and state constitutions forbid the State from enacting any law which imposes punishment for an act which was not punishable when committed or increases the quantum of punishment annexed to the crime when it was committed. U.S. Const. art. 1, § 10; Const. art. 1, § 23; see Weaver v Graham, 450 U.S. 24, 28–29, 67 L. Ed. 2d 17, 101 S. Ct. 960 (1981); In re Powell, 117 Wn.2d 175, 184, 814 P.2d 635 (1991). As we noted in In re Powell, supra, '"[c]ritical to relief under the Ex Post Facto Clause is not an individual's right to less punishment, but the lack of fair notice and governmental restraint when the legislature increases punishment beyond what was prescribed when the crime was consummated."' In re Powell, supra at 184–85 (quoting Weaver, 450 U.S. at 30).

In Calder v Bull, 3 U.S. (3 Dall.) 386, 1 L. Ed. 648 (1798), the United States Supreme Court established the framework for ex post facto analysis. This framework, known as the 'Calder categories', provides in relevant part that a law violates the ex post facto prohibition if it 'changes the punishment, and inflicts a greater punishment, than the law annexed to the crime, when committed.' (Italics ours.) Calder, at 390.

Taking the second part of the test first, we conclude that the sex offender registration statute is retrospective. It was enacted after Ward and Doe committed their offenses and it is being applied to them. *See In re Powell*, 117 Wn.2d at 185; *Weaver*, 450 U.S. at 32–33. As to whether the statute is substantive or procedural, we assume, without deciding, that it is substantive. We hold, however, that appellants are not 'disadvantaged' by the statute because it does not *alter the standard of punishment* which existed under prior law. While the requirement to register as a sex offender may indeed be burdensome, the focus of the inquiry is whether registration constitutes punishment. We conclude that it does not.

The ex post facto prohibition applies only to laws inflicting criminal *punishment*.

. . . To determine whether the sex offender registration statute is punitive or regulatory, we look first to the Legislature's purpose in adopting the law.

When it enacted the statute, the Legislature unequivocally stated that the State's policy is to 'assist local law enforcement agencies' efforts to protect their communities by *regulating* sex offenders by requiring sex offenders to register with local law enforcement agencies as provided in [RCW 9A.44.130].' (Italics ours.) Laws of 1990, Ch 3, § 401. *See also* Laws of 1991, Ch 274, § 1.

Our inquiry, however, does not end with the Legislature's stated purpose. We also examine whether the actual *effect* of the statute is so punitive as to negate the Legislature's regulatory intent.

Appellants argue that because registration carries with it the right of law enforcement agencies to disseminate information to the public, the registration requirement amounts to a 'badge of infamy'. We disagree.

Registration alone imposes no significant additional burdens on offenders. The statute requires an offender to provide the local sheriff with eight pieces of information: name, address, date and place of birth, place of employment, crime for which convicted, date and place of conviction, aliases used, and Social Security number. In addition, the local sheriff must obtain two items: the offender's photograph and fingerprints. We note that at least one criminal justice agency routinely has all of this information on file at the time of an offenders' conviction and sentencing. *See* RCW 10.97.030(1), (3). Thus, only if this information has changed since sentencing could registration require an offender to divulge information which is not already in the hands of the authorities.

We also find that the physical act of registration creates no affirmative disability or restraint. Collecting information about sex offenders in order to aid community law enforcement does not restrain sex offenders in any way. *See, e.g., State v Olivas*, 122 Wn.2d 73, 856 P.2d 1076 (1993) (upholding DNA testing of sex offenders for law enforcement purposes). Sex offenders are free to move within their community or from one community to another, provided they comply with the statute's registration requirements. RCW 9A.44.130(4); *see State v Taylor*, 67 Wn. App. 350, 357, 835 P.2d 245 (1992) (requirement that registrants inform the county sheriff of their current residence does not impede or restrict movement in any way). Moreover, it is inconceivable that filling out a short form with eight blanks creates an affirmative disability. Registration alone imposes burdens of little, if any, significance.

Appellants contend, however, that the dissemination of registrant information creates hostile publicity and, ultimately, has a punitive effect on registrants.

630

They direct our attention to the record which contains three sexual offender notification bulletins received by a resident of Mill Creek, and copies of five newspaper articles, all of which they assert are illustrative of the nature and impact of publicity. No such disclosure, though, appears to have occurred in appellants' cases. Nonetheless, we now examine whether the potential for disclosure of registrant information creates an affirmative disability or restraint.

We begin with the Washington State Criminal Records Privacy Act, RCW 10.97.010 *et seq.* Under RCW 10.97.050(1), criminal justice agencies may release criminal conviction records without restriction. Therefore, the disclosure of conviction information cannot impose an additional burden. It is only where the criminal history record contains nonconviction data, or where the criminal justice agency discloses that the person is a registered sex offender, that dissemination will have the potential for creating an additional restraint.

We hold, however, that because the Legislature has limited the disclosure of registration information to the public, the statutory registration scheme does not impose additional punishment on registrants. The Legislature placed significant limits on (1) whether an agency may disclose registrant information, (2) what the agency may disclose, and (3) where it may disclose the information. The statute regulating disclosure, RCW 4.24.550, provides that '[p]ublic agencies are authorized to release relevant and necessary information regarding sex offenders to the public when the release of the information is necessary for public protection.' RCW 4.24.550(1). The Legislature found that

'[o]verly restrictive confidentiality and liability laws governing the release of information about sexual predators have reduced willingness to release information that could be appropriately released under the public disclosure laws, and have increased risks to public safety. Persons found to have committed a sex offense have a reduced expectation of privacy because of the public's interest in public safety and in the effective operation of government. Release of information about sexual predators to public agencies and *under limited circumstances*, the general public, will further the governmental interests of public safety and public scrutiny of the criminal and mental health systems so long as the information released is *rationally related to the furtherance of those goals.*

Therefore, this state's policy as expressed in [RCW 4.24.550] is to require the exchange of relevant information about sexual predators among public agencies and officials and to authorize the release of *necessary and relevant* information about sexual predators to members of the general public.'

(Italics ours.) Laws of 1990, Ch 3, § 116. The Legislature's pronouncement evidences a clear regulatory intent to limit the exchange of relevant information to the general public to those circumstances which present a threat to public safety.

The first limits to disclosure appear when an agency determines whether to disseminate registrant information. Because the Legislature clearly intended public agencies to disseminate warnings to the public 'under limited circumstances', in many cases, both the registrant information and the fact of registration remain confidential. This cannot impose any additional burdens to that of registration.

For those cases which merit disclosure, the statute requires an agency to have some evidence that the offender poses a threat to the public or, in other words, some evidence of dangerousness in the future. The release of the registrant information must be 'necessary for public protection'. *See* RCW 4.24.550(1). We note that the statute, on its face, requires the disclosing agency to have some evidence that the offender poses a threat to the community. Absent evidence of such a threat, disclosure would serve no legitimate purpose. Therefore, we hold that a public agency must have some evidence of an offender's future dangerousness, likelihood of reoffense, or threat to the community, to justify disclosure to the public in a given case. This statutory limit ensures that disclosure occurs to prevent future harm, not to punish past offenses.

When disclosure is appropriate, the statute also limits what a public warning may contain. As stated above, the statute authorizes release only of 'relevant and necessary' information. This standard imposes an obligation to release registrant information reasonably necessary to counteract the danger created by the particular offender. For example, release of an offender's Social Security number may be unnecessary in many cases, but critical where a potential employer must discover the offender's identity and criminal background. Furthermore, the statutory requirement of 'necessary information' and, for that matter, the Legislature's primary goal of protecting the public, obligates the disclosing agency to gauge the public's potential for violence and draft the warning accordingly. An agency must disclose only that information relevant to and necessary for counteracting the offender's dangerousness.

Finally, the statute limits where an agency may disclose the registrant information. The Legislature dictated that disclosure must be 'rationally related to the furtherance' of the goals of public safety and the effective operation of government. *See* Laws of 1990, Ch 3, § 116. Accordingly, the geographic scope of dissemination must rationally relate to the threat posed by the registered offender. Depending on the particular methods of an offender, an agency might decide to limit disclosure only to the surrounding neighborhood, or to schools and day care centers, or, in cases of immediate or imminent risk of harm, the public at large. The scope of disclosure must relate to the scope of the danger. In addition, the content of a warning may vary by proximity: next-door neighbors or nearby schools might receive a more detailed warning than those further away from harm . . .

Due process
Doe makes a threshold argument that the statute's registration requirement does not apply to him by its own terms. Doe correctly states that the 1990 statute provided that a sex offender register 'within forty-five days of establishing residence in Washington, or if a current resident within thirty days of release from confinement, if any'. Former RCW 9A.44.130(2). Doe argues that he could not register within 30 days of his December 1987 release from confinement because the statute did not yet exist. Doe contends, therefore, that the provisions of the statute do not apply to him. We disagree.

[13] First, the statute explicitly states that '[a]ny adult or juvenile residing in this state who has been found to have committed or has been convicted of any sex offense shall register'. RCW 9A.44.130(1). This definition applies to

632

Doe – an adult residing in Washington who was convicted of a sex offense. Second, the statute defined 'sex offense' to include those offenders like Doe who were released from custody but remained on active supervision on or after February 28, 1990.

A criminal defendant must be informed of all the direct consequences of his plea prior to acceptance of a guilty plea. *State v. Barton*, 93 Wn.2d 301, 305, 609 P.2d 1353 (1980). On the other hand, a defendant need not be advised of all possible *collateral* consequences of his plea.

Because registration was a collateral consequence of Doe's plea, we find no violation of Doe's due process rights.

Equal protection
For purposes of establishing registration deadlines, the statute distinguishes between convicted sex offenders who are under correctional supervision and those who are no longer under supervision. RCW 9A.44.130(3)(a)(i)–(iv) (formerly RCW 9A.44.130(5)). Only those who are under some form of supervision must register. Doe argues that the exemption of other sex offender population groups from the statute violates his equal protection rights under the federal and state constitutions. We disagree.

Constitutional equal protection guarantees require similar treatment under the law for similarly situated persons. U.S. Const. amend. 14, § 1; Const. art. 1, § 12 . . . Where persons of different classes are treated differently, there is no equal protection violation.

Conclusion

In conclusion, we hold that as applied to both Ward and Doe, the requirement to register as a sex offender is not punitive and therefore does not violate the ex post facto prohibitions of the federal and state constitutions. As to Doe, we reject his due process and equal protections claims. The judgments of the trial courts are affirmed.

Since *Ward* was decided, further legal challenges have been brought in the United States, and one or two states have suspended their laws until such time as the constitutional issue of retroactivity has been authoritatively resolved by the United States Supreme Court. The indications for change are not good, however. The Supreme Court has recently held that sex offenders after serving a custodial sentence for their offence can be transferred to a mental hospital on the basis of their 'abnormality', as a form of quarantine, without a diagnosis of mental disorder, and without any evidence that available treatment will alleviate their condition, the majority ruling that confinement in a hospital (like sex offender registration) did not amount to 'punishment' and hence could not be 'cruel or unusual' (Maddox, 1997).

Would comparable arguments brought by a British sex offender now made subject to registration requirements in the Sex Offenders Act 1997 be any more successful in an application under the European Convention on Human Rights? Consider the relevance of Articles 3, 7 and 8 (the text of the

Convention is set out at Extract 1.5.3 above). Article 3 states that 'No one shall be subjected to inhuman or degrading treatment or punishment'. It is very doubtful whether a requirement of registration is in itself a 'punishment'. It certainly amounts to 'treatment', but it hardly seems to be 'degrading' to require registration with the police. The issue of a retrospective registration requirement was referred to above. Article 7 of the Convention, which prohibits the use of retrospective criminal offences and criminal penalties, has been held to apply to provisions in English law where persons convicted of drug trafficking were made subject to laws requiring them to disgorge the proceeds of their offending (*Welch v UK* A 307-A (1995)). In other situations, however, the Court of Human Rights has indicated that orders designed to protect the public, rather than to punish the offender, do not amount to 'penalties' and so cannot infringe Article 7. It seems unlikely that an argument based on Article 7 would succeed. Article 8 declares the right to respect for a person's private and family life, and such right may be infringed where the authorities publicise the name and address of an ex-offender in the locality (see further below), but Article 8 expressly restricts that right where necessary in the interests of public safety, or for the protection of the rights and freedoms of others.

Further questions surround the inclusion on the register of those who have been formally cautioned for a sexual offence alongside those who have been convicted. The rationale and procedure for formal cautioning of offenders was discussed in Chapter 2. Is it appropriate that persons who have been cautioned for their offence, rather than prosecuted, should be required nonetheless to register for five years, as the table in s 1 of the 1997 Act prescribes? What if the police officer administering the caution omits to mention that there will be a registration requirement? Some possible implications for the criminal justice system are explored by Soothill et al (1997):

> It is difficult to predict the outcome of the new legislation at an operational level. How will the police react to the powers which are to be bestowed on them in the Sex Offenders Act and how will the offending population react? Certainly if the police became intrusive in the lives of ex-offenders – using the knowledge of addresses for some proactive police work – the ex-offenders will take evasive action (already, stories in the popular press report sex offenders changing their names by deed poll). There is likely, for instance, to be much greater legal challenge to cautioning, for the stakes will be higher, that is that the inevitablity of being placed on a sex offender register after the caution. There is likely to be more insistence by offenders that the accusation is actually tested in court, for an acquittal may be the only way to prevent the stigma of being included on a sex offender register. So there will be at least two kinds of pressure to avoid using cautioning – the police may want to avoid trouble which might follow from increased scrutiny of and challenge to their use of cautioning, while accused sex offenders may want to exercise their right to a trial and reject the caution option.
>
> On the other hand, there will be other sorts of pressure to make *more* use of cautioning. Certainly, if the sex offender registers are going to be more than simply bureaucratic book keeping and become a more complex part of investigative policing,

then there seems a greater likelihood that cautioning – with its attendant effect of ensuring a person's entry on to the register – will become increasingly popular for both the police and 'victims'. Consequently, there is the danger that increased zeal in the use of the caution will go against the spirit of the established [cautioning] guidelines, particularly in relation to the criteria to have sufficient evidence to support a prosecution.

This developing area of the law provides another good example of the uncertainties which can often surround policy development in criminal justice. Criminal justice agencies (and, in this case, offenders too) may adjust their behaviour in sometimes unexpected ways to accommodate a criminal justice initiative. For further discussion of this point see Chapter 1, at p 59.

(d) Community notification

The sex offender registration statutes came to particular prominence in the state of New Jersey in 1994 with the death of Megan Kanka, a seven year-old girl who was raped and killed by a person with previous convictions for sexual offences against children, who had moved into the street where she lived. New Jersey, which already had a sex offender register, quickly passed a further provision, in force from 1995, which came to be known as 'Megan's Law', allowing the police to inform local communities about the presence of high-risk sex offenders. The subsequently produced 'New Jersey Attorney-General's Guidelines for Law Enforcement for Notification to Local Officials and/or to the Community for the Entry of a Sex Offender into the Community' deploys a 'sex offender risk assessment scale' when deciding on the appropriate level of community notification (Hebenton and Thomas, 1996). In cases which come within the highest risk category, the police visit every house within a quarter of a mile of the ex-offender's house to notify residents of his identity, history and whereabouts. The issue of community notification raises perhaps the most acute issue of concern regarding sex offender registers, and it creates a further point of tension between the police, the ex-offender and the community.

In England and Wales it has long been the practice, when certain offenders are about to be released from prison or mental hospital for Home Office officials to inform the relevant local authority that the ex-offender is intending to relocate in their area. Local authorities have quietly housed such offenders in hostels and housing estates, relying upon social services and probation officers to keep an eye on them. Some, but not all, such offenders are subject to post-release supervision requirements and may be subject to recall to prison. In a case which attracted some media attention in January 1997, a 50 year-old man with convictions for sexual offences against children was driven out of his accommodation by local residents in Scotland after information about the man and his past had been leaked to them by the press (English, 1997). There are a growing number of examples where notification of the whereabouts of sex offenders to local people has generated a lynch mob atmosphere, with the ex-offenders being forced to flee and in some cases being subject to intimidation and assault. Mr Tony Butler, the Chief Constable of Gloucestershire, speaking on behalf of the Association of Chief Police Officers in February 1997, said that the police fully supported the impending introduction of the register, but was concerned that disclosure of information about the whereabouts of convicted sex offenders could be counter-productive and dangerous, by 'driving the offenders underground'. There were, he added, 'real dangers of public over-reaction and violence'.

In *Chief Constable of North Wales Police and Others, ex parte AB and Others* (1997) *The Times* 14 July, the Divisional Court was asked to review a decision of the North Wales police to reveal to the owner of a caravan site near Wrexham of the presence on the site of a married couple who had convictions for rape and indecent assault committed on children, and had served prison sentences of seven years. On their release from prison they had moved from the area where the offences had been committed to the north of England then to Wales, but on each occasion their arrival had been greeted by publicity in the press and hostility from neighbours which had forced them to move again. North Wales police had received information on the couple from Northumberland police that the couple represented a 'considerable risk' to local children, and had alerted the owner of the site. The Divisional Court heard evidence from the Home Office that the police were required to guide their conduct over community notification having regard to the following three principles:

(1) There was a general presumption that information should not be disclosed. That was based on recognition of the potentially serious effect on the ability of convicted people to live a normal life, the risk of violence to them and the risk that disclosure might drive them underground.
(2) There was a strong public interest in ensuring that police were able to disclose information about offenders where it was necessary for the prevention or detection of crime or for the protection of young or other vulnerable people.
(3) Each case should be considered carefully on its own facts, assessing the risk by the offender, the vulnerability of those at risk, and the impact of disclosure on the offender. In making that assessment the police should normally consult other relevant agencies.

The Divisional Court ruled that the conduct of the police in this case was not open to legal challenge. It was clear that the North Wales police had not adopted a blanket policy of disclosure and had considered carefully the consequences of disclosure. The court also rejected the contention that there had been a breach of Article 8 of the European Convention on Human Rights. Lord Bingham, the Lord Chief Justice, presided over the review, and he accepted that the case had 'far-reaching implications'. He said that:

It is not acceptable that those who have undergone the lawful punishment imposed by the courts should be the subject of intimidation and private vengeance, harried from parish to parish like paupers under the old Poor Law. It is not only in their interests but in the interests of society as a whole that they should be enabled, and if need be helped, to live normal, lawful lives. While the risk of repeated offending may in some circumstances justify a very limited measure of official disclosure, a general policy of disclosure can never be justified, and the media should be slow to obstruct the rehabilitation of ex-offenders.

The Divisional Court granted leave to appeal to the House of Lords.

It is important to note that this case pre-dates the implementation of the register under the Sex Offenders Act 1997, and so was concerned with the pre-existing policy of the police. It seems clear, however, that the balance of considerations outlined by the Home Office in that case will continue to provide the basis for community notification now that the register is in operation. The guidance is ceratinly useful, but it leaves a number of important practical issues open. One of the most important is: to whom should the notification be given? Another is: what advice should be given to the person notified about passing on the information? If a decision is made by the police to notify the head teachers of local schools as to the whereabouts of a sex offender in the neighbourhood, how should a head teacher make use of that information? There would seem little to be gained from keeping the information to themselves. If they felt that, in view of the perceived risk to children at the school, they must inform other staff, parents and pupils, how much information, in what form, and in how much detail, should be passed on?

4. DISCRIMINATION IN CRIMINAL JUSTICE

(a) General observations on discrimination

The effects of discrimination have been considered in each of the earlier chapters but this section offers more general observations on the issue. In his review of the literature relating to racial bias, David Smith noted that there are considerable difficulties in interpreting the data about discrimination in the criminal justice process. But, after setting out the nature of the problem, he was able to draw a number of carefully qualified conclusions about the results of current research (see also Hedderman and Gelsthorpe, 1997, p 55, who make similar points in respect of sex discrimination).

Extract 6.4.1

D J Smith, 'Ethnic Origins, Crime, Criminal Justice' in M Maguire, R Morgan and R Reiner (eds), *The Oxford Handbook of Criminology* (1997) 2nd ed, pp 705–707, 749–752

Conceptual issues

The central question to be addressed is how close the criminal justice system comes to constituting a universal framework within which all ethnic groups are treated equally. There is room for considerable discussion about what is meant by equal treatment in this context. It certainly cannot mean that everyone should be treated the same. Obviously, the guilty, and not the innocent, should be punished, and people should be punished more or less severely depending on the seriousness of the offence. Slightly less obviously, someone with a long record of past offending should be punished more severely than someone convicted for the first time. Possibly, although this is more controversial, a person with a stable family life and a steady job should be given a community-based sanction, whereas a person without those supports should be sent to prison. In other words treating people equally must mean that people in like circumstances and categories in relevant respects should be treated equally.

It is common ground that ethnic group should not itself be a criterion that determines how people are treated. But which *other* criteria are relevant and legitimate? And how far, if at all, should their *impact* on different ethnic groups be taken into account? At one extreme there is the view that equal treatment means the impartial application of existing rules and principles regardless of their impact on different ethnic groups. If, on that view, more black than white people are committed to prison because more black people are judged to lack a stable family or a steady job, that does not constitute unequal treatment. At the other extreme, there is the view that any policies, rules, or procedures that have the effect of punishing a higher proportion of one ethnic group than another are unjust, and that law and policy should be adjusted so as to achieve equal outcomes (say, in terms of proportion imprisoned) for different ethnic groups, and also for different social classes.

It is difficult to defend either of these extreme views. Ensuring that equal proportions of different social groups are punished has never been seen as an objective of the criminal justice system, and does not seem a valid interpretation of the ideal of equality before the law. Few would accept the idea that either enforcement or the decisions of the courts should have the aim of achieving equal punishment of different social groups. That would imply unequal treatment of individuals who had committed similar offences and had comparable records. Whenever there was an increase in offending within a particular social group, the system would have to respond by reducing penalties for offenders within that group.

On the other hand, the view that any uneven impact on different ethnic groups should be disregarded seems equally questionable. Apparently neutral rules or criteria may work to the disadvantage of a particular ethnic group, yet perhaps they could be changed without the sacrifice of any fundamental principle. For example, many police forces will not caution juveniles (instead of setting in train a prosecution) if they are known to have committed two or more previous offences. In an area where police law enforcement tends to target black youths (for example, through drugs raids on Reggae clubs) a rule of this kind works to the disadvantage of black people, and, arguably, amounts to treating them unequally. The rule could be relaxed without sacrificing any fundamental principle: after all, police cautions are already given to juveniles who are known to have committed previous offences.

This analysis suggests that equality of treatment within the criminal justice system cannot be interpreted as equality of outcome (say, the same proportion of different ethnic groups committed to prison). Nor can it be interpreted as merely the neutral application of existing rules and criteria, whatever their effect. Instead, it is necessary to adopt an intermediate position. The legitimacy and suitability of existing rules and criteria must be critically reviewed in the light of their impact on different ethnic groups.

These polar views about what constitutes equal treatment are similar to the two opposing models of justice implied in discussion of anti-discrimination law. McCrudden, Smith, and Brown [*Racial Justice at Work: The Enforcement of the 1976 Race Relations Act in Employment* (London: Policy Studies Institute, 1991)] describe them as the *individual justice model* and the *group justice model* of legislation against race and sex discrimination. The aims of these polar models of anti-discrimination legislation conflict in important ways, and the actual legislation represents a compromise between them. The Race Relations Act 1976 and the Sex Discrimination Act 1975 incorporate elements of the group justice model through the concept of *indirect discrimination*: the use of a condition or requirement which is such that a considerably smaller proportion of one than of another group can comply with it, which is to the other's detriment, and where the person using the condition or requirement cannot show it to be justified. The concept of indirect discrimination belongs within the group justice model because it is concerned with the outcomes for groups resulting from the application of some rule or principle. However, conflict with the individual justice model is minimized by the qualification that criteria working to the disadvantage of a particular ethnic group may always be used as long as they can be justified. The statute did not enlarge on what would constitute a justification. In many cases, the condition or requirement is presented as a test of performance or ability. For example, where job applicants are required to take an aptitude test on which members of an ethnic minority tend to score lower than whites, the point at issue is whether the test is a valid and appropriate measure of performance in the job: if it is, then its use is justifiable (and non-discriminatory) even though it works to the disadvantage of the ethnic minority.

At present the decisions at certain key stages of the criminal justice process do not fall within the provisions of the anti-discrimination legislation, although there have been calls for this to be changed (Commission for Racial Equality [Review of the Race Relations Act (London: Commission for Racial Equality, 1991)]). If the scope of the legislation were to be extended to criminal justice, this would highlight the problem of deciding whether particular criteria that work to the disadvantage of an ethnic minority can be justified. On the surface, decision-making criteria within the criminal justice system are often analogous to aptitude tests. For example, a police officer might adopt the practice of stopping and searching any group of two or more young men with long hair and earrings walking on the streets after midnight. This might be justifiable in terms of results, in the sense that young men of this description are often found to be in possession of illicit drugs. Again, wherever a suspect was cheeky or unco-operative, a police officer might decide to arrest and charge him with some offence or other. This also might be justifiable in terms of results, in the sense that cheeky or unco-operative suspects usually end up being convicted of some offence. Yet these examples, of course, illustrate that decision-making criteria within the criminal justice system, unlike employee selection criteria, can seldom be justified purely in terms of results. In the first example, it may be granted that long-haired youths with earrings out after midnight are more likely to be in possession of illicit drugs than pensioners at noon, but invasion of a person's liberty is justified, under English law, only if there is a specific reason to suspect that he has committed an offence. In the second example, the police officer's use of the criterion of cheekiness and lack of co-operation is self-validating, because he or she is in a position to construct the arrest and in most cases to ensure a successful prosecution. Similarly, those who plead guilty are nearly always found guilty, but that does not show that the guilty plea is proof of guilt. Within criminal justice there is no independent test of the results achieved by using a criterion, so that some justification other than results is required . . .

Main findings
First, ethnic minorities – both black people and South Asians – are found to be at higher risk of crime victimization than white people. This difference arises partly because the socio-demographic profile of ethnic minorities tends to increase their risk of victimization, but some difference remains after controlling for the effect of these variables. The elevated risk of victimization is also connected with characteristics of the neighbourhoods where ethnic minorities live. A third factor is that a substantial minority of offences on black people (and to a lesser extent on South Asians) are committed by black people, who probably have an elevated level of offending (see below). However, black-on-black crime is only a small part of the explanation of high black victimization because black people are such a small proportion of the population.

Secondly, at the end of the criminal justice process, black people (Afro-Caribbeans and black Africans) are about six times as likely to be in prison as white people or South Asians.

Thirdly, the pattern of offences for which black people were arrested and imprisoned is consistent with the theory that they tend to be the targets of proactive law enforcement. Also, there is some evidence of bias against black people at various stages: in the targeting of police enforcement; the decision to prosecute juveniles; and sentencing by the Crown Courts. None of this evidence, however, is entirely clear-cut. It can be argued, for example, that the high police stop rate of black people is 'justified' by results (reported offences, arrests, and prosecutions). With regard to decisions to prosecute juveniles, the relevant studies are out of date, and probably did not include all of the relevant variables. With regard to sentencing, the leading study (Hood, 1992) did suggest some racial bias, but its measured effects were rather small, especially when compared with the effects of other variables.

640

Fourthly, at various points, black people are placed at a disadvantage by the application of apparently neutral criteria. The clearest examples are the influence of social background factors on the decision to prosecute rather than caution a juvenile (black children are less likely to have the stable family background that makes cautioning more likely); the influence of social background factors on sentencing; and the lower sentencing tariff for suspects who plead not guilty. The relationship between guilty plea and sentence accounts for a substantial part (perhaps around 15 per cent) of the difference in rate of imprisonment between black and white people.

Fifthly, although some bias against black people has been demonstrated at several stages, and although some apparently neutral criteria have been shown to work to the disadvantage of black people, the magnitude of these effects seems small compared with the stark contrast in rates of arrest and imprisonment between black and white people. A possible theory is that the stark contrast is mainly or entirely caused by cumulative bias and the use of criteria that work to the disadvantage of black people at each different stage of the criminal justice process. That theory has recently received support from the results of a study of young people aged 14–25 (Graham and Bowling [*Young People and Crime*, HORS No 145 (London: Home Office, 1996)]) which showed no difference in rates of self-reported offending between black and white youths. However, those findings do not seem convincing in the light of sampling problems, the inherent limitations of the self-report method in terms of validity and reliability, and the evidence that the truthfulness of self-reports may be systematically related to ethnic group . . . There is a considerable weight of evidence that contradicts the findings of the self-report study, and suggests instead that the stark contrast in rates of imprisonment cannot be mainly the cumulative result of the operations of criminal justice process at each stage.

- The cumulative effects theory would predict a steady increase in the proportion of black people among suspects and offenders from the earliest to the latest stage of the process. In fact, the proportion of black people is about the same among suspects as described by victims, persons arrested, and the prison population.
- Arising directly from the first point, it is impossible to account for the high representation of black people at early stages (for example, according to victims' reports) in terms of bias.
- Even at stages where bias has been demonstrated, its potential impact is fairly limited. For example, proactive law enforcement does target black people to some extent: but most clear-ups do not result from proactive law enforcement, and most proactive law enforcement cannot be targeted on black people. Hence the total effect of this bias must be modest, especially in relation to the stark differences in rates of arrest and imprisonment between black and white people. To take another example, black juveniles are considerably more likely to be prosecuted rather than cautioned compared with comparable white juveniles, but there is no evidence of a similar difference in the case of adult offenders, who account for 90 per cent of the cases coming before the courts. Hence, the bias in cautioning of juveniles, though important, has only a small significance as an explanation of the difference in rates of imprisonment between black and white people.

- Although proactive law enforcement targeted on black people can help to explain the arrest rates for certain offences (notably, robbery) it cannot for others (such as burglary) for which proactive law enforcement cannot for the most part be targeted on black people and is in any case singularly ineffective.
- Contrary to what has been stated by some commentators (for example, Reiner, 1989, 1993) it is not the case that bias has been demonstrated at every stage of the process. Most notably, black people are, if anything, more likely to be acquitted than white people. There is not a steady accumulation of bias from one stage to the next.
- The acquittal rate is only slightly higher among black than white defendants. This is difficult to reconcile with the hypothesis of massive bias against black people at earlier stages, which should lead to the cases against them being relatively weak. Although not conclusive in itself, this argument carries some weight in the context of the rest of the evidence.

A fair assessment of the limited evidence is that although some bias against black people has been demonstrated at several stages of the process, and although some decision-making criteria clearly work to the disadvantage of black people, in large part the difference in rate of arrest and imprisonment between black and white people arises from a difference in the rate of offending.

Fifthly, South Asians – collectively the largest part of the ethnic minority population – are not over-represented among offenders described by victims, persons arrested, or the prison population. No bias has been demonstrated against them at any stage, and at various points they tend to be favoured compared to white or black people. In other contexts, South Asians are just as much subject to racial hostility and discrimination as black people. The bias against black people that has been demonstrated within the criminal justice system is therefore different from that existing in other contexts such as employment. It is not adequately described as part of a generalized 'racism'. More plausibly it springs from a perception of black people specifically, as distinct from other ethnic minorities, as a threat to law and order. However exaggerated, those perceptions are not unconnected with reality, since crime rates are higher than average among black people, but they also help to shape that reality, since racial hostility and discrimination will through a sequence of interactions cause black crime rates to rise still further.

Returning to the broad perspective established at the beginning of this chapter, the process of gaining acceptance for a single, universal standard of law applicable equally to all ethnic groups seems in some ways to be well advanced. Ethnic group is by no means the most important characteristic influencing rates of offending or victimization, or the way people interact with the police, the probation service, or the courts. Sex and age are far more important predictors, and social class is probably more important, too. Although Afro-Caribbeans are considerably more hostile to the police than white people or Asians, the contrast between age groups is much starker. The ethnic minorities do not reject the criminal justice system or deny its legitimacy. As victims of crime, or as bystanders, they are just as likely as white people to report matters to the police.

On the other hand, it cannot be claimed that law enforcement and criminal process have the same impact on black and white people. In the past,

642

claims of unequal treatment have tended to be exaggerated, and hence to lack credibility. There is evidence that law enforcement targets black people, and there is some evidence of bias at various stages of criminal process. Probably more important than bias is the effect of apparently neutral criteria which nevertheless work to the disadvantage of black people. Yet these effects seem much too small to account for the stark difference in rates of imprisonment between black and white people. In large part, this difference probably reflects a difference in rates of offending.

In relation to sex discrimination, the evidence is less comprehensive. We know that far fewer women than men commit crime: the ratio for recorded crime is in the order of 1: 9, with some variation for different offences, but that ratio is reflected in hidden female crime (see Heidensohn, 1996, pp 7–10). Similarly, fewer women than men enter the criminal justice process, with a lower proportion stopped by the police (see Smith and Gray, 1983), and that difference is reflected in sentencing patterns (see Home Office, 1997a). It is not easy to discern discriminatory decision-making in such relatively small numbers (see generally, Heidensohn, 1997). There is evidence that women's experience of the criminal justice process may be different from men's but that may be explained in terms of intervening 'neutral' variables. For example, women may benefit from 'chivalrous' attitudes within the police (see Morris, 1987, but cf Farrington and Morris, 1983) but it could be that this is just one manifestation of the general effect of demeanour on police decision-making, an effect which has an impact on men as well as women (see Harris, 1992; Chapter 2 above). Similarly, there are accounts of women suspects being badly treated by the police, an early example being the response to the suffragette movement (see Strachey, 1978) and a more recent example being the Greenham Common protests (see Young, A, 1991). However, the police are also apt to show little respect for males whom they regard as outsiders – the 'scum' or 'filth' (see Chapter 2 above).

There is similar uncertainty about the extent of sex discrimination by the courts.

Extract 6.4.2

F Heidensohn, *Women and Crime* (1996) 2nd ed, pp 40–42

The courts

Courts tend to present a 'dramatisation of deviance'. In the English adversarial system that tendency is heightened. Many accounts of famous trials, and the daily fare of newspapers illustrate the amount of drama, comic and tragic, which can be culled from courtroom scenes. (In reality of course, many criminal trials are long and boring, taken up with tedious technical evidence or sordid and sickening details.) But the courts do provide dramatic material other than to satisfy curiosity and emotion; from the study of their procedures, the way in which cases are handled, defendants convicted and sentenced, we can learn a good deal, not least about the ways in which women experience criminal justice in them. Fortunately, court proceedings are in public and are a matter of record; there are a number of studies which make use of surveys of court cases, as well as some interviews and observation-based accounts. How then do women and girls experience the administration of justice in the courts and how are they treated by them?

Several accounts suggest that women find courts particularly bewildering, alien and unfair:

'A large proportion of the girls did not understand what was happening during the proceedings; they were not clear who the people were in court, some could not understand the language and some did not understand the court's decision. Many girls, for example, mentioned that they had thought that the clerk of the court was presiding and had initially addressed their remarks to him rather than to the magistrates. Likewise the girls were rarely able to distinguish between costs, compensation and fines and viewed them all as "punishments". Most girls were also confused by the rules of court procedure regarding, for example, when they should speak and when they should sit down or stand up.' [Home Office, *Further Studies of Female Offenders* (London: Home Office, 1975) p 50]

And Dell, whose study might well be retitled 'Bewildered Afraid and Silent in Court' gives these accounts of women who had been committed to Holloway Prison although they had not been legally represented in court:

'One remanded girl, when asked by the interviewer whether she had asked for bail in court, replied "What is bail? Is it the same as legal aid?" . . . one girl put it, "I kept being told to get up and sit down". It is not easy in such circumstances to do justice to one's own defence . . . Frequently the women said that they had not been able to catch what was being said. One woman described her feelings when she was invited to speak in court and failed to respond, much as she wished to: "I was too overawed and frightened . . . I didn't want to make a fool of myself – I would only have cried".' [S Dell, *Silent in Court* (London: Bell, 1971) pp 17–19]

It can, of course, be argued that court appearances are designed to degrade and humiliate the defendant [P Carlen, *Magistrates' Justice* (London: Martin Robertson, 1976)] whether female or male. There are grounds however for believing that the experience can be more traumatic for women and girls. Females are more likely than males to be first offenders and thus literally inexperienced in court affairs. Parker and his colleagues, in one of the few studies comparing male and female juvenile offenders before the courts noted a number of differences in their reactions and perceptions. Girls experienced much lengthier delays than boys in being charged and this added to their sense of injustice and confusion [H Parker, M Casburn and D Turnbull, *Receiving Juvenile Justice* (Oxford: Blackwell, 1981) p 100]. More of the girls, too, although their 'offences were more trivial' were persuaded to plead guilty by their solicitors against their own inclinations and in consequence bore a feeling of unfairness (Parker et al, 1981, p 104):

644

'Moreover passivity may be expected from girl defendants viewed as appropriate behaviour and even encouraged by some court workers . . . Girls may find it doubly difficult to break through this ascribed passivity and speak out in the juvenile court, the more so *since a shame at being on view* and weighed up in the eyes of unknown others featured in these girls' reflections on their juvenile court hearing.' (Parker et al, 1981, p 106)

In contrast, while many of the boys found the court personnel and atmosphere 'sympathetic':

'These boys' feelings were not echoed by the . . . girls we talked with. Rather, for girls the overall impression, it seems was one of feeling "scared" and "frightened" and . . . few seemed to take in what was being said in court because their minds ran on fatalistically to their chances of being "put away".' (Parker et al, 1981, p 108)

Not only did these girls experience and perceive the juvenile court in a different way, they were expected and advised by their solicitors to play a different role from boys:

'Girls, in particular, tended to remember their solicitor advised mute passivity . . . whereas one or two boys say they were encouraged to assert themselves.' (Parker et al, 1981, p 111)

The juvenile court, with social workers and education officers present is rather less likely than a magistrates' court to be a predominantly male environment which some women find particularly intimidating:

'Women are treated badly by the courts – not openly, but in all the male assumptions about how business in court should be conducted.' [A Cook and G Kirk, *Greenham Women Everywhere* (London: Pluto Press, 1983) p 117]

Carlen, in her study of incarcerated women offenders in Scotland noted their feelings of injustice and exclusion. The women in Cornton Vale prison felt that their legal representation had been poorly prepared, their chances of acquittal very poor because the courts were biased towards the police. But most of all 'what had embittered them was their exclusion from the judicial process' [P Carlen, *Women's Imprisonment* (London: Routledge & Kegan Paul, 1983) p 129]. Several of these prisoners felt especially anxious because the judges and lawyers seemed neither to appreciate that they had children, nor to consider who would care for the children if the mother were imprisoned. Some female defendants certainly find their court appearances especially humiliating and oppressive; there is evidence that the trauma can be greater for them than for males although, ironically, their offences tend to be less serious and repeated less frequently.

In his review of racial discrimination in the criminal justice process, cited above (see Extract 6.4.1), Smith (1997, pp 753–754) draws some conclusions that are equally applicable to sex, and indeed any form of, discrimination. First, decision-making criteria should be reviewed in the light of their consequences for particular groups (or gender). Secondly, 'decision-making criteria cannot be validated internally by the results that they produce within the criminal process.' By this, Smith means that early decisions cannot be justified by reference to later decisions. Criteria which appear to predict particular outcomes further downstream, for example, that selecting black suspects will lead to more findings of guilt, are only self-fulfilling prophecies because the later decisions are constrained by the earlier ones. It may be, however, that other criteria (non-discriminatory and non-stereotypical) would produce similar results, so independent reasons are required to show why those criteria should be excluded. Thirdly, Smith stresses the need to consider unexpected side-effects of policies intended to make decision-making more fair.

> The best example here is the decision about whether to caution or charge juvenile suspects. A system for diverting juvenile offenders from the courts is likely to be advantageous to a relatively high-offending group, such as black people. On the face of it, such a system (particularly if operated by the police) is bound to involve a large amount of discretion, subject to minimal oversight and review. This allows scope for direct racial discrimination. The obvious response is to require greater use of formal criteria. Any criteria that fit with the underlying principles of cautioning are, however, likely to work to the disadvantage of a high-offending group, such as black people. That means either adopting inappropriate criteria that have an equal impact on different ethnic groups, which would undermine support for cautioning, or reverting to a more discretionary approach. (Smith, 1997, p 754)

(b) Discrimination within criminal justice agencies

In responding to concerns about discrimination, it is easy to think in terms of ways that the discretion of various actors in the criminal justice process can be externally shaped or controlled. But it may be that the working environment of those actors has an important influence on their sensitivity to discrimination issues. Criminal justice institutions have their own, internal opportunity structures and they are likely to reflect attitudes to discrimination in general. It would be simplistic to suggest that such attitudes are necessarily manifested in the institution's decision-making but it is probable that they can have indirect effects on institutional awareness of discrimination and official willingness to prioritise attempts to solve the problem. For example, in the earlier discussion of policing culture (in Chapter 2), it was noted that racist and sexist remarks are frequently encountered in officers' conversation and humour but that there is little evidence of directly discriminatory decision-making. However, there is equally little evidence of any enthusiasm for responding to the kinds of concern mentioned by Smith above in connection with indirect discrimination. Similarly, the relative absence of women and black people amongst the police or the judiciary does not in itself mean that police and judicial decisions are biased, but they are less likely to reflect much empathy with suspects and defendants who are women or are from racial minorities. There are other reasons, in addition, why the internal structure of

646

criminal justice institutions need to be considered. One is that, from the perspective of the public, the legitimacy of the process cannot be sustained when the process purports to be acting fairly to them but discriminates against its own personnel. Another is that, not least, the rights and interests of those personnel are independently worthy of protection.

During the past two decades, concerted efforts have been made to extend the representativeness of members of criminal justice institutions. In general, the Home Secretary has a duty, under s 95 of the Criminal Justice Act 1991, to publish such information as he considers expedient to facilitate the avoidance of racial, sex or other discrimination; such reports have been only intermittent, however. In the probation service, a Home Office Circular was issued in 1988 giving advice on policy, recruitment, training, employment and provision of service and the service has introduced a system of ethnic monitoring of staff. In 1994, about 7 per cent of officers were from ethnic minority groups, reflecting the proportion of such groups in the national population. As for women, they are well represented in the probation service and, in 1994, the proportion was greater than 50 per cent. There has also been increased awareness of racial discrimination in the courts. The Judicial Studies Board, which is responsible for training judges, now has an Ethnic Minorities Advisory Committee, and the Bar has taken positive steps to recruit more members of ethnic minorities to the profession. There are still relatively few women judges, however.

It is amongst police forces that the greatest efforts have been made to recruit and retain a broader cross-section of the population. But despite over 20 years of recruiting campaigns which have targeted ethnic minorities, there are relatively few police officers from those groups (around 1.6 per cent in 1994). Holdaway suggests that such officers face considerable obstacles, including racist banter from within the force, racist abuse from the public and disapproval from their own communities. For black people especially, joining the police may be seen as joining the opposition (Holdaway, 1991). In 1994, Her Majesty's Inspector of Constabulary published a thematic inspection of equal opportunities in the police service (Her Majesty's Chief Inspector of Constabulary, 1994) and the issue was revisited in the recent inspection on community and race relations. The report demonstrates the close links between racism, recruitment policy and interaction with the public.

Extract 6.4.3

Her Majesty's Chief Inspector of Constabulary, *Winning the Race: Policing Plural Communities* (1996–97) paras 2.62–2.94

Racial incident monitoring

2.62 Forces have much longer experience of monitoring racial incidents which they have been required to record on the basis of a standard definition laid

down by the Association of Chief Police Officers (ACPO) in 1985. That definition has now been broadened to include the widest possible range of incidents
and officers are encouraged to take a similarly broad view . . .

2.63   The figures, though, have been volatile, and recent evidence (FitzGerald
and Hale [*Ethnic Minorities: Victimisation and Racial Harassment: Findings
from the 1988 and 1992 British Crime Surveys* HORS No 154 (London: Home
Office, 1996)]) has confirmed long-standing concerns that these incidents are
significantly under-recorded either because of officers' confusion over what is
expected of them or because of a lack of sympathy with the issue or both.

2.64   Successive reports from the Racial Attacks Group and Select Committees have combined with local pressures (from ACPO rank officers and those
with community relations responsibilities as well as local groups involved with
the police in multi-agency fora) to produce a marked increase in the numbers
recorded. This has itself posed some difficulties. The extent to which any
increase is due to improved recording may be unclear. Even if improved
recording *is* the main reason, it may still be difficult to stop others (including
the media) placing alarmist interpretations on any apparent 'rise'. Associated
with this, force managers may be concerned that the increased numbers
will actually increase perceptions that the police are failing to tackle racial
incidents and that clear-up rates are lower.

2.65   Some forces, however, have been prepared to 'grasp these nettles'. West
Yorkshire, for instance, has a force objective of increasing reports of racial
incidents with a view to encouraging such reports and raising confidence in
their ability to deal with them. Moreover most by now are involved in multi-
agency approaches to address the factors that give rise to such incidents, to
share information in and to establish a clearer picture of local trends, and to
provide co-ordinated support to victims. Where close working relationships
had been established with local authorities, the Race Equality Council and
other voluntary and non-statutory groups (such as SARI in Bristol) these clearly
added considerably to what the force could have done simply in its own right.

2.66   Substantial concerns remain, however. Many officers appear to remain
unaware of the ACPO definition of a racial incident (or its salient points . . .)
and, among those who believe they know, there appears to be widely differing
interpretations of what this means (and of what is required) when such an
incident is reported to them. Moreover, as with other 'indicators', there is the
perennial danger of getting bogged down in questions of quantity rather than
issues of quality.

2.67   The British Crime Survey shows that ethnic minorities as victims of crime
are generally less satisfied than whites with the police response to incidents,
but these levels of dissatisfaction rise significantly where they believe the
crimes they report were racially motivated. While improved recording is important, it will not, of itself, improve the quality of service in response to racial harassment. The quality of response by the police to racial incidents *could* enhance
police community relations, but it seems currently to have the reverse effect in
many cases. Forces are, however, monitoring satisfaction levels amongst those
who have reported incidents (by a sampling mechanism) to judge the level

and quality of police response. Often this function is undertaken independently of the Police Division/Area handling the original complaint.

Complaints

2.68   Finally, a potentially important source of feedback on performance of individuals is complaints against the police and a significant test of a force's commitment to community and race relations is the effectiveness with which they are dealt . . . whether formally through the discipline system or informally as necessary. The lack of faith in the fairness and impartiality of the police complaints procedure was a recurrent theme and its persistence is a major obstacle to progress in this area.

2.69   Unless people trust the investigation processes police/community relations will always be at risk. An isolated incident, if perceived to have been dealt with unsatisfactorily by minority communities, can have wide reaching effects. Clear evidence emerged during the inspection that complaints are being treated seriously and handled professionally. Recently, in Leicestershire and Merseyside, officers have been required to resign following racially offensive behaviour.

2.70   In addition to improving their response to formal complaints, forces should take a positive approach to complaints made about politics, procedures and practices. These are a valuable source of information, particularly when dealing with issues associated with visible ethnic minorities, gay men and lesbian women. Forces should consider designing forms to be made available at community forums/venues as a means of receiving and recording organisational complaints, and they should also have thought through the most appropriate means of responding to these – even where members of the public blame the police for problems for which other agencies are primarily responsible, a perceived failure to respond to the complaint may still be detrimental to the police image.

Staffing issues

2.71   Clearly the progress which needs to be made in police-community and race relations rests critically on the staff who currently deliver force policies and who would be responsible for implementing any necessary changes. The Inspection highlighted three broad areas of concern in relation to staffing, namely: *recruitment and career progression* (both with regard to officers from ethnic minorities and those from the majority (white) population), *the deployment of staff and training*.

2.72   As mentioned previously, the specific issue of ethnic minority recruitment has already been covered separately in the HMIC report 'Developing Diversity in the Police Service' but it is necessary also to acknowledge its importance in the wider context of this report – not least because the recruitment of more officers from the ethnic minorities emerged as a recurring theme of the Inspection. It was recognised within forces and identified as a key issue in raising the confidence of communities in the police service and was seen to provide forces with inherently skilled resources in the area of community and

649

race relations, as well as, reflecting the communities they served . . . Further questions, however, were raised about the retention and wastage of such officers, their experience of prejudice within the force and (not unrelated) their career prospects if they stayed . . .

2.73 Meetings with officers from ethnic minorities in the course of the Inspection confirmed that some had encountered prejudice and felt unsupported by line management and fellow officers in dealing with racist conduct. Such feelings seemed especially acute in one force which was self-consciously proud of its image as one of the pioneers of 'progressive' policies on community and race relations. Very few of these officers had joined the police in order to 'represent' their communities or to be cast in a particular role because of their ethnicity. Above all, they wanted the same respect and career opportunities as their peers *irrespective* of their origins. Moreover, many of their main preoccupations were identical with those of their white colleagues. These included low morale, poor management and career prospects, and a belief that performance indicators were generating a competitive ethos which was increasingly divisive. The establishment of informal networks, in various forms, within forces was regarded as valuable.

2.74 The other side of the recruitment and promotion coin concerns white officers. Although the Inspection was unable to examine these issues in detail, it was not apparent that systematic and effective steps were being taken to screen out recruits whose available skills in dealing with plural communities were in doubt, nor did the proven abilities of serving officers in this field count in their favour in career terms.

2.75 Sergeants were found to constitute the weakest link in the management of community and race relations. They were least likely to understand their responsibilities in this area and the least well prepared for meeting them. HM Inspector found clear examples of their failure to intervene following inappropriate behaviour or the use of racist/discriminatory language . . .

2.76 There were, however, some examples of good practice of which two are worth citing here. One local commander (as members of his staff corroborated independently) routinely made clear to staff posted to his area that, if they thought they might have any difficulty in dealing with an ethnically diverse public, they were free to ask for a transfer – *sooner rather than later*. Also, assessment centres for promotion from constable to sergeant and from sergeant to inspector had begun to test candidates about how they would respond to inappropriate language or behaviour from subordinates. Even if few rose successfully to this challenge, the fact that the question is now being posed is encouraging . . . A further positive sign in some forces was that management expectations with regard to 'sensitivity' were also included in role descriptions and skill profiles.

Deployment of staff

2.77 The Inspection found a major area of concern within forces which corresponded with the view expressed by community groups. This was the frequency with which local community beat officers were abstracted for protracted specialist operations, major events, or routine policing demands. They were, more often than not, the first 'port-of-call' without any real consideration of the consequences for the communities they served. The importance of a continuous community policing presence in gathering community and crime intelligence and as an effective means of preventing and detecting crime was an issue consistently commented upon by members of the public.

2.78 The Inspection demonstrated that where police forces support the indigenous mechanisms that operate within communities, rather than impose policing solutions on them, this can have a more beneficial effect . . .

2.79 The Inspection provided clear evidence that the use of specialist liaison officers, properly supported, in schools and youth projects had a positive effect on police/community relations. Schools liaison continues to be an important first contact with the police for most young people and, as such, still represents the best opportunity to create a positive initial impression. Initiatives include the approach adopted by West Yorkshire, where a teacher is seconded to the police schools liaison unit. This provides the individual with a useful insight and gives mutual support in this vital partnership between two key agencies within the community. It is disappointing that some forces have chosen to withdraw dedicated schools liaison officers . . .

2.80 Youth liaison work, particularly in deprived urban housing estates, can provide further advances in community relations . . .

2.81 In the context of specialist community liaison work, police liaison officers from Steelhouse Lane, Birmingham dealing with gay and lesbian groups provide an opportunity for greater understanding of the difficulties faced by these minorities as part of the wider community. This initiative has led to a positive approach in dealing with homophobic attacks, and thereby gradually improving trust.

2.82 However, the value placed on the work of specialist community liaison officers often appears to be low. Like beat officers, they too may be abstracted to meet other needs within the force, irrespective of the consequences. In one inner city police area, the local Chinese community had developed a good relationship with two dedicated beat officers over a long period. From the community's point of view, their regular attendance at the local community centre and presence in the area provided a vital point of contact for advice and information and in the reporting of racial incidents. From the police perspective the work of these officers stimulated confidence and provided a means to gather intelligence in dealing with local problems. Both officers were abstracted for an extended period during Euro '96 and their absence in the community was acutely felt and perceived as abandonment. The officers themselves echoed this and recognised that it would take a long time to re-establish trust and confidence.

2.83 The Inspection also showed that some specialist community liaison officers were not properly and routinely supervised and allowed to 'do their own thing'. In one force visited, such an officer took on the responsibility of a 'marriage guidance' function to the local Asian community with the potential of causing serious damage to police-community relations and the reputation of the force.

Training

2.84   Appropriate training is essential for all staff (including civilians and special constables) and may be provided in a number of different ways. The Inspection was limited to looking at the provision of *in-force* training. HM Inspector can therefore only comment on the effect of the various sources of national training referred to in the previous chapter insofar as this was evident *within* the forces covered by the Inspection . . .

2.85   Causes for concern at force level were identified in:
• the provision of community and race relations training for those most in need of it
• the content of training
• its evaluation
• the extent to which those who had received national training were able to use this for the benefit of their forces.

2.86   HM Inspector acknowledges the weight of mandatory training (recently and currently) imposed on forces and the limited resources available to meet these needs. Officer protection, investigative interviewing, disclosure issues and legislative changes (among others) compete for part of training budgets along with equal opportunities and community and race relations. All too often, however, specific community and race relations training is relegated to a lowly position on the training agenda, not least because its relevance to meeting operational targets is not clear.

2.87   Some forces claimed to take a 'golden thread' approach, whereby community and race relations training was interwoven within more general training or training on other themes. Yet, in practice, HM Inspector found little evidence of this in the formal content of training programmes or, more importantly, in terms of any post-training effect, for example in tutor-led training of probationer constables or mentoring of newly promoted sergeants.

2.88   By contrast, the service has recognised the need for Equal Opportunity training. Influencing factors include implications for relationships in the workplace and, more generally, the damaging effect and resource demands of forces being taken to Industrial Tribunals. Although HM Inspector fully recognises the importance of such training, it could be argued that these considerations have led to a disproportionate focus on internal equality issues as opposed to quality of service (and non discriminatory) *external* service delivery. Community and race relations training has tended to be viewed as a bolt-on optional extra, de-coupled from questions of service delivery.

2.89   The Inspection of forces revealed that community and race relations training is particularly necessary for two sets of officers:
• those who are beyond their probationary period and are in daily, front-line contact with members of the public;
• those with line management responsibilities.

2.90   The former may discover that their general probationer training did not fully equip them to deal with some of the complex and/or very specific (and sometimes sensitive) situations they now face. They need advice which is tailored to dealing with these situations so that they are better equipped to avoid the behavioural traits and norms of their more cynical peers. Without some counterweight to the 'canteen culture' they may fail to develop their ability to handle such incidents with confidence and sensitivity.

2.91 With regard to some line managers, their indifference (at worst) and lack of confidence (at best) in tackling inappropriate racist behaviour by officers is particularly worrying. Training to equip first line managers to deal appropriately with such behaviour would seem to be a priority (although the influence of leadership and example cannot be overstated). These supervisors are 'key' to combating racist attitudes and behaviour within the service, yet the unfortunate reality is that some actively perpetuate this type of conduct.

2.92 Unfortunately, where specific community and race relations training exists, some officers who attend are not enthusiastic about the topic or overly attentive. Interviews during the course of the Inspection revealed that some officers *assume* that they are already well-versed and successful in community and race relations or that community and race relations is simply a 'matter of common sense' requiring no training whatsoever. Others sincerely expressed the view that they 'treated everyone in the same way' – but this does not obviate the need for any training, and fails to recognise that in some situations, it might be appropriate to handle people differently.

2.93 The Inspection revealed that those officers who are sensitive to dealing with diversity and confident in their handling of different community groups are few in number, and the knowledge and expertise within forces to develop and train staff is limited. Police training in community and race relations poses challenges quite different from training about law enforcement. Many trainers interviewed spoke of insufficient knowledge levels and a lack of self-confidence in delivering such training – the switch from delivering 'technical' to 'social' training proving difficult. Simply providing officers with 'information' on different groups during training is not enough and, may unwittingly foster stereotyping. The newly agreed minimum training needs, in respect of community and race relations training at National Police Training Centres, will help quality assure this type of training for probationer constables.

2.94 The Inspection did not find any examples of good practice in the proper monitoring and evaluation of community and race relations training by appropriately skilled staff. A further cause for concern was the failure of some forces to utilise officers who had received national training for the benefit of the force, or even to give them the opportunity personally to put that training into action. Thus, officers trained . . . by the Specialist Support Unit (SSU), – the Home Office sponsored training facility for Community and Race Relations – at Turvey, were rarely used for in-force training and, in many instances officers who had spent a week at the Holly Royde Conference (aimed at supporting force based projects in the field of community and race relations) working up action plans on community and race relations topics were unsupported in implementing these on their return to force or, worse, were moved to other posts before they could see them through. The training of officers in these ways represents a significant financial investment by forces and yet officers so trained spoke of very ad hoc selection processes and a failure to debrief on return to force.

In respect of sex discrimination in policing, Walklate argues that equal opportunities policies can have an important effect, not only on relationships within the police organisation, but also on the police service's relations with the public.

Extract 6.4.4

S Walklate, 'Equal Opportunities and the Future of Policing' in F Leishman, B Loveday and S Savage (eds), *Core Issues in Policing* (1996) pp 193–199

Women, policing and equal opportunities

In 1981 policewomen accounted for 8.6 per cent of the total force establishment in England and Wales. By 1993 this had risen to 13.2 per cent (HMIC 1993a), though this rise masks marked regional variations from 9.2 per cent in South Wales to 16.1 per cent in the West Midlands . . . [V]ery few senior posts are occupied by women: in December 1993 of 16,571 policewomen, 15,195 were constables, 1,044 were sergeants, 237 were inspectors, 54 were chief inspectors, 27 were superintendents, 11 were chief superintendents, and three were assistant chief constables. Indeed, in 1992, when Alison Halford was pursuing her sex discrimination case, as an assistant chief constable, she was then the highest ranked serving female officer. In 1994, however, three women achieved the rank of deputy chief constable and, in 1995, Britain saw its first woman chief constable with the appointment of Pauline Clare to head the Lancashire police.

These figures in and of themselves suggest that not only are women under-represented in policework, but also that once recruited, their road to the top is certainly a 'greasy pole'! Part of the explanation for the wider under-representation of women in policing lies in the recruitment process: few women apply to become police officers. Why they do not apply may, of course, be connected with the kind of public image that policework has, and the kind of experiences women have of policing both as members of the public and as police officers. We shall discuss the second of these issues first of all.

Kinsey's . . . report of police officers on Merseyside [R Kinsey, *The Merseyside Crime and Police Surveys: Final Report* (Liverpool: Mersey County Council, 1985)] indicates that 43 per cent of those officers under 30 years of age on station duty (the least prestigious job) were women. Coffey, Brown and Savage ['Policewomen's Career Aspirations: Some Reflections on the Role and Capability of Women in Policing in Britain' (1992) 15 *Police Studies* 13–19] report that women were under-represented in many specialist departments and totally absent from others. Brown, Maidment and Bull ['Appropriate Skill-task Matching or Gender Bias in Deployment of Male and Female Officers?' (1993) 3 *Policing and Society* 121–136] found that the deployment patterns of women police officers gravitated towards 'low frequency labour intensive specialised tasks'; for example, supporting rape victims or victims of sexual abuse (an issue which shall be returned to). Anderson, Brown and Campbell [*Aspects of Discrimination Within the Police Service in England and Wales* (London: Home Office Police Research Group, 1993) p 11] state consequently:

'women officers are limited in the amount and type of experience they are able to gain. This in turn affects their job satisfaction and may inhibit their promotion prospects. That fewer women than men achieve promotion in turn can reinforce male stereotypes about women's abilities.'

Some of these stereotypes relate to the presumed physical nature of the job and women's abilities to handle it . . . Others relate to the presumed management problem posed by policewomen; in other words, their short average service record before leaving to have children. Neither of these stereotypes are necessarily supported empirically nor are they insurmountable, but they do relate to the well-documented 'cult of masculinity' which pervades 'cop culture'. This is evidenced in the studies conducted by the PSI (see Smith and Gray [*Police and People in London: IV The Police in Action* (London: Policy Studies Institute)]; Bryant, Dunkerley and Kelland ['One of the Boys?' (1993) 1 *Policing* 236–244]; and Jones ['Making It Work: Some Reflections on the Sex Discrimination Act' (1987) 60 *Police Journal* 294–302]). These attitudes leave many policewomen with the choice of either embracing this male culture as their own or of fulfilling the more traditional expectations associated with their role: what Ehrlich-Martin [*Breaking and Entering: Policewomen on Patrol* (California: University of California Press, 1980)] has referred to as the strategies of POLICEwomen or policeWOMEN – strategies which may, of course, be compounded or challenged by the ways in which equal opportunities policies are, or are not, put in place.

Having established that these are some of the historical and contemporary barriers to an effective and meaningful equal treatment of female officers within the force, is there any evidence to indicate that the experience of policewomen might be changing?

Commentators have suggested that in some respects Alison Halford's sex discrimination case, supported as it was by the EOC, alongside the high profile media coverage that it generated, acted as a catalyst in encouraging other policewomen to speak out about their experiences. Indeed, since 1992 a number of other cases have been similarly reported in the media, though not so extensively. Whether or not the Halford case has had such a catalytic effect is a moot point. What is clear is that there is a greater awareness of the nature and extent of sexual discrimination in the police force. For example, the report produced by Anderson, Brown and Campbell (1993) for the Police Research Group indicates that nine out of ten policewomen experience verbal sexual harassment, six in ten had offensive comments made about their appearance, three in ten were subject to unwanted touching, and one in ten had given serious thought to leaving the police force because of harassment.

Arguably, greater awareness of policewomen's experiences alongside a higher profile stance towards equal opportunities by police forces themselves in the wake of Home Office Circular 87/1989 is likely, in the short term at least, to produce a higher number of cases of sexual discrimination being filed. However, both of these factors are also underpinned by questions of deployment.

As has already been cited, an examination of the deployment patterns of policewomen clearly raises two questions: what assumptions underpin those deployment patterns with respect to the skills of female officers, and how might better use be made of these skills? These assumptions can be discerned in a number of ways; here we shall examine them by overviewing some of the developments which have taken place over the last ten years in police-public relations, the second dimension which equal opportunities policies might be expected to address. We shall pay special attention to those areas in which the police have endeavoured to put in place an improved response to women as 'victims' of crime.

Women as 'victims' of crime and equal opportunities

It has been argued that improved service responses to women as victims of crime were put in place during the 1980s and early 1990s as much as a consequence of the increasing concern to secure public support for policing as they were a product of the concern to address women's needs [J Radford and B Stanko, 'Violence Against Women and Children: The Contradictions of Crime Control Under Patriarchy' in K Stenson and D Colwell (eds), *The Politics of Crime Control* (London: Sage, 1991)]. Whatever the underlying concern, significant policy initiatives have occurred both in the police response to women reporting rape and to 'domestic' violence. In the context of rape, the much publicised televised handling of a rape complainant by the Thames Valley Police (BBC 1, 18 January 1982), and the public outcry which followed it, precipitated Home Office Circular 25/1983. That circular outlined how incidents of rape might be handled more effectively. Consequently, many forces following the lead of the Metropolitan Police proceeded to establish 'rape suites'. To what extent these changes have resulted in substantial changes for women who have reported an incident of rape is, however, subject to some debate. As Smith [*Concerns About Rape*, HORS No 106 (London: HMSO, 1989) p 26] states:

> 'Most police forces have recognised the need to reconsider their own responsiveness to rape. Nevertheless, the evidence from this study of two London boroughs suggests that it is still the classic stereotype of rape which is more likely to be officially recorded as a crime.'

In a later study by Grace, Lloyd and Smith (1992:5) it is reported that:

> 'Alleged acquaintance attacks are the least likely to result in a conviction ... [and] are the most likely cases for women to withdraw their complaints.'

This suggests that there is much work still to be done in this area and perhaps supports the view that such reforms constitute mere 'window dressing' (Radford and Stanko 1991: 196) on the one hand, and the treatment of women as consumers of a service on the other [S Walklate 'Responding to Women as Consumers of Police Service: The UK Experience 1981–1991' in J Vigh and G Katona (eds), *Social Changes, Crime and Police* (Budapest: Eutuos Lorand University Press, 1993)]. The same analysis might also be offered of the recent flurry of policy activity in the area of 'domestic' violence.

Following on from what was considered to be both an innovative and a successful policy response to 'domestic' violence developed by the Metropolitan Police, Home Office Circular 60/1990 gave considerable impetus for other force areas to follow their model. This circular reminded all chief constables of the range of legal strategies under which offenders might be arrested (espousing a 'positive stance' towards arrest for 'domestic' incidents) as well as recommending the establishment of 'dedicated' units through which to support the 'victim' of such incidents.

As was hinted earlier, this circular has prompted a relatively rapid, and certainly imaginative, response from police forces up and down the country as they put efforts in place to take the issue of 'domestic' violence much more seriously than consigning it to the category of 'rubbish' work [K Newman, *Report of the Commissioner for the Metropolis 1982* (London: HMSO, 1984)]; this, despite the fact that both elements of this overall policy stance are fraught with difficulties. One aspect to those difficulties connects the substantive concerns of each of these areas of policing policy activity. These difficulties can be posed as two questions: are these the kinds of policy developments which offer women, as members of the public, the kind of policing policy response they want and/or are entitled to, and who in the police force has acquired the responsibility, for the most part, for delivering these policies? Both of these questions return us to the issue of equal opportunities.

The use and deployment of policewomen in the re-orientation and implementation of policy initiatives in relation to rape and 'domestic' violence has been a significant feature of their respective implementation as policies. The use and deployment of policewomen in this way rests on two assumptions: first, that women would prefer to be dealt with by a female officer; secondly, that female officers are more likely to have the appropriate qualities to offer to women. It is worth commenting on each of these assumptions in greater detail before examining their relevance for equal opportunities policies.

The view that women would prefer to have their case dealt with by a female officer is supported by limited, though not totally convincing, evidence. Heidensohn's study [*Women in Control? The Role of Women in Law Enforcement* (Oxford: Oxford University Press, 1992)] suggests that, from the policewoman's point of view, certain levels of job satisfaction are achieved when involved in work oriented towards supporting women. Moreover, her respondents felt that a certain quality of support was also maintained for the women concerned in these circumstances. Heidensohn's interviewees, however, also pointed out that they could identify police*men* who were equally capable of offering the same kind of quality support. One of the hidden problems here is, of course, that we have very little *gendered* empirical knowledge of what kind of policing the public want on which to base policy practice [S Walklate, 'Jack and Jill Join Up at Sun Hill: Public Images of Police Officers' (1992) 2 *Policing and Society* 219–232].

For example, Radford's . . . survey of women's views of policing [J Radford, 'Policing Male Violence, Policing Women' in J Hammer and M Maynard (eds), *Women, Policing and Social Control* (London: Macmillan, 1987)] revealed that 44 per cent of her sample thought that women officers would be more understanding in relation to violence against women, though 32 per cent thought they would not be. Many said they would prefer to speak to another woman in the context of 'domestic' violence but similarly others recognised that women officers had to be tougher than the men to succeed (Radford 1987: 40–41). Even this evidence, then, displays some understandable ambivalence to the idea that female officers will automatically be more supportive than their male counterparts.

It may be, of course, that what women as 'victims' of crime are asking for is a *quality* of support which is commonly, and stereotypically, associated with women, though the delivery of which is not necessarily guaranteed by them. The apparent ease with which female officers have been most readily accepted as suitable for this kind of work, then, raises questions of not only whether or not this guarantees the kind of service that the public (women) want, but also raises particular and general questions for policewomen as workers in a male-dominated profession. At a particular level it raises the question of how can policewomen take seriously, and encourage their predominantly male colleagues to take seriously, an area of work historically labelled as 'rubbish' work, i.e. not proper policework. At a more general level it foregrounds a potential area of contradiction between espoused policy commitments, especially with respect to equal opportunities and what appears to be the current trend of deployment patterns with respect to 'domestic' violence. In other words, how might it be possible to make sense of the espoused commitment of a police force to equal opportunities alongside its deployment of policewomen in areas traditionally defined as low status work or women's work? Indeed, some of the policy developments discussed here, from one point of view, echo and replicate the role for policewomen in a very similar way to that work done in the old Policewomen's Departments, prior to integration. The question is therefore raised, how and in what ways might equal opportunities policies impact upon such deeply embedded practices?

Heidensohn (1992: 101–102) suggests that equal opportunities policies can impact upon policing in a number of different ways: in keeping the law, in achieving a representative bureaucracy, in bringing a source of innovation and change into policy, in 'feminising' policing, in undermining police tradition and 'proper policing' and in increasing opportunities for individual women and women as a whole. It can be seen that many police forces have made considerable strides towards keeping the law, and that some albeit minimal change appears to be occurring in respect of the promotion opportunities for some policewomen. Moreover, this has certainly been an area in which innovation and change has occurred with respect to policy. However, it is worth exploring in a little more detail the issues raised by Heidensohn (1992) in respect of the questions of 'feminising' policing and 'proper policing'.

The notion of 'feminising' policing can be interpreted in a number of different ways. As Hanmer and Saunders ['Policing Violence Against Women: Implementing Policy Changes', Paper presented to British Criminology Conference, July 1991] observed, when faced with the question of guaranteeing service delivery by policewomen for other women, forces frequently fall back on the statement that they are an 'equal opportunities' employer. Such a statement, couched as it is in a concern to deploy individuals according to their merits, allows forces to advertise specialist posts, for example for a domestic violence officer, openly across the force. Individual officers put themselves forward for such postings. Hypothetically speaking, but rooted in what is already known about 'cop culture', this process allows for a number of complex mechanisms to come into play.

First, fewer male officers are likely to apply for such postings than female officers. This might be as a result of their evaluation of their own skills but also has to be seen alongside the persistent effects of 'cop culture' and the associated definition of what counts as 'proper policing' (to be developed below). Secondly, women do put themselves forward for such work, perhaps seeing such specialist work as an added opportunity for promotion as well as evaluating themselves as having the appropriate skills for such work. Thirdly, selection procedures pay due attention to the kinds of qualities considered appropriate for such work; being sympathetic, supportive, able to listen, able to communicate effectively, etc. The resultant effect of these processes is that more women enter this specialist work. At the same time, a police force is able to defend its equal opportunities policy. As was suggested earlier, these processes certainly seem to be in play in those force areas where efforts are being made to respond seriously to Circular 60/1990. That this for the most part coincides with the (little) evidence we have of what women and local agencies would prefer from policing on this issue may be accidental, but it is, nevertheless, effective. More seriously perhaps, the consequence of relying on such processes can result in the complacent belief that equal opportunity issues have been attended to, but which frequently leaves the reins of change in the hands of those who have perhaps the least interest in seeing change occur: senior policemen. The question remains as to whether such a pessimistic analysis of the cumulative effect of these processes is justified. It is at this juncture that the second area suggested by Heidensohn (1992) demands closer scrutiny: the question of what counts as 'proper policing'.

This can also be interpreted in a number of different ways, from what counts as the central policing task to what count as the central skills associated with the completion of that task. It is clear that the increasing involvement of police forces in a more positive response towards 'domestic' violence raises issues on both these counts. First, police officers are being asked to take the policing of the private domain seriously and, secondly, they are being asked to be sensitive and supportive in their subsequent response to women in violent relationships. Given the evidence and argument presented here, there are (at least) two possible outcomes to these changes in the re-orientation of the policing task.

The first possible outcome to these processes results in the reproduction of police forces prior to integration; in other words, Police Women's Departments are re-constituted in all but name. This outcome endorses the view of all those who believe that general policework is too dangerous for women and that using women for women's and children's issues makes best use of the qualities they have to offer. It leaves the 'dirty work' to the men. It 'ghettoizes' women's issues and leaves the rest of the policework relatively untouched in both style and service delivery. The second possible outcome is one in which both statements on equal opportunities and statements on 'domestic' violence are embraced by all members of a police force, both male and female, in order to create an atmosphere in which male and female officers can pursue their career aspirations in whatever line of work either sex of officer chooses. It has frequently been suggested that such an outcome can only become possible when women make up at least 25 per cent of a total organisation's workforce ... It is clear that police forces in the UK are a long way from achieving that goal. However, what underpins this projected outcome is a certain optimism that if these two areas are seriously embraced then it would demand a fundamental re-examination of what counts as policing. In other words, it would also of necessity challenge men's conceptions of what policing is about, why they became police officers, etc.

It can be seen, therefore, at this moment in time that with respect to women as police officers and women as police customers, a serious commitment to equal opportunities policies has the potential to challenge fundamentally what counts as policework. Whether or not that challenge will actually occur, and if it does, how it will be met, is as yet not wholly clear. Some change is obviously taking place, however, but the extent to which this will result in a genuine re-orientation of police-work is a moot point.

(c) Taking account of racial discrimination in criminal justice decision-making

The existence of a racial motivation for crime has long been recognised as a serious aggravating factor in offence seriousness, relevant across a whole range of offences. Where there appears to be an element of racial motivation underlying a particular crime, that factor may impinge on criminal justice decision-making in a number of different ways. This matter has perhaps received most attention in the sentencing context, where the Court of Appeal has stated on several occasions that considerable weight should be given to racial motivation as a reason for increasing the punishment imposed. An example is *Attorney General's References* (*Nos 29, 30 and 31 of 1994*) (1994) 16 Cr App R (S) 698, where Lord Taylor CJ said that '. . . it cannot be too strongly emphasised by this court that where there is a racial element in a crime of violence, that is a gravely aggravating feature'. The racial motivation makes a given offence worse for two reasons: first, because it increases the harm occasioned to the victim by an additional attack upon his rights as a citizen and, secondly, because there is inevitably a high degree of culpability attaching to offenders who single out victims for the purposes of the attack (see further Ashworth 1995, p 130).

Apart from sentencing, however, evidence of racial motivation may be taken into account at a number of other decision points in the criminal justice system. The Code for Crown Prosecutors, by para 6.4.(i) (see Extract 3.9.1 above) cites motivation 'by any form of discrimination' as a factor to be weighed in favour of prosecution, and the Mode of Trial Guidelines (see Extract 4.2.1 above) indicate that racial motivation may provide a good reason for magistrates committing the defendant for Crown Court trial rather than taking the case themselves. A further question is whether the element of racial motivation should be marked out as part of the definition of an offence, or as forming an 'aggravated' version of certain standard offences, thereby automatically attracting a higher penalty. In *Craney* [1996] 2 Cr App R (S) 336 Lord Taylor CJ, passing a sentence of 11 years in a very serious case of racially motivated assault, commented that:

There is no specific offence of racial violence, although it has been suggested that there should be one. We take the view that it is perfectly possible for the court to deal with any offence of violence which has a proven racial element in it, in a way which makes it clear that that aspect invests the offence with added gravity and therefore must be regarded as an aggravating factor . . . It has been suggested to us . . . that it would be helpful if this court were to indicate to what extent a racialist motive aggravates an offence of violence. It was even suggested in one of the skeleton arguments that the court ought to lay down, by way of guidelines, a series of bands of sentencing in different classes of case. We think it would be wrong for us to do so. The circumstances of cases vary enormously . . .

The creation of a separate offence of racially motivated violence or intimidation arose during the passage of the Criminal Justice and Public Order Bill of 1994, but was rejected by the government on the ground that to define an offence in terms of racial motivation would create an additional element in the offence which it might be difficult for the prosecution to overcome. The issue resurfaced at the Labour Party Conference in October 1997, when it was proposed that there should be a new category of offence of racially motivated offending. The proposal was received with much general acclaim, as being an appropriate and timely response to concerns about racial attacks, but the announcement prompted the following critical leader comment in *The Times* for 3 October 1997:

The Home Secretary's plan to introduce a new category of offence for racially motivated violence is a misuse of the criminal justice system. The government's determination to tackle prejudice is admirable but the Home Secretary should have rejected the lobbying of the Commission for Racial Equality whose determination to effect legislative change will only work against the interests of those whom it wishes to defend. Introducing a racially explicit element into criminal cases in the manner Mr Straw proposes could turn trials into evidential minefields and ideological battlegrounds. The experience of America, most recently in the O.J. Simpson case, shows how dangerous and distorting it can be when questions of racial motivation dominate a trial. . . . How can it be proved satisfactorily that a white man who assaults a black man does so because of his colour rather than, say, resentment at the other's wealth or random indulgence in violence? In cases where black criminals assault white victims and no racial motivation is attributed, those determined to inflame ethnic tensions will allege that the government's legislation discriminates against the majority population . . . The figure of justice is blindfold for a reason. Using the criminal justice system to make symbolic genuflection to political causes, however noble, only undermines the effective operation of the rule and fetters proper judicial discretion.

The relevant provisions are now to be found in the Crime and Disorder Bill. Clause 25 states that an offence is to be regarded as 'racially aggravated' where the defendant at the time of the offence either demonstrated racial hostility by his conduct or where it can otherwise be shown that his offence was motivated by racial hostility. Later clauses create new racially aggravated versions of standard assault, criminal damage, public order, and harassment

661

offences where these motivation is established, these offences attracting higher maximum penalties than for the basic offence. While the creation of such categories of race-based offending might serve to demonstrate the government's commitment to deal steadfastly with such cases, the objections raised in *The Times* leader are matters of real concern. In the United States the development of so-called 'hate crime' laws have generated just these problems (Tonry, 1994, 1995; Hare, 1997).

5. COMPENSATION FOR CRIME VICTIMS

(a) Compensation orders

A victim of crime may receive compensation either from the offender or, if they have suffered physical injury, in some circumstances from the state. Magistrates' courts and the Crown Court have broad powers to make awards of financial compensation for 'injury, loss or damage' occasioned to the victim of the offence (Powers of Criminal Courts Act 1973, s 35). Compensation can be given for stress and anxiety induced by an offence (*Godfrey* (1994) 15 Cr App R 536). This compensation is paid by the offender and so it involves an element of direct reparation between the offender and the victim. The *Criminal Statistics* relating to 1996 (Home Office, 1997a) show that 19 per cent of offenders convicted before the magistrates' court for an indictable offence, and 8 per cent of offenders convicted before the Crown Court were ordered to pay compensation. These figures conceal considerable variation across different offences. Magistrates ordered compensation in 56 per cent of criminal damage cases and 53 per cent of cases involving violence against the person, for example. The maximum award which can be made by a magistrates' court is £5,000 for a single offence, but there is no limit in the Crown Court. In practice, the average level of awards is quite low. The average order imposed in 1996 by a magistrates' court was £194, and in the Crown Court it was £1,072. Where a juvenile has been responsible for the offence, the court can order the parents to pay (Children and Young Persons Act 1969, s 55). Figures for 1996 indicate that parents are required to pay in just over a fifth of the cases where an order is imposed on a juvenile but, of course, the younger the offender the higher the percentage of cases in which a parent is required to pay.

The courts are required by statute to consider the making of a compensation order in every case, and it is not necessary for the victim to apply for it, or for them to be present in court. The court must, however, have the relevant information about the victim's loss before it can make an award. The Victim's Charter (Home Office, 1995; see p 102 above) states that victims should expect the police to provide them with a form on which to detail what they have lost, so that it can be brought to the court's attention by the prosecutor. Although the courts must always consider awarding compensation, we shall see that there are many cases in which this cannot practically be done. If the court does not make an order in the victim's favour the judge or

662

the magistrates must explain why not, thereby providing a useful check that the court has not simply forgotten to consider the victim.

The amount of compensation ordered must, first of all, reflect the degree of loss of the victim. This presents no problem in a straightforward case of criminal damage, such as a broken window. Information is given to the court as to the cost of repair, the matter is readily agreed and an order in that sum can be made. Matters can be more difficult to quantify in other cases, such as where the true value of the property is in dispute, or where the victim has suffered physical injury. If prosecution and defence cannot agree on the extent of the victim's loss, the court can hear evidence to resolve the matter. For cases of physical injury, courts have a table of suggested compensation figures to use as a guideline but, where the issue of compensation is complex and seriously in dispute, the Court of Appeal advises that no order should be made at all. This is especially the case where lay magistrates are involved since, unlike judges, they will have had no experience of the complex task of assessing damages in civil cases. If no compensation order is made in these circumstances, the victim may well end up with nothing, but there is the possibility (at least in theory) of the victim commencing civil proceedings against the offender or, where a 'crime of violence' was involved, making an application to the Criminal Injuries Compensation Board (see p 666 below).

Extract 6.5.1

Magistrates' Association, *Sentencing Guidelines* (1997) p viii

The following guidelines are taken from the Home Office Circular issued in August 1993.

The figures below are only a very general guide and may be increased or decreased according to the medical evidence, the victim's sex, age and any other factors which appear to the court to be relevant in the particular case. If the court does not have enough information to make a decision, then the matter should be adjourned to obtain more facts.

Type of injury		Suggested award
Graze	depending on size	up to £50
Bruise	depending on size	up to £75
Black eye		£100
Cut: no permanent scarring	depending on size and whether stitched	£75–£500
Sprain	depending on loss of mobility	£100–£1,000
Loss of a non-front tooth	depending on cosmetic effect and age of victim	£250–£500
Other minor injury	causing reasonable absence from work (2–3) weeks	£550–£850

Type of injury		Suggested award
Loss of a front tooth		£1,000
Facial scar	however small – resulting in permanent disfigurement	£750+
Jaw	fractured (wired)	£2,750
Nasal	undisplaced fracture of the nasal bone	£750
Nasal	displaced fracture of bone requiring manipulation	£1,000
Nasal	not causing fracture but displaced septum requiring sub-mucous resection	£1,750
Wrist	simple fracture with complete recovery in a few weeks	£1,750–£2,500
Wrist	displaced fracture – limb in plaster for some 6 weeks; full recovery 6–12 months	£2,500+
Finger	fractured little finger; assuming full recovery after a few weeks	£750
Leg or arm	simple fracture of tibia, fibula, ulna or radius with full recovery in three months	£2,500
Laparotomy	stomach scar 6–8 inches long (resulting from exploratory operation)	£3,500

These figures date from 1993 and, perhaps surprisingly, were not increased when the 1997 edition of the Magistrates' Association's *Sentencing Guidelines* was issued. The *Sentencing Guidelines* state that there may be factors in a particular case which could cause any of the listed awards to be revised substantially, such as the effect of an assault on an elderly or disabled person. The figures are derived from the compensation rates issued under the revised Criminal Injuries Compensation Scheme, discussed below.

A second important limitation on the powers of the court to make a compensation order is that the sum ordered must be within the offender's means to pay. This does not mean that it has to be easy for him to pay. A degree of hardship is acceptable, perhaps desirable. In *Workman* (1979) 1 Cr App R (S) 335 it was not unreasonable to expect the offender to sell some items of his property to pay the compensation, but in *Harrison* (1980) 2 Cr App R (S) 313 it was too much to require him to put his house up for sale. Payment can be ordered to be made over a period, by instalments. According to the Magistrates' Association's *Sentencing Guidelines* (Magistrates' Association, 1997) normally the whole order should be paid off within 12 months, but the Court of Appeal has said that in some cases instalments running for up to two or three years are acceptable (*Olliver* (1989) 11 Cr App R (S) 10). Receiving compensation in this way disadvantages the victim, not least in prolonging the effect of the crime, but Shapland et al (1985) found that some victims preferred to be compensated by the offender, even if over a period, rather than receive a lump sum from the state.

If the offender receives a prison sentence for the offence this will effectively deprive him of earning power so, unless he has significant assets, the option of awarding compensation may be lost. The *Criminal Statistics* show that victims are much more likely to receive compensation from a magistrates' court than from the Crown Court due partly, no doubt, to the much more frequent imposition of custodial sentences in the higher court. A compensation order is an 'ancillary order', imposed in addition to the sentence and separate from it. This means that if an order is made this should not affect the sentence to be served by the offender. Sometimes, however, the court might be tempted to suspend the prison sentence, or pass a community sentence instead, in an attempt to ensure that the victim receives compensation. While this may be well motivated, it is contrary to principle since it allows the offender 'to buy his way out' of the punishment for the crime. In *Inwood* (1974) 60 Cr App R 70 Lord Justice Scarman said that:

> Compensation orders were not introduced into our law to enable the convicted to buy themselves out of the penalties for crime. Compensation orders were introduced into our law as a convenient and rapid means of avoiding the expense of resort to civil litigation when the criminal clearly has the means which would enable the compensation to be paid.

This is an important rule, since otherwise the rich offender could avoid imprisonment by paying compensation whilst the poor offender would not have that opportunity, clearly a form of discrimination. Fudging the principle can create another problem, where the offender misleads the court into believing that he has the means to compensate the victim but, after taking his sentence reduction, he admits that he cannot pay. The Court of Appeal has said in *Dando* [1996] 1 Cr App R (S) 155 that in such a case the offender must either find the means to pay, or serve a period in prison in default. One further issue arises where the defendant makes voluntary payment of compensation in advance of the trial. Sentencers may treat such payment as evidence of remorse and reduce the sentence accordingly, but they will want to be assured that the remorse is genuine, and not motivated entirely by self-interest. A further statutory rule in the Powers of Criminal Courts Act 1973, s 35(4A) provides that where the seriousness of the offence indicates that the proper penalty is a fine, and compensation is also appropriate, but where the means of the offender preclude the payment of both in full, the court should give priority to the compensation order, reducing the fine, if necessary to nothing, so that the compensation can be paid. While this may technically infringe the rule in *Inwood*, the objection is not so strong where imprisonment is not in issue. It is a simply a matter of who should have first claim upon the offender's limited resources – and there are good grounds for saying that should be the victim, rather than the state. Section 35(4A) entails that there are some cases where the only response of a criminal court to an offence, apart from the registering of a conviction, is the making of an award of compensation to the victim. Magistrates' courts took this course in about 7 per cent of the cases in which they awarded compensation in 1996.

(b) Criminal injuries compensation

There is also a scheme for state compensation for criminal injuries. Its recent history has been a rather turbulent one. The scheme was first established in England and Wales in 1964, and it continued in existence in a non-statutory form for over 30 years. It operated by making 'ex-gratia payments' out of public funds to victims of 'crimes of violence' who applied to the Criminal Injuries Compensation Board and who complied with a number of qualifying conditions. In one sense the scope of the scheme is much narrower than that covered by awards of compensation made by the criminal courts, since the former is confined to cases of violence while the latter extends to damage to property, and the state scheme has always operated a 'lower limit' to the level of claims which can be considered. In other ways, however, the state scheme is much more effective, in that compensation can be paid irrespective of whether or not the perpetrator was ever caught, prosecuted, or convicted. Also, since the scheme is underwritten by the Treasury, the availability of compensation is not dependent upon the means of the offender.

The rationale for the state scheme has always been in doubt, since it may be questioned why victims of violent crime deserve compensation ahead of victims of other kinds of misfortune (such as many accident victims, or children with birth defects). Crimes of violence account for only a small proportion of injuries and deaths each year. To look at it in another way, why should taxpayers be required to foot this particular bill? One argument is that the state, at least in a general way, is responsible for the social conditions within which criminal offending takes place. According to the European Convention on the Compensation of Victims of Violent Crimes (Council of Europe, 1984), 'the state is bound to compensate the victim because . . . it has failed to prevent the crime by means of an effective criminal policy [and] it introduced policies which failed . . .'. Alternatively, there may be a loose contract-based argument, that where citizens give up their right of private vengeance to the apparatus of state-run criminal justice they are entitled in return to expect the state to protect them from crime or, when crime has occurred, to compensate them for losses incurred. (See further on these arguments Ashworth, 1986; Haldane and Harvey, 1995; and Miers, 1997, pp 2–13). Or it may simply be one of the positive, though politically pragmatic, ways in which the state has recognised the needs of crime victims. According to Miers (1997, p 10):

> What took place in Great Britain in the 1960s was a politicisation of the experience of personal victimisation . . . The critical response to the more liberal ideology which informed penal policy during the 1960s focused on the apparent discrepancies between the State's treatment of offenders, cared for at the taxpayer's expense, while the victim, whose needs were ignored, was sidelined until needed as a Crown witness and then discarded . . . This juxtaposition continues to have a powerful rhetorical pull, especially when played upon by right-wing governments.

It should always be remembered that in many cases no compensation for the crime victim will be forthcoming from the offender. The more devastating the victim's injuries, the less likely it will be that the offender will have a pocket deep enough to provide appropriate compensation.

In 1994 the government, concerned about the rapidly escalating costs of the state scheme, attempted to introduce a new 'tariff' based system, which listed nearly 200 forms of injury and allocated to them compensation values of between £1,000 and £250,000. This was to replace the former system, in place since the scheme's inception, of compensation being assessed on the same basis as of awards of damages in civil cases. The manner in which the government tried to bring in the tariff scheme was challenged by way of judicial review and, in *Home Secretary, ex parte Fire Brigades Union* [1995] 2 AC 513, the House of Lords held that the Home Secretary had exercised his powers unlawfully in doing so. This reversal caused chaos for those claimants whose cases had already been dealt with under the tariff scheme but now had to be considered all over again. The government was then forced to move quickly to introduce a Bill, which became the Criminal Injuries Compensation Act 1995. The Act adopts an 'enhanced tariff' approach, with a simple tariff payment being used for the majority of successful applicants, but additional compensation being payable to those most seriously affected by their injuries. Commending the Bill to Parliament the Secretary of State explained (at HL Deb, Vol 566, col 292, 19 July 1995) that 'Its aim is to provide statutory backing for the payment of compensation to blameless victims of violent crime . . . we believe that the enhanced tariff scheme provides the right balance between the needs of victims and protecting the interests of taxpayers.'

Extract 6.5.2

Criminal Injuries Compensation Scheme, paras 1–16

1. This Scheme is made by the Secretary of State under the Criminal Injuries Compensation Act 1995. Applications received on or after 1 April 1996 for the payment of compensation to, or in respect of, persons who have sustained criminal injury will be considered under this Scheme.

Administration of the Scheme

2. Claims officers in the Criminal Injuries Compensation Authority ('the Authority') will determine claims for compensation in accordance with this Scheme. Appeals against decisions taken on reviews under this Scheme will be determined by adjudicators. Persons appointed as adjudicators are appointed as members of the Criminal Injuries Compensation Appeals Panel ('the Panel'). The Secretary of State will appoint one of the adjudicators as chairman of the Panel. The Secretary of State will also appoint persons as staff of the Panel to administer the provisions of this Scheme relating to the appeal system . . .

Eligibility to apply for compensation

6. Compensation may be paid in accordance with the Scheme:
   (a) to an applicant who has sustained a criminal injury . . .
   (b) where the victim of a criminal injury . . . has since died, to an applicant who is a qualifying claimant for the purposes of paragraph 38 (compensation in fatal cases) . . .

8. For the purposes of this Scheme, 'criminal injury' means one or more personal injuries as described in the following paragraph, being an injury sustained in Great Britain and directly attributable to:
   (a) a crime of violence (including arson, fire-raising or an act of poisoning) or
   (b) an offence of trespass on a railway; or
   (c) the apprehension or attempted apprehension of an offender or a suspected offender, the prevention or attempted prevention of an offence, or the giving of help to any constable who is engaged in any such activity.

9. For the purposes of this Scheme, personal injury includes physical injury (including fatal injury), mental injury (that is, a medically recognised psychiatric or psychological illness) and disease (that is, a medically recognised illness or condition). Mental injury or disease may either result directly from the physical injury or occur without any physical injury, but compensation will not be payable for mental injury alone unless the applicant:
   (a) was put in reasonable fear of immediate physical harm to his own person; or
   (b) had a close relationship of love and affection with another person at the time when that person sustained physical (including fatal) injury directly attributable to conduct within paragraph 8(a), (b) or (c), and
      (i) that relationship still subsists (unless the victim has since died), and
      (ii) the applicant either witnessed and was present on the occasion when the other person sustained the injury, or was closely involved in its immediate aftermath; or

668

(c) was the non-consenting victim of a sexual offence (which does not include a victim who consented in fact but was deemed in law not to have consented); or

(d) being a person employed in the business of a railway, either witnessed and was present on the occasion when another person sustained physical (including fatal) injury directly attributable to an offence of trespass on a railway, or was closely involved in its immediate aftermath. Paragraph 12 below does not apply where mental injury is sustained as described in this sub-paragraph.

10. It is not necessary for the assailant to have been convicted of a criminal offence in connection with the injury, Moreover, even where the injury is attributable to conduct within paragraph 8(a) in respect of which the assailant cannot be convicted of an offence by reason of age, insanity or diplomatic immunity, the conduct may nevertheless be treated as constituting a criminal act.

11. A personal injury is not a criminal injury for the purposes of the Scheme where the injury is attributable to the use of a vehicle, except where the vehicle was used deliberately to inflict, or attempt to inflict, injury on any person.

12. Where an injury is sustained accidentally by a person who is engaged in
(a) any of the law-enforcement activities described in paragraph 8(c); or
(b) any other activity directed to containing, limiting or remedying the consequences of a crime,
compensation will not be payable unless the person injured was, at the time he sustained the injury, taking an exceptional risk which was justified in all the circumstances.

Eligibility to receive compensation

13. A claims officer may withhold or reduce an award where he considers that:
(a) the applicant failed to take, without delay, all reasonable steps to inform the police, or other body or person considered by the Authority to be appropriate for the purpose, of the circumstances giving rise to the injury; or
(b) the applicant failed to co-operate with the police or other authority attempting to bring the assailant to justice; or
(c) the applicant has failed to give all reasonable assistance to the Authority or other body or person in connection with the application; or
(d) the conduct of the applicant before, during or after the incident giving rise to the application makes it inappropriate that a full award or any award at all be made; or
(e) the applicant's character as shown by his criminal convictions (excluding convictions spent under the Rehabilitation of Offenders

Act 1974) or by evidence available to the claims officer makes it inappropriate that a full award or any award at all be made.

14. Where the victim has died since sustaining the injury (whether or not in consequence of it) the preceding paragraph will apply in relation both to the deceased and to any applicant.

15. A claims officer will make an award only where he is satisfied:
   (a) that there is no likelihood that an assailant would benefit if an award were made, or
   (b) where the applicant is under 18 years of age when the application is determined, that it would not be against his interest for an award to be made.

16. Where ... at the time when the injury was sustained the victim and the assailant (whether or not that assailant actually inflicted the injury) were living in the same household as members of the same family, an award will be withheld unless;
   (a) the assailant has been prosecuted in connection with the offence, except where a claims officer considers that there are practical, technical or other good reasons why a prosecution has not been brought, and
   (b) in the case of violence between adults in the family, a claims officer is satisfied that the applicant and the assailant stopped living in the same household before the application was made and are unlikely to share the same household again. For the purposes of this paragraph a man and a woman living together as husband and wife will be treated as members of the same family.

The arrangements for state payment of compensation are complex, and a full account cannot be provided here. Readers seeking a comprehensive discussion are referred to Miers (1997). It is, however, worth considering further ss 13–15 of the Act, the sections which limit the eligibility of 'undeserving applicants' – persons who would otherwise be entitled to criminal injuries compensation, but who can be refused on the basis that their conduct before, during or after the incident giving rise to the application make it inappropriate that they should receive compensation from the state, or that such compensation should be reduced or denied in light of their previous convictions. The following discussion of these interesting and controversial provisions is taken from Miers (1997):

Extract 6.5.3

D Miers, *State Compensation for Criminal Injuries* (1997) pp 156–161, 165–167, 170–176, 182–185

UNDESERVING APPLICANTS

The policy

As noted earlier, the original Scheme 'envisaged that it would be inappropriate for those with significant criminal records or whose own conduct led to their being injured, to receive compensation from public funds' . . . Indeed, the 1961 Working Party noted that while a person's character is not normally taken into account in determining eligibility for State benefits, the matter is different where crime is concerned. Not all victims are 'innocents', and where his mode of life, the company he keeps or the undesirable activities in which he engages are connected with the incident in which he is injured, then, it argued, the State may owe him no moral obligation, at least in the form of compensation for that injury (Home Office, *Compensation for Victims of Crimes of Violence*, Cmnd 1406, London: HMSO, 1961, paras 31 et seq.). It is of course true that many victims have themselves been offenders, a point which has been amply demonstrated in victimisation surveys (Walklate, S, *Victimology*, London: Unwin Hyman, 1989, Ch 2). Thus para 6(c) of the old Scheme provided that the Board could withhold or reduce compensation if it considered that:

> 'having regard to the conduct of the applicant before, during or after the events giving rise to the claim or to his character as shown by his criminal convictions or unlawful conduct – and, in applications under paras 15 and 16 below, to the conduct or character as shown by the criminal convictions or unlawful conduct of the deceased and of the applicant – it is inappropriate that a full award, or any award at all, be granted.'

The continuation of 'a wide power enabling the Board to reduce or refuse compensation on the grounds of the relevant conduct of the victim' was specifically recommended by the Home Office review in 1978 (Home Office, *Review of the Criminal Injuries Compensation Scheme Report of an Interdepartmental Working Party*, 1978, para 61), and it will continue to play a significant role in the new Scheme. Both the formulation and the implementation of this paragraph have occasioned criticism; many of the applications for judicial review of the Board's decisions have concerned the exercise of the discretion given by para 6(c). The central issue turns on the varying conceptions of relevance that have been held by the Board, its supporters and its critics, in particular, concerning what the Board should be able to take into account when considering the relevance to his application of the applicant's biography.

The Board has always regarded 'clean hands' as being of primary importance. In the event of a hearing, the old Scheme imposed on the applicant the obligation to make out his case, and where appropriate this extended, by para 25, 'to satisfying the Board that compensation should not be withheld or reduced under the terms of para 6'. This obligation is present in the new Scheme, para 18(b) of which provides that it is for the applicant to satisfy the claims officer dealing with his application (including an officer reviewing a decision under para 60) that an award should not be withheld or reduced under para 13(d) or (e), equivalent to para 6(c) of the old Scheme. The new Scheme also provides for the reconsideration of a decision before the award has been paid, which envisages the possibility of its being withheld or reduced ... and, where the application comes before the Panel, the applicant must satisfy the adjudicator responsible for determining his appeal, that the award 'should not be reconsidered, withheld or reduced' under this paragraph.

Though quantitatively small (of the 56,869 applications resolved in 1994–95, 4,723 were rejected on this basis: CICB, 1995, App. B), this issue is qualitatively of the first importance. It is the one facet of a compensation scheme which most strikingly brings into focus the assumptions which lie behind the notion of the innocent, and hence deserving victim (Miers, D, 'Compensation and Conceptions of Victims of Crime', *Victimology*, 1983, vol. 8, p 204). The source of the puzzlements which this issue generates goes well beyond the causal problems which may arise in the analogous context of contributory negligence in personal injury actions. Whether damages should be payable to those who are victimised while they are intoxicated by alcohol, solvents or hallucinatory drugs, or who were at the time engaged in unlawful activity, are questions that rarely trouble the courts (e.g., *Hegarty v Shine* (1878) 14 Cox CC 145; *Ashton v Turner* [1981] QB 137; *Pitts v Hunt* [1991] 1 QB 24), even though in recent years retaliatory action by victims of crime has prompted their 'victims' into taking civil action (*Revill v Newbery* [1996] QB 567 (CA)).

The first problem is that because delinquent victims resemble offenders too closely, and may indeed have been formally so defined in the past, the possibility of their receiving compensation threatens the stereotype of the 'innocent' victim for whom such schemes are created. A former Chairman of the Board, Sir Michael Ogden QC, observed (CICB, 1985, para 19):

> 'It is sometimes useful to consider extreme examples. Suppose that Peter Sutcliffe ('The Yorkshire Ripper') had been awarded compensation by the Board for an injury which was wholly unrelated to his crimes, or that an award had been made to the criminal who put a bomb on a coach containing women and children, or made an award to the man who is at the time of writing being hunted by the police in the Dunstable area in connection with extremely nasty offences of rape and other crimes. I would expect that there would be a howl of public outrage; in my view rightly so.'

Despite these observations, the Board has made a full award to a prisoner who sustained severe injuries when attacked in his cell (CICB, 1990, para 26.1: the victim was later pardoned). Public hostility is often expressed about decisions taken by legal bodies; a measure of compatibility between popular sentiment and what the law decides, permits or punishes, is an important factor in the success of any legal system to command the support of those affected by it, but it would be a poor system which used public approval or disapproval of its activities as the determining factor in its decisions. The question is whether it is defensible to refuse compensation to a person because he has a criminal record, but one which is unconnected with the injury complained of. Thousands of people remain eligible for State benefits notwithstanding prior convictions, and if those who are injured in incidents unconnected with their criminal history have been convicted and punished by due process of law, is it right that they should be so disqualified in the future? The Scheme's simple answer to date has been that it is: where offenders commit serious offences, they put themselves, so to speak, beyond the pale of criminal injury compensation. But as the Court of Appeal held in *Revill v Newbery*, a burglar is not to be treated as an outlaw for the purpose of a civil action for damages . . . ; nor should a court reduce exemplary damages where a plaintiff with serious convictions was badly injured by police officers seeking his confession to a series of armed robberies (*Treadway v Chief Constable of West Midlands* (1994) *The Times*, 25 October 1994).

Secondly, the possibility that 'offenders' might, as victims, be eligible for compensation, subverts a prime objective of criminal injury schemes, which is to distinguish victims of crime from offenders where penal regimes are perceived to be too forgiving and too neglectful of the victim. The politicisation of the victim of crime requires that the taxpayer be asked to compensate only those victims who present 'deserving' characteristics, so it therefore becomes necessary to exclude the delinquent victim (however defined) from the Scheme's beneficial provisions . . .

BIBLIOGRAPHY

Abel, G, Becker, J, Cunningham-Rathner, J, Rouleau, J and Murphy, W D (1987) 'Self-Reported Sex Crimes' 2 *Journal of Interpersonal Violence* 3

Abramson, J (1994) *We, the Jury: The Jury System and the Ideal of Democracy* (New York: Basic Books)

Ackroyd, S et al (1992) *New Technology and Practical Police Work: The Social Context of Technical Innovation* (Buckingham: Open University Press)

Adler, Z (1982) 'Rape – The Intention of Parliament and the Practice of the Courts' 45 *Modern Law Review* 664

Alderson, J (1979) *Policing Freedom* (Plymouth: Macdonald and Evans)

Allan, T (1992) 'Fairness, Truth and Silence: The Criminal Trial and the Judge's Exclusionary Discretion' in H Gross and R Harrison (eds), *Jurisprudence: Cambridge Essays* (Oxford: Clarendon Press)

Allan, T (1995) 'The Concept of Fair Trial' in E Attwool and D Goldberg (eds), *Criminal Justice* (Stuttgart: Franz Steiner)

Allen, H (1987) 'Rendering them Harmless: The Professional Portrayal of Women Charged with Serious Violent Crimes' in P Carlen and A Worrall (eds), *Gender, Crime and Justice* (Milton Keynes: Open University Press)

Alschuler, A (1995) 'Racial Quotas and the Jury' 44 *Duke Law Journal* 704

Anderson, R, Brown, J and Campbell, E (1993) *Aspects of Discrimination Within the Police Service in England and Wales* (London: Home Office Police Research Group)

Apex Trust (1994) *Once a Criminal: The Use and Abuse of Criminal Records* (London: Apex Trust)

Ashworth, A (1977) 'Excluding Evidence as Protecting Rights' *Criminal Law Review* 723

Ashworth, A (1984) 'Prosecution, Police and Public – A Guide to Good Gatekeeping' 23 *Howard Journal of Criminal Justice* 65

Ashworth, A (1986) 'Punishment and Compensation: Victims, Offenders and the State' 6 *Oxford Journal of Legal Studies* 86

Ashworth, A (1987) 'Disentangling Disparity' in C Pennington and S Lloyd-Bostock (eds), *The Psychology of Sentencing* (Oxford: Centre of Socio-Legal Studies)

Ashworth, A (1992) 'The Criminal Justice Act 1991' in C Munro and M Wasik (eds), *Sentencing, Judicial Discretion and Training* (London: Sweet & Maxwell)

Ashworth, A (1993a) 'Plea, Venue and Discontinuance' *Criminal Law Review* 830

Ashworth, A (1993b) 'Victim Impact Statements and Sentencing' *Criminal Law Review* 498

Ashworth, A (1994) *The Criminal Process* (Oxford: Clarendon Press)

Ashworth, A (1995) *Sentencing and Criminal Justice*, 2nd ed (London: Butterworths)

Ashworth, A (1996) 'Crime, Community and Creeping Consequentialism' *Criminal Law Review* 220

Ashworth, A and Gibson, B (1994) 'Altering the Sentencing Framework' *Criminal Law Review* 101

Ashworth, A and Hough, M (1996) 'Sentencing and the Climate of Opinion' *Criminal Law Review* 776

Ashworth, A and von Hirsch, A (1997) 'Recognizing Elephants: The Problem of the Custody Threshold' *Criminal Law Review* 187

Ashworth, A, Genders, E, Mansfield, G, Peay, J and Player, E (1984) *Sentencing in the Crown Court: Report of an Exploratory Study* Occasional Paper No 10 (Oxford: Centre for Criminological Research)

Audit Commission (1989) *The Probation Service: Promoting Value for Money* (London: HMSO)

Audit Commission (1990) *Effective Policing – Performance Review in Police Forces* (London: Audit Commission)

Audit Commission (1992), *Police Planning – The New Framework* (London: Audit Commission)

Audit Commission (1993) *Helping with Enquiries: Tackling Crime Effectively* (London: HMSO)

Audit Commission (1994a) *Cheques and Balances: A Framework for Improving Police Accountability* (London: Audit Commission)

Audit Commission (1994b) *A Management Handbook on Police Planning and Financial Delegation* (London: HMSO)

Audit Commission (1996a) *Streetwise – Effective Police Patrol* (London: Audit Commission)

Audit Commission (1996b) *Misspent Youth: Young People and Crime* (London: Audit Commission)

Baldwin, J (1976) 'The Social Composition of the Magistracy' 16 *British Journal of Criminology* 171

Baldwin, J (1992a) *Preparing the Record of Taped Interview* Royal Commission on Criminal Justice Research Study 2 (London: HMSO)

Baldwin, J (1992b) *The Role of Legal Representatives at Police Stations* Royal Commission on Criminal Justice Research Study 3 (London: HMSO)

Baldwin, J (1992c) *Video-Taping Police Interviews With Suspects – An Evaluation* (London: Home Office Police Research Group)

Baldwin, J (1993) 'Police Interview Techniques: Establishing Truth or Proof?' 33 *British Journal of Criminology* 325

Baldwin, J (1997) 'Understanding Judge Ordered and Directed Acquittals in the Crown Court' *Criminal Law Review* 536

Baldwin, J and McConville, M (1977) *Negotiated Justice* (London: Martin Robertson)

Baldwin, J and McConville, M (1979) 'Police Interrogation and the Right to See a Solicitor' *Criminal Law Review* 145

Baldwin, J and McConville, M (1979) *Jury Trials* (Oxford: Oxford University Press)

Baldwin, J and Moloney, T (1992) *Supervision of Police Investigations in Serious Criminal Cases* Royal Commission on Criminal Justice Research Study 4 (London: HMSO)

Baldwin, R and Kinsey, R (1982) *Police Powers and Politics* (London: Quartet)

Ball, C (1992) 'Young Offenders and the Youth Court' *Criminal Law Review* 277

Bankowski, Z and Mungham, G (1981) 'Laypeople and Lawpeople and the Administration of the Lower Courts' 9 *International Journal of the Sociology of Law* 85

Bankowski, Z, Hutton, N and McManus, J (1987) *Lay Justice?* (Edinburgh: T and T Clark)

Bayley, D H (1994) *Police for the Future* (Oxford: Oxford University Press)

Becker, G (1968) 'Crime and punishment: An Economic Analysis' 76 *Journal of Political Economy* 169–174

Becker, G and Landes, W (1975) *Essays in the Economics of Crime and Punishment* (New York: Columbia University Press)

Bedarf, A (1995) 'Examining Sex Offender Community Notification Laws' 83 *California Law Review* 885

Bennett, T (1990) *Evaluating Neighbourhood Watch* (Farnborough: Gower)

Bennett, T (1994) 'Community Policing on the Ground: Developments in Britain' in D P Rosenbaum (ed) *The Challenge of Community Policing: Testing the Promises* (London: Sage Publications)

Bennett, T and Lupton, R (1990) *National Review of Community-Oriented Patrols: Report* Report to the Home Office Research and Planning Unit (Cambridge: Institute of Criminology)

Beyleveld, D (1980) *A Bibliography on General Deterrence Research* (London: Saxon House)

Bieck, W (1977) *Response Time Analysis* (Kansas City: Kansas City Police)

Bindman, D (1977) 'Righting Wrongs' January 15 *Law Society Gazette* 15

Birch, D (1994) 'Excluding Evidence From Entrapment: What is a "Fair Cop"?' *Current Legal Problems* 73

Bittner, E (1967) 'The Police on Skid Row: A Study in Peacekeeping' *American Sociological Review* 699

Bittner, E (1970) 'The Functions of Police in Modern Society' in Egon Bittner (ed), *Aspects of Police Work* (Boston: Northeastern University Press)

Bittner, E (1974) 'A Theory of the Police' in H Jacob (ed), *Potential for Reform of Criminal Justice* (Beverly Hills: Sage Publications)

Blackstone's Criminal Practice (1998) (London: Blackstone Press)

Blakey, 'Does Forensic Science Give Value for Money?' (1995) 35 *Science and Justice* 1

Block, B, Corbett, C and Peay, J (1993) *Ordered and Directed Acquittals in the Crown Court* Royal Commission on Criminal Justice Research Study 15 (London: HMSO)

Bottomley, K and Coleman C (1980) 'Understanding Crime Rates' in R V G Clarke and J M Hough (eds), *The Effectiveness of Policing* (Farnborough: Gower)

Bottomley, K and Coleman, C (1981) *Understanding Crime Rates* (Farnborough: Saxon House)

Bottomley, K, Coleman, C, Dixon, D, Gill, M and Wall, D (1991) 'The Detention of Suspects in Police Custody: The Impact of the Police and Criminal Evidence Act 1984' 31 *British Journal of Criminology* 347

Bottoms, A E (1995) 'The Philosophy and Politics of Punishment and Sentencing' in C Clarkson and R Morgan (eds), *The Politics of Sentencing Reform* (Oxford: Clarendon Press)

Bottoms, A E et al (1990) *Intermediate Treatment and Juvenile Justice* (London: HMSO)

Brants, C and Field, S (1995) 'Discretion and Accountability: A Comparative Perspective on Keeping Crime Out of Court' in P Fennell et al (eds), *Criminal Justice in Europe* (Oxford: Clarendon Press)

Bridges, L (1994) 'Normalising Injustice' 21 *Journal of Law and Society* 20

Bridges, L and Hodgson, J (1995) 'Improving Custodial Legal Advice' *Criminal Law Review* 101

Bridges, L and McConville, M (1994) 'Keeping Faith with their Own Convictions: The Royal Commission on Criminal Justice' 57 Modern Law Review 75

Bright, J (1997) *Turning the Tide: Crime, Community and Prevention* (London: Demos)

British Chamber of Commerce (1997) *Small Firms Survey* (London: British Chamber of Commerce)

Broadhurst, R and Maller, R (1992) 'The Recidivism of Sex Offenders in the Western Australian Prison Population' 32 *British Journal of Criminology* 54

Brogden, A and Brogden, M (1982) 'Postcript: The Toxteth Riots' in M Brogden, *The Police: Autonomy and Consent* (London: Academic Press)

Brown, D (1987) *The Police Complaints Procedure: A Survey of Complainants' Views* Home Office Research Study No 93 (London: HMSO)

Brown, D (1989) *Detention at the Police Station Under the Police and Criminal Evidence Act 1984* Home Office Research Study No 93 (London: HMSO)

Brown, D (1991) *Investigating Burglary: The Effects of PACE* Home Office Research Study No 123 (London: HMSO)

Brown, D (1993) *Detention Under the Prevention of Terrorism (Temporary Provisions) Act 1989: Access to Legal Advice and Outside Contact* Research and Planning Unit Paper 75 (London: Home Office)

Brown, D (1997) *PACE Ten Years on: A Review of the Research* Home Office Research Study No 155 (London: Home Office)

Brown, D, Ellis, T and Larcombe, K (1992) *Changing the Code: Police Detention Under the Revised PACE Codes of Practice* Home Office Research Study No 129 (London: HMSO)

Brown, J M, Maidment, A and Bull, R (1993) 'Appropriate skill-task matching or gender bias in deployment of male and female officers?' 3 *Policing and Society* 121–136

Bryant, L, Dunkerley, D and Kelland, G (1985) 'One of the Boys?' 1 *Policing* 236–244

Butler, A J P (1996) 'Managing the Future: A Chief Constable's View' in F Leishman, B Loveday and S Savage (eds), *Core Issues in Policing* (London: Longman)

Cain, M (1973) *Society and the Policeman's Role* (London: Routledge & Kegan Paul)

Campbell, J Q (1995) 'A Sentencer's Lament on the Imminent Death of the Suspended Sentence' *Criminal Law Review* 293

Cape, E (1991) 'New Duties for Duty Solicitors' *Law Society's Gazette* 19, 13 April

Carlen, P (1976) *Magistrates' Justice* (London: Martin Robertson)

Carlen, P (1983) *Women's Imprisonment* (London: Routledge & Kegan Paul)

Carlen, P (ed) (1976) *The Sociology of Law* (Keele: Keele University)

Carlen, P and Worrall, A (eds) (1987) *Gender, Crime and Justice* (Milton Keynes: Open University Press)

Carter, P (1997) 'Evidence Obtained by Use of a Covert Listening Device' 113 *Law Quarterly Review* 468

Cavadino, P (1988) 'Sentencing Variations in Magistrates' Courts' *Crime UK* 31.

Chambliss, W and Seidman, R (1971) *Law, Order and Power* (Reading, Mass: Addison-Wesley)

Chatterton, M (1976) 'Police in Social Control' in J King (ed), *Control without Custody* (Cambridge: Institute of Criminology)

Chatterton, M (1979) 'The Supervision of Patrol Work under the Fixed Points System' in S Holdaway (ed), *The British Police* (London: Edward Arnold)

Chatterton, M (1983) 'Police Work and Assault Charges' in S Holdaway (ed), *The British Police* (London: Edward Arnold)

Choo, A (1993) *Abuse of Process and Judicial Stays of Criminal Proceedings* (Oxford: Clarendon Press)

Choo, A (1995) 'Halting Criminal Prosecutions: The Abuse of Process Doctrine Revisited' *Criminal Law Review* 864

Choo, A and Mellors, M (1995) 'Undercover Police Operations and What the Suspect Said (or Didn't Say)' 2 *Web Journal of Current Legal Issues* 66

Christie, N (1986) 'The Ideal Victim' in E Fattah (ed), *From Crime Policy to Victim Policy* (London: Macmillan)

Clarke, R (1992) *Situational Crime Prevention* (New York: Harrow & Heston)

Clarkson, C and Morgan, R (eds) (1995) *The Politics of Sentencing Reform* (Oxford: Clarendon Press)

Clarkson, C et al (1994) 'Assaults: The Relationship Between Seriousness, Criminalisation and Punishment' *Criminal Law Review* 4

Clayton, R and Tomlinson, H (1992) *Civil Actions Against the Police*, 2nd edn (London: Sweet & Maxwell)

Coffey, S, Brown, J and Savage, S (1992) 'Policewomen's Career Aspirations: Some Reflections on the Role and Capability of Women in Policing in Britain' 15 *Police Studies* 13–19

Cohen, P (1979) 'Policing the Working Class City' in B Fine et al (eds), *Capitalism and the Rule of Law* (London: Hutchinson)

Cohen, S (1972) *Folk Devils and Moral Panics* (London: Paladin)

Cohen, S (1979) 'The Punitive City: Notes on the Dispersal of Social Control' 3 *Contemporary Crises* 339

Commission for Racial Equality (1991) *Review of the Race Relations Act* (London: Commission for Racial Equality)

Compston, C (1995) 'Local Justice' in N Burnside (ed), *Relational Justice* (Winchester: Waterside Press)

Cook, A and Kirk, G (1983) *Greenham Women Everywhere* (London: Pluto Press)

Cooke, B (1984) 'The Appointment of Justices of the Peace – The Advisory Committee System' *The Magistrate* 69

Corker, D and Levi, M (1996) 'Pre-Trial Publicity and its Treatment in the English Courts' *Criminal Law Review* 622

Council of Europe (1983) *European Convention on the Compensation of Victims of Violent Crimes*, European Treaty Series No 116 (Strasbourg: Council of Europe)

Council of Europe (1984) *The Criminal Record and Rehabilitation of Convicted Persons* (Strasbourg: Council of Europe)

Crawford, A (1997) *The Local Governance of Crime* (Oxford: Clarendon Press)

Cretney, A and Davis, G (1995) *Punishing Violence* (London: Routledge)

Cretney, A and Davis, G (1996) 'Prosecuting Domestic Assault' *Criminal Law Review* 162

Cretney, A and Davis, G (1997a) 'Prosecuting Domestic Assault: Victims Failing Courts or Courts Failing Victims?' 36 *Howard Journal of Criminal Justice* 146

Cretney, A and Davis, G (1997b) 'The Significance of Compellability in the Prosecution of Domestic Assault' 37 *British Journal of Criminology* 75

Cretney, A, Davis, G, Clarkson, C and Shepherd, J (1994) 'Criminalizing Assault: The Failure of the "Offence Against Society" Model' 34 *British Journal of Criminology* 15

Criminal Law Revision Committee (1972) *Eleventh Report: Evidence (General)*, Cmnd 4991 (London: HMSO)

Crisp, D and Moxon, D (1994) *Case Screening by the Crown Prosecution Service: How and Why Cases are Terminated* Home Office Research Study No 137 (London: HMSO)

Crisp, D, Whittaker, C and Harris, J (1995) *Public Interest Case Assessment Schemes* Home Office Research Study No 138 (London: HMSO)

Critchley, T A (1978) *A History of the Police in England and Wales*, 2nd ed (London: Constable)

Cross, R (1995) *Evidence*, C Tapper (ed), 6th ed (London: Butterworths)

Crow, I and Cove, J (1984) 'Ethnic Minorities in the Courts' *Criminal Law Review* 413

Crown Prosecution Service (1993) *Statement on the Treatment of Victims and Witnesses by the Crown Prosecution Service* (London: CPS)

Crown Prosecution Service (1995a) *CPS Policy for Prosecuting Cases of Domestic Violence* (London: CPS)

Crown Prosecution Service (1995b) *The Crown Prosecution Service* (London: CPS)

Crown Prosecution Service (1996) *Annual Report 1995–96* HC 425 (London: HMSO)

Crown Prosecution Service (1997) *Annual Report and Accounts 1996/7* HC 68 (London: Stationery Office)

Currie, E (1988) 'Two Visions of Community Crime Prevention' in T Hope and M Shaw (eds), *Communities and Crime Reduction* (London: HMSO)

Darbyshire, P (1980) 'The Role of the Magistrates' Clerk in Summary Proceedings' 144 *Justice of the Peace* 186

Darbyshire, P (1991) 'The Lamp that Shows that Freedom Lives: Is it Worth the Candle?' *Criminal Law Review* 740

Darbyshire, P (1997a) 'An Essay on the Importance and Neglect of the Magistracy' *Criminal Law Review* 627

Darbyshire, P (1997b) 'For the New Lord Chancellor – Some Causes for Concern About Magistrates' *Criminal Law Review* 861

Darbyshire, P (1997c) 'Previous Misconduct and Magistrates' Courts – Some Tales from the Real World' *Criminal Law Review* 105

Davies, G (1996) 'Mistaken Identification: Where Law Meets Psychology Head On' 35 *Howard Journal of Criminal Justice* 232

Davis, K (1969) *Discretionary Justice: A Preliminary Inquiry* (Baton Rouge: Louisiana State University Press)

Davis, R, Lurigio, A and Skogan, W (1997) *Victims of Crime*, 2nd ed (California: Sage)

Dell, S (1971) *Silent in Court* (London: Bell)

Dennis, I (1993) 'Miscarriages of Justice and the Law of Confessions: Evidentiary Issues and Solutions' *Public Law* 291

Dennis, I (1995) 'Instrumental Protection, Human Right or Functional Necessity? Reassessing the Privilege Against Self-Incrimination' 54 *Cambridge Law Journal* 342

679

Dennis, I 'Reconstructing the Law of Criminal Evidence' (1989) *Current Legal Problems* 21

Devlin, P (1976a) *Report to the Secretary of State for the Home Department on the Departmental Committee on Evidence of Identification in Criminal Cases* HC 338 (London: HMSO)

Devlin, P (1976b) *Trial by Jury* (London: Stevens and Sons)

Devlin, P (1979) *The Judge* (Oxford: Oxford University Press)

Devlin, P (1991) 'The Conscience of the Jury' 107 *Law Quarterly Review* 398

Dholakia, N and Sumner, M (1993) 'Research, Policy and Racial Issues' in B Hudson (ed), *Racism and Criminology* (London: Sage)

Dignan, J (1992) 'Repairing the Damage' 32 *British Journal of Criminology* 453

Dignan, J and Cavadino, M (1996) 'Towards a Framework for Conceptualising and Evaluating Models of Criminal Justice From a Victim's Perspective' 4 *International Review of Victimology* 153

Dignan, J and Wynne, A (1997) '"A Microcosm of the Local Community"? Reflections on the Composition of the Magistracy in a Petty Sessional Division in the North Midlands' 37 *British Journal of Criminology* 184

Dixon, B and Stanko, E (1993) *Serving the People: Sector Policing and Police Accountability* (London: Islington Council)

Dixon, D (1990) 'Politics, Research and Symbolism in Criminal Justice: The Right of Silence and the PACE Act' 20 *Anglo-American Law Review* 27

Dixon, D (1991) 'Common Sense, Legal Advice and the Right of Silence' *Public Law* 233

Dixon, D (1992) 'Legal Regulation and Policing Practice' 1 *Social and Legal Studies* 515

Dixon, D (1997) *Law in Policing: Legal Regulation and Police Practices* (Oxford: Clarendon Press)

Dixon, D, Bottomley, A, Coleman, C, Gill, M and Wall, D (1990) 'Safeguarding the Rights of Suspects in Police Custody' 1 *Policing and Society* 115

Dixon, D, Bottomley, K, Coleman, C, Gill, M and Wall, D (1989) 'Reality and Rules in the Construction and Regulation of Police Suspicion' 17 *International Journal of the Sociology of Law* 185

Dixon, D, Coleman, C and Bottomley, K (1990) 'Consent and the Legal Regulation of Policing' 17 *Journal of Law and Society* 345

Dolinko, D 'Is there a Rationale for the Privilege Against Self-Incrimination?' (1986) 33 *University of California at Los Angeles Law Review* 1063

Doran, S (1989) 'Descent to Avernus' 139 *New Law Journal* 1147

Downes, D and Morgan, R (1997) 'Dumping the "Hostages to Fortune"? The Politics of Law and Order in Post-War Britain' in M Maguire, R Morgan and R Reiner (eds), *The Oxford Handbook of Criminology*, 2nd ed (Oxford: Clarendon Press)

Downes, D and Rock, P (1988) *Understanding Deviance* (Oxford: Clarendon Press)

Drewry, G (1985) 'The Ponting Case – Leaking in the Public Interest' *Public Law* 203

Duff, R (1986) *Trials and Punishments* (Cambridge: Cambridge University Press)

Duff, P (1993) 'The Prosecutor Fine and Social Control' 33 *British Journal of Criminology* 481

Duff, P (1994) 'The Prosecutor Fine' 14 *Oxford Journal of Legal Studies* 565

Duff, P and Findlay, M (1983) 'Jury Vetting – The Jury Under Attack' 3 *Legal Studies* 159

Dunleavy, P and Hood, C (1994) 'From Old Public Administration to New Public Management' 14 *Public Money and Management* 9–16

Dunne, D (1989) *The Birmingham Six* (Dublin: Birmingham Six Committee)

Dunningham, C and Norris, C (1996) 'A Risky Business: The Recruitment and Running of Informers by English Police Officers' 19 *Police Studies* 1

Dworkin, G 'The Serpent Beguiled Me and I Did Eat: Entrapment and the Creation of Crime' (1985) 4 *Law and Philosophy* 17

Dworkin, R (1985) 'Principle, Policy, Procedure' in *A Matter of Principle* (Oxford: Clarendon Press)

Eaton, M (1986) *Justice for Women?* (Milton Keynes: Open University Press)

Edwards, S (1989) *Policing Domestic Violence* (London: Sage)

Ehrlich-Martin, S (1980) *Breaking and Entering: Policewomen on Patrol* (California: University of California Press)

Elliman, S (1990) 'Independent Information for the Crown Prosecution Service' *New Law Journal* 812, 8 June

Elliott, J F (1973) *Interception* (Springfield, Illinois: Charles Thomas)

English, S (1997) 'Jeering Mothers Drive Paedophile off Council Estate', *The Times*, 11 January

Enright, S and Morton, J *Taking Liberties: The Criminal Jury in the 1990s* (London: Weidenfeld and Nicolson)

Erhlich, I (1975) 'Participation in Illegitimate Activities: An Economic Analysis' in G Becker and W Landes (eds), *Essays in the Economics of Crime and Punishment* (New York: Columbia University Press)

Evans, R (1993) 'Comparing Young Adult and Juvenile Cautioning in the Metropolitan Police District' *Criminal Law Review* 572

Evans, R (1994) 'Cautioning: Counting the Cost of Retrenchment' *Criminal Law Review* 566

Evans, R and Ellis, R (1997) *Police Cautioning in the 1990s* Research Findings No 52 (London: Home Office)

Evans, R and Wilkinson C (1990) 'Variations in Police Cautioning Policy and Practice in England and Wales' 29 *Howard Journal of Criminal Justice* 155

Farran, S (1996) *The UK Before the European Court of Human Rights* (London: Blackstone Press)

Farrell, G and Pease, K (1993) *Once Bitten, Twice Bitten: Repeat Victimisation and its Implications for Crime Prevention*, Home Office Police Research Group Paper 46 (London: Home Office)

Farrington, D and Dowds, E (1985) 'Disentangling Criminal Behaviour and Police Reaction' in Farrington D and Gunn J (eds), *Reactions to Crime: The Public, the Police, Courts and Prisons* (Chichester: Wiley)

Farrington, D and Gunn, J (eds) (1985) *Reactions to Crime: The Public, the Police, Courts and Prisons* (Chichester: Wiley)

Farrington, D and Morris, A (1983) 'Sex, Sentencing and Reconviction' 23 *British Journal of Criminology* 229–248

Farrington, D and Tarling, R (1985) *Prediction in Criminology* (Boston: Lexington)

Farrington, D and Walklate, S (eds) (1992) *Offenders and Victims: Theory and Policy* (Oxford: British Society of Criminology)

Faulkner, D (1994) 'The Functioning of Lay Justice' *The Magistrate* 3, 3 February

Faulkner, D (1996) *Darkness and Light: Justice, Crime and Management for Today* (London: Howard League)

Feeley, M (1979) *The Process is the Punishment: Handling Cases in a Lower Criminal Court* (New York: Russell Sage Foundation)

Feeley, M and Simon J (1994) 'Actuarial Justice: The Emerging New Criminal Law' in D Nelken (eds), *The Futures of Criminology* (London: Sage)

Feeley, M and Simon, J (1992) 'The New Penology: Notes on the Emerging Strategy of Corrections and its Implications' 30 *Criminology* 449

Fenwick, H (1995), 'Rights of Victims in the Criminal Justice System' *Criminal Law Review* 843

Field, S (1994) 'Judicial Supervision and the Pre-Trial Process' 21 *Journal of Law and Society* 119

Field, S and Hough, M (1993) *Cash-Limiting the Probation Service: A Case Study in Resource Allocation* Research & Planning Unit Paper 77 (London: Home Office)

Field, S and Thomas, P (eds) (1994) *Justice and Efficiency* (Oxford: Blackwell)

Fielding, N et al (1989) 'Constraints on the Practice of Community Policing' in R Morgan and D Smith (eds), *Coming to Terms with Policing* (London: Routledge)

Fionda, J (1995) *Public Prosecutors and Discretion: A Comparative Study* (Oxford: Clarendon Press)

Fisher, H (1977) *Report of an Inquiry by the Hon Sir Henry Fisher into the Circumstances Leading to the Trial of Three Persons on Charges Arising Out of the Death of Maxwell Confait and the Fire at 27 Doggett Road London SE6* HC 90 (London: HMSO)

Fitzgerald, M (1993) 'Ethnic Minorities in the Criminal Justice System' Royal Commission on Criminal Justice Research Study No 20 (London: HMSO)

Fitzgerald, M and Hale, C (1996) *Ethnic Minorities: Victimisation and Racial Harassment: Findings from the 1988 and 1992 British Crime Surveys* Home Office Research Study No 154 (London: Home Office)

Floud, J and Young, W (1981) *Dangerousness in Criminal Justice* (London: Heinemann)

Foot, P (1993) *Murder at the Farm* (London: Penguin)

Forensic Science Service, *Annual Report and Accounts 1993/4* HC 517 (London: HMSO)

Foster, J (1995) 'Informal Social Control and Community Crime Prevention' 35 *British Journal of Criminology* 563

Freeman, M (1981) 'Why not a Jury Nullification Statute Here Too?' *New Law Journal* 304

Freeman, M (1981) 'The Jury on Trial' *Current Legal Problems* 65

Galligan, D (1988) 'More Scepticism About Scepticism' 8 *Oxford Journal of Legal Studies* 249

Garland, D (1996) 'The Limits of the Sovereign State' 36 *British Journal of Criminology* 459

Gelsthorpe, L (1986) 'Towards a Sceptical Look at Sexism' 14 *International Journal of the Sociology of Law* 125

Genn, H (1988) 'Multiple Victimization' in Maguire M and Pointing J (eds), *Victims of Crime: A New Deal?* (Milton Keynes: Open University Press)

Glidewell, Lord Justice (1992) 'The Judicial Studies Board' in C Munro and M Wasik (eds), *Sentencing, Judicial Discretion and Training* (London: Sweet & Maxwell)

Goldstein, J (1960) 'Police Discretion Not to Invoke the Criminal Justice Process: Low Visibility Decisions in the Administration of Justice' 69 *Yale LJ* 543–589

Gouldner, R, Ritti, R and Ference, T (1977) 'The Production of Cynical Knowledge in Organizations' 42 *American Sociological Review* 539–551

Graham, J and Bowling, B (1996) *Young People and Crime* Home Office Research Study No 145 (London: Home Office)

Grace, S (1995) *Policing Domestic Violence in the 1990s* Home Office Research Study No 139 (London: HMSO)

Grace, S, Lloyd, D and Smith, L (1992) *Rape: From Recording to Conviction* Research and Planning Unit Paper 71 (London: Home Office)

Greenawalt, K (1981) 'Silence as a Moral and Constitutional Right' 23 *William and Mary Law Review* 15

Greer, S (1990) 'The Right to Silence: A Review of the Current Debate' 53 *Modern Law Review* 709

Gregory, J and Lees, S (1996) 'Attrition in Rape and Sexual Assault Cases' 36 *British Journal of Criminology* 1

Gross, S (1987) 'Loss of Innocence: Eyewitness Identification and Proof of Guilt' 16 *Journal of Legal Studies* 395

Gudjonsson, G (1992) *The Psychology of Interrogations, Confessions and Testimony* (Chichester: John Wiley)

Gudjonsson, G and MacKeith, J 'Retracted Confessions: Legal, Psychological and Psychiatric Aspects' (1988) 28 *Medicine, Science and Law* 187

Gudjonsson, G, Clare, I, Rutter, S and Pearse, J (1993) *Persons at Risk During Interviews in Police Custody: The Identification of Vulnerabilities* Royal Commission on Criminal Justice Research Study 12 (London: HMSO)

Haldane, J and Harvey, A (1995) 'The Philosophy of State Compensation' 12 *Journal of Applied Philosophy* 273

Halevy, T (1995) 'Racial Discrimination in Sentencing?' *Criminal Law Review* 267

Hall, D (1991) 'Victims' Voices in Criminal Courts: The Need for Restraint' 28 *American Journal of Criminal Law* 233

Hall, S, Critcher, C, Jefferson, T, Clarke, J and Roberts, B (1978) *Policing the Crisis: Mugging, the State, and Law and Order* (London: Macmillan)

Hanmer, J and Maynard, M (eds) (1987) *Women, Policing and Social Control* (London: Macmillan)

Hanmer, J and Saunders, S (1991) 'Policing Violence Against Women: Implementing Policy Changes' Paper presented to British Criminology Conference, July

Hanna, C (1996) 'No Right to Choose: Mandated Victim Participation in Domestic Violence Prosecutions' 109 *Harvard Law Review* 1849

Hare, I (1997) 'Legislating Against Hate – The Legal Response to Bias Crimes' 17 *Oxford Journal of Legal Studies* 415

Harris, D J, O'Boyle, M and Warbrick, C (1995) *Law of the European Convention on Human Rights* (London: Butterworths)

Harris, R (1992) *Crime, Justice and the Probation Service* (London: Routledge)

Hawkins, K (ed) (1992) *The Uses of Discretion* (Oxford: Clarendon Press)

Healey, M (1985) 'What are Local Government Services For' *Local Government Studies* November/December

Heaton-Armstrong, A and Wolchover, D (1992) 'Recording Witness Statements' *Criminal Law Review* 160

Hebenton, B and Thomas, T (1996) 'Sexual Offenders in the Community: Reflections on Problems of Law, Community and Risk Management in the USA, England and Wales' 24 *International Journal of the Sociology of Law* 427

Hedderman, C and Gelsthorpe, L (eds) (1997) *Understanding the Sentencing of Women* Home Office Research Study No 170 (London: Home Office)

Hedderman, C and Moxon, D (1992) *Magistrates' Court or Crown Court? Mode of Trial Decisions and Sentencing* Home Office Research Study No 125 (London: HMSO)

Heidensohn, F (1986) 'Models of Justice: Portia or Persephone? Some Thoughts on Equality, Fairness and Gender in the Field of Justice' 4 *International Journal of the Sociology of Law* 287

Heidensohn, F (1992) *Women in Control? The Role of Women in Law Enforcement* (Oxford: Oxford University Press)

Heidensohn, F (1996) *Women and Crime*, 2nd ed (London: Macmillan Press)

Heidensohn, F (1997) 'Gender and Crime' in M Maguire, R Morgan and R Reiner (eds), *The Oxford Handbook of Criminology* (Oxford: Clarendon Press)

Henham, R (1986) 'The Influences of Sentencing Principles on Magistrates' Sentencing Practices' 25 *Howard Journal of Criminal Justice* 190

Henham, T (1990) *Sentencing Principles and Magistrates' Sentencing Behaviour* (Aldershot: Avebury)

Her Majesty's Chief Inspector of Constabulary (1993) *Equal Opportunities in the Police Service* (London: HMSO)

Her Majesty's Chief Inspector of Constabulary (1994a) *Report for the Year 1993* HC 446 (London: HMSO)

Her Majesty's Chief Inspector of Constabulary (1994b) *Developing Diversity in the Police Service* (London: HMSO)

Her Majesty's Chief Inspector of Constabulary (1996–7) *Winning the Race: Policing Plural Communities* (London: HMSO)

Her Majesty's Prison Service (1992) *Briefing No 54*, 10 November 1992 (London: Home Office)

Her Majesty's Prison Service (1993) 'In-House Team to Run Manchester' *News Release* 15 July 1993 (London: Home Office)

Her Majesty's Prison Service (1997a) *Annual Report and Accounts April 1995–March 1996* (1997–98) HC 247 (London: HMSO)

Her Majesty's Prison Service (1997b) *Prison Service Annual Report and Accounts April 1996–March 1997* (1997–98) HC 274 (London: HMSO)

Hester, S and Eglin, P (1992) *A Sociology of Crime* (London: Routledge)

Hilson, C (1993) 'Discretion to Prosecute and Judicial Review' *Criminal Law Review* 739

Hodgson, J (1994) 'Adding Injury to Injustice: The Suspect at the Police Station' 21 *Journal of Law and Society* 85

Holdaway, S (ed) (1979) *The British Police* (London: Edward Arnold)

Holdaway, S (1983) *Inside the British Police* (Oxford: Blackwell)

Holdaway, S (1991) 'Race Relations and Police Recruitment' 31 *British Journal of Criminology* 365–382

Home Affairs Committee (1990) *The Crown Prosecution Service* HC 118 (London: HMSO)

Home Affairs Committee (1996a) *Judicial Appointments Procedures, Volume I: Report* HC 52-I (London, HMSO)

Home Affairs Committee (1996b) *Judicial Appointments Procedures, Volume II: Minutes of Evidence and Appendices* HC 52-II (London: HMSO)

Home Affairs Committee (1997) *Police Disciplinary and Complaints Procedures, Volume 1: Report* HC 258-I (London: The Stationery Office)

Home Office (1961) *Compensation for Victims of Violent Crime*, Cmnd 1406 (London: HMSO)

Home Office (1975) *Further Studies of Female Offenders* (London: Home Office)

Home Office (1978) *Review of the Criminal Injuries Scheme: Report of an Indepartmental Working Party* (London: Home Office)

Home Office (1984) *Probation Service in England and Wales: Statement of National Objectives and Priorities* (London: Home Office)

Home Office (1985) *The Cautioning of Offenders* Circular No 14/1985 (London: HMSO)

Home Office (1988) *Report of the Working Group on the Costs of Crime* (London: Home Office)

Home Office (1989) *Magistrates' Courts: Report of A Scrutiny* (London: HMSO)

Home Office (1989a) *Crime Statistics for the Metropolitan Police District by Ethnic Group, 1987: Victims, Suspects and Those Arrested* Home Office Statistical Bulletin 5/89 (London: Home Office)

Home Office (1990) *Crime, Justice and Protecting the Public*, Cm 965 (London: Home Office)

Home Office (1992) *A Guide to Interviewing* (London: Home Office Central Planning and Training Unit)

Home Office (1993a) *Disclosure of Criminal Records for Employment Vetting Purposes* (London: Home Office)

Home Office (1993b) *Police Reform: A Police Service for the Twenty-First Century*, Cm 2281 (London: Home Office)

Home Office (1994) *The Cautioning of Offenders* Circular 18/1994 (London: Home Office)

Home Office (1995) *Criminal Statistics England and Wales 1994*, Cm 3010 (London: HMSO)

Home Office (1995a) *Digest 3: Information on the Criminal Justice System in England and Wales* (London: Home Office)

Home Office (1995b) *Mode of Trial: A Consultation Document*, Cm 2908 (London: HMSO)

Home Office (1996a) *Protecting the Public*, Cm 3190 (London: Home Office)

Home Office (1996b) *Operation of Certain Police Powers Under PACE, England and Wales, 1995* Home Office Statistical Bulletin 12/96 (London: Home Office Research and Statistics Directorate)

Home Office (1996c) *The Victims' Charter: A Statement of the Rights of Victims* (London: Home Office)

Home Office (1996d) *On The Record*, Cm 3308 (London: Home Office)

Home Office (1996e) *Criminal Statistics England and Wales 1995*, Cm 3421 (London: HMSO)

Home Office (1996f) *Sentencing and Supervision of Sex Offenders*, Cm 3304 (London: Home Office)

Home Office (1996g) *Police Complaints and Discipline England and Wales 95/96* Statistical Bulletin 17/96 (London: Home Office Research and Statistics Directorate)

Home Office (1997a) *Criminal Statistics England and Wales 1996*, Cm 3764 (London: Home Office)

Home Office (1997b) *Magistrates' Views of the Probation Service* Research Findings No 48 (London: Home Office)

Home Office (1997c) *No More Excuses – A New Approach to Tackling Youth Crime in England and Wales*, Cm 3809 (London: Home Office)

Home Office (1997d) *Prison Statistics for England and Wales 1996* (London: Home Office)

Home Office (1997e) *Projections of Long Term Trends in the Prison Population to 2005* Statistical Bulletin 7/97 (London: Home Office)

Home Office (1997f) *Review of Delay in the Criminal Justice System: A Report* (London: Home Office)

Home Office (1997g) *Cautions, Court Proceedings and Sentencing England and Wales 1996* Statistical Bulletin 16/97 (London: Home Office Research and Statistics Directorate)

Home Office (1997h) *Race and the Criminal Justice System* (London: Home Office)

Home Office (1997i) *Tackling Youth Crime* (London: Home Office)

Home Office (1997j) *No More Excuses – A New Approach to Tackling Youth Crime in England and Wales*, Cm 3809 (London: Home Office)

Home Office (1997k) *The Three Year Plan for the Probation Service 1997–2000* (London: Home Office)

Home Office (1997l) *Rights Brought Home: The Human Rights Bill*, Cm 3782 (London: Home Office)

Home Office, Northern Ireland Office and Scottish Office (1993) *Inquiry into Police Responsibilities and Rewards*, Cm 2280 (London: HMSO) (Sheehy Report)

Honeycombe, G (1974) *Adam's Tale* (London: Arrow Books)

Hood, C (1991) 'A Public Administration for All Seasons' 69 *Public Administration* 3–19

Hood, R (1962) *Sentencing in Magistrates' Courts* (London: Tavistock)

Hood, R (1972) *Sentencing the Motoring Offender* (London: Heinemann)

Hood, R (1992) *Race and Sentencing* (Oxford: Clarendon Press)

Hood, R (1995) 'Race and Sentencing: A Reply' *Criminal Law Review* 272

Horne, C J (1996) 'The Case for: CCTV Should be Introduced' 1 *International Journal of Risk, Security and Crime Prevention* 317

Horton, C and Smith, D J (1988) *Evaluating Police Work* (London: Policy Studies Institute)

Hough, M (1995) 'Anxiety About Crime: Findings from the 1994 British Crime Survey', Home Office Research Findings No 25 (London: HMSO)

Hough, M (1996) 'The Police Patrol Function: What Research Can Tell Us' in W Saulsbury, J Mott and T Newburn (eds), *Themes in Contemporary Policing* (London: Police Foundation/Policy Studies Institute)

Hough, M and Mayhew, P (1985) *Taking Account of Crime*, Home Office Research Study No 85 (London: HMSO)

Howard, M (1995) 'A Sentencing Policy Backed by Reality' *Law Society's Gazette*, 15 December

Hudson, B (1989) 'Discrimination and Disparity: The Influence of Race on Sentencing' 16 *New Community* 23

Hudson, B (1993) *Racism and Criminology* (London: Sage)

Hudson, B (ed) (1996) *Race, Crime and Justice* (Aldershot: Ashgate)

Humphrey, C (1991) 'Calling on the Experts: the Financial Management Initiative (FMI), Private Sector Management Consultants and the Probation Service' 30 *Howard Journal of Criminal Justice* 1–18

686

Humphrey, C and Pease, K (1992) 'Effectiveness Measurement in the Probation Service: A View from the Troops' 31 *Howard Journal of Criminal Justice* 31–52

Irvine (1997) *Presidential Address to the Magistrates' Association Annual General Meeting*
Irving, B (1980) *Police Interrogation: A Study of Current Practice* Royal Commission on Criminal Procedure Research Study 1 (London: HMSO)

Jackson, J (1993) 'The Royal Commission on Criminal Justice: (2) The Evidence Recommendations' *Criminal Law Review* 817
Jackson, J (1995) 'The Value of Jury Trial' in E Attwool and D Goldberg (eds) *Criminal Justice* ARSP Beiheft 63 (Stuttgart: Franz Steiner)
Jackson, J (1997) 'Judicial Responsibility in Criminal Proceedings' *Current Legal Problems* 59
Jackson, J and Doran, S (1995) *Judge Without Jury: Diplock Trials in the Adversary System* (Oxford: Clarendon Press)
Jackson, J and Doran, S (1997) 'The Case for Jury Waiver' *Criminal Law Review* 155
James, A (1987) 'Performance and the Planning Process' *Social Services Insight*, 6 March
James, A L, Bottomley, A K, Clare, E and Leibling, A (1997) *Privatizing Prisons: Rhetoric and Reality* (London: Sage)
James, D (1979) 'Police–Black Relations: the Professional Solution' in S Holdaway (ed), *The British Police* (London: Edward Arnold)
Jefferson, T & Grimshaw, R (1984) *Controlling the Constable* (London: Muller)
Jefferson, T (1988) 'Race, Crime and Policing: Empirical, Theoretical and Methodological Issues' 16 *International Journal of the Sociology of Law* 521–539
Jefferson, T (1990) *The Case Against Paramilitary Policing* (Milton Keynes: Open University Press)
Jefferson, T (1993) 'The Racism of Criminalization: Policing and the Reproduction of the Criminal Other' in L Gelsthorpe and W McWilliams (eds) *Minority Ethnic Groups and the Criminal Justice System* (Cambridge: University of Cambridge Institute of Criminology)
Jefferson, T and Walker, M (1992) 'Ethnic Minorities in the Criminal Justice System' *Criminal Law Review* 83–95
Jefferson, T and Walker, M (1993) 'Attitudes to the Police of the Ethnic Minorities in a Provincial City' 33 *British Journal of Criminology* 251–266
Jefferson, T, Walker, M and Seneviratne, M (1992) 'Ethnic Minorities, Crime and Criminal Justice: A Study in a Provincial City' in D Downes (ed), *Unravelling Criminal Justice* (London: Macmillan)
Jenkins, S (1995) 'Howard's Crime Waving' *The Times*, 28 September
Johnson, S (1985) 'Black Innocence and the White Jury' 83 *Michigan Law Review* 1611
Jones, C (1993) 'Auditing Criminal Justice' 33 *British Journal of Criminology* 187–202
Jones, S (1987) 'Making it Work: Some Reflections on the Sex Discrimination Act' 60 *Police Journal* 294–302
Jones, T et al (1986) *The Islington Crime Survey: Crime, Victimization and Policing in Inner City London* (Aldershot: Gower)
Joutsen, M (1994) 'Victim Participation in Proceedings and Sentencing in Europe' 3 *International Review of Victimology* 57
JUSTICE (1989) *Miscarriages of Justice* (London: JUSTICE)

JUSTICE (1993) *Negotiated Justice: A Closer Look at the Implications of Plea Bargains* (London: JUSTICE)

JUSTICE (1994a) *Remedying Miscarriages of Justice* (London: JUSTICE)

JUSTICE (1994b) *Unreliable Evidence? Confessions and the Safety of Convictions* (London: JUSTICE)

JUSTICE (1995) *Disclosure, A Consultation Paper: The JUSTICE Response* (London: JUSTICE)

Kamisar, Y (1987) '"Comparative Reprehensibility" and the Fourth Amendment Exclusionary Rule' 86 *Michigan Law Review* 1

Kapardis, A (1985) *Sentencing by English Magistrates as a Human Process* (Nicosia: Asselia Publishers)

Kapardis, A (1997) *Psychology and Law* (Cambridge: Cambridge University Press)

Kassin, S and Wrightsman, L (1985) 'Confession Evidence' in S Kassin and L Wrightsman (eds), *The Psychology of Evidence and Trial Procedure* (London: Sage)

Kaye, T (1991) *'Unsafe and Unsatisfactory'? The Report of the Independent Inquiry into the Working Practices of the West Midlands Police Serious Crime Squad* (London: Civil Liberties Trust)

Kee, R (1989) *Trial and Error* (London: Penguin)

Kelling, G and Pate, T (1980) *The New Jersey Foot Patrol Experiment: Executive Summary* (Washington DC: Police Foundation) (unpublished)

Kemp, C, Norris, C and Fielding, N (1992) 'Legal Manoeuvres in Police Handling of Disputes' in D Farrington and S Walklate (eds), *Offenders and Victims: Theory and Policy* (Oxford: British Society of Criminology)

King, J (ed) (1976) *Control Without Custody* (Cambridge: Institute of Criminology)

King, M (1982) 'Against Summary Trial' *Legal Action*, 14 April

King, M and May, C (1985) *Black Magistrates* (London: Cobden Trust)

King, R D and Maguire, M (eds) (1994) *Prisons in Context* (Oxford: Oxford University Press)

King, R D and McDermott, K (1995) *The State of Our Prisons* (Oxford: Clarendon Press)

Kinsey, R (1985) *The Merseyside Crime and Police Surveys: Final Report* (Liverpool: Mersey County Council)

Kinsey, R, Lea, J and Young, J (1986) *Losing the Fight Against Crime* (Oxford: Basil Blackwell)

Kitsuse, J and Cicourel, A (1963) 'A Note on the Use of Official Statistics' 11 *Social Problems* 131

Kramer, P, Kerr, N and Carroll, J (1990) 'Pretrial Publicity, Judicial Remedies, and Jury Bias' 14 *Law and Human Behaviour* 409

La Trobe (1980) *Guilty, Your Worship* Occasional Monograph No 1 (Bundoora: Legal Studies Department, La Trobe University)

Lacey, N (1994) 'Government as Manager, Citizen as Consumer: The Case of the Criminal Justice Act 1991' (1994) 54 *Modern Law Review* 534–554

Laub, J (1997) 'Patterns of Criminal Victimization in the United States' in R Davis, A Lurigio and W Skogan (eds) *Victims of Crime*, 2nd ed (Califormia: Sage)

Law Commission (1996) *Evidence in Criminal Proceedings: Previous Misconduct of a Defendant* Consultation Paper 141 (London: HMSO)

688

Law Commission (1997) *Criminal Law: Consents to Prosecution* Consultation Paper No 149 (London: Stationery Office)

Laycock, G and Tarling, R (1985) 'Police Force Cautioning: Policy and Practice' 24 *Howard Journal of Criminal Justice* 81

Legal Action Group (1993) *Preventing Miscarriages of Justice* (London: Legal Action Group)

Leigh, L and Zedner, L (1992) *A Report on the Administration of Criminal Justice in the Pre-Trial Phase in France and Germany* Royal Commission on Criminal Justice Research Study 1 (London: HMSO)

Leishman, F, Cope, S and Starie, P (1996) 'Reinventing and Restructuring: Towards a "New Policing Order"' in F Leishman, S Cope and S Savage (eds), *Core Issues in Policing* (London: Longman)

Leng, R (1993) *The Right to Silence in Police Interrogation: A Study of Some of the Issues Underlying the Debate* Royal Commission on Criminal Justice Research Study 10 (London: HMSO)

Leng, R (1994) 'A Recipe for Miscarriage: The Royal Commission and Informal Interviews' in M McConville and L Bridges (eds), *Criminal Justice in Crisis* (Cheltenham: Edward Elgar)

Leng, R (1997) 'Defence Strategies for Information Deficit: Negotiating the CPIA' 1 *International Journal of Evidence and Proof* 215

Lidstone, K and Palmer, C (1996) *Bevan & Lidstone's The Investigation of Crime: A Guide to Police Powers* (London: Butterworths)

Linz, D and Penrod, S (1992) 'Exploring the First and Sixth Amendments: Pretrial Publicity and Jury Decision Making' in D Kagehiro and W Laufer (eds), *Handbook of Psychology and Law* (New York: Springer)

Lloyd, C, Mair, G and Hough, M (1994) *Explaining Reconviction Rates: A Critical Analysis* Home Office Research Study No 136 (London: HMSO)

Lord Chancellor's Department (1991) *Directions for Advisory Committees on Justices of the Peace* (London: Lord Chancellor's Department)

Lord Chancellor's Department (1992) *A New Framework for Local Justice*, Cm 1829 (London: HMSO)

Lord Chancellor's Department (1997) *Judicial Statistics England and Wales for the Year 1996*, Cm 1736 (London: HMSO)

Love, S (1990) *A Guide to Designing Performance Indicators* (Cambridge: HMIC)

Lustgarten, L (1986) *Governance of the Police* (London: Sweet & Maxwell)

Maddox, B (1997) 'US Sex Offenders Face Indefinite Detention', *The Times*, 25 June

Magistrates' Association (1996) 'Judicial Independence' 52 *The Magistrate* 224

Magistrates' Association (1997) *Sentencing Guidelines* (London: Magistrates' Association)

Maguire, M (1991) 'Complaints Against the Police: The British Experience' in A Goldsmith (ed), *Complaints Against the Police – The Trend to External Review* (Oxford: Oxford University Press)

Maguire, M (1997) 'Crime Statistics, Patterns and Trends' in M Maguire, R Morgan, R Reiner (eds) *The Oxford Handbook of Criminology*, 2nd ed (Oxford: Clarendon Press)

Maguire, M 'Effect of the PACE Provisions on Detention and Questioning' (1988) 28 *British Journal of Criminology* 19

Maguire, M and Corbett, C (1987) *The Effects of Crime and the Work of Victim Support Schemes* (Aldershot: Gower)

Maguire, M and Corbett, C (1989) 'Patterns and Profiles of Complaints Against the Police' in R Morgan and D Smith (eds), *Coming to Terms with Policing* (London: Routledge)

Maguire, M and Corbett, C (1991) *A Study of the Police Complaints System* (London: HMSO)

Maguire, M and Norris, C (1992) *The Conduct and Supervision of Criminal Investigations* Royal Commission on Criminal Justice Research Study 5 (London: HMSO)

Maguire, M, Morgan, R and Reiner, R (1997) *The Oxford Handbook of Criminology*, 2nd ed (Oxford: Clarendon Press)

Maguire, M, Noaks, L, Hobbs, R and Brearley, N *Assessing Detective Effectiveness* (Cardiff: Social Research Unit, SOCAS, University of Wales)

Maher, G (1983a) 'Reasonable Doubt and the Jury' *Scots Law Times (News)* 97

Maher, G (1983b) 'Jury Verdicts and the Presumption of Innocence' 3 *Legal Studies* 146

Maher, G (1988) 'The Verdict of the Jury' in M Findlay and P Duff (eds), *The Jury Under Attack* (London: Butterworths)

Mahir, T (1966) 'Managing People' *Police Journal*, August, 1

Mair, G and Mortimer, E (1996) *Curfew Orders with Electronic Monitoring: An Evaluation of the First Twelve Months of the Trials in Greater Manchester, Norfolk and Berkshire* Home Office Research Study No 163 (London: HMSO)

Mair, G and Nee, C (1990) *Electronic Monitoring: The Trials and their Results* Home Office Research Study No 120 (London: HMSO)

Malleson, K (1993) *Review of the Appeal Process* Royal Commission on Criminal Justice Research Study No 17 (London: HMSO)

Malleson, K (1994) 'Appeals Against Conviction and the Principle of Finality' (1994) 21 *Journal of Law and Society* 151

Manning, P (1979) 'The Social Context of Police Work' in S. Holdaway (ed) *The British Police* (London: Edward Arnold)

Mansfield, M and Wardle, T (1993) *Presumed Guilty* (London: Heinemann)

Mark, R (1977) Policing a Perplexed Society (London: Allen and Unwin)

Marshall, G (1978) 'Police Accountability Revisited' in D Downes (ed), *Unravelling Criminal Justice* (London: Macmillan)

Massingham, H (1936) *I Took Off My Tie* (London: Heinemann)

Maung, N and Mirrlees-Black, C (1994) *Racially Motivated Crime: A British Crime Survey Analysis* Home Office Research and Planning Unit Paper 82 (London: Home Office)

Mawby, R (1979) *Policing the City* (Farnborough: Gower)

Maxwell, P and Mallon, D (1997) 'Discrimination Against Ex-Offenders' 36 *Howard Journal of Criminal Justice* 352

May, J (1990) *Interim Report on the Maguire Case* HC 556 (London: HMSO)

May, J (1992) *Second Report on the Maguire Case* HC 296 (London: HMSO)

May, J (1994) *Final Report* HC 449 (London: HMSO)

Mayhew, P et al (1976) *Crime as Opportunity* (London: Home Office)

Mayhew, P, Clarke, R, Burrows, J, Hough, J and Winchester, S (1979) *Crime in Public View* Home Office Research Study No 49 (London: Home Office)

Mayhew, P, Elliott, D and Dowds, L (1989) *The 1988 British Crime Survey* Home Office Research Study No 111 (London: Home Office)

McBarnet, D (1981) *Conviction: Law, the State and the Construction of Justice* (London: Macmillan)

McConville, M (1992) 'Videotaping Interrogations: Police Behaviour On and Off Camera' *Criminal Law Review* 532

McConville, M (1993) *Corroboration and Confessions: The Impact of a Rule Requiring that No Conviction Can Be Sustained on the Basis of Confession Evidence Alone* Royal Commission on Criminal Justice Research Study 13 (London: HMSO)

McConville, M and Baldwin, J (1981) *Courts, Prosecution and Conviction* (Oxford: Clarendon Press)

McConville, M and Baldwin, J (1982) 'The Role of Interrogation in Crime Discovery and Conviction' 22 *British Journal of Criminology* 165

McConville, M and Bridges, L (1993) 'Pleading Guilty Whilst Maintaining Innocence' 143 *New Law Journal* 160

McConville, M and Bridges, L (eds) (1994) *Criminal Justice in Crisis* (Cheltenham: Edward Elgar)

McConville, M and Hodgson, J (1993) *Custodial Legal Advice and the Right to Silence* Royal Commission on Criminal Justice Research Study 16 (London: HMSO)

McConville, M and Shepherd, D (1992) *Watching the Police Watching Communities* (London: Routledge)

McConville, M and Williams, J (1985) *Crime and Punishment: A Radical Rethink* (London: Tawney Society)

McConville, M, Hodgson, J, Bridges, L and Pavlovic, A (1994) *Standing Accused: The Organisation and Practices of Criminal Defence Lawyers in Britain* (Oxford: Clarendon Press)

McConville, M, Sanders, A and Leng, R (1991) *The Case for the Prosecution: Police Suspects and the Construction of Criminality* (London: Routledge)

McConville, M, Sanders, A and Leng, R (1997) 'Descriptive or Critical Sociology? The Choice is Yours' 37 *British Journal of Criminology* 347

McCrudden, C, Smith, D and Brown, C (1991) *Racial Justice at Work: The Enforcement of the 1976 Race Relations Act in Employment* (London: Policy Studies Institute)

McDonald, D (1994) 'Public Imprisonment by Private Means: The Re-emergence of Private Prisons and Jails in the United States, the United Kingdom, and Australia' in R King and M Maguire (eds), *Prisons in Context* (Oxford: Oxford University Press)

McEvoy, K (1995) 'The Reintegration of Offenders in the Light of the Changed Political and Security Circumstances' in the Twentieth Report of the Standing Advisory Commission on Human Rights (1994–95) (London: HMSO)

McEwan, J (1992) *Evidence and the Adversarial Process* (Oxford: Blackwell)

McKenzie, I, Morgan, R and Reiner, R (1990) 'Helping the Police with their Enquiries: The Necessity Principle and Voluntary Attendance at the Police Station' *Criminal Law Review* 22

McLaughlin, E (1994) *Community, Policing and Accountability: The Politics of Policing in Manchester in the 1980s* (Aldershot: Avebury)

McLaughlin, H (1990) 'Court Clerks: Advisers or Decision-Makers?' 30 *British Journal of Criminology* 358

McLean, M (1995) 'Quality Investigation? Police Interviewing of Witnesses' 35 *Medicine Science and Law* 116

Miers, D (1983) 'Compensation and Conceptions of Victims of Crime' 8 *Victimology* 204

691

Miers, D (1992) 'The Responsibilities and Rights of Victims of Crime' 55 *Modern Law Review* 482

Miers, D (1997) *State Compensation for Criminal Injuries* (London: Blackstone Press)

Mills, B (1994) 'Justice for All – And All For Justice' 144 *New Law Journal* 1670

Mirrlees-Black, C, Mayhew, P and Percy, A (1996) *The 1996 British Crime Survey* 1996 Home Office Statistical Bulletin No 19/96 (London: HMSO)

Mirrlees-Black, C, Mayhew, P and Percy, A (1997) *The 1996 British Crime Survey* (London: HMSO)

Moody, R and Tombs, J (1983) 'Plea Negotiations in Scotland' *Criminal Law Review* 297

Morgan, D and Stephenson, G (eds) (1994) *Suspicion and Silence: The Right to Silence in Criminal Investigations* (London: Blackstone Press)

Morgan, J and Zedner, L (1992) *Crime Victims* (Oxford: Oxford University Press)

Morgan, R (1989) 'Policing by Consent: Legitimating the Doctrine' in R Morgan and D J Smith (eds), *Coming to Terms with Policing* (London: Routledge)

Morgan, R (1993) 'Prisons Accountability Revisited' *Public Law* 314

Morgan, R (1997) 'Imprisonment: Current Concerns' in M Maguire, R Morgan and R Reiner (eds) *The Oxford Handbook of Criminology*, 2nd ed (Oxford: Clarendon Press)

Morgan, R and King, D (1987) 'Profiting from Prison' *New Society*, 23 October

Morgan, R and Maggs, C (1985) *Setting the PACE: Police Community Consultation Arrangements in England and Wales* (Bath: Centre for the Analysis of Social Policy, University of Bath)

Morgan, R and Smith, D (eds) (1989) *Coming to Terms with Policing* (London: Routledge)

Morison, J and Leith, P (1992) *The Barrister's World and the Nature of Law* (Milton Keynes: Open University Press)

Morris, A (1987) *Women, Crime and Criminal Justice* (Oxford: Basil Blackwell)

Morris, A (1988) 'Sex and Sentencing' *Criminal Law Review* 163

Morris, A and Gelsthorpe, L (1990) 'Not Paying for Crime' *Criminal Law Review* 839

Morris, A and Gelsthorpe, L (eds) (1981) *Women and Crime* Cropwood Conference Series No 13 (Cambridge: Institute of Criminology)

Morris, A and Wilkinson, C (1983) 'Secure Care: Just an easy Answer?' *Community Care* 22, 8 December

Morris, N and Tonry, M (1990) *Between Prison and Probation: Intermediate Punishments in a Rational Sentencing System* (New York: Oxford University Press)

Morris, P and Heal, K (1981) *Crime Control and the Police* Home Office Research Study No 67 (London: HMSO)

Morrison, T, Erooga, M and Beckett, R C (eds) (1994) *Sexual Offending Against Children* (London: Routledge)

Mortimer, A (1994) 'Why Did You Do It?' *Policing* 103

Mortimer, E and May, C (1997) *Electronic Monitoring in Practice: the Second Year of the Trials of Curfew Orders* (1997) Home Office Research Study No 177 (London: HMSO)

Moston, S and Stephenson, G (1993) *The Questioning and Interviewing of Suspects Outside the Police Station* Royal Commission on Criminal Justice Research Study 22 (London: HMSO)

Moxon, D (ed) (1985) *Managing Criminal Justice* (London: HMSO)

Moxon, D (1988) *Sentencing Practice in the Crown Court* Home Office Research Study No 103 (London: HMSO)

Moxon, D (ed) (1990) *Unit Fines: Experiments in Four Courts*, Home Office Research Study No 43 (London: HMSO)

Moxon, D and Hedderman, C (1994) 'Mode of Trial Decisions and Sentencing Differences Between Courts' 33 *Howard Journal of Criminal Justice* 97

Moxon, D, Jones, P and Tarling, R (1985) *Juvenile Sentencing: Is There a Tariff?* Home Office Research and Planning Unit Paper 32 (London: Home Office)

Mullin, C (1990b) *Error of Judgement: The Truth About the Birmingham Bombings* (revised ed) (London: Chatto and Windus)

Mungham, G and Bankowski, Z (1976) 'The Jury in the Legal System' in P Carlen (ed), *Magistrates' Justice* (London: Martin Robertson)

Munro, C (1992) 'Judicial Independence and Judicial Functions' in C Munro and M Wasik (eds) *Sentencing, Judicial Discretion and Training* (London: Sweet & Maxwell)

NACRO (1997) *Criminal Justice Digest, 1997* (London: NACRO)

Nagel, I and Schulhofer, S (1992) 'A Tale of Three Cities: An Empirical Study of Charging and Bargaining Practices under the Federal Sentencing Guidelines' 66 *Southern California Law Review* 501

Naylor, B (1994) 'Fair Trial or Free Press: Legal Responses to Media Reports of Criminal Trials' 53 *Cambridge Law Journal* 492

Nelken, D (ed) (1994) *The Futures of Criminology* (London: Sage)

Newburn, T and Merry, S (1990) *Keeping in Touch: Police–Victim Communication in Two Areas*, Home Office Research Study No 116 (London: Home Office)

Newman, K (1984) *Report of the Commissioner for the Metropolis 1982* (London: HMSO)

Neyroud, P (1994) 'Wrongs About a Right' April 8 *Police Review* 17

Noaks, L, Levi, M and Maguire, M (1995) *Contemporary Issues in Criminology* (Cardiff: University of Wales Press)

Nobles, R and Schiff, D (1995) 'Miscarriages of Justice: A Systems Approach' 58 *Modern Law Review* 299

Nobles, R, Schiff, D and Shaldon, N (1993) 'The Inevitability of Crisis in Criminal Appeals' 21 *International Journal of the Sociology of Law* 1

Norris, C, Fielding, N, Kemp, C and Fielding, J (1992) 'Black and Blue: An Analysis of the Influence of Race on Being Stopped by the Police' 43 *British Journal of Sociology* 207–224

O'Connor, P (1990) 'The Court of Appeal: Re-Trials and Tribulations' *Criminal Law Review* 615

Ockelton, M (1995) 'Rules of Evidence' in E Attwool and D Goldberg (eds), *Criminal Justice* ARSP Beiheft 63 (Stuttgart: Franz Steiner)

Parker, H, Casburn, M and Turnbull, D (1981) *Receiving Juvenile Justice* (Oxford: Blackwell)

Parker, H, Sumner, M and Jarvis, G (1989) *Unmasking the Magistrates* (Milton Keynes: Open University Press)

Parris, M (1997) 'All-Party Witch Hunt', *The Times*, 24 January

Pattenden, R (1990) *Judicial Discretion and Criminal Litigation* (Oxford: Clarendon Press)

Pattenden, R (1991) 'Should Confessions be Corroborated?' 107 *Law Quarterly Review* 317

Pattenden, R (1995) 'Inferences From Silence' *Criminal Law Review* 602

Pattenden, R (1996) *English Criminal Appeals 1844–1994* (Oxford: Clarendon Press)

Pearson, R (1980) 'Popular Justice and the Lay Magistracy: The Two Faces of Lay Participation' in Z Bankowski and G Mungham (eds), *Essays in Law and Society* (London: Routledge)

Pease, K (1981) *Community Service Orders: A First Decade of Promise* (London: Howard League)

Pease, K (1997) 'Crime Prevention' in M Maguire, R Morgan and R Reiner (eds), *The Oxford Handbook of Criminology*, 2nd ed (Oxford: Clarendon Press)

Pennington, C and Lloyd-Bostock, C (1987) *The Psychology of Sentencing* (Oxford: Centre for Socio-Legal Studies)

Philpotts, G and Lancucki, L (1979) *Previous Convictions, Sentence and Reconviction,* Home Office Research Study No 53 (London: Home Office)

Pickles, J (1988) *Straight From the Bench* (Sevenoaks: Coronet)

Piliavin, I and Briar, S (1964) 'Police Encounters with Juveniles' 70 *American Journal of Sociology* 206–214

Police Complaints Authority (1996) *The 1995/96 Annual Report of the Police Complaints Authority* HC 469 (London: HMSO)

Police Complaints Authority (1997) *The 1996/97 Annual Report of the Police Complaints Authority* HC 95 (London: HMSO)

Police Foundation/Policy Studies Institute (1996) *The Role and Responsibilities of the Police: Report of an Independent Inquiry* (London: Police Foundation/Policy Studies Institute)

Pollard, C (1996) 'Public Safety, Accountability and the Courts' *Criminal Law Review* 152

Powis, D (1977) *Signs of Crime* (London: McGraw Hill)

Pratt, J (1989) 'Corporatism: The Third Model of Juvenile Justice' 29 *British Journal of Criminology* 236

Prison Reform Trust (1993) *The Future of the Prison Education Service* (London: Prison Reform Trust)

Pullinger, H (1985) 'The Criminal Justice System Viewed as a System' in D Moxon (ed) *Managing Criminal Justice* (London: HMSO)

Punch, M (1979) 'The Secret Social Service' in S Holdaway (ed), *The British Police* (London: Edward Arnold)

Punch, M (1983) *Control in the Police Organisation* (London: MIT Press)

Pyle, D (1983) *The Economics of Crime and Enforcement* (London: Macmillan)

Pyle, D (1995) *Cutting the Cost of Crime: the Economics of Crime and Criminal Justice,* Hobart Paper No. 129 (London: Institute of Economic Affairs)

Quinney, R (1970) *The Social Reality of Crime* (Boston: Little Brown)

Radford, J (1987) 'Policing Male Violence, Policing Women' in J Hanmer and M Maynard (eds), *Women, Policing and Social Control* (London: Macmillan)

Radford, J and Stanko, B (1991) 'Violence against Women and Children: The Contradictions of Crime Control under Patriarchy' in K Stenson and D Cowell (eds), *The Politics of Crime Control* (London: Sage)

Raine, J (1989) *Local Justice: Ideals and Realities* (Edinburgh: T and T Clark)

Raine, J and Willson, M (1993) *Managing Criminal Justice* (Hemel Hempstead: Harvester Wheatsheaf)

Redmayne, M (1997) 'Process Gains and Process Values: The Criminal Procedure and Investigations Act 1996' 60 *Modern Law Review* 79

Reiner, R (1985) *The Politics of the Police* (Brighton: Wheatsheaf)

Reiner, R (1988) 'Keeping the Home Office Happy: Can Police Effectiveness Be Measured by Performance Indicators?' 4 *Policing* 28

Reiner, R (1989) 'Race and Criminal Justice' 16 *New Community* 5

Reiner, R (1991) *Chief Constables* (Oxford: Oxford University Press)

Reiner, R (1992a) *The Politics of the Police*, 2nd ed (London: Harvester Wheatsheaf)

Reiner, R (1992b) 'Policing a Postmodern Society' 55 *Modern Law Review* 761

Reiner, R (1993) 'Race, Crime and Justice: Models of Interpretation' in L Gelsthorpe and W McWilliams (eds) *Minority Ethnic Groups and the Criminal Justice System* (Cambridge: University of Cambridge Institute of Criminology)

Reiner, R (1997) 'Media Made Criminality: The Representation of Crime in the Mass Media' in M Maguire, R Morgan and R Reiner (eds), *The Oxford Handbook of Criminology*, 2nd ed (Oxford: Clarendon Press)

Reiner, R and Spencer, S (eds) (1993) *Accountable Policing: Effectiveness, Empowerment and Equity* (London: Institute for Public Policy Research)

Riley, D and Vennard, J (1988) *Triable-Either-Way Cases: Crown Court or Magistrates' Court?* Home Office Research Study No 98 (London: HMSO)

Roberts, P (1996) 'What Price a Free Market in Forensic Science Services?' 36 *British Journal of Criminology* 37

Robertshaw, P and Milne, A (1992) 'The Guilty Plea Discount: Rule of Law or Role of Chance?' 31 *Howard Journal of Criminal Justice* 53

Robertshaw, P, Cox, S and Van Hoen, N (1992) 'Jury Populations and Jury Verdicts' 20 *International Journal of the Sociology of Law* 271

Robertson, B (1989) 'The Looking Glass World of Section 78' *New Law Journal* 1223

Robertson, G (1994) 'Entrapment Evidence: Manna from Heaven or Fruit of the Poisoned Tree?' *Criminal Law Review* 805

Rock, P (1990) *Helping Victims of Crime: The Home Office and the Rise of Victim Support in England and Wales* (Oxford: Oxford University Press)

Rock, P (1993) *The Social World of an English Crown Court* (Oxford: Clarendon Press)

Rock, P (1997) 'Sociological Theories of Crime' in M Maguire, R Morgan and R Reiner (eds), *The Oxford Handbook of Criminology*, 2nd ed (Oxford: Clarendon Press)

Rose, D (1996) *In the Name of the Law: The Collapse of Criminal Justice* (London: Jonathan Cape)

Rose, N (1996) '"The Death of the Social?": Refiguring the Territory of Government' 25 *Economy and Society* 327

Royal Commission on Criminal Justice (1993) *Report*, Cm 2263 (London: HMSO)

Royal Commission on Criminal Procedure (1981) *The Investigation and Prosecution of Criminal Offences in England and Wales: The Law and Procedure*, Cmnd 8092 (London: HMSO)

Royal Commission on the Police (1962) *Final Report*, Cmnd 1728 (London: HMSO)

Rozenberg, J (1992) 'Miscarriages of Justice' in E Stockdale and S Casale (eds), *Criminal Justice under Stress* (London: Blackstone)

Sanders, A (1986) 'Diverting Offenders from Prosecution: Can We Learn from Other Countries?' 150 *Justice of the Peace* 614

Sanders, A (1987) 'Constructing the Case for the Prosecution' 14 *Journal of Law and Society* 229

Sanders, A (1988) 'Rights, Remedies and the Police and Criminal Evidence Act' *Criminal Law Review* 802

Sanders, A (1989) 'The Limits to Diversion from Prosecution' 28 *British Journal of Criminology* 513

Sanders, A (1992) 'Reforming the Prosecution System' 63 *Political Quarterly* 25

Sanders, A (1996) 'Access to Justice in the Police Station: An Elusive Dream?' in R Young and D Wall (eds), *Access to Criminal Justice: Legal Aid, Lawyers and the Defence of Liberty* (London: Blackstone)

Sanders, A and Bridges, L (1990) 'Access to Legal Advice and Police Malpractice' *Criminal Law Review* 494

Sanders, A and Bridges, L (1993) 'The Right to Legal Advice' in C Walker and K Starmer (eds) *Justice in Error* (London: Blackstone Press)

Sanders, A and Young, R (1994) *Criminal Justice* (London: Butterworths)

Sanders, A, Bridges, L, Mulvaney, A and Crozier, G (1989) *Advice and Assistance at Police Stations and the 24 Hour Duty Solicitor Scheme* (London: Lord Chancellor's Department)

Saulsbury, W, Hibberd, M and Irving, B (1994) *Using Physical Evidence* (London: Police Foundation)

Saulsbury, W, Mott, J and Newburn, T (eds) (1996) *Themes in Contemporary Policing* (London: Police Foundation/Policy Studies Institute)

Savage, S (1984) 'Political Control or Community Liaison' 55 *Political Quarterly* 48

Scarman, Lord (1981) *The Brixton Disorders 10–12 April 1981: Report of An Inquiry by the Rt. Hon. the Lord Scarman, OBE*, Cmnd 8427 (London: HMSO)

Scheflin, A and Van Dyke, J (1980) 'Jury Nullification: The Contours of a Controversy' 43(4) *Law and Contemporary Problems* 51

Schulhofer, S (1980) 'Sentencing Reform and Prosecutorial Power' 126 *University of Pennsylvania Law Review* 550

Seabrook, R (1992) *The Efficient Disposal of Business in the Crown Court* (London: General Council of the Bar)

Shapland, J (1981) *Between Conviction and Sentence* (London: Routledge)

Shapland, J (1985) 'The Criminal Justice System and the Victim' 10 *Victimology* 585

Shapland, J, Willmore, J and Duff, P (1985) *Victims in the Criminal Justice System*, Cambridge Studies in Criminology LIII (Aldershot: Gower)

Sharpe, S (1994) 'Covert Police Operations and the Discretionary Exclusion of Evidence' *Criminal Law Review* 793

Shute, S (1994) 'Prosecution Appeals Against Sentence: The First Five Years' 57 *Modern Law Review* 745

Simson, G (1976) 'Jury Nullification in the American System: A Skeptical View' 54 *Texas Law Review* 488

Sinclair, I and Miller, C (1984) *Measures of Police Effectiveness and Efficiency* Research and Planning Unit Paper 25 (London: Home Office)

Skogan, W (1990) *The Police and Public in England and Wales: A British Crime Survey Report* Home Office Research Study No 117 (London: Home Office)

Skogan, W (1994) *Contacts Between Police and Public*, Home Office Research Study No 134 (London: HMSO)

Skolnick, J (1975) *Justice Without Trial*, 2nd ed (New York: Wiley)

Smith, D (1983a) *Police and People in London: II A Survey of Londoners* (London: Policy Studies Institute)

Smith, D (1983b) *Police and People in London: III A Survey of Police Officers* (London: Policy Studies Institute)

Smith, D (1991) 'Police and Racial Minorities' 2 *Policing and Society* 1–15

Smith, D (1997a) 'Case Construction and the Goals of the Criminal Process' 37 *British Journal of Criminology* 319

Smith, D (1997b) 'Ethnic Origins, Crime and Criminal Justice' in M Maguire, R Morgan and R Reiner, *The Oxford Handbook of Criminology*, 2nd ed (Oxford: Clarendon Press)

Smith, D and Gray, J (1983) *Police and People in London: IV The Police in Action* (London: Policy Studies Institute)

Smith, L (1989) *Concerns About Rape* Home Office Research Study No 106 (London: HMSO)

Softley, P, Brown, D, Forde, B, Mair, G and Moxon, D (1980) *Police Interrogation* Home Office Research Study No 61 (London: HMSO)

Soothill, K, Francis, B and Sanderson, B (1997) 'A Cautionary Tale: The Sex Offenders Act 1997' *Criminal Law Review* 482

Southgate, P and Ekblom, P (1986) *Police–Public Encounters* Home Office Research Study No 90 (London: HMSO)

Sparks, R (1970) 'The Use of the Suspended Sentence' *Criminal Law Review* 70

Sparks, R (1992) *Television and the Drama of Crime* (Buckingham: Open University Press)

Sparks, R, Genn, H and Dodd, D (1977) *Surveying Victims* (London: Wiley)

Sprack, J (1995) *Emmins on Criminal Procedure* (London: Blackstone Press)

Stafford, E and Hill, J (1987) 'The Tariff, Social Inquiry Reports and the Sentencing of Juveniles' 27 *British Journal of Criminology* 411

Steer, D (1980) *Uncovering Crime: The Police Role* Royal Commission on Criminal Procedure Research Study 7 (London: HMSO)

Stenson, K and Cowell, D (eds) (1991) *The Politics of Crime Control* (London: Sage)

Stephenson, G (1992) *The Psychology of Criminal Justice* (Oxford: Blackwell)

Stewart Committee (1983) *Keeping Offenders Out of Court: Further Alternatives to Prosecution*, Cm 8027 (Edinburgh: HMSO)

Stewart, J and Walsh, K (1992) 'Change in the Management of Public Services' 70 *Public Administration* 499

Stitt, B and James, G (1984) 'Entrapment and the Entrapment Defense: Dilemmas for a Democratic Society' 3 *Law and Philosophy* 111

Stockdale, E and Casale, S (1992) *Criminal Justice under Stress* (London: Blackstone)

Stockdale, R and Walker, C (1993) 'Forensic Evidence' in C Walker and K Starmer (eds), *Justice in Error* (London: Blackstone Press)

Strachey, R *The Cause* (1978) (London: Virago)

Stuntz, J (1988) 'Self-Incrimination and Excuse' 88 *Columbia Law Review* 1227

Tarling, R (1979) *Sentencing Practice in the Magistrates' Courts* Home Office Research Study No 56 (London: HMSO)

Tarling, R, Moxon, D and Jones, P (1985) 'Sentencing of Adults and Juveniles in Magistrates' Courts' in D Moxon (ed), *Managing Criminal Justice* (London: HMSO)

Taylor, Lord Chief Justice (1993) Address to the Law Society of Scotland *Journal of the Law Society of Scotland* 129

Taylor, M and Pease, K (1989) 'Private Prisons and Penal Purpose' in R Matthews (ed), *Privatizing Criminal Justice* (London: Sage Publications)

Thomas, D (1982) *Current Sentencing Practice* (looseleaf work with regular updating service) (London: Sweet & Maxwell)

Thomas, D (1995) 'Proceeds of Crime Act 1995' 4 *Sentencing News*, 6

Thomas, D (1997) 'Sentencing Legislation – The Case for Consolidation' *Criminal Law Review* 406

Thomas, G and Bilder, M (1991) 'Aristotle's Paradox and the Self-Incrimination Puzzle' 82 *Journal of Criminal Law and Criminology* 243

Thomson Committee (1975) *Criminal Procedure in Scotland (2nd Report)*, Cmnd 6218 (London: HMSO)

Thornton, P (1993) 'Miscarriages of Justice: A Lost Opportunity' *Criminal Law Review* 926

Thornton, P, Mallalieu, A and Scrivener, A (1993) *Justice on Trial: Report of the Independent Civil Liberty Panel on Criminal Justice* (London: Civil Liberties Trust)

Tonry, M (1987) 'Sentencing Guidelines and Sentencing Commissions: The Second Generation' in M Wasik and K Pease (eds), *Sentencing Reform* (Manchester: Manchester University Press)

Tonry, M (1992) 'Judges and Sentencing Policy – The American Experience' in C Munro and M Wasik (eds), *Sentencing, Judicial Discretion and Training* (London: Sweet & Maxwell)

Tonry, M (1994) 'Racial Politics, Racial Disparities and the War on Crime' 40 *Crime and Delinquency* 475

Tonry, M (1995) *Malign Neglect: Race, Crime and Punishment in America* (New York: Oxford University Press)

Tonry, M (1996) *Sentencing Matters* (New York: Oxford University Press)

Trankell, A (1972) *Reliability of Evidence* (Stockholm: Beckmans)

Tuck, M and Southgate, P (1981) *Ethnic Minorities, Crime and Policing: A Survey of the Experiences of West Indians and Whites* Home Office Research Study No 70 (London: HMSO)

Turner, A (1992) 'Sentencing in the Magistrates' Court' in C Munro and M Wasik (eds), *Sentencing, Judicial Discretion and Training* (London: Sweet & Maxwell)

US Department of Justice (1982) *Basic Issues in Police Performance* (Washington DC: National Institute of Justice)

Van Maanen, J (1974) 'Working in the Street: A Developmental View of Police Behaviour' in Jacob, H (ed) (1974) *The Potential for Reform of Criminal Justice* (Beverly Hills, California: Sage)

Vennard, J and Riley, D (1988) 'The Use of Peremptory Challenge and Standby of Jurors and Their Relationship to Trial Outcome' *Criminal Law Review* 731

Victim Support (1995) *The Rights of Victims of Crime* (London: Victim Support)

Vigh, J and Katona, G (eds) (1993) *Social Changes, Crime and Police* (Budapest: Eotuos Lorand University Press)

Vogler, R (1990) 'Magistrates' Courts and the Struggle for Local Democracy 1886–1986' in C Sumner (ed), *Censure, Politics and Criminal Justice* (Buckingham: Open University Press)

von Hirsch, A (1992) 'Incapacitation' in A von Hirsch and A Ashworth (eds), *Principled Sentencing* (Boston: Northeastern University Press)

von Hirsch, A and Ashworth A (1992) *Principled Sentencing* (Boston: Northeastern University Press)

von Hirsch, A and Ashworth, A (1996) 'Protective Sentencing Under Section 2(2)(b): The Criteria for Dangerousness' *Criminal Law Review* 175

von Hirsch, A and Roberts, J (1997) 'Racial Disparity in Sentencing: Reflections on the Hood Study' 36 *Howard Journal of Criminal Justice* 227 von Hirsch, A and Wasik, M (1997) 'Civil Disqualifications Attending Conviction' 56 *Cambridge Law Journal* 599

Waddington, P (1986a) 'Defining Objectives: A Response to Tony Butler' 2 *Policing* 17–25

Waddington, P (1986b) 'The "Objectives" Debate' 2 *Policing* 225

Waddington, P (1987) 'Towards Paramilitarism: Dilemmas in Policing Civil Disorder' *British Journal of Criminology* 37–46

Waddington, P (1993) *Calling the Police: the Interpretation of, and Response to, Calls for Assistance from the Police* (Aldershot: Avebury)

Walker, C and Wall, D (1997) 'Imprisoning the Poor: Television Licence Evaders and the Criminal Justice System' *Criminal Law Review* 173

Walker, M (1988) 'The Court Disposal of Young Males in London in 1983' 28 *British Journal of Criminology* 441

Walker, M (1989) 'The Court Disposals and Remand of White, Afro-Caribbean and Asian Men' 29 *British Journal of Criminology* 353

Walker, M (1987) 'Interpreting Race and Crime Statistics' *Journal of the Royal Statistical Society* A 150, Part 1: 39–56

Walker, M (1992) 'Arrest Rates and Ethnic Minorities: A Study in a Provincial City' *Journal of the Royal Statistical Society* 155, Part 2: 259–272

Walker, N (1972) *Sentencing in a Rational Society* (London: Pelican)

Walker, N (1996) *Dangerous People* (London: Blackstone Press)

Walker, N and Hough, M (eds) (1988) *Public Attitudes to Sentencing: Surveys from Five Countries* (Aldershot: Gower)

Walker, N and Padfield, N (1996) *Sentencing Theory Law and Practice*, 2nd ed (London: Butterworths)

Walklate, S (1989) *Victimology* (London: Unwin Hyman)

Walklate, S (1992) 'Jack and Jill Join Up at Sun Hill: Public Images of Police Officers' 2 *Policing and Society* 219–232

Walklate, S (1993) 'Responding to Women as Consumers of Police Service: The UK Experience 1981–1991' in J Vigh and G Katona (eds), *Social Changes, Crime and Police* (Budapest: Eotuos Lorand University Press)

Walklate, S (1996) 'Equal Opportunities and the Future of Policing' in F Leishman, B Loveday and S Savage (eds), *Core Issues in Policing* (London: Longman)

Wasik, M (1984) 'Sentencing and the Divisional Court' *Criminal Law Review* 272

Wasik, M (1996a) 'Magistrates: Knowledge of Previous Convictions' *Criminal Law Review* 851

Wasik, M (1996b) *The Sentencing Process* (Aldershot: Dartmouth)

Wasik, M (1998) *Emmins on Sentencing* 3rd ed (London: Blackstone Press)

Wasik, M and Pease, K (1987) *Sentencing Reform* (Manchester: Manchester University Press)

Wasik, M and Taylor, R (1995) *Blackstone's Guide to the Criminal Justice Act 1994* (London: Blackstone Press)

Wasik, M and von Hirsch, A (1990) 'Statutory Sentencing Principles: The 1990 White Paper' 53 *Modern Law Review* 508

Wasik, M and von Hirsch, A (1994) 'Section 29 Revised: Previous Convictions in Sentencing' *Criminal Law Review* 409

Waters, I (1996) 'Quality of Service: Politics or Paradigm Shift?' in F Leishman, B Loveday and S Savage (eds), *Core Issues in Policing* (London: Longman)

699

Weatheritt, M (1993) 'Measuring Police Performance: Accounting or Accountability?' in R Reiner and S Spencer (eds), *Accountable Policing: Effectiveness, Empowerment and Equity* (London: Institute for Public Policy Research)

Wells, C (1997) 'Stalking: The Criminal Law Response' *Criminal Law Review* 463

Wells, G (1993) 'What Do We Know About Eyewitness Identification?' 48 *American Psychologist* 553

Welsh, S (1981) 'The Manufacture of Excitement in Police–Juvenile Encounters' 21 *British Journal of Criminology* 257

West, D (1996) 'Sexual Molesters' in N Walker (ed), *Dangerous People* (London: Blackstone Press)

Wilkins, L (1985) 'The Politics of Prediction' in D Farrington and R Tarling (eds), *Prediction in Criminology* (Boston: Lexington)

Williamson, T (1994) 'Reflections on Current Police Practice' in D Morgan and G Stephenson (eds), *Suspicion and Silence: The Right to Silence in Criminal Investigations* (London: Blackstone Press)

Willis, C F (1983) *The Use, Effectiveness and Impact of Police Stop and Search Powers* Home Office Research and Planning Unit Paper No 15 (London: Home Office)

Wilson, J (1968a) 'The Police and the Delinquent in Two Cities' in S Wheeler (ed), *Controlling Delinquents* (New York: John Wiley)

Wilson, J (1968b) *Varieties of Police Behaviour* (Cambridge: Harvard University Press)

Wilson, J Q and Kelling, G (1982) 'Broken Windows: The Police and Neighbourhood Safety' *The Atlantic Monthly* 29–37, March

Wolchover, D (1989) 'Should Judges Sum up on the Facts?' *Criminal Law Review* 781

Woolf, Lord (1991) *Prison Disturbances April 1990*, Cm 1456 (London: HMSO)

Worrall, A (1986) 'Out of Place: Female Offenders in the Court' 28 *Probation Journal* 90

Young, A (1991) *Femininity in Dissent* (London: Routledge)

Young, M (1991) *An Inside Job: Policing and Police Culture in Britain* (Oxford: Oxford University Press)

Young, R and Wall, D (eds) (1996) *Access to Criminal Justice: Legal Aid, Lawyers and the Defence of Liberty* (London: Blackstone Press)

Zander, M (1991) 'What the Annual Statistics Tell us About Pleas and Acquittals' *Criminal Law Review* 252

Zander, M (1993) 'The "Innocent" (?) Who Plead Guilty' 143 *New Law Journal* 85

Zander, M (1993) 'Where the Critics Got It Wrong' 143 *New Law Journal* 1364–1366.

Zander, M (1994) 'Ethics and Crime Investigation by the Police' 10 *Policing* 39

Zander, M and Henderson, P (1993) *Crown Court Study* Royal Commission on Criminal Justice Research Study 19 (London: HMSO)

Zedner, L (1997) 'Victims' in M Maguire, R Morgan and R Reiner (eds), *The Oxford Handbook of Criminology*, 2nd ed (Oxford: Clarendon Press)

Zuckerman, A (1987) 'Illegally Obtained Evidence – Discretion as a Guardian of Legitimacy' *Current Legal Problems* 55

Zuckerman, A (1994) 'Bias and Suggestibility: Is There an Alternative to the Right to Silence' in D Morgan and G Stephenson (eds), *Suspicion and Silence: The Right to Silence in Criminal Investigations* (London: Blackstone Press)

INDEX

703